Hoover's Handbook of

World Business

2011

Austin, Texas

Hoover's Handbook of World Business 2011 is intended to provide readers with accurate and authoritative information about the enterprises covered in it. Hoover's researched all companies and organizations profiled, and in many cases contacted them directly so that companies represented could provide information. The information contained herein is as accurate as we could reasonably make it. In many cases we have relied on third-party material that we believe to be trustworthy, but were unable to independently verify. We do not warrant that the book is absolutely accurate or without error. Readers should not rely on any information contained herein in instances where such reliance might cause financial loss. The publisher, the editors, and their data suppliers specifically disclaim all warranties, including the implied warranties of merchantability and fitness for a specific purpose. This book is sold with the understanding that neither the publisher, the editors, nor any content contributors are engaged in providing investment, financial, accounting, legal, or other professional advice.

The financial data (Historical Financials sections) in this book are from a variety of sources. Morningstar, Inc., provided selected data for the Historical Financials sections of publicly traded companies. For private companies and for historical information on public companies prior to their becoming public, we obtained information directly from the companies or from trade sources deemed to be reliable. Hoover's, Inc., is solely responsible for the presentation of all data.

Many of the names of products and services mentioned in this book are the trademarks or service marks of the companies manufacturing or selling them and are subject to protection under US law. Space has not permitted us to indicate which names are subject to such protection, and readers are advised to consult with the owners of such marks regarding their use. Hoover's is a trademark of Hoover's, Inc.

10 9 8 7 6 5 4 3 2 1

Publishers Cataloging-in-Publication Data

Hoover's Handbook of World Business 2011

    Includes indexes.

    ISBN 978-1-57311-145-4

    ISSN 1055-7199

    1. Business enterprises — Directories. 2. Corporations — Directories.

HF3010 338.7

Hoover's Company Information is also available on the Internet at Hoover's Online (www.hoovers.com). A catalog of Hoover's products is available on the Internet at www.hooversbooks.com.

The Hoover's Handbook series is produced for Hoover's Business Press by:

Sycamore Productions, Inc.
5808 Balcones Drive, Suite 205
Austin, Texas 78731
info@sycamoreproductions.com

Cover design is by John Baker. Electronic prepress and printing are by Sheridan Books, Inc., Ann Arbor, Michigan.

U.S. AND WORLD BOOK SALES

Hoover's, Inc.
5800 Airport Blvd.
Austin, TX 78752
Phone: 512-374-4500
Fax: 512-374-4538
e-mail: orders@hoovers.com
Web: www.hooversbooks.com

EUROPEAN BOOK SALES

William Snyder Publishing Associates
5 Five Mile Drive
Oxford OX2 8HT
England
Phone & fax: +44-186-551-3186
e-mail: snyderpub@aol.com

Hoover's, Inc.

Founder: Gary Hoover
President: Hyune Hand
VP Technology: Mamie Jones
VP Business Excellence: Jeff Cross
VP Product Management and Development: Ken Maranian
Interim VP Marketing: James Rogers
VP Product Development, D&B Digital: Gregory (Greg) Stern
VP Advertising Sales and Operations: Mark Walters
VP Sales: Tom Wickersham
Director Acquisitions: Amy Bible
Senior Director Account Services: Ron M. Chipman
Leader Strategy and Customer Insights: Katherine (Katie) Bullard

(For the latest updates on Hoover's, please visit: http://hoovers.com/global/corp)

EDITORIAL

Director, Editorial: Greg Perliski
Senior Editors: Adrianne Argumaniz, Larry Bills, Jason Cother, Danny Cummings,
Barbara-Anne Mansfield, Barbara Redding, Dennis Sutton
Team Lead: Matt Saucedo
Editors: Chelsea Adams, Adam Anderson, Alex Biesada, Joe Bramhall, James Bryant, Ryan Caione,
Jason Cella, Catherine Colbert, Tami Conner, Nancy Daniels, Bobby Duncan, Lesley Epperson,
Rachel Gallo, Chris Hampton, Stuart Hampton, Jim Harris, Laura Huchzermeyer, Chris Huston,
Jessica Jimenez, Linnea Anderson Kirgan, Sylvia Lambert, Anne Law, Josh Lower, John MacAyeal,
Kathryn Mackenzie, Rebecca Mallett, Michael McLellan, Barbara Murray, Nell Newton,
Lynett Oliver, Tracey Panek, Rachel Pierce, David Ramirez, Diane Ramirez, Mark Richardson,
Melanie Robertson, Patrice Sarath, Amy Schein, Nikki Sein, Lee Simmons, Anthony Staats, Tracy Uba,
Vanessa Valencia, Randy Williams, David Woodruff
QA Editors: Carrie Geis, Rosie Hatch, Diane Lee, John Willis
Editorial Customer Advocates: Adi Anand and Kenny Jones

HOOVER'S BUSINESS PRESS

Distribution Manager: Rhonda Mitchell
Customer Support and Fulfillment Manager: Michael Febonio

ABOUT HOOVER'S, INC. – THE BUSINESS INFORMATION AUTHORITY™

Hoover's, a D&B company, provides its customers the fastest path to business with insight and actionable information about companies, industries, and key decision makers, along with the powerful tools to find and connect to the right people to get business done. Hoover's provides this information for sales, marketing, business development, and other professionals who need intelligence on U.S. and global companies, industries, and the people who lead them. Hoover's unique combination of editorial expertise and one-of-a-kind data collection with user-generated and company-supplied content gives customers a 360-degree view and competitive edge. This information, along with powerful tools to search, sort, download, and integrate the content, is available through Hoover's (http://www.hoovers.com), the company's premier online service. Hoover's is headquartered in Austin, Texas.

Abbreviations

AB – Aktiebolag (Swedish)*
ADR – American Depositary Receipts
AG – Aktiengesellschaft (German)*
AFL-CIO – American Federation of Labor and Congress of Industrial Organizations
AMEX – American Stock Exchange
A/S – Aktieselskab (Danish)*
ASA – Allmenne Aksjeselskaper (Norwegian)*
ATM – asynchronous transfer mode; automated teller machine
CAD/CAM – computer-aided design/computer-aided manufacturing
CASE – computer-aided software engineering
CD-ROM – compact disc – read-only memory
CEO – chief executive officer
CFO – chief financial officer
CMOS – complementary metal-oxide semiconductor
COMECON – Council for Mutual Economic Assistance
COO – chief operating officer
DAT – digital audio tape
DOD – Department of Defense
DOE – Department of Energy
DOT – Department of Transportation
DRAM – dynamic random-access memory
DVD – digital versatile disc/digital video disc
EC – European Community
EPA – Environmental Protection Agency
EPS – earnings per share
EU – European Union
EVP – executive vice president
FCC – Federal Communications Commission
FDA – Food and Drug Administration

FDIC – Federal Deposit Insurance Corporation
FTC – Federal Trade Commission
GATT – General Agreement on Tariffs and Trade
GmbH – Gesellschaft mit beschränkter Haftung (German)*
GNP – gross national product
HDTV – high-definition television
HMO – health maintenance organization
HR – human resources
HTML – hypertext markup language
ICC – Interstate Commerce Commission
IMF – International Monetary Fund
IPO – initial public offering
IRS – Internal Revenue Service
KGaA – Kommanditgesellschaft auf Aktien (German)*
LAN – local-area network
LBO – leveraged buyout
LNG – liquefied natural gas
LP – limited partnership
Ltd. – Limited
MFN – Most Favored Nation
MITI – Ministry of International Trade and Industry (Japan)
NAFTA – North American Free Trade Agreement
Nasdaq – National Association of Securities Dealers Automated Quotations
NATO – North Atlantic Treaty Organization
NV – Naamlose Vennootschap (Dutch)*
NYSE – New York Stock Exchange
OAO – open joint stock company (Russian)
OAS – Organization of American States

OECD – Organization for Economic Cooperation and Development
OEM – original equipment manufacturer
OOO – limited liability company (Russian)
OPEC – Organization of Petroleum Exporting Countries
OS – operating system
OTC – over-the-counter
P/E – price-to-earnings ratio
PLC – public limited company (UK)*
RAM – random-access memory
R&D – research and development
RISC – reduced instruction set computer
ROA – return on assets
ROI – return on investment
SA – Société Anonyme (French)*; Sociedad(e) Anónima (Spanish and Portuguese)*
SA de CV – Sociedad Anónima de Capital Variable (Spanish)*
SEC – Securities and Exchange Commission
SEVP – senior executive vice president
SIC – Standard Industrial Classification
SpA – Società per Azioni (Italian)*
SPARC – scalable processor architecture
SVP – senior vice president
VAR – value-added reseller
VAT – value-added tax
VC – venture capitalist
VP – vice president
WAN – wide-area network
WWW – World Wide Web
ZAO – closed joint stock company (Russian)
z o.o. – z ograniczona odpowiedzialnoscia (Polish)*

* These abbreviations are used in companies' names to convey that the companies are limited liability enterprises; the meanings are usually the equivalent of *corporation* or *incorporated*.

Contents

List of Lists

Companies Profiled

Companies Profiled (continued)

About Hoover's Handbook of World Business 2011

This 18th edition of *Hoover's Handbook of World Business* is focused on its mission of providing you with premier coverage of the global business scene. Featuring 300 of the world's most influential companies based outside of the United States, this book is one of the most complete sources of in-depth information on large, non-US-based business enterprises available anywhere.

Hoover's Handbook of World Business is one of our four-title series of handbooks that covers, literally, the world of business. The series is available as an indexed set, and also includes *Hoover's Handbook of American Business*, *Hoover's Handbook of Private Companies*, and *Hoover's Handbook of Emerging Companies*. This series brings you information on the biggest, fastest-growing, and most influential enterprises in the world.

HOOVER'S ONLINE FOR BUSINESS NEEDS

In addition to Hoover's widely used MasterList and Handbooks series, comprehensive coverage of more than 40,000 business enterprises is available in electronic format on our Web site at www.hoovers.com. Our goal is to provide our customers the fastest path to business with insight and actionable information about companies, industries, and key decision makers, along with the powerful tools to find and connect to the right people to get business done. Hoover's has partnered with other prestigious business information and service providers to bring you all the right business information, services, and links in one place.

We welcome the recognition we have received as the premier provider of high-quality company information — online, electronically, and in print — and continue to look for ways to make our products more available and more useful to you.

We believe that anyone who buys from, sells to, invests in, lends to, competes with, interviews with, or works for a company should know all there is to know about that enterprise. Taken together, this book and the other Hoover's products and resources represent the most complete source of basic corporate information readily available to the general public.

HOW TO USE THIS BOOK

This book has four sections:

1. "Using Hoover's Handbooks" describes the contents of our profiles and explains the ways in which we gather and compile our data.

2. "A List-Lover's Compendium" contains lists of the largest, fastest-growing, and most valuable companies of global importance.

3. The company profiles section makes up the largest and most important part of the book — 300 profiles of major business enterprises, arranged alphabetically.

4. Three indexes complete the book. The first sorts companies by industry groups, the second by headquarters location. The third index is a list of all the executives found in the Executives section of each company profile.

As always, we hope you find our books useful. We invite your comments via phone (512-374-4500), fax (512-374-4538), mail (5800 Airport Boulevard, Austin, Texas 78752), or e-mail (custsupport@hoovers.com).

The Editors,
Austin, Texas,
December 2010

Using Hoover's Handbooks

SELECTION OF THE COMPANIES PROFILED

The 300 profiles in this book include a variety of international enterprises, ranging from some of the largest publicly traded companies in the world — Daimler AG, for example — to Malaysia's largest and oldest conglomerate, Sime Darby Berhad. It also includes many private businesses, such as Bertelsmann AG and LEGO, as well as a selection of government-owned entities, such as Mexico's Petróleos Mexicanos. The companies selected represent a cross-section of the largest, most influential, and most interesting companies based outside the United States.

In selecting these companies, we followed several basic criteria. We started with the global giants, including Toyota and Royal Dutch Shell, and then looked at companies with substantial activity in the US, such as Vivendi and Diageo. We also included companies that dominate their industries (e.g., AB Electrolux, the world's #1 producer of household appliances), as well as representative companies from around the world (an Indian conglomerate, Tata; two firms from Finland, Nokia and Stora Enso Oyj; and two companies from Russia, OAO Gazprom and OAO LUKOIL). Companies that weren't necessarily global powerhouses but that had a high profile with consumers (e.g., IKEA) or had interesting stories (Virgin Group) were included. Finally, because of their truly global reach, we added the Big Four accounting firms (even though they are headquartered or co-headquartered in the US).

ORGANIZATION

The profiles are presented in alphabetical order. You will find the commonly used name of the enterprise at the beginning of the profile; the full, legal name is found in the Locations section. For some companies, primarily Japanese, the commonly translated English name differs from the actual legal name of the company, so both are provided. (The legal name of Nippon Steel Corporation is Shin Nippon Seitetsu Kabushiki Kaisha.) If a company name starts with a person's first name (e.g., George Weston Limited), it is alphabetized under the first name. We've also tried to alphabetize companies where you would expect to find them — for example, Deutsche Lufthansa is in the L's and Grupo Televisa can be found under T.

The annual financial information contained in the profiles is current through fiscal year-ends occurring as late as June 2010. We have included certain nonfinancial developments, such as officer changes, through September 2010.

OVERVIEW

In the first section of the profile, we have tried to give a thumbnail description of the company and what it does. The description will usually include information on the company's strategy, reputation, and ownership. We recommend that you read this section first.

HISTORY

This extended section, which is present for most companies, reflects our belief that every enterprise is the sum of its history and that you have to know where you came from in order to know where you are going. While some companies have limited historical awareness, we think the vast majority of the enterprises in this book have colorful backgrounds. We have tried to focus on the people who made the enterprises what they are today. We have found these histories to be full of twists and ironies; they make fascinating reading.

EXECUTIVES

Here we list the names of the people who run the company, insofar as space allows. We have shown age and pay information where available, although most non-US companies are not required to report the level of detail revealed in the US.

Although companies are free to structure their management titles any way they please, most modern corporations follow standard practices. The ultimate power in any corporation lies with the shareholders, who elect a board of directors, usually including officers or "insiders," as well as individuals from outside the company. The chief officer, the person on whose desk the buck stops, is usually called the chief executive officer (CEO) in the US. In other countries, practices vary widely. In the UK, traditionally, the Managing Director performs the functions of the CEO without the title, although the use of the term

CEO is on the rise there. In Germany it is customary to have two boards of directors: a managing board populated by the top executives of the company and a higher-level supervisory board consisting of outsiders.

As corporate management has become more complex, it is common for the CEO to have a "right-hand person" who oversees the day-to-day operations of the company, allowing the CEO plenty of time to focus on strategy and long-term issues. This right-hand person is usually designated the chief operating officer (COO) and is often the president of the company. In other cases one person is both chairman and president.

We have tried to list each company's most important officers, including the chief financial officer (CFO) and the chief legal officer. For companies with US operations, we have included the names of the US CEO, CFO, and top human resources executive, where available.

The people named in the Executives section are indexed at the back of the book.

The Executives section also includes the name of the company's auditing (accounting) firm, where available.

LOCATIONS

Here we include the company's full legal name and its headquarters, street address, telephone and fax numbers, and Web site, as available. We also list the same information for the US office for each company, if one exists. Telephone numbers of foreign offices are shown using the standardized conventions of international dialing. The back of the book includes an index of companies by head-quarters location.

In some cases we have also included information on the geographic distribution of the company's business, including sales and profit data. Note that these profit numbers, like those in the Products/Operations section below, are usually operating or pretax profits rather than net profits. Operating profits are generally those before financing costs (interest income and payments) and before taxes, which are considered costs attributable to the whole company rather than to one division or part of the world. For this reason the net income figures (in the Historical Financials section) are usually much lower, since they are after interest and taxes. Pretax profits are after interest but before taxes.

PRODUCTS/OPERATIONS

This section lists as many of the company's products, services, brand names, divisions, subsidiaries, and joint ventures as we could fit. We have tried to include all its major lines and all familiar brand names. The nature of this section varies by company and the amount of information available. If the company publishes sales and profit information by type of business, we have included it (in US dollars).

COMPETITORS

In this section we have listed enterprises that compete with the profiled company. This feature is included as a quick way to locate similar companies and compare them. Because of the difficulty in identifying companies that only compete in foreign markets, the list of competitors is still weighted to large international companies with a strong US presence.

HISTORICAL FINANCIALS

Here we have tried to present as much data about each enterprise's financial performance as we could compile in the allocated space. Financial data for all companies is presented in US dollars, using the appropriate exchange rate at fiscal year-end.

While the information presented varies somewhat from industry to industry, it is less complete in the case of private companies that do not release data (although we have always tried to provide annual sales and employment). The following information is generally present.

A five-year table, with relevant annualized compound growth rates, covers:

- Sales — fiscal year sales (year-end assets for most financial companies)
- Net income — fiscal year net income (before accounting changes)
- Net profit margin — fiscal year net income as a percent of sales (as a percent of assets for most financial firms)
- Employees — fiscal year-end or average number of employees
- Stock price — the fiscal year close
- P/E — high and low price/earnings ratio
- Earnings per share — fiscal year earnings per share (EPS)
- Dividends per share — fiscal year dividends per share

The information on the number of employees is intended to aid the reader interested in knowing whether a company has a long-term trend of increasing or decreasing employment. As far as we know, we are the only company that publishes this information in print format.

The numbers on the left in each row of the Historical Financials section give the month and the year in which the company's fiscal year actually ends. Thus, a company with a September 30, 2010, year-end is shown as 9/10.

In addition, we have provided in graph form a stock price history for companies that trade on the major US exchanges. The graphs, covering up to five years, show the range of trading between the high and the low price, as well as the closing price for each fiscal year. For public companies that trade on the OTC or Pink Sheets or that do not trade on US exchanges, we graph net income. Generally, for private companies, we have graphed net income, or, if that is unavailable, sales.

Key year-end statistics in this section generally show the financial strength of the enterprise, including:

- Debt ratio (long-term debt as a percent of shareholders' equity)
- Return on equity (net income divided by the average of beginning and ending common shareholders' equity)
- Cash and cash equivalents
- Current ratio (ratio of current assets to current liabilities)
- Total long-term debt (including capital lease obligations)
- Number of shares of common stock outstanding
- Dividend yield (fiscal year dividends per share divided by the fiscal year-end closing stock price)
- Dividend payout (fiscal year dividends divided by fiscal year EPS)

- Market value at fiscal year-end (fiscal year-end closing stock price multiplied by fiscal year-end number of shares outstanding)
- Fiscal year sales for financial institutions.

Per share data has been adjusted for stock splits. The data for public companies with sponsored American Depositary Receipts has been provided to us by Morningstar, Inc. Other public company information was compiled by Hoover's, which takes full responsibility for the content of this section.

In the case of private companies that do not publicly disclose financial information, we usually did not have access to such standardized data. We have gathered estimates of sales and other statistics from numerous sources.

Hoover's Handbook of

World Business

A List-Lover's Compendium

The 100 Largest Companies by Sales in
Hoover's Handbook of World Business 2011

Rank	Company	Sales ($ mil.)	Rank	Company	Sales ($ mil.)	Rank	Company	Sales ($ mil.)
1	Royal Dutch Shell	285,129	36	Royal Bank of Scotland	89,221	71	Deutsche Bank	60,834
2	BP p.l.c.	246,138	37	Enel S.p.A.	89,104	72	Saint-Gobain	60,674
3	Saudi Arabian Oil	233,300	38	Nissan Motor Co.	86,724	73	ThyssenKrupp	59,181
4	Toyota Motor	204,443	39	Tesco PLC	86,685	74	Nokia Corporation	58,738
5	China Petroleum & Chemical	196,781	40	LG Corp.	86,353	75	Unilever	57,074
6	AXA	180,986	41	Munich Re Group	85,394	76	Groupe Auchan	56,857
7	ING Groep	164,222	42	Telefónica, S.A.	83,665	77	Mitsubishi UFJ Financial Group	56,231
8	TOTAL S.A.	160,738	43	OAO LUKOIL	81,083	78	Robert Bosch	54,711
9	Volkswagen	150,754	44	Statoil ASA	80,101	79	Tokyo Electric	54,115
10	BNP Paribas	134,900	45	Panasonic Corporation	80,025	80	BHP Billiton	52,798
11	Assicurazioni Generali	129,934	46	Hyundai Motor	78,457	81	AEON CO.	51,045
12	Allianz SE	129,920	47	Sony Corporation	77,825	82	Fujitsu Limited	50,483
13	Carrefour SA	123,202	48	Prudential plc	76,603	83	A.P. Møller – Mærsk	50,081
14	Eni S.p.A.	120,883	49	BASF SE	72,653	84	Credit Suisse	49,799
15	Samsung Group	119,229	50	BMW	72,636	85	BBVA	49,576
16	E.ON AG	117,260	51	Fiat S.p.A.	71,806	86	Veolia Environnement	49,519
17	GDF SUEZ	114,525	52	Tata Group	70,800	87	Roche Holding	49,279
18	Daimler AG	113,114	53	Repsol YPF	70,273	88	Bank of China	48,973
19	Siemens	111,834	54	Zurich Financial Services	70,272	89	Renault	48,316
20	Nippon Telegraph and Telephone	109,837	55	Toshiba Corporation	70,210	90	Deutsche Bahn	47,151
21	Banco Santander	107,294	56	Peugeot S.A.	69,391	91	VINCI	46,810
22	Glencore International	106,400	57	ALDI Group	68,700	92	Hannover Re	46,800
23	HSBC Holdings	103,736	58	CNP Assurances	68,627	93	NTT DoCoMo	46,220
24	Nestlé S.A.	103,679	59	Vodafone	67,010	94	GlaxoSmithKline	45,179
25	Lloyds Banking Group	102,737	60	AEGON N.V.	66,513	95	Novartis AG	45,103
26	OAO Gazprom	98,686	61	Philips Electronics	66,469	96	Bouygues SA	44,935
27	Hitachi, Ltd.	96,753	62	Deutsche Post	66,215	97	Bayer AG	44,670
28	Petróleos Mexicanos	96,442	63	RWE	66,201	98	Woolworths Limited	44,497
29	Electricité de France	95,073	64	Japan Tobacco	66,181	99	Wesfarmers Limited	44,380
30	Compañía Española de Petróleos	95,073	65	China Mobile	66,143	100	Mitsui & Co.	44,192
31	Aviva plc	94,096	66	France Telecom	65,847			
32	METRO AG	93,916	67	ArcelorMittal	65,110			
33	Deutsche Telekom	92,588	68	Mitsubishi Corporation	63,179			
34	Honda Motor Co.	92,552	69	Barclays PLC	62,940			
35	PETROBRAS	91,540	70	EADS N.V.	61,373			

SOURCE: HOOVER'S, INC., DATABASE, OCTOBER 2010

The 100 Most Profitable Companies in
Hoover's Handbook of World Business 2011

Rank	Company	Net Income ($ mil.)	Rank	Company	Net Income ($ mil.)	Rank	Company	Net Income ($ mil.)
1	OAO Gazprom	25,722	36	Compañía Española de Petróleos	5,859	71	Toronto-Dominion Bank	2,909
2	China Mobile	16,849	37	HSBC Holdings	5,834	72	Honda Motor Co.	2,896
3	BP p.l.c.	16,578	38	AXA	5,780	73	Nintendo Co.	2,869
4	Barclays PLC	16,385	39	RWE	5,491	74	ACS	2,839
5	PETROBRAS	15,448	40	Vale S.A.	5,349	75	LVMH	2,828
6	Banco Santander	13,489	41	NTT DoCoMo	5,338	76	Taiwan Semiconductor	2,768
7	Vodafone	13,026	42	Rio Tinto	5,335	77	POSCO	2,761
8	BHP Billiton	12,722	43	Nippon Telegraph and Telephone	5,311	78	Christian Dior	2,726
9	Royal Dutch Shell	12,518	44	Unilever	5,296	79	Diageo plc	2,626
10	Bank of China	12,487	45	France Telecom	4,966	80	L'Oréal SA	2,569
11	E.ON AG	12,390	46	Commonwealth Bank of Australia	4,864	81	Assicurazioni Generali	2,532
12	TOTAL S.A.	12,106	47	Anheuser-Busch InBev	4,613	82	Mitsubishi Corporation	2,507
13	Telefónica, S.A.	11,145	48	Lloyds Banking Group	4,502	83	SAP AG	2,505
14	Mizuho Financial	10,785	49	LG Corp.	4,483	84	Repsol YPF	2,500
15	Nestlé S.A.	10,046	50	British American Tobacco	4,321	85	VINCI	2,434
16	Mitsubishi UFJ Financial Group	9,440	51	IBERDROLA, S.A.	4,212	86	Anglo American	2,389
17	Enel S.p.A.	9,158	52	Intesa Sanpaolo	4,211	87	Telecom Italia	2,287
18	China Petroleum & Chemical	9,036	53	Jardine Matheson	3,935	88	National Australia Bank	2,259
19	GlaxoSmithKline	8,809	54	Munich Re Group	3,675	89	Reckitt Benckiser	2,258
20	Novartis AG	8,454	55	Siemens	3,643	90	Groupe Danone	2,180
21	BNP Paribas	8,358	56	Royal Bank of Canada	3,598	91	National Grid	2,093
22	Sanofi-Aventis	8,156	57	Tesco PLC	3,545	92	Novo Nordisk	2,074
23	Samsung Group	8,123	58	Rolls-Royce Group	3,537	93	Crédit Agricole	2,072
24	AstraZeneca	7,521	59	Hyundai Motor	3,469	94	Bouygues SA	2,067
25	Roche Holding	7,499	60	Telstra Corporation	3,374	95	Haci Ömer Sabanci	2,021
26	GDF SUEZ	7,496	61	Rabobank Group	3,279	96	BASF SE	2,021
27	Deutsche Bank	7,127	62	Zurich Financial Services	3,236	97	Teva Pharmaceuticals	2,000
28	OAO LUKOIL	7,011	63	Transocean Ltd.	3,181	98	Gas Natural SDG	1,992
29	BBVA	6,586	64	Hutchison Whampoa	3,180	99	Bayer AG	1,948
30	UniCredit	6,384	65	Statoil ASA	3,152	100	SABMiller	1,910
31	Eni S.p.A.	6,259	66	ABB Ltd	3,136			
32	Endesa, S.A.	6,249	67	Koninklijke KPN	3,122			
33	Allianz SE	6,227	68	Westpac Banking	3,007			
34	Credit Suisse	6,176	69	Vivendi	2,990			
35	Electricité de France	5,859	70	TeliaSonera AB	2,960			

SOURCE: HOOVER'S, INC., DATABASE, OCTOBER 2010

The 100 Largest Employers in
Hoover's Handbook of World Business 2011

Rank	Company	Employees	Rank	Company	Employees	Rank	Company	Employees
1	Carrefour SA	475,976	36	Toshiba Corporation	199,000	71	Bridgestone Corporation	137,135
2	Tesco PLC	472,094	37	Nippon Telegraph and Telephone	195,000	72	FirstGroup plc	133,203
3	Deutsche Post	436,651	38	Woolworths Limited	191,000	73	Nokia Corporation	123,553
4	Siemens	405,000	39	Fiat S.p.A.	190,014	74	IKEA	123,000
5	OAO Gazprom	393,600	40	ThyssenKrupp	187,495	75	Renault	121,422
6	Compass Group	386,170	41	Peugeot S.A.	186,220	76	DENSO CORPORATION	120,812
7	Panasonic Corporation	384,586	42	LG Corp.	186,000	77	Hyundai Motor	120,472
8	Sodexo	379,749	43	France Telecom	181,000	78	EADS N.V.	119,506
9	China Petroleum & Chemical	371,333	44	Honda Motor Co.	176,815	79	Lufthansa	117,521
10	Volkswagen	368,500	45	UniCredit	174,519	80	Schneider Electric	116,065
11	Hitachi, Ltd.	359,746	46	Fujitsu Limited	172,438	81	Anheuser-Busch InBev	116,000
12	Tata Group	357,000	47	Wal-Mart de México	170,014	82	ABB Ltd	116,000
13	Toyota Motor	320,590	48	Banco Santander	169,460	83	Philips Electronics	115,924
14	HSBC Holdings	302,000	49	Canon Inc.	168,879	84	A.P. Møller – Mærsk	115,386
15	ArcelorMittal	287,000	50	Deloitte Touche Tohmatsu	168,651	85	Mitsubishi UFJ Financial Group	115,300
16	METRO AG	286,091	51	Sony Corporation	167,900	86	Infosys Technologies	113,800
17	Nestlé S.A.	278,000	52	Flextronics International	165,000	87	ING Groep	110,325
18	Samsung Group	277,000	53	Electricité de France	164,250	88	Michelin	109,193
19	Robert Bosch	270,687	54	Pricewaterhouse-Coopers	163,545	89	Ricoh Company	108,525
20	Jardine Matheson	270,000	55	Casino Guichard	163,208	90	Bayer AG	108,400
21	Bank of China	262,566	56	Unilever	163,000	91	Wipro Limited	108,071
22	Deutsche Telekom	259,920	57	VINCI	161,746	92	Lloyds Banking Group	107,144
23	Telefónica, S.A.	257,426	58	Nissan Motor Co.	160,422	93	Anglo American	107,016
24	Daimler AG	256,407	59	Société Générale	160,144	94	WPP plc	105,318
25	Groupe Auchan	243,000	60	Allianz SE	153,203	95	Sanofi-Aventis	104,867
26	GDF SUEZ	242,714	61	China Mobile	145,954	96	BASF SE	104,779
27	Deutsche Bahn	240,242	62	Ernst & Young Global	144,441	97	Air France-KLM	104,721
28	Hutchison Whampoa	220,000	63	Barclays PLC	144,200	98	BBVA	103,721
29	Securitas AB	211,459	64	Petróleos Mexicanos	143,421	99	Intesa Sanpaolo	103,718
30	Saint-Gobain	209,175	65	OAO LUKOIL	143,400	100	AXA	103,432
31	Royal Ahold	206,000	66	NEC Corporation	142,358			
32	BNP Paribas	201,740	67	ACS	142,176			
33	Royal Bank of Scotland	201,700	68	KPMG International	140,235			
34	SNCF	200,097	69	Loblaw Companies	139,000			
35	Wesfarmers Limited	200,000	70	Bouygues SA	138,936			

SOURCE: HOOVER'S, INC., DATABASE, OCTOBER 2010

The 100 Fastest-Growing Companies in Five-Year Sales Growth in
Hoover's Handbook of World Business 2011

Rank	Company	Annual % Change*	Rank	Company	Annual % Change	Rank	Company	Annual % Change
1	Aviva plc	72.7	36	Gas Natural SDG	20.1	71	VINCI	11.9
2	Endesa, S.A.	53.7	37	Mitsubishi UFJ Financial Group	19.9	72	Carlsberg A/S	11.6
3	Wesfarmers Limited	48.2	38	PETROBRAS	19.6	73	Petróleos Mexicanos	11.5
4	Hannover Re	47.9	39	Rogers Communications	19.2	74	Bacardi	11.5
5	Tata Group	45.3	40	OAO LUKOIL	18.9	75	Royal Bank of Canada	11.5
6	Dentsu Inc.	44.1	41	PKN ORLEN	18.4	76	National Australia Bank	11.5
7	Lenovo Group	41.8	42	BNP Paribas	18.2	77	Tokio Marine	11.4
8	GDF SUEZ	40.1	43	Pernod Ricard	17.9	78	AEGON N.V.	11.3
9	SOFTBANK CORP.	38.7	44	Hutchison Whampoa	17.6	79	Thomson Reuters	11.0
10	Compañía Española de Petróleos	37.6	45	Sime Darby Berhad	17.4	80	adidas AG	11.0
11	Transocean Ltd.	34.6	46	UniCredit	16.9	81	WPP plc	10.8
12	Imperial Tobacco	33.9	47	Sanofi-Aventis	16.6	82	Commonwealth Bank of Australia	10.7
13	Mitsubishi Corporation	32.8	48	Kirin Holdings	16.2	83	Wal-Mart de México	10.6
14	Nintendo Co.	30.8	49	ITOCHU Corporation	16.1	84	Reckitt Benckiser	10.6
15	Rio Tinto	29.7	50	IKEA	16.1	85	Telenor ASA	10.6
16	CNP Assurances	28.1	51	BBVA	15.2	86	A.P. Møller - Mærsk	10.5
17	Lloyds Banking Group	27.6	52	Telefónica, S.A.	14.5	87	Saint-Gobain	10.3
18	Agrium Inc.	26.9	53	Grupo Bimbo	14.1	88	Sinopec Shanghai Petrochemical	10.1
19	Wipro Limited	26.6	54	E.ON AG	14.0	89	Philips Electronics	10.0
20	Anheuser-Busch InBev	25.8	55	OMV	13.9	90	Pricewaterhouse-Coopers	10.0
21	Saudi Arabian Oil	25.3	56	FirstGroup plc	13.3	91	Schneider Electric	9.9
22	Infosys Technologies	24.7	57	CEMEX	13.3	92	HOCHTIEF AG	9.8
23	Banco Santander	24.3	58	ALDI Group	13.2	93	Airbus S.A.S.	9.8
24	IBERDROLA, S.A.	24.2	59	BAE SYSTEMS	13.1	94	Novartis AG	9.8
25	ArcelorMittal	24.0	60	Christian Dior	13.0	95	Deloitte Touche Tohmatsu	9.7
26	Bank of China	23.7	61	Novo Nordisk	13.0	96	Assicurazioni Generali	9.6
27	Teva Pharmaceuticals	23.7	62	LEGO A/S	12.8	97	Koç Holding	9.6
28	Vale S.A.	23.6	63	Energias de Portugal	12.6	98	Statoil ASA	9.5
29	China Mobile	23.3	64	Woolworths Limited	12.6	99	Barclays PLC	9.4
30	Virgin Group	22.6	65	Toronto-Dominion Bank	12.5	100	Allied Irish Banks	9.4
31	OAO Gazprom	22.1	66	Enel S.p.A.	12.4			
32	Westpac Banking	21.5	67	Prudential plc	12.3			
33	China Petroleum & Chemical	21.3	68	BHP Billiton	12.3			
34	Acer Incorporated	20.4	69	Roche Holding	12.3			
35	Jardine Matheson	20.2	70	ING Groep	12.0			

*These rates are compounded annualized increases, and may have resulted from acquisitions or
one-time gains. If less than 6 years of data are available, growth is for the years available.

SOURCE: HOOVER'S, INC., DATABASE, OCTOBER 2010

The 100 Fastest-Growing Companies in Five-Year Employment Growth in
Hoover's Handbook of World Business 2011

Rank	Company	Annual % Change*	Rank	Company	Annual % Change	Rank	Company	Annual % Change
1	Peugeot S.A.	95.6	36	WPP plc	11.9	71	Marubeni Corporation	8.0
2	Wesfarmers Limited	46.1	37	ArcelorMittal	11.8	72	IKEA	7.9
3	Sime Darby Berhad	32.6	38	Grupo Televisa	11.6	73	ITOCHU Corporation	7.9
4	Gas Natural SDG	31.0	39	Société Générale	11.5	74	Jardine Matheson	7.8
5	Suzuki Motor	30.2	40	SABMiller	11.4	75	SAP AG	7.7
6	adidas AG	29.7	41	Wal-Mart de México	11.2	76	Ricoh Company	7.6
7	Nippon Steel	28.2	42	Tata Group	11.1	77	Lloyd's	7.6
8	Infosys Technologies	25.3	43	Nintendo Co.	11.0	78	Crédit Agricole	7.5
9	Rio Tinto	25.3	44	China Mobile	10.6	79	Ernst & Young Global	7.5
10	Mitsubishi UFJ Financial Group	21.3	45	Ericsson	10.3	80	GDF SUEZ	7.1
11	Teva Pharmaceuticals	20.5	46	Rogers Communications	9.9	81	Alcatel-Lucent	7.1
12	Imperial Tobacco	20.5	47	Kirin Holdings	9.7	82	Tesco PLC	7.1
13	IBERDROLA, S.A.	20.2	48	Carlsberg A/S	9.6	83	Novo Nordisk	6.9
14	Agrium Inc.	19.3	49	UniCredit	9.5	84	Celesio AG	6.8
15	Hyundai Motor	18.8	50	British Sky Broadcasting	9.5	85	Westpac Banking	6.5
16	Wipro Limited	18.4	51	Groupe Auchan	9.4	86	AXA	6.3
17	Transocean Ltd.	17.5	52	Tokio Marine	9.4	87	Grupo Bimbo	6.2
18	Nokia Corporation	17.4	53	Canon Inc.	9.3	88	Bertelsmann AG	6.2
19	MOL Magyar Olaj-és Gázipari	17.1	54	Nikon Corporation	9.3	89	LVMH	6.1
20	BNP Paribas	16.4	55	Pernod Ricard	9.1	90	Banco Santander	6.0
21	Petróleos de Venezuela	15.9	56	Toronto-Dominion Bank	9.0	91	Pricewaterhouse-Coopers	6.0
22	LG Corp.	15.7	57	Lloyds Banking Group	8.9	92	Royal Bank of Canada	5.9
23	Intesa Sanpaolo	15.3	58	Cap Gemini	8.8	93	ACS	5.8
24	FirstGroup plc	14.6	59	Japan Tobacco	8.8	94	Bank of China	5.8
25	Vale S.A.	14.5	60	Anheuser-Busch InBev	8.5	95	Woolworths Limited	5.7
26	Telenor ASA	14.0	61	Assicurazioni Generali	8.5	96	Komatsu Ltd.	5.7
27	Barclays PLC	13.4	62	KPMG International	8.3	97	Enel S.p.A.	5.6
28	Nomura Holdings	13.0	63	Telefónica, S.A.	8.2	98	E.ON AG	5.5
29	SOFTBANK CORP.	12.9	64	Vodafone	8.2	99	Bombardier Inc.	5.4
30	HOCHTIEF AG	12.7	65	PETROBRAS	8.1	100	Aisin Seiki	5.4
31	Roche Holding	12.6	66	BAE SYSTEMS	8.1			
32	TDK Corporation	12.5	67	Royal Bank of Scotland	8.1			
33	Christian Dior	12.4	68	Virgin Group	8.0			
34	Flextronics International	12.4	69	Haci Ömer Sabanci	8.0			
35	CEMEX	12.3	70	Deloitte Touche Tohmatsu	8.0			

*These rates are compounded annualized increases, and may have resulted from acquisitions or one-time gains. If less than 6 years of data are available, growth is for the years available.

SOURCE: HOOVER'S, INC., DATABASE, OCTOBER 2010

Forbes' 100 Largest Public Companies by Market Value

Rank	Company	Country	Market Value* ($ mil.)
1	PetroChina	China	333,840
2	ExxonMobil	US	308,770
3	Microsoft	US	254,520
4	ICBC	China	242,230
5	Wal-Mart Stores	US	205,370
6	China Mobile	Hong Kong/China	199,730
7	BHP Billiton	Australia/UK	192,450
8	Berkshire Hathaway	US	190,860
9	PETROBRAS	Brazil	190,340
10	Apple	US	189,510
11	Procter & Gamble	US	184,470
12	China Construction Bank	China	184,320
13	HSBC Holdings	UK	178,270
14	Johnson & Johnson	US	174,900
15	Nestlé	Switzerland	173,670
16	General Electric	US	169,650
17	Google	US	169,380
18	Royal Dutch Shell	Netherlands	168,630
19	Bank of America	US	167,630
20	BP	UK	167,130
21	IBM	US	167,010
22	JPMorgan Chase	US	166,190
23	AT&T	US	147,550
24	Bank of China	China	147,000
25	Chevron	US	146,230
26	Roche Holding	Switzerland	146,190
27	Vale	Brazil	145,140
28	Pfizer	US	143,230
29	Wells Fargo	US	141,690
30	Cisco Systems	US	140,850
31	Gazprom	Russia	132,580
32	Total	France	131,800
33	Sinopec-China Petroleum	China	130,060
34	Toyota Motor	Japan	127,100
35	Novartis	Switzerland	126,220
36	Oracle	US	123,980
37	Coca-Cola	US	122,790
38	Hewlett-Packard	US	121,330
39	China Life Insurance	China	118,750
40	Rio Tinto	UK/Australia	118,340
41	Merck & Co.	US	116,110
42	Intel	US	115,290
43	Vodafone	UK	112,260
44	Telefónica	Spain	108,190
45	Banco Santander	Spain	107,120
46	PepsiCo	US	99,580
47	Sanofi-Aventis	France	98,070
48	Citigroup	US	96,540
49	GlaxoSmithKline	UK	95,360
50	Samsung Electronics	South Korea	94,480
51	EDF Group	France	92,230
52	Philip Morris International	US	92,040
53	Unilever	Netherlands/UK	91,330
54	BNP Paribas	France	86,670
55	China Shenhua Energy	China	85,420
56	Goldman Sachs Group	US	84,950
57	Abbott Laboratories	US	84,290
58	GDF Suez	France	83,360
59	Rosneft	Russia	83,190
60	ENI	Italy	82,220
61	Verizon Communications	US	82,210
62	Anheuser-Busch InBev	Belgium	81,480
63	Siemens	Germany	80,070
64	Royal Bank of Canada	Canada	78,170
65	Commonwealth Bank	Australia	75,100
66	Schlumberger	Netherlands	73,490
67	Visa	US	73,120
68	ConocoPhillips	US	72,720
69	Statoil	Norway	72,260
70	Mitsubishi UFJ Financial	Japan	72,170
71	América Móvil	Mexico	72,090
72	Saudi Basic Industries	Saudi Arabia	71,200
73	Westpac Banking Group	Australia	70,990
74	Cnooc	Hong Kong/China	70,650
75	Reliance Industries	India	69,360
76	McDonald's	US	69,050
77	Nippon Telegraph & Telephone	Japan	68,680
78	British American Tobacco	UK	68,270
79	E.ON	Germany	68,260
80	Occidental Petroleum	US	65,570
81	United Technologies	US	65,280
82	AstraZeneca	UK	63,560
83	Honda Motor	Japan	63,220
84	L'Oréal Group	France	63,050
85	France Telecom	France	62,390
86	Walt Disney	US	61,170
87	Qualcomm	US	59,760
88	ArcelorMittal	Luxembourg	59,750
89	United Parcel Service	US	58,430
90	BG Group	UK	58,160
91	Sberbank	Russia	57,700
92	3M	US	57,350
93	Bank of Communications	China	57,340
94	Bayer Group	Germany	56,300
95	Deutsche Telekom	Germany	56,250
96	Teva Pharmaceutical Industries	Israel	56,190
97	Barclays	UK	56,150
98	Canon	Japan	55,800
99	Amgen	US	55,720
100	Toronto-Dominion Bank	Canada	55,430

*Most recent fiscal year as of March 1, 2010.

SOURCE: *FORBES*, APRIL 21, 2010

The *FORTUNE* Global 500

Rank	Company	Country	2009 Sales ($ mil.)
1	Wal-Mart Stores	US	408,214
2	Royal Dutch Shell	Netherlands	285,129
3	Exxon Mobil	US	284,650
4	BP	UK	246,138
5	Toyota Motor	Japan	204,106
6	Japan Post Holdings	Japan	202,196
7	Sinopec	China	187,518
8	State Grid	China	184,496
9	AXA	France	175,257
10	China National Petroleum	China	165,496
11	Chevron	US	163,527
12	ING Group	Netherlands	163,204
13	General Electric	US	156,779
14	Total	France	155,887
15	Bank of America Corp.	US	150,450
16	Volkswagen	Germany	146,205
17	ConocoPhillips	US	139,515
18	BNP Paribas	France	130,708
19	Assicurazioni Generali	Italy	126,012
20	Allianz	Germany	125,999
21	AT&T	US	123,018
22	Carrefour	France	121,452
23	Ford Motor	US	118,308
24	ENI	Italy	117,235
25	J.P. Morgan Chase & Co.	US	115,632
26	Hewlett-Packard	US	114,552
27	E.ON	Germany	113,849
28	Berkshire Hathaway	US	112,493
29	GDF Suez	France	111,069
30	Daimler	Germany	109,700
31	Nippon Telegraph & Telephone	Japan	109,656
32	Samsung Electronics	South Korea	108,927
33	Citigroup	US	108,785
34	McKesson	US	108,702
35	Verizon Communications	US	107,808
36	Crédit Agricole	France	106,538
37	Banco Santander	Spain	106,345
38	General Motors	US	104,589
39	HSBC Holdings	UK	103,736
40	Siemens	Germany	103,605
41	American International Group	US	103,189
42	Lloyds Banking Group	UK	102,967
43	Cardinal Health	US	99,613
44	Nestlé	Switzerland	99,114
45	CVS Caremark	US	98,729
46	Wells Fargo	US	98,636
47	Hitachi	Japan	96,593
48	International Business Machines	US	95,758
49	Dexia Group	Belgium	95,144
50	Gazprom	Russia	94,472
51	Honda Motor	Japan	92,400
52	Électricité de France	France	92,204
53	Aviva	UK	92,140
54	Petrobras	Brazil	91,869
55	Royal Bank of Scotland	UK	91,767
56	PDVSA	Venezuela	91,182
57	Metro	Germany	91,152
58	Tesco	UK	90,234
59	Deutsche Telekom	Germany	89,794
60	Enel	Italy	89,329
61	UnitedHealth Group	US	87,138
62	Société Générale	France	84,157
63	Nissan Motor	Japan	80,963
64	Pemex	Mexico	80,722
65	Panasonic	Japan	79,893
66	Procter & Gamble	US	79,697
67	LG	South Korea	78,892
68	Telefónica	Spain	78,853
69	Sony	Japan	77,696
70	Kroger	US	76,733
71	Groupe BPCE	France	76,464
72	Prudential	US	75,010
73	Munich Re Group	Germany	74,764
74	Statoil	Norway	74,000
75	Nippon Life Insurance	Japan	72,051
76	AmerisourceBergen	US	71,789
77	China Mobile Communications	China	71,749
78	Hyundai Motor	South Korea	71,678
79	Costco Wholesale	US	71,422
80	Vodafone	UK	70,899
81	BASF	Germany	70,461
82	BMW	Germany	70,444
83	Zurich Financial Services	Switzerland	70,272
84	Valero Energy	US	70,035
85	Fiat	Italy	69,639
86	Deutsche Post	Germany	69,427
87	Industrial & Commercial Bank of China	China	69,295
88	Archer Daniels Midland	US	69,207
89	Toshiba	Japan	68,731
90	Legal & General Group	UK	68,290
91	Boeing	US	68,281
92	U.S. Postal Service	US	68,090
93	Lukoil	Russia	68,025
94	Peugeot	France	67,297
95	CNP Assurances	France	66,556
96	Barclays	UK	66,533
97	Home Depot	US	66,176
98	Target	US	65,357
99	ArcelorMittal	Luxembourg	65,110
100	WellPoint	US	65,028

SOURCE: *FORTUNE*, JULY 26, 2010

The *FORTUNE* Global 500 (continued)

Rank	Company	Country	2009 Sales ($ mil.)	Rank	Company	Country	2009 Sales ($ mil.)
101	RWE	Germany	64,795	151	Intesa Sanpaolo	Italy	47,282
102	UniCredit Group	Italy	64,709	152	Lowe's	US	47,220
103	Aegon	Netherlands	64,506	153	Roche Group	Switzerland	47,109
104	SK Holdings	South Korea	64,396	154	Renault	France	46,858
105	France Télécom	France	63,860	155	PTT	Thailand	46,220
106	Walgreen	US	63,335	156	China Southern Power Grid	China	45,735
107	Petronas	Malaysia	62,577	157	United Parcel Service	US	45,297
108	Johnson & Johnson	US	61,897	158	Meiji Yasuda Life Insurance	Japan	45,262
109	State Farm Insurance Cos.	US	61,480	159	Lockheed Martin	US	45,189
110	Medco Health Solutions	US	59,804	160	Novartis	Switzerland	45,103
111	EADS	Netherlands	59,520	161	Dow Chemical	US	44,945
112	Hon Hai Precision Industry	Taiwan	59,324	162	Vinci	France	44,378
113	Deutsche Bank	Germany	58,998	163	GlaxoSmithKline	UK	44,240
114	Repsol YPF	Spain	58,571	164	Mitsui	Japan	44,120
115	Microsoft	US	58,437	165	Sears Holdings	US	44,043
116	China Construction Bank	China	58,361	166	Sumitomo Life Insurance	Japan	43,780
117	Itaúsa-Investimentos Itaú	Brazil	57,859	167	International Assets Holding	US	43,604
118	China Life Insurance	China	57,019	168	Bouygues	France	43,579
119	Dai-ichi Life Insurance	Japan	57,018	169	Sanofi-Aventis	France	43,405
120	Nokia	Finland	56,966	170	Bayer	Germany	43,322
121	Unilever	UK/Netherlands	55,352	171	PepsiCo	US	43,232
122	Groupe Auchan	France	55,141	172	Bunge	US	41,926
123	ThyssenKrupp	Germany	54,816	173	Rio Tinto Group	UK	41,825
124	Seven & I Holdings	Japan	54,701	174	MetLife	US	41,098
125	Indian Oil	India	54,288	175	Reliance Industries	India	41,085
126	Mitsubishi UFJ Financial Group	Japan	54,285	176	Safeway	US	40,851
127	AEON	Japan	54,092	177	Deutsche Bahn	Germany	40,774
128	Tokyo Electric Power	Japan	54,026	178	Supervalu	US	40,597
129	Robert Bosch	Germany	53,060	179	Kraft Foods	US	40,386
130	United Technologies	US	52,920	180	Foncière Euris	France	40,385
131	Dell	US	52,902	181	Telecom Italia	Italy	39,764
132	Saint-Gobain	France	52,521	182	Dongfeng Motor	China	39,402
133	China Railway Construction	China	52,044	183	UBS	Switzerland	39,356
134	Goldman Sachs Group	US	51,673	184	Royal Ahold	Netherlands	38,814
135	Banco Bradesco	Brazil	51,608	185	NEC	Japan	38,591
136	JX Holdings	Japan	51,405	186	Tokio Marine Holdings	Japan	38,458
137	China Railway Group	China	50,704	187	China State Construction Engineering	China	38,117
138	Fujitsu	Japan	50,399	188	Centrica	UK	37,927
139	BHP Billiton	Australia	50,211	189	Vivendi	France	37,712
140	Pfizer	US	50,009	190	Freddie Mac	US	37,614
141	Agricultural Bank of China	China	49,742	191	Nippon Steel	Japan	37,563
142	Best Buy	US	49,694	192	Wesfarmers	Australia	37,466
143	Bank of China	China	49,682	193	KDDI	Japan	37,073
144	Marathon Oil	US	49,403	194	Sysco	US	36,853
145	Veolia Environnement	France	49,142	195	Itochu	Japan	36,798
146	Mitsubishi	Japan	48,913	196	Anheuser-Busch InBev	Belgium	36,758
147	A.P. Møller-Mærsk Group	US	48,824	197	Apple	US	36,537
148	Banco do Brasil	Brazil	48,122	198	Woolworths	Australia	36,523
149	Banco Bilbao Vizcaya Argentaria	Spain	48,074	199	Walt Disney	US	36,149
150	Credit Suisse	Switzerland	47,658	200	Cisco Systems	US	36,117

The FORTUNE Global 500 (continued)

Rank	Company	Country	2009 Sales ($ mil.)	Rank	Company	Country	2009 Sales ($ mil.)
201	Mitsubishi Electric	Japan	36,116	251	Swiss Reinsurance	Switzerland	30,745
202	Comcast	US	35,756	252	China National Offshore Oil	China	30,680
203	Sinochem Group	China	35,577	253	JFE Holdings	Japan	30,634
204	China Telecommunications	China	35,557	254	Citic Group	China	30,605
205	FedEx	US	35,497	255	News Corp.	US	30,423
206	Marubeni	Japan	35,326	256	Sberbank	Russia	30,394
207	Northrop Grumman	US	35,291	257	Mizuho Financial Group	Japan	30,346
208	Manulife Financial	Canada	35,144	258	China FAW Group	China	30,237
209	Intel	US	35,127	259	Landesbank Baden-Württemberg	Germany	30,062
210	Aetna	US	34,764	260	HCA	US	30,052
211	Rosneft Oil	Russia	34,695	261	Edeka Zentrale	Germany	29,976
212	DZ Bank	Germany	34,633	262	Alliance Boots	Switzerland	29,848
213	Commerzbank	Germany	34,611	263	Softbank	Japan	29,762
214	SNCF	France	34,585	264	Sharp	Japan	29,682
215	Scottish & Southern Energy	UK	34,357	265	Air France-KLM Group	France	29,644
216	Canon	Japan	34,292	266	Sunoco	US	29,630
217	Iberdrola	Spain	34,136	267	Hess	US	29,569
218	Sumitomo Mitsui Financial Group	Japan	34,104	268	Ingram Micro	US	29,515
219	Franz Haniel	Germany	34,087	269	América Móvil	Mexico	29,233
220	Old Mutual	UK	34,072	270	Fannie Mae	US	29,065
221	New York Life Insurance	US	34,014	271	Power Corp. of Canada	Canada	29,050
222	BT Group	UK	33,860	272	POSCO	South Korea	28,883
223	Shanghai Automotive	China	33,629	273	Koç Holding	Turkey	28,845
224	China Communications Construction	China	33,465	274	Time Warner	US	28,842
225	Rabobank	Netherlands	33,396	275	China South Industries Group	China	28,757
226	AstraZeneca	UK	32,804	276	Baosteel Group	China	28,591
227	Prudential Financial	US	32,688	277	Idemitsu Kosan	Japan	28,560
228	Royal Bank of Canada	Canada	32,610	278	Volvo	Sweden	28,551
229	Caterpillar	US	32,396	279	La Poste	France	28,532
230	Sprint Nextel	US	32,260	280	Johnson Controls	US	28,497
231	Royal Philips Electronics	Netherlands	32,232	281	Cathay Life Insurance	Taiwan	28,315
232	Denso	Japan	32,060	282	State Bank of India	India	28,213
233	Allstate	US	32,013	283	Kansai Electric Power	Japan	28,074
234	General Dynamics	US	31,981	284	Delta Air Lines	US	28,063
235	Danske Bank Group	Denmark	31,851	285	George Weston	Canada	28,009
236	J. Sainsbury	UK	31,828	286	Poste Italiane	Italy	27,935
237	ABB	US	31,797	287	Continental	Germany	27,932
238	BAE Systems	UK	31,773	288	Standard Life	UK	27,803
239	Mitsubishi Heavy Industries	Japan	31,674	289	Bridgestone	Japan	27,750
240	Morgan Stanley	US	31,515	290	Alstom	France	27,739
241	Nippon Mining Holdings	Japan	31,512	291	Delhaize Group	Belgium	27,732
242	Noble Group	China	31,183	292	East Japan Railway	Japan	27,720
243	Liberty Mutual Insurance Group	US	31,094	293	Sabic	Saudi Arabia	27,481
244	Sumitomo	Japan	31,063	294	Merck	US	27,428
245	Coca-Cola	US	30,990	295	Medipal Holdings	Japan	27,421
246	Lufthansa Group	Germany	30,972	296	DuPont	US	27,328
247	Humana	US	30,960	297	Tyson Foods	US	27,165
248	Honeywell International	US	30,908	298	Commonwealth Bank of Australia	Australia	27,162
249	LyondellBasell Industries	Netherlands	30,829	299	Mitsubishi Chemical Holdings	Japan	27,088
250	Abbott Laboratories	US	30,765	300	GS Holdings	South Korea	27,066

Rank	Company	Country	2009 Sales ($ mil.)
301	L.M. Ericsson	Sweden	26,997
302	Hutchison Whampoa	China	26,938
303	Vattenfall	Sweden	26,857
304	American Express	US	26,730
305	National Australia Bank	Australia	26,708
306	Korea Electric Power	South Korea	26,640
307	Bharat Petroleum	India	26,596
308	Suzuki Motor	Japan	26,592
309	PPR	France	26,534
310	Finmeccanica	Italy	26,335
311	TIAA-CREF	US	26,278
312	COFCO	China	26,098
313	China Huaneng Group	China	26,019
314	Hebei Iron & Steel Group	China	25,924
315	China Metallurgical Group	China	25,868
316	Samsung Life Insurance	South Korea	25,805
317	CHS	US	25,730
318	TNK-BP Holding	Russia	25,696
319	Rite Aid	US	25,669
320	Westpac Banking	Australia	25,623
321	KFW Bankengruppe	Germany	25,582
322	Hochtief	Germany	25,563
323	Groupama	France	25,539
324	Cepsa	Spain	25,526
325	Enterprise GP Holdings	US	25,511
326	GasTerra	Netherlands	25,449
327	Quanta Computer	Taiwan	25,429
328	Massachusetts Mutual Life Insurance	US	25,424
329	T&D Holdings	Japan	25,299
330	Aviation Industry Corp. of China	China	25,189
331	Philip Morris International	US	25,035
332	China Minmetals	China	24,956
333	OMV Group	Austria	24,904
334	Raytheon	US	24,881
335	Express Scripts	US	24,749
336	Hartford Financial Services	US	24,701
337	Travelers Cos.	US	24,680
338	Christian Dior	France	24,665
339	Publix Super Markets	US	24,515
340	Amazon.com	US	24,509
341	Wolseley	UK	24,461
342	L'Oréal	France	24,286
343	Staples	US	24,276
344	William Morrison Supermarkets	UK	24,263
345	Bayerische Landesbank	Germany	24,255
346	ACS	Spain	24,245
347	Sun Life Financial	Canada	24,160
348	China North Industries Group	China	24,150
349	CRH	Ireland	24,148
350	Flextronics International	Singapore	24,111
351	Chubu Electric Power	Japan	24,110
352	Sinosteel	China	24,014
353	Wilmar International	Singapore	23,885
354	Hindustan Petroleum	India	23,881
355	Google	US	23,651
356	Shenhua Group	China	23,605
357	Mapfre Group	Spain	23,526
358	Hanwha	South Korea	23,521
359	Fujifilm Holdings	Japan	23,497
360	Macy's	US	23,489
361	KBC Group	Belgium	23,376
362	International Paper	US	23,366
363	Vale	Brazil	23,311
364	Mazda Motor	Japan	23,306
365	Ageas	Belgium/Netherlands	23,254
366	Oracle	US	23,252
367	Norddeutsche Landesbank	Germany	23,201
368	China United Network Communications	China	23,183
369	Accenture	US	23,171
370	3M	US	23,123
371	People's Insurance Co. of China	China	23,116
372	Deere	US	23,112
373	Cosmo Oil	Japan	23,068
374	Migros	Switzerland	22,976
375	Hyundai Heavy Industries	South Korea	22,926
376	Maruhan	Japan	22,843
377	Imperial Tobacco Group	UK	22,760
378	McDonald's	US	22,745
379	Xstrata	Switzerland	22,732
380	Schlumberger	US	22,702
381	Heraeus Holding	Germany	22,545
382	Jardine Matheson	China	22,501
383	Ping An Insurance	China	22,374
384	National Grid	UK	22,331
385	Suncor Energy	Canada	22,327
386	Alfresa Holdings	Japan	22,179
387	British American Tobacco	UK	22,157
388	Aisin Seiki	Japan	22,127
389	Tech Data	US	22,100
390	Lafarge	France	22,078
391	Motorola	US	22,063
392	Bertelsmann	Germany	22,036
393	Fluor	US	21,990
394	Schneider Electric	France	21,952
395	China Resources National	China	21,902
396	Eli Lilly	US	21,836
397	Huawei Technologies	China	21,821
398	PKN Orlen Group	Poland	21,797
399	Australia & New Zealand Banking	Australia	21,778
400	Onex	Canada	21,758

The *FORTUNE* Global 500 (continued)

Rank	Company	Country	2009 Sales ($ mil.)
401	Toronto-Dominion Bank	Canada	21,733
402	Ricoh	Japan	21,716
403	Yamada Denki	Japan	21,714
404	Coca-Cola Enterprises	US	21,645
405	Bristol-Myers Squibb	US	21,634
406	Energie Baden-Württemberg	Germany	21,634
407	Showa Shell Sekiyu	Japan	21,612
408	Northwestern Mutual	US	21,603
409	Nordea Bank	Sweden	21,600
410	Tata Steel	India	21,582
411	DIRECTV	US	21,565
412	China Datang Group	China	21,460
413	Oil & Natural Gas	India	21,448
414	Bank of Nova Scotia	Canada	21,428
415	Jiangsu Shagang Group	China	21,419
416	Japan Tobacco	Japan	21,335
417	MS & AD Insurance Group Holdings	Japan	21,139
418	Alcatel-Lucent	France	21,068
419	Standard Chartered Group	UK	20,941
420	Emerson Electric	US	20,915
421	Anglo American	UK	20,858
422	Danone	France	20,824
423	Nationwide	US	20,751
424	Compass Group	UK	20,747
425	Gas Natural Fenosa	Spain	20,681
426	Michelin	France	20,581
427	Adecco	Switzerland	20,567
428	Wuhan Iron & Steel	China	20,543
429	Kirin Holdings	Japan	20,503
430	Heineken Holding	Netherlands	20,491
431	Compal Electronics	Taiwan	20,448
432	Premafin Finanziaria	Italy	20,424
433	TJX	US	20,288
434	CPC	Taiwan	20,253
435	AMR	US	19,917
436	Aluminum Corp. of China	China	19,851
437	Sodexo	France	19,818
438	Sumitomo Electric Industries	Japan	19,778
439	Fresenius	Germany	19,687
440	Bank of Communications	China	19,568
441	AREVA	France	19,548
442	Tata Motors	India	19,501
443	U.S. Bancorp	US	19,490
444	Co-operative Group	UK	19,477
445	NKSJ Holdings	Japan	19,470
446	Holcim	Switzerland	19,462
447	GMAC	US	19,403
448	Bombardier	Canada	19,366
449	TUI	Germany	19,344
450	Akzo Nobel	Netherlands	19,311
451	PNC Financial Services Group	US	19,231
452	Formosa Petrochemical	Taiwan	19,204
453	Nike	US	19,176
454	Murphy Oil	US	19,138
455	Kimberly-Clark	US	19,115
456	Eiffage	France	18,958
457	Henkel	Germany	18,866
458	Telstra	Australia	18,824
459	Royal KPN	Netherlands	18,777
460	Sistema	Russia	18,750
461	Alcoa	US	18,745
462	Suzuken	Japan	18,692
463	Boehringer Ingelheim	Germany	18,630
464	Plains All American Pipeline	US	18,520
465	Asustek Computer	Taiwan	18,474
466	Erste Group Bank	Austria	18,468
467	Cigna	US	18,414
468	Nippon Yusen	Japan	18,281
469	Aflac	US	18,254
470	Evonik Industries	Germany	18,175
471	Ultrapar Holdings	Brazil	18,064
472	Gruppo Mediolanum	Italy	18,057
473	Kobe Steel	Japan	17,997
474	Tohoku Electric Power	Japan	17,915
475	Thales Group	France	17,905
476	Skanska	Sweden	17,887
477	China Guodian	China	17,871
478	Time Warner Cable	US	17,868
479	Sanyo Electric	Japan	17,850
480	Fomento de Construcciones	Spain	17,652
481	Kajima	Japan	17,635
482	Cie Nationale à Portefeuille	Belgium	17,571
483	United Services Automobile Association	US	17,558
484	J.C. Penney	US	17,556
485	Sumitomo Chemical	Japan	17,458
486	Strabag	Austria	17,447
487	Acer	Taiwan	17,380
488	Magna International	Canada	17,367
489	Daiwa House Industry	Japan	17,339
490	MAN Group	Germany	17,320
491	Exelon	US	17,318
492	Tyco International	Switzerland	17,240
493	Coop	Switzerland	17,238
494	Randstad Holding	Netherlands	17,235
495	Kohl's	US	17,178
496	JBS	Brazil	17,161
497	Shimizu	Japan	17,117
498	Whirlpool	US	17,099
499	Suez Environnement	France	17,091
500	Dai Nippon Printing	Japan	17,053

BusinessWeek's Information Technology 100

Rank	Company	Country	Revenue ($ mil.)	Rank	Company	Country	Revenue ($ mil.)
1	BYD	China	5,777	50	Symantec	US	61
2	Apple	US	42,905	51	MasterCard	US	5,099
3	Tencent Holdings	China	1,821	52	American Tower	US	1,724
4	Amazon.com	US	24,509	53	Genpact	Bermuda	1,120
5	Tata Consultancy	India	6,096	54	Bharti Airtel	India	8,181
6	Priceline.com	US	2,338	55	Totvs	Brazil	501
7	CenturyLink	US	4,974	56	Misys	UK	1,136
8	Cognizant Tech.	US	3,279	57	Dolby Laboratories	US	720
9	Infosys Technologies	India	4,754	58	Red Hat	US	653
10	SOFTBANK	Japan	26,709	59	Itochu Techno-Solutions	Japan	3,070
11	WPG Holdings	Taiwan	5,960	60	FLIR Systems	US	1,147
12	MediaTek	Taiwan	3,499	61	Expedia	US	2,955
13	NTT Data	Japan	11,382	62	Rackspace Hosting	US	629
14	Rakuten	Japan	3,192	63	Atheros Communications	US	542
15	Nintendo	Japan	18,371	64	Phison Electronics	Taiwan	741
16	Samsung Electro-Mechanics	South Korea	4,374	65	Telecom Argentina	Argentina	3,282
17	Wipro	India	5,632	66	Hon Hai Precision	Taiwan	59,341
18	China Mobile	Hong Kong	66,178	67	Intuit	US	3,183
19	Yahoo Japan	Japan	2,655	68	Simplo Technology	Taiwan	1,037
20	Oracle	US	23,252	69	Vistaprint	Bermuda	516
21	Research In Motion	Canada	11,065	70	United Internet	Germany	2,313
22	Google	US	23,651	71	Inmarsat	UK	1,038
23	MphasiS	India	875	72	Capcom	Japan	919
24	Netflix	US	1,670	73	Automatic Data Processing	US	8,867
25	KDDI	Japan	34,947	74	Factset Research	US	622
26	Visa	US	6,911	75	Tw Telecom	US	1,211
27	Baidu	China	651	76	BMC Software	US	1,872
28	ZTE	China	8,823	77	CACI International	US	2,730
29	Lender Processing	US	2,371	78	Flextronics	Singapore	30,949
30	Verizon	US	107,808	79	Shanda Interactive	China	768
31	Fidelity National Information Services	US	3,770	80	Cree	US	567
32	Harris	US	5,005	81	Solera Holdings	US	558
33	Singapore Telecommunications	Singapore	10,392	82	Akamai Technologies	US	860
34	HCL Technologies	India	2,153	83	NII Holdings	US	4,398
35	Freenet	Germany	5,091	84	McAfee	US	1,927
36	Telenet Group	Belgium	1,670	85	LKQ	US	2,048
37	Synnex Technology International	Taiwan	6,685	86	Jardine Cycle	Singapore	10,640
38	Salesforce.com	US	1,077	87	Redecard	Brazil	1,228
39	Software	Germany	1,182	88	Tripod Technology	Taiwan	1,012
40	China Greatwall	China	3,318	89	Vivo	Brazil	8,293
41	Global Payments	US	1,602	90	Aisino	China	1,085
42	Nomura Research	Japan	3,410	91	Yamatake	Japan	2,360
43	Equinix	US	883	92	Autodesk	US	2,315
44	SAIC	US	10,070	93	Chicony Electronics	Taiwan	1,634
45	Kingboard Chemical	Hong Kong	3,067	94	ManTech International	US	2,020
46	Check Point Software	Israel	924	95	B2W Varejo	Brazil	1,922
47	Autonomy	UK	740	96	CA Technologies	Brazil	4,271
48	Crown Castle International	US	1,685	97	Vmware	US	2,024
49	Computer Science	US	16,740	98	Positivo	Brazil	1,100
50	Fiberhome Telecom	China	681	99	KONAMI	Japan	3,095

Note: Rank based on shareholder return, return on equity, revenue growth, and total revenue (revenue for the most recent four quarters available; most recent FY for those companies that do not report quarterly results).

SOURCE: *BUSINESSWEEK*, APRIL 30, 2010

The World's 100 Largest Public Financial Companies

Rank	Company	Country	Assets* ($ mil.)	Rank	Company	Country	Assets ($ mil.)
1	BNP Paribas	France	2,952,220	51	Aegon	Netherlands	428,460
2	Royal Bank of Scotland	UK	2,727,940	52	ANZ Banking	Australia	420,520
3	HSBC Holdings	UK	2,355,830	53	Banco do Brasil	Brazil	406,460
4	Crédit Agricole	France	2,227,220	54	Resona Holdings	Japan	400,470
5	Bank of America	US	2,223,300	55	Bank of Communications	China	392,830
6	Barclays	UK	2,223,040	56	Manulife Financial	Canada	379,500
7	Deutsche Bank	Germany	2,150,600	57	CNP Assurances	France	376,120
8	JPMorgan Chase	US	2,031,990	58	Zurich Financial Services	Switzerland	366,660
9	Mitsubishi UFJ Financial	Japan	1,999,580	59	Prudential	UK	361,500
10	Citigroup	US	1,856,650	60	Bank of Montreal	Canada	360,620
11	ING Group	Netherlands	1,667,620	61	CIC Group	France	351,150
12	Lloyds Banking Group	UK	1,650,780	62	Deutsche Postbank	Germany	325,120
13	Mizuho Financial	Japan	1,538,940	63	SEB-Skand Enskilda Bank	Sweden	323,280
14	Société Générale Group	France	1,468,720	64	Canadian Imperial Bank	Canada	316,510
15	UniCredit Group	Italy	1,438,910	65	DnB NOR	Norway	315,610
16	Banco Santander	Spain	1,438,680	66	Hartford Financial Services	US	307,720
17	ICBC	China	1,428,460	67	Svenska Handelsbanken	Sweden	297,270
18	UBS	Switzerland	1,288,190	68	Berkshire Hathaway	US	297,120
19	Wells Fargo	US	1,243,650	69	Banca MPS	Italy	292,220
20	Commerzbank	Germany	1,202,990	70	Munich Re	Germany	284,210
21	Sumitomo Mitsui Financial	Japan	1,202,590	71	Banco Bradesco	Brazil	281,400
22	China Construction Bank	China	1,106,200	72	US Bancorp	US	281,180
23	AXA Group	France	1,016,700	73	Erste Bank	Austria	278,900
24	Bank of China	China	1,016,310	74	PNC Financial Services	US	269,860
25	Credit Suisse Group	Switzerland	988,910	75	Old Mutual	UK	263,580
26	Intesa Sanpaolo	Italy	877,660	76	Bank of Ireland	Ireland	256,980
27	Fannie Mae	US	869,140	77	State Bank of India Group	India	256,790
28	Goldman Sachs Group	US	849,000	78	Swedbank	Sweden	251,180
29	American International Group	US	847,590	79	Allied Irish Banks	Ireland	249,260
30	Freddie Mac	US	841,780	80	Nomura Holdings	Japan	248,090
31	Allianz	Germany	834,040	81	Standard Life	UK	236,740
32	Dexia	Belgium	828,740	82	Woori Finance Holdings	South Korea	230,520
33	Morgan Stanley	US	771,460	83	China Merchants Bank	China	230,000
34	Natixis	France	769,480	84	Swiss Re Group	Switzerland	221,500
35	BBVA-Banco Bilbao Vizcaya	Spain	760,390	85	Sberbank	Russia	220,620
36	Nordea Bank	Sweden	729,060	86	Sumitomo Trust & Banking	Japan	213,850
37	Royal Bank of Canada	Canada	608,050	87	Banque Nationale de Belgique	Belgium	212,960
38	Generali Group	Italy	607,370	88	KB Financial Group	South Korea	212,400
39	Danske Bank Group	Denmark	597,030	89	Bank of New York Mellon	US	212,220
40	National Australia Bank	Australia	574,410	90	Shinhan Financial	South Korea	208,990
41	Aviva	UK	559,710	91	Deutsche Boerse	Germany	202,770
42	MetLife	US	539,310	92	Landesbank Berlin	Germany	200,800
43	Westpac Banking Group	Australia	519,030	93	Sun Life Financial	Canada	192,100
44	Toronto-Dominion Bank	Canada	517,280	94	Shanghai Pudong Development Bank	China	191,500
45	Commonwealth Bank	Australia	500,200	95	Banco Popular Español	Spain	185,500
46	Prudential Financial	US	480,200	96	SNS Reaal	Netherlands	184,220
47	Legal & General Group	UK	479,640	97	DBS Group	Singapore	184,120
48	KBC Group	Belgium	462,660	98	Lincoln National	US	177,430
49	Bank of Nova Scotia	Canada	460,930	99	SunTrust Banks	US	174,160
50	Standard Chartered Group	UK	435,560	100	China Citic Bank	China	173,840

*Most recent fiscal year as of March 1, 2010.

SOURCE: *FORBES*, APRIL 21, 2010

The World's Top 20 Technology Hardware Companies

Rank	Company	Country	2009 Revenue ($ mil.)
1	Hewlett-Packard	US	116,920
2	Hitachi	Japan	102,700
3	Panasonic	Japan	79,750
4	Sony	Japan	79,390
5	Toshiba	Japan	68,340
6	Hon Hai Precision Industry	Taiwan	59,290
7	Nokia	Finland	58,720
8	Dell	US	52,900
9	Fujitsu	Japan	48,200
10	Apple	US	46,710
11	NEC	Japan	43,290
12	Cisco Systems	US	35,530
13	Ingram Micro	US	29,520
14	Flextronics International	Singapore	29,280
15	Sharp	Japan	29,240
16	Ericsson	Sweden	28,830
17	Quanta Computer	Taiwan	24,890
18	Tech Data	US	22,100
19	Motorola	US	22,040
20	Alcatel-Lucent	France	21,140

SOURCE: *FORBES*, APRIL 21, 2010

The World's Top 20 Consumer Durables Manufacturers

Rank	Company	Country	2009 Revenue ($ mil.)
1	Toyota Motor	Japan	210,840
2	Ford Motor	US	118,310
3	Daimler	Germany	110,060
4	Honda Motor	Japan	102,820
5	Nissan Motor	Japan	86,650
6	Porsche	Germany	81,310
7	BMW Group	Germany	74,090
8	Fiat Group	Italy	71,780
9	Peugeot Groupe	France	69,370
10	Hyundai Motor	South Korea	63,950
11	Renault	France	47,010
12	Denso	Japan	32,280
13	Suzuki Motor	Japan	30,860
14	Volvo Group	Sweden	30,490
15	Johnson Controls	US	29,570
16	Continental	Germany	28,790
17	Bridgestone	Japan	27,940
18	Mazda Motor	Japan	26,040
19	Aisin Seiki	Japan	22,740
20	Michelin Group	France	20,650

SOURCE: *FORBES*, APRIL 21, 2010

The World's Top 20 Telecommunications Companies

Rank	Company	Country	2009 Revenue ($ mil.)
1	AT&T	US	123,020
2	Verizon Communications	US	107,810
3	Nippon Telegraph & Telephone	Japan	106,980
4	Deutsche Telekom	Germany	90,080
5	Telefónica	Spain	79,110
6	China Mobile	Hong Kong/China	66,220
7	France Télécom	France	65,920
8	Vodafone	UK	58,350
9	Telecom Italia	Italy	42,000
10	KDDI	Japan	35,920
11	Sprint Nextel	US	32,260
12	BT Group	UK	30,430
13	América Móvil	Mexico	30,220
14	Softbank	Japan	27,450
15	China Telecom	China	27,420
16	China Unicom (HK)	Hong Kong/China	21,600
17	Telstra	Australia	20,480
18	Royal KPN	Netherlands	19,270
19	BCE	Canada	16,920
20	Telenor	Norway	16,850

SOURCE: *FORBES*, APRIL 21, 2010

The World's Top 20 Marketing Organizations

Rank	Company	Headquarters	2009 Revenue ($ mil.)
1	WPP	Dublin	13,600
2	Omnicom Group	New York	11,720
3	Publicis Groupe	Paris	6,290
4	Interpublic Group of Cos.	New York	6,030
5	Dentsu	Tokyo	3,110
6	Aegis Group	London	2,110
7	Havas	Suresnes, France	2,010
8	Hakuhodo DY Holdings	Tokyo	1,520
9	Acxiom Corp.	Little Rock, AR	750
10	MDC Partners	Toronto	546
11	Alliance Data Systems (Epsilon)	Dallas	514
12	Asatsu-DK	Tokyo	451
13	Edelman	Chicago	440
14	Media Consulta	Berlin	401
15	Photon Group	Sydney	366
16	Sapient Corp. (SapientNitro)	Boston	356
17	Groupe Aeroplan (Carlson Marketing)	Montreal	351
18	IBM Corp. (IBM Interactive)	Armonk, NY	322
19	Cheil Worldwide	Seoul	312
20	Grupo ABC	São Paulo	277

SOURCE: *ADVERTISING AGE*, APRIL 26, 2010

The World's Top 10 Aerospace and Defense Companies

Rank	Company	Country	2009 Revenue ($ mil.)
1	Boeing	US	68,280
2	EADS	Netherlands	61,440
3	Lockheed Martin	US	45,190
4	Northrop Grumman	US	33,760
5	BAE Systems	UK	32,910
6	General Dynamics	US	31,980
7	Raytheon	US	24,880
8	Finmeccanica	Italy	20,940
9	Bombardier	Canada	19,440
10	Thales	France	17,960

SOURCE: *FORBES*, APRIL 21, 2010

The World's Top 10 Oil and Gas Operations

Rank	Company	Country	2009 Revenue ($ mil.)
1	Royal Dutch Shell	Netherlands	278,190
2	ExxonMobil	US	275,560
3	BP	UK	239,270
4	Sinopec-China Petroleum	China	208,470
5	Total	France	160,680
6	Chevron	US	159,290
7	PetroChina	China	157,220
8	ConocoPhillips	US	136,020
9	ENI	Italy	121,010
10	Gazprom	Russia	115,250

SOURCE: *FORBES*, APRIL 21, 2010

The World's Top 10 Software and Services Companies

Rank	Company	Country	2009 Revenue ($ mil.)
1	IBM	US	95,760
2	Microsoft	US	58,690
3	Google	US	23,650
4	Oracle	US	23,230
5	Accenture	Ireland	22,450
6	Computer Sciences	US	16,000
7	SAP	Germany	15,290
8	Capgemini	France	11,990
9	Yahoo	US	6,460
10	Symantec	US	5,920

SOURCE: *FORBES*, APRIL 21, 2010

The World's Top 10 Utilities

Rank	Company	Country	2009 Revenue ($ mil.)
1	E.ON	Germany	117,380
2	GDF Suez	France	114,650
3	EDF Group	France	95,170
4	ENEL	Italy	91,870
5	RWE Group	Germany	66,570
6	Tokyo Electric Power	Japan	60,470
7	Veolia Environnement	France	49,500
8	Scottish & Southern	UK	36,170
9	Iberdrola	Spain	35,150
10	Centrica	UK	34,390

SOURCE: *FORBES*, APRIL 21, 2010

The World's Top 10 Drug and Biotechnology Companies

Rank	Company	Country	2009 Revenue ($ mil.)
1	McKesson	US	108,280
2	Cardinal Health	US	101,660
3	AmerisourceBergen	US	73,760
4	Johnson & Johnson	US	61,900
5	Pfizer	US	50,010
6	Roche Holding	Switzerland	47,350
7	GlaxoSmithKline	UK	45,830
8	Novartis	Switzerland	44,270
9	Sanofi-Aventis	France	41,990
10	AstraZeneca	UK	32,800

SOURCE: *FORBES*, APRIL 21, 2010

The World's Top 10 Chemical Companies

Rank	Company	Country	2009 Revenue ($ mil.)
1	BASF	Germany	72,630
2	Dow Chemical	US	44,880
3	Bayer Group	Germany	43,460
4	Mitsubishi Chemical	Japan	29,880
5	Saudi Basic Industries	Saudi Arabia	27,490
6	EI du Pont de Nemours	US	27,330
7	Akzo Nobel	Netherlands	19,900
8	Sumitomo Chemical	Japan	18,370
9	Air Liquide	France	17,160
10	Linde	Germany	16,090

SOURCE: *FORBES*, APRIL 21, 2010

Forbes' "Richest People in the World" by Net Worth

Rank	Name	Age	Net Worth ($ bil.)	Country	What
1	Carlos Slim Helú & family	70	53.5	Mexico	Telecom
2	William Gates III	54	53.0	US	Microsoft
3	Warren Buffett	79	47.0	US	Berkshire Hathaway
4	Mukesh Ambani	52	29.0	India	Petrochemicals, oil, and gas
5	Lakshmi Mittal	59	28.7	UK	Steel
6	Lawrence Ellison	65	28.0	US	Oracle
7	Bernard Arnault	61	27.5	France	LVMH
8	Eike Batista	53	27.0	Brazil	Mining, oil
9	Amancio Ortega	74	25.0	Spain	Zara
10	Karl Albrecht	90	23.5	Germany	Aldi
11	Ingvar Kamprad & family	83	23.0	Switzerland	Ikea
12	Christy Walton & family	55	22.5	US	Wal-Mart
13	Stefan Persson	62	22.4	Sweden	Hennes & Mauritz
14	Li Ka-shing	81	21.0	Hong Kong	Diversified
15	Jim Walton	62	20.7	US	Wal-Mart
16	Alice Walton	60	20.6	US	Wal-Mart
17	Liliane Bettencourt	87	20.0	France	L'Oréal
18	S. Robson Walton	66	19.8	US	Wal-Mart
19	Prince Alwaleed Bin Talal Alsaud	55	19.4	Saudi Arabia	Investments
20	David Thomson & family	52	19.0	Canada	Inheritance
21	Michael Otto & family	66	18.7	Germany	Retail
22	Lee Shau Kee	82	18.5	Hong Kong	Real estate
23	Michael Bloomberg	68	18.0	US	Bloomberg
24	Sergey Brin	36	17.5	US	Google
24	Charles Koch	74	17.5	US	Manufacturing, energy
24	David Koch	69	17.5	US	Manufacturing, energy
24	Larry Page	37	17.5	US	Google
28	Michele Ferrero & family	83	17.0	Monaco	Chocolates
28	Kwok family	—	17.0	Hong Kong	Real estate
28	Azim Premji	64	17.0	India	Software
31	Theo Albrecht	88	16.7	Germany	Aldi, Trader Joe's
32	Vladimir Lisin	53	15.8	Russia	Steel
33	Steven Ballmer	54	14.5	US	Microsoft
33	Robert Kuok	86	14.5	Hong Kong	Diversified
35	George Soros	79	14.0	US	Hedge funds
36	Anil Ambani	50	13.7	India	Diversified
37	Paul Allen	57	13.5	US	Microsoft, investments
37	Michael Dell	45	13.5	US	Dell
39	Mikhail Prokhorov	44	13.4	Russia	Investments
40	Birgit Rausing & family	86	13.0	Switzerland	Packaging
40	Shashi & Ravi Ruia	66	13.0	India	Diversified
42	Mikhail Fridman	45	12.7	Russia	Oil, banking, telecom
43	Jeffrey Bezos	46	12.3	US	Amazon
44	Savitri Jindal	60	12.2	India	Steel
45	Donald Bren	77	12.0	US	Real estate
45	Gerald Cavendish Grosvenor & family	58	12.0	UK	Real estate
45	John Paulson	54	12.0	US	Hedge funds
48	Abigail Johnson	48	11.5	US	Fidelity
48	Jorge Paulo Lemann	70	11.5	Brazil	Beer
50	Roman Abramovich	43	11.2	Russia	Steel, investments

SOURCE: *FORBES*, MARCH 10, 2010

The World's Top 50 Most Admired Companies

Rank	Company	Country	Rank	Company	Country	Rank	Company	Country
1	Apple	US	21	Costco Wholesale	US	41	Nokia	Finland
2	Google	US	22	BMW	Germany	42	Samsung Electronics	South Korea
3	Berkshire Hathaway	US	22	Target	US	43	Deere	US
4	Johnson & Johnson	US	24	Nike	US	44	L'Oréal	France
5	Amazon.com	US	25	PepsiCo	US	45	AT&T	US
6	Procter & Gamble	US	26	Starbucks	US	46	Lowe's	US
7	Toyota Motor	Japan	27	Singapore Airlines	Singapore	47	General Mills	US
8	Goldman Sachs Group	US	28	Exxon Mobil	US	48	Marriott International	US
9	Wal-Mart Stores	US	29	American Express	US	49	DuPont	US
10	Coca-Cola	US	30	Nordstrom	US	50	Volkswagen	Germany
11	Microsoft	US	31	Intel	US			
12	Southwest Airlines	US	32	Hewlett-Packard	US			
13	FedEx	US	33	UPS	US			
14	McDonald's	US	34	Nestlé	Switzerland			
15	IBM	US	35	Caterpillar	US			
16	General Electric	US	36	Honda Motor	Japan			
17	3M	US	37	Best Buy	US			
18	J.P. Morgan Chase	US	38	Sony	Japan			
19	Walt Disney	US	39	Wells Fargo	US			
20	Cisco Systems	US	40	eBay	US			

SOURCE: *FORTUNE*, MARCH 22, 2010

Hoover's Handbook of

World Business

The Companies

ABB Ltd

You could be forgiven for thinking that ABB is short for A Bunch of Businesses — though that bunch has evolved over some 130 years. ABB engineers power and automation technologies for a broad base of utility, industrial, and commercial customers. Its lines run from robots to light switches. Power products include transmission and distribution components, as well as turnkey substation systems. Automation technologies are used to monitor and control equipment and processes in industrial plants and utilities. ABB has established a presence in about 100 countries, with its core businesses concentrated in power and automation markets.

ABB is shopping for bargain-priced acquisitions (clipped by the economic recession) to boost its product offerings, operations, and geographic reach. In mid-2010 the company acquired K-TEK, a maker of level detection technology used in the oil and gas industry, as well as water and other industries.

Earlier in 2010, ABB purchased Ventyx from Vista Equity Partners. Valued at around $1 billion, the investment scoops up software for managing asset-intensive businesses engaged in the utility, energy, and communications industries. Ventyx joins ABB's network management business and creates an energy management software solutions unit, considerably widening the opportunities for ABB in the utility enterprise management market.

On its heels, ABB has committed $150 million to build up its semiconductor facility based in Lenzburg, Switzerland. As part of the initiative, ABB purchased Polovodice AS, a Czech power semiconductor manufacturer.

In 2009 ABB acquired the assets of Sinai Engineering, a designer and provider of services for electrical generation and transmission systems planning, as well as construction management. ABB also picked up South Africa's Westingcorp (Pty) Ltd. The move ramps up ABB's line of power capacitors and opens the door to local and global electric utilities and mining markets.

HISTORY

Asea Brown Boveri (ABB) was formed in 1988 when two giants, ASEA AB of Sweden and BBC Brown Boveri of Switzerland, combined their electrical engineering and equipment businesses. Percy Barnevik, head of ASEA, became CEO.

ASEA was born in Stockholm in 1883 when Ludwig Fredholm founded Electriska Aktiebolaget to manufacture an electric dynamo created by engineer Jonas Wenstrom. In 1890 the company merged with Wenstrom's brother's firm to form Allmanna Svenska Electriska Aktiebolaget (ASEA), a pioneer in industrial electrification. Early in the 1900s ASEA began its first railway electrification project. By the 1920s it was providing locomotives and other equipment to Sweden's national railway, and by the next decade ASEA was one of Sweden's largest electric equipment manufacturers. In 1962 it bought 20% of appliance maker Electrolux. ASEA created the nuclear power venture ASEA-ATOM with the Swedish government in 1968 and bought full control in 1982.

BBC Brown Boveri was formed in 1891 as the Brown, Boveri, and Company partnership between Charles Brown and Walter Boveri in Baden, Switzerland. It made power generation equipment and produced the first steam turbines in Europe in 1900. BBC entered Germany (1893), France (1894), and Italy (1903) and diversified into nuclear power equipment after WWII.

By 1988 BBC, the bigger company, had a West German network that ASEA, the more profitable company, coveted. Both had US joint ventures. In an unusual merger, ASEA (which became ABB AB) and BBC (later ABB AG) continued as separate entities sharing equal ownership of ABB. Barnevik crafted a unique decentralized management structure under which national subsidiaries were closely linked to their local customers and labor forces. In six years ABB took over more than 150 companies worldwide.

In 1995 ABB merged its transportation segment into Adtranz (a joint venture with Daimler-Benz) to form the world's #1 maker of trains. In 1997 Barnevik gave up the title of CEO, remaining as chairman, and was succeeded by Göran Lindahl, an engineer who had worked his way up the ranks at ASEA. (Barnevik remained chairman until 2001.)

In 1999 ABB acquired Elsag Bailey, a Dutch maker of industrial control systems, for about $1.5 billion, and sold its 50% stake in Adtranz to DaimlerChrysler for about $472 million. ABB and France's ALSTOM combined their power generation businesses to form the world's largest power plant equipment maker. That year ABB AB and ABB AG were at last united under a single stock through holding company ABB Ltd.

ABB scaled back its power plant-related activities in 2000. The company sold its nuclear power business to BNFL for $485 million and its 50% stake in ABB Alstom Power to ALSTOM for $1.2 billion. In 2001 Lindahl resigned and Jörgen Centerman, head of the company's automation business, replaced him.

With economic slowdowns occurring in the company's key markets, ABB announced plans in July 2001 to cut 12,000 jobs, or about 8% of its workforce, over 18 months. Later that year, amid rising numbers of asbestos claims against US subsidiary Combustion Engineering, ABB took a $470 million fourth-quarter charge to cover asbestos liabilities. The claims charged asbestos exposures stemming from products supplied before the mid-1970s by Combustion Engineering, which ABB had acquired in 1990.

In early 2002 ABB found itself embroiled in controversy after revealing not only a record loss but also payments of large pensions to former chairman Barnevik and former chief executive Lindahl. The former executives agreed that year to return a part (about $82 million) of their pension payouts to ABB. That year the company, which faced $4.4 billion in debts after industry slumps had affected its sales of power systems and equipment, industrial automation, and controls, agreed to sell part of its financial services unit to GE Commercial Finance for $2.3 billion.

The day after the company sold its structured finances unit, ABB's chief executive, Jörgen Centerman, resigned and was replaced by the chairman, Jürgen Dormann.

In 2003, as part of its settlement with asbestos plaintiffs, ABB placed Combustion Engineering into bankruptcy. ABB also sold its upstream oil, gas, and petrochemicals unit to Candover Partners, 3i, and J.P. Morgan Partners for $925 million in 2004. Sulzer CEO Fred Kindle succeeded Dormann as ABB's CEO in 2005. (Dormann remained chairman until his retirement in 2007.)

Kindle left ABB in 2008 due to what the company called "irreconcilable differences." Former GE Healthcare CEO Joe Hogan became CEO.

EXECUTIVES

Chairman: Hubertus von Grünberg, age 68
CEO: Joseph M. (Joe) Hogan, age 53, $5,668,287 total compensation
CFO: Michel Demare
Group SVP and Chief Counsel Corporate and Finance: Richard A. Brown
Group SVP and Head Investor Relations: Michel Gerber, age 42
General Counsel: Diane de Saint Victor, age 55, $2,460,061 total compensation
Executive Committee Member, Process Automation: Veli-Matti Reinikkala, age 53, $2,197,596 total compensation
Executive Committee Member, Power Products Division: Bernhard Jucker, age 56, $2,749,290 total compensation
Executive Committee Member, Power Systems Division: Peter Leupp, age 59, $2,738,873 total compensation
Executive Committee Member, Marketing And Customer Solutions: Brice Koch, age 46
Head of Human Resources: Gary Steel, age 57, $2,369,823 total compensation
Head of Discrete Automation and Motion: Ulrich Spiesshofer, age 46, $2,817,246 total compensation
Head Low Voltage Products: Tarak Mehta
Region Manager, North America: Enrique Santacana
VP Corporate Communications and Investor Relations: Julie Lenzner
Auditors: Ernst & Young Ltd.

LOCATIONS

HQ: ABB Ltd
Affolternstrasse 44
8050 Zurich, Switzerland
Phone: 41-43-317-7111   **Fax:** 41-43-317-4420
US HQ: 12040 Regency Pkwy., Cary, NC 06851
US Phone: 203-750-2200   **US Fax:** 203-750-2263
Web: www.abb.com

2009 Sales

	$ mil.	% of total
Europe	13,093	41
Asia	8,684	27
Americas	6,049	19
Middle East & Africa	3,969	13
Total	**31,795**	**100**

PRODUCTS/OPERATIONS

2009 Sales

	$ mil.	% of total
Power Products	9,370	29
Automation Products	7,897	25
Process Automation	7,150	23
Power Systems	6,356	20
Robotics	959	3
Corporate & other	63	—
Total	**31,795**	**100**

Selected Products

Automation Products
 Breakers
 Control products
 DIN-rail components
 Drives
 Enclosures
 Generators
 Instrumentation
 Low-voltage switchgear
 Motors
 Power electronics systems
 Switches
 Wiring accessories
Power Products
 Circuit breakers for all current and voltage levels
 High- and medium-voltage switchgear and apparatus
 Power and distribution transformers
 Sensors

Power Systems
  Power plant automation and electrification solutions
  Transmission and distribution systems
Process Automation
  Automation products and solutions
  Controls
  Industry-specific application knowledge and services
  Plant optimization
Robotics
  Industrial robots
  Industrial software products
  Robot contollers and software

COMPETITORS

ALSTOM	Kawasaki Heavy Industries
AREVA	KUKA
Baldor Electric	Legrand
Bharat Heavy Electricals	Metso
Cooper Industries	Mitsubishi Heavy
Crompton Greaves	Industries
Dürr	Rockwell Automation
Danaher	Schneider Electric
Emerson Electric	Siemens AG
Endress + Hauser	SPX
FANUC	Toshiba
GE	Voith
Hitachi	WEG Indústrias
Honeywell International	Yaskawa Electric
Invensys	Yokogawa Electric

HISTORICAL FINANCIALS

Company Type: Public

Income Statement

FYE: December 31

	REVENUE ($ mil.)	NET INCOME ($ mil.)	NET PROFIT MARGIN	EMPLOYEES
12/09	31,795	3,136	9.9%	116,000
12/08	34,912	3,118	8.9%	120,000
12/07	29,183	3,757	12.9%	112,000
12/06	24,412	1,390	5.7%	108,200
12/05	22,442	740	3.3%	103,500
Annual Growth	9.1%	43.5%	—	2.9%

2009 Year-End Financials

Debt ratio: 15.8%
Return on equity: 25.1%
Cash ($ mil.): 7,119
Current ratio: 1.73
Long-term debt ($ mil.): 2,172

No. of shares (mil.): 2,284
Dividends
  Yield: 2.3%
  Payout: 34.6%
Market value ($ mil.): 43,623

Stock History

NYSE: ABB

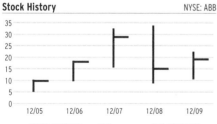

	STOCK PRICE ($) FY Close	P/E High/Low		PER SHARE ($) Earnings	Dividends	Book Value
12/09	19.10	17	9	1.27	0.44	6.04
12/08	15.01	25	7	1.36	0.45	4.89
12/07	28.80	20	10	1.63	0.20	4.80
12/06	17.98	29	16	0.63	0.10	2.64
12/05	9.72	27	15	0.36	—	1.53
Annual Growth	18.4%	—	—	37.0%	63.9%	41.1%

Accor SA

Accor est l'hospitalité. The hospitality company Accor is one of the world's leading hotel operators, owning or managing more than 4,000 properties in nearly 100 countries throughout the world. It serves travelers through upscale brand Sofitel; midscale Novotel, Mercure, and Suitehotel; and economy chains Ibis and all seasons. In addition, budget brand Motel 6 (part of Accor North America) boasts more than 1,000 properties, most of which are franchised. Accor also operates a handful of additional hotel brands. Edenred, formerly the Accor services unit that offered prepaid vouchers, separated from the hotel company in 2010.

Accor split its hotel and services divisions into two separate businesses in 2010 after a long decline in Accor's stock price. The move came in response to shareholder concerns about the struggling hotel division weighing down Accor's growing services operation. Following the demerger, former Accor CFO Jacques Stern was installed as head of Edenred, while CEO Gilles Pélisson continues to oversee the hotel business.

Accor's hospitality division had accounted for about 75% of revenue before the split, and had been experiencing declining revenue, culminating in a net loss for the company in 2009. As part of its turnaround strategy, Accor has been focused primarily on disposals to reduce its adjusted net debt by €2 billion by 2013. The company sold nearly 160 F1 budget hotels (formerly called Formule 1) for €272 million ($398 million) in 2009. Then, in 2010 it announced plans to dispose of 450 hotels over the next three years to further cut costs and reduce debt. It is also shedding noncore assets; it sold its Compagnie des Wagons-Lits onboard rail catering business in 2010.

The strategy appears to be working, as Accor in mid-2010 reported stronger performance for the first half of the year. It posted an increase in revenues, as well as a narrowing of its net loss. It experienced a net loss of €64 million ($81 million), up from a loss of €236 million ($380 million) during the same period in 2009. The company is benefitting from its cost-cutting efforts, as well as from an increased demand for rooms outside of the US after the previous year's crash.

For future hotel growth, meanwhile, in 2010 Accor announced plans to invest €1.4 billion ($1.8 billion) in building new hotels over the next five years. Much of this growth is focused on expansion in Asia. Accor wants to be the number one international operator of hotels in India, with 90 hotels in the country by 2015.

Private equity fund Colony Capital is Accor's largest shareholder, with a nearly 30% stake. Colony's CEO Tom Barrak sits on Accor's board.

HISTORY

Until Gérard Pélisson and Paul Dubrule built their first hotel in 1967, French hotels were generally quaint old inns or expensive luxury hotels. Pélisson and Dubrule's Novotel introduced mid-priced hotels based on the American model. The pair opened the Ibis Hotel in 1973 and bought the Mercure chain in 1975. By 1979, when it opened its first US hotel in Minneapolis, Novotel was Europe's #1 hotel chain, operating 184 hotels on four continents.

Dubrule and Pélisson married their growing hotel business to Jacques Borel International,

forming publicly traded Accor in 1983. Jacques Borel had started out with one restaurant in 1957 and was Europe's #1 restaurateur by 1975, when he took over Belgium's Sofitel chain of luxury hotels. Losses in the hotel game prompted Borel to sell Sofitel to Dubrule and Pélisson in 1980, making their company one of the world's top 10 hotel operators — a list traditionally dominated by US chains. They picked up the rest of Borel's empire in 1983, launching Accor into the restaurant business.

Accor began offering packaged vacations in 1984, after buying a majority stake in Africatours (Africa's largest tour operator), then expanded into the South Pacific, Asia, and the Americas by buying Islands in the Sun (1986), Asietours (1987), and Americatours (1987).

The company opened its first budget hotels (Formule 1) in France in 1985. Accor started marketing Paquet cruises in 1986 and formed the Hotelia and Parthenon chains (Brazilian residential hotels) the next year.

Faced with a mature European market and eager to take advantage of favorable exchange rates, Accor bought Dallas-based budget chain Motel 6 (along with its high debts and poor reputation, which Accor began remedying with an expensive renovation program) in 1990. The next year Accor bought US-based Regal Inns (now part of Motel 6).

Also in 1990 Accor joined Société Générale de Belgique to buy 26.7% of Belgium's Wagons-Lits, owner of about 300 hotels in Europe, Thailand, and Indonesia, as well as restaurants, caterers, and travel agencies in Europe. After a battle involving both Belgian and EC antitrust officials, Accor was allowed to buy a majority stake of Wagons-Lits (later called Wagonlit Travel).

This buy — along with Accor's attempt to increase its share of the luxury market, the continuing burden of its US purchases, and a recession in the travel business — took a financial toll. In response, it began selling assets in 1994, ridding itself of expensive hotel real estate. The company also joined with US-based Carlson Companies to form a joint travel venture called Carlson Wagonlit Travel.

In 1997 co-chairmen Dubrule and Pélisson retired from active management and were succeeded by Jean-Marc Espalioux, formerly of Générale des Eaux (now Vivendi Universal). As part of its strategy to continue to expand internationally, Accor reached an agreement that year with the Moroccan government to develop that country's hotel industry. In 1999 Accor continued hotel acquisitions with US chain Red Roof Inns and hotels in Finland, France, the Netherlands, Poland, and Sweden.

The following year the company opened a luxury Sofitel hotel in downtown Manhattan and began developing other Sofitels in Dallas, Chicago, and Washington, DC. It also sold its EuropCar stake to Volkswagen. In 2001 Accor announced plans for a 370-room Sofitel in the high-tech center of Shenyang, China. Early in 2002 Accor bought a 22% stake in Compagnie Européenne de Casinos, an operator of 24 casinos mostly in France, in a bid to buy out the company. However, after a two-month bidding war with competitor Groupe Partouche, Accor sold its stake to Partouche. Also in 2002 the company acquired a 30% stake in Dorint AG, a German hotel group.

Accor acquired a 29% stake in resorts operator Club Méditerranée (Club Med) in 2004. Later that year it merged its casino operations with Société Hôtelière de la Chaîne Lucien Barrière and

Société des Hôtels et Casinos de Deauville to form Group Lucien Barrière, with Accor holding a 30% stake in the new business. US-based investment firm Colony Capital made a $1.3 billion investment in Accor the following year.

Accor sold its stake in Carlson Wagonlit in 2006. In 2007 the company sold its Red Roof Inns chain, and the following year it sold its stake in Club Med. Accor split its hotel and services divisions into two separate businesses in 2010.

EXECUTIVES

Chairman and CEO: Gilles Pélisson, age 53
Vice Chairman: Philippe Citerne, age 61
Deputy CEO, Accor Services and Finance: Jacques Stern, age 46
COO, Accor Hospitality Americas: Michael Flaxman
COO, Accor Hospitality Europe, Middle East, and Africa; CEO, Sofitel Worldwide: Yann Caillère, age 57
EVP Accor Hospitality Marketing and Distribution: Jean-Luc Chrétien, age 54
EVP Global Human Resources: Patrick Ollivier, age 56
SVP Media Relations: Charlotte Thouvard
SVP Corporate Communications and External Relations: Armelle Volkringer
SVP Marketing and Brands Development: Frederic Josenhans
SVP Investor Relations and Financial Communication: Anthony Mellor
Corporate Secretary: Pascal Quint, age 52
CEO, Lenôtre: Patrick Scicard
CEO, Club Méditerranée: Henri Giscard d'Estaing, age 53
COO, Accor North America and CEO, Motel 6/Studio 6: Olivier Poirot, age 42
COO, Accor Latin America: Roland Bonadona
COO, Accor Asia/Pacific: Michael Issenberg
Auditors: Ernst & Young et Autres

LOCATIONS

HQ: Accor SA
  2, rue de la Mare-Neuve
  91021 Évry, France
Phone: 33-1-69-36-80-80   **Fax:** 33-1-69-36-79-00
US HQ: 4001 International Pkwy., Carrollton, TX 75007
US Phone: 972-360-9000   **US Fax:** 972-360-5821
Web: www.accor.com

2009 Sales

	% of total
Europe	
France	37
Other	38
North America	9
Latin America	8
Other regions	8
Total	**100**

PRODUCTS/OPERATIONS

2009 Sales

	% of total
Hotels	74
Pre-paid services	13
Other	13
Total	**100**

Selected Hotel Brands

All Seasons
Etap Hotel
hotelF1
Ibis
Mercure
Motel 6
Novotel
Pullman
Sofitel
Suitehotel

COMPETITORS

Best Western
Carlson Hotels
Choice Hotels
Four Seasons Hotels
Hyatt
InterContinental Hotels
La Quinta
Marriott
Millennium & Copthorne Hotels
NH Hoteles
Société du Louvre
Sol Meliá
Starwood Hotels & Resorts
Wyndham Worldwide

HISTORICAL FINANCIALS

Company Type: Public

Income Statement

FYE: December 31

	REVENUE ($ mil.)	NET INCOME ($ mil.)	NET PROFIT MARGIN	EMPLOYEES
12/09	9,991	(380)	—	1,190
12/08	10,726	864	8.1%	158,162
12/07	11,812	1,342	11.4%	172,695
12/06	9,938	705	7.1%	170,000
12/05	8,956	431	4.8%	168,623
Annual Growth	**2.8%**	**—**	**—**	**(71.0%)**

2009 Year-End Financials

Debt ratio: —
Return on equity: —
Cash ($ mil.): 1,668
Current ratio: 0.76
Long-term debt ($ mil.): —

No. of shares (mil.): 226
Dividends
  Yield: 6.1%
  Payout: —
Market value ($ mil.): 8,726

Stock History

Euronext Paris: AC

	STOCK PRICE ($) FY Close	P/E High	P/E Low	PER SHARE ($) Earnings	PER SHARE ($) Dividends	PER SHARE ($) Book Value
12/09	38.63	—	—	(1.81)	2.36	20.65
12/08	34.88	15	7	3.65	8.88	20.62
12/07	56.74	14	10	5.56	—	24.05
12/06	54.58	19	14	2.86	—	23.94
12/05	38.78	22	15	1.79	—	22.55
Annual Growth	**(0.1%)**	**—**	**—**	**—**	**(73.4%)**	**(2.2%)**

Acer Incorporated

Acer has more than one PC brand up its sleeve. The company is a leading manufacturer of notebook, desktop, and netbook computers. Other Acer products include servers, storage systems, smart phones, projectors, LCD televisions, digital cameras, and computer displays. The company also provides IT support services, and its Acer eDC facility is the largest stand-alone data center in Asia. Acer, which outsources its manufacturing, sells through resellers and distributors worldwide. In addition to Acer-branded equipment, the company oversees the Gateway, eMachines, and Packard Bell brands. Acer gets about half of its sales in Europe.

The company has significantly expanded its global footprint with acquisitions. Following the purchases of Gateway (2007) and Packard Bell (2008), it trails only Hewlett-Packard in the worldwide PC market.

Acer has maintained a multi-brand strategy that targets specific consumer groups. The Acer brand is targeted toward tech-savvy users; Gateway and Packard Bell computers are designed for brand-conscious consumers in the US and EMEA region, respectively; eMachines is aimed at buyers for whom value is the predominant factor.

Following an industry trend, Acer has developed a line of netbook computers. Larger than a traditional handheld computer but smaller than a notebook PC, netbooks have become a popular choice for users who want a relatively inexpensive computer with limited functionality (primarily Internet access) in a highly portable form factor.

Looking to build on its traditional computer business with mobile devices, Acer acquired E-TEN, a Taiwan-based developer of smart phones, in 2008. E-TEN markets products under its own brand and designs devices for OEMs. In 2009 Acer unveiled a line of Windows-based smart phones with touchscreens.

HISTORY

Acer founder and chairman Stan Shih, respected enough for his business acumen to once be considered for the premiership of Taiwan, designed that country's first desktop calculator in the early 1970s. The company's precursor, Multitech International, was launched in 1976 with $25,000 by Shih and four others who called themselves the "Gardeners of Microprocessing." In 1980 Multitech introduced the Dragon Chinese-language terminal, which won Taiwan's top design award; in 1983 it introduced an Apple clone and its first IBM-compatible PC. Multitech set up AcerLand, Taiwan's first and largest franchised computer retail chain, in 1985.

The company changed its name to Acer (the Latin word for "sharp, acute, able, and facile") in 1987 and went public on the Taiwan exchange the next year. Acer got into the semiconductor market in 1989 when it entered into a joint venture with Texas Instruments (named TI-Acer) to design and develop memory chips in Taiwan. In 1990 Acer's US subsidiary, Acer America, paid $90 million for Altos Computer Systems, a US manufacturer of UNIX systems.

During the prosperous 1980s Acer increased its management layers and slowed the decision-making process. In late 1990 the company restructured, trimming its workforce by 8% (about

400 employees), including two-thirds of headquarters. The layoff was unprecedented — being asked to resign from a job in Taiwan carries a social stigma. Shih wrote a letter to all those affected, explaining the plight of the company. The following year Acer began its decentralization plan to create a worldwide confederation of publicly owned companies.

Acer suffered its first loss in 1991 on revenues of almost $1 billion, partly because of increased marketing budgets in the US and Europe and continuing investment in TI-Acer. The company bounced back in 1993, with 80% of its profit coming from that joint venture.

The Aspire PC, available in shades of gray and green, was unveiled in 1995. In 1996 the company expanded into consumer electronics, introducing a host of new, inexpensive videodisc players, video telephones, and other devices in order to boost global market share. In 1997 Acer purchased TI's notebook computer business. A slowdown in memory chip sales, plus a financial slide at Acer America, cost the firm $141 million, but Acer finished the year in the black.

Shih stepped down as president in 1998 to focus on restructuring. The company ended its venture with TI, buying TI's 33% stake and renaming the unit Acer Semiconductor Manufacturing. The company also began making information appliances, introducing a device able to play CD-ROMs via TV sets and perform other task-specific functions. Continued losses due to a highly competitive US market caused a drop in profits for 1998.

In 1999 Acer sold a 30% stake in its struggling Acer Semiconductor Manufacturing affiliate to Taiwan Semiconductor Manufacturing Company. (TSMC completed its purchase of the remaining 70% of the business, which was renamed TSMC-Acer Semiconductor Manufacturing, the following year.) The competitive heat and the rise of under-$1,000 PCs took a toll that year when Acer cut US jobs, streamlined operations, and withdrew from the US retail market. The company intensified its focus on providing online software, hardware, and support for users, launching a digital services business and a venture capital operation to invest in promising Internet startups.

The company suffered a financial blow in 2000 when large customer IBM cancelled an order for desktop computers. Late that year, after continued losses in a slowing PC market, the company announced it would cut more jobs in the US and Germany and close an unspecified number of plants worldwide.

Acer saw major streamlining in 2001, when it spun off its contract manufacturing operations (renamed Wistron), as well as its consumer electronics and peripherals business (renamed BenQ). Slumping sales in a weakening computer hardware market prompted Acer's restructuring efforts. In addition to clarifying the structure of Acer's sizable operations, the separation of Acer's branded operations and Wistron served to eliminate possible customer concerns about a conflict of interest between the two businesses.

In 2005 president J. T. Wang succeeded Shih as CEO. In 2007 Acer sold its electronic components distribution subsidiary, Sertek, to Yosun Industrial. It also acquired Gateway for $710 million that year. President Gianfranco Lanci took over for Wang as CEO in 2008.

EXECUTIVES

Chairman: J. T. Wang
President, CEO, and Director: Gianfranco Lanci
CFO: Che-Min Tu
SVP; President, ITGO: Jim Wong
SVP; President, SHBG: Aymar de Lencqueaing
SVP and Director; Deputy President, EMEA:
  Walter Deppeler
VP, ITGO: Jackson Lin
VP, ITGO: Towny Huang
VP, EBG: Michael Wang
VP, ITGO: Wayne Ma
VP, EBG: Angelina Hwang
VP, ITGO: Campbell Kan
VP; President, ETBG: Simon Hwang
VP; President, Acer China: Oliver Ahrens, age 45
VP; President, AP: Steve Lin
VP; President, TWN Operation: Scott Lin
VP; President, CBG: James Chiang
VP, Marketing and Branding: Gianpiero Morbello
Associate Director, Investor Relations: Andrew Chang
Director, Product Marketing: Adrian Storp
Manager, Marketing and Communications: Eric Chuang
Auditors: KPMG

LOCATIONS

HQ: Acer Incorporated
8F, 88, Sec. 1, Hsin Tai Wu Rd.
Hsichih, Taipei 221, Taiwan
Phone: 886-2-696-1234   **Fax:** 886-2-696-3535
US HQ: 333 W. San Carlos St., Ste. 1500
  San Jose, CA 95110
US Phone: 408-533-7700   **US Fax:** 408-533-4555
Web: www.acer-group.com/public

2009 Sales

	% of total
Europe	50
North America	26
Asia	18
Taiwan	6
Total	**100**

PRODUCTS/OPERATIONS

Selected Products

Computers (desktop, handheld, notebook, server, tablet)
Digital cameras
Digital projectors
LCD televisions
Monitors (cathode-ray tube and liquid-crystal display)
Smart phones

COMPETITORS

Apple Inc.	NEC
ASUSTeK	Nikon
Canon	Nokia
Dell	Palm, Inc.
Founder Holdings	Panasonic Corp
Fujitsu	Research In Motion
Hewlett-Packard	Samsung Electronics
Hitachi	Sharp Electronics
HTC Corporation	Siemens AG
IBM	Sony
Lenovo	Sony Ericsson Mobile
LG Electronics	Tatung
MEDION	Toshiba
MiTAC Technology	TriGem
Motorola	

HISTORICAL FINANCIALS

Company Type: Public

Income Statement

FYE: December 31

	REVENUE ($ mil.)	NET INCOME ($ mil.)	NET PROFIT MARGIN	EMPLOYEES
12/09	17,805	352	2.0%	6,624
12/08	16,645	358	2.1%	6,727
12/07	14,209	399	2.8%	5,251
12/06	10,763	314	2.9%	5,964
12/05	9,690	258	2.7%	—
Annual Growth	**16.4%**	**8.1%**	**—**	**3.6%**

2009 Year-End Financials

Debt ratio: —	No. of shares (mil.): 2,689
Return on equity: —	Dividends
Cash ($ mil.): 1,663	Yield: 2.1%
Current ratio: 1.29	Payout: 46.2%
Long-term debt ($ mil.): —	Market value ($ mil.): 8,025

Stock History

Taiwan: ACER

	STOCK PRICE ($) FY Close	P/E High/Low		PER SHARE ($) Earnings	Dividends	Book Value
12/09	2.98	23	9	0.13	0.06	1.07
12/08	1.29	15	8	0.14	0.09	0.93
12/07	1.93	14	10	0.17	—	0.88
12/06	2.04	19	9	0.13	—	0.84
Annual Growth	**13.5%**	**—**	**—**	**0.0%**	**(33.3%)**	**8.4%**

ACS

Turning the rains (and the wind) on the plains of Spain into electricity provides the current for growth at ACS Actividades de Construcción y Servicios, one of Spain's largest construction and infrastructure groups. ACS Group operates in four primary business areas: construction, energy, industrial services, and environment and logistics. Activities include civil engineering, installation and maintenance for the energy sector, transport services, and highway management. ACS has grown by investing in such firms as former construction rival Dragados and Germany-based infrastructure giant HOCHTIEF. ACS Group is active in more than 50 countries, mainly in Europe and Latin America.

The group's largest arm is its construction segment. It is engaged in civil, commercial, and residential building, including roads, railways, parking garages, sports facilities, and hospitals. ACS focuses on public-private partnership arrangements for jobs such as public protection housing developments. ACS's concessions unit develops, designs, builds, and maintains infrastructure projects, primarily in Europe and North America. International contracts represent about a quarter of ACS's business.

ACS expanded its construction business in 2009 by acquiring US builder Pulice Construction. The Phoenix-based firm specializes in large public works projects, particularly roads and highways, and is a prime contractor for the Arizona Department of Transportation.

Through Urbaser, Clece Services, and Dragados, the group provides facility management, waste management, and port and logistics chain services. It offers cleaning and management for facilities including health care centers, hotels, office buildings, schools, and courthouses. Industrial services include applied engineering, construction, and maintenance for the energy and communications sectors. The group develops such projects as wind farms and solar energy plants as well as traditional power stations and toll systems.

Other investments include a 29% stake in Abertis, one of the largest infrastructure companies in Europe, and a 12% stake in energy company IBERDROLA.

In 2009 ACS sold its controlling stake in electric utility Unión Fenosa to pay down debts incurred through its investments in HOCHTIEF and IBERDROLA. In 2010 ACS bid to increase its stake in HOCHTIEF from about 30% to more than 50% — it ultimately wants to buy the firm outright.

The global recession hurt construction firms as projects dried up or customers struggled to keep up with payments. ACS was no exception, and it began looking for other noncore assets to sell. It announced plans to sell port operator Dragados Servicios Portuarios y Logisticos to a group of investors for some €720 million (approximately $952 million) in 2010.

HISTORY

In war-torn Europe in 1942, the Spanish construction company Obras y Construcciones Industriales (Ocisa) was born. The company soon began a 50-year association with Spain's hydroelectric industry, marked by the completion of the dam and reservoir project Presa de Bachimana in 1950. The company built nine more dam and reservoir projects in Spain (including Presa de la Llosa, completed in 1997).

As the demand for public works projects decreased and competition increased, Spanish constructors began working abroad, especially in Latin America, where in 1975 Ocisa was contracted to create an irrigation tunnel in Venezuela's Andes.

A six-year economic expansion measured by the success of Spain's "Big Seven" construction companies, including #5 Ocisa, reached its end in 1992 when the Spanish government, the country's biggest builder, was forced to cut spending on infrastructure. This triggered consolidation in Spain's construction industry, including Ocisa's 1993 acquisition of Construcciones Padros, in which Ocisa held a 25% stake. Adopting the new name OCP Construcciones, it also absorbed the assets of its installation and assembly subsidiary, Compania de la Distribucion de Electricidad (Grupo Cobra).

The slowdown in public works projects continued and companies sought additional pooling of resources and diversification of activities at home and abroad. In 1996 OCP bought a 40% stake in the state-owned construction firm Auxini, increased to 100% a year later. Also in 1997 the OCP

group, led by its president, Florentino Perez, acquired Gines Navarro Construcciones, controlled (79%) by the powerful investment group led by brothers Carlos and Juan March. The two companies combined to create Spain's third-largest construction group, Actividades de Construcciones y Servicios, or Grupo ACS.

Perez became chairman of the new group and promised to make it Spain's most profitable public construction company through further diversification, international contracts, and selective investment in real estate. Grupo March, which now controlled about 37% of ACS, joined with OCP shareholders, including former vice president Juan Torres and the Roa family, to offer a portion of their shares on the market, yet retained 50% of the new company among themselves. A public offering of shares in ACS was completed that year following a 4-for-1 share split. ACS began restructuring, placing its construction activities, including Auxini, under its subsidiary Puertos y Obras. In 1998 ACS was first listed on the IBEX-35 index of top Spanish companies.

Grupo ACS benefited from a boom in construction work in Spain led by liberalization of the energy markets and continued international growth, especially in Latin America.

ACS further diversified into transportation in 1999 with the purchase of Continental Auto, a Spanish passenger coach company. The next year the group joined Finnish telecommunications firm Sonera and France's Vivendi to form a consortium to operate under one of Spain's third-generation wireless phone licenses. ACS and Sonera agreed in 2001 to form a new venture to explore additional markets in Europe and the US for 3G wireless operations.

In 2002 ACS took a major step toward expanding further by acquiring the 24% controlling stake in rival Dragados from Banco Santander Central Hispano. The next year Dragados accepted a bid by ACS for another 10% of its shares and the two companies merged to create one of Spain's largest construction companies.

The company acquired a 50% stake in Brazilian port authority Terminal de Santa Catarina for €25.5 million in 2006. ACS has invested further in international port terminals, particularly in Brazil and India.

EXECUTIVES

Chairman and CEO, ACS, Actividades de Construcción y Servicios: Florentino Pérez Rodríguez, age 62
Executive Vice Chairman: Antonio García Ferrer, age 64
Vice Chairman: Pablo Vallbona Vadell
Chairman, Vías y Construcciones: Manuel Pérez Beato
Chairman and CEO Construction, Environment & Logistics and Concesisons; Chairman and CEO Dragados: Marcelino Fernández Verdes
Chairman and CEO, Iridium: Manuel García Buey
Chairman and CEO, Clece: Cristóbal Valderas Alvarado
Chairman and CEO, Services, Communications and Energy; Chairman and CEO of Cobra and Chairman of Etra and Imesapi: Eugenio Llorente Gómez
Chairman and CEO, Urbaser:
Javier Polanco Gómez-Lavín
Chairman Sice Technology and Systems, Dragados Industrial: Juan Enrique Ruiz González
CEO, Geocisa: Alejandro Canga Botteghelz
CEO, Semi and Maessa: Daniel Vega Baladrón
CEO, Vías y Construcciones, SA:
Gonzalo Gomez-Zamalloa Baraibar
CEO, Seis: Botteghelz Canga Botteghelz
CEO Initec, Intecsa and Makiber:
Raúl Llamazares de la Puente

Secretary General, ACS Services, Communications and Energy: José Romero de Ávila González-Albo
Secretary General of Construction, Environment & Logistics and Concesisons: Luis Nogueira Miguelsanz
General Manager, Dragados: Ignacio Segura Surinach
General Manager, Tecsa: José María Aguirre Fernández
Secretary: Jose Luis del Valle Perez
Finance Manager: Jose Zornoza Soto
Director Investments and Management Control:
Christina Aldamiz-Echevarria Gonzalez de Durana
Auditors: Deloitte SL

LOCATIONS

HQ: ACS, Actividades de Construcción y Servicios, S.A.
Avenida Pío XII, No. 102
28036 Madrid, Spain
Phone: 34-91-343-92-00   **Fax:** 34-91-343-94-56
Web: www.grupoacs.com

PRODUCTS/OPERATIONS

2009 Sales

	% of total
Industrial services	43
Construction	39
Environment	17
Concessions	1
Total	**100**

COMPETITORS

Abengoa
Acciona
Aker Solutions
Andrade Gutierrez
Balfour Beatty
Bechtel
Bilfinger Berger
Black & Veatch
Brisa
Cintra
DP World
FCC Barcelona
Ferrovial
Grupo San José
Hyundai Engineering and Construction
Impregilo
Kellogg Brown & Root UK
Odebrecht
OHL
Skanska
TECNOCOM
VINCI

HISTORICAL FINANCIALS

Company Type: Public

Income Statement

FYE: December 31

	REVENUE ($ mil.)	NET INCOME ($ mil.)	NET PROFIT MARGIN	EMPLOYEES
12/09	22,366	2,839	12.7%	142,176
12/08	22,566	1,464	6.5%	141,002
12/07	31,369	3,124	10.0%	132,048
12/06	18,559	1,680	9.1%	118,823
12/05	14,347	750	5.2%	113,273
Annual Growth	11.7%	39.5%	—	5.8%

2009 Year-End Financials

Debt ratio: —
Return on equity: 27.6%
Cash ($ mil.): —
Current ratio: 1.00
Long-term debt ($ mil.): —

No. of shares (mil.): 315
Dividends
  Yield: 5.9%
  Payout: —
Market value ($ mil.): 15,698

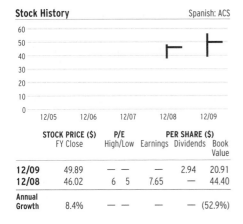

	STOCK PRICE ($)	P/E		PER SHARE ($)		
	FY Close	High/Low		Earnings	Dividends	Book Value
12/09	49.89	—	—	—	2.94	20.91
12/08	46.02	6	5	7.65	—	44.40
Annual Growth	8.4%	—	—	—	—	(52.9%)

Adecco S.A.

Any way you stack it, Adecco is the world's largest employment agency, serving some 100,000 clients from more than 5,500 offices worldwide. The company primarily provides temporary staffing services (more than 90% of sales), but also offers permanent employee placement, project assistance, outsourcing, and other human resources-related services. Besides its core industrial and office staffing services, Adecco maintains six professional lines: Engineering & Technical; Finance & Legal; Human Capital Solutions; Information Technology; Medical & Scientific; and Sales, Marketing & Events. Adecco traces its roots to 1957 and has a history of growing through mergers and acquisitions.

Adecco's list of secondary and specialty brands includes DIS Deutscher Industrie Service, Ajilon Professional, Lee Hecht Harrison Career Services, Altedia, and Office Angels.

Adecco made big waves throughout the staffing industry when it acquired rival MPS Group for $1.3 billion in January 2010. The purchase of MPS Group, an IT staffing leader with a network of more than 220 offices globally, added girth to Adecco's operations worldwide. MPS Group particularly strengthens Adecco's engineering, legal staffing, IT, and finance/accounting offerings. Adecco rolled MPS Group in with its Adecco Group North America division. Company officials said MPS Group subsidiaries (which included Modis, Idea Integration, and Accounting Principals) will function as subsidiaries of Adecco.

The company made a move to expand into the fragmented UK market a few months earlier in October 2009, when it acquired London-based Spring Group for almost $180 million. Spring Group specialized in providing staffing for the information technology industry. Adecco merged Spring Group with its Adecco UK & Ireland operations.

Also in 2009, Adecco appointed a new CEO to lead the company's strategy. Patrick De Maeseneire was tapped as the new CEO. Since 2002, De Maeseneire had served as the CEO of Barry Callebaut, one of the world's top suppliers of industrial chocolate. He is also a former executive from Adecco who worked at the company from 1998 to 2002. As revenue dropped by 26% in 2009 as a result of the economic downturn, Adecco was forced to initiate headcount reductions throughout its offices worldwide during the year.

Before the recession, Adecco in 2008 continued to set its sights on the entire European market when it placed a bid to acquire leading staffing agency Michael Page International, which operates through more than 165 offices spanning almost 30 countries. Michael Page rejected Adecco's first and second offers, however, and Adecco announced in September 2008 that it would not proceed with a takeover attempt. Months later, however, Adecco proved you can't keep an acquisitive company down when it improved its position in the Netherlands through the acquisition of staffing firm DNC De Nederlanden for about $83 million.

HISTORY

Swiss accountant Henri-Ferdinand Lavanchy founded Adia in 1957 when a client asked him to find someone to fill a job. The company expanded internationally in the 1960s with offices in Belgium and elsewhere in Europe and entered the US in 1972. When Adia went public in Switzerland in 1979, Lavanchy retired from active management. Martin Pestalozzi succeeded him. The US operation, Adia Services, went public in 1984.

Pestalozzi's management group was ousted when retailer Asko Deutsche Kaufhaus and Swiss investor Klaus Jacobs bought about 50% of Adia in 1991 after a scandal involving the sale of part of the company to Swiss financier (later fugitive) Werner Ray. Jacobs bought out Asko in 1993, as well as Adia's US investors, bringing US operations under company ownership again.

Adia and Ecco SA, one of the top French employment services companies, merged in 1996 to form Adecco. (Adia chairman Jacobs and Ecco chairman Philippe Foriel-Destezet began a revolving chairmanship and former Adia executive John Bowmer became CEO.) After the merger, Adecco bought ICON Recruitment (IT recruiting, Australia; 1996), Seagate Associates (outplacement consulting, New Jersey; 1997), and Massachusetts-based TAD Resources International, the largest private staffing services company in the US, in 1997. The company bought rival Olsten's staffing and IT business in 2000 to further solidify Adecco as the world's largest temporary staffing firm.

Adecco restructured around four divisions (Adecco Staffing, Ajilon Staffing and Managed Services, Career Services, and e-Recruiting and Executive Search) in 2001. In 2002 Klaus retired from the company; Bowmer became chairman and 10-year company veteran Jérôme Caille took over as CEO. Adecco sold jobpilot, an online job board, to Monster Worldwide in 2004. In 2005 the company acquired French human resources firm Altedia. Caille left the company in 2005 and Jacobs came back on board as chairman and interim CEO. In 2006 Dieter Scheiff was named as the new CEO.

Adecco augmented its German operations in mid-2007 when it acquired German staffing company Tuja Holding GmbH for about $1 billion. Tuja's estimated revenue for 2007 was around $870 million.

After years of acquisitions (and a failed attempt to buy rival Michael Page International), the company appointed Patrick De Maeseneire as the new CEO, effective June 2009. A former Adecco executive, De Maeseneire had served as the CEO of chocolate maker Barry Callebaut since 2002. Adecco made a megadeal in January 2010 with the acquisition of rival MPS Group for $1.3 billion.

EXECUTIVES

Chairman: Rolf Dörig, age 53
Vice Chairman: Thomas O'Neill, age 65
CEO: Baron Patrick G. De Maeseneire, age 53, $3,626,002 total compensation
CFO: Dominik de Daniel, age 35, $2,610,330 total compensation
Chief Sales Officer: Sergio Picarelli, age 43, $656,452 total compensation
Chief Human Resources Officer: Christian Vasino, age 38, $1,320,439 total compensation
CIO: Frank Meyer
Regional Head France, Switzerland, and India: François Davy, age 54, $2,223,374 total compensation
Regional Head North America: Theron I. (Tig) Gilliam Jr., age 46, $1,672,721 total compensation
Regional Head Germany and Austria: Andreas Dinges, age 51, $674,026 total compensation
Regional Head Japan and Asia: Mark Du Ree, $693,770 total compensation
Regional Head Iberia and South America: Enrique Sanchez, age 43, $506,606 total compensation
Regional Head Italy and Eastern Europe: Federico Vione, age 38, $471,389 total compensation
Regional Head Northern Europe: Alain Dehaze, age 47, $247,318 total compensation
Regional Head UK and Ireland: Peter Searle, $137,278 total compensation
General Counsel and Corporate Secretary: Urs Waelchli
Head Group Communications: Stephan Howeg
Global Head, Human Capital Solutions; President, and COO, Lee Hecht Harrison: Peter Alcide
Head of Investor Relations: Karin Selfors-Thomann, age 35
Auditors: Ernst & Young AG

LOCATIONS

HQ: Adecco S.A.
Sägereistrasse 10
8152 Glattbrugg, Zürich, Switzerland
Phone: 41-44-878-88-88   **Fax:** 41-44-829-88-88
US HQ: 175 Broad Hollow Rd., Melville, NY 11747
US Phone: 631-844-7650   **US Fax:** 631-844-7363
Web: www.adecco.com

2009 Sales

	% of total
France	32
US & Canada	16
Japan	9
Germany & Austria	7
UK & Ireland	6
Benelux	5
Italy	5
Iberia	5
Nordics	4
Australia & New Zealand	2
Switzerland	2
Other regions	7
Total	**100**

PRODUCTS/OPERATIONS

2009 Sales

	% of total
Industrial	50
Office	23
Information technology	8
Emerging markets	7
Engineering & technical	4
Finance & legal	2
Human capital solutions	2
Medical & science	2
Sales, marketing & events	2
Total	**100**

COMPETITORS

Administaff
Kelly Services
Manpower
Randstad Holding
Robert Half
SFN Group
Synergie
TAC Worldwide
Volt Information
Westaff

HISTORICAL FINANCIALS

Company Type: Public

Income Statement

FYE: Sunday nearest December 31

	REVENUE ($ mil.)	NET INCOME ($ mil.)	NET PROFIT MARGIN	EMPLOYEES
12/09	21,207	12	0.1%	28,508
12/08	28,141	698	2.5%	36,399
12/07	31,042	1,082	3.5%	36,661
12/06	26,936	806	3.0%	35,007
12/05	21,676	537	2.5%	32,442
Annual Growth	(0.5%)	(61.7%)	—	(3.2%)

2009 Year-End Financials

Debt ratio: 35.8%
Return on equity: —
Cash ($ mil.): 2,090
Current ratio: 1.37
Long-term debt ($ mil.): 1,597

No. of shares (mil.): 192
Dividends
Yield: 0.0%
Payout: —
Market value ($ mil.): 10,520

Stock History

Swiss: ADEN

	STOCK PRICE ($) FY Close	P/E High/Low		PER SHARE ($) Earnings	Dividends	Book Value
12/09	54.82	962	687	0.06	0.00	23.24
12/08	38.76	15	9	3.82	6.77	20.51
12/07	54.36	16	9	5.59	—	22.04
12/06	68.21	18	12	4.14	—	16.95
12/05	45.84	19	15	2.77	—	13.06
Annual Growth	4.6%	—	—	(61.6%)	—	15.5%

adidas AG

Jesse Owens and Muhammad Ali broke records in their adidas athletic shoes. The heart of the adidas product line is athletic shoes, but the company's iconic three-stripe logo appears on apparel and other jock accoutrements. As the #2 maker of sporting goods worldwide behind NIKE, adidas has inked deals with football and basketball athletes, as well as the New York Yankees, and it serves golfers through its TaylorMade-adidas Golf. The company operates some 2,200 retail locations under the adidas and Reebok banners.

Having already put its footprint on athletic shoe history and widely recognized for its expertise in engineering footwear, adidas has been working on making its brand as strong and as global as NIKE's and building a sturdy foundation in the US market. With its noteworthy 2006 Reebok purchase, it has greatly expanded its portfolio of licensed brands, got a leg up on the urban market, and has begun to chip away at NIKE's long-running status as the world's #1 footwear firm. Adding Reebok to adidas offers both companies more bargaining muscle with suppliers and marketers. As far as marketing goes, adidas continues to retain Reebok's image as an athletic shoe engineering company (on the heels of its $250 intelligent shoe debut) and reposition the company as a performance brand in the casual footwear niche.

While the company integrated the adidas and Reebok brands in 2007 and 2008, it streamlined its operations globally. As part of its strategy, adidas bought out Reebok distributors and joint ventures worldwide to regain control over the brands. For its adidas business segment, the company acquired US-based Textronics in 2008. Specializing in making wearable sensors, Textronics has boosted adidas's fitness-monitoring expertise. Also the company expanded its golf business when its TaylorMade-adidas Golf subsidiary purchased golf apparel and accessories maker Ashworth in 2008.

adidas is a top brand name in Europe, North America, Asia, and Latin America. It is concentrating on strengthening its position in major Western European markets while it leverages growth opportunities in the region's emerging markets in Eastern Europe, the Middle East, and Africa. In Latin America, its fastest-growing region, adidas has its eye on becoming a market leader in Argentina, Brazil, Chile, and Mexico.

China, in particular, has been a focus for the athletic shoemaker. Along with its sponsorship of the Beijing Olympics, adidas is looking to one-up NIKE in China by opening its biggest store to date in Beijing.

HISTORY

adidas grew out of an infamous rift between German brothers Adi and Rudi Dassler, who created athletic shoe giants adidas and Puma. As WWI was winding down, Adi scavenged for tires, rucksacks, and other refuse to create slippers, gymnastics shoes, and soccer cleats at home. His sister cut patterns out of canvas. By 1926 the shoes' success allowed the Dasslers to build a factory. At the 1928 Amsterdam Olympics, German athletes first showcased Dassler shoes to the world. In 1936 American Jesse Owens sprinted to Olympic gold in Dassler's double-striped shoes.

Business boomed until the Nazis commandeered the Dassler factory to make boots for soldiers. Although both Rudi and Adi were reportedly members of the Nazi party, only Rudi was called to service. Adi remained at home to run the factory. When Allied troops occupied the area, Adi made friends with American soldiers — even creating shoes for a soldier who wore them at the 1946 Olympics. Rudi came home from an American prison camp and joined his brother; together they scavenged the war-torn landscape for tank materials and tents to make shoes.

Soon a dispute between the brothers split the business. Rumors circulated that Rudi resented that Adi had failed to use his American connections to help spring him from prison camp. Rudi set up his own factory, facing Adi across the River Aurach. The brothers never spoke to each other again, except in court. Rudi's company was named Puma, and Adi's became adidas. Adi added a third stripe to the Dassler's trademark shoe, while Rudi chose a cat's paw in motion. Thus began one of the most intense rivalries in Europe. The children of Puma and adidas employees attended separate elementary schools, and the employees even distinguished themselves by drinking different beers.

With Adi's innovations throughout the late 1940s and 1950s (such as the replaceable-cleat soccer shoe), adidas came to dominate the world's athletic shoe market. In the late 1950s it capitalized on the booming US market, overtaking the canvas sneakers made by P.F. Flyers and Stride Rite (Keds). The company also initiated the practice of putting logos on sports bags and clothing.

In the 1960s and 1970s adidas continued to expand globally to maintain its dominant position. However, a flood of new competitors following the 1972 Munich Olympics and the death of Adi in 1978 signaled the end of an era. As NIKE and Reebok captured the North American market during the 1980s, adidas made one of its biggest missteps — it turned down a sneaker endorsement offer from a young Michael Jordan in 1984.

French politician and entrepreneur Bernard Tapie bought the struggling company in 1989, but he stepped down in 1992 amid personal, political, and business scandals. In 1993 Robert Louis-Dreyfus became CEO. He shifted production to Asia, pumped up the advertising budget, and brought in former NIKE marketing geniuses to re-establish the company's identity.

adidas became adidas-Salomon in 1997 with its $1.4 billion purchase of Salomon, a French maker of skis and other sporting goods. In a 1998 reorganization, Louis-Dreyfus sacked Jean-Francois Gautier as Salomon's president in the wake of disappointing sales, particularly from TaylorMade Golf, Salomon's golf subsidiary.

Amid a 10% slide in revenue, several key executives decided to leave the company in 2000, including adidas America CEO Steve Wynne. Citing poor health, Louis-Dreyfus soon followed (but remained as chairman); he was replaced by the new CEO of adidas America, Ross McMullin, who soon after was diagnosed with cancer.

In 2001 Louis-Dreyfus retired as chairman and in March COO Herbert Hainer became chief executive. Britain's Barclays Bank PLC became adidas' largest shareholder in 2004, raising its stake to 5.4%. The company changed its name in 2006 to adidas AG.

In 2008 adidas AG won a $305 million award from a federal jury in Oregon for trademark violation of its three-stripe design by Collective Brands, the operator of the Payless and Stride Rite shoe-store chains.

EXECUTIVES

Chairman: Igor Landau, age 66
Deputy Chairman: Willi Schwerdtle, age 57
**Deputy Chairwoman; Chairwoman, Central Works
  Council:** Sabine Bauer, age 47
CEO: Herbert Hainer, age 56
Member Executive Board Global Operations:
  Glenn Bennett, age 47
Member Executive Board Finance: Robin Stalker, age 52
Member Executive Board Global Brands:
  Erich Stamminger, age 53
Chief Marketing Officer, adidas Sport Style:
  Hermann Deininger
**Sales Director Customer Service Market Central and
  Director:** Hans Ruprecht, age 56
Senior Investor Relations Manager: Dennis Weber
Senior Reporting Manager: Christelle Paclet
Chief Corporate Communication Officer: Jan Runau,
  age 44
Auditors: KPMG Deutsche Treuhand-Gesellschaft AG

LOCATIONS

HQ: adidas AG
  Adi-Dassler-Strasse 1
  91074 Herzogenaurach, Germany
Phone: 49-9132-84-0   **Fax:** 49-9132-84-2241
US HQ: 5055 N. Greeley Ave., Portland, OR 97217
US Phone: 971-234-2300   **US Fax:** 971-234-2450
Web: www.adidas-group.com

2009 Sales

	% of total
Western Europe	31
North America	23
European Emerging Markets	11
Latin America	10
Greater China	9
Other Asian Markets	16
Total	**100**

PRODUCTS/OPERATIONS

2009 Sales

	% of total
Wholesale	69
Retail	19
Other	12
Total	**100**

Selected Brands

adidas (footwear and apparel for basketball, cycling,
  running, soccer, and tennis)
Ashworth (golf apparel)
Reebok (footwear and apparel)
TaylorMade (golf clubs, accessories)

COMPETITORS

Amer Sports
ASICS
Benetton
Callaway Golf
Converse
Cutter & Buck
Fila USA
Fortune Brands
Head N.V.
Head-Tyrolia-Mares
Huffy Corporation
K-Swiss
Mizuno
New Balance
NIKE
Phillips-Van Heusen
Polo Ralph Lauren
PUMA AG
Rollerblade
Rossignol
Saucony
Trek Bicycle
Under Armour
Victoria's Secret Stores

HISTORICAL FINANCIALS

Company Type: Public

Income Statement

FYE: December 31

	REVENUE ($ mil.)	NET INCOME ($ mil.)	NET PROFIT MARGIN	EMPLOYEES
12/09	14,878	351	2.4%	39,596
12/08	15,221	908	6.0%	36,129
12/07	15,159	817	5.4%	31,344
12/06	13,304	654	4.9%	25,067
12/05	7,859	462	5.9%	15,935
Annual Growth	**17.3%**	**(6.7%)**	**—**	**25.6%**

2009 Year-End Financials

Debt ratio: —
Return on equity: 6.9%
Cash ($ mil.): 1,111
Current ratio: 1.58
Long-term debt ($ mil.): —

No. of shares (mil.): 209
Dividends
  Yield: 1.3%
  Payout: 41.1%
Market value ($ mil.): 11,325

Stock History

OTC: ADDYY

	STOCK PRICE ($) FY Close	P/E High/Low		PER SHARE ($) Earnings	Dividends	Book Value
12/09	54.13	32	18	1.75	0.72	25.87
12/08	38.25	16	7	4.33	—	22.81
12/07	75.45	20	13	3.78	—	21.27
12/06	49.78	10	8	5.94	—	17.83
12/05	47.37	10	7	4.83	—	15.19
Annual Growth	**3.4%**	**—**	**—**	**(22.4%)**	**—**	**14.2%**

AEGON N.V.

Not only has AEGON expanded across Europe, it has also spread Transamerica. The Dutch life insurance giant is using its expertise in acquisition (US rival Transamerica was its largest catch) and consolidation to build a transnational collection of financial service businesses serving 40 million customers worldwide. Its subsidiaries operate primarily in the US, the Netherlands, and the UK, offering personal and commercial life insurance, pensions and annuities, and accident and supplemental health insurance, as well as retirement and savings advice and management services. AEGON also has insurance operations in 15 other countries in the Americas, Europe, and Asia, as well as banking operations in the Netherlands.

The company has established a strong growth pattern for existing and new international markets through strategic acquisitions, though its pace has slowed some due to economic downturns in 2008 and 2009. AEGON, which derives about 60% of its revenues from life insurance premiums, is focused on expanding in the high-growth regions of Asia, central and eastern Europe, and Latin America. In the Asia/Pacific region, AEGON is broadening its operations partially through its Beijing-based insurance joint

venture with the Chinese National Offshore Oil Corporation (CNOOC). It also formed a mutual fund joint venture with China-based Industrial Securities Co. in 2008, and it has an annuities partnership with Sony Life in Japan that began operations in 2009.

To expand in central and eastern European countries, AEGON in 2008 purchased Turkish life and retirement services provider Ankara Emeklilik, Hungarian pension fund UNIQA, and Polish pension fund PTE Skarbiec-Emerytura, as well as stakes in two similar Spanish firms. Then in 2009 it bought out former partner Banca Transilvania's share of BT AEGON, the Romanian pension business set up by the two companies the previous year.

However, the company began scaling back on growth efforts in 2008 due to global economic conditions. Later in 2008, as global financial conditions worsened, AEGON secured a €3 billion ($3.8 billion) capital infusion from the Dutch government to help it ward off economic woes. Association AEGON (or Vereniging AEGON), an independent trust, increased its stake in AEGON from 25% to about 34% through the government infusion transaction.

In 2008 AEGON decided to discontinue an Indian life insurance and asset management joint venture with Ranbaxy. In 2009 it sold its Dutch real estate brokerage business, and in early 2010 AEGON sold its funeral insurance business in the Netherlands.

In mid-2010 the company announced additional restructuring measures to further streamline its operations. To reduce costs and risk exposures, AEGON plans to sharpen its focus on life, pension, and asset management operations, and as such plans to seek a buyer for Transamerica Reinsurance, its US-based global life reinsurance business.

HISTORY

AEGON traces its roots to 1844, when former civil servant and funeral society agent J. Oosterhoff founded Algemeene Friesche, a burial society for low-income workers. The next year a similar organization, Groot-Noordhollandsche, was founded. These companies later became insurers and expanded nationwide. Meanwhile Olveh, a civil servants' aid group, was founded in 1877. The three companies merged in 1968 to form AGO Holding.

AEGON's other operations came from different traditions. Vennootschap Nederland was founded in 1858 as a *tontine* (essentially a death pool, with the survivors taking the pot) by Count A. Langrand-Dumonceau, an ex-French Foreign Legionnaire from Belgium. In 1913 the company merged with Eerste Nederlandsche, whose accident and health division had been previously spun off as Nieuwe Eerste Nederlandsche.

A year after Vennootschap was founded, C. F. W. Wiggers van Kerchem founded a similar scheme, Nillmij, in the Dutch East Indies. The government promoted Nillmij to colonial civil servants and military people, and for a while the company enjoyed a monopoly in the colony. Nillmij's Indonesian operations were nationalized after independence in 1957, but its Dutch subsidiaries continued to operate. All insurers were hit by fast-growing postwar government social programs. As a result, industry consolidation came early to the Netherlands. In 1969 Eerste Nederlandsche, Nieuwe Eerste Nederlandsche, and Nillmij merged to form Ennia.

The shrinking Dutch insurance market forced companies to look overseas. AGO moved into the US in 1979 by buying Life Investors; by 1982 half of its sales came from outside the Netherlands. Ennia, meanwhile, expanded in Europe (it entered Spain in 1980) and the US (buying Arkansas-based National Old Line Insurance in 1981). AGO and Ennia merged in 1983 to form AEGON. The company made more purchases at home and abroad and spent much of the rest of the decade assimilating operations.

AEGON's US units accounted for about 40% of sales in the mid-1980s, and the firm increased that figure with acquisitions.

This left AEGON underrepresented in Europe, as deregulation paved the way for economic union, and social service cutbacks spurred opportunities in private financial planning in the region. So in the 1990s AEGON began buying European companies, including Regency Life (UK, 1991) and Allami Biztosito (Hungary, 1992). It formed an alliance with Mexico's Grupo Financiero Banamex in 1994.

In 1997 AEGON began to concentrate on life insurance and financial services and shed its other operations. It bought the insurance business of Providian (now part of Washington Mutual) and sold noncore lines, such as auto coverage. In 1999 AEGON expanded further in the US with the $9.7 billion purchase of Transamerica and bought the life and pensions businesses of the UK's Guardian Royal Exchange.

Following the Transamerica acquisition, the company divested several assets to focus on life insurance and pensions.

In 2005 the company sold off its German subsidiary AEGON Lebensversicherngs-AG, operating as MoneyMaxx, to Deutscher Ring. In 2006 it acquired a 49% stake in Mexican insurer Seguros Argos.

To expand in central and eastern Europe, AEGON acquired pension fund management company PTE Ergo Hestia in Poland in 2007, as well as Dutch employee benefit and life insurance company OPTAS. Also in 2007 AEGON USA purchased two Merrill Lynch insurance units and insurance services firm Clark Consulting.

EXECUTIVES

Chairman Supervisory Board: Rob J. Routs, age 63
Chairman of the Executive Board and CEO:
 Alexander R. Wynaendts, age 49
CFO and Member Executive Board: Jan Nooitgedagt, age 56
SVP and Head Equities, Capital Management:
 Stephen P. (Steve) Carlin
SVP Fixed-Income Investments, Capital Management:
 Marc Goldfried
Member Management Board; President and CEO, AEGON USA: Mark W. Mullin
CEO AEGON The Netherlands and Member Management Board AEGON N.V.: Marco Keim, age 47
CEO, AGEON Asset Management: Sarah A. C. Russell, age 48
CEO, World Financial Group (WFG): Jack D. Linder
CEO AEGON UK and Member Management Board AEGON: Otto Thoresen, age 54
CEO AEGON Central and Eastern Europe and Member Management Board AEGON N.V.: Gábor Kepecs
President and CEO, Capital Management: Greg Ross
President, World Financial Group (WFG): Joe DiPaola
President, Life and Protection: Tim Stonehocker
Chief Risk Officer, AEGON UK: Mark Laidlaw, age 44
Senior Investment Manager, AEGON Asset Management: Pauline McPherson
Global Head Sustainability: Marc A. van Weede
Global Head Human Resources: Carla Mahieu
Auditors: Ernst & Young Accountants

LOCATIONS

HQ: AEGON N.V.
 Bezuidenhoutseweg 273
 2594 AN The Hague, The Netherlands
Phone: 31-70-344-3210   **Fax:** 31-70-344-8445
US HQ: 4333 Edgewood Rd. NE, Cedar Rapid, IA 52499
US Phone: 319-398-8511
Web: www.aegon.com

2009 Sales

	% of total
Americas	42
UK	32
Netherlands	21
Other countries	5
Total	**100**

PRODUCTS/OPERATIONS

2009 Premiums

	% of total
Life insurance	87
Accident & health insurance	10
General insurance	3
Total	**100**

COMPETITORS

Ageas SA/NV
AIG
Allianz
Allstate
Aviva
AXA
Delta Lloyd
Desjardins Financial Security
Eureko
FMR
Friends Provident
Genworth Financial
Grupo Santander
The Hartford
Industrial Alliance Insurance and Financial Services
ING
Jackson National Life
Legal & General Group
Lincoln Financial Group
Manulife Financial
MAPFRE
Merrill Lynch
MetLife
Nationwide
New York Life
Pacific Mutual
Prudential
Prudential plc
Putnam
RBC Insurance
SNS REAAL
Standard Life
Sun Life
Swiss Life
Zurich Financial Services

HISTORICAL FINANCIALS

Company Type: Public

Income Statement

FYE: December 31

	ASSETS ($ mil.)	NET INCOME ($ mil.)	INCOME AS % OF ASSETS	EMPLOYEES
12/09	428,002	292	0.1%	28,382
12/08	404,892	(1,525)	—	31,425
12/07	462,353	3,755	0.8%	30,414
12/06	415,333	3,680	0.9%	13,544
12/05	368,572	3,236	0.9%	27,159
Annual Growth	**3.8%**	**(45.2%)**	**—**	**1.1%**

2009 Year-End Financials

Equity as % of assets: 6.3%	Dividends
Return on assets: 0.1%	Yield: 0.0%
Return on equity: 1.3%	Payout: —
Long-term debt ($ mil.): 10,728	Market value ($ mil.): 15,949
No. of shares (mil.): 1,736	Sales ($ mil.): 66,513

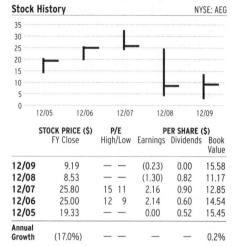

Stock History NYSE: AEG

	STOCK PRICE ($) FY Close	P/E High/Low		PER SHARE ($) Earnings	Dividends	Book Value
12/09	9.19	—	—	(0.23)	0.00	15.58
12/08	8.53	—	—	(1.30)	0.82	11.17
12/07	25.80	15	11	2.16	0.90	12.85
12/06	25.00	12	9	2.14	0.60	14.54
12/05	19.33	—	—	0.00	0.52	15.45
Annual Growth	**(17.0%)**			**—**	**—**	**0.2%**

AEON CO.

Japanese giant AEON CO. has enough retail ventures to last for eons. The holding company has about 155 subsidiaries and owns or franchises more than 5,000 stores worldwide. It runs Japan's largest supermarket chain, with 1,200-plus stores under the MaxValu and other banners, and more than 3,000 MINISTOP convenience stores. AEON also runs a number of specialty chains, including The Body Shop and Laura Ashley stores in Japan. It has a joint venture in Japan with Sports Authority and also operates HapYcom, a leading drugstore chain in Japan. Other operations include shopping center development and financial and credit card services. In 2010 AEON sold its majority stake in clothing chain The Talbots.

In 2008 AEON adopted a holding company structure in a bid to increase its responsiveness to changing (mostly negative) retail trends in Japan, where it rings up 90% of its total sales. A prolonged economic slump, aging population, and weakness in the supermarket and department store sectors have the Japanese retailer looking abroad for future growth and switching focus from opening large-scale general merchandise stores to small and midsized stores at home.

The company is beating a hasty retreat from North America (4% of 2009 sales), with the sale of its roughly 55% stake in Talbots. After merging with BPW Acquisition (a publicly traded shell company), Talbots used some $330 million in merger proceeds, along with funds from a $200 million credit line from GE Capital, to repay nearly $490 million in debt to AEON and take over its holding. AEON is shedding assets in North America to better focus on its retail and financial service operations in China and other Southeast Asian nations.

AEON has stores Australia, China, Malaysia, Singapore, South Korea, and Thailand, where it continues to expand with an emphasis on China.

To that end, it established a subsidiary in Shenzhen and plans to open 100 stores in China, up from about 60 general merchandise stores and supermarkets in 2009. It is also focusing on new shopping mall development in China. In November 2008 the company opened two mall-style shopping centers, located in Beijing and in Huizhou, northeast of Shenzhen. The malls are populated by specialty shops, including AEON-owned banners, such as Jusco and The Body Shop.

At home AEON is trying out new store formats, such as My Basket mini-supermarkets in urban areas. Indeed, AEON plans to increase the number of My Basket stores from about 20 locations in 2009 to 300 within the next two years. In 2009 it rebranded its AEON Welcia drugstores under the new HapYcom banner and began selling nonprescription drugs at deep discounts under the same name.

The stagnant Japanese economy has led the company to cut prices and costs in an effort to become a more efficient operator. It has begun sourcing food and other merchandise directly from suppliers, such as Japanese fisheries and the US consumer goods giant Procter & Gamble. AEON also has a joint venture with SANYO Electric Co. to develop home electronics for sale in its stores. The new line of home electronics debuted in about 500 stores in Japan in the spring of 2008 under AEON's proprietary Topvalu brand. Development of the proprietary label — which covers everything from food to electronics to household goods — is a key element in the company's low-price strategy.

Among Japanese retailers AEON is one of the most proactive in preparing to defend its business from foreign competitors, including the world's #1 retailer Wal-Mart and Britain's Tesco. To compete, it has cut prices and distribution costs, adopted western sales techniques, and has acquired smaller retailers. The company is upgrading its computer systems to rival those of US giant Wal-Mart. Also, AEON beat out Wal-Mart to buy eight hypermarkets in Japan operated by France's Carrefour, which abandoned the Japanese market.

EXECUTIVES

Chairman: Akihiko Harada
President and Director: Motoya Okada, age 58
VP and Director: Naoki Hayashi
VP and Director: Yoshiki Mori
VP: Yoshiharu Nishitani
VP: Hiroshi Yokoo
VP: Kunio Sakano
VP: Mamoru Kuchihiro
VP: Jerry Black
VP: Masaaki Toyoshima
VP: Kunihiko Hisaki
VP: Shouhei Murai
VP: Hideki Wakabayashi
VP: Mitsuko Tsuchiya
VP: Akihito Tanaka
VP: Yutaka Furutani
VP: Atsunobu Agata
VP: Masato Nishimatsu
VP: Kazunori Umemoto
VP: Yuichiro Okauchi
VP: Tsutomu (Tom) Kajita, age 56
Auditors: Deloitte Touche Tohmatsu

LOCATIONS

HQ: AEON CO., LTD.
(Ion Kabushiki Kaisha)
1-5-1 Nakase, Mihama-ku
Chiba 261-8515, Japan
Phone: 81-43-212-6042   **Fax:** 81-43-212-6849
Web: www.aeon.info

2010 Sales

	% of total
Japan	92
North America	3
Asia & other regions	5
Total	**100**

PRODUCTS/OPERATIONS

2010 Sales

	% of total
General merchandise & other retail	70
Service & other operations	18
Specialty store operations	9
Shopping center development	3
Total	**100**

Selected Store Names

Abilities Jusco (CDs, DVDs, and books)
Asbee (shoe stores)
Blue Grass (apparel for teenage girls)
Claire's Nippon (women's clothing)
Cox (family casual clothing)
HapYcom (drugstores)
Home Wide Corp. (home centers)
JUSCO (apparel, food, and household item superstores)
JUS-Photo (film developing)
Laura Ashley Japan (clothing and home furnishings)
Maxvalu (supermarkets)
Mega Sports (Sports Authority stores)
MINISTOP (convenience stores)
MYCAL Corporation (supermarkets)
My Basket (small-scale supermarkets)
Nustep (family footwear stores)
Petcity (pets & pet supplies)
Sports Authority (sporting goods)

COMPETITORS

A.S. Watson
Carrefour
Costco Wholesale
Dairy Farm International
Fast Retailing
The Gap
Heiwado
Isetan Mitsukoshi
Ito-Yokado
METRO AG
Rakuten
Seiyu
Seven & i
Takashimaya
Tesco
Uny

HISTORICAL FINANCIALS

Company Type: Public

Income Statement

FYE: Last day of February

	REVENUE ($ mil.)	NET INCOME ($ mil.)	NET PROFIT MARGIN	EMPLOYEES
2/10	51,045	619	1.2%	76,520
2/09	48,138	(28)	—	74,925
2/08	48,666	414	0.9%	76,624
2/07	40,282	481	1.2%	76,318
2/06	38,092	249	0.7%	71,171
Annual Growth	7.6%	25.6%	—	1.8%

2010 Year-End Financials

Debt ratio: —
Return on equity: 6.9%
Cash ($ mil.): 3,308
Current ratio: 1.10
Long-term debt ($ mil.): —
No. of shares (mil.): 765
Dividends
  Yield: 1.7%
  Payout: 38.6%
Market value ($ mil.): 7,859

Stock History

Tokyo: 82670

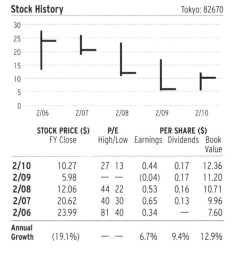

	STOCK PRICE ($) FY Close	P/E High/Low		PER SHARE ($) Earnings	Dividends	Book Value
2/10	10.27	27	13	0.44	0.17	12.36
2/09	5.98	—	—	(0.04)	0.17	11.20
2/08	12.06	44	22	0.53	0.16	10.71
2/07	20.62	40	30	0.65	0.13	9.96
2/06	23.99	81	40	0.34	—	7.60
Annual Growth	(19.1%)	—	—	6.7%	9.4%	12.9%

Agrium Inc.

It's no bull that Agrium is a top producer and marketer of fertilizers in the Americas. A leader in the production of nitrogen, the company operates about 15 plants in North America and Argentina that produce about 10 million tons of nitrogen, potash, and phosphate products per year. In addition to supplying wholesalers, Agrium operates more than 800 fertilizer retail outlets in the US and South America. The company also owns 50% of Profertil, a joint venture with Spain's Repsol YPF that runs Argentina's largest nitrogen plant, and 25% of a nitrogen fertilizers plant in Egypt. After a 2009 bid for CF Industries fell short, Agrium agreed to a $1.2 billion takeover of Australian wheat exporter AWB Ltd. in 2010.

Agrium's bid for AWB was in competiton with, but much higher than, an earlier share-based merger offer by another Australian firm, GrainCorp. When the deal closes, AWB will be the second Australian company acquired by Canada-based Agrium.

Agrium made its $5.2 billion hostile offer for CF Industries amidst a four-company, year-long bidding war that also included Yara Industries and Terra Industries. Agrium withdrew its offer to buy CF Industries after that company successfully acquired Terra.

In 2008 it bought agricultural products retailer UAP for $2.5 billion, including assumed debt. In the latter half of the decade, Agrium has implemented an aggressive expansion strategy by acquiring a number of businesses throughout the Americas. The deal for UAP was the largest by far. It greatly added to Agrium's North American retail operations and also expanded the company's international reach.

Other acquisitions have included agricultural products distributor Royster-Clark and two divisions of Spectrum Brands' Nu-Gro subsidiary.

The Nu-Gro deal formed the base of Agrium's Advanced Technologies unit, which supplies agricultural products and services in North and South America and sells branded micronutrients and other industrial products worldwide (such as control-released fertilizers for the turf grass, horticulture, and consumer agriculture markets).

Agrium purchased 24 retail farm centers in Argentina in 2010 from DuPont Crop Protection. The deal will expand Agrium's Loveland crop-protection products into additional South American countries.

HISTORY

Agrium was formed in 1992 to facilitate the reorganization of Cominco's fertilizer division and to acquire the fertilizer business of the Alberta Energy Company (1993). Cominco was founded in 1896 as the Smelting and Refining Company when Fritz Heinze fired up his first smelter at Trail Creek Landing, British Columbia. Using the ores of the nearby Rossland mines, the company soon diversified into other products (such as fertilizers) and new metallurgical technologies. In 1906 the Smelting and Refining Company, the Rossland mines, and the nearby St. Eugene Mine merged to form the Consolidated Mining and Smelting Company of Canada Limited.

During WWI the Canadian government conscripted all the company's lead, zinc, and chemical production and instructed the company to make explosive-grade ammonium nitrate at its fertilizer plants. Cominco became the company's official name in 1966.

Alberta Energy was formed in 1973 to lessen Alberta's dependence on foreign oil, in response to the OPEC oil embargo. In 1989 its petrochemical division established fertilizer (ammonium nitrate) subsidiaries in the US.

Agrium was established to compete in the rapidly consolidating fertilizer market (the number of North American ammonia producers fell from 55 in 1980 to 26 at the end of 1996). The phosphate and potash industries also consolidated, albeit on a smaller scale.

Between 1993 and 1996 the company expanded its US operations by acquiring Crop Protection Services and Western Farm Service (both retail operations), AG-BIO (the phosphate-based fertilizer business of Imperial Oil), and Nu-West Industries. Agrium expanded into South America in 1995 by opening retail sales units for selling fertilizer, agricultural chemicals, and other services in the farming regions of Argentina.

In 1996 Agrium acquired Viridian, a Canadian fertilizer producer with nitrogen- and phosphate-based fertilizer plants in Alberta. Expanding its supply base, the company bought a phosphate mine in Alberta in 1997. The company also bought back 10% of its shares in 1998. Agrium opened a phosphate rock mine in Ontario in 1999 to reduce its reliance on phosphate rock imported from West Africa.

In 2000 Agrium bought Unocal's nitrogen-based fertilizer operations for around $325 million, thereby increasing its nitrogen production capacity some 60%. Also that year Agrium's Profertil nitrogen plant, a joint venture with Spain's industrial giant Repsol-YPF, began production in Argentina, but the plant was shut down by a government agency following an accidental discharge of ammonia (the plant was reopened later

in 2000). The company continued to expand its retail business in North and South America through acquisitions in 2006 of other agricultural products and services, such as Nu-Gro and Pursell Technologies.

EXECUTIVES

Chairman: Frank W. Proto, age 67
President, CEO, and Director:
  Michael M. (Mike) Wilson, age 58
SVP Finance and CFO: Bruce G. Waterman, age 59
SVP; President, Retail: Richard L. Gearheard, age 59
SVP; President, Agrium Advanced Technologies:
  Andrew K. Mittag, age 49
SVP; President, Wholesale Business Unit:
  Ronald A. (Ron) Wilkinson
SVP Business Development and Chief Legal Officer:
  Leslie A. O'Donoghue
SVP Human Resources: James M. (Jim) Grossett
VP and Treasurer: Patrick J. (Pat) Freeman
VP and Corporate Controller: Angela S. Lekatsas
VP Manufacturing: Charles V. (Chuck) Magro
VP Special Projects: Christopher W. (Chris) Tworek
VP Marketing and Distribution: Kevin R. Helash
Corporate Secretary and Senior Legal Counsel:
  Gary J. Daniel
General Counsel: Joni R. Paulus
Senior Director Corporate and Government Relations:
  Doug Beever
Senior Director Investor Relations: Richard Downey
Auditors: KPMG LLP

LOCATIONS

HQ: Agrium Inc.
  13131 Lake Fraser Dr. SE
  Calgary, Alberta T2J 7E8, Canada
Phone: 403-225-7000   **Fax:** 403-225-7609
US HQ: 4582 S. Ulster St., Ste. 1700, Denver, CO 80237
US Phone: 303-804-4400   **US Fax:** 303-804-4482
Web: www.agrium.com

2009 Sales

	$ mil.	% of total
US	7,146	77
Canada	1,073	12
Europe	495	5
Argentina	283	3
Other	132	1
Adjustment	199	2
Total	**9,328**	**100**

PRODUCTS/OPERATIONS

2009 Sales

	$ mil.	% of total
Retail		
Crop protection products	2,638	28
Crop nutrients	2,522	27
Seeds, services & other	1,004	10
Wholesale		
Nitrogen	1,247	13
Phosphate	436	5
Potash	333	4
Other	1,003	10
Advanced technologies	304	3
Adjustments	(159)	—
Total	**9,328**	**100**

COMPETITORS

BASF SE
CF Industries
K+S
Koch Industries, Inc.
Potash Corp
SQM
Terra Industries
Yara

HISTORICAL FINANCIALS
Company Type: Public

Income Statement

FYE: December 31

	REVENUE ($ mil.)	NET INCOME ($ mil.)	NET PROFIT MARGIN	EMPLOYEES
12/09	9,129	366	4.0%	11,153
12/08	10,031	1,322	13.2%	10,975
12/07	5,270	441	8.4%	6,618
12/06	4,193	33	0.8%	6,554
12/05	3,394	283	8.3%	4,719
Annual Growth	28.1%	6.6%	—	24.0%

2009 Year-End Financials

Debt ratio: 37.0%
Return on equity: 8.4%
Cash ($ mil.): 933
Current ratio: 1.98
Long-term debt ($ mil.): 1,699

No. of shares (mil.): 158
Dividends
  Yield: 0.2%
  Payout: 4.7%
Market value ($ mil.): 9,717

Stock History

NYSE: AGU

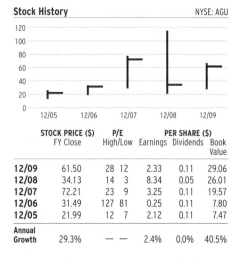

	STOCK PRICE ($) FY Close	P/E High/Low		PER SHARE ($) Earnings	Dividends	Book Value
12/09	61.50	28	12	2.33	0.11	29.06
12/08	34.13	14	3	8.34	0.05	26.01
12/07	72.21	23	9	3.25	0.11	19.57
12/06	31.49	127	81	0.25	0.11	7.80
12/05	21.99	12	7	2.12	0.11	7.47
Annual Growth	29.3%	—	—	2.4%	0.0%	40.5%

Air France-KLM

Air France and KLM represent years of French and Dutch airline tradition, but Air France-KLM represents a first: a holding company made up of two national airlines. Together, Air France-KLM is the largest airline group in Europe and one of the largest in the world. Through its operating units, the company serves about 245 destinations in more than 100 countries around the globe with a fleet of about 640 aircraft. Air France and KLM operate independently from hubs in Paris and Amsterdam, but are working to coordinate their operations, both as sister companies and as members of the SkyTeam alliance, which also includes Alitalia, Delta Air Lines, and Korean Air Lines.

Air France-KLM, along with its industry peers, has been struggling to regain its financial footing following extremely difficult economic conditions in 2008 that have lingered on into 2009. The company lost millions on its fuel-hedging contracts when fuel prices shot up to record prices in mid-2008 and then dropped drastically by the end of the year. (Fuel-hedging is when airlines lock in a pre-determined price for future jet fuel purchases.) Also in 2008 a global recession took hold, causing passenger and cargo demand to plummet.

Like other major airlines, Air France-KLM has cut capacity on its routes and implemented a cost-savings plan. The company enacted a hiring freeze and voluntary reduction and cut its temporary employee ranks, resulting in an almost 6% workforce reduction, which is mild compared to other carriers.

While Air France-KLM also has delayed delivery of about 20 passenger and cargo aircraft to preserve cash, the company took delivery in October 2009 of the first of a dozen new Airbus A380s — the largest passenger plane in the world. The double-decker, fuel-efficient A380, which holds about 540 passengers, entered service for Air France in November 2009, flying between Paris and New York.

Cooperation with other airlines through alliances and joint ventures has helped Air France-KLM weather the tough times. Delta's October 2008 acquisition of Northwest was good news to Air France-KLM, which is involved in a joint venture with the combined company. (Delta completed its integration of Northwest in early 2010.) Air France, KLM, Northwest, and Delta share revenue and split the cost of trans-Atlantic flights between the US, Canada, Mexico, Europe, the Mediterranean, Africa, the Middle East, India, and Latin America.

In early 2009 Air France-KLM acquired a 25% stake in Italian airline Alitalia for about $430 million and is represented on the company's board of directors through three seats. The stake gives Air France-KLM greater access to the Italian market. Alitalia had initially agreed to be acquired by Air France-KLM in March 2008, but Air France-KLM was forced to withdraw its proposal a month later after failing to win the blessing of Alitalia's unions.

Air France and KLM have already combined their air cargo operations as Air France-KLM Cargo, which hauls cargo in dedicated freighters and in the bellies of passenger aircraft. The company's cargo operations suffered the most from the recession, losing some €207 million (about $310 million) in 2008. Air France-KLM cut cargo capacity up to 15% and grounded about six cargo aircraft. KLM's purchase of Martinair in December 2008 has helped the company to retain its lead position in the European cargo market.

Air France-KLM Cargo drew unwelcome attention in 2008 when the company pleaded guilty to charges that its carriers participated in a conspiracy to fix prices for air cargo transportation. Several other airlines pleaded guilty to similar antitrust charges and agreed to pay fines, but the staggering $350 million penalty that Air France-KLM agreed to pay was by far the largest fine in the case.

To navigate the company through this difficult period, Air France-KLM has a new leader. Deputy CEO Pierre-Henri Gourgeon took over as CEO in January 2009 and replaced Jean-Cyril Spinetta, who remained chairman. Gourgeon also replaced Spinetta as CEO of Air France. Spinetta, Air France-KLM's founding chairman and CEO — and one of the chief architects of the airlines' combination — had led Air France since 1997.

The acquisition of KLM by Air France in 2004 allowed the French government, which had been looking for ways to privatize its flag carrier, an opportunity to reduce its majority stake in Air France. The government owns about 16% of the combined company; current and former employees own about 12%.

Talks about merging the two formerly state-owned carriers began informally in 1999 — five years before the deal was completed. Not only did Spinetta and KLM CEO Leo van Wijk have to convince their respective governments the merger was a good idea, but they had to sell it to the European Union, which had several members with their own airlines crying foul. Air France and KLM had to give up some landing slots in Paris and Amsterdam to gain approval for the deal, but regulators saw the consolidation as a move likely to benefit consumers and strengthen the European airline industry as a whole.

EXECUTIVES

Chairman: Jean-Cyril Spinetta, age 66
Vice Chairman: Leo M. van Wijk, age 63
CEO and Director: Pierre-Henri Gourgeon, age 64
SEVP Finance: Philippe Calavia, age 62
EVP Information Systems: Édouard Odier, age 58
SVP Marketing: Christian Herzog, age 54
Auditors: KPMG S.A.

LOCATIONS

HQ: Air France-KLM
45, rue de Paris
95747 Roissy, France
Phone: 33-1-41-56-78-00
Web: www.airfranceklm-finance.com

2010 Sales

	% of total
Europe	41
North & Latin America	22
Asia	16
Africa & Middle East	14
Caribbean & Indian Ocean	7
Total	**100**

PRODUCTS/OPERATIONS

2010 Sales

	% of total
Passenger	77
Cargo	12
Maintenance	6
Other	5
Total	**100**

COMPETITORS

Aer Lingus
Air Berlin
AMR Corp.
Austrian Airlines
British Airways
Brussels Airlines
easyJet
Iberia
Lufthansa
Ryanair
SAS
SNCF
United Continental
Virgin Atlantic Airways

HISTORICAL FINANCIALS

Company Type: Public

Income Statement

FYE: March 31

	REVENUE ($ mil.)	NET INCOME ($ mil.)	NET PROFIT MARGIN	EMPLOYEES
3/10	28,250	(2,097)	—	104,721
3/09	31,659	(1,075)	—	107,000
3/08	38,082	1,211	3.2%	104,600
3/07	30,808	1,184	3.8%	103,050
3/06	26,032	1,118	4.3%	102,422
Annual Growth	**2.1%**	**—**	**—**	**0.6%**

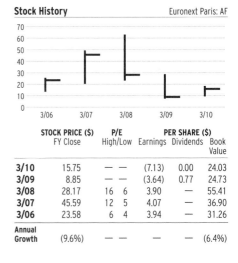

2010 Year-End Financials

Debt ratio: 172.0%	No. of shares (mil.): 300
Return on equity: —	Dividends
Cash ($ mil.): 5,046	Yield: 0.0%
Current ratio: 0.77	Payout: —
Long-term debt ($ mil.): 12,406	Market value ($ mil.): 4,727

Stock History

Euronext Paris: AF

	STOCK PRICE ($) FY Close	P/E High/Low		PER SHARE ($) Earnings	Dividends	Book Value
3/10	15.75	—	—	(7.13)	0.00	24.03
3/09	8.85	—	—	(3.64)	0.77	24.73
3/08	28.17	16	6	3.90	—	55.41
3/07	45.59	12	5	4.07	—	36.90
3/06	23.58	6	4	3.94	—	31.26
Annual Growth	**(9.6%)**	**—**	**—**	**—**	**—**	**(6.4%)**

Air New Zealand

Unlike the kiwi, New Zealand's flightless national bird, Air New Zealand soars far and wide. The company makes most of its money by transporting passengers to destinations in the Asia/Pacific region, Europe, and North America; it also serves about two dozen cities in New Zealand. It operates a fleet of about 100 aircraft, including both jets and turbo-props. Air New Zealand extends its offerings by participating in the Star Alliance, a global marketing and code-sharing network that includes carriers such as Lufthansa and United Airlines. (Code-sharing allows airlines to sell tickets on one another's flights.) The New Zealand government owns 76% of Air New Zealand.

Fuel prices soared to record heights in 2008 and were followed by a global economic recession and dizzying plunge in demand. To stem the tide of losses, the carrier cut jobs and has steadily been slashing capacity on short- and long-haul flights.

The company is working to make its long-haul international service more profitable by adding routes to the US, Europe, and China and by incorporating new, fuel-efficient jets into its fleet. In addition, it is joining with other players in New Zealand's travel industry to promote the country as a tourist destination.

In 2010 the airline announced that it is in talks with Virgin Blue about a possible code-share or joint venture arrangement that would allow the two airlines to better compete with Qantas (the largest trans-Tasman operator) and Emirates on the routes, which more than 1.3 million passengers fly each year. Later that year, however, the Australian Competition and Consumer Commission (ACCC) released a statement with its intention to block the joint venture. Along with the ACCC, airports in the region have voiced concerns over the proposed deal, arguing that the Virgin Blue-Air New Zealand deal would reduce competition and increase fares.

In addition to its scheduled airline operations, Air New Zealand offers aircraft maintenance and ground handling services. Air New Zealand has three wholly owned subsidiary airlines: Mount Cook Airline, Air Nelson, and Eagle Airways.

HISTORY

Created in 1939 as Tasman Empire Airways Limited (TEAL), the company that was to become Air New Zealand began operations in 1940 with two flying boats crossing the Tasman Sea weekly. TEAL was 38%-owned by BOAC (now British Airways) while Qantas Airways held 23% and the New Zealand government had a 20% share. In 1953 the New Zealand and Australian governments took joint control of TEAL.

In 1961 the New Zealand government became sole owner of TEAL, which changed its name to Air New Zealand in 1965. During the 1960s and 1970s, the government invested heavily in Air New Zealand, which expanded its routes to the South Pacific and other areas. In 1978 Air New Zealand merged with state-owned National Airways, formed in 1947 to serve domestic routes.

A year later Air New Zealand experienced a highly publicized setback when a chartered DC-10 crashed at Mount Erebus in Antarctica, killing 257 people.

In 1982 the government appointed Norman Geary as CEO, with a mandate to return Air New Zealand to profitability. Through tough union negotiations and a shrewd marketing campaign, Geary succeeded. He introduced an Auckland-London-Los Angeles route that helped New Zealand become a popular tourism destination in the 1980s. Geary retired in 1988.

Spurring privatization, New Zealand allowed competition in the nation's airline market, including Australian airline Ansett, which secured its first route to New Zealand in 1987. When Air New Zealand went public in 1989, rival Qantas teamed up with American Airlines, Japan Airlines, and Brierley Investments to gain control of the carrier (all three sold their stakes in Air New Zealand during the 1990s). Air New Zealand International became the core business of Air New Zealand, and Air New Zealand National acted as a separate operator for domestic routes.

Air New Zealand International expanded in the 1990s, offering service to Bangkok, Thailand (1990); Taipei, Taiwan (1991); Seoul (1993); Nagoya and Osaka, Japan (1994); and Fukuoka, Japan (1995). Air New Zealand boosted its capacity in 1995 by creating a low-fare express service, Freedom Air, that initially served Australia and Fiji.

In 1996 Air New Zealand acquired from transportation group TNT its 50% stake in Ansett Holdings, which held Qantas archrival Ansett Australia and 49% of Ansett International. Ansett Holdings sold its stake in Ansett New Zealand (Air New Zealand National's domestic rival) to a unit of Rupert Murdoch's News Corp., the co-shareholder of Ansett Holdings.

In 1997 Air New Zealand joined United Airlines to serve US, Australian, and New Zealand routes. The next year Lufthansa and Air New Zealand launched a daily code-share service between Europe and New Zealand, and in 1999 Air New Zealand and United increased their shared flights within the US from 34 per day to 146. Later in 1999 Air New Zealand joined Lufthansa and United Airlines as a full member of the Star Alliance marketing and code-sharing partnership.

Air New Zealand acquired the remaining 50% of loss-making Ansett Holdings from News Corp. in 2000. That year company veteran Jim McCrea, CEO since 1991, hastily departed and former Qantas executive Gary Toomey replaced him. Singapore Airlines acquired 25% of Air New Zealand in 2000.

In 2001 Air New Zealand entered talks to sell Ansett to Qantas, but Qantas decided not to pursue a deal. Air New Zealand then placed Ansett under bankruptcy protection, Toomey resigned, and the Australian carrier's operations were suspended. Two Australian businessmen, Lindsay Fox and Solomon Lew, attempted to purchase Ansett, which would have helped alleviate some of Air New Zealand's debt, but the pair walked away from the deal. The New Zealand government wound up coming to the carrier's rescue — and gaining a controlling stake — with an infusion of $250 million after the Ansett debacle.

Banking industry veteran Ralph Norris took over as CEO in early 2002 and helped guide the airline toward financial stability. Norris stepped down in 2005 and was replaced by Rob Fyfe, chief information officer since 2003.

Air New Zealand reached a code-sharing deal with Qantas that was designed to reduce capacity in the trans-Tasman market (between Australia and New Zealand) but opposition from regulators caused the plan to be withdrawn in 2006.

EXECUTIVES

Chairman: John Palmer, age 62
Deputy Chairman: Roger France, age 65
CEO: Rob Fyfe
Deputy CEO: Norman (Norm) Thompson
CFO and Group General Manager, Corporate: Rob McDonald
Group General Manager, International Airline: Ed Sims
Group General Manager, Shorthaul Airlines: Bruce Parton
Group General Manager, People: Vanessa Stoddart
General Manager, Airline Operations and Safety: David Morgan
General Manager, Marketing and Communications: Mike Tod
General Manager, Strategic Development: Nathan Agnew
General Manager, Airline Operations and Planning: Glen Sowry
Auditors: Deloitte

LOCATIONS

HQ: Air New Zealand Limited
185 Fanshawe St.
Auckland 1010, New Zealand
Phone: 64-9-336-2400　　**Fax:** 64-9-336-2401
Web: www.airnz.co.nz

2010 Sales

	% of total
New Zealand	55
Australia & Pacific Islands	14
North America	11
Asia	10
UK & Europe	10
Total	**100**

PRODUCTS/OPERATIONS

2010 Sales

	% of total
Passengers	82
Cargo	8
Contract services & other revenue	6
Other	4
Total	**100**

COMPETITORS

Air France-KLM	Emirates
AMR Corp.	Japan Airlines
Australian Air Express	Qantas
British Airways	Singapore Airlines
Cathay Pacific	Skywest Airlines
Delta Air Lines	Virgin Blue

HISTORICAL FINANCIALS

Company Type: Public

Income Statement

FYE: June 30

	REVENUE ($ mil.)	NET INCOME ($ mil.)	NET PROFIT MARGIN	EMPLOYEES
6/10	2,815	57	2.0%	—
6/09	2,984	14	0.5%	—
6/08	3,555	166	4.7%	—
6/07	3,307	165	5.0%	—
6/06	2,284	58	2.5%	10,233
Annual Growth	**5.4%**	**(0.3%)**	**—**	**—**

2010 Year-End Financials

Debt ratio: —
Return on equity: —
Cash ($ mil.): 742
Current ratio: 1.05
Long-term debt ($ mil.): —
No. of shares (mil.): 1,084
Dividends
　Yield: 3.3%
　Payout: 40.0%
Market value ($ mil.): 808

Stock History

New Zealand: AIR

	STOCK PRICE ($) FY Close	P/E High/Low	PER SHARE ($) Earnings	Dividends	Book Value
6/10	0.74	18　11	0.05	0.02	1.00
6/09	0.60	64　34	0.01	0.04	0.96
6/08	0.83	15　5	0.16	0.08	1.11
6/07	2.03	15　5	0.16	0.12	1.24
6/06	0.70	17　12	0.06	0.03	0.88
Annual Growth	**1.4%**	**—　—**	**(4.5%)**	**(9.6%)**	**3.3%**

Airbus S.A.S.

Airbus really knows how to pack 'em in. Passengers, that is. The commercial aircraft manufacturer makes the jumbo 525-seat A380, the largest civil airliner in service. It also makes more than a dozen other aircraft models, ranging from single-aisle (A318, A319, A320, A321) to wide-body (A300, A310, A330, A340), with capacities ranging from about 100 to 400 passengers. Airbus vies with Boeing to be the world's #1 commercial jet maker. Its midsized A350 XWB model — due for delivery in 2013 — is expected to compete against Boeing's upcoming 787 Dreamliner. It is also expanding into the military transport aircraft sector with airlifters and aerial tankers. Airbus is owned by EADS.

Airbus Military was formed in 2009 as part of an effort by EADS to streamline operations by integrating its military transport aircraft operations into Airbus. The division will militarize civilian aircraft designs, as well as continue to design new airlifter families. The A400M model, developed for use by European NATO countries and international air forces, made its maiden flight in December 2009.

Aiming to reduce costs in the turbulent global economy, Airbus consolidated eight of its manufacturing centers into four and focused on building strategic relationships with partners in China and India. Other key priorities include increasing its A380 production rate to meet delivery schedules. By the end of 2009, Airbus had received more than 200 orders for the jumbo jet, from customers that include Air France, British Airways, China Southern, Korean Air Lines, Lufthansa, and Virgin Atlantic, among others.

The Asia/Pacific region remains a core market for Airbus. More than 60 airline operators across the region fly its aircraft, and demand in the area was a driving force behind development of the double-deck A380. In 2008 Airbus established a final assembly line in China — its first outside Europe — as evidence of the importance of the region. The facility also gives Airbus better access to the companies in China that are manufacturing composite material parts and components for the A350 and A320 families. The company also supplies parts as a subcontractor under aircraft programs in Australia, China, India, Indonesia, Japan, Malaysia, and South Korea.

HISTORY

In the 1970s three US companies, Boeing, Lockheed, and McDonnell Douglas, dominated the commercial aircraft market. France and the UK had been discussing an alliance to build competing jets since 1965, but political infighting stalled the talks. Finally, in 1969 France and West Germany committed to building the Airbus A300. Airbus Industrie was born in 1970 as a *groupement d'intérêt économique* (grouping of economic interest, a structure used by allied French vineyards). Seed money came from partners Aerospatiale Matra and Deutsche Airbus. CASA joined in 1971.

The A300 entered service with Air France in 1974, but Airbus had trouble selling it outside member countries. The following year the firm hired former American Airlines president George Warde to help market the A300 in the US. His efforts paid off when Eastern Air Lines decided to buy the A300. Also in 1975 Airbus launched the A310, a smaller, more fuel-efficient version of the A300. The UK joined the consortium in 1979.

By 1980 Airbus trailed only Boeing among the world's commercial jet makers. The A320 was introduced in 1984 — it featured a groundbreaking "fly-by-wire" system that allowed pilots to adjust the aircraft's control surfaces via a computer, helping to make it the fastest-selling jetliner in history. The firm launched the A330 and A340, larger planes designed for medium- and long-range flights, in 1987. Two years later Airbus introduced the A321, an elongated version of the A320, and received a $6 billion order from Federal Express.

The German government sold its 20% stake in Deutsche Airbus to Daimler-Benz (now Daimler AG) in 1992. In 1993 Airbus sold only 38 planes, about one-sixth as many as Boeing. Sales rebounded in 1995, and the next year the firm won a contract worth about $5 billion to provide planes to USAir (now US Airways).

Seeking more customers in Asia, Airbus signed parts contracts with Japanese suppliers in 1999 and launched production of its A318, a 107-seat short-haul passenger jet designed to compete with Boeing's 717. Also that year Airbus won a contract worth $946 million to provide British Airways with up to 24 of its A318s.

In 2000 the UK government pledged $836 million in loans to back consortium partner BAE SYSTEMS' participation in the A3XX project, an ambitious plane that would seat more than 550 passengers. That year the German government announced plans to purchase up to 75 Airbus A400M transports valued at around $9.8 billion.

Airbus officially launched the A3XX — and renamed it the A380 — late in 2000. In July Airbus Industrie was incorporated in France as Airbus S.A.S.

Faced with the drastic downturn in the commercial aviation market due to the September 11 attacks, in 2002 the company announced that it would cut full-time equivalent work hours by around 13% (equal to about 6,000 jobs) through voluntary retirement, reduction in part-time work, and cancellation of temporary contracts.

Airbus delivered more planes than Boeing for the first time ever in 2003 (305 to 281) and repeated the feat in 2004 (320 to 285).

Airbus unveiled the first A380 to press and buyers in 2005. In February, Spanish airline Iberia said it planned to buy as many as 79 (30 firm orders and 49 options) A320 planes. Late in 2005 six Chinese airlines agreed to buy 150 A320s — worth about $10 billion — from Airbus.

The A380 made a maiden test flight of nearly four hours on April 27, 2005. However, about a month later Airbus announced that deliveries of the first A380s would be delayed by up to six months. After further dealys the company finally delivered the first A380 in October 2007 — two years late — to Singapore Airlines.

In 2007 the company's cost-cutting measures included 10,000 job cuts in Germany, France, Spain, and the UK; an increase in outsourcing of aerostructure work; and the sale of all or part of six factories.

Airbus faced yet another challenge in 2008 when it won a bid to build tankers for the US Air Force only to have the contract cancelled by the Pentagon four months later so that US competitor Boeing could rebid for the contract. Pentagon officials cited irregularities in the bidding process, but officials at Airbus have claimed the decision is rooted in US political forces that want the Pentagon to maintain a policy of buying US-made products for the military.

EXECUTIVES

President and CEO: Thomas (Tom) Enders, age 51
COO: Fabrice Brégier, age 49
COO, Customers and Chief Commercial Officer: John J. Leahy, age 60
CFO: Harald Wilhelm, age 44
EVP Operations: Gerald Weber, age 60
EVP Procurement: Klaus Richter, age 46
EVP Human Resources: Thierry Baril, age 45
EVP Programmes: Tom Williams, age 57
EVP Engineering: Charles Champion, age 55
Chairman, Airbus Americas: T. Allan McArtor
President, Airbus China: Laurence Barron, age 58
President, Airbus Japan: Stephane Ginoux, age 52
Head, Airbus Military: Domingo Ureña-Raso, age 52

LOCATIONS

HQ: Airbus S.A.S.
1, Rond Point Maurice Bellonte
31707 Blagnac, France
Phone: 33-5-61-93-33-33
US HQ: 198 Van Buren St., Ste. 300, Herndon, VA 20170
US Phone: 703-834-3400   **US Fax:** 703-834-3340
Web: www.airbus.com

PRODUCTS/OPERATIONS

2009 Sales

	% of total
Commercial aircraft	92
Military aircraft	8
Total	**100**

Selected Aircraft

Single-aisle twin-engine jets
A318
A319
A320
A321

Superjumbo four-engine jets
A380 (525-passenger)

Wide-body twin-engine jets
A300-600
A300-600F
A310

Wide-body two- and four-engine jets
A330 (two-engine)
A340 (four-engine)
A340-500
A340-600
A350-800 (270-passenger, scheduled for delivery in 2013)
A350-900 (314-passenger, scheduled for delivery in 2013)
A350-1000 (350-passenger, scheduled for delivery in 2013)

Selected Customers

Aer Lingus
Air Canada
Air France
Alitalia
American Airlines
Arik Air
British Airways
China Southern
DHL
FedEx
Iberia
Jazeera Airways
Korean Airlines
Lufthansa
Qantas Airways
Qatar Airways
Singapore Airlines
Thai Airways
United
US Airways
Virgin Atlantic Airways
Wizzair

COMPETITORS

Boeing
Bombardier
Embraer
Gulfstream Aerospace
Lockheed Martin
Northrop Grumman

HISTORICAL FINANCIALS

Company Type: Subsidiary

Income Statement

FYE: December 31

	REVENUE ($ mil.)	NET INCOME ($ mil.)	NET PROFIT MARGIN	EMPLOYEES
12/09	40,226	—	—	61,987
12/08	38,695	—	—	52,000
12/07	37,115	—	—	56,000
12/06	33,233	—	—	57,000
12/05	26,267	—	—	55,000
Annual Growth	11.2%	—	—	3.0%

Revenue History

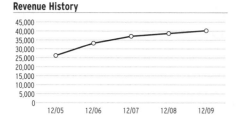

Aisin Seiki

How do you stop Toyota? With Aisin Seiki brake systems, that's how. Aisin Automotive Parts and Systems offers automotive-related products such as transmissions, brakes, and engine and car navigation systems. Its Life and Energy business offers items for more comfortable living, with products that range from heating and cooling systems to toilets with jet sprays; well-care items include electric wheelchairs and reclining beds. Its New Business segment is focused on innovations such as fiber lasers and advances in biotechnology for the automotive market. The company has around 150 consolidated subsidiaries and companies worldwide. Toyota owns 22% of Aisin Seiki and accounts for about 65% of sales.

Aisin Seiki is looking to diversify its customer mix by expanding production overseas to achieve a 50% ratio by 2015. The company pledged $100 million in late 2010 to retool and expand operations at its North Carolina facility to produce automatic transmissions for front-wheel-drive vehicles. The plant, which currently makes transmissions for rear-wheel-drive vehicles, is expected to begin production by late 2011. In an atempt to meet projected demand in Brazil, the company will build a new manufacturing facility in the region and expects to increase its employees in the region by more than 100%. In 2008 the company opened Aisin Thai Automotive Casting in Thailand, established an auto interior parts (auto seat frames and seat covers) manufacturing company in Poland, opened automotive parts production companies in China, started up its second plant in Canada, and launched a facility in the Czech Republic to make aluminum die-cast products. These facilities, along with the rest of the company's manufacturing network, which includes Australia, Belgium, Brazil, India, Indonesia, Mexico, Taiwan, Turkey, and the UK, give the company a firm global footprint.

The company's businesses have worked autonomously in the past; however, Aisin Seiki's view of the present situation is leading it to combine and link its individual businesses, thus strengthening and maximizing the potential of the products and technologies that are cultivated by each company.

The company will continue making automotive components and systems, but it will focus on increasing sales of main products such as transmissions, car navigation systems, and power sliding doors. For the Life segment, it is looking to increase sales of gas heat pump air conditioners and shower toilets.

HISTORY

Aisin Seiki traces its roots to 1943 when Tokai Hikoki was founded to produce airplane engines for the Japanese war effort. After the war the company switched to manufacturing sewing machines and auto parts. Aisin Seiki took its present name in 1965 after Tokai Hikoki merged with Shinkawa Kogyo.

The company's operations were limited to Japan until 1969, when it signed a technical agreement with a German company regarding steering gears. International expansion continued as Aisin Seiki formed Aisin USA (to import aftermarket parts for imported cars) in 1970, Aisin Europe in 1971, and Aisin (UK) and Aisin (Australia) Pty. in 1972. Other operations sprung up in Mexico (1973), Brazil (1974), Singapore (1977), and Germany (1978). In the late 1980s the company worked at expanding the sale of body components, such as sunroofs and seats.

Although Aisin Seiki USA had been formed to import parts for imported cars, by 1990 the unit shipped more parts for domestic cars than it did for imports. In 1996 Aisin Seiki set up Tangshan Aisin Gear, a joint venture with Tangshan Gear Works, to produce manual transmissions in China. The next year the company's Kariya plant, which produced brake and clutch parts used in many Toyotas, burned down. The disruption forced Toyota — which accounted for about 80% of the Kariya plant's sales — to temporarily shut down its 20 Japanese auto plants. Also in 1997 Aisin Seiki formed Aisin GM Allison Co., a joint venture with General Motors, to produce automatic transmissions in Japan and the Pacific Rim region. Aisin GM Allison was dissolved in 2007 as GM geared up to sell Allison Transmission.

In 1998 the company formed Aisin Europe Manufacturing in the UK, its first manufacturing facility in Europe. Also that year it began work on subsidiary Aisin A W Co. to supply engine parts for the Toyota facility in West Virginia. Despite increasing sales, Aisin Seiki announced in 2000 that it would post a loss due to a charge for retirement benefits.

EXECUTIVES

Chairman: Kanshiro Toyoda, age 68
Vice Chairman: Yasuhito Yamauchi, age 66
President and Director: Fumio Fujimori
EVP and Director: Shunichi Nakamura
EVP and Director: Masuji Arai
EVP and Director: Norio Oku, age 64
Senior Managing Director and Director: Yutaka Miyamoto
Senior Managing Director and Director: Naofumi Fujie
Senior Managing Director and Director: Shizuo Shimanuki
Senior Managing Director and Director: Takashi Morita
Senior Managing Director and Director: Toshikazu Nagura
Senior Managing Director and Director: Shinichiro Yamamura

Senior Managing Director and Director: Toshiyuki Mizushima
Senior Managing Director and Director: Makoto Mitsuya
Auditors: ChuoAoyama Audit Corporation

LOCATIONS

HQ: Aisin Seiki Co., Ltd.
2-1, Asahi-machi
Kariya, Aichi 448-8650, Japan
Phone: 81-566-24-8441 **Fax:** 81-566-24-8003
US HQ: 1665 E. 4th St., Seymour, IN 47274
US Phone: 812-524-8144 **US Fax:** 812-524-8146
Web: www.aisin.co.jp

2010 Sales

	% of total
Japan	73
North America	11
Europe	7
Other regions	9
Total	**100**

PRODUCTS/OPERATIONS

2010 Sales

	% of total
Automotive	
Drivetrain	41
Brake & chassis	20
Body-related	19
Engine-related	10
Information-related	6
Life, energy & other	4
Total	**100**

Selected Products

Automotive
Drivetrain products (transmission and clutch systems)
Brake and chassis products (drum brakes, master cylinders, air suspension systems)
Body products (door frames and locks, sunroofs, power seats)
Engine products (water pumps, pistons, exhaust manifolds)
Information and other products (navigation systems, Intelligent Parking Assist)
Aftermarket products
Life and Amenity
Bed, furniture, and fabric (ASLEEP)
Housing equipment
House remodeling service (Livelan)
Home-use sewing machine
Embroidery machine
Facility consulting service (CONTRACT)
Business consulting service (TSS)
Audio equipment
Energy System
GHP
Cogeneration system
Cryopump
Cryocooler
Peltier modules

COMPETITORS

APM Automotive
ArvinMeritor
BorgWarner
Calsonic Kansei
Dana Holding
Delphi Automotive
DENSO
Dura Automotive
Eaton
Faurecia
Haldex
Hitachi America
Lear Corp

Magna International
Mitsubishi Electric
Modine Manufacturing
Panasonic Corp
Robert Bosch
Sumitomo Electric
Tenneco
Torotrak
TRW Automotive
Valeo
Visteon
ZF Friedrichshafen

HISTORICAL FINANCIALS

Company Type: Public

Income Statement				FYE: March 31
	REVENUE ($ mil.)	NET INCOME ($ mil.)	NET PROFIT MARGIN	EMPLOYEES
3/10	22,164	581	2.6%	73,213
3/09	22,763	(156)	—	73,201
3/08	27,196	923	3.4%	73,500
3/07	20,171	567	2.8%	66,000
3/06	18,034	520	2.9%	59,587
Annual Growth	5.3%	2.8%	—	5.3%

2010 Year-End Financials

Debt ratio: —
Return on equity: 8.6%
Cash ($ mil.): 3,048
Current ratio: 1.55
Long-term debt ($ mil.): —

No. of shares (mil.): 281
Dividends
 Yield: 0.6%
 Payout: 29.7%
Market value ($ mil.): 8,502

Stock History

Tokyo: 72590

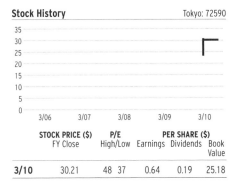

	STOCK PRICE ($) FY Close	P/E High/Low		PER SHARE ($) Earnings	Dividends	Book Value
3/10	30.21	48	37	0.64	0.19	25.18

Akzo Nobel

Akzo Nobel NV is the world's largest paint maker, but it can do more than paint a pretty picture. The company is also among the world's largest chemical manufacturers and a major salt producer. Akzo Nobel divides its business into three lines. The Wood Finishes and Adhesives group produces decorative paints and primarily serves Europe and North America. Akzo Nobel's Industrial Coatings group manufactures marine and protective coatings, packaging coatings, automotive finishes, and industrial coatings. The Functional Chemicals unit makes pulp and paper chemicals, functional chemicals (flame retardants, crop nutrients), industrial chemicals (salt and chlor alkalies), surfactants, and specialty starches.

In 2009 Akzo Nobel acquired the powder coatings business of Dow Chemical Company. The deal brought technological know-how and significant synergy potential to Akzo Nobel's Powder Coatings line, as well as enhancing the company's position in the US.

That same year, Akzo Nobel subsidiary National Starch acquired Penford Australia's specialty grain wet milling and manufacturing facility, expanding National Starch's reach into the Asia/Pacific region. However, in 2010 Corn Products International agreed to acquire National Starch for $2.7 billion.

In what turned out to be a major turning point for the company, Akzo Nobel approached UK coatings and chemicals maker ICI with a $14 bil-

lion takeover offer in late 2007. ICI's board rejected the price tag as insufficient. Akzo Nobel countered, twice, and ended up agreeing to a deal worth $16 billion. As part of the deal, Henkel bought the adhesives and electronic materials businesses of ICI subsidiary National Starch and Chemical. The buy of ICI built up Akzo's coatings business even further. The acquired businesses have great strength in retail decorative paints and in North America, both areas in which Akzo Nobel's coatings business had been lacking.

Another business acquired in the deal was Akzo Nobel's new Chemicals Pakistan division, which was composed of the company's majority holdings in two publicly traded companies. Those subsidiaries made soda ash, polyester fibers, and pure terephthalic acid (PTA).

HISTORY

The Akzo side of Akzo Nobel traces its roots to two companies — German rayon and coatings maker Vereinigte Glanzstoff-Fabriken (founded 1899) and Dutch rayon maker Nederlandsche Kunstzijdebariek (founded 1911 and known as NK or Enka). In 1928 NK built a plant near Asheville, North Carolina, in what later became the town of Enka. The two companies merged in 1929 to create Algemene Kunstzijde-Unie (AKU).

In 1967 two Dutch companies merged to form Koninklijke Zout-Organon (KZO). Two years later KZO bought US-based International Salt and merged with AKU to form Akzo. In the 1980s Akzo focused on building its chemicals, coatings, and pharmaceuticals businesses. Akzo sold its paper and pulp business to Nobel in 1993. A few months later the company reclaimed that business when it bought Nobel.

Best remembered for the prizes that bear his name (which were first awarded in 1901 through a bequest in his will), Alfred Nobel invented the blasting cap in 1863, making it possible to control the detonation of nitroglycerin. He then persuaded Stockholm merchant J. W. Smitt to help him finance Nitroglycerin Ltd. to make and sell the volatile fluid (1864). Nobel's quest to improve nitroglycerin led to his invention of dynamite in 1867.

After Nobel's death in 1896, Nitroglycerin Ltd. remained an explosives maker, and in 1965 it changed its name to Nitro Nobel. In 1978 Swedish industrialist Marcus Wallenberg bought Nitro Nobel for his KemaNord chemical group, known afterward as KemaNobel. Within six years industrialist Erik Penser controlled both KemaNobel and armaments maker Bofors, and he merged them in 1984 as Nobel Industries.

Risky investments led Penser to ruin in 1991. His holdings, including Nobel, were taken over by a government-owned bank and conveyed into Securum, a state-owned holding company (which still owns 18% of Akzo Nobel). In 1992 Nobel spun off its consumer-goods segment.

Akzo bought Nobel in 1994. Although the company had good financial results in 1995, it faced pressure from rising costs for raw materials and a difficult foreign-exchange environment. Akzo announced major closings and layoffs — it sold its polyethylene packaging resin business and moved some clothing-grade rayon operations to Poland.

The merger between Akzo and Nobel was legally completed in 1996. That year the company introduced Puregon, a fertility drug, and Remeron, touted as a replacement for Prozac, in the US and other countries. In 1997 Akzo Nobel put most of its worst-performing segment,

fibers, into a joint venture with Turkish conglomerate Sabanci.

Akzo Nobel acquired Courtaulds (coatings, sealants, and fibers) in 1998 and changed the firm's name to Akzo Nobel UK. Akzo Nobel also bought BASF deco, the European decorative-coatings business of BASF Coatings. Akzo Nobel combined its fiber business with Akzo Nobel UK to form a new division, Acordis. Akzo Nobel then sold Acordis to investment firm CVC Capital Partners in 1999 for $859 million (Akzo Nobel retains a minority share). That year Akzo Nobel bought Hoechst's animal-health unit, Hoechst Roussel Vet, for $712 million.

In 2001 Akzo Nobel sold its medical diagnostics division to French drugmaker bioMérieux-Pierre Fabre. Later that year the company picked up the vehicle refinishes business of MAC Specialty Coatings of the US.

CEO Cees van Lede retired in mid-2003, succeeded by Hans Wijers, who immediately set about restructuring, cutting costs, and erasing debt. By year's end more than 3,300 jobs were cut and Akzo Nobel had sold off three big chemical units: catalysts (to Albemarle), coating resins, and phosphorous chemicals (to Ripplewood Holdings).

The fruits of those sell-offs came with 2005 acquisitions in Germany, France, and Switzerland. The last purchase, of Swiss Lack, made Akzo Nobel the largest paint company in Switzerland as well.

In 2006 Akzo announced plans to split off its pharmaceuticals segment, Organon. It originally planned to float a minority share early in 2007 and then fully separate the new company by 2009. In a surprise move, however, Schering-Plough came in and bought the unit for $14.4 billion.

EXECUTIVES

Chairman: Karel Vuursteen, age 68
Deputy Chairman: Uwe-Ernst Bufe, age 66
Chairman, Board of Management and CEO: G. J. (Hans) Wijers, age 59, $3,531,548 total compensation
CFO: Keith Nichols, age 49, $2,187,990 total compensation
CIO: Peter Schoehuijs, age 45
SVP Human Resources: Heiko Hutmacher
Member, Board of Management, Performance Coatings: Leif Darner, age 58, $2,560,216 total compensation
Member, Board of Management, Decorative Paints: Louis W. (Tex) Gunning, age 60, $1,397,943 total compensation
Member, Board of Management, Specialty Chemicals: Rob Frohn, age 50, $2,334,555 total compensation
Secretary, Investor Relations: Els van der Hulst
Secretary, Board of Management: Graham Wladimiroff
Corporate Director Control: Hans de Vriese, age 45
Corporate Director Internal Audit: Marjo van Ool
Corporate Director Strategy and Mergers and Acquisitions: Jennifer Midura
Corporate Director IP and Special Projects: Piet Schalkwijk
Corporate Director Purchasing: Ton Geurts
Corporate Director Communications: John McLaren
Director Compensation and Benefits: Ralph Wildeman
Director Investor Relations: Huib Wurfbain
General Counsel: Sven Dumoulin
Head of External Relations: Tim van der Zanden
Auditors: KPMG Accountants N.V.

LOCATIONS

HQ: Akzo Nobel N.V.
 Strawinskylaan 2555
 1077 ZZ Amsterdam, The Netherlands
Phone: 31-20-502-7555   **Fax:** 31-20-502-7666
US HQ: 525 W. Van Buren St., Chicago, IL 60607
US Phone: 312-544-7000   **US Fax:** 312-544-7322
Web: www.akzonobel.com

2009 Sales

	% of total
Europe	
Germany	8
UK	6
The Netherlands	6
Sweden	3
Other countries	23
US & Canada	21
Asia	
China	8
Other countries	12
Latin America	9
Other regions	4
Total	**100**

PRODUCTS/OPERATIONS

2009 Sales

	% of total
Specialty chemicals	37
Decorative paints	34
Performance coatings	29
Total	**100**

Selected Products

Specialty chemicals
  Base chemicals
  Functional chemicals
  Polymer chemicals
  Pulp and paper chemicals
  Surfactants

Decorative paints

Performance coatings
  Car refinishes
  Industrial finishes
  Marine and protective coatings
  Powder coatings

COMPETITORS

Alfa SA
Asahi Kasei
BASF SE
Compass Minerals
DuPont
Eastman Chemical
Evonik Degussa
Ferro
Formosa Plastics
H.B. Fuller
Orica
PPG Industries
Sherwin-Williams
Valspar

HISTORICAL FINANCIALS
Company Type: Public

Income Statement
FYE: December 31

	REVENUE ($ mil.)	NET INCOME ($ mil.)	NET PROFIT MARGIN	EMPLOYEES
12/09	19,911	519	2.6%	57,100
12/08	21,727	(1,439)	—	60,000
12/07	15,038	13,779	91.6%	43,000
12/06	18,139	1,523	8.4%	61,880
12/05	15,448	1,142	7.4%	61,340
Annual Growth	**6.6%**	**(17.9%)**	**—**	**(1.8%)**

2009 Year-End Financials

Debt ratio: 44.9%
Return on equity: 4.8%
Cash ($ mil.): 3,050
Current ratio: 1.37
Long-term debt ($ mil.): 4,999

No. of shares (mil.): 233
Dividends
  Yield: 3.7%
  Payout: 141.0%
Market value ($ mil.): 15,521

Stock History

Euronext Amsterdam: AKZA

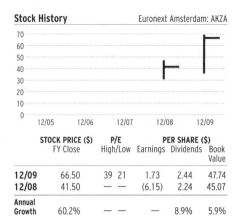

	STOCK PRICE ($) FY Close	P/E High/Low	PER SHARE ($) Earnings	Dividends	Book Value
12/09	66.50	39 21	1.73	2.44	47.74
12/08	41.50	— —	(6.15)	2.24	45.07
Annual Growth	**60.2%**	**— —**	**—**	**8.9%**	**5.9%**

Alcatel-Lucent

Alcatel-Lucent found its calling: supplying high-tech equipment for telecommunications networks. Supplying service providers, the company's core carrier unit offers network switching and transmission systems for wireline and wireless networks, terrestrial and submarine optical systems, microwave radio products, and fixed access equipment. Its enterprise division provides corporate and government clients with unified communications systems, data networking gear, and contact center systems. Alcatel-Lucent's application division develops IP television, payment, messaging, and mobile TV software. The company's services range from application and systems integration to managed services and maintenance.

Alcatel-Lucent has undergone extensive integration and restructuring efforts since its formation in 2006, when Alcatel and Lucent Technologies merged. The company has struggled with organizational changes in a market particularly hard-hit by a weak economy. Key aspects of its turnaround strategy include job cuts; improving margins by cutting manufacturing, supply chain, and procurement costs; and focusing its research and development efforts on its more mature and established technologies such as IP, broadband, and optical products.

Alcatel-Lucent's restructuring measures have largely been focused on its core carrier business, which includes Alcatel-Lucent's wireline, wireless, optics, and IP segments. The company's largest segment, wireline carrier equipment, has been especially vulnerable to decreased spending in the sector. Alcatel-Lucent is looking to burgeoning markets such as China and India, an increased focused on IP networking, and possible spending increases resulting from US economic stimulus packages to provide some growth.

Its wireless carrier business group provides systems based on a variety of standards, including GSM, CDMA, and Wideband CDMA (W-CDMA, also known as UMTS). Alcatel-Lucent's wireless business has suffered from intense competition for GSM share, a declining CDMA market, and pricing pressure in the W-CDMA sector. The company's struggles have led to speculation that Alcatel-Lucent might have to divest its wireless operations.

The company's acquisition and divestiture strategy has aimed at building its service provider product portfolio and jettisoning non-core businesses. It bought French mobile software and application development tool maker OpenPlug in 2010. It also sold its remaining 21% share of defense contractor Thales to airplane maker Dassault Aviation for $2.3 billion.

In 2009 Alcatel-Lucent bought UK-based content delivery network infrastructure and services provider Velocix. The deal is intended to expand the company's portfolio of services for ISPs and media companies.

HISTORY

In 1898 Pierre Azaria combined his electric generating company with three others to form Compagnie Générale d'Électricité (CGE). As one of Europe's pioneer electric power and manufacturing companies, CGE expanded operations in France and abroad through acquisitions. After the French government nationalized electric utilities in 1946, CGE diversified into the production of telecommunications equipment, consumer appliances, and electronics.

In 1970 CGE bought Alcatel, a French communications pioneer founded in 1879 that had introduced digital switching exchanges. CGE combined its telecom division with Alcatel to form CIT Alcatel.

The Mitterrand government nationalized CGE in 1982. The next year the company traded its electronics units for Thomson's communications businesses, making CGE the world's fifth-largest telephone equipment maker. Later, CGE combined Alcatel with ITT's phone equipment operations to form Alcatel NV, a Brussels-based company that started off as the world's second-largest telecom enterprise, after AT&T.

In 1987 the government sold CGE to the public. Two years later CGE and UK-based The General Electric Company, plc (GEC, now Marconi plc) combined their power systems and engineering businesses to create GEC Alsthom NV. The company adopted the Alcatel Alsthom name in 1991 (shortened to Alcatel in 1998) and purchased the transmission equipment unit of US-based Rockwell International (now Rockwell Automation).

Turnaround specialist Serge Tchuruk, the former head of French oil giant TOTAL, was chosen to lead the company in 1995. Deregulation and intense competition in the European telecom market, along with massive writeoffs of bad investments dating back to the 1980s, led to a $5 billion loss in 1995, Alcatel's first loss and one of the largest to date by a French company. As a result Alcatel divested nonstrategic assets and cut its workforce by more than 12,500 employees. The company bounced back with a profit in 1996.

Following the recommendation of the French government, in 1998 Alcatel, Dassault Industries, and Aerospatiale joined forces to buy part of the state's stake in defense electronics group Thomson-CSF (now Thales). Intensifying its telecommunications focus, Alcatel sold its main engineering unit (Cegelec) to GEC Alsthom in 1998 and then spun off the venture as ALSTOM. That year Alcatel bought networking specialists Packet Engines and DSC Communications to further push into the US market.

Alcatel changed the name of its power and communication cables business, one of the world's largest cable manufacturing operations, to Nexans in 2000. The company also sold 20%

of its optical components unit to create the first European tracking stock. Alcatel acquired Genesys Telecommunications Laboratories in 2000. In 2001 Alcatel took control of its satellite communications joint venture with Thales. A market slowdown that year led Alcatel to announce staff cuts of about 10%.

In mid-2001 Alcatel spun off Nexans to the public (it sold its remaining minority stake in the company in 2004), sold its remaining stake in ALSTOM, and bought a controlling stake in its joint venture in China with Shanghai Bell.

That year it sold its semiconductor business, Alcatel Microelectronics, to STMicroelectronics for about $345 million.

In 2006 Alcatel purchased a 28% stake in home networking specialist 2Wire. In 2007 the company divested its stakes in two satellite-related joint ventures it formed with Finmeccanica: Alcatel Alenia Space and Telespazio Holding.

With Alcaltel-Lucent's losses widening, both Tchuruk and Russo stepped down in 2008. Philippe Camus and Ben Verwaayen were named to take over as chairman and CEO, respectively.

EXECUTIVES

Chairman: Philippe Camus, age 61
CEO and Director: Bernardus J. (Ben) Verwaayen, age 58
EVP; President of the Enterprise Product Group: Tom Burns
EVP; President of the Americas Region: Robert Vrij, age 45
EVP; President, Bell Laboratories: Jeong H. Kim, age 49
EVP; President of Quality Assurance and Customer Care: Janet G. Davidson
EVP and CFO: Paul J. Tufano, age 56
EVP Business and Information Technology Transformation: Robin Dargue
SVP Public Affairs: Gabrielle Gauthey
SVP Transformation: Victor Agnellini
SVP Corporate Communications: Caroline Guillaumin
General Counsel: Steve Reynolds
Chief Marketing, Strategy, and Communication Officer: Stephen A. Carter, age 46
Head Operations: John T. Dickson, age 64
Head Corporate Human Resources and Transformation: Pierre Barnabé
President, Wireless Networks Product Division: Wim Sweldens
President, Solutions and Marketing: Kenneth Frank
President, 4G/LTE Wireless Networks: Ken Wirth
Chairman Management Board, Deutschland: Alf H. Wulf, age 47
Auditors: Deloitte & Associés

LOCATIONS

HQ: Alcatel-Lucent
54, rue La Boétie
75008 Paris, France
Phone: 33-1-4076-1010   **Fax:** 33-1-4076-1400
US HQ: 600 Mountain Ave., Murray Hill, NJ 07974
US Phone: 908-508-8080   **US Fax:** 908-508-2576
Web: www.alcatel-lucent.com

2009 Sales

	% of total
Americas	
US	29
Other countries	8
Europe	
France	9
Other Western Europe	20
Other Europe	4
Asia/Pacific	20
Other regions	10
Total	**100**

PRODUCTS/OPERATIONS

2009 Sales

	% of total
Carrier	60
Services	24
Applications software	7
Enterprise	7
Other	2
Total	**100**

Selected Products and Services

Carrier
 CDMA
 Fixed access
 Internet Protocol (IP)
 Maintenance
 Mobile access
 Multicore
 Optics
Services
 Network integration
 Network operations
 Professional services
Enterprise
 Enterprise solutions
 Industrial components
Applications software
 Carrier applications
 Genesys

COMPETITORS

ADC Telecommunications
Avaya
Brocade Communications
Cisco Systems
Corning
ECI Telecom
Ericsson
Fujitsu
Harris Corp.
Hitachi
Huawei Technologies
Juniper Networks
Motorola
NEC
Nokia Siemens Networks
Nortel Networks
Panasonic Mobile Communications
telent
Tellabs
Toshiba
UTStarcom
ZTE

HISTORICAL FINANCIALS

Company Type: Public

Income Statement

	REVENUE ($ mil.)	NET INCOME ($ mil.)	NET PROFIT MARGIN	EMPLOYEES
12/09	21,723	(722)	—	78,373
12/08	23,939	(7,291)	—	77,717
12/07	26,157	(5,173)	—	76,410
12/06	16,217	(232)	—	89,370
12/05	15,617	1,105	7.1%	58,000
Annual Growth	**8.6%**	**—**	**—**	**7.8%**

FYE: December 31

2009 Year-End Financials

Debt ratio: 111.7%
Return on equity: —
Cash ($ mil.): 5,127
Current ratio: 1.35
Long-term debt ($ mil.): 5,989
No. of shares (mil.): 2,260
Dividends
 Yield: 0.0%
 Payout: —
Market value ($ mil.): 10,753

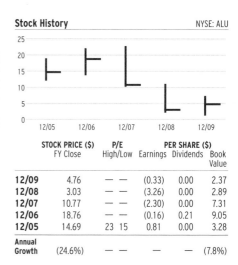

Stock History   NYSE: ALU

	STOCK PRICE ($) FY Close	P/E High/Low		Earnings	PER SHARE ($) Dividends	Book Value
12/09	4.76	—	—	(0.33)	0.00	2.37
12/08	3.03	—	—	(3.26)	0.00	2.89
12/07	10.77	—	—	(2.30)	0.00	7.31
12/06	18.76	—	—	(0.16)	0.21	9.05
12/05	14.69	23	15	0.81	0.00	3.28
Annual Growth	**(24.6%)**	**—**	**—**	**—**	**—**	**(7.8%)**

ALDI Group

ALDI keeps it cheap so shoppers can, too. How has discount food retailer ALDI Group become one of the world's biggest grocery chains, running more than 9,400 stores worldwide? By offering deeply discounted prices on about 1,400 popular food items (a typical grocery store has 30,000). ALDI (short for "Albrecht Discounts") buys cheap land mostly on city outskirts, builds cheap warehouses, employs a tiny staff, and carries mostly private-label items, displaying them on pallets rather than shelves. ALDI has more than 1,000 stores in some 30 US states, but Germany (where ALDI has a network of some 4,200 stores) accounts for about two-thirds of sales. ALDI was co-founded by brothers Karl and the late Theo Albrecht.

The economic downturns in both the US and UK have sent middle-class shoppers flocking to ALDI's discount stores. As a result, while other grocers retrench, ALDI has continued its rapid global expansion by adding hundreds of stores in new and existing markets. After opening about 175 stores in the US in 2009 and 2008, the company entered the Texas market in March 2010 and quickly grew to number more than 25 stores in the Dallas/Fort Worth area. To enable its growth in Texas and nearby Oklahoma, the limited-assortment retailer opened its first warehouse in Denton in 2010. The chain plans to open its first store in Queens, New York, in 2011.

The German discounter entered the US market in 1976 and has grown to ring up annual US sales of about $5.8 billion. Taking an aggressive stance, ALDI is looking to expand into Wal-Mart's territory and to break American shoppers' addiction to big-name brands.

Although Spartan-like, the company's stores do sell housewares, textiles, electronic equipment, and garden supplies. But ALDI is better known for the products and services it doesn't offer, such as in-store banking, pharmacies, liquor, fresh meats and fish, and checkout newsstands. ALDI even charges its customers 5 cents per grocery bag. As penny-pinching as its customers, ALDI doesn't advertise, and about 90% of ALDI's products are private labels. A pair of reclusive billionaires, the Albrecht brothers also co-owned US specialty food retailer Trader Joe's, prior to Theo's death in 2010.

ALDI's 19% share of the grocery market in Germany is being eroded by its European competitors, including compatriot Lidl & Schwarz, which has emulated its low-cost operating methods while offering brand-name products, and stolen customers from ALDI. In response, ALDI has changed its private-label strategy to begin offering more branded items from consumer goods makers such as Procter & Gamble and Unilever. The company has also begun offering more fresh produce.

While ALDI operates in Germany, the US, and more than 15 other countries, it has been missing out on the fast-growing markets in Eastern Europe, where it is not a retail force. However, ALDI recently began opening stores in Hungary and Poland. ALDI is also growing rapidly in Australia, where it has about 150 outlets in New South Wales, Queensland, and Victoria. The international limited-assortment grocery chain is also mulling over a move into the New Zealand market.

HISTORY

Brothers Karl and Theo Albrecht began running their first grocery store in 1948 in the Ruhr Valley, Germany. By the late 1950s the quickly growing company ran about 350 Albrecht Discount stores in Germany, which were later abbreviated to ALDI. As business progressed in the early 1960s, Karl and Theo decided to go their separate ways and divided the company in half. (The company also introduced self-service stores at this time.) Karl began overseeing ALDI Sud (South), which would eventually encompass Australia, Austria, parts of Germany, Ireland, the UK, and the US. Brother Theo took ALDI Nord (North), which would grow to include Belgium, Denmark, France, parts of Germany, Luxembourg, and the Netherlands. (Austrian ALDI stores run under the Hofer banner.)

The firm remained notoriously private and secretive, especially following the 1971 kidnapping of Theo, who was taken by an Italian terrorist group known as the Red Brigade. He was released after the family paid the group's ransom demands.

ALDI broke US ground in 1976 when it opened its first store across the Atlantic. In 1979 the Albrecht brothers bought grocery store Trader Joe's (formerly Pronto Markets) from founder Joseph Coulombe.

The chain opened its first store in the UK in 1990 and had grown to about 250 stores there by the end of the 1990s. In 1999 Karl crossed over the Irish Sea, opening stores in Dublin and Cork. ALDI intends to dot its stores all over the Emerald Isle.

In February 2000 top cereal maker Kellogg agreed to make five cereals under ALDI's own Gletscher Krone brand. ALDI Sud went south literally in 2000, opening its first Australian location in Sydney. Another 100 stores were planned over the next couple of years. The company also opened stores in Spain.

In protest over a new German law imposing a mandatory deposit on aluminum cans and small bottles, ALDI stopped selling canned beer and soft drinks on January 1, 2003. To eliminate inventory, the discounter cut the price of beer to as little as five cents a can at the end of 2002.

Co-founders Theo and Karl Albrecht stepped down as co-CEOs in 2003 and turned over the day-to-day operation of ALDI Sud to Ulrich

Wolters and Norbert Podschlapp. Theo's son Theo Albrecht Jr. is the chief executive of ALDI Nord.

In November 2004 ALDI opened a distribution center in Scotland to support its expansion in the UK.

In a move intended to spark a massive price war in the German market for prepaid cellular service, ALDI launched its own brand of pay-as-you-go wireless phone service in 2005. In partnership with Berge & Meer, the direct sales arm of German travel group TUI, ALDI entered the travel market in 2007. Rival Lidl had recently entered the travel business.

In recent years ALDI has entered markets in Hungary, Slovenia, and Portugal. In the US the company entered Rhode Island and Central Florida in 2008. In 2009 it entered Texas, focusing its growth on the Dallas/Fort Worth area.

Theo Albrecht died in July 2010 at the age of 88.

EXECUTIVES

Co-Chairman: Karl Albrecht, age 86
Co-President: Jason Hart
Co-President: Charles (Chuck) Youngstrom
Group Purchasing Director: Bridget Lehrke
Director, Real Estate, Michigan: David Kapusansky

LOCATIONS

HQ: ALDI Group
　Eckenbergstrasse 16, Postfach 13 01 110
　45307 Essen, Germany
Phone: 49-201-8593-0　　　**Fax:** 49-201-8593-319
US HQ: 1200 N. Kirk Rd., Batavia, IL 60510
US Phone: 630-879-8100　　**US Fax:** 630-879-8152
Web: www.aldi.com

Selected Countries of Operation

Australia
Austria
Belgium
Denmark
France
Germany
Greece
Hungary
Ireland
Luxembourg
The Netherlands
Poland
Portugal
Slovenia
Spain
Switzerland
UK
US

COMPETITORS

ASDA	Musgrave Retail Partners
Carrefour	Netto Foodstores
Casino Guichard	Publix
Coles Group	REWE
Co-operative Group	Royal Ahold
Costco Wholesale	Save-A-Lot Food Stores
Delhaize	Schlecker
Edeka Zentrale	SPAR Handels
E.Leclerc	SUPERVALU
Giant Eagle	Target
ITM Entreprises	Tengelmann
J Sainsbury	Tesco
Kroger	Wal-Mart
Lidl	Winn-Dixie
Marktkauf	Wm Morrison
METRO AG	Supermarkets
Migros	Woolworths Limited
Minyard Group	

HISTORICAL FINANCIALS

Company Type: Private

Income Statement

FYE: December 31

	ESTIMATED REVENUE ($ mil.)	NET INCOME ($ mil.)	NET PROFIT MARGIN	EMPLOYEES
12/09	68,700	—	—	—
12/08	65,700	—	—	—
12/07	48,000	—	—	—
12/06	45,000	—	—	—
12/05	41,900	—	—	—
Annual Growth	13.2%	—	—	—

Revenue History

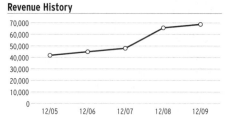

All Nippon Airways

All Nippon Airways (ANA) is one of Japan's leading carriers, along with Japan Airlines. With a fleet of more than 210 aircraft, ANA flies to some 130 domestic destinations and 40 international ones. It extends its network through code-sharing with members of the Star Alliance, an airline marketing partnership that includes such carriers as United Continental's United Airlines and Continental, and Lufthansa. (Code-sharing enables airlines to sell tickets on one another's flights and thus serve more destinations.) Besides passenger service, ANA's air transportation operations include cargo and mail hauling and aircraft maintenance and ground support. The company also sells travel packages and operates hotels.

Domestic passenger flights account for most of the company's air transportation business, but ANA sees international passenger service and cargo operations as its main growth areas.

The company is working to add routes between Japan and China, where it serves additional destinations via its code-sharing partnership with Air China, and to other markets in East Asia. Another key to international growth for ANA is the expansion of Tokyo's Haneda Airport, where a fourth runway is under construction. Along with its benefits for ANA, the new runway is expected to bring more competitors to Haneda, and ANA has indicated that it is considering starting a low-cost carrier in response.

In addition, ANA plans to gradually add freighters to its cargo fleet, which consists of four Boeing 767-300s. Its cargo routes are focused on Asia, but also include US destinations. Up until late 2010 much of the company's cargo service was provided through subsidiaries Air Japan (AJX) and ANA & JP Express (AJV) when it rolled of its cargo operations into Air Nippon Network (AKX); once the merger was complete, AKX was renamed ANA Wings. ANA acquired control of AJV — formerly a joint air cargo venture between ANA and Japan Post, Nippon Express, and Mitsui O.S.K. Lines — in April 2010.

ANA merged AJX and AJV in mid-2010 in order to streamline the operations.

In June 2009 ANA agreed to spin off its helicopter maintenance operations from subsidiary ANA Aircraft Maintenance and sell that division to helicopter manufacturer Eurocopter. Besides All Nippon Airways' primary air transportation, travel, and hotel businesses, the company has interests in information services, logistics, and trading companies.

HISTORY

Two domestic Japanese air carriers that started in 1952 — Nippon Helicopter and Aeroplane Transport and Far East Airlines — consolidated operations in 1957 as All Nippon Airways (ANA).

Throughout the 1960s ANA developed a domestic route network linking Japan's largest cities — Tokyo, Osaka, Fukuoka, and Sapporo — and its leading provincial centers, including Nagoya, Nagasaki, Matsuyama, and Hakodate. During this period domestic traffic grew at an annual rate of 30% to 60%.

In 1970 the Japanese cabinet formulated routes for its major airlines, giving ANA scheduled domestic service and unscheduled international flights. That year Tokuji Wakasa became ANA's chairman, and the company began a program of diversification that led to the establishment of ANA Trading, international charter service (starting with Hong Kong), and a hotel subsidiary. Air Nippon, a regional domestic airline, was started in 1974.

The company established Nippon Cargo Airlines, a charter service set up jointly with four steamship lines, in 1978. ANA carried 19.5 million passengers that year, but its growth slowed between 1978 and 1980. High jet fuel prices caused a $45.6 million loss in 1979, but ANA rebounded a year later. In 1982 ANA opened international charter service to Guam. The company founded ANA Sports in 1984 to manage the company soccer team.

Japan deregulated air routes in 1985, allowing ANA to offer scheduled international flights. The airline offered its first regular flight from Tokyo to Guam in 1986 and soon added service to Los Angeles and Washington, DC. Flights to China, Hong Kong, and Sydney began a year later.

Between 1988 and 1990 ANA added flights to Bangkok, London, Moscow, Saipan, Seoul, Stockholm, and Vienna. In 1988 ANA bought a minority stake in Austrian Airlines and set up the domestic computer reservation system (CRS). The company's international CRS, INFINI (a joint venture with CRS co-op ABACUS), went online in 1990.

ANA started World Air Network Charter (WAC) in 1991 to serve travelers from Japan's smaller cities. That year ANA opened its first European hotel (in Vienna), was listed on the London Stock Exchange, and opened a flight school in the US for its pilots.

In 1992 ANA premiered a hotel in Beijing. In 1995 the airline announced that it would increase its international traffic by more than 30%. As part of this strategy ANA and Air Canada began a code-sharing service in 1996 between Osaka and Vancouver, and a year later ANA became the first Japanese airline to operate a Boeing 777 on an international route (between Tokyo and Beijing).

As the Asian financial crisis sent Japanese airlines to the brink, a pilot strike in 1998 dashed ANA's hopes for a 15% pay cut. To cope, ANA formed alliances with United Airlines (owned by United Continental, formerly UAL Corporation),

Lufthansa, and Brazil's VARIG. ANA extended those partnerships in 1999 by joining the global Star Alliance. To shore up its financial strength, ANA reorganized domestic routes, dropping some unprofitable ones and shifting others to its Air Nippon unit; it also announced plans to launch low-cost air service for international routes in Asia. Competition intensified when Japan fully deregulated domestic fares in 2000, sparking a fare war.

The following year ANA avoided a potentially costly strike and began working toward expanding through partnerships. However, terrorist attacks on the US caused a slump in worldwide air travel, and ANA was forced to cut back on its flights. Then ANA had to trim more routes in response to a worldwide slump in air travel in 2003 due to the SARS outbreak.

In order to develop its own cargo business, ANA sold its 27%-plus stake in Nippon Cargo Airlines to Nippon Yusen Kabushiki Kaisha in 2005. In 2006 ANA formed a hotel management joint venture with hospitality industry leader InterContinental Hotels Group (IHG). The new company, IHG ANA Hotels Group Japan, took over management of ANA's 30 hotel properties.

EXECUTIVES

Chairman: Yoji Ohashi
President, CEO, and Director: Mineo Yamamoto
SEVP Operations and Airport Services and Director: Suguru Omae
SEVP Executive Office, Personnel, Human Resource University Preparatory Office, Employee Relations, and Business Support and Director: Koshichiro Kubo
SEVP Marketing and Sales, CS Promotion and Director: Shinichiro Ito
SEVP Government and Industrial Affairs, Corporate Planning, and Facilities and Director: Hiromichi Toya
EVP: Masao Nakano
EVP: Kenichiro Hamada
EVP Inflight Services and Director: Junko Yamauchi
EVP Corporate Planning and B787 Launch Project and Director: Osamu Shinobe
EVP Flight Operations and Director: Mitsuo Morimoto
EVP General Administration, Public Affairs, and CSR Promotion and Director: Shin Nagase
EVP Engineering and Maintenance and Director: Hiroyuki Ito
EVP Cargo Marketing and Services and Director: Akinori Nomoto
EVP Operations, Airport Services, and Director: Katsumi Nakamura
EVP Investor Relations, Associated Business Development, Financial and Accounting, and Purchasing and Director: Tomohiro Hidema
EVP International and Regulatory Affairs, Alliance and International Affairs, and Information Technology Services and Director: Keisuke Okada
SVP Personnel: Shinya Katanozaka
SVP and President, Air Nippon: Osamu Asakawa
Auditors: Ernst & Young ShinNihon

LOCATIONS

HQ: All Nippon Airways Co., Ltd.
(Zen Nippon Kuyu Kabushiki Kaisha)
Shiodome City Center, 1-5-2 Higashi-Shimbashi, Minato-ku
Tokyo 105-7133, Japan
Phone: 81-3-6735-1000   **Fax:** 81-3-6735-1005
US HQ: 1251 Avenue of the Americas, Ste. 820
New York, NY 10020
US Phone: 212-840-3700
Web: www.ana.co.jp

PRODUCTS/OPERATIONS

2010 Sales

	% of total
Air transportation	81
Travel services	12
Other businesses	7
Total	**100**

2010 Sales

	% of total
Passenger	69
Cargo	7
Other	24
Total	**100**

COMPETITORS

Accor	Delta Air Lines
Air France-KLM	East Japan Railway
American Express	EVA Air
AMR Corp.	Hyatt
British Airways	Japan Airlines
Carlson Wagonlit	Kintetsu
Cathay Pacific	Korean Air
Central Japan Railway	Qantas
China Airlines	Singapore Airlines
China Eastern Airlines	Virgin Atlantic Airways
China Southern Airlines	West Japan Railway

HISTORICAL FINANCIALS

Company Type: Public

Income Statement

FYE: March 31

	REVENUE ($ mil.)	NET INCOME ($ mil.)	NET PROFIT MARGIN	EMPLOYEES
3/10	13,252	(519)	—	12,900
3/09	14,314	(44)	—	33,045
3/08	14,984	646	4.3%	31,345
3/07	12,638	277	2.2%	32,460
3/06	11,643	227	2.0%	30,322
Annual Growth	**3.3%**	**—**	**—**	**(19.2%)**

2010 Year-End Financials

Debt ratio: —
Return on equity: —
Cash ($ mil.): 143
Current ratio: 0.89
Long-term debt ($ mil.): —

No. of shares (mil.): 1,933
Dividends
Yield: 0.0%
Payout: —
Market value ($ mil.): 5,568

Stock History

Pink Sheets: ALNPY

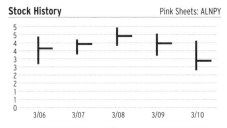

	STOCK PRICE ($) FY Close	P/E High/Low		PER SHARE ($) Earnings	Dividends	Book Value
3/10	2.88	15	9	0.27	0.00	2.64
3/09	3.97	—	—	0.00	0.01	1.71
3/08	4.42	—	—	0.00	0.05	2.36
3/07	3.93	—	—	0.00	—	1.78
3/06	3.65	33	21	0.13	—	1.52
Annual Growth	**(5.8%)**	**—**	**—**	**20.0%**	**—**	**14.8%**

Allianz SE

One of the world's biggest insurers, Allianz SE offers a range of insurance products and services — including life, health, and property/casualty coverage for individuals and businesses — through some 100 subsidiaries and affiliates operating all over the globe (though its key markets are France, Germany, Italy, and the US). In addition to selling insurance, Allianz provides retail and institutional asset management services through Allianz Global Investors, private equity investment through Allianz Capital Partners, and banking services through Allianz Bank. Allianz operates as a Societas Europaea, a joint stock company that is ruled by European Union standards.

The transition to a Societas Europaea took place when Allianz acquired the remainder of its majority-owned subsidiary Ras Holding. Allianz bought out minority shareholders of the firm for about $7 billion in 2006.

To focus on its insurance operations, the company sold its Dresdner Bank subsidiary, one of Germany's largest banks offering both retail and investment banking, to Commerzbank in a $14.4 billion cash and stock transaction in early 2009. The sale did not mark the complete exit of Allianz from the banking world, as it maintains banking operations in Germany under the Allianz Bank name and in other select regions under the Assurbanking unit.

On the insurance front, Allianz has consolidated its worldwide marine insurance operations, including US-based Fireman's Fund, under the Allianz Global Corporate & Specialty brand. The $1 billion unit has offices in more than a dozen locations and is one of the world's largest providers of marine insurance. A substantial portion of the company's property/casualty sales occur through Allianz' subsidiaries in Germany, Italy, France, and the US.

In 2008 Allianz invested $2.5 billion in ailing US insurer Hartford Financial Services. If Allianz were to exercise all options it would own about 20% of Hartford.

While the US and Europe are Allianz's largest markets, the company has significant operations in select Asian countries, and it is expanding its presence in Central and Eastern Europe and the Asia/Pacific region. It sells insurance through the Industrial and Commercial Bank of China, of which it owns a small percentage. Allianz also has a majority holding in Russia's Rosno insurance company and is seeing strong growth in other emerging markets such as India.

Allianz is part of a web of interlocking German corporate ownership. It holds a stake in reinsurance giant Munich Re, which in turn has a small stake in Allianz.

HISTORY

Carl Thieme founded Allianz in Germany in 1890. That year the company took part in the creation of the Calamity Association of Accident Insurance Companies, a consortium of German, Austrian, Swiss, and Russian firms, to insure international commerce.

By 1898 Thieme had established offices in the UK, Switzerland, and the Netherlands. His successor, Paul von der Nahmer, expanded Allianz into the Balkans, France, Italy, Scandinavia, and the US. After a hiatus during WWI, Allianz returned to foreign markets.

In WWII, Allianz insured Auschwitz, Dachau, and other death camps. Company documents show Allianz wasn't worried about risk at the SS troop-guarded camps. After the German defeat, the victors seized Allianz's foreign holdings, except for a stake in Spain's Plus Ultra. In the 1950s Allianz repurchased confiscated holdings in Italian and Austrian companies.

Allianz saturated the German market and began a full-scale international drive in the late 1950s and 1960s. It became Europe's largest insurer through a series of acquisitions beginning in 1973. Allianz formed Los Angeles-based Allianz Insurance in 1977.

In 1981 Allianz launched a takeover (which turned hostile) of the UK's Eagle Star insurance company. After a 1983 bidding joust with Britain's B.A.T Industries (now part of Zurich Financial Services), Allianz withdrew.

The firm consoled itself by shopping. In 1984 it won control of Riunione Adriatica di Sicurtà (Ras), Italy's second-largest insurance company. Two years later the firm bought Cornhill (now Allianz Insurance plc) on its third try. As the Iron Curtain crumbled, Allianz in 1989 acquired 49% of Hungaria Biztosito. Its *drang nach Osten* continued the next year after national reunification, when it gained control of Deutsche Versicherungs AG, East Germany's insurance monopoly. Allianz that year became the first German insurer licensed in Japan; it also bought the US's Fireman's Fund Insurance.

Natural disasters led to large claims and set the company back in 1992, the first time in 20 years it lost money from its German operations. Allianz restructured operations that year.

Allianz set up an asset management arm in Hong Kong in 1996 with an eye to further Asian expansion, getting a license in China the next year. In 1997 after Holocaust survivors sued Allianz and other insurers for failing to pay on life policies after WWII, Allianz agreed to participate in a repayment fund.

In 1998 Allianz bought control of Assurances Générales de France; it was the white knight that prevented Assicurazioni Generali from taking the company. In 1999 Allianz said it would restructure some of its insurance operations, including spinning off its marine and aviation lines, to better compete in the multinational market. In 2000 Allianz bought 70% of PIMCO Advisors Holdings to strengthen its asset management operations.

Allianz remained acquisitive in 2001, buying US investment manager Nicholas-Applegate and taking a majority stake in ROSNO, one of Russia's largest insurers. Also that year, it bought a stake in German banking giant Dresdner and acquired the remainder the following year.

Allianz paid out claims of some $1.3 billion relating to the terrorist attacks on the World Trade Center. The company set up a terrorism insurance unit, offering coverage primarily for companies within the European Union.

After a year of record losses (primarily due to investment losses and Dresdner's struggles), former CEO Henning Schulte-Noelle stepped down and assumed the chair post in 2003. Allianz's stock lost more than 75% of its value in 2002.

Getting out of the red, Allianz rebounded some in 2003, thanks to the upturn in the stock markets and the streamlining of its operations (the company reduced its employee total by some 8,000 people).

The company sold most of its Canadian property/casualty operations to ING Canada in 2004.

EXECUTIVES

Chairman: Henning Schulte-Noelle, age 68
Vice Chairman: Rolf Zimmermann, age 57
Vice Chairman: Gerhard Cromme, age 66
CEO: Michael Diekmann, age 55, $6,567,648 total compensation
Member Management Board and COO; Allianz SE and Allianz Deutschland: Christof Mascher, age 50, $1,438,933 total compensation
Member of the Board of Management, Finance: Paul Achleitner, age 54, $4,760,125 total compensation
Member of the Board of Management, Asset Management Worldwide; Chairman, Allianz Global Investors Italia: Joachim Faber, age 60, $4,751,293 total compensation
Member of the Board of Management, Global Insurance Lines & Anglo Markets: Clement B. Booth, age 56, $4,325,303 total compensation
Member of the Board of Management, Insurance German Speaking Countries and Allianz Banking and Director Labor Relations: Gerhard Rupprecht, age 61, $4,077,163 total compensation
Member of the Board of Management, Insurance Growth Markets: Werner Zedelius, age 53, $4,936,753 total compensation
Member of the Board of Management, Controlling, Reporting, and Risk: Oliver Bäte, age 45, $2,909,000 total compensation
Member of the Board of Management, Insurance Europe I + II, Africa, South America, P/C Sustainability Program: Enrico T. Cucchiani, age 60, $3,830,788 total compensation
CIO, Allianz SE, Allianz Deutschland, and Allianz Managed Operations and Services (AMOS): Ralf Schneider, age 47
Chief Economist: Michael Heise
Chief Risk Officer: Thomas C. Wilson, age 48
CEO, Allianz Re: Clemens F. von Weichs, age 57
CEO, Allianz Real Estate: Olivier Piani
President and CEO, Allianz Life Insurance Company of North America: Gary C. Bhojwani, age 41
President and CEO, Fireman's Fund Insurance Company: Michael E. (Mike) LaRocco, age 53
Head Investor Relations: Oliver Schmidt
Auditors: KPMG Deutsche Treuhand-Gesellschaft AG

LOCATIONS

HQ: Allianz SE
Königinstrasse 28
D-80802 Munich, Germany
Phone: 49-89-3800-0   **Fax:** 49-89-3800-3425
US HQ: 2350 Empire Ave., Burbank, CA 91504
US Phone: 818-260-5000
Web: www.allianz.com

PRODUCTS/OPERATIONS

2009 Sales

	% of total
Life & health insurance	52
Property/casualty insurance	44
Asset management	4
Total	**100**

Selected Holdings

Adriática de Seguros C.A. (Venezuela)
AGF Allianz Argentina Compañía de Seguros Generales S.A.
AGF Brasil Seguros S.A. (73%, Brazil)
Allianz Elementar Versicherung-AG (Austria)
Allianz Fire and Marine Insurance Japan Ltd.
Allianz General Insurance Malaysia Berhad p.l.c.
Allianz Global Corporate & Specialty AG
Allianz Hungária Biztosító Rt (Hungary)
Allianz Insurance Company of Singapore Pte. Ltd.
Allianz Insurance plc (UK)
Allianz Irish Life Holdings p.l.c. (66%)
Allianz Lebensversicherungs-AG (91%)
Allianz Life Insurance Company of North America (US)
Allianz México S.A. Compañía de Seguros
Allianz Nederland Levensverzekering N.V. (The Netherlands)
Allianz pojistóvna, a.s. (Czech Republic)

Allianz Subalpina Società di Assicurazioni e
  Riassicurazioni S.p.A. (Italy)
Allianz Tiriac Asigurari S.A. (52%, Romania)
Assurances Générales de France
Assurances Générales du Laos Ltd. (51%)
Banque AGF S.A. (France)
Deutsche Lebensversicherungs-AG
ELVIA Reiseversicherungs-Gesellschaft AG (Switzerland)
Euler Hermes Kreditversicherungs-AG
Euler Hermes SFAC S.A. (France)
Fireman's Fund Insurance Company (US)
Lloyd Adriatico S.p.A. (Italy)
Mondial Assistance S.A.S. (France)
PT Asuransi Allianz Utama Indonesia Ltd. (75%)
Questar Capital Corporation (US)
Riunione Adriatica di Sicurtà S.p.A. (Italy)
TU Allianz Polska S.A. (Poland)

COMPETITORS

AEGON	Legal & General Group
Ageas SA/NV	MetLife
Allstate	Munich Re Group
Aviva	New York Life
AXA	Nippon Life Insurance
Berkshire Hathaway	Old Mutual
Citigroup	Prudential
CNP Assurances	Prudential plc
ERGO	RSA Insurance
Generali	State Farm
Generali Deutschland	Swiss Re
Groupama	Talanx
The Hartford	Victoria Versicherung
ING	Zurich Financial Services

HISTORICAL FINANCIALS

Company Type: Public

Income Statement

FYE: December 31

	ASSETS ($ mil.)	NET INCOME ($ mil.)	INCOME AS % OF ASSETS	EMPLOYEES
12/09	837,053	6,227	0.7%	153,203
12/08	1,346,884	(3,445)	—	182,865
12/07	1,561,905	11,725	0.8%	181,207
12/06	1,389,521	9,263	0.7%	166,505
12/05	1,181,791	5,187	0.4%	177,625
Annual Growth	(8.3%)	4.7%	—	(3.6%)

2009 Year-End Financials

Equity as % of assets: 6.9%
Return on assets: 0.6%
Return on equity: 11.9%
Long-term debt ($ mil.): 11,411
No. of shares (mil.): 4,539

Dividends
  Yield: 2.1%
  Payout: 27.2%
Market value ($ mil.): 80,991
Sales ($ mil.): 129,920

Stock History

Pink Sheets: AZSEY

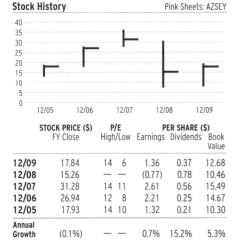

	STOCK PRICE ($) FY Close	P/E High/Low		PER SHARE ($) Earnings	Dividends	Book Value
12/09	17.84	14	6	1.36	0.37	12.68
12/08	15.26	—	—	(0.77)	0.78	10.46
12/07	31.28	14	11	2.61	0.56	15.49
12/06	26.94	12	8	2.21	0.25	14.67
12/05	17.93	14	10	1.32	0.21	10.30
Annual Growth	(0.1%)	—	—	0.7%	15.2%	5.3%

Allied Irish Banks

Allied Irish Banks (AIB), one of Ireland's largest banks and private employers, is looking beyond the Emerald Isle for its proverbial pot o' gold. The company offers retail and commercial accounts and loans, life insurance, financing, leasing, pension, and trust services through some 275 branches in Ireland and another 50 in Northern Ireland, where it operates First Trust Bank. In the UK, AIB focuses on commercial clients through about 35 locations. The company's capital markets division offers commercial treasury services, corporate finance, and investment banking services. In the US, the company has made its mark by specializing in financial services to the not-for-profit sector.

In late 2008 the Irish government injected €2 billion ($2.8 billion) into AIB in exchange for a 25% share in voting rights. Ireland also provided capital for Bank of Ireland and Anglo Irish Bank to help stabilize the Irish financial system, which plunged amidst the global financial crisis. AIB is also seeking capital from the private sector.

The small Irish market and its inevitable ties to the UK's economy made AIB look overseas to remain competitive. Indeed, about a third of AIB's sales, assets, and pre-tax profits now come from outside of Ireland. Meanwhile, its home turf also faces intruders — namely European banks free to do business in the EU-opened Irish market.

In response, the firm positioned itself as an international bank, establishing a presence in Eastern Europe, the Baltic, and southeastern Europe. In the US, AIB owns more than 20% of New York-based M&T Bank. However, it plans to sell its stake in M&T in order to help shore up its capital base.

AIB has been been forced to sell many of its overseas assets in order to boost capital. In 2010 AIB agreed to sell its 70% stake in Poland's Bank Zachodni (which has some 500 branches) to Spain's Grupo Santander for nearly €3 billion ($3.7 billion). It will also sell its stake in Goodbody Holdings, which owns entities including Goodbody Stockbrokers. The proceeds will be used as a source of liquidity.

HISTORY

Allied Irish Banks was formed in 1966 by the "trinity" of Provincial Bank (founded 1825), Munster and Leinster (founded 1885 but with origins back to the late 1600s), and The Royal Bank (founded 1836). Both AIB and its then-larger rival, Bank of Ireland, had to consolidate in order to compete with North American banks entering Ireland. From its start, AIB sought to expand overseas, and by 1968 it had an alliance with Canada's Toronto-Dominion Bank.

In the 1970s AIB expanded its branch network to England and Scotland. The 1980s saw AIB boost its presence in the US market (it had already debuted AIB branches) with the acquisition of First Maryland Bancorp.

The Irish Parliament's Finance Act of 1986 instituted a withholding tax known as the Deposit Interest Retention Tax (DIRT) for Irish residents. Consequently (with a wink and a nod), AIB and other banks let customers create bogus non-resident accounts to avoid paying DIRT. An investigation indicated that, at one point, AIB's branch in Tralee had 14,700 non-resident accounts on its rolls — more than half the local

population. After tax authorities began probing, many of the accounts in question were reclassified as "resident," and customers had to pay the taxes on them. In 1991 AIB was reprimanded, but neither the bank nor its customers have paid the remaining $100 million tax bill.

Tom Mulcahy, who integrated AIB's treasury, investment, and international banking activities, became chief executive in 1994. Mulcahy, a respected leader, envisioned AIB as an international, Ireland-based bank.

In 1995 AIB bought UK-based investment fund manager John Govett from London Pacific Group (now Berkeley Technology Limited). Mulcahy moved AIB the same year into Eastern Europe with a stake in Poland-based Wielkopolski Bank Kredytowy (or WBK).

AIB was busy in 1999. It gained a toehold in Asia by entering a cross-marketing agreement with Singapore's Keppet TatLee bank, a survivor of the region's financial crisis. Liberalized Singapore banking laws allowed AIB the right to buy one-quarter of the bank by 2001. AIB also bought an 80% stake of Bank Zachodni in Poland in 1999.

That year AIB merged First Maryland Bancorp and its other US holdings into the renamed Allfirst Financial, a sizable mid-Atlantic states bank.

To consolidate its power in Eastern Europe, in 2001 AIB merged its Polish banks (Wielkopolski Bank Kredytowy and Bank Zachodni) into Bank Zachodni WBK. That year Mulcahy retired but was appointed by the Irish government to take over as chairman of troubled airline Aer Lingus.

AIB lost nearly $700 million from 1996 to 2002, apparently from bogus foreign exchange transactions made by rogue trader John Rusnak, who pleaded guilty to bank fraud.

In 2003 AIB sold troubled Maryland-based bank Allfirst Financial to M&T Bank Corporation. As part of the deal, AIB assumed ownership of more than 20% of M&T, becoming the company's largest shareholder. Under AIB's direction Allfirst had grown into a major regional player, with about 250 branches in Maryland, Pennsylvania, Virginia, and Washington, DC.

EXECUTIVES

Group Chief Executive and Director: Eugene J. Sheehy, age 55
Chief Operating Officer: Steven Meadows, age 56
CFO, AIB Group: Bernard Byrne
AIB Group Managing Director: Colm E. Doherty, age 51
Managing Director, AIB Poland: Gerry Byrne, age 54
Managing Director, AIB Bank: Robbie Henneberry, age 46
Managing Director Great Britan adn Northern Ireland: Nick Treble, age 50
Manager Group Investor Relations: Rose O'Donovan
Group Press Officer Corporate Relations and Communications: Ronan Sheridan
Manager Youth Market: Kathy McGarry
Secretary: Liam Kinsella
Head Group Strategic Human Resources: Mary Toomey, age 61
Head Corporate Relations and Communications: Catherine Burke
Director; Chairman, AIB Group UK: David Pritchard, age 65
Auditors: KPMG

LOCATIONS

HQ: Allied Irish Banks, p.l.c.
  Bankcentre, Ballsbridge
  Dublin 4, Ireland
Phone: 353-1-660-0311
US HQ: 405 Park Ave., 4th Fl., New York, NY 10022
US Phone: 212-339-8000   **US Fax:** 212-339-8007
Web: www.aibgroup.com

PRODUCTS/OPERATIONS

2009 Sales

	% of total
Interest	
Loans & receivables to customers	64
Financial investments available for sale	12
Other income	2
Noninterest	
Fees & commissions	12
Other	10
Total	**100**

Selected Subsidiaries

AIB Capital Markets plc
AIB Corporate Finance Ltd.
AIB Debt Management Ltd
AIB Funds Management Ltd.
AIB International Financial Services Ltd.
AIB Investment Managers Ltd.
AIB Leasing Ltd.
Bank Zachodni WBK S.A. (Poland)

COMPETITORS

Anglo Irish Bank
Bank Millennium
Bank of America
Bank of Ireland
Bank Pekao SA
Barclays
Citigroup
HSBC
Lloyds Banking Group
Royal Bank of Scotland
SunTrust
Ulster Bank

HISTORICAL FINANCIALS

Company Type: Public

Income Statement

FYE: December 31

	ASSETS ($ mil.)	NET INCOME ($ mil.)	INCOME AS % OF ASSETS	EMPLOYEES
12/09	249,827	(3,458)	—	23,275
12/08	257,719	1,085	0.4%	25,919
12/07	261,481	2,865	1.1%	24,000
12/06	209,326	2,885	1.4%	23,312
12/05	158,294	1,595	1.0%	23,300
Annual Growth	12.1%	—	—	(0.0%)

2009 Year-End Financials

Equity as % of assets: 6.1%
Return on assets: —
Return on equity: —
Long-term debt ($ mil.): 6,573
No. of shares (mil.): 459
Dividends
Yield: 0.0%
Payout: —
Market value ($ mil.): 2,310
Sales ($ mil.): 11,149

Stock History

NYSE: AIB

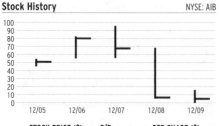

	STOCK PRICE ($) FY Close	P/E High/Low		PER SHARE ($) Earnings	Dividends	Book Value
12/09	5.03	—	—	(6.17)	0.00	33.42
12/08	6.61	29	3	2.33	2.26	27.54
12/07	67.62	15	9	6.37	2.22	31.46
12/06	80.19	13	9	6.45	1.77	24.74
12/05	50.88	15	13	3.55	1.44	18.55
Annual Growth	(43.9%)	—	—	—	—	15.9%

AMP Limited

AMP is on top — down under. The company is one of Australia's largest insurance and investment management groups. Through its AMP Financial Services (AFS) division, more than 2,000 representatives sell the company's financial offerings, which include life, home, vehicle, travel, and business insurance, as well as retirement products, financial planning and advice, superannuation products (professionally managed retirement investment funds), and banking. AMP Capital Investors provides investment management to AFS and to other individual and institutional investors. AMP Limited also provides retail financial services under the Hillcross and Arrive Wealth Management brands.

AMP Limited is active mainly in Australia and New Zealand, but is pursuing expansion in selected parts of Asia. It is also banking on its banking business — which includes savings accounts, home loans, and American Express credit cards — to be an area of growth.

AMP Limited, which has more than A$100 billion of assets under management, claims that approximately one in seven Australians and New Zealanders are AMP customers. And the company aims to increase its presence even more. In 2009 it offered to acquire the operations of AXA Asia Pacific in those two nations. However, rival National Australia Bank entered the fray and outbid AM; regulators nixed the deal, citing antitrust concerns. The winner of AXA Asia Pacific, whose Asian operations are also up for grabs, stands to increase its life insurance and wealth management business.

HISTORY

AMP was conceived in Sydney in 1848 by W. S. Walsh (a clergyman), Thomas Mort (a businessman), and Thomas Holt (a wool trader), who convened with two others to discuss forming a mutual life insurance company in Australia. (Many of the UK's and US's largest mutuals were also founded about this time.) The next year Australian Mutual Provident Society was born; it opened for business with a staff of two: secretary William Perry and a small boy. In its first year the company sold only 42 policies. Luckily, no one died in the first three years of operations and the company was able to build up some reserves. The company grew slowly over the next decade, appointing just two agents — in Auckland, New Zealand, and Hobart, Australia.

Sales took off with the 1860 appointment of the company's first full-time agent, Benjamin Short, who had the novel idea of actively recruiting customers and actually *selling* policies. The company opened an office in New Zealand in 1871; it opened a branch in the UK in 1908.

In the next few decades, the company helped build the Australian economy through investment of its reserves. It funded industry and infrastructure, including farming communities, as part of the South Australian Land Development Scheme. The company grew free of foreign competition, protected by regulations severely restricting the activities of foreign companies in the banking and financial industries in Australia. In 1958 the company formed AMP Fire and General Insurance (changed to AMP General in 1990).

In 1988 AMP moved abroad with the acquisition of London Life Assurance. The following year it made history with its acquisition of funds management group Pearl Assurance, then the largest takeover of a British financial firm by a foreign company.

The company founded AMP Asset Management in 1991 to manage its overseas assets. In 1995 the company expanded its international presence through a joint venture with the financial services arm of UK-based Virgin Group. The company also began offering mortgage and banking products in Australia through a new unit, Priority One.

After a careful inquiry, in 1996 AMP's board recommended demutualization; policyholders approved in 1997, and the conversion was completed the next year with the company taking the name AMP Limited. Trading got off to a rocky start, however, as the company imposed an unusual pricing mechanism by which the official initial stock price was linked to pricing activity over the first five days of trading. This was done to protect individual policyholders from typical opening-day stock gyrations, but institutional investors were unable to value their investments for several days (a technical breach of accounting rules).

AMP bought Citibank's New Zealand retail banking business and UK fund manager Henderson in 1998. The next year AMP battled to buy general insurer GIO Australia Holdings, picking up 57% after resistance to its original low-ball offer; it also bought UK mutual insurer National Provident Institution (NPI).

The company streamlined all of its investment-management operations into a single unit in 1999 and expanded Asian operations with offices in Beijing and Tokyo. In 2000 the problems arising from the GIO takeover resulted in a board shakeup; chairman Ian Burgess resigned.

Local rival Suncorp-Metway bought AMP's domestic general insurance unit in 2001, and Churchill Insurance (a Credit Suisse subsidiary) acquired its similar operations in the UK that year.

AMP split off its UK-based operations as HHG at the end of 2003 (retaining a 10% share). HHG eventually changed its name to Henderson Group plc in 2005. AMP sold its shares in Henderson later that year.

EXECUTIVES

Chairman: Peter Mason, age 63
Managing Director and CEO: Craig Dunn, age 46
CFO: Paul Leaming
CIO: Lee Barnett
Managing Director, AMP Financial Services: Craig Meller, age 47
Managing Director, AMP Capital Investors: Stephen Dunne
Chief Economist and Head of Investment Strategy, AMP Capital Investors: Shane Oliver
Secretary and General Counsel: Brian Salter
Executive Business Development Manager, AMP Capital Investors: Andrew Bennett
Head of Asia Pacific Equities, AMP Capital Investors: Kerry Series
Head of Property Funds Management, AMP Capital Investors: Chris Judd
General Manager Group Strategy: Jonathan Deane
General Manager Human Resources: Fiona Wardlaw
General Manager Public Affairs: Matthew Percival
Auditors: Ernst & Young

HQ: AMP Limited
33 Alfred St., Level 24
Sydney 2000, Australia
Phone: 61-2-9257-5000   **Fax:** 61-2-9257-7178
Web: www.amp.com.au

PRODUCTS/OPERATIONS

2009 Sales

	% of total
Investment gains	75
Fee revenue	12
Life insurance premiums & related revenue	10
Other	3
Total	**100**

COMPETITORS

ageas SA/NV
Australia and New Zealand Banking
Aviva
AXA Asia Pacific
Commonwealth Bank of Australia
Macquarie Group
National Australia Bank
QBE
RSA Insurance
St. Andrew's Australia

HISTORICAL FINANCIALS

Company Type: Public

Income Statement

FYE: December 31

	ASSETS ($ mil.)	NET INCOME ($ mil.)	INCOME AS % OF ASSETS	EMPLOYEES
12/09	80,209	646	0.8%	3,500
12/08	59,884	400	0.7%	3,600
12/07	94,941	863	0.9%	4,100
12/06	77,214	721	0.9%	3,500
12/05	62,389	1,152	1.8%	3,500
Annual Growth	**6.5%**	**(13.5%)**	**—**	**0.0%**

2009 Year-End Financials

Equity as % of assets: 2.9%
Return on assets: 0.9%
Return on equity: 34.9%
Long-term debt ($ mil.): —
No. of shares (mil.): 2,094

Dividends
Yield: 2.1%
Payout: 39.4%
Market value ($ mil.): 12,661
Sales ($ mil.): 8,232

Stock History

Australian: AMP

	STOCK PRICE ($) FY Close	P/E High/Low	PER SHARE ($) Earnings	Dividends	Book Value
12/09	6.04	19 10	0.33	0.13	1.10
12/08	3.74	32 16	0.21	0.17	0.67
12/07	8.71	21 17	0.46	0.19	0.81
12/06	7.96	21 15	0.39	—	0.91
12/05	5.61	18 14	0.32	—	0.98
Annual Growth	**1.9%**	**— —**	**0.8%**	**(17.3%)**	**2.9%**

Anglo American

Anglo American's name might be a little misleading — it's never been American. The UK-based company owns significant stakes in global producers of platinum (75% of Anglo Platinum) and diamonds (45% of De Beers S.A.). In addition, Anglo American has interests in ferrous and base metals and industrial minerals; it also is among the world's largest coal miners. The company has spent much of the decade reorganizing its portfolio and has narrowed its focus. Though it used to have a majority stake in AngloGold Ashanti, Anglo American divested its remaining shares in 2009. The founding Oppenheimer family no longer controls Anglo American, though Nicky Oppenheimer, who chairs De Beers, sits on the board.

In 2009 the company set up new units along product and geographical lines. The new divisions consist of platinum (South Africa), copper (Chile), nickel (Brazil), metallurgical coal (Australia), thermal coal (South Africa), Kumba Iron Ore (of which Anglo American owns 63%, South Africa), and Iron Ore Brazil. The change capped off several year of reorganization and divestment.

In divesting its gold interests, Anglo American seemed to capitulate to demands from the investor community and the idea that the gold industry is sufficiently different from the rest of the mining industry as to necessitate separate management. It sold its 20% stake in Gold Fields to Norilsk Nickel in 2004 and reduced its stake in Anglo Gold Ashanti to 42% from its former 51% in 2006, then to below 20% the following year, and finally entirely in 2009.

Additionally, Anglo American has made several other divestitures. It and partner BHP Billiton sold their joint venture, chrome miner and manufacturer Samancor, in 2005, and the company rid itself of subsidiary Boart Longyear in 2007.

Other divestitures have included selling its 80% stake in Highveld Steel (to Evraz) in 2006-2007 and spinning off its paper and packaging businesses, Mondi, which had accounted for more than 20% of sales. In 2009 the company also divested its nearly 50% interest in South African sugar company Tongaat Hulett, spinning off the stake to institutional investors and gaining $500 million. In 2010 Anglo American agreed to sell its zinc assets in Namibia and South Africa to Vedanta Resources in a $1.3 billion deal.

The company, formerly Anglo American Corporation of South Africa, moved to the UK and began trading on the London Stock Exchange in an effort to reach international investors. When it was based in South Africa, Anglo American was unable to send its money overseas (the result of boycotts connected to that country's apartheid policies), so it bulked up on South African interests. Anglo American has evolved such that it can depend on product and geographic diversity to weather global economic turmoil. South African operations now make up less than half of the company's total sales.

HISTORY

In 1905 the Oppenheimers, a German family with a major interest in the Premier Diamond Mining Company of South Africa, began buying some of the region's richest gold-bearing land. The family formed Anglo American Corporation of South Africa in 1917 to raise money from

J. P. Morgan and other US investors. The name was chosen to disguise the company's German background during WWI.

Under Ernest Oppenheimer the company bought diamond fields in German Southwest Africa (now Namibia) in 1920, breaking the De Beers hegemony in diamond production. Oppenheimer's 1928 negotiations with Hans Merensky, the person credited with the discovery of South Africa's "platinum arc," led to Anglo American's interest in platinum.

The diamond monopoly resurfaced in 1929 when Anglo American won control of De Beers, formed by Cecil Rhodes in 1888 with the help of England's powerful Rothschild family.

Anglo American and De Beers had become the largest gold producers in South Africa by the 1950s. They were also major world producers of coal, uranium, and copper. In the 1960s and 1970s, Anglo American expanded through mergers and cross holdings in industrial and financial companies. It set up Luxembourg-based Minorco to own holdings outside South Africa and help the company avoid sanctions placed on firms doing business in the apartheid country.

Minorco sold its interest in Consolidated Gold Fields in 1989, and in 1990 it bought Freeport-McMoRan Gold Company (US). In 1993 Minorco bought Anglo American's and De Beers' South American, European, and Australian operations as part of a swap that put all of Anglo American's non-African assets, except diamonds, in Minorco's hands. Some analysts claimed the company had moved the assets to protect them from possible nationalization by the new, black-controlled South African government. The company spun off insurer African Life to a group of black investors in 1994.

Anglo American bought a stake in UK-based conglomerate Lonrho (now Lonmin) in 1996. In 1997 Anglo American made mining acquisitions in Zambia, Colombia, and Tanzania and began reorganizing its gold and diamond operations.

The company left its homeland for London in 1999, changed its name to Anglo American plc, and wrapped up the acquisitions of many of its minority interests including Amcoal, Amgold, Amic, and Minorco.

In 2000 the company bought UK building materials company Tarmac plc and later sold Tarmac America to Greece-based Titan Cement for $636 million. That year De Beers paid $590 million for Anglovaal Mining's stake in De Beers' flagship Venetia diamond mine and $900 million for Royal Dutch Shell's Australian coal mining business. On the disposal side, Anglo American sold its 68% stake in LTA. Harry Oppenheimer died that year at the age of 92.

In a surprising move, in early 2001 Anglo American announced that it had formed a consortium with Central Holding (the Oppenheimer family) and Debswana Diamond to acquire De Beers. In February De Beers agreed to be acquired in a deal worth about $17.6 billion. The deal — giving Anglo American and Central Holding 45% each and Debswana a 10% stake — was completed in June 2001.

In 2002 Anglo American and Japan-based conglomerate Mitsui pooled their Australian coal resources; Anglo American owns 51% of the joint venture. The company also completed a $1.3 billion deal that year for Chilean copper assets (two mines and a smelter) formerly owned by Exxon Mobil. In 2003 the company eyed the red hot iron ore market when it acquired a controlling stake in South Africa-based iron producer Kumba Resources.

EXECUTIVES

Chairman: Sir John Parker, age 67
CEO and Board Member: Cynthia B. Carroll, age 53
Director Finance and Board Member: René Médori, age 53
Chief Medical Officer: Brian Brink
Group Head Safety and Sustainable Development: Dorian Emmett, age 57
Group Director Strategy and Business Development: Peter Whitcutt, age 44
Group Director Mining and Technology: Brian Beamish, age 53
Group Director Human Resources and Communications: Mervyn Walker, age 50
Group Head Corporate Communications and Branding: Anik Michaud
Group Director Business Performance and Projects: David Weston, age 51
Group Director Non-Core Assets: Duncan Wanblad, age 43
Executive Director Anglo American South Africa: Godfrey G. Gomwe, age 52
Head Investor and Corporate Affairs: Nick von Schirnding
Head Sustainable Development and Energy: Samantha Hoe-Richardson
Head Safety: Mike Oswell
Manager International Social and Community Development: Jonathan Samuel
CEO, Kumba Iron Ore: Chris Griffith, age 45
CEO, Thermal Coal: Norman B. Mbazima, age 52
CEO, Iron Ore Brazil: Stephan Weber, age 48
CEO, Metallurgical Coal: Seamus French, age 47
CEO, Copper: John MacKenzie, age 41
CEO, Anglo Nickel: Walter De Simoni, age 54
CEO, Anglo Platinum: Neville F. Nicolau, age 50
Auditors: Deloitte LLP

LOCATIONS

HQ: Anglo American plc
20 Carlton House Terrace
London SW1Y 5AN, United Kingdom
Phone: 44-20-7968-8888   **Fax:** 44-20-7968-8500
Web: www.angloamerican.co.uk

PRODUCTS/OPERATIONS

2009 Sales

	$ mil.	% of total
Platinum	4,535	19
Copper	3,967	16
Iron	3,419	14
Thermal coal	2,490	10
Metallurgical coal	2,239	9
Diamonds	1,728	7
Nickel	348	1
Other mining & industrial	5,911	24
Adjustments	(4,092)	—
Total	**20,545**	**100**

Selected Industries and Subsidiaries

Platinum
  Anglo Platinum Corporation Limited (75%, South Africa)
Base Metals
  Black Mountain (copper, lead, and zinc; South Africa)
  Empresa Minera de Mantos Blancos SA (copper, Chile)
  Gamsberg Zinc Corporation (zinc, South Africa)
  Hudson Bay Mining and Smelting Co. (copper and zinc, Canada)
  Minera Loma de Níquel, CA (91%, nickel, Venezuela)
  Minera Quellaveco SA (80%, copper, Peru)
  Minera Sur Andes Limitada (copper, Chile)
Coal
  Anglo Coal (South Africa)
  Anglo Coal (Callide) Pty Limited (Australia)
Ferrous Metals and Industries
  Kumba Resources Limited (66%; coal, iron ore, heavy minerals; South Africa)
  Scaw Metals (iron, steel, engineering work; South Africa)

Industrial Minerals
  Bilfinger Berger Baustoffe GmbH (construction materials, Germany)
  Copebras Limitada (73%, phosphate products, Brazil)
  Lausitzer Grauwacke GmbH (construction materials, Germany)
  Midland Quarry Products Limited (50%, construction materials, UK)
  Steetley Iberia SA (construction materials, Spain)
  Tarmac France SA (construction materials, France)
  Tarmac Group Limited (construction materials, UK)
  Tarmac Severokamen AS (construction materials, Czech Republic)
  WKSM SA (construction materials, Poland)
Diamonds
  De Beers S.A. (45%)

COMPETITORS

BHP Billiton
Centromin
Freeport-McMoRan
Impala Platinum
Norilsk Nickel
Peñoles
Rio Tinto Limited
Teck
Vale
Xstrata

HISTORICAL FINANCIALS

Company Type: Public

Income Statement

FYE: December 31

	REVENUE ($ mil.)	NET INCOME ($ mil.)	NET PROFIT MARGIN	EMPLOYEES
12/09	20,545	2,389	11.6%	107,016
12/08	26,114	5,176	19.8%	105,013
12/07	25,325	7,263	28.7%	116,000
12/06	24,926	6,170	24.8%	162,000
12/05	29,436	3,521	12.0%	195,000
Annual Growth	**(8.6%)**	**(9.2%)**	**—**	**(13.9%)**

2009 Year-End Financials

Debt ratio: —   No. of shares (mil.): 2,633
Return on equity: 9.7%   Dividends
Cash ($ mil.): 3,220   Yield: 0.0%
Current ratio: —   Payout: —
Long-term debt ($ mil.): —   Market value ($ mil.): 90,911

Stock History

Pink Sheets: AAUKF

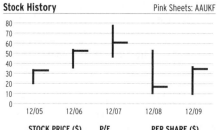

	STOCK PRICE ($) FY Close	P/E High/Low		PER SHARE ($) Earnings	Dividends	Book Value
12/09	34.53	—	—	—	0.00	10.50
12/08	16.82	—	—	—	0.46	8.20
12/07	60.63	—	—	—	0.57	9.19
12/06	52.53	—	—	—	1.13	10.28
12/05	32.88	—	—	—	0.38	10.47
Annual Growth	**1.2%**	**—**	**—**	**—**	**—**	**0.1%**

Anheuser-Busch InBev

Pull up a barstool, there's plenty of brew to go around (or to go a round or two). Anheuser-Busch InBev (ABInBev) is the largest beer producer in the world by volume. The Belgian company produced some 365 million hectoliters (more than 9.6 billion gallons) of beer in 2009. It upped its brewing output considerably with its $52 billion purchase of the US's Anheuser-Busch (A-B) in 2008. The company has a product list of more than 200 brands, including global best-sellers Budweiser, Stella Artois, and Beck's. It has a long list of regional beers, including Leffe and Hoegaarden, as well as a slew of local favorites, such as Michelob, Skol, and Brahma. ABInBev has operations in 23 countries around the world.

Shrewdly, ABInBev has expanded in emerging markets, particularly in Asia. The company owns the brewing operations of Malaysia's Lion Group and a controlling interest in the KK Group, both of which brew popular beers in China. It owns controlling interests in Chinese brewers Zhejiang Shiliang Brewery, Fujian Sedrin, and Hunan Debier Brewery. In South Korea the company owns Oriental Brewery, that country's second-largest beer maker. In its biggest sales segment, North America, the company owns 35% of the US's Craft Brewers Alliance, which makes the Redhook Ale, Widmer, Kona, and Goose Island beer brands. It also owns 50.2% of Mexico's largest beer company, GRUPO MODELO, maker of Corona.

However, despite its #1 position, its long list of labels, and a desire to expand, ABInBev is saddled with enormous debt as the result of its buyout of A-B. So, in 2009 ABInBev went on a selling spree. It sold 20% of its 27% holding in Chinese brewer, Tsingtao, to Asahi Breweries, bringing Asahi's holdings in Tsingtao to 40% (which subsequently changed to 20% through a deal between Tsingtao and Asahi). The company used proceeds from the sale — about $667 million — to pay down debt. Later that same year, it sold its remaining 7% share of Tsingtao to Chinese national and private investor, Chen Fashu. It sold Labatt USA to KPS Capital Partners. It also sold Oriental Brewery to the investment firm, Kohlberg Kravis Roberts, for some $1.8 billion.

Still in selling mode, in October 2009 ABInBev sold its operations in Central Europe and the Balkans to private investment firm CVC Capital Partners for $2.3 billion in cash, bonds, and minority shares.

In a move to eliminate operations not relevant to beer making, in 2009 the company sold the part of its subsidiary, Metal Container Corporation, that makes soda cans and lids to Ball Corporation for $577 million. A-B retained the seven plants that make beer containers. It also sold Busch Entertainment (theme parks) to the Blackstone Group in 2009 for $2.7 billion, including $2.3 billion in cash, a tidy amount that put another dent in its debt.

A group made up of members of the Artois and Piedboeuf families (who took over ownership of the then-private company during the 1920s) control 45% of ABInBev's voting rights.

HISTORY

Monks at the Leffe Abbey in Belgium were brewing beer as early as 1240, and surviving records from 1366 mention Belgium's Den Horen brewery. Belgian master brewer Sebastien

Artois (best known for his Stella Artois lager) took over Den Horen in 1717. In 1853 the Piedboeuf family founded a brewery at Liege and established the Jupiler lager. Albert Van Damme assumed management of that brewery in 1920.

Over the years, the Artois and Piedboeuf families took over or established operations both in and outside Belgium. Direct descendants (the clans de Spoelberch, Van Damme, and de Mevius) of the two families were still managing the companies in 1987 when they decided the key to survival in the fragmented European beer market was to merge.

Artois-Piedboeuf-Interbrew acquired the Hoegaarden brewery in Belgium in 1989. The company changed its name to Interbrew three years later, acquired another Belgian brewery (Belle-Vue), and bought stakes in breweries in Bulgaria, Croatia, and Hungary. In 1995 Dommelsche Bierbrouwerij bought Allied Breweries Nederland, an Allied Domecq subsidiary, and Interbrew acquired the Oranjeboom breweries in the Netherlands.

The company purchased John Labatt Ltd. for $2 billion in 1995. As a result of the deal, Interbrew gained control of Latrobe Brewing (Rolling Rock beer, US), 22% of Mexico's FEMSA Cerveza (increased to 30% in 1998), the Toronto Argonauts football team, 90% of the Toronto Blue Jays (it sold an 80% stake in the baseball team to cable firm Rogers Communications in 2000) and various broadcast properties.

Interbrew sold many noncore assets, including Lehigh Valley Dairies (US) and John Labatt Retail (pubs, UK), in 1996. In 1998 Interbrew paid $250 million for 50% of the Doosan Group's Oriental Brewery, South Korea's second-largest brewer, and bought a majority stake in Russian brewer Rosar. The next year it combined its Russian operations with Sun Brewing, forming Russian brewer Sun-Interbrew. Hugo Powell was named CEO of Interbrew that year.

Interbrew bought Britain's third-largest brewer, Whitbread Beer Company, in 2000 for $590 million. Having gained a foothold in the UK market, the company then bought Bass Brewers from Bass PLC in 2000 for more than $3 billion. Interbrew went public on the Euronext (Brussels) exchange in 2000.

In 2001 Baron Paul De Keersmaeker retired as chairman and was replaced by Pierre Jean Everaert. Interbrew sold Carling, which controls about 18% of the UK beer market, to Coors for $1.7 billion, after being ordered to remedy unfair competition advantages related to the Bass Brewers purchase. John Brock, former COO of Cadbury Schweppes became CEO of Interbrew in 2003. In 2004 Interbrew purchased a 70% stake in Chinese brewer Zhejiang Shiliang.

InBev was created through a 2005 merger of Interbrew and AmBev. By creating InBev, Interbrew gave up interest in distributing FEMSA beer brands in the US. In return, Interbrew retained full control of the US division of Labatt. InBev merged Labatt U.S.A. with what was Beck's North America to create its US operations.

In 2005 InBev acquired Russian premium brewer Tinkoff and sold its stake in soft-drink company Bremer Erfrischungsgetränke to Coca-Cola. It sold its minority stake in Spanish brewer Damm as well. At year-end Carlos Brito, formerly zone president for the company's North American operations, succeeded John Brock as CEO of InBev.

In 2006 it paid some $1 billion to increase its stake in Quinsa, an Argentine brewer, to 90% from 57% that year.

EXECUTIVES

Chairman: Peter Harf, age 64
CEO: Carlos Brito, age 50
CFO: Felipe Dutra, age 45
Global Head Mergers and Acquisitions:
Robert J. (Bob) Golden
Global Brand Director, Beck's: Jorn Socquet
Global VP Brands: Frank Abenante
Chief Legal and Corporate Affairs Officer; Secretary:
Sabine Chalmers, age 45
Chief Marketing Officer: Chris Burggraeve, age 46
Chief People and Technology Officer: Claudio Garcia
Chief Procurement Officer: Tony Milikin
Chief Supply Officer: Claudio Braz Ferro, age 41
VP Budweiser: Jason Warner
VP Purchasing: Thomas J. (Tom) Adamitis
VP Investor Relations: Robert Ottenstein
VP Marketing: Keith S. Levy
VP Sales and Distribution: Evan C. Athanas
VP Finance: David Almeida, age 33
Director Global External Communications:
Gwendoline Ornigg
President, Anheuser-Busch: David A. (Dave) Peacock, age 41
Auditors: KPMG Bedrijfsrevisoren-Réviseurs d'Entreprises

LOCATIONS

HQ: Anheuser-Busch InBev SA/NV
Brouwerijplein 1
3000 Leuven, Belgium
Phone: 32-16-27-61-11   **Fax:** 32-16-50-61-11
Web: www.inbev.com

2009 Sales

	$ mil.	% of total
North America	15,486	42
Latin America		
North	7,649	21
South	1,899	5
Europe		
Western	4,312	12
Central & Eastern	2,492	7
Asia Pacific	1,985	5
Other	2,936	8
Total	**36,758**	**100**

PRODUCTS/OPERATIONS

Selected Brands

Global flagship brands
Beck's
Budweiser
Leffe
Stella Artois
Global specialty brands
Cuvée
Hoegaarden
Local brands
Argentina — Andes, Brahma, Norte, Patagonia, Quilmes
Belgium — Belle-Vue, Jupiter
Bolivia — Ducal, Paceña, Taquiña
Brazil — Antarctica, Bohemia, Brahma, Skol
Canada — Alexander Keith's, Bud Light, Kokanee, Labatt, Luc
Chile — Baltica, Becker, Brahma
China — Double Deer, Harbin, Jinling, Jinlongquan, KK, Sedrin, Shiliang
Cuba — Bucanero, Cristal, Mayabe
France — Boomerang, Loburg
Germany — Diebels, Franziskaner, Haake-Beck, Hasseröder, Löwenbräu
Italy — Franziskaner, Löwenbräu, Spaten
Mexico — Corona, Bud Light
The Netherlands — Dommelsch, Jupiter, Hertog Jan
Paraguay — Baviera, Brahma, Ouro Fino, Pilsen
Peru — Brahma, Zenda
Russia — Bagbier, Brahma, Klinskoye, Löwenbräu, Sibirskaya Korona
UK — Bass, Boddingtons, Brahma
Uruguay — Pilsen, Norteña, Patricia
US — Bass, Brahma, Bud Light, Busch, Michelob, Natural Light

COMPETITORS

Anchor Brewers
Asahi Breweries
Asia Pacific Breweries
Bavaria S.A.
Beijing Enterprises
Big Rock Brewery
Boston Beer
Carlsberg
Central European Distribution
Coca-Cola
Coca-Cola FEMSA
Constellation Brands
Craft Brewers Alliance
Diageo
FEMSA
FEMSA Cerveza
Foster's Group
Fraser & Neave
Grolsch
Heineken
Holsten-Brauerei
Kirin Holdings Company
Lion Nathan
Molson Coors
Pyramid Breweries
Radeberger Gruppe
SABMiller
San Miguel Corporation
Sapporo
Suntory Holdings
Thai Beverage
Tsingtao
UB Group
Yanjing
Yuengling & Son

HISTORICAL FINANCIALS

Company Type: Public

Income Statement

FYE: December 31

	REVENUE ($ mil.)	NET INCOME ($ mil.)	NET PROFIT MARGIN	EMPLOYEES
12/09	36,758	4,613	12.5%	116,489
12/08	23,507	1,927	8.2%	119,874
12/07	21,097	4,456	21.1%	88,690
12/06	17,549	2,804	16.0%	85,617
12/05	13,749	1,654	12.0%	77,366
Annual Growth	27.9%	29.2%	—	10.8%

2009 Year-End Financials

Debt ratio: 161.7%   No. of shares (mil.): 1,591
Return on equity: —   Dividends
Cash ($ mil.): 3,689   Yield: 0.8%
Current ratio: 0.76   Payout: 9.7%
Long-term debt ($ mil.): 49,028   Market value ($ mil.): 57,904

Stock History

NYSE: BUD

	STOCK PRICE ($) FY Close	P/E High/Low		PER SHARE ($) Earnings	Dividends	Book Value
12/09	36.40	13	6	2.90	0.28	19.06
12/08	16.58	32	5	1.93	2.85	14.11
12/07	57.00	13	9	5.25	—	12.52
12/06	49.94	16	11	3.03	—	10.16
12/05	36.77	21	14	1.77	—	8.50
Annual Growth	(0.3%)	—	—	13.1%	(90.2%)	22.3%

A.P. Møller – Mærsk

Big metal boxes mean money for A.P. Møller – Mærsk. The company's container shipping units, led by Maersk Line, maintain a fleet of more than 500 containerships, and subsidiary APM Terminals is a major container terminal operator. Other vessels in the fleet include tankers and oil field supply and specialty ships. In addition to its shipping-related activities, A.P. Møller – Mærsk offers supply chain management and freight forwarding services (through Damco), oil and gas drilling (primarily in the North Sea), and it owns one of Denmark's largest grocery and general merchandise chains. Other units build ships and shipping containers and provide air cargo services.

Despite cost-cutting initiatives and reorganizations to focus on its core operations, A.P. Møller – Mærsk still experienced significant reductions in revenue for 2009. Decreased freight sales, crude prices, and overall demand handed the company a DKK 5.5 billion ($1 billion) loss for the year.

A.P. Møller – Mærsk's cost-cutting initiatives, launched in 2008, involved streamlining its route network, optimizing its fuel cost structure, and simplifying its product portfolio and the process by which its customers interact with its sales force. It also combined its Maersk Logistics and Damco divisions in 2009, branding the new entity Damco, and sold its ferry holdings and UK grocery store operations. The company decided to phase out ship building activities at its Odense Steel Shipyards.

At the same time, high fuel prices count as a benefit for the company's oil and gas segment. Among A.P. Møller – Mærsk's major oil and gas assets is a stake in the Dansk Undergrunds Consortium (DUC), which is engaged in exploration and production in the Danish sector of the North Sea. As fields in the North Sea mature, the company's Maersk Oil unit is investing in properties elsewhere, including Qatar, Angola, and the Gulf of Mexico.

Founded by Peter Mærsk Møller and his son Arnold Peter Møller, A.P. Møller – Mærsk styles its name as "Mærsk" but uses "Maersk" for the names of most of its subsidiaries.

HISTORY

Arnold Peter Møller and his father, sea captain Peter Mærsk Møller, founded Aktieselskabet Dampskibsselskabet Svendborg (Steamship Company Svendborg) in 1904 in Svendborg, Denmark. Their first ship, a second-hand steamer, bore on its funnel a white seven-pointed star on a blue background, which had been on Peter's first ship. Later known as the Maersk star, the logo adorned all subsequent ships of the company, as well as ships of a second company formed eight years later — Dampskibsselskabet af 1912, Aktieselskab (Steamship Company of 1912). At that point, six ships were in the Maersk fleet.

In 1917 the company began building its own ships after establishing the Odense Steel Shipyard. It launched regular liner service between the US and the Far East in 1928, calling the operation the Maersk Line. With the addition of its first tankers that year, Maersk owned 35 ships.

Mærsk Mc-Kinney Møller, A.P.'s son, became a partner in the company in 1940. That year, with Germany occupying Denmark, he fled to the US with his bride on one of the last ships out. Refusing to take orders from the Nazis, A.P. transferred control of the company to the US, where the 26-year-old Mærsk had established operations. Most of the Maersk fleet flew under British or US flags during the war, which took the life of 148 Maersk seamen and claimed 25 ships. Mærsk Mc-Kinney Møller returned to Denmark in 1947.

A.P. Møller formed the Maersk Company in 1951 in London as a shipbroker; it became one of the world's largest shipowners. The early 1960s saw A.P. Møller diversifying as it moved into oil and gas exploration and production in Denmark in 1962 and established supermarket chain Dansk Supermarked in 1964. A.P. died the next year, having run the company for more than 60 years. Prior to his death, he had created three foundations to hold most of the company's shares. His son Mærsk took command of A.P. Møller and the Maersk fleet, which contained 88 ships. Under his leadership the company expanded even further and became more international; his business savvy became apparent when he sold some of the company's tanker fleet in the 1970s, just prior to prices going down.

In 1970 A.P. Møller established domestic carrier Maersk Air. A.P. Møller began seeing its first oil production in the North Sea in 1972. The next year the company acquired its first container vessel, the *Svendborg Maersk*.

Maersk Container Industri was formed in 1991 to produce intermodal containers. That year Maersk and rival Sea-Land entered into a transpacific vessel-sharing agreement, which was expanded into a global alliance in 1995. In 1999, just months after buying South Africa's Safmarine Container Lines, Maersk bought Sea-Land's international liner services and 18 terminals. The Maersk Line and Sea-Land operations were merged to form Maersk Sealand.

In 2001 Maersk Air and Scandinavian Airlines System (SAS) were together fined $45 million by the European Commission for infringing on the EC's competition rules by entering into a secret deal to monopolize certain air routes in Scandinavia. As a result, Maersk Air's chairman and managing director stepped down and were replaced.

A.P. Møller, which through the years had continued to operate through two separately listed companies — Aktieselskabet Dampskibsselskabet Svendborg and Dampskibsselskabet af 1912, Aktieselskab — reorganized in 2003 and wound up with a single publicly traded company — A.P. Møller – Mærsk A/S — at its head.

A.P. Møller – Mærsk purchased the majority of Kerr-McGee's North Sea oil assets in late 2005. Also that year, the passenger transportation business of Maersk Air was sold to an Icelandic investment group.

Maersk Line was launched as a brand in 2006, as a result of the combined operations of Maersk Sealand and Royal P&O Nedlloyd, which was acquired by A.P. Møller – Mærsk in 2005. Consolidating the businesses proved to be more difficult than expected, however. The container shipping operations lost money in 2006 before posting a small profit in 2007. That year CEO Jess Søderberg stepped down two years ahead of schedule, and Nils Smedegaard Andersen, CEO of brewer Carlsberg and a director of A.P. Møller – Mærsk, replaced him.

EXECUTIVES

Chairman: Michael P. Rasmussen, age 55
Vice Chairman: Poul J. Svanholm, age 77
Vice Chairman: Ane Mærsk Mc-Kinney Uggla, age 62
Group CEO and Partner: Nils Smedegaard Andersen, age 52
Group CFO: Trond Ø. Westlie, age 49
Partner; CEO, Maersk Drilling and Maersk FPSOs: Claus V. Hemmingsen, age 48
Partner; CEO, Maersk Line and Container Business: Eivind Kolding, age 51
Partner; CEO, Maersk Tankers: Søren Skou, age 46
CEO, Safmarine: Tomas Dyrbye
CEO, Danish Supermarked: Erling Jensen, age 62
CEO, Damco: Rolf Habben-Jansen
CEO, Rosti: Stig Hoffmeyer
CEO, Maersk Supply Service: Carsten P. Andersen, age 53
CEO, Maersk Oil: Jakob Thomasen, age 48
President and CEO, Maersk Fluid Technology: Klaus-Werner Damm
Investor Relations Manager: Hans Christian Aagaard
Auditors: Grant Thornton

LOCATIONS

HQ: A.P. Møller – Mærsk A/S
Esplanaden 50
1098 Copenhagen K, Denmark
Phone: 45-3363-3363   **Fax:** 45-3363-4108
Web: www.maersk.com

2009 Sales

	% of total
Denmark	24
US	10
Qatar	9
UK	8
Singapore	1
Other regions	48
Total	

PRODUCTS/OPERATIONS

2009 Sales

	% of total
Shipping	
Container shipping	41
Tankers & offshore	11
Oil & gas	22
Retail	18
APM terminals	5
Other	3
Total	**100**

Selected Operating Units

Container shipping
  APM Terminals B.V.
  Maersk Line
  Safmarine Container Lines N.V.

Tankers and offshore
  Maersk Contractors
  Maersk Supply Service
  Maersk Tankers

Retail
  Dansk Supermarked Group

Oil and gas
  Maersk Oil

Other
  Damco A/S (supply chain management and freight forwarding services)
  Maersk Container Industri A/S (manufacturing of refrigerated shipping containers)
  Odense Staalskibsvaerft A/S Group (shipbuilding)
  Star Air A/S (air cargo transportation)

HISTORICAL FINANCIALS

Company Type: Public

Income Statement

FYE: December 31

	REVENUE ($ mil.)	NET INCOME ($ mil.)	NET PROFIT MARGIN	EMPLOYEES
12/09	50,081	(1,057)	—	115,386
12/08	59,059	3,341	5.7%	119,599
12/07	55,049	3,683	6.7%	117,319
12/06	46,835	2,863	6.1%	108,530
12/05	33,058	3,201	9.7%	—
Annual Growth	10.9%	—	—	2.1%

2009 Year-End Financials

Debt ratio: —
Return on equity: —
Cash ($ mil.): 1,608
Current ratio: 0.93
Long-term debt ($ mil.): —

No. of shares (mil.): 4
Dividends
  Yield: 1.8%
  Payout: —
Market value ($ mil.): 30,982

Stock History

OMX Copenhagen: MAERSKB

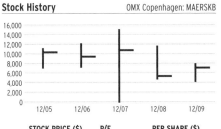

	STOCK PRICE ($) FY Close	P/E High/Low	PER SHARE ($) Earnings	PER SHARE ($) Dividends	PER SHARE ($) Book Value
12/09	7,049.16	— —	(322.41)	125.19	6,961.88
12/08	5,322.14	15 6	780.71	—	6,444.28
12/07	10,738.56	17 —	855.33	—	6,207.01
12/06	9,411.08	18 11	668.86	—	5,193.97
12/05	10,327.68	14 9	773.47	—	4,447.60
Annual Growth	(9.1%)	— —	—	—	11.9%

ArcelorMittal

Many metal makers lack the mettle of ArcelorMittal. The company is easily the largest steelmaking entity in the world, producing more than 74 million tons annually. Operating in more than 60 countries — though strongest in Europe — ArcelorMittal manufactures the full range of steel products: slabs and coil, coated steel and tinplate, wire rod and rebar, and billets and blooms, as well as all manner of stainless and electrical steel products. CEO and founder Lakshmi Mittal controls nearly half of ArcelorMittal and has blazed through this decade making a number of gigantic acquisitions, the largest being the Franco-Belgian amalgam Arcelor, to make his firm far and away the leader in the global steel industry. The combined company is 43% owned by the Mittal family.

ArcelorMittal, which operates through subsidiaries in Europe, Africa, and the Americas, has laid plans for Asian expansion, as well.

Since its consolidation of Arcelor and Mittal Steel, the company has been working to gather its Brazilian steel operations into one cohesive unit. ArcelorMittal Brasil is among that country's largest steel producers now. In 2008 ArcelorMittal agreed to pay London Mining $810 million to buy its Brazilian iron ore mining unit. The idea behind the deal is to integrate more fully ArcelorMittal's steel operations by providing its own raw materials.

In 2009 ArcelorMittal completed its acquisition of the laser-welding steel activities of Noble International, a leader in the niche industry. Arcelor Mittal initially received $300 million from Noble in 2007 in exchange for its laser-welding operations; it acquired the balance of the company when Noble filed for bankruptcy two years later. It also acquired Mexican steel producer Sicarsta for nearly $1.5 billion, an acquisition that, combined with its Lazaro Cardenas, created Mexico's largest steel company.

In 2010 ArcelorMittal sought to buy Zimbabwe Iron and Steel Works, but was rejected by the Zimbabwean government, which owns a controlling stake in the operation. Government officials said they were looking for a smaller company to partner with the state-owned operation.

HISTORY

ArcelorMittal is the product of decades of steelmaking by India's Mittal family. In 1967 patriarch Mohan Mittal unsuccessfully tried to open a steel mill in Egypt. He and his four younger brothers then set up a steel company in India, but squabbles pushed Mohan to chart his own course, eventually giving rise to an empire that flourished under the Ispat name. Mohan's son Lakshmi began working part-time at the family steel mill while in school; he started full-time at 21, after graduating in 1971.

Mohan set up an operation in Indonesia in 1975 (Ispat Indo) and put Lakshmi in charge. The next year, fueled by ambitions and held back by government regulations in India, Lakshmi formed Ispat International in Jakarta, Indonesia, to focus on expansion through acquisitions. He spent the next decade strengthening the Indonesian operations and perfecting the minimill process using direct-reduced iron (DRI).

Ispat took advantage of the recessionary late 1980s and early 1990s by making a string of acquisitions. In 1988 it took over the management

of Trinidad and Tobago's state steel companies (bought in 1994; renamed Caribbean Ispat).

In 1992 Ispat bought Mexico's third-largest (albeit bankrupt) steel and DRI producer. Two years later it acquired Canada's Sidbec-Dosco steelmaker. Also that year Lakshmi took exclusive control of international operations, leaving his brothers Pramod and Vinod to control the Indian divisions.

The mid-1990s brought more acquisitions: In 1995 Ispat bought Germany's Hamburger Stahlwerks and a mill in Kazakhstan. In 1997 the company bought the long-product (wire rod) division of Germany's Thyssen AG (renamed Ispat Stahlwerk Ruhrort and Ispat Walzdraht Hochfeld). It also completed a $776 million IPO — the steel industry's biggest, outside of privatizations.

Ispat acquired Chicago-based Inland Steel in 1998. In 1999 Ispat formed a joint venture with Mexican steelmaker Grupo Imsa to make flat-rolled steel to sell throughout most of the Americas. That year Ispat Inland became the target of a US federal criminal grand jury investigation and a related civil lawsuit for allegedly defrauding the Louisiana Highway Department. (The case was settled for $30 million.)

The present company was forged in 2004 when Ispat International (of which the Mittal family owned 70%) purchased LNM Holdings (wholly owned by the Mittals) for $13 billion.

In 2006 the former Mittal Steel agreed to buy rival Arcelor for about $34 billion to create ArcelorMittal. Mittal Steel had established its hold on the world steel market through its 2005 purchase of the US-based International Steel Group (ISG) for $4.5 billion. The purchase made the company the largest steel producer in the US (ahead of U.S. Steel and Nucor). Once the deal closed, the company combined ISG's operations with those of subsidiary Ispat Inland to form a single North American entity, Mittal Steel USA.

Also in 2005 Mittal Steel acquired a 93% stake in Ukrainian state-run steel company KryvorizhStal with the winning $4.84 billion bid in an auction held by the Ukrainian government.

The company also began to broaden its portfolio outside the steel industry, dipping its toe into the energy business. In mid-2005 Mittal formed two joint ventures with India's government-controlled Oil & Natural Gas Corporation: one to buy stakes in foreign oil and gas projects, the other involved in oil and gas trading and shipping. The ventures began to look for business in places like Indonesia, Kazakhstan, Angola, and Trinidad and Tobago.

After consolidating his family's various steel interests in the early part of this decade, Mittal began work on the steel industry as a whole and was soon the world's largest steel producer.

By 2006, Mittal Steel no longer was content to be merely the world's largest steel producer; it wanted to dominate the market. The company announced an offer to the shareholders of Arcelor, then the industry's #2 player, to buy that company and, in the process, create the world's first 100-million-ton steel producer. Arcelor, and seemingly half the governments of Western Europe, initially fought the attempt.

Mittal improved its proposed price, however, and Arcelor's board finally approved the offer when Mittal also made ownership/corporate governance concessions. After a few months of a transitional management team arrangement, Lakshmi Mittal took over as CEO of the combined company toward the end of 2006.

EXECUTIVES

Chairman and CEO: Lakshmi N. Mittal, age 59
CFO and Member Group Management Board:
Aditya Mittal, age 34
Member Group Management Board, Long Products, China, Stainless, Tubular Products, Corporate Responsibility, and ArcelorMittal Foundation, and Chairman, Investment Allocation Committee:
Gonzalo Urquijo, age 49
Member Group Management Board, Shared Services:
Davinder K. Chugh, age 53
Member Group Management Board, Corporate Finance, Mergers and Acquisitions and Business Development including India (chapter 1), and Risk Management:
Sudhir Maheshwari, age 46
Member Group Management Board, Flat Europe, Distribution Solutions, Product Development and R&D, and Global Customers: Michel Wurth, age 55
Member Group Management Board, Technology and Projects, Asia and Africa: Christophe Cornier, age 57
SEVP; Head, Mining: Peter G. J. Kukielski, age 53
EVP and CTO: Pierre Gugliermina, age 58
EVP; Head, Mining Projects and Exploration:
Philippus F. (Phil) du Toit, age 57
EVP and Head Human Resources: Willie Smit
EVP and Head, Finance: Bhikam C. Agarwal, age 57
EVP; CEO, USA: Michael G. (Mike) Rippey, age 52
EVP and Head, Strategy: Bill Scotting, age 51
EVP and Head, Marketing and Commercial Coordination: Michael B. Pfitzner, age 60
Secretary: Henk Scheffer
Corporate Communications: Nicola Davidson
Director Investor Relations: Daniel Fairclough
Auditors: Deloitte S.A.

LOCATIONS

HQ: ArcelorMittal
19 avenue de la Liberté
L-2390 Luxembourg, Luxembourg
Phone: 352-4792-1   **Fax:** 352-4792-2675
US HQ: 1 S. Dearborn St., 19th Fl., Chicago, IL 60603
US Phone: 312-899-3440
Web: www.arcelormittal.com

2009 Sales

	$ mil.	% of total
Europe	33,662	52
Americas	20,013	31
Asia & Africa	11,435	17
Total	**65,110**	**100**

PRODUCTS/OPERATIONS

2009 Sales

	$ mil.	% of total
Flat Carbon Products		
Europe	19,981	26
Americas	13,340	18
Long Carbon Americas & Europe	16,767	22
Steel Solutions & Services	13,524	18
Asia, Africa & CIS	7,627	10
Stainless Steel	4,234	6
Adjustments	(10,363)	—
Total	**65,110**	**100**

Segments and Selected Products

Flat Carbon Europe
  Coated products
  Coil
    Cold-rolled
    Hot-rolled
  Plate
  Slab
  Tin plate
Flat Carbon Americas
  Coated products
    Steel
    Plate
  Coil
    Cold-rolled
    Hot-rolled
  Slabs

Long Carbon Americas and Europe
  Billets
  Blooms
  Rebar
  Sections
  Wire rod
Asia, Africa, and Comonwealth of Independent States
  Flat products
  Long products
  Pipes
  Tubes
ArcelorMittal Steel Solutions and Services (in-house trading and distribution arm)
Stainless Steel (flat and long stainless steel and alloy products)

COMPETITORS

AK Steel Holding Corporation
Baosteel
BHP Billiton
BlueScope Steel
China Steel
Essar Group
Evraz
Gerdau
JFE Holdings
Mechel OAO
Nippon Steel
Nucor
POSCO
Severstal
Shougang Corp.
Tata Steel
Tenaris
Ternium
ThyssenKrupp Steel
United States Steel

HISTORICAL FINANCIALS

Company Type: Public

Income Statement

FYE: December 31

	REVENUE ($ mil.)	NET INCOME ($ mil.)	NET PROFIT MARGIN	EMPLOYEES
12/09	65,110	118	0.2%	287,000
12/08	124,936	9,399	7.5%	316,000
12/07	105,216	10,368	9.9%	311,466
12/06	58,870	5,226	8.9%	319,578
12/05	28,132	3,365	12.0%	224,286
Annual Growth	**23.3%**	**(56.7%)**	**—**	**6.4%**

2009 Year-End Financials

Debt ratio: 33.9%
Return on equity: 0.2%
Cash ($ mil.): 5,919
Current ratio: 1.39
Long-term debt ($ mil.): 20,677
No. of shares (mil.): 1,561
Dividends
Yield: 1.4%
Payout: 800.0%
Market value ($ mil.): 71,412

Stock History

NYSE: MT

	STOCK PRICE ($) FY Close	P/E High/Low		PER SHARE ($) Earnings	Dividends	Book Value
12/09	45.75	588	204	0.08	0.64	39.11
12/08	24.59	15	2	6.78	1.39	35.36
12/07	77.35	11	5	7.40	1.30	36.32
12/06	42.18	8	5	5.28	0.50	26.99
12/05	26.33	9	5	4.89	0.30	6.50
Annual Growth	**14.8%**	**—**	**—**	**(64.2%)**	**20.9%**	**56.6%**

AstraZeneca

AstraZeneca's products run the gamut from A (top-selling breast cancer drug Arimidex) to Z (migraine treatment Zomig). One of the world's major pharmaceutical firms, AstraZeneca specializes in drugs for gastrointestinal, cardiovascular, neurology, respiratory, infection, and oncology therapeutic areas. The firm's biggest seller is acid reflux remedy Nexium. For matters of the heart, AstraZeneca makes hypertension and heart failure drug Atacand and cholesterol reducer Crestor. The company's other top drugs include anti-psychotic Seroquel and Symbicort and Pulmicort for asthma. AstraZeneca also markets FluMist, a nasal influenza vaccine. The company's drugs are sold in more than 100 countries.

AstraZeneca's other businesses include Aptium Oncology, which operates cancer treatment centers in the US, and Astra Tech, which manufactures such medical devices as urinary catheters and dental implant systems.

CEO David Brennan is making a concerted effort to boost the company's industry position ahead of patent expirations by strengthening AstraZeneca's drug development pipeline. AstraZeneca also intends to reduce the number of disease targets within its core therapy areas, focusing on the major maladies in each segment.

To help combat upcoming patent loss and fund initiatives to strengthen its pipeline, the company has announced plans to reduce its worldwide workforce by as many as 23,000 positions (roughly 32%) by the end of 2014. By the end of 2009, about 12,600 positions had already been eliminated, primarily from its R&D and supply chain organizations.

AstraZeneca is working hard to keep the bestsellers coming. Faced with patent expirations of market leaders Prilosec, Zestril, and Nolvadex, the company has answered the challenge with several promising new drugs. Its purple Prilosec follow-up, Nexium, soared to the top of its offerings, earning some $5 billion annually.

Its neuroscience segment has skyrocketed as earnings from schizophrenia and bipolar treatment Seroquel have reached nearly $5 billion. But Seroquel's profit margin received a hit in 2010 after AstraZeneca agreed to pay about $520 million to settle US Department of Justice claims it marketed the drug for unapproved uses such as a treatment for anxiety, attention deficit hyperactivity disorder, and bipolar maintenance.

The company's pipeline includes about 145 drugs in various development stages. In 2009 the company submitted new regulatory filings for Brilinta (acute coronary syndromes), Certriad (submitted with Abbott Labs for lipid abnormalities), Vimovo (arthritic pain), and Onglyza, a diabetes treatment.

AstraZeneca also partners with smaller development firms to boost its R&D operations. For example, it has a partnership with biotech firm Targacept to help feed its neurological drug pipeline. The two companies expanded their relationship in 2009 when AstraZeneca agreed to pay up to $1.2 billion for rights to Targacept's antidepressant candidate TC-5214.

In 2009 the company agreed to acquire Paris-based Novexel, a developer of drugs designed to fight antibiotic-resistant infections in a deal worth up to about $425 million. The buy gives AstraZeneca a built-in alliance with Forest Laboratories, which is co-developing Novexel's two most advanced drug candidates.

HISTORY

AstraZeneca forerunner Imperial Chemical Industries (ICI) was created from the 1926 merger of four British chemical companies — Nobel Industries; Brunner, Mond and Company; United Alkali; and British Dyestuffs — in reaction to the German amalgamation that created I. G. Farben. ICI plunged into research, recruiting chemists, engineers, and managers and forming alliances with universities. Between 1933 and 1935, at least 87 new products were created, including polyethylene.

Fortunes declined as competition increased after WWII. In 1980 ICI posted losses and cut its dividend for the first time. In 1982 turnaround artist John Harvey-Jones shifted ICI from bulk chemicals to high-margin specialty chemicals such as pharmaceuticals and pesticides. That business became Zeneca, which ICI spun off in 1993.

The takeover specter loomed large over the company during its first year. Zeneca had several drugs in its pipeline, but it also had expiring patents on others, making them fair game for competitors. Bankrolled by its agrochemical business, Zeneca forged alliances with other pharmaceutical firms. In 1994 it entered a marketing alliance with Amersham International (now Amersham) to sell Metastron, a nuclear-medicine cancer agent. The next year Zeneca formed a joint venture with Chinese companies Advanced Chemicals and Tianli to make textile-coating chemicals.

In 1995 Glaxo was forced to sell a migraine drug candidate to complete its merger with Wellcome. Zeneca's gamble in buying the then-unproven drug (Zomig) paid off when the product gained US FDA approval two years later.

By 1997 Zeneca completed its gradual acquisition of Salick Health Care, formed to create more humane cancer treatment programs. The purchase followed a trend of large drug firms moving into managed care, which raised concerns that centers might be pressured to use their parent companies' drugs, but Zeneca maintained that Salick would remain independent except to the extent that it offered an opportunity to evaluate treatments.

In 1998 Zeneca got the FDA's OK to sell its brand of tamoxifen (Nolvadex) to women at high risk of contracting breast cancer. In 1999 it sued Eli Lilly to protect Nolvadex against Lilly's marketing claim that its osteoporosis treatment Evista reduced breast cancer risk, a use for which it was not approved.

In 1999 Zeneca completed its purchase of Sweden's Astra to form AstraZeneca. That year the firm sold its specialty chemicals unit, Zeneca Specialties, to Cinven Group and Investcorp. With its agricultural business stagnated due to crippled markets in Asia and Europe, AstraZeneca merged the unit with the agrochemicals business of Novartis and spun it off as Syngenta.

In 2001 AstraZeneca sold its genetic diversity testing services subsidiary, Cellmark Diagnostics, to Orchid Cellmark.

Chief executive Sir Tom McKillop retired at the close of 2005 and was succeeded by marketing expert David Brennan.

The company in 2007 bought US biotech firm MedImmune for more than $15 billion. The acquisition expanded AstraZeneca's capability for vaccination research, as well as its research in oncology, infection, and respiratory disorders; it also added manufacturing facilities.

The MedImmune purchase dovetailed with AstraZeneca's $1.3 billion acquisition of Cambridge Antibody Technology in 2006.

EXECUTIVES

Chairman: Louis Schweitzer, age 68, $504,000 total compensation
CEO and Director: David R. Brennan, age 56, $4,937,000 total compensation
CFO and Director: Simon Lowth, age 49, $2,209,000 total compensation
Chief Medical Officer: Howard Hutchinson
EVP Operations: David Smith
EVP Development: Anders Ekblom
EVP Human Resources and Corporate Affairs: Lynn Tetrault
EVP Global Marketing; CEO, North America: Tony P. Zook
President, AstraZeneca Japan: Masuhiro Kato
President and CEO, AstraZeneca Canada: Marion McCourt
President and CEO, AstraZeneca UK: Mark Jones
President, North America: Rich Fante
President, Research and Development: Martin Mackay
General Counsel: Jeff Pott
Auditors: KPMG Audit Plc

LOCATIONS

HQ: AstraZeneca PLC
15 Stanhope Gate
London W1K 1LN, United Kingdom
Phone: 44-20-7304-5000   **Fax:** 44-20-7304-5151
US HQ: 1800 Concord Pike, Wilmington, DE 19850
US Phone: 302-886-3000   **US Fax:** 302-886-2972
Web: www.astrazeneca.com

2009 Sales

	$ mil.	% of total
United States	14,778	45
Western Europe	9,277	28
Japan	2,341	7
Canada	1,203	4
Emerging Europe	1,091	3
China	811	3
Emerging Asia/Pacific	780	2
Other countries	2,523	8
Total	32,804	100

PRODUCTS/OPERATIONS

2009 Sales

	$ mil.	% of total
Cardiovascular		
Crestor	4,502	14
Seloken/Toprol-XL	1,443	4
Atacand	1,436	4
Tenormin	296	1
Plendil	241	1
Zestril	184	1
Other cardiovascular	274	1
Gastrointestinal		
Nexium	4,959	15
Losec/Prilosec	946	3
Other gastrointestinal	106	—
Neuroscience		
Seroquel	4,866	14
Local anesthetics	599	2
Zomig	434	2
Other neuroscience	338	1
Oncology		
Arimidex	1,921	6
Zoladex	1,086	3
Casodex	844	3
Iressa	297	1
Other oncology	370	1
Respiratory		
Symbicort	2,294	7
Pulmicort	1,310	4
Rhinocort	528	1
Infection & other		
Synagis	1,082	3
Merrem	872	3
Non Seasonal Flu	389	1
Other products	288	—
Astra Tech	506	2
Aptium Oncology	393	2
Total	32,804	100

Selected Products

Cardiovascular
Atacand (angiotensin II antagonist for hypertension and heart failure)
Crestor (statin for cholesterol-lowering drug)
Plendil (calcium antagonist for hypertension and angina)
Seloken/Toprol-XL (beta-blocker for blood pressure, heart failure, angina)
Tenormin (beta-blocker for hypertension, angina pectoris, other)
Zestril (ACE inhibitor for hypertension, other)
Gastrointestinal
Entocort (anti-inflammatory for inflammatory bowel disease)
Losec/Prilosec (acid reflux disease)
Nexium (acid reflux disease)
Neuroscience
Carbocaine (local anesthetic)
Citanest (local anesthetic)
Diprivan (general anesthetic)
Naropin (local anesthetic)
Seroquel (anti-psychotic for schizophrenia and bipolar)
Xylocaine (local anesthetic)
Zomig (migraines)
Oncology
Arimidex (aromatase inhibitor for breast cancer)
Casodex (anti-androgen for prostate cancer)
Faslodex (oestrogen receptor antagonist for breast cancer)
Iressa (kinase inhibitor for non-small cell lung cancer)
Nolvadex (breast cancer)
Zoladex (LHRH agonist for prostate and breast cancer)
Respiratory
Accolate (oral leukotriene receptor antagonist for asthma)
Bambec, Oxeol (asthma)
Oxis (beta-agonist for asthma and chronic obstructive pulmonary disease)
Pulmicort (anti-inflammatory for asthma)
Rhinocort (topical nasal anti-inflammatory)
Symbicort (anti-inflammatory and bronchodilator in one inhaler for asthma and chronic obstructive pulmonary disease)
Infection and Other Products
FluMist (nasal flu vaccine)
Merrem/Meronem (intravenous antibiotic for serious hospital infections)
Synagis (humanized monoclonal antibody for respiratory syncytial virus)

COMPETITORS

Abbott Labs
Amgen
Aptium Oncology
Bard
Bayer AG
Bristol-Myers Squibb
Elan
Eli Lilly
Genentech
Gilead Sciences
GlaxoSmithKline
Johnson & Johnson
Memorial Sloan-Kettering
Merck
Novartis
Pfizer
Ranbaxy Laboratories
Roche Holding
Sanofi-Aventis
Teva Pharmaceuticals
US Oncology
Zimmer Holdings

HISTORICAL FINANCIALS

Company Type: Public

Income Statement

FYE: December 31

	REVENUE ($ mil.)	NET INCOME ($ mil.)	NET PROFIT MARGIN	EMPLOYEES
12/09	32,804	7,521	22.9%	63,000
12/08	31,601	6,101	19.3%	66,100
12/07	29,559	5,595	18.9%	67,900
12/06	26,475	6,043	22.8%	66,000
12/05	23,950	4,706	19.6%	64,900
Annual Growth	8.2%	12.4%	—	(0.7%)

2009 Year-End Financials

Debt ratio: 1.2%
Return on equity: 41.1%
Cash ($ mil.): 9,918
Current ratio: 1.35
Long-term debt ($ mil.): 244

No. of shares (mil.): 1,425
Dividends
  Yield: 4.5%
  Payout: 40.3%
Market value ($ mil.): 66,911

Stock History

NYSE: AZN

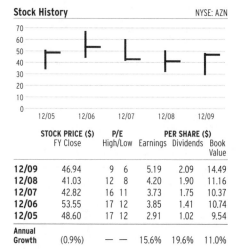

	STOCK PRICE ($) FY Close	P/E High	P/E Low	PER SHARE ($) Earnings	PER SHARE ($) Dividends	PER SHARE ($) Book Value
12/09	46.94	9	6	5.19	2.09	14.49
12/08	41.03	12	8	4.20	1.90	11.16
12/07	42.82	16	11	3.73	1.75	10.37
12/06	53.55	17	12	3.85	1.41	10.74
12/05	48.60	17	12	2.91	1.02	9.54
Annual Growth	(0.9%)	—	—	15.6%	19.6%	11.0%

Atos Origin

Atos Origin has a firm toehold on Europe's IT services mountain. The company provides services such as facilities management, e-commerce consulting, and systems design, implementation, and integration. Atos Origin also offers data and transaction processing services, website hosting, and outsourcing services for such functions as customer relationship management and enterprise resource planning. Formed from the combination of Atos and Origin (the computer services division of Philips Electronics), Atos Origin targets clients in the financial services, manufacturing, retail, and telecommunications industries, along with governments and utilities. The company gets most of its revenues in Europe.

Atos Origin is expanding its overseas presence through acquisitions. The company bought India-based payment services specialist Venture Infotek in 2010 and it acquired China-based Shanghai Covics Business Solution Ltd. the previous year. Shanghai Covics specialized in SAP software consulting and systems integration services. In 2007 the company raised its profile in the health care IT sector by acquiring Uni-Medecine.

The International Olympic Committee is using Atos Origin as its global IT systems integrator through 2016, including the Summer Games to be held in London and Rio de Janeiro.

HISTORY

Atos Origin's lineage is a story of mergers. The company's predecessor, Groupe Sligos, was itself the product of a merger — the 1973 union of Sliga (Crédit Lyonnais' data processing services subsidiary) with Cegos Informatique, a management systems development and consulting company started in 1962.

In 1981 Sligos debuted the first bank/retailer network switching system. It acquired Soliac, France's largest credit card maker, in 1983. Sligos went public in 1986 and two years later acquired a majority stake in CMG (acquired by rival Logica plc in 2002), one of France's leading computer engineering companies.

During the early 1990s Sligos focused on international growth, gaining majority interests in banking systems companies. It bought a controlling interest in Marben Group, a systems integration and networking firm, in 1993.

In 1996 Sligos joined with CyberCash, a (now defunct) US-based transaction processing company, to develop a secure Internet payment method for the European market. It sold CMG (by then a PC retailing subsidiary) to Infopoint and its Soliac magnetic strip and smartcard unit to Schlumberger.

In 1997 Sligos merged with French IT services company Axime. (Axime was created by the 1991 merger of IT service providers FITB, Segin, and Sodinforg. Bernard Bourigeaud joined Axime that year and became its chairman and CEO in 1992.)

Following the Sligos-Axime merger the company changed its name to Atos, with Axime's Bourigeaud assuming the role of chairman. Atos spent the last half of 1997 (and the first half of 1998) reorganizing its operations around four key areas: systems integration, outsourcing, multimedia, and services.

In 1998 Atos pared off its networking services and direct marketing subsidiaries. That year the company doubled the size of its Italian operation by acquiring IT services firm Sesam from Fiat and Digital Equipment (later acquired by Compaq Computer, now a part of Hewlett-Packard), and it bought French customer relationship management specialist Statilogie. Atos in 1999 bought a controlling interest in France-based Odyssée, a consulting specialist in the financial services market. The next year the company developed a joint venture with ParisBourse to offer online stock trading and electronic banking.

In 2000 the company merged with Origin, the computer services arm of Philips Electronics. Bourigeaud became chairman and CEO of the merged company, named Atos Origin. In 2002 Atos Origin acquired KPMG's British and Dutch operations for $617 million, moving the company into high-end consulting and the realm of Capgemini and IBM. Late the same year, Philips ended up taking a sizeable write-off on its stake in Atos Origin.

In 2004 Atos Origin acquired the SEMA Group, the IT services arm of Schlumberger, for about $1.5 billion, a purchase that significantly increased its annual revenues. After the purchase of the SEMA Group, the company began selling businesses considered either geographically or commercially noncore. These included its US-based Cellnet business and operations in the Middle East and the Nordic region.

Bourigeaud was replaced by Philippe Germond as CEO in 2007. Germond was replaced the following year by Thierry Breton, who previously held the positions of finance minister for France and CEO of France Telecom.

EXECUTIVES

Chairman and CEO: Thierry Breton, age 54, $2,763,693 total compensation
SEVP Operations: Charles Dehelly, age 58, $1,064,963 total compensation
SEVP Global Functions: Gilles Grapinet, age 46, $1,018,762 total compensation
CFO: Michel-Alain Proch, age 42
Group CIO: Tarek Moustafa
General Secretary and Chief of Staff to CEO: Philippe Mareine, age 40
Chief Procurement Officer: Enguerrand de Pontevès
Board Member; Director Human Resources, Atos Origin UK: Jean Fleming, age 40
EVP; CEO, Atos Origin North America: Paul Stewart
EVP Telecom and Media: Bruno Fabre
SVP Internal Audit: Daniel Milard
SVP Global Public Relations: Marie-Tatiana Collombert
VP Investor Relations and Financial Communications: Gilles Arditti
Head Rest of World Group Business Unit and Major Events: Patrick Adiba
Head Global Innovation and Business Development and Strategy: Marc-Henri Desportes, age 38
Head Global Consulting: Hervé Payan, age 43
Head Talent Management and Communications: Marc Meyer, age 51
Head Global Managed Services: Éric Grall, age 49
Head Global Systems Integration: Francis Meston, age 49
Head Strategic Sales and Strategic International Customers: Francis Delacourt, age 54
General Counsel: Eric Sandrin
Auditors: Deloitte & Associés

LOCATIONS

HQ: Atos Origin S.A.
  Tour Les Miroirs — Bâtiment C, 18, avenue d'Alsace
  92926 Paris, France
Phone: 33-1-55-91-20-00   **Fax:** 33-1-55-91-20-05
US HQ: 5599 San Felipe St., Ste. 300
  Houston, TX 77056
US Phone: 713-513-3000   **US Fax:** 713-403-7204
Web: www.atosorigin.com

2009 Sales

	% of total
Europe, Middle East & Africa	
France	22
Benelux	20
UK	18
Germany & Central Europe	11
Other countries	16
Iberia & South America	8
Other regions	5
Total	**100**

PRODUCTS/OPERATIONS

2009 Sales

	% of total
Managed services	38
Systems integration	37
High technology transaction services	17
Consulting	5
Medical business process outsourcing (BPO)	3
Total	**100**

2009 Sales by Industry Sector

	% of total
Public services	28
Financial services	22
Telecommunications & media	14
Manufacturing	13
Retail	10
Utilities	9
Other	4
Total	**100**

Selected Services

Systems Integration
  Application and data migration
  Application lifecycle management
  Configuration management
  Enterprise architecture
  Enterprise resource planning
  eServices
  Operations design, roll-out, and support
  Systems development
Managed Operations
  Business continuity
  Data and application hosting
  IT support outsourcing
  On-demand services
  Security services
Consulting
  Business intelligence
  Business strategy
  Customer relationship management
  Enterprise security
  Financial management solutions
  Knowledge services
  Supply chain management
  Transformation management

COMPETITORS

Altran Technologies
ARES
Aubay
BT
Bull
Capgemini
CBGI
CIBER
Computacenter
Computer Sciences Corp.
CS Communication
Devoteam
Dimension Data
Fujitsu Services
Getronics
GFI Informatique
HP Enterprise Services
IBM Global Services
Imtech
Infosys
Logica
Morse Ltd.
Parity Group
Siemens IT Solutions and Services
Sogeti
Sopra
Steria
TEAMLOG
Triple P
Umanis
Unisys

HISTORICAL FINANCIALS

Company Type: Public

Income Statement

FYE: December 31

	REVENUE ($ mil.)	NET INCOME ($ mil.)	NET PROFIT MARGIN	EMPLOYEES
12/09	7,348	51	0.7%	49,036
12/08	7,926	41	0.5%	50,975
12/07	8,619	93	1.1%	51,704
12/06	7,120	(327)	—	49,847
12/05	6,465	291	4.5%	47,684
Annual Growth	3.3%	(35.2%)	—	0.7%

2009 Year-End Financials

Debt ratio: —
Return on equity: —
Cash ($ mil.): 766
Current ratio: 1.12
Long-term debt ($ mil.): —

No. of shares (mil.): 70
Dividends
  Yield: 0.0%
  Payout: —
Market value ($ mil.): 3,207

Stock History

Euronext Paris: ATO

	STOCK PRICE ($) FY Close	P/E High/Low		PER SHARE ($) Earnings	Dividends	Book Value
12/09	45.98	87	38	0.63	0.00	33.99
12/08	25.25	126	47	0.45	0.56	—
12/07	52.03	79	47	1.03	—	35.70
12/06	59.28	—	—	(5.16)	—	31.68
12/05	65.91	18	13	4.12	—	31.81
Annual Growth	(8.6%)	—	—	(37.5%)	—	1.7%

Groupe Auchan

Auchan's mammoth markets make room for more than meals. France's second-largest food retailer (behind Carrefour), Auchan operates about 495 hypermarkets (French for supercenters) and some 745 supermarkets in about a dozen countries. France is Auchan's largest market, but it has stores throughout Europe and in China, Dubai, Russia, and Taiwan. (Auchan exited the US, Mexico, and Morocco in recent years.) Its hypermarkets carry up to 100,000 products, including groceries, apparel, consumer electronics, and fast food. They also provide travel services. Auchan's other core businesses include banking (Banque Accord), and shopping mall development (Immochan). The founding Mulliez family controls Auchan.

The Mulliez family, one of the richest in the world, also owns Tapis Saint-Maclou, France's largest carpet company, and about 80 Kiabi clothing stores in France, Spain, and Italy.

At the end of 2008, nearly two-thirds of Auchan's stores were located outside of France and international markets accounted for 50% of the company's revenue. Specifically, the company expansion beyond France has been focused primarily on Central and Eastern Europe, as well as in Asia, where it opened or acquired about 50 hypermarkets, a dozen supermarkets, and 20 shopping centers in 2008. In Dubai the French firm formed a partnership with Nakheel Group to begin opening Auchan hypermarkets in the Gulf States in 2009. Auchan planned on opening about 60 new stores in 2009.

The company's hypermarkets operate under the names Auchan, Alcampo, Marjane, and RT Mart (in China); its supermarkets operate under various banners including Atac and Simply Market in France, and Sabeco in Spain. In addition to its 745 company-owned supermarkets, another 1,500 supermarkets are operated as partnerships or franchises.

Auchan's banking subsidiary, Banque Accord, provides financial services to more than 6 million Auchan customers in 10 countries, including 3.1 million in France; and its real estate subsidiary, Immochan, operates about 290 shopping centers in a dozen countries. Other business activities include online shopping (Auchandirect), and home furnishings and appliance stores under the Alinéa and Little Extra banners.

HISTORY

Gerard Mulliez opened his first grocery store in Roubaix, France, in 1961. Seven years later he opened a store (under the Auchan banner) in Roncq — the store was the first modern hypermarket. For the next decade Mulliez expanded his retail operations across France, opening 26 stores.

In 1967 he started an employee shareholding program. Reaching outside the grocery and basic consumer goods market, the company acquired a 50% stake in home improvement retailer Leroy Merlin in 1979.

Auchan entered the international market in 1981, opening an Alcampo hypermarket in Spain. By 1988 the company had one store in the US and a few in Italy. In 1996 Auchan opened hypermarkets in Poland, Mexico, Portugal, and Luxembourg. Also that year Auchan doubled in size by acquiring French grocery retailer Docks de France (including Mammouth hypermarkets and Atac supermarkets) and bought Pao de Açucar, which added more stores in Spain and Portugal. In 1997 it opened stores in Thailand and Argentina, followed by a hypermarket in Hungary in 1998. In 1999 Auchan opened its first store in China.

In April 2000 the company sold 407 small grocery and convenience stores to rival French food retailer Casino Guichard-Perrachon (the stores were obtained when Auchan bought Docks de France). Also in 2000 Auchan opened its second US store (also in Houston) and it bought 68% of retailer RT Mart Taiwan.

Though having announced plans for expansion into Morocco and Russia, Auchan agreed in April 2001 to sell its only hypermarket in Thailand to its rival Casino. Also in 2001 Auchan launched e-commerce sites in France and Spain and acquired Billa, a Polish chain of 11 supermarkets. Overall, the company added 44 supermarkets and 51 hypermarkets that year.

In 2002 Auchan expanded into Russia with the opening of two hypermarkets in the Moscow area.

Auchan closed its hypermarkets in Mexico and shuttered its two remaining US outlets in Houston in March 2003, citing a sharp rise in competition in the Houston area. Overall in 2003, the company opened 31 new stores (nine hypermarkets and 22 supermarkets) in Europe and two hypermarkets in Beijing and Chengdu, China.

Despite a difficult year in France and Italy, Auchan opened 23 new hypermarkets and enlarged another 17 locations in 2005. The retailer also opened its first Atak supermarket in Russia.

Vianney Mulliez took over as chairman in 2006, succeeding his second cousin Gerard. Gerard Mulliez passed over his son to promote Vianney, who had been head of the Immochan unit.

In 2007 Auchan signed an agreement with Az SpA to operate franchised hypermarkets in the Calabria region of Italy. It also signed a partnership agreement with the Furshet Group for stores in the Ukraine and is eyeing ventures in India. In August 2007 Auchan sold its stake in its Moroccan supermarkets and hypermarkets to its partner, Morocco's ONA group, for about $39 million.

EXECUTIVES

Chairman: Vianney Mulliez
Director Group Finance: Xavier de Mézerac
Member Supervisory Board; Chairman, Hypermarkets, France: Arnaud Mulliez
Chairman, Hypermarkets, Russia and Poland: François Colombié
Chairman, Supermarkets, Russia: Philippe Delalande
Chairman, Hypermarkets, Spain: Patrick Coignard
Chairman, Banque Accord: Jérôme Guillemard
Chairman, Mainland China and Taiwan, Auchan, Hypermarkets: Bruno Mercier
Chairman and General Manager, Hypermarkets: Christophe Dubrulle
Chairman, Gallerie Commerciali Italia, Italy: Hans Mautner
Chairman, Hypermarkets, Portugal: Eduardo Igrejas
Chairman and Managing Director, Italy; Chairman, Hypermarkets, Romania: Philippe Le Grignou
Chairman, Supermarkets; Managing Director, Supermarkets, Italy: Benoist Cirotteau
Vice Chairman, Hypermarkets, France; Chairman, Hypermarkets, Hungary: Henri Mathias
Investor Relations: Isabelle Boulainghier
Auditors: KPMG Audit

LOCATIONS

HQ: Groupe Auchan S.A.
40, avenue de Flandre, BP 139
59964 Croix, France
Phone: 33-3-2081-6800   **Fax:** 33-3-2081-6909
Web: www.groupe-auchan.com

2009 Sales

	% of total
France	47
Rest of Western Europe	29
Asia, Central & Eastern Europe	24
Total	**100**

PRODUCTS/OPERATIONS

2009 Sales

	% of total
Hypermarkets	80
Supermarkets	17
Other	3
Total	**100**

2009 Stores

	No.
Supermarkets	739
Hypermarkets	515
Total	**1,254**

COMPETITORS

Carrefour	Lidl
Casino Guichard	Migros
E.Leclerc	Tengelmann
Galeries Lafayette	Tesco
Guyenne et Gascogne	Wal-Mart
ITM Entreprises	

HISTORICAL FINANCIALS

Company Type: Private

Income Statement   FYE: December 31

	REVENUE ($ mil.)	NET INCOME ($ mil.)	NET PROFIT MARGIN	EMPLOYEES
12/09	56,857	998	1.8%	243,000
12/08	55,653	1,049	1.9%	209,000
12/07	54,041	1,122	2.1%	186,443
12/06	46,162	1,001	2.2%	174,644
12/05	39,802	1,156	2.9%	174,584
Annual Growth	**9.3%**	**(3.6%)**	**—**	**8.6%**

Net Income History

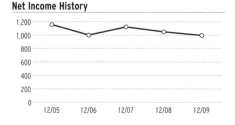

Aviva plc

In the consolidating European insurance industry, Aviva is a lively player. As the top insurance provider in the UK and a leading insurance firm worldwide, Aviva offers both life and general insurance. Its long-term savings segment focuses on life insurance, pensions, unit trusts, and other products; its general insurance segment includes the stuff which is called "non-life" or "property/casualty" elsewhere: home, auto, and fire coverage. Its Aviva Investors arm provides asset management globally. In the UK it also offers private medical insurance through employers. While most of the company's businesses operate under the Aviva banner, it also operates local businesses under other brands, including RAC.

The company has spent years shaping itself into a global company through acquisitions in both mature and developing markets. It now distributes its products in more than 25 countries. To gain access to emerging markets, Aviva acquired smaller insurers in Belgium, Hungary, and the Netherlands. Extending its distribution channels, Aviva has teamed up with banks all across Europe (including tie-ups with ABN AMRO and Royal Bank of Scotland).

Aviva spent $2.9 billion to acquire US rival AmerUs Group in 2006. The company had earlier exited a less profitable portion of the market when it sold its US general insurance operations to White Mountains Insurance Group (2001). Its activities in the US are limited to life insurance and annuities, while in Canada, the company sticks to general (property/casualty) insurance. Eventually, it hopes to offer both types of insurance on either side of the US and Canada border.

Aviva aims to grow its long-term savings business and to expand into central and eastern Europe. The company struck a deal to purchase the Russian pension fund operations of ING in 2009.

While the company professes a desire to grow its business in Asia, its progress in that region has been erratic. Aviva moved more of its back-office operations to India and Sri Lanka, but then reversed the trend in 2008 when it sold the business process outsourcing units to WNS. In 2010 it announced it would re-enter the Singaporean insurance market after a five-year absence.

After its purchase of Fortis' Australian operations made Aviva one of that country's top 10 insurers, it decided that wasn't quite good enough. The company sold its Aviva Australia insurance and wealth management operations business to National Australia Bank in 2009 for $825 million.

To loosen up a bit more cash, Aviva has announced that it will offer up as much as 30% of its Netherlands-based Delta Lloyd subsidiary in an initial public offering. The company hopes that the sale will raise upwards of $1.5 billion.

Former finance director Andrew Moss stepped up as CEO in early 2007 when Richard Harvey stepped down after a difficult 2006.

HISTORY

When insurers hiked premiums after the 1861 Great Tooley Street Fire of London, merchants formed Commercial Union Fire Insurance (CU). It opened offices throughout the UK and in foreign ports and soon added life (1862) and marine (1863) coverage.

Over the next 20 years, CU's foreign business thrived. The firm had offices across the US by the 1880s. In the 1890s CU entered Australia, India, and Southeast Asia. Foreign business eventually accounted for some 75% of CU's sales.

CU went shopping in the 20th century, adding accident insurer Palatine Insurance Co. of Manchester in 1900 and rescuing two companies ruined by San Francisco's 1906 earthquake and fire. CU recovered from the Depression with the help of a booming auto insurance market, and spent most of the 1930s and WWII consolidating operations to cut costs.

Profits suffered in the 1950s as CU faced increased competition in the US. To boost sales, it merged with both multiline rival North British and Mercantile and life insurer Northern and Employers Assurance in the early 1960s. While US business continued to lag in the 1970s, the company's European business grew.

From 1982 to 1996, CU cut its operations in the US, entered new markets (Poland, 1992; South Africa and Vietnam, 1996), and sold its New Zealand subsidiaries (1995). As competition in the UK increased, the company in 1997 reorganized and merged with General Accident in 1998.

General Accident & Employers Liability Assurance Association (GA) was formed in 1885 in Perth, Scotland, to sell workers' compensation insurance. Within a few years, GA had branches in London and Scotland. It diversified into insurance for train accidents (1887), autos (1896), and fire (1899); in 1906 its name changed to General Accident Fire and Life Assurance.

GA expanded into Australia, Europe, and Africa at the turn of the century. After WWI, the company's auto insurance grew along with car ownership. During the 1930s the company entered the US auto insurance market. WWII put a stop to GA's growth.

The company expanded after the war, forming Pennsylvania General Fire Insurance Association (1963) and acquiring the UK's Yorkshire Insurance Co. (1967). By the 1980s about one-third of its sales came from the US.

After 1986 GA acquired some 500 real estate brokerage agencies to cross-sell its home and life insurance. To increase presence in Asia and the Pacific, in 1988 it acquired NZI Corp., a New

Zealand banking and insurance company whose failing operations cost GA millions.

As the industry consolidated, the company bought nonstandard auto insurer Sabre (1995), life insurer Provident Mutual (1996), and General Insurance Group Ltd. in Canada (1997). Unable to compete on its own, GA merged with Commercial Union to form CGU in 1998.

After the merger, CGU added personal pension plans and entered alliances to sell insurance in Italy and India. Merger costs and exceptional losses for 1998 hit operating profits hard. In 1999 CGU upped its stake in French bank Société Générale to about 7% to help it fend off a hostile takeover attempt by Banque Nationale de Paris (now BNP Paribas).

In 2000 CGU merged with rival Norwich Union to form CGNU and made plans to exit the Canadian life and the US general insurance businesses. In an attempt to strengthen its brand name, the company changed its name to Aviva in 2002. Aviva also made changes to its Asian operations in 2004, selling its general insurance business in Asia to Mitsui Sumitomo Insurance.

Aviva acquired UK-based automotive service company RAC in 2005 to gain access to its auto insurance and loan businesses. Aviva stripped off RAC's noncore businesses, including its fleet services, which it sold to VT Group in 2006.

EXECUTIVES

Chairman: Lord Colin M. Sharman, age 67, $969,309 total compensation
CEO and Director: Andrew Moss, age 52, $4,972,783 total compensation
CFO and Director: Patrick C. (Pat) Regan, age 44
Director; CEO, Aviva UK: Mark Hodges, age 45, $2,131,015 total compensation
Director; CEO, Europe, Middle East, and Africa: Andrea Moneta, age 45, $2,562,493 total compensation
Deputy CFO and Chief Capital Officer: Tim Harris
Chief Risk Officer: Robin Spencer, age 40
CEO, Aviva Investors: Alain Dromer, age 55
CEO and Managing Director, Aviva Life Insurance: T.R. (Ram) Ramachandran
CEO, Aviva USA: Christopher J. (Chris) Littlefield, age 43
CEO, Global Markets, Aviva Investors: Paula Allen
CEO, Aviva France: Jean-Pierre Menanteau, age 45
CEO, Investors North America: Greg Boal
CEO, Aviva North America: Igal Mayer, age 49
Company Secretary: Graham Jones
Chief Marketing and Communications Officer: Amanda Mackenzie, age 46
Group Director Human Resources: John Ainley, age 53
Head Investor Relations: Jessie Burrows
Auditors: Ernst & Young LLP

LOCATIONS

HQ: Aviva plc
St. Helen's, 1 Undershaft
London EC3P 3DQ, United Kingdom
Phone: 44-20-7283-2000   **Fax:** 44-20-7662-2753
Web: www.aviva.com

2009 Sales

	% of total
Europe	
UK	32
Other countries	48
North America	14
Asia/Pacific	6
Total	**100**

PRODUCTS/OPERATIONS

Selected Subsidiaries
Aviva Italia SpA (Italy)
Aviva Sigorta (Turkey)
Aviva Vida y Pensiones, Sociedad Anonima de Seguros y Reaseguros (Spain)
Aviva Vie (France)
Aviva USA (US)
CGNU Life Assurance (UK)
Eurofil (France)
RAC plc (UK)
Woori Aviva (South Korea)

COMPETITORS

Allianz
AXA
Generali
ING
Legal & General Group
Prudential plc
QBE
Royal Bank of Scotland
RSA Insurance
Standard Life
Zurich Financial Services

HISTORICAL FINANCIALS
Company Type: Public

Income Statement
FYE: December 31

	ASSETS ($ mil.)	NET INCOME ($ mil.)	INCOME AS % OF ASSETS	EMPLOYEES
12/09	564,403	1,728	0.3%	46,327
12/08	513,158	(1,324)	—	54,758
Annual Growth	10.0%	—	—	(15.4%)

2009 Year-End Financials

Equity as % of assets: 2.9%	Dividends
Return on assets: 0.3%	Yield: 7.5%
Return on equity: 10.6%	Payout: 80.0%
Long-term debt ($ mil.): 23,889	Market value ($ mil.): 17,775
No. of shares (mil.): 2,805	Sales ($ mil.): 94,096

Stock History
London: AV

	STOCK PRICE ($) FY Close	P/E High/Low		PER SHARE ($) Earnings	Dividends	Book Value
12/09	6.34	14	4	0.60	0.48	5.99
12/08	5.64	—	—	(0.53)	0.51	5.81
Annual Growth	12.4%	—	—	—	(5.9%)	3.2%

AXA

The insurance world revolves around this AXA. The company, which started as a sleepy collection of mutual insurance companies, is today one of the world's largest insurers and a financial management powerhouse. In the US, AXA owns AXA Financial, which controls life insurance firm AXA Equitable and investment manager AllianceBernstein. The company also has major subsidiaries in the UK (AXA UK), Germany (AXA Konzern), Japan (AXA Life), Australia (AXA Asia/Pacific), and Belgium (AXA Belgium). The companies offer life insurance, personal and commercial property and casualty insurance, financial services, and asset management services.

Rather than trying to run a cross-border organization, AXA instead buys and builds up businesses in each country, rebranding them under the AXA name. The company serves some 96 million customers in 90 countries primarily in Europe, North America, and the Asia/Pacific region, as well as in Africa, Latin America, and the Middle East.

To expand its insurance operations in emerging markets, AXA bought out its Turkish joint venture partner, pension fund Oyak, for $525 million in 2008. Later that year the company purchased #3 Mexican life insurance company ING Seguros (now AXA Seguros) for $1.5 billion from ING Groep.

To further expand in the targeted high-growth regions of Central and Eastern Europe, in 2010 AXA entered the Romanian life insurance market with the buy of Omniasig Life. The deal followed AXA's buy of minority interests in Omniasig's Hungarian, Czech, and Polish subsidiaries from the European Bank for Reconstruction and Development in late 2009.

In 2010 AXA sold parts of its UK life insurance business (including traditional life and pension, corporate pension, and annuity operations) to acquisition vehicle Resolution Ltd. for €3.3 billion ($4.1 million). Resolution added the acquired operations to another insurance firm, Friends Provident, picked up in 2009; the former AXA operations are now known as Friends Life.

Mutuelles AXA (two mutuals) controls AXA through a more than 20% stake. In 2010 AXA voluntarily delisted its stock from the NYSE to focus on its larger-volume listing on the Euronext Paris exchange.

HISTORY

AXA dates to the 1817 formation of regional fire insurer Compagnie d'Assurances Mutuelles contre l'incendie in Rouen, France (northwest of Paris). In 1881 France's first mutual life insurer was founded: Mutuelle Vie.

In 1946 these two operations and the younger Anciennes Mutuelles Accidents (founded 1922) were brought together by Sahut d'Izarn (general manager of Compagnie d'Assurances) as the Groupe Ancienne Mutuelle. Later members included Ancienne Mutuelle of Calvados (1946), Ancienne Mutuelle of Orleans (1950), Mutualité Générale (1953), and Participation (1954).

A long-term thinker, d'Izarn named not only his successor, Lucien Aubert, but also Aubert's successor: Claude Bébéar, a 23-year-old friend of d'Izarn's son. Never having held a job, Bébéar found the whole thing amusing and decided to try it.

Groupe Ancienne Mutuelle prospered during the 1960s, thanks to d'Izarn's disciplined management, but his technophobia kept the company from entering the computer age.

D'Izarn died in 1972. Aubert capitulated to worker demands during a series of strikes in the early 1970s; Bébéar ended a 1974 strike by threatening to use force against an employee sit-in, then ousted Aubert.

Bébéar spent the rest of the 1970s upgrading the firm's technology. During this period the company became known as Mutuelles Unies.

Bébéar then began building the firm through a series of spectacular acquisitions. In 1982 Mutuelles Unies gained control of crisis-ridden stock insurer Drouot. Two years later the company's name became AXA (which has no meaning and was chosen because it is pronounced the same in most Western languages). When another old-line insurer, Providence, went on the market, AXA went after it. Providence's management was entertaining another offer when AXA bought tiny, inactive Bayas Tudjus, which held the right to a seat on the Providence board. Bébéar capitalized on small stockholders' dissatisfaction to spark a bidding war and used a new issue of Drouot stock in 1986 to buy Providence — France's first hostile takeover.

AXA bought lackluster US firm Equitable (later named AXA Financial) in 1991, infusing $1 billion into the firm in return for the right to own up to 50% of its stock upon demutualization in 1992. AXA moved into Asia with the purchase of Australia's National Mutual in 1995.

Bébéar consolidated the operations into a global organization. In 1996 AXA bought the ailing Union des Assurances de Paris, which had done poorly since its 1994 privatization. It bought the 52% of Belgian insurer Royale Belge SA it didn't already own, as well as Belgian savings bank Anhyp in 1998.

Bébéar raised hackles when he supported the Société Générale-Paribas bank merger, then supported BNP's hostile takeover attempt of both (which garnered only Paribas). In 2000 Bébéar stepped down from the management board but took over as chairman of the Supervisory Board.

In an attempt to strengthen its US retail insurance and annuity business, AXA, through subsidiary AXA Financial, bought MONY Group for some $1.5 billion in 2004. The deal was opposed by some of MONY's shareholders, but it ultimately gained approval. On the down side, AXA discontinued its slumping US-based reinsurance operations. Also in 2004 the company exited its operations in Uruguay, thus exiting the South American market, and sold its Dutch brokerage and health insurance subsidiaries and its German mortgage lending business.

AXA made a major coup in the insurance industry when it acquired the Winterthur Group from Credit Suisse Group for €7.9 billion ($11 billion) in 2006. Winterthur added subsidiaries in 17 countries with 13 million customers and especially strengthened AXA's European operations.

In 2007 the company's property fund division, AXA Investment Managers, announced plans to invest more than $15 billion in Asian real estate by 2013. In addition, AXA established the AXA Research Fund in 2008 to invest $500 million in social science research institutions over five years.

After a long career at the center of AXA's operations, Bébéar retired as chairman of the supervisory board in 2008, but retained the title of honorary chairman of the company.

EXECUTIVES

Chairman and CEO: Henri de Castries, age 56
Vice Chairman: Norbert Dentressangle, age 56
COO: Veronique Weill
Group CFO: Gerald Harlin, age 54
Chief Risk Officer: Jean-Christophe Menioux
Deputy CEO and Board Member: Denis Duverne, age 56
Member Management Board and Head Property and Casualty Insurance: François Pierson, age 63
SVP and Head Investor Relations: Mattieu Rouot
SVP External Affairs, AXA Equitable: Chris Winans
SVP and Head Investor Relations: Etienne Bouas-Laurent
VP, US Investor Relations: George Guerrero
Head Human Resources: Shu Khoo
President and CEO, AXA Financial and Global Head Life and Savings and Health: Christopher M. (Kip) Condron, age 62
CEO, Japan Asia/Pacific Business Unit: John R. Dacey
CEO Insurance, Switzerland: Phillippe Egger
CEO, AXA Life Japan and AXA Japan Holdings: Mark Pearson, age 51
CEO, France: Nicolas Moreau, age 45
CEO, AXA Asia/Pacific Holdings Australia: Andrew (Andy) Penn, age 46
CEO, AXA Konzern AG: Frank Keuper, age 57
CEO, AXA Investment Managers: Dominique Carrel-Billiard, age 44
Chairman and CEO, Alliance Bernstein: Peter Kraus
Auditors: PricewaterhouseCoopers Audit

LOCATIONS

HQ: AXA
25 avenue Matignon
75008 Paris, France
Phone: 33-1-40-75-57-00   **Fax:** 33-1-40-75-57-95
US HQ: 1290 Avenue of the Americas
New York, NY 10104
US Phone: 212-554-1234   **US Fax:** 212-707-1746
Web: www.axa.com

2009 Insurance Sales

	% of total
Northern Central & Eastern Europe	25
France	25
Mediterranean	15
North America	12
Asia/Pacific	11
UK & Ireland	8
International insurance	3
Other	1
Total	**100**

PRODUCTS/OPERATIONS

2009 Sales

	% of total
Life & savings	64
Property/casualty	29
Asset management	3
International insurance	3
Banking & other	1
Total	**100**

Selected Subsidiaries

Insurance (life, savings, and property/casualty)
AXA Asia/Pacific Holdings Limited (53%, Australia)
AXA Belgium SA
AXA Canada Inc. (Canada)
AXA China Region Limited (Hong Kong)
AXA Financial, Inc. (US)
  AXA Advisers, LLC (US)
  AXA Equitable Life Insurance Company (US)
AXA France Assurance
AXA Holding A.S. (Turkey)
AXA Holding Maroc (Morocco)
AXA Italia S.p.A
AXA Japan Holding Co. Ltd (98%)
  AXA Life Insurance Company Limited (Japan)
AXA Konzern AG (Germany)
AXA Luxembourg SA
AXA Mediterranean Holding S.A. (Spain)
AXA Czech Republic Pension Funds
AXA Portugal Companhia de Seguros SA
AXA Seguros, S.A. de Compania de Valores (Mexico)
AXA UK plc
AXA Versicherungen AG (Germany)
Kyobo AXA General Insurance (Kyobo Automobile Insurance, 92%, South Korea)
Reso Garantia (39%, Russia)

Asset Management
AXA Investment Managers (95%)
AXA Real Estate Investment Managers
AllianceBernstein (62%)
AXA Rosenberg (75%)

International Insurance (subsidiaries with global activities)
AXA Assistance SA
AXA Cessions
AXA Corporate Solutions Assurance (99%)

Banking & Other
AXA Bank AG (Germany)
AXA Bank Europe (Belgium)
AXA Banque (France)

COMPETITORS

ACE Limited
AEGON
AIG
Allianz
Allstate
Aviva
Bank of America
Berkshire Hathaway
BNP Paribas
CIGNA
Citigroup
CNP Assurances
Dai-ichi Mutual Life
Eureko
Fortis Insurance
Generali
The Hartford
ING
JPMorgan Chase
Legal & General Group
Merrill Lynch
MetLife
Munich Re Group
Nationwide
New York Life
Nippon Life Insurance
Prudential
Prudential plc
State Farm
Sumitomo Life
Talanx
Travelers Companies
Zurich Financial Services

HISTORICAL FINANCIALS

Company Type: Public

Income Statement

FYE: December 31

	ASSETS ($ mil.)	NET INCOME ($ mil.)	INCOME AS % OF ASSETS	EMPLOYEES
12/09	1,015,067	5,780	0.6%	103,432
12/08	949,321	1,742	0.2%	109,304
12/07	1,064,076	9,407	0.9%	174,935
12/06	959,863	7,597	0.8%	96,009
12/05	682,965	4,943	0.7%	78,800
Annual Growth	10.4%	4.0%	—	7.0%

2009 Year-End Financials

Equity as % of assets: 6.5%
Return on assets: 0.6%
Return on equity: 9.7%
Long-term debt ($ mil.): 14,633
No. of shares (mil.): 2,290

Dividends
Yield: 2.4%
Payout: 26.4%
Market value ($ mil.): 54,285
Sales ($ mil.): 180,986

Stock History

Pink Sheets: AXAHY

	STOCK PRICE ($) FY Close	P/E High/Low		PER SHARE ($) Earnings	Dividends	Book Value
12/09	23.71	13	4	2.16	0.57	28.93
12/08	22.33	61	25	0.62	1.71	23.04
12/07	40.32	13	9	4.05	0.00	29.34
12/06	40.46	12	9	3.38	0.00	27.21
12/05	32.28	46	8	2.59	0.00	17.50
Annual Growth	(7.4%)	—	—	(4.4%)	—	13.4%

Axel Springer

The paper trail has been a path to success for Axel Springer. Germany's leading newspaper company and one of Europe's largest media concerns, Axel Springer publishes more than 170 newspapers and magazine titles in more than 30 countries. Its flagship paper *Bild* is Germany's #1 newspaper. Other papers include *Die Welt* and the tabloid *Welt Kompakt*. Axel Springer's magazine operations include *Auto Bild, Computer Bild*, and *TV Digital*. In addition to publishing, the company has holdings in online content, printing, real estate, and television. The family of founder Hinrich Springer owns about 50% of the company.

Axel Springer's newspaper and magazine operations have been suffering from declines in circulation and a weak advertising market. As a result of the global economic downturn, in 2009 the company's net profit almost halved. In order to raise money, in 2009 Axel Springer sold stakes in some regional papers, and the previous year it sold its stake in broadcaster ProSiebenSat.1 Media. It also increased the cover price for some of its publications.

The troubled print publishing business has also led Axel Springer to invest heavily in digital media

holdings. The company was one of the first German publishers to provide a paid-for application for Apple's iPhone; it launched the application at the end of 2009. The company is also developing applications for Apple's iPad. In addition, its Digital Window (a joint venture with Swiss firm PubliGroupe) purchased Buy.at from AOL in 2010. It is using the acquisition to expand in the digital marketing services space.

HISTORY

Hinrich Springer, whose newspaper business had been closed by the Nazi government in 1941, and his son Axel launched Axel Springer Verlag in 1946 with the magazine *Nordwestdeutsche Hefte*. In 1948 the company unveiled *Hamburger Abendblatt*, which became Hamburg's best-selling newspaper by 1950. Axel Springer eventually took over the business and introduced the tabloid *Bild Zeitung* (later renamed *Bild*) in 1952. The success of the paper helped fund the company's expansion.

Axel Springer bought the daily *Die Welt* in 1953 and *Berliner Morgenpost* in 1959. The company moved its headquarters to Berlin in 1966. Fiercely supportive of the reunification of Germany, Springer built the company's headquarters immediately next to the Berlin Wall. In the 1970s the company expanded into the regional newsletter and magazine market. Axel Springer's growing control over German media did not go unnoticed, however, and opposition to the company's power was demonstrated when its Hamburg office was bombed in 1972 (the company was the target of arson again in 1998). Springer considered selling the entire company, but opted to sell several individual publications instead.

The company expanded beyond print media in 1984, investing in satellite consortium SAT.1 Satelliten Fernsehen. In 1985 it acquired stakes in cable TV and bought two Munich radio stations. After taking the company public that year, founder Axel Springer died. In 1989 German media firm KirchGruppe (later TaurusHolding) began buying shares in Axel Springer Verlag.

In 1996 Axel Springer entered the Czech and Slovak newspaper markets with the purchase of a 49% stake in Dutch firm Ringier-Taurus. The company formed a joint venture in 1998 with Infoseek (later absorbed by Disney Online) and other partners to launch a German-language Web search service. It also bought 95% of German book publisher ECON + LIST Verlagsgesellschaft. August Fischer, former chief executive of News Corp.'s News International, was appointed chairman and CEO that year. A 1998 bid to buy UK-based media firm Mirror Group (now Trinity Mirror) proved unsuccessful.

In 1999 Axel Springer acquired stakes in several TV production companies, including a 90% interest in Schwartzkopff TV-Productions. The following year the company merged its 41%-owned TV station SAT.1 with German TV station operator Pro Sieben Media to create ProSiebenSAT.1 Media, Germany's largest commercial TV group. Fischer retired at the end of 2001 and was replaced by Mathias Döpfner. The company began investing in new online ventures, including a portal built around *Bild*. TaurusHolding sold its shares in the company in 2003 to Deutsche Bank.

In 2003 it agreed to sell the paperback unit of its Ullstein Heyne List book group to Random House. The company also sold off several of its stakes in TV production companies as it sought to focus on its main publishing unit. In 2004 it

took a 49% stake in Stepstone Deutschland, a Web-based employment agency in Germany.

Axel Springer bid $3 billion in 2005 to acquire ProSiebenSat.1 from media mogul Haim Saban, but the deal was blocked by antitrust regulators. Investment firms Permira and Kolberg Kravis Roberts acquired control of the TV broadcaster the following year; Axel Springer later sold its remaining stake in the business in 2007.

EXECUTIVES

Chairman: Giuseppe Vita, age 75
Deputy Chairwoman: Friede Springer
Deputy Chairman and Head of Printing and Logistics Division: Rudolf Knepper, age 65
CEO; Head of Subscription Paper Division and International Divisions: Mathias Döpfner, age 47
COO and CFO: Lothar Lanz, age 61
Head of BILD Division and Magazines: Andreas Wiele, age 48
Head of Communications BILD Group: Tobias Fröhlich
Head of Communications Digital and International Media: Christian Garrels
Head of Corporate Communications: Edda Fels
Head of Investor Relations: Claudia Thomé, age 40
Auditors: Ernst & Young AG

LOCATIONS

HQ: Axel Springer Aktiengesellschaft
Axel-Springer-Strasse 65
10888 Berlin, Germany
Phone: 49-30-2591-0
Web: www.axelspringer.de

2009 Sales

	% of total
Germany	79
Other countries	11
Total	**100**

PRODUCTS/OPERATIONS

2009 Sales

	% of total
Newspapers	41
Magazines	18
Digital media	17
Printing	11
Other	14
Total	**100**

Selected Operations

Newspapers
Bild
Die Welt
Euro am Sonntag
Welt am Sonntag
Welt Kompakt
Magazines
Auto Bild
Bild der Frau
Bildwoche
Computer Bild
Euro
Fonds&Co.
Frau von Heute
Funk Uhr
Hörzu
Jolie
Mädchen
Markt und Mittelstand
Maxim
Metal Hammer
Musikexpress
Popcorn
Rolling Stone
Sport Bild
Starflash
TV Digital
TV GUIDE
TVneu
Yam!

HISTORICAL FINANCIALS

Company Type: Public

Income Statement

FYE: December 31

	REVENUE ($ mil.)	NET INCOME ($ mil.)	NET PROFIT MARGIN	EMPLOYEES
12/09	3,743	450	12.0%	10,740
12/08	3,853	805	20.9%	10,666
12/07	3,801	(425)	—	12,944
12/06	3,135	372	11.9%	9,733
12/05	2,832	268	9.5%	10,166
Annual Growth	7.2%	13.8%	—	1.4%

2009 Year-End Financials

Debt ratio: —	No. of shares (mil.): 30
Return on equity: 28.0%	Dividends
Cash ($ mil.): 283	Yield: 5.9%
Current ratio: 1.37	Payout: 43.2%
Long-term debt ($ mil.): —	Market value ($ mil.): 3,205

Stock History

German: SPR

	STOCK PRICE ($) FY Close	P/E High	P/E Low	PER SHARE ($) Earnings	PER SHARE ($) Dividends	PER SHARE ($) Book Value
12/09	107.56	8	4	14.60	6.31	57.56
12/08	72.43	5	2	26.13	—	50.15
12/07	144.25	—	—	(14.28)	—	59.85
12/06	177.45	—	—	—	—	78.74
12/05	127.90	—	—	—	—	46.67
Annual Growth	(4.2%)	—	—	—	—	5.4%

Bacardi

You want proof? The people at Bacardi Global Brands will pour it out for you — from a bottle. One of the world's leading wine and spirits makers, Bacardi produces 10 varieties of its namesake rum (of which it sells some 20 million cases every year). However, rum is not the only potable offered by Bacardi. The company's portfolio consists of more than 200 brands and labels, including Bombay Sapphire Gin, Martini Vermouth, Dewar's Scotch Whisky, B&B and Bénédictine liqueurs, and Grey Goose Vodka. Other types of spirits in its portfolio include tequila, vermouth, cognac, and sparkling wine. Serving more than 100 countries, the company operates 27 production sites around the world.

In 2008 Séamus McBride, a former executive with the Colgate-Palmolive Company, was appointed president and CEO of the company. He replaced Andreas Gembler, who retired.

To round out its portfolio, the distiller has been expanding its line of premium liquors through acquisitions, including one of Mexico's leading premium tequilas, Tequila Cazadores. It continues to do so with its 2009 introduction of Barcardi O, an orange-flavored rum.

Steeped in liquor lore, Bacardi Limited claims the first Cuba Libre (rum and cola) was made using its rum in 1898. Its bottles feature Bacardi's trademark bat logo, said to have been inspired by bats (an omen of good luck) that lived in the company's first distillery.

The descendants of founder Facundo Bacardi y Massó own Bacardi.

HISTORY

Facundo Bacardi y Massó immigrated to Cuba from Spain in 1830. He started in the liquor business as a rum salesman for John Nunes, an Englishman who owned a small distillery in Santiago, Cuba. In 1862 Facundo, his brother José, and a French wine merchant bought Nunes' distillery and began producing a smoother rum from a formula created by Facundo after years of trial and error. The more mixable quality of Bacardi's rum proved to be a key to its success. In 1877 Facundo passed company leadership to his sons; the eldest, Emilio, took over running the company (and spent some of his spare time in jail for his anti-Spanish activities).

Bacardi Limited struggled during the 1890s as Cuba's economy foundered. The business was thrown into even greater turmoil when revolutionary leader José Marti began what would be the final fight for Cuban independence. One of Marti's biggest supporters was Emilio, who earned another stay in jail and then exile for his sympathies. After Cuba gained its independence in 1902, Bacardi grew rapidly, getting a further boost from Prohibition as Havana became "the unofficial US saloon." (Prohibition did, however, end a venture in the US.)

The company moved into brewing in the 1920s and expanded its rum operations in the 1930s, opening a distillery in Mexico (1931) and another in Puerto Rico (1935). In 1944 it opened Bacardi Imports in the US and built up its overseas operations during the 1950s.

Amid all its success, Bacardi again became embroiled in Cuban politics during the late 1950s. Although some company leaders showed open opposition to Cuban leader Fulgencio Batista and support for Fidel Castro, others opposed Castro. As a result of the 1959 revolution, the Bacardi family was forced into exile, fleeing to the US and Europe. Castro seized Bacardi's assets in 1960. However, the expropriation was not a fatal blow since both the Mexican and Puerto Rican operations had been out-earning the Cuban operations since the 1940s. Bacardi continued to enjoy explosive growth during the 1960s and 1970s. In 1977 some family members sold about 12% of the Bacardi empire to Hiram Walker.

By 1980 Bacardi was the #1 liquor brand in the US, but family squabbles and bad decisions threatened the company. Bacardi Capital, set up to manage the empire's money, lost $50 million in 1986. That year the empire's leadership started to buy up shares in Bacardi companies, including those sold to Hiram Walker and the 10% of Bacardi Corporation that had been sold to the public in 1962.

In an effort to diversify and to increase its European markets, the company bought a majority stake in Martini & Rossi in 1993. Two years later it launched Bacardi Limon, a citrus-flavored rum, and Hatuey (pronounced "ah-tway") beer. In 1996 family lawyer George Reid became president and CEO, the first nonfamily member to head the company.

Bacardi acquired the rights to the Havana Club trademark in 1997 from the Arechabala family. The move exacerbated a dispute with France's Pernod Ricard, which had partnered with the Cuban government to use the Havana Club name. Bacardi bought the Dewar's Scotch whisky and Bombay gin brands from Diageo in 1998.

In 2000 Reid resigned and Ruben Rodriguez was appointed president and CEO. Rodriguez added chairman to his titles when Manuel Jorge Cutillas retired later in the year. In 2000 Bacardi (along with partner Brown-Forman) also lost the bidding war for Seagram's alcoholic drinks business (Glenlivet, Sterling Vineyards, Martell Cognac) to rival bidding duo Diageo and Pernod Ricard.

In 2002 Bacardi acquired Tequila Cazadores, a leader in Mexico's Agave Reposado segment. Javier Ferran, an 18-year company veteran, left Bacardi in 2004 after serving as CEO for only about 18 months. Ferran was replaced by Andreas Gembler, a Philip Morris veteran.

Also in 2004 Bacardi topped off its liquor offerings with the purchase of premium vodka brand, Grey Goose. Rodriguez retired in 2005 as the company's chairman. Bacardi named Facundo Bacardi, a great-grandson of the company's founder, as chairman. Rodriguez remained a board member. In 2006 the company acquired New Zealand spirits company 42 BELOW, known for its vodka, for approximately $91 million.

EXECUTIVES

LOCATIONS

2009 Sales

	% of total
Europe, the Middle East & Africa	52
North America	39
Latin America	9
Total	**100**

PRODUCTS/OPERATIONS

2009 Sales

	% of total
Global spirits brands	55
Other group brands	29
Other	16
Total	**100**

Selected Brands

Brandy
VIEJO VERGEL

Clear flavored rum and spirits
BACARDI APPLE
BACARDI BIG APPLE
BACARDI CÓCO
BACARDI GRAND MELÓN
BACARDI LIMÓN
BACARDI O
BACARDI PEACH RED
BACARDI RAZZ / BERRY

Cognac
GASTON DE LA GRANGE
OTARD 1795 Extra
OTARD 55
OTARD Napoleón
OTARD VSOP
OTARD XO
OTARD XO Gold

Gin
BOMBAY
BOMBAY SAPPHIRE
BOSFORD

Liqueur
B&B
BÉNÉDICTINE
CHINA MARTINI
GET 27/31
NASSAU ROYALE

Rum
BACARDI 151
BACARDI 1873
BACARDI 1873 Solera
BACARDI 8
BACARDI Añejo
BACARDI Black / Select
BACARDI Gold / Oro
BACARDI Reserva
BACARDI Reserva Limitada
BACARDI Superior
CASTILLO Añejo
CASTILLO Gold
CASTILLO Silver
CASTILLO Spiced
ESTELAR
PALMAS

Scotch whiskey
Blended
DEWAR'S 12 Year Old
DEWAR'S 18 Year Old
DEWAR'S Signature
DEWAR'S WHITE LABEL
WILLIAM LAWSON'S Finest Blended
WILLIAM LAWSON'S SCOTTISH GOLD
Single malt
ABERFELDY 12 Year Old
ABERFELDY 21 Year Old
AULTMORE
CRAIGALLACHIE
GLEN DEVERON 10 Year Old
ROYAL BRACKLA

Sparkling wine
GRANDI AUGURI
MAGICI ISTANTI
MARTINI Asti
MARTINI Brut
MARTINI Prosecco
MARTINI Riesling

Tequila
CAMINO REAL
CAZADORES Añejo
CAZADORES Blanco
CAZADORES Reposado
CORZO Añejo
CORZO Blanco
CORZO Reposado
CUATRO VIENTOS

Vermouth
French
NOILLY PRAT Ambre
NOILLY PRAT Blanc
NOILLY PRAT Rouge
Italian
MARTINI Bianco
MARTINI D'Oro
MARTINI Dry
MARTINI Rosé
MARTINI Rosso

Vodka
ERISTOFF
ERISTOFF Black
ERISTOFF Red
GREY GOOSE
GREY GOOSE La Poire
GREY GOOSE Le Citron
GREY GOOSE L'Orange
NATASHA
RUSSIAN PRINCE

COMPETITORS

Angostura
Beam Global Spirits & Wine
Blavod
Brown-Forman
C&C
Cabo Wabo
Constellation Brands
Corby Distilleries
De Vere Group
Diageo
E. & J. Gallo
Fortune Brands
Heaven Hill Distilleries
Jackson Family Wines
Jose Cuervo
LVMH
Martini & Rossi
McCormick Distilling
Morrison Bowmore
Paramount Distillers
Pernod Ricard
Rémy Cointreau
Skyy

HISTORICAL FINANCIALS

Company Type: Private

Income Statement

FYE: March 31

	REVENUE ($ mil.)	NET INCOME ($ mil.)	NET PROFIT MARGIN	EMPLOYEES
3/09	5,336	805	15.1%	6,000
3/08	5,546	795	14.3%	6,000
3/07	4,967	730	14.7%	6,000
3/06	4,558	658	14.4%	6,000
Annual Growth	**5.4%**	**7.0%**	**—**	**0.0%**

Net Income History

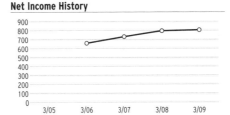

BAE SYSTEMS

BAE SYSTEMS, which helped win the Battle of Britain with its Mosquito and Spitfire fighters, is a leading military contractor and a major foreign player in the US defense market. BAE's four operating groups — Electronics, Intelligence & Support; Land & Armaments; Programs & Support; and International — provide avionics, military aircraft, armored vehicles, air defense systems, missiles, artillery locators, communications and navigation systems, radar, ships, and space systems. BAE's fighter aircraft include the Harrier, Hawk, Tornado, and the next-generation Eurofighter Typhoon. North America is BAE's biggest market, with the US Department of Defense its largest single customer.

The company operates in the US through BAE Systems, Inc. In the fall of 2010, the company agreed to purchase the Intelligence Services division of L-1 Identity Solutions for $300 million.

Like its competitors, BAE SYSTEMS is preparing for a hit from announced cuts in defense spending by the US and UK governments. BAE SYSTEMS has tried to stay ahead of market swings by selling some of its smaller, older aerospace businesses. In addition, it has been redeploying its resources into defense-related technology assets by purchasing units from Lockheed Martin.

Simultaneously, the defense giant is targeting several naval support and upgrade contracts on the horizon with the US Navy and other maritime customers. It expanded its ship repair business in mid-2010 by acquiring Atlantic Marine.

BAE SYSTEMS isn't putting all of its defense systems in one regional basket, either. The group has core operations in Australia, Saudi Arabia, South Africa, Sweden, and the UK. In 2010 it added India to the list by entering into a joint venture with Mahindra & Mahindra to build a factory in that country to produce artillery guns. With a plant in India, BAE SYSTEMS will be able to bid on potential India armed forces contracts valued at $4 billion to supply defense equipment. The company also plans to expand its presence in Saudi Arabia, where demand for its products continues to increase; the country accounts for over 9% of the company's total revenues.

In the meantime, BAE SYSTEMS has struggled with litigation. In spring 2010 the company pled guilty to "knowingly and willfully making false statements to US government agencies" between 2000 and 2002. It faced charges of not complying with the anti-bribery provisions of the Foreign Corrupt Practices Act (FCPA), and violating the Arms Control Export Act and International Traffic in Arms Regulations. The Court ordered BAE SYSTEMS to pay a $400 million fine, one of the largest criminal fines the US has ever levied against a company for business-related violations. The US subsidiary was not involved in any of the actions.

HISTORY

Post-Wright brothers and pre-WWII, a host of aviation companies sprang up to serve the British Empire — too many to survive after the war when the empire contracted. Parliament took steps in 1960 to save the industry by merging companies to form larger, stronger entities — Hawker-Siddeley Aviation and British Aircraft Corporation (BAC).

Hawker-Siddeley, made up of aircraft and missiles divisions, was created by combining A.V. Roe, Gloster Aircraft, Hawker Aircraft, Armstrong Whitworth, and Folland Aircraft. It attained fame in the 1960s for developing the Harrier "jump jet."

BAC was formed from the merger of Bristol Aeroplane, Vicker-Armstrong, and English Electric. In 1962 it joined France's Aerospatiale to build the supersonic Concorde and became a partner in ventures to develop the Tornado and Jaguar fighters. The cost of these ventures, plus the commercial failure of the Concorde, was more than the company could bear. Realizing British aviation was again in trouble, the British government nationalized BAC and Hawker-Siddeley in 1976 and merged them in 1977 with Scottish Aviation to form British Aerospace (BAe).

BAe joined the Airbus consortium in 1979. A partial privatization of the company began in 1981 when the government sold 52% to the public (the remaining stake sold in 1985). Also in 1981 BAe announced a joint venture with Comsat General and announced that it would be the prime contractor for L-SAT-1, the European Space Agency's telecommunications satellite.

In 1987 BAe bought Steinheil Optronik (optical equipment) and Ballast Nedam Groep (civil and marine engineering). In 1990 BAe formed Ballast Nedam Construction.

BAe began to restructure its troubled regional aircraft division in 1992 by laying off thousands of workers and closing a major plant. The company sold Ballast Nedam and its corporate jet business to Raytheon and won a $7.5 billion contract from Saudi Arabia for Tornado jets in 1993. BAe sold its satellite business in 1994.

Matra BAe Dynamics, the world's third-largest maker of tactical missiles, was formed in a 1996 merger between BAe and Lagardère subsidiary Matra Hachette.

BAe's emphasis on large jetliners led to the 1998 breakup of Aero International, its two-year-old regional-aircraft joint venture with Aerospatiale (France) and Alenia (Italy). Shortly thereafter, BAe spent $454 million for a 35% stake in Swedish military jet maker Saab AB. In 1999 BAe bought the electronic systems defense unit of Marconi Electronic Systems (MES) for $12.7 billion (including US-based Tracor). The company changed its name to BAE SYSTEMS to remove the British influence from its name.

In 2000 the UK government agreed to loan BAE about $836 million to support the Airbus A3XX superjumbo airliner project. The prime contractor for the UK's new Type 45 destroyer, BAE was named to build two of the first three Type 45s. Late in the year BAE spent about $1.67 billion for a group of Lockheed Martin's defense electronics businesses, including its Sanders airborne electronics unit.

BAE SYSTEMS took a 29% stake in Alvis, maker of the Challenger main battle tank, in 2003. In March 2004 General Dynamics made a 280-pence-a-share bid for Alvis; BAE topped that offer in early June with a bid of 320 pence a share (about $650 million) and a deal was struck.

In February of 2005 BAE reduced its stake in SAAB AB from 35% to 22%. In the summer of 2005 BAE acquired US armored vehicle maker United Defense Industries (UDI) in a deal worth about $4.2 billion.

The company then closed its commercial aerospace unit and sold off its stake in Airbus, as well as its aerostructures business; BAE essentially became a military contractor.

In 2007 BAE bought Armor Holdings for about $4.5 billion.

EXECUTIVES

Chairman: Richard L. (Dick) Olver, age 63
CEO and Board Member: Ian King, age 54
COO; President and CEO, BAE Systems, Inc.; Acting President, Electronics, Intelligence, and Support (EI&S): Linda P. Hudson
President, Electronics, Intelligence and Support: Mike Heffron
President, Land and Armaments Operating Group: Robert T. (Bob) Murphy
Director Group Finance: George W. Rose, age 58
Group Managing Director Programmes and Support: Nigel Whitehead
Director Media Relations, Electronics and Integrated Solutions: Bart Greer
Director Group Business Development: Alan Garwood
Director Investor Relations: Andrew Wrathall
Group General Counsel: Phillip Bramwell
Director Group HR: Alastair Imrie
Director Audit: Grenville Hodge
Director Group Strategy: Andrew Davies
Director Group Media Relations: John Neilson
Director Group Business Development: Alan Garwood, age 55
Director Group Communications: Charlotte Lambkin
Secretary: David Parkes
Chief of Staff: Fiona Davies
Chairman, BAE Systems, Inc.:
Gen. Anthony C. (Tony) Zinni, age 66
Auditors: KPMG Audit Plc

LOCATIONS

HQ: BAE SYSTEMS plc
Stirling Square, Carlton Gardens
London SW1Y 5AD, United Kingdom
Phone: 44-1252-373-232 **Fax:** 44-1252-383-991
US HQ: 1601 Research Blvd., Rockville, MD 20850
US Phone: 301-838-6000 **US Fax:** 301-738-4643
Web: www.baesystems.com

2009 Sales

	% of total
US	49
Europe	
UK	19
Other countries	12
Middle East	
Saudi Arabia	12
Other countries	1
Canada	1
Asia/Pacific	4
Africa & Central & South America	2
Total	**100**

PRODUCTS/OPERATIONS

2009 Sales

	% of total
Land & Armaments	29
Programs & Support	27
Electronics, Intelligence & Support	25
International businesses	19
Total	**100**

Selected Products and Services

Electronics, Intelligence, and Support
  Advanced airborne reconnaissance system
  Avionics support equipment
  Communications jamming
  Doppler navigation systems
  Laser transmitters and receivers

Integrated Systems and Partnerships
  Air-to-air missiles
  Combat and radar systems
  Naval sonar
Land and Armaments
  All terrain vehicles (Bv206)
  Armored personnel carriers (Warrior, Piranha)
  Battle tanks (Challenger 2)
  Naval gun system (Mk 45)
  Recovery vehicles (Beach Recovery Vehicle)
Programs
  Astute class submarine
  Eurofighter Typhoon
  Hawk
  Nimrod
  Type 45 destroyers
Support
  Military services and support

COMPETITORS

Astronautics	ITT Corp.
Boeing	L-3 Communications
Bombardier	Lockheed Martin
EADS	Meggitt USA
Fabbrica D'Armi Pietro	Navistar International
Beretta	Northrop Grumman
Finmeccanica	Park Air Systems
GenCorp	Rockwell Collins
General Dynamics	RUAG Holding
Goodrich Corp.	Thales
Honeywell International	Ultra Electronics
Horstman Defence Systems	United Technologies

HISTORICAL FINANCIALS

Company Type: Public

Income Statement

FYE: December 31

	REVENUE ($ mil.)	NET INCOME ($ mil.)	NET PROFIT MARGIN	EMPLOYEES
12/09	32,448	(107)	—	721
12/08	24,128	2,559	10.6%	105,000
12/07	28,565	1,841	6.4%	88,000
12/06	24,151	3,210	13.3%	79,000
12/05	18,957	955	5.0%	478
Annual Growth	**14.4%**	**—**	**—**	**10.8%**

2009 Year-End Financials

Debt ratio: 66.6%
Return on equity: —
Cash ($ mil.): 5,881
Current ratio: 0.73
Long-term debt ($ mil.): 4,939

No. of shares (mil.): 3,585
Dividends
  Yield: 4.2%
  Payout: —
Market value ($ mil.): 20,526

Stock History

Pink Sheets: BAESY

	STOCK PRICE ($) FY Close	P/E High/Low		PER SHARE ($) Earnings	Dividends	Book Value
12/09	5.73	—	—	(0.03)	0.24	2.07
12/08	5.45	10	6	0.72	0.20	2.92
12/07	9.94	20	15	0.53	0.24	3.32
12/06	8.34	9	7	0.96	0.21	2.25
12/05	6.57	22	13	0.30	0.17	1.34
Annual Growth	**(3.4%)**	**—**	**—**	**—**	**9.0%**	**11.5%**

Banco Santander

Banco Santander is the leader in the running of Spanish banks. However, the company's reach spreads far beyond its home country. Santander offers retail banking and consumer finance in Portugal, the UK, and other parts of Europe, as well as the US. Subsidiaries such as Banco Santander Chile, Banco Santander (Brasil), Santander Río in Argentina, and Grupo Financiero Santander make it a top banking group in Latin America, where it has operations in about 15 countries. Banco Santander also offers asset management, private banking, corporate and investment banking, and insurance.

One of Santander's target areas for growth is Latin America, where profit for the company has grown recently. In 2010 it announced plans to take full control of its Mexico unit by acquiring Bank of America's 25% stake in Grupo Financiero Santander for €2 billion ($2.5 billion).

In addition to Latin America, Banco Santander also wants to be a big player the US. The company's American holdings include Northeast regional bank Sovereign Bank. In 2009 Santander acquired the approximately three-quarters of Sovereign it didn't already own. Also in 2009, Santander purchased a more than €3 billion ($4 billion) US car loan portfolio and a loan servicing platform from HSBC Holdings. The next year Santander agreed to buy a €2.5 billion ($3 billion) auto loan portfolio from Citigroup. The moves provided Santander additional platforms in the US market.

In the UK Santander operates as Santander UK — an amalgamation of the Abbey National, Bradford & Bingley, and Alliance & Leicester (all of which were acquired by Santander). In 2010 Santander announced plans to buy nearly 320 Royal Bank of Scotland branches in the UK for nearly €2 billion ($3 billion).

In 2007 the company, along with Royal Bank of Scotland and Fortis, acquired the Netherlands-based ABN AMRO (the international retail banking giant with more than 4,350 branches) for around €71 billion ($87 billion). As part of the bid, Banco Santander took ABN AMRO's Brazilian operations, doubling its market share in Brazil.

The Botín family has led Grupo Santander since its founding in 1857. Emilio Botín Sanz de Sautuola y García de los Ríos, Spain's richest man (depending on whom you ask), has been chairman since 1986.

HISTORY

Banco Santander Central Hispano (BSCH) was created by the 1999 merger of Banco Santander and Banco Central Hispano (BCH).

In 1857 a group of Basque businessmen had formed Banco Santander to finance Latin American trade. The emergence of Cantabria as a leading province after WWI helped the bank expand, first regionally and then nationally.

The Botín family has been closely identified with the bank for decades. Emilio Botín served first as a board member and then for a few years as chairman before his death in 1923. The post was held by his son Emilio Botín-Sanz de Sautuola from 1950 to 1986, when *his* son Emilio Botín Sanz de Sautuola y García de los Ríos (known as Don Emilio) took over.

Spanish banks were spared the worst of the Great Depression (thanks to their isolation and the country's shunning the gold standard), but Spain's civil war was draining. In the early 1940s Santander expanded into Madrid and other major Spanish cities and merged with a few rivals. In the 1950s and 1960s, as interest rates were controlled and mergers halted, banks competed by building branch networks and investing overseas, particularly in Latin America. In 1965 Santander joined with Bank of America to form Bankinter (it divested most of its stake by the mid-1990s).

Tight economic controls were relaxed in the 1970s after Franco's death. Despite global recession, Santander continued to invest in Latin America through the mid-1980s.

In the late 1980s Santander prepared to compete in a deregulated Spain and Europe, forming alliances with Royal Bank of Scotland, Kemper (now part of Zurich Financial Services), and Metropolitan Life Insurance. In 1989 the bank jump-started competition by introducing Spain's first high-interest account.

Santander focused on home in the 1990s. Spurned by Banco Hispano Americano (BHA), Santander acquired a 60% stake in the ailing Banco Español de Crédito (Banesto), which became wholly owned in 1998. The bank took a hit when Latin America plunged into an economic crisis that year. With profit margins falling, the bank merged with BCH in 1999.

BCH was formed by the 1991 merger of Banco Central and BHA. BHA had been established in 1900 by investors in Latin America; Central had been founded in 1919. The mixed banks offered both commercial and investment banking; they funded industrialization and investment in Latin America and became two of Spain's largest banks before the civil war.

After the war BHA sold its Latin American assets when the currency dried up, while Central used mergers and acquisitions to expand across Spain. Isolated from WWII by Franco, the two banks used their dual strategies to fund overseas investment and domestic-branch growth.

After Franco's death, the banks faced increased competition at home and abroad. Central bought BHA in 1991 to remain competitive as Spain entered the European Economic Community (now the EU) in 1992.

Following the merger, BCH trimmed 20% of its branches, fired some 10,000 employees, and sold unprofitable holdings. Focused on Latin America, the bank took small stakes in small banks. Losing its edge, BCH merged with Santander in 1999.

In 2000 the newly merged BSCH focused on expanding in Europe and Latin America. Among its European moves was its alliance with Société Générale to buy investment-fund management firms, particularly in the US. Executive infighting saw ex-Santander chairman Emilio Botín triumph over ex-BCH chairman José María Amusátegui for control of BSCH's helm. Soon after, the bank started doing business as simply Santander Central Hispano.

In one of Europe's largest cross-border bank mergers ever, Santander paid more than €12 billion ($15 billion) for British bank Abbey National in 2004. It solidified its UK operations through the approximately €1.25 billion ($2.6 billion) purchase of Alliance & Leicester.

In 2009 the Venezuelan government took over Banco Santander subsidiary Banco de Venezuela, the third-largest bank in the country. The government paid €755 million ($1 billion) to nationalize the bank.

EXECUTIVES

Chairman:
Emilio Botín Sanz de Sautuola y García de los Ríos, age 76

First Vice Chairman: Fernando de Asúa Álvarez, age 78

Second Vice Chairman and CEO: Alfredo Sáenz Abad, age 67

Third Vice Chairman: Matías Rodríguez Inciarte, age 60

Fourth Vice Chairman: Manuel Soto Serrano, age 70

EVP Technology and Operations: José M. Fuster, age 52

EVP Financial Management and Investor Relations: José A. Álvarez, age 50

EVP and Vice-Secretary General: Jaime P. Pérez Renovales, age 42

EVP America: Jesús M. Zabalza, age 52

EVP Financial Accounting and Control: José M. Tejón, age 59

EVP Strategy and Director; Vice Chairman, Santander UK: Juan R. Inciarte, age 57

EVP and General Secretariat: Ignacio Benjumea, age 58

EVP America and Director: Francisco Luzón López, age 62

EVP Santander Branch Network, Spain: Enrique García Candelas, age 57

EVP America: Marcial Portela, age 65

EVP Global Private Banking and Asset Management: Javier Marín, age 44

EVP Human Resources: José Luis G. Alciturri, age 61

EVP Communications, Corporate Marketing, and Research: Juan M. Cendoya, age 43

EVP and General Secretariat: César Ortega, age 56

EVP Consumer Finance: Magda Salarich, age 54

EVP Insurance and Global Direct Banking: Jorge Morán, age 46

Director; Chairwoman, Banesto: Ana P. Botín, age 50

CEO, Santander UK and Alliance & Leicester: António H. Osorio, age 46

LOCATIONS

HQ: Banco Santander, S.A.
Avda. de Cantabria s/n, Boadilla del Monte
28660 Madrid, Spain
Phone: 34-902-11-22-11
Web: www.gruposantander.com

PRODUCTS/OPERATIONS

2009 Sales

	% of total
Interest & exchange rates	26
Transaction banking	26
Equities	18
Lending	18
Treasury & portfolios	10
Investment banking	2
Total	**100**

COMPETITORS

Banco Comercial Português
Banco do Brasil
Banco Popular Español
Bank of America
Bankinter
BBVA
Citigroup
Deutsche Bank
Espírito Santo
HSBC
JPMorgan Chase

HISTORICAL FINANCIALS

Company Type: Public

Income Statement

FYE: December 31

	ASSETS ($ mil.)	NET INCOME ($ mil.)	INCOME AS % OF ASSETS	EMPLOYEES
12/09	1,591,611	13,489	0.8%	169,460
12/08	1,479,456	13,154	0.9%	170,961
12/07	1,342,109	13,320	1.0%	131,819
12/06	1,101,086	10,030	0.9%	129,800
12/05	961,433	7,391	0.8%	129,196
Annual Growth	13.4%	16.2%	—	7.0%

2009 Year-End Financials

Equity as % of assets: 6.5%
Return on assets: 0.9%
Return on equity: 14.7%
Long-term debt ($ mil.): 52,748
No. of shares (mil.): 8,229

Dividends
Yield: 3.9%
Payout: 61.1%
Market value ($ mil.): 193,886
Sales ($ mil.): 107,294

Stock History

NYSE: STD

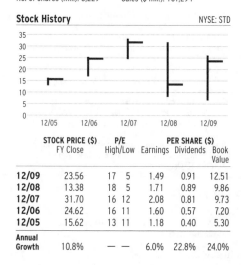

	STOCK PRICE ($) FY Close	P/E High/Low		PER SHARE ($) Earnings	Dividends	Book Value
12/09	23.56	17	5	1.49	0.91	12.51
12/08	13.38	18	5	1.71	0.89	9.86
12/07	31.70	16	12	2.08	0.81	9.73
12/06	24.62	16	11	1.60	0.57	7.20
12/05	15.62	13	11	1.18	0.40	5.30
Annual Growth	10.8%	—	—	6.0%	22.8%	24.0%

Bank of China

The Bank of China (BOC) has its sights set on global conquest — of the financial kind. One of the largest banks in the world's most populous country, BOC is a financial giant. It has more than 10,000 domestic branches as well as foreign offices in about 30 countries. Commercial banking (including corporate and retail banking and treasury operations) accounts for about 90% of its revenues. BOC Investment provides investment banking services in China, the UK, the US, and Singapore. BOC Group Insurance sells general and life insurance products in China. The group provides aviation financing through BOC Aviation. China's government owns about 70% of BOC, one of the nation's four state-owned commercial banks.

In early 2009 BOC faced sell-offs by major investors as several subprime-battered financial institutions lined up to divest their stakes in the bank. UBS sold its entire 1% stake, Bank of America its 3% stake, and Royal Bank of Scotland its 4% stake. The two banks then cut their strategic partnership ties.

The bank's 2006 IPO was said to be the world's largest in six years. The successful IPO was fraught with symbolism for the banking industry in China, which had been struggling. China

had to bail out two of the country's top banks, BOC and China Construction Bank, three times within six years. For decades, money in China's state banks was used to support failing state companies, leaving the banks with a mountain of bad loans.

HISTORY

The Bank of China (BOC) has always had strong ties to the government of China. Established as a central bank in 1912, right after the establishment of the Provisional Government of the Republic of China, BOC became a government-chartered international exchange bank in 1928. Their first overseas branch was opened in London in 1929, leading to a global network of 34 overseas branches over the next two decades.

After WWII the bank specialized in foreign exchange, supporting foreign trade and the development of China's national economy. Between 1984 and 2001 BOC issued bonds in the international capital market 27 times. In 1993, when China initiated reform in its foreign exchange system, BOC played a key role in the unification of exchange rates, foreign exchange purchases and sales, and the incorporation of foreign-funded enterprises into the foreign exchange sales system.

In 1994 BOC began to transform from a specialized bank to a wider-based, state-owned commercial bank by issuing its first BOC Hong Kong dollar notes and then Macao pataca notes. The issue of both notes helped stabilize their respective markets.

BOC International Holdings, a wholly owned subsidiary of BOC specializing in investment banking, was incorporated in Hong Kong in 1998. Three years later, the group restructured its Hong Kong operations by merging 10 of its member banks into Bank of China (Hong Kong) Limited, a locally registered bank that successfully listed on the Hong Kong Stock Exchange in July 2003.

The bank was not free of scandal. A 2002 probe into BOC's New York branch by the US Office of the Comptroller of the Currency revealed that preferential treatment was given to certain customers who had personal relationships with some members of the bank's previous management. Regulators from the US and China fined BOC $20 million for "unsafe and unsound" business practices.

In 2005 the Royal Bank of Scotland (RBS) formed a consortium that bought a 10% stake in BOC. In exchange, BOC agreed to distribute the Scottish bank's credit cards and other products. RBS sold its stake in 2009, and the banks ended their partnership agreement.

BOC went public in 2006. Its IPO was estimated to be the world's largest in six years. Foreign banks and investors scrambled for a piece of the action; Saudi investor Prince Alwaleed bin Talal invested $2 billion in the bank.

To increase its non-interest income, BOC acquired Singapore Aircraft Leasing (since renamed BOC Aviation) for $965 million in late 2006. The BOC Aviation portfolio includes more than 75 aircraft in about 20 countries.

BOC announced plans in 2008 to acquire 20% of French private bank La Compagnie Financiere Edmond de Rothschild, but dropped those plans in 2009 after failing to get approval from Chinese regulators.

EXECUTIVES

Chairman, Board of Supervisors: Liu Ziqiang, age 60
Honorary Chairperson: Chen Muhua
Chairman: Xiao Gang, age 51, $181,895 total compensation
Vice Chairman and President: Li Lihui, age 56
Executive Director and EVP: Li Zaohang, age 53
Executive Director and EVP: Zhou Zaiqun, age 57
EVP: Chen Siqing, age 48
EVP: Zhang Yanling, age 57
EVP: Zhu Min, age 56
EVP: Wang Yongli, age 44
Chief Audit Officer: Ng Peng Khian, age 53
Secretary to the Board of Directors: Zhang Bingxun, age 59
Secretary, Party Discipline Committee: Zhang Lin, age 52
Chief Credit Officer: Chim Wai Kin, age 48
Auditors: PricewaterhouseCoopers

LOCATIONS

HQ: Bank of China Limited
(Zhongguo Yinhang Gufen Youxien Gongsi)
1 Fuxingmen Nei Dajie
Beijing 100818, China
Phone: 86-10-6659-2638 **Fax:** 86-10-6659-4568
US HQ: 410 Madison Ave., New York, NY 10017
US Phone: 212-935-3101 **US Fax:** 212-593-1831
Web: www.boc.cn

2009 Branches

	No.
Eastern China	3,388
Central & southern China	2,688
Western China	1,571
Northern China	1,451
Northeastern China	890
Hong Kong & Macau	862
Other overseas	111
Total	**10,961**

PRODUCTS/OPERATIONS

2009 Sales

	% of total
Interest	
Loans	60
Investment debt securities	16
Other	8
Noninterest	
Agency commissions	3
Credit commitment fees	3
Other	10
Total	**100**

Selected Subsidiaries

Bank of China Group Insurance Company Limited
BOC Aviation Private Limited
BOC Hong Kong (Group) Limited
Bank of China Group Investment Limited
Chiyu Banking Corporation Limited (commercial banking, 47%)
Nanyang Commercial Bank, Limited (commercial banking, 66%)
Tai Fung Bank Limited (commercial banking, 50.3%)

COMPETITORS

Agricultural Bank of China
Bank of East Asia
Cathay Financial Holding
China Construction Bank
China Development Bank
China Merchants Bank
China Minsheng Banking
Chuo Mitsui Trust
CITIC International Financial
Hang Seng Bank
HSBC
Industrial and Commercial Bank of China
Shanghai Pudong Development Bank

HISTORICAL FINANCIALS

Company Type: Public

Income Statement

FYE: December 31

	ASSETS ($ mil.)	NET INCOME ($ mil.)	INCOME AS % OF ASSETS	EMPLOYEES
12/09	1,280,409	12,487	1.0%	262,566
12/08	1,014,836	9,494	0.9%	249,278
12/07	819,592	8,478	1.0%	237,379
12/06	681,102	6,031	0.9%	232,632
12/05	587,634	4,039	0.7%	209,265
Annual Growth	21.5%	32.6%	—	5.8%

2009 Year-End Financials

Equity as % of assets: 6.2%
Return on assets: 1.1%
Return on equity: 16.4%
Long-term debt ($ mil.): 11,236
No. of shares (mil.): 271,545

Dividends
  Yield: 3.1%
  Payout: 40.0%
Market value ($ mil.): 166,854
Sales ($ mil.): 48,973

Stock History

Hong Kong: 3988

	STOCK PRICE ($) FY Close	P/E High/Low		PER SHARE ($) Earnings	Dividends	Book Value
12/09	0.61	16	6	0.05	0.02	0.29
12/08	0.31	17	7	0.04	0.03	0.27
12/07	0.52	24	15	0.03	—	0.23
12/06	0.55	24	17	0.02	—	0.20
Annual Growth	3.5%	—	—	35.7%	(33.3%)	25.1%

Bank of Montreal

Bank of Montreal is bilingual — it speaks Canadian *and* American business. Also known as BMO Financial Group (or, more familiarly, BMO, pronounced "bee-moe"), the company is one of Canada's oldest and biggest banks. Serving individuals, government agencies, and businesses large and small, it has about 900 branches that provide deposits, mortgages and loans, life insurance, credit cards, investments, and wealth management services. In the US, it owns Chicago's Harris Bankcorp, which performs similar services through more than 300 branches, primarily in the Midwest. Another subsidiary, BMO Capital Markets, offers institutional brokerage and investment banking services mainly in Canada and the US.

BMO Financial is focused on building its business through acquisitions as well as organic growth, and would like to continue to build its Harris Bank franchise; the company's goal is to have up to 1,000 branches in the US. As part of that initiative, Harris acquired the failed AMCORE Bank in 2010 in an FDIC-facilitated transaction. The company also bought First National Bank & Trust in Indiana in 2007 and Wisconsin's Merchants and Manufacturers Bancorporation and Ozaukee Bank the following

year. It has made modest forays into Florida and Arizona as well.

BMO Financial is also emphasizing growth in its Private Client segment, which includes money manager BMO Nesbitt Burns, online brokerage BMO InvestorLine, and BMO Harris Private Bank, by adding new products and services such as exchange-traded funds. In 2009 the company bought American International Group's Canadian life insurance business, adding about 400,000 clients and expanding BMO's distribution channel.

Also that year, BMO Financial Group bought the North American operations of Diners Club from Citigroup, doubling its corporate credit card business.

HISTORY

Montreal was a key port for fur and agriculture trade by the early 1800s. To finance these activities, the Montreal Bank (Canada's first) opened in 1817. Chartered in 1822, the bank officially became Bank of Montreal. Its ties with the US were strong, and nearly 50% of its original capital came from Yanks.

When the fur trade shifted northward to Hudson Bay in the 1820s, the bank diversified. In 1832 Bank of Montreal financed Canada's first railroad, the Champlain & St. Lawrence. The bank also grew through acquisitions, including the Bank of Canada (1831) and the Bank of the People (1840). It opened a branch in New York in 1859.

Canada united as a confederation in 1867, and Bank of Montreal expanded west. During the 1860s, it became Canada's de facto central bank until the 1935 creation of the Bank of Canada. By 1914 Bank of Montreal was the nation's largest. It bought the British Bank of North America (1918), Merchants Bank of Canada (1922), and Molsons Bank (1925). During the Depression, however, its growth ground to a halt.

WWII pumped up Canada's economy and the company's finances. Bank of Montreal enjoyed even greater growth during the postwar boom. It began expanding internationally, particularly in Latin America. But the bank failed to capitalize on the growth of consumer and small-business lending during the 1960s and was the last major Canadian bank to issue a credit card (in 1972). In 1975 it hired William Mullholland, a Morgan Stanley veteran, to run the company. Mullholland closed unprofitable branches and modernized operations.

The bank bought Chicago-based Harris Bankcorp in 1984. As Canada's banking industry deregulated, Bank of Montreal moved into investment banking, acquiring one of Canada's largest brokerage firms, Nesbitt Thomson, in 1987.

The Latin American debt crisis and the recession of the late 1980s and early 1990s hit Bank of Montreal hard. It tumbled into the red in 1989, partly because of loan defaults. The next year Matthew Barrett replaced Mullholland as chairman and began overhauling operations, focusing on consumer and middle-market business banking and on cutting costs.

By 1994 nonperforming assets were down, and Bank of Montreal began growing again. It bought brokerage Burns Fry and merged it with Nesbitt Thomson to form Nesbitt Burns, thus increasing its presence in merchant and investment banking and securities. It added to its Harris Bank network with the purchase of Suburban Bancorp. The next year Bank of Montreal

expanded its private banking business for wealthy individuals; it also began targeting aboriginal Canadians.

Eyeing international growth, Bank of Montreal bought an interest in Mexico's Grupo Financiero Bancomer in 1996 (now called BBVA Bancomer; it has since sold its interest) and opened branches in Beijing (1996) and Dublin, Ireland (1997). It agreed in 1998 to merge with Royal Bank of Canada, but Canada's finance minister rejected the merger.

Barrett stepped down as CEO and chairman in 1999; the firm named Anthony Comper its new CEO. The bank realigned its operations to focus on retail and commercial banking, investment banking, and wealth management and cut some 2,450 jobs. Eyeing growth in the US, Bank of Montreal in 2000 agreed to buy Florida's Village Banc of Naples, as well as Seattle brokerage Freeman Welwood.

Continuing its southward push, it bought Chicago-area community banks Lakeland Community Bank and New Lenox State Bank, as well as Indiana-based Mercantile Bancorp in 2004.

Bank of Montreal sold US-based online brokerage Harrisdirect to E*TRADE in 2005. Comper retired in 2007 and was succeeded as CEO by former COO William Downe.

EXECUTIVES

Chairman: David A. Galloway, age 66
Vice Chairman: Kevin G. Lynch
President, CEO, and Director: William A. (Bill) Downe, age 57
CFO: Russel C. Robertson
SEVP, Head Human Resources, and Senior Leadership Advisor: Rose M. Patten
EVP Technology Development and Enterprise Infrastructure: Karen L. Metrakos
EVP and Chief Risk Officer: Thomas E. (Tom) Flynn
EVP and General Counsel: Simon A. Fish
EVP and Head Commercial Banking, Harris: David R. Casper
EVP Finance: Pierre O. Greffe, age 57
SVP, Deputy General Counsel, Corporate Affairs and Corporate Secretary: Blair F. Morrison
SVP and Chief Marketing Officer: Susan M. Payne
Group Head Technology and Operations: Barry K. Gilmour, age 62
President and CEO, Personal and Commercial Banking Canada: Franklin J. (Frank) Techar, age 48, $668,000 total compensation
President and CEO, BMO Life Insurance: Gordon J. Henderson
President and CEO, BMO Life Assurance: Peter C. McCarthy
President, BMO Capital Markets: Eric C. Tripp
President and Director, Private Client Division, BMC Nesbit Burns: Dean Manjuris
President and CEO, Private Client Group: Gilles G. Ouellette
President and CEO, Personal and Commercial Banking US and Harris Financial: Ellen M. Costello, age 54
Chairman, BMO Nesbitt Burns; President, Quebec: L. Jacques Ménard, age 64
Auditors: KPMG LLP

LOCATIONS

HQ: Bank of Montreal
  100 King St. West, 1 First Canadian Place
  Toronto, Ontario M5X 1A1, Canada
Phone: 416-867-5000   **Fax:** 416-867-6793
US HQ: 111 W. Monroe St., Chicago, IL 60690
US Phone: 312-461-7745   **US Fax:** 312-461-3869
Web: www.bmo.com

PRODUCTS/OPERATIONS

2009 Sales

	% of total
Interest	
Loans	48
Securities	15
Deposits with banks	1
Noninterest	
Securities commissions & fees	6
Securitization revenues	6
Deposit & payment service charges	5
Trading revenues	4
Lending fees	3
Mutual fund revenues	3
Other	9
Total	**100**

COMPETITORS

Bank of America
Caisses centrale Desjardins
CIBC
Citigroup
Fifth Third
JPMorgan Chase
Laurentian Bank
National Bank of Canada
Northern Trust
RBC Financial Group
Scotiabank
TD Bank

HISTORICAL FINANCIALS

Company Type: Public

Income Statement

FYE: October 31

	ASSETS ($ mil.)	NET INCOME ($ mil.)	INCOME AS % OF ASSETS	EMPLOYEES
10/09	362,237	1,666	0.5%	36,173
10/08	344,073	1,636	0.5%	37,000
10/07	383,934	2,233	0.6%	36,000
10/06	285,388	2,376	0.8%	35,000
10/05	252,754	2,039	0.8%	34,000
Annual Growth	**9.4%**	**(4.9%)**	**—**	**1.6%**

2009 Year-End Financials

Equity as % of assets: 5.2%
Return on assets: 0.5%
Return on equity: 9.9%
Long-term debt ($ mil.): 5,022
No. of shares (mil.): 563

Dividends
Yield: 6.0%
Payout: 90.9%
Market value ($ mil.): 24,338
Sales ($ mil.): 14,983

Stock History

NYSE: BMO

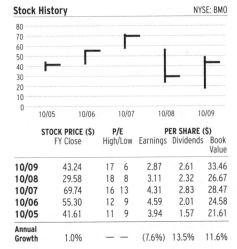

	STOCK PRICE ($) FY Close	P/E High/Low		PER SHARE ($) Earnings	Dividends	Book Value
10/09	43.24	17	6	2.87	2.61	33.46
10/08	29.58	18	8	3.11	2.32	26.67
10/07	69.74	16	13	4.31	2.83	28.47
10/06	55.30	12	9	4.59	2.01	24.58
10/05	41.61	11	9	3.94	1.57	21.61
Annual Growth	**1.0%**	**—**	**—**	**(7.6%)**	**13.5%**	**11.6%**

Barclays PLC

Raising the bar for global finance, Barclays owns one of Europe's largest banks, a top market-making investment bank, the top UK credit card, and an international wealth management firm. Its flagship Barclays Bank has some 1,700 branches in the UK as well as operations throughout Europe, Africa, the Middle East, and the US. Its Barclaycard arm has more than 20 million credit cards and provides consumer lending and payment processing services, primarily in Europe. Barclays Capital is one of the largest investment banks in the world (thanks largely to its acquisition of the North American operations of Lehman Brothers). Altogether, Barclays serves more than 48 million customers in more than 50 countries.

Barclays operates through two primary segments — Global Retail and Commercial Banking (GRCB) and Investment Banking and Investment Management. Its GRCB units provide consumer banking, Woolwich-branded mortgages, insurance, leasing, and card services in Europe, the US, and Africa. The investment banking/management units include Barclays Capital and Barclays Wealth.

To weather the global economic crisis, Barclays sold some businesses, cut costs through branch closures and workforce reductions, and restructured its credit market exposures. The group chose not to participate in the UK's bank bailouts in late 2008 but pursued its own capital raising plan (through which sovereign investment fund Qatar Investment Authority became its largest shareholder).

In 2008 Barclays sold noncore business Barclays Life and its portfolio of some 760,000 life and pension policies to Swiss Re for £753 million ($1.5 billion).

In 2009 Barclays shut down US-based subprime mortgage lender EquiFirst. Later that year, it sold a majority of Barclays Global Investors to American money manager BlackRock for £9.5 billion ($15 billion). In exchange, it holds a 20% stake in the new BlackRock.

Barclays has also worked to expand internationally, mostly in the US and emerging markets, to offset some of its exposure to the UK economy. It paid £1 billion ($1.8 billion) for Lehman Brothers' North American operations, a deal which made Barclays Capital one of the world's largest investment banks. However, Lehman Brothers questions the parameters of the transaction and is battling the bank in court to win back some of its lost profits.

To boost its retail and commercial banking operations, the company bought Standard Life Bank from Scottish insurer Standard Life, which exited the banking business, for £226 million ($368.5 million) in 2010.

In a surprise shakeup, Barclays announced in 2010 that CEO John Varley will step down from the position the following year. He will be replaced by Bob Diamond, an American and Barclays' president and investment banking chief.

HISTORY

Barclays first spread its wings in 1736 when James Barclay united his family's goldsmithing and banking businesses. As other family members joined the London enterprise, it became known as Barclays, Bevan & Tritton (1782).

Banking first became regulated in the 19th century. To ward off takeovers, 20 banks combined with Barclays in 1896. The new firm, Barclay & Co., began preying on other banks. Within 20 years it bought 17, including the Colonial Bank, chartered in 1836 to serve the West Indies and British Guiana (now Guyana). The company, renamed Barclays Bank Ltd. in 1917, weathered the Depression as the UK's #2 bank.

Barclays began expanding again after WWII, and by the late 1950s it had become the UK's top bank. It had a computer network by 1959, and in 1966 it introduced the Barclaycard in conjunction with Bank of America's BankAmericard (now Visa).

In 1968 the UK's Monopolies Commission barred Barclays' merger with two other big London banks, but had no objections to a two-way merger, so Barclays bought competitor Martins.

Barclays moved into the US consumer finance market in 1980 when it bought American Credit, 138 former Beneficial Finance offices, and Bankers Trust's branch network.

During the 1980s London banks faced competition from invading overseas banks, local building societies, and other financial firms. Banking reform in 1984 led to formation of a holding company for Barclays Bank PLC.

To prepare for British financial deregulation in 1986, Barclays formed Barclays de Zoete Wedd (BZW) by merging its merchant bank with two other London financial firms. Faced with sagging profits, Barclays sold its California bank in 1988 and its US consumer finance business in 1989.

In 1990 Barclays bought private German bank Merck, Finck & Co. and Paris bank L'Européenne de Banque. The company countered 1992's bad-loan-induced losses by accelerating a cost-cutting program begun in 1989. To appease stockholders, chairman and CEO Andrew Buxton (a descendant of one of the bank's founding families) gave up his CEO title, hiring Martin Taylor (previously CEO of textile firm Courtaulds) for the post.

The company sold its Australian retail banking business in 1994, then began trimming other operations, including French corporate banking and US mortgage operations. In 1997 it sold BZW's European investment banking business to Credit Suisse First Boston, retaining the fixed-income and foreign exchange business.

Losses in Russia and a $250 million bailout of US hedge fund Long-Term Capital Management hit Barclays Capital in 1998. Taylor resigned that year in part because of his radical plans for the bank. Sir Peter Middleton stepped in as acting CEO; Barclays later tapped Canadian banker Matthew Barrett for the post. (Middleton also became chairman upon Buxton's retirement.)

In 2000 the bank ruffled feathers when it announced the closure of about 170 mostly rural UK branches. In 2004 chief executive Barrett was named Barclays' chairman, succeeding Peter Middleton.

After exiting the South African market in 1987 over apartheid concerns, Barclays returned in 2005, buying a majority stake in the Absa Group, one of the country's largest retail banks.

The company entered the US credit card market when it bought Juniper Financial from Canadian Imperial Bank of Commerce in 2004.

Marcus Agius succeeded the retiring Matthew Barrett as chairman in 2007. Barclays bought Russian bank Expobank from Petropavlovsk Finance. Expobank has one of the largest ATM networks in Russia and is part of the booming consumer banking industry there.

EXECUTIVES

Chairman: Marcus Agius, age 63
Vice Chairman: Sir Richard Broadbent, age 56
Group Chief Executive and Director: John S. Varley, age 53, $2,070,665 total compensation
President and Director; CEO, Investment Banking and Investment Management: Robert E. (Bob) Diamond Jr., age 58, $430,100 total compensation
Group Finance Director and Director: Christopher (Chris) Lucas, age 49, $2,870,679 total compensation
Chief Executive, Global Retail and Commercial Banking: Frederik (Frits) Seegers, age 51, $3,633,310 total compensation
Chief Executive, UK Retail Banking: Deanna W. Oppenheimer
CEO, Barclays Wealth: Thomas L. (Tom) Kalaris
CEO, Barclays Commercial Bank: Eduardo Eguren
CEO, Barclays Shared Services: Sameer Chadha
CEO, Global Retail Banking: Antony Jenkins
President, Barclays Capital and Co-CEO Corporate and Investment Banking: Jerry del Missier
Co-CEO Corporate and Investment Banking: Rich Ricci
Chief Economist, Barclays Wealth: Michael Dicks
Group Risk Officer: Robert Le Blanc, age 52
Group General Counsel: Mark Harding
Group Treasurer: Jon Stone
Secretary: Lawrence Dickinson
Director Human Resources: Cathy Turner
Auditors: PricewaterhouseCoopers LLP

LOCATIONS

HQ: Barclays PLC
1 Churchill Place
London E14 5HP, United Kingdom
Phone: 44-20-7116-1000
US HQ: 745 7th Ave., New York, NY 10119
US Phone: 212-412-4000
Web: www.barclays.com

PRODUCTS/OPERATIONS

2009 Sales

	% of total
Interest	44
Fees & commissions	21
Principal transactions	15
Net trading income	15
Net insurance contract premiums	2
Other	3
Total	**100**

COMPETITORS

AXA UK
Bank of New York Mellon
CIBC
Citigroup
Deutsche Bank
Grupo Santander
HSBC
Invesco
JPMorgan Chase
Lloyds Banking Group
Mitsubishi UFJ Financial Group
Mizuho Financial
RBC Financial Group
Royal Bank of Scotland
Standard Chartered
UBS
The Vanguard Group

HISTORICAL FINANCIALS

Company Type: Public

Income Statement

FYE: December 31

	ASSETS ($ mil.)	NET INCOME ($ mil.)	INCOME AS % OF ASSETS	EMPLOYEES
12/09	2,196,082	16,385	0.7%	144,200
12/08	3,008,162	6,420	0.2%	156,300
12/07	2,443,405	8,793	0.4%	141,885
12/06	1,953,366	8,958	0.5%	133,529
12/05	1,593,563	6,622	0.4%	113,300
Annual Growth	**8.3%**	**25.4%**	**—**	**6.2%**

2009 Year-End Financials

Equity as % of assets: 3.4%
Return on assets: 0.6%
Return on equity: 25.4%
Long-term debt ($ mil.): 260,226
No. of shares (mil.): 3,011
Dividends
Yield: 0.2%
Payout: 1.2%
Market value ($ mil.): 84,405
Sales ($ mil.): 62,940

Stock History

NYSE: BCS

	STOCK PRICE ($) FY Close	P/E High/Low		PER SHARE ($) Earnings	Dividends	Book Value
12/09	28.03	8	1	5.20	0.06	25.00
12/08	14.18	18	3	3.33	1.98	17.82
12/07	80.59	23	14	5.33	2.59	15.40
12/06	113.85	22	15	5.47	2.18	12.88
12/05	72.39	22	18	3.62	1.68	9.98
Annual Growth	**(21.1%)**	**—**	**—**	**9.5%**	**(56.5%)**	**25.8%**

BASF SE

The world is BASF's ester. BASF is the world's largest chemical company, ahead of Dow and DuPont. It has more than 150 major manufacturing facilities and does business worldwide through six business segments: plastics (including polyolefins and polystyrene), performance products (value-added chemicals and dyes), chemicals (plasticizers and solvents), oil and gas exploration and production (through subsidiary Wintershall AG), functional solutions (catalysts, coatings, and construction chemicals), and agricultural products (additives, herbicides, and fertilizers).

BASF uses what it calls *Verbund* strategy throughout its facilities — plants are both customers and suppliers of each other. While the company still gets more than half its sales from Europe, it continues to expand overseas, particularly in Asia. It saw early on that the chemicals market in Asia would be the equal of that in Europe and wanted a healthy piece of the action.

In 2009 BASF spent about $4 billion to acquire Swiss chemicals giant Ciba. Following a review phase of Ciba's operations and their fit within the structure of BASF, the company has begun to integrate Ciba into its performance products segment; this will entail the sale or closure of almost half of Ciba's 55 manufacturing facilities and the loss of about 3,700 of its employees. As part of that strategy, BASF SE sold the Regulatory and Safety Testing businesses of Ciba's Expert Services unit to London-based Intertek Group in 2010.

Also in 2010 BASF agreed to acquire specialty chemicals company Cognis GmbH in a €3.1 billion ($3.8 billion) deal. BASF beat out Lubrizol Corp. for control of Cognis despite the US chemical company's higher offer. Concerns over financing scuttled Lubrizol's chances to win over shareholders. Cognis will give BASF a boost in entering several high-margin business lines, such as personal care and cosmetics.

The company legally changed its name from BASF Aktiengesellschaft to BASF SE in 2008. The move made formal BASF's transition to a European company, as opposed to one organized in Germany.

HISTORY

Originally named Badische Anilin & Soda-Fabrik, BASF AG was founded in Mannheim, Germany, by jeweler Frederick Englehorn in 1861. Unable to find enough land for expansion in Mannheim, BASF moved to nearby Ludwigshafen in 1865. The company was a pioneer in coal tar dyes, and it developed a synthetic indigo in 1897. Its synthetic dyes rapidly replaced more expensive organic dyes.

BASF scientist Fritz Haber synthesized ammonia in 1909, giving BASF access to the market for nitrogenous fertilizer (1913). Haber received a Nobel Prize in 1918 but was later charged with war crimes for his work with poison gases. Managed by Carl Bosch, another Nobel Prize winner, BASF joined the I.G. Farben cartel with Bayer, Hoechst, and others in 1925 to create a German chemical colossus. Within the cartel BASF developed polystyrene, PVC, and magnetic tape. Part of the Nazi war machine, I.G. Farben made synthetic rubber and used labor from the Auschwitz concentration camp during WWII.

After the war I.G. Farben was dismantled. BASF regained its independence in 1952 and rebuilt its war-ravaged factories. Strong postwar domestic demand for basic chemicals aided its recovery, and in 1958 BASF launched a US joint venture with Dow Chemical (BASF bought out Dow's half in 1978). The company moved into petrochemicals and became a leading manufacturer of plastic and synthetic fiber.

In the US the company purchased Wyandotte Chemicals (1969), Chemetron (1979), and Inmont (1985), among others. To expand its natural gas business in Europe, in 1991 the company signed deals with Russia's Gazprom and France's Elf Aquitaine. BASF bought Mobil's polystyrene-resin business and gained almost 10% of the US market.

BASF bought Imperial Chemical's polypropylene business in 1994 and became Europe's second-largest producer of the plastic. The next year the company paid $1.4 billion for the pharmaceutical arm of UK retailer Boots.

In 1997 BASF formed a joint venture with PetroFina (now TOTAL S.A.); in 2001 the venture opened the world's largest liquid steam cracker, in Port Arthur, Texas.

In 1999 the US fined the company $225 million for its part in a worldwide vitamin price-fixing cartel (in 2001 the European Commission fined it another $260 million, bringing the total expected cost of fines, out-of-court settlements, and legal expenses to about $800 million). BASF also faced a class-action suit as a result of the scheme. That year BASF merged its textile operations into Bayer and Hoechst's DyStar joint venture, forming a $1 billion company that is a world-leading dye maker.

In 2000 BASF expanded its superabsorbents business by paying $656 million for US-based Amcol International's Chemdal International unit. Rather than attempt to compete in the rapidly consolidating pharmaceutical industry, in 2001 BASF sold its midsized Knoll Pharmaceutical unit to Abbott Laboratories for about $6.9 billion. It also announced that it would close 10 plants and cut about 4,000 jobs (4% of its workforce).

BASF in 2003 bought a portion of Bayer's agchem businesses for $1.3 billion when European antitrust regulators mandated the Bayer divestment following its acquisition of Aventis CropScience. BASF also acquired Honeywell Specialty Materials' engineering plastics business in exchange for its fibers division.

That year also brought chairman Jürgen Hambrecht's announcement that the company would push forward with a restructuring of its North American business. Included among the steps were job cuts of approximately 1,000 and the relocation of its North American headquarters (though remaining in New Jersey) in late 2004.

BASF sold Basell, its petrochemical JV with Shell, in 2005. Investment group Access Industries came in with the winning bid of about $5.7 billion.

The company opened two Verbund sites in Asia — one in Nanjing, China, and the other in Kuantan, Malaysia. The Chinese site delivered its first product in early 2005 and began operating fully in the middle of that year. It's the centerpiece and primary operation of BASF-YPC, a joint venture with Sinopec that was formed in 2000. BASF's goal is to achieve 70% of its sales in the region from local production by 2015; that figure hovered at about 60% in 2008.

EXECUTIVES

Chairman of the Supervisory Board: Eggert Voscherau, age 66
Chairman of the Works Council and Deputy Chairman of the Supervisory Board: Robert Oswald, age 54
Deputy Chairman of the Supervisory Board: Michael Diekmann, age 55
Chairman, Board of Executive Directors: Jürgen Hambrecht, age 63
CFO and Director; Chairman and CEO, BASF Corporation: Kurt W. Bock, age 52
Member of the Board of Executive Directors, Performance Polymers, Polyurethanes, and Styrenics Division and Asia/Pacific Regional Division: Martin Brudermuller, age 49
Member, Board of Executive Directors, Construction Chemicals, Dispersion and Pigments, Care Chemicals, Nutrition and Health, Paper Chemicals, Performance Chemicals, and the Competence Center Polymer Research: John Feldmann, age 61
Member, Board of Executive Directors, Inorganics, Petrochemicals, Intermediates, Chemicals Research and Engineering, and BASF Future Business: Andreas Kreimeyer, age 55
Member, Board of Executive Directors, Competence Centers, Human Resources, Environment, Health and Safety, Engineering and Maintenance and Verbund Site Management Europe and Director Industrial Relations; Site Director, Ludwigshafen: Harald Schwager, age 50
Member, Board of Executive Directors, Oil and Gas Division, the Europe Regional Division, Competence Center, and Global Procurement and Logistics Division: Hans-Ulrich Engel, age 51

Member, Board of Executive Directors, Crop Protection, Coatings and Specialty Chemicals Research Division, BASF Plant Science, South America Regional Division: Stefan Marcinowski, age 57
President, Global Integration and CEO, Ciba: Michael Heinz, age 46
Chief Compliance Officer: Eckart Sünner
Head Communications and Government Relations, BASF Group: Elisabeth Schick, age 44
Chairman of the Board of Executive Directors, Wintershall: Rainer Seele, age 50
Auditors: KPMG Deutsche Treuhand-Gesellschaft AG

LOCATIONS

HQ: BASF SE
  Carl-Bosch Strasse 38
  67056 Ludwigshafen, Germany
Phone: 49-621-60-0   **Fax:** 49-621-60-425-25
US HQ: 100 Campus Dr., Florham Park, NJ 07932
US Phone: 973-245-6000   **US Fax:** 973-895-8002
Web: www.basf.com

2009 Sales by Region

	% of total
Europe	
Germany	43
Other countries	17
North America	18
Asia/Pacific	16
South America/Africa/Middle East	6
Total	**100**

PRODUCTS/OPERATIONS

2009 Sales

	% of total
Oil & Gas	22
Performance Products	18
Chemicals	15
Plastics	14
Functional Solutions	14
Agricultural Solutions	7
Other	10
Total	**100**

Selected Products

Oil and Gas
  Crude oil and natural gas exploration
  Natural gas distribution and trading
Chemicals
  Inorganics (ammonia, formaldehyde, melamine, sulfuric acid, and urea)
  Intermediates
  Performance chemicals (water-based resins, etc.)
  Petrochemicals (feedstocks, industrial gases, and plasticizers)
  Specialty chemicals
Plastics
  Engineering plastics
  Foams
  Polyurethane
  Polyamide and intermediates
  Styrenics
Functional Solutions
  Catalysts
  Coatings
    Automotive coatings
    Decorative paints
    Industrial coatings
    Pigments
  Construction chemicals
Performance Products
  Automotive fluids
  Care Chemicals
  Printing systems
  Surfactants
  Textile chemicals
Agricultural Solutions
  Agricultural products (fungicides, herbicides, and insecticides)
  Fine chemicals (fragrances, pharmaceutical ingredients, UV absorbers, and vitamins)

COMPETITORS

3M
Air Products
Akzo Nobel
Albemarle
Ashland Inc.
Bayer AG
BP
Cargill
Cognis
Dow Chemical
DSM
DuPont
Eastman Chemical
Evonik Degussa
Exxon Mobil
FMC
Formosa Plastics
Henkel
INEOS
LANXESS
LG Group
Monsanto Company
Royal Dutch Shell
SABIC
TOTAL

HISTORICAL FINANCIALS

Company Type: Public

Income Statement

FYE: December 31

	REVENUE ($ mil.)	NET INCOME ($ mil.)	NET PROFIT MARGIN	EMPLOYEES
12/09	72,653	2,021	2.8%	104,779
12/08	87,818	4,105	4.7%	96,924
12/07	85,299	5,984	7.0%	95,175
12/06	69,468	4,246	6.1%	95,247
12/05	50,792	3,573	7.0%	80,945
Annual Growth	**9.4%**	**(13.3%)**	**—**	**6.7%**

2009 Year-End Financials

Debt ratio: 71.2%   No. of shares (mil.): 919
Return on equity: 8.1%   Dividends
Cash ($ mil.): 2,630   Yield: 4.5%
Current ratio: 1.68   Payout: 126.2%
Long-term debt ($ mil.): 17,835   Market value ($ mil.): 57,210

Stock History

Pink Sheets: BASFY

	STOCK PRICE ($) FY Close	P/E High/Low		PER SHARE ($) Earnings	Dividends	Book Value
12/09	62.29	29	13	2.21	2.79	27.27
12/08	39.09	34	6	4.41	—	26.96
12/07	149.27	25	17	6.12	—	30.65
12/06	97.43	23	18	4.20	—	25.95
12/05	76.64	23	17	3.39	—	22.05
Annual Growth	**(5.1%)**	**—**	**—**	**(10.1%)**	**—**	**5.5%**

Bayer AG

You could get a headache trying to name all of Bayer AG's products. The company, which created aspirin in 1897, makes health care products (pharmaceuticals, OTC drugs, and animal health care), specialty materials (plastics and high-performance materials), and agricultural products (for crop protection and home garden care). It operates in the US through Bayer Corporation. Aside from its line of Bayer aspirin, the company's best-known consumer brands include Aleve, Alka-Seltzer, and One-A-Day vitamins. Its top selling pharmaceuticals include multiple sclerosis treatment Betaseron and birth control pill Yasmin.

Bayer is growing its core businesses (health care, high-tech materials, and crop nutrition) by enhancing its strong position in key markets and by expanding into new areas by investing in emerging technologies. MaterialScience opened a new plant in China in 2009, the world's largest methylene diphenyl diisocyanate (MDI, an ingredient in polyurethane) factory. It plans to have several more Chinese facilities online by 2011. CropScience is also investing in production; it will spend about €30 million ($42 million) to expand its German production facilities by 2011. The unit has also picked up AgroGreen's crop protection business and US-based biotech company Athenix, for which it paid about $365 million.

Between 2008 and 2009, the company acquired a handful of companies (medical device maker Possis Medical and biotech firm DIREVO) as well as entered into numerous collaboration agreements including one with Genzyme to co-develop and promote multiple sclerosis drugs. The deal also licenses Bayer blood cancer products to Genzyme.

Bayer HealthCare also zeroed in on its core development programs by purchasing two potential oncology drug candidates from Swiss pharma firm Nycomed. A deal with Polish drugmaker Bioton in 2009 gave Bayer the right to distribute Bioton's insulin in China. In the US, Bayer netted itself two prescription dermatology product lines from SkinMedica (Desonate for dermatitis and NeoBenz for acne).

The consumer part of HealthCare added OTC cough and cold remedies from Topsun Science and Technology Qidong Gaitianli Pharmaceutical to increase the group's standing in China.

In 2009 Bayer instituted temporary plant shutdowns, production cutbacks, and short-term reductions in working hours and compensation at MaterialScience division plants in Germany. Also in 2009 Marijn Dekkers, formerly head of Thermo Fisher Scientific, was appointed to lead Bayer.

HISTORY

Friedrich Bayer founded Bayer in Germany in 1863 to make synthetic dyes. Research led to such discoveries as Antinonin (synthetic pesticide, 1892), aspirin (1897), and synthetic rubber (1915).

Under Carl Duisberg, Bayer allegedly made the first poison gas used by Germany in WWI. During the war the US seized Bayer's US operations and trademark rights and sold them to Sterling Drug.

In 1925 Bayer, BASF, Hoechst, and other German chemical concerns merged to form I.G. Farben Trust. Their photography businesses, combined as Agfa, also joined the trust. Between wars Bayer developed polyurethanes and the first sulfa drug, Prontosil (1935).

During WWII the trust took over chemical plants of Nazi-occupied countries, used slave labor, and helped make Zyklon B gas used to kill people at Auschwitz. At war's end Bayer lost its 50% of Winthrop Laboratories (US) and Bayer of Canada (to Sterling Drug). The 1945 Potsdam Agreement called for the breakup of I.G. Farben, and Bayer AG emerged in 1951 as an independent company with many of its original operations, including Agfa.

After rebuilding in West Germany, Bayer AG and Monsanto formed a joint venture (Mobay, 1954); Bayer AG later bought Monsanto's share (1967). In the 1960s the company offered more dyes, plastics, and polyurethanes, and added factories worldwide. Agfa merged with Gevaert (photography, Belgium) in 1964; Bayer AG retained 60%. Over the next 25 years it acquired Miles Labs (Alka-Seltzer, US, 1978), the rest of Agfa-Gevaert (1981), Compugraphic (electronic imaging, US, 1989), and Nova's Polysar (rubber, Canada, 1990).

Bayer AG integrated its US holdings under the name Miles in 1992 (renamed Bayer Corporation in 1995). It regained US rights to the Bayer brand and logo in 1994 by paying SmithKline Beecham $1 billion for the North American business of Sterling Winthrop.

Bayer AG formed a joint venture with Swiss rival Roche Holding in 1996 to market over-the-counter Roche drugs in the US. In 1997 Bayer, Baxter International, Rhône-Poulenc Rorer, and Green Cross agreed to a $670 million settlement over blood products that infected thousands of hemophiliacs with HIV during the 1980s. In 1998 it bought US-based Chiron's diagnostics operations for $1.1 billion and formed a research alliance with Millennium Pharmaceuticals.

Bayer, Hoechst, and BASF merged their textile activities in 1999 to form the world's largest dye-making company. The next year Bayer boosted its polyurethane business by paying $2.5 billion for US-based Lyondell Chemical's polyols unit.

In 2001 Bayer had to recall Baycol (known as Lipobay in Europe), its popular cholesterol-lowering drug that has been linked to more than 100 deaths worldwide.

In a bid to bolster its agrochemical business, Bayer acquired Aventis CropScience in 2002 for about $5 billion plus $2 billion in debt.

In mid-2003 the company, along with partner GlaxoSmithKline, launched Levitra, its rival to Pfizer's $1 billion-earning Viagra.

Late in 2003 Bayer announced that it would spin off its chemicals business (along with parts of Bayer MaterialScience). The separation of its former chemicals subgroup was completed in 2005 when Bayer spun off the unit as a publicly traded company called LANXESS.

The company's OTC drugs unit got much larger in 2005 when Bayer bought Roche's consumer health unit for nearly $3 billion. The deal created one of the world's top three non-prescription drugs companies, combining Bayer's aspirin, Alka-Seltzer, and Midol brands with Roche's Aleve pain relievers, among others.

In 2006 Bayer acquired Schering AG for about $20 billion after a hostile bidding war with Merck. Schering AG was merged with Bayer's existing prescription drug business to create Bayer Schering Pharma AG. Bayer purchased Schering to strengthen its presence in the specialty pharmaceuticals business, especially women's health.

EXECUTIVES

Honorary Chairman, Supervisory Board:
Hermann Josef Strenger
Chairman, Supervisory Board: Manfred Schneider, age 71
Deputy Chairman, Supervisory Board: Thomas de Win, age 51
Chairman, Board of Management: Marijn E. Dekkers, age 53
CFO and Member, Board of Management:
Werner Baumann, age 48
Executive Chairman, Board of Management, Bayer Business Services: Daniel Hartert
Chairman, Board of Management, Bayer CropScience:
Sandra E. Peterson, age 51
Chairman, Board of Management, Bayer Schering Pharma: Andreas Fibig, age 48
Chairman, Board of Management, Bayer MaterialScience: Patrick W. Thomas, age 53
Member, Management Board, Strategy and Human Resources and Americas, Africa, and Middle East: Richard Pott, age 57
Member, Management Board, Innovation, Technology, and Environment and Asia/Pacific: Wolfgang Plischke, age 59
Member, Board of Management, Bayer CropScience: Achim Noack, age 51
Head Public Policy/Environment: Dirk Frenzel
Head Communications: Michael Schade
Head Investor Relations: Alexander Rosar
Head Corporate Policy and Media Relations:
Michael Preuss
Managing Director, Currenta: Klaus Schäfer
Managing Director, Bayer Technology Services:
Dirk Van Meirvenne, age 47
President and CEO, Bayer Corporation; President and CEO, Bayer MaterialScience LLC:
Gregory S. (Greg) Babe, age 53
Auditors: PricewaterhouseCoopers AG

LOCATIONS

HQ: Bayer AG
Bayerwerk, Gebäude W11, Kaiser-Wilhelm-Allee 51368 Leverkusen, Germany
Phone: 49-214-30-1   **Fax:** 49-214-30-663-28
US HQ: 100 Bayer Rd., Pittsburgh, PA 15205
US Phone: 412-777-2000   **US Fax:** 412-777-2034
Web: www.bayer.de

2009 Sales

	% of total
Europe	40
North America	29
Asia/Pacific	16
Latin America/Africa/Middle East	15
Total	**100**

PRODUCTS/OPERATIONS

2009 Sales

	% of total
Health Care	
Pharmaceuticals	34
Consumer Health	18
MaterialScience	24
CropScience	
Crop Protection	17
Environmental Science, Bioscience	3
Other	4
Total	**100**

Selected Operations and Products

HealthCare
Animal health products
Diabetes care products
Consumer care products (over-the-counter drugs)
Pharmaceuticals

MaterialScience
Coatings
Colorants
Plastics
Polyurethanes

CropScience
  BioScience (biotechnology and seeds)
  Crop protection (insecticides and herbicides)
  Environmental science (lawn care and non-
    agricultural pesticides)

Selected Brands
HealthCare
  Adalat (cardiovascular medication)
  Advantage (animal health)
  Aleve/Naproxen (analgesic)
  Alka-Seltzer (analgesic and antacid)
  Ascensia (diabetes care glucose meters)
  Aspirin (analgesic)
  Avalox/Avelox (antibiotic)
  Bepanthen/Bepanthol (skin care treatment)
  Betaferon/Betaseron (multiple sclerosis medication)
  Baytril (animal health infections)
  Canesten (antifungal)
  Cipro/Ciprobay (antibiotic)
  Diane (contraceptive)
  Glucobay (diabetes treatment)
  Iopamiron (diagnostic imaging)
  Kogenate (hematology/cardiology)
  Levitra (impotence drug)
  Magnevist (diagnostic imaging)
  Mirena (contraceptive)
  Nexavar (oncology)
  One-A-Day (vitamins)
  Rennie (heartburn)
  Supradyn (multivitamin)
  Ultravist (diagnostic imaging)
  Yasmin/Yasminelle/ZAZ (contraceptive)
MaterialScience
  Baydur (polyurethane)
  Bayflex (polyurethane)
  Desmodur/Desmophen (isocyanates, polyesters and
    polyols for polyurethanes)
  Makrolon (polycarbonate resin)
CropScience
  Betanal (herbicides)
  Confidor/Gaucho/Admire/Merit (insecticides/seed
    treatment)
  Decis/K-Othrine (insecticides)
  Flint/Stratego/Sphere (fungicides)
  Folicur/Raxil (fungicides/seed treatment)
  Poncho (seed treatment)
  Proline (fungicides)
  Puma (herbicides)

COMPETITORS
3M
Abbott Labs
Akzo Nobel
AstraZeneca
BASF SE
Boehringer Ingelheim
Bristol-Myers Squibb
Celanese
Dow Chemical
DSM
DuPont
Eastman Chemical
Eli Lilly
Evonik Degussa
GE Healthcare
GlaxoSmithKline
Johnson & Johnson
Merck
Merck KGaA
Merial
Mitsubishi Chemical
Monsanto Company
Novartis
Pfizer
Ranbaxy Laboratories
Rhodia
Roche Holding
Sanofi-Aventis
Syngenta
Teva Pharmaceuticals
Watson Pharmaceuticals

HISTORICAL FINANCIALS
Company Type: Public

Income Statement
FYE: December 31

	REVENUE ($ mil.)	NET INCOME ($ mil.)	NET PROFIT MARGIN	EMPLOYEES
12/09	44,670	1,948	4.4%	108,400
12/08	46,398	2,430	5.2%	108,600
12/07	47,668	6,942	14.6%	106,200
12/06	38,235	2,238	5.9%	96,594
12/05	32,539	1,896	5.8%	93,700
Annual Growth	8.2%	0.7%	—	3.7%

2009 Year-End Financials
Debt ratio: 65.3%
Return on equity: 8.4%
Cash ($ mil.): 3,001
Current ratio: 1.24
Long-term debt ($ mil.): 15,212
No. of shares (mil.): 827
Dividends
  Yield: 2.5%
  Payout: 82.4%
Market value ($ mil.): 66,323

Stock History
Pink Sheets: BAYRY

	STOCK PRICE ($) FY Close	P/E High/Low	PER SHARE ($) Earnings	Dividends	Book Value
12/09	80.20	33 21	2.44	2.01	28.19

BBVA

It's not Cortez revisited, but Banco Bilbao Vizcaya Argentaria (BBVA) — one of Spain's top banks — is conquering the New World. Although much of its business activity is in Spain (about 60% of its loans), the company also operates in about 10 Latin American countries through subsidiaries BBVA Bancomer in Mexico; Banco Bilbao Vizcaya Argentaria, Chile; and BBVA Banco Francés in Argentina. With some 7,500 offices in more than 30 countries, the bank offers retail, corporate, and institutional banking; investment banking; asset management; insurance; and Internet banking. BBVA also operates in other European countries and is expanding in China, as well as in the US, where it owns Compass Bank.

Adding on to its US operations, BBVA acquired the failed Guaranty Financial Group in 2009. The deal, which was facilitated by the FDIC, fit in with BBVA's strategy of expanding in the Sunbelt, especially Texas. BBVA began to really grow in the US in order to capture more of the lucrative business transacted between the US and Mexico and to access the exploding Spanish-speaking market in the states. Its 2007 acquisition of Compass (now operating as BBVA Compass) for about €7 billion ($9 billion) added more than 400 branches to BBVA's US network. BBVA merged its previously acquired State National Bancshares, Laredo National Bancshares, and Texas Regional Bancshares into Compass.

BBVA has also targeted Asia as another growth market, forming an alliance with China-based CITIC Group. In accordance, the company owns a 30% stake in CITIC International Financial Holdings and in 2009 increased its stake in China Citic Bank to 15%. The move reinforced BBVA's China strategy, increasing its commitment to the region.

In South America BBVA also is expanding. The bank is buying Credit Uruguay Banco from Credit Agricole. The deal will make BBVA one of the largest financial institutions in Uruguay, and expand its branch network by nearly 40 locations.

Bad loans in BBVA's home market of Spain led to lower revenues during the recession. Spain's economy as a whole remained weak through 2010. However, bright spots in places such as Mexico helped lift BBVA. Commercial and residential mortgages began to grow in Mexico in 2010, after the economy contracted a year before.

HISTORY

Banco Bilbao Vizcaya Argentaria (BBVA) is the progeny of the 2000 merger of Banco Bilbao Vizcaya (BBV) and Argentaria, Caja Postal y Banco Hipotecario. BBV formed when Banco de Bilbao and Banco de Vizcaya merged in 1988, while Argentaria, Caja Postal y Banco Hipotecario coalesced from the 1991 merger of six government-owned banks.

In 1857 a group of Basque businessmen banded together to offer loans and other banking services to businesses. The bank — eventually Banco de Bilbao — helped fund the region's industrialization. Its first foray beyond the Basque region was Paris, not Madrid, in 1902. It later entered London, Madrid, and other major European cities.

Franco's rise to power and the isolation of WWII deterred industrial growth. In protectionist Spain, Bilbao bought 16 banks between 1941 and 1943 and formed a unit to focus on US and Latin American partnerships.

In the 1960s Bilbao reorganized and formed a unit focused on industrial growth. It rolled with the punches as banking rules continued to change in the 1970s and 1980s. The bank expanded consumer services, began issuing credit cards (1971), and bought banks that couldn't cope with changing regulations.

To compete in financially deregulated Europe, Spain's overpopulated banking industry began to consolidate in the early 1990s. After #3 Bilbao failed to take over #2 Banco Español de Crédito, it merged with regional rival Banco de Vizcaya.

Formed in 1901 by Basque merchants, Banco de Vizcaya expanded through purchases and had some 200 branches by 1935, including offices in Europe's leading cities. During the post-WWII bust, it bought weaker banks and invested in Spain's industrial complex.

In the 1960s and 1970s, Vizcaya added industrial banking, insurance, personal investment management, and leasing. The bank refocused on international growth, opening branches in London, Mexico City, New York, and other cities. It entered consumer banking and became another participant in the branch race; by 1980 Vizcaya had some 900 offices. Looking to be a strong player in deregulated Europe, the bank merged with Bilbao in 1988; together, the two banks had nearly 3,400 branches.

The merger almost unraveled after Vizcaya chair Pedro Toledo (set to lead the new bank with Bilbao chair José Ángel Sánchez Asiain) died in 1989. The two banks fought over Toledo's replacement until the Bank of Spain suggested in

1990 that Bilbao executive Emilio Ybarra y Churruca become the only chair.

Until 1992 government regulations and strong unions prevented BBV from cutting some 5,000 jobs and 600 branches. After Europe's 1992 deregulation, the company targeted Latin America, buying banks in Mexico and Peru (1995); Argentina, Colombia, and Venezuela (1996); and Brazil and Chile (1997). The merger of rivals Banco Santander and Banco Central Hispanoamericano in 1999 prompted BBV to merge with Argentaria in 2000.

Also in 2000 BBVA bought 30% of Mexico's #2 bank, Grupo Financiero Bancomer, and merged it into its existing Mexican bank, Grupo Financiero BBV-Proburza; the resulting Grupo Financiero BBVA-Bancomer is the country's largest bank. The bank completed the renaming of its subsidiaries to reflect their position as BBVA subsidiaries in 2002.

In 2004 BBVA bought the 40% of Mexico's BBVA Bancomer that it did not already own. To finance about half of the approximately $4 billion bid, the company issued 195 million new shares.

The next year BBVA tried to buy the rest of Italian bank Banca Nazionale del Lavoro (BNL) (it already owned 15%). However, Italian regulatory bodies nixed the deal and BNP Paribas bought BNL. BBVA later sold its stake in the Italian bank.

To break into the US market, BBVA purchased Texas banks Laredo National Bancshares for $850 million in 2005, Texas Regional Bancshares for more than $2 billion in 2006, and State National Bancshares for $480 million in 2007. BBVA expanded its US operations again when it bought Compass Bank in 2007. Two years later BBVA acquired the failed Guaranty Financial Group.

EXECUTIVES

Chairman and CEO: Francisco González Rodríguez, age 66, $5,394,427 total compensation
President and COO: Ángel Cano Fernández, age 49
Head Finance Division: Manuel González Cid
Head Innovation and Technology: Ramón Monell Valls
Head South America: Vicente Rodero Rodero
Head Wholesale Banking and Asset Management: Jose Barreiro Hernández
Head Investor Relations: Tomas Blasco Sánchez
Head Human Resources and Services: Juan Ignacio Apoita Gordo
Head United States: José María García Meyer-Dohner
Head Mexico: Ignacio Deschamps González
Head Legal, Tax, Audit, and Compliance: Eduardo Arbizu Lostao
Head Risk: Manuel Castro
Head Brand and Communication: Gregorio Panadero Illera, age 41
Head Corporate and Business, Spain and Portugal: Juan Asúa Madariaga
Head Strategy and Development: Carlos Torres Vila
Secretary: Domingo Armengol Calvo
Director Investor Relations: Pedro Barahona
Auditors: Deloitte SL

LOCATIONS

HQ: Banco Bilbao Vizcaya Argentaria, S.A.
Plaza San Nicolás, 4
48005 Bilbao, Vizcaya, Spain
Phone: 34-944-875-555 **Fax:** 34-944-876-161
US HQ: 1345 Avenue of the Americas, 45th Fl.
New York, NY 10105
US Phone: 212-728-1500 **US Fax:** 212-333-2906
Web: www.bbva.com

2009 Sales

	% of total
Spain & Portugal	34
Mexico	26
South America	18
USA	12
Other	10
Total	**100**

PRODUCTS/OPERATIONS

2009 Sales

	% of total
Interest	69
Fees & commissions	15
Net gains on financial assets	3
Dividends	1
Other	12
Total	**100**

Selected Subsidiaries and Affiliates

Bancomer (Mexico)
BBVA Banco Francés (Argentina)
BBVA Banco Provincial de Venezuela
BBVA Chile
BBVA Colombia
BBVA Compass (US)
BBVA Continental Group
BBVA Luxinvest, S.A.
BBVA Panama
BBVA Patrimonios (private bank)
BBVA Portugal
BBVA Provincial Group
BBVA Puerto Rico
BBVA Seguros, S.A.
BBVA USA Banshares Group
CITIC International Financial Holdings Limited (Hong Kong, 30%)
Dinero Express
Seguros Bancomer (Mexico)
Uno-e Bank, S.A. (online services)

COMPETITORS

ABN AMRO Group
Banamex
Banco Comercial Português
Banco de la Nación Argentina
Banco do Brasil
Banco Galicia
Banco Popular Español
Bankinter
Banorte
Barclays
BNP Paribas
Credit Suisse
DEPFA BANK
Deutsche Bank
Espírito Santo
Grupo Santander
HSBC
JPMorgan Chase
Santander Río
Société Générale

HISTORICAL FINANCIALS

Company Type: Public

Income Statement

FYE: December 31

	ASSETS ($ mil.)	NET INCOME ($ mil.)	INCOME AS % OF ASSETS	EMPLOYEES
12/09	766,855	6,586	0.9%	103,721
12/08	764,865	7,590	1.0%	108,972
12/07	738,309	9,006	1.2%	111,913
12/06	543,914	6,254	1.1%	95,000
12/05	466,263	4,523	1.0%	94,681
Annual Growth	**13.2%**	**9.8%**	**—**	**2.3%**

2009 Year-End Financials

Equity as % of assets: 5.5%
Return on assets: 0.9%
Return on equity: 16.8%
Long-term debt ($ mil.): 168,855
No. of shares (mil.): 3,748
Dividends
Yield: 1.5%
Payout: 24.7%
Market value ($ mil.): 96,903
Sales ($ mil.): 49,576

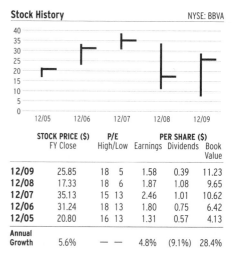

Stock History

NYSE: BBVA

	STOCK PRICE ($) FY Close	P/E High/Low		PER SHARE ($) Earnings	Dividends	Book Value
12/09	25.85	18	5	1.58	0.39	11.23
12/08	17.33	18	6	1.87	1.08	9.65
12/07	35.13	15	13	2.46	1.01	10.62
12/06	31.24	18	13	1.80	0.75	6.42
12/05	20.80	16	13	1.31	0.57	4.13
Annual Growth	**5.6%**	**—**	**—**	**4.8%**	**(9.1%)**	**28.4%**

BCE Inc.

BCE is the Biggest Communications Enterprise in Canada. The company (BCE actually stands for Bell Canada Enterprises) owns Bell Canada, the incumbent provider of long-distance and local telephone access in Ontario and Quebec, with more than 7 million lines in service. It also provides broadband Internet access to 2 million subscribers under the Bell Internet banner and digital video subscriptions to about 2 million viewers via Bell TV. BCE's mobile holdings include wireless carrier Bell Mobility (about 6 million subscribers) and subsidiary Virgin Mobile Canada. Additionally, it owns 44% of Bell Aliant, which serves more than 3 million local phone and 700,000 broadband Internet customers in eastern Canada.

In response to the limited growth potential offered by its traditional wireline voice segment, BCE said in 2009 that it plans to improve customer retention and increase sales of premium services through continued investment in its high-speed data network infrastructure. The company intends to extend the reach of DSL and fiber-optic broadband Internet connections in order to boost its capacity to provide such data-centric services as broadband television.

Late in 2010 BCE acquired the data hosting services business of Quebec-based Hypertec in order to expand its colocation and managed data center services business.

The company bought electronics chain The Source from bankrupt US-based retailer Circuit City in 2009. BCE hopes that the expanded retail presence will give a quick and relatively inexpensive boost to sales of wireless, digital TV, Internet, and home phone services. The Source has about 750 stores located across Canada.

The company announced in 2010 that it would buy the remaining 85% of CTVglobemedia that it did not already own. The deal pays about $1.5 billion in equity and $1.7 billion in debt to

The Woodbridge Company Limited (the Toronto-based holding company of the Thomson family), Ontario Teachers Pension Plan, and Torstar Corporation. CTV operates Canada's top television network with 27 stations nationwide and 30 specialty channels.

HISTORY

Alexander Graham Bell experimented with the telephone in his native Canada before moving to the US in the mid-1870s. His father sold his Canadian patent rights to National Bell Telephone which combined with Canada's Hamilton District Telegraph to form Bell Telephone Company of Canada. Known as Bell Canada, it received a charter in 1880 and settled in Montreal. By 1882 it had 40 exchanges. AT&T owned 48% of the company in 1890, but by 1925 Canadians owned 95% of Bell Canada. (AT&T severed all ties in 1975.)

As telecommunications needs grew, the company began buying smaller exchanges (1954). It acquired a 90% stake in telecom equipment maker Northern Electric in 1957 and the remainder in 1964. After Bell Canada reduced its stake in 1973, Northern became Northern Telecom in 1976 (now Nortel Networks). Bell Canada also invested in a satellite joint venture (Telesat, 1970) and formed Bell Canada International (BCI) to provide international telecom consulting (1976).

In 1983, responding to proposed legislation that would have calculated manufacturing profits in phone rate formulas, Bell created Bell Canada Enterprises (renamed BCE in 1988) as a holding company to separate unregulated businesses from phone carriers. BCE branched out with stakes in gas pipelines (1983) and real estate (1985) but dropped out of the ventures to focus on its core telecom business (1989). It began providing wireless phone service in 1985.

As deregulation rolled into Canada in the 1990s, Bell Canada had to maintain high long-distance rates to subsidize its regulated local service. In 1993 it was denied a rate increase and took a large loss. In 1994 regulators allowed local rate increases. The next year BCE announced 10,000 job cuts and began offering Internet access.

BCE took a loss in 1997, writing down assets in preparation for full competition. Also that year it floated part of BCI, following contracts for cellular systems in Brazil and India. BCE began staging a comeback in 1998 when it sold its shares in Jones Intercable and C&W. It made new investments, including 100% of Telesat Canada, a part of fONOROLA's fiber network, and more than 40% of computer consulting firm CGI Group. Insider Jean Monty (who had steered Nortel's turnaround) became CEO.

Through an alliance with MCI WorldCom (later WorldCom), the company gained access to a global network in 1999. Also that year Ameritech (which became SBC Ameritech) bought a 20% stake in Bell Canada. Bell Canada bought a 20% stake in Manitoba Telecom Services (MTS) that year (it sold its stake in MTS in 2004).

In 2000 Bell Canada spun off nearly all of its 40% Nortel stake to shareholders. That year it bought broadcaster CTV, and went on to buy global broadband services provider Teleglobe in a $5 billion stock deal. BCE combined its broadcasting and Internet portal assets with Thomson's *The Globe and Mail* newspaper to form a new company, Bell Globemedia (now CTVglobemedia), in 2001 (Thomson sold its stake in 2003).

BCE sold US-based long-distance operator Excel Communications to VarTec Telecom in 2002. BCE took full ownership of Internet portal Sympatico in 2002, acquiring the 29% formerly held by Lycos.

A lack of demand for its broadband services forced BCE to reconsider the value of its Teleglobe unit. In 2002 BCE discontinued long-term funding for Teleglobe, which began working to restructure its debt under bankruptcy protection. As 2002 ended Teleglobe was sold to a unit of Ernst & Young, the court-appointed creditors' monitor.

In 2004 BCE sold its Bell Canada directories business to Kohlberg Kravis Roberts & Co. and a unit of the Ontario Teachers' Pension Plan. In the deal, valued at C$3 billion, BCE kept a 10% stake in the new company. BCE then used the proceeds from this sale to buy back the 16% of Bell Canada owned by AT&T Inc. It also bought the 40% of Bell West it did not own.

In an effort to return focus to its core phone business, in late 2006 BCE sold its Telesat Canada unit to Loral Space & Communications and PSP Investments for approximately $3.42 billion. It also sold its stake in CTV globemedia in that year for $1.36 billion. The company sold its Telesat direct-to-home satellite television unit to Loral Space and Communications the following year for about $3 billion.

EXECUTIVES

Chairman, BCE and Bell Canada:
Thomas C. (Tom) O'Neill, age 64
President, CEO, and Director, BCE and Bell Canada:
George A. Cope, age 48
EVP and CFO, BCE and Bell Canada: Siim A. Vanaselja
EVP Field Services, Bell Canada: Mary Ann Turcke
EVP and CIO, Bell Canada: Michael Cole
EVP Corporate Services, BCE and Bell Canada:
David Wells
EVP Network, Bell Canada: J. Trevor Anderson
EVP and Chief Legal and Regulatory Officer, BCE and Bell Canada: Martine Turcotte
EVP Strategic Initiatives, Bell Canada: Charles Brown
SVP Operations, Bell Mobility: John Watson
Chief Brand Officer, Bell Canada; President, Bell Mobility: Wade Oosterman
Group President, Systems and Technology, Bell Canada: Eugene Roman, age 52
President, Wholesale, Bell Canada: Tom Little
President, Wholesale, Bell Canada: John Sweeney
President, Bell Business Markets, Bell Canada:
Stéphane Boisvert
President, Residential Services, Bell Canada:
Kevin W. Crull, age 43
Chief Talent Officer, BCE and Bell Canada:
Léo W. Houle, age 63
Head of Investor Relations: Thane Fotopoulos
Auditors: Deloitte & Touche LLP

LOCATIONS

HQ: BCE Inc.
  1, carrefour Alexander-Graham-Bell, Bldg. A, 8th Fl.
  Verdun, Quebec H3E 3B3, Canada
Phone: 514-870-8777   **Fax:** 514-786-3970
Web: www.bce.ca

PRODUCTS/OPERATIONS

2009 Sales

	% of total
Bell	
Bell Wireline	58
Bell Wireless	26
Bell Aliant	16
Total	**100**

COMPETITORS

Canada Payphone
CanWest Global Communications
COGECO
Globalive
MTS Allstream
Primus Telecommunications
Quebecor
Rogers Communications
Shaw Broadcast Services
Shaw Communications
Skype
Sprint Nextel
TELUS
Vonage
Yak Communications

HISTORICAL FINANCIALS

Company Type: Public

Income Statement

FYE: December 31

	REVENUE ($ mil.)	NET INCOME ($ mil.)	NET PROFIT MARGIN	EMPLOYEES
12/09	16,900	1,656	9.8%	50,662
12/08	14,473	772	5.3%	50,102
12/07	18,193	4,131	22.7%	54,000
12/06	15,187	1,721	11.3%	54,434
12/05	16,384	1,683	10.3%	60,001
Annual Growth	0.8%	(0.4%)	—	(4.1%)

2009 Year-End Financials

Debt ratio: 72.5%
Return on equity: 13.0%
Cash ($ mil.): 655
Current ratio: 0.69
Long-term debt ($ mil.): 9,814

No. of shares (mil.): 756
Dividends
  Yield: 5.7%
  Payout: 75.1%
Market value ($ mil.): 19,880

Stock History

NYSE: BCE

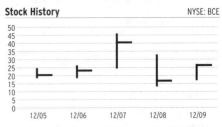

	STOCK PRICE ($) FY Close	P/E High/Low		PER SHARE ($) Earnings	Dividends	Book Value
12/09	26.31	13	9	2.01	1.51	21.41
12/08	16.76	39	17	0.83	0.61	18.74
12/07	40.47	9	5	4.96	1.45	23.22
12/06	23.15	13	10	1.93	1.24	15.17
12/05	20.44	13	10	1.91	1.22	16.71
Annual Growth	6.5%	—	—	1.3%	5.5%	6.4%

Benetton Group

If Benetton had a theme song, it could be "We Are the World." Italy's largest clothing maker, The Benetton Group pushes a global attitude in its ads while colorfully dressing customers in about 120 countries through some 6,300 franchised Benetton stores, department stores, and megastores. Benetton's clothing — primarily casual knitwear and sportswear for men, women, and children — bears labels such as United Colors of Benetton (about 50% of sales) and upscale Sisley and Sisley Young, which ring up about 15% of sales. Other brands include Playlife and Killer Loop. Complementing its fashion apparel business, Benetton's textile division makes and sells fabrics, yarns, and labels to third parties.

The worldwide financial crisis and weak retail environment clipped Benetton's sales and profits. Gerolamo Caccia Dominioni stepped down as CEO in April 2010 after just three years at the helm. The CEO's duties have been split between two new directors: Biagio Chiarolanza and Franco Furnò. Luciano and Alessandro Benetton serve as chairman and executive deputy chairman and together with Chiarolanza and Furnò constitute the executive management of the firm. Members of the Benetton family own about two-thirds of the business.

Despite its global outlook, more than 80% of Benetton Group's sales are still rung up in Europe, which continues to be plagued by a sluggish economy and weak demand. Consequently, Benetton has been looking to new markets for growth in Asia (China, India, and South Korea), Eastern Europe (Russia), and the Mediterranean (Greece, Spain, and Turkey). In a bid to enter the Mexican market, the Italian firm has signed a deal with Sears Roebuck de México to develop its brand there. The company expects sales from other emerging markets (China, India, and Turkey) to triple by mid-2011.

The company operates about 100 stores in China (including flagship stores in Beijing and Shenzhen), and has plans to add 150 Sisley stores there by 2011. In the Middle East, Benetton has plans to open 60 new stores in Dubai. During 2008 it opened its first Benetton Man store in New Delhi.

Benetton is also focused on attracting younger customers to its stores. The retailer has expanded its low-priced collections of denim, polo shirts, and sweatshirts. It also launched the Benetton Baby label in 2007. The company now operates about 35 Benetton Baby stores.

Benetton's multimedia enterprises fall under the Fabrica umbrella, which Benetton describes as a "communication research and development center," that the company founded in 2000. Fabrica produces films, funds avant-garde music projects, and publishes the magazine *Colors*.

HISTORY

Luciano Benetton began selling men's clothing while still in his teens in post-WWII Treviso, Italy. His younger, artistic sister, Giuliana, knitted colorful and striking sweaters for a small, local clientele. In 1955 the two pooled their skills. Giuliana sold Luciano's accordion and a younger brother's bicycle, raising enough money to purchase a knitting machine. Luciano then marketed her moderately priced sweaters.

Demand for their clothes grew, and the pair did so well that 10 years later they built a factory in Ponzano, near Treviso. Siblings Gilberto and bicycleless Carlo joined the business, and the first Benetton store opened in Belluno, in the Alps, in 1968. By 1975 Benetton had 200 stores in Italy and had set up headquarters in a 17th-century villa. In 1979 the company opened five stores in the US.

Through the early to mid-1980s, the company averaged one store opening a day; Benetton was the first Western retailer to enter Eastern Europe. The company's controversial advertising program began in 1984 with ads depicting such provocative images as then-president Ronald Reagan with AIDS lesions.

When it went public in 1986, Benetton had almost 600 stores in the US. That year it established a factory in the US. In the late 1980s Edizione Holding, the family's investment firm, also bought a hotel chain and ski equipment maker Nordica.

Benetton began losing US market share during the late 1980s. Competition from The Gap and The Limited hurt, and overexpansion brought complaints from franchisees that the stores were cannibalizing each other's sales. (In New York City there were seven stores on Fifth Avenue alone.) In the early 1990s The Gap established stores in the already-mature European market, and Benetton began looking for new markets.

Edizione increased its investments in those years, acquiring 80% of Prince Manufacturing, a US maker of tennis equipment, and purchased a 50% interest in the TWR group, a race car manufacturer. In 1995 Benetton won its second lawsuit against German retailers that refused to pay for merchandise because they said sales had been hurt by the company's shock advertising. The next year it opened a United Colors of Benetton megastore on Fifth Avenue in New York City, the first to combine Edizione's clothing, sporting goods, and accessories under one roof.

Benetton bought Edizione's sports equipment and apparel collection, Benetton Sportsystem. Trying to win back US consumers, Benetton in 1998 cut a deal to sell Benetton USA-brand clothing in Sears, Roebuck & Co. stores. In early 2000, however, Sears yanked the Italian goods from its store after customers complained about Benetton's anti-death-penalty ad campaign. Soon after, Benetton and controversial ad man Oliviero Toscani parted ways.

In 2001 Benetton announced plans to recapture the US market share it once held by opening megastore formats (starting with three new stores in Manhattan). Later, Carlo Gilardi stepped down as joint managing director, and Luigi de Puppi (former CEO of Electrolux Zanussi) was named his successor.

Just weeks before its 2003 shareholders meeting, the company announced that de Puppi would step down, since his mandate to clear out Benetton's ailing sports divisions was completed with sales of Rollerblade, Nordica, and Prince.

In May 2005 Alessandro Benetton, son of Chairman Luciano Benetton, was named deputy chairman of the company's board, a title he now shares with his uncle Carlo.

In 2006 CEO Silvano Cassano resigned abruptly after having completed a three-year reorganization plan, according to the company. Cassano remained on the board. Gerolamo Caccia Dominioni, most recently vice chairman and COO of Warner Music Group's Warner unit, was named to the CEO post in March 2007.

In January 2008 Benetton's shares were delisted from the NYSE.

EXECUTIVES

Chairman: Luciano Benetton, age 75
Executive Deputy Chairman: Alessandro Benetton, age 46
Deputy Chairman: Carlo Benetton, age 66
COO and Director: Biagio Chiarolanza, age 48
Executive Director: Franco Furnò
CFO: Alberto Nathansohn, age 52
CIO and CTO: Adolfo Pastorelli, age 54
Director Worldwide Human Resources: Giovanni Di Vaio, age 55
Head Press and Communication: Federico Sartor
Head Administration and Reporting: Lorenzo Zago
Head Legal and Corporate Affairs: Andrea Pezzangora
Head Investor Relations: Mara Di Giorgio
Auditors: PricewaterhouseCoopers SpA

LOCATIONS

HQ: Benetton Group S.p.A.
Villa Minelli
31050 Ponzano Veneto, Treviso, Italy
Phone: 39-0422-519036   **Fax:** 39-0422-519930
US HQ: 597 5th Ave., New York, NY 10017
US Phone: 212-593-0290   **US Fax:** 212-371-1438
Web: www.benetton.com

2009 Sales

	% of total
Europe	
Italy	48
Other countries	34
Asia	14
Americas	3
Other regions	1
Total	**100**

PRODUCTS/OPERATIONS

2009 Sales by Brand

	% of total
United Colors of Benetton (UCB) Adult	51
UCB Kids	31
Sisley	16
Playlife	2
Total	**100**

2009 Sales

	% of total
Apparel	95
Textile	5
Total	**100**

Selected Brands

Casual wear
    Sisley (higher-fashion men's and women's clothing)
    United Colors of Benetton

Sportswear
    Killer Loop (snowboarding clothing)
    Playlife (sporty leisure wear)

Selected Products

Baby products
Dresses
Handbags
Hats
Knitwear
Perfume
Shirts
Shoes
Socks
Sportswear
Sunglasses
Underwear
Watches

HISTORICAL FINANCIALS

Company Type: Public

Income Statement

FYE: December 31

	REVENUE ($ mil.)	NET INCOME ($ mil.)	NET PROFIT MARGIN	EMPLOYEES
12/09	2,937	169	5.8%	9,511
12/08	2,999	222	7.4%	9,766
12/07	3,069	221	7.2%	8,896
12/06	2,523	165	6.5%	8,894
12/05	2,097	133	6.3%	7,978
Annual Growth	8.8%	6.2%	—	4.5%

2009 Year-End Financials

Debt ratio: 29.5%
Return on equity: 8.5%
Cash ($ mil.): 193
Current ratio: 1.54
Long-term debt ($ mil.): 607

No. of shares (mil.): 183
Dividends
  Yield: 4.5%
  Payout: 39.2%
Market value ($ mil.): 1,634

Stock History

Pink Sheets: BNGPY

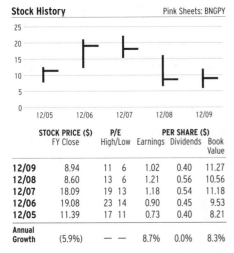

	STOCK PRICE ($) FY Close	P/E High/Low		PER SHARE ($) Earnings	Dividends	Book Value
12/09	8.94	11	6	1.02	0.40	11.27
12/08	8.60	13	6	1.21	0.56	10.56
12/07	18.09	19	13	1.18	0.54	11.18
12/06	19.08	23	14	0.90	0.45	9.53
12/05	11.39	17	11	0.73	0.40	8.21
Annual Growth	(5.9%)	—	—	8.7%	0.0%	8.3%

Bertelsmann AG

This company is so big, it takes up space on the bookshelf, the magazine stand, and on television. Bertelsmann is one of the world's leading media conglomerates with operations in publishing and TV. It owns about 90% of RTL Group, Europe's #1 TV broadcaster with more than 40 channels operating in a dozen countries. Bertelsmann also owns Random House, the world's top trade book publisher, as well as 75% of magazine publisher Gruner + Jahr. In addition, its arvato unit is a leading provider of distribution, manufacturing, and other business services to media companies. Carl Bertelsmann founded the company in 1835. His descendants, the Mohn family, control the business through the Bertelsmann Stiftung foundation.

Bertelsmann is certainly one of the largest, but also one of the very few, media conglomerates to dominate the European continent: While its TV and publishing businesses range across dozens of countries, most of the company's nearest competitors restrict their activities to one or two countries.

But being a global powerhouse in publishing and broadcasting has made Bertelsmann vulnerable during the global recession. Advertising revenue suffered steep declines in many markets, while many of Gruner + Jahr's magazine titles struggle to hold on to readers in the age of digital distribution and expanding competition.

The company's response to the economic challenge during 2009 was to curtail costs through layoffs and other restructuring efforts. Its Random House unit, hit especially hard by a downturn in worldwide book sales, cut staff across several imprints, including Crown Publishing and Knopf Doubleday. Similarly, Gruner + Jahr trimmed its employee count by about 10%.

RTL Group is working to diversify away from commercial advertising by expanding its pay-TV and digital media operations. The broadcasting group is also buoyed by its FremantleMedia production unit, responsible for spawning *Pop Idol*, *American Idol*, and all the other *Idol* competition programs around the world. Random House, meanwhile, is eyeing growth of electronic publishing thanks to popular reading devices such as the Amazon Kindle and the Apple iPad.

Bertelsmann's arvato services unit, normally an anchor of strength and stability, also dealt with the challenge of recessionary pressure as demand for commercial printing declined and worldwide DVD sales plunged. The company sees future growth coming from expanding markets in Asia, including China and India. During 2009 arvato launched a 51%-owned supply chain management joint venture in China with telecommunications providers Telling Group and Sinomaster Group.

Another growth area for the company is music publishing royalties. In 2008 Bertelsmann launched BMG Rights Management, a joint venture with US-based private equity firm KKR, which controls the rights to more than 75,000 songs. BMG acquired US-based publisher Cherry Lane Music Publishing the following year. Bertelsmann had abandoned the music business earlier in 2008 when the company sold its 50% stake in Sony BMG Music Entertainment (now Sony Music Entertainment) to former joint venture partner Sony for $1.2 billion in cash. In 2006 it sold BMG Music Publishing to Universal Music Group for $2.1 billion.

HISTORY

Carl Bertelsmann founded his publishing company C. Bertelsmann Verlag in Gütersloh, Germany, in 1835. The company primarily published hymnals and religious materials, expanding into newspapers during the 1860s. Heinrich Mohn, a fourth-generation descendant, took over the company in 1921 and expanded its operations to include popular fiction, which helped Bertelsmann expand to more than 400 employees by 1939.

During WWII the company published books and propaganda material for the German army, but was closed by the Nazi government in 1944 as it was not considered important to the war effort. (The company had maintained for decades it was closed because it produced religious materials, but contrary evidence was uncovered in 2000 by historians working at the behest of the company.) After WWII Mohn's son, Reinhard (who had been captured by the Allies and interned in a Kansas POW camp), returned to Germany determined to rebuild the company.

Bertelsmann boosted book sales by launching book clubs in Germany during the 1950s and bought Germany's UFA (TV and film production) in 1964. It took a minority interest in publisher Gruner + Jahr in 1969, taking a controlling stake in 1973. In the US, Bertelsmann bought 51% of Bantam Books in 1977 (and the rest in 1981) and Arista Records in 1979. In 1986 it took control of Doubleday Publishing and bought RCA Records (forming Bertelsmann Music Group the next year). Mohn transferred substantial non-voting shares in the company to the Bertelsmann Foundation (Bertelsmann Stiftung) in 1993.

Bertelsmann acquired book publisher Random House in 1996. In addition, Thomas Middelhoff became chairman and CEO in 1998. The next year Bertelsmann acquired some 85% of scientific publisher Springer Verlag. Also in 1999 Reinhard Mohn transferred his controlling shares in the company to Bertelsmann Verwaltungsgesellschaft, a firm controlled by Bertelsmann executives and the Mohn family.

In 2000 Bertelsmann merged CLT-Ufa with Pearson TV to form RTL Group. (Bertelsmann got a 37% stake.) Bertelsmann bought Groupe Bruxelles Lambert's 30% stake in RTL Group in 2001. As part of the deal Bruxelles gained a 25% stake in Bertelsmann, with the understanding that it would be able to float its interest to the public in four years. Also that year, it bought Pearson's 22% stake in RTL Group.

The company's board fired Middelhoff in 2002, citing disagreements over the direction of the company. He was replaced by Gunter Thielen, chairman of Bertelsmann's arvato business unit. Music subsidiary BMG Entertainment merged with Sony Music in 2004 to create Sony BMG Music Entertainment, a joint venture with Sony Corporation.

After a contentious few months in 2006 when Groupe Bruxelles Lambert almost forced an IPO of the notoriously private media firm, the Mohn family bought out Lambert's interest in the company for $5.7 billion (leaving the Mohns with a 23% interest in Bertelsmann, and the Bertelsmann Foundation owning the rest). Later that year, the company sold BMG Music Publishing (which was not part of the BMG-Sony Music merger) to Universal Music Group for $2.1 billion.

Thielen stepped down as CEO of Bertelsmann at the beginning of 2008 and was replaced by Hartmut Ostrowski.

EXECUTIVES

Chairman and CEO Supervisory Board: Gunter Thielen, age 68
Vice Chairman Supervisory Board: Jürgen F. Strube, age 42
Chairman Executive Board and CEO:
Hartmut Ostrowski, age 52
EVP Corporate Treasury and Finance: Roger Schweitzer
EVP, Direct Group: Gerd Bührig
EVP, Bertelsmann US (BInc.): Rob Sorrentino
EVP, Bertelsmann Digital Media Investments:
Richard Sarnoff, age 51
EVP Audit and Consulting: Marc Wössner
EVP Financial Reporting and Accounting:
Martin Rembde
EVP Bertelsmann China and Bertelsmann Asia Investment: Annabelle Long
EVP Controlling and Strategy: Günther Grüger, age 59
EVP Education and Corporate Development:
Dirk Refäuter
EVP Legal Department: Urlich Koch
EVP Corporate Communications: Thorsten Strauß
EVP Tax Department: Michael Beisheim, age 45
EVP Human Resources: Immanuel Hermreck, age 38
Chairman and CEO, Random House: Markus Dohle, age 41
CEO, RTL Group: Gerhard Zeiler, age 55
CEO, Gruner + Jahr AG: Bernd Buchholz, age 49
Board Member; Vice CEO, Bertelsmann Stiftung, and Chairwoman, Bertelsmann Verwaltungsgesellschaft:
Liz Mohn
Auditors: KPMG Deutsche Treuhand-Gesellschaft AG

LOCATIONS

HQ: Bertelsmann AG
Carl-Bertelsmann-Strasse 270
D-33311 Gütersloh, Germany
Phone: 49-5241-80-0   **Fax:** 49-5241-80-62321
US HQ: 1540 Broadway, 35th Fl., New York, NY 10036
US Phone: 212-541-2800   **US Fax:** 212-541-2810
Web: www.bertelsmann.de

2009 Sales

	% of total
Europe	
Germany	35
Other countries	48
US	12
Other regions	5
Total	**100**

PRODUCTS/OPERATIONS

2009 Sales

	% of total
Products	46
Advertising	27
Services	18
Rights & royalties	9
Total	**100**

2009 Sales

	% of total
RTL Group	34
arvato	31
Gruner + Jahr	16
Random House	11
DirectGroup	8
Total	**100**

Selected Operations

arvato (media services)
DirectGroup (direct consumer sales)
Gruner + Jahr (75%, magazine publishing)
Random House (book publishing, US)
RTL Group (91%, television broadcasting and production, Luxembourg)

COMPETITORS

Amazon.com
Axel Springer
Bauer Verlagsgruppe
CANAL+
Cinram
Disney
Hearst Corporation
ITV
Lagardère
NBC Universal
News Corp.
ProSiebenSat
Time Warner
Verlagsgruppe Georg von Holtzbrinck
Viacom

HISTORICAL FINANCIALS

Company Type: Private

Income Statement

FYE: December 31

	REVENUE ($ mil.)	NET INCOME ($ mil.)	NET PROFIT MARGIN	EMPLOYEES
12/09	22,020	50	0.2%	102,983
12/08	22,718	381	1.7%	106,083
12/07	18,758	405	2.2%	102,397
12/06	25,459	3,198	12.6%	97,132
12/05	21,187	1,233	5.8%	91,559
Annual Growth	**1.0%**	**(55.1%)**	**—**	**3.0%**

Net Income History

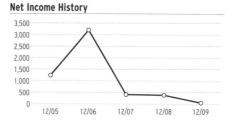

BHP Billiton

Two heads — or headquarters — are better than one. Aussie minerals and oil company BHP Limited acquired UK miner Billiton plc in 2001. The result is a two-headquartered, dual-listed company that is run as a single entity with the same board of directors and management. On the Melbourne side is BHP Billiton Limited; the London side is BHP Billiton Plc, and they collectively are known as BHP Billiton. The company ranks among the world's top producers of iron ore and coal (thermal and metallurgical) and is a major producer of petroleum products such as crude oil and natural gas. Other units produce aluminum, base metals, diamonds, manganese, and stainless steel materials. BHP Billiton has operations worldwide.

Full pockets allowed BHP Billiton to jump on the potash bandwagon in 2010, making a blockbuster $39 billion offer for Potash Corporation of Saskatchewan. Potash's board immediately rejected the offer, calling it inadequate. Following the Potash board's actions, BHP Billiton upped the ante, making a direct pitch to Potash shareholders. Potash later filed suit in US federal court to block the takeover bid.

Potash is a primary raw material in the manufacture of fertilizers and has been a top priority for the global titans of mining, such as Vale. Earlier in 2010 BHP Billiton acquired Athabasca Potash Inc. (API) for about C$340 million ($320 million US). API's projects are located in Saskatchewan, in close proximity to BHP Billiton's own potash operations.

Due to the strong demand, BHP Billiton has increased production of iron ore, coking coal, and manganese. The shifting nature of the market, though, changes the company's highest-grossing segments. On the petroleum side, the company is continuing to acquire oil and gas exploration leases in the Gulf of Mexico.

The company has tried several times to make a major move since the beginning of 2008, when it first approached chief rival Rio Tinto with an offer that valued that company at almost $150 billion. Rio Tinto's board rejected the notion out of hand, but BHP Billiton seemed intent on pursuing the deal, which would create the world's largest minerals company and one of the largest regardless of industry. Months later, at the end of 2008 and amid the global economic meltdown, BHP Billiton announced that the deal no longer provided value to its shareholders and called it off.

The company also operates a coal producing joint venture with Mitsubishi that has projects in Australia. In 2008 BHP Billiton Mitsubishi Alliance (BMA) spent $2.4 billion to buy the Saraji East metallurgical coal project from New Hope Corporation. Each of BMA's owners paid $1.2 billion to New Hope for the project, which lies adjacent to one of BMA's coal mines.

HISTORY

In 1883 Charles Rasp, a boundary rider for the Mt. Gipps sheep station, believed valuable ore lay in the Broken Hill outcrop in New South Wales, Australia. He gathered a few young speculators, and The Broken Hill Proprietary Company (BHP) was incorporated in 1885. BHP immediately found a massive lode of silver, lead, and zinc. None of the founders knew how to run a mine, so they recruited US engineers William Patton and Herman Schlapp. From the beginning, labor and management clashed. The founding directors set up the head office in Melbourne, far from the mine, and gambled with gold sovereigns in the boardroom. But the miners worked in dangerous conditions. An 1892 labor strike was the first of BHP's bitter strikes.

In 1902 the new general manager, Guillaume Delprat, invented a flotation process that recovered valuable metals from iron ore waste. Delprat also foresaw a future in steel, although Australia had no steel industry. BHP commissioned the Newcastle steelworks in 1915 and soon became the country's largest steel producer. BHP's 1935 purchase of Australian Iron and Steel, its only competitor, gave it a virtual steel monopoly, while high tariffs protected it from outside competition. Its exhausted Broken Hill mine was closed that year.

In the 1960s BHP got into oil when it partnered with Esso Standard, the Australian subsidiary of Standard Oil of New Jersey, for offshore exploration. In 1967 the partners found oil in the Bass Strait, which soon supplied 70% of Australia's petroleum. In the 1960s and 1970s, BHP began expanding its iron ore, manganese, and coal interests. Meanwhile, public opposition mounted to BHP's market power and labor practices, and in 1972 the government took steps to limit BHP's power, removing some subsidies and tax breaks.

The weak steel market of the 1970s and 1980s caused BHP to lay off almost a third of its steelworkers in 1983, but with government intervention, BHP radically improved its steel productivity. In 1984 BHP bought Utah International's mining assets from General Electric (including Chile's rich Escondida copper mine). In 1986 corporate raider Robert Holmes à Court took a run at BHP; BHP decided to become an international mining company to prevent further raids. Its acquisitions in the late 1980s included ERG Inc. and Monsanto Oil (combined into BHP Americas), Aquila Steel, and Pacific Refining in Hawaii.

A peace deal with Holmes à Court gave BHP about 37% of Foster's Brewing, but in 1992 BHP took a $700 million write-down after Foster's stock declined. With new worries over Asia's economic troubles, BHP soon was struggling. In 1997 BHP sold most of its stake in Foster's, and three senior executives resigned.

As BHP's woes continued, CEO John Prescott resigned; Paul Anderson was recruited from Duke Energy to succeed Prescott. In 1999 D. R. Argus took over as chairman, replacing Jeremy Ellis. In a restructuring move, the company sold its engineering, power, insurance and information technology businesses in 1999 and 2000. BHP began to sell $2 billion worth of steel operations (including its long product unit, OneSteel). In 2000 the company shortened its official name to BHP Limited.

BHP acquired Billiton in 2001, forming BHP Billiton Ltd. and BHP Billiton plc. In order to focus on its minerals and oil and gas operations, in 2002 BHP Billiton spun off its steel business as BHP Steel.

In 2005, BHP Billiton acquired metals and minerals company WMC Resources, which had been the target of the Swiss mining heavyweight Xstrata. Its offer of $7.3 billion surpassed Xstrata's and was accepted and endorsed by the WMC board. The addition of WMC added significantly to BHP Billiton's copper, nickel, and uranium operations.

EXECUTIVES

Chairman: Jacques A. (Jac) Nasser, age 62
CEO and Director: Marius Kloppers, age 48
Group Executive and CFO: Alex Vanselow, age 48
CIO: Chris Crozier
Group Executive and Chief People Officer:
Karen J. Wood, age 54
Group Executive and Chief Executive, Ferrous and Coal: Marcus P. Randolph, age 54
Group Executive and Chief Commercial Officer:
Alberto Calderon, age 50
Group Executive and Chief Executive, Petroleum:
J. Michael (Mike) Yeager, age 57
Group Executive and Chief Executive, Non-Ferrous:
Andrew Mackenzie, age 52
Group Company Secretary and Director:
Jane F. McAloon, age 46
President, Manganese: Tom Schutte
President, Marketing: Mike Henry
President, Stainless Steel Materials: Glenn Kellow
President, Manganese: Peter Beaven
President, Iron Ore: Ian R. Ashby
President and COO, New Mexico Coal: Jac Fourie
Investor Relations, Americas: Scott Espenshade
Media Relations Australia: Samantha Evans
Auditors: KPMG Audit Plc

LOCATIONS

HQ: BHP Billiton Limited
180 Lonsdale St., BHP Billiton Centre
Melbourne 3000, Australia
Phone: 61-3-9609-3333   **Fax:** 61-3-9609-3015
US HQ: 1360 Post Oak Blvd., Ste. 150
Houston, TX 77056
US Phone: 713-961-8500   **US Fax:** 713-961-8400
Web: www.bhpbilliton.com

2010 Sales

	$ mil.	% of total
Asia		
China	13,236	25
Japan	5,336	10
Other countries	9,840	19
Europe	9,843	19
North America	5,547	11
Australia	4,515	9
South America	2,013	4
Southern Africa	1,227	2
Other regions	1,241	2
Total	**52,798**	**100**

PRODUCTS/OPERATIONS

2010 Sales

	$ mil.	% of total
Iron ore	11,139	21
Base metals	10,409	20
Coal		
Metallurgical coal	6,059	11
Energy coal	4,265	8
Petroleum	8,782	17
Aluminum	4,353	8
Stainless steel materials	3,617	7
Manganese	2,150	5
Diamonds & specialty products	1,272	2
Other	752	1
Total	**52,798**	**100**

Selected Divisions

Coal
  Metallurgical
  Energy
Iron ore
Petroleum
  Crude oil
  Ethane
  LPG
  Natural gas
Base metals
  Copper
  Gold
  Lead
  Silver
  Zinc
Aluminum
  Alumina
  Aluminum
  Bauxite
Manganese
Stainless steel materials
  Cobalt
  Ferrochrome
  Nickel
Diamonds and specialty products
  Diamonds
  Potash
  Titanium minerals

COMPETITORS

Alcoa
Anglo American
ArcelorMittal
BP
Chevron
Chinalco
Codelco
ConocoPhillips
Corus Group
Exxon Mobil
Fortescue Metals
Freeport-McMoRan
Koch Industries, Inc.
Kumba Iron Ore
Marathon Oil
Newmont Mining
Nippon Steel
Norsk Hydro ASA
Repsol YPF
Rio Tinto Limited
Royal Dutch Shell
Teck
TOTAL
Vale
Xstrata

HISTORICAL FINANCIALS

Company Type: Public

Income Statement

FYE: June 30

	REVENUE ($ mil.)	NET INCOME ($ mil.)	NET PROFIT MARGIN	EMPLOYEES
6/10	52,798	12,722	24.1%	39,570
6/09	50,211	5,877	11.7%	40,990
6/08	59,473	15,390	25.9%	41,732
6/07	39,498	13,416	34.0%	39,947
6/06	32,153	10,450	32.5%	40,002
Annual Growth	13.2%	5.0%	—	(0.3%)

2010 Year-End Financials

Debt ratio: 28.9%
Return on equity: —
Cash ($ mil.): 12,456
Current ratio: 1.93
Long-term debt ($ mil.): 14,042

No. of shares (mil.): 3,358
Dividends
  Yield: 2.7%
  Payout: 36.4%
Market value ($ mil.): 208,185

Stock History

NYSE: BHP

	STOCK PRICE ($) FY Close	P/E High/Low		PER SHARE ($) Earnings	Dividends	Book Value
6/10	61.99	18	11	4.56	1.66	14.45
6/09	54.73	37	12	2.11	1.64	11.90
6/08	85.19	17	9	5.50	1.12	11.41
6/07	59.75	13	8	4.58	0.77	8.83
6/06	43.07	15	8	3.45	0.64	7.21
Annual Growth	9.5%	—	—	7.2%	26.9%	19.0%

Grupo Bimbo

Do not take this Bimbo lightly. In Mexico — where *pan Bimbo* is synonymous with soft, white sandwich bread — Grupo Bimbo is that country's largest commercial baking operation. It is one of the top bakers in the world as well, with some 35% of its sales taking place outside of Mexico. Offering 7,000 products under 150 brand names, Grupo Bimbo produces bread, cookies, and tortillas under the Tía Rosa, Bimbo, Wonder, and Marinela brands. It also makes salty snack foods under the Barcel brand and candies under the Ricolino brand. Not content with dominating the Latin American bread markets, the company owns Texas-based Mrs. Baird's and Bimbo Bakeries USA, both of which serve the southwestern US.

In a bid to bolster its position in Mexico's confectionery market, the baker in 2010 agreed to acquire confectioner Dulces Vero, a maker of lollipops, gumdrops, taffy, and other sweets that are staples in Mexican schools and sold by street vendors. Once the deal is complete, Dulces Vero will become part of Bimbo's Barcel snacks division. The pending purchase follows Bimbo's 2009 acquisition of US fresh baking business Weston Foods. It paid a whopping US$2.5 billion in cash for the bread maker. The purchase added the Arnold, Brownberry, Entenmann's, Freihofer, Stroehmann, and Thomas' brand names to Bimbo's US offerings and expanded the company's distribution platform and product portfolio; it also made Bimbo a top player in the competitive US bread market.

The company has expanded northward through acquisitions and the introduction of its brands to the growing US Hispanic population. Its Bimbo Bakeries USA offers the Arnold, Boboli, Brownberry, Marinela, Mrs. Baird's, Orowheat, and Tía Rosa brands. The company also has a presence in China, selling bread and pastries under the Bimbo brand from its operations in Beijing. It is player in Europe's gummy-candy market, owning a candy plant in the Czech Republic. In addition, Grupo Bimbo makes industrial baking ovens.

Grupo Bimbo is majority-owned by CEO Daniel Servitje and the Servitje family, which founded it in 1945 and named it for the bear in the company logo.

HISTORY

Starting with 10 trucks and bread in cellophane wrappers, in 1945 Lorenzo Servitje and associates, including Jaime Jorba, began deliveries of their Bimbo-brand breads around Mexico City.

Two years later distribution spread to three other cities. Steady growth for Grupo Industrial Bimbo followed during the 1950s and 1960s, with new plants opening in Guadalajara and Monterrey. In 1962 Jorba left the company, returned to Spain, and created Bimbo España. In 1964, when Continental Bakeries introduced Wonder Bread to Mexico, Bimbo countered with a similarly positioned bread line using the licensed US Sunbeam brand.

By 1972 the company was firmly established as the bread-market leader in Mexico when it began making corn tortillas. The next year the company founded Frexport, its jam and jelly unit.

The company went public in 1980 but remained firmly under the control of the Servitje family. A major leap in the company's vision for itself came when it created a bun for McDonald's. Bimbo won the exclusive contract to supply buns to Mexico's McDonald's in 1985. In 1986 Bimbo acquired rival Continental Bakeries' Wonder Bread brand in Mexico, thus securing a virtual monopoly on the Mexican packaged-bread market. Future growth would come from international expansion.

During the 1990s Bimbo began a steady stream of acquisitions and construction of plants in Guatemala (1990), Chile (1992), Venezuela (1993), and Peru (1998). Daniel Servitje Montull was named CEO of Bimbo in 1997.

In the mid-1990s Bimbo began doing contract work for German confectioner Park Lane, leading up to its 1998 purchase of Park Lane, and it established a factory in the Czech Republic. However, the company's boldest move was its 1998 purchase of Mrs. Baird's, the largest family-owned US bakery, based in Fort Worth, Texas. The company formed Bimbo Bakeries USA to control the Mrs. Baird's business and move closer to its US competition. In 1999 it acquired the Four-S bakery business in California. Four-S came with the popular local Weber brand of bread.

In 1999 the company shortened its name to Grupo Bimbo. That year it was awarded the exclusive contract to supply buns to McDonald's in Colombia, Peru, and Venezuela.

During 2000 Grupo Bimbo completed the spinoff of its flour mills and processed jellies units, with the agreement that they would continue supplying Grupo Bimbo. Roberto Servitje Achutegui, grandson of founder Lorenzo Servitje, left the company that year to run a new company, Grupo Altex. In 2001 Grupo Bimbo purchased a bread baking operation in Costa Rica from tortilla-giant and rival Gruma.

In 2002 Grupo Bimbo purchased five western US Orowheat production facilities from George Weston. The acquisition gave the company access to some well-known consumer brands including Thomas' English Muffins, Entenmann's, and Boboli. That year it also closed its Mrs. Baird's bakery facility in Dallas.

As part of its strategy to concentrate on its consumer businesses, in 2003 Bimbo sold its 42% stake in packaging business Novacel to French aluminum company Pechiney (now a part of Rio Tinto Alcan) for $38 million. It also closed its Dallas Orowheat bakery that year. Bimbo, along with a consortium of other companies, took over Argentinean bakery business Compania de Alimentos de Fargo in 2003. Bimbo's stake in Fargo is 30%.

In 2004 the company bought three Mexican confectionery companies: Joyco de México, Alimentos Duval, and Lolimen. Bimbo expanded into frozen bakery-product manufacturing that year, as well, when it formed a joint venture with Rich Products to produce frozen and partially baked goods under the Fripan brand name.

During 2005 the company bought Colombian bread maker Lalo, Chilean pastry manufacturer Lagos el Sur, Mexican pastry manufacturer Pastelerías El Globo, and Mexican confectioner La Corona. It purchased two Uruguayan bakery companies in 2006: Walter M. Doldan y Cia and Los Sorchantes.

Marking its entry into China, in 2006 the company purchased the Chinese unit of Spanish baker Panrico SA.

EXECUTIVES

Chairman: Roberto Servitje, age 82
CEO and Alternate Chairman: Daniel Servitje, age 51
President: Javier Augusto González, age 54
CFO: Guillermo Quiroz, age 56
Chief Human Relations Officer: Javier Millán, age 61
Chief Commercial Officer: Rosalío Rodriguez, age 57
SEVP: Pablo Elizondo, age 56
Secretary: Luis Miguel Briola
Director, Marketing: José Manuel González
Director Institutional Relations:
  Martha Eugenia Hernández
Director Investor Relations: Armando Giner
President, Barcel, S.A. de C.V.: Gabino Gómez
President, Latin America Division (OLA): Alberto Díaz, age 59
President, Bimbo Bakeries USA, Inc. (BBU):
  Reynaldo Reyna, age 54
Auditors: Galaz, Yamazaki, Ruiz Urquiza, S.C.

LOCATIONS

HQ: Grupo Bimbo, S.A.B. de C.V.
  Prolongación Paseo de la Reforma No. 1000,
  Colonia Peña Blanca Santa Fe
  Delegación Álvaro Obregón
  01210 México, D.F., Mexico
Phone: 52-55-5268-6600   **Fax:** 52-55-5268-6697
Web: www.grupobimbo.com

2009 Sales

	% of total
Mexico	45
US	43
Latin America	12
Total	**100**

PRODUCTS/OPERATIONS

Selected Brands

China
  Bimbo (bread products, pastries)
  Million Land (prepared food)
Latin America
  Mexico
    Barcel (confectionery, salty snacks)
    Bimbo (bread products)
    Coronado (confectionery)
    Del Hogar (bread products)
    El Globo (Mexican pastries)
    El Molino (Mexican pastries)
    Gabi (bread products)
    Juicee Gummee (confectionery)
    La Balance (Mexican pastries)
    La Corona (confectionery)
    Lara (crackers, cookies)
    Lonchibon (bread products)
    Marinela (pastries)
    Orowheat (bread products)
    Suandy (cookies, cakes, pastries)
    Tía Rosa (tortillas and other Mexican-style grain products)
    Wonder (licensed, bread products)
  Other Countries
    Ana Maria (bread products)
    Breddy (bread products)
    El Maestro Cubano (bread products and cookies)
    Galletas Lido (cookies)
    Los Sorchanges (bread products)
    Nutrella (bread products and cookies)
    Pan Catalan (bread products)
    Panificio Laura (bread products and cookies)
    Plucky (confectionery)
    Pullman (bread)
    Ricard (confectionery)
    Schmidt (bread)
    Tulipan (bread)
    Winni (cupcakes)

US
- Arnold (bread products)
- Bimbo (bread products)
- Boboli (licensed, pizza crust)
- Brownberry (bread products)
- Entenmann's (pastries)
- Freihofer (bread products)
- Marinela (pastries)
- Mrs. Baird's (bread products)
- Oroweat (bread products)
- Stroehmann (bread products)
- Thomas' (English muffins)
- Tia Rosa (tortillas and other Mexican-style grain products)

COMPETITORS

Awrey Bakeries
Azteca Foods
Chattanooga Bakery
Chupa Chups
Flowers Foods
Frito-Lay
George Weston
Glisten plc
Gonnella Baking
Greyston Bakery
Gruma
Grupo Corvi
HARIBO
Haribo of America
Heinemann's Bakeries
Hershey
Hostess Brands
Jelly Belly Candy
King's Hawaiian
Klosterman Baking
Kraft Foods
La Tortilla Factory
Lance Snacks
Lewis Bakeries
Mars, Incorporated
McKee Foods
Minsa
Otis Spunkmeyer
Pepperidge Farm
Perfection Bakeries
Procter & Gamble
Roman Meal
Rubschlager Baking
Sara Lee
Schwebel Baking
Spangler Candy
Stroehmann Bakeries, L.C.
Tasty Baking
Tootsie Roll
United States Bakery
Yamazaki Baking

HISTORICAL FINANCIALS

Company Type: Public

Income Statement

FYE: December 31

	REVENUE ($ mil.)	NET INCOME ($ mil.)	NET PROFIT MARGIN	EMPLOYEES
12/09	8,923	466	5.2%	100,000
12/08	5,974	323	5.4%	108,000
12/07	6,619	358	5.4%	91,000
12/06	5,881	335	5.7%	85,000
12/05	5,206	270	5.2%	81,000
Annual Growth	14.4%	14.7%	—	5.4%

2009 Year-End Financials

Debt ratio: —
Return on equity: —
Cash ($ mil.): 382
Current ratio: 1.04
Long-term debt ($ mil.): —

No. of shares (mil.): 1,176
Dividends
  Yield: 0.0%
  Payout: —
Market value ($ mil.): 7,683

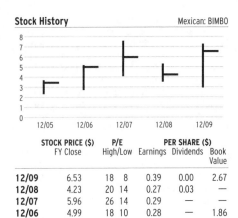

Stock History

Mexican: BIMBO

	STOCK PRICE ($) FY Close	P/E High/Low		Earnings	PER SHARE ($) Dividends	Book Value
12/09	6.53	18	8	0.39	0.00	2.67
12/08	4.23	20	14	0.27	0.03	—
12/07	5.96	26	14	0.29	—	—
12/06	4.99	18	10	0.28	—	1.86
12/05	3.44	16	11	0.22	—	—
Annual Growth	17.4%	—	—	15.4%	—	12.7%

BMW

In the world of automobiles, few acronyms evoke as much awe as BMW. Short for Bayerische Motoren Werke, the company is one of the world's top 10 automakers. BMW's premium lineup includes sedans, coupés, convertibles, and sport wagons in the 1, 3, 5, 6, and 7 Series. Other models include the M3 coupe and convertible, the X5 sport active, and the Z4 roadster. In addition, BMW is known for the automotive MINI and Rolls-Royce brands, as well as its motorcycles K 1200 GT, R 1200 RT, and F 800 S models, among others. Financial services bolster the company's bottom line, as well, with purchase financing and leasing, asset management, dealer financing, and corporate fleets.

Like its automotive OEM brethren, BMW's activities continue to be negatively impacted by the global recession. As a result, BMW has shifted direction in several areas. It trimmed vehicle production by more than 10% to align with lower demand, reduced its workforce, as well as cut back on R&D by some 8%, and capital investments by 20%.

Nonetheless, several plants in Germany and its plant in the US still received upgrades and expansions. The company's joint venture with SGL Group gained momentum in 2010. SGL is investing $100 million to open a carbon fiber manufacturing plant in Washington's Moses Lake. Production of the light-weight carbon fiber reinforced plastics (CFRP) is dedicated to BMW's newest green line, the Megacity Vehicle. Simultaneously, BMW is working with SB Limotive, a JV between Bosch and Samsung SDI, to source the battery cells that will power the Megacity.

Other green initiatives include the roll out of 49 models in 2009 that meet the EU5 emissions standard. In 2009 BMW added numerous new car models. The MINI E was launched on a trial basis, giving BMW experience in delivering lithium-ion technology. Rolls-Royce got the Ghost, a coupe version of the Phantom.

BMW's remapping includes its dealer network, which has expanded in the developing markets of China and India. Underpinning the effort, it has opened up a joint venture in China (with Brilliance China Automotive Holdings) for production of BMWs. Moreover, a manufacturing and dealer presence coupled with a new finance subsidiary in India looks to bolster its strategy to tap Asia's growing automotive market. BMW is also hunting for opportunities in Eastern Europe, as nations there join the European Union.

BMW is more than 45% owned by the widow and children of Herbert Quandt, an industrialist. The family is one of Germany's richest family dynasties.

HISTORY

BMW's logo speaks to its origin: a propeller in blue and white, the colors of Bavaria. In 1913 Karl Rapp opened an aircraft-engine design shop near Munich. He named it Bayerische Motoren Werke (BMW) in 1917. The end of WWI brought German aircraft production to a halt, and BMW shifted to making railway brakes until the 1930s. BMW debuted its first motorcycle, the R32, in 1923, and the company began making automobiles in 1928 after buying small-car company Fahrzeugwerke Eisenach.

In 1933 BMW launched a line of larger cars. The company built aircraft engines for Hitler's Luftwaffe in the 1930s and stopped all auto and motorcycle production in 1941. BMW chief Josef Popp resisted and was ousted. Under the Nazis, the company operated in occupied countries, built rockets, and developed the world's first production jet engine.

With its factories dismantled after WWII, BMW survived by making kitchen and garden equipment. In 1948 it introduced a one-cylinder motorcycle, which sold well as cheap transportation in postwar Germany. BMW autos in the 1950s were large and expensive and sold poorly. When motorcycle sales dropped, the company escaped demise in the mid-1950s by launching the Isetta, a seven-foot, three-wheeled "bubble car."

Herbert Quandt saved the enterprise in 1959 by buying control for $1 million. Quandt's BMW focused on sports sedans and released the first of the "New Range" of BMWs in 1961. Success of the niche enabled BMW to buy automaker Hans Glas in 1966.

In the 1970s BMW's European exports soared, and the company set up a distribution subsidiary in the US. The company also produced larger cars that put BMW on par with Mercedes-Benz.

Rapid export growth in the US, Asia, and Australia continued in the 1980s, but Japanese bikes and poor demand hurt motorcycle sales. The launch of the company's luxury vehicles in 1986 heated up the BMW-Mercedes rivalry. US sales peaked that year and fell 45% by 1991. However, in 1992 BMW outsold Mercedes in Europe for the first time and became the first European carmaker to operate a US plant since Volkswagen pulled out in 1988.

BMW teamed with the UK's Rolls-Royce aerospace firm in 1990 to make jet engines for planes that included executive business-travel jets such as the Gulfstream V.

The company bought UK carmaker Rover from British Aerospace and Honda in 1994. BMW offered to buy the luxury Rolls-Royce auto unit (including the Bentley) from UK-based Vickers in 1998, but lost out when Volkswagen (VW) countered with a higher offer. The company fared better, however, when aircraft engine maker Rolls-Royce sold the Rolls-Royce auto brand name and logo to BMW for $66 million. (VW got to use the name until 2003.)

Also in 1998 BMW, along with other German companies, was hit by a class-action lawsuit brought by Holocaust survivors seeking compensation for their work as slave laborers during WWII. (BMW participated in a settlement agreement late the following year.)

In mid-1998 BMW began cutting jobs at its money-losing Rover unit. As Rover's plants continued their downward trend in 1999, BMW's board forced out chairman Bernd Pischetsrieder, who spearheaded the Rover acquisition in 1994. The UK later pledged to help pay for renovations at Rover's Longbridge plant to save about 14,000 jobs and prevent it from moving operations to Hungary.

The company in 2000 sold its Land Rover SUV operations to Ford in a deal worth about $2.7 billion. In 2001 BMW launched its MINI brand in the UK; other European markets soon followed. BMW brought the MINI Cooper to US shores in 2002. The following year BMW took control of the Rolls-Royce brand from Volkswagen.

Despite selling the operations of Rover in 2000, BMW still retained the rights to the brand. In 2006 Ford said it would exercise its right of first refusal agreement with BMW and take control of the brand for about $11 million.

EXECUTIVES

Chairman Supervisory Board: Joachim Milberg, age 66, $238,403 total compensation
Deputy Chairman Supervisory Board: Jürgen F. Strube, age 42, $163,476 total compensation
Deputy Chairman Supervisory Board: Stefan Schmid, $176,628 total compensation
Deputy Chairman Supervisory Board: Stefan Quandt, $163,476 total compensation
Deputy Chairman Supervisory Board: Manfred Schoch, $163,476 total compensation
Chairman Management Board: Norbert Reithofer, age 54, $3,638,223 total compensation
Member Management Board Finance:
  Friedrich Eichiner, age 55, $1,939,874 total compensation
Member Management Board, Sales and Marketing:
  Ian Robertson, age 52, $1,885,196 total compensation
Member Management Board, Purchasing and Supplier Network: Herbert Diess, age 52, $1,907,984 total compensation
Member Management Board Production:
  Frank-Peter Arndt, age 54, $1,812,728 total compensation
Member Management Board, Development:
  Klaus Draeger, age 54, $1,894,545 total compensation
Member Management Board Human Resources and Industrial Relations Director: Harald Krüger, age 45, $1,917,664 total compensation
Head Development, Small Classes Product Line and Member Supervisory Board: Anton Ruf, $885,495 total compensation
CEO, Rolls-Royce Motor Cars Limited:
  Torsten Müller-Ötvös
Auditors: KPMG AG Wirtschaftsprüfungsgesellschaft

LOCATIONS

HQ: Bayerische Motoren Werke AG
  Petuelring 130
  D-80788 Munich, Germany
Phone: 49-89-382-0
US HQ: 300 Chestnut Ridge Rd.
  Woodcliff Lake, NJ 07677
US Phone: 201-307-4000 **US Fax:** 201-307-4095
Web: www.bmwgroup.com

2009 Sales

	% of total
Europe	
Germany	23
Other countries	25
North America	23
Asia/Oceania	17
UK	8
Other regions	4
Total	**100**

PRODUCTS/OPERATIONS

2009 Sales

	% of total
Automobiles	72
Financial services	26
Motorcycles	2
Total	**100**

Selected Products

Automobiles
  BMW models
    1 Series
      3-door
      5-door
      Convertible
      Coupé
    3 Series
      Convertible
      Coupé
      Sedan
      Touring
    5 Series
      Gran Turismo
      Sedan
      Touring
    6 Series
      Convertible
      Coupé
    7 Series
      Active Hybrid
      Sedan
    M Models
      M3 Convertible
      M3 Coupé
      M3 Sedan
      M6 Convertible
      M6 Coupé
      X5, X6
      Z4 M Roadster
    X (1, 3, 5, 6, Active Hybrid 6)
    Z4 Models
      Z4 Roadster
  MINI
    John Cooper Works (Hardtop, Convertible, Clubman)
    MINI Cooper
    MINI Cooper Clubman
    MINI Cooper Convertible
    MINI Cooper S
    MINI Cooper S Clubman
    MINI Cooper S Convertible
  Rolls-Royce
    Ghost
    Phantom
    Phantom Coupé
Motorcycles
  Enduro
  High Performance
  Sport
  Tour
  Urban

COMPETITORS

Chrysler
Daimler
Ducati
Fiat
Ford Motor
General Motors
Harley-Davidson
Honda
Kawasaki Heavy Industries
Mazda
Nissan
Renault
Saab Automobile
Suzuki Motor
Toyota
Ultra Motorcycle
Volkswagen
Yamaha
Yamaha Motor

HISTORICAL FINANCIALS

Company Type: Public

Income Statement

FYE: December 31

	REVENUE ($ mil.)	NET INCOME ($ mil.)	NET PROFIT MARGIN	EMPLOYEES
12/09	72,636	301	0.4%	96,230
12/08	74,981	465	0.6%	100,041
12/07	82,453	4,613	5.6%	107,539
12/06	64,644	3,792	5.9%	106,575
12/05	55,255	2,652	4.8%	105,798
Annual Growth	7.1%	(42.0%)	—	(2.3%)

2009 Year-End Financials

Debt ratio: —
Return on equity: 1.1%
Cash ($ mil.): 11,132
Current ratio: 1.08
Long-term debt ($ mil.): —
No. of shares (mil.): 602
Dividends
  Yield: 0.9%
  Payout: 97.7%
Market value ($ mil.): 27,436

Stock History

German: BMW

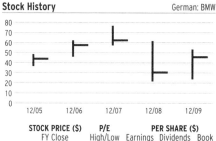

	STOCK PRICE ($) FY Close	P/E High/Low	Earnings	PER SHARE ($) Dividends	Book Value
12/09	45.58	118 56	0.44	0.43	47.41
12/08	30.46	88 33	0.69	1.49	47.45
12/07	62.33	11 8	7.04	—	53.14
12/06	57.40	11 8	5.78	—	41.92
12/05	43.88	12 10	3.94	—	33.39
Annual Growth	1.0%	— —	(42.2%)	(71.1%)	9.2%

BNP Paribas

One of Europe's largest banks, BNP Paribas operates about 2,200 retail branches in France and has approximately 4,000 additional locations in some 85 other countries. The company and its myriad subsidiaries specialize in retail banking, corporate and investment banking, and asset management. It operates in Italy through BNL banca commerciale. BNP Paribas acquired a 75% stake in beleaguered Fortis Banque, adding some 1,450 retail branches in Belgium and Luxembourg and further cementing BNP Paribas as a top European bank. BNP Paribas owns BancWest (the parent of Bank of the West and First Hawaiian Bank) in the US. The company earns more than half of its revenue outside of France.

After a couple of false starts and a seven-month saga, BNP Paribas acquired control of Fortis Banque (also known as Fortis Bank) in 2009. Fortis' Dutch operations were excluded from the transaction. Fortis Bank was nationalized in October 2008 to prevent its collapse, and the takeover by BNP Paribas was delayed and revised to satisfy Fortis shareholders and other interested parties. Upon the closing of the deal, BNP Paribas became the market leader in Belgium and Luxembourg. The Belgian government gained more than 10% of BNP Paribas in the transaction.

Other BNP Paribas units include BNP Paribas Asset Management, consumer lender Cetelem, private bank BNP Paribas Banque Privée, online brokerage Cortal Consors, and insurance firms BNP Paribas Assurance and Pinnacle Insurance. The latter operations got a boost from the tie-up with Fortis Bank, as BNP Paribas also acquired a 25% stake in umbrella organization Fortis Insurance. Also in 2009, the company acquired a majority of private bank Insinger de Beaufort. It holds a controlling stake in real estate firm Klépierre, as well.

BNP Paribas has exhibited a rapacious appetite for international growth in recent years, expanding its operations into some 10 new countries since 2004. In addition to the Fortis and BNL acquisitions, BNP Paribas has acquired Sahara Bank in Libya and a 51% stake in UkrSibbank, one of Ukraine's leading banks. BNP Paribas also owns Banque Internationale pour le Commerce et l'Industrie, which is active in six African nations, and a majority of Türk Ekonomi Bankasi in Turkey. BNP Paribas has been expanding in China, Egypt, Israel, and Russia as well.

In 2010 BNP Paribas acquired US investment bank Hill Street Capital, which became part of BNP Paribas Securities.

HISTORY

BNP Paribas Group's predecessor Banque Nationale de Paris (BNP) is the progeny of two state banks with parallel histories; each was set up to jump-start the economy after a revolution in 1848.

For a century, Paris-based Comptoir National d'Escompte de Paris (CNEP) bounced between private and public status, depending on government whim. It was the #3 bank in France from the late 19th century through the 1950s.

Banque National pour le Commerce et l'Industrie (BNCI) started in Alsace, a region that was part of Germany from the Franco-Prussian War until WWI. BNCI served as an economic bridge between Germany and France, which had to give the bank governmental resuscitation during the Depression. By the 1960s BNCI had passed CNEP in size.

French leader Charles de Gaulle expected banking to drive post-WWII reconstruction, and in 1945 CNEP and BNCI were nationalized. In 1966 France's finance minister merged them and they became BNP. That year the company started an association with Dresdner Bank of Germany, under which the two still operate joint ventures, primarily in Eastern Europe.

By 1993 privatization was again in vogue, and BNP was cut loose by the government. It expanded outside France to ameliorate the influences of the French economy and government. Even before it was privatized, BNP was involved in such politically charged actions as the bailout of OPEC money repository Banque Arabe and the extension of credit to Algeria's state oil company Sonatrach.

The privatized BNP looked overseas in the late 1990s. In 1997 alone, it won the right to operate in New Zealand, bought Laurentian Bank and Trust of the Bahamas, took control of its joint venture with Egypt's Banque du Caire, and opened a subsidiary in Brazil.

BNP bought failed Peregrine Investment's Chinese operations in 1998. That year the bank also expanded in Peru, opened an office in Algeria, opened a representative office in Uzbekistan, set up an investment banking subsidiary in India,

and bought Australian stock brokerage operations from Prudential.

After a decade of globe-trotting, BNP brought it on home in 1999 and set off a year of tumult in French banking. As France's other two large banks (Société Générale and Paribas) made plans to merge, BNP decided it would absorb both banks as a means to get a bigger chunk of the to-be-privatized Crédit Lyonnais and to protect France from Euro-megabank penetration by creating the globe's largest bank.

Executives at Société Générale (SG) had other ideas, forming a cartel called "Action Against the BNP Raid." Meanwhile, BNP tried to boost to controlling stakes its holdings in the two banks. (In Europe's cross-ownership tradition, the target banks also owned part of BNP.) France's central bank tried unsuccessfully to negotiate a deal (the government supported the triumvirate merger). A war of words was played out in the media, and finally shareholders had to vote on the proposals. In the end, BNP won control of Paribas, but not SG. As BNP prepared to integrate a reluctant Paribas into its operations, regulators ordered BNP to relinquish its stake in SG. The newly merged company was dubbed BNP Paribas Group.

In 2000 BNP Paribas bought 150 shopping centers from French retailer Carrefour and the 40% of merchant bank Cobepa that it didn't already own. In 2001 it took full control of US-based BancWest. BNP bought United California Bank from UFJ Holdings the following year.

The bank opened up a second "home market" when it bought Italy's Banca Nazionale del Lavoro (BNL) for $11 billion in 2006.

In 2008, as the world's economies struggled to stay afloat, the French government agreed to inject €10.5 billion ($14 billion) into the nation's top six banks, including BNP Paribas. The government didn't receive shares in the banks it assisted; rather, the capital injections were meant to help reenergize lending activities in France. A year after receiving the cash, BNP Paribas announced plans to repay the government's aid.

EXECUTIVES

Chairman: Michel Pébereau, age 68
Vice Chairman: Jean-Louis Beffa, age 69
President, CEO, and Director: Baudouin Prot, age 58
Managing Director: Jean Clamon, age 58
Co-COO: Georges Chodron de Courcel, age 60
Co-COO: Jean-Laurent Bonnafé, age 49
SEVP and Head Group Finance and Development: Philipe Bordenave
Global Head Prime Brokerage Sales, BNP Paribas Corporate and Investment Banking: Samuel Hocking
Global Head Fixed Income Trading: Guillaume Amblard
Global Head Primary Markets and Origination: Martin Egan
Global Head Credit Research and Strategy: Robert McAdie
Managing Director Wealth Management: Pascal Grundrich
Managing Director and Head, GES Americas: John Bohan
Head French Retail Banking: François Villeroy de Galhau
Head, Investor Relations and Financial Information (IRFI): Béatrice Belorgey
Head Group Human Resources: Frédéric Lavenir
Director Corporate Social Responsibility: Laurence Pessez
Chairman Asset Management: Gilles Glicenstein
Chairman, Securities Services: Jacques d'Estais
Auditors: Deloitte & Associés

LOCATIONS
HQ: BNP Paribas
  16, boulevard des Italiens
  75009 Paris, France
Phone: 33-1-40-14-45-46
US HQ: 787 7th Ave., New York, NY 10019
US Phone: 212-841-2000   **US Fax:** 212-841-3251
Web: www.bnpparibas.com

PRODUCTS/OPERATIONS

2009 Sales by Segment

	% of total
Retail Banking	
French retail banking	14
Personal finance	11
BNL banca commerciale	7
Other	12
Corporate & Investment Banking	
Advisory & capital markets	23
Financing	8
BNP Paribas-Fortis	13
Investment Solution	12
Total	**100**

COMPETITORS

ABN AMRO Group	HSBC
Banco Popular Español	JPMorgan Chase
Bank of America	Natixis
Barclays	Société Générale
BBVA	UBS
Citigroup	U.S. Bancorp
Crédit Agricole	Wells Fargo
Deutsche Bank	

HISTORICAL FINANCIALS
Company Type: Public

Income Statement
FYE: December 31

	ASSETS ($ mil.)	NET INCOME ($ mil.)	INCOME AS % OF ASSETS	EMPLOYEES
12/09	2,949,093	8,358	0.3%	201,740
12/08	2,925,489	4,258	0.1%	170,000
12/07	2,494,067	11,513	0.5%	162,687
12/06	1,900,245	9,641	0.5%	141,911
12/05	1,489,943	6,931	0.5%	109,780
Annual Growth	18.6%	4.8%	—	16.4%

2009 Year-End Financials

Equity as % of assets: 3.4%
Return on assets: 0.3%
Return on equity: 9.6%
Long-term debt ($ mil.): 1,359,498
No. of shares (mil.): 1,185
Dividends
  Yield: 1.8%
  Payout: 19.2%
Market value ($ mil.): 94,960
Sales ($ mil.): 134,900

Stock History
Euronext Paris: BNP

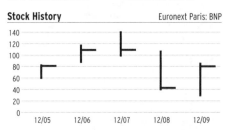

	STOCK PRICE ($) FY Close	P/E High/Low		PER SHARE ($) Earnings	Dividends	Book Value
12/09	80.12	11	4	7.45	1.43	84.04
12/08	42.64	25	9	4.31	4.72	63.30
12/07	109.24	11	8	12.39	—	66.81
12/06	109.04	11	8	10.49	—	55.11
12/05	80.95	10	7	8.25	—	40.68
Annual Growth	(0.3%)	—	—	(2.5%)	(69.7%)	19.9%

Bombardier Inc.

Bombardier carries the torch for the rail and aerospace industries. The company's Aerospace division manufactures commercial and business aircraft. It is the #1 regional aircraft maker with its CRJ and Q series, and is a leading maker of business jets (Global, Challenger, Learjet). Bombardier's Transportation division is one of the world's largest railway equipment makers. About 95% of its revenues are derived outside of Canada with 28% of its sales made in North America. Its Flexjet division offers fractional jet ownership services (customers buy flight time without buying interest in an aircraft). The company, which is controlled by the Bombardier family, designed the torch for the Vancouver 2010 Olympics.

The business and civil aircraft markets experienced their most turbulent conditions since the aftermath of September 11, due to the global recession and credit crisis in 2009. The perpetually dicey financial condition of the airline industry — due to fluctuating fuel prices and shifts in consumer spending — affects demand for commercial aircraft. Bombardier has a limited number of customers, many of which are government agencies or publicly held companies, and those entities have seen their own revenues fall due to the recession.

Bombardier has adapted by reducing its production of business jets and CRJ regional aircraft and reducing its workforce by 4,700 (about 13%). Even with the economic challenges, Bombardier was able to increase its revenue market share in business and commercial aircraft.

The company did not pull back on its investment in the development of a 100- to 149-seat CSeries aircraft for the regional airline market. Scheduled for flight in 2013, the CSeries uses lighter-weight materials along with Bombardier's trademarked PurePower PW1000G engine to yield a reduction in fuel and emissions of 20%. Also scheduled for a 2013 unveiling is the Learjet 85. The business aircraft will be composed of all composite materials and can achieve speeds of Mach 0.82 (about 624 mph).

Bombardier's Transportation division experienced a multi-billion-dollar contract year in 2009 that proved to be a mitigating factor in the Aerospace division's challenges. Bombardier's expansion into emerging markets (China, India, and Russia) is paying off. In conjunction with its partner CSRSifang Locomotive and Rolling Stock Ltd., it landed a $4 billion contract with the Chinese Railway Ministry to build 80 high-speed trains.

France's railway Société Nationale des Chemins de Fer Français (SNCF) ponied up approximately $11 billion in 2010 for Bombardier's double-decker trains. At home, the Toronto Transit Commission awarded the company a $1.2 billion contract to build the city's new low-floor light rail vehicles, which will replace its aging fleet of street cars.

Bombardier's new Savil plant in India started producing its first Delhi MOVIA metro trains in 2009. The facility gives the company a solid foothold in the Asia/Pacific region.

Bombardier's Transportation division is focused on light rail and commuter and regional trains, as well as on lucrative service contracts for existing rail infrastructure. The company continues to develop its very high speed (VHS) ZEFIRO 380 train; the "380" refers to its speed of 380 kilometers per hour (about 236 mph).

HISTORY

Bombardier got its start in the 1920s when mechanic Joseph-Armand Bombardier began converting old cars into snowmobiles. He founded L'Auto-Neige Bombardier Limited in 1942 to make commercial snow vehicles. In 1959 Bombardier introduced the first personal snowmobile, the Ski-Doo.

At age 27, Laurent Beaudoin became the company's president in 1966. Bombardier went public in 1969. When the bottom dropped out of the snowmobile business due to the energy crisis in 1973, Beaudoin diversified, and in 1974 Bombardier won its first mass-transit contract to build Montreal subway cars. Expanding further into mass transportation, Bombardier merged with MLW-Worthington Limited, a builder of diesel engines and diesel-electric locomotives. In 1978 the company became Bombardier Inc.

During the 1980s Bombardier continued to diversify. It expanded into military vehicles and became the leading supplier to the North American rail transit industry. The company entered the European railcar market in 1986, the same year it acquired Canadair, Canada's largest aerospace company, from the national government.

Founded in 1920 as the aircraft division of Canadian Vickers, Canadair became a separate company producing military and civilian aircraft in 1944. Acquired by Electric Boat (which became part of General Dynamics) in 1947, it was nationalized by the Canadian government in 1976. In 1978 Canadair introduced its Challenger 600 business jet, which became a major seller.

Bombardier began development of a commuter aircraft, the Canadian Regional Jet (a 50-seat derivative of the Challenger), in 1989.

In 1990 the company bought US-based Learjet and its service centers, and two years later it acquired a stake in de Havilland, a regional aircraft maker, which it jointly owns with the Province of Ontario. In 1996 Amtrak selected an international consortium headed by Bombardier to produce high-speed trains, electric locomotives, and train-maintenance facilities.

Bombardier doubled the size of its European operations in 1998 by buying German railcar maker Deutsche Waggonbau.

The company sold its 50% stake in Shorts Missile Systems to Thomson-CSF in 2000. Bombardier also inked a $2 billion deal to make 94 regional jets for Delta Air Lines; the Delta order includes options for an additional 406 aircraft through 2010.

To start off 2001, Bombardier signed a deal with SkyWest worth about $1.4 billion for 64 Canadair regional jets. Completing an agreement made the year before, Bombardier acquired Daimler AG's Adtranz rail systems unit for about $725 million. In September the company announced that it would lay off about 10% of its aerospace workforce (it also said that it would cut another 7% of that workforce if demand did not grow).

Bombardier divested its Recreational Products unit (snowmobiles and personal watercraft) in 2003.

CEO Paul Tellier resigned in December 2004 amid rumored boardroom differences with Laurent Beaudoin, who assumed the CEO duties.

In 2005 the company sold its inventory finance division, which provided equipment financing, to GE Commercial Finance for $2.4 billion.

Laurent Beaudoin maintained his role as chairman when, in 2008, he handed over the president and CEO titles to his son Pierre.

EXECUTIVES

Chairman: Laurent Beaudoin, age 71
Vice Chairman: Jean-Louis Fontaine, age 70
President and CEO: Pierre Beaudoin, age 51
EVP and President, Bombardier Transportation:
  André Navarri, age 57
SVP and CFO: Pierre Alary
SVP and General Counsel: Daniel Desjardins
**SVP, Strategy and Corporate Audit Services and Risk
  Assessment:** Richard C. Bradeen
SVP, Public Affairs and Human Resources:
  John Paul MacDonald
CIO: Robert Proulx
Corporate Secretary: Roger Carle
Director, Investor Relations: Shirley Chénier
Director, Communications: Isabelle Rondeau
President and COO, Bombardier Aerospace:
  Guy C. Hachey, age 54
Auditors: Ernst & Young LLP

LOCATIONS

HQ: Bombardier Inc.
  800 René-Lévesque Blvd. West
  Montreal, Quebec H3B 1Y8, Canada
Phone: 514-861-9481   **Fax:** 514-861-2420
Web: www.bombardier.com

2010 Sales

	% of total
Americas	
US	23
Canada	5
Other countries	2
Europe	
Germany	10
France	8
UK	8
Sweden	3
Italy	3
Spain	3
Russia	3
Switzerland	3
Netherlands	2
Other countries	8
Asia	
China	7
India	2
Other countries	5
Africa	2
Oceania	
Australia	3
Total	**100**

PRODUCTS/OPERATIONS

2010 Sales

	% of total
Transportation	52
Aerospace	48
Total	**100**

2010 Sales

	% of total
Manufacturing	76
Services	14
Other	10
Total	**100**

Selected Operations

Aerospace
  Amphibious aircraft
    415 turboprop (Superscooper)
  Business aircraft
    Challenger 300, 605, 850
    Global 5000
    Global Express XRS
    Learjet 40 XR, 45 XR, 60 XR, 85
  Defense services
    Flying training
    Military aircraft technical service
  Regional aircraft
    CRJ 200, 700, 705, 900, 1000 NextGen
    CS100, 300
    Q200, 300, 400

Flexjet
  Fractional ownership
  Whole aircraft ownership and management
Transportation
  Freight cars
  Locomotives for passenger trains
  Monorails
  Rapid-transit cars
  Single-level and bi-level railcars
  Subway cars
  Trams
  Tram-trains
  Turbotrains
  Vehicles with tilting systems

COMPETITORS

AeroCentury
Airbus
ALSTOM
Blue Star Jets
Boeing
Cessna
Dassault Aviation
EADS
Embraer
Finmeccanica
Flight Options
Greenbrier Companies
Gulfstream Aerospace
Hawker Beechcraft
Kawasaki Rail Car
Meggitt Training Systems
Mitsubishi Heavy Industries
NetJets
Piper Aircraft
Siemens AG
Thales
XOJET

HISTORICAL FINANCIALS

Company Type: Public

Income Statement

FYE: January 31

	REVENUE ($ mil.)	NET INCOME ($ mil.)	NET PROFIT MARGIN	EMPLOYEES
1/10	19,366	698	3.6%	62,900
1/09	19,721	1,008	5.1%	66,700
1/08	17,506	317	1.8%	60,000
1/07	14,816	268	1.8%	56,000
1/06	14,726	249	1.7%	47,860
Annual Growth	7.1%	29.4%	—	7.1%

2010 Year-End Financials

Debt ratio: 124.1%
Return on equity: 25.1%
Cash ($ mil.): 3,372
Current ratio: 0.99
Long-term debt ($ mil.): 4,162

No. of shares (mil.): 1,753
Dividends
  Yield: 2.3%
  Payout: 28.2%
Market value ($ mil.): 8,833

Stock History

Toronto: BBD.B

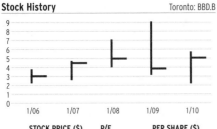

	STOCK PRICE ($) FY Close	P/E High/Low		PER SHARE ($) Earnings	Dividends	Book Value
1/10	5.04	14	6	0.39	0.11	2.11
1/09	3.85	16	6	0.56	0.02	1.45
1/08	4.96	44	26	0.16	0.00	1.78
1/07	4.48	33	19	0.14	0.00	1.56
1/06	3.02	28	18	0.13	0.00	1.38
Annual Growth	13.7%	—	—	31.6%	—	11.1%

Bouygues SA

If all roads lead to Bouygues, that's because the company built them. Bouygues (pronounced "bweeg") operates in five industries: road work, construction, property development, media, and telecommunications. Subsidiaries include Colas (road construction and maintenance, about 40% of sales) and Bouygues Construction (around 30%). Bouygues Immobilier is the company's property development arm, with interests in commercial and residential development. The company has increased its stake in Bouygues Telecom (France's #3 mobile phone carrier) to around 90%, and it also owns more than 40% of TF1 (France's #1 TV channel). Bouygues has a 30% stake in ALSTOM, which builds rail cars, ships, and power plants.

Subsidiary Bouygues Construction is a force in itself, with several subsidiaries performing civil construction and electrical/maintenance work. The group focuses on public-private partnerships, those lucrative partnerships that governments use to build roads, prisons, schools, and other infrastructure. Bouygues has increasingly participated in sustainable development projects, with investments in training, research, and resources. It also is broadening its operations in electrical contracting and property development, and expects to expand its presence in Europe, as well.

Other Bouygues units have been busy, too. In 2008 property developer Bouygues Immobilier expanded with the acquisition of Urbis, a French rival. That year Colas bought the Gouyer Group of companies (distribution of construction materials) in Martinique and Guadeloupe, while Bouygues Telecom acquired a fixed-line network that allowed it to launch the Bbox broadband router and Internet services that include VoIP, e-mail, Internet access, and television; the telecom unit also gained the previously denied right to offer the iPhone 3G.

Chairman Martin Bouygues and his brother Olivier, sons of the company's founder, own about 18% of Bouygues through holding company SCDM; however, they control more than a quarter of the voting rights.

HISTORY

With the equivalent of $1,700 in borrowed money, Francis Bouygues, son of a Paris engineer, started Entreprise Francis Bouygues in 1952 as an industrial works and construction firm in the Paris region of France. Within four years his firm had expanded into property development.

By the mid-1960s Bouygues had entered the civil engineering and public works sectors and developed regional construction units across France. In 1970 it was listed on the Paris stock exchange. Four years later the company established Bouygues Offshore to build oil platforms.

In 1978 the firm built Terminal 2 of Paris' Charles de Gaulle airport. Three years later it won the contract to construct the University of Riyadh in Saudi Arabia (then the world's largest building project at 3.2 million sq. ft.), which was completed in 1984. That year Bouygues acquired France's #3 water supply company, Saur, and power transmission and supply firm ETDE.

Expansion continued in 1986 with the purchase of the Screg Group, which included Colas, France's top highway contractor. The next year the company led a consortium to buy 50% of newly privatized network Société Télévision Française 1 (TF1). Bouygues became the largest shareholder with a 25% stake (increased to 40% by 1999). In 1988 the company began building the Channel Tunnel (completed in 1994) and moved into its new ultramodern headquarters, dubbed Challenger, in Saint-Quentin-En-Yvelines, outside Paris.

After rumors of failing health, Francis Bouygues resigned as chairman in 1989. His son Martin took over as chairman and CEO, although the patriarch, called France's "Emperor of Concrete," remained on the board until his death in 1993.

Despite fears that the group would suffer without its founder's leadership, Bouygues continued to grow with the 1989 acquisition of a majority interest in Grands Moulins de Paris, France's largest flour milling firm (sold in 1998). In 1990 it purchased Swiss construction group Losinger.

The company entered the telecom industry in 1993 with a national paging network and added a mobile phone license a year later. In 1996 the group listed 40% of Bouygues Offshore's shares on the New York and Paris stock exchanges. Also that year it launched mobile phone operator Bouygues Telecom and entered a partnership with Telecom Italia.

By 1999 Bouygues Telecom had reached 2 million customers, and Bouygues bought back a 20% share held by the UK's Cable and Wireless to increase its stake to nearly 54%. That year Bouygues Offshore bought Norwegian engineering firm Kvaerner, and the group spun off its construction sector, creating Bouygues Construction.

After word circulated that Deutsche Telekom wanted to acquire the group's telecom unit, Bouygues became the target of takeover rumors. Francois Pinault, France's richest businessman, became Bouygues' largest non-family shareholder when he increased his stake to 14% (later reduced to about 2%). Pinault's biggest rival, Bernard Arnault, upped his stake to more than 9% of the group, fueling speculation of a battle over control of the board.

In 2001 the company pulled out of France's auction for a third-generation wireless license and remained the only European incumbent mobile carrier without a major domestic investment in 3G technology (until 2009). The next year the company agreed to buy Telecom Italia's stake in Bouygues Telecom, increasing Bouygues' ownership in the mobile operator from 54% to more than 65%. In 2002 the company sold its 51% stake in oil field platform construction unit Bouygues Offshore to Italian oil services group Saipem, which announced plans to bid for the remaining shares.

However, talks with German utility giant E.ON over the sale of Bouygues' Saur subsidiary failed that year, after E.ON decided to focus instead on its electricity and gas operations.

In 2005 Bouygues was more successful when it sought to sell Saur piecemeal. It sold several divisions of the subsidiary (Coved, Saur France, Saur International, and Stereau) to French private equity firm PAI Partners but retained the African and Italian (Sigesa-Crea) divisions of the firm.

Bouygues bought the French government's 21% stake in ALSTOM for $2.5 billion in 2006. The deal was approved on the condition that it not try to control the company for at least three years. Bouygues did build up its holding after the acquisition, though.

EXECUTIVES

Chairman and CEO: Martin Bouygues, age 58
Deputy CEO and Director: Olivier Bouygues, age 58
CFO: Philippe Marien, age 54
EVP Information Systems and New Technologies and Director: Alain Pouyat, age 66
SVP Human Resources and Administration: Jean-Claude Tostivin, age 63
Director; Head Purchasing, TF1: Jean-Michel Gras, age 39
Director Group Corporate Communications: Blandine Delafon
Director; Quality and Environment Manager, Bouygues Bâtiment International: Thierry Jourdaine, age 47
Director; Chairman, CEO, and Director, Bouygues Construction: Yves Gabriel, age 60
Director; Chairman and CEO, TF1: Nonce Paolini, age 61
Director; Chairman, CEO, and Director, Bouygues Immobilier: François Bertière, age 60
Director; Chairman, CEO, and Director, Colas: Hervé Le Bouc, age 58
CEO and Director, Bouygues Telecom: Olivier Roussat, age 46
Corporate Secretary: Jean-François Guillemin, age 57
Auditors: Mazars & Guérard

LOCATIONS

HQ: Bouygues SA
32, avenue Hoche
75008 Paris, France
Phone: 33-1-4420-1000   **Fax:** 33-1-3060-4861
Web: www.bouygues.fr

2009 Sales

	% of total
Europe	
France	69
Other countries	15
US & Canada	6
Africa & Middle East	5
Asia/Pacific	4
Central & South America	1
Total	**100**

PRODUCTS/OPERATIONS

2009 Sales

	% of total
Colas	36
Bouygues Construction	30
Bouygues Telecom	17
Bouygues Immobilier	9
TFI	7
Other	1
Total	**100**

Selected Subsidiaries and Affiliates

Construction
Autoroute de liaison Seine-Sarthe SA (33%)
Bouygues Bâtiment Ile-de-France SA (99.97%)
Bati-Rénov SA (99.3%)
Bouygues Bâtiment International SA (99.97%)
Bouygues Thaï Ltd (49%)
DTP Singapour Pte Ltd (99.97%)
Kohler Investment SA (Luxembourg, 99.97%)
Bouygues Construction SA (99.97%)
ETDE SA (99.97%)
Exprimm IT (99.97%)
Icel Maidstone Ltd (UK, 99.97%)
Quille SA (99.97%)
Westminster Local Education Partnership Ltd (UK, 80%)
Property
Bouygues Immobilier
Entreprises Île-de-France
Parque Empresearial Cristalia SL

Roads
Cofiroute (16%)
Colas Guadeloupe (96.6%)
Colas Hungaria (96.6%)
Colas Polska (96.6%)
Colas SA (96.6%)
Spac (96.6%)
Telecoms and Media
Bouygues Telecom SA (89.6%)
Métro France Publications (14.8%)
Télévision Française 1 SA (TF1, 43%)
TF1 Vidéo (43%)
TV Breizh (43%)

COMPETITORS

Alarko	Fluor
AMEC	Foster Wheeler
Atlantia	France Telecom
AWG Plc	GDF SUEZ
Balfour Beatty	Groupe SNEF
Bechtel	HOCHTIEF
Bilfinger Berger	Hyundai Engineering
Bovis Lend Lease	MWH Global
CANAL+	Severn Trent
CSCEC	SFR
Dragados	Skanska
EIFFAGE	SUEZ Environnement
FCC Barcelona	Technip

HISTORICAL FINANCIALS

Company Type: Public

Income Statement

FYE: December 31

	REVENUE ($ mil.)	NET INCOME ($ mil.)	NET PROFIT MARGIN	EMPLOYEES
12/09	44,935	2,067	4.6%	138,936
12/08	46,109	2,376	5.2%	145,150
12/07	43,587	2,345	5.4%	137,500
12/06	34,840	2,087	6.0%	122,561
12/05	28,510	1,229	4.3%	115,441
Annual Growth	**12.0%**	**13.9%**	**—**	**4.7%**

2009 Year-End Financials

Debt ratio: —
Return on equity: 16.8%
Cash ($ mil.): 6,755
Current ratio: 1.02
Long-term debt ($ mil.): —
No. of shares (mil.): 354
Dividends
Yield: 4.4%
Payout: 42.4%
Market value ($ mil.): 18,494

Stock History

Euronext Paris: EN

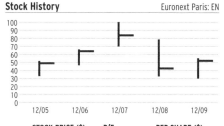

	STOCK PRICE ($) FY Close	P/E High/Low		PER SHARE ($) Earnings	Dividends	Book Value
12/09	52.20	10	6	5.40	2.29	39.35
12/08	42.57	13	6	6.12	—	30.05
12/07	83.90	17	12	5.80	—	29.05
12/06	64.16	14	10	4.75	—	19.91
12/05	48.91	18	12	2.87	—	15.48
Annual Growth	**1.6%**	**—**	**—**	**17.1%**	**—**	**26.3%**

BP p.l.c.

BP is also BO (Big Oil). It is the world's third-largest integrated oil concern, behind Exxon Mobil and Royal Dutch Shell. BP explores for oil and gas in 30 countries and has proved reserves of 18.3 billion barrels of oil equivalent. BP is the largest oil and gas producer in the US and also a top refiner, with stakes in 16 refineries, processing 4 million barrels of crude oil per day. BP markets its products in more than 80 countries and operates 22,400 gas stations worldwide. The company's reputation took a major hit in 2010 when one of its deepwater rigs, working less than 50 miles south of Louisiana, exploded and killed 11 workers. Millions of gallons of crude gushed into the Gulf of Mexico for months.

The spill developed into a major political, economic, and public relations crisis for the company as it struggled to cap the leaking well, clean up the massive oil spill, and mollify Gulf Coast communities that saw their fishing industry decimated and their coastlines inundated by oil. In late May, US scientists declared the spill the worst in US history. Eight weeks after the accident BP shares had lost 50% of the value they had before the incident as costs and liability claims on the company mounted. To address the growing crisis, in June 2010 the company agreed to establish an escrow account of $20 billion, managed by third party, to reimburse claims from people and businesses financially damaged by the oil spill.

As the crisis continued BP was reported to be looking at selling shares to significant institutional investors and major oilfield assets to other oil companies in order to generate cash. In July BP sold assets in Canada, Egypt, and the Permian Basin in the US, to fellow explorer Apache for about $7 billion. That year it also agreed to sell its Colombian assets to Talisman Energy and Ecopetrol for $1.9 billion. It also agreed to sell assets in Venezuela and Vietnam to TNK-BP for $1.8 billion.

On July 15, 2010, the company stopped the oil flow from the broken well in the Gulf of Mexico with a containment cap. Subsequently, Tony Hayward stepped down as CEO in October 2010, and was replaced by BP veteran Robert Dudley (the first American CEO in BP's history). For the second quarter of 2010 the company took a pre-tax charge of $32.2 billion related to the oil spill.

Prior to the *Deepwater Horizon* rig disaster BP announced a medium-term exploration and development strategy focused on growing its operations in three areas: deep-water production, global natural gas production, and managing a number of the world's major oilfields where it has established a leadership position over the past 20 years.

HISTORY

Today's BP (formerly BP Amoco) was born on two sides of the Atlantic. In the US, Amoco emerged from Standard Oil Trust, organized by John D. Rockefeller in 1882. In 1886 he bought Lima (Ohio) oil, a high-sulfur crude, anticipating the discovery of a sulfur-removing process. Such a process was, indeed, patented in 1887, and in 1889 Standard organized Standard Oil of Indiana, which later established such innovations as company-owned service stations and a research lab at the refinery.

Overseas, British Petroleum (BP) was a twinkle in the eye of English adventurer William D'Arcy, who began oil exploration of Persia in 1901. In 1908, bankrolled by Burmah Oil, D'Arcy's firm was the first to strike oil in the Middle East. D'Arcy and Burmah Oil formed Anglo-Persian Oil in 1909, and the British government took a 51% stake in 1914.

Back in the US, Standard was broken up into 34 independent oil companies in 1911. Standard Oil of Indiana kept its oil refining and US marketing operations. In 1925 it added a few Mexican and Venezuelan firms, including Pan American Petroleum and Transport, which held half of American Oil Co., known for Amoco antiknock gasoline. It began Amoco Chemicals in 1945.

Anglo-Persian took the BP name in 1954 and bought its own Standard Oil: After making a strike in Alaska in 1969, BP swapped Alaskan reserves for a 25% interest (later upped to 55%) in Standard Oil of Ohio (SOHIO). BP also struck North Sea oil in 1970. But falling oil and copper prices in the mid-1980s and a dry hole in the Beaufort Sea hurt earnings. Under Robert Horton, SOHIO sold off units. BP also bought livestock feed producer Purina Mills (1986, sold 1998) and the rest of SOHIO (1987).

Standard Oil of Indiana had its own problems, including being kicked out of Iran after the Islamic revolution and causing a major oil spill off the French coast in 1978. The firm, which became Amoco in 1985, bought Canada's Dome Petroleum in 1988, making it the largest private owner of North American gas reserves, but the big purchase proved hard to swallow.

In 1992 Amoco hurled itself into overseas oil exploration. It was the first foreign oil company to explore the Chinese mainland. In 1995 John Browne, often compared to Rockefeller, became BP's CEO. In 1996 the British government sold its remaining stake in BP.

As oil prices tumbled in 1998, BP merged with Amoco in a $52 billion deal that formed BP Amoco. The new oil major agreed the following year to buy US-based Atlantic Richfield (ARCO).

In 2000 BP Amoco and Shell Oil sold their stakes in Altura Energy to Occidental Petroleum for $3.6 billion. The company adopted BP as its main worldwide brand in 2000, and it officially shortened its name the next year.

In 2005 BP sold its petrochemical unit, Innovene, to INEOS for a reported $9 billion. Also that year an explosion and fire at BP's Texas City refinery killed 15 workers and injured many more. In 2006 BP sold its 28% stake in the Shenzi field in the Gulf of Mexico to Repsol for $2.2 billion.

In 2006 the discovery of corrosion in a major oil pipeline forced BP to close down part of its Prudhoe Bay oilfield (which represents 8% of daily US crude production) for several weeks.

In 2007 the company sold its Coryton refinery in the UK to Petroplus Holdings for $1.4 billion.

BP's long-term chief executive John Browne was forced to step down in 2007 over a personal scandal and was replaced by BP veteran Tony Hayward. In 2007 BP agreed to pay US authorities $373.5 million in fines relating to the 2005 Texas City refinery explosion, the 2006 Alaska oil spill, and a propane price-fixing scandal.

In 2009 BP announced the discovery of a major oil field in the Gulf of Mexico containing 3 billion barrels of oil, promising to boost its production by 50%, to 600,000 barrels per day. The next year BP agreed to buy Devon Energy's international assets for $7 billion, in a deal that, among other things, gives BP a foothold in the emerging major oil play of offshore Brazil.

EXECUTIVES

Chairman: Carl-Henric Svanberg, age 58
Group Chief Executive and Director:
Robert W. (Bob) Dudley, age 54,
$3,442,166 total compensation
Executive Director; Chief Executive, Refining and Marketing: Iain C. Conn, age 47,
$3,673,192 total compensation
COO, BP Exploration and Production:
Douglas J. (Doug) Suttles
COO Gulf Coast Restoration Organization: Mike Utsler
CFO and Executive Director: Byron E. Grote, age 61,
$6,903,205 total compensation
EVP and Group Chief of Staff: Steve Westwell, age 51
EVP Global Human Resources: Sally T. Bott, age 60
SVP Exploration and Production: Kent Wells
Group VP Digital and Communications Technology and CIO: Dana S. Deasy, age 48
Group General Counsel: Rupert Bondy, age 48
Group Head Research and Technology: David Eyton
Company Secretary: David J. Jackson, age 57
Head Claims: Darryl Willis
Head of Region, Europe and South Africa:
Jean-Baptiste Renard, age 46
Head Investor Relations: Fergus MacLeod
Chairman and President, BP America: H. Lamar McKay, age 51
President, BP Exploration (Alaska): John Mingé
CEO, BP Solar: Reyad Fezzani
Auditors: Ernst & Young LLP

LOCATIONS

HQ: BP p.l.c.
1 St. James's Sq.
London SW1Y 4PD, United Kingdom
Phone: 44-20-7496-4000 **Fax:** 44-20-7496-4630
US HQ: 501 Westlake Park Blvd., Houston, TX 77079
US Phone: 281-366-2000
Web: www.bp.com

2009 Sales

	$ mil.	% of total
US	83,982	34
Other countries	155,290	64
Other	4,693	2
Total	**243,965**	**100**

PRODUCTS/OPERATIONS

2009 Sales

	$ mil.	% of total
Refining & marketing	212,229	87
Exploration & production	25,086	10
Other	6,650	3
Total	**243,965**	**100**

Major Operations

Refining and marketing
  Marketing
  Refining
  Supply and trading
  Transportation and shipping
Exploration and production
  Field development
  Gas processing and marketing
  Oil and gas exploration
  Pipelines and transportation
    Alyeska Pipeline Service Co. (47%)
      Trans Alaska Pipeline System
      Valdez terminal
Gas and power
  Natural gas marketing and trading
  Natural gas liquids

Chemicals
  Chemical intermediates
  Feedstock
  Performance products
  Polymers
Other
  Coal mining
  Solar power

COMPETITORS

Apache
Ashland Inc.
BASF SE
Bayer AG
BG Group
BHP Billiton
Cargill
Chevron
Dow Chemical
DuPont
Eni
Exxon Mobil
Hess Corporation
Huntsman International
Imperial Oil
Koch Industries, Inc.
Norsk Hydro ASA
Occidental Petroleum
PEMEX
PETROBRAS
Petróleos de Venezuela
Royal Dutch Shell
Shell Aviation
Sinclair Oil
Sunoco
TOTAL

HISTORICAL FINANCIALS

Company Type: Public

Income Statement

FYE: December 31

	REVENUE ($ mil.)	NET INCOME ($ mil.)	NET PROFIT MARGIN	EMPLOYEES
12/09	243,965	16,578	6.8%	80,300
12/08	365,700	21,157	5.8%	92,000
12/07	288,951	20,845	7.2%	98,100
12/06	270,602	22,315	8.2%	97,000
12/05	243,948	22,026	9.0%	96,200
Annual Growth	**0.0%**	**(6.9%)**	**—**	**(4.4%)**

2009 Year-End Financials

Debt ratio: 25.1%
Return on equity: 17.2%
Cash ($ mil.): 8,339
Current ratio: 1.14
Long-term debt ($ mil.): 25,518

No. of shares (mil.): 3,132
Dividends
  Yield: 5.8%
  Payout: 64.0%
Market value ($ mil.): 181,536

Stock History

NYSE: BP

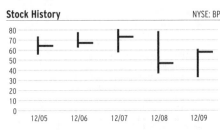

	STOCK PRICE ($) FY Close	P/E High/Low		PER SHARE ($) Earnings	Dividends	Book Value
12/09	57.97	11	6	5.25	3.36	32.45
12/08	46.74	12	6	6.69	3.30	29.16
12/07	73.17	12	9	6.47	2.54	29.92
12/06	67.10	12	10	6.63	2.30	27.02
12/05	64.22	12	9	6.18	2.09	25.44
Annual Growth	**(2.5%)**	**—**	**—**	**(4.0%)**	**12.6%**	**6.3%**

Bridgestone Corporation

Bridgestone is one rolling stone that gathers no moss. Vying with Michelin to be the world's largest tire maker, Bridgestone helps vehicles traverse almost any type of terrain. The company supplies tires to most major car makers; it also makes tires for the construction, highway, mining, and aviation industries. Non-tire products include chemical and industrial products (foam and rubber products), sporting goods (golf balls), and bicycles. Tires account for more than 80% of Bridgestone's revenues, with about three-quarters of its sales made overseas. It has a global production and sales network that focuses on supplying local markets in more than 150 countries worldwide.

Faced with plummeting demand in its core tire business in a weak global economy, Bridgestone sought to curb investment and other expenses, reduce inventory, and streamline operations by strengthening its vertically integrated supply chain (the company controls most aspects of its business, from raw materials to tire sales outlets) and closing down underperforming plants. Bridgestone announced plans in February 2010 to sell two steel cord production facilities for approximately $100 million to Bekaert, a steel cord producer based in Belgium. The timing is in line with Bridgestone's $36 million investment to add production of bus and truck tires at its Indore (India) plant, which is in keeping with the company's desire to expand into emerging markets. In 2009 it closed factories in New Zealand and Adelaide, Australia.

The company is focusing on specialty tires such as runflat and UHP (ultra-high-performance) replacement tires. In its diversified businesses, which also struggled with falling demand, Bridgestone is developing eco-friendly products, including adhesive films for solar cells, which hold promise for growth. The company is rolling out an eco-friendly tire as well, the ECOPIA.

Bridgestone is also encouraging a strong bicycle industry in Japan through its Bridgestone Cycle subsidiary, which makes everything from carriers and helmets to mud guards and tool sets to go with its variety of adult and children's sport, electric, folding, and special order bicycles.

In mid-2009 the company announced its plans to build a plant in Thailand to produce rubber parts for retread tires. In 2007 Bridgestone purchased Bandag, a retread company in the US with international production facilities.

HISTORY

In 1906 Shojiro Ishibashi and his brother Tokujiro assumed control of the family's clothing business. They focused on making *tabi,* traditional Japanese footwear, and in 1923 began working with rubber for soles. In 1931 Shojiro formed Bridgestone (Ishibashi means "stone bridge" in Japanese) to make tires, and during that decade the company began producing auto tires, airplane tires, and golf balls. Bridgestone followed the Japanese military to occupied territories, where it built plants. The company's headquarters moved to Tokyo in 1937.

Although Bridgestone lost all of its overseas factories during WWII, its Japanese plants escaped damage. The company began making bicycles in 1946 and signed a technical assistance pact with Goodyear five years later, enabling Bridgestone to import badly needed technology. In the 1950s and 1960s, Bridgestone started making nylon tires and radials and again set up facilities overseas, mostly elsewhere in Asia. The company benefited from the rapid growth in Japanese auto sales in the 1970s. Shojiro died at age 87 in 1976.

In 1983 Bridgestone bought a plant in LaVergne, Tennessee, from tire maker Firestone. Five years later Bridgestone topped Italian tire maker Pirelli's bid and bought the rest of Firestone for $2.6 billion, valuing the tire manufacturer at a lofty 26 times its earnings.

Bridgestone/Firestone (currently Bridgestone Americas Holding and soon to be renamed Bridgestone Americas Inc.) became Bridgestone's largest subsidiary. Harvey Firestone had founded his tire business in 1900 and expanded with the auto industry in the US. In the 1920s he leased 1 million acres in Liberia for rubber plantations and established a chain of auto supply and service outlets. After WWII Firestone started making synthetic rubber and automotive components, expanded overseas, and acquired US tire producers Dayton Tire & Rubber and Seiberling.

At the time of Firestone's purchase, General Motors (GM) dropped it as a supplier. Bridgestone/Firestone compensated for this loss in volume by selling more tires through mass-market retailers. It began selling tires to GM's Saturn Corporation in 1990.

The following year new Bridgestone/Firestone chairman Yoichiro Kaizaki moved to cut production costs, alienating union workers. He became company head in 1993. Tensions in the US rose in 1995 when the company hired 2,300 permanent replacement workers during a plant strike. In 1996, after United Rubber Workers members had become part of United Steelworkers of America, the two sides approved a new contract.

Expanding its markets, Bridgestone opened a retail outlet in Moscow in 1999 and acquired a radial tire plant in China from South Korea's Kumho Industrial Company in 2000. That year the company recalled approximately 6.5 million Firestone ATX, ATX II, and Wilderness AT tires after dozens of incidents where the tires came apart at road speeds. The affected tires had been used on light trucks and SUVs since 1990, many of them as original equipment on the Ford Explorer. Not long after the recall, Bridgestone/Firestone chairman and CEO Masatoshi Ono retired and was replaced by John Lampe. The fallout and ensuing blame-game (improper inflation guidelines/unstable vehicle vs. faulty tires) essentially ended Bridgestone's 95-year relationship with Ford (Bridgestone still does business with Ford outside the Americas).

In 2001 Bridgestone replaced president Yoichiro Kaizaki with SVP Shigeo Watanabe. Then, in June, while revealing that it would face its first loss since listing 30 years previously, Bridgestone announced that it would close the Decatur, Illinois, plant at which many of the recalled tires were made. The plant employed about 1,500 workers. Later in the year the company announced that it would recall an additional 3.5 million tires.

In 2005 Bridgestone purchased the Indonesian rubber plantations from Goodyear.

Watanabe stepped down as chairman, president, and CEO the next year; he was replaced by EVP Shoshi Arakawa.

EXECUTIVES

Chairman, President, and CEO: Shoshi Arakawa, age 63
Corporate Officer and Group CEO: Hidekazu Ishibashi
President: Kazuhisa Saikai
Treasurer, CFO, and CIO: Takahashi Yasushi Osamu
Managing Director, Tire Business Operations and Chief, International Tire Business: Takashi Urano
VP and Officer, Vice Chairman, Bridgestone Americas: Narumi (Nick) Zaitsu
VP and Officer; Chairman Bridgestone Americas: Asahiko (Duke) Nishiyama
VP, Senior Officer, and Director; Chairman, President, and CEO, Bridgestone Europe: Toru Tsuda
Corporate Officer and Head, Product Development and Development Manager: Hiroshi Yamaguti
Corporate Officer, Retail Business Development Director: Shiniti Sato
Corporate Officer, Tire Business Division: Shimizu Minoru
Corporate Officer, Tire Product Strategist: Masato Hiruma
Corporate Officer, Direct Tire Sales Demand: Yongdu Yasuo
Corporate Officer, Chemicals Products Business Contact: Natsuki Huzii
Corporate Officer, Deputy Human Resources Representative and the Central Research Institute: Hideki Yokoyama
Corporate Officer, Bridgestone Americas Inc. (Akron) Dispatch: Hideo Hara
Auditors: Deloitte Touche Tohmatsu

LOCATIONS

HQ: Bridgestone Corporation
10-1, Kyobashi 1-chome, Chuo-ku
Tokyo 104-8340, Japan
Phone: 81-3-3567-0111   **Fax:** 81-3-3535-2553
US HQ: 535 Marriott Dr., Nashville, TN 37214
US Phone: 615-937-1000   **US Fax:** 615-937-3621
Web: www.bridgestone.co.jp

2009 Sales

	% of total
The Americas	43
Japan	26
Europe	14
Other countries	17
Total	**100**

PRODUCTS/OPERATIONS

2009 Sales

	% of total
Tires	83
Diversified products	17
Total	**100**

Selected Products

Tires and Tubes
  Agricultural machinery
  Aircraft
  Buses
  Cars
  Commercial vehicles
  Construction and mining vehicles
  Monorails
  Motorcycles
  Race cars
  Scooters
  Trucks

Diversified Products
  Bicycles and bicycle accessories
  Chemical and Industrial
    Adhesive and anti-reflective film for glass and flat-panel displays
    Conveyor belts
    Electronic paper for still image display
    High-performance films
    Hydraulic hoses
    Marine fenders
    Panel type water tank
    Polyurethane foam
    Rubber tracks
    Seismic isolators
    Single crystal wafers for semiconductor devices
  Sporting Goods
    Golf apparel
    Golf balls
    Golf clubs
    Tennis goods

COMPETITORS

3M
Acushnet
Callaway Golf
Continental AG
Cooper Tire & Rubber
Goodyear Tire & Rubber
Hankook Tire
Huffy Corporation
Kumho Tire
Marangoni
Michelin
Pirelli
Sime Darby
Sumitomo Rubber

HISTORICAL FINANCIALS

Company Type: Public

Income Statement

FYE: December 31

	REVENUE ($ mil.)	NET INCOME ($ mil.)	NET PROFIT MARGIN	EMPLOYEES
12/09	28,154	218	0.8%	137,135
12/08	35,786	115	0.3%	137,981
12/07	30,176	1,172	3.9%	133,752
12/06	25,115	715	2.8%	126,326
12/05	22,834	1,534	6.7%	123,727
Annual Growth	5.4%	(38.6%)	—	2.6%

2009 Year-End Financials

Debt ratio: —
Return on equity: 1.9%
Cash ($ mil.): 1,719
Current ratio: 1.67
Long-term debt ($ mil.): —

No. of shares (mil.): 784
Dividends
  Yield: 1.0%
  Payout: 121.4%
Market value ($ mil.): 13,825

Stock History

Pink Sheets: BRDCY

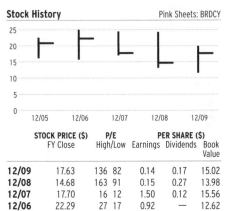

	STOCK PRICE ($) FY Close	P/E High/Low	PER SHARE ($) Earnings	Dividends	Book Value
12/09	17.63	136 82	0.14	0.17	15.02
12/08	14.68	163 91	0.15	0.27	13.98
12/07	17.70	16 12	1.50	0.12	15.56
12/06	22.29	27 17	0.92	—	12.62
12/05	20.83	12 9	1.92	—	12.21
Annual Growth	(4.1%)	— —	(48.0%)	19.0%	5.3%

British Airways

A member of the royal family of European airlines, British Airways (BA) serves about 150 destinations in some 75 countries from hubs at London's Heathrow and Gatwick airports. The carrier operates a fleet of more than 240 aircraft, consisting mainly of Airbus and Boeing jets. BA extends its network to more than 300 destinations via code-sharing relationships, chiefly with AMR's American Airlines and other members of the Oneworld global marketing alliance, such as Iberia and Qantas. Among Europe's flag carriers, BA is outranked only by the combined Air France-KLM and by Lufthansa. In November 2009 BA agreed to merge with Iberia, Spain's #1 airline.

Under its terms, the carriers would form a joint holding company, International Airlines Group. BA would own 56% and Iberia would hold 44%. Iberia chairman Antonio Vazquez will serve as chair of the new board, while BA head Willie Walsh will become CEO of the new company. Each carrier would retain its brand and hub. The new entity would join Air France-KLM and Lufthansa (which owns Austrian, bmi, Brussels, and SWISS) as an operator of multiple national flag carriers, creating Europe's third-largest airline by revenue.

In the meantime BA, Iberia, and American Airlines are rolling out a transatlantic joint venture that defends their routes between the US and UK. The joint venture, a step up from their code-sharing alliance, opens the way for coordinating routes, schedules, and prices.

The recession caused revenues across the airline industry to take a nosedive after fuel prices soared to record heights in 2008 followed by a sharp plunge in demand caused by the global financial downturn. After massive losses in 2008, in May 2009 British Airways asked its 40,000 employees to work without pay for up to a month, take unpaid leave, or drop down to part-time work. More than 800 workers agreed to work for free in July and another 7,000 or so said they would take pay cuts or unpaid leave. Additionally, the company reduced its workforce by 1,750, including one-third of its managerial staff. CEO Willie Walsh, CFO Keith Williams, and all 11 board members also forewent their salaries in July.

British Airways faced continued difficulty in 2010 with the eruption of the Iceland volcano Eyjafjallajokull in April. The airline sustained estimated losses of £15 million to £20 million per day due to airspace closure. Although the EU agreed that national governments could compensate airlines for the losses incurred, the UK's new transport minister ruled out compensation by the UK government.

HISTORY

British Airways has a jet trail winding back to 1916 and its biplane-flying ancestor, Aircraft Transport and Travel, which in 1919 launched the world's first daily international air service (between London and Paris). Concerned about subsidized foreign competition, British authorities in 1924 merged Aircraft Transport and Travel successor Daimler Airways with other fledgling British carriers — British Air Marine Navigation, Handley Page, and Instone Air Line — to form Imperial Airways.

Imperial pioneered routes from London to India (1929), Singapore (1933), and — in partnership with Qantas Empire Airways — Australia (1934). Competition on European routes emerged in the 1930s from upstart British Airways; in 1939 the government, troubled by the threat to Imperial, nationalized and merged the two airlines to form British Overseas Airways Corporation (BOAC).

After WWII, BOAC continued as the UK's international airline, but state-owned British European Airways (BEA) took over domestic and European routes. In 1972 the government combined the duo to form British Airways (BA).

BA and Air France jointly introduced supersonic passenger service in 1976 with the Concorde — a PR victory that contributed to years of losses. Colin Marshall became CEO in 1983 and reduced manpower and routes.

In 1987 the government sold BA to the public, and the airline bought chief UK rival British Caledonian. Hoping to become a globe-spanning carrier, in 1992 BA tried to gain a 44% stake in USAir (which became US Airways). American Airlines, United, and Delta strongly objected, demanding equal access to UK markets. BA settled for a 25% stake, the maximum foreign ownership allowed by US law, in 1993.

That year BA settled a libel suit brought by UK competitor Virgin Atlantic Airways, which accused BA of waging a smear campaign against it. The settlement cost BA about $5 million, and Virgin Atlantic followed with a $1 billion antitrust suit in the US (dismissed in 1999). In 1994 BA paid out $4 million to settle yet another Virgin Atlantic suit, this one claiming BA had done sloppy maintenance on Virgin aircraft.

In 1996 Marshall turned over the CEO job to Bob Ayling, who had joined BA in 1985. BA and American Airlines agreed to coordinate prices and schedules and to share market data for their transatlantic routes. Though the deal met regulatory obstacles from the start, in 1997 BA sold its stake in US Airways.

Ayling resigned in 2000, and Marshall stepped in as temporary CEO before Rod Eddington, a veteran of Cathay Pacific and Ansett, was appointed. Also that year BA took a 9% stake in Iberia and sold its interest in France's Air Liberté.

BA grounded its Concordes in 2000 (flights resumed in 2001), three weeks after the crash of an Air France Concorde outside Paris in which 113 people were killed. (BA retired its Concorde fleet, a longtime symbol of the airline's transatlantic dominance, for good in 2003.)

BA laid off 5,200 employees in 2001 as a result of decreased demand for air travel after the terrorist attacks in New York and Washington, DC. The layoffs were on top of 1,800 job cuts the airline made earlier in the year, reducing BA's workforce by 10%.

Eddington stepped down as CEO in 2005, and former Aer Lingus chief Willie Walsh was named to replace him.

In 2006 BA was a target of an investigation by US and UK government agencies into alleged price-fixing on fuel surcharges by airlines. Commercial director Martin George and communications head Iain Burns, were placed on leave and then resigned in connection with the inquiry. The next year BA settled the charges by agreeing to pay fines of about $300 million to the US and about $247 million to the UK.

BA moved to augment its transatlantic service in 2008 by launching a new carrier, OpenSkies, which began operations by flying between Paris and New York.

EXECUTIVES

Chairman: Martin F. Broughton, age 63
Chief Executive and Director:
 William M. (Willie) Walsh, age 48
CFO and Director: Keith Williams, age 54
Director Operations: Andy Lord
Director Flight Operations: Stephen Riley
Director Corporate Communications: Julia Simpson
Director Sales and Marketing: Andrew Crawley
Director Engineering: Garry Copeland
Director People and Organizational Effectiveness:
 Tony McCarthy
Director Strategy and Business Units: Robert Boyle,
 age 44
Director Investments and Alliances: Roger P. Maynard,
 age 67
Acting Director Customer: Silla Maizey
Secretary: Alan K. Buchanan, age 52
Head Investor Relations: George Stinnes
Auditors: Ernst & Young

LOCATIONS

HQ: British Airways Plc
 Waterside (HAA3), Harmondsworth
 London UB7 0GB, United Kingdom
Phone: 44-0844-493-0787
US HQ: 75-20 Astoria Blvd., Jackson Heights, NY 11370
US Phone: 347-418-4000   **US Fax:** 347-418-4204
Web: www.british-airways.com

2010 Sales

	% of total
Europe	
UK	46
Other countries	16
The Americas	
US	18
Other countries	2
Africa, Middle East & Indian sub-continent	9
Asia/Pacific & Australia	9
Total	**100**

PRODUCTS/OPERATIONS

2010 Sales

	% of total
Passenger	93
Cargo	7
Total	**100**

COMPETITORS

Air France-KLM
All Nippon Airways
British Midland
Delta Air Lines
easyJet
Flybe
Japan Airlines
Lufthansa
Ryanair
SAS
Singapore Airlines
United Continental
US Airways
Virgin Atlantic Airways

HISTORICAL FINANCIALS

Company Type: Public

Income Statement

FYE: March 31

	REVENUE ($ mil.)	NET INCOME ($ mil.)	NET PROFIT MARGIN	EMPLOYEES
3/10	12,045	274	2.3%	41,494
3/09	12,777	(509)	—	40,627
3/08	17,454	1,384	7.9%	45,140
3/07	16,707	862	5.2%	43,501
3/06	14,827	785	5.3%	49,957
Annual Growth	**(5.1%)**	**(23.1%)**	**—**	**(4.5%)**

2010 Year-End Financials

Debt ratio: 180.1%	No. of shares (mil.): 1,154
Return on equity: —	Dividends
Cash ($ mil.): 1,184	Yield: 0.0%
Current ratio: 0.71	Payout: —
Long-term debt ($ mil.): 5,192	Market value ($ mil.): 4,224

Stock History

Pink Sheets: BAIRY

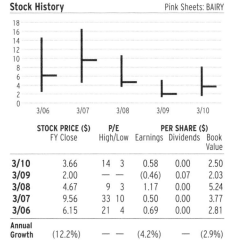

	STOCK PRICE ($) FY Close	P/E High/Low		PER SHARE ($) Earnings	Dividends	Book Value
3/10	3.66	14	3	0.58	0.00	2.50
3/09	2.00	—	—	(0.46)	0.07	2.03
3/08	4.67	9	3	1.17	0.00	5.24
3/07	9.56	33	10	0.50	0.00	3.77
3/06	6.15	21	4	0.69	0.00	2.81
Annual Growth	**(12.2%)**	**—**	**—**	**(4.2%)**	**—**	**(2.9%)**

British American Tobacco

When people pick up smoking, British American Tobacco (BAT) picks up steam. Spun off with the reorganization of B.A.T. Industries, BAT is the world's #2 tobacco company (behind Marlboro maker Altria Group). The firm makes about 715 billion cigarettes each year and sells them in more than 150 countries. BAT's global cigarette brands include Dunhill, Kent, Lucky Strike, and Pall Mall — just four in a portfolio of some 300. The company also makes loose tobacco and regional cigarette brands. Its former US unit, Brown & Williamson (Kool and GPC cigarettes), merged with R.J. Reynolds Tobacco (RJRT) in 2004. Reinet Investments SCA, controlled by South African billionaire Johann Rupert, is BAT's largest shareholder.

BAT's four global brands — Dunhill, Kent, Lucky Strike, and Pall Mall — posted a volume increase of 16% in 2008 to number 187 billion cigarettes. (This percentage represents a 64% increase in volume since 2004.) Driving growth of these four important brands is key to BAT's overall growth strategy.

BAT owns 42% of Reynolds American, which was created by the Brown & Williamson/RJRT merger. BAT now looks to emerging markets in South Korea, Vietnam, and Nigeria, as well as other countries for growth. To that end, BAT in 2009 acquired Indonesia's fourth-largest cigarette maker, PT Bentoel Internasional Investama, and merged it with its Indonesian arm, BAT Indonesia, in 2010. A year earlier, BAT acquired the cigarette business assets of Tekel, the Turkish state-owned tobacco company.

The cigarette maker has scaled back the number of factories it operates from 83 to 49, including acquisitions, since 2000. In 2008 it shuttered plants in the Netherlands and South Africa, while adding factories as a result of the Tekel and Skandinavisk Tobakskompagni (ST) acquisitions. The purchase of ST's cigarette business in mid-2008 increased BAT's volume in Europe.

In response to health concerns and lawsuits brought against the tobacco industry in the US, BAT has been test-marketing a Swedish product called snus, a pasteurized tobacco product that resembles a small teabag. BAT markets it as more than 100 times less harmful than cigarettes — selling in South Africa under the Peter Stuyvesant brand and in Sweden under the Lucky Strike brand.

Jan du Plessis stepped down as chairman of BAT in November 2009, and was succeeded by Richard Burrows. Nicandro Durante was named CEO-designate in September 2010.

HISTORY

After a year of vicious price-cutting between Imperial Tobacco (UK) and James Buchanan Duke's American Tobacco in the UK, Imperial counterattacked in the US. To end the cigarette price war in the UK, the firms created British American Tobacco (BAT) in 1902. The truce granted Imperial the British market, American the US market, and they jointly owned BAT in the rest of the world.

With Duke in control, BAT expanded into new markets. In China it was selling 25 billion cigarettes a year by 1920. When the Communist revolution ended BAT's operations in China, the company lost more than 25% of its sales (although China later reemerged as a major export market for the company's cigarettes).

A 1911 US antitrust action forced American to sell its interest in BAT and opened the US market to the company. BAT purchased US cigarette manufacturer Brown & Williamson in 1927 and continued to grow through geographic expansion until the 1960s. In 1973 BAT and Imperial each regained control of its own brands in the UK and Continental Europe. Imperial sold the last of its stake in BAT in 1980.

Fearing that mounting public concern over smoking would limit the cigarette market, BAT acquired nontobacco businesses; it changed its name to B.A.T Industries in 1976. The acquisitions of retailers Saks (1973), Argos (UK, 1979), Marshall Field (1982), and later, insurance firms, diversified the company's sales base. After a 1989 hostile takeover bid from Sir James Goldsmith, it sold its retail operations, and retained its tobacco and financial services.

In 1994 B.A.T acquired the former American Tobacco for $1 billion. In 1997 the company acquired Cigarrera de Moderna (with 50% of Mexico's cigarette sales) and formed a joint venture with the Turkish tobacco state enterprise, Tekel.

B.A.T's tobacco operations were spun off in 1998 as British American Tobacco (BAT). The financial services operations were merged with Zurich Insurance in a transaction that created two holding companies: Allied Zurich (UK) and Zurich Allied (Switzerland). With the changes, Martin Broughton became chairman of BAT.

The company in 1999 paid $8.2 billion to buy Dutch cigarette company Rothmans International (Rothmans, Dunhill) from Switzerland's Compagnie Financiere Richemont and South Africa's Rembrandt Group — both controlled by Anton Rupert. With the purchase, BAT received a controlling stake in Canada's Rothmans, Benson & Hedges (RBH).

In early 2000 BAT bought the 58% of Canada's Imasco it didn't already own. Imasco sold off its financial services and BAT received Imasco's Imperial Tobacco unit (not related to the UK's Imperial Tobacco Group) in the deal. (Formerly called Imperial Tobacco Company of Canada, Imasco was created in 1908 with help from BAT.) BAT also unloaded its share of RBH via a public offering.

In 2001 Broughton announced that the Chinese government had approved development plans that would allow the company to build a factory in China. The company also announced it would build the first foreign-owned cigarette factory in South Korea, at that time the world's #8 tobacco market.

Increasing its Latin American regional presence, BAT purchased a controlling stake in Peru's top tobacco company, Tabacalera Nacional, and several of its suppliers in 2003. However, two months later BAT said it would not make the million-dollar investment in the company. The announcement came soon after Peru raised taxes on cigarettes. By the end of the year, BAT had purchased tobacco manufacturer Ente Tabacchi Italiani S.p.A. from the Italian government. BAT sold the distribution end of its Italian business to Compañía de Distribución Integral Logista in 2004, the same year that Broughton retired; the company named Jan du Plessis as chairman and Paul Adams as CEO.

In June 2009 the company acquired an 85% stake in Indonesia's fourth largest cigarette maker PT Bentoel Internasional Investama Tbk for £303 million ($494 million) from Rajawali Group.

EXECUTIVES

Chairman: Richard Burrows, age 64
CEO Designate and Board Member: Nicandro Durante, age 53, $1,728,299 total compensation
COO and Board Member: John Daly, age 53
Managing Director: David Waterfield
CIO, Director Finance, and Board Member: Ben Stevens, age 50, $1,354,787 total compensation
Group Marketing Director: Jean-Marc Lévy
Legal Director and General Counsel: Neil Withington
Director, Asia Pacific: David Fell, age 49
Director, Eastern Europe: Des Naughton, age 43
Director, Western Europe: Jack M. H. D. Bowles, age 46
Director, Operations and IT: Peter Taylor, age 56
Director Human Resources: Rudi Kindts
Director Corporate and Regulatory Affairs: Michael Prideaux, age 58
Head Investor Relations: Ralph Edmondson
Head, Science and Regulation: Christopher (Chris) Proctor
President and CEO, Imperial Tobacco Canada: Ian Muir
Auditors: PricewaterhouseCoopers LLP

LOCATIONS

HQ: British American Tobacco p.l.c.
Globe House, 4 Temple Place
London WC2R 2PG, United Kingdom
Phone: 44-20-7845-1000   **Fax:** 44-20-7240-0555
Web: www.bat.com

2009 Sales

	% of total
Western Europe	27
Asia/Pacific	23
Americas	22
Africa & Middle East	16
Eastern Europe	12
Total	**100**

PRODUCTS/OPERATIONS

2009 Cigarettes Sold

	No. (billions)
Pall Mall	68
Kent	61
Dunhill	41
Lucky Strike	26
Other international brands	147
Total	**343**

Selected International Cigarette Brands
Barclay
Benson & Hedges (Asia/Pacific, Middle East, Africa)
Capri
Carlton
Dunhill
John Player Gold Leaf
Kent
Kool
Lucky Strike
Misty
Pall Mall
Peter Stuyvesant
Player's
Rothmans
State Express 555
Viceroy
Winfield

COMPETITORS

Altria
Imperial Tobacco
Japan Tobacco
Lorillard
Philip Morris International
Reemtsma Cigarettenfabriken
Santa Fe Natural Tobacco
Swedish Match
Swisher International
Tiedemanns
Universal Corporation
Vector Group

HISTORICAL FINANCIALS

Company Type: Public

Income Statement

FYE: December 31

	REVENUE ($ mil.)	NET INCOME ($ mil.)	NET PROFIT MARGIN	EMPLOYEES
12/09	22,628	4,321	19.1%	95,710
12/08	17,762	3,600	20.3%	56,170
12/07	52,226	4,240	8.1%	53,000
12/06	49,362	3,716	7.5%	55,145
12/05	41,348	3,054	7.4%	96,952
Annual Growth	**(14.0%)**	**9.1%**	**—**	**(0.3%)**

2009 Year-End Financials

Debt ratio: 142.0%
Return on equity: —
Cash ($ mil.): 3,442
Current ratio: 1.17
Long-term debt ($ mil.): 15,467

No. of shares (mil.): 1,013
Dividends
  Yield: 2.8%
  Payout: 67.3%
Market value ($ mil.): 104,284

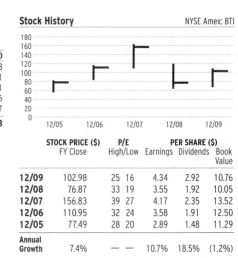

| Stock History | | | | | NYSE Amex: BTI |

	STOCK PRICE ($) FY Close	P/E High/Low	PER SHARE ($) Earnings	Dividends	Book Value
12/09	102.98	25 16	4.34	2.92	10.76
12/08	76.87	33 19	3.55	1.92	10.05
12/07	156.83	39 27	4.17	2.35	13.52
12/06	110.95	32 24	3.58	1.91	12.50
12/05	77.49	28 20	2.89	1.48	11.29
Annual Growth	**7.4%**	**— —**	**10.7%**	**18.5%**	**(1.2%)**

British Broadcasting Corporation

You might say "The Beeb" puts Britain on the air. British Broadcasting Corporation (BBC) is a publicly financed broadcasting company and the dominant force in TV and radio in the UK. It operates eight television services offering a mix of programming that includes general entertainment, news, current affairs, and sports. Its 10 radio services offer music, news, and sports programming throughout the country. The BBC also keeps the world informed through its BBC World Service radio network. In addition to broadcasting, the company creates and distributes television programs and distributes pay-TV channels to international markets through BBC Worldwide. The BBC was established by royal charter in 1922.

Public financing in the form of a license fee accounts for about 80% of the BBC's revenue. The monthly mandatory fee is paid by all TV set owners in the UK and supports both radio and television operations. The company is governed by the BBC Trust, a 12-member board appointed by the Queen to represent the public interest. Within the UK media landscape, the BBC is the publicly financed counterpoint to commercial broadcast networks ITV and Channel 5 (which is owned by Northern and Shell). Its radio services operate alongside commercial broadcasters Global Radio and TIML Radio (Absolute Radio).

While the BBC is still a beloved institution, the public broadcaster often finds its existence called into question by both political and commercial interests. Challenging the license fee is a favorite sport of conservative politicians and commercial broadcasters who charge that the public subsidy gives the BBC an unfair advantage. The BBC Trust responded to some of those concerns early in 2009 with indications that BBC Worldwide would scale back some of its international expansion activities.

The BBC continues to looks to the future, however, by investing in several interactive media initiatives to reach audiences through the Internet. Its website, offering streaming video and audio content, reaches more than 20 million users each week.

Another priority for the BBC has been to broaden its content offering as it relates to the other nations within Great Britain (that is, Scotland, Northern Ireland, and Wales).

The BBC responded to the economic recession in 2009 with a number of measures to reduce expenses. Those efforts included some job cuts and executive pay freezes. Later that year, the BBC furthered those efforts by suspending executive bonuses indefinitely and cutting some salaries for presenters, actors, and other talent.

HISTORY

Established as the British Broadcasting Company Limited in 1922, the BBC was founded by a group of radio manufacturers aiming to block any single manufacturer from grabbing a broadcasting monopoly. Under general manager John Reith, BBC radio programming grew to include news, cultural events, sports, and weather. A burgeoning social and cultural presence led to its reestablishment in 1927 under a new royal charter. The organization was renamed the British Broadcasting Corporation, and the charter ensured it would remain outside the control of the British Parliament.

By 1935 BBC radio had reached about 95% of the British population. TV broadcasting debuted the next year, but the cost of TV sets limited audience numbers to about 20,000. Those who could afford a TV got to see the coronation of King George VI and Wimbledon. TV broadcasting would be short-lived, however: Beginning in 1939 and throughout WWII, the signal was blacked out when the transmitter proved a good aircraft direction finder.

Although TV screens went dark, BBC radio served a vital role during WWII. Its broadcasts to occupied territories and the airing of Prime Minister Winston Churchill's wartime speeches elevated the BBC's reputation as a news broadcaster.

BBC TV transmission resumed in 1946. The 1953 broadcast of the coronation of Queen Elizabeth II helped launch the television age of the 1950s. In 1955 commercial broadcaster Independent Television Network became the BBC's first rival for viewers. The BBC introduced its second public TV channel (BBC Two) in 1964. By 1969 both BBC One and BBC Two were broadcasting in color.

The corporate culture of the BBC during the 1970s and 1980s was dominated by financial upheaval. Budget cuts combined with growing competition prompted the formation of a committee to review the BBC's financing alternatives. Although the committee's 1986 report did not permit commercial advertising on the BBC, it did lead to more flexibility in funding.

Sir John Birt was appointed the BBC's director general in 1992, and the reorganization and cost-cutting program he instituted fueled the debate over the company's move toward commercialization. Through BBC Worldwide, the BBC inched away from its public service roots. In 1997 the BBC privatized its domestic TV and radio transmission business and launched a 24-hour cable news channel. UKTV (a commercial TV joint venture with Flextech — later called Virgin Media Television) also went on the air that year. In 1998 the BBC teamed with Discovery Communications to launch BBC America, a US cable channel.

In 1999 Greg Dyke, who had been chief executive of Pearson Television, was named to succeed Birt, who left in January 2000. Shortly after Dyke took the reins, he announced a massive restructuring of the organization designed to cut costs (eliminating hundreds of jobs), form more partnerships with private entities, and increase the amount spent on programming.

Both Dyke and chairman Gavyn Davies resigned from the BBC in 2004 following a British judge's ruling that a controversial BBC story accusing Prime Minister Tony Blair of exaggerating Iraq's weapons of mass destruction capabilities was riddled with errors. Television executive Michael Grade became chairman, and former Channel Four CEO Mark Thompson became the new director general.

The BBC started 2005 with a renewal of its royal charter that will keep the company in business until 2016. However, the UK government forced the company to create an independent board of trustees to oversee its operation. The following year the BBC suffered a blow when Grade left the organization to head commercial broadcasting firm ITV. Thompson took over executive management of the BBC, while Sir Michael Lyons was appointed chairman of the BBC Trust.

EXECUTIVES

Director-General and Chair, Executive Board:
Mark Thompson, age 53,
$1,640,812 total compensation
COO and Executive Director: Caroline Thomson,
age 53, $812,537 total compensation
CFO and Executive Director: Zarin Patel,
$844,015 total compensation
CTO: John Linwood, $352,099 total compensation
COO, Journalism: Dominic Coles,
$399,754 total compensation
Executive Director; CEO, BBC Worldwide:
John B. Smith, age 52
Director, BBC North: Peter Salmon, age 53,
$611,555 total compensation
Group General Counsel and Secretary, BBC and Non-Executive Director, BBC Worldwide: Andy Griffee,
$342,874 total compensation
Group Financial Controller: Chris Day,
$330,441 total compensation
Human Resources Director: Clare Dyer,
$255,855 total compensation
Employee Relations and People Strategy Director:
Mike Gooddie, $298,045 total compensation
Creative Director: Alan Yentob, age 63,
$319,180 total compensation
Director Brand and Planning: Jacky Brandreth-Potter,
$263,607 total compensation
Director, Procurement and Revenue Management:
Beverley Tew, $267,909 total compensation
Director Communications: Ed Williams,
$352,199 total compensation
Director Nations and Regions: Pat Loughrey,
$495,973 total compensation
Director Policy and Strategy: John Tate,
$282,977 total compensation
Director Marketing, Communications, and Audiences and Executive Director: Sharon Baylay
Director World Service: Peter Horrocks,
$295,263 total compensation
Head Rights and Business Affairs: James Lancaster,
$262,581 total compensation
Head Legal and Business Affairs: John Moran,
$150,017 total compensation
Auditors: KPMG LLP

LOCATIONS

HQ: British Broadcasting Corporation
Broadcasting House, Portland Place
London W1A 1AA, United Kingdom
Phone: 44-20-7580-4468   **Fax:** 44-20-7637-1630
Web: www.bbc.co.uk

PRODUCTS/OPERATIONS

2010 Revenue Sources

	% of total
License fees	72
Commercial businesses	21
Government grants	6
Other	1
Total	**100**

Selected Operations

Broadcasting
 Radio
  1Xtra (contemporary urban music)
  5 Live (news and sports)
  5 Live Sports Extra
  6 Music
  Asian Network (ethnic radio programming)
  BBC World Service (international news and
   information)
  Radio 1
  Radio 2
  Radio 3 (classical music)
  Radio 4 (news and current affairs programming)
  Radio 7 (scripted radio programming)
 Television
  BBC One (general programming)
  BBC Two (general programming)
  BBC Three (young adults)
  BBC Four (factual and arts programming)
  BBC News
  BBC Parliament
  BBC Red Button (on-demand programming)
  CBBC (children's programming)
  CBeebies (kid's programming)
BBC Worldwide
 BBC America
 BBC Canada
 BBC Entertainment
 BBC HD
 BBC Kids (Canada)
 BBC Knowledge
 BBC Lifestyle
 BBC World News (international news and information)
 UKTV (pay-TV channels)

COMPETITORS

Absolute Radio
Bauer Radio
BSkyB
Channel 4
Five.tv
Global Radio
ITV
stv group
UTV Media

HISTORICAL FINANCIALS

Company Type: Government-owned

Income Statement				FYE: March 31
	REVENUE ($ mil.)	NET INCOME ($ mil.)	NET PROFIT MARGIN	EMPLOYEES
3/10	7,218	720	10.0%	22,861
3/09	6,544	361	5.5%	22,874
3/08	8,804	203	2.3%	23,101
3/07	8,197	119	1.5%	23,037
3/06	6,967	6	0.1%	25,377
Annual Growth	0.9%	226.9%	—	(2.6%)

Net Income History

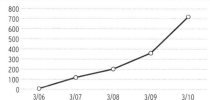

British Sky Broadcasting

The lofty British Sky Broadcasting Group (BSkyB) is one of the UK's leading pay-TV providers. BSkyB distributes entertainment, news, and sports programming to subscribers in the UK and Ireland via its digital direct-to-home (DTH) satellite service, primarily through its Sky Digital brand. It also licenses some channels to cable operators including Virgin Media. In addition, BSkyB provides broadband Internet services through Sky Broadband and resells residential telephony service. In 2010 the company sold its business-to-business broadband Internet and data services business Easynet to Lloyds TSB Development Capital for about £100 million (around $150 million).

Looking to add more content, in mid-2010 BSkyB bought Virgin Media Television (renamed Living TV Group) from Virgin Media for about £105 million (around $158 million). The acquisition includes a small portfolio of cable and satellite TV networks that consist of reality-based and scripted entertainment programming, along with related websites.

To boost brand awareness, BSkyB broadcasts three channels — Sky News, Sky Sports News, and Sky Travel — over Freeview, a free-to-air TV service. (Freeview and services like it are also referred to as digital terrestrial television, or DTT, services.) With millions of untapped homes in the UK, the company is hoping increased brand awareness will bring in more subscriber revenue.

BSkyB provides its own free-to-air satellite TV offering, known as Freesat from Sky, to take further advantage of the popularity of the Freeview service. With the purchase of a set of reception equipment, customers have access to about 200 TV and radio channels with no subscription fees. BSkyB also holds broadcast rights to the leading football leagues in England and Scotland, and has minority stakes in several clubs.

News Corp. owns 39% of BSkyB. In June 2010 News Corp. announced a proposal to buy the remaining shares of the company, though it has not made a formal offer.

HISTORY

Australian-born media czar Rupert Murdoch, after taking control of several British newspapers, moved into satellite TV service in the UK in 1989 when his News Corp. holding company started Sky Network Television. Broadcasting SkyTV's four channels via satellites owned by the Luxembourg-based Astra group allowed Murdoch to avoid restrictions of the British Broadcasting Act, which prohibited owners of national newspapers from owning more than 20% of a TV company.

In 1990 a consortium of companies, including Chargeurs, Granada, and Pearson, set up rival service British Satellite Broadcasting. The rivals faced a consumer market slow to adapt to new technology and a shrinking advertising base caused by an economic recession; both companies posted huge losses (SkyTV's weekly losses grew to more than $20 million in 1990). In the wake of such financial hemorrhaging, the firms merged that year and became British Sky Broadcasting (BSkyB), a slimmer operation with five channels.

The small stake held by Chargeurs was later transferred to its Pathé communications unit.

In 1993 BSkyB teamed up with US media group Viacom to produce a Nickelodeon channel (children's programming) for the UK market. Then the firm allied with home shopping channel QVC to launch QVC UK (BSkyB sold its stake in the company in 2004). By the end of 1993, more than 3 million UK homes were receiving BSkyB's programs.

BSkyB sold about 20% of itself to the public in 1994, dropping News Corp.'s stake from 50% to 40%. That year it reinforced its position as the top UK sports broadcaster by launching Sky Sports 2. BSkyB teamed with rival BBC in 1995 to acquire more sports programming. It also formed an alliance with international news agency Reuters in an effort to strengthen its Sky News Channel.

In 1997 BSkyB began developing digital satellite TV and interactive services in the UK through British Interactive Broadcasting, a joint venture with British Telecommunications (now BT Group), HSBC Holdings, and Matsushita Electric Industrial. (The service, Sky Digital, was launched in 1998 and offers subscribers about 150 channels.)

Managing director Sam Chisholm and his deputy, David Chance, resigned in 1997, opening the door for Murdoch's 29-year-old daughter, Elisabeth, to take a greater role at BSkyB. (She left the company in 2000.) Mark Booth (formerly with Murdoch's Japanese Sky Broadcasting) became CEO. BSkyB launched digital pay-per-view TV in the UK in 1997.

In 1999 the government blew the whistle on BSkyB's plan to buy UK soccer team Manchester United for $1 billion, saying it would have reduced competition in soccer broadcasting. (BSkyB retained its minority stake in the team.)

Fox/Liberty Networks CEO Tony Ball replaced Booth as CEO in 1999 after Booth was named to head a News Corp.-backed new media company. French conglomerate Vivendi (now Vivendi Universal) bought Pathé's stake in BSkyB, along with those of Granada and Pearson, and Rupert Murdoch took over as chairman of BSkyB, replacing Pathé's Jerome Seydoux. Vivendi announced in 2000 that it would sell its BSkyB stake to clear regulatory hurdles in its bid to acquire Canada's Seagram and take over the Universal entertainment group.

News Corp. in 2000 spun off its satellite holdings, including BSkyB, to form a new company, Sky Global Networks, in large part to accommodate Murdoch's acquisition of US-based DIRECTV. Ball stepped down as CEO in 2003. In November of the same year, eyebrows were raised when Rupert Murdoch's son James was brought in to fill the CEO spot. At least in part because he was only 30 years old at the time, there were many grumblings of nepotism.

The company scored big points when it acquired exclusive broadcasting rights to the Premier League football games in 2003, but the deal prompted the European Commission to scrutinize the situation as a possible violation of European competition rules.

In 2006 the company acquired a nearly 18% stake in ITV (formerly Granada), a leading European TV broadcasting and production company, in a deal valued at about $2 billion. In 2007 it acquired set-top box maker Amstrad. The deal added in-house design and development of such products to BSkyB's roster of services. Also that year, the company sold its stake in BSkyB Nature Limited.

EXECUTIVES

Chairman: James R. Murdoch, age 37, $150,270 total compensation
CEO and Director: Jeremy Darroch, age 49, $4,627,335 total compensation
COO: Mike Darcey, age 46
CFO and Director: Andrew Griffith, age 39, $2,090,389 total compensation
CTO: Didier Lebrat, age 50
Managing Director, Entertainment and News: Sophie Turner-Laing, age 49
Managing Director, Sky Sports: Barney Francis, age 38
Managing Director, Enterprise Business: David S. Rowe, age 51
Managing Director, Customer Group: Andrea Zappia
General Counsel: James Conyers, age 45
Group Director Business Performance: William Mellis, age 53
Group Director Brand Marketing: Andy Brent, age 49
Group Director Strategic Project Delivery: Alun Webber, age 44
Group Director Corporate Affairs: Graham McWilliam, age 38
Director Strategic Product Development: Gerry O'Sullivan
Director Product Design and TV Product Development: Brian Lenz
Director Sports and Marketing: David Murdin
Director Brand Strategy and Marketing: Robert Tansey
Director People: Deborah Baker, age 50
Director Corporate Communications: Robert Fraser
Director Investor Relations: Robert Kingston
Secretary: Grant Way
Auditors: Deloitte LLP

LOCATIONS

HQ: British Sky Broadcasting Group plc
Grant Way, Isleworth
London TW7 5QD, United Kingdom
Phone: 44-20-7705-3000 **Fax:** 44-20-7705-3008
Web: www.sky.com

PRODUCTS/OPERATIONS

2009 Sales

	% of total
Subscription	
Retail	78
Wholesale	4
Advertising	6
Installation, hardware & service	4
Sky Bet	1
Other	7
Total	**100**

Selected Channels

The Amp (music programming)
Artsworld
Bravo (entertainment programming for men)
Challenge (game shows)
Flaunt (music programming)
LIVING (entertainment programming)
LIVINGit (reality-based programming)
Scuzz (music programming)
Sky Box Office (pay-per-view programming)
Sky Cinema (classic cinema programming)
Sky Movies
Sky News
Sky One (general entertainment programming)
Sky Sports
Sky Travel (travel programming)
Sky Vegas Live (interactive entertainment)

COMPETITORS

BBC	RTL Group
BT	stv group
Carphone Warehouse	Tiscali
Channel 4	Virgin Media
Five.tv	Vodafone
ITV	Yorkshire-Tyne Tees
Orange	Television Holdings

HISTORICAL FINANCIALS

Company Type: Public

Income Statement

FYE: June 30

	REVENUE ($ mil.)	NET INCOME ($ mil.)	NET PROFIT MARGIN	EMPLOYEES
6/09	8,851	428	4.8%	14,922
6/08	9,893	(254)	—	14,145
6/07	9,125	1,001	11.0%	13,087
6/06	7,529	1,001	13.3%	11,216
6/05	7,289	765	10.5%	9,958
Annual Growth	5.0%	(13.5%)	—	10.6%

2009 Year-End Financials

Debt ratio: —
Return on equity: —
Cash ($ mil.): 1,339
Current ratio: 0.88
Long-term debt ($ mil.): 3,873

No. of shares (mil.): 438
Dividends
Yield: 2.5%
Payout: 126.5%
Market value ($ mil.): 21,727

Stock History

Pink Sheets: BSYBY

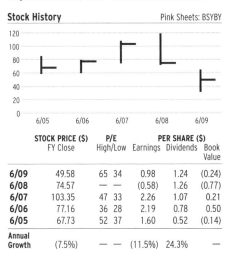

	STOCK PRICE ($) FY Close	P/E High/Low	PER SHARE ($) Earnings	Dividends	Book Value
6/09	49.58	65 34	0.98	1.24	(0.24)
6/08	74.57	— —	(0.58)	1.26	(0.77)
6/07	103.35	47 33	2.26	1.07	0.21
6/06	77.16	36 28	2.19	0.78	0.50
6/05	67.73	52 37	1.60	0.52	(0.14)
Annual Growth	(7.5%)	— —	(11.5%)	24.3%	—

BT Group

Once upon a time, BT Group's rivals could have fit into one of the company's signature red phone booths. Though competition has taken a toll, BT Group still wears the crown as the UK's top telecommunications carrier, with about 15 million customers. BT Group offers local and long-distance phone service and provides Internet access and other data and IT services. Major corporate clients are served by its BT Global Services division (which also accounts for most international business), while its Retail division oversees consumer services. Its BT Wholesale and Open-reach divisions address the broadband and local network needs of other carriers. BT Group operates primarily in the UK, but its operations span 170 countries.

BT has responded to the growing global demand for business services with the acquisition of service providers from a range of disciplines in Europe and the US. In 2008 BT bought German information technology firms Stemmer and SND from net AG to boost its presence in the region. The company also acquired UK online classified advertising specialist Ufindus, which became part of BT's online directory business.

Also that year, it bought US videoconferencing specialist Wire One Holdings to improve the capability and geographic reach of its conferencing unit, and it picked up Silicon Valley-based integrated communications software developer Ribbit Corporation.

BT announced in 2010 that it would take over management of the broadband network of France-based rival Orange, which is experiencing a declining subscriber base. As established carriers face mounting competition in the high-speed Internet space from the likes of Virgin Media and TalkTalk, some are looking to form partnerships to shore up their online businesses.

BT was chosen by the International Olympic Committee to provide communications services for the 2012 Olympic Games in London.

HISTORY

In 1879 the British Post Office (now known as Royal Mail and formerly Consignia) got the exclusive right to operate telegraph systems. When private firms tried to offer phone service, the government objected, arguing in court that its telegraph monopoly was imperiled. The courts agreed, and the Post Office was empowered to license private phone companies, collect a 10% royalty, and operate its own systems.

The private National Telephone Company emerged as the leading phone outfit, competing with the Post Office. When National's license expired in 1911, the Post Office took over and became the monopoly phone company. In 1936 the phone system introduced its familiar red public call offices (phone booths), designed for King George V's jubilee.

Under a 1981 law, telecommunications were split off from the Post Office and placed under the newly created British Telecommunications (BT) company. The government also allowed competitor Mercury Communications — formerly One 2 One and now known as T-Mobile (UK) — to compete. The Thatcher government soon called for BT's privatization.

After the Telecommunications Act of 1984, BT went public in one of the largest UK stock offerings in history. The act set up the regulatory Office of Telecommunications (OFTEL). The next year Cellnet, BT's joint venture with Securicor, launched its mobile phone network. To become a multinational concern, BT bought control of Canadian phone equipment maker Mitel (1986, sold in 1992) and 20% of firm McCaw Cellular (1989, sold to AT&T in 1994).

In 1990 the British government opened the UK to more phone competition and BT responded with improvements to its network and a workforce reduction. The government sold almost all of its remaining shares in BT in 1993. The next year the company bought a 20% stake in MCI, the #2 US long-distance carrier.

In 1996 BT announced a plan to buy out MCI, but as losses mounted from MCI's expansion into the US local market, BT in 1997 lowered its bid and lost MCI to upstart WorldCom.

In 1999 BT expanded in continental Europe, Latin America (a 20% stake in IMPSAT), Asia (with AT&T, a 30% stake in Japan Telecom), and the US, where it bought systems integration firm Syntegra (USA) (formerly Control Data Systems and now part of BT Americas) and Yellow Book USA. At home BT bought out Securicor's stake in Cellnet. UK regulators also ordered the company to upgrade its UK phone network and open it to rivals by 2001.

BT bought Ireland's Esat Telecom in 2000. That year the government sold its remaining stake in BT and the company bought Telenor's share of VIAG Interkom; early the next year the company took full ownership of the German mobile phone company. Also in early 2001, BT sold its stakes in Japan Telecom and J-Phone Communications to Vodafone, which later that year bought BT's Airtel Móvil (now known as Vodafone España) interest.

BT Group countered increasing competition and mounting debt woes through restructuring that included the 2001 spinoff of its domestic and international wireless businesses. The decision left BT Group as the only top-tier European telecom firm without a wireless network.

To further its restructuring, the company in 2002 sold its Yellow Pages unit, Yell, to two buy-out firms: Hicks, Muse, Tate & Furst (now HM Capital Partners) and Apax Partners.

In a major reorganization, BT Group turned itself into a holding company. Ordered to upgrade and open its domestic networks, it split its UK fixed-line network operations into separate wholesale and retail businesses. BT Group also expanded its information communications technology (ICT) services offered to multisite corporations in the US. It signed its largest IT services deal to date, valued at $3 billion over eight-and-a-half years, with the Reuters Group.

The company in 2005 acquired SkyNet Systems, a provider of Internet protocol-based LAN systems. To expand its global professional services offerings, the company made several purchases in 2006 including US-based Counterpane Internet Security, a provider of managed networked security services.

BT acquired Fiat's Italian telecom subsidiary Atlanet in early 2006, and later that year BT bought Fiat's Brazilian telecom business Telexis.

In 2007 the company purchased Comsat International, a data communication services provider, expanding its presence in Latin America. Also in 2007, BT bought the IT infrastructure division of France-based CS Communication & Systèmes. Meanwhile, it increased its North American presence with the acquisition of IT consulting and software provider International Network Services.

EXECUTIVES

Chairman: Sir Michael D. V. (Mike) Rake, age 62
Chief Executive and Board Member: Ian P. Livingston, age 45
Group Finance Director and Board Member: Anthony E. A. (Tony) Chanmugam, age 56
VP Global Portfolio, BT Global Services: Neil Sutton
VP Global Services Transformation Programmes, BT Innovate & Design: Jacqueline Steed
VP European Affairs: Adrian Whitchurch
VP Trade and International Affairs: Tilman Kupfer
VP, BT Latin America: João Macias Gomes
Programme Manager Community Investment: Beth Courtier
Managing Director, Retail Strategy: Sean M.G. Williams
CEO, Global Services: Jeffrey D. (Jeff) Kelly, age 54
Chief Executive, BT Wholesale: Sally Davis, age 55
Chief Executive, BT Operate: Roel Louwhoff, age 45
Chief Executive, BT Retail: Gavin Patterson, age 42
Director Marketing and Brand: Suzi Williams
Director Group Public Policy: Dorothy Smith
Company Secretary: Andrew Parker, age 50
Manager Public Affairs: Christine van der Steur
Auditors: PricewaterhouseCoopers LLP

LOCATIONS

HQ: BT Group plc
81 Newgate St.
London EC1A 7AJ, United Kingdom
Phone: 44-20-7356-5000 **Fax:** 44-20-7356-5520
US HQ: 620 8th Ave., 45th Fl., New York, NY 10018
US Phone: 212-205-1800
Web: www.btplc.com

2010 Sales

	% of total
UK	77
Europe, Middle East & Africa	16
Americas	6
Asia/Pacific	1
Total	**100**

PRODUCTS/OPERATIONS

2010 Sales

	% of total
BT Global Services	32
BT Retail	31
Openreach	20
BT Wholesale	17
Total	**100**

Selected Subsidiaries and Affiliates

Basilica Computing Limited (IT services)
British Telecommunications plc (telecommunication related services and products)
BT Americas Inc. (telecommunication related services and products, US)
BT Australasia Pty Limited (telecommunication related services and products, Australia)
BT Centre Nominee 2 Limited (property holding company)
BT Communications Ireland Limited (telecommunications services)
BT Conferencing Inc. (Audio, video, and Web conferencing services, US)
BT Convergent Solutions Limited (communications related services and products)
BT ESPAÑA, Compañía de Servicios Globales de Telecomunicacions, S.A. (telecommunication-related services and products, Spain)
BT Fleet Limited (fleet management)
BT France SA (telecommunication related services and products)
BT Frontline Pte Ltd (communications related services and products, Singapore)
BT (Germany) GmbH & Co. oHG (telecommunication related services and products)
BT Global Services Limited (international telecommunications network systems)
BT Holdings Limited (investment holding company)
BT Hong Kong Limited (telecommunication related services and products)
BT Infrastructures Critiques (IT systems and network services, France)
BT INS Inc (Information telecommunication consulting and software, US)
BT Italia SpA (telecommunications related services and products, Italy, 97%)
BT Limited (international telecommunication network systems provider)
BT Nederland NV (telecommunication related services and products, The Netherlands)
BT US Investments Limited (investments holding company, US)
Communications Global Network Services Limited (telecommunication related services and products, Bermuda)
Communication Networking Services (UK) (telecommunication related services and products)
Infonet Services Corporation (global managed network services provider, US)
Infonet USA Corporation (global managed network services provider, US)
Radianz Americas Inc. (global managed network services provider, US)

COMPETITORS

Accenture	KPN
AT&T	Telecom Italia
Cable & Wireless	Telefónica
Capgemini	Telenor
COLT Group	TeliaSonera
Deutsche Telekom	T-Home
France Telecom	Verizon
Global Crossing	Virgin Media
IBM Global Services	Vodafone

HISTORICAL FINANCIALS

Company Type: Public

Income Statement

FYE: March 31

	REVENUE ($ mil.)	NET INCOME ($ mil.)	NET PROFIT MARGIN	EMPLOYEES
3/10	32,003	1,549	4.8%	97,800
3/09	30,875	(118)	—	107,021
3/08	41,892	3,456	8.3%	111,858
3/07	39,914	5,625	14.1%	106,200
3/06	34,010	2,697	7.9%	104,400
Annual Growth	**(1.5%)**	**(12.9%)**	**—**	**(1.6%)**

2010 Year-End Financials

Debt ratio: —
Return on equity: —
Cash ($ mil.): 2,188
Current ratio: 0.60
Long-term debt ($ mil.): 15,454

No. of shares (mil.): 815
Dividends
Yield: 1.7%
Payout: 24.2%
Market value ($ mil.): 22,980

Stock History

NYSE: BT

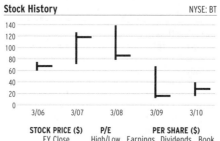

	STOCK PRICE ($) FY Close	P/E High/Low		PER SHARE ($) Earnings	Dividends	Book Value
3/10	28.19	20	9	1.94	0.47	(4.90)
3/09	15.87	—	—	(0.16)	2.34	0.25
3/08	85.95	33	19	4.21	3.02	13.20
3/07	118.06	19	11	6.61	2.46	10.26
3/06	67.60	23	19	3.15	1.92	3.33
Annual Growth	**(19.6%)**	**—**	**—**	**(11.4%)**	**(29.7%)**	**—**

Canadian Imperial Bank of Commerce

Canadian Imperial Bank of Commerce (CIBC) is both Canadian and imperial when it comes to growing its business. CIBC has more than 1,000 domestic branches that offer a range of consumer and business financial services, including deposits, loans, investments, and insurance. It operates in two main segments: CIBC Retail Markets (consumer and small business banking, credit cards, wealth management) and wholesale banking arm CIBC World Markets (capital markets and corporate and investment banking

services). Internationally, CIBC owns a majority of FirstCaribbean International Bank.

CIBC also offers investment management services in Hong Kong and Singapore. Active mainly in North America, CIBC World Markets has operations in Asia, Australia, and Europe, as well.

Operating units within CIBC's business lines include retail brokerage CIBC Wood Gundy. CIBC is selling its stake in trust and custody services provider CIBC Mellon to its partner in the joint venture, The Bank of New York Mellon, for an undisclosed amount.

CIBC does not have a substantial retail banking presence in the US like larger competitors Toronto-Dominion, Bank of Montreal, and Royal Bank of Canada. The company has been content to focus on its retail business in Canada, adding new products, opening branches, and extending business hours. In 2010 CIBC strengthened its credit card business in Canada through the acquisition of a $2 billion credit card portfolio from Citigroup. The deal, which made CIBC Canada's largest credit card issuer, is part of CIBC's strategy to grow its core Canadian operations.

However, in 2010 CIBC also made a move that may signal that it is looking for acquisitions abroad as well. That year it agreed to buy a 23% stake in Bermuda-based Bank of N.T. Butterfield. The acquisition may be small but it is a shift from CIBC's previous cost-cutting approach. The bank restructured its World Markets unit by separating its corporate lending and investment banking businesses. The unit shed some of its US operations in a sale to Oppenheimer Holdings in 2008. It has identified electronic trading as an area of possible growth.

HISTORY

In 1858 Bank of Canada was chartered; Toronto financier William McMaster bought the charter in 1866 when investors failed to raise enough money to open it and changed the name to Canadian Bank of Commerce.

The firm opened in 1867, bought the Gore Bank of Hamilton (1870), and expanded within seven years to 24 branches in Ontario, as well as Montreal and New York. Led by Edmund Walker, the bank spread west of the Great Lakes with the opening of a Winnipeg, Manitoba, branch in 1893 and joined the Gold Rush with branches in Dawson City, Yukon Territory, and Skagway, Alaska, in 1898.

As the new century began, the bank's purchases spanned the breadth of Canada, from the Bank of British Columbia (1901) to Halifax Banking (1903) and the Merchants Bank of Prince Edward Island (1906). More buys followed in the 1920s; the bank's assets peaked in 1929 and then plunged during the Depression. It recovered during WWII.

In 1961 Canadian Bank of Commerce merged with Imperial Bank of Canada to become Canadian Imperial Bank of Commerce (CIBC). Imperial Bank was founded in 1875 by Henry Howland; it went west to Calgary and Edmonton and became known as "The Mining Bank." It bought Barclays Bank (Canada) in 1956.

As the energy and agriculture sectors declined in the early 1980s, two of CIBC's largest borrowers, Dome Petroleum and tractor maker Massey-Ferguson, defaulted on their loans. Deregulation opened investment banking to CIBC, which in 1988 bought a majority share of Wood Gundy, one of Canada's largest investment dealers; CIBC also purchased Merrill Lynch Canada's retail brokerage business.

In 1992 CIBC added substantially to its loss reserves (resulting in an earnings drop of 98%) to cover real estate losses from developer Olympia & York and others. This launched more cost-cutting as the company reorganized by operating segments.

Deregulation allowed CIBC to begin selling insurance in 1993; the company built a collection of life, credit, personal property/casualty, and nonmedical health companies.

In 1996 the bank formed Intria, a processing and technical support subsidiary. The next year CIBC Wood Gundy became CIBC World Markets, and CIBC bought securities firm Oppenheimer & Co. and added its stock underwriting and brokerage abilities to CIBC World Markets.

In 1998 increasing foreign competition prompted CIBC and Toronto-Dominion to plan a merger (as did Royal Bank of Canada and Bank of Montreal); the government halted both plans, citing Canada's already highly concentrated banking industry.

Spurned, the bank overhauled its operations to spark growth in the late 1990s. To cut costs it eliminated some 4,000 jobs and sold its more than $1-billion real estate portfolio. It teamed with the Winn-Dixie (1999) and Safeway (2000) supermarket chains to operate electronic branches in the US. The firm scaled back its disappointing international operations and began selling its insurance units.

In 2002 the company snagged US-based Merrill Lynch's Canadian retail brokerage, asset management, and securities operations, renaming it CIBC Asset Management Inc. That same year CIBC merged its Caribbean banking business with that of UK-based Barclays to create FirstCaribbean Bank.

The next year CIBC sold the Oppenheimer private client and asset-management divisions to Fahnestock Viner (now Oppenheimer Holdings). It sold Juniper Financial, a Delaware-based credit card issuer, to Barclays for some $293 million in 2004.

In 2004 and again in 2006, CIBC was sued by creditors of Internet telecommunications company Global Crossing, stating that the bank had engaged in insider trading to the tune of $2 billion. Creditors demanded a return of the proceeds. CIBC denied the claims, but in 2006 two units of the bank agreed to pay $17.4 million to investors in the ill-fated telecom.

More trouble came in 2005 when CIBC agreed to pay some $2.4 billion in an investor class-action suit to resolve claims that the company helped notorious energy trader Enron to conceal losses.

EXECUTIVES

Chairman: Charles Sirois, age 55
President, CEO, and Director:
Gerald T. (Gerry) McCaughey, age 53
SEVP and CFO: J. David Williamson, age 49,
$1,852,196 total compensation
SEVP; President, CIBC Retail Markets:
Sonia A. Baxendale, $2,958,823 total compensation
SEVP: Ron A. Lalonde, $3,059,671 total compensation
SEVP and Chief Risk Officer: Tom D. Woods, age 57,
$2,251,623 total compensation
SEVP Corporate Development; Deputy Chairman and Managing Director, CIBC World Markets:
Richard E. Venn, age 59
Chief Administrative Officer and General Counsel, Administrative Division: Michael G. Capatides

EVP Governance and Control: Kevin J. Patterson
EVP, Finance Shared Services: Kevin Glass
EVP, Finance Business Support: David Arnold
EVP Technology and Operations: Mike J. Boluch
EVP Marketing, Communications, and Public Affairs:
Stephen J. Forbes
EVP Human Resources: Jacqueline Moss
VP, Corporate Secretary, and Associate General Counsel: Michelle Caturay
VP Investor Relations: John P. Ferren
VP, Ombudsman, and Chief Privacy Officer:
Kimberly McVittie
Senior Economist: Benjamin Tal
Senior Director Communications and Public Affairs:
Rob Mcleod
Director Investor Relations: Valentina Wong
Chairman and CEO, CIBC World Markets:
Richard W. Nesbitt, age 54,
$4,136,858 total compensation
President, CIBC Asset Management: Steve Geist
Auditors: Ernst & Young LLP

LOCATIONS

HQ: Canadian Imperial Bank of Commerce
Commerce Court
Toronto, Ontario M5L 1A2, Canada
Phone: 416-980-2211   **Fax:** 416-980-5028
US HQ: 425 Lexington Ave., 3rd Fl.
New York, NY 10017
US Phone: 212-667-8301   **US Fax:** 212-667-4590
Web: www.cibc.com

PRODUCTS/OPERATIONS

2009 Sales

	% of total
Interest	
Loans	52
Securities & other	15
Noninterest	
Deposit & payment fees	6
Mutual fund fees	5
Securitized assets	4
Foreign exchange, other than trading	4
Underwriting & advisory fees	3
Commissions on securities transactions	3
Investment management & custodial fees	3
Other	5
Total	**100**

2009 Assets

	% of total
Cash & equivalents	2
Trading securities	4
Other securities	28
Loans	
Residential mortgages	26
Personal	10
Credit card	4
Business & government	11
Derivative instruments	7
Other	8
Total	**100**

COMPETITORS

Barclays
BMO Financial Group
Caisses centrale Desjardins
Citigroup
Goldman Sachs
JPMorgan Chase
National Bank of Canada
RBC Financial Group
Scotiabank
TD Bank

HISTORICAL FINANCIALS

Company Type: Public

Income Statement

FYE: October 31

	ASSETS ($ mil.)	NET INCOME ($ mil.)	INCOME AS % OF ASSETS	EMPLOYEES
10/09	313,268	1,095	0.3%	28,928
10/08	292,700	(1,704)	—	39,698
10/07	358,431	3,452	1.0%	40,457
10/06	271,123	2,360	0.9%	39,100
10/05	238,174	(27)	—	37,016
Annual Growth	**7.1%**	**—**	**—**	**(6.0%)**

2009 Year-End Financials

Equity as % of assets: 3.3%
Return on assets: 0.4%
Return on equity: 11.2%
Long-term debt ($ mil.): 4,809
No. of shares (mil.): 391
Dividends
  Yield: 7.6%
  Payout: 164.4%
Market value ($ mil.): 20,818
Sales ($ mil.): 12,897

Stock History

NYSE: CM

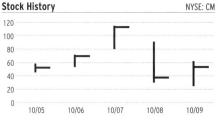

	STOCK PRICE ($) FY Close	P/E High/Low		PER SHARE ($) Earnings	Dividends	Book Value
10/09	53.27	25	11	2.47	4.06	34.06
10/08	37.48	—	—	(4.87)	2.87	29.27
10/07	113.05	12	8	9.65	3.24	36.16
10/06	69.46	11	8	6.63	2.46	28.12
10/05	52.17	—	—	(0.39)	2.23	23.33
Annual Growth	**0.5%**	**—**	**—**	**—**	**16.2%**	**9.9%**

Canon Inc.

Canon is still banging away at the document reproduction market. The company makes printers and other computer peripherals for home and office use. Its other well-known lines include copiers, fax machines, and scanners. Canon's industrial segment features products used in such diverse applications as semiconductor manufacturing equipment, television broadcast lenses, and devices used for eye examinations. Canon still operates its original camera business, which makes digital cameras, camcorders, LCD projectors, lenses, and binoculars. The company, which generates about three-quarters of its revenues outside Japan, continues to emphasize its product development and marketing efforts in Europe and North America.

The global recession took its bite from Canon's sales, which fell by nearly one-quarter during 2009. The company posted its lowest profit in a decade as a result. While Canon operates in highly competitive markets in consumer, industrial, and office products, its brand retains a significant presence around the world. Counterfeiting of Canon products is on the rise, and the poor quality of many counterfeit products could affect the company's brand image and operating results. Canon depends on a small number of large distributors to circulate its products in Europe and North America; those distributors could play a role in reducing the company's power over pricing in those regions. At the same time, the proliferation of Internet-based retailers may make conventional distribution channels obsolete.

Canon's office products, its largest segment, include printers, copiers, scanners, and multifunction devices for the consumer and enterprise markets. Canon sells branded products and supplies partners that resell under their own brands. Partner/competitor Hewlett-Packard accounts for approximately 20% of its sales. The company is targeting color office products for growth in this segment.

Perhaps still best known for its cameras, Canon has seen its photographic business steadily decline. However, the company remains a leader in the digital camera market, where it is concentrating on high-end single-lens-reflex (SLR) devices. Industry, Canon's third primary product group, encompasses a diverse portfolio including semiconductor production equipment, LCD components, medical imaging equipment, lenses, and large-format printers.

Canon adheres to the *kyosei* philosophy (living and working together for the common good), which stresses respect for local cultures and customs and more local control of subsidiaries. Customers in Europe account for nearly a third of its revenues. Accounting for almost 30% of sales, its next largest geographic segment, the Americas, is served by subsidiaries including Canon U.S.A. and Canon Canada.

In 2009 Canon agreed to acquire Océ, Europe's largest manufacturer of printers, to solidify its position in that key geographic market.

HISTORY

Takeshi Mitarai and a friend, Saburo Uchida, formed Seiki Kogaku Kenkyusho (Precision Optical Research Laboratory) in Tokyo in 1933 to make Japan's first 35mm camera. In 1935 the camera was introduced under the brand name Kwanon (after Quan Yin, the Buddhist goddess of mercy) — but later renamed Canon. In response to a pre-WWII military buildup, the company made X-ray machines for the Japanese.

In 1947 the company became Canon Camera Company as the brand name gained popularity. Canon opened its first overseas branch, in New York, in 1955. It diversified into business equipment by introducing the first 10-key electronic calculator (1964) and a plain-paper photocopier (1968) independent of Xerox's patented technology. Canon dropped "Camera Company" from its name in 1969.

The company invented the "liquid dry" copying system, which used plain paper and liquid developer, in 1972. It failed to produce new cameras and was surpassed by Minolta (now defunct) as Japan's top camera exporter. Sales were sluggish in the early 1970s, and in 1975 Canon suspended dividends for the first time since WWII.

At that time Canon's managing director, Ryuzaburo Kaku, convinced Mitarai that the company's problems stemmed from indecisive leadership and weak marketing. Kaku turned Canon around, unleashing the electronic AE-1 in a media blitz that in 1976 included the first-ever

TV commercials for a 35mm camera. With automated features, the AE-1 appealed to the clumsiest photographers. Its success catapulted Canon past Minolta as the world's #1 camera maker.

In 1979 Canon introduced the first copier to use a dry developer. As the copier market matured in the early 1980s, Canon shifted to making other automated office equipment, including laser printers and fax machines.

Mitarai died in 1984. Minolta the next year again displaced Canon as the world's #1 camera maker, when it introduced a fully automated model. But Canon came back in 1987 with the electronic optical system (EOS) auto-focus camera, which returned the company to preeminence in 1990. That year the company initiated an ink cartridge recycling program. Canon teamed up with IBM in 1992 to produce portable PCs. In 1993 Takeshi Mitarai's son Hajime, who joined Canon in 1974, was named president and began expanding product development.

In 1995 Canon introduced the world's first color ferroelectric LCD designed to replace cathode ray tubes in computer and TV screens as the industry standard. When Hajime died that year, cousin Fujio Mitarai, a 34-year Canon employee who served as the head of Canon U.S.A. in the 1980s, was named president and CEO. In 1996 the company made Canon Latin America a direct subsidiary of Canon U.S.A., with the *kyosei* idea that regionalized control would make the subsidiary more efficient.

Canon stopped making PCs in 1997. The next year the company unveiled its Hyper Photo System, which combines a scanner, PC server, and printer to produce photo prints, and expanded its copier remanufacturing operations. In 1999, after 16 years of production, Canon stopped making optical memory cards. The company also opened a research and development facility in the US.

In 2000 Canon and Toshiba began working together to develop technology for flat-panel displays. Canon expanded its line of digital cameras in 2001.

In 2004 Canon formed a joint venture with Toshiba to develop surface-conduction electron-emitter display (SED) products. Canon acquired Toshiba's stake in the company in 2007.

EXECUTIVES

Chairman and CEO: Fujio Mitarai, age 75
President and COO: Tsuneji Uchida, age 68
EVP and CFO; Senior General Manager, Policy and Economy Research Center: Toshizo Tanaka, age 70
EVP and CTO; Group Executive, Corporate R&D Headquarters, Chief Executive, Optical Products Operations: Toshiaki Ikoma, age 69
Board Member; President and CEO SED Inc.: Kazunori Fukuma, age 60
Board Member; President and CEO, Canon (China) Co. Ltd.: Hideki Ozawa
Chief Executive Image Communication Products Operations and Board Member: Masaya Maeda, age 58
Senior Managing Director; President and CEO, Canon USA: Yoroku (Joe) Adachi, age 62
Senior Managing Director; Chief Executive, Peripheral Products Operations: Yasuo Mitsuhashi, age 60
Senior Managing Director; Group Executive Corporate Planning Development: Kunio Watanabe, age 66
Senior Managing Director; Group Executive External Relations, Group Executive Human Resources Management and Organization: Akiyoshi Moroe, age 66
Senior Managing Director; Group Executive Corporate Intellectual Property and Legal: Nobuyoshi Tanaka, age 64

Executive Officer; Group Executive Corporate Intellectual Property and Legal Headquarters: Kenichi Nagasawa
Executive Officer; Group Executive, Human Resources Management and Organization: Kengo Uramoto
Auditors: Ernst & Young ShinNihon

LOCATIONS

HQ: Canon Inc.
30-2, Shimomaruko 3-chome, Ohta-ku
Tokyo 146-8501, Japan
Phone: 81-3-3758-2111   **Fax:** 81-3-5482-9680
US HQ: 1 Canon Plaza, Lake Success, NY 11042
US Phone: 516-328-5000
Web: www.canon.com

2009 Sales

	% of total
Europe	31
Americas	28
Japan	22
Other regions	19
Total	**100**

PRODUCTS/OPERATIONS

2009 Sales

	% of total
Office	50
Consumer	39
Industrial & other	11
Total	**100**

Selected Products

Office
  Business information
    Document scanners
    Fax machines
    Handy terminals (handheld computers)
  Computer peripherals
    Consumables
    Printers (bubble jet and laser)
    Scanners
  Office imaging
    Consumables
    Office
    Personal

Consumer
  Cameras
    Digital
    Film
  Lenses
  Liquid-crystal display projectors
  Video camcorders

Industrial and Other
  Broadcasting equipment
  Digital radiography
  Encoders
  Eye care systems
  Medical imaging systems
  Semiconductor production equipment
  Transceivers

COMPETITORS

Agfa	NEC
ASML	Nikon
Barco	Océ
CASIO COMPUTER	Oki Electric
Citizen	Olympus
Eastman Kodak	Panasonic Corp
Epson	Philips Electronics
FUJIFILM	Ricoh Company
Fujitsu	Samsung Electronics
Hewlett-Packard	SANYO
Hitachi	Sharp Corp.
Hoya Corp.	Sony
IBM	Toshiba
Konica Minolta	Victor Company of Japan
Kyocera	Xerox
Lexmark	

HISTORICAL FINANCIALS

Company Type: Public

Income Statement

FYE: December 31

	REVENUE ($ mil.)	NET INCOME ($ mil.)	NET PROFIT MARGIN	EMPLOYEES
12/09	34,791	1,427	4.1%	168,879
12/08	45,173	3,411	7.6%	166,980
12/07	40,003	4,359	10.9%	131,352
12/06	34,932	3,827	11.0%	118,499
12/05	31,880	3,262	10.2%	115,583
Annual Growth	2.2%	(18.7%)	—	9.9%

2009 Year-End Financials

Debt ratio: 0.2%
Return on equity: 4.9%
Cash ($ mil.): 8,619
Current ratio: 2.57
Long-term debt ($ mil.): 53

No. of shares (mil.): 1,334
Dividends
  Yield: 0.0%
  Payout: —
Market value ($ mil.): 612

Stock History

NYSE: CAJ

	STOCK PRICE ($) FY Close	P/E High/Low	PER SHARE ($) Earnings	Dividends	Book Value
12/09	0.46	— —	1.16	0.00	21.85
12/08	0.35	— —	2.72	0.57	22.00
12/07	0.41	— —	3.36	1.01	19.56
12/06	0.48	— —	2.87	0.83	18.82
12/05	0.33	— —	2.45	0.57	16.58
Annual Growth	8.7%	— —	(17.0%)	—	7.1%

Cap Gemini

Technology and outsourcing are the twin pillars of Cap Gemini. The company, known globally as Capgemini Group, is one of the world's leading providers of systems integration and consulting services, with operations in more than 35 countries. It offers systems development and implementation, as well as analysis and consulting services to help large businesses outfit themselves with technology. Capgemini provides a range of business process outsourcing services in such areas as customer relationship management, finance, human resources, and supply chain management. It also offers traditional management consulting. The Sogeti division provides support and consulting to smaller customers through local offices.

Companies in the public sector make up its largest customer segment, accounting for almost 30% of customers. Most of these customers are located in Europe, including the UK tax authority Her Majesty's Revenue & Customs (HMRC), Royal Mail (UK), and EDF (France).

Capgemini continues to grow through acquisitions, buying four companies in 2010. In February it bought Swedish purchasing software firm IBX and incorporated it into its Capgemini Procurement Services division. In June subsidiary

Capgemini Financial Services bought Plaisir Informatique, a French company that performs data migrations for the banking and insurance sector. Also that month, Capgemini bought the remaining 51% of UK-based Strategic Systems Solutions (SSS) that it did not already own to bolster its international business.

In July it bought Skvader Systems AB for its Smart Energy Services segment. The Smart Energy Services segment, created in 2010, provides energy efficient practices for smart metering, smart grid, smart home solutions, and smart analytics.

Targeting a different hemisphere altogether, the company acquired a 55% controlling stake in leading Brazilian IT services provider CPM Braxis for €233 million ($322 million) to tap into growth in the region.

HISTORY

Serge Kampf founded software house Sogeti in 1967 in Grenoble, France. He had an economics degree and had held a variety of jobs — from selling bakery ovens and computers to working for the French national telephone company. Frustrated as an executive with French computer company Groupe Bull, he resigned and started Sogeti.

Believing the future of information technology (IT) would be in support rather than hardware, Kampf focused on providing computer services to companies outside Paris that were being overlooked by his larger competitors. He was immediately successful, and three years later opened a Paris branch. In 1973 Kampf changed the focus of the company, abandoning the more specialized activities of data processing for general consulting, software, and technical assistance.

Cap Gemini Sogeti was created two years later by merging Sogeti with two French software service companies, C.A.P. (Computerized Applications Programming, started in 1962) and Gemini (1969). At first it operated as a "body shop," a loose organization of freelance programmers offering temporary help to computer users. It set up a consulting team in the US in 1978 and began a series of US acquisitions that led to the formation of Cap Gemini America (1981).

The company acquired a 42% stake in French competitor Sesa in 1982; six years later it bought the rest as part of a new strategy to become a global operator with a range of services. Cap Gemini Sogeti's 1990 purchase of Hoskyns Group, the UK's largest computer services company, was just one of a string of acquisitions aimed at fulfilling that dream. (Over a five-year period, it bought 22 European and American companies for $1.1 billion.) To raise money for his international expansion plans, Kampf sold 34% of the company to German carmaker Daimler-Benz (now Daimler) in 1991.

As Cap Gemini Sogeti expanded around the world, its decentralized network of operations rarely shared business or expertise. In 1993, on the heels of its first loss, the company launched a restructuring program that set up seven strategic business areas with dual regional and segment roles and modified product lines. Cap Gemini Sogeti returned to profitability in 1995.

The mid-1990s brought more than a dozen partnerships, including deals with French chemical conglomerate Rhône-Poulenc (now Sanofi-Aventis, 1995) and British Steel (now Corus Group, 1996).

In 1997 Daimler-Benz sold its stake (then 24%) in Cap Gemini to Compagnie Générale

d'Industrie et de Participations. The next year Cap Gemini bought the UK finance and commerce arm of AT&T. Expanding further into the US, the company bought telecommunications specialist Beechwood in 1999.

Geoff Unwin took over as CEO in 2000 while Serge Kampf remained as chairman. Like other consultancies, the firm was hit hard by the long technology downturn that was ushered in shortly after the turn of the new millennium. The effects were felt especially hard at Cap Gemini in part because of its acquisition in 2000 of Ernst & Young's consulting arm. Unwin and Kampf came under fire for pursuing the $11 billion deal, but under their leadership the company (which changed its name to Cap Gemini Ernst & Young) weathered the storm and emerged as a more streamlined operation.

The next year, the slowdown in IT spending (primarily in the US) caused the company to cut 5,400 jobs. Later that year Unwin announced his retirement as CEO, and was succeeded by COO Paul Hermelin. In 2002 another 5,500 jobs (about 10% of its workforce) were cut, mainly in its telecom and financial services units. The appointment of Alexandre Haeffner as COO launched major managerial restructuring. (He was replaced by Pierre Danon in 2005.)

In 2004 the company simplified its name to Capgemini as part of an overall reorganization effort. Soon after, the company's struggling US division got a shot in the arm when it signed a 10-year, $3.5 billion business and computer consulting services contract with power company TXU Corp. Capgemini also acquired consulting firm Transiciel (now Sogeti-Transiciel).

Capgemini sold its North American health care consulting practice in 2005 to Accenture. Later that year, COO Pierre Danon, credited with helping to turn around Capgemini's North American operations, was fired after news leaked he was seeking the CEO position at hotelier Accor.

In 2007 Capgemini invested in the expansion of its financial services and insurance offerings when it bought global IT services firm Kanbay International in a deal valued at $1.25 billion.

EXECUTIVES

Chairman: Serge Kampf, age 75
Vice Chairman and CEO: Paul Hermelin, age 58
Deputy General Manager and CFO: Nicolas Dufourcq
Managing Director, Global Financial Services: Bertrand Lavayssière
Global Head Consulting Services (Capgemini Consulting): Pierre-Yves Cros
Head Local Professional Services; Chairman and CEO, Sogeti: Luc-François Salvador
Head Public Sector: Stanislas Cozon
Head Managed Business Services: Bertrand Barthélemy
Head Sales and Alliances: Olivier Picard
Head Outsourcing Services: Paul Spence
Head Human Resources: Jeremy Roffe-Vidal, age 39
Head Marketing and Communications: Philippe Grangeon
Head Legal Affairs: Isabelle Roux-Chenu
Head Investor Relations: Manuel Chaves d'Oliveira, age 46
Group Director Technology Innovation: Andy Mulholland
Group Director Technical and Support Services: François Hucher
General Secretary: Alain Donzeaud
CEO, Financial Services Global Business Unit: Aiman Ezzat, age 48
CEO, Financial Services Global Business Unit: Raymond J. Spencer, age 59
CEO, Capgemini China: Bo Chen
CEO, Latin America, Spain, and Portugal: Eric Morgan
Senior Advisor: Jean-Pierre Durant des Aulnois
Auditors: PricewaterhouseCoopers Audit

LOCATIONS

HQ: Cap Gemini S.A.
Place de l'Etoile, 11 rue de Tilsitt
75017 Paris, France
Phone: 33-1-4754-5000   **Fax:** 33-1-4754-5086
US HQ: 623 5th Ave., 33rd Fl., New York, NY 10022
US Phone: 212-314-8000   **US Fax:** 212-314-8001
Web: www.capgemini.com

2009 Sales

	% of total
France	23
UK & Ireland	22
North America	19
Benelux	17
Germany & Central Europe	6
Nordic countries	6
Southern Europe & Latin America	5
Asia/Pacific	2
Total	**100**

PRODUCTS/OPERATIONS

2009 Sales

	% of total
Technology	40
Outsourcing	36
Sogeti	17
Consulting	7
Total	**100**

Selected Services

Application management
Business information services
Business process outsourcing
Cloud computing
Customer relationship management
Enterprise resource planning
Finance and employee transformation
Global help desk
Information technology consulting
Infrastructure outsourcing
IT security
Knowledge management
Management consulting
Outsourcing
Program management
Software development
Strategy consulting
Supply chain management
Systems integration
Testing
Training

COMPETITORS

Accenture
Affiliated Computer Services
Atos Origin
Bain & Company
Booz Allen
Bull
Capita
CGI Group
CSC UK
Deloitte Consulting
Dimension Data
Getronics
GFI Informatique
HP Enterprise Business
HP Enterprise Services
IBM Global Services
Infosys
Logica
McKinsey & Company
Perot Systems
Satyam
Sopra
Specialist Computer Holdings
Steria
Tata Consultancy
Unisys
Wipro Technologies

HISTORICAL FINANCIALS

Company Type: Public

Income Statement

FYE: December 31

	REVENUE ($ mil.)	NET INCOME ($ mil.)	NET PROFIT MARGIN	EMPLOYEES
12/09	11,997	255	2.1%	90,516
12/08	12,277	636	5.2%	91,621
12/07	12,810	648	5.1%	83,508
12/06	10,159	387	3.8%	67,889
12/05	8,236	167	2.0%	61,036
Annual Growth	9.9%	11.2%	—	10.4%

2009 Year-End Financials

Debt ratio: —
Return on equity: 4.4%
Cash ($ mil.): 708
Current ratio: 1.65
Long-term debt ($ mil.): —
No. of shares (mil.): 155
Dividends
  Yield: 3.1%
  Payout: 81.7%
Market value ($ mil.): 7,103

Stock History

Euronext Paris: CAP

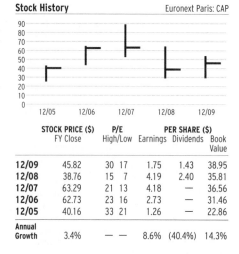

	STOCK PRICE ($) FY Close	P/E High/Low		PER SHARE ($) Earnings	Dividends	Book Value
12/09	45.82	30	17	1.75	1.43	38.95
12/08	38.76	15	7	4.19	2.40	35.81
12/07	63.29	21	13	4.18	—	36.56
12/06	62.73	23	16	2.73	—	31.46
12/05	40.16	33	21	1.26	—	22.86
Annual Growth	3.4%	—	—	8.6%	(40.4%)	14.3%

Carlsberg A/S

If any company has thirst-quenching down to a science, it's Carlsberg A/S, the owner of Carlsberg Breweries. In addition to the worldwide brewing operations of its flagship subsidiary, Carlsberg A/S also operates the Carlsberg Research Center, which houses 80 beer-brewing laboratories. Although most of the company's revenue comes from the sale of Carlsberg beers, the group also sells the Tuborg brand (one of the best-selling beers in Norway). The group is controlled by the Carlsberg Foundation, established in 1876 by founder J.C. Jacobsen. The company is majority-owned by the Carlsberg Foundation, which promotes the arts, sciences, and social work in Denmark.

While the global economic downturn has been tough for some brewers, Carlsberg has used the 2009 recession to fine-tune its products portfolio and cater to brew buyers whose purchases are recession-proof. In order to concentrate on its more profitable core brands in Germany, the company in 2009 sold its Braunschweig beer operations to German brewer Oettinger Brauerei. Also that year, it launched one of the world's most expensive beers, Jacobsen Vintage No. 2, which costs some €250 (or about $370) a bottle.

In 2008 Carlsberg and Heineken acquired Scottish brewer Scottish & Newcastle (now Heineken UK) for $15.3 billion. Upon completion of the takeover, Carlsberg took 100% control of Baltic Beverage Holdings (BBH), its 50-50 joint venture with Scottish & Newcastle (S&N) and a leading Russian brewer, as well as S&N's French, Greek, Vietnamese, and Chinese operations, including Mythos in Greece and Brasseries Kronenbourg in France. (Heineken took over the US, Indian, UK, and other European operations of S&N. Later in 2008 Carlsberg acquired Estonian brewer AS Saku Olletehas.) On the heels of these moves in 2008, it invested in China again. In 2010 it agreed to acquire about a 12% stake in Chongqing Brewery Co. Ltd. for more than 2 billion Danish kroner ($340 million) to boost its presence in China's fast-growing beer market.

Carlsberg's portfolio of more than 500 brands includes a goodly number of local beer brands, such as Feldschlösschen (Sweden), Okocim (Poland), Wusu (China), and Baltika (Russia). Its soft drink sales are generated mainly from licenses to produce drinks from Coca-Cola, but the company also produces its own soft drinks, cider, and water.

HISTORY

Carlsberg stems from the amalgamation of two proud Danish brewing concerns. Captain J. C. Jacobsen founded the first of these in Copenhagen; his father had worked as a brewery hand before acquiring his own small brewery in 1826. Studious and technically minded, J. C. inherited the brewery in 1835. He opened the Carlsberg Brewery (named for his son Carl) in 1847 and exported his first beer (to the UK) in 1868. J. C. established the Carlsberg Foundation in 1876 to conduct scientific research and oversee brewery operations.

Carl, who conflicted with his father over brewery operations, opened a new facility (New Carlsberg) adjacent to his dad's in 1881. Both men bestowed gifts upon their city, such as a church, an art museum, a royal castle renovation, and Copenhagen Harbor's famous Little Mermaid statue. Father and son willed their breweries to the foundation, which united them in 1906.

Tuborgs Fabrikker was founded in 1873 by a group of Danish businessmen who wanted to establish a major industrial project (including a brewery) at Tuborg Harbor. Philip Heyman headed the group and in 1880 spun off all operations but the brewery.

Carlsberg and Tuborg became Denmark's two leading brewers. After WWII, both began marketing their beers outside the country. Between 1958 and 1972 they tripled exports and established breweries in Europe and Asia. Both brewers' desire to grow internationally influenced their decision to merge, which they did in 1969 as United Breweries.

During the 1980s the firm diversified, forming Carlsberg Biotechnology in 1983 to extend its research to other areas. It strengthened its position in North America through licenses with Anheuser-Busch (1985) and John Labatt (1988). United Breweries reverted to the old Carlsberg name in 1987.

Carlsberg and Allied-Lyons (which became Allied Domecq before being acquired by Pernod Ricard in 2005) combined their UK brewing, distribution, and wholesaling operations under the name Carlsberg-Tetley (now Carlsberg UK) in 1992, creating the UK's third-largest brewer (behind Bass and Courage).

The firm teamed up with India's United Breweries in 1995 to distribute Carlsberg beer on the subcontinent. Bass acquired Allied's 50% of Carlsberg-Tetley in 1996 but sold its stake to Carlsberg in 1997 upon orders from regulators. Also in 1997 Carlsberg and Coca-Cola set up Coca-Cola Nordic Beverages to bottle and distribute soft drinks in Nordic countries. That year Poul Svanholm retired after 25 years as CEO; he was replaced by Jørn Jensen.

Carlsberg acquired a 60% stake in Finnish brewer Sinebrychoff in 1998. Carlsberg then sold a 60% stake in Vingaarden to Finland's Oy Rettig (1999), sold its remaining 43% share of the Tivoli amusement park to Danish tobacco group Skandinavisk Tobakskompagni (2000), and reduced its 64% holding in Royal Scandinavia to 28% (2000). Carlsberg bought the beverage operations of Swedish firm Feldschlösschen Hürlimann in 2000 and agreed to combine brewing businesses with Norway-based Orkla in a deal worth $1.5 billion; Carlsberg Breweries was formed in February 2001 after both agreed to divest several brands and distribution rights to gain regulatory approval.

Carlsberg stopped production at Coca-Cola Nordic Beverages (the company still exists but has no operations) in 2001 because of conflicts with Orkla's Pepsi bottling contracts in Sweden and Norway; Carlsberg and Coca-Cola continued to produce and sell Coke in Denmark and Finland. Nils S. Andersen became the company's president and CEO that year.

In 2003 Carlsberg Breweries acquired an additional 27.5% stake in Pirinsko Pivo, a Bulgarian brewery, bringing its overall ownership to 94.5%. That same year, it purchased the Chinese brewers Dali and Kunming. The following year the group acquired the Germany-based beer brewer and distributor Holsten-Brauerei.

In 2007 Nils Andersen became CEO at A.P. Møller – Mærsk; Jørgen Rasmussen replaced him.

EXECUTIVES

Chairman: Prof Povl Krogsgaard-Larsen, age 69
Deputy Chairman: Jess Søderberg, age 65
President and CEO: Jørgen B. Rasmussen, age 55
Deputy CEO and CFO: Jørn P. Jensen, age 46
SVP Corporate Supply Chain: Kasper Madsen
SVP, Asia: Roy Bagattini, age 47
SVP, Northern Europe: Jørn T. Rohde, age 49
SVP, Western Europe: Jesper Friis, age 41
SVP, Eastern Europe; President, Baltika Brewery, Russia: Anton Artemiev, age 50
SVP Innovation, Group Sales, and Marketing: Khalil Younes, age 46
VP and CIO: Kenneth E. Schmidt
VP Group Human Resources: Thomas Ekvall, age 51
VP Group Treasury: Lars Cordi
VP Group Communications: Anne-Marie Skov
VP Investor Relations: Peter Kondrup
VP Legal Counseling and Risk Management and General Counsel: Ulrik Andersen
Communications Director, Carlsberg Danmark: Jens Bekke
Human Resources Director, Carlsberg Danmark: Thomas Kolber
Auditors: KPMG C. Jespersen

LOCATIONS

HQ: Carlsberg A/S
100 Ny Carlsberg Vej
DK-1760 Copenhagen, Denmark
Phone: 45-3327-3300   **Fax:** 45-3327-4808
US HQ: 3 Forest St., New Canaan, CT 06840
US Phone: 203-972-7900
Web: www.carlsberg.com

2009 Sales

	% of total
Western & Northern Europe	62
Eastern Europe	31
Asia	7
Total	**100**

COMPETITORS

Anheuser-Busch InBev
Asahi Breweries
Asia Pacific Breweries
Brau Union
Danone Water
Diageo
Grolsch
Heineken
Kingway Brewery
Kirin Holdings Company
Lion Nathan
Molson Coors
Nestlé Waters
PepsiCo
Royal Unibrew
SABMiller
San Miguel Corporation
Sapporo
Snow Breweries
Suntory International
Tiger Brands
Tsingtao

HISTORICAL FINANCIALS

Company Type: Public

Income Statement

FYE: December 31

	REVENUE ($ mil.)	NET INCOME ($ mil.)	NET PROFIT MARGIN	EMPLOYEES
12/09	11,437	803	7.0%	43,271
12/08	11,353	607	5.3%	45,505
12/07	8,834	513	5.8%	33,276
12/06	7,268	384	5.3%	31,680
12/05	6,027	217	3.6%	30,000
Annual Growth	**17.4%**	**38.6%**	**—**	**9.6%**

2009 Year-End Financials

Debt ratio: —
Return on equity: 7.3%
Cash ($ mil.): 527
Current ratio: 0.59
Long-term debt ($ mil.): —
No. of shares (mil.): 153
Dividends
Yield: 0.9%
Payout: 14.7%
Market value ($ mil.): 11,503

Stock History

OMX Copenhagen: DCARLB

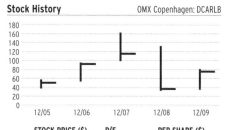

	STOCK PRICE ($) FY Close	P/E High/Low		PER SHARE ($) Earnings	Dividends	Book Value
12/09	75.40	17	8	4.55	0.67	75.11
12/08	36.36	31	8	4.20	—	68.93
12/07	115.08	27	17	5.92	—	24.10
12/06	91.99	21	13	4.35	—	20.41
12/05	49.90	24	17	2.31	—	18.66
Annual Growth	**10.9%**			**18.5%**	**—**	**41.6%**

Carrefour SA

At the junction of groceries, merchandise, and services, you'll find Carrefour (which means "crossroads"). The world's second-largest retailer (behind Wal-Mart), Carrefour operates more than 15,600 stores under various banners, including hypermarkets (Carrefour), supermarkets (Carrefour Market, formerly Champion), convenience stores (City, Express), discount stores (Dia, Ed), and cash-and-carry outlets (Promocash) in about 35 countries in Europe, Latin America, and Asia. France, with more than 5,400 Carrefour stores, accounts for more than 40% of the retailer's sales. Carrefour secured its spot as the #1 European retailer when it merged with food retailer Promodès and raised its banner over those stores.

Carrefour, which pioneered the hypermarket format, has over the past decade seen its business suffer, particularly in France, as shoppers shun its huge stores in favor of specialty shops and discount chains. To right the business, Carrefour has recruited CEO Lars Olofsson, who joined the business from Nestlé in 2009. Olofsson is attempting to quell investor discontent with Carrefour's recent performance by fixing its retail operations in France while accelerating expansion in select international markets.

Other efforts to revive its retail business include the sale of $1.2 billion worth of assets — including its stores in Japan and Mexico — in order to lower prices and attract new shoppers, and to fund the construction of new stores.

Unable to build new stores in its homeland due to regulations protecting smaller stores, Carrefour expands through acquisitions at home and abroad. Carrefour in 2010 acquired Ipek, a Turkish grocery chain with more than 25 locations in Istanbul, for €24 million (about $30 million). In 2009 it acquired about half a dozen stores from the Brazilian supermarket chain Gimenes, which complemented its 2007 purchase of hypermarket operator Atacadao (worth about $1 billion), which made Carrefour the largest food seller in Brazil.

Carrefour is China's largest foreign retailer (ahead of Wal-Mart), with more than 500 hypermarkets and discount stores there in 20-plus cities. Furthering its expansion there, Carrefour acquired a majority stake in Chinese hypermarket operator Baolongcang in mid-2010. Baolongcang operates about a dozen hypermarkets in Hebei, near Beijing. The French retailer in 2008 acquired an additional 25% stake in its Guangzhou Jiaguang Supermarket joint venture from Guangzhou Grandbuy.

Closer to home, subsidiary Carrefour Italia is struggling and is exploring exiting the market in the south of the country. Carrefour also said it was pulling up stakes because the Russian market does not offer enough growth prospects. It looks to shutter at least 25 locations in its chain of more than 220 supermarkets in Poland, as well. However, in 2010 it announced the formation of a new joint venture company with long-time partner Marinopoulous to develop Carrefour in the Balkans.

The Halley family has ceded control of Carrefour to Blue Capital, an investment vehicle jointly owned by Groupe Arnault, the investment company owned by Bernard Arnault, head of LVMH Moët Hennessy Louis Vuitton, and US private equity fund Colony Capital, that is now Carrefour's largest shareholder.

HISTORY

Although its predecessor was actually a supermarket opened by Marcel Fournier and Louis Defforey in a Fournier's department store basement in Annecy, France, the first Carrefour supermarket was founded in 1963 at the intersection of five roads (Carrefour means "crossroads"). That year Carrefour opened a vast store, dubbed a "hypermarket" by the media, in Sainte-Genevieve-des-Bois, outside Paris.

The company opened additional outlets in France and moved into other countries, including Belgium (1969), Switzerland (1970 — the year it went public), Italy and the UK (1972), and Spain (1973). Carrefour stepped up international expansion during the mid-1970s after French legislation limited its growth within the country.

Carrefour exported its French-style hypermarkets to the US (Philadelphia) in 1988. Scant advertising, limited selection, and a union strike led Carrefour to close its US operations in 1993. Carrefour paid over $1 billion for two rival chains (the bankrupt Montlaur chain and Euromarché) in 1991.

Daniel Bernard replaced Michel Bon, the hard-charging expansion architect, in 1992 after a 50% drop in first-half profits. A year later Carrefour partnered with Mexican retailer Gigante to open a chain of hypermarkets in Mexico. It expanded into Poland in 1997 and the Czech Republic in 1998. That year Carrefour acquired French supermarket operator Comptoirs Modernes (with about 800 stores under the Stoc, Comod, and Marché Plus flags).

In August 1999 Carrefour announced a deal even bigger than the one for Comptoirs Modernes — a $16.3 billion merger with fellow French grocer Promodès, which operated more than 6,000 hypermarkets, supermarkets, convenience stores, and discount stores in Europe. Paul-Auguste Halley and Leonor Duval Lemonnier founded Promodès in Normandy, France, in 1961. Initially a wholesale food distributor, Promodès opened its first supermarket in 1962. This was followed by a cash-and-carry wholesale outlet (1964), a hypermarket (1970), and convenience stores (Shopi and 8 à Huit, during the 1970s). To gain regulatory approval for the acquisition, Carrefour divested its stake in the Cora chain and sold nearly 40 other stores in France and Spain. The Promodès acquisition was completed in 2000.

In 2005 Luc Vandevelde, the former chairman of troubled British retailer Marks and Spencer, succeeded Daniel Bernard as non-executive chairman of Carrefour. Bernard had been with Carrefour for 13 years. No stranger to the company, Vandevelde was chief executive of Promodès when it merged with Carrefour in 1999. Concurrently, ex-CFO José-Luis Duran was named CEO.

Also in 2005 Carrefour exited the Japanese market with the sale of its eight hypermarkets there to Japanese retail giant AEON CO. In 2006 the company pulled out of South Korea, selling its 32 stores there to local fashion retailer E.Land for about $1.9 billion.

In 2007 Vandevelde resigned his position as non-executive chairman after a falling out with the controlling Halley family.

In 2008 the Halley family split its 13% stake in Carrefour into two separate holding companies, thereby ceding control of the French retail giant to Blue Capital. In May, Robert Halley stepped down as chairman of the company's supervisory board and was replaced by the deputy chairman Amaury de Sèze. In 2009 Duran stepped down and Lars Olofsson took over as top executive.

EXECUTIVES

Chairman, Supervisory Board: Amaury-Daniel de Sèze, age 64
Vice Chairman, Supervisory Board: Jean-Martin Folz, age 63
CEO and Director: Lars Olofsson, age 58
CFO: Pierre B. Bouchut, age 54
Group CIO: Hervé Thoumyre
Executive Director Hypermarkets France: Guillaume Vicaire
Executive Director Supermarkets France: Alexandre Falck
Executive Director, Carrefour Property: Pascal Duhamel
Executive Director, France: James McCann, age 40
Executive Director Convenience Stores and Promocash: Gérard Dorey
Executive Director Group Financial Services and Insurance: Gauthier Durand Delbècque
Group Financial Control Director: Albin Jacquemont
Group Human Resources Director: Cécile Cloarec
Group Director Merger and Acquisitions: Vincent Abello
Group General Counsel: Franck Tassan
Group Communications Director: Florence Baranes Cohen
Group Marketing Director: Patrick Rouvillois
Group Chief Commercial Officer: José C. Gonzales-Hurtado, age 46
Director Financial Communications and Investor Relations: Patrice Lambert-de Diesbach, age 53
General Secretary: Pierre Alexandre Teulie
Auditors: KPMG Audit

LOCATIONS

HQ: Carrefour SA
26, quai Michelet, TSA 20016
92695 Levallois-Perret, France
Phone: 33-1-55-63-39-00   **Fax:** 33-1-55-63-39-01
Web: www.carrefour.com

2009 Sales

	% of total
Europe	
France	43
Other countries	36
Latin America	14
Asia	7
Total	**100**

2009 Stores

	No.
France	5,440
Rest of Europe	7,941
Latin America	1,275
Asia	718
Partner stores	287
Total	**15,661**

PRODUCTS/OPERATIONS

2009 Sales

	% of total
Hypermarket	62
Supermarket	22
Hard discount	11
Other	5
Total	**100**

2009 Stores

	No.
Hard discount stores	6,475
Convenience	4,698
Supermarkets	2,949
Hypermarkets	1,395
Cash & Carry	144
Total	**15,661**

Selected Operations and Banners

Hypermarkets
  Carrefour
Supermarkets
  Champion
  GB
  Globi
  GS
  Marinopoulos
  Norte
  Super GB
  Super GS
  Unic
Hard discount stores
  Dia
  Ed
  Minipreco
Other stores
  Cash-and-carry stores
  Docks Market
  Promocash
  Puntocash
Convenience stores
  8 à Huit
  Di per Di
  GB Express
  Marché Plus
  Proxi
  Shopi

Other Operations

Carfuel (petroleum products)
Comptoirs Modernes (supermarkets)
Costco UK (20%, warehouse club)
Erteco (hard-discount stores)
Financiera Pryca (46%, consumer credit, Spain)
Fourcar B.V. (investments, The Netherlands)
GlobalNetXchange (Internet-based supply exchange joint venture)
Ooshop (online shopping)
Prodirest (catering)
Providange (auto centers)
S2P (60%, consumer credit)

COMPETITORS

AEON
ALDI
Auchan
Brasileira de Distribuição
Casino Guichard
China Nepstar
Dairy Farm International
Delhaize
Edeka Zentrale
E.Leclerc
Eroski
Falabella
Galeries Lafayette
Generale Supermercati
Globex Utilidades
H&M
ITM Entreprises
Ito-Yokado
La Rinascente
Lianhua Supermarket
Lidl
Lotteshopping
Marui Group
METRO AG
Migros
Primisteres Reynoird
Rallye
REWE
Royal Ahold
SHV Holdings
Super Indo
Tengelmann
Tesco
Wal-Mart
WuMart
Zara

HISTORICAL FINANCIALS

Company Type: Public

Income Statement

FYE: December 31

	REVENUE ($ mil.)	NET INCOME ($ mil.)	NET PROFIT MARGIN	EMPLOYEES
12/09	123,202	626	0.5%	475,976
12/08	122,580	2,169	1.8%	495,287
12/07	120,914	3,649	3.0%	490,000
12/06	102,775	3,208	3.1%	456,295
12/05	88,227	1,814	2.1%	436,747
Annual Growth	8.7%	(23.3%)	—	2.2%

2009 Year-End Financials

Debt ratio: —
Return on equity: 4.1%
Cash ($ mil.): 4,731
Current ratio: 0.71
Long-term debt ($ mil.): —

No. of shares (mil.): 705
Dividends
Yield: 3.2%
Payout: 224.6%
Market value ($ mil.): 33,905

Stock History

Euronext Paris: CA

	STOCK PRICE ($) FY Close	P/E High/Low		PER SHARE ($) Earnings	Dividends	Book Value
12/09	48.10	71	46	0.69	1.55	22.60
12/08	38.79	28	13	2.58	1.52	20.32
12/07	78.44	22	16	3.93	—	22.27
12/06	60.61	20	14	3.47	—	17.75
12/05	46.87	16	14	3.06	—	14.09
Annual Growth	0.6%	—	—	(31.1%)	2.0%	12.5%

Casino Guichard

You won't hit the jackpot at Casino, Guichard-Perrachon, but odds are you'll go home with the groceries. One of the world's leading food retailers, the company owns and operates more than 9,250 hypermarkets (mostly Géant), supermarkets (Casino and Monoprix, to name a few), restaurants (Casino Cafétéria), and discount stores (Leader Price). Casino is the third-largest food retailer (behind Carrefour and Auchan), and the #1 convenience store operator in France (primarily Petit Casino, but other banners include Franprix, Vival, and Spar). Most of its stores are in France, but it has more than 1,700 outlets in about 10 countries in Asia and South America.

France accounts for two-thirds of Casino's sales, down from three-quarters not long ago. About 90% of its growing international business comes from the fast-growing South American and Asian markets, where Casino is placing its bets. Indeed, Casino holds leadership positions in both regions, where it operates a total of 1,570 stores, including 290 hypermarkets. Casino owns a stake in Brazil's #1 retailer Companhia Brasileira de Distribuição (CBD), operator of the Pão de Açucar chain there. The French retailer

also operates in the Indian Ocean region, where it owns a majority stake in Vindémia, an operator of supermarkets and hypermarkets in Asia and Africa.

At home, price competition from discounters has hurt Casino and its rival Carrefour as French shoppers eschew their traditional hypermarkets and supermarkets for discount stores. In response, Casino has strengthened its position in the convenience and discount store markets. Indeed, convenience and discount stores are the retailer's most popular formats, accounting for 61% of sales and 71% of profits in France.

Casino is shoring up its balance sheet through a plan to dispose of some €1 billion ($1.3 billion) of assets by the end of 2010. The divestments included the sale of 42 superette, Casino supermarket, and Franprix-Leader price stores in 2008. Future divestments will include the sale of €334 million ($424 million) of soon-to-be-built real estate to Mercialys, a property company spun off by Casino in 2006. The French retailer also sold its Polish hypermarkets to METRO AG and its Leader Price supermarkets there to Britain's Tesco for a total of about $1.2 billion.

The company's 115-plus Géant hypermarkets (warehouse-style stores that sell groceries and other merchandise) and convenience stores together contribute more than 50% of revenues. Casino Cafétéria operates about 275 eating places in varying size and cuisines, including Poncholito (Tex-Mex) and La Pastaria (Italian). Casino is also active in e-commerce (Cdiscount.com).

Casino is controlled by Euris, which is controlled by Jean-Charles Naouri, Casino's chairman and CEO.

HISTORY

Frenchman Geoffroy Guichard married Antonia Perrachon, a grocer's daughter, in 1889 in Saint-Étienne, France. Three years later Geoffroy took over his father-in-law's general store (a converted "casino" or musical hall). In 1898 the company became Société des Magasins du Casino. By 1900, when it became a joint stock company, Casino had 50 stores; it opened its 100th store in 1904. That year the company introduced its first private-label product: canned sardines. In 1917 Guichard named his two sons, Mario and Jean, as managers.

By WWI there were about 215 branches, more than 50 in Saint-Étienne. From 1919 to the early 1920s, the company opened several factories to manufacture goods such as food, soap, and perfumes. In 1925 the elder Guichard retired, leaving the day-to-day operations of Casino to his two sons. (Geoffroy died in 1940.) WWII took a heavy toll on the company: About 70 Casino stores were leveled and another 450 were damaged.

The company began opening cafeterias in 1967, and in 1976 it formed Casino USA to run them. Casino USA bought an interest in the California-based Thriftimart volume retailer in 1983, renaming the company after Thriftimart's Smart & Final warehouse stores.

Casino grew by acquiring companies across France, including CEDIS (16 hypermarkets, 116 supermarkets, and 722 smaller stores in eastern France; 1985) and La Ruche Meridionale (18 hypermarkets and 112 supermarkets in southern France, 1990). Casino bought nearly 300 hypermarkets and supermarkets from Rallye SA in 1992, giving Rallye about 30% of the company. The company opened its first hypermarket in Warsaw, Poland, in 1996.

Rival Promodès made a roughly $4.5 billion hostile takeover bid for Casino in 1997. Guichard family members voted against the Promodès offer, instead backing a $3.9 billion friendly offer from Rallye (increasing their stake to nearly 50%). Casino also launched a massive counterattack — buying more than 600 Franprix and Leader Price supermarket stores from food manufacturer TLC Beatrice and acquiring a 21% stake in hypermarket chain Monoprix. Promodès withdrew its bid four months later.

Casino expanded internationally in the late 1990s, acquiring stakes in food retailers in Argentina (Libertad), Uruguay (Disco), Colombia (Almacenes Exito SA), Brazil (Companhia Brasileira de Distribuição), and Thailand (Big C, the country's largest retailer).

Casino acquired 100 Proxi convenience stores in southeast France in 2000 from Montagne and more than 400 convenience stores (Eco Service and others) from Auchan. Casino also bought 51% of French online retailer Cdiscount.com. It also increased its ownership of Monoprix to 49%. In July 2002 Casino bought a 38% stake in Laurus NV, its financially troubled Dutch rival.

Chief executive Pierre Bouchut unexpectedly left Casino in March 2005. Jean-Charles Naouri, the company's chairman and controlling shareholder, replaced him. Casino spun off some of its shopping center assets in an October IPO for part of its real estate assets in France.

In January 2006 Casino increased its stake in Colombia's biggest retailer Exito to nearly 39%. The company in July sold its 19 hypermarkets in Poland to METRO AG, its German rival, for about $1.1 billion as part of its asset disposal program.

In May 2007 Casino sold its 55% stake of the California-based Smart & Final warehouse grocery chain to Apollo Management for $813 million, thereby exiting the US market.

In 2008 Casino acquired French textile maker International Textiles Associes (or INTEXA) from members of the Broyer family.

In November 2009 Casino acquired the remaining shares of Leader Price and Franprix chains from the Baud family, bringing its ownership stake up to 100% in both chains.

EXECUTIVES

Chairman and CEO: Jean-Charles Naouri, age 61
CFO: Michel A. M. Favre, age 51
Chairman, Asinco, EMC, and IRTS: Jean-Michel Duhamel
Secretary of the Board: Jacques Dumas, age 58
Secretary to Executive Committee: Camille De Verdelhan
Group Director Legal: Thierry Levantal
Director Human Resources: Yves Desjacques, age 42
Director Corporate Development and Holdings: Hakim L. Aouani
Director Real Estate and Expansion: Jacques Ehrmann, age 50
Director Neighbourhood Stores and Supermarkets: François Duponchel
Executive Deputy Managing Director French Networks and Group Marketing: Jacques-Edouard Marie Charret
General Manager Hypermarkets Network and Non-food Purchasing: Jean Henri A. Duboc
Manager Supply Chain; Chairman, Cdiscount: Hervé Daudin
Auditors: Cabinet Didier Kling & Associés

LOCATIONS

HQ: Casino, Guichard-Perrachon
  1, Esplanade de France
  42008 Saint-Étienne, France
Phone: 33-4-77-45-31-31 **Fax:** 33-4-77-45-38-38
Web: www.casino.fr

2009 Sales

	% of total
France	66
Latin America	25
Asia	6
Indian Ocean	3
Total	**100**

2009 Stores

	No.
France	9,254
Other countries	1,730
Total	**10,984**

PRODUCTS/OPERATIONS

2009 Stores (France)

	No.
Hypermarkets	117
Supermarkets	761
Convenience stores	7,540
Discount stores	559
Cafeterias	277
Total	**9,254**

Selected Operations

Banque du Groupe Casino (60%, financial services)
Big C (63%, Thailand)
Casino Enterprise (non-food operations)
Cativen (66%, Venezuela)
Cdiscount.com (67%, e-commerce)
Companhia Brasileira de Distribuição (34%, Brazil)
Devoto (97%, supermarkets, Uruguay)
Exito Colombia SA (55%, supermarkets)
Franprix (100%, supermarkets)
Géant (hypermarkets)
Imagica (photo and digital imaging processing)
Leader Price (100%, supermarkets)
Libertad (100%, hypermarkets, Argentina)
Vindémia (100%, supermarkets; Madagascar, Mauritius, Réunion)

COMPETITORS

ALDI
A.P. Møller – Mærsk
Auchan
Carrefour
E.Leclerc
Groupe Flo
Guyenne et Gascogne
IGA
ITM Entreprises
Kingfisher
METRO AG
Migros
Primistères Reynoird
Royal Ahold
Tesco
Wal-Mart

HISTORICAL FINANCIALS

Company Type: Public

Income Statement

FYE: December 31

	REVENUE ($ mil.)	NET INCOME ($ mil.)	NET PROFIT MARGIN	EMPLOYEES
12/09	38,348	1,234	3.2%	163,208
12/08	40,458	846	2.1%	173,367
12/07	36,756	1,354	3.7%	159,946
12/06	30,029	958	3.2%	192,948
12/05	27,299	515	1.9%	208,403
Annual Growth	**8.9%**	**24.4%**	**—**	**(5.9%)**

2009 Year-End Financials

Debt ratio: —
Return on equity: 12.6%
Cash ($ mil.): 3,893
Current ratio: 0.94
Long-term debt ($ mil.): —
No. of shares (mil.): 110
Dividends
  Yield: 4.0%
  Payout: 48.9%
Market value ($ mil.): 9,897

Stock History

Euronext Paris: CO

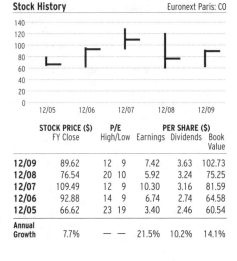

	STOCK PRICE ($) FY Close	P/E High/Low		PER SHARE ($) Earnings	Dividends	Book Value
12/09	89.62	12	9	7.42	3.63	102.73
12/08	76.54	20	10	5.92	3.24	75.25
12/07	109.49	12	9	10.30	3.16	81.59
12/06	92.88	14	9	6.74	2.74	64.58
12/05	66.62	23	19	3.40	2.46	60.54
Annual Growth	**7.7%**	**—**	**—**	**21.5%**	**10.2%**	**14.1%**

CASIO COMPUTER

CASIO COMPUTER wants a watch on every wrist and a handheld computer in every pocket. The firm makes a wide range of electronics for consumers, including calculators, cell phones, digital cameras, portable TVs, watches, and musical keyboards. CASIO COMPUTER also manufactures computing and communications devices, like PDAs and electronic cash registers. The company seeks out superlatives when creating products: The G-Shock watch (launched in 1983) boasted it was the toughest (able to survive a three-story drop) and the EXILIM camera (2002) claimed to be the world's thinnest (roughly the size of a credit card). The three younger brothers of late founder Tadao Kashio continue to run CASIO COMPUTER.

CASIO typically generates about 90% of its revenue from sales of consumer electronics (such as calculators, label printers, and electronic dictionaries), and the balance is derived from electronic components (including liquid crystal displays (LCDs) and bump-processing consignments). Revenues had appeared to be on an upswing in recent years, but in fiscal 2009 the company was hurt by slumping demand for consumer electronics amid the global financial crisis. CASIO looks to turn around its fortunes, focusing its business on four primary product categories: digital cameras, electronic dictionaries, timepieces, and cell phones. Timepieces and electronic dictionaries have been relatively strong revenue generators, but CASIO's digital camera and cell phone businesses have suffered from intense competition and falling prices.

Directing its attention to small and midsized displays, CASIO in early 2010 formed joint venture Ortus Technology with Toppan Printing (80% owner) to manufacture organic light-emitting diode (OLED) and thin-film-transistor (TFT) LCDs. As part of the deal, CASIO transferred facilities and personnel involved in OLED and TFT

LCD displays development to the company, as well as ownership of its Kochi Casio subsidiary.

A joint venture formed in 2010 merged the mobile phone businesses of CASIO, NEC Corp., and Hitachi. The newly formed company, which operates under the name NEC Casio Mobile Communications, was created to reduce expenses between the firms and shore up eroding cell phone demand. (NEC will hold a 71% stake, Casio 20%, and Hitachi 9%.) It plans to compete with Sharp for the top spot in the handset market, aiming to sell some 5 million smart phones in North America and Australia by 2012.

HISTORY

In 1942 Tadao Kashio started a Tokyo-based machine shop, Kashio Manufacturing. His brother, Toshio, later joined him. After reading about a 1946 computing contest in which an abacus bested an electric calculator, Toshio, an inventor, wrote a note to himself: "Abacus is human ability; calculator is technology." In 1950 he began developing a calculator. The other Kashio brothers — Yukio, a mechanical engineer, and Kazuo, who took over sales — joined the company in the 1950s.

The brothers incorporated in 1957 as CASIO COMPUTER, an Anglicization of the family name. That year the company launched its first product, an electric calculator featuring an innovative floating decimal point display; it was the first Japanese-built electric calculator. CASIO COMPUTER took advantage of new transistor technology to create electronic calculators, and in 1965 it introduced the first electronic desktop calculator with memory. The company began exporting to the US in 1970.

In the 1970s only CASIO COMPUTER and Sharp emerged as significant Japanese survivors of the fierce "calculator war." CASIO COMPUTER's strategy of putting lots of new functions on a proliferation of small models and selling them at rock-bottom prices worked not only with calculators but with digital watches as well. The company introduced its first digital watch in 1974 and went on to dominate that market.

CASIO COMPUTER expanded its product line into electronic music synthesizers (1980), pocket TVs (1983), and thin-card calculators (1983). Determined to break away from the production of delicate timepieces, CASIO COMPUTER introduced shock-resistant (G-Shock) digital watches in 1983. In the mid-1980s sales were hurt by a rising yen and stiff price competition from developing Asian nations. The company responded by releasing sophisticated calculators for such specialized users as architects and insurance agents. To offset the effects of the yen's heightened value in the late 1980s, CASIO COMPUTER moved manufacturing to Taiwan, Hong Kong, South Korea, California, and Mexico. Kazuo Kashio was named president in 1988.

In 1990 CASIO COMPUTER established CASIO COMPUTER Electronic Devices to sell LCDs and chip-on-film components. In 1991 the company acquired a capital interest in Asahi, a producer of communications equipment and light electrical appliances. CASIO COMPUTER moved much of its production overseas in 1994, primarily to Thailand and Malaysia, after the high yen contributed to a nearly 28% drop in exports.

The company introduced its first digital camera in 1995. The next year CASIO COMPUTER launched its CASSIOPEIA handheld PC, and in

1997 it entered the US pager market. In 1998 the company formed subsidiary CASIO Soft to develop Microsoft-based software for handheld PCs and other mobile devices.

In 2000 the company restructured its management system, and cut expenses (particularly research and development). The following year it instituted a three-year plan designed to strengthen its digital imaging, mobile networking, and electronic components businesses.

The company launched a joint venture with Hitachi in 2004; the new business unit, Casio Hitachi Mobile Communications Co., produces mobile phone handsets. In a bid to expand its presence in key markets worldwide, CASIO COMPUTER established several new subsidiaries in 2006, including Miami-based Casio Latin America; Casio Espana SL, in Barcelona, Spain; and Casio Benelux, in the Netherlands.

CASIO COMPUTER and NTT DoCoMo partnered in 2007 to establish joint venture CXD NEXT Co. The company services CASIO's NetRegi, an electronic cash register that offers virtual private network capability, among other features. The joint venture is focused on electronic cash register technologies, such as electronic settlements and sales data management services. Its goal is to allow retailers to monitor shop sales through a website and to transfer sales data to cell phones.

EXECUTIVES

Chairman: Toshio Kashio
President and CEO: Kazuo Kashio
EVP and Representative Director: Yukio Kashio
Senior Managing Director: Yozo Suzuki
Senior Managing Director: Fumitsune Murakami
Managing Director: Susumu Takashima
Managing Director: Akira Kashio
Managing Director: Akinori Takagi
Director: Kouichi Takeichi
Director: Tadashi Takasu
Auditors: KPMG AZSA & Co.

LOCATIONS

HQ: CASIO COMPUTER CO., LTD.
(Casio Keisanki Kabushiki Kaisha)
6-2, Hon-machi 1-chome, Shibuya-ku
Tokyo 151-8543, Japan
Phone: 81-3-5334-4111
US HQ: 570 Mount Pleasant Ave., Dover, NJ 07801
US Phone: 973-361-5400   **US Fax:** 973-537-8910
Web: world.casio.com

2010 Sales

	% of total
Asia	
Japan	52
Other countries	19
North America	15
Europe	14
Total	**100**

PRODUCTS/OPERATIONS

2010 Sales

	% of total
Electronics	
Consumer	38
Mobile network solutions	25
Timepieces	18
System equipment	8
Electronic components	5
Other	6
Total	**100**

Selected Products

Electronics
  Consumer products
    Calculators
    Digital cameras
    Electronic dictionaries
    Electronic musical instruments
    Label printers
  Mobile Network Solutions
    Cell phones
    Pocket PCs
  System Equipment
    Electronic cash registers
    Office computers
    Printers
    Data projectors
  Timepieces
    Analog watches
    Clocks
    Digital watches
Electronic Components and Other Products
  Electronic components
    Bump processing consignments
    Carrier tape
    LCDs
    TCP assembly and processing consignments
  Other
    Factory automation
    Molds
    Toys

COMPETITORS

Canon
Fujitsu
Hewlett-Packard
Hitachi
IBM
LG Electronics
Motorola
NEC
Nikon
Palm, Inc.
Panasonic Corp
Philips Electronics
Ricoh Company
Roland Corporation
Samsung Group
SANYO
Seiko
Sharp Corp.
Sony
Swatch
Timex
Toshiba
Yamaha

HISTORICAL FINANCIALS

Company Type: Public

Income Statement

FYE: March 31

	REVENUE ($ mil.)	NET INCOME ($ mil.)	NET PROFIT MARGIN	EMPLOYEES
3/10	4,617	(178)	—	12,247
3/09	5,325	(238)	—	12,358
3/08	6,275	123	2.0%	13,202
3/07	5,267	213	4.1%	13,013
3/06	4,936	202	4.1%	12,673
Annual Growth	**(1.7%)**	**—**	**—**	**(0.9%)**

2010 Year-End Financials

Debt ratio: —
Return on equity: —
Cash ($ mil.): 569
Current ratio: 1.80
Long-term debt ($ mil.): —

No. of shares (mil.): 276
Dividends
  Yield: 1.9%
  Payout: —
Market value ($ mil.): 2,140

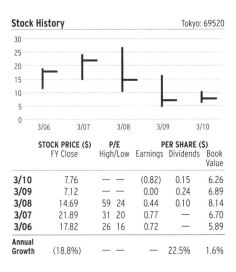

Stock History

Tokyo: 69520

	STOCK PRICE ($) FY Close	P/E High/Low		PER SHARE ($) Earnings	Dividends	Book Value
3/10	7.76	—	—	(0.82)	0.15	6.26
3/09	7.12	—	—	0.00	0.24	6.89
3/08	14.69	59	24	0.44	0.10	8.14
3/07	21.89	31	20	0.77	—	6.70
3/06	17.82	26	16	0.72	—	5.89
Annual Growth	**(18.8%)**	**—**	**—**	**—**	**22.5%**	**1.6%**

Celesio AG

Celesio likes being a middleman when it comes to pharmaceuticals. The company is one of Europe's largest drug wholesalers, holding market-leading positions in several of the countries it serves. Its largest wholesale markets are France, Germany, and the UK. In addition to more than 140 wholesale distribution branches, Celesio owns retail chains consisting of 2,300 pharmacies in Europe, including Norway, Italy, and the UK. The company also offers marketing, logistics, and transportation solutions to pharmaceutical manufacturers through its manufacturer solutions division (and its Movianto and pharmexx units). German conglomerate Franz Haniel & Cie. owns a majority stake in Celesio, which was founded in 1835.

While Celesio already has subsidiaries and operations in more than 25 countries, acquisitions remain part of its growth strategy. The firm is focused on expanding its activities across Europe, as well as into additional regions. Margins for the wholesale business, however, continue to be threatened by government price controls in many of the countries where Celesio operates, especially in the core UK market.

In 2009 Celesio announced plans to open its own chain of more than 100 pharmacies in Sweden following the implementation of a new law there that opened the door for private companies to establish pharmacies. The law ended a nearly 40-year government monopoly on the country's state-run Apoteket pharmacies. Celesio also expanded its Belgian operations by acquiring distribution firm Laboratoria Flandria and logistics firm Dirk Raes in 2009.

In 2007 Celesio acquired Apotheke DocMorris, a mail-order pharmacy based in Germany. Apotheke DocMorris remains an independent subsidiary of Celesio, and has built up partnerships with some 150 pharmacies in Germany that now stock the strong DocMorris brand of products. Following the acquisition, Apotheke DocMorris extended its mail order pharmacy business into the UK and Norway.

Celesio acquired a majority stake in Panpharma, Brazil's largest wholesale pharmaceuticals company, in 2009. The move is part of

Celesio's strategy to expand outside Europe, especially in emerging growth markets. The deal includes the option for Celesio to increase its initial 54% holding at a later time.

HISTORY

Merchant Franz Ludwig Gehe formed his Gehe & Co. chemist and dye wholesale business in Dresden in 1835. At a time when pharmaceuticals were a luxury, Gehe supplied unprocessed raw materials to pharmacists to help make drugs more affordable. The company sold its products through traveling sales agents working around the world. Thirty years later the company opened its first factory.

In 1882 Gehe died, and control of his firm passed to his nephew, Rudolph Luboldt, who had joined in 1859. Under the watch of Luboldt's successor son, Walter, Gehe & Co. published its first catalog of drugs in 1894. Almost 10 years later the firm became a joint-stock company. In 1910 it published a drug reference book for doctors and pharmacists.

Over the next 20 years, the company opened offices in eastern Germany and Poland. It bought a Czech chemicals factory (1924) and set up subsidiaries in Germany, Poland, and Spain in the 1930s. After WWII it lost its Dresden headquarters and most of its branches (its eastern German operations eventually became Jenapharm, a drug company owned by the East German government); Gehe & Co. rebuilt in West Germany, moving its main office to Munich.

Gehe & Co. achieved record sales through most of the 1950s and 1960s. During this time it opened new offices and bought a few German rivals, including Heitzer & Co. Growth continued in the 1970s; when family-owned conglomerate Franz Haniel & Cie. snapped up a majority holding in the firm in 1973, the firm acquired four of Haniel's existing wholesale units, boosting its German market share. Gehe & Co. also began investing in technology as its industry automated.

Growth continued in the 1980s as it continued buying drug wholesalers. In 1981 the firm moved its headquarters again, this time to Stuttgart, and changed its name to GEHE AG. The company diversified when it bought mail-order office equipment firm Kaiser & Kraft Group in 1985; it supplemented this new division with further purchases. In 1989 GEHE returned to drug manufacturing when it bought a stake in generics maker Azuchemie.

The reunification of Germany also brought the company a reunification: In 1991 it bought Jenapharm, bringing it back into the family. Two years later GEHE restructured, becoming a holding company with divisions for its wholesale, drug production, and mail-order operations. Also in 1993 new German government regulations to control the soaring cost of public health care caused the firm's sales to plummet 20%. To escape price controls at home, it focused on expanding in Europe in a big way. Among its purchases were leading wholesaler Office Commerciale Pharmaceutique (now OCP) and AAH, which controlled 30%-40% of the wholesale market in Ireland and the UK. AAH brought with it a chain of retail pharmacies, which GEHE grew by buying Lloyds Chemists in 1997.

As laws governing ownership of pharmacies in some European countries changed in the late 1990s, the firm bought retail chains in Italy and the Czech Republic. In 1999 it opted to refocus on its pharmaceutical operations; GEHE spun off its Kaiser & Kraft mail-order business as TAKKT and sold its health care services (rehabilitation equipment). The next year it expanded into Austria when it bought wholesale market leader Herba Chemosan Apotheker. In 2001 GEHE extended its pharmacy operations into the Netherlands, Norway, Ireland, and Belgium.

The company became Celesio AG after changing its name in 2003. The name change from GEHE to Celesio was made to distinguish the parent company from its similarly named subsidiaries. In 2005 Celesio advanced its pharmacy business by purchasing over 100 UK Cohens and Scholes pharmacies.

The company expanded into Denmark through its 2006 acquisitions of distribution companies K.V. Tjellesen and Max Jenne. It also enhanced its manufacturer solutions division, which provides logistics and transportation services, by investing in pharmexx, a sales and marketing services provider.

EXECUTIVES

Chairman, Supervisory Board: Jürgen Kluge, age 57
Deputy Chairman, Supervisory Board: Ihno Goldenstein
Chairman, Management Board and CEO: Fritz Oesterle, age 58
Member Management Board and CFO: Christian Holzherr, age 46
CEO, pharmexx: Reto Flückiger, age 45
COO, pharmexx: Georg Nagl, age 45
Head Manufacturer Solutions and Head Global Strategic Marketing and Business Innovation Unit: Michael Lonsert
Group Managing Director, Celesio Wholesale: Wolfgang Mähr, age 52
Latin America and South East Asia, pharmexx: Michael Schomaker, age 55
Head Corporate Communications: Rainer Berghausen
Director Investor Relations: Michaela Wanka
Auditors: Ernst & Young AG

LOCATIONS

HQ: Celesio AG
Neckartalstrasse 155
70376 Stuttgart, Germany
Phone: 49-711-5001-00   **Fax:** 49-711-5001-1260
Web: www.celesio.com

2009 Sales

	% of total
France	32
UK	22
Germany	19
Austria	5
Norway	4
Brazil	2
Other	16
Total	**100**

PRODUCTS/OPERATIONS

2009 Sales

	% of total
Wholesale	55
Retail pharmacies	43
Manufacturing solutions	2
Total	**100**

Selected Subsidiaries

Wholesale (distribution, also known as Pharmacy Solutions division)
AAH Pharmaceuticals Ltd. (UK)
AFM S.p.A. (Italy)
Cahill May Roberts Group Ltd (Ireland)
GEHE Pharma Handel GmbH (Germany)
GEHE Pharma Praha, spol. S r.o. (Czech Republic)
Herba Chemosan Apotheker AG (Austria)
Kemofarmacija d.d. (Slovenia, Romania, and Croatia)
Laboratoria Flandria NV (Belgian)
Norsk Medisinaldepot AS (Norway)
OCP Repartition (France)
OCP Portugal, Produtos Farmacêuticos SA (Portugal)
Panpharma Participacoes S.A. (Brazil)
Pharma Belgium SA
Rudolf Spiegel GmbH (Germany)
Tjellesen Max Jenne A/S (Denmark)

Pharmacies (retail, also known as Patient and Consumer Solutions division)
Admenta Italia S.p.A.
DocMorris Kooperationen GmbH (mail order)
Lékárny Lloyds s.r.o. (Czech Republic)
Lloyds Apotheken B.V. (Netherlands)
Lloyds Pharmacy Limited (UK)
Lloydspharma SA (Belgium)
Unicare Pharmacy Limited (Ireland)
Vitusapotek AS (Norway)

Solutions (sales and logistics, also known as Manufacturer Solutions division)
Evolution Homecare
Movianto
pharmexx

COMPETITORS

Alliance Boots
Andreae-Noris Zahn
Cardinal Health
Co-operative Group
Mawdsleys
Mediq
PHOENIX Pharma
Profarma Distribuidora
Sigma Pharmaceuticals
Superdrug
United Drug
waymade

HISTORICAL FINANCIALS

Company Type: Public

Income Statement

	REVENUE ($ mil.)	NET INCOME ($ mil.)	NET PROFIT MARGIN	EMPLOYEES
12/09	30,810	3	0.0%	46,095
12/08	30,770	(26)	—	37,746
12/07	32,897	641	1.9%	37,516
12/06	28,456	558	2.0%	36,442
12/05	24,268	498	2.1%	35,407
Annual Growth	**6.1%**	**(71.5%)**	**—**	**6.8%**

FYE: December 31

2009 Year-End Financials

Debt ratio: —
Return on equity: 0.1%
Cash ($ mil.): 183
Current ratio: 1.40
Long-term debt ($ mil.): —
No. of shares (mil.): 170
Dividends
Yield: 2.7%
Payout: —
Market value ($ mil.): 4,315

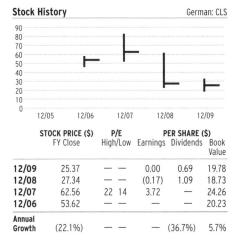

	STOCK PRICE ($) FY Close	P/E High/Low		PER SHARE ($) Earnings	Dividends	Book Value
12/09	25.37	—	—	0.00	0.69	19.78
12/08	27.34	—	—	(0.17)	1.09	18.73
12/07	62.56	22	14	3.72	—	24.26
12/06	53.62	—	—	—	—	20.23
Annual Growth	(22.1%)	—	—	—	(36.7%)	5.7%

CEMEX

You certainly couldn't accuse CEMEX of being stuck in the mud. The building materials company is one of the top cement makers in the world (along with Lafarge and Holcim). The majority of its sales come from cement; the company has more than 60 cement plants and an annual production capacity of more than 95 million tons. It also produces, markets and distributes ready-mix concrete, aggregates, and clinker, an intermediate product used to make portland cement. CEMEX operates in North America (through CEMEX Inc.), as well as in Africa, Asia, Europe, the Middle East, and South America. The US, Mexico, and Europe account for about 80% of revenues.

Before the global economic crisis hit, CEMEX was focused on growth by making diverse acquisitions around the world. One of its first major acquisitions came when it bought European cement giant RMC Group — one of the world's largest cement makers and the largest supplier of ready-mix concrete — for some $5.75 billion in 2005. The RMC deal helped expand CEMEX's operations beyond Latin America and the US. The company also acquired Rinker, Australia's biggest building material manufacturer for more than $14 billion — a price tag that dwarfed the RMC transaction.

Although acquisitions helped make CEMEX a global force, they also gave the company a pile of debt at time when construction activity plummeted. The company's profits and sales sank in 2008 and 2009 as demand for building products dwindled. CEMEX was forced to take steps to regain financial flexibility by selling assets and refinancing debt to better position itself for the economic recovery.

CEMEX cut costs by suspending operations at several facilities and reduced its capital expenditures by halting plant expansion projects. With debt reduction a priority, CEMEX also began selling off assets. In 2008 it sold most of its stake in telecom company Axtel and later its Canary Islands operations, garnering a combined $474 million for debt payments. The following year it sold its Australian operations to Holcim for nearly $2 billion. It also attempted to sell its Austrian and Hungarian business to STRABAG. However, STRABAG later withdrew its offer after it appeared that Austrian authorities might not approve the deal. CEMEX's Austrian assets are still up for sale.

The company continues to cut non-core assets as it prepares for recovery and growth in other markets. Future demand will likely be driven by government-funded infrastructure projects in the US and a recovering housing market. As such, CEMEX is buying Ready Mix USA's interest in the companies' two joint ventures, which have operations in the Southeast US. It also may be focusing more on emerging markets such as the Middle East, Africa, and Asia, which reported record sales for the company during the downturn.

In 2009, per a new Mexican law, the company changed its corporate name to CEMEX, S.A.B. (Sociedad Anónima Bursátil, or Publicly Held Company) de C.V.

HISTORY

The foundation of CEMEX began with — what else? — cement. Lorenzo Zambrano founded Cementos Hidalgo in northern Mexico in 1906. In 1931 the company merged with Cementos Portland Monterrey and was renamed Cementos Mexicanos, from which its current name, CEMEX, is derived.

During the 1960s the company expanded into the cities of Ciudad Valles and Torreon by building plants; it moved into Merida in 1966 by acquiring Cementos Maya. The founder's grandson, also named Lorenzo Zambrano, joined the company in 1968. CEMEX became a true national force during the 1970s by acquiring more plants, including one in central Mexico.

CEMEX went public in 1976. With its acquisition of Cementos Guadalajara and its three plants, it became Mexico's top cement maker. After serving in several engineering positions and as vice president of operations, Zambrano was named CEO in 1985. He had worked at CEMEX as a teenager in the early 1960s and claims he knew he wanted to work for CEMEX since he was 14.

Zambrano set about making CEMEX an international player. Already an exporter, the company boosted its exporting business by purchasing Cementos Anáhuac in 1987. Two years later CEMEX sealed its position as the top Mexican cement maker by acquiring that country's #2 cement company, Cementos Tolteca. CEMEX then bought its first non-Mexican operations in 1992, adding Valenciana de Cementos and Sanson, Spain's largest cement makers. Two years later CEMEX added Vencemos (Venezuela's top cement business), Cemento Bayano (Panama), and a plant in Texas.

The globalization of CEMEX helped the company weather several peso devaluations during the 1990s, including one in late 1994. The company continued to expand abroad, adding Cementos Nacionales (Dominican Republic) in 1995 and Cementos Diamante and Samper (both in Colombia) in 1996. Those deals made the company the world's third-largest cement producer.

After claiming more of the European and Latin American cement markets, CEMEX turned its attention to the Pacific Rim, where it made investments in Rizal Cement Company in the Philippines in 1997 and PT Semen Gresik in Indonesia in 1998 (it sold its 25% stake in 2006).

A booming US economy fueled residential and commercial construction in fiscal 1999, lifting CEMEX to record sales. In 2000 CEMEX gained significant size when it acquired US cement maker Southdown for $2.8 billion. The company sold its Kentucky and Missouri operations to Rinker Materials, a unit of Australia's CSR Ltd, in 2001.

In mid-2002 CEMEX bought Puerto Rican Cement Company (PRCC) for around $180 million. The next year CEMEX acquired Mineral Resource Technologies and Dixon-Marquette Cement in the US. In March of 2005 CEMEX added extensive European operations with the acquisition of UK-based ready-mix cement giant RMC Group. The deal, worth about $5.8 billion, instantly made CEMEX a leader in Europe.

The company also acquired Rinker, Australia's biggest building material manufacturer for more than $14 billion in 2007. However, two years later CEMEX (struggling under the weight of debt and facing declining sales) sold its Australian operations to Holcim for nearly $2 billion.

EXECUTIVES

Chairman and CEO: Lorenzo H. Zambrano, age 65
CFO: Rodrigo Treviño
EVP Administration: Victor M. Romo, age 50
EVP Planning and Finance: Fernando A. González, age 54
President, Europe, Middle East, Africa, and Asia: Juan Romero Torres, age 51
President, Americas Region: Francisco Garza, age 53
General Counsel and Secretary: Ramiro G. Villarreal
Analyst Relations: Luis Garza
Investor Relations: Eduardo Rendón
Media Relations: Jorge Pérez
Chief Comptroller: Rafael Garza
Auditors: KPMG Cárdenas Dosal, S.C.

LOCATIONS

HQ: CEMEX, S.A.B. de C.V.
　Avenida Ricardo Margáin Zozaya 325, Colonia del Valle Campestre
　66265 San Pedro Garza García, Nuevo León, Mexico
Phone: 52-81-8888-8888　　**Fax:** 52-81-8888-4417
US HQ: 920 Memorial City Way, Ste. 100
　Houston, TX 77024
US Phone: 713-650-6200　　**US Fax:** 713-653-6815
Web: www.cemex.com

2009 Sales

	% of total
Mexico	22
US	20
Europe	
UK	8
Spain	6
Other countries	24
Central/South America	10
Africa & Middle East	7
Asia	3
Total	**100**

PRODUCTS/OPERATIONS

2009 Sales

	% of total
Cement	46
Ready-mix concrete	37
Aggregates	14
Other	3
Total	**100**

Selected Subsidiaries

CEMEX México, S. A. de C.V.
  CEMEX España, S.A. (Spain)
    Assiut Cement Company (Egypt)
    Cement Bayano, S.A. (Panama)
    CEMEX Asia Holdings Ltd. (Singapore)
      APO Cement Corporation (Philippines)
      CEMEX (Thailand) Co., Ltd.
      Solid Cement Corporation (Philippines)
    CEMEX Colombia S.A.
    CEMEX (Costa Rica), S.A.
    CEMEX de Puerto Rico Inc
    CEMEX Dominicana, S.A. (Dominican Republic)
    CEMEX France Gestion (S.A.S.)
    CEMEX, Inc. (US)
    CEMEX Venezuela, S.A.C.A.
CEMEX U.K.
  CEMEX Austria plc.
  CEMEX Czech Operations, s.r.o.
  CEMEX Deutschland, AG. (Germany)
  CEMEX Holdings (Israel) Ltd.
  CEMEX Investments Limited (UK)
  CEMEX Polska sp. Z.o.o. (Poland)
  CEMEX SIA (Latvia)
  CEMEX Topmix LLC, Gulf Quarries LLC,
    CEMEX Supermix LLC and CEMEX Falcon LLC
  Dalmacijacement d.d. (Croatia)
  Danubiusbeton Betonkészító Kft. (Hungary)
  Readymix PLC. (Ireland)

COMPETITORS

Aggregate Industries
Ash Grove Cement
Buzzi Unicem USA
Cementos Portland Valderrivas
CRH
Eagle Materials
Essroc
HeidelbergCement
Holcim
Italcementi
Italmobiliare
Lafarge
Martin Marietta Materials
Siam Cement
Sumitomo Osaka Cement
Taiheiyo Cement
Tarmac
Trinity Industries
TXI
Ube-Mitsubishi Cement
U.S. Concrete
Vulcan Materials

HISTORICAL FINANCIALS

Company Type: Public

Income Statement

FYE: December 31

	REVENUE ($ mil.)	NET INCOME ($ mil.)	NET PROFIT MARGIN	EMPLOYEES
12/09	15,169	127	0.8%	47,624
12/08	17,649	165	0.9%	56,791
12/07	21,656	2,389	11.0%	66,612
12/06	18,260	2,380	13.0%	54,905
12/05	15,143	2,087	13.8%	26,679
Annual Growth	0.0%	(50.4%)	—	15.6%

2009 Year-End Financials

Debt ratio: 96.1%
Return on equity: 0.8%
Cash ($ mil.): 1,082
Current ratio: 1.15
Long-term debt ($ mil.): 15,757

No. of shares (mil.): 891
Dividends
  Yield: 0.0%
  Payout: —
Market value ($ mil.): 777

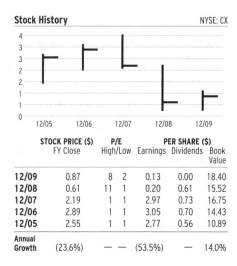

	STOCK PRICE ($) FY Close	P/E High/Low		PER SHARE ($) Earnings	Dividends	Book Value
12/09	0.87	8	2	0.13	0.00	18.40
12/08	0.61	11	1	0.20	0.61	15.52
12/07	2.19	1	1	2.97	0.73	16.75
12/06	2.89	1	1	3.05	0.70	14.43
12/05	2.55	1	1	2.77	0.56	10.89
Annual Growth	(23.6%)	—	—	(53.5%)	—	14.0%

Centrica plc

Centrica is centered on energy. The UK's largest gas supplier, Centrica serves 15.6 million residential electricity and gas customers in that country, primarily under the British Gas brand. It also supplies electricity, gas, and energy related services to more than 1 million businesses. Other operations include gas and electricity production, wholesale energy marketing, international retail energy marketing, drain cleaning services, and appliance sales. Through its Direct Energy subsidiary, the company supplies gas and power to residential customers in Canada and the US. Centrica also has operations in Continental Europe, Egypt, Nigeria, and Trinidad & Tobago.

Through Centrica Energy, Centrica has proved and probable reserves of almost 2 trillion cu. ft. of natural gas. It is expanding gas exploration and production operations in the UK and North America to support its supply businesses; Centrica also has gas storage operations.

The company has gained some 5.1 million retail power and gas supply customers, including more than 800,000 in the purchase of two Texas retail electric providers from American Electric Power and 1 million through the purchase of Canadian Utilities' retail businesses.

In a move to dramatically boost its energy production and provide an entrance to the nuclear sector, in 2009 Centrica acquired 20% of nuclear power operator British Energy. Centrica has also acquired Electricity Direct, a UK commercial retail supplier serving nearly 1 million customers.

In order to secure more natural gas resources, in 2009 the company acquired a 67% stake in the undeveloped York gas fields in the southern North Sea from Hess Limited. Centrica also acquired North Sea explorer Venture Production. In 2010 the company agreed to acquire Royal Dutch Shell's 10% stake in the Statfjord field in the Norwegian sector of the North Sea, for $225 million, increasing its holdings in the field to 19%.

HISTORY

William Murdock invented gas lighting in 1792. In 1812 the Gas Light and Coke Company of London was formed as the world's first gas supplier to the public, and by 1829 the UK had 200 gas companies. In the second half of the 19th century, the gas industry began looking for new uses for the fuel. Gas stoves were introduced in 1851, the geyser water heater was invented in 1868, and in 1880 the first gas units to heat individual rooms were developed.

Gas companies countered the emerging electricity industry by renting gas stoves at low prices and installing gas fittings (stove, pipe, and lights) in poor homes with no installation charges or deposits. By 1914 the UK had 1,500 gas suppliers.

The electricity industry soon made major strikes against the gas industry's dominance. In 1926 the government began reorganizing the fragmented electricity supply industry, building a national power grid and establishing the Central Electricity Generating Board to oversee it.

The gas industry was nationalized in 1949, and 1,050 gas suppliers were brought under the control of the British Gas Council. Still, the gas industry was losing. Supplying gas was more expensive than generating electricity: Gas was seen as a power supply of the past. The Gas Council sought to change that image through an aggressive marketing campaign in the 1960s, touting gas as a modern, clean fuel. Other factors played a part in its re-emergence: The Clean Air Act of 1956 steadily reduced the use of coal for home heating, liquefied natural gas was discovered in the North Sea, and OPEC raised oil prices in the 1970s. When natural gas was introduced, most of the old gasworks were demolished, and the British Gas Council (which became the British Gas Corp. in 1973) set about converting, free of charge, every gas appliance in the UK to natural gas.

As Margaret Thatcher's government began privatizing state industries, the British Gas Corp. was taken public in 1986. Freed from government control, British Gas expanded its international exploration and production activities. When the US gas industry began deregulating, British Gas formed joint venture Accord Energy in 1994 with US gas trader Natural Gas Clearinghouse (now NGC) to sell gas on the wholesale market.

With the opening of the UK gas-supply market (which began regionally in 1996 and went nationwide in 1998), British Gas split into two public companies to avoid a conflict of interest between its supply business and its monopoly transportation business. In 1997 it spun off Centrica, the retail operations, and BG (now BG Group), which received the transportation business and the international exploration and production operations.

The UK electricity supply market began opening up to competition in 1998, and Centrica won 750,000 UK electricity customers, most of them also gas customers. In 1999 it bought The Automobile Association, which it sold to venture capitalists in 2004. In 2000 Centrica began offering telecom services in the UK.

Centrica moved into North America in 2000 by purchasing two Canadian companies: natural gas retailer Direct Energy Marketing and gas production company Avalanche Energy. It gained a 28% stake in US marketing firm Energy America through the Direct Energy transaction and purchased the remaining 72% from US firm Sempra Energy the next year. Continuing its non-domestic strategy, Centrica bought a 50% interest in Belgium energy supplier Luminus.

The firm purchased 60% of the 1,260-MW Humber Power station in 2001, its first domestic power plant interest. It also acquired the UK operations of Australia's One.Tel, and it bought Enron's European retail supply business, Enron Direct, for $137 million.

In 2002 Centrica purchased the retail energy services business of Canadian pipeline company Enbridge for $637 million; it also agreed to acquire another Enron-controlled company, US retail energy supplier NewPower Holdings, for $130 million. But Centrica withdrew its offer to buy NewPower a month after the deal was announced because of concerns about NewPower's potential Enron-related liabilities. Later that year Centrica acquired 200,000 retail customer accounts in Ohio and Pennsylvania from NewPower.

In 2007 Centrica acquired Newfield Exploration's North Sea assets for $486 million and in 2008 it acquired its first gas and oil assets in the Norwegian North Sea for $375 million (from Marathon Oil).

EXECUTIVES

Chairman: Roger M. Carr, age 63
Chief Executive: W. Samuel H. (Sam) Laidlaw, age 54
Director Group Finance: Nick Luff, age 42
President, Direct Energy Business: Maura J. Clark, age 50
President, Home and Business Services, Direct Energy: Eddy Collier
President, Wholesale Energy, Direct Energy: Badar Khan
Board Member; Managing Director, British Gas: Phillip K. (Phil) Bentley, age 51
Managing Director, Communities and New Energy, British Gas: Gearoid Lane
Managing Director, Centrica Energia, Spain: Enrique Giménez
Managing Director, Centrica Energy and Europe and Board Member: Mark Hanafin
Group Director Human Resources: Anne Minto
Group Director Health, Safety, and Environment: Graeme Collinson
Group General Counsel and Company Secretary: Grant Dawson
Director, Europe: Rob Leonard
Director Public Relations, Direct Energy: Joshua Orzech
Director Investor Relations: Andrew Page
Group Director Corporate Affairs: Catherine May
Director; President and CEO, Direct Energy and Board Member: Chris Weston
Auditors: PricewaterhouseCoopers LLP

LOCATIONS

HQ: Centrica plc
Millstream, Maidenhead Road
Windsor SL4 5GD, United Kingdom
Phone: 44-1753-494-000 **Fax:** 44-1753-494-001
Web: www.centrica.co.uk

2009 Sales

	% of total
UK	69
North America	
US	18
Canada	10
Other regions	3
Total	**100**

PRODUCTS/OPERATIONS

2009 Sales

	% of total
UK	
Downstream	
Residential energy supply	33
Business energy supply & services	14
Residential services	6
Upstream	
Industrial & commercial	8
Power generation	6
Gas & oil	5
Storage	1
North America	
Residential energy supply	11
Business energy supply	11
Upstream & wholesale energy	3
Residential & business services	2
Total	**100**

COMPETITORS

AGL Resources	Green Mountain Energy
Calor	IBERDROLA
Community Energy	RWE npower
Constellation Energy Group	Scottish and Southern Energy
Dominion Resources	Southern Company
EDF Energy	STASCO
Electrabel	United Utilities
E.ON Ruhrgas	Viridian Group
E.ON UK	Western Power Distribution
Gasunie	

HISTORICAL FINANCIALS

Company Type: Public

Income Statement

FYE: December 31

	REVENUE ($ mil.)	NET INCOME ($ mil.)	NET PROFIT MARGIN	EMPLOYEES
12/09	34,978	890	2.5%	34,125
12/08	30,893	(208)	—	32,817
12/07	32,624	3,008	9.2%	33,908
12/06	32,212	(302)	—	33,933
12/05	23,136	1,743	7.5%	35,410
Annual Growth	**10.9%**	**(15.5%)**	**—**	**(0.9%)**

2009 Year-End Financials

Debt ratio: —
Return on equity: 13.8%
Cash ($ mil.): 2,061
Current ratio: 1.13
Long-term debt ($ mil.): —
No. of shares (mil.): 5,132
Dividends
Yield: 4.4%
Payout: 76.9%
Market value ($ mil.): 22,975

Stock History

Pink Sheets: CPYYY

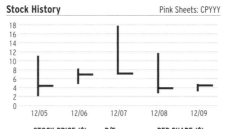

	STOCK PRICE ($) FY Close	P/E High/Low		PER SHARE ($) Earnings	Dividends	Book Value
12/09	4.48	18	13	0.26	0.20	1.30
12/08	3.85	—	—	(0.05)	0.17	1.22
12/07	7.16	22	9	0.80	0.20	1.29
12/06	6.94	—	—	(0.08)	0.18	0.60
12/05	4.38	24	5	0.46	0.14	0.80
Annual Growth	**0.6%**	**—**	**—**	**(13.3%)**	**9.3%**	**12.9%**

China Mobile

China Mobile Limited sees unlimited potential. The company serves about 450 million subscribers making it China's (and the world's) leading wireless operator by subscribers. In terms of sales, it trails UK-based global leader Vodafone Group. China Mobile offers domestic and international phone service, text messaging, and other mobile data services such as streaming news and entertainment content. In addition to its flagship postpaid GoTone brand, the company targets the youth and budget-concious markets with M-zone and Easyown prepaid services. State-controlled China Mobile Communications Corporation indirectly holds a majority stake of 74% through intermediary subsidiary China Mobile (Hong Kong) Group.

China Mobile Limited has invested heavily in the past few years to update its existing wireless network with implenting a newer 3G (third generation) network across the country to enable higher-bandwidth mobile data services such as broadband Internet and streaming video. These upgrades paid off in 2008 when China Mobile Limited served as the wireless services provider for the Beijing Olympics, boosting the company's profile before a global audience.

Meanwhile, China Mobile Limited's organic growth has been fueled in large part by the adoption of mobile communications in rural areas where, in some cases, there were previously no wired or wireless telephone services. Additionally, the company has catered increasingly to corporate clients in a search for higher-margin contracts. It has targeted commercial and government customers with enhanced customer and calling services packages. Key industries for China Mobile Limited in 2008 included agriculture and education.

Other efforts to grow its business included the acquisition of state-run fixed-line carrier China Tietong Telecommunications in 2008 as part of a broader restructuring of the telecom industry in China, which also involved former rival China Unicom selling its wireless operations to China Telecom. The previous year it grew globally as well, with the acquisition of nearly 90% of Pakistani wireless company Paktel Ltd. for about $284 million.

These purchases continued the company's history of using acquisitions to expand operations. From 1998 to 2004 China Mobile purchased 29 regional telecom service providers. The company acquired China Resources Peoples Telephone (later renamed China Mobile Peoples Telephone), a Hong Kong-based telecom service provider, for $436 million in 2006.

Executive director and VP Li Yue was named CEO in August 2010, replacing Wang Jianzhou (who remained as chairman).

EXECUTIVES

Chairman and Executive Director: Wang Jianzhou, age 61
CEO and Executive Director: Li Yue, age 51
VP, CFO, and Executive Director: Xue Taohai, age 54
VP and Executive Director: Liu Aili, age 46
VP and Executive Director: Sha Yuejia, age 52
VP and Executive Director: Lu Xiangdong, age 50
VP and Executive Director: Xin Fanfei, age 53
VP and Executive Director: Huang Wenlin, age 56
Executive Director: Xu Long, age 53
Auditors: KPMG

LOCATIONS

HQ: China Mobile Limited
(Zhongguo Yidongsi Gufen Youxien Gongsi)
60th Fl., The Center, 99 Queen's Rd. Central
Hong Kong
Phone: 852-3121-8888 **Fax:** 852-2511-9092
Web: www.chinamobileltd.com

PRODUCTS/OPERATIONS

2009 Sales

	% of total
Usage & monthly fees	67
Value-added service fees	29
Other	4
Total	**100**

COMPETITORS

China Telecom Corporation Limited
China Unicom
City Telecom
Hutchison Telecommunications
PCCW Ltd.
Vodafone

HISTORICAL FINANCIALS

Company Type: Public

Income Statement

FYE: December 31

	REVENUE ($ mil.)	NET INCOME ($ mil.)	NET PROFIT MARGIN	EMPLOYEES
12/09	66,143	16,849	25.5%	145,954
12/08	60,161	16,457	27.4%	138,368
12/07	48,793	11,901	24.4%	127,959
12/06	37,741	8,436	22.4%	111,998
12/05	31,349	6,907	22.0%	99,104
Annual Growth	**20.5%**	**25.0%**	**—**	**10.2%**

2009 Year-End Financials

Debt ratio: 6.6%
Return on equity: 24.3%
Cash ($ mil.): 11,542
Current ratio: 1.37
Long-term debt ($ mil.): 4,909

No. of shares (mil.): 4,013
Dividends
  Yield: 23.5%
  Payout: 38.3%
Market value ($ mil.): 27,256

Stock History

NYSE: CHL

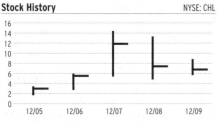

	STOCK PRICE ($) FY Close	P/E High/Low		PER SHARE ($) Earnings	Dividends	Book Value
12/09	6.79	2	1	4.15	1.59	18.48
12/08	7.42	3	1	4.04	1.62	16.08
12/07	11.88	5	2	2.93	1.06	12.73
12/06	5.53	3	1	2.10	0.78	10.16
12/05	2.98	2	1	1.67	0.59	8.77
Annual Growth	**22.9%**	**—**	**—**	**25.6%**	**28.1%**	**20.5%**

China Petroleum & Chemical

China Petroleum and Chemical Corporation (Sinopec Corp.) is the largest refiner and petrochemical producer in China. Its parent, state-owned China Petrochemical (Sinopec Group), reorganized in 2000 and pooled the best of its assets as Sinopec Corp. Sinopec Corp.'s businesses include oil and gas exploration and production; crude oil processing; oil products trading, transportation, distribution, and marketing; and petrochemicals manufacturing. It has proved reserves of 4 billion barrels of oil and more than 7 trillion cu. ft. of gas, and owns more than 29,000 gas stations. The government of China controls about 75% of the company through the Sinopec Group.

In a major international expansion move (and China's largest foreign corporate takeover to date), in 2009 the company acquired Addax Petroleum, which has reserves in Africa and the Middle East, for $7.5 billion.

In a further expansion, in 2010 Sinopec agreed to buy ConocoPhillips' 9% stake in Canadian oil sands operator Syncrude for $4.6 billion.

In 2007 the company formed a $5 billion joint venture with Exxon Mobil and Saudi Aramco to expand an oil refinery in Fujian and add on a chemicals plant; the project remains on schedule. In fact, the company is in the process of building a number of new refineries and petrochemical facilities throughout the country.

EXECUTIVES

Chairman, Board of Supervisors: Wang Zuoran, age 59
Vice Chairman, Board of Supervisors: Zhang Youcai, age 68
Chairman: Su Shulin, age 47
Vice Chairman and President: Wang Tianpu, age 47, $106,214 total compensation
Vice Chairman: Zhang Yaocang, age 56
CFO: Wang Xinhua, age 54, $51,937 total compensation
SVP and Director: Dai Houliang, age 46, $105,482 total compensation
SVP and Director: Cai Xiyou, age 48, $105,482 total compensation
SVP and Director: Zhang Jianhua, age 45, $89,332 total compensation
SVP and Director: Wang Zhigang, age 52, $92,216 total compensation
VP and Director General Development and Planning Department: Lei Dianwu, age 47, $52,961 total compensation
VP and Director General Engineering Department: Zhang Kehua, age 56, $73,681 total compensation
VP: Jiao Fangzheng, age 47, $67,148 total compensation
VP: Zhang Haichao, age 52, $65,047 total compensation
Secretary: Chen Ge, age 47, $53,108 total compensation
Auditors: KPMG Huazhen

LOCATIONS

HQ: China Petroleum & Chemical Corporation
(Zhongguo Shiyou Huagong Gufen Youxien Gongsi)
22 Chaoyangmen North St., Chaoyang District
Beijing 100728, China
Phone: 86-10-5996-0028 **Fax:** 86-10-5996-0386
Web: www.sinopec.com.cn

PRODUCTS/OPERATIONS

2009 Sales

	% of total
Marketing & distribution	58
Chemicals	15
Refining	7
Exploration & production	3
Corporate & other	17
Total	**100**

COMPETITORS

Bangchak Petroleum Public
BP
Chevron
CNOOC
CPC
Exxon Mobil
Furmanite
PetroChina
Royal Dutch Shell
TOTAL

HISTORICAL FINANCIALS

Company Type: Public

Income Statement

FYE: December 31

	REVENUE ($ mil.)	NET INCOME ($ mil.)	NET PROFIT MARGIN	EMPLOYEES
12/09	196,781	9,036	4.6%	371,333
12/08	211,862	4,343	2.1%	358,304
12/07	164,691	7,727	4.7%	334,337
12/06	136,902	6,889	5.0%	340,886
12/05	101,984	5,071	5.0%	364,528
Annual Growth	**17.9%**	**15.5%**	**—**	**0.5%**

2009 Year-End Financials

Debt ratio: 38.8%
Return on equity: 17.6%
Cash ($ mil.): 1,280
Current ratio: 0.64
Long-term debt ($ mil.): 21,335

No. of shares (mil.): 867
Dividends
  Yield: 8.1%
  Payout: 10.0%
Market value ($ mil.): 11,171

Stock History

NYSE: SNP

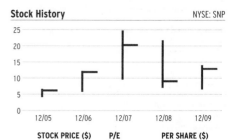

	STOCK PRICE ($) FY Close	P/E High/Low		PER SHARE ($) Earnings	Dividends	Book Value
12/09	12.88	1	1	10.39	1.04	63.39
12/08	9.02	5	2	4.38	2.03	55.31
12/07	20.26	3	1	8.89	2.19	48.47
12/06	11.85	1	1	7.93	1.65	38.74
12/05	6.15	1	1	5.82	1.49	31.95
Annual Growth	**20.3%**	**—**	**—**	**15.6%**	**(8.6%)**	**18.7%**

Christian Dior

This is not your grandmère's Christian Dior. Under head designer John Galliano, the fashion house has gone from outfitting ladies who lunch to women who rock. The holding company's operating unit, Christian Dior Couture, designs and makes some of the world's most coveted haute couture, as well as luxury ready-to-wear fashion and accessories for men and women. Christian Dior operates more than 235 boutiques worldwide with plans to open more. Don't let the pious name fool you, though; Christian Dior is a wolf in very tight-fitting clothing due to its roughly 40% stake in luxury goods giant LVMH. Chairman and LVMH CEO Bernard Arnault and family control Christian Dior.

Capitalizing on its brand's reputation for timeless elegance, the company has been busy growing its network of swank boutiques in markets such as Russia, Asia, and the Middle East. It plans to continue building its presence in these regions, specifically targeting China and Singapore in 2010. Christian Dior in 2009 opened four new shops in China along with single locations in Dubai, UAE; St. Petersburg, Russia; Singapore; and Macau. In 2008 the company opened five shops in China and single locations in Qatar and Bahrain. Europe (including France) remains Christian Dior's largest market, but Asia (including Japan) is closing in quickly on the lead.

Declining couture sales, not surprising given the global economic downturn, have Dior Couture closing underperforming boutiques while it focuses on investing in places such as China and Russia. The remainder of the company's sales come from its stake in LVMH, the world's leading luxury goods group. LVMH's umbrella of brands includes fashion and leather goods (Dior, Donna Karan, Givenchy, Emilio Pucci, Louis Vuitton, Marc Jacobs), watches and jewelry (Chaumet, De Beers, Omas, TAG Heuer, Zenith), spirits and wines (Château d'Yquem, Dom Pérignon, Hennessy, Moët & Chandon, Veuve Clicquot Ponsardin), and fragrances and cosmetics (Bliss, BeneFit, Guerlain, Hard Candy, Parfums Christian Dior, Parfums Givenchy, Parfums Kenzo).

Before head designer John Galliano came aboard in 1996, Dior was known for its conservative cut. Galliano quickly turned the staid fashion house on its head with his own brand of controversy — one Galliano line was based on the rags worn by homeless people. Christian Dior Couture in 2008 acquired a majority stake in John Galliano SA, a company specializing in the creation and concession of fashions and other luxury goods by the designer.

HISTORY

Christian Dior, a trained architect, opened his own fashion house in 1947 with the backing of flamboyant textile king Marcel Boussac. Dior brightened up a bleak postwar Paris in 1948 when he launched his "New Look" designs. After years of slim cuts (to conserve fabric) and drab colors, Dior's looks were feminine, glamorous, and opulent (skirts often used 40 or more yards of fabric).

Dior opened a store in New York in 1948 and pioneered the concept of licensing with hosiery and ties. Dior died unexpectedly from a stroke in 1957 and was succeeded by 21-year-old assistant Yves Saint-Laurent. By 1960, when Marc Bohan succeeded Saint-Laurent, the house of Dior had dressed such famous women as Brigitte Bardot, Marlene Dietrich, and Eva Perón.

But mismanagement by Boussac took its toll, and the company sold its trademark for perfume and cosmetics — potentially its most lucrative licenses — to Moët-Hennessy in 1972. Boussac drained the profits from Dior to finance his company's other struggling divisions, and in 1978 the Boussac group was purchased by (also struggling) textile and retailing company Agache-Willot. Agache-Willot wound up in the hands of the French government with the dubious distinction of being France's largest bankruptcy since the war.

In 1984 ambitious but little-known real estate executive Bernard Arnault beat out several more prominent suitors to buy Agache-Willot from the French government; he put up $15 million of his own money and $45 million from investors and renamed the company Financiere Agache. He then laid off 9,000 people, sold factories, and made the company profitable within three years.

Christian Dior SA was born in 1988 when Arnault sold 42% of it to the public to finance his victorious battle for control of newly formed luxury goods conglomerate LVMH Moët Hennessy Louis Vuitton. Meanwhile, Arnault had to deal with the fact that Christian Dior's traditional business, Dior Couture, was losing its luster. Part of the problem was overlicensing — more than 250 licenses existed for everything Dior, from sunglasses to sheets. What's more, Dior Couture simply looked dowdy compared to other hot young designers.

To turn things around, Arnault lured Beatrice Bongibault from Chanel and made her managing director of Dior Couture. She quickly cut nearly a quarter of the company's licenses and centralized control of those that remained, improving quality and cutting costs. (Her techniques were quickly copied by other design houses.) She also replaced designer Bohan with Italian Gianfranco Ferré in 1989. Arnault ousted Bongibault in 1990. Dior Couture accused her of embezzlement, but the parties settled out of court.

Dior Couture bought back most of its remaining licenses in 1994 and 1995. In 1996 Dior Couture turned to controversial designer John Galliano — already head of LVMH's house of Givenchy — to capitalize on the publicity that followed Galliano's eccentric, sometimes bizarre creations.

Aided by its retail expansion, Dior Couture bounced back from a 1997 loss with a profit in 1998. The fashion house opened 19 more boutiques in 2000 and introduced the Dior Homme collection of menswear — designed by Hedi Slimane — in January 2001 (now designed by Kris Van Assche).

In 2005 the company launched the perfume brands Miss Dior Chérie and Dior Homme. Christian Dior reclaimed the Baby Dior business in 2006, which had been operated under license. The fashion house celebrated its 60th anniversary in 2007.

In 2008, Christian Dior Couture acquired 87% of the shares of John Galliano SA, a company specializing in the creation and concession of fashions and luxury items by the designer. To mark its entrance into the Chinese market, the company hosted a major exhibition in Beijing.

EXECUTIVES

Chairman: Bernard Arnault, age 61
Vice Chairman: Eric Guerlain, age 70
CEO and Director: Sidney Toledano, age 59
CFO: Florian Ollivier
President, LVMH Perfumes and Cosmetics, North
America: Pamela Baxter
Auditors: Mazars & Guérard

LOCATIONS

HQ: Christian Dior SA
30 Avenue Montaigne
75008 Paris, France
Phone: 33-1-44-13-24-98   **Fax:** 33-1-44-13-27-86
US HQ: 712 Fifth Ave., 37th Fl., New York, NY 10019
US Phone: 212-582-0500   **US Fax:** 212-582-1063
Web: www.dior.com

2009 Sales

	% of total
Asia (excluding Japan)	23
Europe (excluding France)	22
US	22
France	15
Japan	10
Other regions	8
Total	**100**

PRODUCTS/OPERATIONS

2009 Sales

	% of total
Fashion & leather goods	36
Selective retailing	26
Perfumes & cosmetics	15
Wines & spirits	15
Watches & jewelry	4
Couture	4
Total	**100**

2009 Sales

	% of total
Retail & other	76
Wholesale	19
License	5
Total	**100**

Principal Holdings

Christian Dior Couture SA
  Accessories
  Haute couture
  Luxury ready-to-wear
LVMH Moët Hennessy Louis Vuitton (42%)
  Fragrances and cosmetics
  Leather and fashion
  Retailing
  Watches and jewelry
  Wine and spirits

COMPETITORS

Armani	L'Oréal
Bill Blass	Oscar de la Renta
Bulgari	Polo Ralph Lauren
Calvin Klein	PPR SA
Chanel	Prada
Dolce & Gabbana	Puig
Escada	Richemont
Estée Lauder	Salvatore Ferragamo
Gianni Versace	Shiseido
Hermès	Valentino Fashion
IT Holding	Vera Wang
Krizia	

HISTORICAL FINANCIALS

Company Type: Public

Income Statement

FYE: December 31

	REVENUE ($ mil.)	NET INCOME ($ mil.)	NET PROFIT MARGIN	EMPLOYEES
12/09	25,432	2,726	10.7%	80,510

2009 Year-End Financials

Debt ratio: —
Return on equity: 18.4%
Cash ($ mil.): 3,630
Current ratio: 1.70
Long-term debt ($ mil.): —

No. of shares (mil.): 182
Dividends
Yield: 2.2%
Payout: 41.4%
Market value ($ mil.): 18,690

Stock History

Euronext Paris: CDI

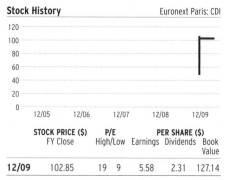

	STOCK PRICE ($) FY Close	P/E High/Low		PER SHARE ($) Earnings	Dividends	Book Value
12/09	102.85	19	9	5.58	2.31	127.14

Club Med

At least one company knows there is something medicinal about a beach vacation. Club Méditerranée, popularly known as Club Med, owns 150 leisure operations in some 40 countries in Europe, North and South America, and the Asia/Pacific region. Its holdings include about 80 all-inclusive resort villages and a cruise ship operation. Club Med locations offer different resort styles that focus on areas such as sports, culture, the family, and spas. All total, the company hosts more than 1 million visitors annually. The company was founded in 1949 by Olympic medalist Gérard Blitz (a former Belgian water polo champion) and French businessman Gilbert Trigano.

Hobbled by a reputation that had become passé, Club Med has spent the last two decades revamping its 1970s "sea, sex, and sun" image to become more upscale and family-oriented. The company spent more than $500 million through 2008 to renovate and upgrade its villages and resorts. It also introduced its new Bar & Snacking Included service to its villages and created Club Med Baby Welcome and Club Med Passworld in order to better cater to families.

The company is looking toward China for growth. It has adopted a development strategy of launching one village a year in China between 2010 and 2014 through partnerships. It first plans to open a Club Med boutique in Shanghai in 2010. United Arab Emirates has also emerged as an area of focus, with Abu Dhabi a top contender to host Club Med's first resort in that region.

Wanting to focus solely on its chain of holiday resorts, in late 2008 Club Med sold its Jet Tours operations to Thomas Cook Group, a leading travel services conglomerate, for $110 million. Jet Tours served about 270,000 clients each year and operated under the Jet Tours, Club Eldorado, and Austral Lagons brand names. At the same time, it also sold a majority stake in its Club Med Gym operations to private equity fund 21 Central Partners.

HISTORY

Belgian diamond cutter Gérard Blitz dreamed up the Club Méditerranée concept as an escape from the post-WWII doldrums in Europe. In 1950 he convened a gathering of charter members on the island of Majorca, where the group slept in tents, cooked their own food, and had a great deal of fun. The Club Med philosophy was born — vacation villages in exotic locations, combining low prices and simple amenities with community spirit and entertainment.

Frenchman Gilbert Trigano, who provided the tents for that first gathering, came on board as the managing director of the company in 1954 and launched a major expansion drive. Polynesian-style huts replaced the tents at the newly opened location in Greece in 1954, and in 1956 the company set up its first ski resort in Leysin, Switzerland. Club Méditerranée was incorporated the following year.

The Rothschild Group was the company's main shareholder from 1961 until 1988, providing the capital for much of Club Méditerranée's expansion. The company went public in 1966.

Club Méditerranée expanded into the cruise line business during the late 1960s, but surly crews and the outbreak of the Arab-Israeli War in 1967 scuttled plans. In the late 1960s Club Méditerranée gained a foothold in the US, opening an office in New York and a hotel in Northern California. In the 1970s the company became one of the biggest leisure groups in France through a series of mergers and acquisitions. The 1970s and 1980s also saw the company hone its freewheeling, anything-goes image.

Club Med, Inc., was set up in New York in 1984 to handle the company's business in the Americas and Asia. Trigano relaunched the cruise line concept in 1990. Club Méditerranée's expansion came to a crashing halt in 1991 as the company suffered its first-ever loss. Political unrest in its prime tourist locations plagued operations, leading in 1993 to another major loss and Trigano's resignation (though he remained as a director). His son Serge took over as chairman that year and set about cutting costs. Lawsuits beset the company in 1996 — one involving the fatal crash of a Club Med plane, the other involving a blackface minstrel show.

Board members looking to turn around losses created a new position for Serge Trigano in 1997 and replaced him as chairman with Philippe Bourguignon, who had helped revive Euro Disney. To boost profits, the company sold its *Club Med 1* cruise ship, as well as other assets that were outside the scope of its core resort business. It also phased out its lower-priced Club Aquarius resorts as part of its efforts to refocus on a single brand. But Club Med suffered record losses in 1997, and Trigano and his father later resigned.

With its restructuring plan in full swing in 1998, Club Med made its way back into the black. The company began renovating its village resorts and consolidating and centralizing its administrative offices. Club Med also implemented a new advertising campaign in 1998 and announced plans to open new ski resorts in the US and Canada, as well as Club Med at Paris Bercy, a recreational center in Paris. In 1999 Club Med bought French travel company Jet Tours Holding.

In 2000 it branched into e-commerce through its creation of Internet subsidiary Club Med On Line. It also purchased its third US village in 2000 in Crested Butte, Colorado. Club Med branched into the body building business in 2001 when it purchased Gymnase Club, a chain of 200 fitness clubs, renamed Club Med Gym.

However, the company closed 17 of its resorts (12 just for the winter) following September 11, 2001, to help cut costs in a diminished market for tourism. Amid losses for a second consecutive year, Bourguignon resigned in 2002.

Striving to cut costs and focus primarily on its holiday resorts operations, in 2008 Club Med sold off its Jet Tours and Club Med Gym operations.

EXECUTIVES

Chairman and CEO: Henri Giscard d'Estaing, age 53
Vice Chairman: David Dautresme, age 76
EVP Finance: Michel Wolfovski
VP, Latin America: Janyck Daudet
VP Sales and Marketing, New Markets, Europe and Africa: Sylvain Rabuel
VP Strategic Marketing and Quality: Katia Hersard
VP Villages, Europe and Africa: Patrick Calvet
VP Communications and External Relations: Thierry Orsoni
VP Sales and Marketing, France, Belgium, and Switzerland: Anne Yannic
VP, Asia-Pacific and Development: Caroline Puechoultres
VP Human Resources: Olivier Sastre
Director Sustainable Development: Agnes Weil
Director Investor Relations and Financial Communications: Carol Bruel
Director Public Relations and Press: Emmanuelle Errera
Director Public Relations, Club Med Americas: Kate Moeller
Auditors: Deloitte & Associés

LOCATIONS

HQ: Club Méditerranée
11 rue Cambrai
75957 Paris, France
Phone: 33-1-53-35-35-53   **Fax:** 33-1-53-35-36-16
Web: www.clubmed.com

2009 Sales

	% of total
Europe	
France	48
Other	27
Asia	12
America	11
Other regions	2
Total	**100**

PRODUCTS/OPERATIONS

Selected Brands

Club Med
Club Med Baby Welcome
Club Med Business
Club Med Cruises
Club Med Discovery
Club Med Passworld
Club Med Voyages
Club Med World

HISTORICAL FINANCIALS

Company Type: Public

Income Statement

FYE: October 31

	REVENUE ($ mil.)	NET INCOME ($ mil.)	NET PROFIT MARGIN	EMPLOYEES
10/09	1,990	(79)	—	13,716
10/08	1,950	(38)	—	8,442
10/07	2,489	(12)	—	23,139
10/06	2,136	6	0.3%	22,398
10/05	1,917	12	0.6%	22,831
Annual Growth	0.9%	—	—	(12.0%)

2009 Year-End Financials

Debt ratio: —	No. of shares (mil.): 28
Return on equity: —	Dividends
Cash ($ mil.): 253	Yield: —
Current ratio: 0.63	Payout: —
Long-term debt ($ mil.): —	Market value ($ mil.): 579

Stock History

Pink Sheets: CLMDY

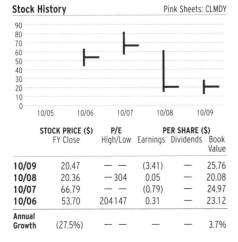

	STOCK PRICE ($) FY Close	P/E High/Low		PER SHARE ($) Earnings	Dividends	Book Value
10/09	20.47	—	—	(3.41)	—	25.76
10/08	20.36	— 304		0.05	—	20.08
10/07	66.79	—	—	(0.79)	—	24.97
10/06	53.70	204 147		0.31	—	23.12
Annual Growth	(27.5%)	—	—	—	—	3.7%

CNP Assurances

Running to the post office and the bank? Buy some insurance while you're out. CNP Assurances is France's top personal life insurer. In addition to life insurance and other savings products, it sells health, death and disability, and other personal risk coverage and pensions. CNP sells its products primarily through about 20,000 outlets of La Poste, the French postal service, and La Caisse Nationale des Caisses d'Epargne, the state savings banks; together these two channels account for about 75% of CNP's sales. These partners are also shareholders in the company, together owning about 35%. Another French paragovernmental organization, Caisse des Dépôts et Consignations, owns more than 39%.

The firm has distribution deals with France's Treasury and its civil service mutual insurance companies, and such financial institutions as Mutualité Française, the umbrella organization for France's mutual health insurers. CNP also has operations abroad, taking stakes in neighboring countries' leading insurers (primarily in Portugal) as they are privatized; it also works in Italy, Spain, and China.

In 2008 the company announced a restructuring plan to turn its growth gaze overseas, primarily South America, Southern Europe, and the Mediterranean. CNP is looking for both organic growth and acquisitions to meet its goals.

During 2009 CNP made good on its plan, moving into Cyprus and Greece. It paid €145 million ($191 million) for 50.1% of Marfin Insurance Holdings, the insurance branch of Marfin Popular Bank Group, Cyprus' second largest bank. Together, the bank and CNP hold four companies, with a total of more than 315 branches selling life and property insurance in the two island nations.

HISTORY

CNP Assurances traces its origins to three government insurance entities established in the mid-19th century. Caisse nationale d'assurance en cas d'accident ("accident insurance") was formed in 1868. Caisse nationale d'assurance en cas de décès ("death and disability insurance") was formed in 1848, while Caisse de retraite pour la vieillesse ("retirement pensions") followed two years later. These two organizations were merged in 1949, forming Caisse nationale d'assurance sur la vie. Ten years later it was merged with the government's accident insurance bureau to form Caisse Nationale de Prévoyance ("provident society"). CNP was put under the domain of the French government's investment banking arm, Caisse des Dépôts et Consignations (CDC).

Over the years CNP earned a reputation for specializing in certain risks, introducing a variety of life and personal risk insurance and pension and savings products. During the 1980s the company enjoyed a healthy growth rate, around 20% annually, as more French individuals and companies began investing in insurance products.

In 1987 CNP became a national public establishment, making it independent from, though still owned by, the government. The next year the company teamed with Centre National des Caisses d'Epargne et de Prévoyance (now La Caisse Nationale des Caisses d'Epargne, or Caisses d'Epargne) to form Ecureuil-Vie, a joint venture to sell CNP's insurance and savings products in the national savings banks. That year it partnered with Portugal's Caixa Geral de Depósitos to create new products.

In the early 1990s CNP was among several entities the government announced it would privatize. To prepare for the change, the company reorganized and became CNP Assurances; the government sold a large chunk of the firm to CDC, La Poste, and Caisses d'Epargne, reducing its stake to 42%. During this time CNP passed rival Union des Assurances de Paris (now part of AXA) to become France's top life insurer.

Privatization lurched along until 1995, when it was put on hold for elections; the Socialist government that came to power was less enthusiastic about the sale of government assets than its predecessor. The process hit another snag two years later when some workers protested, fearing they'd lose their status as civil servants and the perks associated with it. Also in 1997 CNP became the major shareholder of Polish life insurer Polisa-Zycie when it raised its stake from 26% (purchased 1996) to 46%. By 1998 privatization was back on track, and the government sold a 22% stake in CNP to the public. CDC, La Poste, and Caisses d'Epargne raised their interests to their current levels. Before the year's end, CNP bought majority stakes in Portuguese insurers Global and Global Vida.

Expansion abroad continued in 1999 when CNP announced plans to set up operations in China. That year it teamed with the UK's Prudential for cobranded insurance products. In 2000 the company extended its selling arrangement with Caisses d'Epargne to 2005. In 2003 it sold off its share of Italian bancassurance company Carivita.

EXECUTIVES

Chairman: Edmond Alphandéry, age 67
CEO: Gilles Benoist, age 62
Director Finance and Deputy CEO: Antoine Lissowski
Director International Operations and Deputy CEO: Xavier Larnaudie-Eiffel
Director Press Relations: Sophie Messager
Director Redaction: Agathe Sanson
Director Management and Innovation: Jean-Pierre Walbaum, age 63
Director Partnerships and Business Development: Gérard Méneroud, age 62
Head of Investor Relations: Jim Root
Auditors: KPMG Audit

LOCATIONS

HQ: CNP Assurances SA
4, place Raoul Dautry
75716 Paris, France
Phone: 33-1-42-18-88-88   **Fax:** 33-1-42-18-86-55
Web: www.cnp.fr

2009 Premium Revenue

	% of total
France	81
Italy	10
Brazil	6
Other countries	3
Total	**100**

PRODUCTS/OPERATIONS

2009 Sales

	% of total
Premiums	68
Investment & other income	32
Total	**100**

2009 Premium Revenue

	% of total
Life insurance	52
Financial instruments	40
Property/casualty insurance	8
Total	**100**

Selected Subsidiaries

Caixa Seguros (52%, insurance, Brazil)
CNP Holding Brasil
CNP IAM
CNP International (reinsurance)
CNP Seguros de Vida (76%, insurance, Argentina)
CNP UniCredit Vita (57%, insurance, Italy)
CNP Vida (94%, insurance, Spain)
Global (83%, insurance, Portugal)
Global Vida (83%, insurance, Portugal)
Investissement Trésor Vie (insurance)
La Banque Postale Prévoyance (50%, insurance)
Marfin Insurance Holdings Ltd. (50%, insurance, Cyprus)
Préviposte

COMPETITORS

Allianz
Assurances Générales de France
AXA
BNP Paribas
Crédit Agricole
Eureko
Groupama
ING

HISTORICAL FINANCIALS

Company Type: Public

Income Statement

FYE: December 31

	ASSETS ($ mil.)	NET INCOME ($ mil.)	INCOME AS % OF ASSETS	EMPLOYEES
12/09	432,650	1,609	0.4%	4,628
12/08	379,951	1,148	0.3%	4,400
12/07	407,234	2,030	0.5%	3,261
Annual Growth	3.1%	(11.0%)	—	19.1%

2009 Year-End Financials

Equity as % of assets: 4.1%
Return on assets: 0.4%
Return on equity: 10.1%
Long-term debt ($ mil.): —
No. of shares (mil.): 2,367

Dividends
Yield: 4.2%
Payout: 41.8%
Market value ($ mil.): 57,474
Sales ($ mil.): 68,627

Stock History

Euronext Paris: CNP

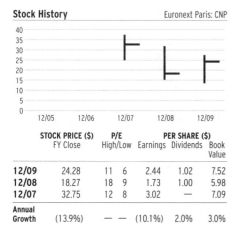

	STOCK PRICE ($) FY Close	P/E High/Low		PER SHARE ($) Earnings	Dividends	Book Value
12/09	24.28	11	6	2.44	1.02	7.52
12/08	18.27	18	9	1.73	1.00	5.98
12/07	32.75	12	8	3.02	—	7.09
Annual Growth	(13.9%)	—	—	(10.1%)	2.0%	3.0%

Commonwealth Bank of Australia

Commonwealth Bank of Australia (CBA), one of Australia's Big Four banks, offers retail and commercial banking, insurance, and investment services, including credit cards, home loans, deposit accounts, and mutual funds. CBA's brands include wealth manager Colonial First State, master trust services provider FirstChoice, online brokerage CommSec, and ASB Bank, which provides banking, investment, and financial services that reach Asia, Europe, and the US. CBA has approximately 1,000 branch offices in Australia (plus more than 3,800 Australia Post locations), as well as operations that reach Asia, Europe, and the US.

In late 2008 the company acquired Australia-based BankWest from British bank HBOS (now part of Lloyds Banking Group). The US$1.5 billion deal included insurer and asset manager St.

Andrew's and bolstered CBA's presence in western Australia.

CBA is also focused on international expansion. In addition to ASB Bank in New Zealand, the company owns Commonwealth Bank Indonesia and minority stakes in banks in China and Vietnam. In 2010 CBA entered the Chinese insurance market with the launch of a joint venture with Bank of Communications. Customer service and business banking are also areas of focus for the bank.

HISTORY

The Commonwealth Bank Act of 1911 allowed Australian banks to conduct both savings bank and central bank functions and paved the way for the founding of the Commonwealth Bank of Australia the next year. The bank initially operated through a single main office and in nearly 500 post offices in Victoria; it spread out through the entire country over the next few years.

The young bank was drafted during WWI to help the federal government organize war loans and a merchant shipping fleet. In 1919 the bank took over responsibility for issuing notes from the Federal Treasury. In 1928 it created the Commonwealth Savings Bank.

Australia — heavily indebted to British lenders — was devastated by the Great Depression. As banks failed, the Commonwealth Bank picked up several other institutions, including the state banks in Western Australia and New South Wales. During those years Commonwealth took on more and more of the functions of a central bank.

During WWII the bank again came to the aid of its country, acting as an agent for the federal government. After the war, when the Australian economy stabilized, the bank began offering home loans.

After years of controversy, in 1959 two bank acts formally separated the Commonwealth Bank's central bank and savings functions. The Reserve Bank of Australia took over the central bank functions in 1960, and the trading and savings operations were taken over by the new Commonwealth Development Bank, later renamed the Commonwealth Banking Corporation (a subsidiary of Commonwealth Bank of Australia).

The bank concentrated on expansion and diversification in the 1970s, establishing travel, home insurance, and financing (CBFC, 1978); it set its sights on technology in the 1980s, expanding its credit card offerings and introducing electronic banking.

The US's 1987 stock market crash again affected Australia's banks, which spent almost a decade recovering. Luckily for Commonwealth Bank, it wasn't the hardest hit.

In 1988 Commonwealth Bank moved into life insurance and investment services, forming subsidiaries Commonwealth Life and Commonwealth Management Services (now together known as CBA Financial Services). In 1989 it bought 75% of New Zealand-based ASB Bank.

Commonwealth faced a bevy of challenges, including banking deregulation that began in 1982, foreign competition, and 1990's banking-law amendments allowing banks to be publicly traded. All of these factors influenced Commonwealth's decision to reorganize. The government sold approximately 30% of its stake in 1991, in part to help Commonwealth fund its acquisition of the State Bank of Victoria. The government sold the rest of its stake in 1996.

That year the company's push into electronic banking bore fruit — some 60% of all its bank-

ing transactions were online; that figure later rose to 80%. The company moved into e-commerce in 1999, putting out a call for an overseas partner; Commonwealth's stated goal was to generate one-quarter of its income outside Australia. Also that year Commonwealth and a division of The Bank of Nova Scotia joined forces to form a commodities trading group specializing in metals. In 2000 the company bought Australian financial services firm Colonial Limited.

EXECUTIVES

Chairman: David J. Turner, age 65
Managing Director and CEO: Ralph J. Norris, age 60
CFO and Group Executive, Financial and Risk Management: David Craig
Group Executive, Enterprise Services and CIO: Michael R. Harte
Group Executive, Human Resources and Group Services: Barbara Chapman
Group Executive, Business and Private Banking: Ian Narev
Group Executive, Retail Banking Services: Ross McEwan
Group Executive, Institutional Banking and Markets: Ian Saines
Group Executive, Wealth Management: Grahame A. Petersen
Group Executive, International Financial Services: Simon Blair
Group Executive Risk Management and Chief Risk Officer: Alden Toevs
Chief Executive, Colonial First State Global Asset Management: Mark J. Lazberger
Head of UK and Europe: Paul Orchart
General Counsel: David Cohen
Company Secretary: Carla F. Collingwood
Investor Relations: Louise Amos
President Director, PT Commonwealth Life: Simon Bennett
CEO, CommFinance: Jiang Guo-Xiong
CEO, First State Investments (UK): Charles Metcalf
Auditors: Ernst & Young

LOCATIONS

HQ: Commonwealth Bank of Australia
Ground Floor, Tower 1, 201 Sussex St.
Sydney C3 2060, Australia
Phone: 61-9118-1335
Web: www.commbank.com.au

PRODUCTS/OPERATIONS

2010 Sales

	% of total
Banking	
Interest	63
Other	22
Funds management	10
Insurance	5
Total	**100**

2010 Sales by Segment

	% of total
Retail banking services	40
Institutional banking & markets	19
Business & private banking	15
Wealth management	12
New Zealand	6
Bankwest	1
Other	7
Total	**100**

COMPETITORS

AMP Limited	Lloyds Banking Group
Asteron	Macquarie Group
Australia and New Zealand Banking	National Australia Bank
AXA Asia Pacific	QBE
HSBC	Suncorp-Metway
	Westpac Banking

HISTORICAL FINANCIALS

Company Type: Public

Income Statement

FYE: June 30

	ASSETS ($ mil.)	NET INCOME ($ mil.)	INCOME AS % OF ASSETS	EMPLOYEES
6/10	553,452	4,864	0.9%	45,025
6/09	499,089	3,824	0.8%	44,218
6/08	468,313	4,632	1.0%	39,621
6/07	360,773	3,816	1.1%	37,873
6/06	269,408	2,890	1.1%	36,664
Annual Growth	19.7%	13.9%	—	5.3%

2010 Year-End Financials

Equity as % of assets: —
Return on assets: 0.9%
Return on equity: —
Long-term debt ($ mil.): —
No. of shares (mil.): 1,549

Dividends
  Yield: 4.8%
  Payout: 68.6%
Market value ($ mil.): 64,512
Sales ($ mil.): 35,781

Stock History

Australian: CBA

	STOCK PRICE ($) FY Close	P/E High/Low		PER SHARE ($) Earnings	Dividends	Book Value
6/10	41.65	18	11	2.93	2.01	19.38
6/09	31.38	16	8	2.42	2.14	16.06
6/08	38.58	18	11	3.35	2.52	15.89
6/07	46.89	17	13	2.88	2.01	13.11
6/06	32.41	15	12	2.25	1.50	9.82
Annual Growth	6.5%	—	—	6.8%	7.6%	18.5%

Compass Group

Look in almost any direction and you'll likely see a foodservice operation run by this company. Compass Group is the world's largest contract foodservices provider, with operations in more than 50 countries. It provides hospitality and foodservice for a variety of businesses and such public-sector clients as cultural institutions, hospitals, and schools. It also offers vending, catering, concessions, and security services for a number of events and sports venues. Its foodservice brands include Chartwells, Crothall, and Levy Restaurants. In addition, Compass is a franchisee of such well-known chains as Burger King and Starbucks.

Compass Group became the leader in its industry through aggressive expansion and numerous acquisitions over the years. It continued to grow in 2010 with the acquisition of IDA Service A/S, an operator of food and support services in Denmark. Earlier in the year it bought family-owned Tirumala Hospitality Services (THS), a strong regional actor in the foodservice industry in western India. THS provides catering services to the business and industry sector in its home country. It got into the safety business in 2010 when it agreed to acquire VSG Group Limited (VSG), a security services firm, from Lloyds Development Capital for $81 million.

Earlier in the year, Compass Group bought Southeast Service Corporation in the US and France's Caterine Restauration. In 2009, the firm added US-based Kimco and Medi-Dyn, as well as Germany's Plural, which provide janitorial and related support services for business and industrial clients and health care facilities. It also snapped up the remaining 50% of shares it didn't already own in Brazil's GR SA and purchased several McColls retail locations in the UK.

While the global recession and credit crisis have caused hardships in many industries, the contract foodservices segment has continued to grow as companies look for new ways to outsource and cut costs. As such, Compass Group is focused on winning new services contracts and expanding its business relationships with existing customers.

Compass Group has also been mindful of costs itself, pulling out of some unprofitable global markets, streamlining operations, and strengthening financial controls throughout its expansive network of worldwide subsidiaries.

HISTORY

Compass Group was formed in 1987 when management bought out the catering business of London-based food and spirits giant Grand Metropolitan (now Diageo) for $260 million. The company went public the next year, listing on the London Stock Exchange. Gerry Robinson, CEO at the time, left in 1991 to take a position with British TV programming giant Granada Group (renamed ITV plc in 2004), where he helped that company diversify into foodservice operations. Finance director Francis Mackay took over as CEO.

Believing that real growth in the catering industry could come from size and economies of scale, Mackay orchestrated a $2.5 billion acquisition plan over the next five years. In 1992 Compass bought Traveller's Fare (now Upper Crust) — a railway caterer — from British Rail. The company expanded into airports the following year with the acquisition of Scandinavian Airlines System's catering operations. Then in 1994 Compass bought Canteen Corporation, the US's third-largest vending and foodservice company.

Compass achieved its goal of becoming the world's largest caterer in 1995 with the acquisition of France's Eurest International, putting it ahead of Sodexho Alliance and Granada. Mackay calmed London investors nervous about the pace of Compass' acquisitions by selling off its hospital management operations and paying lip service to focusing on organic growth. Later that year Compass was awarded the world's largest foodservice contract, a $250-million, five-year deal with IBM.

By 1996 the company seemed to have forgotten all about organic growth, buying Service America, and then Daka International and France's SHRM in 1997. French subsidiary Eurest later snatched a $40 million contract from rival Sodexho (later Sodexo) to supply the staff restaurants at Euro Disney, one of France's top three catering contracts. The next year Compass solidified its position in the airport markets with a five-year licensing deal for use of the T.G.I. Fridays brand, joining Taco Bell, Pizza Hut, Burger King, and Harry Ramsden's fish and chip shops in Compass' quiver of branded airport outlets.

In 1999 CEO Mackay became group chairman, leaving the reins to Compass' chief of North American operations, Michael Bailey. The company's US acquisitions quickly paid off that year with a contract to serve 90% of the food venues at the 2002 Winter Olympics in Salt Lake City. In 2000 the company merged with UK hospitality giant Granada Group (the combined firm became Granada Compass), which then spun off its media operations as a separate company, Granada Media. Late that year it bought Boston-based bakery/café chain Au Bon Pain for about $108 million.

The new company got a quick divorce in 2001 when Granada Compass decided to demerge and make Compass Group public again. Compass Group later sold the Le Meridien hotel operations it gained from the Granada merger to Nomura International for nearly $3 billion. (The firm kept the Travelodge chain.) The company then began making purchases, including Morrison Management Specialists for $563 million, the 66% it didn't already own in Selecta Group, UK vending machine company Vendepac, and health care services management company Crothall Services. Compass lost seven operating sites during the September 11 terrorist attacks on the World Trade Center.

In 2002 Compass signed arguably the industry's largest contract ever, a $200 million a year deal to feed Chevron employees around the world. In 2003 the company sold its Travelodge motel business and Little Chef diners to private equity firm Permira for $1.14 billion, a 5% discount to the asking price. Compass became the first non-Chinese company to provide food in stations and on trains operated by the Shanghai Railway Administration in 2004. In addition, the firm bought Creative Host Services in 2004.

In 2005 Compass sold a 75% stake in Au Bon Pain back to a management group, retaining a 25% interest in the quick-casual chain. The following year it sold its travel hospitality businesses, including Creative Host (now SSP America) and UK motorway operator Moto, to private investors for more than $3 billion. Compass sold its European vending business, Selecta, to German financial giant Allianz for $1.5 billion in 2007.

EXECUTIVES

Chairman: Sir Roy A. Gardner, age 65
Group Chief Executive and Board Member:
  Richard J. Cousins, age 51
Group Finance Director and Board Member:
  Andrew Martin, age 50
Group Managing Director, USA, Canada, and Mexico and Board Member: Gary R. Green, age 52
General Counsel and Secretary: Mark J. White
Auditors: Deloitte LLP

LOCATIONS

HQ: Compass Group PLC
  Compass House, Guildford Street
  Chertsey, Surrey KT16 9BQ, United Kingdom
Phone: 44-1932-573-000   **Fax:** 44-1932-569-956
US HQ: 2400 Yorkmont Rd., Charlotte, NC 28217
US Phone: 704-329-4000   **US Fax:** 704-329-4160
Web: www.compass-group.com

	% of total
North America	44
Europe	
UK	14
Other countries	25
Other regions	17
Total	**100**

PRODUCTS/OPERATIONS

Selected Operating Units

All Leisure (sports and leisure venues)
Bon Appétit Management Company (on-site dining services)
Canteen (vending services)
Chartwells (education foodservices)
Crothall (health care facilities management)
ESS (offshore and remote foodservices)
Eurest (corporate foodservice)
FLIK (upscale foodservices)
Levy Restaurants (fine dining, sports and leisure events)
Medirest (health care services)
Morrison Management Specialists (health care foodservice)
Restaurant Associates Managed Services (corporate dining and sporting and leisure events)
Scolarest (education foodservices)

COMPETITORS

ARAMARK	Healthcare Services
Autogrill	Reliance Security
Centerplate	SectorGuard
Delaware North	Securiplan
Elior	Sodexo
Farsight Security Services	

HISTORICAL FINANCIALS

Company Type: Public

Income Statement

FYE: September 30

	REVENUE ($ mil.)	NET INCOME ($ mil.)	NET PROFIT MARGIN	EMPLOYEES
9/09	21,402	933	4.4%	386,170
9/08	20,785	805	3.9%	388,181
9/07	21,016	1,054	5.0%	365,630
9/06	19,222	534	2.8%	389,240
9/05	17,754	344	1.9%	410,074
Annual Growth	4.8%	28.4%	—	(1.5%)

2009 Year-End Financials

Debt ratio: —
Return on equity: 23.2%
Cash ($ mil.): 936
Current ratio: —
Long-term debt ($ mil.): —

No. of shares (mil.): 1,854
Dividends
  Yield: 3.2%
  Payout: —
Market value ($ mil.): 11,282

Stock History

Pink Sheets: CMPGF

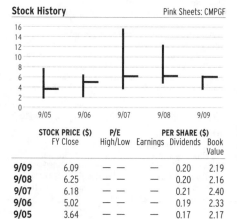

	STOCK PRICE ($) FY Close	P/E High/Low		PER SHARE ($) Earnings	Dividends	Book Value
9/09	6.09	—	—	—	0.20	2.19
9/08	6.25	—	—	—	0.20	2.16
9/07	6.18	—	—	—	0.21	2.40
9/06	5.02	—	—	—	0.19	2.33
9/05	3.64	—	—	—	0.17	2.17
Annual Growth	13.7%	—	—	—	4.1%	0.2%

Crédit Agricole

The name suggests a country farmer's credit union, but Crédit Agricole's scope is much greater. France's largest bank, Crédit Agricole owns a 25% stake each in about 40 regional banks, which in turn own more than half of Crédit Agricole. It offers retail and business banking, lending, and deposit services at more than 9,000 locations throughout the country, including those of subsidiary Le Crédit Lyonnais (LCL). The company also is involved in investment banking and capital markets (through its Crédit Agricole CIB unit), in addition to insurance, leasing, and private banking. Crédit Agricole combined its asset management operations with those of rival French bank Société Générale to form Amundi.

Crédit Agricole owns 75% of the new unit, which has more than €590 billion ($800 billion) of client assets under management. Credit Agricole has renamed and restructured other units as well, in an effort to strengthen its brand: Calyon was renamed Crédit Agricole Corporate and Investment Bank (CIB), and consumer finance company Sofinco and private label credit card issuer Finaref were combined to create Crédit Agricole Consumer Finance. Crédit Agricole also has specialized units devoted to private equity, real estate, factoring, and asset servicing.

Beyond France, Crédit Agricole operates retail banks Cariparma and FriulAdria, which were acquired from Intesa Sanpaolo in 2007; they have more than 700 branches in Italy. In 2010 Crédit Agricole arranged to acquire up to an additional 200 locations in Cariparma's and FriulAdria's markets from Intesa Sanpaolo. Crédit Agricole also owns about two-thirds of Emporiki Bank of Greece and has stakes in banks in Poland, Serbia, and the Ukraine. It is active in several African nations as well. International activities account for about half of the company's net income.

In 2008 Crédit Agricole found itself ensnared along with its colleagues in the worsening economic crisis and credit crunch. To encourage banks to loosen their purse strings, the French government acquired billions of euros worth of debt securities from Crédit Agricole and five peers with the intention that they use the funds to increase their lending.

The bank reported quarterly profits during 2009, but those numbers still didn't meet those of the year before. Crédit Agricole's CEO, Georges Pauget, stepped down in 2010. He was replaced by Jean-Paul Chifflet, who was deputy chairman of both Crédit Agricole and SAS Rue La Boétie, the company's largest shareholder.

HISTORY

In the mid-1800s France's farmers were suffering from crop failures and a lack of credit. The government tried to meet the credit crunch without much success until in 1894 it created an agricultural credit company, Crédit Agricole, that was tax-exempt and provided state-subsidized farm loans (a monopoly it enjoyed until 1989). Five years later the government established the regional banks as intermediaries between it and the local banks. By the turn of the century, Crédit Agricole's three-tiered structure was in place.

The first 30 years of the 20th century were a time of growth for the bank. The government allowed Crédit Agricole to expand its lending to include long-term personal loans to encourage the growth of rural farming (1910) and loans to businesses involved in other industries (1919). The bank survived WWI and the drop in farm production largely through government support. After the war Crédit Agricole funded rural electrification and other infrastructure.

After WWII the bank grew as it issued loans to finance the modernization of France's farms. In 1959 the government allowed Crédit Agricole to begin writing mortgages; expansion of the bank's operations continued in the 1960s as it was permitted to broaden its lending scope and create subsidiaries, including one to finance individual investments (Union d'Etudes et d'Investissements). In 1967 it began keeping deposits (previously it had transferred them to the French Treasury) and used the assets to fuel its national growth.

The early 1970s saw the bank continue to expand its lending operations. Its diversification came under fire from both the government, which wanted the bank to focus on agriculture, and rival banks, which resented their tax-exempt competitor. Crédit Agricole expanded beyond France in the mid-1970s, offering mainly agricultural loans and funds to export firms. It opened its first international office in Chicago in 1979.

In the early 1980s the government continued to allow Crédit Agricole to broaden its lending scope, but at a price: The bank lost its tax-exempt status. Crédit Agricole continued diversifying; it established such subsidiaries as Predica (life insurance, 1986) and bought stakes in two brokerage firms (1988). As the 1980s closed, it became a mutual company when the government sold 90% of the bank to the regional banks.

In 1991 the last restrictions on Crédit Agricole's lending were removed, and the bank began transforming itself into a financial services firm. It expanded its lending operations around the world and added subsidiaries offering a variety of financial services. In 1996 it bought Banque Indosuez (which became Crédit Agricole Indosuez), fueling its growth in international wholesale banking. In the late 1990s the bank sought partnerships to expand its operations.

Its expansion was slowed by financial turmoil in Russia and Asia, and the bank closed its emerging markets business. The next year Crédit Agricole teamed with Spain's Banco Bilbao Vizcaya Argentaria and Commercial Bank of Greece as part of its plans to expand its presence in the Mediterranean and southern Europe; it already owned sizable stakes in Italy's Banca Intesa (now IntesaBci) and major banks in Lebanon, Morocco, and Portugal.

In 2000 the bank bought a majority share in Poland-based Europejski Fundusz Leasingowy, but declined an offer to become the controlling shareholder of fellow French bank Crédit Lyonnais, which it eventually acquired in 2003. Crédit Agricole went public on the Euronext Paris Exchange at the end of 2001.

Under pressure from the US government, Crédit Lyonnais admitted in 2003 to illegally acquiring Executive Life, the Californian insurance company, in the early 1990s. Crédit Lyonnais agreed to pay a fine of nearly $772 million to avoid criminal prosecution. It was allowed to keep its US banking license.

EXECUTIVES

Chairman: René Carron, age 68
Deputy Chairman and CEO: Jean-Paul Chifflet, age 61
CFO: Bertrand Badré, age 41
Head, Group IT and Process Development:
 Alain Deschenes
Deputy CEO, Finance and Strategy Division:
 Jacques Lenormand, age 62
Deputy CEO, Specialized Business Lines Division:
 Jean-Frédéric de Leusse, age 52
**Deputy CEO, The Regional Banks Development,
 Payment Systems, and Insurance:** Jean-Yves Hocher,
 age 55
Deputy CEO, Retail Banking Activities: Bernard Mary,
 age 63
Head, Regional Banks Development:
 Jean-Pierre Vauzanges
Head, Italy: Ariberto Fassati, age 63
Head, Insurance Unit; CEO, Predica: Bernard Michel,
 age 61
Head, Specialised Financial Services: Jérôme Brunel,
 age 56
Head, Private Banking, Private Equity and Real Estate:
 Gilles de Margerie, age 54
Head, International Retail Banking: Marc Carlos, age 51
Head, Group Strategy: Paul de Leusse
Head, CASA Group Communications: Alexandra Rocca
Chief Economist: Jean-Paul Betbèze, age 61
Director; CEO, CRCAM Nord de France: Alain Diéval,
 age 61
Director; CRCAM Anjou et du Maine: Bruno de Laage,
 age 59
**Chairman and CEO, Crédit Agricole Asset Management
 (CAAM) and CAAM Group:** Yves Perrier, age 55
**Chairman and CEO, Crédit Agricole Cheuvreux (CA
 Cheuvreux):** Jean-Claude Bassien, age 47
Auditors: PricewaterhouseCoopers Audit

LOCATIONS

HQ: Crédit Agricole S.A.
 91-93 Boulevard Pasteur
 75015 Paris, France
Phone: 33-1-43-23-52-02 **Fax:** 33-1-43-23-34-48
Web: www.credit-agricole-sa.fr

COMPETITORS

ABN AMRO Group
BNP Paribas
BPCE
Citigroup
Commerzbank
Credit Suisse
Deutsche Bank
Generale de Belgique
HSBC
Société Générale
UBS

HISTORICAL FINANCIALS

Company Type: Public

Income Statement

FYE: December 31

	ASSETS ($ mil.)	NET INCOME ($ mil.)	INCOME AS % OF ASSETS	EMPLOYEES
12/09	2,231,983	2,072	0.1%	89,172
12/08	2,330,214	1,784	0.1%	88,933
12/07	2,081,595	6,706	0.3%	86,866
12/06	1,664,028	7,017	0.4%	77,063
12/05	1,257,067	5,032	0.4%	62,112
Annual Growth	15.4%	(19.9%)	—	9.5%

2009 Year-End Financials

Equity as % of assets: 3.3%
Return on assets: 0.1%
Return on equity: 3.1%
Long-term debt ($ mil.): —
No. of shares (mil.): 2,376

Dividends
 Yield: 3.6%
 Payout: 88.9%
Market value ($ mil.): 42,091
Sales ($ mil.): 5,234

Stock History

Euronext Paris: ACA

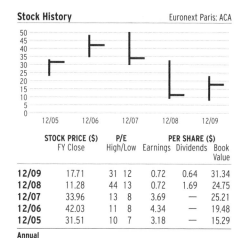

	STOCK PRICE ($) FY Close	P/E High/Low		PER SHARE ($) Earnings	Dividends	Book Value
12/09	17.71	31	12	0.72	0.64	31.34
12/08	11.28	44	13	0.72	1.69	24.75
12/07	33.96	13	8	3.69	—	25.21
12/06	42.03	11	8	4.34	—	19.48
12/05	31.51	10	7	3.18	—	15.29
Annual Growth	(13.4%)	—	—	(31.0%)	(62.1%)	19.7%

Credit Suisse

Credit Suisse is one of Switzerland's top financial services groups, though a distant second to behemoth rival firm UBS. The group provides investment management, private banking, and asset management services to clients around the world. Investment banking offerings include debt and equity underwriting, M&A advisory, and other securities services. The group provides wealth management services in Switzerland through subsidiary Clariden Leu; internationally, it operates under the Credit Suisse brand. Credit Suisse offers asset management services to individual, institutional, and government clients. The group has more than 250 retail branches in Switzerland and operates in more than 50 countries.

Globally, the investment banking industry was hit hard by the US subprime mortgage crisis, and Credit Suisse was no exception. It reported a net loss of €5.4 billion in 2008, the worst in its history. Credit Suisse turned down a bailout offer from the Swiss government in 2008, but it did receive a capital injection of CHF10 billion ($8.7 billion) from private investors. However, the capital infusion couldn't prevent losses as global credit markets froze and consumer and shareholder confidence fell. The company cut more than 5,000 jobs, or some 11% of its workforce, mostly from its investment banking unit. It also reviewed its results for 2007 and, among its findings, discovered rogue traders in its ranks à la the beleaguered Société Générale.

The company's strategy as the economy recovers includes expanding its roster of high-networth customers around the world and, in Switzerland, adding commercial clients of all sizes. Outside of Switzerland, its asset management business will concentrate on alternative investments including private equity, hedge funds, and real estate — vehicles that have remained desirable to many investors. In 2010, the company agreed to buy a 30% stake in US hedge fund York Capital Management.

Credit Suisse has also focused on emerging markets. In 2008 it expanded its Middle East franchise when it bought majority ownership in

joint venture Saudi Swiss Securities. The company is also planning to open a joint venture securities firm in China. It has added Shariah-compliant banking for Islamic clients.

In 2008 it bought an 80% stake in US firm Asset Management Finance Corporation, a division of National Bank of Canada.

HISTORY

In 1856, shortly after the creation of the Swiss federation, Alfred Escher opened Credit Suisse (CS) in Zurich. Primarily a venture capital firm, CS helped fund Swiss railroads and other industries. It later opened offices in Italy and helped establish the Swiss Bank Corporation.

CS shifted its focus to commercial banking in 1867 and sold most of its stock holdings. By 1871 it was Switzerland's largest bank, buoyed by the nation's swift industrialization. In 1895 CS helped create the predecessor of Swiss utility Electrowatt. Foreign activity grew in the 1920s. A run on banks in the Depression forced CS to sell assets at a loss and dip into reserves of unreported retained profits.

Trade declined in WWII, but neutrality left Switzerland's institutions intact and made it a major banking center, partly due to CS's role as a conduit for the Nazis' plundered gold. Foreign exchange and gold trading became important activities for CS after WWII. Mortgage and consumer credit acquisitions fueled domestic growth in the 1970s.

In 1978 the bank took a stake in US investment bank First Boston and, with it, formed London-based Credit Suisse-First Boston (CSFB). CS created 44%-owned holding company Credit Suisse First Boston to own First Boston, CSFB, and Tokyo-based CS First Boston Pacific.

The stock market crash of 1987 led a damaged First Boston to merge with CSFB the next year. In 1990 CS (renamed CS Holding) injected $300 million into CSFB and shifted $470 million in bad loans from its books, becoming the first foreign owner of a major Wall Street investment bank.

In the early 1990s CS Holding strengthened its insurance business with a Winterthur Insurance alliance. In 1993 and 1994 acquisitions helped it gain share in its overbanked home market.

In 1996 CS Holding reorganized as Credit Suisse Group and grew internationally, including further merging the daredevil US investment banking operations into Credit Suisse's more staid and relationship-oriented corporate banking. It bought Winterthur (Switzerland's #2 insurer) in 1997, as well as Barclays' European investment banking business.

Credit Suisse and other Swiss banks came under fire in 1996 for refusing to relinquish assets from Jewish bank accounts from the Holocaust era and for gold trading with the Nazis. In 1997 the banks agreed to establish a humanitarian fund for Holocaust victims. A stream of lawsuits by American heirs and boycott threats from US states and cities led in 1998 to a tentative $1.25 billion settlement (unpopular in Switzerland), with Credit Suisse on the hook for about a third of that.

CS in 1998 expanded its investment banking by buying Brazil's Banco de Investimentos Garantia; it also moved to expand US money management operations by allying with New York-based Warburg Pincus Asset Management. By 1999 that joint venture — which was to give the investment firm access to CS's mutual fund distribution channels in Europe and Asia — had morphed into CS's $650 million purchase of Warburg Pincus Asset Management.

Japan revoked the license of the company's financial products unit for obstructing an investigation (the harshest penalty ever given to a foreign firm at the time); it also accused the company of helping 60 others hide losses and cover up evidence.

In 2000 the company decided to allow searches of Holocaust-era accounts. The company expanded Credit Suisse First Boston when it bought US investment firm Donaldson, Lufkin & Jenrette in 2000, and renamed it Credit Suisse First Boston (USA).

The collapse of Credit Suisse's share price, along with what proved to be an over-ambitious acquisition strategy, brought about the downfall of CEO Lukas Mühlemann, who was pressured out by shareholders in 2002. In 2005 Credit Suisse merged with its Credit Suisse First Boston subsidiary, creating a global Credit Suisse brand.

In 2007 Credit Suisse sold its life and non-life insurance subsidiary Winterthur to insurance giant AXA for nearly $10 billion.

The company named Brady Dougan CEO in 2007. Dougan is the first non-German speaker to hold the position.

EXECUTIVES

Chairman: Hans-Ulrich Doerig, age 70
Honorary Chairman: Rainer E. Gut, age 78
Vice Chairman: Urs Rohner, age 51
Vice Chairman: Peter Brabeck-Letmathe, age 65
CEO, Credit Suisse Group and Credit Suisse: Brady W. Dougan, age 51
CFO: David Mathers, age 45
Chief Economist: Alois Bättig
Chief Talent, Branding, and Communications Officer: Pamela A. Thomas-Graham, age 46
General Counsel: Romeo Cerutti, age 48
Corporate Secretary: Béatrice Fischer
CIO and Director: Karl Landert, age 51
Chief Risk Officer: D. Wilson Ervin, age 50
Corporate Secretary: Pierre Schreiber
CEO Founder Securities: Neil Ge
CEO, Private Banking: Walter Berchtold, age 48
Managing Director; Head, U.S. Equity Research: Lara Warner
Managing Director and Head, Global Hedge Fund: Erin M. Callan, age 44
Managing Director, Investment Banking; CEO, Credit Suisse UK: James H. Leigh-Pemberton
Co-Head Global Financial Institutions Group; Vice Chairman, Investment Banking Department: Vikram Gandhi
Co-Head Global Financial Institutions Group: Ewen Stevenson
Co-Head Global Investment Banking and Head Global Mergers and Acquisitions: Marc D. Granetz
Co-Head Global Investment Banking and Head Global Market Solutions Group: James L. (Jim) Amine
Chairman, Investment Bank: Paul Calello, age 49
CEO, Investment Bank: Eric Varvel, age 47
Auditors: KPMG Klynveld Peat Marwick Goerdeler SA

LOCATIONS

HQ: Credit Suisse Group AG
Paradeplatz 8
8070 Zurich, Switzerland
Phone: 41-44-212-16-16   **Fax:** 41-44-332-25-87
US HQ: 11 Madison Ave., New York, NY 10010
US Phone: 212-325-2000   **US Fax:** 212-325-6665
Web: www.credit-suisse.com

PRODUCTS/OPERATIONS

2009 Sales

	% of total
Interest & dividends	49
Commissions & fees	27
Trading	23
Other	1
Total	**100**

COMPETITORS

AEGON
Barclays
Citigroup
Deutsche Bank
Goldman Sachs
Grupo Santander
HSBC
ING
JPMorgan Chase
Mitsubishi UFJ Financial Group
Mizuho Financial
Morgan Stanley
Nomura Securities
TD Bank
UBS

HISTORICAL FINANCIALS

Company Type: Public

Income Statement

FYE: December 31

	ASSETS ($ mil.)	NET INCOME ($ mil.)	INCOME AS % OF ASSETS	EMPLOYEES
12/09	993,677	6,176	0.6%	47,600
12/08	1,108,087	(7,781)	—	47,800
12/07	1,206,406	5,598	0.5%	48,100
12/06	1,031,264	9,321	0.9%	44,871
12/05	1,020,691	4,448	0.4%	63,523
Annual Growth	(0.7%)	8.6%	—	(7.0%)

2009 Year-End Financials

Equity as % of assets: 3.6%
Return on assets: 0.6%
Return on equity: 18.5%
Long-term debt ($ mil.): 153,532
No. of shares (mil.): 1,184

Dividends
Yield: 0.2%
Payout: 2.2%
Market value ($ mil.): 56,089
Sales ($ mil.): 49,799

Stock History

NYSE: CS

	STOCK PRICE ($) FY Close	P/E High/Low		PER SHARE ($) Earnings	Dividends	Book Value
12/09	47.36	12	4	4.95	0.11	30.52
12/08	26.76	—	—	(7.41)	2.36	25.82
12/07	53.34	11	8	6.18	2.36	32.34
12/06	57.26	7	5	8.06	1.59	30.22
12/05	38.72	11	8	3.81	1.16	27.11
Annual Growth	5.2%	—	—	6.8%	(44.5%)	3.0%

Dai Nippon Printing

A leading commercial printer, Dai Nippon Printing (aka DNP) has diversified well beyond the business of spreading ink on paper. The global firm still produces books and magazines, dictionaries, catalogs, and business forms, and it has added items such as CD-ROMs, holograms, and smart cards to the mix. DNP's Lifestyle and Industrial Supplies segment makes decorative materials for use in fixtures and furniture, along with packaging for consumer products. The company's electronics products include photomasks used in the manufacture of integrated circuits and color filters for liquid crystal displays. DNP subsidiary CHI Group sells electronic books. Also, DNP owns a majority stake in Hokkaido Coca-Cola Bottling.

Like other leading printing companies, DNP has branched out from publishing and commercial printing into such fields as environmentally friendly packaging, decorative materials for floors and windows, display-related products, and electronics. Indeed, the firm is working to market itself as a complete provider of information communications services, offering clients marketing and promotional support, communications software, and cross-media services.

Aiming to boost education and publishing operations, DNP acquired a majority stake in bookseller Junkudo, which operates about 30 shops in major Japanese cities. It also invested in Shufunotomo Co., a women's magazine publisher, to beef up its publishing operations by buying common shares of the company's stock and raising its stake in Shufunotomo to about 40%. DNP combined its resources and influence with three other Japanese publishers, agreeing to acquire a roughly 30% stake in secondhand bookseller Bookoff. The chain operates through about 1,000 stores across Japan.

Responding to the shrinking publishing market in Japan and beyond, DNP is working to streamline its operations by merging several of its subsidiaries under the newly established holding company, CHI Group Co. The group was formed in 2010 by the merger of DNP's bookstore chain Maruzen with library service provider TRC Inc. Junkudo will also be integrated into CHI Group. The newly formed group is the focus of DNP's effort to accelerate the development of its electronic publishing efforts. Digital publishing is one of the few bright spots in an otherwise dismal publishing arena.

In February 2010, DNP launched a tender offer to acquire the remaining shares of Intelligent Wave, a publicly traded Japanese firm engaged in network connection, authorization and other processing systems for credit card payments. The two firms, which already cooperate to provide security services to financial institutions, want to strengthen their financial ties in order to expand.

Electronics had been DNP's fastest-growing business. Because it makes products for both the interior (photomasks) and exterior (displays) of high-tech equipment, the company believes it is well-positioned for additional growth. However, the global financial crisis led to a sharp slump in demand and price declines for DNP's electronics products. Hokkaido Coca-Cola Bottling's beverage sales have also lost their fizz as a result of weak consumer spending and intense competition.

HISTORY

In 1876 Shueisha, the predecessor to Dai Nippon Printing (DNP), was established in central Tokyo. As the only modern printing firm in Japan, it was well-positioned to attract the business of the emerging newspaper and book industries. The company originally used a movable-type hand printer, but became the first private industry to use steam power in Japan when it updated its presses in 1884.

Following Japanese victories over China and Russia at the turn of the century, Japan embarked on a period of military and economic expansion. This was matched by a growing demand for printing. In 1927 Japan published 20,000 book titles and 40 million magazines. The country's first four-color gravure printing system was inaugurated the following year. In 1935 Shueisha changed its name to Dai Nippon Printing following its merger with Nisshin Printing.

The 1930s and 1940s were lean times for printers; Japan's repressive military government suppressed publishers and banned books. WWII devastated the publishing industry, along with the rest of the Japanese economy, but the publishing industry recovered soon after the end of the war. DNP was assisted in its recovery by government contracts; in 1946 it was designated by the Ministry of Finance to print 100-yen notes. In 1949 the company entered the securities printing business, and in 1951 it expanded into packaging and decorative interiors production. DNP reemerged in 1958 as Japan's largest printing firm.

In 1963 DNP followed Toppan in setting up an office in Hong Kong. Both Hong Kong and Singapore had become havens for Shanghai printing entrepreneurs who had emigrated in the face of the Communist takeover of China in 1949. These cities became centers for low-cost, high-quality color printing for British and American book publishers. In 1973 DNP overtook R. R. Donnelley as the world's largest printer. The next year the company set up a subsidiary in the US, DNP (America), Inc.

DNP moved into the information processing business in the 1980s, developing a credit card-sized calculator in 1985, a digital color printer system in 1986, and a Japanese-language word processor in 1987. The company launched Hi-Vision Static Pictures in 1989 to market a process that converted data into a form used by high-definition TV. In 1990 DNP bought a controlling stake in Tien Wah Press, the #1 printer in Singapore.

The next year DNP completed the first construction stage of its Okayama plant, dedicated to information media supplies (mainly transfer ribbons for color printers). The second stage, specializing in interior decorative materials, was completed in 1993.

In 1994 the company launched its Let's Go to an Amusement Park! virtual reality software system. Two years later DNP produced an integrated circuit card for about a tenth of current costs, giving it a major competitive edge in the magnetic card market.

In 1999 the company began selling CD-ROMs online through subsidiary TransArt. The following year Dai Nippon formed partnerships or joint ventures with Toshiba (to develop printed circuit boards), Microsoft (to develop Windows-based smart cards), and Numerical Technologies (to develop advanced phase-shifted photomasks). In 2002 the company joined with Toshiba and Takara to develop and promote a lightweight educational computer called an Ex-Pad.

EXECUTIVES

President: Yoshitoshi Kitajima
EVP: Koichi Takanami
EVP: Masayoshi Yamada
EVP: Satoshi Saruwatari
EVP: Yoshinari Kitajima
Senior Managing Director: Masahiko Wada
Senior Managing Director: Yujiro Kuroda
Senior Managing Director: Teruomi Yoshino
Senior Managing Director: Osamu Tsuchida
Senior Managing Director: Mitsuhiko Hakii
Senior Corporate Officer: Tatsuro Kitayuguchi
Senior Corporate Officer: Tatsuya Nishimura, age 61
Senior Corporate Officer: Koichi Hashimoto
Auditors: Meiji Audit Corporation

LOCATIONS

HQ: Dai Nippon Printing Co., Ltd.
(Dai Nippon Insatsu Kabushiki Kaisha)
1-1-1, Ichigaya-Kagacho, Shinjuku-ku
Tokyo 162-8001, Japan
Phone: 81-3-3266-2111   **Fax:** 81-3-5225-8239
US HQ: 335 Madison Ave., 3rd Fl., New York, NY 10017
US Phone: 212-503-1095   **US Fax:** 212-286-1505
Web: www.dnp.co.jp/index_e.html

PRODUCTS/OPERATIONS

2010 Sales

	% of total
Information Communication	46
Lifestyle & Industrial Supplies	34
Electronics	16
Beverages	4
Total	**100**

Selected Products and Services

Information Communication
  Bank notes
  Books
  Business forms
  Catalogs
  CD-ROMs and DVDs
  Direct mail
  Magazines
  Plastic cards
  Promotional publications
Lifestyle and Industrial Supplies
  Decorative materials
  Packaging
Electronics
  Color filters for liquid crystal displays
  Photomasks
  Projection TV screens
  Shadowmasks for color TVs
Beverages

COMPETITORS

3M
Asahi Breweries
Cookson Group
Graphic Packaging Holding
Hitachi
LG Display
Photronics
Quad/Graphics
R.R. Donnelley
Sapporo
Siemens AG
Suntory Holdings
Toppan Printing
TSMC

HISTORICAL FINANCIALS

Company Type: Public

Income Statement

FYE: March 31

	REVENUE ($ mil.)	NET INCOME ($ mil.)	NET PROFIT MARGIN	EMPLOYEES
3/10	17,082	460	2.7%	10,539
3/09	16,291	(215)	—	40,317
3/08	16,275	455	2.8%	38,657
3/07	13,216	465	3.5%	37,740
3/06	12,823	555	4.3%	35,596
Annual Growth	**7.4%**	**(4.6%)**	**—**	**(26.2%)**

2010 Year-End Financials

Debt ratio: —
Return on equity: 4.8%
Cash ($ mil.): 1,644
Current ratio: 1.57
Long-term debt ($ mil.): —
No. of shares (mil.): 661
Dividends
  Yield: 2.4%
  Payout: 84.6%
Market value ($ mil.): 9,011

Stock History

Pink Sheets: DNPCF

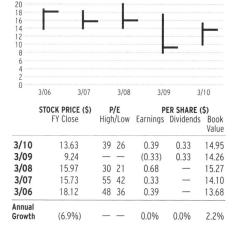

	STOCK PRICE ($) FY Close	P/E High/Low		PER SHARE ($) Earnings	Dividends	Book Value
3/10	13.63	39	26	0.39	0.33	14.95
3/09	9.24	—	—	(0.33)	0.33	14.26
3/08	15.97	30	21	0.68	—	15.27
3/07	15.73	55	42	0.33	—	14.10
3/06	18.12	48	36	0.39	—	13.68
Annual Growth	**(6.9%)**	**—**	**—**	**0.0%**	**0.0%**	**2.2%**

The Daiei, Inc.

Japan's economic woes put The Daiei on a diet. The company (whose name is pronounced die-ay) and its subsidiaries operate more than 1,000 supermarkets, department stores, and specialty shops. Other operations include food processing and distribution, property management, and credit card services. Daiei, which diversified haphazardly during the 1980s, came close to bankruptcy due to massive debts and failure to innovate. New management worked to stem losses and closed about 2,000 retail outlets, but it struggled to revive the business. To help remake the retailing giant, trading company Marubeni teamed up with supermarket operator AEON in 2006. Together they control about 50% of Daiei.

The partnership came together after the Industrial Revitalization Corp. of Japan (IRCJ), the government agency formed to turn around struggling Japanese companies, ended its long involvement with Daiei in mid-2006. IRCJ sold its one-third stake in the company to Marubeni for about $610 million. AEON, Japan's largest supermarket operator, was chosen over Wal-Mart to help Marubeni rebuild Daiei.

Fierce competition among supermarket operators in Japan has put pressure on Daiei to reduce costs to revive its business. To counter slumping revenues and dreary sales forecasts, the company said it will close about 10% of its directly owned stores, or about 20 retail outlets, by 2013. While it typically shutters a handful of unprofitable locations annually, the decision marks Daiei's most significant operations move since 2006, when it closed some 50 stores.

In 2010 Michio Kuwahara was named CEO. He replaced Tooru Nishimi, who retired.

In addition to Marubeni's and AEON's own stakes, the private equity firm Advantage Partners owns about 30% of Daiei.

HISTORY

Daiei founder Isao Nakauchi narrowly escaped death and the law before launching his first Daiei corner drugstore. As a Japanese soldier serving in the Philippines in WWII, he came under heavy fire but survived. He later thanked sloppy American engineering (the bombs that fell near him did not explode) for his survival. After the war he and his brother made a fortune selling penicillin above the legal price; his brother was arrested for his part in the dealings.

Nakauchi launched his Housewives' Store Daiei in Osaka in 1957 at the depth of the post-Korean War depression. The low prices of a discount drugstore appealed to hard-pressed consumers, and the success of the first store prompted Nakauchi to open others in the Osaka area. He also took advantage of the depression at the wholesale level, buying up surplus goods from cash-strapped manufacturers.

In 1958 the company opened in Sannomiya and introduced the concept of the discount store chain to Japan. Over the next three decades, Daiei diversified its offerings while staying focused on its "for the customers" philosophy, i.e., very low prices.

The company expanded into Tokyo in 1964 with the purchase of Ittoku and opened its first suburban store in 1968 near Osaka. By 1972 Daiei was not only a nationwide chain, it was also Japan's #1 supermarket operator (with 75 stores) and #2 retailer. In 1974 the company overtook Mitsukoshi to become Japan's top retailer. A year later Daiei opened its first convenience store, Lawson.

Showing an increasing interest in sourcing from international businesses, Daiei teamed up with J. C. Penney (1976) and Marks and Spencer (1978) for retailing and Wendy's and Victoria Station (both in 1979) for restaurants. The retailer entered the US market with the 1980 purchase of Holiday Mart, a three-store discount chain in Hawaii, where it also set up its first purchasing office.

Daiei entered the hotel business in 1988 by winning the contract for a $2.2 billion recreation center in Fukuoka. In 1992 the company opened the first American-style membership warehouse in Japan (Kobe), Kuo's Wholesale Membership Club. That year Daiei acquired 42% of major retailer Chujitsuya. The company launched private-label products in 1994. Also that year Daiei merged with retail affiliates Chujitsuya, Uneed Daiei, and Dainaha, establishing Japan's first nationwide network of stores.

When Japan lifted a 50-year ban on holding companies in 1997, Daiei was the first to take advantage of the relaxed laws, forming K.K.

Daiei Holding Corporation to oversee its non-retail businesses. In 1999 Tasdasu Toba became president, replacing founder Nakauchi, who remained chairman of Daiei.

Amid allegations of an insider-trading scandal, Toba resigned as president and Nakauchi resigned as chairman and CEO in 2000. Hiroshige Sasaki, a former managing director, became acting president and Kunio Takagi was named to replace him as the head of Daiei in 2001.

In early 2002 Daiei was rescued by a bank-led bailout and the company announced a three-year restructuring plan that included 60 store closures and reducing its workforce by about 5,000 employees. The state-run Development Bank of Japan announced a new $480 million funding plan in October 2002 to aid Daiei in its restructuring. To that end, Daiei closed 60 unprofitable stores and refurbished others in the hope of engineering a turnaround.

In May 2004 five of the 15 members of the company's board of directors, including chairman Jiro Amagai, left the board. In October Daiei's next chairman — Heihachiro Yoshino — and president Kunio Takagi both announced their resignations, just days after Daiei's lenders forced the struggling retailer to seek a government bailout. Takagi assumed the largely symbolic post of chairman of the company. He was succeeded as president by Toshio Hasumi.

In 2007 Daiei sold stakes in its supermarket unit Maruetsu (to AEON) and credit card service unit OMC Card (to Sumitomo Mitsui Banking Corp.).

In May 2008 AEON director Yoshiharu Kawato became chairman of Daiei.

EXECUTIVES

Chairman: Yoshiharu Kawato
President: Michio Kuwahara, age 61
Accountant: Akinori Yamashita
Treasurer: Akira Minami
Chief Commodity Supply Food: Hisashi Mori
Chief Planning and Operations: Masahiko Touyama
Chief Justice: Kazu Teraoka Sun
Chief Logistics: Makoto Watanabe
Corporate Auditor: Eisuke Nagai
Director Household Products Supply: Masao Ogata
Director Human Resources: Yoshiaki Takahashi, age 54
Auditors: Deloitte Touche Tohmatsu

LOCATIONS

HQ: The Daiei, Inc.
    4-1-1, Minatojima Nakamachi, Chuo-ku
    Kobe 650-0046, Japan
Phone: 81-78-302-5001   **Fax:** 81-3-3433-9226
Web: www.daiei.co.jp

COMPETITORS

AEON
Carrefour
Daimaru
Fast Retailing
Isetan Mitsukoshi
Ito-Yokado
Keiyo Company
Marui Group
MYCAL
Seiyu
Takashimaya
Tokyu Department Store
Uny

HISTORICAL FINANCIALS

Company Type: Public

Income Statement

FYE: February 28

	REVENUE ($ mil.)	NET INCOME ($ mil.)	NET PROFIT MARGIN	EMPLOYEES
2/10	10,175	(134)	—	25,246
2/09	9,871	(242)	—	—
2/08	9,157	379	4.1%	—
2/07	8,741	345	3.9%	—
Annual Growth	5.2%	—	—	—

Net Income History

Tokyo: 82630

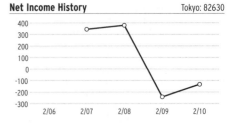

Daimler AG

After nearly 10 years of irreconcilable differences, Daimler and Chrysler called it quits. They joined forces in 1998 in a $37 billion deal, but the marriage never worked. In 2007 Daimler sold 80% of Chrysler to Cerberus Capital Management for about $7.4 billion. Daimler's passenger car business, Mercedes-Benz Cars, includes the Mercedes, Maybach, and smart brands. Its Daimler Trucks North America unit is a leading heavy-truck maker in the US, and with its Fuso, Mercedes-Benz, and Sprinter brands, Daimler is the world's leading maker of commercial vehicles. The company controls about a 22% stake in EADS, the European aerospace and defense consortium. Daimler gets about half of its sales in Europe.

The global downturn in the automotive industry is particularly depressing for sales of Daimler's premium passenger cars and heavy-duty commercial vehicles. The company delisted and deregistered from the New York Stock Exchange and the SEC in May 2010. This comes after a miserable year; in 2009 the company's worldwide car sales fell across most geographic markets, excluding China where Mercedes-Benz is the fastest-growing premium brand.

Daimler's problems chiefly stemmed from the Chrysler side of the business, which — like Ford and General Motors — was struggling with too much capacity, too few models that impress consumers, and high costs for parts and labor. In 2009 Daimler agreed to give up its remaining stake in Chrysler to investment firm Cerberus and to forgive loans to Chrysler. Daimler also agreed with the federal Pension Benefit Guaranty Corporation to make payments of $600 million over three years into Chrysler's pension plans.

In 2010 Daimler entered a partnership agreement with Nissan and Renault. The three companies will share small-car technology and powertrains, and work together to develop electric cars. As part of the three-way deal, the companies will take equity stakes in each other. Renault and Nissan will each acquire a 1.55% stake in Daimler; the combined 3.1% stake in

Daimler is estimated to be worth about €1.2 billion ($1.6 billion). Daimler will acquire a 3.1% stake in both Renault and Nissan.

Expanding into developing economies, too, in mid-2010 the company entered into a joint venture with Chinese automaker BYD (partially held by Warren Buffett) to develop electric vehicles for the Chinese market.

In another growing region, Eastern Europe, Daimler inked a deal with Uzavtosanoat, an automotive holding company, to create a joint venture that will assemble and sell a range of Mercedes-Benz branded bus models to Uzbekistan and neighboring markets.

Generating cash in 2009, Daimler sold an equity stake of about 9% to Aabar Investments, an Abu Dhabi-based firm, for nearly €2 billion ($2.7 billion). Aabar, controlled by the International Petroleum Investment Company (IPIC) of Abu Dhabi, became Daimler's largest shareholder as a result, overtaking the government of Kuwait, which owns almost 7% of the automaker.

HISTORY

Daimler-Benz was formed by the merger of two German motor companies — Daimler and Benz — in 1926. Daimler-Benz bought Auto Union (Audi) in 1958 (sold to Volkswagen in 1966). The company's Mercedes cars gained international fame, and sales expanded worldwide in the 1970s.

Daimler-Benz diversified in the 1980s, buying aerospace, heavy truck (Freightliner), and consumer and industrial electrical companies. Although diversification continued, sales slowed. Losses at its aerospace unit forced Daimler-Benz into the red in 1995. Also that year the company and ABB Asea Brown Boveri formed joint venture Adtranz, the #1 train maker in the world, and Jürgen Schrempp became chairman of the management board (CEO).

In 1998 Daimler-Benz acquired Chrysler and introduced a subcompact car, the smart, in Europe. DaimlerChrysler rolled both companies' financial services units into DaimlerChrysler Interservices (DEBIS) and acquired the remaining shares of Adtranz in 1999.

North American influence in the company began to fade in 2000 with the exit of US management, including co-chairman Robert Eaton. Prior to his retirement, Eaton announced DaimlerChrysler's goal to become the world's #1 carmaker through partnerships or acquisitions.

In 2000 DaimlerChrysler agreed to buy a controlling $2.1 billion stake in Mitsubishi Motors. DaimlerChrysler bought Canada-based truck maker Western Star Holdings and paid about $473 million for the 79% of Detroit Diesel (heavy-duty truck engines) that it didn't already own. The company also agreed to sell its rail systems unit, Adtranz, to Bombardier (completed in 2001 for about $1.1 billion).

Also in 2000, in an effort to turn things around at its money-losing Chrysler division, James Holden was replaced with Dieter Zetsche, who immediately began making personnel changes. Days after Zetsche was installed, billionaire investor Kirk Kerkorian filed an $8 billion lawsuit seeking to undo the 1998 Daimler-Benz/Chrysler merger on grounds that portraying the deal as a "merger of equals" was misrepresentative.

Zetsche announced early in 2001 that Chrysler would eliminate almost 26,000 North American jobs over three years (largely through retirement and attrition) and make wholesale changes in the group's senior management positions overseeing the Chrysler and Mercedes divisions.

In 2004 DaimlerChrysler sold its 10% stake in Hyundai Motor. Also that year it received Chinese regulatory approval to build cars in China with joint venture partner Beijing Automotive Industry Holding Co. Ltd. (BAIC).

In 2005 DaimlerChrysler sold its remaining stake in Mitsubishi Motors to Goldman Sachs.

Early in 2006 DaimlerChrysler said it would eliminate 6,000 administrative jobs, or 20% of its worldwide administrative workforce, in order to streamline operations. Later that year the company formed a joint venture with Chinese Fujian Motor Industry Group and Taiwanese China Motor Corporation for the manufacture of the Mercedes-Benz Sprinter and Vito vans for the Chinese market.

In October 2007 Daimler officially changed its name from DaimlerChrysler to Daimler AG.

The company reduced its 15% stake in EADS by selling 7% early in 2007 to German state-owned development bank KfW. Daimler, however, retained the stake's voting rights.

EXECUTIVES

Chairman Supervisory Board: Manfred Bischoff, age 68
Deputy Chairman, Supervisory Board: Erich Klemm, age 56
Chairman Management Board and Head Mercedes-Benz Car Group: Dieter Zetsche, age 56, $6,226,137 total compensation
Member Management Board, Head, Daimler Trucks: Andreas Renschler, age 52, $1,421,855 total compensation
Member Management Board, Group Research and Mercedes-Benz Cars Development: Thomas Weber, age 56, $2,434,523 total compensation
Member Management Board, Finance and Controlling, Daimler Financial Services: Bodo Uebber, age 50, $2,480,748 total compensation
Member Management Board, Manufacturing and Procurement Mercedes-Benz Cars: Wolfgang Bernhard, age 50
Member Management Board, Human Resources and Labor Relations Director: Wilfried Porth, age 51
General Counsel and Chief Compliance Officer: Gero Herrmann
EVP; Management Board Member, Daimler Financial Services AG, Human Resources, Sales, and Financial Services: Margarete Haase, age 57
EVP; Management Board Member, Daimler Financial Services AG, Europe, Africa, and Asia/Pacific: Alwin Epple, age 47
EVP and Head Global External Affairs and Public Policy: Martin Jaeger, age 45
EVP and Chief Accounting Officer: Robert Köthner
EVP; President and CEO, Mercedes-Benz UK: Wilfried Steffen, age 55
EVP Design, Mercedes Car Group: Gorden Wagener
SVP and Head, Investor Relations and Treasury: Michael Mühlbayer
President and CEO, Mercedes-Benz US International: Markus Schaefer
Head Sales and Marketing: Marc Langenbrinck
Head Communications: Joerg Howe
Head of Daimler Trucks North America: Martin Daum, age 50
Auditors: KPMG Deutsche Treuhand-Gesellschaft AG

LOCATIONS

HQ: Daimler AG
Mercedesstrasse 137
70327 Stuttgart, Germany
Phone: 49-711-17-0   **Fax:** 49-711-17-22244
Web: www.daimler.com

2009 Sales

	% of total
Western Europe	
Germany	24
Other countries	22
Americas	
US	21
Other countries	8
Asia	16
Other regions	9
Total	**100**

PRODUCTS/OPERATIONS

2009 Sales

	% of total
Mercedes-Benz Cars	51
Daimler Trucks	21
Daimler Financial Services	15
Mercedes-Benz Vans	8
Daimler Buses	5
Total	**100**

Selected Divisions and Brands

Mercedes-Benz Cars
Maybach
57 / 57 S
62 / 62 S
Landaulet
Mercedes-Benz
A-Class
A-Class Coupe
B-Class
C-Class Estate
C-Class Saloon
CL-Class
CLC-Class
CLS-Class
E-Class Coupe
E-Class Estate
E-Class Saloon
G-Class
G-Class Cabriolet
GL-Class
GLK-Class
M-Class
R-Class
S-Class
SL-Class
SLK-Class
SLS-AMG
smart
fortwo coupe
fortwo cabrio
Daimler Trucks
Freightliner
Mercedez-Benz
Mitsubishi Fuso
Western Star Trucks
Mercedes-Benz Vans
Daimler Buses
Mercedes-Benz (city buses, coaches, interurban, minibuses)
Mercedes-Benz chassis
Mitsubishi Fuso (large buses, midi-sized buses, minibuses)
Orion (city buses)
Setra (coaches, interurban buses)
Thomas Built Buses (hybrid school bus, school and activity buses)

COMPETITORS

BMW	PACCAR
Fiat	Peugeot
Ford Motor	PROTON Holdings
Fuji Heavy Industries	Renault
General Motors	Saab Automobile
Honda	Scania
Isuzu	Toyota
Land Rover	Volkswagen
MAN	Volvo
Navistar International	Zipcar
Nissan	

HISTORICAL FINANCIALS

Company Type: Public

Income Statement

FYE: December 31

	REVENUE ($ mil.)	NET INCOME ($ mil.)	NET PROFIT MARGIN	EMPLOYEES
12/09	113,114	(3,789)	—	256,407
12/08	135,653	2,001	1.5%	273,216
12/07	146,130	5,850	4.0%	272,382
12/06	200,165	4,266	2.1%	360,385
12/05	177,974	3,388	1.9%	382,724
Annual Growth	(10.7%)	—	—	(9.5%)

2009 Year-End Financials

Debt ratio: 109.9%
Return on equity: —
Cash ($ mil.): 14,045
Current ratio: 1.14
Long-term debt ($ mil.): 47,665

No. of shares (mil.): 1,024
Dividends
　Yield: 1.1%
　Payout: —
Market value ($ mil.): 78,228

Stock History

German: DAI

	STOCK PRICE ($) FY Close	P/E High/Low		PER SHARE ($) Earnings	Dividends	Book Value
12/09	76.39	—	—	(3.77)	0.86	42.35
12/08	53.96	63	17	1.97	2.87	43.13
12/07	140.76	29	16	5.59	2.21	52.71
12/06	81.02	20	15	4.14	1.90	44.04
12/05	60.43	20	14	3.32	1.76	42.29
Annual Growth	6.0%	—	—	—	(16.4%)	0.0%

Groupe Danone

You say Danone, I say Dannon; let's call the whole thing one of the largest dairy food and water producers in the world. The company is organized around its core activities: fresh dairy products, water, and infant and medical nutrition. The company, #1 maker of fresh dairy products worldwide, offers dozens of worldwide and regional yogurt brands, including the Dannon, Activia, and organic yogurt Stonyfield Farm. The company's Evian, Volvic, Aqua, and other water brands make it #2 worldwide in bottled water. Danone became a player in the baby-food sector with its 2007 purchase of Royal Numico and is now the world's #2 baby nutrition company. Its medical nutrition products are #1 in Europe.

The company agreed to merge its Russian dairy business with local producer Unimilk. The company, to be named Danone-Unimilk, will serve markets in Russia, the Ukraine, Kazakhstan, and Belarus, and will make Russia Danone's second-largest market after France. The deal, expected to close by the end of 2010, complements the company's strategy to become a major player in emerging markets, particularly those in Asia and Eastern Europe.

In Western Europe, Danone is focused on enhancing its fruit offerings. The company in 2010 acquired Immedia, the third-largest smoothie maker in France. Also that year it formed a joint venture with banana-giant Chiquita to market fruit beverages throughout the region.

The company acquired full control of its South African joint venture, Danone Clover in 2009. It purchased Clover's 45% stake for R1,085 ($145 million) in cash. (Clover is one of South Africa's largest dairy companies.) Other partnerships include a joint venture with Weight Watchers formed in 2008. The 51% Weight Watchers-49% Danone operation provides weight-management services to the People's Republic of China.

In 2008 the company divested itself of its French baby milk and baby drinks businesses by selling them to Groupe Lactalis. That year it also sold its subsidiary, Frucor, a maker of non-alcoholic beverages in New Zealand and Australia, as well as its international brands V and Mizone (with the exception of in China and Indonesia) to Suntory for some €600 million ($780 million).

The company hit a snag with one of its Chinese operations in 2010. Due to continuing disagreements over control of the Hangzhou Wahaha Group, a Chinese soft-drink joint venture established in 1996 in which Danone owned 51%, Wahaha and Danone parted ways, with Wahaha giving the yogurt giant a cash settlement estimated to be in the $555 million range.

HISTORY

In 1965 Antoine Riboud replaced his uncle as chairman of family-run Souchon-Neuvesel, a Lyons, France-based maker of glass bottles. Antoine quickly made a mark in this field — he merged the firm with Boussois, a major French flat-glass manufacturer, creating BSN in 1966.

Antoine enlarged BSN's glass business and filled the company's bottles by acquiring well-established beverage and food concerns. In 1970 BSN purchased Brasseries Kronenbourg (France's largest brewer), Société Européenne de Brasseries (another French brewer), and Evian (mineral water, France). The 1972 acquisition of Glaverbel (Belgium) gave BSN 50% of Europe's flat-glass market. The next year BSN merged with France's Gervais Danone (yogurt, cheese, Panzani pasta; founded in 1919 and named after founder Isaac Carasso's son Daniel). This moved the company into pan-European brand-name foods.

Increasing energy costs depressed the company's flat-glass earnings, so BSN began divesting its flat-glass businesses. In the late 1970s it acquired interests in brewers in Belgium, Spain, and Italy.

BSN bought Dannon, the leading US yogurt maker (co-founded by Daniel Carasso, who had continued making Danone yogurt in France until WWII), in 1982. It established a strong presence in the Italian pasta market by buying stakes in Ponte (1985) and Agnesi (1986). BSN also purchased Generale Biscuit, the world's #3 biscuit maker (1986), and RJR Nabisco's European cookie and snack-food business (1989).

In a series of acquisitions starting in 1986, BSN took over Italy and Spain's largest mineral water companies and several European pasta makers and other food companies. Adopting the name of its leading international brand, BSN became Groupe Danone in 1994.

Antoine's son, Franck, succeeded him as chairman in 1996 and restructured the company to focus on three core businesses: dairy, beverages (specifically water and beer), and biscuits.

By 1997 Danone had begun shedding non-core grocery products. Danone in 1999 completed a merger and subsequent sale of part of its BSN Emballage glass-packaging unit to UK buyout firm CVC Capital Partners for $1.2 billion; Danone retained 44% ownership.

Thirsty for the #2 spot in US bottled water sales, Danone gulped down McKesson Water (the #3 bottled water firm in the US after Nestlé and Suntory) for $1.1 billion in 2000. Also that year Danone's joint venture Finalrealm (which includes several European equity firms), along with Burlington Biscuits, Nabisco, and HM Capital Partners (then called Hicks, Muse, Tate & Furst), acquired 87% of leading UK biscuit maker United Biscuits. Danone then bought Naya (bottled water, Canada) and sold its brewing operations (#2 in Europe) to Scottish & Newcastle for more than $2.6 billion.

During 2001 Danone announced restructuring would shutter two LU biscuit plants and eliminate about 1,800 jobs; the move met with strikes and legal battles. That same year, having been bumped to the #2 spot in the US yogurt market (after General Mills' Yoplait brand), Danone acquired 40% of Stonyfield Farm, the #4 yogurt brand in the US, and ultimately came to own 85% of the company. Antoine Ribaud died in 2002 at the age of 83.

In 2005 Danone got out of the brewing business altogether, with the sale of its 33% stake in Spanish brewer Mahou. It sold its HP Foods Group, including Amoy, Lea & Perrins, and HP sauce brands, to Heinz, and its biscuits businesses in the UK and Ireland.

Danone sold its biscuit operations to Kraft Foods in 2007. Strengthening its business in Asia, Danone acquired all of the Japanese joint venture with Ajinomoto and Calpis that it did not already own.

Following its acquisition of a controlling interest in a venture with Russia's Unimilk, Danone sold its 18.4% stake in Wimm-Bill-Dann Foods back to the Russian dairy and juice producer for $470 million.

EXECUTIVES

Chairman and CEO: Franck Riboud, age 54
Vice Chairman and Co-COO: Jacques Vincent, age 64
Deputy General Manager and Co-COO; Director: Emmanuel Faber, age 46
Deputy General Manager and Co-COO; Director: Bernard Hours, age 54
CFO: Pierre-André Térisse, age 43
EVP Waters: Thomas Kunz, age 53
EVP and General Manager, Danone Research: Sven Thormahlen, age 53
Co-EVP Fresh Dairy Products: Felix Martin Garcia, age 49
Co-EVP Fresh Dairy Products: Jordi Constans, age 45
General Manager, Baby Food: Christian Neu, age 53
General Manager Medical Nutrition: Flemming Morgan, age 54
General Manager Evian Volvic Export: Elio Pacheco
General Manager Human Resources: Muriel Pénicaud, age 54
Director Investor Relations: Antoine Guttinger
Chairman, President, and CEO, Stonyfield Farm: Gary Hirshberg, age 56
President and General Manager Waters, America (DWA): Nick Krzyzaniak
President and CEO, Dannon Co.: Gustavo Valle
Auditors: Mazars

LOCATIONS

HQ: Groupe Danone
17, Boulevard Haussmann
75009 Paris, France
Phone: 33-1-44-35-20-20   **Fax:** 33-1-42-25-67-16
US HQ: 10 Burton Dr., Londonderry, NH 03053
Web: www.danonegroup.com

2009 Sales

	% of total
Europe	60
Asia	12
Rest of the world	28
Total	**100**

2009 Production Sites

	No. of plants
Europe	
Western	36
Central	19
Asia/Pacific	50
Africa & Middle East	15
North America	6
Total	**126**

PRODUCTS/OPERATIONS

2009 Sales

	% of total
Fresh dairy	57
Water	17
Baby nutrition	20
Medical nutrition	6
Total	**100**

Selected Products and Brands

Fresh dairy
　Africa (Clover)
　Argentina (La Serenissima, Ser)
　China (Bright Dairy)
　France (Danette, Danone, Senjà)
　International (Actimel, Danone)
　Japan (Danone, Yakult)
　Latin America (Corpus, La Serenisima, Mastellone)
　US (Activia, Dannon, Stonyfield Farm)

Bottled water
　Argentina (Villa del Sur)
　Asia/Pacific (Aqua)
　Canada (Crystal Springs, Evian, Labrador, Naya)
　France (Badoit, Salvetat, Arvie)
　International (Evian, Volvic)
　Mexico (Bonafont)
　Spain (Font Vella)
　Turkey (Hayat)
　US (Dannon, Evian)

Baby nutrition
　Bebelac
　blédina
　Cow & Gate
　Dumex
　Gallia
　Mellin
　milupa
　NUTRICIA

Medical nutrition
　FortiCare
　Fortimel
　Fortisip
　Neocate
　Nutricia
　Nutrini

COMPETITORS

Abbott Nutrition	Irish Dairy Board
Ajinomoto	Kellogg
American Dairy	Kerry Group
Arla Foods	Kraft Foods
Associated British Foods	Lactalis
Beech-Nut	Leche Pascual
China Mengniu Dairy	Mead Johnson
Coca-Cola	Metagenics
Dairy Crest	Nestlé
Dairy Farm International	Novartis
Dairygold	Parmalat
Dean Foods	PepsiCo
Dr Pepper Snapple Group	Pfizer
Fonterra	Shanghai Bright Dairy & Food
FrieslandCampina	
General Mills	Sodiaal
Gerber Products	Unilever NV
Glanbia plc	Wessanen
Granarolo	Wimm-Bill-Dann
Heinz	Yili Group

HISTORICAL FINANCIALS

Company Type: Public

Income Statement

FYE: December 31

	REVENUE ($ mil.)	NET INCOME ($ mil.)	NET PROFIT MARGIN	EMPLOYEES
12/09	21,472	2,180	10.2%	80,976
12/08	21,453	2,102	9.8%	80,143
12/07	18,805	6,385	34.0%	76,044
12/06	18,583	1,787	9.6%	88,124
12/05	15,476	1,985	12.8%	88,184
Annual Growth	**8.5%**	**2.4%**	**—**	**(2.1%)**

2009 Year-End Financials

Debt ratio: 44.9%
Return on equity: 14.0%
Cash ($ mil.): 923
Current ratio: 0.75
Long-term debt ($ mil.): 8,539
No. of shares (mil.): 615
Dividends
　Yield: 2.8%
　Payout: 48.5%
Market value ($ mil.): 37,780

Stock History

Pink Sheets: GDNNY

	STOCK PRICE ($) FY Close	P/E High/Low		PER SHARE ($) Earnings	Dividends	Book Value
12/09	61.38	18	13	3.55	1.72	30.87
12/08	60.86	23	14	3.86	1.55	19.80
12/07	90.37	7	6	12.82	—	21.57
12/06	75.73	22	15	3.65	—	12.49
12/05	52.26	16	12	3.48	—	10.19
Annual Growth	**4.1%**	**—**	**—**	**0.5%**	**11.0%**	**31.9%**

Deloitte Touche Tohmatsu

This company is "deloitted" to make your acquaintance, particularly if you're a big business in need of accounting services. Deloitte Touche Tohmatsu (or Deloitte) is one of accounting's Big Four, along with Ernst & Young, KPMG, and PricewaterhouseCoopers. Deloitte operates through some 150 independent firms around the world, including US-based Deloitte LLP and its accounting arm, Deloitte & Touche LLP. Each independent member firm works in a specific geographic area offering audit, tax, consulting, risk management, and financial advisory services, in addition to human resources and technology services. Deloitte Touche Tohmatsu coordinates its member firms but does not provide services to clients.

Deloitte found out that its business was not necessarily recession-proof as member firm revenues declined slightly in 2009. The company was impacted by the global economic crisis and clients' ability to remain financially flexible during the downturn. Revenues from consulting remained strong during the recession, while tax and audit revenues were flat.

The company continues to prepare for growth over the long term; it foresees expanding its presence in emerging markets such as China, India, Brazil, southeast Asia, and the Middle East. Deloitte has worked to establish new member firms in those regions and attract employees.

In 2009 Deloitte acquired the North American public services practice of BearingPoint, which had filed for Chapter 11 bankruptcy protection. The deal helped position Deloitte as a top provider of professional services for the US government.

Deloitte made a rather unusual acquisition in 2010 when it bought Simulstrat, a scenario simulation program (commonly known as war gaming) for the public and private sectors. The program is a spinoff from the Department of War Studies at Kings College of London. Based on military methodology, Simulstrat helps organizations prepare for complex future political, economic, social, environmental, technological, legal, and regulatory events.

Also that year Deloitte bought IM Global, a specialist in identity and access management. The acquisition added to Deloitte's information and technology risk unit.

HISTORY

In 1845 William Deloitte opened an accounting office in London, at first soliciting business from bankrupts. The growth of joint stock companies and the development of stock markets in the mid-19th century created a need for standardized financial reporting and fueled the rise of auditing, and Deloitte moved to the new field. The Great Western Railway appointed him as its independent auditor (the first anywhere) in 1849.

In 1890 John Griffiths, who had become a partner in 1869, opened the company's first US office in New York City. Four decades later branches had opened throughout the US. In 1952 the firm partnered with Haskins & Sells, which operated 34 US offices.

Deloitte aimed to be "the Cadillac, not the Ford" of accounting. The firm, which became Deloitte Haskins & Sells in 1978, began shedding its conservatism as competition heated up; it was the first of the major accountancy firms to use aggressive ads.

The firm spent the 1980s and 1990s pursuing a strategy of using accountants and consultants in concert to provide seamless service in auditing, accounting, strategic planning, information technology, financial management, and productivity. In 1984 Deloitte Haskins & Sells tried to merge with Price Waterhouse, but the deal was dropped after Price Waterhouse's UK partners objected.

In 1989 Deloitte Haskins & Sells joined the flamboyant Touche Ross (founded 1899) to become Deloitte & Touche. Touche Ross's Japanese affiliate, Ross Tohmatsu (founded 1968) rounded out the current name. The merger was engineered by Deloitte's Michael Cook and Touche's Edward Kangas, in part to unite the former firm's US and European strengths with the latter's Asian presence. Cook continued to oversee US operations, with Kangas presiding over international operations. Many affiliates, particularly in the UK, rejected the merger and defected to competing firms.

As auditors were increasingly held accountable for the financial results of their clients, legal action soared. In the 1990s Deloitte was sued because of its actions relating to Drexel Burnham Lambert junk-bond king Michael Milken, the failure of several savings and loans, and clients' bankruptcies.

Nevertheless, in 1995 the SEC chose Michael Sutton, the firm's national director of auditing and accounting practice, as its chief accountant. That year Deloitte & Touche formed Deloitte & Touche Consulting to consolidate its US and UK consulting operations; its Asian consulting operations were later added to facilitate regional expansion. Deloitte Consulting became Deloitte's fastest-growing line, offering strategic and management consulting in addition to information technology and human resources consulting services.

Increasingly, though, Deloitte and its peers came under fire for their combined accounting/consulting operations; regulators and observers wondered whether accountants could maintain objectivity when they were auditing clients for whom they also provided consulting.

In 1999 the firm sold its accounting staffing service unit to its managers and Evercore Partners, citing possible conflicts of interest with its core audit business. Also that year Kangas stepped down as CEO to be succeeded by James Copeland.

In 2001 the SEC forced Deloitte & Touche to restate the financial results of Pre-Paid Legal Services. In an unusual move, Deloitte & Touche publicly disagreed with the SEC's findings.

The accountancy put some old trouble to bed in 2003 when it agreed to pay $23 million to settle claims it had been negligent in its auditing of failed Kentucky Life Insurance, a client in the 1980s. Later that year the UK's High Court found Deloitte negligent in audits related to the failed Barings Bank; however, the ruling was considered something of a victory for the accountancy because it essentially cleared Deloitte of the majority of charges against it and effectively limited its financial liability in the matter.

Copeland retired from the global CEO's office that year and handed the reins over to Bill Parrett, who had formerly served as managing director for the US and the Americas. Parrett was succeeded in 2007 by James Quigley, who'd served as CEO of Deloitte's US arm.

EXECUTIVES

Chairman: John P. Connolly
CEO: James H. (Jim) Quigley, age 58
CFO: Jeffrey P. (Jeff) Rohr
Chief Information Officer: Wolfgang Richter
Chief Knowledge Officer: Tracey Edwards
Global Managing Partner Consulting and Executive Member, US: Ainar D. Aijala Jr.
Global Managing Partner Strategic Client Program: Otmar Thoemmes
Global Managing Partner Financial Advisory Services and Executive Member, Canada: Frank Vettese
Global Managing Partner Tax: Dan Lange
Global Managing Partner Talent and Executive Member, United Kingdom: Vassi Naidoo
Global Managing Partner Brand and Executive Member, Belgium: Ludo de Keulenaer
Global Managing Partner Services and M&A and Executive Member, US: Jerry P. Leamon
Global Managing Partner Regulatory and Risk and Executive Member, US: Jeffrey K. (Jeff) Willemain
Global Brand and Marketing Director: Luis Gallardo
Director Global PR and CEO Communications: Madonna Jarrett
General Counsel: Philip Rotner
Human Resources Operations: Peter May
Executive Member and Country Leader, United States: Barry Salzberg, age 56

LOCATIONS

HQ: Deloitte Touche Tohmatsu
1633 Broadway, New York, NY 10019
Phone: 212-489-1600   **Fax:** 212-489-1687
Web: www.deloitte.com/view/en_GX/global

2009 Sales by Region

	% of total
Americas	48
Europe/Middle East/Africa	39
Asia/Pacific	13
Total	**100**

PRODUCTS/OPERATIONS

2009 Sales

	% of total
Audit	46
Consulting	25
Tax	22
Financial advisory services	7
Total	**100**

2009 Sales by Industry

	% of total
Financial services	26
Consumer business & transportation	20
Manufacturing	14
Telecommunications, media & technology	11
Energy & resources	8
Public sector	8
Life sciences	7
Other	6
Total	**100**

Selected Products and Services

Audit
  Auditing services
  Global offerings services
  International financial reporting conversion services
Consulting
  Enterprise applications
  Human capital
  Outsourcing
  Strategy and operations
  Technology integration

Tax
  Corporate tax
  Global tax compliance
  Indirect tax
  International assignment services
  International tax
  M&A transaction services
  Research and development credits
  Tax publications
  Tax technologies
  Transfer pricing
Financial Advisory
  Corporate finance
  Forensic services
  Reorganization services
  Transaction services
  Valuation services
Sustainability and Climate Change
  Assurance services
  Consulting
  Financial advisory
  Risk services
  Tax
Merger and Acquisition Services
Other
  Enterprise Risk Services
    Capital markets
    Control assurance
    Corporate responsibility and sustainability
    Internal audit
    Regulatory consulting
    Security and privacy services

COMPETITORS

Accenture
BDO International
Booz Allen
Boston Consulting
Capgemini
Ernst & Young Global
Grant Thornton International
HP Enterprise Services
KPMG
Marsh & McLennan
McKinsey & Company
PricewaterhouseCoopers

HISTORICAL FINANCIALS

Company Type: Private

Income Statement

	REVENUE ($ mil.)	NET INCOME ($ mil.)	NET PROFIT MARGIN	EMPLOYEES
5/09	26,100	—	—	168,651
5/08	27,400	—	—	165,000
5/07	23,100	—	—	146,600
5/06	20,000	—	—	135,000
5/05	18,200	—	—	121,283
Annual Growth	**9.4%**	**—**	**—**	**8.6%**

FYE: May 31

Revenue History

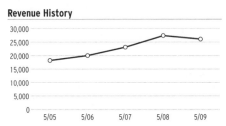

DENSO CORPORATION

DENSO CORPORATION knows: When building cars, the whole is very little without its parts. Among the largest automotive parts manufacturers, DENSO supplies OEM and aftermarket components and systems for most of the world's carmakers. It drives six product groups that make systems for powertrain control, information and safety, electric, electronic, small motors, and thermal systems. Its lines range from automotive air conditioning systems to radiators and spark plugs. The Information and Safety Systems arm develops car navigation and collision avoidance systems. Non-auto, industrial systems and consumer products are also made; subsidiary DENSO WAVE churns out robots and programmable logic controllers.

DENSO's holistic perspective is demonstrated in all aspects of its automotive business, from product development and design to manufacturing and sales. The company touts collaborative efforts with local car manufacturers and suppliers that support each customer's specific regional requirements. Although the company has a global presence, with operations in more than 30 countries, more than half of its sales depend on the Japanese economy.

DENSO, however, has not been spared the consequences of the auto industry's dramatic slump and snail-like recovery. No geographic market has been immune; DENSO's ratchet back in spending and streamlining of operations in 2008 and 2009 has not been enough to offset dwindling automobile production and weak currency exchange rates. DENSO is responding by aggressively curbing capital investments in production, while simultaneously pushing new product compliance, and management processes that aim to shrink costs in all divisions.

The company is pinning its future growth, foremost, on product research and development that boosts fuel efficiency and reduces carbon dioxide emissions. To this end DENSO has partnered with Toyota Motor to develop a new starter for idle-stop systems, and various hybrid technologies, including microchips that control the electric motor and gas engine. In late 2008 the company introduced an air-conditioning unit for compact cars, featuring approximately a 20% smaller footprint. Its intelligent sensing, monitoring, and navigation technologies are advancing, too, with components that promise to help reduce car accidents.

Cost control measures are playing an equally dominant role in DENSO's operations. The company is shifting its concentration from products for mature markets and premium vehicles to producing low-cost lines that cater to rising demand in developing markets, particularly for compact cars. Business systems at DENSO are evolving as well; more projects are addressed on an interdepartmental basis, allowing resources to be pooled and leveraged.

Former parent Toyota owns about 23% of DENSO. Toyota also accounts for about half of the company's sales.

HISTORY

Originally the in-house parts supplier for Toyota Motor, Nippondenso Co. (the predecessor to DENSO) was spun off in 1949 because Toyota no longer wanted the burden of Nippondenso's troubled financial performance. Nippondenso remained dependent upon Toyota for sales, and members of Toyota's controlling family, the Toyodas, remained involved in management. Nippondenso established a technological partnership with Germany's Robert Bosch in 1953.

As part of its plan to become a major supplier to North American carmakers, in 1966 Nippondenso established a sales office in Chicago and branch offices in Los Angeles and Detroit. It then turned to Europe, establishing a branch office in Stuttgart, Germany, in 1970. The following year the company established its first overseas subsidiary, Nippondenso of Los Angeles (now DENSO Sales California). In 1972 the company established three more foreign subsidiaries, in Australia, Canada, and Thailand. A European subsidiary (now DENSO Europe) was established in the Netherlands in 1973.

Nippondenso began consignment production for what is now known as Asmo Co., a maker of electric motors, in 1978. In 1984 the company joined with Allen Bradley Co. (US) to develop factory automation equipment. That year the predecessor to DENSO Manufacturing Michigan, one of the company's largest international subsidiaries, was established. Nippondenso expanded into Spain in 1989 by opening a plant in Barcelona.

In 1990 the company formed NDM Manufacturing (now DENSO Manufacturing UK), a joint venture (25%-owned) with Magneti Marelli of Italy, for the manufacture of automotive air conditioning and heating systems. The following year Nippondenso and AT&T formed a joint venture for the development of integrated circuit (IC) cards.

Nippondenso established several Chinese manufacturing joint ventures during the mid-1990s. In 1994 the company was recognized by the *Guinness Book of Records* as the maker of the world's smallest car, the DENSO Micro Car.

The company changed its name to DENSO CORPORATION in 1996. In 1999 DENSO acquired the rotating machines business of Magneti Marelli of Italy. The next year DENSO agreed to buy out Magneti Marelli's share in the companies' automotive air conditioning and heating joint venture (deal completed in 2001).

In 2001 DENSO ceased production of wireless phones in order to focus on making onboard car information systems. Also in 2001 the company merged its industrial equipment subsidiaries (bar code scanners and factory automation robots), and spun them off as majority-owned subsidiary DENSO Wave.

DENSO joined forces with Robert Bosch GmbH in 2003 to form a joint venture for the development of car navigation and multimedia systems.

In 2006 DENSO added four new Chinese production facilities that make navigation systems, air conditioner compressors, instrument panels, and oil filters. DENSO has also established a technical center in China, and is setting up another one in Thailand. The Thai technical center will support DENSO operations in China and India.

EXECUTIVES

Chairman: Koichi Fukaya
President and CEO: Nobuaki Katoh
EVP and Director: Kenji Ohya
EVP and Director: Hiromi Tokuda
Senior Managing Director, Engineering Research and Development Center and Thermal Systems Business Group and Board Member: Hikaru Sugi
Senior Managing Director Sales Group and Board Member: Kazuo Hironaka
Senior Managing Director, Electronic Systems Business Group and Board Member: Shinji Shirasaki
Senior Managing Director, Overall Electronic Business and Director: Mitsuharu Kato
Senior Managing Director, Corporate Center, Procurement Group and North America Region and Board Member: Koji Kobayashi
Senior Managing Director, Overall Production Affairs and Production Promotion Center and Board Member: Sojiro Tsuchiya
Managing Officer; President, DENSO Europe B.V.; President, DENSO Automotive Deutschland GmbH: Shigehiro Nishimura
Managing Officer; President and CEO, DENSO International America: Yoshiki (Steve) Sekiguchi
Managing Officer; President, DENSO International Asia: Yasushi Nei
Auditors: Deloitte Touche Tohmatsu

LOCATIONS

HQ: DENSO CORPORATION
1-1, Showa-cho
Kariya, Aichi 448-8661, Japan
Phone: 81-566-25-5511   **Fax:** 81-566-25-4860
US HQ: 24777 Denso Dr., P.O. Box 5047,
Southfield, MI 48086
US Phone: 248-350-7500   **US Fax:** 248-213-2337
Web: www.globaldenso.com

2010 Sales

	% of total
Japan	51
Americas	18
Asia & Oceania	17
Europe	14
Total	**100**

PRODUCTS/OPERATIONS

2010 Sales

	% of total
Automotive	
Thermal systems	30
Powertrain control systems	23
Information & safety systems	18
Electronic systems	10
Electric systems	9
Small motors	8
Industrial systems & consumer products	1
Other	1
Total	**100**

Selected Products

Automotive
  Thermal systems
    Air conditioning systems
    Air purifiers
    Cooling fans
    Cooling modules
    Front end modules
    Oil coolers
    Radiators
    Truck refrigeration units
  Powertrain control systems
    Diesel engine management systems
    Gasoline engine management systems
    Transmission control components
  Information and safety systems
    Multi-information display
    Radar system for detecting obstacles in front of
      vehicle
    Remote touch controller
  Electronic systems
    Car security systems
    Instrument clusters
    Integrated climate control panels
    Rear and corner sonars
    Remote keyless entry controllers
    Smart keys
  Electric systems
    ABS actuators
    Airbag sensors
    Alternators
    Electric power steering motors
    Starters
  Small motors
    Power window motors
    Windshield washer systems
    Windshield wiper systems
Industrial and consumer
  Bar code readers
  Industrial robots
  Programmable logic controllers

COMPETITORS

Adept Technology
Aisin Seiki
APM Automotive
Delphi Automotive
Johnson Controls
Key Safety Systems
KUKA
Prestolite Electric
Robert Bosch
TRW Automotive
Valeo
Visteon

HISTORICAL FINANCIALS

Company Type: Public

Income Statement

FYE: March 31

	REVENUE ($ mil.)	NET INCOME ($ mil.)	NET PROFIT MARGIN	EMPLOYEES
3/10	32,113	854	2.7%	120,812
3/09	32,304	(864)	—	119,919
3/08	40,537	2,462	6.1%	119,000
3/07	30,625	1,741	5.7%	112,262
3/06	27,120	1,443	5.3%	—
Annual Growth	4.3%	(12.3%)	—	2.5%

2010 Year-End Financials

Debt ratio: —
Return on equity: 4.4%
Cash ($ mil.): 6,199
Current ratio: 2.30
Long-term debt ($ mil.): —
No. of shares (mil.): 806
Dividends
  Yield: 0.9%
  Payout: 28.6%
Market value ($ mil.): 24,213

Stock History

Pink Sheets: DNZOY

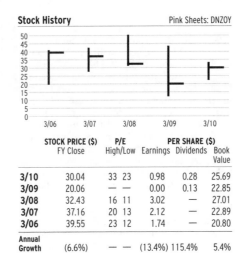

	STOCK PRICE ($) FY Close	P/E High/Low		PER SHARE ($) Earnings	Dividends	Book Value
3/10	30.04	33	23	0.98	0.28	25.69
3/09	20.06	—	—	0.00	0.13	22.85
3/08	32.43	16	11	3.02	—	27.01
3/07	37.16	20	13	2.12	—	22.89
3/06	39.55	23	12	1.74	—	20.80
Annual Growth	(6.6%)	—	—	(13.4%)	115.4%	5.4%

Dentsu Inc.

Unlike Godzilla, Dentsu is one monster that doesn't leave Japan in ruins. One of the largest advertising conglomerates in the world, Dentsu is the #1 ad firm in Japan. Its numerous agencies operate in about 25 countries and provide creative services for more than 6,000 clients, although sales outside of Japan only account for a small percentage of revenue. Dentsu also offers a host of other services, including public relations, media and event planning, and market research. The company has expanded its operations in Asia through a partnership with US-based Young & Rubicam and owns a 15% stake in ad conglomerate Publicis Groupe. Dentsu has offices in 30 cities in Japan and about 40 cities internationally.

As Japan's largest ad conglomerate Dentsu controls about 30% of Japan's advertising market. While Dentsu has outdistanced its closest domestic rivals, Hakuhodo and Asatsu-DK, the company has designs on becoming a global powerhouse on par with ad conglomerates such as WPP Group and Omnicom, but currently only about 10% of Dentsu's revenues are generated outside of Japan.

Dentsu's future growth plans include expanding its operations in Asia (particularly in China) using the Dentsu brand, and maintaining a grip in the US and Europe through its partnership with Publicis. Maintaining this strategy, in mid-2009 it launched Dentsu Sports America, a sports marketing firm in the US. The new agency will sponsor such events as the International Association of Athletics Federations (IAAF) World Championship in Athletics and the FINA World Championships.

Dentsu has organized itself along four business lines representing the company's current position and the lines it would like to grow. The company's domestic advertising services comprise the bulk of Dentsu's operations, while advertising related markets (consisting of specialized marketing, interactive, and sales promotion services), new markets (consisting of sports and entertainment marketing services), and overseas operations represent Dentsu's growth objectives.

Right out of the gate in 2010, Dentsu made a move to expand its digital advertising operations when it acquired Innovation Interactive LLC, a provider of services and technology used for search marketing, social media, and audience targeting. Owning nine offices in four countries, Innovation is comprised of three operating units: 360i (digital marketing agency), SearchIgnite (paid search technology platform), and Netmining (provider of audience targeting tools). The deal strengthened Dentsu's position in the cutting-edge digital arena and increased its presence in the US and Europe.

HISTORY

Seeing a need for a Japanese wire service, Sino-Japanese war correspondent Hoshiro Mitsunaga founded Telegraphic Service Co. in 1901. Mitsunaga let newspapers pay their wire service bills with advertising space, which his advertising agency, Japan Advertising (also founded in 1901) resold. He merged the two companies as Nihon Denpo-Tsushin Sha (Japan Telegraphic Communication Company) in 1907. Known as Dentsu for short (the name was officially changed in 1955), the company gained Japanese rights to the United Press wire in 1908 and began extracting even more favorable advertising rates from its clients.

With its mix of content and advertising, Dentsu became a leading Japanese communications business. But in 1936 Japan's government consolidated all news services into its propaganda machine, Domei, taking half of Dentsu's stock. During WWII all of Japan's advertising agencies were combined into 12 entities. Following the war, US occupation forces dismantled Domei, and its 50% holding in Dentsu stock was transferred to two new press agencies, Kyodo and Jiji.

Hideo Yoshida, who became president of Dentsu in 1947, began the task of rebuilding the company, currying favor by employing the sons of politicians and business leaders. He also helped build the television industry in Japan by investing in start-up broadcasters. Their gratitude translated into preferential treatment for Dentsu, leading to its decades-long domination of Japanese TV advertising.

By 1973 Dentsu had become the world's largest advertising agency, but the company's growth stalled with the slowing Japanese economy. Slow to expand overseas, foreign billings accounted for just 7% of revenues in 1986 (and despite growth initiatives the company has yet to make lasting progress in this area). The next year Saatchi & Saatchi passed Dentsu as the world's #1 advertising group. Young & Rubicam/Dentsu later joined with Havas' Eurocom to form HDM Worldwide (named after Havas, Dentsu, and Y&R's Marsteller).

Dentsu rebounded with Japan's economic boom in the late 1980s, but the company continued to struggle abroad. Eurocom pulled out of HDM Worldwide in 1990, and the newly named Dentsu, Young & Rubicam Partnerships reorganized to focus on North America, Asia, and Australia. Dentsu joined with Collett Dickenson Pearce to maintain its presence in Europe after HDM's demise. Restructuring in 1996 created several new units, including one to focus on the Olympics, and in 1997 the company set up the Interactive Solution Center to focus on digital media.

The company agreed to buy UK ad agency Harari Page in 1998 and announced plans for its own public offering. Dentsu took a 20% stake in Bcom3 (formerly BDM) in 2000, the new advertising holding company formed by the merger of The Leo Group and MacManus Group. It also formed a Japanese Internet services joint venture with US consulting company marchFIRST. After marchFIRST's demise Dentsu gained full ownership of the company and renamed it DentsuFUSE.

The following year Dentsu reorganized its US and European units and purchased US ad firm Oasis International Group and became a publicly listed company in late 2001.

In April 2009 chairman and CEO Tateo Mataki retired, making way for Tatsuyoshi Takashima, who was the company's president and COO.

EXECUTIVES

President, CEO, and Director: Tatsuyoshi Takashima
Senior Manager Corporate Communications: Yukihiro Oguchi
Chairman, Dentsu UK and Regional Director, Dentsu Europe: Jim Kelly
Director Sports; President and CEO, Dentsu Sports America: Kiyoshi Nakamura
Executive Officer; President and CEO, Dentsu Holdings USA and Dentsu America: Timothy P. (Tim) Andree
COO, Dentsu India: Satish Sathyanarayana
Senior Corporate Auditor: Kimiharu Matsuda
Auditors: Deloitte Touche Tohmatsu

LOCATIONS

HQ: Dentsu Inc.
1-8-1, Higashi-shimbashi, Minato-ku
Tokyo 105-7001, Japan
Phone: 81-3-6216-5111 **Fax:** 81-3-5551-2013
US HQ: 32 Avenue of the Americas, 16th Fl.
New York, NY 10013
US Phone: 212-397-3333
Web: www.dentsu.com

2010 Sales

	% of total
Japan	91
Other countries	9
Total	**100**

PRODUCTS/OPERATIONS

2010 Sales by Business Category

	% of total
Television spot	26
Television time	22
Marketing promotion	13
Creative	12
Newspapers	9
Content services	6
Interactive media	3
Magazines	3
Out-of-home media	3
Radio	1
Other	2
Total	**100**

2010 Sales by Industry

	% of total
Information & communications	15
Beverages & cigarettes	11
Cosmetics & toiletries	8
Foodstuffs	7
Automobiles & related products	6
Finance & insurance	6
Distribution & retail	6
Pharmaceuticals & medical supplies	6
Food services & other services	5
Hobbies & sporting goods	5
Home electric appliances & AV equipment	5
Government organizations	4
Transportation & leisure	4
Real estate & housing facilities	3
Publications	2
Other	8
Total	**100**

COMPETITORS

Asatsu-DK
Grey Group
Hakuhodo
Havas
Interpublic Group
Omnicom
Publicis Groupe
Video Research
WPP

HISTORICAL FINANCIALS

Company Type: Public

Income Statement

FYE: March 31

	REVENUE ($ mil.)	NET INCOME ($ mil.)	NET PROFIT MARGIN	EMPLOYEES
3/10	18,109	387	2.1%	18,255
3/09	19,398	389	2.0%	17,921
3/08	20,722	365	1.8%	17,000
3/07	17,765	260	1.5%	16,224
3/06	16,700	264	1.6%	15,337
Annual Growth	**2.0%**	**10.1%**	**—**	**4.5%**

2010 Year-End Financials

Debt ratio: — No. of shares (mil.): 249
Return on equity: 7.8% Dividends
Cash ($ mil.): 1,012   Yield: 1.0%
Current ratio: 1.23   Payout: 20.3%
Long-term debt ($ mil.): — Market value ($ mil.): 6,604

Stock History

Tokyo: 43240

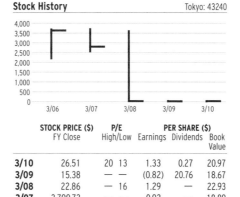

	STOCK PRICE ($) FY Close	P/E High/Low	Earnings	PER SHARE ($) Dividends	Book Value
3/10	26.51	20 13	1.33	0.27	20.97
3/09	15.38	— —	(0.82)	20.76	18.67
3/08	22.86	— 16	1.29	—	22.93
3/07	2,799.72	— —	0.92	—	18.89
3/06	3,632.06	— —	0.95	—	17.79
Annual Growth	**(70.8%)**	**— —**	**8.8%**	**(98.7%)**	**4.2%**

Deutsche Bahn

One of Europe's largest transportation providers, Deutsche Bahn gets freight and passengers from Punkt A to Punkt B. The company's DB Schenker group encompasses logistics and rail operations. More than half of the company's sales come from freight transport and logistics, led by Schenker AG. The company's railway division carries more than 1.9 billion passengers yearly throughout Germany and into neighboring countries over a network of about 34 million km of track. Deutsche Bahn operates bus services in Germany and holds interests in passenger rail franchises in Europe. Other divisions manage the company's train stations and provide track infrastructure services. Deutsche Bahn is owned by the German government.

Raising cash through privatization has been a long-held goal for Deutsche Bahn, and in 2008 its passenger and freight transportation and logistics businesses were spun off as a new company, DB Mobility Logistics, in preparation for an IPO. Plans called for just under 25% of DB Mobility Logistics to be sold to the public, while parent Deutsche Bahn (and thus the German government) would maintain a controlling stake. However, the IPO was postponed in late 2008, due to the international financial crisis.

In the meantime, Deutsche Bahn — and DB Mobility Logistics — have businesses to run, particularly freight transportation and logistics operations, which have surpassed passenger transportation to become Deutsche Bahn's largest business segment. The company strengthened its logistics business in 2006 by acquiring US-based freight forwarder BAX Global, which was integrated into DB Schenker USA. Buying BAX Global expanded Deutsche Bahn's logistics network in the Asia/Pacific region and the Americas, and the company hopes to gain additional business from Asian and transpacific trade. Deutsche Bahn plans to continue to invest in its logistics operations, and in 2008 it acquired a majority stake in Spanish logistics company Transportes Ferroviarios Especiales (Transfesa), which specializes in arranging the transportation of freight by rail and by road.

The company also is moving to extend its rail freight operations, which are conducted primarily under the DB Schenker Rail brand. The UK is an appealing market since its transport industry was deregulated some years ago, spurring companies to become more international in their operations.

In 2007 Deutsche Bahn bought English Welsh & Scottish Railway, the UK's leading rail freight carrier, for about $560 million. In 2008 it acquired Laing Rail from construction firm John Laing. The company gained interests in three rail operations, including full ownership of Chiltern Railways, which operates between London and Birmingham. With plans to capitalize on the liberalization of the European transportation industry, Deutsche Bahn paid around £1.5 billion (more than $2 billion) in 2010 to buy Arriva, one of the UK's largest bus and rail operators. European antitrust laws, however, are dashing Deutsche Bahn's hopes and forcing it to divest Arriva's German bus business along with Arriva's other German activities.

In May 2009 Rüdiger Grube took over as chairman of the company's management board and CEO, replacing Hartmut Mehdorn. Grube has served on the boards of Daimler and EADS.

HISTORY

In 1989 the Federal Cabinet of West Germany adopted a resolution to set up an independent government railway commission. That year the wall between East Germany and West Germany came down, and the two nations were united into the Federal Republic of Germany in 1990.

In 1993 the cabinet endorsed a railway reform plan submitted by the federal minister of transport, and later that year the plan won approval from the German Parliament and the Federal Council. Deutsche Bahn was then established in 1994 to unify Germany's western (Deutsche Bundesbahn) and eastern (Deutsche Reichsbahn) railway systems as a public company. The Federal Republic of Germany was sole shareholder.

The next year Deutsche Bahn created a subsidiary, DBKom, to offer telecom services in competition with Deutsche Telekom. In 1996 a consortium led by German conglomerate Mannesmann bought a 50% stake in DBKom. By 1997 Deutsche Bahn had been transformed from a government department into a registered company and split into four operating units: tracks, freight, local passenger services, and intercity passenger services. That year Deutsche Bahn also bought Lufthansa's 33% stake in tour operator Deutsches Reisebüro (DER), giving it full ownership of the company, as well as DER's 20% stake in tour group TUI.

Trouble came in 1998: Deutsche Bahn sent its 59 first-generation high-speed InterCityExpress (ICE) trains for inspections after one of the trains crashed and killed 98 passengers. Investigators believed a broken wheel caused the crash.

Deutsche Bahn and French state-owned railway SNCF announced plans in 1999 to develop a high-speed train capable of traveling up to 320 km (198 miles) per hour. Also that year Hartmut Mehdorn, credited with turning around printing equipment manufacturer Heidelberger Druck and DaimlerChrysler's aerospace unit, became Deutsche Bahn's new CEO. Mehdorn pledged to make Deutsche Bahn more efficient by cutting losses and raising productivity. That year the company sold its stake in TUI to conglomerate Preussag and its DER unit to supermarket giant Rewe.

In 2000 Germany's transport minister postponed plans to float Deutsche Bahn after it posted losses for the first time since 1994.

Hoping to take advantage of Deutsche Bahn's financial troubles, Connex, then a subsidiary of French conglomerate Vivendi, offered in 2001 to acquire Deutsche Bahn's long-distance express passenger trains. But Mehdorn refused the offer, saying the company did not want to give up its long-distance traffic. Deutsche Bahn did agree in 2001 to form a railway telematics (communications system) joint venture with Mannesmann Arcor, a company controlled by Vodafone. The agreement called for Deutsche Bahn to keep its 18% stake in Arcor but lose its minority veto rights, which Deutsche Bahn had used earlier that year to block an Arcor IPO.

Deutsche Bahn sold its 83% stake in bus unit Deutsche Touring GmbH to Eurosur SA of Spain for an undisclosed amount in 2005.

Deutsche Bahn enhanced its logistics business in 2006 by acquiring US-based freight forwarder BAX Global. The next year Deutsche Bahn snatched up English Welsh & Scottish Railway and rebranded it DB Schenker Rail UK.

EXECUTIVES

Honorary Chairman, Supervisory Board:
Gunther Saßmannshausen
Chairman, Supervisory Board: Werner Müller
Deputy Chairman, Supervisory Board:
Alexander Kirchner
CEO and Chairman: Rüdiger Grube, age 59
CFO: Richard Lutz, age 45
Member Management Board, Technology, Integrated Systems, Services and Infrastructure; Chairman, Rail Technology and Services, CTO: Volker Kefer
Member Management Board, Economic and Political Affairs: Otto Wiesheu, age 65
Member Management Board, Compliance, Privacy, and Legal Affairs: Gerd T. Becht, age 58
Member Management Board, Personnel Division:
Norbert Hansen, age 57
Member Management Board, Human Resources:
Ulrich Weber, age 60
Member Management Board, Infrastructure and Services: Stefan Garber, age 55
Auditors: PwC Deutsche Revision AG

LOCATIONS

HQ: Deutsche Bahn Aktiengesellschaft
Potsdamer Platz 2
D-10785 Berlin, Germany
Phone: 49-30-297-0   **Fax:** 49-30-297-6-19-19
Web: www.db.de

2008 Sales

	% of total
Europe	
Germany	64
Other countries	23
Asia/Pacific	6
North America	6
Other regions	1
Total	**100**

PRODUCTS/OPERATIONS

2008 Sales

	% of total
Transport & logistics	
Schenker	44
Rail freight	14
Passenger transport	
Regional	20
Long-distance	11
Local	5
Infrastructure & services	
Track infrastructure	2
Energy	2
Passenger stations	1
Other	1
Total	**100**

COMPETITORS

Air Berlin
Air France
British Airways
DHL
Expeditors
FedEx
Geodis
KLM Royal Dutch Airlines
Kuehne + Nagel International
Lufthansa
National Express Group
Panalpina
SNCF
UPS Supply Chain Solutions
Veolia Environnement

HISTORICAL FINANCIALS

Company Type: Government-owned

Income Statement

FYE: December 31

	REVENUE ($ mil.)	NET INCOME ($ mil.)	NET PROFIT MARGIN	EMPLOYEES
12/08	47,151	1,862	3.9%	240,242
12/07	46,084	2,526	5.5%	237,078
12/06	39,649	2,216	5.6%	229,200
12/05	31,654	724	2.3%	216,389
12/04	35,314	246	0.7%	233,657
Annual Growth	7.5%	65.9%	—	0.7%

2008 Year-End Financials

Debt ratio: 115.9%   Current ratio: —
Return on equity: 11.2%   Long-term debt ($ mil.): 19,850
Cash ($ mil.): —

Net Income History

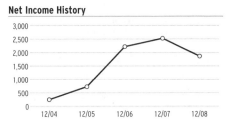

Deutsche Bank

Deutsche Bank AG is one of the top financial groups in the world and the largest bank in its home country of Germany, where it operates about 1,000 retail branch locations. It has another 1,000 branches in more than 70 countries in Europe, the Americas, Asia, the Pacific Rim, and Africa. Deutsche Bank operates through three primary segments: Corporate and Investment Bank, Corporate Investments, and Private Clients and Asset Management. The massive and far-flung Deutsche Asset Management subsidiary, which includes US-based companies Deutsche Bank Securities, RREEF, and DWS Investments (formerly DWS Scudder), serves private and institutional clients and has some €700 billion ($975 billion) in assets under management.

To boost its lending operations in the US, the company bought MortgageIT, a real estate investment trust, for some €285 million ($430 million) in 2007. The timing wasn't great: the subsidiary suffered a major loss, a victim of the US subprime mortgage crisis. Also that year Deutsche Bank acquired Abbey Life from Lloyds Banking Group for some €1 billion ($2 billion.) This acquisition fared better than MortgageIT, finishing out the year in the black.

In 2008 the bank established an outpost in China and built up its stake in China-based mutual fund manager Harvest Fund to 30%, hoping to take advantage of the giant country's growing economy. It later paid some €3 billion ($4 billion) for a 25% stake in fellow German bank Deutsche Postbank. The acquisition, which included an option to acquire a majority stake, strengthens Deutsche Bank's consumer banking offerings.

Although Deutsche Bank held strong throughout the earlier part of the global economic crisis, it suffered a fourth-quarter loss of €4.8 billion in

2008. Its corporate and investment banking and corporate investments segments lost money that year, and profits in the private client and asset management businesses declined. Executives announced plans to reshape business by focusing on volume transactions such as commodities trading, interest rates, currencies and stocks.

In 2010 it acquired the bulk of European asset manager Sal. Oppenheim Group for about €1 billion ($1.5 billion). The deal aligned Deutsche Bank with one of Germany's strongest private banking brands as it attempts to boost its distressed wealth management business.

Also in 2010, Deutsche Bank's once-canceled deal to buy parts of ABN AMRO's commercial banking operations in the Netherlands was finally completed. The acquisition was part of the company's strategy to expand in Europe. The company also set its sights on the Middle East. It formed a shariah-compliant joint venture, Deutsche Gulf Finance, in Saudi Arabia. The unit, which is 60% owned by a group of Saudi investors, offers home financing.

HISTORY

Georg von Siemens opened Deutsche Bank in Berlin in 1870. Three years later the firm opened an office in London and was soon buying other German banks. In the late 1800s Deutsche Bank helped finance Germany's electrification (carried out by Siemens AG) and railroad construction in the US and the Ottoman Empire. Von Siemens ran the bank until his death in 1901.

The bank survived post-WWI financial chaos by merging with Disconto-Gesellschaft and later helped finance the Nazi war machine. After the war, the Allies split the company into 10 banks; it became extinct in Soviet-controlled East Germany.

The bank was reassembled in 1957 and primarily engaged in commercial banking, often taking direct interests in its customers. It added retail services in the 1960s. In 1975, to prevent the Shah of Iran from gaining a stake in Daimler-Benz (now Daimler), the bank bought 29% of that company.

The firm opened an investment banking office in the US in 1971 and a branch office in 1978. In the 1980s it expanded geographically, buying Bank of America's Italian subsidiary (1986) and UK merchant bank Morgan Grenfell (1989); it also moved into insurance, creating life insurer DB Leben (1989).

Terrorists killed chairman Alfred Herrhausen, a symbol of German big business, in 1989. After German reunification in 1990, successor Hilmar Kopper oversaw the bank's reestablishment in eastern Germany.

In 1994 Deutsche Bank bought most of ITT's commercial finance unit. That year the company suffered scandal when real estate developer Jurgen Schneider borrowed more than DM1 billion and disappeared; he was later found and returned to Germany.

The company grew its global investment banking operations in 1995 under its Morgan Grenfell subsidiary. Corporate culture clashes prompted Deutsche Bank to take greater control of the unit and restructure it in 1998.

Deutsche Bank's global aspirations suffered a setback in 1998 when losses on investments in Russia trimmed its bottom line. Still trying to put WWII behind it, the bank accepted responsibility for its wartime dealing in gold seized from Jews but has rejected liability to compensate victims of Nazi forced labor who toiled in industrial companies in which it holds stakes.

In 1999 the bank acquired Bankers Trust. Despite a decision to divest its industrial portfolio, that year the company bought Tele Columbus, the #2 cable network in Germany, and Piaggio, the Italian maker of the famed Vespa motor scooter.

Deutsche Bank's reorganization in 2001 saw the bank eliminate 2,600 jobs worldwide and realign its businesses into two divisions. Deutsche Bank also bought Banque Worms from French insurer AXA.

Looking for a steady supply of cash, in 2001 Deutsche Bank's Morgan Grenfell Private Equity bought 3,000 English pubs owned by UK-based Whitbread plc. In 2004 Deutsche Bank acquired Berkshire Mortgage, one of the top multifamily residential lenders in the US. The next year it bought Russian financial services company United Financial Group.

The year 2006 was a bad year for the company from a public relations standpoint. Fallout from former chairman Rolf Breuer's remarks regarding the financial stability of banking client Kirch Holding led to a shakeup in the executive suite and the board that year. Later, UK financial regulators charged the bank an $11.1 million fine for market misconduct related to trading activity in 2004. In the US the IRS investigated the bank for alleged abusive tax shelters.

The bank also took a public relations hit when its CEO, Josef Ackermann, went on trial for illegal bonuses during his tenure at Mannesmann.

EXECUTIVES

Chairman, Supervisory Board: Clemens A.H. Börsig, age 62
Deputy Chairman: Karin Ruck, age 44
Chairman, Management Board and Group Executive Committee: Josef Ackermann, age 62, $9,551,530 total compensation
COO: Hermann-Josef Lamberti, age 54, $4,254,891 total compensation
CFO: Stefan Krause, age 47, $4,015,767 total compensation
Chief Risk Officer: Hugo Bänziger, age 53, $5,288,926 total compensation
Head, Global Markets; Joint Head, Corporate and Investment Bank: Anshuman (Anshu) Jain, age 47, $7,793,860 total compensation
Head, Regional Management Worldwide: Jürgen Fitschen, age 62, $3,099,236 total compensation
Head, Private and Business Clients: Rainer Neske, age 46, $3,228,194 total compensation
Head, Global Rates and Commodities: Michele Faissola
Head, Asset Management: Kevin Parker, age 50
Head, Credit Portfolio Management and Prime Brokerage, Global Rates: Fredrik Gentzel
Head, Global Investment Solutions: Kevin Lecocq
Head, Global Transaction Banking: Werner Steinmüller
Global Head, Company Research: Guy Ashton
CEO, Deutsche Bank Americas; Chairman, Americas Executive Committee: Seth Waugh
Auditors: KPMG Deutsche Treuhand-Gesellschaft AG

LOCATIONS

HQ: Deutsche Bank Aktiengesellschaft
Theodor-Heuss-Allee 70
60486 Frankfurt, Germany
Phone: 49-69-910-00 **Fax:** 49-69-910-34-225
US HQ: 60 Wall St., New York, NY 10005
US Phone: 212-250-2500 **US Fax:** 212-797-0291
Web: www.deutsche-bank.de

2009 Sales

	% of total
Europe, Middle East & Africa	
Germany	26
Other countries	41
Americas	22
Asia/Pacific	11
Total	**100**

PRODUCTS/OPERATIONS

2009 Sales

	% of total
Interest	
Financial assets at fair value through profit or loss	32
Loans	25
Other	6
Noninterest	
Commission & fee income	20
Other	14
Total	**100**

COMPETITORS

Barclays	KfW
BNP Paribas	Landesbank Berlin
Citigroup	Merrill Lynch
Citigroup Global Markets	Mizuho Financial
Commerzbank	Morgan Stanley
Cortal Consors	National Australia Bank
Credit Suisse	Rabobank
DZ BANK	Société Générale
Goldman Sachs	TD Bank
Grupo Santander	UBS
HSBC	UniCredit Bank AG
JPMorgan Chase	

HISTORICAL FINANCIALS

Company Type: Public

Income Statement

FYE: December 31

	ASSETS ($ mil.)	NET INCOME ($ mil.)	INCOME AS % OF ASSETS	EMPLOYEES
12/09	2,150,752	7,127	0.3%	77,053
12/08	3,116,269	(5,426)	—	80,456
12/07	2,970,188	9,518	0.3%	78,291
12/06	1,487,128	7,844	0.5%	68,849
12/05	1,178,950	4,194	0.4%	63,427
Annual Growth	16.2%	14.2%	—	5.0%

2009 Year-End Financials

Equity as % of assets: 2.4%	Dividends
Return on assets: 0.3%	Yield: 0.7%
Return on equity: 14.9%	Payout: 6.5%
Long-term debt ($ mil.): 188,870	Market value ($ mil.): 63,101
No. of shares (mil.): 621	Sales ($ mil.): 60,834

Stock History

NYSE: DB

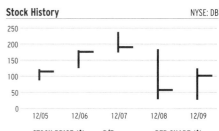

	STOCK PRICE ($) FY Close	P/E High/Low		PER SHARE ($) Earnings	Dividends	Book Value
12/09	101.63	11	3	10.88	0.71	84.59
12/08	57.35	—	—	(10.73)	6.33	69.97
12/07	190.48	12	9	19.21	4.64	87.71
12/06	175.78	12	8	15.24	2.59	69.77
12/05	114.72	14	11	8.23	1.63	57.29
Annual Growth	(3.0%)	—	—	7.2%	(18.8%)	10.2%

Deutsche Post

Deutsche Post has outgrown its mailbox origins. Through its DHL operations, the company is one of the world's leading providers of express delivery and logistics services, including freight forwarding, transportation management, and warehousing and distribution. Overall, DHL-branded businesses account for more than half of the parent company's sales. Although Deutsche Post still handles the mail in Germany, that part of the business is being de-emphasized. In addition to traditional postal operations, the company provides mail process outsourcing at home and abroad. About two-thirds of Deutsche Post's sales come from outside its home country.

Deutsche Post is working to counter the negative effects of the global recession by implementing a number of companywide initiatives. In fall 2010 the company broke ground in the online advertising market by purchasing nugg.ad. The business acquisition is an independent targeting service provider used by advertising agencies and marketers.

Deutsche Post, in the meantime, is reevaluating its legacy operations. Demand for mail delivery has trended downward; the company plans to substitute mail shipped by air for less-costly ground transportation. In addition, Deutsche Post cut costs in 2010 by transferring 277 postal branches to its Deutsche Postbank affiliate. Deutsche Post will sell the remaining 80 branches by the end of 2011. It sold its domestic express operations in France and the UK, as well. The divestment followed a restructuring of the Express division in an attempt to make operations leaner and more streamlined.

In the US where FedEx and UPS lead the market, Deutsche Post is narrowing its express delivery operations. In late 2008 it slashed 9,500 US jobs — around 73% of its DHL Express (USA) workforce and closed hundreds of offices. DHL Express (USA) subsequently eliminated air and ground services within the US. The company maintains its international shipping services to and from the US.

To focus on its core logistics operations, as well as raise cash, Deutsche Post in early 2009 sold a minority stake in its Deutsche Postbank unit to rival Deutsche Bank. The deal, in which Deutsche Bank paid about $3.9 billion for nearly 30% of Postbank, included options for both parties that could result in Deutsche Bank acquiring the remainder of Deutsche Post's shares in the financial services unit.

The company's direction is being overseen by Frank Appel. Appel, a former McKinsey consultant who had run several Deutsche Post units as a member of the company's management board, replaced Klaus Zumwinkel as CEO in 2008. Zumwinkel resigned after he was questioned in connection with a government investigation of alleged tax evasion.

Under Zumwinkel, who had led the company since 1990, Deutsche Post evolved from a government-owned mail service to a publicly traded company with worldwide delivery and logistics operations. The German government controls a 31% stake in Deutsche Post.

HISTORY

The German postal system was established in the 1490s when German emperor Maximilian I ordered a reliable and regular messenger service to be set up between Austria (Innsbruck, where the emperor had his court) and the farther reaches of his Holy Roman Empire: the Netherlands, France, and Rome. The von Tassis (later renamed Taxis) family of Italy was responsible for running the network. Family members settled in major cities across Europe to expand the postal business.

Although the family operated what was officially an exclusively royal mail service, by the early 1500s the company was also delivering messages for private patrons. In 1600 a family member who served as general postmaster was authorized to collect fees for private mail deliveries. By the early 19th century, Thurn und Taxis, as the company was then called, was the leading postal service in the Holy Roman Empire, serving more than 11 million people.

The dissolution of the Holy Roman Empire, prompted by Napoleon's military adventures, led to the creation of a federation of 39 independent German states. Thurn und Taxis had to make agreements with members of the separate states, including Austria and Prussia. After Austria's defeat in 1866 by Prussia, the confederation was dissolved and all Thurn und Taxis postal systems were absorbed by Prussia. When Bismarck's Prussian-led German Reich was established in 1870, the new postal administration (Reichspostverwaltung) began issuing postage stamps valid across Germany.

After Germany was defeated in WWII and split into two nations in 1949, two postal systems were established: Deutsche Post (East Germany) and Deutsche Bundespost (West Germany). The fall of the Berlin Wall in 1989 preceded a reunion of the two German states in 1990. That year Deutsche Post, led by chairman Klaus Zumwinkel, was integrated into Deutsche Bundespost. The merger resulted in losses and a huge backlog of undelivered mail. Zumwinkel initiated the company's first steps to recovery by cutting 140,000 jobs.

The heavy costs of reunification (it was 1994 before Deutsche Bundespost posted a profit again) prompted the German government to set the postal system on a course toward privatization. In 1995 the postal system was restructured as Deutsche Post AG and placed under the management of executives from the private sector.

In 1998 a new postal law reaffirmed Deutsche Post's monopoly on traditional letter delivery until 2002. However, other special mail delivery options (such as same-day delivery of letters) were granted to private companies. That year Deutsche Post acquired shares in parcel delivery companies in Europe and the US, including a stake of nearly 25% in DHL. In 1999 it acquired Deutsche Postbank, the former retail banking arm of Deutsche Bundespost, as part of a strategy to make it more attractive for an IPO.

Deutsche Post added more units in 2000, including US-based airfreight forwarder Air Express International, which was integrated into Danzas. The German government sold a minority stake in Deutsche Post to the public in 2000. (Further share sales followed, and by 2006 the government had reduced its stake in Deutsche Post to about 35%.)

In 2002 the company took full ownership of DHL. The next year Deutsche Post (through DHL) paid about $1 billion for the ground delivery network of US-based Airborne.

Klaus Zumwinkel resigned in 2008 after he was questioned during a government investigation into alleged tax evasion. Management board member Frank Appel succeeded him.

EXECUTIVES

Chairman, Supervisory Board:
Wulf von Schimmelmann
Deputy Chairman, Supervisory Board: Andrea Kocsis
Chairman, Board of Management and CEO:
Frank Appel, age 49
Member Board of Management and CFO:
Lawrence A. Rosen, age 52
Member Board of Management, Global Forwarding and Freight: Hermann Ude, age 49
Member Board of Management; CEO, DHL Express:
Ken Allen, age 55
Member Board of Management, Personnel:
Walter Scheurle, age 57
Member Board of Management, Mail: Jürgen Gerdes
Member Board of Management, Supply Chain and Corporate Information Solutions, DHL Worldwide Network: Bruce A. Edwards, age 55
CEO, DHL Global Mail: Thomas Kipp
Head, Corporate Communications: Christof Ehrhart, age 42
Auditors: PricewaterhouseCoopers AG Wirtschaftsprufungsgesellschaft

LOCATIONS

HQ: Deutsche Post AG
    Charles-de-Gaulle-Str. 20
    53113 Bonn, Germany
Phone: 49-228-182-6-3636   **Fax:** 49-228-182-6-3199
Web: www.dpwn.de

2009 Sales

	% of total
Europe	
Germany	34
Other countries	36
Americas	14
Asia/Pacific	12
Other regions	4
Total	**100**

PRODUCTS/OPERATIONS

2009 Sales

	% of total
Mail	29
Supply Chain	27
Global Forwarding/Freight	22
Express	22
Total	**100**

Selected Services

Air freight
Contract logistics
Dialog marketing services
European road freight
International express
National and international mail and parcel services
Ocean freight
Outsourcing and system solutions for the mail business

COMPETITORS

CEVA Logistics	La Poste
Commerzbank	Nippon Express
DB Schenker	Panalpina
Deutsche Bank	Poste Italiane
DZ BANK	Royal Mail
Expeditors	TNT
FedEx	UniCredit Bank AG
Hays plc	UPS
HSBC	US Postal Service
Kuehne + Nagel International	UTi Worldwide

HISTORICAL FINANCIALS
Company Type: Public

Income Statement
FYE: December 31

	REVENUE ($ mil.)	NET INCOME ($ mil.)	NET PROFIT MARGIN	EMPLOYEES
12/09	66,215	993	1.5%	436,651
12/08	76,781	(2,789)	—	447,626
12/07	93,483	2,775	3.0%	536,350
12/06	79,877	3,011	3.8%	—
12/05	52,813	2,647	5.0%	—
Annual Growth	5.8%	(21.7%)	—	(9.8%)

2009 Year-End Financials

Debt ratio: —
Return on equity: 8.7%
Cash ($ mil.): 4,391
Current ratio: 1.03
Long-term debt ($ mil.): —

No. of shares (mil.): 1,209
Dividends
  Yield: 4.4%
  Payout: 113.2%
Market value ($ mil.): 23,366

Stock History
German: DPWX

	STOCK PRICE ($) FY Close	P/E High/Low		PER SHARE ($) Earnings	Dividends	Book Value
12/09	19.33	26	12	0.76	0.86	9.81
12/08	16.79	—	—	(1.97)	1.27	9.12
12/07	34.60	23	17	1.69	—	13.46
12/06	30.13	15	12	2.11	—	12.24
12/05	24.25	11	8	2.36	—	10.49
Annual Growth	(5.5%)	—	—	(24.7%)	(32.3%)	(1.7%)

Deutsche Telekom

Operating the *autobahn* on the global information superhighway, Deutsche Telekom is a leading telecom company in Europe and one of the largest carriers in the world. The company serves about 128 million wireless phone customers through its T brand. It is also Germany's #1 fixed-line telephone operator; it provides domestic and international wireline long-distance voice services to about 34 million access lines also under the T banner. It is additionally a leading ISP with about 15 million broadband subscribers, offering other data and multimedia services such as Entertain-branded Internet television. Deutsche Telekom's T-Systems International division specializes in IT services for businesses.

Deutsche Telekom's domestic T brand is led by its wireless unit, one of the country's leading wireless telecom providers, which serves more than 26 million subscribers. Its key international wireless subsidiaries are T-Mobile USA and T-Mobile (UK).

The company in 2010 combined its T-Mobile (UK) subsidiary with the UK business of France Telecom's Orange-branded wireless operations to create a joint venture that is the largest mobile carrier in the UK. T-Mobile and Orange each own 50% of the venture.

In 2009 the company absorbed its T-Mobile International subsidiary, which formerly oversaw the operations of its US and UK wireless businesses, in a move to simplify both its corporate structure and its sales and marketing efforts. The reorganization resulted in the US and UK businesses coming under the direct supervision of Deutsche Telekom.

The company bought Strato, the Web-hosting services unit of freenet, for €275 in 2009 in a bid to boost its presence in the data network services market. The deal helped Deutsche Telekom to gain ground on market leader United Internet.

The company's underperforming IT services unit, T-Systems International, provides information and communications technology services primarily to German-based multinational customers. Deutsche Telekom, which had previously said that it might combine T-Systems with a future acquisition, in 2008 formed a partnership with US-based IT services provider Cognizant in order to cut operational costs and to expand T-Systems' potential European customer base for systems integration services. The deal included the transfer of staff from T-Systems' unit in India to Cognizant's Indian operations.

The German government holds about 15% of the company; German state-owned development bank KfW owns about 17%.

HISTORY

Deutsche Telekom was formed by the 1989 separation of West Germany's telecommunications services from the nation's postal system. Dating back to the 15th century (when the Thurn und Taxis private postal system was created for German principalities), the service expanded to cover Austria, France, the Netherlands, and most of Germany by the 1850s. After the 1866 Austro-Prussian War, it became part of the North German Postal Confederation. When the German Empire was formed in 1871, the postal operation became the Deutsche Reichspost (later the Bundespost). Shortly thereafter, the newly invented telephone was introduced in Germany.

Post-WWI inflation shook the Bundespost, and the government allowed it to try new organizational structures. A 1924 law allowed the state-run service to operate as a quasi-commercial company.

Hitler came to power in 1933, and the postal service became an instrument of Nazi surveillance. After WWII, occupation forces began rebuilding Germany's badly damaged infrastructure. In 1947 the American-British zone returned postal authority to Germans, and in 1949 the USSR established the state of East Germany.

Only by the 1960s did West Germany's postal and phone services meet modern standards. Privatization of the Bundespost became a political cause when many complained about the monopoly's cost and inefficiency. Efforts to privatize the agency (named Deutsche Telekom in 1989) intensified with the 1990 German reunification. But faced with updating the antiquated phone system of the former East Germany, political opposition to taking Deutsche Telekom public faded.

The company began operating T-D1, its mobile phone network, in 1992, and the next year it launched T-Online, now Germany's largest online service provider. In 1996 Deutsche Telekom finally went public and raised more than $13 billion in Europe's largest IPO. It also launched Global One with France Telecom and Sprint; as part of the partnership, Deutsche Telekom took a 10% stake in Sprint.

In 1998 European Union (EU) member countries opened their phone markets to competition, and Deutsche Telekom's long-distance market share quickly eroded. Under EU pressure, in 1999 Deutsche Telekom said it would sell its cable network, which it divided into nine regional units.

Deutsche Telekom bought French fixed-line carrier SIRIS and UK wireless provider One 2 One (now T-Mobile UK). In 2000 the company sold its stake in Global One to France Telecom, as did Sprint. (In the fallout from the unwinding of the Global One partnership, Deutsche Telekom in 2001 sold its stake in Sprint PCS and sold its interest in France Telecom the next year.)

T-Mobile International moved into the US mobile phone market in 2001 with the acquisitions of VoiceStream Wireless and Powertel, now known as T-Mobile USA. The German government's stake in Deutsche Telekom decreased by 17% largely to accommodate US regulators for the VoiceStream and Powertel acquisitions.

With competition flourishing in Germany, Deutsche Telekom worked hard to lose its bureaucratic image and reposition itself as a slimmer, customer-friendly organization. To cut costs and eliminate debt, it reduced its workforce by 22,000 jobs, or 9%, over two years.

As the company's share price slumped amid the general telecom industry downturn, CEO Ron Sommer was forced to resign in July 2002.

Until 2003 Deutsche Telekom was Germany's #1 cable provider through the company's six regional cable TV operations, which it sold for $1.87 billion to a group of US investors that included Apax Partners, the Goldman Sachs Group, and Providence Equity Partners.

The company boosted its T-Mobile USA holdings through the $2.5 billion acquisition in 2005 of wireless networks serving California and Nevada from Cingular Wireless.

Deutsche Telekom in 2007 began to reduce costs by cutting the pay and extending the hours of about 50,000, or one-third, of its employees.

EXECUTIVES

Chairman: Ulrich Lehner, age 63
Deputy Chairman: Lothar Schröder
CEO: René Obermann, age 47,
$4,016,588 total compensation
Member Management Board and CFO:
Timotheus (Tim) Höttges, age 47,
$1,620,801 total compensation
Member Management Board, T-Home Sales and Service: Niek Jan van Damme, age 49,
$13,711,623 total compensation
Member Management Board, South Eastern Europe:
Guido Kerkhoff, age 43, $1,174,231 total compensation
Member Management Board Data Privacy, Legal Affairs, and Compliance: Manfred Balz, age 65,
$1,181,514 total compensation
Member Management Board and Chief Technology and Innovation Officer: Edward R. (Ed) Kozel, age 55
Head Business Customers; CEO, T-Systems:
Reinhard Clemens, age 50,
$2,293,981 total compensation
SEVP Corporate Communications: Philipp Schindera, age 39
SVP Personal and Social Networking; CEO, Scout24:
Martin Enderle
Chief Product and Innovation Officer:
Thomas Kiessling
Chief Human Resources Officer: Thomas Sattelberger, age 61
President and CEO, T-Mobile USA: Philipp Humm, age 50
Auditors: Ernst & Young
Wirtschaftsprüfungsgesellschaft

LOCATIONS

HQ: Deutsche Telekom AG
Friedrich-Ebert-Allee 140
53113 Bonn, Germany
Phone: 49-228-181-0
US HQ: 32 Avenue of the Americas, 20th Fl.
New York, NY 10013
US Phone: 212-658-6200 **US Fax:** 212-658-6250
Web: www.deutschetelekom.com

2009 Sales

	% of total
Europe	
Germany	43
Other countries	32
North America	24
Other countries	1
Total	**100**

PRODUCTS/OPERATIONS

2009 Sales

	% of total
Telecommunications	90
Systems solutions	10
Total	**100**

COMPETITORS

Belgacom
BT
Cable & Wireless
COLT Group
France Telecom
Freenet
HP Enterprise Services
Invitel
KPN
QSC
Swisscom
TDC
Tele Columbus
Tele2
Telecom Italia
Telefónica
Telefónica O2 Germany
Telekom Austria
Telenor
TeliaSonera
United Internet
Versatel
Vodafone
Vodafone D2

HISTORICAL FINANCIALS

Company Type: Public

Income Statement

FYE: December 31

	REVENUE ($ mil.)	NET INCOME ($ mil.)	NET PROFIT MARGIN	EMPLOYEES
12/09	92,588	506	0.5%	259,920
12/08	87,253	2,098	2.4%	234,887
12/07	91,907	837	0.9%	244,000
12/06	81,006	4,179	5.2%	248,000
12/05	70,825	6,636	9.4%	243,695
Annual Growth	**6.9%**	**(47.5%)**	**—**	**1.6%**

2009 Year-End Financials

Debt ratio: 115.0%
Return on equity: 0.9%
Cash ($ mil.): 7,198
Current ratio: 0.93
Long-term debt ($ mil.): 59,908

No. of shares (mil.): 4,361
Dividends
Yield: 5.3%
Payout: 1,018.2%
Market value ($ mil.): 91,878

	STOCK PRICE ($) FY Close	P/E High/Low		PER SHARE ($) Earnings	Dividends	Book Value
12/09	21.07	197	134	0.11	1.12	11.95
12/08	21.57	68	34	0.48	0.87	12.98
12/07	31.90	175	124	0.19	1.06	14.20
12/06	24.01	25	18	0.98	0.91	14.10
12/05	19.69	17	12	1.55	0.73	12.55
Annual Growth	**1.7%**	**—**	**—**	**(48.4%)**	**11.3%**	**(1.2%)**

Diageo plc

Diageo's company parties must be the talk of the town. It is the leading premium spirits business in the world by volume, net sales, and operating profit. The company produces eight of the world's top 20 spirits brands. It is also one of the few international beverage companies that spans the entire alcoholic drinks sector, offering beer, wine, and spirits. Diageo's best-known brands include Smirnoff vodka, Baileys Irish Cream liqueur, Johnnie Walker Scotch whisky, José Cuervo tequila, Tanqueray gin, Captain Morgan rum, Guinness beer, and wines from Sterling Vineyards and Beaulieu Vineyard. While its products are marketed worldwide, its Diageo North America subsidiary generates the most sales (about 40%).

Having a toehold in the premium white spirits sector in China, Diageo upped its stake in ShuiJingFang, China's leading white spirits maker, to 53% in 2010. It intends to use the controlling interest as a platform to grow its share in the largest, most profitable, and fastest growing Chinese spirits sector.

Efforts to expand into emerging Asian markets have been mixed. A deal to acquire 15% of India's market-leading distiller United Spirits fell apart in 2009 when the parties couldn't agree on a price. Later that year, however, Diageo inked a partnership with China-based spirits maker Shui Jing Fang. The companies will work to produce a premium vodka, Shanghai White, in China.

The company has been cultivating its interests in vodka elsewhere, as well. In 2008 Diageo formed a 50-50 joint venture with Dutch vodka maker Ketel One, paying €610 million ($900 million) for its interest.

Signaling an increased interest in liqueurs, Diageo in mid-2010 boosted its ownership in the London Group, which supplies the premium NUVO brand of liqueurs, to 70%.

Pointing to falling prices and demand, Diageo is paring down the operations of Diageo Chateau & Estate Wines, its US wine division. In 2010 the drinks giant announced that it would cut jobs and sell some noncore wine brands, including Barton & Guestier to France's Castel Freres.

In 2000 Lord James Blyth of Rowington stepped down as chairman. He was replaced by Dr. Franz Humer, who previously served as CEO of F. Hoffmann-La Roche.

Although it has operations worldwide, Diageo's principal production facilities are located in the UK, Ireland, Italy, Canada, and the US. It owns wineries in France, Argentina, and the US; it also owns the Gleneagles Resort, a hotel and golf complex located in Scotland. The company owns about 35% of Moët Hennessy, the spirits and wine subsidiary of LVMH.

HISTORY

Diageo — from the Latin word for "day" and the Greek word for "world" — was born from Guinness and GrandMet's 1997 merger to fight flat liquor sales and spirited competitors.

Guinness began business in 1759 when Arthur Guinness leased a small brewery in Dublin, Ireland. Guinness began specializing in porters in 1799. Managed by the third generation of Guinnesses, the company went public as a London-based firm in 1886.

In the 1950s managing director Hugh Beaver was credited with conceiving the *Guinness Book of World Records*. During the 1970s Guinness bought more than 200 companies, with disappointing results. Guinness refocused on brewing and distilling operations in the late 1980s by selling noncore businesses and acquiring firms such as Schenley (Dewar's). In 1988 and 1989 it bought 24% of LVMH Moët Hennessy Louis Vuitton (later exchanged for 34% of LVMH's wine and spirits business). More acquisitions followed in the 1990s, capped by Guinness' 1997 announcement of its $19 billion merger with Grand Metropolitan.

GrandMet was established by Maxwell Joseph. In 1931 he began acquiring properties for resale, but WWII slowed his progress. He started buying hotels in 1946, and by 1961 GrandMet had gone public.

Diversification began in 1970 with the purchases of catering firms, restaurants, and betting shops. In the early 1970s, in what was the largest British takeover up to that time, GrandMet bought brewer Truman Hanburg, followed by Watney Mann, which owned International Distillers & Vintners, makers of Bailey's, Bombay Gin, and J&B.

GrandMet looked overseas through the 1970s, taking over the Liggett Group, a US cigarette maker (sold in 1986) whose Paddington unit was the US distributor of J&B Scotch. In 1987 it bought Heublein (Smirnoff, Lancers, José Cuervo). Two years later it bought The Pillsbury Company (Burger King and Green Giant) in a hostile takeover.

In 1997 Guinness and GrandMet combined, creating Diageo and dividing the companies and brands among four divisions: The Pillsbury Company, Burger King, Guinness, and United Distillers & Vintners.

In 2000 COO Paul Walsh, a former Pillsbury CEO, took over as CEO of both Diageo and its newly combined alcoholic beverage division, Guinness/UDV. Also that year Diageo, along with fellow wine and spirits producer Pernod Ricard, agreed to pay $8.2 billion to Vivendi for the Seagram's drinks business that holds several brands, including Crown Royal, VO Canadian whiskies, and Sterling Vineyards.

In 2001 Diageo sold its Guinness World Records business to media company Gullane Entertainment for $63 million. That year the company also completed its sale of Pillsbury to General Mills. After months of wrangling with the FTC, Diageo finally won regulatory approval for the Seagram's drinks purchase from Vivendi in 2001. The company gained the Crown Royal, and VO Canadian brands through this purchase.

In 2002 Diageo completed the sale of its Malibu rum brand to Allied Domecq for about $796 million. Diageo discontinued marketing its Captain Morgan Gold rum drink in the US later that year because of disappointing sales.

Also in 2002 Diageo sold Burger King for $1.5 billion to a group composed of Texas Pacific Group, Bain Capital, and Goldman Sachs Capital Partners. In 2003 Diageo joined with Heineken to purchase 30% of InBev's Nambia Breweries in southern Africa.

In 2005 Diageo and Heineken formed a partnership for the production and distribution of Guinness in Russia. It also acquired Netherlands distiller Ursus Vodka for an undisclosed amount and added Bushmills Irish whiskey to its stable, with the purchase of the brand from Pernod Ricard for $363 million.

In 2007 the company acquired about a 45% stake in Quanxing, which distills the traditional premium Chinese liquor, baijiu.

EXECUTIVES

Chairman: Franz B. Humer, age 64
CEO and Director: Paul S. Walsh, age 55
CFO and Director: Dierdre Mahlan
Chief Marketing Officer: Andy Fennell, age 43
Chief Customer Officer: Ron Anderson
General Counsel: Timothy D. (Tim) Proctor, age 60
EVP Corporate Relations: Guy L. Smith, age 61
President, Diageo Europe: Andrew Morgan, age 54
President, Diageo Asia-Pacific: Gilbert Ghostine
Global Category Director, Whisk(e)y: David Gates
Global Category Director, Vodka, Gin, and Rums: Edward Pilkington
Managing Director, Global Supply: David Gosnell, age 52
Company Secretary: Paul D. Tunnacliffe, age 48
Director Human Resources: Gareth Williams, age 57
Head Financial Communications: James Crampton
President and CEO, Diageo North America; Chairman, Asia Pacific: Ivan M. Menezes, age 51
President, Diageo International: Stuart R. Fletcher, age 53
President, Diageo USA: Larry Schwartz
Auditors: KPMG Audit Plc

LOCATIONS

HQ: Diageo plc
8 Henrietta Place
London W1G 0NB, United Kingdom
Phone: 44-20-7927-5200   **Fax:** 44-20-7927-4600
US HQ: 801 Main Ave., Norwalk, CT 06851
US Phone: 203-229-2100   **US Fax:** 203-229-8901
Web: www.diageo.com

2010 Sales

	% of total
North America	34
Europe	28
Asia/Pacific	11
Other	27
Total	**100**

PRODUCTS/OPERATIONS

2010 Sales

	% of total
Scotch	27
Beer	22
Vodka	11
Ready-to-drink	8
Rum	6
Whiskey	6
Wine	6
Liqueur	5
Gin	3
Tequila	3
Other	3
Total	**100**

Selected Brands

Global priority brands
  Baileys Original Irish Cream liqueur
  Captain Morgan rum
  Guinness stout
  J & B scotch whiskey
  Johnnie Walker scotch whiskies
  José Cuervo tequila
  Smirnoff ready-to-drink products
  Smirnoff vodka
  Tanqueray gin
Other beer
  Harp lager
  Malta Guinness non-alcoholic malt
  Red Stripe lager
  Smithwick's ale
  Tusker lager
Other spirits
  Bell's Extra Special whiskey
  Buchanan's De Luxe whiskey
  Bundaberg rum Cacique rum
  Bushmills Irish whiskey
  Crown Royal Canadian whiskey
  Gordon's gin and vodka
  Ketel One vodka
  Old Parr whiskey
  Seagram's whiskey
  Windsor Premier whiskey
Wine
  Beaulieu Vineyard
  Blossom Hill
  Chalone Vineyard
  Piat d'Or
  Rosenblum Cellars
  Sterling Vineyards

COMPETITORS

Angostura	Grupo Modelo
Anheuser-Busch	Heaven Hill Distilleries
Anheuser-Busch InBev	Heineken
Asahi Breweries	Kirin Holdings Company
Asia Pacific Breweries	Lion Nathan
Bacardi	Martini & Rossi
Bavaria S.A.	Maxxium
Beam Global Spirits &	Molson Coors UK
Wine	Paramount Distillers
Blavod	Pernod Ricard
Brown-Forman	Quinsa
Cabo Wabo	Rémy Cointreau
Campari	SABMiller
Carlsberg A/S	Sapporo
Cervecerías Unidas	Sidney Frank Importing
Constellation Brands	Skyy
E. & J. Gallo	The Trump Organization
FEMSA	Tsingtao
Foster's Group	Yuengling & Son

HISTORICAL FINANCIALS

Company Type: Public

Income Statement

FYE: June 30

	REVENUE ($ mil.)	NET INCOME ($ mil.)	NET PROFIT MARGIN	EMPLOYEES
6/10	14,736	2,626	17.8%	23,287
6/09	15,378	2,849	18.5%	24,270
6/08	16,162	3,191	19.7%	24,373
6/07	15,000	2,985	19.9%	22,520
6/06	13,176	3,463	26.3%	22,619
Annual Growth	**2.8%**	**(6.7%)**	**—**	**0.7%**

2010 Year-End Financials

Debt ratio: 204.1%
Return on equity: 46.2%
Cash ($ mil.): 2,189
Current ratio: 1.76
Long-term debt ($ mil.): 12,320

No. of shares (mil.): 626
Dividends
  Yield: 2.4%
  Payout: 56.9%
Market value ($ mil.): 59,212

Stock History

NYSE: DEO

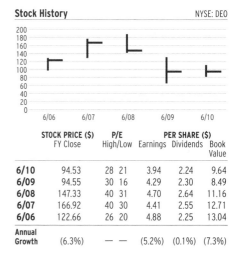

	STOCK PRICE ($) FY Close	P/E High/Low		PER SHARE ($) Earnings	Dividends	Book Value
6/10	94.53	28	21	3.94	2.24	9.64
6/09	94.55	30	16	4.29	2.30	8.49
6/08	147.33	40	31	4.70	2.64	11.16
6/07	166.92	40	30	4.41	2.55	12.71
6/06	122.66	26	20	4.88	2.25	13.04
Annual Growth	**(6.3%)**	**—**	**—**	**(5.2%)**	**(0.1%)**	**(7.3%)**

EADS N.V.

European Aeronautic Defence and Space Company (EADS) is an international marriage of moguls: Daimler Aerospace (DASA, Germany), Aerospatiale Matra (France), and Construcciones Aeronáuticas SA (CASA, Spain). The group is Europe's largest supplier of aerospace, defense and related services. On the global stage it rivals Boeing. EADS' largest holding is Airbus; it ranks among the top two makers of large commercial aircraft, and with Airbus Military, manufactures tankers, and transport and mission aircraft. Other operations launch Eurocopter's helicopters, Astrium's satellites, Arianespace's commercial satellite launchers, and Defense & Security's business and military defense jets.

In its race to be the world's #1 commercial plane manufacturer, EADS has aimed for more aggressive Airbus sales by ramping up production. Its strategy took a hit in lower profit margins but drew higher sales.

Contributing about two-thirds of the company's business, Airbus lends a powerful brand synonymous for making commercial aircraft. Its A320 family includes single-aisle aircraft; staggering sales worldwide make this the top selling commercial jetliner. Airbus A330/A340 twin-aisle jets include tankers that cater to markets wanting a plane that can lift more passengers/cargo and go farther.

EADS' Eurocopter operation reins in more than 50% of the civil and public/private enterprise helicopter market's sales. Number one in this marketplace, the group's choppers, including a growing military share, account for 30% of the world's total helicopter fleet. This segment experienced a market downturn for smaller, commercial helicopters; the company responded by implementing a restructuring program, which included cutting costs, reducing inventories, and boosting technology, to help the civil helicopter business weather the crisis.

The Astrium space group supplies satellites, launchers, and space services to Europe's institutional and military space programs. Astrium has driven the design and development of high-profile projects such as Galileo, the European satellite navigation system, and the International Space Station's Columbus space laboratory and unmanned Automated Transfer Vehicle.

Its second largest unit is its Defense & Security Division, which leads EADS' armed forces and civil security operations. Its activities range broadly from producing the Eurofighter (combat aircraft) to missile systems, defense communication systems, and electronics. Its MBDA subsidiary is recognized as the world's largest missile company. US contracts are on this unit's wish list, but the company is eyeing India in particular as a prime target for expansion.

The company won its first big US military contract in 2008 when Airbus North America was tapped to make US Army light utility helicopters.

EADS strengthened its position in the Japanese marketplace in mid-2009 when it established a new subsidiary to drive regional marketing and industrial and aerospace alliances.

Daimler AG owns about 22.5% of EADS. SOGEPA (a French state holding company) and France-based Lagardère SCA together own approximately 22.5%. Spain owns 5%.

HISTORY

The growth of the European Aeronautic Defence and Space Company — EADS — is overshadowed by the long history of its components and by the obstacles overcome to cement the deal: The French and the Germans historically aren't overly fond of each other, so how did it come to pass that Germany's Daimler Aerospace and France's Aerospatiale Matra put aside their differences to band together with Spain's Construcciones Aeronáuticas SA (CASA)?

The US aerospace sector in the 1990s saw many companies consolidate, scrambling to make their way in the post-Cold War era. Boeing, the largest aerospace company in the world, got that way by acquiring a slew of operations, including Rockwell International's aerospace and defense operations (1995), and most importantly, McDonnell Douglas in a $16 billion deal (1997). In the same era, defense giant Lockheed merged with Martin Marietta (1995) and acquired Loral (1997). These US companies had it relatively easy — they all paid taxes to Uncle Sam, but acquisition deals in Europe were stymied by concerns over national security and privatization because much of Europe's defense industry was government-owned.

Spurred into action by their US rivals, in 1997 DASA and British Aerospace (now BAE SYSTEMS) — partners in Airbus — began merger talks. Fearful of being left out in the cold, France's

government-owned Aerospatiale — another Airbus partner — began talks to merge with Matra, a French defense company controlled by Lagardère. Weeks after the Aerospatiale-Matra deal was announced in 1998, the chairman of DASA's parent company, Jürgen Schrempp, met with Lagardère's CEO, Jean-Luc Lagardère, and proposed a three-way deal. It never occurred and in 1999 the BAE SYSTEMS and DASA deal fell through as well.

Later that year Schrempp and Lagardère met again and laid the groundwork for a merger between DASA and Aerospatiale Matra. Less than three weeks after the Aerospatiale-Matra merger was completed, Lagardère found himself pitching the DASA/Aerospatiale Matra merger idea to a stunned French government (which still held a 48% stake in Aerospatiale Matra). Marathon negotiations ensued. Late in the year Spain's Construcciones Aeronáuticas SA (CASA) agreed to become part of EADS.

In 2000 EADS went public. The next year EADS began pushing for a consolidation of army and naval equipment manufacturing among EU countries similar to the aerospace consolidation that created EADS. For Airbus, the long-sought switch from consortium to corporation finally occurred in July 2001 when Airbus S.A.S. was incorporated.

EADS bought out BAE SYSTEMS' 25% share in their Astrium joint venture in 2003. In 2004 EADS agreed to acquire US defense electronics maker Racal Instruments as part of its plan to increase defense sales in the US.

Also in 2004 EADS and BAE SYSTEMS gave Airbus the green-light to build the A350, a plane that competes directly with Boeing's upcoming 787 Dreamliner. In 2005 EADS was given preferred bidder status for the UK's Royal Air Force aerial refueling tanker contract. The program is expected to be worth about $25 billion.

In 2006 Daimler announced plans to gradually reduce its stake in EADS from about 30% to about half that amount. Russian bank Vneshtorgbank (100% controlled by the Russian government) also purchased a 5% stake in EADS for about $1.17 billion. The move was expected to strengthen cooperation between EADS and the re-emerging Russian aerospace industry.

EXECUTIVES

Chairman: Bodo Uebber, age 50
CEO and Director: Louis Gallois, age 66
CFO: Hans Peter Ring, age 59
CTO: Jean J. Botti, age 53
Chief Compliance Officer: Pedro Montoya, age 46
Chief Strategy and Marketing Officer: Marwan Lahoud, age 44
Head Corporate Media Relations: Alexander Reinhardt
Head Corporate Communications: Pierre Bayle
Head Investor Relations: Nathalie Errard
Head Airbus Military: Domingo Ureña-Raso, age 52
Head Human Resources: Jussi Itävuori, age 54
Chairman, North America: Ralph D. Crosby Jr., age 63
President, EADS Japan: Vincent Larnicol
President and CEO, Airbus: Thomas (Tom) Enders, age 51
President and CEO, Eurocopter: Lutz Bertling, age 48
CEO, EADS Astrium: François Auque, age 54
CEO, North America: Sean C. O'Keefe, age 54
CEO, Defence and Security Systems Division: Stefan Zoller, age 53
Auditors: KPMG Accountants N.V.

LOCATIONS

HQ: European Aeronautic Defence and Space Company EADS N.V.
Mendelweg 30
2333 CS Leiden, The Netherlands
Phone: 31-20-655-4800
Web: www.eads-nv.com

2009 Sales

	% of total
Europe	50
Asia/Pacific	20
The Americas	19
Middle East	9
Other	2
Total	**100**

PRODUCTS/OPERATIONS

2009 Sales

	% of total
Airbus	64
Defence & Security	12
Astrium	11
Eurocopter	10
Other	3
Total	**100**

Selected Operations and Interests

Business aircraft (Dassault Aviation, 46%)
Commercial airplanes (Airbus)
Helicopters (Eurocopter SAS)
Jet fighters (Dassault Aviation, 46%; Eurofighter, 43%)
Missile systems (MBDA, 38%)
Satellites (Astrium)

COMPETITORS

AgustaWestland
BAE SYSTEMS
BAE Systems Inc.
Boeing
Bombardier
E'Prime Aerospace
GenCorp
Lockheed Martin
Northrop Grumman
Orbital Sciences
Raytheon
RUAG Holding
Textron

HISTORICAL FINANCIALS

Company Type: Public

Income Statement

				FYE: December 31
	REVENUE ($ mil.)	NET INCOME ($ mil.)	NET PROFIT MARGIN	EMPLOYEES
12/09	61,373	(1,078)	—	119,506
12/08	60,982	2,251	3.7%	118,349
12/07	57,585	(643)	—	116,493
12/06	52,025	152	0.3%	116,805
12/05	40,510	2,025	5.0%	113,210
Annual Growth	**10.9%**	**—**	**—**	**1.4%**

2009 Year-End Financials

Debt ratio: —	No. of shares (mil.): 811
Return on equity: —	Dividends
Cash ($ mil.): 10,087	Yield: 1.4%
Current ratio: 1.00	Payout: —
Long-term debt ($ mil.): —	Market value ($ mil.): 16,363

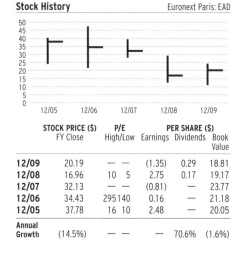

	STOCK PRICE ($) FY Close	P/E High/Low	PER SHARE ($) Earnings	Dividends	Book Value
12/09	20.19	— —	(1.35)	0.29	18.81
12/08	16.96	10 5	2.75	0.17	19.17
12/07	32.13	— —	(0.81)	—	23.77
12/06	34.43	295 140	0.16	—	21.18
12/05	37.78	16 10	2.48	—	20.05
Annual Growth	(14.5%)	— —	—	70.6%	(1.6%)

Electricité de France

While France has been slow to open its own doors to competition in the utilities industry, state-owned Electricité de France (EDF) has been quick to expand into global deregulated markets. One of the world's top electric utilities (as well as one of the last major state-controlled energy giants in Europe), EDF has a generating capacity of more than 127,100 MW (primarily from nuclear energy sources) and provides power to 28 million French customers and 10 million customers in other countries (primarily in Europe). The company operates power plants in Europe, Africa, the Americas, Asia, and the Middle East. The French government owns 85% of the company.

EDF is investing aggressively abroad, and is banking on a global revival in the use of nuclear energy for power plants. In a move to boost its position as both a major energy and a nuclear power player in Europe, in 2009 EDF acquired British Energy, with its 1.1 million customer accounts, for about $18 billion. Expanding its presence and its position as a nuclear power provider in the US, in 2009 EDF unit EDF Development acquired 49.99% of Constellation Energy's Constellation Energy Nuclear Group, LLC, for $4.5 billion.

To help pay down debt EDF put its three UK distribution grids up for sale. Hong Kong's Cheung Kong Infrastructure and Hongkong Electric, both controlled by Hong Kong-based billionaire Li Ka-shing, made an offer in 2010 to acquire the grids for about $9 billion.

Nuclear plants provide more than 86% of EDF's domestic power supply; other sources include hydroelectric and fossil-fueled plants. Making use of its extensive experience, especially in developing nuclear power, EDF builds power plants and provides plant management and consulting services worldwide.

Subsidiary EDF Trading markets electricity, natural gas, coal, and oil throughout Europe. The company's 34%-owned Dalkia unit (Veolia Environnement — formerly Vivendi Environnement — owns 66%) offers energy management and industrial services.

EDF is auctioning off capacity rights to some of its domestic generation facilities to comply with EU regulations; it is also working to create partnerships with other European utilities (including Enel and Electrabel) to allow more access to the French market.

The company is also developing renewable energy facilities. Not to be left out in the competitive renewable energy market, EDF is seeking to boost its wind and solar energy output from a few hundred MW in 2008 to 4,000 MW by 2012.

HISTORY

The French government nationalized hundreds of regional private firms to form Electricité de France (EDF) in 1946 as part of an effort to rebuild the nation's badly shaken post-war economy. This was a marked difference from the notoriously complex and inefficient pre-war electrical industry.

By the 1950s EDF had taken advantage of the centralized control and developed massive hydroelectric projects. Hydroelectric power would account for more than 70% of EDF's power.

But in France as elsewhere, hydro wasn't enough to keep up with the growing demand for electricity, and fossil fuels became an increasingly important power source. Then came the oil shortages of the 1970s, and France — with limited domestic supplies of oil and gas — began searching for alternatives to fossil-fueled plants. Nuclear power was determined to be the answer.

The government moved to invest billions of dollars in developing its relatively small nuclear power production facilities. Muddled with Malthusian predictions of power shortages and a preoccupation with having enough energy to be self-reliant, France found its nuclear operations left the government with more energy than it could use and more debt than it wanted. The company began to build a cable connecting the Continent to the UK in 1981. With the power grids of the two countries connected in 1986, EDF was finally able to start exporting its power to the Brits.

The 1990s brought with them deregulation. EDF fought to keep the UK-France grid closed to other energy sellers. After the government forbade the utility from diversifying into areas other than electricity in 1995, the company turned its attention to foreign investment, especially in Latin America.

The company faced increasing deregulatory pressures from without in the late 1990s. The newly formed European Union required open competition from member states. Begrudgingly and behind schedule, EDF opened about 30% of its market to competition in 2000.

Other members of the EU complained that EDF was trying to play it both ways: It was making aggressive acquisitions in the UK liberalized market (it bought London Electricity in 1999), while resisting a competition-enabling breakup or even allowing a foreign competitor to buy a stake in the French market.

EDF in 2001 expanded its stake in Italy's Montedison, a conglomerate with substantial energy holdings, by forming a consortium (Italenergia) with Italian automaker Fiat and some Italian banks to wrest control of Montedison from Italian bank MEDIOBANCA. Although the consortium owns 94% of Montedison, EDF has only 2% of voting rights. (Montedison changed its name to Edison in 2002.)

EDF also purchased a 35% interest in German utility Energie Baden-Württemberg in 2001, and it merged its energy services unit with Dalkia, a unit of Vivendi Environnement (now Veolia Environnement), taking a 34% stake in Dalkia (which will eventually be increased to 50%). EDF subsidiary London Electricity agreed to buy $2.4 billion in UK assets from TXU Europe that year, including a 2,000 MW power plant, TXU's Eastern Electricity distribution unit, and its interest in TXU/EDF joint venture 24seven; the deals were completed in 2001 and 2002.

In 2002 EDF increased its stake in Brazilian utility Light Serviços de Eletricidade to 88% by swapping Light's interest in Sao Paulo utility Eletropaulo for AES's 24% interest in Light. Later that year EDF purchased UK electric and gas utility SEEBOARD (1.9 million customers) from US utility AEP in a $2.2 billion deal.

Deregulation of 70% of the French market took effect in July 2004. Between 2000 and 2004, only 30% of the market was deregulated, just more than the percentage required by European Union (EU) rulings.

EDF acquired Edison SpA (Italy's second-largest power group) in partnership with Italian utility company AEM SpA in 2005 for an estimated $15.4 billion.

EXECUTIVES

Chairman and CEO: Henri Proglio, age 61
CFO: Daniel Camus, age 57
SEVP Strategy and Coordination: Philippe V. Huet
SEVP Customers: Jean-Pierre Benqué, age 57
SEVP Customers: Pierre Lederer, age 61
Chief Human Resources and Communication Officer: Dominique Lagarde
Corporate Secretary: Marianne Lagneau, age 45
Chairman and CEO, Edison S.p.A.: Umberto Quadrino, age 64
CEO, EnBW: Hans-Peter Villis, age 52
CEO, EDF Energy: Vincent de Rivaz, age 53
COO, Integration and Deregulated Operations: Jean-Louis Mathias, age 63
Auditors: KPMG Audit

LOCATIONS

HQ: Electricité de France
22-30, avenue de Wagram
75008 Paris, France
Phone: 33-1-40-42-22-22   **Fax:** 33-1-40-42-79-40
Web: www.edf.fr

2009 Sales

	% of total
Europe	
France	51
UK	17
Germany	11
Italy	7
Other countries	5
Other	9
Total	**100**

COMPETITORS

Business Group Benelux
Centrica
ELETROBRÁS
Endesa S.A.
Enel
Energias de Portugal
E.ON
GDF SUEZ
Hydro-Québec
IBERDROLA
International Power
RWE
Scottish and Southern Energy
Vattenfall
Veolia Environnement

HISTORICAL FINANCIALS

Company Type: Public

Income Statement

FYE: December 31

	REVENUE ($ mil.)	NET INCOME ($ mil.)	NET PROFIT MARGIN	EMPLOYEES
12/09	95,073	5,859	6.2%	164,250
12/08	90,601	4,983	5.5%	104,929
12/07	87,780	8,527	9.7%	158,640
12/06	77,749	7,622	9.8%	156,524
12/05	60,460	3,967	6.6%	161,560
Annual Growth	12.0%	10.2%	—	0.4%

2009 Year-End Financials

Debt ratio: —
Return on equity: 14.8%
Cash ($ mil.): 10,007
Current ratio: 1.03
Long-term debt ($ mil.): —

No. of shares (mil.): 1,849
Dividends
Yield: 2.9%
Payout: 55.7%
Market value ($ mil.): 110,126

Stock History

Euronext Paris: EDF

	STOCK PRICE ($) FY Close	P/E High/Low		PER SHARE ($) Earnings	Dividends	Book Value
12/09	59.56	21	12	3.07	1.71	25.37
12/08	58.49	45	19	2.64	1.89	17.58
12/07	119.93	28	17	4.53	—	21.66
12/06	72.83	19	10	4.05	—	16.63
12/05	37.87	17	16	2.33	—	12.27
Annual Growth	12.0%	—	—	7.1%	(9.5%)	19.9%

AB Electrolux

AB Electrolux has a hunting license for dust bunnies. The firm, a top maker of household appliances worldwide, operates through two segments: consumer durables (residential kitchen, fabric care, and cleaning) and professional products (industrial kitchens, restaurants, and laundries). It cranks out washing machines, stoves, refrigerators, and freezers under the AEG, Electrolux, Eureka, Frigidaire, and Zanussi names. It's also the #1 maker globally of vacuum cleaners (Electrolux, Eureka brands). Electrolux's presence in the commercial market has it making foodservice and laundry equipment under the Electrolux and Zanussi labels.

In 2011 current COO Keith McLoughlin will succeed CEO Hans Straberg. Previously head of Electrolux Major Appliances North America, McLoughlin brings with him expertise in R&D, manufacturing, and purchasing, as well as 20 years of experience at DuPont.

The company boasts a global reach, as Electrolux's products are sold in more than 150 markets. Its largest markets are Europe and North America. Looking beyond established markets to emerging markets in Central and Eastern Europe, the company has agreed to acquire a washing machine factory in Ukraine. Turning to another lucrative emerging market, it also agreed to acquire 52% of the Egyptian company Olympic Group in 2010. Olympic is the largest manufacturer of washing machines, refrigerators, and cookers (stoves) in the Middle East and North Africa.

Its breadth has made Electrolux a behemoth in the household appliances industry. Electrolux sells some 40 million products worldwide; nearly half of them were sold under its namesake brand.

With declining housing starts in the US and retailers struggling to lure shoppers to buy products, Electrolux has seen the US market stagnate. Tax incentives to entice US consumers to purchase energy efficient large appliances helped to offset sales declines. With 60% of Electrolux's appliances in the US being sold by roughly four big box retailers (Lowe's, Sears, Home Depot, and Best Buy), it may be some time before the company realizes gains again in North America.

Meanwhile, Electrolux is keeping a close eye on its operations to ensure it maintains its top spot. Citing production costs, Electrolux closed its Swedish factory (moving manufacturing to Hungary), as well as some operations in France and in the US in Michigan and Texas. The company eventually relocated many of its North American and European plants to Asia, Mexico, and Eastern Europe and divested its Indian operations. And, to boot, Electrolux laid off some 3,000 employees worldwide in 2009.

Through Investor AB — which also has stakes in Saab and other multinational companies — the Wallenberg family controls about 26% of Electrolux's voting power.

HISTORY

Swedish salesman Axel Wenner-Gren saw an American-made vacuum cleaner in a Vienna, Austria, store window in 1910 and envisioned selling the cleaners door-to-door, a technique he had learned in the US. Two years later he worked with fledgling Swedish vacuum cleaner makers AB Lux and Elektromekaniska to improve their existing designs. The two companies merged to form AB Electrolux in 1919. When the board of the new company balked at Wenner-Gren's suggestion to mass-produce vacuum cleaners, he guaranteed Electrolux's sales through his own sales company.

In the 1920s the company used the "Every home — an Electrolux home" slogan as Wenner-Gren drove his sales force on and launched new sales companies in Europe and North and South America. He scored a publicity coup by securing the blessing of Pope Pius XI to vacuum the Vatican, gratis, for a year. By the end of the 1920s, Electrolux had purchased most of Wenner-Gren's sales companies (excluding Electrolux US) and had gambled on refrigerator technology and won. By buying vacuum cleaner maker Volta (Sweden, 1934), it gained retail distribution.

Despite the loss of Eastern European subsidiaries during WWII, the company did well until the 1960s, when it backed an unpopular refrigeration technology. Swedish electrical equipment giant ASEA, controlled by Marcus Wallenberg, bought a large stake in Electrolux in 1964, and in 1967 he installed Hans Werthén as chairman. Werthén slashed overhead and sold the company's minority stake in Electrolux US to Consolidated Foods. (The US Electrolux business was taken private in 1987.)

Since 1970 Electrolux has bought more than 300 companies (many of them troubled appliance makers), updated their plants, and gained global component manufacturing efficiencies. Acquisitions included National Union Electric (Eureka vacuum cleaners, US, 1974), Tappan (appliances, US, 1979), Zanussi (appliances, industrial products; Italy; 1984), White Consolidated Industries (appliances, industrial products; US; 1986), and Lehel (refrigerators, Hungary, 1991). By 1996 the company had acquired a 41% interest in Refrigeração Paraná, Brazil's #2 manufacturer of appliances. (Electrolux owned it all by 1998.)

To better focus on its "white goods" (washers, refrigerators, etc.), in 1996 Electrolux began selling noncore businesses. In 1997, under new CEO Michael "Mike the Knife" Treschow, the company launched a restructuring plan involving the closing of about 25 plants and the elimination of more than 12,000 jobs, mostly in Europe. The plan worked: Electrolux's profits more than quadrupled in 1998.

Electrolux acquired the European operations of chainsaw maker McCulloch in 1999. To strengthen its Asian presence, Electrolux teamed up with Toshiba for future collaboration on household appliances. Also that year the company said it would sell its vending machine unit and professional refrigeration business.

In 2002 Electrolux CEO Michael Treschow resigned (but remained as a director) and was replaced by board member Hans Stråberg.

As part of a restructuring to combat the effects of diminishing consumer demand and higher material costs, Electrolux cut nearly 5,000 jobs (about 6% of its workforce) during 2003.

Electrolux relaunched its flagship brand of vacuum cleaners in North America during 2004, having bought the rights from long-unaffiliated vacuum maker Electrolux LLC (now Aerus). Also that year former CEO Michael Treschow reappeared in a leadership position, assuming the role of chairman. Treschow left the company again in 2007.

The firm exited its outdoor segment, which consisted of chainsaws and lawn and garden equipment and diamond tools through a spinoff in 2006.

EXECUTIVES

Chairman: Marcus Wallenberg, age 54
Deputy Chairman: Peggy Bruzelius, age 60
President, CEO, and Director: Hans Stråberg, age 53
CFO: Jonas Samuelson, age 42
EVP and Head Professional Products: Alberto Zanata, age 50
EVP and Head of Electrolux Major Appliances, Europe: Enderson Guimaraes, age 50
EVP and Head Floor Care and Small Appliances: Morten Falkenburg
EVP; Head, Major Appliances, Latin America: Ruy Hirschheimer, age 61
EVP, Head Research and Development, Purchasing and Manufacturing, Major Appliances: Keith R. McLoughlin, age 54
EVP; Head, Electrolux Major Appliances Asia/Pacific: Gunilla Nordström, age 51
EVP; President and CEO Major Appliances, North America: Kevin Scott
SVP and General Counsel: Cecilia Vieweg, age 54
SVP Corporate Communications and Head Group Staff Communications: Anders Edholm
SVP Group Staff Human Resources and Organizational Development, Electrolux Group: Carina Malmgren Heander
VP Investor Relations and Financial Information: Peter Nyquist
Auditors: PricewaterhouseCoopers AB

LOCATIONS

HQ: AB Electrolux
S:t Göransgatan 143
S 105 45 Stockholm, Sweden
Phone: 46-8-738-60-00 **Fax:** 46-8-656-7461
Web: www.electrolux.com

PRODUCTS/OPERATIONS

2009 Sales

	% of total
Consumer durables	93
Professional products	7
Total	**100**

Selected Products and Brands

Consumer durables
  Core A
  Floorcare products
Professional products
  Foodservice equipment
  Laundry equipment

COMPETITORS

Ali SpA	Indesit
BISSELL	LG Electronics
BSH Bosch und Siemens	Miele
Fisher & Paykel Appliances	Philips Electronics
Franke Group	Royal Appliance
GE Appliances & Lighting	Samsung Group
Gree Electrical Appliances	SEB
Haier Group	Whirlpool
Hobart Corp.	WinWholesale

HISTORICAL FINANCIALS

Company Type: Public

Income Statement
FYE: December 31

	REVENUE ($ mil.)	NET INCOME ($ mil.)	NET PROFIT MARGIN	EMPLOYEES
12/09	15,180	363	2.4%	50,633
12/08	13,497	47	0.3%	56,000
12/07	16,359	457	2.8%	56,896
12/06	15,151	561	3.7%	55,471
12/05	16,261	221	1.4%	69,523
Annual Growth	(1.7%)	13.1%	—	(7.6%)

2009 Year-End Financials

Debt ratio: 54.4%
Return on equity: 15.3%
Cash ($ mil.): 1,327
Current ratio: 1.34
Long-term debt ($ mil.): 1,425

No. of shares (mil.): 309
Dividends
  Yield: —
  Payout: —
Market value ($ mil.): 7,198

Stock History
Pink Sheets: ELUXY

	STOCK PRICE ($) FY Close	P/E High	P/E Low	PER SHARE ($) Earnings	PER SHARE ($) Dividends	PER SHARE ($) Book Value
12/09	23.30	20	6	1.27	—	8.48
12/08	8.60	83	40	0.17	—	6.83
12/07	16.95	18	10	1.61	—	8.11
12/06	19.99	18	7	1.94	—	6.23
12/05	25.94	35	23	0.75	—	10.53
Annual Growth	(2.6%)	—	—	14.1%	—	(5.2%)

Endesa, S.A.

Endesa provides power to more than 24 million customers in 11 countries (50% Spanish customers) on three continents. A subsidiary of Italian power giant Enel, Endesa is Spain's #1 electric utility and has a generating capacity of 39,700 MW from nuclear, fossil-fueled, hydroelectric, and renewable energy plants. Endesa is the primary electricity company in Chile, Argentina, Colombia and Peru and also operates in Brazil. It is a major player in the Mediterranean region, especially Italy, and is active in other countries. Endesa serves more than 397,200 natural gas customers in Spain. The company is also investing heavily in renewable energy to meet Spain's commitment to greenhouse gas reduction.

In 2009 Endesa had a generating capacity of more than 3,700 MW of wind power, or about 10% of the Spanish wind power market. In another major move to promote renewable energy, in 2010 the company agreed to develop about 550 recharging locations in Barcelona, Madrid, and Seville to power electric cars.

The company found itself the target of takeover bids by other European power companies seeking to bulk up in the wake of the deregulation of the European power and gas markets. In 2007 E.ON and Gas Natural made bids of $47-plus billion and $26-plus billion, respectively, for Endesa. That year Enel and Acciona jumped into the fray, buying about 70% and 25% of the company, respectively, when Gas Natural dropped out of the bidding. E.ON dropped out in 2008 in return for buying some power plants and shareholdings in Italy, Spain, and France from Endesa. In 2009 Enel bought Acciona's stake.

Formerly a state-owned firm, Endesa branched out into new territories to prepare for the deregulation of Spain's electric utility market, which took full effect in 2003.

HISTORY

When dictator Francisco Franco set about rebuilding Spain after the Civil War, Empresa Nacional de Electricidad (Endesa) was formed in 1944 under the state-run Instituto Nacional de Industria (INI). The nation's lack of power facilities sparked the company into building hydroelectric plants. In the 1950s the US, fighting the Cold War, financed Spain's industrial boom, which Endesa aided by building coal-fired plants, including Compostilla (on line in 1961).

When inflation plagued Spain in the late 1950s, the government cut off INI's funding. INI and its companies then borrowed heavily from banks. Spain then passed the Stabilization Act in 1959 to make INI companies self-financing, though they were still government-owned. In the 1960s many of Spain's rural areas were undeveloped, so the government instituted and funded a plan to build power infrastructure.

In 1972 Endesa acquired the As Pontel and Teruel facilities, where it began constructing fossil fuel plants. However, the energy crisis of the early 1970s kept the plants from operating until 1976 and 1979, respectively.

After Franco's death in 1975, King Juan Carlos moved Spain into Europe's free market union. In preparation for the liberalization of the energy markets, INI and Endesa reorganized in 1983 and shifted INI's holdings in regional electric utilities (Eneco, Enher, Gesa, and Unelco) to Endesa.

After the government halted its nuclear power program in 1984, many private electric companies were left with bad investments. Endesa was brought in to bail them out by taking over power plants; to repay Endesa, they were forced to buy Endesa's electricity. The 1985 asset swaps also brought regional power companies Erz and Fecsa into Endesa's grasp.

In 1986 Spain joined the European Community; two years later the government sold 20% of Endesa to the public. In the early 1990s Endesa went into coal production when it purchased ENCASUR (1990), and it continued buying interests in private power companies, including Viesgo and Sevillana.

The government floated more of the company in 1997, and the utility became Endesa, S.A. Its eye on Latin American opportunity, Endesa bought a 29% stake in Chile's largest power company, Enersis. It also branched into telecommunications by grabbing a small stake in Retevisión.

Endesa was fully privatized in 1998, the year Spain's deregulation process began. The next year Endesa paid some $2.6 billion to buy the outstanding shares of its regional units and merge them into the company, as part of its larger effort to reorganize and cut its costs and workforce. Endesa also increased its stake in Enersis to more than 60%.

In 2000 Endesa began restructuring its regional electric utilities into separate generation and distribution units. Also that year, Endesa, Telecom Italia, and Unión Fenosa combined their Spanish telecom holdings to form the Auna joint venture. (Telecom Italia later sold its stake to Santander Central Hispano.) Endesa also agreed to acquire rival Spanish utility Iberdrola, but the companies cancelled the transaction in 2001.

In 2001 Endesa completed the purchase of a 30% interest in French generation company SNET. The company also acquired one of Italian utility Enel's power production units (Elettrogen). Endesa sold its New Viesgo unit (a spinoff composed of regional electric utility Electra de Viesgo, which served 500,000 customers and had 2,400 MW of generation assets) to Enel in 2002.

In 2005 Endesa sold its major stake in Auna to France Telecom.

EXECUTIVES

Chairman: Borja Prado Eulate, age 54
CEO and Director: Rafael Miranda Robredo, age 61
Director and Deputy CEO: Esteban Morrás Andrés
EVP, Latin America, General Management Electricity Business: Pedro Larrea Paguaga
CFO and SVP: Paolo Bondi
SVP Legal: Francisco de Borja Acha Besga
SVP Human Resources: Germán Medina Carrillo
SVP Corporate Services: Antonio Pareja Molina
General Manager Purchasing: Francesco Buresti
General Manager, Spain and Portugal:
  José Damián Bogas Gálvez
Auditors: Deloitte SL

LOCATIONS

HQ: Endesa, S.A.
  Ribera del Loira, 60
  28042 Madrid, Spain
Phone: 34-91-213-1000 **Fax:** 34-91-563-8181
US HQ: 410 Park Ave., Ste. 410, New York, NY 10022
US Phone: 212-750-7200 **US Fax:** 212-750-7433
Web: www.endesa.es

2009 Sales

	% of total
Spain & Portugal	68
Latin America	32
Total	**100**

COMPETITORS

AES	International Power
Business Group Benelux	PPL Corporation
Edison	Red Eléctrica de España
Electricité de France	RWE
Energias de Portugal	Sempra Energy
E.ON	Telefónica
Gas Natural SDG	Tractebel Engineering
HC Energía	Vattenfall
IBERDROLA	

HISTORICAL FINANCIALS

Company Type: Public

Income Statement

FYE: December 31

	REVENUE ($ mil.)	NET INCOME ($ mil.)	NET PROFIT MARGIN	EMPLOYEES
12/09	35,017	6,249	17.8%	26,305
12/08	30,626	11,431	37.3%	27,581
12/07	25,248	5,127	20.3%	—
12/06	27,151	5,011	18.5%	—
Annual Growth	8.9%	7.6%	—	(4.6%)

2009 Year-End Financials

Debt ratio: —	No. of shares (mil.): 1,059
Return on equity: 24.4%	Dividends
Cash ($ mil.): 2,634	Yield: 26.3%
Current ratio: 1.01	Payout: 194.6%
Long-term debt ($ mil.): —	Market value ($ mil.): 36,334

Stock History

Pink Sheets: ELEYY

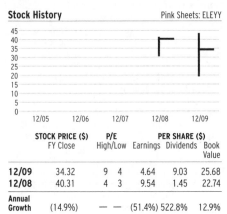

	STOCK PRICE ($) FY Close	P/E High/Low		PER SHARE ($) Earnings	Dividends	Book Value
12/09	34.32	9	4	4.64	9.03	25.68
12/08	40.31	4	3	9.54	1.45	22.74
Annual Growth	(14.9%)	—	—	(51.4%)	522.8%	12.9%

Enel S.p.A.

Arrivederci, monopolio! Buongiorno, diversified energy player. Italy's largest electric utility, Enel, has given up its monopoly status and raced into the deregulated global power marketplace. Enel distributes electricity and gas to about 61 million customers in more than 20 countries and has more than 96,000 MW of primarily fossil-fueled and hydroelectric generating capacity. The second largest gas distributor in Italy (after Italgas), Enel serves 2.7 million customers in Italy. It also has renewable and international power generation assets. The Italian government owns about a third of Enel.

Enel hasn't just been sipping cappuccino while competitors rush in: The company has moved to become a global multi-utility. Internationally, Enel has built and acquired independent power plants, primarily in Europe and the Americas.

The company has also divested noncore assets, including some real estate holdings and most of its water distribution operations, to focus on its energy operations, particularly on building up its renewable energy portfolio. In 2008 the company set Enel Green Power to develop wind, solar, geothermal and biomass projects. By 2009 it was operating alternative energy plants worldwide with a generating capacity of 4,700 MW. In 2010 Enel Green Power acquired Pagoda Wind Power, which is developing 4,000 MW of wind projects in California.

The company took control of Spain's power giant Endesa in 2007, increasing its market share as a European power player. Hoping to pay down what had become a heavy debt load, the company in 2009 sold an 80% stake in gas distributor Enel Rete Gas for $666 million.

Italy's Ministry of Economy and Finance directly owns about 14% of Enel; it owns another 17% indirectly through the government-controlled bank Cassa Depositi e Prestiti.

HISTORY

Italy's energy consumption doubled in the 1950s as the country experienced a period of rapid industrialization and urbanization. A tight-knit oligopoly controlled the electric power industry and included Edison, SADE, La Centale, SME, and Finelettrica. The economic boom pushed into the 1960s, and the Italian government created Enel (Ente Nazionale per l'Energia Elettrica) in 1962 to nationalize the power industry. In 1963 Enel began gradually buying some 1,250 electric utilities. About 160 municipal utilities and the larger independents, such as Edison, were left out of the takeover.

The company spent the late 1960s and early 1970s connecting Italy's unwieldy transmission network and building new power plants, including the La Spezia thermoelectric plant (600 MW). Construction costs, coupled with the high prices Enel was required to pay for its takeover targets, caused the utility to become steeped in debt. The Arab oil embargoes of the early 1970s made matters worse, and the Italian government helped Enel with an endowment in 1973.

The energy crisis also prompted Enel to build its first nuclear power plant, Caorso, which came on line in 1980. However, nuclear power was short-lived in Italy: After the 1986 Chernobyl accident, a national referendum forced Enel to de-activate its nukes in 1987. The firm also stepped up its development of renewable energy sources in the 1980s.

Meanwhile, Enel opened its Centro Nazionale de Controllo (CNC) in Rome in 1985 to supervise Italy's power grid. The next year the company turned its first profit.

To begin disassembling Enel's monopoly, the Italian government in 1992 opened the power generation market to outside producers and converted Enel into a joint stock company (with the state holding all of the shares). Following the European Union's 1997 directive to deregulate Europe's power industry, Enel unbundled its utility activities and began trimming its staff. Italy's Bersani Decree (passed in 1999) outlined the restructuring process: Enel was ordered to divest 15,000 MW of its generating capacity, a state-controlled operator was set up to oversee Italy's grid, and large users were allowed to choose their own suppliers.

In response, Enel began to diversify in 1998. It started Wind Telecomunicazioni, a joint venture with France Telecom and Deutsche

Telekom. (Deutsche Telekom sold its stake to the other partners in 2000.) Wind began offering fixed-line and mobile telecom services to corporations in 1998 and extended the services to residential users the next year. Enel also began building water infrastructure to serve local distributors and purchased three water operations in southern Italy.

Also in 1999 the government floated 32% of Enel in one of the world's largest IPOs at the time. The next year the company transferred control of its transmission network to an independent government-owned operator (Gestore della Rete di Trasmissione Nazionale), while retaining ownership of the assets.

Enel bought fixed-line telephone company Infostrada from Vodafone in 2001, acquired two more Italian gas distributors, and sold its 5,400-MW Elettrogen generation unit to Spain's Endesa for $2.3 billion. Enel also put its 7,000-MW Eurogen generation unit on the auction block in 2001. The high bidder, with a $2.6 billion offer, was a consortium backed by Fiat and Électricité de France; the sale was completed in 2002.

Also in 2002 Enel purchased Camuzzi Gazometri's gas distribution business (Italy's second-largest) for $870 million from Mill Hill Investments, and it bought Endesa's Viesgo unit (2,400 MW of generating capacity and 500,000 power customers) for about $1.8 billion.

Enel sold its final generation divestment company, Interpower (2,600 MW), to a consortium of utilities (including Belgian utility Electrabel and Italian utility ACEA) in 2003.

That year Enel purchased France Telecom's 27% stake in Wind for $1.4 billion, making the unit a wholly owned subsidiary. (It sold the unit in 2006 to the Egypt-based Weather Investments consortium.)

The Italian government began the second round of Enel's privatization process in 2003 by selling a 7% stake to Morgan Stanley for more than $2.3 billion. In 2004 the government further reduced its stake by nearly 20% through a public offering of shares.

With Italian regulators requiring that Enel divest 80% of its Terna subsidiary (which holds the company's power transmission assets) by 2007, Enel spun off 50% of the unit in an IPO in 2004. The following year it divested another 44%, and the company reduced its holding to about 5% by January 2006.

EXECUTIVES

Chairman: Piero Gnudi, age 72
CEO and Director: Fulvio Conti, age 62
CFO; Chairman, Enel Green Power: Luigi Ferraris
Head, Information and Communication Technology: Silvio Sperzani
Head, Regulatory and Environment: Simone Mori, age 46
Head, Human Resources: Massimo Cioffi, age 49
Head, Legal: Salvatore Cardillo, age 60
Head, External Communications: Gianluca Comin, age 47
Head, Group Risk Management: Claudio Machetti, age 51
Head, Procurement and Services: Antonio Cardani, age 60
Engineering and Innovation Division Director: Livo Vido, age 61
Chairman, Endesa: Borja Prado Eulate, age 54
CEO, Endesa: Andrea Brentan, age 61
CEO, Enel Green Power: Francesco Starace, age 55
President and CEO, Enel North America: Toni Volpe, age 38
Auditors: KPMG S.p.A.

LOCATIONS

HQ: Enel S.p.A.
 Viale Regina Margherita, 137
 00198 Rome, Italy
Phone: 39-06-8305-1 **Fax:** 39-06-8305-3771
Web: www.enel.com

2009 Sales

	% of total
Europe	
Italy	50
Russia	3
Other countries	34
Americas	13
Total	**100**

PRODUCTS/OPERATIONS

2009 Sales

	% of total
Iberia & Latin America	28
Sales (Italy)	26
Generation & energy management (Italy)	24
Infrastructure & networks (Italy)	9
International	7
Renewable energy	2
Other	4
Total	**100**

COMPETITORS

A2A
ABB
ACEA
Acque Potabili
Edison
Electricité de France
Eni
E.ON
ERG S.p.A.
HC Energía
IBERDROLA
International Power
Italgas
Risanamento
RWE
Tractebel Engineering

HISTORICAL FINANCIALS

Company Type: Public

Income Statement — FYE: December 31

	REVENUE ($ mil.)	NET INCOME ($ mil.)	NET PROFIT MARGIN	EMPLOYEES
12/09	89,104	9,158	10.3%	81,208
12/08	86,239	8,505	9.9%	75,981
12/07	64,282	6,201	9.6%	73,500
12/06	51,157	4,091	8.0%	58,548
12/05	40,336	4,894	12.1%	51,778
Annual Growth	**21.9%**	**17.0%**	**—**	**11.9%**

2009 Year-End Financials

Debt ratio: —
Return on equity: 19.8%
Cash ($ mil.): 5,976
Current ratio: 0.89
Long-term debt ($ mil.): —

No. of shares (mil.): 9,403
Dividends
 Yield: 9.6%
 Payout: 68.3%
Market value ($ mil.): 54,548

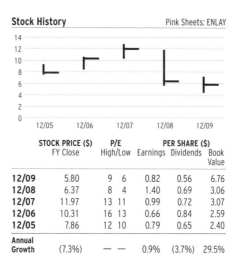

Stock History — Pink Sheets: ENLAY

	STOCK PRICE ($) FY Close	P/E High	P/E Low	Earnings	Dividends	Book Value
12/09	5.80	9	6	0.82	0.56	6.76
12/08	6.37	8	4	1.40	0.69	3.06
12/07	11.97	13	11	0.99	0.72	3.07
12/06	10.31	16	13	0.66	0.84	2.59
12/05	7.86	12	10	0.79	0.65	2.40
Annual Growth	**(7.3%)**	**—**	**—**	**0.9%**	**(3.7%)**	**29.5%**

Energias de Portugal

If you're from Portugal, you plug into EDP — Energias de Portugal, the state-controlled holding company for utilities that generate, transmit, and distribute electricity. EDP's distribution unit serves customers across Portugal and has stakes in Brazilian power distributors. In total, EDP serves 9.9 million electric customers. Other operations include a majority stake in Spanish utility HC Energía, gas distribution (790,000 customers), utility metering and billing, engineering, and water and wastewater projects. EDP has a combined generating capacity of more than 15,600 MW from its domestic hydroelectric, fossil-fueled, and wind-driven plants. The Portuguese government controls about 20% of EDP.

Branching out across the peninsula, EDP has boosted its interest in HC Energía from 40% to 96% by purchasing the shares owned by German utility Energie Baden-Württemberg and Spanish banks Cajastur and Cáser. It also controls 95% of Spanish gas utility Naturgas (acquiring 25% in 2010 for $803 million).

Since 2007 the company has sold much of its holdings in a variety of companies, including a 30% stake in Portugal's national transmission grid operator, Rede Eléctrica Nacional (REN); a 40% stake in TURBOGÁS — Produtora Energética, the company behind the construction of gas power station Tapada do Outeiro; and a 27% stake in PORTUGEN — Energia, which is in charge of operating Tapada do Outeiro.

HISTORY

EDP — Energias de Portugal has its roots in the several power enterprises that sprouted throughout the country during the infancy of electricity. The first recorded event in Portugal's electrification was the import of six voltaic arc lamps in 1878. The nation's first large-scale project saw the light in 1893 when the city of Braga was illuminated by the Sociedade de Electricidade do Norte de Portugal.

Electricity grew throughout the 1900s in the form of municipal concession contracts for distribution and government-licensed power plants. Large-scale power stations were not in effect in Portugal until after 1947, when Companhia Nacional de Electricidade was formed to interconnect the small generating systems dotting the nation. From the 1950s to mid-1970s, new companies were formed to bring electricity to various parts of Portugal.

The original Electricidade de Portugal was founded in the wake of a leftist revolution during the 1970s in Portugal. In what became known as the Captain's Revolution, military officers overthrew the Portuguese government, which had been a dictatorship since 1933. The new government, dominated by Marxists, nationalized Portugal's industries, including its generation, transmission, and distribution companies, in 1975. The next year the Portuguese government created Electricidade de Portugal to unify the recently nationalized companies.

A new Social Democrat government came to power in 1987 and decided to denationalize Portuguese industry, including EDP. The company reorganized into four major sectors in 1994: production (headed by its CPPE subsidiary), transmission, distribution, and services (led by its REN subsidiary, which operated the national grid, four regional utilities, and 10 services units). EDP was the holding company.

Seeking opportunities opened up by the privatization of Brazil's state-owned electricity distributor, EDP joined a consortium with Spain's Endesa and Chile's Chilectra to buy 70% of Rio de Janeiro distributor CERJ in 1996. The next year EDP gained a license to help build a hydro plant in Brazil. By 1998 the Endesa-led consortium had gained control of another Brazilian distributor, Coelce.

The Portuguese government floated 30% of EDP in 1997, raising $1.76 billion. In a joint venture with the UK's PowerGen and Germany's Siemens, EDP formed Turbogás to operate a power plant that would produce 20% of Portugal's electricity.

In 1998 EDP forged an alliance with Spain's Iberdrola and bought 80% of Guatemalan utility EEGSA. That year EDP and São Paulo utility CPFL gained control of São Paulo distributor Bandeirante. In 1999 EDP acquired stakes in two other Brazilian distributors. It also joined the UK's Thames Water to develop projects in Portugal, Chile, and Brazil and bought 45% of Chilean water and sewage company Essel. (EDP exchanged its stake in Essel for Thames Water's interest in the Portuguese joint venture in 2002.) The Portuguese state reduced its stake in EDP to about 50% in 1999.

Stepping up its telecommunications activities in 2000, EDP made its telecom unit, Onitelecom (ONI), fully operational and agreed to share a fiber-optic network on the Iberian Peninsula with Spain's Iberdrola. (In 2006, however, the company sold its stake in ONI.) Also in 2000 the Portuguese government acquired a majority stake in EDP's REN unit, and EDP combined its four power distribution utilities into one unit (EDP Distribuição).

In 2001 EDP and Spanish savings bank Cajastur jointly bid to buy Hidrocantábrico, one of Spain's leading utilities. EDP won control of 20% of Hidrocantábrico, while German utility Energie Baden-Württemberg (EnBW) won control of 60%. The following year, after a fierce bidding war, the two companies agreed that EDP would control the majority share (40%), while EnBW would own only 35%.

The company changed its name from EDP — Electricidade de Portugal to EDP — Energias de Portugal in 2004.

EXECUTIVES

Chairman, Supervisory Board: António de Almeida, age 72
Vice Chairman: Alberto J. C. de Castro, age 57
CEO: António L. G. N. Mexia, age 52
Executive Director and CFO: Nuno Alves, age 51
Executive Director: Ana Maria M. Fernandes, age 46
Executive Director: António M. Pita de Abreu, age 60
Executive Director: António Martins da Costa, age 54
Executive Director: João M. Manso Neto, age 51
Executive Director: Jorge M. Pragana da Cruz Morais, age 53
General Manager Information Systems: José Salas
Director Corporate Marketing: Inês Lima
Director Financial Management: Magda A. Magid Vakil
Director Investor Relations: Miguel Viana
Director Brand and Communication: Paulo C. Costa
Director Operational Management of Human Resources and Labour Relations: Eugénio A. Purificação Carvalho
Director Sustainability and the Environment: António Neves de Carvalho
Director Risk Management: José A. de Lima
Director of Chairman of the CAE's Office and Institutional Relations: João P. Mateus
Director Regulation and Competition: Maria J. Mano Pinto Simões
Director Organisational Development: Rui Ferin Cunha
Director Business Analysis: Miguel S. Andrade
Secretary: Noélia Rocha
Auditors: KPMG & Associados, SROC, SA

LOCATIONS

HQ: EDP — Energias de Portugal, S.A.
Praça Marquês de Pombal, 12
1250-162 Lisbon, Portugal
Phone: 351-21-001-2500   **Fax:** 351-21-002-1403
Web: www.edp.pt

2009 Sales

	% of total
Europe	
Portugal	59
Spain & other countries	25
Americas	
Brazil	14
US	2
Total	**100**

PRODUCTS/OPERATIONS

2009 Sales

	% of total
Electricity	91
Gas	8
Other	1
Total	**100**

COMPETITORS

AES
Cemig
Electrabel
Electricité de France
ELETROBRÁS
Endesa S.A.
Enel
E.ON
IBERDROLA
Jazztel
RWE

HISTORICAL FINANCIALS

Company Type: Public

Income Statement

FYE: December 31

	REVENUE ($ mil.)	NET INCOME ($ mil.)	NET PROFIT MARGIN	EMPLOYEES
12/09	17,805	1,674	9.4%	12,096
12/08	19,588	1,709	8.7%	12,245
12/07	16,443	1,501	9.1%	13,097
12/06	13,618	1,342	9.9%	13,575
12/05	10,987	1,268	11.5%	14,141
Annual Growth	**12.8%**	**7.2%**	**—**	**(3.8%)**

2009 Year-End Financials

Debt ratio: 249.1%
Return on equity: 17.2%
Cash ($ mil.): 3,138
Current ratio: 0.76
Long-term debt ($ mil.): 26,028

No. of shares (mil.): 3,657
Dividends
Yield: 3.6%
Payout: 40.0%
Market value ($ mil.): 16,288

Stock History

Pink Sheets: EDPFY

	STOCK PRICE ($) FY Close	P/E High	P/E Low	PER SHARE ($) Earnings	PER SHARE ($) Dividends	PER SHARE ($) Book Value
12/09	4.45	11	8	0.40	0.16	2.86
12/08	3.80	16	7	0.42	—	2.45
12/07	6.58	20	15	0.37	—	2.52
12/06	5.07	15	10	0.34	—	2.02
12/05	3.08	9	7	0.34	—	1.57
Annual Growth	**9.6%**	—	—	**4.1%**	—	**16.2%**

Eni S.p.A.

It's not teeny, it's Eni — and it's huge. One of Italy's largest companies, Eni operates in the oil and natural gas, petrochemicals, and oil field services industries and has expanded into power generation. Its main subsidiaries and affiliates include EniPower (power generation), Italgas (natural gas transmission), Saipem (oil field services), pipeline operator Snam Rete Gas, and Snamprogetti (contracting, engineering). As one of the world's leading oil enterprises, in 2008 Eni had proved reserves of 6.6 billion barrels of oil equivalent, most of it in Italy and in Africa. The Italian government owns about 30% of Eni but is considering selling the holding.

The company's oil and gas holdings and exploration and production efforts extend into more than 30 countries on five continents. Eni has expanded outside its traditional bases of Africa and Italy, with ventures in the Americas, the Asia/Pacific region, Europe, and the Middle East.

In response to the opening up of Italy's energy markets, Eni is increasing its natural gas holdings and adding electricity generating power units. In 2007 the company bought Dominion Resources' US oil and gas assets in the Gulf of Mexico for $4.75 billion. To expand its Asian and Algerian holdings, in 2008 Eni acquired Burren

Energy and agreed to buy First Calgary Petroleums. It was able to benefit from SUEZ's acquisition of Gaz de France by buying up GDF SUEZ's majority stake in Belgian gas company Distrigas. Eni now owns 99% of Distrigas.

In 2009 the company sold its 20% stake in Gazprom Neft to Gazprom for $4.2 billion. It also signed a broad strategic partnership with Gazprom to jointly develop energy opportunities both in and outside Russia.

That year Eni consolidated its gas divisions, and sold Italgas and Stogit (gas storage) to subsidiary Snam Rete Gas.

Expanding its Central European market share, in 2010 it acquired Exxon Mobil's 135 gas stations and other downstream assets in Austria.

HISTORY

Although the Italian parliament formed Ente Nazionale Idrocarburi (National Hydrocarbon Agency) in 1953, Enrico Mattei is the true father of Eni. In 1945 Mattei, a partisan leader during WWII, was appointed northern commissioner of Agip, a state-owned petroleum company founded in 1926 by Mussolini, and ordered to liquidate the company. Mattei instead ordered the exploration of the Po Valley, where workers found methane gas deposits in 1946.

When Eni was created in 1953, Mattei was named president. His job was to find energy resources for an oil-poor country. He initiated a series of joint ventures with several Middle Eastern and African nations, offering better deals than his large oil company rivals, which he dubbed the Seven Sisters.

Mattei didn't stick to energy: By the time he died in a mysterious plane crash in 1962, Eni had acquired machinery manufacturer Pignone, finance company Sofid, Milan newspaper *Il Giorno,* and textile company Lane Rossi. Eni grew during the 1960s, partly because of a deal made for Soviet crude in 1958 and a joint venture with Esso in 1963. It also expanded its chemical activities.

By the early 1970s losses in Eni's chemical and textile operations, the oil crisis, and the Italian government's dumping of unprofitable companies on Eni hurt its bottom line. Former finance minister Franco Reviglio took over in 1983 and began cutting inefficient operations.

EniChem merged with Montedison, Italy's largest private chemical company, in 1988, but clashes between the public agency and the private company made Montedison sell back its stake in 1990. Eni became a joint stock company in 1992, but the government retained a majority stake.

Franco Bernabe took over Eni following a 1993 bribery scandal and began cutting noncore businesses. The Italian government began selling Eni stock in 1995. In 1996 Eni signed on to develop Libyan gas resources and build a pipeline to Italy. A year later the company merged its Agipa exploration and production subsidiary into its main operations. Eni also took a 35% stake in Italian telecom company Albacom (which has since been sold to British Telecom Group).

The government cut its stake in Eni from 51% to 38% in 1998. That year Vittorio Mincato, a company veteran, succeeded Bernabe as CEO. In 1999 Eni and Russia's RAO Gazprom, the world's largest natural gas production firm, agreed to build a controversial $3 billion natural gas pipeline stretching from Russia to Turkey. Eni agreed to invest $5.5 billion to develop oil and gas reserves in Libya; it also sold interests in

Saipem and Nuovo Pignone, as well as some of its Italian service stations.

In 2000 Eni paid about $910 million for a 33% stake in Galp, a Portuguese oil and gas company that also has natural gas utility operations. Also that year Eni bought British-Borneo Oil & Gas in a $1.2 billion deal, and in 2001 it paid $4 billion for UK independent exploration and production company LASMO, topping a bid by US-based Amerada Hess.

The Italian government sold off another 5% of Eni in 2001, reducing its stake to about 30%, and announced that it was considering selling its entire investment. In an effort to reduce noncore holdings, the company sold property management subsidiary Immobiliare Metanopoli to Goldman Sachs. Also that year Eni sold a minority stake in its gas pipeline unit, Snam Rete Gas, to the public.

In 2002 Eni entered discussions to acquire Enterprise Oil, but lost out to a rival bid from Royal Dutch Shell. Later that year Eni's oil field services unit Saipem gained control of Bouygues Offshore.

EXECUTIVES

Chairman: Roberto Poli, age 72
Deputy Chairman and CEO, Saipem: Pietro Franco Tali, age 60
CEO: Paolo Scaroni, age 64
COO Refining and Marketing: Angelo Fanelli, age 58
COO Exploration and Production Division: Claudio Descalzi, age 55
COO Gas and Power Division: Domenico Dispenza, age 64
Chief Corporate Operations Officer: Salvatore Sardo, age 58
SEVP Legal Affair Department and General Counsel: Massimo Mantovani, age 47
SEVP Public Affairs and Communication: Stefano Lucchini, age 48
SEVP Internal Control System: Rita Marino, age 46
SEVP Corporate Affairs and Governance and Secretary: Roberto Ulissi, age 48
SVP External Communication: Gianni Di Giovanni
VP and New York Representative: V. De Luca
Director Supplies; CEO, Syndial: Sergio Polito, age 61
Chairman, Stogit: Federico Spiller
CEO, Stogit: Paolo Bacchetta
Chairman, Syndial: Leonardo Bellodi
Assistant to the Chairman: Francesca Dionisi Vici
Executive Assistant to CEO: Rafaella Leone, age 48
Auditors: PricewaterhouseCoopers SpA

LOCATIONS

HQ: Eni S.p.A.
Piazzale Enrico Mattei 1
00144 Rome, Italy
Phone: 39-06-5982-1 **Fax:** 39-06-5982-2141
US HQ: 485 Madison Ave., New York, NY 10022
US Phone: 646-264-2250 **US Fax:** 646-264-2222
Web: www.eni.it

PRODUCTS/OPERATIONS

2009 Sales

	% of total
Refining & marketing	31
Gas & power	30
Exploration & production	24
Engineering & construction	10
Petrochemicals	4
Corporate & financial	1
Total	**100**

Major Subsidiaries and Affiliates

EniPower SpA (power generation)
Italgas SpA (natural gas supply)
Saipem SpA (43.4%, oil field services)
Snam Rete Gas SpA (55.9%, gas pipeline)
Snamprogetti SpA (contracting and engineering)

COMPETITORS

A2A
Anonima Petroli Italiana
Ashland Inc.
BASF SE
BG Group
BP
Chevron
ConocoPhillips
Edison
ERG S.p.A.
Exxon Mobil
Hellenic Petroleum
Marathon Oil
Occidental Petroleum
PEMEX
PETROBRAS
Petróleos de Venezuela
Royal Dutch Shell
Sunoco
TOTAL

HISTORICAL FINANCIALS

Company Type: Public

Income Statement

FYE: December 31

	REVENUE ($ mil.)	NET INCOME ($ mil.)	NET PROFIT MARGIN	EMPLOYEES
12/09	120,883	6,259	5.2%	78,417
12/08	153,450	13,472	8.8%	78,880
12/07	129,494	14,718	11.4%	75,862
12/06	114,731	12,171	10.6%	73,572
12/05	88,557	10,443	11.8%	72,258
Annual Growth	**8.1%**	**(12.0%)**	**—**	**2.1%**

2009 Year-End Financials

Debt ratio: 39.2%	No. of shares (mil.): 2,003
Return on equity: 9.7%	Dividends
Cash ($ mil.): 2,305	Yield: 3.3%
Current ratio: 1.02	Payout: 68.3%
Long-term debt ($ mil.): 25,889	Market value ($ mil.): 145,263

Stock History

NYSE: E

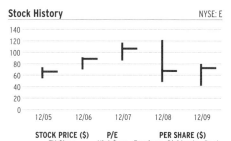

	STOCK PRICE ($) FY Close	P/E High/Low	PER SHARE ($) Earnings	Dividends	Book Value
12/09	72.53	23 13	3.47	2.37	32.97
12/08	67.40	18 7	6.85	3.43	31.27
12/07	106.61	14 11	8.04	3.64	29.68
12/06	88.76	14 11	6.57	3.25	25.73
12/05	66.06	13 10	5.54	3.38	21.88
Annual Growth	**2.4%**	**— —**	**(11.0%)**	**(8.5%)**	**10.8%**

E.ON AG

E.ON has transformed itself from a regional conglomerate into a multi-utility and a global player with 30 million customers. Subsidiary E.ON Energie is one of Germany's top two power companies (running neck and neck with RWE), with some 17 million electricity, gas, and water customers; the unit also has about 28,750 MW of electric generating capacity across Germany and Central Europe. E.ON operates E.ON Ruhrgas, Germany's #1 natural gas supplier. Non-German utility subsidiaries include E.ON UK and E.ON Nordic. In response to tightening European regulations regarding carbon emissions, E.ON has announced plans to obtain 24% of its generating capacity from renewable energy sources by 2030.

Taking advantage of deregulation across Europe's energy markets, E.ON has emerged as one of the Continent's leading integrated gas and power service provider through a series of acquisitions (including Ruhrgas, and UK-based Powergen and it US unit LG&E Energy), and strategic alliances.

In 2009, to counter EDF's acquisition of British Energy, E.ON and RWE formed a joint venture to develop 6,000 MW of nuclear power capacity in the UK.

That year, prompted by the regulatory requirements of the European Commission, E.ON and GDF SUEZ agreed to swap generating assets to allow for more competition in their major markets. It sold 860 MW of Germany-based conventional power plants, 132 MW of hydroelectric plants, and access to 770 MW of nuclear power. In return GDF SUEZ sold to E.ON a similar amount of power generation capacity in France and the Benelux countries. In 2010, also to meet EU anti-monopoly regulations, it sold grid operator Transpower to Dutch giant TenneT for $1.1 billion and it swapped 5,000 MW of generation capacity with EDF and EnBW.

In 2010 the company announced plans to sell E.ON U.S., which operates Kentucky's two major utilities, for $7.2 billion.

HISTORY

VEBA (originally Vereinigte Elektrizitats-und Bergwerks AG) was formed in 1929 in Berlin to consolidate Germany's state-owned electricity and mining interests. These operations included PreussenElektra, an electric utility formed by the German government in 1927; Hibernia, a coal mining firm founded in 1873; and Preussag, a mining and smelting company founded in 1923.

In the 1930s VEBA produced synthetic gasoline (essential to the German war machine) from coal at its Hibernia plant. In 1938 the company and chemical cartel I. G. Farben set up Chemische Werke Hüls to make synthetic rubber. After WWII, VEBA's assets in western Germany were transferred to the government, and several executives were arrested. Preussag was spun off in 1959.

In 1965 the government spun off VEBA to the public. That year the company entered trading and transportation by buying Stinnes, one of West Germany's largest industrial companies. In 1969 VEBA transferred its coal mining interests to Ruhrkohle and a few years later moved into oil exploration and development. The company shortened its name to VEBA in 1970.

The West German government sold its remaining stake in VEBA in 1987. In a changed regulatory environment, large investors were able to accumulate big portions of stock, and their dissatisfaction with the company's lackluster results made it a takeover target. In response, new chairman Ulrich Hartmann began cutting noncore businesses and reducing staff.

In 1990 VEBA began accumulating mobile communications, networking, and cable TV companies. It allied with the UK's Cable and Wireless (C&W) in 1995 to develop a European mobile phone business, but in 1997 C&W sold its interest to VEBA (as part of the deal, VEBA gained a 10% stake in C&W, which it sold in 1999). In anticipation of the 1998 deregulation of the German telecom market, VEBA and RWE merged their German telecom businesses in 1997.

VEBA acquired a 36% stake in Degussa, a specialty chemicals company, in 1997; two years later Degussa merged with Hüls to form a separately traded chemical company called Degussa-Hüls, in which VEBA took a 62% stake. VEBA sold a 30% stake in Stinnes to the public in 1999. The company's telecom venture sold its fixed-line telephone business, its cable TV unit, and its stake in mobile phone operator E-Plus.

These moves, however, were just the prelude to a bigger deal: a $14 billion merger agreement between VEBA and fellow German conglomerate VIAG. The partners announced plans to dump noncore businesses and beef up their energy and chemicals holdings. VEBA and VIAG completed their merger in 2000, and the combined company adopted the name E.ON. The companies' utilities businesses were combined into E.ON Energie, and their chemicals units were brought together as Degussa.

To gain regulatory approval to form E.ON, VEBA and VIAG agreed to sell their stakes in German electric utilities Bewag and VEAG and coal producer LAUBAG. E.ON sold its VEAG and LAUBAG interests, along with semiconductor and electronics distribution units, in 2000 and sold Bewag in 2001.

That year E.ON agreed to buy UK electricity generator Powergen (now E.ON UK), and it announced plans to sell off nonutility operations, including Degussa and Veba Oel. Later that year E.ON agreed to swap a 51% stake in Veba Oel for BP's 26% stake in German natural gas supplier Ruhrgas (now E.ON Ruhrgas).

In 2002 E.ON sold its VAW Aluminum unit to Norwegian conglomerate Norsk Hydro in a $2.8 billion deal. Regulators moved to prevent E.ON from acquiring BP's stake in Ruhrgas in 2002, but BP agreed to pay for the Veba Oel stake in cash if necessary, and the swap was completed later that year. E.ON also acquired Vodafone and ThyssenKrupp's stakes in Ruhrgas in 2002, and it sold its remaining stake in Veba Oel to BP.

Also in 2002 E.ON completed its purchase of Powergen for about $8 billion. In late 2002 E.ON acquired the UK energy supply and generation businesses of TXU Europe in a $2.5 billion deal.

The following year E.ON swapped its majority stake in chemical maker Degussa with coal group

RAG for RAG's 18% interest in Ruhrgas. It completed its acquisition of Ruhrgas by purchasing the combined 40% stake held by Royal Dutch Shell, Exxon Mobil, and TUI (formerly Preussag).

In 2007 E.ON acquired Ireland-based wind farm company Airtricity for $1.4 billion. Also that year it acquired Russia-based power utility OGK-4 for almost $6 billion.

Expanding its business portfolio in 2008 the company moved into the energy trading market with the establishment of E.ON Energy Trading.

EXECUTIVES

Chairman of the Supervisory Board: Ulrich Hartmann, age 72
Deputy Chairman: Erhard Ott
Chairman Management Board and CEO: Johannes Teyssen, age 50
Member Board of Management, Finance, Accounting, Controlling and Corporate Planning, Mergers and Acquisitions, Tax, GLOBE: Marcus Schenck, age 44
Member Board of Management, E.ON Academy, Facility Management, Real Estate, OneE.ON, and Human Resources/Organization and Chief Human Resources Officer: Christoph Dänzer-Vanotti, age 55
Member Board of Management, Group Human Resources, IT, Group Procurement, Legal and Compliance, Corporate Incident and Crisis Management, Real Estate/Mining, Facility Management, and E.ON Academy: Regine Stachelhaus, age 55
Member Board of Management, Research and Development, New Build and Technology, Corporate Responsibility, Health/Safety and Environment; Chairman, E.ON Energie: Klaus-Dieter Maubach, age 48
Member Board of Management, Mergers and Acquisitions, Legal Affairs, Corporate Development, and New Markets: Lutz Feldmann, age 53
Member Board of Management: Bernhard Reutersberg, age 56
Member Board of Management, Upstream/Generation, Trading, and Optimization: Jørgen Kildahl, age 47
EVP Investor Relations: Kiran Bhojani
EVP: Heinrich Montag
EVP: Gert von der Groeben
SVP Political Affairs and Corporate Communications: Guido Knott
Chairman, CEO and President, E.ON US: Vic Staffleri
Chairman and CEO, E.ON Espana: Miguel Antonanzas
CEO, E.ON Ruhrgas: Klaus Schäfer, age 43
CEO, E.ON España; President, E.ON Italia: Miguel Antoñanzas
CEO, E.ON Energy Trading: Tony Cocker
CEO, E.ON UK: Paul Golby, age 58
CEO, E.ON Italia: Luca Dal Fabbro, age 44
Auditors: PricewaterhouseCoopers AG

LOCATIONS

HQ: E.ON AG
E.ON-Platz 1
40479 Düsseldorf, Germany
Phone: 49-211-4579-0   **Fax:** 49-211-4579-501
US HQ: 220 W. Main St., Louisville, KY 40202
US Phone: 502-589-1444   **US Fax:** 502-627-3629
Web: www.eon.com

2009 Sales

	% of total
Europe	
Germany	52
Other EU countries	15
Other countries	31
US	2
Total	**100**

PRODUCTS/OPERATIONS

2009 Sales

	% of total
Central Europe	33
Energy Trading	33
Pan-European Gas	16
UK	8
New Markets	6
Nordic countries	2
US Midwest	2
Total	**100**

COMPETITORS

AGIV
BASF SE
Bayer AG
Business Group Benelux
Deutsche Telekom
Dow Chemical
DuPont
Electricité de France
EnBW
Endesa S.A.
Enel
Eni
EVN
France Telecom
GDF SUEZ
RWE
Vattenfall

HISTORICAL FINANCIALS

Company Type: Public

Income Statement

	REVENUE ($ mil.)	NET INCOME ($ mil.)	NET PROFIT MARGIN	EMPLOYEES
12/09	117,260	12,390	10.6%	91,010
12/08	122,278	2,261	1.8%	93,538
12/07	101,165	11,369	11.2%	87,815
12/06	84,695	6,672	7.9%	80,612
12/05	61,411	8,780	14.3%	75,173
Annual Growth	17.6%	9.0%	—	4.9%

FYE: December 31

2009 Year-End Financials

Debt ratio: 76.0%   No. of shares (mil.): 1,905
Return on equity: 23.3%   Dividends
Cash ($ mil.): 6,034   Yield: 5.1%
Current ratio: 1.05   Payout: 34.0%
Long-term debt ($ mil.): 43,938   Market value ($ mil.): 79,824

Stock History

Pink Sheets: EONGY

	STOCK PRICE ($) FY Close	P/E High/Low		PER SHARE ($) Earnings	Dividends	Book Value
12/09	41.89	7	4	6.32	2.15	30.35
12/08	40.09	76	33	0.96	1.93	25.50
12/07	71.43	40	26	1.81	—	38.14
12/06	45.22	41	32	1.12	—	33.13
12/05	34.50	24	17	1.48	—	27.65
Annual Growth	5.0%	—	—	43.8%	11.4%	2.4%

ERGO Insurance Group

ERGO Insurance Group thinks logically: people need insurance, ergo they sell it! The company comprises a number of firms specializing in life, health, property, casualty, and legal expenses insurance, as well as pensions. Property/casualty and life policies are offered under the ERGO brand, while health, legal, and travel insurance are provided through the DKV, D.A.S., and ERV divisions. The company targets individuals and small to midsized businesses. ERGO is controlled by reinsurance giant Munich Re; the two companies have formed joint venture MEAG MUNICH ERGO AssetManagement to provide financial services.

ERGO sells its products through a vast network of self-employed agents, direct sales employees, and brokers. ERGO's marketing efforts target private individuals, who account for the lion's share of premiums.

In 2009 the company consolidated its property/casualty and life operations under the ERGO brand, withdrawing the Victoria and Hamburg-Mannheimer brands from the German market. ERGO also renamed its majority-owned KarstadtQuelle Insurance subsidiary, which provides insurance and financial advice to department stores and mail-order customers through a partnership with Arcandor (formerly Karstadt Quelle), as ERGO Direct. ERGO also has cooperative agreements with banker HVB.

ERGO's health insurance and legal expenses products are its biggest sellers in Germany and Europe. In 2009 the company introduced a new product in those markets, the "Home and Walkies" insurance package, which covers liabilities related to dogs (such as fights with others' dogs while out for a walk or doggie messes left on apartment rugs or hotel floors).

ERGO has been strengthening its foreign operations through acquisitions and joint ventures. The company operates in approximately 30 countries; focus areas for growth include Eastern Europe, including Poland and Turkey, as well as Asian countries such as India and China. To that end, ERGO acquired a majority stake in Turkish insurer ISVICRE and formed an Indian joint venture, HDFC Ergo General Insurance, with Housing Development Finance Corporation.

It expanded its Baltic States operations in 2008 by forming a European Public Company to offer health insurance, and then merging its existing life insurance operations into the new company, becoming the first non-government health insurer in the Baltics. The company operates in Estonia and Lithuania.

HISTORY

In 1843 Otto Crelinger applied for a royal license to create a railway insurance company in Prussia; King Friedrich Wilhelm IV of Prussia granted it 10 years later. By 1861 the company was selling life insurance as well, and in 1875 it took the name VICTORIA.

VICTORIA was the first German company to offer life insurance to the public without the need to see a doctor (a plan modeled after Prudential's operations in the UK), and it gradually extended its reach to several other European countries and expanded into other areas of insurance, including property, casualty and automobile. By 1900 it was Germany's largest insurance company, and on the eve of WWI, it was the largest in Europe.

The war took a severe toll on VICTORIA, but careful planning kept it on its feet. By 1927 it was back to prewar asset levels. In 1932 the company accounted for 80% of foreign premiums collected by German insurance companies.

WWII would prove to be an even more trying period for VICTORIA. Among the company's many misfortunes was the destruction of its main offices in Berlin. However, cautious planning again kept the company afloat. By 1953 it was back on top of its game, now mainly operating from Düsseldorf.

West Germany's economy flourished in the 1960s. During this decade VICTORIA bought D.A.S., then a relatively small legal expenses insurer that would grow to be the market leader. The 1970s saw a downturn in the world economy, but VICTORIA weathered the decade well, even expanding into the health insurance market.

In 1997 German reinsurer Munich Re decided to bring together three insurance companies in which it held stakes: VICTORIA, Hamburg-Mannheimer (primarily a life and accident insurer), and DKV (a health insurer). The group instantly became Germany's second-largest insurer, behind Allianz. All of these companies served mostly individual customers in Germany and abroad, with secondary focuses on small to midsized businesses and some government institutions. Munich Re owned about 54% of the new holding company, which was called ERGO Insurance Group (Versicherungsgruppe). ERGO shares went public in February 1998. Later that year Munich Re increased its stake to about 63%.

The new insurance conglomerate continued strengthening its international presence, acquiring Spain's fifth-largest insurer, Previasa. In 1999 ERGO acquired the Netherlands' health insurer Levob and Spain's Nordica. In 2000 the company acquired Italy's Bayerische Vita (life insurance) and Bayerische Assicurazioni (property and casualty insurance), an additional Netherlands insurer, and majority stakes in Poland's Compensa Zycie (a life insurer) and a new life and accident insurer in Slovakia.

Also in 2000 the company's joint venture with Munich Re, MEAG MUNICH ERGO AssetManagement, began providing financial services, and ERGO forged a strategic partnership with Deutsche Telekom to develop an online marketplace for insurance and financial services. The company, together with affiliate Österreichische Volksbanken, also made a bid for the Austrian Post Office Savings Bank.

In 2001 ERGO took a majority stake in PREVENTA, Lithuania's third biggest insurer.

Since then the company has been focused on continuing to grow its foreign operations, primarily through acquisitions. To that end, the company has made about five major buys over the past few years.

EXECUTIVES

Chairman, Supervisory Board: Nikolaus von Bomhard, age 54
Chairman, Management Board: Torsten Oletzky, age 44
Management Board Member, Finances, Investments, and Life Insurance: Daniel von Borries, age 45
Management Board Member, Composite Segment; Chairman, Victoria Versicherung and Hamburg-Mannheimer Sachversicherungs: Christian Diedrich, age 53
Management Board Member, Health Segment; CEO, DKV Deutsche Krankenversicherung and Chairman, Victoria Krankenversicherung: Günter Dibbern, age 64
Management Board Member, International Operations: Jochen Messemer, age 44

Management Board Member, Customer Service, Company Organisation, and IT: Bettina Anders
Management Board Member, Accounting, Taxes, Controlling, and Risk Management: Rolf Ulrich, age 53
Management Board Member, Domestic Human Resources, General Services, Facility and Materials Management, Purchasing, and Logistics: Ulf Mainzer, age 45
Management Board Member, Sales: Jürgen Vetter, age 53
Head of External Communication, Investor and Rating Relations, and Press: Alexander Becker
Auditors: KPMG Bayerische Treuhandgesellschaft AG

LOCATIONS

HQ: ERGO Insurance Group
Victoriaplatz 2
40198 Düsseldorf, Germany
Phone: 49-211-4937-0   **Fax:** 49-211-4937-1500
Web: www.ergo.com

2009 Sales

	% of total
Germany	70
Other countries	30
Total	**100**

PRODUCTS/OPERATIONS

2009 Sales

	% of total
Health	31
Life	29
Direct/travel	23
Property/casualty	17
Total	**100**

COMPETITORS

AEGON	Generali
Allianz	Generali Deutschland
AOK	Helvetia Group
AWD	Prudential plc
AXA	Vienna Insurance Group
Fortis Insurance	Zurich Financial Services

HISTORICAL FINANCIALS

Company Type: Public

Income Statement				FYE: December 31
	ASSETS ($ mil.)	NET INCOME ($ mil.)	INCOME AS % OF ASSETS	EMPLOYEES
12/09	194,235	248	0.1%	33,152
12/08	187,530	130	0.1%	31,508
12/07	188,118	1,149	0.6%	29,127
12/06	164,174	1,195	0.7%	28,310
12/05	145,592	897	0.6%	29,227
Annual Growth	7.5%	(27.5%)	—	3.2%

2009 Year-End Financials

Equity as % of assets: —
Return on assets: 0.1%
Return on equity: —
Long-term debt ($ mil.): —
Sales ($ mil.): 31,106

Net Income History
German: EVG2

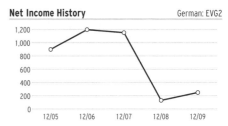

Ericsson

Ericsson opens all lines of communication. The world's leading maker of mobile broadband infrastructure gear provides the equipment that telecom carriers use to build and expand networks. The company also provides wireline broadband, metro area Ethernet, and optical transport equipment. Its services unit handles operations ranging from systems integration to network management. Ericsson's multimedia arm provides content-related products such as Internet television systems. The company's joint venture with Sony, Sony Ericsson Mobile Communications, ranks among the top providers of cell telephones. Another joint venture with ST Microelectronics, ST-Ericsson, makes semiconductors mainly for wireless applications.

Ericsson is using acquisitions to bolster its product portfolio and expand further into international markets to capitalize on booming demand for the mobile broadband services that its equipment enables. In 2009 the company acquired parts of bankrupt Nortel's North American wireless business for $1.1 billion in a bid to boost its profile as a provider of CDMA-based mobile networking gear to wireless carriers on the continent.

The company went on in 2010 to pay $242 million in cash for a controlling stake (50% plus one share) in Nortel's joint venture with Seoul-based LG Electronics, LG-Nortel. The deal boosted Ericsson's profile in South Korea's robust telecom market, particularly in the areas of sales and R&D. South Korea boasts the highest per capita broadband penetration on the planet.

Ericsson's best known joint venture, Sony Ericsson, accounts for its cell phone operations. Each company owns 50% of the business, which has experienced declining demand for its handsets due to an aging product line-up, the weakened global economy, and steadily mounting competition from relative newcomers from Asia, including Samsung and HTC. The company's ST Ericsson joint venture with Geneva-based STMicroelectronics, which produces semiconductors and related products for wireless phones, has also been hit by weak demand.

Both Sony Ericsson and ST Ericsson have enacted cost-cutting measures including staff cuts and the consolidation of R&D operations. New chairmen and chief executives have also been appointed for both ventures in hopes of turning the businesses around.

Ericsson's professional services unit handles consulting, customer support, network design and integration, and training, as well as managed services such as application hosting and network operations. In 2009 the company signed a deal to manage Sprint Nextel's daily network operations and maintain its physical infrastructure in a deal valued at as much as $5 billion.

In 2010 EVP/CFO Hans Vestberg took over as CEO, succeeding Carl-Henric Svanberg, who resigned to become chairman of BP.

Ericsson's largest investors are Investor AB, the investment vehicle for the Wallenberg family, and AB Industrivärden, which control 19% and 13% of the voting power, respectively.

HISTORY

Lars Magnus Ericsson opened a telegraph repair shop in Stockholm in 1876, the same year Alexander Graham Bell applied for a US patent on the telephone. Within two years Ericsson was making telephones. His company grew rapidly, supplying equipment first to Swedish phone companies and later to other European companies. In 1885 Ericsson crafted a combination receiver-speaker in one handset.

In 1911 Ericsson and SAT, the Stockholm telephone company, merged under the Ericsson banner. The company adopted its present name in 1926. In 1930 international financier Ivar "The Match King" Kreuger, owner of the Swedish Match Co., won control of Ericsson. His triumph was short-lived. Krueger committed suicide in 1932 and one of his creditors, Sosthenes Behn's ITT, took over.

ITT in 1960 sold its interest in Ericsson to the top Swedish industrialist family, the Wallenbergs. In 1975 Ericsson introduced its computer-controlled exchange, called AXE. Buoyed by AXE's success, the company unveiled the "office of the future" in the early 1980s, diversifying into computers and office furniture.

However, Ericsson's timing was off: The demand for office automation never materialized and profits plunged. Electrolux chairman Hans Werthen was recruited to split his time between the two companies and rescue Ericsson. The company sold its computer business to Nokia in 1988 and refocused on telephone equipment. It dusted off its aging AXE system for the burgeoning cellular market and quickly won key contracts.

In 1998 manager Sven-Christer Nilsson was appointed CEO. He reorganized the company and laid off 14,000 workers.

After Ericsson fought bitterly with rival QUALCOMM over wireless standards and patents, the companies settled in 1999, agreeing to push for the standardization of third-generation technology based on QUALCOMM's code-division multiple access technology. As a part of the deal, Ericsson purchased QUALCOMM's infrastructure business.

By mid-1999 Nilsson was pushed out for moving too slowly on restructuring plans and was replaced as CEO by chairman Lars Ramqvist, who put many of the duties on president Kurt Hellström. Hellström immediately set out to simplify the company's managerial and accounting structure, trim its workforce and slow-growth businesses, and push new phone models to market.

Fierce competition, an industrywide slowdown in handset sales, and manufacturing glitches led Ericsson to outsource the manufacture of its phones to Flextronics and form a joint venture (Sony Ericsson Mobile Communications) with Sony to link the development and marketing of their handsets in 2001. Ericsson also sold its direct enterprise sales and service unit, outsourced IT operations in Europe to EDS, and cut more than 20,000 jobs that year. Hellström became CEO in 2001.

Chairman Ramqvist became honorary chairman in 2002; Electrolux CEO Michael Treschow was named as the acting chairman. Ericsson announced 20,000 more layoffs in 2002.

Ericsson sold its optoelectronic components business in 2003. Hellström retired later that year and Carl-Henric Svanberg, former CEO of Assa Abloy, was appointed CEO.

In 2005 Ericsson acquired certain telecom hardware assets from troubled Marconi (later renamed telent), for about $2.1 billion.

The company acquired Redback Networks ($1.9 billion) and TANDBERG Television ($1.4 billion) in 2007. Looking to broaden its multimedia offerings, the company purchased Mobeon, a Swedish provider of IP-based voice and video mail.

EXECUTIVES

Chairman: Michael Treschow, age 67
Deputy Chairman: Sverker Martin-Löf, age 67
Deputy Chairman: Marcus Wallenberg, age 54
President, CEO, and Director: Hans Vestberg, age 45, $2,528,431 total compensation
EVP, CFO, and Head Group Function Finance: Jan Frykhammar, age 44
EVP and Head Business Unit Networks: Johan Wibergh, age 47
Chief Brand Officer; Head Market Unit South East Europe: Cesare Avenía, age 59
SVP, General Counsel, and Head Group Function Legal Affairs: Carl Olof Blomqvist, age 58
SVP Group Function Sales and Marketing: Torbjörn Possne, age 56
SVP, CTO, and Head Group Function Technology and Portfolio Management; Head Ericsson in Silicon Valley: Håkan Eriksson, age 48
SVP and Head Group Function Human Resources and Organization: Bina Chaurasia
SVP and Head Group Function Strategy: Douglas L. Gilstrap, age 47
SVP and Head Business Unit Multimedia: Jan Wäreby, age 53
SVP and Head CDMA Mobile Systems: Rima Qureshi, age 44
SVP and Head Group Function Communications: Henry Sténson, age 54
VP and Head Investor and Analyst Relations: Åse Lindskog
President, Sony Ericsson Mobile Communications: Bert Nordberg, age 53
Head North America Region; President and CEO, Ericsson North America: Angel Ruiz
Head Corporate Public and Media Relations: Ola Rembe
Auditors: PricewaterhouseCoopers AB

LOCATIONS

HQ: Telefonaktiebolaget LM Ericsson
Torshamnsgatan 23, Kista
SE-164 83 Stockholm, Sweden
Phone: 46-10-719-0000
US HQ: 6300 Legacy Dr., Plano, TX 75024
US Phone: 972-583-0000
Web: www.ericsson.com

2009 Sales

	% of total
Asia/Pacific	32
Central & Western Europe, Middle East & Africa	25
Western Europe	21
North America	12
Latin America	10
Total	**100**

PRODUCTS/OPERATIONS

2009 Sales

	% of total
Networks	66
Professional services	27
Multimedia	6
Other	1
Total	**100**

COMPETITORS

Accenture
Alcatel-Lucent
Amdocs
Cisco Systems
Comverse Technology
Harmonic
HP Enterprise Services
HTC Corporation
Huawei Technologies
IBM
Juniper Networks
LG Electronics
Motorola
Nokia Siemens Networks
Oracle
QUALCOMM
Samsung Electronics
Sharp Corp.
Tata Consultancy
Tech Mahindra
Technicolor
ZTE

HISTORICAL FINANCIALS

Company Type: Public

Income Statement

FYE: December 31

	REVENUE ($ mil.)	NET INCOME ($ mil.)	NET PROFIT MARGIN	EMPLOYEES
12/09	28,721	511	1.8%	82,500
12/08	26,910	1,452	5.4%	78,750
12/07	29,328	3,410	11.6%	74,011
12/06	25,914	3,827	14.8%	63,781
12/05	19,091	3,058	16.0%	56,055
Annual Growth	10.7%	(36.1%)	—	10.1%

2009 Year-End Financials

Debt ratio: 21.4%
Return on equity: 2.7%
Cash ($ mil.): 3,171
Current ratio: 2.13
Long-term debt ($ mil.): 4,172
No. of shares (mil.): 3,198
Dividends
Yield: 20.1%
Payout: 162.5%
Market value ($ mil.): 4,088

Stock History

NASDAQ (GS): ERIC

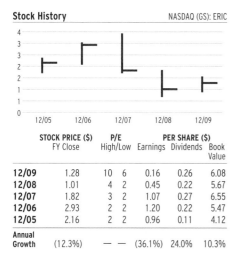

	STOCK PRICE ($) FY Close	P/E High	P/E Low	PER SHARE ($) Earnings	PER SHARE ($) Dividends	PER SHARE ($) Book Value
12/09	1.28	10	6	0.16	0.26	6.08
12/08	1.01	4	2	0.45	0.22	5.67
12/07	1.82	3	2	1.07	0.27	6.55
12/06	2.93	2	2	1.20	0.22	5.47
12/05	2.16	2	2	0.96	0.11	4.12
Annual Growth	(12.3%)	—	—	(36.1%)	24.0%	10.3%

Ernst & Young Global

Accounting may actually be the *second*-oldest profession, and Ernst & Young is one of the oldest practitioners. Ernst & Young is also one of the world's Big Four accounting firms (third in revenue behind PricewaterhouseCoopers and Deloitte Touche Tohmatsu, ahead of KPMG). It has some 700 offices providing auditing and accounting services in 140 countries. The firm also provides legal services and advisory services relating to emerging growth companies, human resources issues, and corporate transactions (mergers and acquisitions, public offerings, and the like). Ernst & Young has one of the world's largest tax practices, serving multinational clients that have to comply with multiple local tax laws.

Ernst & Young offers its services to companies in a vast range of industries, including asset management, life sciences, mining, media and entertainment, retail, technology, and hotel and leisure. The company's financial reporting segment offers an IFRS/GAAP comparison so companies can compare and contrast the international and US accounting standards. Ernst & Young's tax business has grown as the economy has become increasingly globalized and companies face more complicated international compliance issues.

The group is organized in five geographic areas, with divisions covering Europe, the Middle East, India, and Africa; the Americas (Ernst & Young LLP); Oceania; Japan; and the Far East. The structure allows the company to develop and strengthen its cross-country operations within integrated regions.

Ernst & Young hands out an Entrepreneur of the Year award annually. Past recipients include CEO of Rosetta Stone Tom Adams, Dr. Jean-Paul Clozel, founder of Swiss pharmaceuticals company Actelion, and Cirque du Soleil founder Guy Laliberté.

HISTORY

In 1494 Luca Pacioli's *Summa di Arithmetica* became the first published text on double-entry bookkeeping, but it was almost 400 years before accounting became a profession.

In 1849 Frederick Whinney joined the UK firm of Harding & Pullein. His ledgers were so clear that he was advised to take up accounting, which was a growth field as stock companies proliferated. Whinney became a name partner in 1859 and his sons followed him into the business. The firm became Whinney, Smith & Whinney (WS&W) in 1894. After WWII, WS&W formed an alliance with Ernst & Ernst (founded in Cleveland in 1903 by brothers Alwin and Theodore Ernst), with each firm operating on the other's behalf across the Atlantic.

Whinney merged with Brown, Fleming & Murray in 1965 to become Whinney Murray. In 1979 Whinney Murray, Turquands Barton Mayhew (also a UK firm), and Ernst & Ernst merged to form Ernst & Whinney.

But Ernst & Whinney wasn't done merging. Ten years later, when it was the fourth-largest accounting firm, it merged with #5 Arthur Young, which had been founded by Scotsman Arthur Young in 1895 in Kansas City. Long known as "old reliable," Arthur Young fell on hard times in the 1980s because its audit relationships with failed S&Ls led to expensive litigation (settled in 1992 for $400 million).

Thus the new firm of Ernst & Young faced a rocky start. In 1990 it fended off rumors of collapse. The next year it slashed payroll, even thinning its partner roster. Exhausted by the S&L wars, in 1994 the firm replaced its pugnacious general counsel, Carl Riggio, with the more cost-conscious Kathryn Oberly.

In the mid-1990s Ernst & Young concentrated on consulting, particularly in software applications, and grew through acquisitions. In 1996 the firm bought Houston-based Wright Killen & Co., a petroleum and petrochemicals consulting firm, to form Ernst & Young Wright Killen. It also entered new alliances that year, including ones with Washington-based ISD/Shaw, which provided banking industry consulting, and India's Tata Consulting.

In 1997 Ernst & Young was sued for a record $4 billion for its alleged failure to effectively handle the 1993 restructuring of the defunct Merry-Go-Round Enterprises retail chain (it settled for $185 million in 1999). On the heels of a merger deal between Coopers & Lybrand and Price Waterhouse, Ernst & Young agreed in 1997 to merge with KPMG International. But Ernst & Young called off the negotiations in 1998, citing the uncertain regulatory process they faced.

The firm reached a settlement in 1999 in lawsuits regarding accounting errors at Informix and Avis Budget Group and sold its UK and southern African trust and fiduciary businesses to Royal Bank of Canada (now RBC Financial Group).

In 2000 Ernst & Young became the first of the (then) Big Five firms to sell its consultancy, dealing it to France's Cap Gemini Group for about $11 billion. The following year the UK accountancy watchdog group announced it would investigate Ernst & Young for its handling of the accounts of UK-based The Equitable Life Assurance Society. The insurer was forced to close to new business in 2000 because of massive financial difficulties.

Ernst & Young made headlines and gave competitors plenty to talk about in 2002 when closely held financial records were made public during a divorce case involving executive Rick Bobrow (who in 2003 abruptly retired as global CEO after just a year on the job).

Also in 2002 the firm allied with former New York City mayor Rudy Giuliani to launch a business consultancy bearing the Giuliani name. Ernst & Young later helped the venture to build its investment banking capabilities by selling its corporate finance unit (as well as its stake in Giuliani Partners) to that firm in 2004.

With the collapse of rival Andersen in 2002, Ernst & Young boosted its legal services, assembling some 2,000 lawyers in dozens of countries.

But the firm faced Andersen-style trouble of its own as client suits against auditors became more common in the wake of corporate scandals at Enron and other troubled companies. Both Avis Budget Group, Inc. (formerly Cendant) and HealthSouth sued Ernst & Young in connection with alleged accounting missteps in 2004.

In 2005 Ernst & Young's UK arm emerged victorious from a torrid legal battle with insurer Equitable Life, which in 2003 had sued the accountancy for professional negligence related to work performed when Ernst & Young was its auditor. Another highlight for that year was the fee bonanza fueled by changes in international accounting standards required by the Sarbanes-Oxley Act in the US.

EXECUTIVES

Chairman and CEO: James S. (Jim) Turley, age 55
Global Vice Chair, Advisory: Norman Lonergan
Global Vice Chair Assurance: Christian Mouillon
Global Vice Chair Transaction Advisory Services (TAS):
 Pip McCrostie
Global Vice Chair Tax: Mark A. Weinberger
Global COO: John Ferraro
Global Managing Partner Markets: John Murphy
Global Managing Partner Quality and Risk
 Management: Victoria Cochrane
Global Managing Partner Operations and Finance:
 Jeffrey H. (Jeff) Dworken
Global Managing Partner People: Sam Fouad
Global Managing Partner EMEIA Integration:
 Patrick Gounelle

LOCATIONS

HQ: Ernst & Young Global Limited
 Becket House, 1 Lambeth Palace Rd.
 London SE1 7EU, United Kingdom
Phone: 44-20-7951-2000   **Fax:** 44-20-7951-1345
US HQ: 5 Times Sq., New York, NY 10036
US Phone: 212-773-3000   **US Fax:** 212-773-6350
Web: www.ey.com

2009 Sales

	$ mil.	% of total
Europe, Middle East, India, Africa	9,636	45
Americas	8,647	41
Japan	1,196	6
Far East	1,144	5
Oceania	817	3
Total	**21,440**	**100**

PRODUCTS/OPERATIONS

2009 Sales by Service Line

	$ mil.	% of total
Assurance	10,141	47
Tax	5,822	27
Advisory	3,589	17
Transaction Advisory Services	1,888	9
Total	**21,440**	**100**

Selected Services

Assurance and Advisory
 Actuarial services
 Audits
 Accounting advisory
 Business risk services
 Internal audit
 Real estate advisory services
 Technology and security risk services
Emerging Growth Companies
 Corporate finance services
 Mergers and acquisitions advisory
 Operational consulting
 Strategic advisory
 Transactions advisory
Human Capital
 Compensation and benefits consulting
 Cost optimization and risk management
 Transaction support services
Law
 Corporate and M&A
 Employment
 Finance
 Information technology services
 Intellectual property
 International trade and antitrust
 Litigation and arbitration
 Real estate
Tax
 Global tax operations
 Indirect tax
 International tax

Transactions
 Capital management
 Corporate development advisory
 Financial and business modeling
 M&A advisory
 Post-deal advisory
 Strategic finance
 Transaction management
 Valuation

COMPETITORS

Baker Tilly International
BDO International
Crowe Horwath International
Deloitte
Grant Thornton International
KPMG
Moore Stephens International
PKF International
PricewaterhouseCoopers

HISTORICAL FINANCIALS

Company Type: Private

Income Statement

FYE: June 30

	REVENUE ($ mil.)	NET INCOME ($ mil.)	NET PROFIT MARGIN	EMPLOYEES
6/09	21,440	—	—	144,441
6/08	24,500	—	—	135,000
6/07	21,160	—	—	121,000
6/06	18,400	—	—	114,000
6/05	16,902	—	—	106,650
Annual Growth	**6.1%**	**—**	**—**	**7.9%**

Revenue History

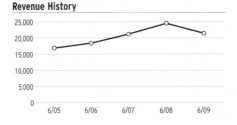

Compañía Española de Petróleos

Compañía Española de Petróleos (Cepsa) has its foot on the gas, the oil, and petrochemicals, too. Cepsa, the second-largest oil company in Spain (behind Repsol YPF), refines 121,900 barrels of crude oil daily, primarily in three refineries. Its oil exploration and production efforts are focused on Algeria, Colombia, Egypt, Peru, and Spain. It has proved reserves of 172.5 million barrels of oil equivalent. Cepsa's marketing network includes more than 1,800 gas stations in Spain and Portugal. It also produces a range of chemical products (including polyester precursors, phenol, plasticizers, and polypropylene) and has gas and power interests. Spain's TOTAL controls 49% of Cepsa and 47% of Abu Dhabi's IPIC.

In 2009 IPIC acquired the stakes in the company formerly held by Banco Santander and Unión Fenosa.

A significant part of the company's exploration and production activities is conducted through a production-sharing arrangement with Algeria's state-owned oil company, Sonatrach. The two companies are working together to develop reserves in the eastern part of the Sahara Desert. In 2009 the companies were given the go-ahead by Algerian authorites to drill 40 wells in the lucrative Timimoun Gas Field in southwestern Algeria. Cepsa has another joint venture with Sonatrach to promote an Algeria-Spain pipeline to meet Europe's rising demand for natural gas.

HISTORY

Compañía Española de Petróleos, S.A. (Cepsa) was founded in 1929 as Spain's first oil company listed on the Madrid stock exchange. The company built its first refinery the next year (Tenerife) and branched out into exploration and production in the 1940s. Cespa continued to grow, creating its lubricant supply operations in 1950 and entering the petrochemical sector in 1954.

The company would wait until 1967, however, to gain its next refinery, La Rábida. A refinery in Gibraltar followed in 1969. (In the 1960s and 1970s Franco pushed for more refineries in Spain, which supported his larger goal — to bulk up the country's heavy industry sector.)

Franco's legacy within Spain's oil industry was a non-diversified energy supply. Spain's reliance on oil meant that when two energy crises arose in the 1970s, the country was plunged into a recession that lasted until the mid-1980s. Cespa expanded outside Spain in 1987, building a storage facility in Portugal.

Almost a quarter of Cepsa's oil was derived from the United Arab Emirates, and that country's International Petroleum Investment Corp. (IPIC) bought a 10% stake in the oil company in 1989. France's Elf Aquitane (later absorbed into TOTAL FINA ELF) followed suit by acquiring a 25% stake in 1990. A year later Cepsa bought smaller Spanish refiner Ertoil from Elf Aquitane. As part of the deal, Elf increased its ownership in Cepsa from 25% to 33%, and Cepsa got its second refinery in Gibraltar.

Cepsa sold its part of chemical storage joint venture Proquimica in 1994, the same year that Banco Central Hispano sold half of its 36% stake in the company to an international fund managed by Morgan Grenfell. In 1995 Endesa, Spain's largest energy concern, invested in Cepsa, but sold its holdings four years later after buying a stake in rival oil company Repsol (now Repsol YPF).

In 2000 the company expanded into Canada by building a petrochemical factory in Quebec to produce purified terephthalic acid (PTA), a material used in plastics such as soft drink bottles. Cepsa also formed another joint venture with Sonatrach to promote an Algeria-Spain natural gas pipeline.

Cepsa and TOTAL FINA ELF (later renamed TOTAL) received regulatory approval in 2001 to merge their Spanish natural gas supply units. The resulting joint venture company, CEPSA Gas Comercializadora, accounted for about 5% of Spain's liberalized natural gas market in 2002.

In 2005 the company formed CEPSA Marine Fuels to supply fuels to the shipping market.

To streamline operations, in 2008 Cepsa set up CEPSA Química as an umbrella company to handle all of its petrochemical operations.

EXECUTIVES

Chairman: Santiago Bergareche Busquet
Vice Chairman: Michel Bénézit
Vice Chairman: Alfredo Sáenz Abad, age 67
SVP Corporate Technical Division: Pedro Miró Roig
SVP Exploration and Production, Natural Gas and Corporate Management: Fernando Maravall Herrero
SVP Petrochemicals: Fernando Iturrieta Gil
SVP Oil Marketing and CEO: Dominique de Riberolles
SVP Human Resources, Legal Affairs, and Property Asset Management: Juan Rodríguez Fidalgo
VP Corporate Communications and Institutional Relations: Luis Calderón Castro
VP Specialties: Federico Bonet Pla
VP Retail and Wholesale Operations: Francisco Calderón Pareja
VP Refining: José Maria García Aguado
VP Supply, Trading, Bunkering, and Aviation: Iñigo Diaz de Espada Soriano
VP Planning, Control, and Distribution and Secretary of the Executive Management Committee: José E. Aranguren Escobar
VP Exploration and Production: Luis Travesedo Loring
Auditors: Deloitte SL

LOCATIONS

HQ: Compañía Española de Petróleos, S.A.
Campo de las Naciones, Avenida del Partenón 10
28042 Madrid, Spain
Phone: 34-91-337-60-00   **Fax:** 34-91-725-4116
Web: www.cepsa.es

COMPETITORS

BP	Hess Corporation
Eni	IBERDROLA
Exxon Mobil	Repsol YPF
Gas Natural SDG	Royal Dutch Shell

HISTORICAL FINANCIALS

Company Type: Public

Income Statement

FYE: December 31

	REVENUE ($ mil.)	NET INCOME ($ mil.)	NET PROFIT MARGIN	EMPLOYEES
12/09	26,321	560	2.1%	11,703
12/08	35,400	410	1.2%	11,815
12/07	31,249	1,126	3.6%	11,398
12/06	27,319	1,071	3.9%	—
12/05	21,755	1,197	5.5%	10,912
Annual Growth	4.9%	(17.3%)	—	1.8%

2009 Year-End Financials

Debt ratio: —	No. of shares (mil.): 268
Return on equity: 7.5%	Dividends
Cash ($ mil.): 858	Yield: 4.6%
Current ratio: 1.42	Payout: 71.1%
Long-term debt ($ mil.): —	Market value ($ mil.): 8,349

Stock History

Spanish: CEP

	STOCK PRICE ($) FY Close	P/E High/Low	PER SHARE ($) Earnings	Dividends	Book Value
12/09	31.20	49 15	2.01	1.43	28.67
12/08	95.28	68 65	1.45	0.56	27.42
Annual Growth	(67.3%)	— —	38.6%	155.4%	4.6%

EXOR S.p.A.

Controlled by the wealthy Agnelli family through parent firm Giovanni Agnelli and C., holding company EXOR (formerly IFI — Istituto Finanziario Industriale) owns stakes in a variety of enterprises. The company owns about 30% of automotive giant Fiat (which the Agnellis founded and still control); 60% of one of Italy's top soccer clubs, Juventus; more than 70% of US real estate giant Cushman & Wakefield; some 15% of Swiss testing equipment manufacturer SGS; and about a quarter of Sequana Capital, which owns European papermakers Arjowiggins and Antalis. EXOR owns 100% of Italy-based Alpitour, which operates tours and hotels.

Minority stakes in Italian banks and a France-based TV production company help round out its holdings.

Most of the former IFI's portfolio was owned through holding company Ifil. In order to simplify its structure, IFI in 2009 acquired the approximately 30% of Ifil that it did not already own, forming EXOR.

HISTORY

Istituto Finanziario Industriale (IFI) was formed by Giovanni Agnelli in 1927 as a family "safe" for his stakes of various industrial businesses. Automaker Fiat immediately became and remains the centerpiece of IFI's holdings.

Fiat benefited from Mussolini's protectionist policies in the 1930s, but Agnelli remained a liberal. During WWII, when Axis defeat appeared imminent, Agnelli slowed war production and put Italian resistance members on his payroll. At the end of the war, Fiat executives — unable to wait for the Marshall Plan — traveled to the US to seek reconstruction loans.

Upon Agnelli's death in 1945, ownership of IFI passed to his Agnelli and Nasi family heirs. In 1958 IFI gained control of Finanziaria di Partecipazioni (Ifil), another industrial holding company.

Ten years later IFI formed Infint (renamed EXOR Group in 1994) to manage IFI's foreign shares. Also in 1968 IFI stock was offered to the public to fund company expansion. The Agnelli and Nasi families' shares decreased throughout the 1970s and 1980s as more capital was sought.

The 1970s saw IFI dispose of noncore holdings, such as Società Assicuratrice Industriale, in order to cut debt.

IFI and Ifil bought back shares of Fiat in the 1980s while Ifil began to invest more widely. Parent company Giovanni Agnelli e C. S.a.p.az. (G.A. e C.), controlled solely by the Agnelli and Nasi families, formed in 1987 and bought IFI.

In 1999 G.A. e C. and IFI upped their stakes in EXOR Group. Two years later IFI sold its stake in the Rockefeller Center to T. Speyer & Crown. In 2003 the junior Giovanni Agnelli died; Umberto Agnelli succumbed the following year.

IFI in 2009 acquired the approximately 30% of Ifil that it did not already own, forming EXOR.

EXECUTIVES

Chairman: John P. Elkann, age 34
Honorary Chairman: Gianluigi Gabetti, age 83
Vice Chairman: Tiberto Ruy Brandolini d'Adda, age 62
Vice Chairman: Pio Teodorani-Fabbri
CEO and Director: Carlo Barel di Sant'Albano, age 46
CFO: Enrico Vellano
Managing Director: Pierre Marinet
Managing Director: Alessandro Potestá
Managing Director: Steven Geller
Secretary: Pierluigi Bernasconi
Chief Administration Officer: Aldo Mazzia
Auditors: Deloitte & Touche S.p.A.

LOCATIONS

HQ: EXOR S.p.A.
Corso Matteotti, 26
10121 Turin, Italy
Phone: 39-011-509-0266   **Fax:** 39-011-535-600
Web: www.exor.com

PRODUCTS/OPERATIONS

Selected Holdings

Alpitour (tourism)
Banjay Holding (17%, TV production, France)
Cushman & Wakefield (72%)
Fiat (30%)
Gruppo Banca Leonardo (10%)
Juventus F.C. S.p.A. (60%)
Sequana Capital (27%, France)
SGS (15%, Switzerland)

COMPETITORS

Bastogi
Gemina
Investor AB
Italmobiliare
Madison Dearborn
Mittel
Wendel

HISTORICAL FINANCIALS

Company Type: Public

Income Statement

FYE: December 31

	REVENUE ($ mil.)	NET INCOME ($ mil.)	NET PROFIT MARGIN	EMPLOYEES
12/09	3,478	(578)	—	16,950
12/08	3,755	603	16.1%	17,885
12/07	3,911	979	25.0%	17,461
12/06	7,301	528	7.2%	18,239
12/05	6,430	1,508	23.4%	18,458
Annual Growth	(14.2%)	—	—	(2.1%)

2009 Year-End Financials

Debt ratio: —	No. of shares (mil.): 160
Return on equity: —	Dividends
Cash ($ mil.): 903	Yield: 4.6%
Current ratio: 2.38	Payout: —
Long-term debt ($ mil.): —	Market value ($ mil.): 2,297

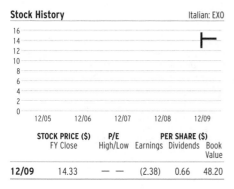

	STOCK PRICE ($) FY Close	P/E High/Low	PER SHARE ($) Earnings	Dividends	Book Value
12/09	14.33	— —	(2.38)	0.66	48.20

Fiat S.p.A.

The country that gave us Sophia Loren and Leonardo da Vinci also gave us the century-old Fiat. The group's cars range from models like the popular Fiat Nuova 500 to the Alfa Romeo, Ferrari (85% owned), and Maserati brands. Fiat divides its business into autos; agricultural and construction equipment (led by CNH Global); commercial vehicles (Iveco); and components, which includes Magneti Marelli, FPT Powertrain Technologies, 85%-owned engine part maker Teksid, and industrial automation supplier Comau. It is also involved in publishing and communications through newspaper *La Stampa* and ad firm Pulikompass. In 2009 Fiat took a 20% stake in Chrysler, assuming management control of the US carmaker.

Fiat announced in 2010 that it plans to spin off its farm and construction equipment and heavy truck businesses into a new company. The spinoff will yield Fiat Industrial S.p.A., comprised of CHN agriculture and construction equipment, Iveco, and FPT Industries and Marine operations. Reinvented and free of its industrial operations, "New Fiat" aims to drive an unadulterated auto company, able to manufacture six million cars by 2014. Its primary brands will include Fiat, Alfa, Lancia, Maserati, and Ferrari.

Fiat earlier reached a deal with Chrysler and its majority owner at the time, Cerberus Capital Management, on a broad cooperative agreement that would give the Italian carmaker a 20% equity stake in Chrysler, which it can increase to 35% once certain milestones are reached; Fiat looks to eventually increase its ownership to 49% of Chrysler. Fiat will provide technology and vehicle platforms to the American carmaker, allowing Chrysler to build and sell smaller, more fuel-efficient cars in North America.

Chrysler was able to complete new agreements with its labor unions, and most of its lenders were willing to swap their debt for a cash payout proposed by the Obama administration's auto task force. A group of lenders held out on the deal, however, and Chrysler filed for Chapter 11 protection from creditors.

Chrysler and Fiat went forward with their plans when the American carmaker exited from bankruptcy reorganization, six weeks after its filing. Fiat appointed three of the nine directors on Chrysler's new board. Fiat CEO Sergio Marchionne became the CEO of Chrysler Group (as

the restructured company is known), succeeding Robert Nardelli.

In 2009 the company set up a €400 million ($570 million) joint venture with Guangzhou Automobile Group to make cars and engines for the Chinese market. Its first China-made model is planned for a 2011 launch.

The founding Agnelli family, through holding company EXOR, owns about 30% of Fiat.

HISTORY

Ex-cavalry officer Giovanni Agnelli founded Fabbrica Italiana di Automobili Torino (Fiat) in 1899. Between 1903 and 1918 the automaker expanded into trucks, railcars, aviation, and tractors. Protected by tariffs, Fiat became Italy's dominant auto company.

WWII boosted Fiat's fortunes, but bombs damaged many of its plants. With US support, Fiat rebuilt and survived by exporting and by building plants abroad. As growth in Italy resumed, Fiat began making steel and construction equipment.

After the European Community forced Italy to lower tariffs in 1961, Fiat lost market share, although foreign sales helped offset its woes. Giovanni Agnelli II (the founder's grandson) became chairman in 1966. Fiat then bought high-end Italian carmakers Lancia and Ferrari in 1969.

The company formed Fiat Auto S.p.A. in 1979, bringing together the Fiat, Lancia, Autobianchi, Abarth, and Ferrari lines. The next year Cesare Romiti became managing director and cut 23,000 jobs and broke union influence at Fiat. The company closed its unprofitable US car operations in 1983. Fiat and British Ford combined their truck operations in 1986, and Fiat also bought Alfa Romeo that year.

Fiat and Ford merged their farm and construction equipment divisions in 1991 to form Fiat subsidiary New Holland (renamed CNH Global in 1999).

Slow car sales in Italy prompted Fiat to temporarily lay off about 74,000 workers in 1996, and chairman Agnelli stepped down. In 1997 Agnelli's successor, Romiti, and financial director Paolo Mattioli were convicted of falsifying records and illegally financing political parties. They were barred from employment at Fiat.

Paolo Fresco, former vice chairman of General Electric, replaced Romiti as head of Fiat in 1998. The next year New Holland bought agricultural and construction equipment maker Case for around $4.3 billion and changed its name to CNH Global. Also, Fiat began making light commercial trucks in China with Yuejin Motor.

To expand its auto business outside Europe, Fiat agreed in 2000 to trade a 20% stake in its car unit for a 5.1% stake in GM. That year ALSTOM agreed to buy a 51% stake in Fiat's rail unit. Also in 2000 Fiat began selling off the divisions of Magneti Marelli. The company's bid (with a consortium including Electricité de France) of about $5.5 billion for control of agro-energy group Montedison was accepted in July.

In 2002 Fiat announced it would lay off as many as 5,600 workers, and it sold its entire stake in GM to an unnamed investment bank for nearly $1.2 billion. A provision of the 2000 deal that gave GM 20% (later reduced to 10%) of Fiat Auto also gave the Italian automaker a "put" option to force GM to buy the remaining 90% as early as 2004 (or as late as 2009). Gianni Agnelli, Fiat's honorary chairman and grandson of the company's founder, died at the age of 81 in early 2003. Later that year Fiat sold its Fiat Avio avia-

tion unit to The Carlyle Group and Italian defense group Finmeccanica for about $1.8 billion.

Fiat chairman Umberto Agnelli died in 2004, plunging the company into management chaos. When the board named Ferrari and Maserati chairman Luca Cordero di Montezemolo chairman of Fiat instead of Fiat CEO Giuseppe Morchio, Morchio suddenly quit. The company named turnaround specialist Sergio Marchionne as Fiat S.p.A.'s fifth CEO in two years.

In early 2005 GM claimed the previously negotiated "put" option was rendered invalid when Fiat Auto restructured and GM's stake was reduced to 10%. Fiat insisted GM's claim was false. After a month of very private negotiations early in 2005, GM finally agreed to pay Fiat $2 billion to settle the dispute, and thereby avoid having to buy Fiat Auto. After the messy divorce from General Motors, Fiat replaced the CEO of beleaguered Fiat Auto, Hebert Demel, with Fiat CEO Sergio Marchionne, marking the first time since 1899 that a single person ran both the Fiat holding company and Fiat Auto.

In mid-2009 Fiat took a 20% stake in Chrysler, assuming management control of the US carmaker. Fiat had reached a deal with Chrysler and its majority owner at the time, Cerberus Capital Management, on a broad cooperative agreement that would give the Italian carmaker a 20% equity stake in Chrysler, which it could increase to 35% once certain milestones were reached. Reeling from turmoil in the auto industry in the midst of a global economic downturn, Chrysler sought loans from the US government's auto task force to hold it over until the deal with Fiat could be completed. While most of Chrysler's lenders agreed to swap their debt for a cash payout from the US administration, a group of lenders held out on the deal; Chrysler filed for Chapter 11 bankruptcy protection early in 2009. Fiat and Chrysler were able to complete the deal when Chrysler emerged from bankruptcy six weeks after its filing. Fiat CEO Sergio Marchionne took over as CEO of Chrysler Group (as the restructured company is known).

EXECUTIVES

Chairman: John P. Elkann, age 34
CEO and Director; CEO, Fiat Group Automobiles; CEO, Chrysler Group LLC: Sergio Marchionne, age 58
EVP, Controller, and Interim CFO: Alessandro Baldi, age 57
EVP Human Resources: Paolo Raimondi
SVP Industrial Relations: Paolo Rebaudengo, age 62
SVP Manufacturing and Chief Manufacturing Officer: Stefan Ketter, age 50
SVP GEC Coordinator and Group ICT: Gilberto Ceresa, age 44
SVP Communications: Simone Migliarino, age 62
VP Investor Relations: Marco Auriemma
Group Treasurer: Camilo Rossotto, age 48
Head of Product Portfolio Planning and Product Concept: Sergio Cravero, age 49
Head, Fiat Brand: Andrea Formica
Head International Operations and Fiat Professional: Lorenzo Sistino
Statutory Auditor — Chairman: Riccardo Perotta
Secretary and Director: Franzo Grande Stevens
CTO; CEO, Maserati, Abarth, and Alfa Romeo: Harald J. Wester, age 51
CEO, Lancia Automobiles: Olivier François, age 49
CEO, Fiat Research Center: Nevio Di Giusto
CEO, Comau and Teksid: Riccardo Tarantini, age 60
CEO, Ferrari: Jean Todt, age 64
CEO, CNH: Harold D. Boyanovsky, age 66
CEO, Ferrari: Amedeo Felisa, age 64
CEO, Iveco: Alfredo Altavilla, age 47
CEO, Magneti Marelli: Eugenio Razelli, age 59
Auditors: Deloitte & Touche S.p.A.

LOCATIONS

HQ: Fiat S.p.A.
250 Via Nizza
10126 Turin, Italy
Phone: 39-011-006-1111   **Fax:** 39-011-006-3798
Web: www.fiatgroup.com

2009 Sales

	% of total
Italy	25
Brazil	18
US	9
Germany	8
France	8
UK	4
Spain	3
Poland	3
Turkey	2
Other countries	20
Total	**100**

PRODUCTS/OPERATIONS

2009 Sales

	% of total
Autos	
Core (Fiat, Lancia, Alfa Romeo)	46
Ferrari	3
Maserati	1
Agricultural & Construction Equipment (CNH)	18
Trucks & Commercial Vehicles (Iveco)	13
FPT Powertrain Technologies	9
Components (Magneti Marelli)	8
Production Systems (Comau)	1
Metallurgical Products (Teksid)	1
Total	**100**

Selected Brands

Abarth
  500
  Grande Punto
Alfa Romeo
  8C
  147
  159
  Brera
  GT
  MiTo
  Spider
Ferrari
  Eight Cylinder
    430 Scuderia
    F430 Spider
    Ferrari California
  12 Cylinder
    599 GTB Fiorano
    612 Scaglietti
    FXX
Fiat
  500
  600
  Bravo
  Grande Punto 3
  Multipla
  Nuova Croma
  Panda
  Punto Classic
  Qubo
  Sedici
  Ulysse
Lancia
  Delta
  Musa
  Phedra
  Thesis
  Ypsilon
Maserati
  Gran Turismo
  Gran Turismo S
  Quattroporte
  Quattroporte S
  Quattroporte Sport GT S

COMPETITORS

AGCO	Mazda
AUDI	Navistar International
BMW	Nissan
Caterpillar	Oshkosh Truck
Daimler	PACCAR
Deere	Peugeot
FMC	Porsche Automobil
Ford Motor	Holding
General Motors	PROTON Holdings
Halliburton	Renault
Honda	Saab Automobile
Ingersoll-Rand	Suzuki Motor
Isuzu	Toyota
JLG Industries	Volkswagen
Kia Motors	

HISTORICAL FINANCIALS

Company Type: Public

Income Statement

FYE: December 31

	REVENUE ($ mil.)	NET INCOME ($ mil.)	NET PROFIT MARGIN	EMPLOYEES
12/09	71,806	(1,215)	—	190,014
12/08	83,696	2,426	2.9%	198,348
12/07	86,149	3,023	3.5%	185,227
12/06	68,437	1,407	2.1%	172,012
12/05	55,307	1,581	2.9%	173,695
Annual Growth	**6.7%**	**—**	**—**	**2.3%**

2009 Year-End Financials

Debt ratio: 208.1%   No. of shares (mil.): 1,092
Return on equity: —   Dividends
Cash ($ mil.): 17,522   Yield: 0.0%
Current ratio: 2.25   Payout: —
Long-term debt ($ mil.): 30,729   Market value ($ mil.): 16,045

Stock History

Italian: F

	STOCK PRICE ($) FY Close	P/E High/Low		PER SHARE ($) Earnings	Dividends	Book Value
12/09	14.69	—	—	(0.97)	0.00	13.52
12/08	6.47	14	4	1.80	0.56	13.36
12/07	26.05	16	9	2.25	0.23	14.29
12/06	19.10	20	9	1.04	0.00	11.32
12/05	8.72	6	4	1.48	0.00	9.44
Annual Growth	**13.9%**	**—**	**—**	**—**	**—**	**9.4%**

FirstGroup plc

FirstGroup was not the first group to get stakes in the UK's deregulated bus and train industries, but it is one of the nation's largest diversified transportation enterprises. The company operates the First Capital Connect, First Great Western, First ScotRail, and TransPennine Express railway franchises in the UK, and its trains carry about 285 million people annually. FirstGroup provides public bus services throughout the UK that carry some 3 million passengers daily. Its

FirstGroup America unit provides school bus services, operates public bus systems, and manages vehicle fleets in North America. Greyhound, North America's leading intercity bus company, is part of FirstGroup America.

As with most transportation companies, FirstGroup suffered as fuel prices hit an all-time high in 2008. The company lost some £23 million (about $35 million) during the fiscal year that ended in March 2009 on fuel-hedging contracts. (Fuel-hedging is when transportation companies lock in a predetermined price for future fuel purchases.)

The global recession has hurt FirstGroup's Greyhound business in the US and its UK bus operations, while its school bus and rail operations have remained steady. The company's mix of contract-backed and passenger sales is helping to insulate it from ups and downs in consumer demand. To guard against further losses, FirstGroup is trimming £200 million ($308 million) from its operating costs by reducing the frequency on lower-performing routes and laying off 4,400 workers (about 3%).

With its four UK rail franchises, FirstGroup operates First Hull Trains (intercity passenger services). The company has seen strong demand for rail transportation, and its First Great Western and First Capital Connect units have absorbed new operations. To keep pace, FirstGroup is investing in the infrastructure of its systems. At the same time, it is exploring opportunities to acquire rail businesses in Europe.

FirstGroup pulled off a coup in February 2010 by beating out some 80 companies to be named the preferred bidder for bus contracts to transport spectators during the 2012 Summer Olympics in London. Under the deal, which is worth £20 million ($30 million), FirstGroup will provide about 900 vehicles.

To reduce its debt, the company sold cargo hauler First GB Railfreight in mid-2010. French freight transporter Groupe Eurotunnel paid about £26.3 million ($38.2 million) to consolidate its European freight train position. Since the deregulation in the European rail freight sector, British and European buyers have been acquiring companies to create pan-continental networks.

HISTORY

FirstGroup was created when large Badgerline, which ran buses through northern and southwestern England and in the Midlands, acquired small Aberdeen bus company GRT in 1995. But the bus companies that make up the group date back decades.

The Transport Act of 1947 nationalized Britain's bus companies and brought rail, road, and canal transport under one governing body, the British Transport Commission. The UK's buses were operated by the state-controlled National Bus Company.

Under free enterprise champion Margaret Thatcher, public transportation became one of the first of the UK's national industries to be privatized. The country's express coach system was deregulated in 1980. In 1985 the Transport Act authorized bus deregulation outside London and led the way to the breakup of National Bus Company, which operated 70 bus subsidiaries.

Trevor Smallwood was an executive of Bristol Omnibus in 1983 when it split into four companies. He became managing director of Bristol Country Bus (which later changed its name to Badgerline). In 1986 Smallwood led a management LBO of Badgerline. The company soon acquired other bus lines, and by 1993, when it went public, Badgerline was operating 2,300 buses in Birmingham, Bristol, Chelmsford, London, Plymouth, and Swansea.

GRT was bought out by its management in 1989 (becoming the first Scottish company to be privatized). To become a national player, GRT acquired English coach line Midland Bluebird in 1990, and three years later expanded further with the acquisition of Northampton and Leicester bus companies. The buyouts boosted its fleet from 200 to 730 buses, and GRT went public in 1994.

Following the industry trend toward consolidation, in 1995 Badgerline, then the #3 bus operator, acquired GRT, the #7 bus company. The new company, FirstBus, became the second-largest UK bus firm, behind Stagecoach.

FirstBus made a series of bus acquisitions in 1996 and 1997, including Great Yarmouth Transport, Greater Manchester Buses, Portsmouth Transit, and Strathclyde Buses. Picking up on opportunities created by British Rail's privatization, FirstBus won a seven-year franchise in 1997 to operate the Great Eastern Railway. It moved into another deregulating industry, airport management, with the acquisition of a 51% stake in Bristol International Airport. The company changed its name from FirstBus to FirstGroup in 1997, reflecting its expansion into new transportation markets.

In 1998 FirstGroup bought control of bus operator Mainline Partnership and partnered with New World Development to operate bus services in Hong Kong. Also that year, FirstGroup acquired the Great Western and North Western rail franchises. Expanding into the US, in 1999 the company bought Ryder System's school bus unit.

Exiting some of its operations in 2000, the company sold its 26% stake in its joint venture with New World Development. FirstGroup sold its 51% stake in the Bristol airport to a joint venture between Spain's Cintra and Australia's Macquarie Bank. At the same time, it bought the Hertz Group school bus operations in Canada.

The next year the company expanded its US school bus operations by acquiring companies in Maine and Wisconsin. In October 2007 FirstGroup made an even bigger move to expand in the US when it acquired Laidlaw International, North America's leading bus operator.

EXECUTIVES

Chairman: Martin J. Gilbert, age 54
Deputy Chairman and Chief Executive; Chairman Executive Safety Committee: Sir Moir Lockhead, age 65
COO and Deputy Chief Executive: Timothy T. (Tim) O'Toole, age 54
Finance Director: Jeff Carr, age 49
Managing Director, Aircoach: Allen Parker
Managing Director, FRS — Rail Replacement: Maurice Duckworth
Managing Director, FCC: Jim Morgan
Managing Director, Potteries: Kenneth Poole
Managing Director, FGW: Mark Hopwood
Managing Director, First ScotRail: Steve Montgomery
Managing Director, UK Rail and Interim Managing Director, Rail Division: Mary Grant
Commercial Director and Company Secretary: Sidney (Sid) Barrie, age 58
Director Group Corporate Communications: Rachael Borthwick
Director Group Public Affairs and Communications: Paul Moore
Auditors: Deloitte LLP

LOCATIONS

HQ: FirstGroup plc
395 King St.
Aberdeen AB24 5RP, United Kingdom
Phone: 44-1224-650-100   **Fax:** 44-1224-650-140
US HQ: 600 Vine St., Ste. 1400, Cincinnati, OH 45202
US Phone: 513-241-2200   **US Fax:** 513-419-3242
Web: www.firstgroup.com

2010 Sales

	% of total
UK	53
US	40
Canada	7
Total	**100**

PRODUCTS/OPERATIONS

2010 Sales

	% of total
North America	37
UK Rail	35
UK Bus	18
Greyhound	9
Total	**100**

COMPETITORS

Arriva
Atlantic Express
Go-Ahead Group
National Express Group
Stagecoach
Veolia Environnement
Virgin Rail

HISTORICAL FINANCIALS

Company Type: Public

Income Statement

FYE: March 31

	REVENUE ($ mil.)	NET INCOME ($ mil.)	NET PROFIT MARGIN	EMPLOYEES
3/10	9,522	199	2.1%	133,203
3/09	8,792	204	2.3%	135,807
3/08	9,387	240	2.6%	105,685
3/07	7,297	180	2.5%	74,233
3/06	5,278	187	3.5%	70,747
Annual Growth	**15.9%**	**1.5%**	**—**	**17.1%**

2010 Year-End Financials

Debt ratio: —
Return on equity: 15.8%
Cash ($ mil.): 505
Current ratio: —
Long-term debt ($ mil.): —
No. of shares (mil.): 481
Dividends
Yield: 5.4%
Payout: —
Market value ($ mil.): 2,602

Stock History

London: FGP

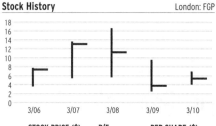

	STOCK PRICE ($) FY Close	P/E High/Low		PER SHARE ($) Earnings	Dividends	Book Value
3/10	5.41	—	—	—	0.29	2.85
3/09	3.80	—	—	—	0.25	2.38
3/08	11.23	—	—	—	0.32	2.92
3/07	13.06	—	—	—	0.29	2.48
3/06	7.39	—	—	—	0.23	1.20
Annual Growth	**(7.5%)**	—	—	—	**6.0%**	**24.1%**

Flextronics International

Having factories on four continents would make you flexible, too. Flextronics International offers turnkey manufacturing services to the world's leading electronics companies, including Cisco Systems, Eastman Kodak, Ericsson, Hewlett-Packard, Microsoft, Research In Motion, and Sony-Ericsson. The company's services range from design engineering, through manufacturing and assembly, to distribution and warehousing. It manufactures and assembles printed circuit boards, electromechanical components, subsystems, and complete systems for a wide range of makers of networking and telecommunications equipment, computers, consumer electronics, and medical instrumentation.

Constantly struggling with its profitability in a low-margin business, Flextronics is restructuring its operations. The company is closing some plants and reducing the workforce at others as it tries to find the right mix of manufacturing to make money. In 2009 it sold its stake in Aricent, a privately held communications software company, to investment firms KKR and CPP Investment Board for about $250 million. The sale is part of a plan to sell noncore assets as Flextronics tries to bolster its balance sheet.

The global recession and credit crisis exposed Flextronics to financially troubled customers and suppliers, some of which are in bankruptcy reorganization, such as Nortel Networks.

The company has a limited number of customers — the top 10 of which account for almost half of sales — and a limited number of global competitors, while also contending with other rivals that have a regional or product-specific focus, and original design manufacturers, which design their own electronics products and tailor them for specific customers.

In 2009 Flextronics acquired SloMedical S.R.O., a leading maker of disposable medical devices for the European market. In addition to adding disposable devices for the medical and surgical market in Eastern Europe, SloMedical, which is based in Slovenia, gives Flextronics an FDA-compliant, clean room-enabled production site with low production costs.

The preceding year the company acquired contract disposable device maker Avail Medical Products to further the expansion of its Flextronics Medical segment.

HISTORY

Flextronics International, formed in 1990, follows two earlier contract manufacturers named Flextronics formed in 1969 and 1980. The latter iteration used acquisitions to expand throughout Asia and the US. In 1988 it opened the first US-managed contract electronics plant in China, and that year sales topped $200 million.

But acquisitions had burdened Flextronics with debt and left it with disparate operations. It divested its US-based manufacturing operations and laid off 75% of its workforce. The company brought in a management team to sell its healthy Asian operations to pay off debt. These operations formed Flextronics International.

A revitalized Flextronics, based in Singapore, went public in 1994. It quickly joined the industry rush toward consolidation and globalization.

Acquisitions included nCHIP (California, 1996), FICO Plastics (Hong Kong, 1997), Neutronics Electronic Industries (Austria, 1997), and Kyrel EMS Oyj (Finland and France, 1999).

In early 2000 Flextronics acquired rival The DII Group, which propelled the company to the #4 spot in contract manufacturing (behind Solectron, SCI Systems, and Celestica). The company was also selected by Microsoft to build the software juggernaut's Xbox video game console. Later in 2000 Motorola and Flextronics signed one of the largest outsourcing deals ever, worth an estimated $30 billion over five years. The company expanded further in Asia when it acquired JIT Holdings, a Singapore-based electronics manufacturer.

Early in 2001 Flextronics announced a deal with telecommunication giant Ericsson; under the pact Flextronics assumed management of Ericsson's mobile phone manufacturing operations worldwide. Later that year the company announced that it would cut its workforce by about 10%, and that the multibillion-dollar deal with Motorola had unraveled due to a continuing market slowdown. Flextronics also repurchased Motorola's 5% stake in the company.

Also in 2001 Flextronics bought Telcom Global Solutions, a supplier of planning and design services for telecommunications providers. Flextronics later announced a deal with Xerox to acquire Xerox facilities in Brazil, Canada, Malaysia, and Mexico for about $220 million, and to provide manufacturing services to Xerox for five years. Later that year the company announced that it would lay off 10,000 workers — about 15% of its staff — in a cost-cutting move.

In 2002 the company announced a deal with CASIO COMPUTER, under which Flextronics bought two CASIO plants in Asia, then supplied the Japanese electronics maker with finished products in a three-year deal. Also that year the company significantly expanded its presence in southern China with the purchase of Hong Kong-based NatSteel Broadway (printed circuit boards, plastic and metal components).

In 2004 Flextronics took over optical, wireless, and enterprise manufacturing, as well as optical design operations from Nortel Networks in a four-year supply deal generating about $2.5 billion in annual revenues. Flextronics later closed several former Nortel facilities in Canada, France, and Northern Ireland.

Flextronics also acquired a majority ownership stake in India-based software services provider Hughes Software Systems (HSS) in 2004. Flextronics purchased Agilent's mobile communications camera module business early in 2005. The company sold its semiconductor division to AMIS Holdings (now part of ON Semiconductor), and its Flextronics Network Services (FNS) division was merged with a company called Telavie and renamed Relacom; Flextronics retained a 30% stake.

To focus on its core electronics manufacturing services business in 2006, Flextronics sold its Flextronics Software Systems business to an affiliate of Kohlberg Kravis Roberts (KKR) for about $900 million. Flextronics retained a 15% stake in the software development business.

In 2007 Flextronics purchased rival contract manufacturer Solectron in a deal valued at $3.6 billion. The combination vaulted the company into the position of the second largest contract electronics manufacturer in the world.

EXECUTIVES

Chairman: H. Raymond (Ray) Bingham, age 64
CEO and Director: Michael M. (Mike) McNamara, age 53, $7,755,768 total compensation
CFO: Paul Read, age 45, $2,020,046 total compensation
President, Computing: Sean P. Burke, age 49, $1,676,627 total compensation
President, Infrastructure: Michael J. Clarke, age 56, $1,608,678 total compensation
President, Global Operations: Francois Barbier, age 51, $1,192,170 total compensation
President, Mobile Market: Gernot Weiss
President, Multek: Werner Widmann, age 58
SVP and General Counsel: Carrie L. Schiff, age 44, $1,354,839 total compensation
SVP Investor Relations: Warren Ligan
SVP Finance: Christopher (Chris) Collier, age 42
Auditors: Deloitte & Touche LLP

LOCATIONS

HQ: Flextronics International Ltd.
2 Changi South Lane
486123, Singapore
Phone: 65-6890-7188
Web: www.flextronics.com

2010 Sales

	$ mil.	% of total
Asia	11,595.4	48
Americas	7,831.0	33
Europe	4,684.3	19
Total	**24,110.7**	**100**

PRODUCTS/OPERATIONS

Selected Services

Assembly and manufacturing
 Complex electromechanical components
 Printed circuit boards (PCBs)
 Subsystems (including those that incorporate PCBs)
Distribution
 Just-in-time delivery
Engineering
 Design
 Prototyping
 Test development
Materials procurement and management
 Planning
 Purchasing
 Warehousing
Network support
 Installation and maintenance of telecommunications
  systems and corporate networks
Packaging
Plastic and metal components
Testing
 Computer-aided testing of PCBs, subsystems, and
  systems

COMPETITORS

ASUSTeK	MiTAC
Benchmark Electronics	Nam Tai
Cal-Comp Electronics	Plexus
Celestica	Quanta Computer
Changhong Electric	Sanmina-SCI
Compal Electronics	SYNNEX
Elcoteq	Tech Data
Fabrinet	TTM Technologies
Hana Microelectronics	Universal Scientific
Hon Hai	Venture Corp.
IBM Canada	Viasystems
Ingram Micro	WBL Corp.
Jabil	Wistron
Kimball International	

HISTORICAL FINANCIALS

Company Type: Public

Income Statement

FYE: March 31

	REVENUE ($ mil.)	NET INCOME ($ mil.)	NET PROFIT MARGIN	EMPLOYEES
3/10	24,111	19	0.1%	165,000
3/09	30,949	(6,086)	—	160,000
3/08	27,558	(639)	—	162,000
3/07	18,854	509	2.7%	116,000
3/06	15,288	141	0.9%	99,000
Annual Growth	**12.1%**	**(39.8%)**	**—**	**13.6%**

2010 Year-End Financials

Debt ratio: 100.3%
Return on equity: 1.0%
Cash ($ mil.): 1,928
Current ratio: 1.26
Long-term debt ($ mil.): 1,990
No. of shares (mil.): 766
Dividends
 Yield: —
 Payout: —
Market value ($ mil.): 6,007

Stock History

NASDAQ (GS): FLEX

	STOCK PRICE ($) FY Close	P/E High/Low		PER SHARE ($) Earnings	Dividends	Book Value
3/10	7.84	419	149	0.02	—	2.59
3/09	2.89	—	—	(7.41)	—	2.39
3/08	9.39	—	—	(0.89)	—	10.66
3/07	10.94	16	11	0.85	—	8.06
3/06	10.35	60	37	0.24	—	6.99
Annual Growth	**(6.7%)**	**—**	**—**	**(46.3%)**	**—**	**(22.0%)**

Formosa Plastics

Formosa Plastics Corporation (FPC) is foremost in its industry. Taiwan's top petrochemical company and among the world's largest producers of polyvinyl chloride (PVC), FPC is a member of industrial giant Formosa Plastics Group. Additionally, the company makes acrylic acid, polyolefins like LLDPE and HDPE, caustic soda, chlorine, calcium carbonates, and hydrochloric acid. FPC subsidiaries include Formosa Plastics Corporation, U.S.A., which produces PVC in the US and is involved in basic chemical manufacturing (products like caustic soda). Other members of the Formosa Plastics Group include Formosa Asahi Spandex and Nan Ya Plastics.

The Taiwanese government fears the country's industry might become too dependent on its business in China and regulates the issue closely. Despite this fact, Formosa Plastics, along with FPG's other units, has continued to invest in mainland China.

Founder and former chairman Yung-Ching Wang was one of Taiwan's wealthiest industrialists. He stepped down in 2006, leaving the company in the control of his family; Wang died in 2008.

HISTORY

In 1932 Yung-Ching Wang borrowed $200 from his father, a Taiwanese tea merchant, to buy a rice mill near the town of Jiayi. The mill was destroyed by Allied bombs in 1944, but Wang went on to make a fortune in timber and founded Formosa Plastics, a small polyvinyl chloride (PVC) plant, in 1954. He bought the technology from the Japanese, later joking that he didn't even know then what the "P" in PVC stood for.

At first Wang had trouble finding buyers for his PVC resins. In 1958 he set up his own resin processor, Nan Ya Plastics, and later formed Formosa Chemicals & Fibre to make rayon backing for PVC leather (1965). For the next 15 years, the company grew into the Formosa Plastics Group (FPG), an exclusively Taiwanese enterprise.

Between 1980 and 1988 Wang bought 14 US PVC manufacturers, including Imperial Chemical's vinyl chloride monomer plant (1981), Stauffer Chemical's PVC plant (1981), and Manville Corporation's PVC businesses (1983). He started building a Texas PVC plant in 1981 and cut construction costs up to 40% by importing equipment from Taiwan. When the PVC market became saturated in the mid-1980s, Wang diversified, building plants to make semiconductor chemicals.

Wang bought several Texas-based oil and gas properties in 1988, including 218 producing wells, a gas-processing plant, and a pipeline firm. Faced with stricter pollution controls in Taiwan, Wang began building an ethylene plant in Point Comfort, Texas, in 1988.

In 1992 Wang wanted to build an ethylene complex in mainland China, where there were no pollution controls. Taiwan balked at the proposal, suggesting that FPG build at home. Attempting to circumvent a Taiwanese law against direct investment in the mainland, Wang sought Chinese approval through subsidiary Formosa Plastics Corporation, U.S.A. In 1993 Chinese authorities rejected a plan that would require them to finance up to two-thirds of a $7 billion petrochemical complex.

Formosa Plastics bought bankrupt US computer maker Everex Systems in 1993. Meanwhile, the group's focus again turned to mainland China when Nan Ya Plastics made plans in 1994 to build three plants along China's Long River.

The 1995 death of Wang's mother (at age 108) set off a power struggle between family factions. The company won licenses in 1996 to build power plants, which would make FPG Taiwan's first private-sector power supplier and end a 50-year government utility monopoly. That year, in defiance of Taiwan's policy of limiting investment in China, FPG announced it would build a power plant there. Pressure from the Taiwanese government put the project on hold in 1997.

FPG upped its investment in a new Taiwanese petrochemical complex in 1998. It formed ventures with Asahi Chemical to make spandex fiber and with France's Renault to make hybrid (gasoline/electric) cars. Also that year the group admitted to combining mercury-laden waste with cement and sneaking the toxic mixture to Cambodia disguised as 3,000 tons of cement block. FPG apologized after villagers living near the dump became ill.

Undaunted by a history of animosity between the two countries, Formosa Plastics and FPG's other flagship companies in 1999 invested a 60% stake in the production of power plants in the Chinese province of Fujian.

Wang retired in 2006, leaving control of the company in the hands of his children and other family members.

EXECUTIVES

Chairman and President: Chih-Tsun Lee
Executive Director: Jui-hua Wang
Executive Director: Wilfred Wang
Executive Director: Wen-yuan Wang
Executive Director: Z. L. Yang
EVP and Director: Jason Lin
EVP Formosa Plastics Corporation U.S.A.: C. L. Tseng
SVP and Director: Tsung-Chang Lee
SVP Operations and Director: T. J. Huang
SVP Research and Development and Director: Jerome C. L. Ko
VP Plastics Division: Cheng-Jung Lin
VP Engineering and Construction Division: Fu-Shou Xie
VP Tairylan Division: Bing-Chin Chen
VP Finance Division: Benny Chang
VP Chemicals Division: Guo-Hong Wei
VP Carbide Division: Wen-Song Chang
VP Polypropylene Division: Han-Fu Lin
VP Polyolefin Division: Tze-Fong Chang

LOCATIONS

HQ: Formosa Plastics Corporation
(Taiwan Shujiao Gongye Gufeng Youxian Gongsi)
201 Tung Hwa North Rd.
Taipei, Taiwan
Phone: 886-2-2712-2211   **Fax:** 886-2-2717-5287
Web: www.fpc.com.tw

PRODUCTS/OPERATIONS

Selected Products

Acrylic acid
Acrylic staple fiber
Calcium carbide
Calcium carbonate
Carbon fiber
Caustic soda
Esters
Flake caustic soda
Hydrochloric acid
Hydrochlorofluorocarbons
Liquid caustic soda
Petrochemical production
Plastic modifiers
Polyethylene
  High-density (HDPE)
  Linear low-density (LLDPE)
  Low-density (LDPE)
Polypropylene
Polyvinyl chloride (PVC) resins
Vinyl chloride monomer

COMPETITORS

Akzo Nobel
BASF SE
Dow Chemical
DuPont
INEOS
LG Group
Occidental Chemical
Shin-Etsu Chemical
Sinopec Shanghai Petrochemical
Yizheng Chemical

HISTORICAL FINANCIALS

Company Type: Public

Income Statement

FYE: December 31

	REVENUE ($ mil.)	NET INCOME ($ mil.)	NET PROFIT MARGIN	EMPLOYEES
12/09	5,586	854	15.3%	4,986
12/08	6,099	601	9.8%	5,023
12/07	5,953	1,470	24.7%	4,927
12/06	4,765	955	20.0%	4,909
12/05	4,119	—	—	4,892
Annual Growth	7.9%	(3.6%)	—	0.5%

2009 Year-End Financials

Debt ratio: —
Return on equity: 13.7%
Cash ($ mil.): 254
Current ratio: 2.27
Long-term debt ($ mil.): —
No. of shares (mil.): 6,121
Dividends
Yield: 2.7%
Payout: 42.9%
Market value ($ mil.): 12,778

Stock History

Taiwan: FPC

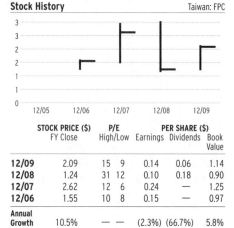

	STOCK PRICE ($) FY Close	P/E High/Low	Earnings	PER SHARE ($) Dividends	Book Value
12/09	2.09	15 9	0.14	0.06	1.14
12/08	1.24	31 12	0.10	0.18	0.90
12/07	2.62	12 6	0.24	—	1.25
12/06	1.55	10 8	0.15	—	0.97
Annual Growth	10.5%	— —	(2.3%)	(66.7%)	5.8%

Foster's Group

Foster's offers "dinki-di" ("something good from Australia"). Grateful thirsty folks say "Good on ya." (No translation needed.) Foster's Group makes a long list of beer, wine, and to a lesser extent, spirit labels. Its beers include Foster's and Crown lagers; Wolf Blass and Yellowglenn wines, Bulmers cider, and Black Jack whiskey. It also offers Cascade soda and Torquay bottled water. What more could a mate and his Sheila need? Beer and wine account for most of the company's sales, bringing in 96% of its 2010 sales. Its beverages are available worldwide. Focusing on its wine operations, the company has decided to split off its beer, cider, and spirits operations and is looking to sell that part of the business.

While Foster's has declined to name any potential suitors for its non-wine business, SABMiller, which owns the rights to Foster's in the US, and Japan's Asahi Breweries and Suntory (which are nearer to Foster's turf) are believed to be circling. Analysts have valued its beer operations at up to A$12 billion ($10 billion). Molson Coors, which owns a 5% stake in Foster's, was another potential suitor; however, the Canadian brewer's interest has recently cooled.

The separation of beer and spirits and wine businesses has been an ongoing company project during the past three years. In 2009, in order to realize cost savings and improve performance in its most important region (Australia), Foster's implemented a strategy of higher efficiency, increased capability, and growth. The strategy involved the creation of a dedicated Australian beer, cider, and spirits business (Carlton & United Breweries, or CUB) in order to improve management focus and simplicity. The strategy also involved the creation of a dedicated, stand-alone Australian and New Zealand wine operation, which leverages Foster's wine market insight and winemaking skills. The restructuring involved executive changes, including the appointment of new managing directors for CUB, the Australia and New Zealand wine operations, and Foster's Americas.

In September 2010 Foster's Group rejected an offer to purchase its wine business, despite the fact that sales have dropped as a result of the global financial malaise. (Several US private equity firms were believed to be among the suitors.)

HSBC Custody Nominees (Australia) Limited owns 27% of the company; J.P. Morgan Nominees Australia Limited owns 19%; and National Nominees Limited owns 17%.

HISTORY

Upon finding that Australia's only beers were English-styled ales served at room temperature, American emigrants W. M. and R. R. Foster built a lager brewery near Melbourne in 1888 and gave customers ice to chill their Foster's Lager. The brothers began exporting in 1901 when Australians left to serve in the Boer War in South Africa. Carlton and United Breweries Proprietary (CUB) was formed in 1907 when the brothers merged their operations with five other breweries, including Victoria and Carlton.

Over the years, CUB acquired stakes in trading company Elder Smith Goldsbrough Mort and Henry Jones (IXL), a diversified food company owned by John Elliott. Faced with a takeover, in 1981 Elder Smith was merged into Henry Jones, forming Elders IXL. CUB became that firm's largest stockholder, with 49%, in 1983. Elders bought the rest of CUB in 1984.

Elders expanded internationally with its purchases of UK's Courage Breweries (1986) and Canada's Carling O'Keefe Breweries (1987). In 1989 Carling O'Keefe and Molson formed a joint venture, Molson Breweries. To fight possible takeover attempts, that year Harlin Holdings (led by Elliott) offered to buy a 17% stake of Elders from two companies, but regulators forced the firm to extend its offer to all shareholders. As a result, Harlin ended up with more than 55% of Elders. The deal saddled Elders with debt, and in 1990 the company began selling its non-brewing assets. Also that year Elliott resigned as chairman and CEO, and Elders changed its name to Foster's Brewing Group.

Foster's purchased the brewing interests of Grand Metropolitan (now Diageo) in 1991. Elliott's investment firm went bankrupt in 1992 and Australian conglomerate Broken Hill Proprietary (BHP), which also owned 19% of Elders, assumed control of its shares. (BHP sold its stake in 1997.) Also in 1992 Molson Breweries chief Ted Kunkel became CEO. He wrote off over $2 billion in non-brewing assets that were still on the books and sold 10% of the brewer's interest in Molson.

In 1995 Foster's sold its UK brewing operations to Scottish & Newcastle. The next year it entered the wine business, buying Mildara Blass and Rothbury Wines, and in 1997 it entered the Australian wine club business with the purchase of Cellarmaster Wines. The next year Foster's bought wine clubs Bourse du Vin International (the Netherlands) and 51% of Germany's Heinrich Maximilian Pallhuber (later acquiring the rest).

Also in 1998 Foster's sold its Canadian brewing interests — 50% of Molson Breweries and 25% of Coors Canada — to The Molson Companies (but retained a 25% interest in Molson USA). In July 1998 Foster's acquired the Austotel Trust hotel chain from Brierly Investments, making it the largest operator of hotels in Australia.

Subsidiary Mildara Blass acquired the US direct wine marketer Windsor Vineyards in 2000; also, subsidiary Cellarmaster Wines bought a 25% interest in online wine retailer Wine Planet (increased in mid-2001 to about 90%). Foster's bought Beringer Wine Estates, a leading California winery, for about $1.2 billion. Wine profits for Foster's doubled in the year following the company's 2000 purchase of Beringer.

In 2001 the company dropped "Brewing" from its official name, becoming Foster's Group Limited. In 2002 Beringer Blass Wine Estates agreed to buy the Carmenet brand from Napa-based Chalone Wine Group (now part of Diageo Chateau & Estate Wines Company). In 2002 sales of wine surpassed those of the company's beers for the first time.

Foster's spun off its Australian Leisure and Hospitality group in November 2003, which included pubs, liquor shops, and interests in hotels and real estate development. That division became a separate company known as the Australian Leisure & Hospitality Group Ltd.

In 2005 Foster's acquired its rival, the premium winemaker Southcorp. The acquisition, which added such brands as Lindemans, Penfolds, and Rosemount wines to Foster's portfolio, created one of the world's biggest global wine companies. In 2006 the company sold its namesake brand in Europe to Scottish & Newcastle; it also sold its loss-making Shanghai Brewery to Suntory that year.

In 2008 the company was fined AUD$1 million (about the same in US dollars) for failing to repair a machine that caused a worker's death. The accident happened at Foster's Abbotsford brewery in 2006 when, in a repeat of a similar incident several years earlier, a machine operator's head became jammed in a bottling machine. Foster's pleaded guilty to failing to maintain a safe workplace and failing to provide adequate worker training and supervision.

EXECUTIVES

Chairman: David A. Crawford, age 66
CEO and Director: Ian Johnston
Chief Human Resources Officer: Sue Smith
Chief Supply Officer: Michael Brooks
Chief Legal and Company Secretary: Paul Conroy
Managing Director, Australian and New Zealand Wine: David Dearie
Managing Director, Americas: Stephen Brauer
Managing Director, Europe, the Middle East, and Africa: Peter Jackson
Managing Director, Carlton and United Breweries: John Pollaers, age 48
Director, Transformation: Donna Watt
VP Investor Relations: Chris Knorr
Auditors: PricewaterhouseCoopers

LOCATIONS

HQ: Foster's Group Limited
77 Southbank Blvd.
Southbank, Victoria 3006, Australia
Phone: 61-3-8626-2000   **Fax:** 61-3-8626-2002
Web: www.fostersgroup.com

2010 Sales

	% of total
Australia	65
Americas	21
Europe, Middle East & Africa	8
Other regions	6
Total	**100**

PRODUCTS/OPERATIONS

2010 Sales

	% of total
Beer	54
Wine	42
Other	4
Total	**100**

Selected Products and Brands

Beer
  1664
  Abbotsford
  Asahi
  Bitter
  Brown
  Brown Ale
  Carlsberg
  Carlton
  Corona
  Crown
  Foster's Lager
  Harp Lager
  Hoegaarden
  KB Lager
  Kent Old
  Kronenbourg
  Matilda Bay
  Melbourne
  Newcastle
  Power's
  Pure Blonde
  Resch's
  Shanghai Lager
  Stella Artois
Cider
  Bulmers
  Mercury
  Original
  Strongbow
Non-alcohol
  Cascade
  Cottonwood Valley Water
  Delite Mineral Water
  Perrier Water
  Real Juice
  Torquay
  Vittel
Spirits and pre-mixes
  100 Pipers
  Barossa Brandy
  The Black Douglas
  Boomerang Vodka
  Chateau Napoleon
  Cinzano Spirit
  Continental Liquers
  Cougar
  Coyote Tequila
  Czarina Vodka
  Dalmore 12 year Whiskey
  Karloff
  Old Oak Brandy
  Prince Albert Gin
  Ratu's Rum
  Regal
  SKYY

Wine
Andrew Garrett   Matthew Lang
Beringer   Matua Valley
Campanile   Meridian
Cellar no. 8   Mildara
Chateau St Jean   Minchinbury
Coldstream Hills   Penfolds
Devils Lair   Queen Adelaide
Fonseca Port   Robertsons Well
Fortitude   Rosemount
Great Western   Saltram
Greg Norman Estates   Sbragia Family
Half Mile Creek   Secret Stone
Heemskerk   St Clement
Ingoldby   St Huberts
Jamiesons Run   Stags' Leap
Lindemans   Taylor's Port
The Little Penguin   Taz
Maglieri   Yarra Ridge
Maison de Grande Esprit   Yellowglen

COMPETITORS

Accor
Anheuser-Busch InBev
Asahi Breweries
Asia Pacific Breweries
Boston Beer
Brown-Forman
Carlsberg
Coca-Cola Amatil
Constellation Brands
Diageo
E. & J. Gallo
FEMSA
Gambrinus
Heineken
Jackson Family Wines
Kirin Holdings Company
Lion Nathan
LVMH
Marriott
Molson Coors
Pabst
Pernod Ricard
Premier Pacific
Ravenswood Winery
SABMiller
San Miguel Corporation
Starwood Hotels & Resorts
Terlato Wine
Trinchero Family Estates
Tsingtao
Wine Group

HISTORICAL FINANCIALS

Company Type: Public

Income Statement

FYE: June 30

	REVENUE ($ mil.)	NET INCOME ($ mil.)	NET PROFIT MARGIN	EMPLOYEES
6/10	3,826	(397)	—	6,125
6/09	3,779	356	9.4%	6,612
6/08	4,412	113	2.6%	6,373
6/07	4,185	823	19.7%	6,588
6/06	4,302	854	19.8%	10,100
Annual Growth	(2.9%)	—	—	(11.8%)

2010 Year-End Financials

Debt ratio: —   No. of shares (mil.): 1,931
Return on equity: —   Dividends
Cash ($ mil.): 203   Yield: 4.8%
Current ratio: 1.78   Payout: —
Long-term debt ($ mil.): —   Market value ($ mil.): 9,341

Stock History

Pink Sheets: FBRWY

	STOCK PRICE ($) FY Close	P/E High/Low		PER SHARE ($) Earnings	Dividends	Book Value
6/10	4.84	—	—	(0.21)	0.23	1.20
6/09	4.14	27	19	0.18	0.21	1.56
6/08	4.87	120	83	0.06	0.24	1.90
6/07	5.41	15	11	0.41	0.19	2.02
6/06	3.99	10	9	0.42	0.15	1.68
Annual Growth	4.9%	—	—	—	11.3%	(8.2%)

France Telecom

France Telecom hopes it can do for telecommunications services what its countrymen have done for wine: make it the product of choice. The company provides fixed-line and wireless voice and data services, primarily through its Orange brand, to consumers and commercial clients. It serves about 190 million customers in 32 countries. France Telecom is a leading European wireless operator and broadband service provider, with about 130 million mobile customers and 13 million broadband subscribers. It also has 46 million wireline customers. The company's services for corporate clients are provided by its Orange Business Services unit, which offers a wide range of managed business networking and data services.

The company appointed its head of French operations, Stéphane Richard, as its new CEO in 2010. The company has said that its strategy for the next two years will include efforts to simplify its products and services by redesigning its customer-facing technology and improving customer service and marketing operations. It also continues to look beyond France for new business, particularly in Europe, Africa, and the Middle East.

The company's key acquisitions during 2009 included an increase in its stake in France Telecom España from 80% to nearly 100% through a series of purchases. It also bought a 49% stake in Tunisia-based Divona Telecom for €95 million and renamed the business Orange Tunisie. The previous year, France Telecom bought a controlling stake in Hits Telecom Uganda, renaming it Orange Uganda, for €71 million. Outside of France, the company's largest geographic markets are the UK, Spain, and Poland.

France Telecom in 2010 formed a joint venture with Deutsche Telekom that combined the UK mobile and broadband Internet businesses of both companies. Each company owns half of the venture which was conceived as part of a plan to cut operational costs and expand the reach of its Orange brand through partnerships with other European carriers. France Telecom's UK business is composed primarily of Orange Personal

Communications Services, Orange Retail, and Orange Home UK.

France Telecom made a move to expand into Egypt as well, agreeing in 2009 to buy Orascom Telecom's controlling stake in wireless services provider Mobinil. France Telecom will pay $300 million to acquire Egypt's biggest wireless carrier. As part of the deal Mobinil will also pay $130 million for Orascom's LINKdotNET and Link Egypt Internet assets. The agreement follows years of bitter legal wrangling by the companies for control of Mobinil.

The company in 2010 agreed to pay $840 million for a 40% stake in Moroccan network operator Meditel in another move to push further into emerging markets. Also that year France Telecom bought submarine communications cable laying and maintenance specialist Elettra from Telecom Italia to expand its capacity to install and service undersea networks.

The French government owns about 27% of France Telecom.

HISTORY

Shortly before he abdicated, King Louis Philippe laid the groundwork for France's state-owned telegraphic service. Established in 1851, the operation became part of the French Post Office in the 1870s, about the time Alexander Graham Bell invented the telephone. The French government licensed three private companies to provide telegraph service, and during the 1880s they merged into the Société Générale de Téléphones (SGT). In 1883 the country's first exchange was initiated in Rheims. Four years later an international circuit was installed connecting Paris and Brussels. The government nationalized SGT in 1889.

By the turn of the century, France had more than 60,000 phone lines, and in 1924 a standardized telephone was introduced. Long-distance service improved with underground cabling, and phone exchanges in Paris and other leading cities became automated during the 1930s.

WWII proved a major setback to the French government's telephone operations, Direction Générale des Télécommunications (DGT), because a large part of its equipment was destroyed or damaged. For the next two decades France lagged behind other nations in telephony infrastructure development. An exception to this technological stagnation was Centre National d'Etudes des Télécommunications (CNET), the research laboratory formed in 1944 that eventually became France Telecom's research arm.

In 1962 DGT was a key player in the first intercontinental television broadcast, between the US and France, via a Telstar satellite. The company began to catch up with its peers when it developed a digital phone system in the mid-1970s. In 1974 CNET was instrumental in the launch of France's first experimental communications satellite. In another technological advance, DGT began replacing its paper directories with the innovative Minitel online terminals in 1980.

The French government created France Telecom in 1988. In 1993 France Telecom and Deutsche Telekom (DT) teamed up to form the Global One international telecommunications venture, and Sprint joined the next year. Global One was formally launched in 1996.

In 1997 the government sold about 20% of France Telecom to the public. With Europe's state telephone monopolies ending in 1998, France Telecom reorganized and brought prices in line with those of its competitors.

In 2000 France Telecom paid $4.3 billion to DT and Sprint to take full ownership of Global One. Later in 2000 France Telecom snatched up UK mobile phone operator Orange in a $37.5 billion cash and stock deal after Vodafone was forced to divest the company before merging with Mannesmann. France Telecom also invested $4.5 billion in UK cable operator NTL and sold its stake in Mexican telecom giant Telmex.

In 2001 the company sold its 49.9% stake in Noos, France's #1 cable TV operator. It sold its nearly 11% stake in Greek mobile carrier Vodafone-Panafon to Vodafone Group for €311 million the following year.

France Telecom took full ownership of Orange and Wanadoo, a European directory publisher and ISP, in 2004. In 2006 the company sold its 54% stake in directories business PagesJaunes Groupe to Kohlberg Kravis Roberts & Co. in a deal valued at about $4.2 billion. Also that year, it acquired the remaining shares that it did not already own of Dutch-based carrier Equant.

The company in 2007 sold the mobile phone unit of France Telecom España to Deutsche Telekom in return for that company's Ya.com Internet unit. It also acquired a controlling stake in security network specialist Silicomp.

EXECUTIVES

Chairman: Didier Lombard, age 68
CEO: Stéphane Richard, age 48
Deputy CEO, Finance, Information Systems, and UK JV: Gervais Pellissier, age 50
Deputy CEO, Quality, Corporate Social Responsibility: Jean-Philippe Vanot, age 58
EVP, Group General Secretary, and France Carriers Division: Pierre Louette, age 47
EVP New Growth Businesses: Raoul Roverato, age 39
EVP Networks and Carriers and Research and Development: Thierry Bonhomme, age 53
EVP Africa, the Middle-East, and Asia: Marc Rennard, age 53
EVP Marketing and Innovation: Jean-Paul Cottet, age 55
EVP Group Human Resources: Bruno Mettling, age 52
EVP Enterprise Communication Services; CEO, Orange Business Services: Vivek Badrinath, age 41
EVP and Deputy French Operations: Delphine Ernotte, age 43
EVP Strategic Initiatives and Partnerships: Georges Penalver, age 53
EVP Communication, Philanthropy, and Content Strategy: Christine Albanel, age 54
EVP Operations in Europe (except France) and Sourcing: Olaf Swantee, age 43
Secretary: Cédric Testut
Principal Accounting Officer: Valérie Thérond
Auditors: Deloitte & Associés

LOCATIONS

HQ: France Telecom
6, place d'Alleray
75505 Paris, France
Phone: 33-1-44-44-22-22   **Fax:** 33-1-44-44-95-95
US HQ: 225 Liberty St., Ste. 4301, New York, NY 10281
US Phone: 212-332-2100
Web: www.francetelecom.com

2009 Sales

	% of total
France	46
UK	10
Spain	8
Poland	7
Other countries	16
Enterprise	14
International carriers & shared services	2
Adjustments	(3)
Total	**100**

PRODUCTS/OPERATIONS

Selected Operations

Enterprise Communication Services (communication services to companies)
Home Communication Services (residential communication services, especially fixed-line broadband)
Personal Communication Services (communication services for individuals using mobile devices)
Content (partnerships with content providers and development of related technology platforms)
Health (services to the health care industry)
Audience and advertising (Internet advertising business)

COMPETITORS

AT&T	Jazztel
Belgacom	KPN
Bouygues	SFR
BT	Tele2
Cable & Wireless	Telecom Italia
COLT Group	Telefónica
CompleTel	Telefónica Europe
Deutsche Telekom	Tiscali
Equinix Europe	T-Online
HP Enterprise Services	Unisys
Hutchison Whampoa	Vodafone
IBM Global Services	

HISTORICAL FINANCIALS

Company Type: Public

Income Statement

FYE: December 31

	REVENUE ($ mil.)	NET INCOME ($ mil.)	NET PROFIT MARGIN	EMPLOYEES
12/09	65,847	4,966	7.5%	181,000
12/08	75,682	5,758	7.6%	182,793
12/07	77,857	9,262	11.9%	187,331
12/06	68,270	5,466	8.0%	191,036
12/05	58,270	6,784	11.6%	203,008
Annual Growth	**3.1%**	**(7.5%)**	**—**	**(2.8%)**

2009 Year-End Financials

Debt ratio: 122.7%
Return on equity: 13.0%
Cash ($ mil.): 5,660
Current ratio: 0.58
Long-term debt ($ mil.): 45,761
No. of shares (mil.): 2,649
Dividends
Yield: 3.6%
Payout: 79.6%
Market value ($ mil.): 95,814

Stock History

NYSE: FTE

	STOCK PRICE ($) FY Close	P/E High/Low		PER SHARE ($) Earnings	Dividends	Book Value
12/09	36.17	25	19	1.62	1.29	14.08
12/08	39.56	25	13	2.17	2.65	14.74
12/07	52.44	17	11	3.47	1.75	16.57
12/06	36.54	18	13	2.07	1.30	13.36
12/05	29.42	15	11	2.61	0.68	11.15
Annual Growth	**5.3%**	**—**	**—**	**(11.2%)**	**17.4%**	**6.0%**

FUJIFILM Holdings

FUJIFILM Holdings no longer dwells only on the negatives. Its FUJIFILM unit makes color photographic films and papers, digital cameras, photofinishing equipment, and chemicals. It leads the film market in Japan and has hammered away at rival Eastman Kodak's lead in the US. FUJIFILM Holdings's other businesses include document solutions (copy machines, printers, paper) and information solutions (medical imaging products, flat-panel display materials, optical devices). FUJIFILM Holdings operates in Europe, Australia, Asia, and North and South America, although 60% of its sales come from Japan. It adopted a holding company structure and changed its name from Fuji Photo Film to FUJIFILM Holdings in 2006.

Like Kodak, FUJIFILM Holdings has chosen to diversify far beyond the film industry and to invest more in digital technologies and less in traditional film. To that end, the company's Brazilian unit, FUJIFILM do Brasil, acquired the San Paolo-based medical product sales agency NDT Comercial in 2010. NDT had already marketed FUJIFILM's medical products, such as X-ray films, across Brazil. After the acquisition NDT became a subsidiary of FUJIFILM. Previous purchases include Santa Clara, California-based Dimatix, a maker of inkjet printer parts, in 2006. (On the whole, FUJIFILM generates more than 40% of its revenues through a joint venture with Xerox — called Fuji Xerox Co. — that makes and markets printers and office copiers.)

To meet increasing demand from consumers for digital images, FUJIFILM has adopted what it calls "hybrid imaging" to combine its expertise in imaging with the latest electronics, such as flat-panel displays and camera-equipped cell phones. The company has entered into a joint venture partnership with SVA Electron Co. of China to make color filters used in thin film transistor liquid crystal displays, which are widely used in computer monitors and flat-screen televisions. FUJIFILM has also broken into the nucleic acid extraction market with its tabletop DNA/RNA isolation system.

FUJIFILM is also expanding into medical sales. It acquired the remaining shares of Fuji Medical Systems France S.A. (a medical imaging products distributor) in 2006 and bought TSR Holding S.A. (a medical equipment service and maintenance supplier). The company's Toyama Chemical Co. subsidiary develops pharmaceuticals including anti-infective agents (such as new flu medications for treating the H1N1 virus and other strains), CNS and cardiovascular agents, and anti-inflammatory agents.

HISTORY

Mokichi Morita, president of Japan's leading celluloid maker (Dainippon Celluloid Company, founded 1919), decided to start making motion picture film in the early 1930s. Movies were becoming popular in Japan, but there was no domestic film supplier. Working with a grant from the government, Dainippon Celluloid established Fuji Photo Film Co., an independent company, in 1934 in Minami Ashigara Village, near Mount Fuji.

At first the company had trouble gaining acceptance in Japan as a quality film producer. However, German emulsion specialist Dr. Emill

Mauerhoff helped Fuji overcome its product deficiencies, producing black-and-white photographic film (1936) and the first Japanese-made color film (1948). In the meantime Fuji added 35mm photographic film, 16mm motion picture film, and X-ray film to its product line. By the early 1940s the company was operating four factories and a research laboratory in Japan. Its first overseas office, opened in Brazil in 1955, was followed by offices in the US (1958) and Europe (1964).

Fuji continued to expand its product line, adding magnetic tape in 1960. Two years later it formed Fuji Xerox, a Japanese joint venture with Xerox, to sell copiers in Japan and the Pacific Rim. It operated as a private-label film supplier in the US and did not market its products under its own brand name until 1972.

International marketing VP Minoru Ohnishi became Fuji's youngest president in 1980 at age 55. To decrease dependence on Japanese film sales, he built sales in the US (agreeing to sponsor the 1984 Los Angeles Olympics, after Eastman Kodak refused to, was key) and pumped money into the production of videotapes, floppy disks, and medical diagnostic equipment. Fuji introduced Fujicolor Quicksnap, the world's first 35mm disposable camera, in 1986. It began establishing manufacturing operations in the US two years later.

The company created the FUJIFILM Microdevices subsidiary to produce image-processing semiconductors in 1990. In 1992 Fuji scientists completed a crude artificial "eye" (a possible forerunner of more efficient eyes for robots). The following year it launched the Pictrostat instant print system, which produces color prints in one minute from photos, slides, and objects.

Fuji was forced to temporarily raise US prices in 1994 after Kodak accused it of illegally dumping its photographic paper exported to the US. But Fuji skirted the problem in 1995 by making the paper at its US plant. That year Kodak asked for economic sanctions against Fuji and the Japanese government, saying that the government encouraged Fuji to use exclusive contracts to control film distribution, thus keeping Kodak from selling film in many stores. (The case was rejected by the World Trade Organization in 1997.)

The firm unveiled the Advanced Photo System (co-developed with Kodak and three other companies) in 1996, combining conventional photography with digital-image processing and printing technology. Also that year Fuji bought six off-site wholesale photofinishing plants from Wal-Mart and won contracts to provide supplies to all of Wal-Mart's in-store one-hour photo labs.

In 1999 Fuji introduced a high-quality image sensor for digital cameras (Super CCD) and Instax, an instant picture camera. Fuji and Sony launched HiFD, a floppy disk with 140 times the storage capacity of traditional disks, in early 2000. Fuji later announced plans to develop more efficient, low-cost ink jet printers through an alliance with Xerox and Sharp Corp. In March 2001 Fuji acquired half of Xerox's 50% stake in the companies' Fuji Xerox joint venture.

It bought Sericol from Saratoga Partners in 2005 for $230 million and Avecia Inkjet in 2006 for $260 million.

In January 2008 FUJIFILM Holdings acquired Germany's IP Labs GmbH, a developer of online photo service systems. The consolidation of Toyama Chemical into a consolidated subsidiary in March marked the holding company's entry into the pharmceutical business. In November it purchased Empiric Systems LLC, a US-based maker of radiology information systems.

EXECUTIVES

President, CEO, and Director: Shigetaka Komori
EVP, CFO, and Director: Toshio Takahashi
Corporate VP, General Manager, Corporate Planning Headquarters, and Director; President and CEO, FUJIFILM Recording Media U.S.A.: Toru Takahashi, age 68
Corporate VP and Director: Nobuaki Inoue
Corporate VP: Sumito Yamada
Corporate VP: Kouichi Suematsu
Corporate VP: Kazuhiko Furuya
Corporate VP: Makio Watanabe
Corporate VP: Kouichi Tamai
Corporate VP: Toshiaki Suzuki
Corporate VP and Director: Nobuoki Okamura
Corporate VP: Hiroyuki Sakai
General Manager, Recording Media Products Division: Norio Shibata
General Manager, Procurement Division: Makoto Kawaguchi
President, FUJIFILM Holdings America Corporation and President and CEO, FUJIFILM North America Corporation: Ryutaro (Ray) Hosoda
Auditors: Ernst & Young ShinNihon

LOCATIONS

HQ: FUJIFILM Holdings Corporation
7-3, Akasaka 9-chome, Minato-ku
Tokyo 107-0052, Japan
Phone: 81-3-6271-1111
US HQ: 200 Summit Lake Dr., Valhalla, NY 10595
US Phone: 914-789-8100   **US Fax:** 914-789-8295
Web: www.fujifilmholdings.com

2009 Sales

	% of total
Japan	60
Americas	16
Europe	12
Other regions	12
Total	**100**

PRODUCTS/OPERATIONS

2009 Sales

	% of total
Document solutions	44
Information solutions	39
Imaging solutions	17
Total	**100**

Selected Products

Document solutions
  Digital color printers
  Digital photo printers
  Photographic papers, equipment, and chemicals
Information solutions
  Data storage media
  Graphic systems
  LCD materials
  Medical imaging products
  Miscellaneous industrial materials and equipment
  Office automation systems
Imaging solutions
  Electronic imaging systems
  Magnetic products
  Motion picture films
  Optical products
  Photo lab equipment
  Photographic films

COMPETITORS

Agfa
Bayer AG
Canon
Datapulse Technology
Eastman Kodak
Electronics for Imaging
GlaxoSmithKline
Hewlett-Packard
Imation
Iomega
Konica Minolta
Kyocera
Mitsubishi Paper Mills
Nikon
Novartis
Olympus
Pfizer
Philips Electronics
Ricoh Company
Sony

HISTORICAL FINANCIALS

Company Type: Public

Income Statement

FYE: March 31

	REVENUE ($ mil.)	NET INCOME ($ mil.)	NET PROFIT MARGIN	EMPLOYEES
3/09	25,023	108	0.4%	76,252
3/08	28,537	1,047	3.7%	77,000
3/07	23,622	292	1.2%	76,358
3/06	22,882	318	1.4%	75,845
3/05	23,562	788	3.3%	75,638
Annual Growth	**1.5%**	**(39.1%)**	**—**	**0.2%**

2009 Year-End Financials

Debt ratio: 14.5%
Return on equity: 0.6%
Cash ($ mil.): 2,776
Current ratio: 2.44
Long-term debt ($ mil.): 2,611
No. of shares (mil.): 489
Dividends
  Yield: 91.0%
  Payout: 95.5%
Market value ($ mil.): 110

Stock History

Tokyo: 49010

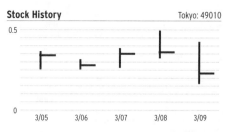

	STOCK PRICE ($) FY Close	P/E High/Low		Earnings	Dividends	Book Value
3/09	0.23	2	1	0.22	0.21	36.95
3/08	0.36	—	—	1.95	0.14	39.44
3/07	0.35	1	—	0.55	0.15	34.34
3/06	0.28	—	—	0.62	0.16	34.47
3/05	0.34	—	—	1.54	0.19	35.28
Annual Growth	**(9.3%)**	**—**	**—**	**(38.5%)**	**2.5%**	**1.2%**

Fujitsu Limited

Fujitsu Limited's supply of high-tech offerings seems almost limitless. The company provides customers worldwide with products ranging from computers and electronic components to air conditioners and bar code scanners. Fujitsu's computer products include PCs, servers, storage systems, and peripherals. One of the top IT services firms in the world, it provides consulting, infrastructure management, and systems integration. Other lines include a wide range of software, telecommunications transmission equipment, consumer electronics, and semiconductors. Fujitsu also owns Nifty, one of Japan's leading ISPs.

Fujitsu was hard hit by the global economic slump. The company experienced revenue declines in each of its product groups in fiscal 2009, and reported a loss for the year.

The company generates most of its revenues in Japan, but its growth strategy includes strengthening its international operations. To that end the company acquired KAZ Group, the IT arm of Australian telecom Telstra, in 2009. It also bought out Siemens' stake in their European computer joint venture, Fujitsu Siemens, for €450 million ($570 million) in 2009. The unit is now called Fujitsu Technology Solutions. Fujitsu's efforts to strengthen its North America operations have included consolidating a number of its subsidiaries in the region. In 2009 the company combined three of its US-based subsidiaries — Fujitsu Consulting, Fujitsu Computer Systems, and Fujitsu Transaction Solutions — to form Fujitsu America.

The company's technology services operations generate the largest portion of its revenue. In addition to consulting and outsourcing, it provides systems integration, migration, and optimization services. Fujitsu Services is among the company's key IT services subsidiaries. Fujitsu's software offerings include customer relationship management (CRM), supply chain management (SCM), and enterprise resource planning (ERP) applications.

Fujitsu's Ubiquitous Products division is responsible for products including handheld and notebook PCs, mobile phones, disk drives, servers, and mainframes.

The company said in mid-2010 that it would combine its cell phone business with that of key rival Toshiba in hopes that the new business (it will be the largest cell phone maker in Japan) will be better able to compete with industry leader Nokia, as well as top players in North America and Asia; Fujitsu will own a controlling stake in the new company.

Fujitsu spun off its advanced semiconductor business as a separate subsidiary, Fujitsu Microelectronics (now Fujitsu Semiconductor), in 2008. The following year it sold its hard-disk drive business to Toshiba.

In 2010 Fujitsu promoted SVP Masami Yamamoto to president, succeeding Michiyoshi Mazuka, who remained chairman after serving less than a year in the top executive post at the company. Mazuka became president in 2009 when Kuniaki Nozoe unexpectedly resigned, citing illness. The company later revealed that Nozoe resigned for reasons other than illness. Nozoe publicly challenged his dismissal in 2010, petitioning a court to regain his seat on Fujitsu's board. The court rejected his request for a preliminary injunction, however.

HISTORY

Fiemens and Furukawa Electric created Fuji Electric in 1923 to produce electrical equipment. Fuji spun off Fujitsu, its communications division, in 1935. Originally a maker of telephone equipment, Fujitsu produced anti-aircraft weapons during WWII. After the war it became one of four major suppliers to state-owned monopoly Nippon Telegraph and Telephone (NTT) and continued to benefit from Japan's rapid economic recovery in the 1950s and 1960s.

With encouragement from Japan's Ministry of International Trade and Industry (MITI), Fujitsu developed the country's first commercial computer in 1954. MITI erected trade barriers to protect Japan's new computer industry and in the early 1960s sponsored the production of mainframe computers, directing Fujitsu to develop the central processing unit. The company expanded into semiconductor production and factory automation in the late 1960s. Its factory automation business was spun off as Fujitsu Fanuc in 1972.

Fujitsu gained badly needed technology when it bought 30% of IBM-plug-compatible manufacturer Amdahl in 1972. By 1979 Fujitsu had passed IBM to become Japan's #1 computer manufacturer. In Europe, Fujitsu entered into computer marketing ventures with Siemens (1978) and UK mainframe maker ICL (1981). In the US it teamed with TRW to sell point-of-sale systems (1980), assuming full control of the operation in 1983. Fujitsu released its first supercomputer in 1982.

Fujitsu bought 80% of ICL (from the UK's Standard Telephones & Cables) in 1990 for $1.3 billion. In 1993 it formed a joint venture with Advanced Micro Devices to make flash memory products.

The company doubled its share of Japan's PC market in 1995 to more than 18% and the next year expanded its PC business globally. In 1997 Fujitsu paid about $878 million for the 58% of Amdahl it didn't already own. The next year it bought the 10% of ICL it didn't own. Fujitsu's 1998 earnings suffered from a slump in the semiconductor market, Amdahl-related expenses, and a weak Asian economy.

Also in 1998 Naoyuki Akikusa, son of a former NTT president, became head of Fujitsu. He began trimming some operations, while ramping up the company's Internet activities. Fujitsu in 1999 became full owner of online services provider Nifty Serve, making it Japan's largest Internet service provider. Also that year Siemens and Fujitsu combined their European computer operations in a joint venture.

Akikusa's reorganization continued in 2000. Fujitsu overhauled its server business (subsidiary Amdahl ceased production of IBM-compatible mainframes) and accelerated production of flash memory. Responding to a global slump in its markets, in 2001 Fujitsu announced that it would cut more than 16,000 jobs — about 10% of its workforce — to control costs. Soon after, it announced the cutting of an additional 4,500 jobs.

In 2003 the company formed a joint venture with AMD called Fujitsu AMD Semiconductor Ltd., to manufacture flash memory. (Renamed Spansion in 2004, it went public in 2005.)

Early in 2005 Fujitsu sold Hitachi its stake in Fujitsu Hitachi Plasma Display, a company it formed with Hitachi to develop plasma display panels for televisions. Fujitsu sold its liquid crystal display (LCD) business, Fujitsu Display Technologies, to Sharp in 2005.

EXECUTIVES

Chairman: Michiyoshi Mazuka, age 67
President: Masami Yamamoto, age 56
SEVP; President, Global Business Group; Chairman, Fujitsu Telecommunications Europe Limited; Chairman, Fujitsu Technology Solutions: Richard Christou, age 65
SEVP and Director: Masami Fujita
SEVP: Hideyuki Saso
SEVP: Kenji Ikegai
SEVP and Director: Kazuo Ishida
EVP and Director: Masahiro Koezuka
EVP and Director: Kazuhiko Kato
Managing Director, Applications, United Kingdom and Ireland: John Hanley
President and CEO, Fujitsu America: Anthony P. (Tony) Doye, age 52
Auditors: Ernst & Young ShinNihon

LOCATIONS

HQ: Fujitsu Limited
Shiodome City Center, 1-5-2, Higashi-Shimbashi, Minato-ku
Tokyo 105-7123, Japan
Phone: 81-3-6252-2220   **Fax:** 81-3-6252-2783
US HQ: 1250 E. Arques Ave., Sunnyvale, CA 94085
US Phone: 408-746-6200   **US Fax:** 408-746-6260
Web: www.fujitsu.com

2010 Sales

	% of total
Asia/Pacific	
Japan	66
Other countries	7
Europe, Middle East & Africa	21
Americas	6
Total	**100**

PRODUCTS/OPERATIONS

2010 Sales

	% of total
Technology Solutions	
Services	
Infrastructure services	28
Solutions & systems integration	24
System platforms	
System products	7
Network products	6
Ubiquitous Product Solutions	
PCs & mobile phones	16
Hard disk drives	1
Device solutions	
LSI devices	6
Other	5
Other	7
Total	**100**

Selected Products and Services

Technology Solutions
  Services
    Infrastructure services
    Systems integration
  System platforms
    Network products
    System products
Ubiquitous Product Solutions
  Hard disk drives
  Mobile phones
  PCs
Device Solutions
  Electronic components
  LSI devices

HISTORICAL FINANCIALS

Company Type: Public

Income Statement

FYE: March 31

	REVENUE ($ mil.)	NET INCOME ($ mil.)	NET PROFIT MARGIN	EMPLOYEES
3/10	50,483	556	1.1%	172,438
3/09	48,239	164	0.3%	166,000
3/08	53,687	485	0.9%	167,374
3/07	637,150	869	0.1%	160,977
3/06	40,756	583	1.4%	158,491
Annual Growth	5.5%	(1.2%)	—	2.1%

2010 Year-End Financials

Debt ratio: —	No. of shares (mil.): 2,067
Return on equity: 6.8%	Dividends
Cash ($ mil.): 3,482	Yield: 1.0%
Current ratio: 1.20	Payout: 9.8%
Long-term debt ($ mil.): —	Market value ($ mil.): 13,648

Stock History

Pink Sheets: FJTSY

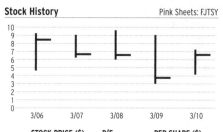

	STOCK PRICE ($) FY Close	P/E High/Low		PER SHARE ($) Earnings	Dividends	Book Value
3/10	6.60	12	7	0.61	0.06	4.17
3/09	3.75	—	—	(0.56)	0.03	3.72
3/08	6.57	48	31	0.20	—	4.62
3/07	6.66	23	17	0.38	—	3.59
3/06	8.45	36	19	0.25	—	3.77
Annual Growth	(6.0%)	—	—	25.0%	100.0%	2.5%

Galp Energia

Portugal's primary oil and gas group, Galp Energia (formerly Petróleos de Portugal), produces, transports, refines, distributes, and sells crude oil, natural gas, and oil products. It operates mainly in Portugal and Spain, but also has operations in a half-dozen former Portuguese colonies. Although Galp Energia is primarily a refining and marketing company with more than 1,450 gas stations, it is seeking to expand its exploration and production efforts. The company has significant exploration and production activities in Angola, Brazil, and Portugal and holds gas and power infrastructure assets in Portugal. Italian energy giant Eni and Portuguese investment firm Amorim Energia each own 33% of the company.

In a bid to reposition itself as a multinational energy firm, the company is expanding its natural gas and refined products distribution operations on the Iberian peninsula and is beefing up its international portfolio, particularly in Brazil, where it has active assets in the lucrative Santos Basin.

In 2008 Galp Energia expanded its downstream assets in Spain and Portugal, acquiring Exxon Mobil's Iberian subsidiaries (Esso Portuguesa, Esso Espanola, and a part of ExxonMobil Petroleum & Chemical).

HISTORY

Galp Energia (formerly Petróleos de Portugal — Petrogal) was formed in 1976 after the 1975 nationalization and subsequent merger of four oil companies: Sonap, Sacor, Cidla, and Petrosul.

For the first 40 years of the 20th century, oil exploration and production in Portugal was dominated by international companies, most significantly Vacuum Oil (a Standard Oil company). Queiroz Pereira, the first Portuguese-owned oil company, was formed in 1930. It merged with Sociedade Nacional de Petróleos (Sonap) in 1933. The company subsequently engaged in marketing and distribution operations in Portugal and its colonies. In 1938 the Sociedade Anónima Concessionária de Refinação em Portugal (Sacor) was formed as a refining monopoly. Two years later Sacor opened the first oil refinery in Portugal, located near Lisbon. Sacor also operated as a marketing and distribution company in Portugal and its African colonies. Cidla, a subsidiary of Sacor, was set up in 1939 to distribute and market butane and propane gas.

In 1957 Sacor formed Sociedade Portuguesa de Petroquímica to utilize the surplus gases from refineries. Commercial operation began in 1961; the company manufactured ammonia, hydrogen, and other inorganic chemicals. Sacor units also moved into the production of organic chemicals and fertilizers in the 1960s and 1970s.

Sacor brought Portugal's second refinery, near Oporto, into operation in 1969. Petrosul, owned by Sonap and financial group Mello, was incorporated in 1972 and awarded the construction of the third and largest refinery to be built in Portugal, the Sines Industrial Complex refinery. Following the 1974 political revolution in Portugal that overthrew the authoritarian government, radical changes swept across Portuguese society, including the granting of independence to colonies and the nationalization of the oil sector and other industries.

Following the creation of Petrogal in 1976, the company completed the Sines refinery, which went into production in 1978. In 1981 Petrogal built and opened its aromatics plant, which was integrated within the Oporto refinery complex. Petrogal became a public liability company in 1989, but remained 100% state-controlled. Moving toward privatization as per the rulings of the EU, 25% of the company's shares were sold to Petrocontrol, a private consortium. Petrogal completed the reconversion of the Sines complex in 1994 and closed down its aging Lisbon refinery that year.

The Portuguese government diluted its stake in Petrogal to 55% in 1995. Two years later Petrogal established Petrogal Moçambique to operate in that country's oil and natural gas sectors. Its assets include a retail sales network and Mozambique's only liquid petroleum gas distributor.

In 1999, as part of the restructuring of the Portuguese energy sector, the government formed the GALP Petróleos e Gas de Portugal (GALP SGPS) holding company — which included Petrogal — and natural gas concerns Gas de Portugal and Transgás. In 2000 Italian energy giant Eni acquired a 33% stake in GALP SPGS.

A year later Galp Energia purchased two oil exploration licenses in Brazil, in collaboration with state-owned PETROBRAS.

In 2007 the company announced a new oil discovery in waters off the coast of Angola.

EXECUTIVES

Chairman: Francisco L. Murteira Nabo
Vice Chairman and CEO: Manuel Ferreira De Oliveira
Vice Chairman and CFO: Francesco Antonietti
Executive Director, Power and Board Member: André Freire de Almeida Palmeiro Ribeiro
Executive Director, Natural Gas and Board Member: Enrico Grigesi
Executive Director, Oil Distribution, Iberia and Board Member: João Pedro de Figueiredo Brito
Executive Director, Refining, Supply, and Logistics and Board Member: José António Marques Gonçalves
Executive Director, Exploration, Production, and Oil Distribution, Africa and Board Member: Fernando Manuel dos Santos Gomes
Secretary: Rui Maria Diniz Mayer
Deputy Secretary: Maria Helena Claro Goldschmidt
Auditors: Deloitte & Associados, SROC, SA

LOCATIONS

HQ: Galp Energia SGPS, S.A.
Edifício Galp Energia, Rua Tomás da Fonseca
1600-209 Lisbon, Portugal
Phone: 351-21-724-2500   **Fax:** 351-21-724-2965
Web: www.galpenergia.com

PRODUCTS/OPERATIONS

2009 Sales

	% of total
Refining & marketing	88
Gas & power	12
Total	**100**

Selected Subsidiaries

Galp Power (electricity generation and sales)
Galpgeste (management and operation of service stations)
GDP Gás de Portugal
Petróleos de Portugal (Petrogal; exploration and production, refining, transport, distribution, and sales of oil products)
Sacor Maritima (marine transport)
Sopor (51%, distribution and sale of oil products)
Transgás Armazenagem (natural gas underground storage)

COMPETITORS

BP	Repsol YPF
Endesa S.A.	Royal Dutch Shell
Exxon Mobil	TOTAL

HISTORICAL FINANCIALS

Company Type: Public

Income Statement

FYE: December 31

	REVENUE ($ mil.)	NET INCOME ($ mil.)	NET PROFIT MARGIN	EMPLOYEES
12/09	16,809	506	3.0%	7,493
12/08	20,945	165	0.8%	7,817
12/07	18,300	1,150	6.3%	5,798
12/06	16,108	996	6.2%	5,869
12/05	13,190	830	6.3%	5,909
Annual Growth	6.2%	(11.6%)	—	6.1%

2009 Year-End Financials

Debt ratio: —
Return on equity: 15.5%
Cash ($ mil.): 349
Current ratio: 1.13
Long-term debt ($ mil.): —

No. of shares (mil.): 829
Dividends
 Yield: 1.6%
 Payout: 46.7%
Market value ($ mil.): 14,357

Stock History

Euronext Lisbon: GALP

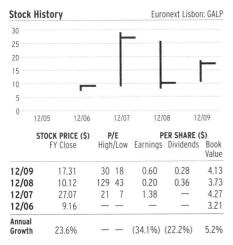

	STOCK PRICE ($) FY Close	P/E High/Low		PER SHARE ($) Earnings	Dividends	Book Value
12/09	17.31	30	18	0.60	0.28	4.13
12/08	10.12	129	43	0.20	0.36	3.73
12/07	27.07	21	7	1.38	—	4.27
12/06	9.16	—	—	—	—	3.21
Annual Growth	23.6%	—	—	(34.1%)	(22.2%)	5.2%

Gas Natural SDG

A latter-day Spanish *conquistador*, Gas Natural is venturing into markets in both the Old World and the New. Gas Natural operates a group of energy companies that supply natural gas and electricity, serving 20 million customers primarily in Spain, but also in France, Italy, and Latin America. The largest natural gas supplier in Spain, Gas Natural is also a leading liquefied natural gas (LNG) supplier. The company has interests in utilities across Latin America and has a generating capacity of 17,000 MW. In 2009 Gas Natural greatly expanded its power business, acquiring Spanish utility Unión Fenosa in a $26 billion deal, and in 2010 adopted Gas Natural Fenosa as its new corporate brand name.

The Unión Fenosa purchase boosted the company's profile as an integrated gas and power enterprise and extended Gas Natural's operations to more than 20 countries. In order to comply with antitrust regulations, the terms of the deal included having the company selling 600,000 gas customer connections, 2,000 MW of installed power capacity, and its remaining stake in Enagas, Spain's gas transportation and storage enterprise. Previously Gas Natural had spun off 65% of Enagas to comply with the 1998 Hydrocarbons Law.

To help pay down debt related to the Unión Fenosa acquisition, in 2009 the company sold power assets in Mexico to Mitsui and Tokyo Gas for $1.2 billion.

Before the deal Criteria owned 37% of Gas Natural; Repsol YPF, 31%; and a bank syndicate, 32%.

In response to the deregulation of Spain's retail gas market, which took full effect in 2003, Gas Natural has been working to become a multi-utility by developing domestic fiber-optic telecommunications and electricity generation and supply operations. The company has also turned to the Americas for growth: Gas Natural has interests in gas suppliers and distributors in Argentina, Brazil, Colombia, Mexico, and Puerto Rico. It also trades natural gas in Europe, operates a gas pipeline in Morocco, and has formed an Italian gas marketing unit and acquired an Italian gas distributor.

In a more ambitious plan, Gas Natural is creating a liquefied natural gas (LNG) joint venture with Repsol YPF that will have a marketing capacity of 12 million metric tons of LNG a year. The joint venture will also use a fleet of 10-plus LNG carriers.

HISTORY

Gas Natural SDG was created in 1992 when Spanish oil giant Repsol and the bank La Caixa merged their interests in natural gas distributors Catalana de Gas (of Barcelona) and Gas Madrid into a national company and gave it Repsol's gas pipelines. Catalana de Gas' leader, Pere Duran Farell, who in the 1960s had led efforts to introduce natural gas to Spain, became chairman (serving until 1997).

Repsol's formation was the result of Spain's efforts to organize its fragmented energy industry. After an era of dependency on foreign investment before and during Francisco Franco's dictatorship (1939-75), Spain in 1979 set up the Instituto Nacional de Hidrocarburos (INH), which placed all state-owned gas and oil firms under one agency in 1981.

Spain entered the European Economic Community (or EEC, which became the European Union) in 1986. A year later Repsol was created to bring the state oil companies into a unified company to meet European liberalization goals. Repsol offered a 26% stake to the public in 1989.

Under pressure from the EEC to open up Spain's markets to foreign competition, Repsol and La Caixa formed Gas Natural in 1992 to create a gas distributor big enough to compete effectively. Gas Natural had a 40% market share. The European Union subsidized its pipeline construction, and the Spanish government assisted its rapid growth by promoting natural gas as electric utility fuel in lieu of imported oil.

Gas Natural became a fully integrated company in 1995 when it acquired Empresa Nacional de Gas (Enagas), the country's national gas grid operator, from INH. The purchase of the much larger Enagas, which was building expensive pipelines, was made possible only by INH taking on part of the pipeline cost. Enagas was the sole industrial supplier, and Gas Natural the largest commercial and residential supplier; the two combined became the #3 distributor in Europe, behind British Gas (now BG) and Gaz de France.

In 1997 Gas Natural, which had acquired Gas de Buenos Aires Norte when it was newly formed, won the bid for Rio de Janeiro gas utilities auctioned off by Brazil's government. It also won concessions in Colombia and Mexico.

That year electric utility Iberdrola, Repsol, and Gas Natural agreed to build power plants jointly. But Gas Natural was forced out of the partnership when other power companies, for whom Gas Natural was the sole gas supplier, complained.

In 1998, as the Hydrocarbons Law kicked off a liberalization plan for the Spanish gas market, Gas Natural planned to build two power plants, much to the chagrin of the electric companies. Gas Natural cut a deal with the leading electric company, Endesa, under which Endesa agreed to buy gas from Gas Natural in return for participating in Gas Natural's power projects. The two also agreed to combine some of their gas utilities and pursue international projects together.

The next year Repsol, which had gained control of giant Argentine oil company YPF, became Repsol YPF. Gas Natural also made plans in 1999 to restructure operations and unbundle its services in compliance with the Hydrocarbons Law. In 2000 Gas Natural made an unsolicited bid to buy Spanish utility Iberdrola, which instead agreed to be acquired by Endesa. The following year Gas Natural signed an agreement with Italian energy giant Enel to explore joint marketing and sales negotiations for liquefied natural gas internationally.

In 2002 Repsol YPF sold a 23% interest in Gas Natural to institutional investors (it retained a 24% stake in the company). Later that year Gas Natural spun off 65% of Enagas in an IPO. In September 2005 Gas Natural made a €22.5 billion (more than $26 billion) takeover bid for Endesa. To ease some concerns authorities may have about that bid, Gas Natural divested its distribution and transport operations in October 2005.

EXECUTIVES

Chairman: Salvador Gabarró Serra, age 75
Vice Chairman: Antonio Brufau Niubó, age 62
CEO and Director: Rafael Villaseca Marco, age 59
CFO: Carlos J. Álvarez Fernández, age 47
Chief Corporate Officer: Antonio Gallart Gabás, age 50
Managing Director Retail Business:
 Josep Moragas Freixa, age 51
Managing Director Regulated Business:
 Antonio Peris Mingot, age 54
Managing Director Wholesale:
 Manuel Fernandez Álvarez, age 49
Managing Director Gas Management:
 José M. Egea Krauel, age 56
Managing Director Latin America:
 Sergio Aranda Moreno, age 51
Manager Strategy and Development:
 Antonio Basolas Tena, age 43
Manager Communications and Head Presidential
 Office: Jordi García Tabernero, age 46
Manager Legal Services: Manuel García Cobaleda, age 42
Auditors: PricewaterhouseCoopers Auditores S.L.

LOCATIONS

HQ: Gas Natural SDG, S.A.
 Plaça del Gas, 1
 08003 Barcelona, Spain
Phone: 34-902-199-199
Web: www.gasnatural.com

2009 Sales

	% of total
Europe	
Spain	63
Other countries	6
Latin America	27
North America	
USA	2
Puerto Rico	1
Other regions	1
Total	**100**

PRODUCTS/OPERATIONS

2009 Sales

	% of total
Wholesale & retail	39
Electricity generation	25
Gas distribution	20
Electricity distribution	11
Upstream & midstream	2
Other	3
Total	**100**

COMPETITORS

BG Group
BP
CEPSA
Endesa S.A.
HC Energía
IBERDROLA
Italgas
MetroGAS
Royal Dutch Shell
TGS

HISTORICAL FINANCIALS

Company Type: Public

Income Statement

FYE: December 31

	REVENUE ($ mil.)	NET INCOME ($ mil.)	NET PROFIT MARGIN	EMPLOYEES
12/09	21,325	1,992	9.3%	19,803
12/08	19,090	1,652	8.7%	21,130
12/07	14,856	1,554	10.5%	6,953
12/06	13,652	1,128	8.3%	6,686
12/05	10,099	887	8.8%	6,717
Annual Growth	**20.5%**	**22.4%**	**—**	**31.0%**

2009 Year-End Financials

Debt ratio: —
Return on equity: 15.1%
Cash ($ mil.): 844
Current ratio: 1.06
Long-term debt ($ mil.): —

No. of shares (mil.): 922
Dividends
  Yield: 5.8%
  Payout: 0.6%
Market value ($ mil.): 19,928

Stock History

Pink Sheets: GASNF

	STOCK PRICE ($) FY Close	P/E High/Low		PER SHARE ($) Earnings	Dividends	Book Value
12/09	21.62	—	—	207.81	1.26	18.93
12/08	27.19	11	8	3.33	0.61	9.75
Annual Growth	**(20.5%)**	**—**	**—**	**6,140.5%**	**106.6%**	**94.2%**

OAO Gazprom

Gazprom, Russia's largest company, produces 83% of the nation's natural gas, controls 17% of the world's reserves, and is also the world's largest gas producer. The company is engaged in gas exploration, processing, transport, and marketing. It operates Russia's domestic gas pipeline network and delivers gas to countries across Central Asia and Europe. Gazprom relies heavily on Western exports. It also holds stakes in Russian financial institutions, a polypropylene plant, and its own telecom network. The Russian government has boosted its stake in Gazprom from 38% to just more than 50%. The company accounts for about 25% of Russia's tax revenues.

In 2008 former Gazprom chairman Dmitri Medvedev was elected president of Russia.

Exports to Europe are critical to Gazprom, burdened by debt because of the insolvency of Russian consumers and hordes of nonpaying customers. Gazprom holds strategic partnerships with Western energy companies, including Germany's E.ON Ruhrgas, which owns almost 4% of the company's shares. Other partners include Royal Dutch Shell, Eni of Italy, and Finland's Fortum. Gazprom has also announced a deal with German chemical conglomerate BASF that grants BASF minority shares in both the proposed North Europe Gas Pipeline and the West Siberia field that will feed it.

To boost its exploration and production assets, Gazprom formed a strategic alliance in 2007 with TNK-BP. It also teamed up with TOTAL to develop the vast Shtokman gas field in the Barents Sea. In 2008 Gazprom acquired a 25% stake in Daltransgaz, a part owner of a natural gas pipeline in Russia's Far East, from Rosneft.

The company became embroiled in a pricing dispute with neighbor Ukraine in 2009, resulting in the disruption of gas supplies to Ukraine and, because of its transnational pipelines, to dozens of other countries in Europe.

Wanting to expand its Russian and international assets, in 2009 Gazprom acquired Italian energy titan ENI's 20% share in Gazprom Neft. ENI had acquired its stake in 2007 following the bankruptcy of YUKOS. Gazprom had the option to buy ENI's stake within two years and exercised that right in 2009, paying just more than $4 billion to ENI. Gazprom now directly owns or indirectly controls through subsidiaries about 95% of Gazprom Neft.

That year the company made its first entry into the US market when it began trading and marketing natural gas though Gazprom Marketing & Trading USA.

HISTORY

Following the breakup of the Soviet Union in the early 1990s, one of the first priorities of the Russian government was to move some state monopolies toward a free-market economic system. A presidential decree in 1992 called for the formation of a Russian joint-stock company to explore for and produce gas, gas condensates, and oil; provide for gas processing; operate gas wells; and build gas pipelines and storage facilities.

By 1993 the government had converted its natural gas monopoly, Gazprom, into a joint-stock company; the company had dated back to the 1940s, and the USSR Ministry of the Gas Industry had kept all of its assets when it became a corporation in 1989.

The new Gazprom was 15%-owned by Gazprom workers and 28% by people living in Russia's gas-producing regions. The state retained about a 40% share (boosted to 51% in 2003). The company inherited all of the export contracts to Western and Central Europe of the Commonwealth of Independent States.

Thanks to the power of Viktor Chernomyrdin (Gazprom's former Soviet boss and gas industry minister, who became Russia's prime minister in 1992), the company was able to enjoy large tax breaks and maintain its role as a monopoly — even as other industries were being more deeply privatized. However, the privatization of Gazprom was later attacked as being manipulated to profit the company's top management, including Chernomyrdin. Top managers were rumored to have each received 1%-5% of shares — holdings potentially worth $1.2 billion-$10 billion each.

Needing to raise cash, in 1996 Gazprom offered 1% of its stock to foreigners, the first sale of stock to foreign investors. In 1997 Gazprom and Royal Dutch/Shell formally became partners. That year Gazprom began building its Blue Stream pipeline across the Black Sea to Turkey. Italian group Eni helped back the project and became a partner by 1999.

In 1998 Gazprom acquired a stake in Promostroibank, Russia's fourth-largest financial institution. German energy powerhouse Ruhrgas acquired a 3% stake in Gazprom in 1998, which it increased to nearly 4% the next year. Also in 1999 Gazprom started building its Yamal-Europe pipeline, which was to stretch to Germany for exports to Europe.

The next year an attempt by Gazprom to muscle into Hungary's chemicals sector by offering cheaper raw materials was blocked by Hungary's TVK and Borsodchem and their allies. Also in 2000 Gazprom became embroiled in a politically controversial issue when it called for the country's leading private media holding group, Media-MOST, to sell shares to the gas giant in order to settle millions of dollars of debt. Because Media-MOST held NTV television, a major critic of Russian President Vladimir Putin, the deal was alleged to have been directed by the Kremlin.

The alignment of Gazprom's board changed in 2000 after the annual shareholder's meeting. For the first time in Gazprom's history, company managers did not have a majority of seats. A new chairman, Dmitri Medvedev, second in command to Putin, was elected to replace Chernomyrdin. In 2001 the board fired CEO Rem Vyakhirev and replaced him with Deputy Energy Minister Alexei Miller, a Putin ally.

In 2005 Gazprom abandoned plans to merge with Rosneft (which would have effectively given the Russian government control of Gazprom) and acquired Sibneft in an effort to add significant oil operations to its business. Millhouse Capital, a holding company controlled by Russian oligarch Roman Abramovich, sold its majority stake in what was then a major exploration and production company called Sibneft (now Gazprom Neft) to Gazprom for a reported $13 billion.

In 2006 Gazprom signed long-term contracts for gas deliveries with Austrian energy giant OMV. Again in 2006 Royal Dutch/Shell agreed to give control of the $22 billion Sakhalin-2 project (run by Sakhalin Energy Investment) in Russia's Far East to Gazprom.

EXECUTIVES

Chairman: Victor A. Zubkov, age 69
Deputy Chairman and CEO: Alexey B. Miller, age 48
Deputy Chairman, Management Committee:
Alexander N. Kozlov, age 57
Deputy Chairman, Management Committee:
Valery A. Golubev, age 58
Deputy Chairman, Management Committee; Director General, Gazprom Corporate Security Service:
Sergey F, Khomyakov
Deputy Chairman, Management Committee and Chief Accountant: Elena A. Vasilyeva, age 51
Deputy Chairman, Management Committee; Director General, OOO Gazprom export: Alexander I. Medvedev, age 55
Deputy Chairman, Management Committee and Head, Finance and Economics Department:
Andrey V. Kruglov, age 41
Director; Deputy Chairman and Head Administration, Management Committee: Mikhail L. Sereda, age 40
Director; Deputy Chairman, Management Committee:
Alexander G. Ananenkov, age 57
Member, Management Committee; Head, Strategic Development Department: Vlada V. Rusakova, age 56
Member, Management Committee; Head, Asset Management and Corporate Relations Department:
Olga P. Pavlova, age 57
Member, Management Committee; Head, Investment and Construction Department: Yaroslav Y. Golko, age 49
Member, Management Committee; Head, Legal Department: Nikolay N. Dubik, age 38
Head, Administrative Department and Management Committee Administration: Pyotr A. Myagkov
Head, Information Policy Department:
Alexander D. Bespalov, age 60
Head, International Business Department:
Stanislav E. Tsygankov, age 44
Head, Technological Process Control Systems Automation Department: Nikolai F. Stolyar, age 57
Head, Personnel Management Department:
Elena Kasyanova, age 49
Auditors: ZAO PricewaterhouseCoopers Audit

LOCATIONS

HQ: OAO Gazprom
16 Nametkina St.
117997 Moscow GSP-7, Russia
Phone: 7-495-719-30-01   **Fax:** 7-495-719-83-33
Web: www.gazprom.ru

2009 Gas Sales

	% of total
Russia	25
Former Soviet republics	19
Other countries	56
Total	**100**

PRODUCTS/OPERATIONS

2009 Sales

	% of total
Gas	56
Oil	23
Transportation & other	21
Total	**100**

COMPETITORS

BP
Centrica
E.ON Ruhrgas
Gasunie
LUKOIL
Qatar Petroleum
Rosneft
Sakhalin Energy
Surgutneftegas
Tatneft

HISTORICAL FINANCIALS

Company Type: Public

Income Statement

FYE: December 31

	REVENUE ($ mil.)	NET INCOME ($ mil.)	NET PROFIT MARGIN	EMPLOYEES
12/09	98,686	25,722	26.1%	393,600
12/08	107,597	24,330	22.6%	376,300
12/07	98,636	26,785	27.2%	436,100
12/06	83,755	20,983	25.1%	432,000
12/05	42,836	7,078	16.5%	396,757
Annual Growth	**23.2%**	**38.1%**	**—**	**(0.2%)**

2009 Year-End Financials

Debt ratio: —
Return on equity: 14.8%
Cash ($ mil.): 8,401
Current ratio: —
Long-term debt ($ mil.): —

No. of shares (mil.): 5,925
Dividends
  Yield: —
  Payout: —
Market value ($ mil.): 151,088

Stock History

Pink Sheets: OGZPY

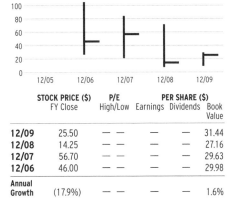

	STOCK PRICE ($) FY Close	P/E High/Low	PER SHARE ($) Earnings	Dividends	Book Value
12/09	25.50	— —	—	—	31.44
12/08	14.25	— —	—	—	27.16
12/07	56.70	— —	—	—	29.63
12/06	46.00	— —	—	—	29.98
Annual Growth	**(17.9%)**	**— —**	**—**	**—**	**1.6%**

GDF SUEZ

GDF SUEZ is one of Europe's big boys. It is engaged in the purchasing, production, and marketing of natural gas and electricity; the development and maintenance of major natural gas and electricity infrastructures; and the creation and marketing of energy and environmental services. With operations in more than 40 countries, GDF SUEZ is the world's leading independent power producer with 68,400 MW of installed capacity. It is Europe's top importer of liquefied natural gas (LNG), its largest supplier of natural gas, the continent's leading supplier of multi-technical energy services, and a leading global supplier of water and waste management services. The French government controls 36% of the company.

French energy and environmental services giants came together when SUEZ merged with Gaz de France in 2008 to form GDF SUEZ. GDF SUEZ is looking to harness its global size and its presence in a mix of energy areas (nuclear, natural gas, LNG, coal, and renewables) with its water sanitation and waste management expertise to deliver energy in a way that preserves the environment.

In a move to expand geographically, in 2008 GDF SUEZ acquired a 90% stake in Izmit Gaz Dagitim San Ve Tic AS (Turkey's third-largest natural gas distributor) for $232 million. In 2009

the company made further geographic realignments, prompted by the regulatory requirements of the European Commission, for GDF SUEZ and Germany's E.ON to allow for more competition in their major markets by swapping some generation capacity.

In 2010 the company's GDF SUEZ Energy International made a bid to acquire UK-based International Power. The $21.5 billion deal will create the world's largest global independent power generation company. When completed, GDF SUEZ will hold 70% of New International Power, which will have generation capacity of 66,000 MW.

In order to pay down debt, in 2010 the company sold its 5% stake in Spanish energy firm Gas Natural for about $686 million.

HISTORY

The first canal in Egypt was dug in the 13th century BC, but it was Napoleon who revived the idea of a shorter trade route to India: a canal through Egypt linking the Gulf of Suez with the Mediterranean. Former French diplomat and engineer Ferdinand de Lesseps formed Compagnie Universelle du Canal Maritime de Suez in 1858 to build and eventually operate the canal, which opened 11 years later. Egypt's modernization had pushed it into debt and increased its ties to the British government, which, by 1875, had acquired a 44% stake in the company.

For more than 80 years the Suez Canal was a foreign enclave, protected by the British Army since 1936. After Egypt's puppet government fell, and as Gamal Abd Al-Nasser assumed power in 1956, British troops exited the Canal Zone, which Egypt quickly nationalized. Israel, Britain, and France attacked, but the United Nations arranged a truce and foreign forces withdrew, leaving the Suez in Egypt's control.

With no canal to operate, Universelle du Canal Maritime de Suez became Compagnie Financière de Suez in 1958. A year later it created a bank (which became Banque Indosuez in 1974).

In 1967 Financière de Suez became the largest shareholder in Société Lyonnaise des Eaux et de L'Eclairage, a leading French water company. Formed in 1880, Lyonnaise des Eaux had stakes in water (Northumbrian Water) and energy (Elyo). After France's energy firms were nationalized in 1946, Lyonnaise des Eaux dipped deeper into the water industry by acquiring Degrémont (now Ondeo-Degrémont) in 1972. It also purchased stakes in waste management (SITA, 1970) and heating systems (Cofreth, 1975).

In the 1980s Lyonnaise des Eaux expanded in Spain, the UK, and the US, and diversified into cable TV (1986) and broadcast TV (1987).

Meanwhile, Financière de Suez became a financial power when it won a controlling stake in Société Générale de Belgique (SGB) in 1988 and bought Groupe Victoire in 1989. But the two buys left the firm (renamed Compagnie de Suez in 1990) deeply in debt.

Losing money, Compagnie de Suez disposed of Victoire (1994) and then the valuable Banque Indosuez (1996). In 1996 the company bought a controlling stake in Belgium's top utility, Tractebel (now SUEZ-TRACTEBEL). Compagnie de Suez and Lyonnaise des Eaux merged in 1997 to create Suez Lyonnaise des Eaux.

In 2000 Suez Lyonnaise bought United Water Resources (now United Water). The next year the company shortened its name to Suez (later modified to SUEZ).

SUEZ divested most of its 11% stake in Belgian insurance firm Fortis for nearly $2 billion in 2003. In 2003 the company merged Tractebel and SGB (Tractebel's former holding company) to form SUEZ-TRACTEBEL.

Gaz de France was founded in 1946 by the French government to consolidate the more than 500 (mostly coal-fired) gas works that had existed before WWII. From 1949 on, Gaz de France focused on upgrading gas plants and local transmission networks. Its first long-distance pipeline was built in 1953, linking Paris to the Lorraine coal gas fields. With the development of the Lacq gas field in southwestern France, annual gas sales increased by 300% between 1957 and 1962.

By 1965 nearly half of the French population was supplied with natural gas. Spurred on by the loss of its Algerian colony, which held major oil and gas assets, the French government pushed for new gas supplies to supplement its Lacq resources. Gaz de France was able to secure a contract with Algerian natural gas supplier Sonatrach in 1965, and in 1967 it signed an import contract with Dutch supplier Gasunie. The company also diversified in the 1960s, helping to build a natural gas liquefaction plant in Algeria and a receiving terminal in Le Havre.

Following the price shock of the Arab oil embargo of the early 1970s, Gaz de France stepped up its search for alternative suppliers, including contracts with Russia's largest gas producer Soyouzgazexport and four separate Norwegian producers, Efofisk (1977), Stafjord (1985), Heimdal (1986), and Gullfaks (1987).

For the first time in its history, Gaz de France became an offshore field operator in 2000 by acquiring exploration and production company TransCanada International Netherlands and a 39% stake in Noordgastransport BV, an offshore gas pipeline operator.

In 2001, through the purchase of a 10% interest in Petronet LNG, Gaz de France embarked on a project to import liquefied natural gas from Qatar to India.

EXECUTIVES

Chairman and CEO; Chairman, SUEZ-TRACTEBEL, GDF SUEZ Energy Services, and SUEZ Environnement: Gérard Mestrallet, age 61
Vice Chairman and President: Jean-François Cirelli, age 52
EVP and CFO: Gérard Lamarche, age 49
EVP, Energy Europe and International; CEO, Electrabel: Dirk Beeuwsaert, age 62
EVP Global Gas and LNG Business Line: Jean-Marie Dauger, age 58
Executive Member; EVP Suez Environnement: Jean-Louis Chaussade, age 58
Executive Member and General Secretary: Yves de Gaulle, age 59
Executive Member, Communications, Financial Communications, and Public Affairs: Valérie Bernis, age 51
Executive Member, Infrastructures: Jean-Claude Depail, age 61
Executive Member, Senior Managers Department: Emmanuel van Innis, age 63
Executive Member, Energy France: Henri Ducré, age 54
Executive Member, Business Strategy and Sustainable Development: Alain Chaigneau, age 59
Executive Member, Audit and Risks: Philippe Jeunet
Executive Member, Energy Services: Jérôme Tolot
Executive Member, Human Resources: Philippe Saimpert, age 56
Executive Member, Energy Europe and International: Pierre Clavel, age 51
Executive Member, Integration, Synergies, and Performance: Emmanuel Hedde, age 62
President, Energy Policy Committee: Jean-Pierre Hansen, age 62
Auditors: Mazars

LOCATIONS

HQ: GDF SUEZ
16-26, rue du Docteur Lancreaux
75008 Paris, France
Phone: 33-1-57-04-0000
Web: www.gdfsuez.com

2009 Sales

	% of total
Europe	
France	38
Belgium	15
Other EU countries	31
Other countries	2
North America	6
Asia, Middle East & Oceania	4
South America	3
Africa	1
Total	**100**

PRODUCTS/OPERATIONS

2009 Sales

	% of total
Energy Europe & International	30
Global Gas & LNG	22
Energy France	15
Energy Services	14
SUEZ Environment	13
Infrastructures	6
Total	**100**

COMPETITORS

BG Group
Bouygues
CANAL+
Centrica
Covanta
Dragados
Electricité de France
Electricité de Strasbourg
Enel
Eni
E.ON
Gas Natural SDG
Gasunie
Gazprom
Italgas
National Grid
RWE
SABESP
United Utilities
Vattenfall
Veolia Environnement

HISTORICAL FINANCIALS

Company Type: Public

Income Statement

FYE: December 31

	REVENUE ($ mil.)	NET INCOME ($ mil.)	NET PROFIT MARGIN	EMPLOYEES
12/09	114,525	7,496	6.5%	242,714
12/08	95,739	7,881	8.2%	199,964
12/07	69,879	6,795	9.7%	146,350
12/06	36,468	3,065	8.4%	139,814
12/05	26,521	2,062	7.8%	157,639
Annual Growth	**44.2%**	**38.1%**	**—**	**11.4%**

2009 Year-End Financials

Debt ratio: —
Return on equity: —
Cash ($ mil.): 14,796
Current ratio: 1.12
Long-term debt ($ mil.): —
No. of shares (mil.): 2,261
Dividends
  Yield: 5.3%
  Payout: 78.7%
Market value ($ mil.): 98,154

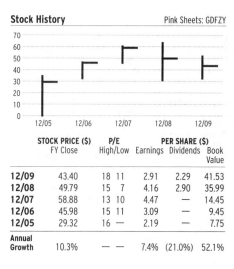

	Stock History						Pink Sheets: GDFZY

	STOCK PRICE ($) FY Close	P/E High/Low		PER SHARE ($) Earnings	Dividends	Book Value
12/09	43.40	18	11	2.91	2.29	41.53
12/08	49.79	15	7	4.16	2.90	35.99
12/07	58.88	13	10	4.47	—	14.45
12/06	45.98	15	11	3.09	—	9.45
12/05	29.32	16	—	2.19	—	7.75
Annual Growth	**10.3%**	**—**	**—**	**7.4%**	**(21.0%)**	**52.1%**

Assicurazioni Generali

Italy's largest insurance company (and one of the largest in Europe), Assicurazioni Generali writes insurance for risks as varied as space launches and corporate package policies. Some 450 companies in about 65 countries make up the Generali group. Its core members are involved primarily in insurance (including life, accident, health, motor, fire, marine/aviation, and reinsurance); the rest concentrate on other financial services and real estate. Generali is noted for being a leading insurer of satellite and space missions, which it has been covering since 1964. In more earthbound realms, the company targets individuals and small to midsized businesses, and has been in business since 1831.

Italy, France, Spain, and Germany are Generali's largest markets. The insurer has entrenched itself in Germany after acquiring a controlling interest in one of the country's largest insurers, AMB Generali (formerly Aachener und Munchener), and establishing an alliance with Commerzbank.

With its place in Western Europe cemented, the company has begun to probe areas such as Eastern Europe, Latin America, India, and China as areas for investment and growth. Generali is focusing its services around individual life and group pension schemes; it has also boosted its non-insurance operations by forming Banca Generali, a banking organization that provides personal financial services.

As part of its expansion plans, in 2009 Generali picked up about a quarter of Czech private equity firm PPF Partners, which is known for its hostile takeovers. The two had formed a 51-49 joint venture, known as Generali PPF Holding, in 2008.

That year Generali received a license to offer life insurance in the United Arab Emirates. It hoped to tap expatriates (80% of the population) who may be in search of insurance. In 2008 it moved into Belarus and Romania and began opening outlets in India, with plans to eventually have 300 locations there. In 2009 the company was granted a license to sell life insurance in Vietnam, marking its entry into that market.

The company completed its acquisition of Swiss Life subsidiary Banca del Gottardo in 2008 for $1.65 billion. The purchase boosted Generali's asset management operations; Gottardo was combined with Generali's international private banking unit, BSI.

While Generali has been focused on restructuring its international operations to make room for its many acquisitions, the company also made a move to reorganize and streamline its domestic operations in 2009. The company acquired the remaining shares of majority-owned Italian life insurance firm Alleanza Assicurazioni. Generali then merged Alleanza with its Italian property/casualty subsidiary, Toro Assicurazioni, into a new company named Alleanza Toro. The new entity holds a good chunk of Generali's domestic operations, serving over 3 million customers, and continues to offer products under the Alleanza and Toro brands. Generali aims to use the combined sales and marketing force to better compete in its home market.

Generali shareholders include Italy's secretive and powerful MEDIOBANCA (15%) and Banca d'Italia (about 5%). Overall, Italian shareholders account for about 70% of the company's shares.

HISTORY

Assicurazioni Generali was founded as Assicurazioni Generali Austro-Italiche in 1831 by a group of merchants led by Giuseppe Morpurgo in the Austro-Hungarian port of Trieste. Formed to provide insurance to the city's bustling trade industry, the company offered life, marine, fire, flood, and shipping coverage. That year Morpurgo established what he intended to be Generali's headquarters in Venice. (While the company maintained offices in both cities, Trieste ultimately won out.)

By 1835 Generali had opened 25 offices in Central and Western Europe; it had also expelled Morpurgo. The firm moved into Africa and Asia in the 1880s. In 1900 Generali began selling injury and theft insurance. In 1907 Generali's Prague office provided the young, experimental writer Franz Kafka his first job. (He found it disagreeable and quit after a few months.)

During WWI the firm's Venice office pledged allegiance to Italy, while the office in Trieste (still part of Austria-Hungary) stayed loyal to the Hapsburgs. After the war Trieste was absorbed by the new Italian republic. Under Edgardo Morpurgo, Generali expanded further in the 1920s, managing 30 subsidiaries and operating in 17 countries. As fascist Italy aligned itself with Germany in the 1930s, adoption of anti-Semitic laws caused Morpurgo and a number of other high-ranking Jewish employees to flee the country. In 1938 Generali moved its headquarters to Rome (but moved them back to Trieste after war's end).

The firm maintained steady business both before and during Nazi occupation in WWII; in 1945, however, the Soviets seized all Italian properties in Eastern Europe, including 14 Generali subsidiaries. In 1950 Generali invaded the US market, offering shipping and fire insurance and reinsurance. Generali established a cooperative agreement with Aetna Life and Casualty (now Aetna Inc.) in 1966, further cementing its US connections.

In 1988 Generali tried to acquire French insurer Compagnie du Midi. Foreshadowing Generali's later dealings with Istituto Nazionale delle Assicurazioni (INA), Midi escaped Generali's grasp through a merger with AXA. As the Iron Curtain frayed in 1989, Generali formed AB Generali Budapest through a joint venture with a Hungarian insurer. In 1990 the firm opened an office in Tokyo through an agreement with Taisho Marine and Fire Insurance (which became Mitsui Marine & Fire Insurance and is now Mitsui Sumitomo Insurance). By 1993 Generali had become Italy's largest insurer.

In 1997 the firm was accused, along with other major European insurers, of not paying on policies of Holocaust victims. (It moved to settle claims in 1999.)

The company focused on the German and Swiss markets in 1998, acquiring controlling interests in insurer AMB Aachener und Munchener (now AMB Generali) and in Banca della Svizzera Italiana.

In 1999 Generali succeeded in a hostile takeover of INA, its largest domestic competitor. The move pre-empted INA's proposed merger with San Paolo IMI, which would have knocked Generali to second place among the country's insurers. Avoiding violation of the EU's antitrust laws in connection with the INA acquisition, the company sold four subsidiaries (including Italian insurers Aurora and Navale) in 2000.

In 2002 Generali rolled together three securities investments firms — Altinia, Ina Sim, and Prime Consult Sim — into Banca Generali.

EXECUTIVES

Chairman: Cesare Geronzi, age 75
Vice Chairman: Gabriele Galateri di Genola, age 63
Vice Chairman: Vincent Bolloré, age 58
Vice Chairman: Francesco G. Caltagirone, age 67
Managing Director, CEO, and Board Member: Giovanni Perissinotto, age 56
General Manager and CFO: Raffaele Agrusti, age 53
Managing Director and Board Member: Sergio Balbinot, age 51
Secretary and Deputy General Manager, Legal, Corporate Affairs, and Privacy: Vittorio Rispoli, age 50
Head Research and Development: Lorenzo Savorelli, age 51
Head Mergers and Acquisitions: David Glavina
Head Group Internal Audit: Alessandro Busetti
Head Investor Relations: Paola Buratti
Head Corporate Public Affairs: Mauro Giusto, age 50
Assistant General Manager and Chief Risk Officer: Amerigo Borrini
Assistant General Manager, Group Legal and Corporate Affairs: Oliviero E. Pessi
Deputy General Manager, Human Resources, Organization, Communication, and Information Technology Coordinator: Lodovico Floriani, age 66
Auditors: PricewaterhouseCoopers SpA

LOCATIONS

HQ: Assicurazioni Generali SpA
Piazza Duca degli Abruzzi, 2
34132 Trieste, Italy
Phone: 39-040-671-111   **Fax:** 39-040-671-600
US HQ: 1 Liberty Plaza, 29th Fl., New York, NY 10006
US Phone: 212-602-7600   **US Fax:** 212-587-9537
Web: www.generali.com

2009 Revenues

	% of total
Europe	
Italy	28
France	17
Germany	13
Central & Eastern Europe	16
Other countries	20
Other regions	6
Total	**100**

PRODUCTS/OPERATIONS

2009 Sales

	% of total
Life insurance	59
Property/casualty insurance	31
Financial services	10
Total	**100**

COMPETITORS

Ageas SA/NV
AIG
Allianz
Assurances Générales de France
AXA
Camfin
ERGO
Eureko
FonSai
ING
Milano Assicurazioni
Swiss Re
UniCredit
Unipol
Zurich Financial Services

HISTORICAL FINANCIALS

Company Type: Public

Income Statement

FYE: December 31

	ASSETS ($ mil.)	NET INCOME ($ mil.)	INCOME AS % OF ASSETS	EMPLOYEES
12/09	607,414	2,532	0.4%	85,322
12/08	541,161	1,500	0.3%	84,000
12/07	563,066	4,967	0.9%	67,306
12/06	498,221	3,776	0.8%	66,003
12/05	409,239	2,855	0.7%	61,561
Annual Growth	10.4%	(3.0%)	—	8.5%

2009 Year-End Financials

Equity as % of assets: 4.7%
Return on assets: 0.4%
Return on equity: 11.4%
Long-term debt ($ mil.): —
No. of shares (mil.): 1,557
Dividends
  Yield: 0.8%
  Payout: 15.8%
Market value ($ mil.): 41,993
Sales ($ mil.): 129,934

Stock History

Italian: G

	STOCK PRICE ($) FY Close	P/E High/Low		PER SHARE ($) Earnings	Dividends	Book Value
12/09	26.97	21	10	1.33	0.21	18.34
12/08	27.47	50	27	0.90	1.32	10.24
12/07	45.63	16	13	3.11	1.15	13.98
12/06	39.90	19	14	2.27	0.74	12.89
12/05	31.78	20	15	1.63	0.53	10.61
Annual Growth	(4.0%)	—	—	(5.0%)	(20.7%)	14.7%

George Weston

George Weston Limited fuels Canadians through those long winters. More than 90% of the company's sales come from its 63%-owned Loblaw Companies Limited, Canada's largest supermarket operator (with more than 1,400 stores under more than a dozen banners including Loblaws, Provigo, and Zehrs) and the country's largest wholesale food distributor. The rest comes from Weston Foods, with operations in Canada and the US that focus on freshly baked goods, frozen dough, biscuits, and other bakery products. (Its Interbake Foods division is a major supplier of Girl Scout cookies in the US.) Chairman and president Galen Weston owns about 63% of the company, which was founded by his grandfather in 1882.

Both Loblaw and Weston Foods are facing challenges resulting from changing consumer preferences concerning what to eat and where to shop. In response, George Weston has been restructuring both businesses to better match changing tastes.

In 2009 George Weston sold its US-based fresh baked and baked goods business Dunedin Holdings to Mexico's Grupo Bimbo for about $2.5 billion. The sale included the Arnold, Brownberry, Entenmann's, Freihofer, Stroehmann, and Thomas' brand names. Previously, George Weston sold its Neilson Dairy business to Saputo in a deal that closed in late 2008.

In a bid for higher-margin products, George Weston acquired Keystone Bakery Holdings, a US-based provider of frozen cupcakes, doughnuts, and cookies for in-store bakeries and foodservice companies, in 2010. Aside from sweet treats, George Weston is looking to shift its product mix to include more whole grains as an increased focus on healthier breads has hurt sales of white-flour-based products.

Loblaw is facing increased competition from non-traditional rivals, such as Wal-Mart Canada and Costco Wholesale Canada, which are claiming a growing share of the retail grocery market. In response, the company is cutting prices and sprucing up its retail stores. It's also aggressively expanding its low-price Real Canadian Superstore format, which numbers more than 100 stores, to better compete with foreign superstore operators. In a bid to boosts its portfolio of ethnic products, Loblaw acquired T&T Supermarket, Canada's largest retailer of Asian food, in mid-2009.

HISTORY

A baker's apprentice, George Weston began delivering bread in Toronto with a single horse in 1882. He added the Model Bakery in 1896 and began making cookies and biscuits in 1908.

Upon George's death in 1924, his son Garfield gained control of the company and took it public as George Weston Limited in 1928. Having popularized the premium English biscuit in Canada, Garfield acquired bakeries in the UK to make cheap biscuits (uncommon at the time). He grouped the bakeries as a separate public company called Allied Bakeries in 1935 (it later became Associated British Foods and is still controlled by the Weston family).

Expansion-minded Garfield led the company into the US with the purchase of Associated Biscuit in 1939. By the late 1930s George Weston was making cakes, breads, and almost 500 kinds of candy and biscuits.

During the 1940s the company made a number of acquisitions, including papermaker E.B. Eddy (1943; sold 1998 to papermaker Domtar, giving it a 20% stake in Domtar), Southern Biscuit (1944), Western Grocers (1944, its first distribution company), and William Neilson (1948, chocolate and dairy products).

In 1953 it acquired a controlling interest in Loblaw Groceterias, Canada's largest grocery chain. George Weston continued its acquisitions during the 1950s and 1960s, adding grocer National Tea and diversifying into packaging (Somerville Industries, 1957) and fisheries (British Columbia Packers, 1962; Conners Bros., 1967).

By 1970, when Garfield's son Galen became president, the company's holdings were in disarray. Galen brought in new managers, consolidated the food distribution and sales operations under Loblaw Companies Limited, and cut back on National Tea (which shrank from over 900 stores in 1972 to 82 in 1993). When Garfield died in 1978, Galen became chairman.

Ever since Galen, a polo-playing chum of Prince Charles, was the target of a failed kidnapping attempt by the Irish Republican Army in 1983, the family has kept a low public profile.

George Weston became the #1 chocolate maker in Canada with its purchase of Cadbury Schweppes' Canadian assets in 1987. The 1980s concluded with a five-year price war in St. Louis among its National Tea stores, Kroger, and a local grocer. This ultimately proved fruitless, and Loblaw sold its US supermarkets in 1995, ending its US retail presence. As part of its divestiture of underachieving subsidiaries, the company sold its Neilson confectionery business back to Cadbury Schweppes in 1996 and sold its chocolate products company in 1998.

In early 1998 Loblaw set its sights on Quebec, buying Montreal-based Provigo. Other George Weston acquisitions in the late 1990s included Oshawa Foods' 80-store Agora Foods franchise supermarket unit in eastern Canada and its Fieldfresh Farms dairy business, the frozen-bagel business of Quaker Oats, Pennsylvania-based Maier's Bakery, and Bunge International's Australian meat processor, Don Smallgoods. It also sold its British Columbia Packers fisheries unit.

Early in 2001 George Weston surprised analysts when it won Unilever's Bestfoods Baking Company (Entenmann's, Oroweat) with a bid of $1.8 billion. The company reduced its stake in Loblaw by 2% and sold its Connors canned seafood business to fund the purchase, which was completed in July 2001. To help pay down debt, in early 2002 the company sold its Orowheat business in the western US to Mexican bread giant Grupo Bimbo for $610 million.

In 2003 Weston's food distribution business introduced about 1,500 private label products. It sold its fisheries operations in Chile at a loss in 2004, for about $20 million. That September the company purchased Quebec-based Boulangerie Gadoua Ltée, a family-owned baking business.

The company restructured its US biscuit operations and opened a new fresh bakery plant in Orlando, Florida, in 2005 as part of its push to increase its business in the southeastern US. A new bakery in the midwestern US began production of bread and English muffins in late 2006.

In early 2007 Weston's Loblaw subsidiary announced it was writing down its operations in Quebec to the tune of $768 million tied to its struggling Provigo grocery stores.

EXECUTIVES

Chairman and President: W.G. Galen Weston, age 70
Deputy Chairman: Allan L. Leighton, age 56
CFO: Paviter S. (Pavi) Binning, age 50
EVP Corporate Development: Robert G. (Bob) Vaux, age 61
EVP, Secretary, and General Counsel: Gordon A. M. Currie, age 51
EVP Finance: Louise M. Lacchin, age 50
SVP Pension and Benefits: Lucy J. Paglione, age 50
SVP Tax: J. Bradley Holland, age 46
SVP Shared Services: Geoffrey H. (Geoff) Wilson, age 54
SVP Labor Relations: Roy R. Conliffe, age 59
SVP Finance: Jeremy Roberts
SVP Risk Management and Audit Services: Manny J. DiFilippo, age 50
SVP, Legal Counsel, and Assistant Secretary: Robert A. Balcom, age 48
VP Commodities: David Farnfield
VP and Treasurer: Lisa R. Swartzman, age 39
VP Corporate Systems: Kirk W. Mondesire, age 49
VP and Legal Counsel: Adam Walsh
VP and Controller: Lina Taglieri
Senior Director Environmental: Walter Kraus
Auditors: KPMG LLP

LOCATIONS

HQ: George Weston Limited
22 St. Clair Ave. East
Toronto, Ontario M4T 2S7, Canada
Phone: 416-922-2500 **Fax:** 416-922-4395
Web: www.weston.ca

2009 Sales

	% of total
Canada	98
US	2
Total	**100**

PRODUCTS/OPERATIONS

2009 Sales

	% of total
Loblaw	95
Weston Foods	5
Total	**100**

Selected Operating Divisions

Food Distribution (selected Loblaw banners)
 Atlantic Superstore
 Extra Foods
 Fortinos
 Loblaws
 Maxi
 Maxi & Co.
 no frills
 Provigo
 The Real Canadian Superstore
 The Real Canadian Wholesale Club
 SuperValu
 valu-mart
 Your Independent Grocer
 Zehrs Markets
Food Processing (selected units)
 Interbake Foods Inc. (cookies and crackers, US)
 Maplehurst Bakeries, Inc. (frozen bakery products, US)
 Weston Bakeries Limited (freshly baked goods)
 Weston Fruitcake Company

COMPETITORS

Bridgford Foods	Kellogg U.S. Snacks
Campbell Canada	Lanes Biscuits
Canada Safeway	Maple Leaf Foods
Costco Wholesale Canada	METRO
Flowers Foods	Otis Spunkmeyer
Grupo Bimbo	Sobeys
Hostess Brands	Tasty Baking
IGA	Wal-Mart Canada
Jim Pattison Group	

Company Type: Public

Income Statement   FYE: December 31

	REVENUE ($ mil.)	NET INCOME ($ mil.)	NET PROFIT MARGIN	EMPLOYEES
12/09	30,321	986	3.3%	6,000
12/08	26,242	680	2.6%	6,000
12/07	33,416	573	1.7%	140,000
12/06	27,580	104	0.4%	155,000
12/05	26,897	599	2.2%	17,500
Annual Growth	3.0%	13.3%	—	(23.5%)

2009 Year-End Financials

Debt ratio: 77.5%
Return on equity: 17.2%
Cash ($ mil.): 3,209
Current ratio: 1.89
Long-term debt ($ mil.): 5,124

No. of shares (mil.): 129
Dividends
  Yield: 2.2%
  Payout: 18.7%
Market value ($ mil.): 8,232

Stock History   Toronto: WN

	STOCK PRICE ($) FY Close	P/E High/Low		PER SHARE ($) Earnings	Dividends	Book Value
12/09	63.77	9	7	7.31	1.37	51.24
12/08	49.03	11	7	4.97	1.18	37.55
12/07	55.14	21	13	3.99	1.47	38.94
12/06	64.82	174	133	0.45	1.23	34.62
12/05	74.02	23	16	4.38	1.23	34.01
Annual Growth	(3.7%)	—	—	13.7%	2.7%	10.8%

GlaxoSmithKline

GlaxoSmithKline (GSK) calms your nerves and helps you breathe easier. One of the top five pharmaceutical firms in the world, GSK's bestsellers include central nervous system therapies, respiratory and cardiovascular drugs, and antivirals, as well as vaccines. The company's top product is asthma medication Advair, which combines two of the company's other products, Flovent and Serevent. Other products include herpes treatment Valtrex, epilepsy treatment Lamictal, antidepressant Paxil, prostate enlargement therapy Avodart, and antibiotic Augmentin. The company's consumer products include Tums for sour stomachs, dental care products Aquafresh and Sensodyne, and smoking-cessation products NicoDerm and Nicorette.

As sales in GSK's largest market, the US, account for about a third of pharmaceutical sales, maintaining a rich portfolio of US patent-protected products can make or break the company's future. Examples of GSK drugs that have experienced sales slumps due to patent losses include its extended-release Paxil CR in 2008, and bestsellers Imitrex and Valtrex, which began facing generic competition in 2009. Other products feeling the heat from generics include Zofran, Flonase, and Coreg.

The development of new potential blockbusters is the best way to alleviate these losses, and GSK's development efforts include about 150 different clinical stage projects, about 30 of which are in late-phase trials. Drug candidates nearing the end of the development stage include therapies for rheumatoid arthritis, type-2 diabetes, lupus, heart disease, and various cancers. Successful development programs have included cancer drug Arzerra, which was launched in the US in 2009, and infant rotavirus vaccine Rotarix and blood disorder treatment Promacta, both of which were approved by the FDA in 2008. Another highlight of GSK's development program is its pandemic vaccine program, which has delivered vaccines for H5N1 (avian bird) flu and H1N1 (swine) flu.

In 2009 GSK widened its offering of dermatology products by acquiring Stiefel Laboratories from the Stiefel family and other investors (including the Blackstone Group) for some $2.9 billion. The company is also engaged in several key collaboration projects to grow its pipeline, including a licensing deal worth up to $2.1 billion with biotech firm Genmab to co-develop and market cancer antibody therapies and a $1 billion agreement with Synta Pharmaceuticals to develop a late-stage melanoma candidate. It has similar development deals with OncoMed (cancer treatments), Galapagos (anti-infectives), and Theravance (gastrointestinal drugs).

The company launched a restructuring program in 2009 to cut operational costs in all areas, including manufacturing, sales, research, and infrastructure. The program includes job cuts, and comes on top of previous cost-cutting programs that resulted in an approximate 8% workforce reduction during 2007 and 2008.

In mid-2010 GlaxoSmithKline and Pfizer said they would open all of the products in their HIV joint venture, called ViiV Healthcare, to generic drugmakers working in undeveloped or low-income countries, including the whole of sub-Saharan Africa, which accounts for 80% of people living with HIV.

HISTORY

Englishman Joseph Nathan started an import-export business in New Zealand in 1873. He obtained the rights to a process for drying milk and began making powdered milk in New Zealand, selling it as baby food Glaxo. Nathan's son Alec, dispatched to London to oversee baby food sales in Britain, increased Glaxo's name recognition by publishing the Glaxo Baby Book, a guide to child care. After WWI the company began distribution in India and South America.

In the 1920s Glaxo launched vitamin D-fortified formulations. It entered the pharmaceutical business with its 1927 introduction of Ostelin, a liquid vitamin D concentrate, and continued to grow globally in the 1930s, introducing Ostermilk (vitamin-fortified milk).

Glaxo began making penicillin and anesthetics during WWII; it went public in 1947. A steep drop in antibiotic prices in the mid-1950s led Glaxo to diversify; it bought veterinary, medical instrument, and drug distribution firms.

In the 1970s the British Monopolies Commission quashed both a hostile takeover attempt by Beecham and a proposed merger with retailer and drugmaker Boots. Glaxo launched US operations in 1978.

In the 1980s Glaxo shed nondrug operations to concentrate on pharmaceuticals. A 1981 marketing blitz launched antiulcer drug Zantac (to vie with SmithKline's Tagamet) in the US, where Glaxo's sales had been small. The company boosted outreach by contracting to use Hoffmann-La Roche's sales staff. The Zantac sales assault gave Glaxo leadership in US antiulcer drug sales.

Under CEO Sir Richard Sykes, Glaxo in 1995 made a surprise bid for UK rival Wellcome. Founded in 1880 by Americans Silas Burroughs and Henry Wellcome to sell McKesson-Robbins' products outside the US, Burroughs Wellcome and Co. began making its own products two years later. By the 1990s the company, which fostered Nobel Prize-winning researchers, led the world in antiviral medicines. Its primary drug products were Zovirax (launched 1981) and Retrovir (1987). Though an earlier bid by Glaxo had been rejected, Sykes won the takeover with backing from Wellcome Trust, Wellcome's largest shareholder.

The FDA in 2000 approved Glaxo's Lotronex for irritable bowel syndrome, but several hospitalizations linked to the drug prompted the FDA to ask the company to withdraw it from the US market. Later that year Glaxo completed its merger with former UK rival SmithKline Beecham to create GlaxoSmithKline (GSK); Jean-Pierre Garnier took over as CEO.

In 2006 GSK settled a tax dispute with the IRS for $3.1 billion, the largest single tax payment in IRS history, over international profit allocation in taxes filed by Glaxo Wellcome (prior to the 2001 Glaxo Wellcome/SmithKline Beecham merger) from 1989 through 2000. The payment also includes taxes owed from 2001 through 2005.

In 2008 Jean-Pierre Garnier was replaced as CEO by Andrew Witty, who had been with the company for more than 20 years and was previously president of GSK's European pharmaceuticals division.

Later in 2009 GSK sold US marketing rights to antidepressant Wellbutrin XL, which began facing generic competition in 2006 and has thus seen lower sales volumes, to fellow drugmaker Valeant Pharmaceuticals (formerly Biovail) for $510 million.

EXECUTIVES

Chairman: Sir Christopher Charles (Chris) Gent, age 61
CEO and Director: Andrew Witty, age 45
CFO and Director: Julian Heslop, age 56
Executive Director and CFO Designate: Simon Dingemans
CIO: Bill Louv
Chief of Staff: Daniel J. (Dan) Phelan, age 60
Chief Strategy Officer: David Redfern
SVP and General Counsel: Dan Troy
SVP Medicines Discovery and Development: Patrick Vallance
SVP, Company Secretary, and Corporate Compliance Officer: Simon M. Bicknell
SVP Global Communications: Philip (Phil) Thomson
SVP Medicines Development: Allan Baxter, age 58
SVP Global Communications: Duncan Learmouth
SVP Human Resources: Claire Thomas
SVP Biopharm Development: Carlo Russo
SVP Worldwide Business Development, Research and Development: Adrian Rawcliffe
SVP Managed Markets: Dennis White

Chairman, Research and Development and Director:
Moncef Slaoui, age 50
President, North America Pharmaceuticals:
Deirdre P. Connelly, age 49
Chairman and CEO, Stiefel Laboratories:
Charles W. (Charlie) Stiefel
President, Global Manufacturing and Supply:
David Pulman
President and General Manager, Biologicals:
Jean Stéphenne, age 61
President, Emerging Markets: Abbas Hussain
Auditors: PricewaterhouseCoopers LLP

LOCATIONS

HQ: GlaxoSmithKline plc
980 Great West Rd., Brentford
London TW8 9GS, United Kingdom
Phone: 44-20-8047-5000   **Fax:** 44-20-8990-4321
US HQ: 1 Franklin Plaza, Philadelphia, PA 19101
US Phone: 215-751-4000   **US Fax:** 215-751-3233
Web: www.gsk.com

2009 Sales

	% of total
US pharmaceuticals	32
Europe pharmaceuticals	27
Emerging markets pharmaceuticals	11
Asia/Pacific & Japan pharmaceuticals	10
Other trading pharmaceuticals	4
Consumer health care	16
Total	**100**

PRODUCTS/OPERATIONS

2009 Sales

	% of total
Pharmaceuticals	
Respiratory	25
Antivirals	14
Vaccines	13
Cardiovascular & urogenital	8
Central nervous system	7
Antibacterials	6
Metabolic	4
Oncology & emesis	2
Other	5
Consumer health care	
OTC medicines	8
Oral care	5
Nutritional health care	3
Total	**100**

Selected Pharmaceuticals

Respiratory
  Beconase (allergies)
  Flixonase/Flonase (allergies)
  Flixotide/Flovent (asthma and chronic obstructive
    pulmonary disease)
  Seretide/Advair (asthma and chronic obstructive
    pulmonary disease)
  Serevent (asthma and chronic obstructive pulmonary
    disease)
  Veramyst (rhinitis)
Antivirals
  Agenerase (protease inhibitor for HIV/AIDS)
  Epivir/3TC (reverse transcriptase inhibitor for
    HIV/AIDS)
  Epizicom/Kivexa (combination of Epivir and Ziagen
    for HIV/AIDS)
  Lexiva/Telzir (protease inhibitor for HIV/AIDS)
  Relenza (influenza)
  Valtrex/Zelitrex (shingles and genital herpes)
  Zeffix/Septavir/Heptodin/Epivir HBV (hepatitis B)
  Ziagen (reverse transcriptase inhibitor for HIV/AIDS)
  Zovirax (herpes infections, shingles, chicken pox, and
    cold sores)
Vaccines
  Engerix-B (hepatitis B)
  Fluarix (influenza)
  FluLaval (influenza)
  Havrix (hepatitis A)
  Rotarix (rotavirus)
  Twinrix (hepatitis A and hepatitis B)

Cardiovascular and urogenital
  Arixtra (deep vein thrombosis and pulmonary
    embolism)
  Avodart (prostatic hyperplasia)
  Flolan (blood-clotting inhibitor)
  Levitra (erectile dysfunction, with Schering-Plough)
  Lovaza (coronary heart disease)
  Vesicare (overactive bladder)
Central nervous system disorders
  Imigran/Imitrex (migraines)
  Lamictal (epilepsy and bipolar disorder)
  Naramig/Amerge (migraines)
  Seroxat/Paxil (depression)
  Wellbutrin SR (depression)
  Zyban (smoking-cessation aid)
Antibacterials
  Augmentin (antibiotic)
  Bactroban (skin infections)
  Malarone (malaria)
  Zinnat (community-acquired respiratory infections)
Metabolic and gastrointestinal
  Avandamet (type 2 diabetes)
  Avandia (type 2 diabetes)
  Zantac (stomach ulcers)
Oncology and emesis
  Bexxar (non-Hodgkin's lymphoma)
  Hycamtin (ovarian, cervical, and small cell lung
    cancers)
  Promacta/Revolade (blood therapy)
  Tykerb/Tyverb (advanced and metastatic breast cancer)
  Zofran (cancer therapy-induced nausea)

COMPETITORS

Abbott Labs
Amgen
AstraZeneca
Bayer AG
Biogen Idec
Bristol-Myers Squibb
Dr. Reddy's
Elan
Eli Lilly
Forest Labs
Genzyme
Gilead Sciences
Hoffmann-La Roche
Johnson & Johnson
Merck
Mylan
Novartis
Novo Nordisk
Pfizer
Ranbaxy Laboratories
Roche Holding
Sanofi-Aventis
Takeda Pharmaceutical
Teva Pharmaceuticals
UCB

HISTORICAL FINANCIALS
Company Type: Public

Income Statement

FYE: December 31

	REVENUE ($ mil.)	NET INCOME ($ mil.)	NET PROFIT MARGIN	EMPLOYEES
12/09	45,179	8,809	19.5%	99,913
12/08	35,245	6,820	19.3%	99,003
12/07	45,223	10,380	23.0%	103,000
12/06	45,513	10,561	23.2%	102,695
12/05	37,342	8,083	21.6%	100,728
Annual Growth	**4.9%**	**2.2%**	**—**	**(0.2%)**

2009 Year-End Financials

Debt ratio: 147.8%
Return on equity: 64.3%
Cash ($ mil.): 10,424
Current ratio: 1.45
Long-term debt ($ mil.): 23,548

No. of shares (mil.): 2,595
Dividends
  Yield: 2.8%
  Payout: 55.4%
Market value ($ mil.): 174,642

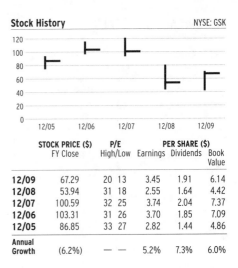

Stock History   NYSE: GSK

	STOCK PRICE ($) FY Close	P/E High/Low		PER SHARE ($) Earnings	Dividends	Book Value
12/09	67.29	20	13	3.45	1.91	6.14
12/08	53.94	31	18	2.55	1.64	4.42
12/07	100.59	32	25	3.74	2.04	7.37
12/06	103.31	31	26	3.70	1.85	7.09
12/05	86.85	33	27	2.82	1.44	4.86
Annual Growth	**(6.2%)**	**—**	**—**	**5.2%**	**7.3%**	**6.0%**

Glencore International

Glencore International trades in the stuff of which stuff is made. The company is a commodities trader (metals and minerals, agricultural products, and energy) and a diversified natural resources conglomerate with interests in companies involved in mining, smelting, and refining. In the energy sector, the company markets such products as coal, crude oil, jet fuel, and gasoline. Glencore's ownership stakes include a 35% share in Xstrata, a 44% interest in Century Aluminum, three-quarters ownership of Australian nickel miner Minara Resources, and a 32% share in French base metals refiner Recylex. Founded in 1974 and owned by its employees, Glencore has offices in more than 40 countries worldwide.

Low commodity prices amid a recessionary economy drove both revenues and profits down for Glencore in 2009. Sales dropped 30% from 2008, and net income dipped 42%. However, Glencore's profitability did show a steady quarter-to-quarter improvement in 2009, with both revenues and profits trending toward recovery in the first half of 2010 due to higher prices for raw materials, particularly in the metals sector.

The company is extremely active in the mergers and acquisitions game, though it tends to hold onto investments for the long term rather than looking for short-term gains. In 2009 it divested its majority stake in a Colombian oil refinery, selling the 51% share in Refineria de Cartagena — which sells its petroleum products throughout the Americas — to Ecopetrol for $550 million. It then spent about $235 million to buy 51% of Chemoil Energy, which supplies marine fuels worldwide, and also took a majority stake in Swiss biofuels producer Biopetrol Industries.

Also in 2009 the company sold its Prodeco coal business to Xstrata for about $2 billion. The deal acted as Glencore's participation in an Xstrata rights issue, and the company made sure to include a buy-back right. About a year after it sold Prodeco, Glencore exercised that right and bought back Prodeco for about $2.25 billion. In 2010 Glencore acquired the Italian metals warehousing business of the Pacorini Group, which it will operate as a subsidiary. It also bought the remaining 60% of shares it did not already own in Vasilkovskoje Gold for some $200 million.

EXECUTIVES

Chairman: Willy R. Strothotte, age 64
CEO: Ivan Glasenberg, age 53
CFO: Steven Kalmin
CIO, US Division: Blandine Lewine
Spokesman: Marc Ocskay
Project/CIO Office Manager: Vikki Marshall
HR, US Division: Drew Thompson
Officer; Manager, Public Relations:
  Lotti Grenacher Hagmann

LOCATIONS

HQ: Glencore International AG
  Baarermattstrasse 3
  CH-6340 Baar, Zug, Switzerland
Phone: 41-41-709-2000   **Fax:** 41-41-709-3000
Web: www.glencore.com

PRODUCTS/OPERATIONS

Selected Investments

Century Alumina (44%, US aluminum processor)
Mopani (73%, Zambian copper and cobalt miner)
Moreno Group (Argentine agricultural firm)
Sherwin Alumina (US alumina refiner)
Sinchi Wayra (Bolivian lead and zinc miner)
Recylex (32%, French lead and zinc refiner)
Rusal (10%, integrated Russian aluminum producer)
Xstrata (35%, diversified Swiss metals company)

Selected Operations

Agricultural Products
  Barley
  Corn
  Meals
  Rice
  Sugar
  Wheat
Energy Products
  Coal
  Oil
Metals and Minerals
  Copper
  Ferroalloys
  Lead
  Nickel
  Zinc

COMPETITORS

ADM
Anglo American
BHP Billiton
Noble Group Limited
Norsk Hydro ASA
Rio Tinto Limited

HISTORICAL FINANCIALS

Company Type: Private

Income Statement

FYE: December 31

	REVENUE ($ mil.)	NET INCOME ($ mil.)	NET PROFIT MARGIN	EMPLOYEES
12/09	106,400	—	—	50,000
12/08	152,200	—	—	50,000
12/07	142,300	—	—	62,000
12/06	116,500	—	—	50,000
12/05	91,000	—	—	50,000
Annual Growth	4.0%	—	—	0.0%

Revenue History

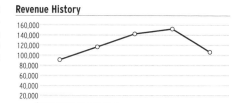

	12/05	12/06	12/07	12/08	12/09

Haci Ömer Sabanci

Haci Ömer Sabanci is one of Turkey's largest industrial and financial conglomerates, with interests in the energy, banking, retail, cement, tire and automotive, and other industries. Its primary holding is a 40% stake in Turkish banking firm Akbank, which provides commercial, retail, and private banking as well as investment and foreign trade services. Other holdings include a 50% stake in domestic energy company Enerjisa and supermarket operator Carrefoursa. Sabanci's portfolio spans some 20 countries in Europe, Africa, Asia, and the Americas. The company has several partnerships with multinationals such as Bridgestone, Mitsubishi Motor, and Philip Morris. The wealthy Sabanci family owns 60% of the company.

Sabanci has over the years increased its focus on its core businesses, including energy and retail. It has invested in Enerjisa's continued growth, buying new gas, wind, and hydroelectric plants for the unit. The group's retail venture with Carrefour has also grown, with more than 150 supermarkets serving more than 90 million customers annually. On the other hand, Sabanci sold its stake in the Toyotasa automobile distribution venture and spun off noncore units of Akbank during 2009.

HISTORY

Haci Ömer Sabanci's eponymous empire traces back to the 1930s. Sabanci left his native village Akcakaya at the age of 14 to become a laborer in a cotton plantation in the Adana region of Turkey in 1921. By 1932 he had become a shareholder in a cotton ginning plant. During the next decade he grabbed stakes in two vegetable oil plants: Türk Nebati Yaglar Fabrikasi (1943) and Marsa (1946; renamed in 1993 as Marsa KJS, a joint venture with Kraft).

Quickly broadening his portfolio, Sabanci, along with more than 80 citizens of Adana and surrounding regions, became a founding shareholder in Akbank (named for Sabanci's native village) in 1948. He further diversified with investments in Bossa, a flour and cotton ginning mill, in 1951. Sabanci's second financial holding, the Aksigorta insurance business, was formed in 1960 as a subsidiary of Akbank.

By the time Sabanci died in 1966, Akbank had opened its 100th branch office. Sabanci's five sons took the helm of their father's companies and moved the group's headquarters to the more cosmopolitan Istanbul in 1974, in accordance with Sabanci's growing stance as a global entity. Domestic operations continued to grow, however; fabric producer Yünsa was founded in 1973,

and the Çimsa unit began producing cement two years later.

The 1980s marked the Haci Ömer Sabanci group's emergence as a multinational and the beginnings of its signature business style: growth through partnerships with major players. In 1985 Akbank joined with Banque Nationale de Paris (now BNP Paribas) to create BNP-Ak Bank; leading German bank Dresdner joined the companies three years later to form BNP-Ak-Dresdner Bank. A joint venture with DuPont in 1987 created nylon yarn producer Dusa. The following year the company renamed its Lassa tire manufacturing concern Brisa, after sealing a deal with Bridgestone of Japan. By the end of the decade, the Sabanci family were billionaires.

The group continued developing powerful partnerships in the next decade. Two joint ventures with Philip Morris (1991 and 1994) involved Haci Ömer Sabanci in the manufacturing, marketing, and selling of the maker's cigarettes in Turkey. A trinational deal in 1997 with US conglomerate Koch Industries and Mexican billionaire Isaac Saba's Imasab created Sakosa, a polyester tire cord and industrial yarn manufacturer. Another joint venture with DuPont in 1999 (DuPontsa BV) linked the companies' operations to create Europe's largest polyester producer.

An attempt to break into telecommunications stalled that year when the almost $3 billion price tag in Turkey's mobile phone license auction proved too steep for the Sabanci group. However, the company was able to purchase Turk.Net, Turkey's largest ISP, for $25 million. By 2000 Haci Ömer Sabanci had ceased seeking out partnerships and ventures in disparate sectors, planning instead to narrow its focus to select industries, including energy, the Internet, and telecommunications.

In 2001 the company teamed up with DuPont to form global nylon industrial yarn and tire cord joint venture DUSA International. It also sold its stake in automotive joint venture Toyota sa to partner Toyota.

Chairman Sakip Sabanci's lifelong dream of creating a world-class museum in Turkey was realized in 2002 with the opening of the Sakip Sabanci Museum. Sabanci died two years later.

Also in 2004 Sabanci bought BNP Paribas and Dresdner Bank out of their BNP-Ak-Dresdner Bank venture.

Belgian partner Bekaert bought out Sabanci's share of their Beksa steel cord and metal fiber joint venture in 2008. Sabanci sold stakes in other holdings, including its edible oils operations, financial services companies, and another joint venture with Toyota.

The group teamed up with Austria-based Verbund to own and operate a regional electricity distributor in Turkey in 2008. The landmark $1 billion deal was part of the Turkish government's plan to privatize and transform the country's power industry.

EXECUTIVES

Chairman and Managing Director: Güler Sabanci
Vice Chairman: Erol Sabanci, age 71
CEO: Zafer Kurtul
CFO: Faruk Bilen, age 40
CIO: Ergun Hepvar
Secretary General: Nedim Bozfakioglu
Chief Legal Officer: Metin Reyna
Chief Economist: Barbaros Ineci
Chief Risk Officer: Tamer Saka

President, Tire, Tire Reinforcement Materials and
  Automotive: Mehmet N. Pekarun
President, Energy: Selahattin Hakman, age 57
President, Cement: Mehmet Gocmen
President, Food and Retailing: Haluk Dinçer, age 47
President, Financial Services: Akin Kozanoglu, age 61
President, Strategy and Business Development:
  Hakan Akbas, age 41
Director, Corporate Affairs: Kürsat Darbaz
Director, Corporate Strategy and Planning: Volkan Kara
Director, Institutional Investor Relations:
  Fikret Cömert
Director, Human Resources: A. Merve Ergün
Auditors: PricewaterhouseCoopers

LOCATIONS

HQ: Haci Ömer Sabanci Holding A.S.
  Sabanci Center 4 Levent
  34330 Istanbul, Turkey
Phone: 90-212-385-80-80   **Fax:** 90-212-385-88-88
Web: www.sabanci.com.tr/En

PRODUCTS/OPERATIONS

Selected Investments

Cement
  Akçansa (40%)
  Çimsa (58%)

Energy
  Enerjisa DisCo (50%)
  Enerjisa GenCo (50%)

Financial Services
  Akbank (41%)
  Aksigorta (62%)
  Avivasa (49.8%)

Retail
  Carrefoursa (39%)
  Diasa (40%)
  Teknosa (70%)

Tires and Automotive
  Bria (44%)
  Kordsa Global (91%)
  Temsa Global (49%)

Other
  Bimsa
  Dönkasan (50%)
  Philip Morrissa (25%)
  Philsa (25%)
  Olmuksa (44%)
  Tursa (99.5%)

COMPETITORS

Alarko
Berkshire Hathaway
Dogan Holding
Global Yatirim
Koç
Yazicilar

HISTORICAL FINANCIALS

Company Type: Public

Income Statement

FYE: December 31

	REVENUE ($ mil.)	NET INCOME ($ mil.)	NET PROFIT MARGIN	EMPLOYEES
12/09	12,457	2,021	16.2%	55,201
12/08	12,997	1,528	11.8%	51,120
12/07	16,420	823	5.0%	—
12/06	11,892	347	2.9%	—
12/05	10,600	514	4.8%	—
Annual Growth	4.1%	40.8%	—	8.0%

2009 Year-End Financials

Debt ratio: —   No. of shares (mil.): 2,040
Return on equity: 20.3%   Dividends
Cash ($ mil.): 10,795   Yield: 1.2%
Current ratio: 0.68   Payout: 11.9%
Long-term debt ($ mil.): —   Market value ($ mil.): 7,686

Stock History

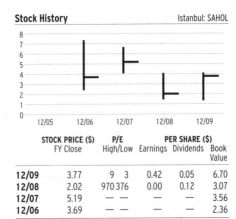

	STOCK PRICE ($) FY Close	P/E High/Low		PER SHARE ($) Earnings	Dividends	Book Value
12/09	3.77	9	3	0.42	0.05	6.70
12/08	2.02	970	376	0.00	0.12	3.07
12/07	5.19	—	—	—	—	3.56
12/06	3.69	—	—	—	—	2.36
Annual Growth	0.7%	—	—	—	(58.3%)	41.7%

Hannover Re

Who insures insurance companies over and over? Hannover! Hannover Rückversicherung (Hannover Re) is the second-largest German reinsurance company (Münchener Rückversicherungs-Gesellschaft, better known as Munich Re, is #1) and the fourth-largest such company in the world. Through a host of subsidiaries, the company provides property and casualty (Hannover Re's largest segment), financial, life, and health reinsurance products worldwide. Hannover Re is 50%-owned by German mutual insurance group Talanx AG.

The property/casualty unit of the ever-diversifying Hannover Re accounts for more than 60% of all premiums and is geared toward markets in the US, Germany, and Japan. Its life/health business is marketed through subsidiary Hannover Life Re and focuses on treaty (groups of risks) rather than facultative (individual risk) policies.

To boost its presence in the US, the company purchased a portfolio of life reinsurance from Scottish Re in 2009. The deal gave Hannover a business it attempted to buy from ING Groep in 2004, but lost out to Scottish Re.

Financial reinsurance is provided through Hannover Re Advanced Solutions, a Dublin-based consortium managed jointly with HDI Reinsurance (Ireland); both Hannover Re and HDI Reinsurance (Ireland) are subsidiaries of HDI Haftpflichtverband der Deutschen Industrie.

While Hannover Re's traditional *brot und butter* has been property and casualty reinsurance, the firm has expanded its life and health lines. Hannover Re has also adopted American accounting practices and become more transparent in order to remain a compelling stock in investors' eyes.

HISTORY

Hannover Rückversicherung (Hannover Re) was founded in 1966 as the Aktiengesellschaft für Transport und Rückversicherung (ATR) by the Feuerschadenverband Rheinisch-Westfaelischer

Zechen (FSV), a mutual insurer specializing in fire damage, in the town of Bochum. Within five years, ATR had expanded into international reinsurance markets. In 1970 FSV merged with another mutual, HDI Haftpflichtverband der Deutschen Industrie, which owned reinsurer Eisen und Stahl Rückversicherungs-AG. ATR's headquarters relocated to Hannover, and six years later it was renamed Hannover Rückversicherungs-Gesellschaft.

Jointly managed by HDI, Hannover Re and Eisen und Stahl operated separately until 1996: Hannover Re targeted international markets, while Eisen und Stahl operated mostly within Germany. Hannover Re maintained its foreign focus throughout the 1970s and 80s, expanding in Europe and South Africa, and making its first forays into the US. In 1990 the firm acquired US life insurer Reassurance Company of Hannover.

Hannover Re went public in 1994, selling 25% of its stock. Also that year the firm formed an Australian subsidiary. The next year Hannover Re acquired Eisen und Stahl (renamed E+S Ruck 1996), which then assumed total control of the company's domestic business.

In 1998 Hannover Re became the first reinsurer to securitize life insurance business (reinsurers often securitize non-life policies to protect against natural catastrophe risks) through an agreement with Interpolis, an Irish reinsurance subsidiary of the Netherlands' Rabobank. Also that year the firm expanded its financial reinsurance business, reorganizing the Irish consortium it formed with another subsidiary of HDI into Hannover Re Advanced Solutions.

As natural disasters offset earnings in Hannover Re's property & casualty division in 1998 and 1999, its life and health segment boomed. To facilitate further growth, the firm restructured these operations into a new subsidiary, Hannover Life Re. Also in 1999 the firm acquired the Clarendon Insurance Group of New York. In 2001 Hannover Re joined Inreon, an online reinsurance trading exchange set up by rivals Munich Re and Swiss Re. Also in 2001 the company established a Bermuda-based subsidiary, focused on catastrophe business. The following year Hannover Re split its stock in order to stimulate demand and become a more widely held company.

Like many other insurers, the company was hit hard by the attacks of September 11, 2001, falling stock markets, and, in 2005, damages in the Gulf of Mexico caused by hurricanes Katrina and Rita.

Late in 2006 China loosened its regulation of a number of industries, and insurance was one of them — Hannover Re was one of the first to gain permission to enter the Chinese market for life and health reinsurance.

At about the same time, the company announced plans to cut down on its noncore business operations. The first move in this direction was the sale of its US-based Praetorian Group subsidiary to QBE's US-based subsidiary for a sum in excess of $800 million. Hannover Re used the proceeds to shore up its property/casualty and life/health reinsurance businesses.

EXECUTIVES

Supervisory Chairman: Wolf-Dieter Baumgartl
Deputy Chairman, Supervisory Board: Klaus Sturany, age 63
CEO: Ulrich Wallin, age 49
CFO: Roland Vogel

Executive Board Member, Non-life, Advanced Solutions: Jürgen Gräber, age 54
Executive Board Member, Non-life: Michael Pickel, age 49
Executive Board Member, Non-life: André Arrago, age 60
Executive Board Member, Hanover Life Re, Northern and Central Europe: Klaus Miller, age 50
Senior Manager Investor Relations: Klaus Paesler
Head Corporate Communications: Karl Steinle, age 39
CEO, Hannover Life Re: Wolf Becke, age 63
EVP and CFO, Hannover Life Reassurance Company of America: David A. Wheat
Auditors: KPMG AG Wirtschaftsprüfungsgesellschaft

LOCATIONS

HQ: Hannover Rückversicherung AG
Karl-Wiechert-Allee 50
30625 Hannover, Germany
Phone: 49-511-5604-0   **Fax:** 49-511-5604-1188
US HQ: 800 N. Magnolia Ave., Ste. 1400
Orlando, FL 32803
US Phone: 407-649-8411   **US Fax:** 407-649-8322
Web: www.hannover-re.com

2009 Premiums Written

	% of total
Europe	
UK	17
Germany	13
France	5
Other countries	12
North America	
US	28
Other countries	4
Asia	8
Australia	4
Africa	3
Other regions	6
Total	**100**

COMPETITORS

Everest Re
General Re
Lloyd's
Munich Re Group
PartnerRe
Reinsurance Group of America
SCOR
Swiss Re
XL Group plc

HISTORICAL FINANCIALS

Company Type: Public

Income Statement

FYE: December 31

	ASSETS ($ mil.)	NET INCOME ($ mil.)	INCOME AS % OF ASSETS	EMPLOYEES
12/09	60,573	1,106	1.8%	1,984
12/08	53,564	(190)	—	1,790
12/07	54,561	1,251	2.3%	1,825
Annual Growth	**5.4%**	**(6.0%)**	**—**	**4.3%**

2009 Year-End Financials

Equity as % of assets: 10.1%
Return on assets: 1.9%
Return on equity: 21.9%
Long-term debt ($ mil.): —
No. of shares (mil.): 121
Dividends
Yield: 1.9%
Payout: —
Market value ($ mil.): 5,654
Sales ($ mil.): 46,800

Stock History

Pink Sheets: HVRRY

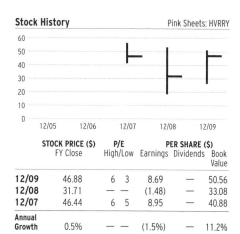

	STOCK PRICE ($) FY Close	P/E High/Low		PER SHARE ($) Earnings	Dividends	Book Value
12/09	46.88	6	3	8.69	—	50.56
12/08	31.71	—	—	(1.48)	—	33.08
12/07	46.44	6	5	8.95	—	40.88
Annual Growth	**0.5%**	**—**	**—**	**(1.5%)**	**—**	**11.2%**

Heineken N.V.

Smaller brewers are green with envy. Heineken, one of the world's brewing giants, sells its namesake beer in its signature green bottle in just about every country on the planet. The Dutch brewer operates more than 125 breweries in 70-plus countries. Its other well-known brands include Amstel and Kingfisher. In addition to its own brands, the company boasts about 170 international, regional, and specialty beers, including Murphy's Irish Red (Europe), Cordoba (Argentina), and Tiger (Asia). As part of its business, Heineken also distributes wine, soft drinks and other beverages.

To get a leg up in Latin America, Heineken acquired the Mexican brewer of Sol and Tecate beers — FEMSA Cerveza — in 2010. Heineken paid Cerveza's former parent company, Fomento Económico Mexicano, €3.8 billion (about $5.4 billion) in an all-share deal. As a result, Heineken became a stronger, more competitive player in the Latin American beer market — one of the most profitable and fastest-growing market niches in the world. The deal added Cerveza's beer brands, including Dos Equis, Sol, and Tecate, to Heineken's global brand portfolio.

The deal was on the heels of a smaller buy the previous year. In 2009 it undertook a €25 million (about $37 million) purchase of Fraser and Neave's portion of the joint venture, Asia Pacific Breweries (APB) India, that they both owned. The purchase made APB India a wholly owned subsidiary of Heineken.

As Heineken continues to invest in its core beer market, it is selling other assets. To that end, in mid-2010 it agreed to sell its UK drinks distribution unit WaverleyTBS to a private investment firm. (WaverleyTBS subsidiary United Wine Merchants, operating in Northern Ireland, is not included in the sale and will remain part of Heineken UK.) Following the sale, WaverleyTBS will retain commercial distribution agreements with Heineken.

In 2008 Heineken and Denmark's Carlsberg acquired Scottish & Newcastle (S&N), which it renamed Heineken UK, after much haggling and back and forth of unsolicited offers between the parties. Once completed, the $15.3 billion takeover resulted in Heineken owning the US,

Indian (37% of United Breweries, maker of Kingfisher beer), UK, and other European operations of the noted Irish brewer. Carlsberg took over 100% ownership of Baltic Beverage Holdings (BBH), the 50-50 joint venture it has with S&N, as well as its Chinese, French, Greek, and Vietnamese operations. Also as a result of its S&N purchase, Heineken became the world's biggest cider producer.

The founding Heineken family remains in control of the company.

HISTORY

Every Sunday morning Gerard Heineken's mother was appalled by crowds of drunken Dutchmen who had consumed too much gin the night before. Heineken, who wanted his mother's financial backing, insisted that drunkenness would decrease if people drank beer instead of gin and pointed out that there were no good beers in Holland. His strategy worked. In 1863 Heineken's mother put up the money to buy De Hooiberg (The Haystack), a 271-year-old brewery in Amsterdam.

Gerard proved his aptitude for brewing and within 10 years had established a brewery in Rotterdam. He named the business Heineken in 1873 and launched the company's lucrative foreign trade by exporting beer in 1876 to France. (By the 1950s half the beer brewed by the company was for export.) The company perfected a yeast strain (Heineken A-yeast) in 1886 that is still in use today.

In 1917 Gerard's son Dr. Henri Pierre Heineken inherited the firm and expanded operations to the US. Making a voyage to that country, Henri Pierre met Leo van Munching, a ship's bartender who displayed a remarkable knowledge of beer. Recognizing van Munching's talent, Henri Pierre hired him as Heineken's US importer. Prohibition killed the US operations, although the company entered new markets elsewhere; after repeal, Heineken was the first foreign beer to re-enter the US market.

After WWII, Henri Pierre sent his son, Alfred, to learn the business under van Munching, who had created a national distribution system in the US. Alfred succeeded his father in 1953 and stepped down in 1989.

Heineken bought the Amstel Brewery in Holland (founded 1870) in 1968. Two years later it became a producer of stout through the acquisition of James J. Murphy in Cork, Ireland. Facing a consolidation of the European market, Heineken launched a campaign in the 1980s to expand its European beer operations, purchasing breweries in France, Greece, Ireland, Italy, and Spain.

In 1991 Heineken bought a majority interest in Hungarian brewer Komaromi Sorgyar, its first Eastern European investment. Two years later Karel Vuursteen was appointed chairman.

The firm cut more than 1,300 jobs in 1993 and sold its spirits and wine operations the next year. In 1995 Heineken began a major spending spree, acquiring Interbrew Italia and 66% of Zlaty Bazant, the largest Slovakian brewery and maltworks (it acquired the rest in 1999). The company bought Birra Moretti, Italy's third-largest brewery, in 1996.

In 2002 vice president Anthony Ruys replaced Vuursteen as CEO. It also signed a deal allowing Belgium's Interbrew (now Anheuser-Busch InBev) to brew and sell Murphy's Irish Stout in Britain. Heineken also gained EU approval that year to buy a stake in German brewer Karlsberg.

Also in 2002 Heineken purchased Russian brewer Bravo International (which changed its name to Heineken Brewery in 2003). In 2003 it purchased Austrian brewer BBAG Österreich-ische Brau-Beteiligungs-AG for $1.7 billion.

Making a strong play for the growing US Hispanic market, Heineken inked a three-year deal with FEMSA Cerveza in 2004, making it the sole importer of FEMSA's Mexican beers Tecate, Sol, Dos Equis, Carta Blanca, and Bohemia. In 2004 it joined its Chinese operations with those of Asia Pacific Breweries to form Heineken Asia Pacific Breweries China (HAPBC); and that year HAPBC bought an approximate 21% stake in China's Kingway Brewery Holding.

In 2005 the company formed a partnership with Diageo to produce and distribute Guinness in Russia. In 2006 its Asian joint venture with Fraser and Neave, Asia Pacific Breweries, acquired the Fosters brewing assets in Vietnam.

Heineken was one of three Dutch brewers (along with Grolsch and Bavaria Brewery) that in 2007 were fined by the European Commission for price fixing surrounding sales to Dutch bars and restaurants in the late 1990s. Heineken's fine amounted to €219 million ($297 million).

EXECUTIVES

Chairman, Supervisory Board: Cees van Lede, age 68
Vice Chairman, Supervisory Board: Jan M. de Jong, age 65
Chairman, Executive Board and CEO: Jean-François M. L. van Boxmeer, age 49
Member, Executive Board and CFO: René Hooft Graafland, age 55
Group Legal Affairs: Steven van Maasakker
Group Business Development: Marc Koster
Group Internal Audit: Joop Brakenhoff, age 45
Group Finance: Robin H. von Konijnenburg
Director Group Human Resources: Michael O'Hare, age 43
Director Group Commerce: Alexis Nasard, age 44
Director Group Control and Accounting: Floris van Woerkom, age 47
Director Group Corporate Relations: Sean O'Neill, age 46
Group Strategy: John Hunt
Secretary: Francis Tjaarda
Business Process and Technology: Peter Brickley
Managing Director Scottish and Newcastle UK: Stefan Orlowski, age 44
President and CEO, USA: Dolf van den Brink
Head External Communications: John G. Clarke
Auditors: KPMG Accountants N.V.

LOCATIONS

HQ: Heineken N.V.
Tweede Weteringplantsoen 21
1017 ZD Amsterdam, The Netherlands
Phone: 31-20-523-9239   **Fax:** 31-20-626-3503
Web: www.heinekeninternational.com

2009 Sales

	% of total
Western Europe	55
Central & Eastern Europe	21
Africa & the Middle East	12
The Americas	10
Asia/Pacific	2
Total	**100**

PRODUCTS/OPERATIONS

Selected European Brands

France
  33 Export
  Adelscott
  Amstel
  Buckler
  Desperados
  Dorelei
  Fisher tradition
  Heineken
  Kriska
  Murphy's Irish Stout
  Pelforth
  St. Omer
Germany
  Arnegger
  Bären Pilsner
  Desperados
  Edel-Weizen
  Export
  Fürstenberg
  Goldköpfle
  Grape
  Hacker-Pschorr
  Hefe Weisbier
  Hoepfner
  Judelbier
  Karslberg
  Keller-Weisbier
  Kräusen
  Kulmbacher
  Leicht
  Maibock
  Mixery
  Mönchshof
  Paulaner
  Porter
  QOWAZ
  Radler
  Riegeter
  Sternquell
  UrPils
Italy
  Amstel
  Birra Messina
  Birra Moretti
  Budweiser
  Classica von Wunster
  Dreher
  Heineken
  Ichnusa
  McFarland
  Murphy's Irish Stout
  Prinz
  Sans Souci
The Netherlands
  Amstel
  Heineken
  Lingen's Blond
  Murphy's Irish Red
  Vos
  Wieckse
Russia
  Botchkarov
  Heineken
  Löwenbräu
  Ochota
  Okskoye
  Rusich
  Shikan
  Sobol
  Solyanaya Pristan
  Volga
UK
  Amstel
  Coors Light
  Foster's
  Heineken
  Jacques
  John Smiths
  Kronenbourg
  McEwan's
  Murphy's Irish Stout
  Newcastle
  Strongbow (apple cider)

COMPETITORS

Anheuser-Busch InBev
Asahi Breweries
Asia Pacific Breweries
Bavaria S.A.
Boston Beer
Carlsberg A/S
Cervecerías Unidas
Constellation Brands
Danone Water
Diageo
FEMSA
Grolsch
Holsten-Brauerei
Kirin Holdings Company
Lion Nathan
Mendocino Brewing
Molson Coors
Nestlé Waters
SABMiller
San Miguel Corporation
Sapporo
Taiwan Tobacco & Wine

HISTORICAL FINANCIALS

Company Type: Public

Income Statement

FYE: December 31

	REVENUE ($ mil.)	NET INCOME ($ mil.)	NET PROFIT MARGIN	EMPLOYEES
12/09	21,128	1,459	6.9%	55,301
12/08	20,183	295	1.5%	56,208
12/07	18,493	1,188	6.4%	54,004
12/06	15,606	1,598	10.2%	65,648
12/05	12,786	901	7.0%	64,305
Annual Growth	**13.4%**	**12.8%**	**—**	**(3.7%)**

2009 Year-End Financials

Debt ratio: 138.3%
Return on equity: 20.9%
Cash ($ mil.): 745
Current ratio: 0.78
Long-term debt ($ mil.): 10,607

No. of shares (mil.): 576
Dividends
Yield: 1.8%
Payout: 28.5%
Market value ($ mil.): 27,457

Stock History

Pink Sheets: HINKY

	STOCK PRICE ($) FY Close	P/E High/Low		PER SHARE ($) Earnings	Dividends	Book Value
12/09	47.67	17	9	2.98	0.85	13.31
12/08	30.87	103	45	0.61	1.04	10.94
12/07	65.09	30	22	2.43	—	13.81
12/06	47.53	15	11	3.26	—	11.47
12/05	31.72	18	16	1.84	—	8.16
Annual Growth	**10.7%**	**—**	**—**	**12.8%**	**(18.3%)**	**13.0%**

Hellenic Petroleum

It's not refined Greek thought, but refined Greek oil that makes Hellenic Petroleum the leading oil refining company in Greece and neighboring Macedonia. Greece's largest company, Hellenic Petroleum operates four refineries: at Aspropyrgos, Elefsina, and Thessaloniki in Greece, and Skopje in Macedonia. It also operates about 1,525 gas stations in Albania, Bulgaria, Cyprus, Georgia, Greece, Montenegro, and Serbia. It has 1,200 gas stations in Greece (23% of the retail market). Its other businesses include petrochemical production, oil and gas exploration, and infrastructure development. Hellenic Petroleum is owned by Paneuropean Oil and Industrial Holdings S.A. (35.89%) and the Greek government (35.5%).

Hellenic Petroleum markets gasoline under the brands EKO, ELDA, and MAMIDAKIS.

One of Greece's leading producers of petrochemicals and chemicals (including PVC, solvents, naphtha, and hexane), Hellenic Petroleum has recently completed a polypropylene plant in Thessaloniki and a propylene splitter in Aspropyrgos. It has a 25% interest in a company, Denison Mines, that has exploration rights in a 1,600-sq.-km. area in the North Aegean.

Subsidiary Asprofos, originally established to upgrade and expand the Aspropyrgos Refinery, also works on industrial projects outside the company and has emerged as one of the largest infrastructure engineering companies in southeastern Europe. Involved in pipeline construction and operation as well, Hellenic Petroleum constructed an oil pipeline from its refinery in Macedonia to the Greek port of Thessaloniki.

Hellenic Petroleum is deepening the vertical integration of its businesses while expanding its presence within Greece and the Balkans. Investing heavily in the growth market of natural gas, Hellenic Petroleum owns 35% of Greek natural gas company DEPA. Through joint ventures, Hellenic Petroleum has expanded its oil and gas exploration in the Balkans and the Middle East.

In 2008 the company acquired Opet Aygaz Bulgaria, which operates a network of 17 gas stations in Bulgaria. Building its assets at home, in 2009 Hellenic Petroleum acquired BP's network of 1,200 gas stations in Greece for about €360 million ($515 million US). Formerly called BP Hellas, the company has been rebranded Hellenic Fuels, though the service stations will retain the BP brand for at least five years.

HISTORY

Following discovery of the South Kavala gas field and Prinos oil field in the North Aegean Sea, the Greek government formed its own exploration company, Public Petroleum Corp. (DEP), in 1975. The company subsequently acquired control of the Hellenic Aspropyrgos Refinery (ELDA), a major refinery near Athens.

During the 1980s the state bought the Greek assets of Esso (now ExxonMobil), including a refinery and chemicals and marketing units. This Esso business (renamed EKO) set up two new oil-related enterprises: DEP-EKY (exploration and production) and DEPA (natural gas import and distribution). DEP retained control over crude imports, refining, and product trading. The company also set up engineering unit Asprofos, originally as a joint venture with Foster Wheeler Italiana, to upgrade and expand the

Aspropyrgos Refinery. (Foster Wheeler sold its stake in 1988.) The refinery branched into petroleum marketing with the formation of another unit, ELDA-E.

Between 1991 and 1997 EKO expanded, establishing marketing activities in Georgia and acquiring Greek liquefied petroleum gas firm Petrolina. DEP and ELDA formed a petrochemical venture, and DEP-EKY joined a consortium to explore for oil and gas in western Greece.

In 1998 the Greek government restructured the oil and gas industry. DEP became Hellenic Petroleum Company, and other oil- and gas-related enterprises were merged into it. As part of the restructuring, EKO and ELDA merged their marketing segments to form EKO-ELDA, which acquired marketing unit G.MAMIDAKIS later that year. Although 85% of the natural gas company, DEPA, was transferred back to the government, Hellenic Petroleum retained the option to buy back shares.

Hellenic Petroleum was partially privatized in 1999, and the government kept a 75% stake (later reduced to 35%). Expanding in the Balkans, the company acquired control of the oil refinery in Skopje, Macedonia, that year, and bought 75% (later boosted to 86%) of Global, a petroleum marketing company in Albania. It also upped its stake in DEPA to 35% and began construction of polypropylene and propylene units.

In 2002 Hellenic Petroleum completed a crude oil pipeline linking its Macedonian refinery to its refinery at the Greek port of Thessaloniki. In 2003 it absorbed the operations of refining rival Petrola Hellas.

EXECUTIVES

Chairman: Efthymios N. Christodoulou, age 78
CEO and Director: John Costopoulos
CFO: Andreas N. Siamsiis
Executive Member, Board: Nikolaos Lerios, age 67
Executive Member, Board: Theodoros Vardas
Director Corporate Planning and Development: George Alexopoulos
Director Accounting: Pantelis Tikkas
Director Public Relations and Corporate Affairs: Evangelos Stranis
Investor Relations Officer: George Grigoriou
Auditors: PricewaterhouseCoopers SA

LOCATIONS

HQ: Hellenic Petroleum S.A.
(Ellenika Petrelaia)
8A Chimarras St.
GR 151 25 Maroussi, Greece
Phone: 30-210-6302-000   **Fax:** 30-210-6302-510
Web: www.hellenic-petroleum.gr

PRODUCTS/OPERATIONS

2009 Sales

	% of total
Refining	96
Petrochemicals	4
Total	**100**

Selected Subsidiaries and Affiliates

ASPROFOS S.A. (infrastructure engineering company)
DEPA S.A. (35%, natural gas importation and distribution)
DIAXON A.B.E.E. (polypropylene film production)
GLOBAL PETROLEUM ALBANIA ShA. (99.9%, petroleum marketing)
OKTA CRUDE OIL REFINERY A. D. (51%, crude oil refinery, Macedonia)
VOLOS PET INDUSTRY S.A. (VPI, 35%, polyethylene terephthalate production)

COMPETITORS

Eni
Koç
LUKOIL
OMV
Royal Dutch Shell
Statoil
TOTAL

HISTORICAL FINANCIALS

Company Type: Public

Income Statement				FYE: December 31
	REVENUE ($ mil.)	NET INCOME ($ mil.)	NET PROFIT MARGIN	EMPLOYEES
12/09	8,847	233	2.6%	5,148
12/08	14,280	41	0.3%	5,184
12/07	12,567	537	4.3%	5,251
12/06	10,715	357	3.3%	5,425
12/05	7,879	404	5.1%	5,516
Annual Growth	2.9%	(12.8%)	—	(1.7%)

2009 Year-End Financials

Debt ratio: 25.7%
Return on equity: —
Cash ($ mil.): —
Current ratio: —
Long-term debt ($ mil.): 871

Net Income History

Athens: ELPE

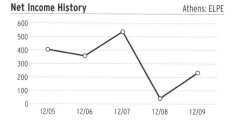

Henkel KGaA

Henkel focuses on home and hearth. The international company makes branded products for laundry and home care (Persil, Purex, Pril), cosmetics and toiletries (Schwarzkopf, Fa, Dial), and adhesives (Loctite, Ceresit, Teroson). Most of Henkel's operations are centered in Europe, although its ownership of The Dial Corporation gives it access to the US market. Henkel serves customers in more than 125 countries from offices extending nearly everywhere but Greenland and Australia. Relatives of the founding Henkel family control the company, which began in 1876. Amid an economic downturn in the US and abroad, Henkel in 2009 initiated a long-term strategy with financial targets that extend into 2012.

In recent years Henkel has made strategic acquisitions and shed noncore businesses as it focuses on its long-term plans and creates a more balanced portfolio. In 2008 the company sold its industrial water treatment unit to BK Giulini, part of Israel Chemical. Henkel considered the unit noncore in light of its plans to focus on home care, personal care, and adhesives and sealants. Later, to supplement its adhesives business, Henkel in April 2008 acquired the adhesives and electronic materials units of National Starch and Chemical Company from Akzo Nobel for about $5 billion. To help finance the National Starch purchase, Henkel divested its roughly 30% stake in Minnesota-based Ecolab. (The selloff ended a partnership that began in 1989.) Also, Henkel's India unit sold a trio of brands — soap brands Aramusk and Moloy and hair oil Mahabringol — to VVF, a maker of personal care products and oleochemicals, as well as its Tiljala plant.

Henkel boasts production in more than 55 countries. Its largest includes its plant in Dusseldorf, Germany, where it makes detergents and cleaning products, adhesives, and industrial items. Manufacturing for the company's cosmetics and toiletries unit is performed in Wassertrudingen, Germany.

HISTORY

In 1876 Fritz Henkel, a chemical plant worker, started Henkel & Cie in Aachen, Germany, to make a universal detergent. He moved the business to Düsseldorf in 1878 and launched Henkel's Bleaching Soda, one of Germany's first brand-name products. In the 1880s the company began making water glass, an ingredient of its detergent, which differs from soap in the way it emulsifies dirt. Henkel debuted Persil, a detergent that eliminated the need for rubbing or bleaching clothes, in 1907. Persil became a leading detergent in Germany.

Henkel set up an Austrian subsidiary in 1913. In response to a postwar adhesives shortage, the company started making glue for its own packaging and soon became Europe's leading glue maker. Henkel began making cleansers with newly developed phosphates in the late 1920s.

When Fritz died in 1930, Henkel stock was divided among his three children. In the 1930s the company sponsored a whaling fleet that provided fats for its products, and by 1939 the firm had 16 plants in Europe.

During WWII Henkel lost most of its foreign plants and made unbranded soap in Germany. After the war the company retooled its plants, branched out into personal care products, and competed with Colgate-Palmolive, Procter & Gamble, and Unilever for control of the German detergent market. (By 1968 Henkel dominated, with close to a 50% share.)

In 1960 Henkel bought its first US company, Standard Chemicals (renamed Henkel Corp. in 1971). Konrad Henkel, who took over in 1961, modernized the company's image by making changes in management structure and marketing techniques. Henkel patented a substitute for environmentally harmful phosphates, acquired 15% of Clorox in 1974, and bought General Mills' chemical business in 1977.

Henkel, owned at the time by 66 family members, went public with nonvoting shares in 1985. It bought US companies Nopco (specialty chemicals) and Parker Chemical (metal surface pretreatment) in 1987 and Emery, the #1 US oleochemicals maker, in 1989.

In 1991 Henkel formed a partnership with Ecolab (of which it owned 24% — later expanded to 50%). In 1994 Henkel expanded into China and bought 25% of a Brazilian detergent maker.

The company's 1995 acquisition of Hans Schwarzkopf GmbH made Henkel the #1 hair-coloring manufacturer in Germany. The next year Henkel paid $1.3 billion for US adhesive giant Loctite, its biggest purchase to date.

Henkel picked up Yamahatsu Sangyo, a Japanese maker of hair colorants, in 2000. The company sold its Substral unit (fertilizer and plant care) to Scotts Company (now Scotts Miracle-Gro). In 2001 Henkel bought TOTAL's metal-treatment

chemicals business. In addition, the company sold its Cognis specialty chemicals unit to private equity funds Schroeder Ventures and Goldman Sachs Capital Partners for about $2.2 billion. Also in 2001 Henkel said it would cut 2,500-3,000 jobs (about 5% of its workforce) over the next two years. That year the company also sold its stake in joint venture Henkel-Ecolab to Ecolab for about $430 million.

In 2004 Henkel and US bleach giant Clorox agreed to a deal (in the form of an asset swap) that dissolved Henkel's nearly 30% stake in Clorox. The $2.8 billion transaction involved Henkel's purchase of Clorox's 20% stake in Henkel Iberica, a joint venture between the two in Portugal and Spain. Henkel also bought Clorox's stake in a pesticide company as part of the transaction and added Combat insecticides and Soft Scrub bathroom cleaner to its brand portfolio.

Henkel bought 70% of Coventry's Chemtek, an independent firm that specializes in formulating and manufacturing liquid cleaners, in 2004. The balance of the share is owned by Charteredbrands of Edinburgh.

To strengthen its foothold in the electronics market in China, Henkel in 2005 bought a majority stake in Huawei Electronics Co., a maker of epoxy molding compounds for semiconductors.

In 2006 the company sold its rubber-to-substrate bonding and rubber coating business to North Carolina-based LORD Corporation. Also that year Dial added the Right Guard, Soft & Dri, and Dry Idea brands previously owned by Procter & Gamble and Gillette for about $420 million. Henkel sold Dial's Armour-branded products (Treet, Vienna sausages), corn starch, and boxed pizza to Pinnacle Foods Group for $183 million.

Henkel in 2008 sold its 30% stake in Ecolab through a public offering. Ecolab itself paid Henkel $300 million for a portion of the shares.

EXECUTIVES

Chairwoman, Supervisory Board: Simone Bagel-Trah
Vice Chairman, Supervisory Board: Winfried Zander, age 55
Chairman and CEO, Management Board: Kasper B. Rorsted, age 48
EVP Purchasing, Information Technology, Legal and CFO: Lothar Steinebach, age 62
EVP Laundry & Home Care: Friedrich Stara, age 61
EVP Adhesive Technologies: Thomas Geitner, age 55
EVP, Cosmetics and Toiletries: Hans Van Bylen, age 49
SVP and Chief Compliance Officer: Dirk-Stephan Koedijk
SVP Adhesive Technologies and Financial Director: Matthias Schmidt
SVP Human Resources: Juliane Wiemerslage
SVP Global Purchasing: Bertrand Conquéret
SVP Adhesive Technologies, Supply Chain & Operations: Libor Kotlik
SVP Information Technology: Peter Wroblowski
SVP Finance and Controlling: Wolfgang Beynio
SVP; President, Dial Corporation North America and Henkel Consumer Goods, Inc.: Bradley A. (Brad) Casper, age 49
SVP Adhesive Technologies Research: Ramón Bacardit
SVP Cosmetics, Toiletries, Financial Director and Corporate Controlling: Carsten Knobel
SVP Law: Thomas Gerd Kühn
SVP Financial Operations: Joachim Jäckle
VP Corporate Communications, North America: Cindy Demers
Chief Communications Officer: Carsten Tilger, age 42
Chief Strategy Officer: Marcus Kuhnert
President, CFO, and Director, Henkel Corporation; President and Director, Henkel of America: John E. Knudson
Auditors: KPMG Deutsche Treuhand-Gesellschaft AG

LOCATIONS

HQ: Henkel KGaA
Henkelstrasse 67
40589 Düsseldorf, Germany
Phone: 49-211-797-0   **Fax:** 49-211-798-0
US HQ: 2200 Renaissance Blvd., Ste. 200
Gulph Mills, PA 19406
US Phone: 610-270-8100   **US Fax:** 610-270-8103
Web: www.henkel.com

2009 Sales

	% of total
Western Europe	39
Growth Regions (Eastern Europe, Africa/Middle East, Latin America, Asia excluding Japan)	38
North America	19
Japan/Australia/New Zealand	2
Corporate	2
Total	**100**

PRODUCTS/OPERATIONS

2009 Sales

	% of total
Adhesive Technologies	46
Laundry & Home Care	30
Cosmetics/Toiletries	22
Corporate	2
Total	**100**

Selected Products

Adhesives
  Consumer and craftsmen adhesives
  Engineering adhesives
  Industrial and packaging adhesives
Cosmetics and toiletries
  Bath and shower products
  Dental care and oral hygiene products
  Deodorants
  Hair colorants
  Hair salon products
  Hairstyling and permanent-wave products
  Perfumes and fragrances
  Shampoos and conditioners
  Skin care products
  Skin creams
Detergents and household cleansers
  Bath and toilet cleansers
  Dishwashing products
  Fabric softeners
  Floor and carpet care products
  Furniture and kitchen care products
  Glass cleaners
  Heavy-duty detergents
  Household cleansers
  Plant care products
  Specialty detergents
Industrial and institutional hygiene and surface technologies

COMPETITORS

3M	Estée Lauder
Alticor	H.B. Fuller
Avon	Johnson & Johnson
BASF SE	Kimberly-Clark
Bayer AG	L'Oréal
Beiersdorf	Procter & Gamble
Church & Dwight	Reckitt Benckiser
Clorox	Sara Lee
Colgate-Palmolive	S.C. Johnson
Dow Chemical	Shiseido
DuPont	Unilever

HISTORICAL FINANCIALS

Company Type: Public

Income Statement

FYE: December 31

	REVENUE ($ mil.)	NET INCOME ($ mil.)	NET PROFIT MARGIN	EMPLOYEES
12/09	19,453	900	4.6%	51,361
12/08	19,918	1,738	8.7%	55,513
12/07	19,244	1,356	7.0%	52,303
12/06	16,808	1,128	6.7%	51,716
12/05	14,181	897	6.3%	52,565
Annual Growth	8.2%	0.1%	—	(0.6%)

2009 Year-End Financials

Debt ratio: —
Return on equity: 9.7%
Cash ($ mil.): 1,591
Current ratio: 1.13
Long-term debt ($ mil.): —
No. of shares (mil.): 260
Dividends
  Yield: 1.6%
  Payout: 36.9%
Market value ($ mil.): 11,598

Stock History

German: HEN

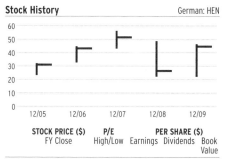

	STOCK PRICE ($) FY Close	P/E High/Low		PER SHARE ($) Earnings	Dividends	Book Value
12/09	44.64	23	12	1.98	0.73	36.10
12/08	26.43	12	6	3.93	0.72	35.18
12/07	51.44	—	—	—	—	31.97
12/06	43.19	—	—	—	—	27.86
12/05	31.00	—	—	—	—	24.48
Annual Growth	9.5%	—	—	(49.6%)	1.4%	10.2%

Hitachi, Ltd.

Hitachi, which means "risen sun," is looking for a new dawn of profits from its galaxy of businesses. The company's power and industrial systems (power plant equipment) brings in the most revenue; it is also a world-leading maker of corporate transaction-oriented mainframes, as well as semiconductors, servers, and other information system and telecommunications equipment. Hitachi also makes elevators and escalators, industrial robots and control systems, and computer mother boards. Other products include metals, wire, and cable. Hitachi's consumer goods range from TVs to refrigerators and washing machines; the company also has operations in financial services, property management, and logistics.

The economic downturn and slow recovery continues to force change across Hitachi's businesses. In a move aimed at improving its ability to compete in an increasingly global marketplace, in mid-2010 Hitachi announced an alliance with Mitsubishi Heavy Industries (MHI) and Mitsubishi Electric Corp. The three companies plan to spin off and integrate their hydroelectric power businesses into a joint venture that will be created in 2011. The joint venture is

seen as a way for Hitachi and its partners to better compete for international projects against market leaders such as Toshiba and Voith Hydro (a joint venture between Voith and Siemens). The domestic market for hydroelectric power systems in Japan has stopped growing, which has forced companies there to rely on maintenance services to stay afloat.

Through Hitachi Plant Technologies, the company announced plans in January 2010 to purchase a 20% stake in Malé Water and Sewerage, which is owned by the Maldives government and services approximately 40% of the island nation. The acquisition gives Hitachi Plant a chance to cut its teeth in the overseas water business, garnering experience and expertise, so that it might better compete against larger water businesses.

Hitachi, NEC Corp., and CASIO COMPUTER created a joint venture in hopes of trimming costs, shoring up eroding cell phone demand, and minimizing the damage of the loss-making business on the bottom line. Operated by Hitachi and Casio, the new company has been dubbed NEC Casio Mobile Communications. It merges the mobile phone divisions of the three partners, with Hitachi holding a 9% stake, Casio 20%, and NEC owning 71%. Plans are for NEC Casio Mobile Communications to compete with Sharp for top spot in the handset market, aiming to sell about 5 million smart phones in North America, Mexico, and Australia by 2012.

Takashi Kawamura became chairman, president, and CEO of Hitachi in 2009, succeeding Kazuo Furukawa. Kawamura, a Hitachi employee since 1962, previously served as chairman of Hitachi Maxell and Hitachi Plant Technologies.

HISTORY

Namihei Odaira, an employee of Kuhara Mining in the Japanese coastal city of Hitachi, wanted to prove that Japan did not have to depend on foreigners for technology. In 1910 he began building electric motors in Kuhara's engineering and repair shop. Japanese power companies were forced to buy Odaira's generators when WWI made imports scarce. Impressed, they reordered, and in 1920 Hitachi (meaning "risen sun") became an independent company.

During the 1920s acquisitions and growth turned Hitachi into a major manufacturer of electrical equipment and machinery. In the 1930s and 1940s, Hitachi developed vacuum tubes and light bulbs and produced radar and sonar for the Japanese war effort. Postwar occupation forces removed Odaira and closed 19 Hitachi plants. Reeling from the plant closures, war damage, and labor strife, Hitachi was saved from bankruptcy by US military contracts during the Korean War.

In the 1950s Hitachi became a supplier to Nippon Telegraph and Telephone (NTT), the state-owned telecommunications monopoly. Japan's economic recovery led to strong demand for the company's communications and electrical equipment. Hitachi began mass-producing home appliances, radios, TVs, and transistors. The group spun off Hitachi Metals and Hitachi Cable in 1956 and Hitachi Chemical in 1963.

With the help of NTT, the Ministry of International Trade and Industry, and technology licensed from RCA (bought by General Electric in 1986), Hitachi produced its first computer in 1965. Hitachi built factories in Southeast Asia and started manufacturing integrated circuits.

Hitachi launched an IBM-compatible computer in 1974. The company sold its computers

in the US through Itel until 1979, when Itel was bought by National Semiconductor, and afterward through National Semi's National Advanced Systems (NAS) unit. In 1982 FBI agents caught Hitachi staff buying documents allegedly containing IBM software secrets. Settlement of a civil lawsuit required Hitachi to make payments to IBM for eight years as compensation for the use of IBM's software.

When the rising Japanese yen hurt exports in the late 1980s, Hitachi focused on its domestic market and invested heavily in factory automation. But a recession at home caused earnings to fall. In 1988 the company and Texas Instruments joined in the costly development and production of 16-megabyte DRAMs. In 1989 Hitachi bought 80% of NAS, giving it direct control of its US distribution. Despite its rivalry with IBM, in 1991 Hitachi began to resell IBM notebook PCs under its own name in Japan.

Tokyo police in 1997 began investigating Hitachi, charging that the company and others had paid off a corporate racketeer. Etsuhiko Shoyama became president in 1999, replacing Tsutomu Kanai, who became chairman. Hitachi posted its then-worst loss in history in 1999; the firm combined some subsidiaries and announced layoffs.

Hitachi teamed with Sun Microsystems in 2002 in a multibillion-dollar storage software distribution and cross-licensing agreement. The company also formed a joint venture with IBM for Hitachi to acquire IBM's disk drive operations, which was launched the following year as Hitachi Global Storage Technologies.

Hitachi announced plans for an LCD television joint venture with Toshiba and Matsushita Electric in 2004, and a plasma television joint venture with Matsushita Electric in 2005.

Etsuhiko Shoyama, president and CEO of Hitachi since mid-2003, became chairman and CEO of the company in 2006.

Hitachi decided to exit the consumer PC market in late 2007. The company scaled back production of PCs at its factory in Toyokawa, Japan, to focus on manufacturing computer servers for business applications.

EXECUTIVES

Chairman, CEO, and Representative Executive Officer: Takashi Kawamura, age 70

President, Representative Executive Officer, and Director: Hiroaki Nakanishi, age 64

Representative Executive Officer; SVP and Executive Officer, Finance and Corporate Pension System: Toyoaki Nakamura, age 58

Representative Executive Officer; EVP and Executive Officer, Corporate Planning, High Functional Materials and Components and Production Engineering; General Manager, Corporate Quality Assurance Division and Supervisory Office, MONOZUKURI; Chairman, Hitachi Metals: Nubuo Mochida, age 63

Representative Executive Officer; EVP and Executive Officer, Urban Planning and Development Systems Business; Defense Systems Business; Corporate Planning; Environmental Strategies; Human Capital; Legal and Corporate Communications; Corporate Brand and Corporate Auditing: Takashi Hatchoji, age 61

Representative Executive Officer; EVP and Executive Officer, Information and Telecommunication Business; Information and Control Systems Business; Research and Development and Information Technology; Hitachi Group CTO, Chief Innovation Officer, and Chief Information Security Officer: Naoya Takahashi, age 60

Representative Executive Officer; EVP and Executive Officer, Automotive Systems Business, Motor Power Systems, Battery Systems Business, Sales Operations, Hitachi Group Global Business, Procurement, Medical Systems Business and Business Incubation; General Manager, Supervisory Office for Sales: Kazuhiro Mori, age 62

Representative Executive Officer; EVP and Executive Officer, Management Reform, Finance, Corporate Pension System Business Development and Consumer Business; Deputy General Manager, Supervisory Office for Management Reforms and Chief Hitachi Group Headquarters: Takashi Miyoshi, age 63

Chief Marketing Officer, Sales and Marketing Division, Industrial and Social Infrastructure Systems: Kiyoshi Kinugawa

President and CEO, Hitachi America: Chiaki Fujiwara

Auditors: Ernst & Young ShinNihon

LOCATIONS

HQ: Hitachi, Ltd.
(Hitachi Seisakusho Kabushiki Kaisha)
6-6, Marunouchi 1-chome, Chiyoda-ku
Tokyo 100-8280, Japan
Phone: 81-3-3258-1111   Fax: 81-3-4564-2148
US HQ: 50 Prospect Ave., Tarrytown, NY 10591
US Phone: 914-332-5800   US Fax: 914-332-5555
Web: www.hitachi.com

2010 Sales

	% of total
Asia/Pacific	
Japan	66
Other countries	18
Europe	7
North America	7
Other regions	2
Total	**100**

PRODUCTS/OPERATIONS

2010 Sales

	% of total
Information & telecom systems	17
Infrastructure & industrial systems	12
High-functional materials & components	12
Electronic systems & equipment	10
Digital media & consumer products	9
Power systems	6
Other	34
Total	**100**

Selected Products and Services

Power and industrial systems
Air-conditioning equipment
Automotive equipment
Construction machinery
Elevators
Environmental control systems
Escalators
Hydroelectric power plants
Industrial machinery and plant construction
Nuclear power plants
Rolling stock
Thermal power plants

Information and telecommunication systems
Computer peripherals
Fiber-optic components
Mainframes
RAID storage systems
Servers
Software
Switches

High-functional materials and components
Cables
Carbon products
Chemical products
Copper products
Electrical insulating materials
Fine ceramics
Magnetic materials
Malleable cast-iron products
Printed circuit boards
Specialty steels
Synthetic resins

Digital media and consumer products
Batteries
Fluorescent lamps
Information storage media
Kitchen appliances
LCD projectors
Mobile phones
Optical storage drives
Refrigerators
Room air conditioners
TVs
VCRs
Videotapes
Washing machines

Electronic devices
LCDs
Medical electronics equipment
Multipurpose semiconductors
Semiconductor manufacturing equipment
System LSIs
Testing and measurement equipment

COMPETITORS

Alcatel-Lucent	Motorola
ALSTOM	NEC
Applied Materials	Nippon Steel
AREVA	Nokia
Babcock & Wilcox	Nortel Networks
Canon	Oki Electric
Dell	Panasonic Corp
Ericsson	Philips Electronics
Fluor	Samsung Group
Fujitsu	SANYO
GE	Sharp Corp.
Hewlett-Packard	Siemens AG
IBM	Sony
Intel	TDK
Johnson Controls	Texas Instruments
Kyocera	Toshiba
LG Group	Truly International
McDermott	Unisys
Micron Technology	United Technologies
Mitsubishi Electric	Whirlpool
Mitsubishi Heavy	
Industries	

HISTORICAL FINANCIALS

Company Type: Public

Income Statement

FYE: March 31

	REVENUE ($ mil.)	NET INCOME ($ mil.)	NET PROFIT MARGIN	EMPLOYEES
3/10	96,753	(1,154)	—	359,746
3/09	102,794	(8,093)	—	361,796
3/08	112,538	(582)	—	347,810
3/07	87,136	(279)	—	384,444
3/06	80,694	318	0.4%	355,879
Annual Growth	**4.6%**	**—**		**0.3%**

2010 Year-End Financials

Debt ratio: 125.5%   No. of shares (mil.): 452
Return on equity: —   Dividends
Cash ($ mil.): 6,231   Yield: 0.0%
Current ratio: 1.21   Payout: —
Long-term debt ($ mil.): 17,390   Market value ($ mil.): 181

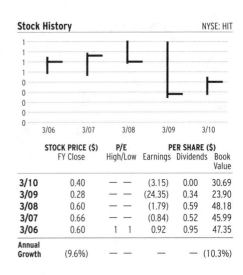

Stock History

NYSE: HIT

	STOCK PRICE ($) FY Close	P/E High/Low		PER SHARE ($) Earnings	Dividends	Book Value
3/10	0.40	—	—	(3.15)	0.00	30.69
3/09	0.28	—	—	(24.35)	0.34	23.90
3/08	0.60	—	—	(1.79)	0.59	48.18
3/07	0.66	—	—	(0.84)	0.52	45.99
3/06	0.60	1	1	0.92	0.95	47.35
Annual Growth	**(9.6%)**	**—**	**—**	**—**	**—**	**(10.3%)**

HOCHTIEF AG

HOCHTIEF is a giant in Germany and beyond. In addition to doing business throughout Europe, the construction-related services provider operates in the Americas and the Asia/Pacific region and is among the world's largest general builders. US subsidiaries Turner and Flatiron provide building and infrastructure construction. Leighton Holdings, based in Australia, provides engineering and construction services for the infrastructure and mining industries.

HOCHTIEF aims to provide services that span the lifecycle of a construction project. The company is known for building private projects such as warehouses and retail complexes. But its growing concessions and public-private partnership (PPP) division works on major federal, state, and municipal projects such as power plants, toll roads, tunnels, and water treatment facilities. HOCHTIEF is continually growing and has its sights set on areas of growth, especially in places where the PPP market is expanding, as it is in North America.

Through its concessions division the group also is active in airport projects and it runs public buildings such as schools, hospitals, and prisons in the UK. HOCHTIEF AirPort has grown to become one of the world's largest independent airport managers. The division also takes ownership stakes in projects; its portfolio encompasses principal airports in Athens; Budapest, Hungary; Düsseldorf and Hamburg, Germany; Sydney; and Tirana, Albania. HOCHTIEF is considering an initial public offering for its profitable concessions division.

The company also is involved in real estate development and management. HOCHTIEF Projektenwicklung plans, develops, and markets large properties such as hotels, office buildings, and retail and residential projects in Europe. HOCHTIEF Property Management is a leading management company in Germany.

In addition to building and developing properties HOHTIEF also makes sure those properties stay running. Its services division includes facility management and energy management providers. The division specializes in servicing the automotive industry, chemical and pharmaceutical plants, financial services facilities, airports, and health care and event facilities.

Spanish construction group Actividades de Construcciones y Servicios (ACS) is HOCHTIEF's largest shareholder, with an approximately 30% stake. In 2010 ACS placed a bid to increase its stake to more than half, and it eventually plans to acquire the firm outright.

HISTORY

Brothers Philipp and Balthasar Helfmann, mill and farm workers from Kelsterbach, Germany, started construction company Fa. Gebr. Helfmann, Bauunternehmer in Frankfurt am Main in 1875. The firm primarily built houses until 1878, when it was contracted to build the university at Giessen.

In 1884 the company was made a general partnership. Projects of this era included Frankfurt's Hotel Continental and Wiesbaden's Hotel Kaiserhof. When Balthasar died in 1896 Philipp converted the business to a joint stock company and renamed it Actien-Gesellschaft für Hoch- und Tiefbauten. Three years later, with new capital for expansion, the company won its first contract abroad — construction of a pneumatic conveyer-equipped granary in the harbor at Genoa (its first reinforced-concrete project).

Philipp Helfmann died in 1899, but the company continued operating. The battlefields of WWI took away most of the workforce, and construction slowed to a near halt. But in the years following the war the company grew. In 1921 German industrialist Hugo Stinnes began buying stakes in the company and was its major shareholder by 1923. The company decided in 1922 to relocate to Essen, closer to the Stinnes Group's operations, and in 1923 it was renamed HOCHTIEF Aktiengesellschaft für Hoch- und Tiefbauten vorm. Gebr. Helfmann.

Stinnes died in 1924, and two years later his empire collapsed. But German banks helped keep HOCHTIEF alive and operating as an independent company. That year Rheinisch-Westfälische-Elektrizitätswerke AG (RWE), the electric utility that Stinnes helped create, became the main shareholder in HOCHTIEF, with a 31% stake.

Many of RWE's facilities were damaged during WWII, including its Essen headquarters, and the RWE staff used the HOCHTIEF building until 1961. Post-war reconstruction kept the company active, including Germany's first nuclear reactor built by HOCHTIEF and commissioned in 1966. After the war RWE began increasing its stake in HOCHTIEF until it became the majority shareholder (56%) in 1989.

As a division of the RWE Group, HOCHTIEF began acquiring former state-owned companies throughout Germany. By 1996 it had added financing and operation of major projects to its services. That year it led a consortium to build and operate an international airport in Athens. In 1997 it teamed with Ireland's Aer Rianta to build new terminals and manage the airport in Düsseldorf, Germany. The next year HOCHTIEF won a bid to build and operate Berlin's new airport, but a rival's allegations of bidding irregularities led to a raid by prosecutors on HOCHTIEF's headquarters. Charges were dismissed, but the company was disqualified from the project.

HOCHTIEF, like many of its competitors, expanded abroad in 1999 by helping engineer Canadian firm Armbro's takeover of rival BFC (and then grabbing a 49% share in the merged firm, now Aecon Group) and by acquiring US construction giant Turner.

It secured a contract to build a rail tunnel under the River Thames in London in 2001. Also that year it merged its building and civil units into HOCHTIEF Construction and made plans to join former rival IVG Immobilien to bid on building Berlin's new airport, Berlin-Brandenburg.

In 2004 longtime shareholder and German energy giant RWE sold its 56% stake in HOCHTIEF to European and US institutional investors. It was the largest such transaction involving a German stock.

HOCHTIEF subsidiary Leighton and joint venture partner Downer EDI won a contract to build a four-lane highway in New Zealand in 2006.

In 2007 the company acquired the energy contracting business of Vattenfall Europe, adding to its existing service portfolio of energy contracting and management operations. Also that year, HOCHTIEF acquired Flatiron Construction from Royal BAM Group. That deal provided the group with entry into infrastructure PPP markets in the US and Canada.

EXECUTIVES

Chairman, Supervisory Board: Martin Kohlhaussen
Deputy Chairman, Supervisory Board: Gerhard Peters
Chairman, Executive Board: Herbert Lütkestratkötter, age 59
CFO and Member, Executive Board: Burkhard Lohr, age 47
Member, Executive Board; Head, Real Estate and Services Divisions: Martin Rohr, age 55
Member, Executive Board; Head, HOCHTIEF Europe, Global Procurement, and Insurance: Frank Stieler, age 52
Member, Executive Board; Chairman, HOCHTIEF Concessions and HOCHTIEF Asia Pacific Divisions: Peter Noé, age 52
CEO, HOCHTIEF AirPort: Reinhard Kalenda
CEO, Flatiron Construction: Tom Rademacher
CEO and Director, Leighton Holdings: Wal M. King, age 65
President and CEO, Turner Construction: Peter J. Davoren
Chairman and CEO, Aecon Group: John M. Beck, age 69
Managing Director, Leighton Contractors: Peter McMorrow
Head, Corporate Communications and Group Spokeswoman: Jutta Hobbiebrunken
Head, Investor Relations: Lars Petzold
Auditors: Deloitte & Touche GmbH

LOCATIONS

HQ: HOCHTIEF AG
Opernplatz 2
45128 Essen, Germany
Phone: 49-201-824-0   **Fax:** 49-201-824-2777
Web: www.hochtief.de

2009 Sales by Region

	% of total
Americas	37
Australia	35
Europe	
Germany	12
Other countries	6
Asia	10
Total	**100**

PRODUCTS/OPERATIONS

2009 Sales

	% of total
Construction services	
Asia/Pacific	47
Americas	33
Europe	13
Real estate	3
Services	3
Concessions	1
Total	**100**

Selected Subsidiaries and Associates

Airport
HOCHTIEF AirPort Capital Verwaltungs GmbH & Co. KG
HOCHTIEF AirPort GmbH

Construction Services Americas
Flatiron Construction Corp. (US)
HOCHTIEF Americas GmbH
HOCHTIEF do Brasil S.A. (92%)
The Turner Corporation (US)

Construction Services Asia Pacific
HOCHTIEF Asia Pacific GmbH
Leighton Holdings Limited (Australia, 55%)

Construction Services Europe
DURST-BAU GmbH (Austria)
HOCHTIEF Construction AG

Development
Deutsche Bau- und Siedlungs-Gesellschaft mbH
HOCHTIEF Aurestis Beteiligungsgesellschaft mbH
HOTCHTIEF Projektentwicklung GmbH

COMPETITORS

Acciona
Avionic Services International
BAA
BE&K
Bechtel
Bilfinger Berger
Bouygues
Cheung Kong Infrastructure
Dragados
Fluor
Parsons Corporation
PCL Employees Holdings
Peter Kiewit Sons'
Skanska
STRABAG SE
Tutor Perini
VINCI

HISTORICAL FINANCIALS

Company Type: Public

Income Statement

	REVENUE ($ mil.)	NET INCOME ($ mil.)	NET PROFIT MARGIN	EMPLOYEES
12/09	26,036	585	2.2%	66,178
12/08	26,926	482	1.8%	64,527
12/07	24,215	207	0.9%	52,449
12/06	20,404	118	0.6%	46,847
12/05	16,170	80	0.5%	41,469
Annual Growth	**12.6%**	**64.4%**	**—**	**12.4%**

FYE: December 31

2009 Year-End Financials

Debt ratio: —
Return on equity: 15.6%
Cash ($ mil.): 2,536
Current ratio: 1.14
Long-term debt ($ mil.): —
No. of shares (mil.): 70
Dividends
    Yield: 2.6%
    Payout: 47.9%
Market value ($ mil.): 5,372

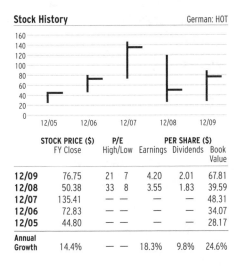
	STOCK PRICE ($)	P/E		PER SHARE ($)		
	FY Close	High/Low		Earnings	Dividends	Book Value
12/09	76.75	21	7	4.20	2.01	67.81
12/08	50.38	33	8	3.55	1.83	39.59
12/07	135.41	—	—	—	—	48.31
12/06	72.83	—	—	—	—	34.07
12/05	44.80	—	—	—	—	28.17
Annual Growth	14.4%	—	—	18.3%	9.8%	24.6%

Honda Motor Co.

*Accord*ing to Honda, you might be in your *Element* if you buy a *Ridgeline*. Honda Motor is Japan's #2 automaker (after Toyota) and the world's largest motorcycle producer. The company's car models include the Accord, CR-V, Civic, Element, and Ridgeline, as well as gasoline-electric hybrid versions of the Civic and Accord. Honda's line of motorcycles includes everything from scooters to superbikes. The company also makes a line of ATVs and personal watercraft. Honda's power products division makes commercial and residential machinery (lawn mowers, snow blowers, and tillers); portable generators; and outboard motors. About 80% of Honda Motor sales are from outside Japan.

Like its rival Toyota, Honda is facing questions about the quality of its cars. The company has recalled more than 1.2 million vehicles in the US since January 2010. Problems range from air bags that may not deploy and soft brake pedals to electric switches that can catch fire when wet and a power-steering hose that could deteriorate prematurely when exposed to high temperatures and lead to a fire. The recalls, many related to its Acura models, have not received as much media attention as the Toyota recalls.

In 2009 Honda increased its commitment to hybrid vehicles by signing a joint venture contract with GS Yuasa to establish a new company, Blue Energy. GS Yuasa Power Supply, a wholly owned subsidiary of GS Yuasa, owns a 51% stake and Honda Motor owns a 49% stake. The two companies decided that Blue Energy will manufacture lithium-ion batteries, and drive sales and R&D. Lithium-ion batteries are lighter and hold almost double the energy of a standard battery, which may optimize the performance of next-generation hybrid vehicles.

In its home region of Asia, Honda's automotive focus is the same as everyone else's — China and India. To meet the increasing demand, Honda added capacity to one of its Chinese factories and opened new facilities in both India and Thailand. Its Dongfeng Honda Automobile unit, a 50/50 joint venture with Dongfeng Motor, has announced it will build a second factory in China in order to keep up with surging demand in the region.

Honda began marketing its FCX Clarity, a zero-emissions hydrogen fuel cell sedan, in 2008. It also introduced the Insight Hybrid at the Paris Motor Show that year. The Insight is Honda's answer to Toyota's popular Prius. Honda executives are acting on their belief that dedicated hybrid vehicles like the Insight will perform better than hybridized current models. The company began selling the Insight in Europe, Japan, and the US in 2009.

Honda is enjoying brisk motorcycle sales, particularly in Asia where motorcycles are a popular mode of transportation. It is beefing up production capacity in India to keep up with demand. Honda is adding on to its two existing Indian factories and is building a third one.

In mid-2009 Takeo Fukui stepped down as Honda Motor's president and CEO and was succeeded in those posts by senior managing director Takanobu Ito. Fukui remained on the company's board and assumed the traditional ex-CEO's role of company advisor. Ito joined Honda in 1978.

HISTORY

Soichiro Honda spent six years as an apprentice at Tokyo service station Art Shokai before opening his own branch of the repair shop in Hamamatsu in 1928. He also raced cars and in 1931 received a patent for metal spokes that replaced wood in wheels.

Honda started a piston ring company in 1937. During WWII the company produced metal propellers for Japanese bombers. When bombs and an earthquake destroyed most of his factory, Honda sold it to Toyota in 1945.

In 1946 Honda began motorizing bicycles with war-surplus engines. When this proved popular, Honda began making engines. The company was renamed Honda Motor Co. in 1948 and began producing motorcycles. Soichiro Honda hired Takeo Fujisawa in 1949 to manage the company so Honda could focus on engineering. Honda's innovative overhead valve design made its early 1950s Dream model a runaway success. In 1952 the smaller Cub, sold through bicycle dealers, accounted for 70% of Japan's motorcycle production.

Funded by a 1954 public offering and Mitsubishi Bank, Honda expanded capacity and began exporting. American Honda Motor Company was formed in Los Angeles in 1959, accompanied by the slogan "You meet the nicest people on a Honda" in a campaign crafted to counter the stereotypical biker image. Honda added overseas factories in the 1960s and began producing lightweight trucks, sports cars, and minicars.

The company began selling its tiny 600 model in the US in 1970, but it was the Civic, introduced in 1973, that first scored with the US car market. Three years later Honda introduced the Accord, which featured an innovative frame adaptable for many models. In 1982 Accord production started at the company's Ohio plant.

Ex-Honda engineer Nobuhiko Kawamoto was named president in 1990, a year before Soichiro Honda died. Kawamoto cut costs and continued to expand the company internationally. That year the Big Three US automakers (General Motors, Ford, and Chrysler), clamoring for trade sanctions against Japanese carmakers, threw Honda out of the US carmakers' trade association.

In 1997 Honda bought Peugeot's plant in Guangzhou, China, and boosted its US vehicle production by opening an all-terrain vehicle (ATV) plant in South Carolina in 1998. American Honda agreed in 1998 to pay $330 million to settle a class-action lawsuit filed by 1,800 dealers who accused Honda of delivering popular models only to dealers who paid bribes (18 executives from American Honda were convicted). That year Hiroyuki Yoshino, an engineer with US management experience, succeeded Kawamoto as CEO.

In 2000 Honda announced that its super-low-emission engine (as called for by US regulators) would make its mass-market debut in 2001, well ahead of competitor versions. Also, Honda recalled 500,000 cars in Japan due to problems with audio systems and engine oil seals.

Honda announced in 2001 that it would introduce diesel-powered vehicles in Europe by 2003. Later that year Honda's R&D unit set up a solar-powered hydrogen production station in California as part of its efforts to develop renewable-energy fuel-cell vehicles.

In 2006 Honda announced it would enter the aviation market with the introduction of what Honda CEO Takeo Fukui called the "Honda Civic of the sky."

As vehicle sales slowed in 2008 Honda cut production by 12% in Japan and North America.

EXECUTIVES

President and Board Member, Honda Motor and Honda R&D: Takanobu Ito, age 57
Managing Officer; President and Director, Honda America Mfg.: Hidenobu Iwata
Operating Officer; EVP and Director, American Honda Motor: Takashi Sekiguchi
Senior Managing Director and Board Member; President and Director, Honda North America; COO, Regional Operations, North America: Tetsuo Iwamura, age 59
Senior Managing Director and Board Member; COO, Motorcycle Operations; Chief Officer of Driving Safety Promotion Center: Tatsuhiro Oyama, age 60
Senior Managing Director, COO Production Operations, Risk Management Officer, General Supervisor Information Systems, and Board Member: Akio Hamada, age 61
Senior Managing Director and Board Member; President and Director, Honda Motor Europe; COO, Regional Operations (Europe, Middle East and Africa): Shigeru Takagi, age 58
Senior Managing Director, Government and Industrial Affairs, and Compliance Officer and Board Member: Mikio Yoshimi, age 63
Managing Officer, Quality, Certification and Regulation Compliance: Koichi Fukuo
Managing Officer; EVP and Director, Honda Motor Europe; President and Director; Honda U.K. Manufacturing: Suguru Kanazawa
Managing Officer Regional Operations, CIS countries, the Middle & Near East and Africa (Europe, the Middle & Near East and Africa): Manabu Nishimae
Managing Director, COO Purchasing Operations, and Board Member: Masaya Yamashita, age 57
Managing Director and Board Member; President and Director, Honda R&D: Tomohiko Kawanabe, age 58
Auditors: KPMG AZSA & Co.

LOCATIONS

HQ: Honda Motor Co., Ltd.
(Honda Giken Kogyo Kabushiki Kaisha)
1-1, 2-chome, Minami-Aoyama, Minato-ku
Tokyo 107-8556, Japan
Phone: 81-3-3423-1111   **Fax:** 81-3-5412-1515
US HQ: 156 West 56th St., 20th Fl.
New York, NY 10022
US Phone: 212-707-9920
Web: world.honda.com

2010 Sales

	% of total
North America	44
Asia	
Japan	18
Other countries	18
Europe	9
Other regions	11
Total	**100**

PRODUCTS/OPERATIONS

2010 Sales

	% of total
Automobiles	77
Motorcycles	13
Financial services	7
Power products & other	3
Total	**100**

Selected Honda Car and Truck Models

Passenger cars
  Accord
  City
  Civic
  Insight
  Inspire
  Legend

Minivans, multi-wagons, sport utility vehicles
  Airwave
  Crossroad
  CR-V
  CR-Z
  Element
  Elysion
  Fit
  FREED
  FR-V
  Jazz
  Odyssey
  Partner Pilot
  Ridgeline
  Step Wagon
  Stream

Mini cars
  Acty
  Life
  Vamos
  Zest

Selected Motorcycle Models

CBR600RR
CBR1000RR
Elite (scooter)
Fury
Gold Wing
Interstate
NT700V
Nighthawk
PCX (scooter)
Ruckus (scooter)
Sabre
SH150i (scooter)
Shadow RS
Silver Wing (scooter)
Stateline
ST1300
VFR1200F

COMPETITORS

BMW
Briggs & Stratton
Brunswick Corp.
Caterpillar
Chrysler
Daihatsu
Daimler
Deere
Exmark Manufacturing
Fiat
Ford Motor
Fuji Heavy Industries
General Motors
Harley-Davidson
Hyundai Motor
Indian Motorcycle
Isuzu
Kawasaki Heavy Industries
Kia Motors
Land Rover
Mahindra Renault
Mazda
Mitsubishi Motors
Nissan
Peugeot
Renault
Saab Automobile
Suzuki Motor
Tata Motors
Textron
Toro Company
Toyota
Triumph Motorcycles
Viper Motorcycle
Volkswagen
Volvo
Yamaha Motor

HISTORICAL FINANCIALS

Company Type: Public

Income Statement

FYE: March 31

	REVENUE ($ mil.)	NET INCOME ($ mil.)	NET PROFIT MARGIN	EMPLOYEES
3/10	92,552	2,896	3.1%	176,815
3/09	102,906	1,408	1.4%	181,876
3/08	120,318	6,015	5.0%	178,960
3/07	94,273	5,037	5.3%	167,231
3/06	84,473	5,090	6.0%	144,785
Annual Growth	**2.3%**	**(13.2%)**	**—**	**5.1%**

2010 Year-End Financials

Debt ratio: 53.4%	No. of shares (mil.): 1,811
Return on equity: 6.6%	Dividends
Cash ($ mil.): 12,082	Yield: 0.0%
Current ratio: 1.35	Payout: —
Long-term debt ($ mil.): 24,953	Market value ($ mil.): 690

Stock History

NYSE: HMC

	STOCK PRICE ($) FY Close	P/E High/Low	PER SHARE ($) Earnings	Dividends	Book Value
3/10	0.38	— —	1.60	0.00	25.78
3/09	0.24	— —	0.78	0.10	22.74
3/08	0.29	— —	3.33	0.64	25.15
3/07	0.30	— —	2.75	0.56	21.04
3/06	0.26	— —	2.76	0.42	19.42
Annual Growth	**10.0%**	**— —**	**(12.7%)**	**—**	**7.3%**

HSBC Holdings

HSBC would be a real alphabet soup if the company's name reflected its geographic diversity. One of the world's largest banking groups by assets, HSBC Holdings owns subsidiaries throughout Europe, Hong Kong and the rest of the Asia/Pacific region, the Middle East and Africa, and the Americas. All told, HSBC has some 8,000 locations in more than 80 countries. The group's activities include consumer and commercial banking, credit cards, asset management, private banking, securities underwriting and trading, insurance, and leasing. Its North American operations include HSBC USA, credit card issuer HSBC Finance, and HSBC Bank Canada.

With turmoil and instability in the US and European markets, HSBC has increasingly turned toward emerging markets in Asia and elsewhere for growth. In 2008 it acquired a majority stake in India brokerage firm IL&FS Investsmart. The following year it acquired a majority stake in Indonesian lender Bank Ekonomi Raharja, doubling its retail branches in the nation.

HSBC has always had a bent toward international expansion, even from its inception. Founded in Hong Kong in 1865, HSBC owns all or parts of The Hongkong and Shanghai Banking Corporation, HSBC France, The Saudi British Bank, Hong Kong's Hang Seng Bank, and The Bank of Bermuda.

HSBC was also one of the first foreign banks to receive regulatory approval to incorporate in China. It owns about 20% of Bank of Communications, one of China's largest commercial banks, and was paid some $1.5 billion by the Taiwanese government to take over the 36 branches of the failed Chinese Bank.

In the West, HSBC dealt with losses by shutting down or selling various businesses. The group closed its Decision One US-based wholesale subprime lending unit in 2007 and, the following year, placed its US vehicle lending business in run-off. In 2009 it closed its North American consumer lending business, placing related portfolios (excluding credit cards) in run-off. To further reduce its exposure to consumer credit, it sold a $4 billion US car loan portfolio and servicing platform to Santander.

In 2010 HSBC sold HSBC Insurance Brokers to Marsh & McLennan in a £135 million ($218 million) cash-and-stock deal. As part of the transaction, the companies entered into a strategic partnership under which Marsh will market insurance and risk-management services to HSBC's corporate and private clients ahead of other providers.

HSBC announced in 2010 that chairman Stephen Green will step down to become the UK trade minister. The company is searching to find a replacement for Green, who has worked for HSBC for nearly 30 years.

HISTORY

Scotsman Thomas Sutherland and other businessmen in 1865 opened the doors to Hongkong & Shanghai Bank, financing and promoting British imperial trade in opium, silk, and tea in East Asia. It soon established a London office and created an international branch network emphasizing China and East Asia. It claims to have been the first bank in Thailand (1888).

War repeatedly disrupted, but never demolished, the bank's operations. During WWII the headquarters were temporarily moved to London. (They moved back on a permanent basis in 1991.) The bank's chief prewar manager, Sir Vandeleur Grayborn, died in a Japanese POW camp. After the Communists took power in China in 1949, the bank gradually withdrew; by 1955 only its Shanghai office remained, and it was later closed. The bank played a key role in Hong Kong's postwar growth by financing industrialists who fled there from China.

In the late 1950s Hongkong & Shanghai Bank's acquisitions included the British Bank of the Middle East (founded 1889; now The Saudi British Bank) and Mercantile Bank (with offices in India and Southeast Asia). In 1965 the company bought 62% of Hang Seng, Hong Kong's #2 bank. It also added new subsidiaries, including Wayfoong (mortgage and small-business finance, 1960) and Wardley (investment banking, Hong Kong, 1972).

In the late 1970s and into the 1980s, China began opening to foreign business. The bank added operations in North America to capitalize on business between China, the US and Canada. Acquisitions included Marine Midland Bank (US, 1980), Hongkong Bank of Canada (1981), 51% of treasury securities dealer Carroll McEntee & McGinley (US, 1983), most of the assets and liabilities of the Bank of British Columbia (1986), and Lloyds Bank Canada (1990).

Following the 1984 agreement to return Hong Kong to China, Hongkong & Shanghai Bank began beefing up in the UK, buying London securities dealer James Capel & Co. (1986) and the UK's #3 bank, Midland plc (1992). In 1993 the company formed London-based HSBC Holdings and divested assets, most notably its interest in Hong Kong-based Cathay Pacific Airways.

HSBC then began expanding in Asia again, particularly in Malaysia, where its Hongkong Bank Malaysia became the country's first locally incorporated foreign bank. The company returned to China with offices in Beijing and Guangzhou.

Latin American banks acquired in 1997 were among the non-Asian operations that cushioned HSBC from the worst of 1998's economic crises. Nonetheless, The Hong Kong Monetary Authority took a stake in the bank to shore up the stock exchange and foil short-sellers.

In 1999 China's government made HSBC a loan for mainland expansion. That year the company bought the late Edmond Safra's Republic New York Corporation and his international bank holding company, Safra Republic Holdings.

In 2000 the company bought CCF (then called Crédit Commercial de France, now HSBC France). In response to the slowing economy, it froze the salaries of 14,000 employees in 2001.

HSBC expanded its consumer finance operations with the purchase of US-based Household International (now HSBC Finance) in 2003.

The following year HSBC acquired The Bank of Bermuda, as well as Marks and Spencer Financial Services (aka M&S Money), one of the UK's leading credit card issuers. It bought US credit card company Metris the following year.

The company expanded its presence in Central America and the Caribbean with the 2006 purchase of Panama-based Banistmo.

HSBC in 2008 canceled its proposed $6 billion acquisition of Lone Star's 51% stake in Korea Exchange Bank, an acquisition that had been held up for months by an investigation by the South Korean government. The company cited weakened asset values in the global financial markets for the cancellation.

EXECUTIVES

Group Chairman: Stephen K. Green, age 61
CFO and Executive Director Risk and Regulation; Chairman, HSBC Finance: Douglas J. Flint, age 54
Director: Sir Simon Robertson, age 68
Director; Chairman, Europe, Middle East, and Global Businesses, HSBC Private Banking Holdings (Suisse), HSBC Bank Middle East, and HSBC France; CEO, Global Banking and Markets: Stuart T. Gulliver, age 50
Group Managing Director and Group Chief Technology and Services Officer: Kenneth M. (Ken) Harvey, age 49
Group Managing Director, CEO, HSBC Bank plc: Paul A. Thurston, age 56
Group General Manager; CEO, Global Private Banking: C. M. Meares, age 52
Group General Manager and Director Communications: Richard S. Beck, age 44
Group Managing Director and Group Chief Risk Officer: Brian Robertson, age 55
Group General Manager and Group General Counsel: R. E. T. Bennett, age 58
Group General Manager and Group Chief Accounting Officer: Russell C. Picot, age 52
Group Managing Director; CEO, HSBC North America: Niall S. K. Booker, age 51
Group Company Secretary and Group General Manager: Ralph G. Barber, age 59
Group Managing Director and Group Head Human Resources: Ann Almeida, age 53
Group General Manager; President and CEO, HSBC Bank USA: I. M. Dorner, age 55
Manager Investor Relations: Alastair Brown
Auditors: KPMG Audit Plc

LOCATIONS

HQ: HSBC Holdings plc
8 Canada Sq., 42 Fl.
London E14 5HQ, United Kingdom
Phone: 44-20-7991-8888   **Fax:** 44-20-7992-4880
US HQ: 26525 N. Riverwoods Blvd., 4 North East
Mettawa, IL 60045
US Phone: 224-544-2000
Web: www.hsbc.com

2009 Sales

	% of total
Europe	38
Asia/Pacific	
Hong Kong	29
Other countries	24
Latin America	6
Middle East	3
Total	**100**

PRODUCTS/OPERATIONS

2009 Sales

	% of total
Interest	58
Fees	20
Net earned insurance premiums	10
Net trading income	9
Other	3
Total	**100**

Selected Subsidiaries

HSBC Bank plc
HSBC Asset Finance (UK) Ltd.
HSBC Bank A.S.
HSBC Europe BV
HSBC Bank International Limited (99.8%)
HSBC Bank Malta p.l.c. (70%)
HSBC Private Banking Holdings (Suisse) S.A.
HSBC France (99.99%)
HSBC Germany Holdings GmbH
HSBC Trinkaus & Burkhardt AG
Marks and Spencer Retail Financial Services Holdings Limited

HSBC Finance (Netherlands)
HSBC Holdings BV
HSBC Asia Holdings (UK) Ltd.
Hang Seng Bank Ltd (62%)
The Hongkong and Shanghai Banking Corporation Ltd
HSBC Bank Malaysia Berhad
HSBC Insurance (Asia) Ltd.
HSBC Latin America Holdings (UK) Ltd.
HSBC Bank Brasil S.A. — Banco Multiplo
HSBC Latin America B.V.
HSBC Bank Argentina S.A. (99.99%)
HSBC Mexico S.A., Institucion de Banca Multiple, Grupo Financiero HSBC (99.99%)
HSBC Overseas Holdings (UK) Ltd
HSBC Bank Canada
HSBC North America Holdings Inc.
HSBC Investments (North America) Inc.
HSBC Bank USA, N.A.
HSBC Finance Corporation
HSBC Securities (USA) Inc.

COMPETITORS

Bank of America	JPMorgan Chase
Bank of China	Lloyds Banking Group
Barclays	Mitsubishi UFJ Financial
BBVA	Mizuho Financial
CIBC	Prudential plc
Citigroup	RBC Financial Group
Credit Suisse	Royal Bank of Scotland
Deutsche Bank	Standard Chartered
Hutchison Whampoa	UBS
Intesa Sanpaolo	

HISTORICAL FINANCIALS

Company Type: Public

Income Statement

FYE: December 31

	ASSETS ($ mil.)	NET INCOME ($ mil.)	INCOME AS % OF ASSETS	EMPLOYEES
12/09	2,364,452	5,834	0.2%	302,000
12/08	2,527,465	5,728	0.2%	325,000
12/07	2,354,266	19,133	0.8%	330,000
12/06	1,860,758	15,789	0.8%	312,000
12/05	1,501,970	15,081	1.0%	284,000
Annual Growth	**12.0%**	**(21.1%)**	**—**	**1.5%**

2009 Year-End Financials

Equity as % of assets: 5.4%
Return on assets: 0.2%
Return on equity: 5.3%
Long-term debt ($ mil.): 257,466
No. of shares (mil.): 3,502
Dividends
Yield: 3.0%
Payout: 100.0%
Market value ($ mil.): 199,929
Sales ($ mil.): 103,736

Stock History

NYSE: HBC

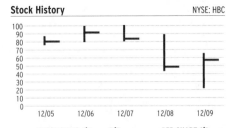

	STOCK PRICE ($) FY Close	P/E High/Low		PER SHARE ($) Earnings	Dividends	Book Value
12/09	57.09	38	13	1.70	1.70	36.64
12/08	48.67	38	19	2.35	4.65	26.73
12/07	83.71	12	10	8.15	4.35	36.60
12/06	91.65	14	12	6.95	3.80	30.94
12/05	80.47	13	11	6.75	3.45	26.39
Annual Growth	**(8.2%)**	**—**	**—**	**(29.2%)**	**(16.2%)**	**8.5%**

Hutchison Whampoa

Hutchison Whampoa has a hand in just about everything in Hong Kong. The company, one of Hong Kong's oldest *hongs* (trading companies), has extensive holdings in retailing (A.S. Watson & Co), ports, energy (Hongkong Electric, Husky Energy), telecommunications (3G mobile phone and paging services), and infrastructure (power plants, toll roads, and construction materials). In addition, Hutchison Whampoa owns hotels and a sizable portfolio of Hong Kong properties. Outside Hong Kong, the company has operations in about 55 countries, including China and elsewhere in the Asia/Pacific region, as well as in Europe and the Americas. Hutchison Whampoa is controlled by Li Ka-shing, one of the world's wealthiest men.

Hutchison Whampoa's retail and manufacturing subsidiary, A.S. Watson & Co. (ASW), accounts for about 40% of revenues with more than 8,300 retail stores spread among a dozen chains. Operations include supermarkets (Park'N Shop), health and beauty stores (Watson's Your Personal Store, Drogas, Kruidvat), Fortress electrical appliance stores in Hong Kong, soft drink and water bottling operations, and wine retailing (Watson's Wine Cellar). Already the world's largest operator of health and beauty stores (by store count), with outlets throughout Europe and Asia, ASW has expanded its health and beauty business with the acquisition of the French retail perfume chain Marionnaud Parfumeries and the 120-door The Perfume Shop chain in the UK. Its Chinese retail arm, Watsons China, operates about 400 stores in some 65 cities on the Mainland.

With about 300 berths in some 50 ports, Hutchison Port Holdings (HPH) is one of the world's biggest container terminal operators. HPH operates in six of the nine busiest container ports in the world, including three key ports on Britain's east coast and ports on both ends of the Panama Canal. In addition to owning a controlling interest in Hongkong International Terminals, HPH has large investments in terminal operations in southern China.

Hutchison Whampoa is a leading competitor in mobile telecommunications, offering wireless service to some 16 million customers throughout Australia, Europe, and Hong Kong. Hutchison Telecommunications International Limited (HTIL) provides fixed-line and mobile communications services to customers primarily in Southeast Asia. Hutchison Whampoa took the company private on May 25, 2010.

Hutchison Whampoa has strong connections to the Chinese government, thanks to its rags-to-riches chairman, Li, who has spent years building business relationships inside China. His Cheung Kong (Holdings) Limited is a substantial shareholder in Hutchison Whampoa. In turn, Hutchison Whampoa owns about 85% of Cheung Kong Infrastructure.

HISTORY

Hongkong and Whampoa Dock was the first registered company in Hong Kong. The enterprise was founded in 1861, when it bought dry docks in Whampoa (near present-day Guangzhou, China) after the kidnapping and disappearance of the docks' owner, John Couper, during the Second Opium War (1856-60). It bought docks in Hong Kong in 1865.

Founded in 1880 by John Hutchison, Hutchison International became a major Hong Kong consumer goods importer and wholesaler. It took control of Hongkong and Whampoa Dock and A.S. Watson (drugstores, supermarkets, soft drinks) during an acquisition spree in the 1960s. The purchases entailed a complex web of deals that fell apart in the mid-1970s. To save Hutchison International, the Hongkong & Shanghai Bank took a large stake in the company and brought in Australian turnaround specialist Bill Wyllie. Wyllie slashed expenses, sold 103 companies in 1976, and bought the rest of Hongkong and Whampoa Dock in 1977. The company became Hutchison Whampoa that year.

In a surprise move, in 1979 Hongkong & Shanghai Bank sold its 23% stake in Hutchison to Cheung Kong Holdings: Cheung Kong founder Li Ka-shing, who began his career at age 14 by selling plastic flowers, became the first Chinese to control a British-style hong. Wyllie left in 1981.

In the 1980s Hutchison redeveloped its older dockyard sites, which had become prime real estate. The company's International Terminals unit grew with Hong Kong's container traffic into the world's largest privately owned container terminal operator. In the 1980s the firm diversified into energy (buying stakes in utility Hongkong Electric and Canada-based Husky Oil) and precious metals and mining. It also moved into telecommunications, buying Australian paging and UK mobile telephone units in 1989.

The following year the hong launched the AsiaSat I satellite in a venture with Cable & Wireless (C&W) and China International Trust & Investment. More acquisitions followed, including European mobile phone businesses and telecom equipment makers. In 1996 the firm reorganized its Hong Kong telecom operations into Hutchison Telecommunications and launched its European wireless operations as a new public company, Orange. In 1998 Hutchison Telecommunications made a move into the US when it bought a 20% stake in Western Wireless' digital PCS unit, VoiceStream.

In 1999 the company and C&W sold their stakes in AsiaSat. Hutchison Whampoa also traded its stake in Orange to Mannesmann, acquiring 10% of the German conglomerate, which was later acquired by Vodafone. Also in 1999 Hutchison Whampoa and Global Crossing formed a $1.2 billion telecom joint venture to build a fiber-optic network in China (in 2002 the company purchased the remaining 50%).

In 2001 Hutchison Whampoa sold its stake in US-based mobile phone operator VoiceStream to Deutsche Telekom for $5.1 billion in cash.

In 2004 the company sold the remaining 20% stake in its joint venture in China with household products giant Procter & Gamble to P&G for $1.8 billion. Also in 2004 Hutchison Whampoa's fixed-line telecommunications group acquired Vanda Systems, and became a listed company on the Hong Kong Stock exchange under the new name Hutchison Global Communications Holdings (HGCH). In October the company combined its 52% stake in HGCH with its interests in the 2G cellular businesses under a single parent company, Hutchison Telecommunications International Limited (HTIL), and took HTIL public on the Hong Kong and New York stock exchanges.

In 2008 the company launched a new division, Hutchison Water, a provider of water production and treatment solutions.

Ports and related services
  Hongkong International Terminals Limited (53%,
    container terminal operations)
  Hongkong United Dockyards Limited (50%, ship
    repair and general engineering)
  Shanghai Mingdong Container Terminals Limited
    (40%, China)
  Yantian International Container Terminals Limited
    (38%, China)
Telecommunications
  3 Italia S.p.A. (97%, 3G mobile multimedia services)
  Hutchison 3G UK Limited (3G mobile multimedia
    services)
  Hutchison Telecommunications (Australia) Limited
    (52%, holding company and multimedia services)
  Hutchison Telecommunications (Hong Kong) Limited
    (60%)
Property and hotels
  Harbour Plaza Hotel Management (International)
    Limited (50%)
  Hutchison Whampoa Properties Limited (holding
    company)
Finance and investments
  Hutchison Whampoa (Europe) Limited (consulting
    services, UK)
Other
  TOM Group Limited (24%, Internet portal)

COMPETITORS

Aldeasa
Alliance Boots
AT&T
BT
Cable & Wireless
Carrefour
China Mobile
China Unicom
Dairy Farm International
Deutsche Telekom
DFS Group
DP World
France Telecom
Hopewell Holdings
Jardine Matheson
KP
Orange
Orient Overseas
PCCW Ltd.
PSA International
Road King Infrastructure
Schlecker
Sime Darby
SkyTel
Sprint Nextel
Swire Pacific
Verizon
Wharf

HISTORICAL FINANCIALS
Company Type: Public

Income Statement

	REVENUE ($ mil.)	NET INCOME ($ mil.)	NET PROFIT MARGIN	EMPLOYEES
12/09	26,915	2,802	10.4%	220,000
12/08	30,375	3,180	10.5%	220,000
12/07	28,019	4,210	15.0%	230,000
12/06	23,620	2,907	12.3%	220,000
12/05	23,553	1,850	7.9%	200,000
Annual Growth	3.4%	10.9%	—	2.4%

FYE: December 31

2009 Year-End Financials

Debt ratio: —
Return on equity: 7.0%
Cash ($ mil.): 11,926
Current ratio: 1.68
Long-term debt ($ mil.): —

No. of shares (mil.): 4,263
Dividends
  Yield: 3.2%
  Payout: 51.2%
Market value ($ mil.): 29,346

Stock History

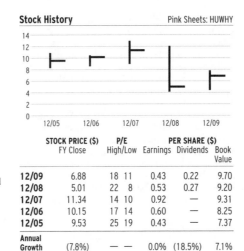

	STOCK PRICE ($) FY Close	P/E High/Low		PER SHARE ($) Earnings	Dividends	Book Value
12/09	6.88	18	11	0.43	0.22	9.70
12/08	5.01	22	8	0.53	0.27	9.20
12/07	11.34	14	10	0.92	—	9.31
12/06	10.15	17	14	0.60	—	8.25
12/05	9.53	25	19	0.43	—	7.37
Annual Growth	(7.8%)	—	—	0.0%	(18.5%)	7.1%

Hyundai Motor

South Korea's leading carmaker, Hyundai Motor produces compact and luxury cars, SUVs, and minivans, as well as trucks, buses, and other commercial vehicles. The company re-established itself as South Korea's leading carmaker in 1998 by acquiring a 51% stake in Kia Motors (since reduced to about 34%). Selling cars in the US since 1986, Hyundai started selling its heavy trucks stateside in 1998. Hyundai's models for the North American market include the Accent and Sonata; models sold elsewhere include the GRD and Equus.

With auto sales in its home market stagnant, Hyundai is looking to key overseas markets for growth. The company is targeting regions that include China, Eastern Europe, India, and North America. In the US, its Hyundai Motor America unit has benefited from the company's highly publicized Hyundai Assurance vehicle return program. The company has plans to leave Japan, however, unable to compete with the Japanese customer's preference for domestic (primarily Toyota and Honda) and European nameplates.

Since opening its first Chinese plant in 2002, Hyundai doubled its production in that country. It entered into an agreement with China-based Baotou Bei Ben Heavy-Duty Truck in December 2009 to start a 50/50 joint venture to manufacture trucks in China; together the companies plan to invest $400 million in the venture. Having announced its plans in 2010 to open a third plant in China (targeted completion in 2012), Hyundai is looking to have a 20% share of the Chinese market by year-end, as well as to sell 100,000 heavy trucks by 2014. To that end the automaker signed a $1.2 billion deal to form a joint venture with Guangzhou Motor Group, giving Hyundai access to the commercial vehicle market in China.

To keep pace with markets in Europe, Hyundai chose the Czech Republic for the site of a $1.2 billion manufacturing complex. The facilities were completed in 2008 and are capable of producing 200,000 vehicles per year, with an ultimate annual capacity of 300,000 vehicles.

Hyundai is a leading brand in India as well, trailing domestic player Maruti Suzuki India.

This is no small feat, as the Korean company only entered the market in the mid-1990s.

Despite his legal woes and the opposition of one of the company's largest shareholders (the National Pension Service), Chung Mong-Koo was re-elected chairman in 2008. Chung owns about 5% of Hyundai Motor.

HISTORY

Hyundai Motor Company was established in 1967, and it initially began manufacturing cars and light trucks through a technology collaboration with Ford's UK operations. By the early 1970s Hyundai was ready to build cars under its own nameplate. The company debuted the subcompact Hyundai Pony in 1974 at Italy's annual Turin Motor Show.

The Pony was an instant domestic success and soon propelled Hyundai to the top spot among South Korea's carmakers. During the mid-1970s the company began exporting the Pony to El Salvador and Guatemala.

By the 1980s Hyundai was ready to shift into high gear and begin high-volume production in anticipation of penetrating more overseas markets. The company began exporting to Canada in 1983.

Hyundai introduced the Hyundai Excel in 1985. That year the company established its US subsidiary, Hyundai Motor America. By 1986 Hyundai was exporting Excels for sale in the US. Sales of the Excel soared the next year, so Hyundai decided to build a factory in Bromont, Quebec.

But by the time the factory was finished in 1989, consumers were tiring of the aging compact car and the quality problems that came with it. Hyundai closed the plant after just four years of operation.

The company introduced its first sports car, the Scoupe, in 1990. The following year it developed the first Hyundai-designed engine, called the Alpha. By 1998 Hyundai was beginning to feel the pinch of the Asian economic crisis as domestic demand dropped drastically. However, the decrease in Korean demand was largely offset by exports. That year Hyundai took a controlling stake in Korean competitor Kia Motors.

In hopes of increasing its share of the Asian automotive market, Daimler AG took a 10% stake in Hyundai in 2000 (sold in 2004). The deal included the establishment of a joint venture to manufacture commercial vehicles, as well as an agreement among Hyundai, Daimler, and Mitsubishi Motors to develop small cars for the global market.

The following year Daimler announced it would exercise its option to take a 50% stake in Hyundai's heavy truck business.

In 2004 Hyundai CEO Kim Dong-Jin was indicted in South Korea on charges that he violated campaign finance laws and engaged in managerial negligence. The charges stemmed from a general crackdown on campaign finance violations, during which more than a dozen members of South Korea's parliament were either indicted or detained. Later in 2004 Kim was convicted of the charges against him and sentenced to a suspended two-year prison term.

To increase its presence in the US, Hyundai completed construction of a new manufacturing plant, Hyundai Motor Manufacturing Alabama, in 2005.

In 2006 Hyundai's legal woes persisted when two executives were arrested as part of a Korean bribery investigation. The pair were accused of creating a slush fund that was allegedly used to fund a lobbyist who sought favors for Hyundai from the South Korean government. Officials were also investigating whether the slush fund was created at the behest of Hyundai chairman Chung Mong-Koo.

Chung Mong-Koo was indicted on charges that he embezzled Hyundai company cash to finance bribes for Korean government officials in exchange for corporate favors. Chung was convicted early in 2007. Under Korean law, Chung faced a potential life sentence, but received only a three-year prison term as the judge in the case said Chung contributed hugely to the development of the Korean economy. Three other Hyundai officials were also convicted, but they received suspended sentences. Chung's son, Kia Motors boss Chung Eui-Sun, also was under investigation, but prosecutors did not indict him.

Later in 2007 Chung's three-year prison sentence was suspended by an appeals court, with a three-judge panel citing his importance to South Korea's economy. The appellate judges, however, required the Hyundai executive to maintain a clean record for five years to avoid prison and to fulfill a promise he made to donate $1.1 billion of his personal assets to society.

EXECUTIVES

Chairman and Co-CEO: Chung Mong-Koo, age 61
Vice Chairman: Chung Eui-Sun, age 39
Vice Chairman, President, and CEO, Mobis: Suk Soo Chung, age 57
Vice Chairman and President, Europe: Kim Yong-Hwan, age 53
President and Co-CEO: Yang Seung Suk
Co-CEO and VP: Kang Ho Don, age 57
Auditors: Deloitte HanaAnjin LLC

LOCATIONS

HQ: Hyundai Motor Company
(Hyundai Jadongcha Chusik Hoesa)
231 Yangjae-dong, Seocho-gu
Seoul 137-938, South Korea
Phone: 82-2-3464-1114
US HQ: 10550 Talbert Ave., Fountain Valley, CA 92728
US Phone: 714-965-3000   **US Fax:** 714-965-3148
Web: worldwide.hyundai.com

2009 Sales

	% of total
South Korea	22
North America	18
Europe	16
Other regions	44
Total	**100**

PRODUCTS/OPERATIONS

2009 Sales

	% of total
Automotive	94
Financial services	6
Total	**100**

Selected Models

Commercial vehicles
  Aero (large city bus)
  Aero Town (medium bus)
  County (small bus)
  e-Mighty (light commercial truck)
  Super Aero City (bus)
  Universe (large coach bus)

Passenger cars
  Accent (compact coupe)
  Atos Prime (subcompact)
  Avante XD
  Azera (sedan)
  Elantra (sedan)
  Entourage (minivan)
  Equus/Centennial (premium sedan)
  Genesis (premium coupe)
  Getz (compact sedan)
  Santa Fe (SUV)
  Sonata (sedan)
  Tiburon (coupe)
  Tucson (SUV)
  Trajet (SUV)
  Veracruz (SUV)

COMPETITORS

Chery Automobile
Chrysler
Daihatsu
Daimler
Dongfeng Motor
Fiat
Ford Motor
General Motors
GM Daewoo Auto & Technology
Honda
Isuzu
Maruti Suzuki
Mazda
Nissan
Peugeot
Renault
Ssangyong Motor
Tata Motors
Toyota
Volkswagen

HISTORICAL FINANCIALS

Company Type: Public

Income Statement

FYE: December 31

	REVENUE ($ mil.)	NET INCOME ($ mil.)	NET PROFIT MARGIN	EMPLOYEES
12/09	78,457	3,469	4.4%	120,472
12/08	62,992	863	1.4%	97,686
12/07	74,334	1,709	2.3%	74,900
12/06	67,722	1,340	2.0%	54,115
12/05	57,636	2,277	3.9%	68,000
Annual Growth	**8.0%**	**11.1%**	**—**	**15.4%**

2009 Year-End Financials

Debt ratio: 80.3%
Return on equity: —
Cash ($ mil.): —
Current ratio: —
Long-term debt ($ mil.): 19,944

Net Income History

Korea: 005380

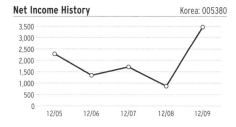

IBERDROLA, S.A.

Once just a force in Spain, IBERDROLA has established itself as a major global player in the power industry over the past few years. In 2009 it served more than 28 million customers in Europe and the Americas, and it owns hydroelectric, fossil-fueled, nuclear, and renewable power generation facilities with a capacity of about 44,000 MW (including 26,400 MW in Spain, 6,700 MW in the UK, 3,800 MW in the US, and 5,550 MW in Mexico and Guatemala). The company is putting a major focus on being the world leader in developing renewable energy plants (10,000 MW in 2009, with more than 56,600 MW in its product pipeline).

The company's long-term strategy is to focus on the development of its portfolio of clean energy plants and to upgrade its network of transmission and distribution grids to more efficiently harness the new power coming online.

In 2010 IBERDROLA announced plans to invest about $4.8 billion in wind power, smart grid and distribution network developments in the UK between 2010 and 2012. It also secured a contract with partner Vattenfall to build one of the world's largest marine wind farms in the world (in offshore UK) with a capacity of 7,200 MW, capable of supplying clean energy to 5 million homes.

Despite the impact of the global recession, which weakened demand and saw the company's revenues dip slightly in 2009, IBERDROLA still managed to increase its new capacity that year by 1,500 MW of primarily wind powered generation plants.

IBERDROLA became a major global force in 2007 with the friendly takeover of Scottish Power for $22.5 billion. Scottish Power was the third-largest electricity distributor and largest wind power producer in the UK. In 2008, in a major move into the US power market, IBERDROLA acquired Energy East (now Iberdrola USA) for $4.5 billion. Iberdrola USA distributes and markets power and natural gas to Connecticut, Maine, Massachusetts, New Hampshire, and New York.

HISTORY

The 1992 merger of two private utilities — Hidroeléctrica Española (Hidrola) and Hidroeléctrica Iberia Iberduero — created IBERDROLA. Iberduero's forebear, Hidroeléctrica Ibérica, was born in 1901 in Spain's industrialized north; its first power plant began operations in 1904.

In 1918 Saltos del Duero began producing hydroelectric power along the Duero River. The two companies merged to become Iberduero in 1944, five years after the reign of Gen. Francisco Franco began. Neither Iberduero nor Hidrola (founded in 1907 to electrify Madrid and Valencia) grew much during Spain's isolationist years.

Hoping to make friends, the US pumped money into Spain in the 1950s. As industrial production picked up, both Hidrola and Iberduero completed construction on several large power plants between 1957 and 1969.

Dependent on imported oil, Spain was shaken by the 1970s oil crisis. In 1975, a few months before Franco died, the government began to promote nuclear energy. Both firms invested heavily in nukes, but by 1984 overcapacity, high building costs, and inflation led the government to freeze nuclear construction. Hidrola, Iberduero, and other private utilities were left deeply in debt.

In the late 1980s the government arranged nuclear and hydro asset swaps to spread the debt around. Ultimately, more power was shifted to the state utility, Endesa. In 1992, with Endesa gobbling up smaller utilities and European deregulation in the wings, Iberduero and Hidrola merged in self-defense. The result was IBERDROLA, Spain's largest privately owned utility and Endesa's only real competition. IBERDROLA and Endesa stayed at odds, particularly over stranded costs from the stalled nuclear program and the government's mandate that the private utilities buy Endesa's energy to repay Endesa for taking over their power plants. Finally, in 1996 the government agreed to issue bonds to cover most of the debt.

IBERDROLA began piling up Latin American interests in 1992 by buying stakes in Argentina's Gas Litoral and the Güemes power plant. It soon grabbed holdings in Bolivian electricity distributors Electropaz and Elfeo (1995), two Chilean utilities (1996), gas and electric companies in Brazil, and a gas company in Colombia (1997).

To create a more horizontal business structure, in 1995 IBERDROLA created Iberinco, an engineering firm, and Iberener to manage Latin American energy holdings. It formed telecom joint venture Utilitel with Telefónica in 1997 and founded data management firm Iberdrola Sistemas in 1998.

IBERDROLA agreed to cooperate with oil company Repsol on developing energy projects in 1997, a year before Spain's deregulation began. With Electricidade de Portugal and the US's TECO Energy, it acquired Guatemala's Empresa Eléctrica in 1998, and with Telefónica bought interests in Brazilian wireless phone companies.

In 1999 IBERDROLA took over US company Energy Works (which managed electricity buys for industrial customers), allied with German giant RWE to compete throughout Europe, and made plans to exit the Utilitel venture.

IBERDROLA bought Brazilian electric distributor CELPE for $1 billion in 2000. Later that year the company itself agreed to be acquired by rival Endesa for $12.9 billion, but the deal was abandoned in 2001. Also in 2001 IBERDROLA sold its Latin American telecommunications interests to Telefónica.

In 2002 the company sold controlling stakes in its Spanish water utilities (Pridesa and Ondagua) to RWE's Thames Water unit for $96 million. IBERDROLA also sold its power transmission assets to Infraestructuras de Alta Tension (INALTA), which is owned by CVC Capital Partners (75%) and Red Eléctrica de España (25%).

IBERDROLA expanded in Latin America to include electric generation and distribution companies in Brazil, Bolivia, Chile, Guatemala, and Mexico.

The company sold off noncore assets, including some domestic water utility and real estate assets, its Latin American gas businesses, and two Chilean hydroelectric plants. Spanish construction giant ACS acquired 10% of IBERDROLA in 2006 for $2.7 billion. That year the company acquired two UK-based wind power projects with a combined power capacity of more than 20MW, its first such acquisition in the UK.

EXECUTIVES

Chairman and CEO: José Ignacio Sánchez Galán, age 60
Vice Chairman: Víctor de Urrutia Vallejo, age 68
CFO: José Sáinz Armada
Head Non Energy Business: Pedro Velasco
Head, Renewables: Xabier Viteri
Head Latin America: Gonzalo Pérez Fernández
Head Liberalized Business, Spain and Portugal:
  Francisco Martínez Córcoles
Director, Iberia and Latin America: José Luis San Pedro
Director Development: Pedro Azagra Blázquez
Director Internal Audit: Luis Javier Aranaz Zuza
Director Strategy and Studies: José L. del Valle Doblado
Director Operations: José L. San Pedro Guerenabarrena
Director International: Amparo Moraleda Martínez
Legal Counsel: Federico San Sebastián Flechoso
Secretary: Julián Martínez Simancas Sanchez
CEO, Iberdrola Engineering and Construction:
  Alberto Sicre
Auditors: Ernst & Young, S.L.

LOCATIONS

HQ: IBERDROLA, S.A.
  8 Cardenal Gardoqui
  48008 Bilbao, Vizcaya, Spain
Phone: 34-944-151-411   **Fax:** 34-944-154-579
US HQ: 201 King of Prussia Rd., Ste. 500,
  Radnor, PA 19087
US Phone: 610-254-9783
Web: www.iberdrola.es

2009 Sales

	% of total
Europe	
Spain	46
UK	31
US	12
South America	
Mexico/Guatemala	6
Other countries	5
Total	**100**

COMPETITORS

AES	Energias de Portugal
Avánzit	Enersis
Cemig	E.ON UK
CEPSA	Gas Natural SDG
Constellation Energy	HC Energía
Group	International Power
Edison	Navitas Energy
Electricité de France	Plambeck Neue Energien
ELETROBRÁS	PPL Corporation
EnBW	Red Eléctrica de España
Endesa S.A.	Sempra Energy
Enel	Tractebel Engineering

HISTORICAL FINANCIALS
Company Type: Public

Income Statement

	REVENUE ($ mil.)	NET INCOME ($ mil.)	NET PROFIT MARGIN	EMPLOYEES
12/09	35,198	4,212	12.0%	32,711
12/08	35,514	4,184	11.8%	32,993
12/07	25,711	3,465	13.5%	23,159
12/06	14,535	2,190	15.1%	16,923
12/05	13,902	1,637	11.8%	17,009
Annual Growth	26.1%	26.7%	—	17.8%

FYE: December 31

2009 Year-End Financials

Debt ratio: —
Return on equity: 11.3%
Cash ($ mil.): 1,563
Current ratio: 1.09
Long-term debt ($ mil.): —
No. of shares (mil.): 5,382
Dividends
  Yield: 4.9%
  Payout: 58.7%
Market value ($ mil.): 51,448

	STOCK PRICE ($) FY Close	P/E High/Low		Earnings	PER SHARE ($) Dividends	Book Value
12/09	9.56	12	8	0.80	0.47	7.73
12/08	9.22	19	8	0.82	0.17	6.12
Annual Growth	3.7%	—	—	(2.4%)	176.5%	26.3%

IKEA

How Swede it is. One of the world's top furniture retailers, IKEA sells Scandinavian-style home furnishings and other housewares in about 300 stores in more than 35 countries. To cut transportation costs, IKEA uses flat packaging; customers assemble the products at home. The company designs its own furniture, which is made by about 1,220 suppliers in some 55 countries. IKEA's stores feature playrooms for children and Swedish cuisine restaurants. It also sells by mail order and online. An acronym for founder Ingvar Kamprad and his boyhood home, Elmtaryd, Agunnaryd, IKEA began operating in Sweden in 1943. It is owned by Kamprad's Netherlands-based charitable foundation, Stichting Ingka.

While the downturn in the global economy and housing crises in the UK and US have depressed furniture sales overall, IKEA's low-price retail concept helped it grow its market share in all of its retail markets.

IKEA operates more than 35 stores in the US, where it says it will add another three to five stores a year despite the worst sales environment for home decor in decades. IKEA is counting on strength as a purveyor of value-priced furniture to carry it through the economic downturn here. It has eight distribution centers in North America and in 2008 opened its first US manufacturing plant in Virginia.

In Asia, IKEA is growing in Japan and China. After entering Japan — the world's second-largest consumer market after the US — in 2006, IKEA's presence has grown to about half a dozen locations there. The company has stores in Beijing, Chengdu, and six other cities in China. However, IKEA is under pressure from cheaper Chinese household goods suppliers. In mid-2009 IKEA announced it is putting all new investment plans in Russia on hold, citing pervasive corruption and the demand for bribes. IKEA, which operates as both a retailer and shopping center developer there, opened its first store in Russia in 2000. Looking ahead, the company hopes to begin opening stores in India and has been leaning on government agencies there to soften their regulations.

IKEA's manufacturing arm, The Swedwood Group, makes wood-based furniture and components at more than 45 factories and sawmills in nine countries. IKEA, Sweden's largest food exporter, is replacing its non-organic offerings with organic fare, including cheese, coffee, and jams.

To house all of its furniture, the Swedish furniture king has begun selling prefabricated homes in Sweden, Norway, Finland, Denmark, and England. The company's BoKlok ("live smart") prefab houses are available in two styles: single-family villas (available only in Sweden), and two-story timber-frame buildings containing six apartments. To date, IKEA has sold more than 3,500 homes and aims to move that figure to 500 per year.

HISTORY

At the age of 17, Ingvar Kamprad formed his own company in Sweden in 1943, peddling fish, vegetable seeds, and magazines by bicycle. He called the company IKEA, an acronym for his name and the village in which he grew up (Elmtaryd, Agunnaryd). Four years later he added the newly invented ballpoint pen to his product assortment and started a mail-order catalog.

In 1950 Kamprad added furniture and housewares to his mail-order products, and in 1953 he bought a furniture factory and opened a small showroom. The showroom was a hit with price-conscious Swedes and was replaced by the first official IKEA store in 1958. The first store outside Sweden was established in 1963 in Norway. Two years later the company opened its flagship store in Stockholm, a 150,000-sq.-ft. marvel whose round design was inspired by the Guggenheim Museum in New York. The store featured a nursery, a restaurant, a bank, and parking spaces for 1,000 cars. By 1969 two more stores were opened in Sweden and another in Denmark.

A fire badly damaged the Stockholm store in 1973, but the subsequent fire sale pulled in more shoppers than the store's grand opening. That year IKEA expanded beyond Scandinavia, opening stores in Switzerland and Germany. In 1976 it opened a store in Canada, its first store outside Europe, and it entered Australia, the Canary Islands, Hong Kong, Iceland, Kuwait, Saudi Arabia, and Singapore during the late 1970s and early 1980s.

To avoid questions of succession after his death, Kamprad in 1980 transferred ownership of the company to a charitable foundation. IKEA opened its first US store (in Philadelphia) in 1985. Anders Moberg was named president of IKEA in 1986. By 1991 there were seven outlets in the US and 95 total in 23 countries. IKEA began its push into Eastern Europe two years later, but at the same time struggled with economic downturns in its major markets, Germany and Scandinavia.

Kamprad's reluctant announcement that he had associated with pro-Nazi groups in the 1940s and 1950s brought a torrent of bad press. The revelation prompted IKEA to reconsider opening a store in Israel, believing the Israeli government would not sanction the investment. Instead, Jewish groups claimed the company was deliberately avoiding the country. IKEA agreed in 1995 to open an Israeli store and finally granted a license for a franchise to Blue Square — Israel Ltd. in 1997.

That year IKEA announced plans to build about 20 plants over five years in the Baltics, Bulgaria, and Romania, a move designed to reduce its dependence on contract manufacturers and nearly double its own manufacturing capacity. Also in 1997 it began offering prefab housing in Sweden with construction firm Skanska.

IKEA opened its largest store (400,000 sq. ft.) outside Europe in Chicago in 1998 and announced plans to open more stores in Russia, China, and Eastern Europe. In 2000 the company opened its first store in Moscow, with plans for more Russian locations.

In December 2002 IKEA Netherlands received a letter with a bomb threat and temporarily shut down 10 of its retail locations. Explosives were discovered in two stores in the Netherlands and detonated; two IKEA employees were minimally injured. Federal authorities confirmed that the motive behind the attacks was extortion.

The Swedish home furnishings group opened 18 new stores in fiscal year 2005 (15 in Europe and three in North America). The following year IKEA added 16 new stores worldwide, including its first in Japan.

EXECUTIVES

Chairman and CEO: Thomas Bergström
President and CEO, IKEA Group: Mikael Ohlsson
VP and CFO, IKEA Group: Sören Hansen
Managing Director, Swedwood: Gunnar Korsell
Managing Director, IKEA Sweden: Torbjörn Lööf
Retail Region Manager, Europe North: Werner Weber
Retail Region Manager, Europe East: Per Kaufmann
Retail Region Manager, US and Canada: Noel Wijsmans
Retail Region Manager, China, Japan, and Australia:
  Ian Duffy, age 52
Group Human Resources Manager:
  Pernille Spiers-Lopez
Manager Sustainability: Thomas Bergmark
Information Manager, IKEA Group: Helen Duphorn
Senior Adviser: Ingvar Kamprad, age 84

LOCATIONS

HQ: Inter IKEA Systems B.V.
  Olof Palmestraat 1
  2616 Delft, The Netherlands
Phone: 31-15-215-0750   **Fax:** 31-15-219-0533
US HQ: 9930 Franklin Square Dr., Baltimore, MD 21236
US Phone: 610-834-0180
Web: franchisor.ikea.com

2009 Sales

	% of total
Europe	80
North America	15
Asia & Australia	5
Total	**100**

PRODUCTS/OPERATIONS

Selected Products

Armchairs
Bath accessories
Bath suites
Bean bags
Bed linens
Beds and bedroom suites
Bookcases
Boxes
CD storage
Ceiling lamps
Children's furniture
Clocks
Coffee tables
Cookware
Cord management
Desk accessories
Dining tables and chairs
Dinnerware
Entertainment units
Floor lamps
Frames
Kitchen organizers
Kitchen units
Leather sofas
Lighting
Mattresses

Mirrors
Musical instruments for children
Office chairs and suites
Posters
Rugs
Sofas and sofa beds
Spotlights
Stools
Table lamps
Toy storage
TV cabinets and stands
Utility storage
Video storage
Wall shelves and systems
Wardrobe units
Window treatments

COMPETITORS

ASDA
Ashley Furniture
Bassett Furniture
Bed Bath & Beyond
Container Store
Cost Plus
Design Within Reach
Euromarket Designs
Eurway
Gruppo Coin
Harvey Norman Holdings
Home Retail
Horten
Howden
Hulsta-Werke Huls
Jennifer Convertibles
John Lewis
Kmart
La Rinascente
Marks & Spencer
METRO AG
Otto Group
Pier 1 Imports
Restoration Hardware
Rooms To Go
Wal-Mart
Williams-Sonoma
Zara

HISTORICAL FINANCIALS

Company Type: Private

Income Statement				FYE: August 31
	REVENUE ($ mil.)	**NET INCOME** ($ mil.)	**NET PROFIT MARGIN**	**EMPLOYEES**
8/09	32,475	—	—	123,000
8/08	31,098	—	—	127,800
8/07	27,017	—	—	118,000
8/06	22,194	—	—	104,000
8/05	18,089	—	—	90,000
Annual Growth	**15.8%**	—	—	**8.1%**

Revenue History

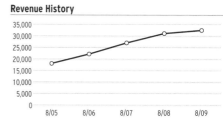

Imperial Oil

Imperial Oil, Canada's largest oil company, holds sway over a vast empire of oil and gas resources. It has proved reserves of 63 million barrels of oil, 1,661 million barrels of bitumen, 691 million barrels of synthetic oil, and 590 billion cu. ft. of natural gas. Imperial is one of Canada's top natural gas producers, the #1 refiner and marketer of petroleum products, and a major supplier of petrochemicals. It sells petroleum products, including gasoline, heating oil, and diesel fuel, under the Esso name and other brand names. Most of the company's production comes from fields in Alberta and the Northwest Territories. Exxon Mobil owns about 70% of Imperial.

Imperial owns 25% of Syncrude Canada, which operates the world's largest oil sands development, with synthetic oil and bitumen/heavy oil end products. The oil company sells gasoline to motorists at 1,850 Esso gas stations (540 company-owned or leased) across Canada.

Imperial's petroleum products and chemicals business operates four refineries (with a collective capacity to process 500,000 gallons a day) and has an extensive network of wholesale outlets (in addition to its gas station chain) in every region of Canada. The company's chemicals segment operates a manufacturing plant in Sarnia, Ontario, and a number of distribution centers across Canada.

Expanding its exploration and production assets, in 2007 Imperial and ExxonMobil Canada acquired exploration rights for a development parcel in the Beaufort Sea, and in 2008, in the Horn River area of northeastern British Columbia. At Cold Lake, Alberta, the company uses steam to recover very heavy crude and related products from oil sands deposits (120,000 barrels per day in 2009) through its participation in Syncrude Project. Management is seeking to boost production from its plentiful oil sands holdings; its research laboratories in Ontario and Alberta are focused on developing technology for finding better ways to recover heavy oil.

In 2009 the company reported depressed earnings, an effect of the global recession that reduced oil and gas prices and demand.

HISTORY

London, Ontario, boomed from the discovery of oil in the 1860s and 1870s, but when the market for Canadian kerosene became saturated in 1880, 16 refiners banded together to form the Imperial Oil Company.

The company refined sulfurous Canadian oil, nicknamed "skunk oil" for its powerful smell. Imperial faced tough competition from America's Standard Oil, which marketed kerosene made from lighter, less-odorous Pennsylvania crude. Guided by American expatriate Jacob Englehart, Imperial built a better refinery and hired a chemist to develop a process to clean sulfur from the crude.

By the mid-1890s Imperial had expanded from coast to Canadian coast. Cash-starved from its expansion, the company turned to old nemesis Standard Oil, which bought a controlling interest in Imperial in 1898. That interest is today held by Exxon Mobil.

After the turn of the century, Imperial began producing gasoline to serve the new automobiles. The horseless carriages were spooking the workhorses at the warehouse where fuel was sold, so an Imperial manager in Vancouver opened the first Canadian service station in 1907. The company marketed its gas under the Esso banner borrowed from Standard Oil.

An Imperial crew discovered oil in 1920 at Norman Wells in the remote Northwest Territories. In 1924 a subsidiary sparked a new boom with a gas well discovery in the Turner Valley area northeast of Edmonton. But soon Imperial's luck ran as dry as the holes it was drilling; it came away empty from the next 133 consecutive wells. That string ended in 1947 when it struck oil in Alberta at the Leduc No. 1. To get the oil to market, Imperial invested in the Interprovincial Pipe Line from Alberta to Superior, Wisconsin.

The company began research in 1964 to extract bitumen from the oil sands in Cold Lake, Alberta. During the 1970s oil crisis, Imperial continued to search for oil in northern Canada. It found crude on land near the Beaufort Sea (1970) and in its icy waters (1972). The company formed its Esso Resources Canadian Ltd. subsidiary in 1978 to oversee natural resources production.

In 1989 Texaco (acquired by Chevron in 2001), still reeling from a court battle with Pennzoil, sold Texaco Canada to Imperial. To diminish debt and comply with regulators, Imperial agreed to sell some of Texaco Canada's refining and marketing assets in Atlantic Canada, its interests in Interhome Energy, and oil and gas properties in western Canada.

Imperial reorganized in 1992, centralizing several units, and in 1993 closed its refinery at Port Moody, British Columbia. It sold most of its fertilizer business in 1994, disposed of 339 unprofitable gas stations in 1995, and the next year closed down Canada's northernmost oil refinery at Norman Wells.

In 1997 Imperial announced an ambitious program to expand Syncrude's oil sands bitumen upgrading plant. In 1998 Exxon agreed to buy Mobil, which had substantial Canadian oil assets. In 1999 Canada preapproved the potential merger of Imperial Oil and Mobil Canada. Later that year Exxon completed its purchase of Mobil to form Exxon Mobil.

EXECUTIVES

Chairman, President, and CEO: Bruce H. March, age 53, $3,264,452 total compensation
SVP Finance and Administration and Treasurer: Paul J. Masschelin, age 55
SVP Resources Division: T. G. (Glenn) Scott
VP, General Counsel, and Corporate Secretary: Brian W. Livingston
VP Human Resources: Brian G. Hallamore
VP; General Manager, Fuels Marketing: Simon M. Smith, $2,143,291 total compensation
VP; General Manager, Refining and Supply: Chris W. Erickson, $2,310,910 total compensation
Director Corporate Planning: George E. Bezaire
Public Affairs: Kimberley Fox
Controller: Sean R. Carleton
Investor Relations: Mark Stumpf
Assistant Secretary: Brent Latimer
Auditors: PricewaterhouseCoopers LLP

LOCATIONS

HQ: Imperial Oil Limited
237 4th Ave. SW
Calgary, Alberta T2P 3M9, Canada
Phone: 800-567-3776   **Fax:** 800-367-0585
Web: www.imperialoil.ca

PRODUCTS/OPERATIONS

2009 Sales

	% of total
Refining & marketing	79
Exploration & production	17
Chemicals	4
Total	**100**

COMPETITORS

Abraxas Petroleum
Ashland Inc.
Barnwell Industries
BHP Billiton
BP
Canadian Natural
ConocoPhillips
Devon Energy
Dominion Resources
DuPont
Encana
Eni
Hunting
Husky Energy
Koch Industries, Inc.
Marathon Oil
Murphy Oil
Occidental Petroleum
PEMEX
PETROBRAS
Petróleos de Venezuela
Pioneer Natural Resources
Royal Dutch Shell
Suncor
Sunoco
Talisman Energy
TOTAL

HISTORICAL FINANCIALS

Company Type: Public

Income Statement

FYE: December 31

	REVENUE ($ mil.)	NET INCOME ($ mil.)	NET PROFIT MARGIN	EMPLOYEES
12/09	20,390	1,505	7.4%	5,015
12/08	25,825	3,172	12.3%	4,850
12/07	25,909	3,246	12.5%	4,800
12/06	21,253	2,610	12.3%	4,900
12/05	24,196	2,230	9.2%	5,100
Annual Growth	(4.2%)	(9.4%)	—	(0.4%)

2009 Year-End Financials

Debt ratio: 30.4%
Return on equity: 18.3%
Cash ($ mil.): 489
Current ratio: 0.93
Long-term debt ($ mil.): 2,735

No. of shares (mil.): 848
Dividends
   Yield: 1.0%
   Payout: 21.7%
Market value ($ mil.): 31,225

Stock History

NYSE Amex: IMO

	STOCK PRICE ($) FY Close	P/E High/Low	Earnings	PER SHARE ($) Dividends	Book Value
12/09	36.84	23 15	1.75	0.38	10.61
12/08	27.58	14 5	3.57	0.31	8.75
12/07	55.78	18 9	3.47	0.36	9.52
12/06	31.58	13 10	2.67	0.27	7.49
12/05	28.48	15 7	2.17	0.27	6.71
Annual Growth	6.6%	— —	(5.2%)	8.9%	12.1%

Imperial Tobacco

The UK's #1 cigarette maker, Imperial Tobacco Group has traded up to an even bigger throne. Its acquisition of Spain's Altadis in 2008 added the Montecristo and Ducados brands. Its purchase of German tobacco firm Reemtsma (Davidoff and West cigarettes) doubled its size and made it one of the world's top tobacco firms. Imperial's other brands include Lambert & Butler, the UK's #1 cigarette, as well as Castella cigars, and Amphora and St Bruno pipe tobacco. Its Drum brand is the #1 hand-rolling tobacco worldwide, and Rizla is a top cigarette paper. Acquisitions in Australia and New Zealand have assured Imperial's presence in emerging markets. It bought Commonwealth Brands, the #4 US tobacco company, in 2007.

Adding Altadis, owner of the world's largest cigar operation, to its portfolio created the second-largest European cigarette company (behind British American Tobacco). As a result of the acquisition, Altadis' cigarette operation will be combined with Imperial's, while Imperial's cigar business will be integrated into Altadis' cigar operations and remain headquartered in Madrid. In a follow-on purchase, Imperial acquired Altadis' separately listed distribution unit, Cia. de Distribucion Integral Logista, adding a new business segment to its activities. Logistica delivers tobacco products for international manufacturers, including Imperial, to tobacconists and other sales outlets across Southern Europe. As part of the deal with Altadis, Imperial Tobacco sold its fine cut tobacco brand Interval and several other brands to Philip Morris International.

In mid-2008 Imperial announced a three-year restructuring project in Europe to integrate its business with that of Altadis. To that end, about 2,400 jobs (equal to about 6% of the combined workforce of the two companies) were cut in the aftermath of the acquisition.

The Altadis acquisition and that of Commonwealth Brands in the US greatly increased Imperial's global presence and portfolio of brands in both cigarettes and other tobacco products, including cigars and fine cut tobacco. In addition to a strong presence in mature markets (the company controls about 46% of the UK cigarette market), Imperial has upped its exposure to emerging markets in Africa, Asia, Eastern Europe, and the Middle East. In China, Imperial has signed a 10-year deal to produce and sell cigarettes. Worldwide the company operates more than 30 cigarette factories, about 15 tobacco product factories, eight tobacco processing plants, and several facilities that manufacture rolling papers and tubes.

Like rivals British American Tobacco and Gallaher, Imperial was spun off from a conglomerate eager to distance itself from increasingly litigious tobacco operations. (It was part of Hanson until that group's 1996 four-way split.) In 2005 Imperial restructured its European production, resulting in the closure of its operations in Dublin, Ireland, and nearly 100 job cuts.

In May 2010 COO Alison Cooper succeeded the retiring Gareth Davis as CEO of the company. Cooper joined Imperial Tobacco Group in 1999.

HISTORY

Imperial Tobacco Group was formed in 1901 to fight American Tobacco's invasion of the UK. American Tobacco had become the dominant US tobacco company partly by using a large cash reserve to undercut competitors. When it bought UK tobacco and cigarette factory Ogden's that year, 13 UK tobacco firms responded by registering as The Imperial Tobacco Company. The firms (including Wills, Lambert & Butler, and John Player & Sons) continued to make and sell their products separately.

As expected, American Tobacco cut prices, and Imperial fought back, acquiring the Salmon & Cluckstein tobacco shop chain and offering bonuses to retailers that sold its products. When Imperial threatened US expansion in 1902, American Tobacco surrendered: It gave Ogden's to Imperial and halted its Ireland and Great Britain business in exchange for Imperial's pledge to stay out of the US (except for buying tobacco leaf). The two formed the British American Tobacco Company (BAT) to sell both firms' cigarettes overseas. But when American Tobacco split into four companies in 1911 and sold its BAT interest, the agreement was modified to let Imperial sell some of its brands in the US.

By the 1950s Imperial controlled more than 80% of the UK tobacco market, but its share decreased during the 1960s due to competition from Gallaher Group (Benson & Hedges). Imperial diversified, buying companies such as Golden Wonder Crisps snack food (1961) and the Courage & Barclay brewery (1972).

In 1973 BAT and Imperial agreed that each firm would control its own brands in the UK and Continental Europe. Imperial sold the last of its stake in BAT in 1980. Conglomerate Hanson Trust paid $4.3 billion for Imperial in a 1986 hostile takeover. Hanson reduced Imperial's tobacco brands from more than 100 to five brand families (a move that decreased its UK market share to 33% by 1990). It also sold Imperial's drinks unit, including Courage and John Smith beer, to Elders IXL (now Foster's Brewing). Between 1986 and 1993 Hanson cut Imperial's tobacco operations from five factories and 7,500 employees to three factories and 2,600 employees; it also sold Imperial's restaurant and food operations.

As UK cigarette consumption dropped, Imperial began expanding overseas in 1994. By 1996 exports had risen to 15% of sales. That year Gareth Davis became CEO of Imperial.

Facing further declining UK cigarette sales and a government tax hike, Imperial bought the world's #1 cigarette paper brand, Rizla (1997), and Sara Lee's cut-tobacco unit, Douwe Egberts Van Nelle (1998). In 1999 it added a bevy of Australian and New Zealand brands (Horizon, Brandon, Flagship, Peter Stuyvesant) from BAT.

Imperial expanded operations in Africa in 2001 with the acquisition of 75% of Tobaccor. It also began distributing the Marlboro brand in the UK. The company bought 90% of Reemtsma in 2002 for $5.1 billion.

In 2004 Imperial cut 940 jobs as it closed manufacturing plants in Hungary, Slovakia, and Slovenia. The company shifted production to Germany and Poland. More cuts arrived in 2005 with the closing of a plant in Dublin.

In February 2007 Imperial Tobacco acquired the Commonwealth Brands cigarette division of Houchens Industries for $1.9 billion.

In January 2008 the company completed the purchase of Altadis for $18.2 billion. In May it completed the purchase of Altadis's Logista tobacco and tobacco products distribution business. In April Imperial sold its nearly 50% stake in the Aldeasa, a duty-free retailer based in Spain, to Autogrill Espana for about €355 million ($496 million).

EXECUTIVES

Chairman: Iain J. G. Napier, age 61, $859,614 total compensation
CEO and Board Member: Alison J. Cooper, age 44, $2,125,773 total compensation
Finance Director and Board Member: Robert (Bob) Dyrbus, age 58, $4,432,688 total compensation
Group Sales and Marketing Director and Board Member: Graham L. Blashill, age 63, $2,377,613 total compensation
General Counsel, Secretary, and Board Member: Matthew Phillips, age 39
Group Human Resources Director: Kathryn A. Turner, age 54
Group Press Officer: Simon Evans
Director Manufacturing: Gary L. Aldridge
Head Corporate Communications: Alex Parsons
Manager Investor Relations: John Nelson-Smith
CEO, Commonwealth Brands: Jonathan Cox
CEO, Reemtsma Cigarettenfabriken: Richard Gretler
COO, Cigar Business Unit: Fernando Domínguez, age 50
General Manager, Altadis: Dominic Brisby
Auditors: PricewaterhouseCoopers LLP

LOCATIONS

HQ: Imperial Tobacco Group PLC
   Upton Road
   Bristol BS99 7UJ, United Kingdom
Phone: 44-117-963-6636   **Fax:** 44-117-966-7405
Web: www.imperial-tobacco.com

2009 Sales

	% of total
European Union	82
Americas	5
Other	13
Total	**100**

PRODUCTS/OPERATIONS

2009 Sales

	% of total
Tobacco (manufacturing, marketing & sale)	66
Logistics (distribution of tobacco products)	34
Total	**100**

Selected Products and Brands

Cigarettes
   Bastos
   Cohiba
   Davidoff (flagship brand)
   Drum (roll-your-own tobacco)
   Ducados
   Embassy
   Excellence
   Fortuna
   Gauloises
   Gitanes
   Golden Virginia (launched in the UK in 1877)
   Horizon
   John Player (Blue, Special)
   Lambert & Butler (discount brand)
   Montecristo
   Prima
   R1
   Regal
   Richmond (discount brand)
   Rizla (rolling paper)
   Route 66 (American blend sold in France, Belgium, and Eastern Europe)
   Superkings
   West (sold in more than 100 countries)

Cigars
  Antonio y Cléopatra
  Cadena
  Castella
  Classic
  Farias
  Hav-A-Tampa
  Montecristo
  Panama
Rolling paper and tobacco
  Amphora
  Drum
  Rizla (rolling paper)
  St Bruno

COMPETITORS

Altria
British American Tobacco
General Cigar
Gudang Garam
Japan Tobacco
JT International
Lorillard
Philip Morris International
Reynolds American
Swedish Match
Swisher International
UST llc

HISTORICAL FINANCIALS

Company Type: Public

Income Statement

FYE: September 30

	REVENUE ($ mil.)	NET INCOME ($ mil.)	NET PROFIT MARGIN	EMPLOYEES
9/09	23,477	1,055	4.5%	39,664
9/08	18,380	778	4.2%	32,316
9/07	6,713	1,852	27.6%	14,221
9/06	5,920	1,593	26.9%	14,486
9/05	5,504	1,382	25.1%	14,428
Annual Growth	43.7%	(6.5%)	—	28.8%

2009 Year-End Financials

Debt ratio: —
Return on equity: 9.6%
Cash ($ mil.): 1,649
Current ratio: —
Long-term debt ($ mil.): —

No. of shares (mil.): 1,016
Dividends
  Yield: 3.5%
  Payout: —
Market value ($ mil.): 29,255

Stock History

Pink Sheets: ITYBY

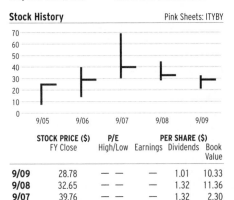

	STOCK PRICE ($) FY Close	P/E High/Low	PER SHARE ($) Earnings	Dividends	Book Value
9/09	28.78	— —	—	1.01	10.33
9/08	32.65	— —	—	1.32	11.36
9/07	39.76	— —	—	1.32	2.30
9/06	28.89	— —	—	1.09	1.10
9/05	24.81	— —	—	0.91	1.22
Annual Growth	3.8%	— —	—	2.6%	70.5%

Infosys Technologies

Infosys emphasizes every aspect of IT. One of India's leading technology services firms, Infosys Technologies provides software development and engineering to corporate clients through a network of development centers in Asia, Europe, and North America. It also provides data management, systems integration, project management, support, and maintenance services. Subsidiary Infosys BPO offers business process outsourcing (BPO) services, and US-based Infosys Consulting provides strategic consulting. Infosys gets effectively all of its sales from international markets, with North America accounting for two-thirds of the total. Clients come mainly from the financial services, manufacturing, telecom, and retail industries.

Geographic expansion is the key component of Infosys' growth strategy. The percentage of total company sales that comes from North America, for example, continues to rise as the demand for outsourced IT services grows. Meanwhile, sales to customers in Western Europe have declined at a similar rate in recent years. The company has identified Australia, China, Eastern Europe, and Latin America as growth areas.

The company established a new subsidiary called Infosys Public Services in 2010 to address the market for outsourcing and consulting services to the US government. Infosys added to its US holdings the previous year with the purchase of Atlanta-based BPO specialist McCamish Systems for $38 million. The deal served to bolster its portfolio of services for the insurance and financial services industries, which account for about one third of sales. Infosys said later in 2009 that it plans to double its workforce in the US where it forsees a continued increase in demand for outsourcing contracts.

Infosys added to its operations in Europe during 2009 when it established a regional subsidiary in Sweden. This followed a snag in European expansion plans the previous year when the company lost out to rival HCL Technologies in a bid to acquire UK-based Axon Group.

Closer to home the company is investing in its infrastructure to handle the increased demands on human resources required by the growth of its business. Infosys opened a new training facility in India in 2010 to prepare more personnel for their development and support duties.

Narayana Murthy, Infosys' high-profile founder and chairman, owns about 4% of the company.

HISTORY

After receiving a master's degree in electrical engineering from one of India's highly regarded Institutes of Technology (Kanpur) in the 1960s, Narayana Murthy left for France and a job developing software for the air traffic control system at Paris' Charles de Gaulle airport.

During college Murthy had developed the belief that communism was the answer to his country's problems with poverty and corruption, a stance that was fortified during his time spent with Paris leftists in the 1970s. But while hitchhiking back to India in 1974, Murthy's Marxist sympathies eroded quickly after he was jailed in Hungary for allegedly disclosing state secrets while talking with Austrian tourists on a train.

Murthy became a socialist at heart but capitalist in practice, setting out on a mission to create wealth rather than redistribute poverty.

That mission officially began in 1981, when Murthy convinced six fellow software engineers to start their own company. Infosys was founded that year with $250 in capital (mostly borrowed from their wives) and no idea of what it would sell.

From the beginning Murthy looked for business outside India, where he was able to sell customizable, inexpensive software to multinational corporations, such as Reebok and Nordstrom. But a lack of reputation and government regulations made business difficult for Infosys during the 1980s — it took nine months just to get the company's first telephone line, and three years to import new computers. Infosys opened its first US office in 1987.

Many of the government regulations that had kept India's economy stagnant were lifted when reform swept the country in 1991. But this also opened the door for companies such as IBM (which had been asked to leave in 1977) and Digital Equipment (later acquired by Compaq) to enter India and lure away its best engineers. While no Indian company had ever done this before, Murthy initiated a stock option plan and other perks to retain his employees. Infosys went public in 1993. Morgan Stanley swooped in to salvage the undersubscribed IPO in a move that would later reap millions when Infosys' stock began to soar.

In 1995 Infosys lost its biggest customer, General Electric, which had accounted for more than 20% of sales. Murthy took it as a lesson to never let one client or product drive more than 10% of a business. Infosys responded quickly by inking big deals with Xerox, Levi Strauss, and Nynex. By 2003 the company's biggest customer accounted for only about 6% of revenues.

Infosys grew rapidly in the mid-1990s by signing short-term pilot projects that it leveraged into more extensive contracts for managing mainframe upgrades, designing custom software, and implementing e-commerce systems.

In the late 1990s Infosys established offices in Canada, Japan, and the UK to better market its offshore development capabilities. The move paid off — by the end of fiscal 1999, sales had reached $121 million. That year Infosys became the first Indian company to list its shares on Nasdaq, an offering timed perfectly with the surge in demand for technology stocks. Infosys' market cap ballooned to more than $17 billion in 2000.

The company that year inked a long-term pact with Microsoft to dedicate more than 1,200 engineers to build e-commerce, financial services, and customer relationship management applications for the software giant.

Not immune to the slowing economy, Murthy saw his wealth drastically decrease in 2001; he lost more than $100 million due to Infosys' declining share value. In 2002 Murthy stepped down from the daily management of the company; co-founder Nandan Nilekani took over as CEO, while Murthy remained chairman.

Also in 2002 Infosys launched a new subsidiary, Progeon, to provide business process outsourcing services. The company launched Infosys Consulting in 2004 in hopes of capturing additional business in the US.

Nilekani was replaced as CEO by Kris Gopalakrishnan in 2007.

EXECUTIVES

Chairperson and Chief Mentor: N. R. Narayana Murthy, age 64
CEO, Managing Director, and Head, Executive Council: S. (Kris) Gopalakrishnan, age 55
COO and Director: S. D. Shibulal, age 55
SVP and CFO: V. Balakrishnan, age 45
SVP and Group Head, Human Resources: Nandita Mohan Gurjar
SVP and Head, Infrastructure Management Services: Priti Jay Rao, age 50
SVP and Head, India Business: Binod H. Rangadore, age 47
SVP Communication, Media, and Entertainment and Head, Global Sales, Alliances, and Marketing: Subhash B. Dhar, age 44
VP Information Systems: K. (Sury) Suryaprakash, age 41
Chief Risk Officer: M. D. (Ranga) Ranganath, age 44
Director and Head, Administration, Education and Research, Finance, Human Resources Development, and Infosys Leadership Institute: T. V. Mohandas (Mohan) Pai, age 51
Director and Head, Quality, Information Systems, and Communication Design Group; Chairman, Infosys Australia: Krishnaswamy Dinesh, age 56
Head, Consulting Solutions; CEO and Managing Director, Infosys Consulting: Stephen R. (Steve) Pratt
Head, Legal: Samuel M. Kallupurakal
Company Secretary and Compliance Officer: Parvatheesam Kanchinadham
Senior Manager Investor Relations, United States: Sandeep Mahindroo
Auditors: KPMG

LOCATIONS

HQ: Infosys Technologies Limited
Electronics City, Hosur Road
Bangalore, Karnataka 560 100, India
Phone: 91-80-2852-0261   **Fax:** 91-80-2852-0362
Web: www.infosys.com

2010 Sales

	% of total
North America	66
Europe	23
India	1
Other regions	10
Total	**100**

PRODUCTS/OPERATIONS

2010 Sales

	% of total
Financial services	34
Manufacturing	20
Telecommunications	16
Retail	13
Other	17
Total	**100**

Selected Services

Business process management
Custom application development
Engineering
Information technology consulting
Infrastructure management
Maintenance and production support
Management consulting
Operations and business process consulting
Package evaluation and implementation
Software re-engineering
Systems integration
Testing

COMPETITORS

Accenture
Atos Origin
Capgemini
Cognizant Tech Solutions
Computer Sciences Corp.
Deloitte Consulting
Genpact
HCL Technologies
HP Enterprise Business
HP Enterprise Services
IBM Global Services
Keane
Logica
MindTree
Oracle
Patni Computer Systems
Perot Systems
SAP
Satyam
Tata Consultancy
Wipro Technologies
WNS (Holdings)

HISTORICAL FINANCIALS

Company Type: Public

Income Statement

FYE: March 31

	REVENUE ($ mil.)	NET INCOME ($ mil.)	NET PROFIT MARGIN	EMPLOYEES
3/10	4,804	1,313	27.3%	113,800
3/09	4,663	1,281	27.5%	104,900
3/08	4,176	1,155	27.7%	91,200
3/07	3,090	850	27.5%	72,200
3/06	2,152	555	25.8%	52,700
Annual Growth	**22.2%**	**24.0%**	**—**	**21.2%**

2010 Year-End Financials

Debt ratio: —
Return on equity: 28.7%
Cash ($ mil.): 2,698
Current ratio: 6.56
Long-term debt ($ mil.): —
No. of shares (mil.): 571
Dividends
  Yield: 0.8%
  Payout: 20.0%
Market value ($ mil.): 33,592

Stock History

NASDAQ (GS): INFY

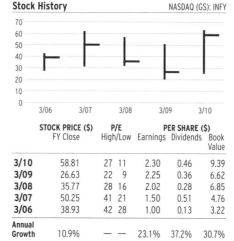

	STOCK PRICE ($) FY Close	P/E High/Low		PER SHARE ($) Earnings	Dividends	Book Value
3/10	58.81	27	11	2.30	0.46	9.39
3/09	26.63	22	9	2.25	0.36	6.62
3/08	35.77	28	16	2.02	0.28	6.85
3/07	50.25	41	21	1.50	0.51	4.76
3/06	38.93	42	28	1.00	0.13	3.22
Annual Growth	**10.9%**	**—**	**—**	**23.1%**	**37.2%**	**30.7%**

ING Groep

ING Groep is a Dutch hybrid of bank*ing*, in*suring*, and asset-manag*ing* services. One of the world's largest insurance and financial services companies, its operations are focused on its home Benelux market, as well as the rest of Europe, the Asia/Pacific region, and North America. Key products include life and non-life insurance, pensions, and retirement services. The company's banking operations include wholesale and retail banking, mortgage lending, and online retail banking (ING Direct). ING provides asset management for individuals and institutions through both its insurance and banking units. The firm has announced plans to spin or sell off its insurance operations to repay government bailout loans.

Amid the global financial crisis of 2008, ING accepted a €10 billion (more than $13 billion) loan from the Dutch government. The bailout was intended to shore up the company's capital position and reassure wary investors. Strategic measures were taken in 2009 to further offset losses and repay debt, including layoffs (starting with CEO Michael Tilmant, who stepped down and was replaced by former chairman Jan Hommen) and asset sales. By the end of 2009 job cuts totaled about 10% of its workforce, and the company announced plans to split the company in half after determining that more drastic measures would be necessary.

ING's restructuring plan encompasses the sale of the entire insurance division, which includes businesses in Europe, the Americas, and the Asia/Pacific. The plan also includes the divestiture of the company's insurance-related investment management operations, the ING Direct USA business, and select banking operations in the Netherlands. Through its restructuring measures and stock rights issuances the company was able to repay half of the funds received through the Dutch government bailout at the end of 2009.

Asset divestitures resulting from the initiatives have thus far included the early 2010 sales of the company's Swiss Private Banking unit to Julius Baer for $506 million and its Asian Private Banking unit (operating in Hong Kong, the Philippines, and Singapore) to OCBC Bank for nearly $1.5 billion. In addition, the company sold its North American reinsurance operations to RGA and most of its US insurance brokerage operations to Lightyear Capital in early 2010. ING has also agreed to sell its stake in one of its Chinese life insurance ventures (Pacific Antai with China Pacific Insurance) to China Construction Bank.

Prior to the economic meltdown, ING took aim at becoming a financial services player in all four corners of the world and made acquisitions accordingly. Along with much of the insurance industry, it shifted its base from traditional life insurance products to investment-backed products, which favor companies that can sell through banks. ING utilized its owns banks to distribute such products.

In more mature markets like North America and Europe, the company has had the aging population in its sights and placed retirement planning and pensions as sources of future growth. In 2008 the company acquired CitiStreet, a leading US administrator of defined-contribution retirement savings, pension, health, and other plans; it paid about $900 million for the firm.

HISTORY

ING Groep's roots go back to 1845 when its earliest predecessor, the Netherlands Insurance Co., was founded. The firm began expanding geographically; in 1903 it added life insurance. In 1963 it merged with the century-old Nationale Life Insurance Bank to form Nationale-Nederland (NN). Over the next three decades, the company grew primarily through acquisitions in Europe, North America, and Australia. In 1986 NN became the first European life insurance company to be licensed in Japan.

Another predecessor, the Rijkspostspaarbank, was founded in 1881 to provide Dutch citizens with simple post office savings accounts. In 1918 the Postcheque-en Girondienst (giro) system was established to allow people to use vouchers drawn on their savings accounts to pay bills. This system became the main method of settling accounts (instead of bank checking accounts).

Rijkspostspaarbank and Postcheque merged in 1986 to become Postbank. Postbank merged in 1989 with the Nederlandse Middenstandsbank (founded 1927) to become NMB Postbank. The vast amounts of cash tied up in the post office savings and giro systems fueled NMB's business.

In 1991, as the European economic union became a reality and barriers between banking and insurance began to fall, NN merged with NMB Postbank to form Internationale Nederland Groep (ING). ING began cutting costs, shedding redundant offices and unprofitable operations in both its segments. In the US, where insurance and banking were legally divided, the company "debanked" itself in order to keep its more lucrative insurance operations (but retained the right to provide banking services to those operations).

ING sought to increase its investment banking and finance operations in the 1990s. In 1995 it took over UK-based Barings Bank (personal banker to the Queen of England) after Nicholas Leeson, a trader in Barings' Singapore office, lost huge sums of money in derivatives trading. The acquisition gave the firm a higher profile but left it embroiled in lingering legal actions.

In 1997 ING expanded its securities business by acquiring investment bank Furman Selz, doubled its US life insurance operations by purchasing Equitable of Iowa, and listed on the NYSE. In 1998 ING's acquisition strategy again involved Europe and North America: It bought Belgium's Banque Bruxelles Lambert and Canadian life insurer Guardian Insurance Co.

ING turned eastward in 1999, kicking off asset management operations in India and buying a minority stake in South Korea's HC&B (formerly Housing & Commercial Bank). In 2000 the company bulked up its North American operations with the purchase of 40% of Savia SA, a Mexican insurance concern. It also bought US firm ReliaStar Financial in a $6 billion deal.

The company struggled with investment banking arm ING Barings. The unit was reorganized and streamlined for cost-savings purposes, but ultimately was put on the block. Its Asian equities operations were sold to Macquarie Bank in 2004. Barings Private Equity Partners unit was sold to its management. The Barings investment management operations were sold to MassMutual in 2005, while Northern Trust bought up its fund administration, trust, and custody operations.

In 2005 ING turned over its US life reinsurance operations to Scottish Re. ING acquired a 20% stake in the Bank of Beijing as part of a strategic alliance. In 2006 the company sold off its UK brokerage business, Williams de Broë, to The Evolution Group.

EXECUTIVES

Chairman Supervisory Board: Peter A. F. W. Elverding, age 62
Chairman Executive Board: Jan H. M. Hommen, age 67
Member Executive Board and CFO: Patrick Flynn, age 50, $650,673 total compensation
CEO, Commercial Banking; Vice Chairman, Management Board Banking: Eric Boyer de la Giroday, age 57, $1,278,414 total compensation
Member Executive Board and Chief Risk Officer: Koos Timmermans, age 50, $978,813 total compensation
CEO, Retail Banking Direct and International, Management Board Banking: Eli P. Leenaars, age 48, $396,996 total compensation
COO Insurance; Management Board Insurance: Thomas J. (Tom) McInerney, age 53, $579,013 total compensation
Management Board Banking: Hans van der Noordaa, age 48, $396,996 total compensation
Management Board, Insurance: Matthew J. Rider
President, U.S. Retail Life Distribution: Daniel P. (Dan) Mulheran, age 60
President, ING Advisors Network: Valerie Brown
CEO, ING Insurance U.S.: Rob Leary
CEO, ING Investment Management: Gilbert Van Hassel
Chief Financial and Risk Officer, ING Investment Management, Europe: Jonathan Atack, age 46
Head Media Relations: Peter Jong
Head Group Investor Relations: Dorothy Hillenius, age 40
Head of Operations and Information Technology Banking: Steve Van Wyk
Chairman, Vysya Bank: K. R. Ramamoorthy
Auditors: Ernst & Young Accountants

LOCATIONS

HQ: ING Groep N.V.
ING House, Amstelveenseweg 500
1081 KL Amsterdam, The Netherlands
Phone: 31-20-541-5411 **Fax:** 31-20-541-5497
US HQ: 1325 Avenue of the Americas
New York, NY 10019
US Phone: 646-424-6000 **US Fax:** 646-424-6060
Web: www.ing.com

2009 Sales

	% of total
Europe	
The Netherlands	25
Belgium	9
Other European countries	15
North America	30
Asia	17
Latin America	2
Australia	2
Total	**100**

PRODUCTS/OPERATIONS

2009 Sales

	% of total
Insurance	
Life premiums	61
Non-life premiums	4
Commission income	4
Investment & other	7
Banking	24
Total	**100**

Selected Subsidiaries and Affiliates

Insurance operations
ING Afore S.A. de C.V. (Mexico)
ING America Insurance Holdings, Inc. (US)
ING Asigurari de Viata S.A. (Romania)
ING Greek Life Insurance Company S.A.
ING Nationale-Nederlanden Magyarorszagi Biztosito Rt. (Hungary)
ING Nationale-Nederlanden Polska S.A.
ING North America Insurance Corporation (US)
ING Verzekeringen N.V.
ING Zivotna Poistovna a.s. (Slovakia)
Lion Connecticut Holdings Inc. (US)
Movir N.V.

Nationale Nederlanden Generales, Compañía de Seguros y Reaseguros S.A. (Spain)
Nationale-Nederlanden Levensverzekering Maatschappij N.V.
ReliaStar Life Insurance Company (US)
RVS Levensverzekering N.V.
RVS Schadeverzekering N.V.
Security Life of Denver Insurance Company (US)
Banking operations
Bank Mendes Gans N.V.
ING Bank N.V.
ING Bank A.S. (Turkey)
ING Bank Deutschland A.G.
ING Bank Slaski S.A. (Poland)
ING België N.V. (Belgium)
ING Direct N.V.
ING Financial Holdings Corporation (US)
ING Middenbank Curaçao N.V. (Netherlands Antilles)
ING Vysya Bank Ltd. (India)

COMPETITORS

ABN AMRO Group	The Hartford
Achmea	HSBC
AEGON	KBC
AIG	Legal & General Group
Allianz	Lincoln Financial Group
Aviva	MetLife
AXA	Nationwide
Barclays	Principal Financial
Citigroup	Prudential
CNP Assurances	Prudential plc
Credit Suisse	Rabobank
Deutsche Bank	RSA Insurance
Deutsche Bundesbank	Swiss Life
Fortis Insurance	UBS
Generali	Zurich Financial Services

HISTORICAL FINANCIALS

Company Type: Public

Income Statement

FYE: December 31

	ASSETS ($ mil.)	NET INCOME ($ mil.)	INCOME AS % OF ASSETS	EMPLOYEES
12/09	1,662,472	(2,209)	—	110,325
12/08	1,884,207	(1,031)	—	124,661
12/07	1,929,568	13,586	0.7%	120,282
12/06	1,619,275	10,157	0.6%	118,243
12/05	1,376,770	8,930	0.6%	115,328
Annual Growth	**4.8%**	**—**	**—**	**(1.1%)**

2009 Year-End Financials

Equity as % of assets: 3.1%
Return on assets: —
Return on equity: —
Long-term debt ($ mil.): 236,055
No. of shares (mil.): 3,832
Dividends
Yield: 0.0%
Payout: —
Market value ($ mil.): 53,871
Sales ($ mil.): 164,222

Stock History

NYSE: ING

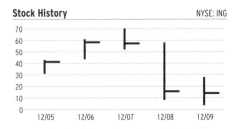

	STOCK PRICE ($) FY Close	P/E High/Low		PER SHARE ($) Earnings	Dividends	Book Value
12/09	14.06	—	—	(1.07)	0.00	13.51
12/08	15.65	—	—	(0.51)	2.19	10.09
12/07	57.27	11	8	6.30	2.05	14.28
12/06	58.27	13	10	4.66	1.57	13.26
12/05	41.24	11	8	3.93	1.35	11.92
Annual Growth	**(23.6%)**	**—**	**—**	**—**	**—**	**3.2%**

Intesa Sanpaolo

Intesa Sanpaolo is the result of the mega-merger of the former Banca Intesa and Sanpaolo IMI, which joined forces at the beginning of 2007. The combined institution provides retail and commercial banking services through its Banca dei Territori division. The company operates from approximately 6,300 branches throughout Italy, plus more than 1,900 locations in Central and Eastern Europe, as well as the Mediterranean basin. Intesa Sanpaolo also performs investment banking, public and infrastructure finance, factoring, and trade financing services. The company's Eurizon Financial Group unit includes life insurer Eurizon Vita, asset manager Eurizon Capital, and financial planner Banca Fideuram.

Intesa Sanpaolo is selling up to 200 of its branches to France-based Crédit Agricole; the divestiture was ordered by antitrust authorities after the Intesa and Sanpaolo IMI merger. In late 2008 the Italian banking group sold 36 branches to Veneto Banca for €274 million ($401 million). The company sold its securities services arm to US money manager State Street in 2010, and has been exploring a possible sale or spinoff of Fideuram.

A good portion of its branches were acquired in 2007 when Intesa Sanpaolo increased its stake in Banca CR Firenze to some 60% in preparation for taking over the bank outright. Banca CR Firenze added about 550 locations in Tuscany and surrounding regions to Intesa Sanpaolo's network. The next year the bank upped its stake in Cassa dei Risparmi di Forlì e della Romagna to about 70%, increasing its influence in northern Italy. During more reshuffling of assets, Intesa Sanpaolo sold a 30% stake in Cassa di Risparmio di Fano to Credito Valtellinese in 2009.

Intesa Sanpaolo is working to strengthen its main Banca dei Territori division, which handles domestic commercial banking and is responsible for retail customers, individual customers and small businesses. It has agreed to buy a majority stake in Banca Monte Parma, which operates some 70 branches in central Italy. The company is also strategically expanding in foreign markets. In 2008 it opened its first branch in Dubai and entered the Ukraine market for the first time.

HISTORY

In Italy charity begins at home, and often heads to the financial institutions. In 1563 Turin citizens founded Compagnia di San Paolo, a foundation that provided education and dowries to orphaned girls and aid to impoverished nobility. In 1579 the organization began a pawn shop, the Monte di Pietà, or Mountain of Mercy (founded in 1519 and reopened by the Compagnia). The foundation grew over the next 200 years, fattened by bequests and inheritances from wealthy Piedmontese families.

The French Republican government in Piedmonte gradually took control of the foundation's operations and closed it in 1802. The Monte di Pietà was reopened in 1804 and under the French influence became more bank-like. In 1848 the charitable and financial operations were formally divided.

Industrialization came slowly to Italy after its unification in the 1860s (the country remained largely agricultural until after WWII), and the organization survived a banking crisis from 1887 to 1894 by operating conservatively. It contributed to the WWI effort by purchasing government bonds. In 1928 the foundation separated Monte di Pietà's credit and pawn operations and adopted the name Istituto di San Paolo di Torino — Beneficenza e Credito (San Paolo).

Specialized institutions were founded in the 1920s to finance utilities and transportation; one of them, La Centrale Societa per il Finanziamento di Imprese Elettriche e Telefoniche, was formed in 1925 to help finance Italy's energy and telecommunications industries. In 1965 this entity enlarged its focus and changed its name to La Centrale Finanziaria Generale, a forerunner of Banca Intesa. La Centrale's interests in energy were transferred to ENEL, the state holding company, in 1985, leaving it with banking, finance, and insurance holdings. That year the bank merged with Nuovo Banco Ambrosiano, formerly Banco Ambrosiano.

Banco Ambrosiano was founded in 1896 by Guiseppi Tovino, whose good works and sturdy faith made him a saint (he was beatified in 1998). Betraying his legacy, in 1981 chairman Roberto Calvi was found hanging under the Blackfriars Bridge in London. Calvi, called "God's Banker" for his connections to the Vatican, left behind a tangle of debt, phony holding companies, and fraud that implicated the Catholic Church, brought down an archbishop, and involved a secretive Masonic lodge. Banco Ambrosiano was taken over by a group of creditor banks and its name was changed to Nuovo Banco Ambrosiano.

In 1989, Nuovo Banco Ambrosiano merged with its subsidiary, Banco Cattolica del Veneto, and became known as Banco Ambroveneto. It bought La Cassa di Risparmio delle Provincie Lombarde (Cariplo), Italy's biggest savings bank, in 1997; they merged to form Banca Intesa the following year. Cariplo was founded by the Austro-Hungarian government in 1823, when the region was still recovering from Napoleon's depredations. Count Giovanni Pietro Porro wanted to allow artisans and day laborers to set aside money, and the company remained true to that mission throughout Italy's unification and two world wars.

Italy began its race toward privatization in 1990 to counter the growing interest of foreign banks in the Italian market and help the nation meet the criteria for joining the European Union. In 1992 San Paolo was one of the first banks to sell a 20% stake in itself (it sold another 20% in 1997). The bank bought several regional and national banks over the next few years and in 1998 merged with investment bank Istituto Mobiliare Italiano, or IMI (founded 1931), to form Sanpaolo IMI.

Banca Intesa was the product of a combination of the staid Cassa di Risparmio delle Provincie Lombarde (Cariplo) and the somewhat more colorful Banco Ambroveneto, whose history helped inspire the plot of *The Godfather, Part III*. It took over Banca Commerciale Italiana (BCI, or Comit) in 2000, creating one of Italy's largest banks. Banca Intesa integrated BCI to form IntesaBci the following year, and then in late 2002 rebranded as Banca Intesa.

Banca Intesa and Sanpaolo IMI merged in 2007.

EXECUTIVES

Chairman: Giovanni Bazoli, age 77
Deputy Chairman: Mario Bertolissi, age 62
Deputy Chairwoman: Elsa Fornero, age 62
Chairman Management Board: Enrico Salza, age 73
Deputy Chairman Management Board: Orazio Rossi, age 77
CEO, Managing Director, and Member Management Board: Corrado Passera, age 55
COO: Pier Luigi Curcuruto, age 60
CFO: Carlo Messina, age 48
Co-General Manager; Head of the Corporate and Investment Banking Division: Gaetano Miccichè, age 60
Chief Lending Officer: Eugenio Rossetti, age 54
Chief Risk Officer: Bruno Picca, age 60
Head Planning and Control: Lucia Ariano
Head Compliance: Piero Boccassino
Head Human Resources: Marco Vernieri
Head Loan Recovery: Stefano Marchetti
Head Investor Relations: Andrea Tamagnini
Head Lending Decisions: Luigi Aricò
Head Risk Management: Davide Alfonsi
Head Legal Affairs: Elisabetta Lunati
Head Corporate Affairs: Piero Luongo, age 55
Head of Administration and Tax: Ernesto Riva
Head of Research: Gregorio de Felice
Head of Corporate Relationship Management and International Network: Giuseppe Castagna
Head Investment Banking: Fabio Canè
Head Rating Agencies: Marco Delfrate
Treasurer: Stefano Del Punta
Auditors: Reconta Ernst & Young S.p.A.

LOCATIONS

HQ: Intesa Sanpaolo S.p.A.
Piazza San Carlo, 156
10121 Turin, Italy
Phone: 39-011-555-1
US HQ: 1 William St., New York, NY 10004
US Phone: 212-607-3500   **US Fax:** 212-607-3883
Web: www.group.intesasanpaolo.com

PRODUCTS/OPERATIONS

2009 Sales by Segment

	% of total
Banca dei Territori	59
Corporate & Investment Banking	20
International Subsidiary Banks	13
Banca Fideuram	4
Public Finance	2
Eurizon Capital	2
Total	**100**

COMPETITORS

Banca Popolare di Milano
Banco Popolare
BBVA
BNL bc
Dexia
Mediobanca
Monte dei Paschi di Siena
UniCredit

HISTORICAL FINANCIALS

Company Type: Public

Income Statement				FYE: December 31
	ASSETS ($ mil.)	NET INCOME ($ mil.)	INCOME AS % OF ASSETS	EMPLOYEES
12/09	895,526	4,211	0.5%	103,718
12/08	896,629	3,780	0.4%	108,310
12/07	843,254	10,827	1.3%	98,112
12/06	384,947	3,521	0.9%	99,953
12/05	323,948	3,709	1.1%	58,703
Annual Growth	28.9%	3.2%	—	15.3%

2009 Year-End Financials

Equity as % of assets: 8.6%
Return on assets: 0.5%
Return on equity: 5.7%
Long-term debt ($ mil.): —
No. of shares (mil.): 11,849

Dividends
  Yield: 0.0%
  Payout: —
Market value ($ mil.): 53,495
Sales ($ mil.): 32,087

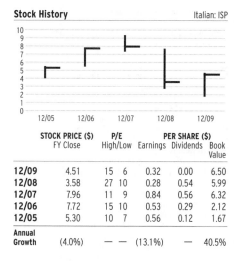

Stock History

Italian: ISP

	STOCK PRICE ($) FY Close	P/E High/Low		PER SHARE ($) Earnings	Dividends	Book Value
12/09	4.51	15	6	0.32	0.00	6.50
12/08	3.58	27	10	0.28	0.54	5.99
12/07	7.96	11	9	0.84	0.56	6.32
12/06	7.72	15	10	0.53	0.29	2.12
12/05	5.30	10	7	0.56	0.12	1.67
Annual Growth	(4.0%)	—	—	(13.1%)	—	40.5%

Invensys plc

Invensys maintains a broad inventory of ways to keep its customers in control. The company operates through three units: Controls (used in industrial equipment, HVAC systems, and appliances), Rail Group (signaling, communication, and control systems for railroads and subways), and Operations Management (which combines its Process Systems automation technology, Wonderware automation software, and Eurotherm monitoring systems divisions). Invensys operates in more than 60 countries throughout the world. Clients include BP, Chevron, Exxon Mobil, London Underground, Network Rail, Samsung, and Sub-Zero.

Invensys is moving away from customized control equipment and developing standardized control systems based on open operating systems that offer customers increased automation and flexibility. The company is aggressively targeting key international markets for growth, with new business development teams going into regions such as Southeast Asia, the Middle East, India, Germany, and Latin America — and emerging with new clients, including Codelco (Chile), ONTRACK (New Zealand), and Petrobras (Brazil).

Invensys Operations Management division acquired India-based Skelta Software in April 2010. Skelta brings its BPM (business process management) and workflow software to the Invensys' portfolio. The acquisition offers new workflow capabilities to the company's Wonderware System Platform and its InFusion Enterprise Control System. Financial terms of the deal were not disclosed.

The company continues to make acquisitions to boost niche markets in its Rail and Operations Management sectors, including Quantum Engineering (2008, £20 million, onboard train control equipment) and SAT Corporation (August 2008, £30 million, remote workflow hardware and software).

HISTORY

Immigrant Austrian artillery officer Augustus Siebe founded Siebe in London in 1819. A lifelong inventor, Siebe's creations included breechloading rifles, carbon arc lamps, the world's first diving suit, and early ice-making machines.

From the 1890s to the early 1970s, Siebe made a name for itself in marine engineering and as a maker of breathing apparatuses, developing products such as submarine escape and diving equipment for Britain's Royal Navy. General Dynamics veteran Barrie Stephens took over management of the struggling Siebe in 1963. Stephens cut costs, restructured, terminated half the workforce, and in the late 1960s, started making acquisitions.

With its 1972 purchase of European safety equipment specialist James North & Sons, Siebe began transforming from a marine-based engineer to a controls and engineering company. It expanded into continental Europe and in 1982 moved into North America with the purchase of Tecalemit (garage equipment).

Included in the Tecalemit buy were two healthy electronic controls businesses, which Stephens tried, but failed, to sell. When Siebe acquired CompAir (air compressors) in 1985 (sold 2002), the deal included three pneumatic controls companies. Without trying, Siebe had established a controls presence. That segment was strengthened further in 1986 when it bought Robertshaw (appliance controls, US). The following year's additions of US concerns Ranco and Barber-Colman added automotive, industrial, and commercial building controls.

In 1990 Siebe hit the jackpot with the $650 million acquisition of Foxboro, which had developed a UNIX-based system capable of controlling entire oil refineries and automobile plants. With the Foxboro purchase, Siebe's control business began to seriously challenge Honeywell.

Mid-to-late-1990s acquisitions included AVP (food and drinks industry equipment), Wonderware (factory application software), Eurotherm (temperature controls), and Electronic Measurement (industrial power supply). To offset costs associated with these acquisitions, Siebe began restructuring in 1998 and sold its North Safety Products Business (personal safety and life support products) to Norcross Safety Products (acquired in 2008 by Honeywell).

In 1999 Siebe acquired engineering rival BTR plc in a $6 billion deal that nearly tripled Siebe's size; the combined company changed its name to BTR Siebe and later to Invensys. Also that year the company sold more than a dozen businesses, including its automotive and aerospace operations. It also sold 90% of its Paper Technology Group to investment firm Apax Partners in a deal valued at about $800 million. Invensys' 1999 acquisitions included Best Power (uninterruptible power supplies), purchased from industrial products maker SPX for around $240 million.

Invensys formed a pact with Microsoft in early 2000 to develop standards for connecting home appliances to the Internet. Later that year the company gained control of Netherlands-based Baan Company, a near-bankrupt maker of software that allowed manufacturers to manage their internal operations, in a $709 million deal.

Early in 2002 Invensys sold its energy storage business for $425 million. That May the company reorganized and sold its flow control business to US-based Flowserve Corporation for

$535 million. Invensys also sold its Invensys Sensor Systems business to Honeywell for $415 million in cash. In late 2003 Invensys divested its metering business for about $650 million. The following year Invensys sold its Powerware subsidiary (uninterruptible power supplies and power management systems) to Eaton for $560 million.

Late in 2005 Invensys sold its power supply business, which included a majority-owned JV called Densei-Lambda, to TDK for $235 million. It also sold the European and Middle Eastern operations of its Invensys Building Systems (IBS) unit to Schneider Electric for $150 million.

The following year it sold its remaining IBS operations in the US and Asia/Pacific to Schneider for nearly $300 million. Also in 2006 the company sold foodservice equipment maker APV Baker (now Baker Perkins) to private investors. The company sold its other APV operations to SPX Corporation in 2008.

In 2007 Invensys acquired US software provider CIMNET for $23 million; CIMNET was integrated into the Wonderware business. The same year Invensys also sold its fire safety division for $44 million to United Technologies Corporation.

EXECUTIVES

Chairman: Sir Nigel R. Rudd, age 63
CEO and Director: Ulf Henriksson, age 47, $3,760,118 total compensation
COO: Gary Freburger
CFO and Director: Wayne Edmunds
Chief Human Resources Officer: Paula Larson
Chief Legal Officer and Company Secretary: Victoria Hull
Chief of Staff: Anthony Gajadharsingh
EVP and Head Corporate Communications: Steve Devany
SVP Environment, Health, and Safety: Angel Alcala
President, Invensys Controls: Mark Balcunas
President, Invensys Operations Management: Sudipta Bhattacharya
President and CEO, Rail Systems: James Drummond
Auditors: Ernst & Young LLP

LOCATIONS

HQ: Invensys plc
Portland House, Bressenden Place
London SW1E 5BF, United Kingdom
Phone: 44-20-7834-3848　　**Fax:** 44-20-7834-3879
US HQ: 5601 Granite Pkwy., Ste. 1000, Plano, TX 75024
US Phone: 469-365-6400　　**US Fax:** 469-365-6401
Web: www.invensys.com

2010 Sales

	% of total
Europe	
UK	14
Other countries	28
North America	30
Asia/Pacific	16
South America	6
Africa & Middle East	6
Total	**100**

PRODUCTS/OPERATIONS

2010 Sales

	% of total
Operations management	45
Rail Group	31
Controls	24
Total	**100**

2010 Sales by Market

	% of total
Rail transportation	31
Consumer cyclical	21
Oil & gas	12
General industries	12
Utilities & power	6
Discrete manufacturing	6
Petrochemicals	4
Basic materials	2
Pharmaceuticals	2
Other	4
Total	**100**

COMPETITORS

ABB
Eaton
Emerson Electric
Endress + Hauser
FWMurphy
GE
Honeywell International
Johnson Controls
Parker Hannifin
Rockwell Automation
Schlumberger
Schneider Electric
Siemens AG
Smiths Group
SPX
Tomkins
Yokogawa Electric

HISTORICAL FINANCIALS

Company Type: Public

Income Statement

FYE: March 31

	REVENUE ($ mil.)	NET INCOME ($ mil.)	NET PROFIT MARGIN	EMPLOYEES
3/10	3,380	222	6.6%	20,357
3/09	3,245	185	5.7%	22,139
3/08	4,204	666	15.8%	26,002
3/07	3,933	407	10.4%	27,313
3/06	4,278	33	0.8%	28,434
Annual Growth	(5.7%)	60.8%	—	(8.0%)

2010 Year-End Financials

Debt ratio: —	No. of shares (mil.): 807
Return on equity: 28.7%	Dividends
Cash ($ mil.): 548	Yield: 0.7%
Current ratio: —	Payout: —
Long-term debt ($ mil.): —	Market value ($ mil.): 4,143

Stock History

Pink Sheets: IVNYY

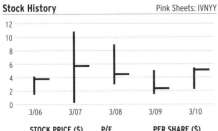

	STOCK PRICE ($) FY Close	P/E High/Low	PER SHARE ($) Earnings	Dividends	Book Value
3/10	5.13	— —	—	0.04	0.78
3/09	2.36	— —	—	0.00	1.13
3/08	4.49	— —	—	0.00	1.10
3/07	5.72	— —	—	0.00	(0.34)
3/06	3.78	— —	—	0.00	(1.28)
Annual Growth	7.9%	— —	—	—	—

Isuzu Motors

Isuzu Motors has been trucking along since 1916 as one of Japan's first automobile manufacturers. The company is one of the world's top commercial truck makers, with heavy-, medium-, and light-duty models. Isuzu is also a leading diesel engine manufacturer for such automakers as Adam Opel, GM, and Renault; its engines are used in automotive as well as industrial and marine applications. Other vehicle products include sightseeing and private buses, passenger pickup trucks, and SUVs. Its D-MAX pickup is particularly popular in Thailand and South America.

Even in light of General Motors filing for bankruptcy, Isuzu has agreed to maintain its alliance with the company. Isuzu and GM are partnered to produce diesel engines in the US and Poland.

The company, once a pioneer in the American SUV market, announced it would stop selling its pickups and SUVs in the US in 2009 after an eight-year slide in US sales. Longtime partner GM produced the two vehicles Isuzu had been selling in the US — the Ascender SUV and the i-Series pickups. GM began reducing its 49% stake in Isuzu Motors around 2002. In 2006 Toyota Motor Corp. acquired 5.9% of Isuzu after GM sold its remaining shares.

Commercial truck and bus demand is forecast to grow in developing markets, specifically China, Russia, and India (where Isuzu has established a new production facility). In 2010 Isuzu signaled a truck sales joint venture in China with Qingling Motors (Group). The venture builds on a manufacturing tie-up, started in 1985, which fostered co-production of trucks, sport utility vehicles, and diesel engines, and sales on behalf of Isuzu by Qingling Motors. It plans to double its annual capacity of trucks in China to 200,000 units by around 2015. The company also plans to construct new sales facilities in South America and the Middle East.

At home, it is maintaining a strong domestic market position, especially with its N Series light-duty line of trucks, which was launched at the end of 2006. Isuzu is also attempting to hold on to, if not surpass, its spot as the world's #4 manufacturer of diesel engines (by production volume) by continuing to invest in research and development of advanced diesel technology.

Major shareholders include Mitsubishi Corporation and two Japanese trust accounts; each hold about 9% stakes in Isuzu Motors. ITOCHU Corporation holds just under 8%.

HISTORY

After collaborating on car and truck production for 21 years, Tokyo Ishikawajima Shipbuilding and Engineering and Tokyo Gas and Electric Industrial formed Tokyo Motors, Inc. in 1937. The partners began producing the A truck (1918) and the A9 car (1922) under licenses from Wolseley (UK).

Tokyo Motors made its first truck under the Isuzu nameplate in 1938. It spun off Hino Heavy Industries in 1942. By 1943 the company was selling trucks powered by its own diesel engines, mostly to the Japanese military.

By 1948 the company was Japan's premier maker of diesel engines. It was renamed Isuzu (Japanese for "50 bells") in 1949. With generous public- and private-sector financing and truck orders from the US Army during the Korean War,

Isuzu survived and refined its engine- and truck-making prowess. A pact with the Rootes Group (UK) enabled Isuzu to enter automaking. Beginning in 1953, Isuzu built Rootes' Hillman Minx in Japan.

Despite its strong reputation as a truck builder, Isuzu suffered financially, and by the late 1960s its bankers were shopping the company around to more stable competitors. GM, after witnessing rapid Japanese progress in US and Asian auto markets, bought about 34% of Isuzu in 1971. During the 1970s Isuzu launched the popular Gemini car and gained rapid entry to the US through GM, exporting such vehicles as the Chevy Luv truck and the Buick Opel.

As exports to GM waned, Isuzu set up its own dealer network in the US in 1981. That year GM CEO Roger Smith told a stunned Isuzu chairman Toshio Okamoto that Isuzu lacked the global scale GM was seeking. Smith asked Okamoto for help in buying a piece of Honda. After Honda declined and GM settled for 5% of Suzuki, Isuzu extended its GM ties, building the Geo Storm and establishing joint production facilities in the UK and Australia.

Despite a high-profile advertising campaign featuring Joe Isuzu, the company suffered in the 1980s in its efforts to gain any kind of significant share of the US passenger car market. Post-1985 yen appreciation hurt exports. Subaru-Isuzu Automotive, a joint venture with Fuji Heavy Industries, initiated production of Rodeos in Lafayette, Indiana, in 1989.

After Isuzu lost nearly $500 million in 1991 and 1992, it called on GM for help. GM responded by sending Donald Sullivan, a strategic business planning expert, to become Isuzu's #2 operations executive. Isuzu signed a joint venture with Jiangxi Automobile Factory and ITOCHU in 1993 to build light-duty trucks in China.

Isuzu weathered a public relations storm in 1996 when *Consumer Reports* magazine claimed that the top-selling Trooper sport utility vehicle was prone to tip over at relatively low speeds. Isuzu dismissed the report as unscientific, and the National Highway Traffic Safety Administration sided with the automaker. In 1997 the company sued the magazine for defamation. (Isuzu lost the case in 2000.) Also in 1997 Isuzu agreed to develop GM's diesel engines.

The next year GM and Isuzu announced a joint venture to make diesel engines in the US. Also in 1998 Isuzu announced restructuring plans that included cutting 4,000 jobs and reducing the number of its domestic marketing subsidiaries. In 1999 GM boosted its stake in Isuzu to 49%. Isuzu also agreed to form a joint venture with Toyota to manufacture buses.

Amid mounting losses and pressure from GM, Isuzu announced a management shake-up in 2001 that included naming GM chairman John Smith Jr. as special advisor and installing Randall Schwarz (GM truck group) as vice president.

Isuzu had some rocky going in the early part of the 21st century. The company asked its creditor banks to forgive 100 billion yen (about $750 million) in debt in exchange for stakes in the company. As part of the plan, GM wrote off its entire stake in Isuzu, and reinfused the ailing carmaker with $84 million. The deal resulted in a recapitalized Isuzu and reduced GM's stake to 8%. Early in 2006 GM sold its stake to entities including Mitsubishi Corporation, ITOCHU Corporation, and Mizuho Corporate Bank.

As 2006 wound near its close, Toyota Motor picked up a 5.9% stake in Isuzu Motors from Mitsubishi and ITOCHU.

EXECUTIVES

Chairman and Director: Yoshinori Ida
President and Director: Susumu Hosoi
EVP and Director: Yoshihiro Tadaki
Managing Executive Officer and Director:
Yasuaki Shimizu
Managing Executive Officer and Director:
Ryozo Tsukioka
Managing Executive Officer and Director:
Eizou Kawasaki
Senior Executive Officer and Director:
Masanori Katayama
Senior Executive Officer and Director:
Chikao Mitsuzaki
Senior Executive Officer and Director: Shunichi Satomi
Senior Executive Officer and Director: Ryo Sakata,
age 59
Senior Executive Officer: Toshio Sasaki
Senior Executive Officer: Shunichi Tokunaga
Senior Executive Officer: Masaru Odajima
Senior Executive Officer: Tsutomu Yamada
Senior Executive Officer: Kazuhiko Ito
Senior Executive Officer: Kazuharu Shimizu
Senior Executive Officer: Yoshiyuki Miyatake
Senior Executive Officer: Katsumasa Nagai
Auditors: Ernst & Young ShinNihon

LOCATIONS

HQ: Isuzu Motors Limited
(Isuzu Jidosha Kabushiki Kaisha)
6-26-1 Minami-oi, Shinagawa-ku
Tokyo 140-8722, Japan
Phone: 81-3-5471-1141 **Fax:** 81-3-5471-1042
US HQ: 13340 183rd St., Cerritos, CA 90702
US Phone: 562-229-5000 **US Fax:** 562-229-8825
Web: www.isuzu.co.jp

2010 Sales

	% of total
Asia	
Japan	63
Other countries	28
North America	5
Other regions	4
Total	**100**

PRODUCTS/OPERATIONS

Selected Vehicles and Brands

Buses
Erga heavy-duty bus
Erga Mio medium-duty bus
Gala large tour bus
Gala Mio midsize tour bus
Commercial vehicles
C&E Series heavy-duty trucks & tractors
F Series medium-duty trucks
N Series light-duty trucks
Diesel engines
Pickup trucks & SUVs
D-MAX
MU-7 (Thailand)
Panther (Indonesia)

Selected Subsidiaries and Affiliates

Anadolu Isuzu Otomotiv Sanayi Ve Ticaret AS (Turkey)
DMAX Ltd. (US)
Isuzu Australia Limited
Isuzu Benelux N.V. (Belgium)
Isuzu (China) Holding Co., Ltd.
Isuzu Commercial Truck of America, Inc.
Isuzu Commercial Truck of Canada, Inc.
Isuzu Motors America, Inc.
Isuzu Motors Asia Ltd. (Singapore)
Isuzu Motors Co., (Thailand) Ltd.
Isuzu Motors Germany GmbH
Isuzu Motors Polska Sp. zo. o. (Poland)
Isuzu Philippines Corporation
Isuzu Truck (UK) Ltd.
P.T. Isuzu Astra Motor Indonesia
Qingling Motors Co., Ltd. (China)

COMPETITORS

Ashok Leyland	MAN
China Yuchai	Mitsubishi Fuso
Cummins	Navistar International
Daimler	PACCAR
Daimler Trucks North	Renault
America	Scania
Ford Motor	UD Trucks
General Motors	Volkswagen
Hino Motors	Volvo

HISTORICAL FINANCIALS

Company Type: Public

Income Statement

FYE: March 31

	REVENUE ($ mil.)	NET INCOME ($ mil.)	NET PROFIT MARGIN	EMPLOYEES
3/10	11,661	115	1.0%	24,440
3/09	14,645	157	1.1%	24,671
3/08	19,385	1,232	6.4%	23,200
3/07	14,108	784	5.6%	20,000
3/06	13,455	502	3.7%	20,000
Annual Growth	(3.5%)	(30.8%)	—	5.1%

2010 Year-End Financials

Debt ratio: —
Return on equity: 3.8%
Cash ($ mil.): 1,681
Current ratio: 1.21
Long-term debt ($ mil.): —
No. of shares (mil.): 1,694
Dividends
Yield: 1.1%
Payout: 60.0%
Market value ($ mil.): 4,625

Stock History

Pink Sheets: ISUZY

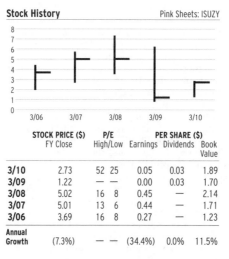

	STOCK PRICE ($) FY Close	P/E High/Low		PER SHARE ($) Earnings	Dividends	Book Value
3/10	2.73	52	25	0.05	0.03	1.89
3/09	1.22	—	—	0.00	0.03	1.70
3/08	5.02	16	8	0.45	—	2.14
3/07	5.01	13	6	0.44	—	1.71
3/06	3.69	16	8	0.27	—	1.23
Annual Growth	(7.3%)	—	—	(34.4%)	0.0%	11.5%

ITOCHU Corporation

If you drive it, eat it, fly it, or wear it, there's a good chance this company is involved with it. ITOCHU Corporation is a leading Japanese *sogo shosha* (general trading company), along with Mitsui & Co. and Mitsubishi, and has business interests in such diverse areas as aerospace, equipment manufacturing, food distribution, and clothing production. It also has interests and operations in chemicals, energy and mining, financial services, and retailing. The conglomerate has more than 150 offices in about 75 countries and operates through its approximately 500 subsidiaries and affiliated companies around the world.

ITOCHU has invested the past few years in streamlining its business divisions and focusing on growth industries. It is looking to expand its involvement in new energy resources, pharmaceutical marketing, and environmental services, as well as communications, logistics, and technology services.

Geographically, the company continues to increase its presence in China and North America; however, its domestic operations still account for almost two-thirds of its revenue.

The company acquired 85% of US-based solar power systems maker Solar Net LLC in 2009. In 2010 it bought China-based daily goods wholesaler Hangzhou New Huahai Business & Trading, boosting ITOCHU's presence in that market. That same year, ITOCHU agreed to acquire a 15% stake in Kalahari Minerals PLC, which holds uranium, gold, copper, and other base metal interests in Namibia. That same year, the company formed a business alliance with Composites Unlimited, an aircraft cabin interior component manufacturer. ITOCHU took a 20% stake in the company.

In 2008 the company partnered with BayCorp Holdings and Energy Management to form American Renewables to develop, build, and operate biomass-fueled power-generation facilities in the US. It also plans to make and sell bioethanol in Brazil. Also that year it acquired 41% of Medical Collective, a Japanese company that provides marketing assistance to pharmaceutical companies.

Masahiro Okafuji was named president of ITOCHU in 2010. He replaced Eizo Kobayashi, who was named the company's chairman. Okafuji was previously ITOCHU's executive vice president.

HISTORY

Chubei Itoh was only 18 when he organized his own wholesale linen business, C. Itoh & Co., in 1858. As Japan opened to foreign trade in the 1860s, the company prospered and was one of Osaka's largest textile wholesalers by the 1870s. C. Itoh established a trade office in San Francisco in 1889.

By 1919 C. Itoh had trading offices in New York, Calcutta, Manila, and four cities in China. Although it was not one of the *zaibatsu* (industrial groups) that flourished in Japan during the period between the world wars, C. Itoh benefited from the general increase in trade.

C. Itoh merged in 1941 with two other trading operations, Marubeni and Kishimoto, into a new company, Sanko Kabushiki Kaisha. C. Itoh and Marubeni were separated in 1949. C. Itoh supplied UN troops with provisions during the Korean War; profits were used to diversify into petroleum, machinery, aircraft, and automobiles.

After the oil crisis of 1973 demonstrated Japan's vulnerability to oil import disruptions, C. Itoh actively participated in the development of petroleum production technology. To prevent the failure of Japan's 10th-largest trading company, Ataka, the Japanese government arranged a merger in 1977, making C. Itoh the third-largest *sogo shosha*.

The company established Japan Communications Satellite (JCSAT) with Mitsui and Hughes Communications in 1985. JCSAT launched its first two satellites in 1989 and 1990. The following year C. Itoh and Toshiba joined Time Warner in a limited partnership, Time Warner Entertainment Company, to produce and distribute movies and television programs and to operate cable TV systems in the US. C. Itoh, Time Warner, and Toshiba formed another joint venture to distribute Warner Bros. films and develop amusements parks in Japan.

C. Itoh changed its name to ITOCHU, a transliteration of its Japanese name, in 1992. After sales dropped the next year, ITOCHU began selling poorly performing subsidiaries, reducing its investment portfolio by more than one-third.

In 1996 the company formed an alliance with US oil company Atlantic Richfield to buy Coastal Corp.'s western US coal operations, and it took a stake in a massive project led by Amoco and British Petroleum to develop oil and gas deposits in the Caspian Sea. That year PerfecTV! (a joint venture with Sumitomo and other Japanese companies) began satellite broadcasting. Also in 1996 ITOCHU bought stakes in the Asia Broadcasting and Communications Network, a satellite communications company.

To help cover its losses from the Asian currency crisis, the company sold 40% of its stake in Time Warner in 1998; in 1999 ITOCHU sold its remaining stake. ITOCHU also sold lowperforming real estate investments and laid plans to divest about one-third of its subsidiaries.

Two of ITOCHU's agricultural subsidiaries were liquidated in 2000. The company also sought out partnerships in order to offset costs incurred in new ventures: it joined with Japan's other top trading companies and Brazil's Petrobras to develop oil fields in South America. And in response to the rapid consolidation of Japan's steel industry, ITOCHU and Marubeni agreed to integrate their steel operations in 2001 to better compete.

In 2002 ITOCHU formed a partnership with Bally International to expand the European fashion brand's presence in Japan. In 2004 the company sold its interest in Utah-based Canyon Fuel Co. to Arch Coal, Inc. for $112 million, and dissolved its subsidiary, ITOCHU Coal International Inc. Also that year the company formed a joint venture with Ishimori Shotaro Pro Inc. to establish Ishimori Entertainment, which produces movies, television programs, and publications based on Shotaro Ishimori titles, including the popular MASKED RIDER.

ITOCHU established a fund with Turner Broadcasting to finance Japanese animation in 2005. It also acquired two US medical-device-distribution companies, Products for Surgery and Flanagan Instruments, marking ITOCHU's first step into that market.

EXECUTIVES

Chairman: Eizo Kobayashi, age 61
President: Masahiro Okafuji, age 60
CFO: Tadayuki Seki
Chief Corporate Planning Officers and CIO:
Koji Takayanagi
Senior Managing Director; President, Energy, Metals & Minerals Company: Yoichi Kobayashi
Managing Director; President, Finance, Realty, Insurance & Logistics Services Company: Kenji Okada
Managing Director; President, Aerospace, Electronics & Multimedia Company: Hiroo Inoue
Managing Director; Chief Officer, New Business Development: Takanobu Furuta
President, Chemicals, Forest Products and General Merchandise Company: Satoshi Kikuchi
President, Machinery: Toru Nomura
President, Food Company: Yoshihisa Aoki
President and CEO, China; Chairman, ITOCHU (China) Holding, ITOCHU Shanghai:
Nobuo Kuwayama

COO, Textile Material & Fabric: Shuichi Koseki
COO, Metals, Minerals Resources, & Coal:
Ichiro Nakamura
COO, Forest Products & General Merchandise:
Tomofumi Yoshida
EVP Energy, Metal & Minerals Company; COO, Energy Development: Yoshio Matsukawa
EVP and COO, Overseas Operations: Toshihito Tamba
Deputy Chief Administration Officer and General Manager, Human Resources Division:
Kazutoshi Maeda
Auditors: Deloitte Touche Tohmatsu

LOCATIONS

HQ: ITOCHU Corporation
(Itochu Shoji Kabushiki Kaisha)
5-1, Kita-Aoyama 2-chome, Minato-ku
Tokyo 107-8077, Japan
Phone: 81-3-3497-2121   **Fax:** 81-3-3497-4141
US HQ: 335 Madison Ave., Bank of America Plaza, 22nd-23rd Fls., New York, NY 10017
US Phone: 212-818-8000   **US Fax:** 212-818-8543
Web: www.itochu.co.jp

2009 Sales

	% of total
Japan	63
US	16
Australia	6
Other countries	15
Total	**100**

PRODUCTS/OPERATIONS

Selected Major Subsidiaries and Associated Companies

Energy, metals, and minerals
Galaxy Energy Group Ltd. (25%, British Virgin Islands)
IPC (USA) Inc. (50%)
ITOCHU Minerals & Energy of Australia Pty. Ltd.
ITOCHU Non-Ferrous Materials Co. Ltd.
ITOCHU Oil Exploration Co., Ltd. (96%)
ITOCHU Petroleum Japan Ltd.
NISSHO Petroleum Gas Corporation (25%)

Machinery
Auto Investment, Inc. (US)
ITOCHU Automobile Corporation
ITOCHU CONSTRUCTION MACHINERY CO.
ITOCHU Texmac Corporation
MCL GROUP LTD. (UK)
PROMAX Automotive (US)

Textiles
CORONET CORPORATION
Hunting World Japan Co., Ltd.
ITOCHU HOME FASHION CORPORATION
Prominent Apparel Ltd. (Hong Kong, China)
Thai Shikibo Co., Ltd. (30%, Thailand)
Tianjin Huada Garment Co., Ltd. (China)
Unico Corporation
Unimax Saigon Co.. Ltd. (80%, Vietnam)

Chemicals, forest products, and general merchandise
ALBANY PLANTATION FOREST COMPANY OF AUSTRALIA (28%)
BRUNEI METHANOL COMPANY SDN. BHD. (25%)
CIPA Lumber Co., Ltd. (Canada)
Daishin Plywood Co., Ltd.
GALLEHER CORPORATION (US)
ITOCHU Forestry Corp.
ITOCHU Kenzai (87%)
ITOCHU PLASTICS INC.
ITOCHU Pulp & Paper
ITOCHU Windows Co., Ltd.
PrimeSource Building Products, Inc. (US)
Shanghai Baoling Plastics Co., Ltd. (22%, China)
SHOWA ALUMINUM POWDER K.K. (85%)
Tetra Chemicals (Singapore) Pte. Ltd. (40%)
THAITECH RUBBER CORPORATION LTD. (33%, Thailand)

Food
Al Beverage Holding Co. Ltd. (20%)
CGB ENTERPRISES, INV. (50%, US)
Family Corporation Inc.
FamilyMart Co., Ltd. (31%)
FUJI Oil Co., Ltd. (25%)
ITOCHU Feed Mills Co., Ltd. (86%)
ITOCHU FRESH Corporation
ITOCHU Sugar Co., Ltd.
JAPAN Foods Co., Ltd. (35%)
OILSEEDS INTERNATIONAL LTD. (US)
Prima Meat Packers, Ltd. (40%)
P.T. ANEKA TUNA INDONESIA (47%)
Universal Food Co., Ltd. (98%)
WINNER FOOD PRODUCTS LTD. (26%, Hong Kong)
Yayoi Foods Co., Ltd. (93%)

Aerospace, electronics, and multimedia
Excite Japan Co., Ltd. (60%)
ITC NETWORKS CORPORATION (61%)
ITOCHU Airlease B.V. (The Netherlands)
ITOCHU Techno-Solutions Corporation (51%)
NANO Media Inc. (52%)
SPACE SHOWER NETWORKS INC. (51%)
SUNCALL CORPORATION (22%)

Finance, real estate, insurance, and logistics services
Beijing Pacific Logistics Co., Ltd. (China, 50%)
CENTURY 21 REAL ESTATE OF JAPAN LTD (55%)
EURASIA SPED Kft (Hungary, 60%)
Guangzhou Global Logistics Corp. (57%, China)
ITOCHU Finance Corporation (99%)
ITOCHU Housing Co., Ltd
ITOCHU Property Development, Ltd
ITOCHU Urban Community Ltd.
Naigai Travel Service Co., Ltd. (97%)

COMPETITORS

ADM	Mitsubishi Corp.
Altria	Mitsui
AOL	Nestlé
Balli	Nippon Steel
Dow Chemical	Nippon Television
Exxon Mobil	NTT
Fluor	Panasonic Corp
Google	Rio Tinto plc
Hutchison Whampoa	Samsung Group
Ito-Yokado	Sharp Corp.
JX Nippon Mining & Metals	Sojitz
Kanematsu	Sumitomo
Klöckner	Sumitomo Metal Mining
LG Group	ThyssenKrupp
Lockheed Martin	Tokyo Broadcasting System
Marubeni	TOTAL
Marui Group	Unilever
	Yahoo Japan

HISTORICAL FINANCIALS

Company Type: Public

Income Statement

FYE: March 31

	REVENUE ($ mil.)	NET INCOME ($ mil.)	NET PROFIT MARGIN	EMPLOYEES
3/09	35,145	1,700	4.8%	55,431
3/08	28,815	2,201	7.6%	48,657
3/07	22,459	1,502	6.7%	45,690
3/06	18,868	1,264	6.7%	42,967
3/05	18,570	726	3.9%	40,890
Annual Growth	17.3%	23.7%	—	7.9%

2009 Year-End Financials

Debt ratio: 227.7%   No. of shares (mil.): 1,582
Return on equity: 18.3%   Dividends
Cash ($ mil.): 6,464   Yield: 1.7%
Current ratio: 1.37   Payout: 7.5%
Long-term debt ($ mil.): 19,884 Market value ($ mil.): 7,773

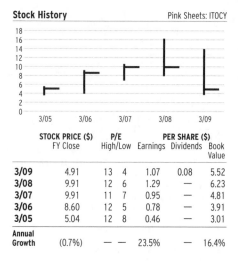
J Sainsbury

J Sainsbury's trolley is filled with more than groceries. The UK's third-largest food retailer (after Tesco and ASDA) operates the Sainsbury's Supermarkets chain of some 535 grocery stores throughout the UK. Its fast-growing Sainsbury's online home delivery shopping service covers about 90% of the UK population. In addition to supermarkets, it operates about 335 convenience stores under the Sainsbury's Local banner. The firm also owns half of Sainsbury's Bank (in a 50-50 joint venture with Scottish bank HBOS) and a property development company. Sainsbury also sells apparel and home goods, including cookware and bedding, in its supermarkets and online.

After a rough patch in the early- and mid-2000s when Sainsbury strayed from its core competency — and made an ill-fated foray into the US market — the company has renewed its focus on supplying UK customers with the staples of everyday life with considerable success. With non-food sales growing three times as fast as food sales, Sainsbury is eager to add more. To that end, the company doubled its clothing warehouse capacity to meet increased demand for its TU clothing range (launched in 2004). Sainsbury's TU childrenswear line has grown to rank seventh in the UK market by volume, where it competes with ASDA's George line of apparel.

Under the leadership of CEO Justin King, who joined Sainsbury in 2004, Sainsbury has posted increasing sales in each of the past five years.

To narrow the gap between Sainsbury and its larger competitors, in mid-2009 the company said it will raise £445 million (about $720 million) to fund the growth of its retail footprint. (New stores are planned for England, Scotland, and Northern Ireland.) Sainsbury has attributed its recent strong performance to strong demand for its private-label brand products. It has also cut prices and stepped up promotions in a bid to lure cash-strapped shoppers from more upscale rivals such as Marks & Spencer and Waitrose.

Real estate investment group Delta Two, which is backed by Qatar Holding, has about a 26% stake in Sainsbury.

HISTORY

Newlyweds John James and Mary Ann Sainsbury established a small dairy shop in their London home in 1869. Customers flocked to the clean and efficient store, a far cry from most cluttered and dirty London shops. They opened a second store in 1876. By 1914, 115 stores had been opened, and the couple's sons had entered the business.

During WWI the company's stores established grocery departments to meet demand for preserved products, such as meat and jams, which were sold under the Sainsbury's label.

Mary Ann died in 1927 and John James the next year. Son John Benjamin, wholly devoted to the family business, took charge. (He is reported to have said on his deathbed, "Keep the stores well lit.") In the 1930s he engineered the company's first acquisition, the Thoroughgood stores.

Sales dropped by 50% during WWII, and some shops were destroyed by German bombing. Under third-generation leader Alan John Sainsbury, the company opened its first self-service store in 1950 in Croydon. The 75,000-sq.-ft. store opened in 1955 in Lewisham was considered to be the largest supermarket in Europe.

J Sainsbury went public in 1973. It established a joint venture with British Home Stores in 1975, forming the Savacentre hypermarkets (the company bought out its partner in 1989).

Sainsbury partnered with Grand Bazaar Innovation Bon Marche of Belgium in 1979 to establish Homebase, a do-it-yourself chain. (It bought the remaining 25% in 1996 and then sold the company in 2001, retaining only 18%.)

By 1983 most of Sainsbury's 229 stores were clustered in the south of England. A mature market and stiff competition forced the company to look elsewhere for growth — both overseas and closer to home. It began buying into US-based Shaw's Supermarkets in New England and in 1984 opened its first Scottish hypermarket. By 1987 the grocer owned 100% of Shaw's, which had 60 stores in Massachusetts, Maine, and New Hampshire.

In 1991 Sainsbury came under competitive pressure from Tesco and the Argyll Group (later renamed Safeway plc), which also began building superstores. It responded with an expansion drive of its own, including opening its first Scottish supermarket (in Glasgow) the next year.

In 1996 the company opened Sainsbury's Bank. David Sainsbury — a great-grandson of the founders — retired as chairman in 1998 to pursue politics, marking the first time a Sainsbury had not headed up the company in its more-than-a-century history.

As a cost-cutting effort in 1999, Sainsbury cut 2,200 jobs, more than half in management. It also launched its convenience store concept, called Sainsbury's Local. Also that year Sainsbury bought the 53-store Star Markets chain of Massachusetts, merging it into its Shaw's operations. In 2000 Sir Peter Davis took over as CEO of Sainsbury's Supermarkets, replacing David Bremner. In 2001 Sainsbury acquired 19 Grand Union stores in the US (17 of which were converted to the Shaw's banner). The company also sold its home-and-garden chain Homebase to private equity firm Permira.

Justin King (formerly of Marks & Spencer) joined Sainsbury as its CEO in March 2004, succeeding Sir Peter Davis, who became chairman of the board. In April Sainsbury sold JS USA Holdings, which operated 203 Shaw's and Star Markets stores in New England, to US grocery chain Albertson's in a deal worth about $2.4 billion.

Davis stepped down as chairman of Sainsbury on July 1, 2004, one year ahead of schedule and following a prolonged dispute with investors that culminated in a fight over his compensation.

Philip Hampton (former finance director of Lloyds TSB, BT Group, and BG Group) joined Sainsbury as its new chairman on July 19, 2004. In September Sainsbury agreed to pay ex-chairman Davis £2.6 million. At that time Lord Levene of Portsoken and Keith Butler-Wheelhouse, both non-executive directors of the company and members of the remuneration committee, resigned from the board.

In 2007 the company sold 5% of its majority stake in Sainsbury's Bank to its joint venture partner HBOS for about £21 million ($40 million). As a result, the bank became a 50-50 joint venture between the two firms. In 2008 Qatar Holding-backed investment group Delta Two increased its stake in Sainsbury to about 25%, fueling speculation that it may attempt to take over the British grocer.

The company welcomed David Tyler, formerly chairman of Logica, as its new chairman in 2009. Tyler succeeded Sir Philip Hampton.

EXECUTIVES

Chairman: David A. Tyler, age 57
CEO and Director: Justin King, age 48
CFO and Director: John Rogers
Company Secretary: Tim Fallowfield
Commercial Director: Michael (Mike) Coupe, age 49
Group Development Director: Darren Shapland, age 43
Director Commercial Services: Neil Sachdev
Customer Director: Gwyn Burr
Human Resources Director: Imelda Walsh
IT and Change Director: Angela Morrison
Convenience Director: Helen Buck
Director Supermarket Finance: Jonny Mason
Managing Director Non-Food: Luke Jensen
Retail and Logistics Director: Roger Burnley
Change Director: Hamish Elvidge
Head Clothing Design: Tracey Hodgson
Head Investor Relations: Elliot Jordan
Head Public Affairs: Erica Zimmer
Divisional Merchandise Manager, Home and Lifestyle Division: John Cooper
Divisional Head Buying, Home and Lifestyle Division: Claire Sollis
Executive Chef: John Wood
Auditors: PricewaterhouseCoopers LLP

LOCATIONS

HQ: J Sainsbury plc
33 Holborn
London EC1N 2HT, United Kingdom
Phone: 44-20-7695-6000   **Fax:** 44-20-7695-7610
Web: www.j-sainsbury.co.uk

PRODUCTS/OPERATIONS

2010 Stores

	No.
Sainsbury's Supermarkets	537
Convenience stores	335
Total	**872**

Store Formats

Sainsbury's at Bells Stores (convenience stores)
Sainsbury's Central (convenience stores averaging 10,000 sq. ft. and 6,500 product lines)
Sainsbury's Local (convenience stores averaging 3,000 sq. ft. and 2,500 product lines)
Sainsbury's Supermarkets (full-service supermarkets averaging 20,000-30,000 sq. ft. and 17,000 product lines)
Superstores (full-service supermarkets averaging 30,000-50,000 sq. ft. and 26,000 product lines, plus amenities such as restaurants, dry cleaners, and gasoline stations)

COMPETITORS

ALDI
Alliance Boots
ASDA
Co-operative Group
Costcutter Supermarkets
First Quench
Iceland Foods
Lidl
Marks & Spencer
METRO AG
Musgrave Retail Partners
Netto Foodstores
One Stop Stores
Tesco
Waitrose
Wm Morrison Supermarkets

HISTORICAL FINANCIALS

Company Type: Public

Income Statement — FYE: Third Saturday in March

	REVENUE ($ mil.)	NET INCOME ($ mil.)	NET PROFIT MARGIN	EMPLOYEES
3/10	30,082	882	2.9%	99,600
3/09	26,871	411	1.5%	148,500
3/08	35,569	656	1.8%	151,000
3/07	33,743	639	1.9%	146,900
3/06	27,967	111	0.4%	153,300
Annual Growth	1.8%	67.7%	—	(10.2%)

2010 Year-End Financials

Debt ratio: —
Return on equity: 12.9%
Cash ($ mil.): 1,261
Current ratio: —
Long-term debt ($ mil.): —
No. of shares (mil.): 1,861
Dividends
Yield: 4.2%
Payout: —
Market value ($ mil.): 9,184

Stock History

Pink Sheets: JSAIY

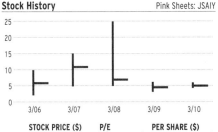

	STOCK PRICE ($) FY Close	P/E High/Low	PER SHARE ($) Earnings	Dividends	Book Value
3/10	4.94	— —	—	0.20	4.02
3/09	4.45	— —	—	0.18	3.34
3/08	6.84	— —	—	0.21	5.29
3/07	10.81	— —	—	0.16	4.60
3/06	5.79	— —	—	0.14	3.71
Annual Growth	(3.9%)	— —	—	9.3%	2.0%

Japan Tobacco

Japan Tobacco (JT) has plenty to puff about. The company controls about 65% of the cigarette market in a country where about 40% of the male population smokes. JT is the world's #3 tobacco firm, trailing Philip Morris International and BAT. Its JT International unit, which acquired Britain's Gallaher Group for $15 billion in 2007, makes and markets Camel, Salem, and Winston brands (outside the US) and is its parent company's growth engine. JT also has holdings in the food, beverage, and pharmaceuticals industries. A state-owned monopoly until 1985, the Japanese Finance Ministry now owns about half the firm.

With domestic demand for cigarettes on the decline, JT is looking abroad — and to a lesser extent to other industries — for growth.

Britain's Tribac Leaf has operations in Malawi, Zambia, China, and India, while the Brazilian units operate in their home country. The recent purchases in Brazil and a separate transaction to form a new tobacco sourcing company with US leaf suppliers, represent an attempt by JT to keep the price and quality of its tobacco leaf supply under control. The new joint venture — called JTI Leaf Services — is with Hail & Cotton and J.E.B. International, both of the US. In recent years, sharp price increases of various crops have caused leaf tobacco costs to stay high and have contributed to price volatility.

JT acquired Gallaher to boost its shares of Western and European markets, seek smokers outside Japan, and maintain its position as one of the world's top tobacco companies. The purchase added the Silk Cut and Benson & Hedges cigarette brands to its portfolio. Indeed, with Gallaher under its umbrella JT made more than 610 billion cigarettes in 2009. JTI has expanded into 70 markets worldwide.

In a country where the average smoker burns through a pack each day, JT makes nine of the nation's top 10 brands, including such favorites as Mild Seven, Caster, and Seven Stars. Two new brands, Icene Super Cooling Menthol and LUCIA Citrus Fresh Menthol are being touted as producing less odor and smoke than conventional brands.

Beyond tobacco, JT has controlling stakes in several Japanese companies in the frozen and processed foods and seasonings businesses, including Fuji Foods and Katokichi (now called TableMark), both acquired in 2008. Its Japan Beverage subsidiary makes canned coffee (under the Roots brand), and operates beverage vending machines. The company is also active in the research and development of new drugs through its growing pharmaceutical arm, Torii Pharmaceutical Co. Ltd.

HISTORY

In 1898, roughly 325 years after tobacco was introduced in Japan, the nation's Ministry of Finance formed a bureau to monopolize its production to fund military and industrial expansion.

During WWII, Japan's tobacco leaf imports from North and South America grew scarce and led to cigarette rationing. In 1949 the government began operating the tobacco production bureau as a business: the Japan Tobacco and Salt Public Corporation (in 1905 the bureau also became responsible for a salt monopoly).

The company launched Hope, the first Japanese-made filter cigarette, in 1957, and it became the world's best seller a decade later. In 1972 it began printing mild packaging "warnings": "Be careful not to smoke excessively for your health."

Japan Tobacco and Salt began selling Marlboro cigarettes licensed from Philip Morris in 1973. The Mild Seven brand (its current bestseller) went on sale in 1977; it became the world's #1 cigarette in 1981 but dropped to #2 (behind Marlboro) in 1993.

When its tobacco monopoly ended in 1985, the government established the firm as Japan Tobacco (a government-owned joint stock company). As competition from foreign imports increased, the firm came up with new means of making yen. It formed Japan Tobacco International (cigarette exports mainly to the US and Southeast Asia), moved into agribusiness and real estate operations, and, in 1986, created JT Pharmaceutical. In 1987 cigarette import tariffs ended, and importers lowered prices to match the company's; its sales and market share subsequently declined. During the late 1980s it introduced HALF TIME beverages and its first low-tar cigarettes.

In 1992 Japan Tobacco bought its first overseas production facility, Manchester Tobacco (closed in 2001). Former Ministry of Finance official Masaru Mizuno became CEO that year — and soon took up smoking. Also in 1992 the company and Agouron Pharmaceuticals agreed to jointly develop immune system drugs; in 1994 they added antiviral drugs. The government sold about 20% of the firm's stock to the public in 1994 and 13% in 1996. The firm began operating Burger King restaurants in Japan in 1996. Japan Tobacco bought Pillsbury Japan in 1998.

Japan Tobacco in 1999 paid nearly $8 billion for R.J. Reynolds International, the international tobacco unit of what was then RJR Nabisco. It then renamed the unit JT International.

Slowing sales prompted Japan Tobacco to announce in 2000 that it would reduce its workforce by 6,100 by 2005. Company exec Katsuhiko Honda became CEO that year (Mizuno remained as chairman) and said he'd push the government to sell its stake. In May Mizuno stepped down as chairman and was replaced by Takashi Ogawa.

In 2001 Japan's Ministry of Finance recommended that it cut its holdings in the company from 66% to 50%; it would also allow the company to sell additional shares, which could further dilute the government's stake to as little as 33%.

Japan Tobacco's Canadian subsidiary filed for bankruptcy protection in August 2004 following a billion-dollar smuggling claim by the Canadian government. Canada said that the company owed $1.4 billion in Canadian back taxes for allegedly smuggling cigarettes in 1998 and 1999.

Japan Tobacco in 2005 ended its agreement with Philip Morris to make and sell Marlboro cigarettes. Honda retired as chairman in 2006. He was succeeded by Yoji Wakui.

The company closed 13 of its 25 manufacturing plants and six of its 30 sales branches in 2006 as part of an effort to increase profits. These reductions slashed as many as 4,000 jobs as demand for cigarettes, partly depressed by higher taxes, continued to decline. In 2008 the company acquired a majority stake in Katokichi Co. for about $900 million. It then sold a 49% stake in the business to Nissin Foods.

In 2009 Japan Tobacco acquired the UK's Tribac Leaf and Brazil-based leaf suppliers Kannenberg & Cia and Kannenberg, Barker, Hail & Cotton Tabacos.

EXECUTIVES

Chairman: Yoji Wakui
President, CEO, and Director: Hiroshi Kimura, age 54
Executive Deputy President; President, Tobacco Business; and Director: Mitsuomi Koizumi
Executive Deputy President and Chief Communications Officer, Assistant to CEO in CSR and General Administration, and Director: Masakazu Shimizu
Executive Deputy President and Assistant to CEO in Compliance, Finance and Food Business, and Director: Munetaka Takeda
Executive Deputy President and Assistant to CEO in Strategy, HR, Legal and Operational Review and Business Assurance, and Director: Masaaki Sumikawa
SEVP and Chief Legal Officer: Ryuichi Shimomura
SEVP; President, Pharmaceutical Business; and Director: Noriaki Okubo
EVP and Chief Research and Development, Tobacco Business: Tadashi Iwanami
EVP; President, Food Business; and Director: Sadao Furuya
EVP and Chief Marketing and Sales Officer, Tobacco Business: Yoshihisa Fujisaki
EVP, Chief Strategy Officer, and Head Manufacturing General Division, Tobacco Business: Mutsuo Iwai
SVP and Chief Financial Officer and Head Global Tax Group: Hideki Miyazaki
SVP and Head Central Pharmaceutical Research Institute, Pharmaceutical Business: Junichi Haruta
SVP and Chief Human Resources Officer: Satoshi Matsumoto
SVP and Head Tobacco Business Planning Division and Chief Corporate, Scientific and Regulatory Affairs Officer, Tobacco Business: Akira Saeki
Chief General Affairs Officer: Ryoji Chijiiwa
President and CEO, JTI: Pierre de Labouchere
Auditors: Deloitte Touche Tohmatsu

LOCATIONS

HQ: Japan Tobacco Inc.
(Nihon Tabako Sangyo)
2-1, Toranomon 2-chome, Minato-ku
Tokyo 105-8422, Japan
Phone: 81-3-3582-3111   **Fax:** 81-3-5572-1441
Web: www.jti.co.jp

PRODUCTS/OPERATIONS

2010 Sales

	% of total
Tobacco	
Japan	50
Other countries	43
Foods	6
Pharmaceuticals	1
Total	**100**

Selected Cigarette Brands

BB Slugger
Benson & Hedges
Bitter Valley
Cabin and Cabin Mild
Camel (outside the US)
Caster and Caster Mild
Frontier
Fuji Renaissance
Hi-Lite Menthol
Hope Menthol
Icene Super Cooling Menthol
LD
LUCIA Citrus Fresh Menthol
Mild Seven (regular, Lights, Super Lights)
Salem (outside the US)
Seven Stars
Silk Cut
Winston (outside the US)

Selected Divisions and Operations

Agribusiness
Beverage business
Engineering
Food business
Pharmaceuticals
Real estate
Tobacco

COMPETITORS

Ajinomoto
Altadis
Asahi Breweries
British American Tobacco
Coca-Cola
Imperial Tobacco
Kraft International
Mitsubishi Chemical
Nestlé
Nisshin Seifun Group
Philip Morris International
Reemtsma Cigarettenfabriken
Suntory Holdings
Unilever
Vector Group

HISTORICAL FINANCIALS

Company Type: Public

Income Statement

FYE: March 31

	REVENUE ($ mil.)	NET INCOME ($ mil.)	NET PROFIT MARGIN	EMPLOYEES
3/10	66,181	1,271	1.9%	49,665
3/09	70,229	1,268	1.8%	47,977
3/08	64,552	2,404	3.7%	47,500
3/07	40,464	1,788	4.4%	33,428
3/06	39,448	1,714	4.3%	31,476
Annual Growth	**13.8%**	**(7.2%)**	**—**	**12.1%**

2010 Year-End Financials

Debt ratio: —
Return on equity: 7.5%
Cash ($ mil.): 1,677
Current ratio: 1.09
Long-term debt ($ mil.): —
No. of shares (mil.): 10
Dividends
Yield: 1.5%
Payout: 36.8%
Market value ($ mil.): 35,969

Stock History

Tokyo: 29140

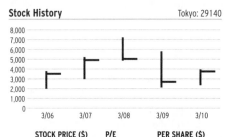

	STOCK PRICE ($) FY Close	P/E High/Low		PER SHARE ($) Earnings	Dividends	Book Value
3/10	3,754.22	25	16	155.87	57.39	1,857.50
3/09	2,692.01	43	17	132.39	26.73	1,666.33
3/08	5,025.43	28	20	250.93	—	2,182.44
3/07	4,912.24	27	16	186.66	—	1,735.81
3/06	3,521.48	4	2	893.85	—	1,564.76
Annual Growth	**1.6%**	**—**	**—**	**(35.4%)**	**114.7%**	**4.4%**

Jardine Matheson

The British no longer rule Hong Kong, but don't tell Jardine Matheson Holdings (JMH), which governs the many interests of its affiliate Jardine Strategic Holdings, one of the oldest of the Hong Kong *hongs* (diversified trading companies) and one of the few still in British hands. JMH's subsidiaries include Jardine Pacific and Jardine Motors Group, Asian supermarket operator Dairy Farm, and Hongkong Land, which owns prime real estate in Hong Kong. Other businesses include financial services, hotels (Mandarin Oriental), construction, mining, and transport services. Members of the Keswick family, descendants of the co-founder William Jardine, control JMH and Jardine Strategic through a complex ownership structure.

JMH owns about 81% of Jardine Strategic, while Jardine Strategic owns more than 50% of JMH. (The cross-shareholding between the two companies is designed to repel takeovers. JMH created Jardine Strategic in 1986 in an anti-takeover transaction.)

JMH also has numerous investments in China and throughout Asia. The company has diversified geographically, but the Asia/Pacific region is where the money is — about 90% of the company's revenues come from that part of the world. To maintain its footing in the region's uncertain economic times, JMH is working to control costs. The company is also buying up additional shares in its affiliates, and focusing on building its businesses in Southeast Asian countries including Indonesia, Malaysia, and Singapore. Dairy Farm, with some 4,650 supermarkets, convenience and health and beauty stores, and restaurants throughout Asia, is growing rapidly in China, Malaysia, and Indonesia. Through Jardine Cycle & Carriage (JC&C) the group now owns about 50% of carmaker Astra International of Indonesia, making it a subsidiary of the group. JC&C is also investing in Vietnam. Jardine Motors is expanding its Mercedes-Benz network in Southern China and developing its Hyundai passenger car business in Hong Kong. In the UK it is going up-market, a strategy that hurt the company as the recession took hold in England.

Across the Pacific, Jardine Matheson is expanding its Mandarin Oriental chains of some two dozen hotels, with three slated to open in 2009. The group has also added Moscow and Atlanta to its development portfolio of 18 properties. Current unfavorable economic conditions have delayed some of the projects.

HISTORY

Scotsmen William Jardine and James Matheson met in Bombay in 1820. In 1832 they founded Jardine Matheson in Canton, the only Chinese city then open to foreigners. The company started shipping tea from China to Europe and smuggling opium from India to China. In 1839 Chinese authorities tried to stop the drug trade, seizing 20,000 chests of opium, 7,000 of them Jardine's. Jardine persuaded Britain to send gunboats to China, precipitating the First Opium War. China lost the war and ceded Hong Kong to Britain in 1842.

Jardine moved to Hong Kong and resumed trading opium. The Second Opium War (1856-60) resulted in the opening of 11 more ports and the legalization of opium imports. Jardine flourished and later branched into the more legitimate fields of brewing, textiles, banking, insurance, and sugar. It formed Hongkong Land (HKL), a real estate company; introduced steamships to China; and built the country's first railroad line (1876). The company earned the sobriquet "the Princely *Hong*" because of its high-society officers with free-spending habits.

The Sino-Japanese War and WWII shut the company down. In 1945, with China gripped by civil war, Jardine reopened in Hong Kong. Attempts to re-establish operations in China ended in 1954 after the Communist takeover. The company went public in 1961 and was run during the 1960s by members of the Keswick family. Henry Keswick was succeeded by *Taipan* (big boss) David Newbigging in 1972.

The costs incurred in an acquisition program begun in the 1970s made Jardine a takeover target by 1980. Newbigging defended the company by erecting a bulwark of crossholdings of it and HKL stock. The resulting debt pushed Jardine to the brink of bankruptcy, forcing it to sell assets.

Simon Keswick — Henry's younger brother — succeeded Newbigging in 1984 and reorganized the company, making investments in Mercedes-Benz distributorships and fast-food franchises that helped turn Jardine around. As the UK and China negotiated the transfer of Hong Kong to Chinese control, Keswick moved Jardine's legal home to Bermuda. Jardine continued to be plagued by takeover attempts, however, particularly by Li Ka-shing, who was assisted by China's investment organization, CITIC. In a 1986 anti-takeover transaction, the company created Jardine Strategic Holdings to hold interests in HKL and its spinoffs. When the Chinese army put down student demonstrations in Beijing two years later, Keswick called the Chinese government "a thuggish, oppressive regime."

To increase its holdings outside of Hong Kong, Jardine bought 26% of Trafalgar House in 1993 but sold its stake in the troubled British conglomerate in 1996, which contributed to lower profits. Jardine delisted five of its companies from the Hong Kong stock exchange in 1994. Continuing to expand geographically, the company acquired 20% of India's Tata Industries and bought London's Hyde Park Hotel in 1996.

Hong Kong was returned to China in 1997, and in a display of public fence-mending, Chinese Vice Premier Zhu Rongji welcomed Jardine's participation in mainland ventures. But Jardine's stormy relationship with China continued even as Jardine's profits dropped during the Asian economic crisis. In 1999 China closed down Jardine's Beijing and Guangzhou brokerage offices (and banned the two chief China officers from the business for life), claiming that Jardine was engaging in unauthorized activities.

In 2000 and again in 2001 the Keswicks — Simon and his brother Henry — turned back attempts by US-based Brandes Investment Partners, which owns about 10% of Jardine, to seize control of the company.

In 2005 JMH acquired a 20% stake in Rothschilds Continuation, a holding company with financial services interests, including investment bank N M Rothschild & Sons.

Managing director Percy Weatherall retired in March 2006. Weatherall was succeeded by Anthony Nightingale, chairman of Jardine Cycle & Carriage, Jardine Motors, Jardine Pacific, and MCL Land.

In July 2008 Jardine Cycle & Carriage acquired a 20% stake in Truong Hai Automotive Corp., a Vietnamese automaker.

EXECUTIVES

Chairman: Henry Keswick
Managing Director; Chairman, Jardine Cycle & Carriage, Jardine Motors Group, and Jardine Pacific: Anthony J. L. Nightingale
Group General Counsel: Giles White
Group Treasurer: Simon Dixon
Group Legal Manager: Stephen Hopkins
Group Financial Controller: P. M. Kam
Group Corporate Secretary and Director Group Corporate Affairs: Neil M. McNamara
Group Taxation Manager: Betty Chan
Group Strategy Director: Mark S. Greenberg
Group Head of Human Resources: Ritchie Bent
Head of Group Audit and Risk Management: Eric van der Hoeven
Director; Managing Director, Jardine Cycle & Carriage: Benjamin W. (Ben) Keswick
Director; Chairman, Dairy Farm, Hongkong Land, and Mandarin Oriental: Simon L. Keswick, age 67
Director; Chief Executive, Jardine Pacific and Jardine Motors: Adam P. C. Keswick
Auditors: PricewaterhouseCoopers LLP

LOCATIONS

HQ: Jardine Matheson Holdings Limited
48th Fl., Jardine House
Hong Kong
Phone: 852-2843-8288   **Fax:** 852-2845-9005
Web: www.jardines.com

2009 Sales

	$ mil.	% of total
Southeast Asia	14,675	65
Greater China	6,300	28
UK	1,339	6
Rest of world	187	1
Total	**22,501**	**100**

PRODUCTS/OPERATIONS

2009 Sales

	$ mil.	% of total
Astra (automotive, financial services, agribusiness, heavy equipment & other)	9,537	42
Dairy Farm	7,029	31
Jardine Motors Group	2,522	11
Jardine Cycle & Carriage	1,103	5
Jardine Pacific	1,082	5
Hongkong Land	801	4
Mandarin Oriental	438	2
Other	2	—
Adjustment	(13)	—
Total	**22,501**	**100**

Selected Major Subsidiaries and Affiliates

Astra International (automobile distribution and manufacturing, financial and IT services, heavy machinery)
Cycle & Carriage Ltd (69%, motor trading, Singapore)
Dairy Farm International Holdings Ltd (78%; supermarkets, hypermarkets, health and beauty and home furnishings stores, convenience stores and restaurants)
Hongkong Land Holdings Ltd (50%, real estate)

Jardine Lloyd Thompson plc (32%, insurance and brokerage, UK)
Jardine Motors Group Holdings Ltd. (auto distribution, sales, and service, China, Hong Kong, Macau, and the UK)
Jardine Pacific Holdings Ltd. (100%, transport services, engineering and construction, restaurants, and IT services)
Jardine Strategic Holdings Ltd. (81%, holding company)
Mandarin Oriental International Ltd. (74%, hotels)

COMPETITORS

Accor
Carrefour
Cheung Kong Holdings
Chevalier
China Resources Enterprise
Daiei
Hopewell Holdings
HSBC
Hutchison Whampoa
Hyatt
ITOCHU
Kumagai Gumi
Marriott
Marubeni
McDonald's
Samsung Group
Seiyu
Sime Darby
Swire Pacific
Tesco

HISTORICAL FINANCIALS

Company Type: Public

Income Statement

FYE: December 31

	REVENUE ($ mil.)	NET INCOME ($ mil.)	NET PROFIT MARGIN	EMPLOYEES
12/09	22,501	3,935	17.5%	270,000
12/08	22,362	1,643	7.3%	110,000
12/07	19,445	2,884	14.8%	240,000
12/06	16,281	2,054	12.6%	240,000
12/05	11,929	1,820	15.3%	200,000
Annual Growth	**17.2%**	**21.3%**	**—**	**7.8%**

2009 Year-End Financials

Debt ratio: 60.0%
Return on equity: 43.3%
Cash ($ mil.): 4,093
Current ratio: 1.46
Long-term debt ($ mil.): 5,946

Net Income History

London: JAR

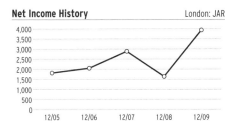

Kao Corporation

More than a century after Kao affixed a lunar logo to its name, Japanese consumers still think the company's products hang the moon. Kao (pronounced "cow") is Japan's #1 maker of personal care, laundry, and cleaning products. Its brand names include Attack (a top laundry detergent in Japan), Bioré (skin care), Family Kyukyutto (dishwashing detergent), Asience (shampoo), Laurier (sanitary napkins), Merries (disposable diapers), and ALBLANC (cosmetics). The company also manufactures Healthya brand beverages (green tea and water), cooking oils and fatty chemicals, printer and copier toner products, and plastics used in products such as athletic shoe soles.

Although popular in Japan, Kao is striving to attain the international scope of rivals like Procter & Gamble (P&G) and Unilever. Indeed, in a move aimed at strengthening its position in Europe, the company in mid-2009 acquired a premium hair care product plant in Darmstadt, Germany, owned by Reichardt International through its Kao Corp. GmbH unit. Other foreign subsidiaries include Kao Professional Salon Services, which makes hair care products in Europe and markets them to salons, and Kao Brands, a maker of skin care and hair care products, including Jergens brand items, in North America. Kao's consumer products generate the majority of its revenue, and North America accounts for about 7%. To bring new products to market, Kao invests heavily in research and development.

Kao brought its fat-reducing Econa cooking oil to the US in 2003. Introduced in Japan in 1999, Econa is marketed as Enova in the US through a joint venture with Archer Daniels Midland Co. However, the company temporarily stopped selling Econa-related products, including cooking oils and dressings, in fall 2009 due to health concerns regarding the safety of glycidol fatty acid esters contained in fats and oils.

Indeed, health concerns over Econa products are just one of Kao's concerns. Slumping sales in its key prestige cosmetics division and weak demand for industrial chemicals are hurting the company's results. Bright spots for the company include: strong demand for its fabric and home care products due to successful new product launches, such as Attack Neo ultra-concentrated detergent; and growing sales of its beverages and disposable diapers.

HISTORY

Tomiro Nagase founded the Kao Soap Company in 1887; shortly afterward, he began selling bars under the motto, "A Clean Nation Prospers." Kao's longtime rivalry with Procter & Gamble (P&G) was foreshadowed when it adopted a moon trademark in 1890 strikingly similar to the one chosen by P&G eight years earlier.

Kao moved into detergents in the 1940s. In the 1960s the company struck upon an idea that would vertically integrate it and set it apart from other consumer products manufacturers: It set up a network of wholesale distributors ("hansha") who sell only Kao products. The hansha system improved distribution time and cut costs by eliminating middlemen.

Yoshio Maruta, one of several chemical engineers to run Kao, took over as president in 1971. Maruta presented himself as more Buddhist scholar than corporate honcho; during his 19 years at the top, he gave the company a wider vision through his emphasis on creativity and his insistence on an active learning environment. To encourage sharing of ideas, the company used open conference rooms for meetings and anyone interested could attend and participate in any meeting.

Under Maruta, Kao launched a string of successful products in new areas in the 1980s. In 1982 the company introduced its Sofina cosmetics line, emphasizing the line's scientific basis in a break from traditional beauty products marketing. The next year its Super Merries diapers (with a new design that reduced diaper rash) trounced P&G's Pampers in Japan. Its popular Attack laundry detergent (the first concentrated laundry soap) led the market within six months of its 1987 debut.

Seeking a way to enter the US market, Kao bought the Andrew Jergens skin care company — based in Cincinnati, as is P&G — in 1988. (It also purchased a chemical company to supply the materials to make Jergens' products.) P&G and Unilever braced themselves for the new competition, but Kao didn't deliver, releasing products like fizzy bath tablets that didn't sell well in a nation of shower-takers. In 1989 it bought a 75% interest in Goldwell, a German maker of hair care and beauty products sold through hair stylists. (By 1994 Kao owned all of Goldwell, which is now called Kao Professional Salon Services.)

In the mid-1980s Kao built a name for itself in the floppy disk market and became the top producer of 3.5-in. floppy disks in North America by 1990. However, competition crowded the field and drove the price of disks down. In 1997 the company stopped production of floppy disks in the US.

Chemical engineer Takuya Goto took over as president that year. Kao looked to other Asian markets and the US for potential consumers and found a willing audience in the US for its Bioré face strips. In 1998 Kao purchased Bausch & Lomb's skin care business, gaining the Curel and Soft Sense lotion brands.

In 2000 Kao established a joint venture with Novartis to make baby foods and over-the-counter drugs such as stomach medicines and other pain relief drugs. In 2001 Kao lost out on its offer for Clairol to P&G. Also in 2001 it formed a joint venture with Archer Daniels Midland to produce an anti-obesity diacylglycerol oil (used in margarine, cooking oil, salad dressing, and mayonnaise) and in 2002 began marketing it in the US under the brand name Enova. That year Kao dissolved its OTC-medicine-manufacturing joint venture with Novartis and renamed its Sofina cosmetics brand Prestige Cosmetics. Additionally in 2002 Kao acquired John Frieda Professional Hair Care through Andrew Jergens. (Andrew Jergens became Kao Brands in 2004.)

In 2004 Goto became chairman and Motoki Ozaki was promoted from president of the Global Fabric and Home Care division to president and CEO. The same year Kao broke off talks to purchase Kanebo.

In 2008 the company sold its fatty amine business to Akzo Nobel Surface Chemistry, a unit of Akzo Nobel.

EXECUTIVES

President, CEO, and Director: Motoki Ozaki
President, Global Food and Beverage: Takuji Yasukawa
President, Global Human Health Care Business: Katsuhiko Yoshida
President, Global Chemical Business and Director: Toshihide Saito
SEVP Global Production and Engineering, Strategic Environment and Safety Management, Logistics, and Director: Takua Goto, age 70
Director; SEVP Kao Customer Marketing, Prestige Cosmetics: Mikio Nakano
EVP Global Legal and Compliance, Global Corporate Communications, Global Information Systems and Director: Shunichi Nakagawa
EVP and Director; President and CEO, Kao Customer Marketing: Tatsuo Takahashi
EVP Global Research and Development, Product Quality Management and Director: Toshiharu Numata
EVP Global Business Development and Director: Norihiko Takagi
EVP Global Consumer Products, Global Beauty Care Business Unit: Hiroshi Kanda
VP Global Accounting and Finance and Director: Shinichi Mita
VP Corporate Strategy; President and CEO, Kao Brands Company: William J. (Bill) Gentner
VP, Global Beauty Care Business; President, Global Prestige Cosmetics and Global Premium Skin Care: Masumi Natsusaka
VP Global Human Capital Development: Yasushi Aoki
VP Global Marketing Development and Global Research: Shigeru Koshiba
VP Global Business Development and Director: Masato Hirota
VP Global Procurement and Director: Ken Hashimoto
Auditors: Deloitte Touche Tohmatsu

LOCATIONS

HQ: Kao Corporation
14-10 Nihonbashi Kayabacho, 1-chome, Chuo-ku
Tokyo 103-8210, Japan
Phone: 81-3-3660-7111   **Fax:** 81-3-3660-8978
Web: www.kao.co.jp/en

2010 Sales

	% of total
Asia & Oceania	
Japan	76
Other countries	9
Europe	9
North America	6
Total	**100**

PRODUCTS/OPERATIONS

2010 Sales

	% of total
Consumer	
Beauty care	46
Fabric & home care	23
Human health care	16
Chemical	15
Total	**100**

Selected Products

Fatty chemicals and edible oils
Hygiene and bath products
Laundry and cleaning products
Personal care products and cosmetics

Selected Brand Names

Attack (laundry detergent)
Ban (deodorant)
Bioré (skin care)
Bub (shower gel)
Econa (cooking oil)
Family Kyukyutto (dishwashing detergent)
Jergens (skin care)
Laurier (sanitary napkins)
Merries (disposable diapers)
Quickle Wiper (electrostatic duster)

HISTORICAL FINANCIALS

Company Type: Public

Income Statement

FYE: March 31

	REVENUE ($ mil.)	NET INCOME ($ mil.)	NET PROFIT MARGIN	EMPLOYEES
3/10	12,777	552	4.3%	34,913
3/09	13,119	663	5.1%	33,745
3/08	13,279	670	5.0%	32,900
3/07	10,451	598	5.7%	32,175
3/06	8,261	605	7.3%	29,908
Annual Growth	11.5%	(2.3%)	—	3.9%

2010 Year-End Financials

Debt ratio: —
Return on equity: 9.4%
Cash ($ mil.): 757
Current ratio: 1.41
Long-term debt ($ mil.): —

No. of shares (mil.): 537
Dividends
  Yield: 2.3%
  Payout: 70.7%
Market value ($ mil.): 13,719

Stock History

Pink Sheets: KAOCF

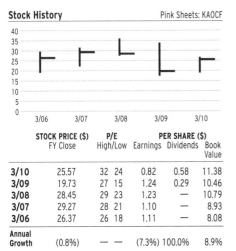

	STOCK PRICE ($) FY Close	P/E High/Low		PER SHARE ($) Earnings	Dividends	Book Value
3/10	25.57	32	24	0.82	0.58	11.38
3/09	19.73	27	15	1.24	0.29	10.46
3/08	28.45	29	23	1.23	—	10.79
3/07	29.27	28	21	1.10	—	8.93
3/06	26.37	26	18	1.11	—	8.08
Annual Growth	(0.8%)	—	—	(7.3%)	100.0%	8.9%

Kesko Corporation

You name it, Kesko sells it. The Finnish firm is big in importing, distributing, and wholesaling in its homeland and in Estonia, Latvia, Lithuania, Norway, Sweden, and now Russia and Belarus. Its largest division, Kesko Food (about 45% of sales) includes more than 1,000 of its own "K" food stores (operating in a variety of formats mostly in Finland and in the Baltic countries). Kesko also operates about 870 other retail outlets — from department stores and home and specialty shops (shoes and sporting goods), to stores selling hardware, builders' supplies, agriculture goods, and machinery. Kesko also is a wholesaler and imports vehicles made by Volkswagen and Audi through its VV-Auto division.

In Finland, where the company claims to have about a third of the grocery market, sales at its K-food stores increased by more than 5% in 2009 vs. 2008. (Food sales posted a more modest 2.4% increase across all of Kesko's markets.) However, the performance of Kesko's more economically sensitive businesses — including building and home improvment retail, and sales of cars and machinery — posted double-digit declines in 2009. The company blamed the global recession for the weakness and laid off employees in those divisions. Across the entire business, Kesko posted about a 12% drop in net sales in 2009 vs. 2008.

To grow in Finland, Kesko is building more stores in urban areas, and is continuing its expansion in Russia and the Baltic countries with acquisitions and new-store openings. Its building and home improvement supplies subsidiary Rautakesko owns a majority interest in Norgros AS, Norway-based owner of about 115 Byggmakker hardware and building materials stores. (Byggmakker is the largest building and home improvement store chain in Norway.) Rautakesko will focus its expansion particularly on Russia in the next few years.

Kesko's Anttila department store division operates about 30 stores and is the leading home and specialty goods retailer in Finland. Anttila's full-scale department stores sell apparel, entertainment and home goods. It also operates about 10 Kodin Ykkönen department stores that specialize in interior decor and home goods. Its e-commerce operation, NetAnttila, sells products in Finland, Estonia, and Latvia.

Most of the 330 PLUS stores in Kesko's Hardware and Builders' Supplies unit fly the K-rauta and Rautia flags in Estonia, Finland, Latvia, Russia, and Sweden. The Kekso Agriculture and Machinery unit includes K-agriculture stores selling heavy machinery for commercial use, as well as light machinery and boating products.

Kesko Agro operates some 90 stores in Finland. They sell animal feed and agricultural chemicals and machinery.

HISTORY

Kesko sprung from four Finnish wholesalers and retailers (Kauppiaitten Oy, Keski-Suomen Tukkukauppa Oy, Maakauppiaitten Oy, and Savo-Karjalan Tukkuliike) in 1940. To centralize their purchasing and business needs, the foursome merged. Kesko was up and running early the next year with some 5,800 retail members. In 1947 the company formed a retail group and Kesko's signature K-emblem made its debut.

In the 1950s Kesko's K-emblem appeared on about 3,700 member stores, and the company expanded into the agricultural and construction supplies industry.

The company listed on the Helsinki Stock Exchange in 1960. That decade Kesko added fresh foods to its general stores, which later helped it evolve into a grocery retailer. Self-service became the norm in the mid 1960s, permanently changing the Finnish retailing landscape. A centralized distribution center was established near Helsinki, and Kesko began selling its industrial operations.

In the 1970s Kesko developed its first supermarket and started selling home products, specialty merchandise (opening sporting goods retailer Kesport), and hardware items.

Investments (and divestments) were Kesko's game in the 1980s; it bought new offices, a new warehouse site, and a few large retail units. The company continued to sell most of its industrial operations, which had grown to include a flour-mill, match and bicycle factories, and a rye crisp business. Kesko kept its most profitable unit — a coffee roastery (Viking Coffee). That decade Kesko introduced its first private-label food brand (Pirkka).

Kesko's sales slumped in the early 1990s in response to recessions in Finland and the world. By 1994, though, all was well again. The company began expanding into Sweden and then Russia, opening stores under a variety of formats. In 1996 Kesko acquired Kaukomarkkinat Oy (commercial trading house), sold metal distributor Keskometalli Oy, and tried acquiring Finnish supermarket chain Tuko. But Finland's European Commission stopped the deal from going through to protect the country's smaller merchants. The following year Kesko bought information technology firm Academica Oy.

The 1990s also saw Kesko acquiring Anttila Oy, a department store operator. In 1999 the company appointed Matti Honkala as its new CEO (the former was Eero Utter). The company controlled 50% of the Finnish market.

In 2000 Kesko announced it would open four hypermarkets in Latvia by 2004. In early 2001 Kesko turned its foods unit and home and specialty goods group into wholly owned subsidiaries, and said it would do the same with its hardware and builders' supplies unit and the agriculture and machinery segment later in 2001. Also that year it acquired 17 Saastumarket stores in Estonia, opened two more, and announced plans to build at least 10 more.

In 2004 Matti Halmesmäki replaced the retiring Matti Honkala as CEO.

In July 2005 Rautakesko acquired the Stroymaster DIY chain in Russia and converted them to the K-rauta banner in August 2006.

In January 2006 Konekesko sold its warehouse technology (forklifts and warehouse racks) business in Finland to BT Industries of Sweden for a gain of about €2.6 million. In December Kesko Food sold its 50% stake in Rimi Baltic AB to ICA Baltic AB for E190 million.

In March 2008 Kesko sold its interest in Tähti Optikko Group, an optical goods chain. In April it sold its export/import firm Kauko-Telko to Aspo. Kauko-Telko (formerly Kaukomarkkinat) traded in home electronics, technical products, optical items, sporting goods, and watches.

EXECUTIVES

Chairman: Heikki Takamäki, age 63
Deputy Chair: Seppo Paatelainen, age 66
President and CEO: Matti Halmesmäki, age 58
SVP and CFO: Arja Talma, age 48
SVP Corporate Communications: Paavo Moilanen, age 58
SVP Human Resources: Riitta Laitasalo, age 55
Chief Risk Officer: Seppo Aakio
VP and Corporate Controller: Jukka Erlund, age 36
VP and CIO: Arto Hiltunen, age 34
VP and General Counsel: Anne Leppälä-Nilsson, age 57
Group Treasurer: Heikki Ala-Seppälä, age 48
Director Internal Audit: Pasi Mäkinen, age 50
Information Technology Manager: Satu Koskinen, age 35
President, UAB Senuku Prekybos Centras, Lithuania: Arturas Rakauskas, age 38
President, Musta Pörssi: Leena Havikari, age 51
President, K-citymarket and Anttila Oy: Ari Akseli, age 38
President, Indoor Group: Jussi Mikkola, age 54
President, Rautakesko: Jari Lind, age 52
President, Kesko Food: Terho Kalliokoski, age 49
President, VV-Auto Group Oy: Pekka Lahti, age 55
President, Kenkäkesko: Martti Toivanen, age 49
President, Intersport Finland: Juha Nurminen, age 47
President, Home and Specialty Goods; Head e-Marketing and Services: Matti Leminen, age 59
Auditors: SVH Pricewaterhouse Coopers Oy

LOCATIONS

HQ: Kesko Corporation
Satamakatu 3
00016 Helsinki, Finland
Phone: 358-10--5311   **Fax:** 358-9-657-465
Web: www.kesko.fi

2009 Sales

	% of total
Finland	83
Other Nordic countries	8
Baltic countries	6
Other countries	3
Total	**100**

PRODUCTS/OPERATIONS

2009 Sales

	% of total
Food	44
Building & home improvement	27
Home & specialty goods	18
Car & machinery	11
Total	**100**

Selected Kesko Divisions

Kesko Agro Ltd. (agriculture and machinery)
Kesko Food Ltd. (groceries)
Anttila (department stores, home and specialty goods)
Rautakesko Ltd. (building supplies, interior decoration, and hardware)
VV-Auto (auto dealerships)

COMPETITORS

Axfood
ICA AB
IKEA
Kooperativa Förbundet
Lähikauppa
Leroy Merlin
Lidl
Rautakirja
Royal Ahold
Tengelmann

HISTORICAL FINANCIALS

Company Type: Public

Income Statement

FYE: December 31

	REVENUE ($ mil.)	NET INCOME ($ mil.)	NET PROFIT MARGIN	EMPLOYEES
12/09	13,747	226	1.6%	19,184
12/08	13,532	339	2.5%	21,327
12/07	14,033	420	3.0%	—
12/06	11,543	486	4.2%	—
12/05	9,382	215	2.3%	21,603
Annual Growth	**10.0%**	**1.3%**	**—**	**(2.9%)**

2009 Year-End Financials

Debt ratio: —
Return on equity: 7.9%
Cash ($ mil.): 106
Current ratio: 1.56
Long-term debt ($ mil.): —

No. of shares (mil.): 99
Dividends
  Yield: 4.3%
  Payout: 44.5%
Market value ($ mil.): 3,263

Stock History

OMX Helsinki: KESBV

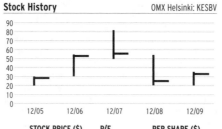

	STOCK PRICE ($) FY Close	P/E High/Low		PER SHARE ($) Earnings	Dividends	Book Value
12/09	33.08	11	7	3.21	1.43	30.07
12/08	25.09	17	7	3.16	2.26	28.09
12/07	55.52	—	—	—	—	28.49
12/06	52.80	—	—	—	—	23.41
12/05	28.36	—	—	—	—	17.78
Annual Growth	**3.9%**			**1.6%**	**(36.7%)**	**14.0%**

Kingfisher plc

Kingfisher is a big fish in do-it-yourself (DIY) retail. Europe's leading home improvement retail group and the third-largest in the world, Kingfisher operates more than 820 home improvement stores in about eight countries in Europe and Asia. The company's DIY portfolio includes B&Q stores in the UK, Ireland, and China (among other countries), and Castorama and Brico Dépôt in France, Poland, and now Russia. (The UK-based chain has exited the Italian market, citing rosier growth prospects elsewhere.) Kingfisher's other DIY stores include Brico Dépôt in Spain, and 50%-owned Koçtas in Turkey. Kingfisher's Screwfix business is the UK's largest direct and online supplier of tools to the trade.

Kingfisher's rapid expansion in China, where it had grown to number more than 60 B&Q outlets (the Beijing B&Q is the world's biggest), led to operational difficulties in that lucrative market. As a result, Kingfisher is reducing its store count in China by about a third (to some 40 stores), and downsizing about half of the remaining locations in an attempt to cut its losses and right the business. It is also remerchandising its China stores to focus more on home decor, soft furnishings, and accessories to cater to the growing population of apartment dwellers there.

Russia is a growth market on Kingfisher's global itinerary. The company currently has about a dozen Castorama stores there, but plans to build many more. To that end, Kingfisher has appointed a former IKEA executive, Peter Partma, as the country manager for Castorama Russia. Kingfisher hopes to replicate its success in Poland, where it has about 50 outlets and plans to increase that number to more than 60 in the near future, in Russia.

At home, Kingfisher is attempting to reverse the slump in DIY sales brought on by the recession and housing market crash. To that end, Kingfisher is remodeling 110 of its biggest B&Q warehouse stores in Britain. The company is also looking to expand its considerable acreage within the UK, with plans to expand its building trade-oriented chain that would bring its French Brico into the country, as well as drilling in deeper with Screwfix. In addition to the websites of its banners, Kingfisher reels in more business online through Screwfix Direct, which operates a website that offers next-day delivery of tools and other hardware products.

In France, the company's second-largest market behind the UK, sales have held up relatively well, as French consumers are much less indebted than the British.

Kingfisher owns about a fifth of Hornbach Holding, the parent company of German DIY warehouse retailer Hornbach-Baumarkt, with more than 120 stores across Europe.

HISTORY

The beginning of Kingfisher is directly tied to the former US Woolworth chain (now Foot Locker). With the success of F.W. Woolworth general merchandise stores in the US, founder Frank Woolworth expanded overseas, first to Canada, then in 1909 to Liverpool, England. By 1914 Woolworth's UK subsidiaries had 31 stores.

Growing quickly, the company went public in 1931, with its US parent retaining a 53% stake. The company spent most of the postwar years rebuilding bombed stores and had 762 stores by 1950.

The company opened its first Woolco Department Store, modeled after the US Woolco stores of its parent, in 1967. However, other retailers had cut into sales, and by 1968 it lost its place as Britain's leading retailer to Marks and Spencer. In 1973 it opened Shoppers World, a catalog showroom. It made its first takeover in 1980, buying B&Q, a chain of 40 do-it-yourself stores.

An investment group acquired Woolworth in 1982 using the vehicle Paternoster Stores. (The US parent sold its stake in Woolworth.) The company, renamed Woolworth Holdings, closed unprofitable Woolworth stores and sold its Shoppers World stores in 1983 and its Ireland Woolworth stores in 1984. It also acquired Comet, a UK home electronics chain, and continued to expand B&Q.

Two years later all of its F.W. Woolworth stores were renamed Woolworths, and food and clothing lines were abandoned. Also in 1986 the company sold its Woolco stores and bought record and tape distributor Record Merchandisers (later renamed Entertainment UK). The next year Woolworth Holdings acquired Superdrug, a chain of 297 discount drugstores. Adding to its Superdrug chain, in 1988 the company acquired and integrated two UK pharmacy chains: 110-store Tip Top Drugstores and 145-store Share Drug.

To reflect its growing diversity of businesses, the company was renamed Kingfisher in 1989. Also that year it bought drug retailer Medicare. Expanding further into electronics, in 1993 Kingfisher acquired Darty, with 130 stores.

Following the lead of rival Dixons, in 1999 Kingfisher launched its own free Internet access service in France called Libertysurf. Soon thereafter, Libertysurf acquired 70% of Objectif Net and its website, Nomade.fr.

Kingfisher demerged Woolworths Group in 2001 in a public offering. With Woolies went electronic entertainment companies EUK, MVC, VCI, and Streets Online.

CEO Geoffrey Mulcahy stepped down in 2002 and was replaced by Gerry Murphy, formerly CEO for Carlton (now ITV plc), in 2003. Kingfisher sold its 20 retail parks for $1.1 billion to a consortium that includes real estate firms Pillar Property and Capital & Regional Properties the same year. Also in 2003 Kingfisher sold ProMarkt, with about 190 stores in Germany, to its former owners, Michael and Matthias Wegert.

To focus on DIY, Kingfisher floated its electrical businesses as a new company, Kesa Electricals, in 2003. Kingfisher sold two home improvement chains that year. Réno-Dépôt, which operates about 20 home-improvement stores in Canada, was sold to RONA.

In 2005 the company acquired its biggest competitor in Asia, OBI Asia, which added about a dozen stores in China and its first outlet in South Korea. In 2006 Kingfisher entered Russia, with its first Castorama store there. In May, Sir Francis Mackay retired as chairman of the company and was succeeded by Peter Jackson.

In January 2008 Kingfisher named Ian Cheshire as its new chief executive succeeding Gerry Murphy, who resigned in late 2007. Cheshire joined B&Q in 1998. In 2008 Kingfisher sold its Italian Castorama business to France's Groupe ADEO for $871 million.

Daniel Bernard took over the chairman's seat from Jackson in 2009.

EXECUTIVES

Chairman: Daniel Bernard, age 64
CEO and Director: Ian Cheshire, age 50
Group Finance Director and Board Member: Kevin O'Byrne, age 45
Group Innovation Director: Andy Wiggins
Group Property Director: Ian Playford
Group Communications Director: Ian Harding, age 45
Group Commercial Director: Veronique Laury-Deroubaix
Director, Corporate Affairs: Nick Folland, age 44
CEO, B&Q China: Loic Dubois
CEO, Castorama Poland: Janusz Lella
CEO, Screwfix: Steve Willett
CEO, Castorama Russia: Oleg Pisklov
CEO, UK Division: Euan A. Sutherland, age 41
CEO, France: Phillipe Tible, age 58
CEO, International: Peter Høgsted, age 41
Head, Investor Relations: Sarah Gerrand
Auditors: PricewaterhouseCoopers LLP

LOCATIONS

HQ: Kingfisher plc
3 Sheldon Sq., Paddington
London W2 6PX, United Kingdom
Phone: 44-20-7372-8008   **Fax:** 44-20-7644-1001
Web: www.kingfisher.co.uk

2010 Sales

	% of total
UK & Ireland	42
France	41
Rest of Europe & China	17
Total	**100**

2010 Stores

	No.
UK	477
France	201
Poland	56
China	43
Turkey	26
Spain	16
Russia	12
Total	**831**

COMPETITORS

Focus (DIY)
Grafton Group
Grafton Merchanting
Homebase Limited
Leroy Merlin
METRO AG
MPS Builders and Merchants
Praktiker
Saint-Gobain Building Distribution
Tengelmann
Travis Perkins
Wolseley

HISTORICAL FINANCIALS

Company Type: Public

Income Statement

FYE: January 31

	REVENUE ($ mil.)	NET INCOME ($ mil.)	NET PROFIT MARGIN	EMPLOYEES
1/10	16,786	620	3.7%	80,010
1/09	14,572	304	2.1%	85,000
1/08	18,006	545	3.0%	85,000
1/07	17,028	661	3.9%	80,200
1/06	14,155	247	1.7%	75,500
Annual Growth	**4.4%**	**25.9%**	**—**	**1.5%**

2010 Year-End Financials

Debt ratio: —
Return on equity: 8.3%
Cash ($ mil.): 2,014
Current ratio: —
Long-term debt ($ mil.): —

No. of shares (mil.): 2,362
Dividends
   Yield: 2.5%
   Payout: —
Market value ($ mil.): 8,014

Stock History

Pink Sheets: KGFHY

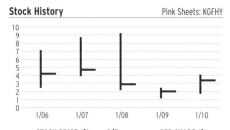

	STOCK PRICE ($) FY Close	P/E High/Low		PER SHARE ($) Earnings	Dividends	Book Value
1/10	3.39	—	—	—	0.09	3.35
1/09	2.02	—	—	—	0.08	2.95
1/08	2.90	—	—	—	0.21	3.98
1/07	4.70	—	—	—	0.21	3.67
1/06	4.20	—	—	—	0.19	3.23
Annual Growth	**(5.2%)**	**—**	**—**	**—**	**(17.0%)**	**0.9%**

Kirin Holdings

You might say this company makes good-luck beer. Named for a unicorn, which is a Japanese symbol of good fortune, Kirin Holdings is a top beer maker in Japan through its Kirin Brewery Co. In addition to its domestic Kirin-branded beers, the company owns brewers that serve overseas markets, such as Australia's Lion Nathan. The beer brewer also makes the alcoholic fruit drink chu-hi and owns some 50% of Japanese wine producer Mercian Corporation. Expanding beyond beverages, Kirin also has operations in the health- and functional-food, and pharmaceutical-manufacturing sectors.

Kirin Holdings revamped its top management in 2010 to foster growth. To that end, early in the year it named company veteran Senji Miyake president and CEO of the Japanese brewer, among other top management changes. Miyake joined Kirin Brewery Company in 1970.

The company began talks with rival Japanese brewer Suntory Holdings in 2009 about a possible merger of the two companies. However, negotiations were cancelled in early 2010.

Kirin is overhauling its operations in Japan to gear up for future mergers and acquisitions. Representing its first significant acquisition since the failed Suntory deal, Kirin in July 2010 inked a deal with Fraser & Neave, based in Singapore, valued at $970 million for about a 15% stake in the firm. The complementary company boasts brewery operations (37 breweries in 14 countries) and soft drinks businesses spanning Malaysia, Thailand, and Singapore.

Kirin took 100% control of Lion Nathan in 2009. It paid A$3.5 billion (about $3.2 billion) to acquire the 54% of Lion that it did not already own. The purchase was part of Kirin's long-term strategy of investing in other countries. It does so because of Japan's demographics (i.e., more people are dying there than are being born). Australia presents Kirin with a stable customer base. In the same vein, Kirin also acquired 48% of Filipino beer maker San Miguel Brewery for some $1.2 billion in 2009.

In the US Kirin owns soft-drink bottler Coca-Cola Bottling Company of Northern New England, bourbon maker Four Roses Distillery in Kentucky, and Raymond Vineyards in California. Other international holdings include a minority stake in San Miguel Corporation, the leading food and beverage company in the Philippines . The company is expanding its presence in China with the development of a brewery in Zhuhai City, and through alliances with local breweries in the Yangtze River Delta area and northeast China.

Kirin Holdings has operations that make coffee and tea drinks and mineral water. It is also involved in potato growing and cut-flower production. The company's pharmaceutical products include treatments for renal anemia and leucopenia; in the development pipeline are treatments for kidney-cell cancer and other kidney diseases.

HISTORY

American William Copeland went to Yokohama, Japan, in 1864 and five years later established the Spring Valley Brewery, the first in Japan, to provide beer for foreign nationals. Lacking funds to continue the brewery, Copeland closed it in 1884. The next year a group of foreign and Japanese businessmen reopened it as

Japan Brewery. The business created the Kirin label in 1888 and was soon profitable.

The operation was run primarily by Americans and Europeans at first, but by 1907 Japanese workers had filled the ranks and adopted the Kirin Brewery Company name. Sales plummeted during WWII when the government limited brewing output. After the war, the US occupation forces inadvertently assisted Kirin when they split Dai Nippon Brewery (Kirin's main competitor) into two companies (Asahi and Sapporo Breweries) while leaving Kirin intact. The company became Japan's leading brewer during the 1950s.

During the 1970s Kirin introduced several soft drinks and in 1972 branched into hard liquor through a joint venture with Seagram (Kirin-Seagram). The firm bought several Coca-Cola bottling operations in New England and Japan in the 1980s. Kirin also entered the pharmaceuticals business, in part through a joint venture with US-based Amgen. In 1988 the brewer signed an agreement with Molson to produce Kirin beer for the North American market. In 1989 Kirin bought Napa Valley's Raymond Vineyards.

In 1991 Kirin formed a partnership to market Tropicana drinks in Japan. It also entered an alliance with Sankyo (Japan's #2 drug company) in 1991 to market Kirin's medication for anemia, which it had developed with Amgen.

Chairman Hideyo Motoyama resigned in 1993 after four company executives were arrested for allegedly paying a group of racketeers who had threatened to disrupt Kirin's annual meeting. Joint venture Kirin-Amgen won the rights to make thrombopoietin (TPO), a blood platelet growth stimulator, in 1995.

Yasuhiro Satoh became president of Kirin in 1996. The brewer moved into China that year through an agreement with China Resources (Shenyang) Snowflake Brewery. To brew its beers in the US, the company formed Kirin Brewery of America, also in 1996.

In response to losing market share to Asahi, Kirin cut its workforce in 1998 and introduced Tanrei, a cheaper, low-malt beer that quickly captured half of its market. Building on its presence in China, Kirin bought 46% of brewer Lion Nathan (based in Australia and New Zealand) for $742.5 million that year. It became a licensed brewer of Anheuser-Busch in 1999.

Like other Japanese brewers, Kirin struggled against dwindling demand for its most expensive brews in 2000. Koichiro Aramaki was named president of the company the following year and began to expand and diversify Kirin's operations to overcome slow growth domestically. In 2002 the company bought 15% of Philippine food and drink giant San Miguel for about $530 million. It also boosted ties with beverage giant Pernod Ricard by purchasing 32% of SIFA, a French food services firm, for an estimated $155 million. In 2002 Kirin launched its new Pure Blue brand of "shochu" distilled liquor.

In 2006 Aramaki stepped down as president (he remained chairman) and turned the reins over to former managing director Kazuyasu Kato. The company added to its international dairy holdings with its 2007 acquisition of Australian milk and cheese producer National Foods. The following year National Foods acquired Australian dairy company Australian Co-operative Foods Limited for about $763 million.

In 2010 EVP Senji Miyake was named CEO, suceeding Kato, who was named chairman.

EXECUTIVES

Chairman: Kazuyasu Kato, age 65
President, CEO, and Director: Senji Miyake
Managing Director and CFO: Yoshiharu Furumoto
Managing Director: Yuji Owada
Managing Director: Etsuji Tawada
EVP and Director: Kazuhiro Sato
VP, Pharmaceutical Research Laboratories:
 Junichi Koumegawa
Auditor: Teruo Ozaki
Auditor: Toyoshi Nakano
Auditor: Kazuo Tezuka
Corporate Auditor: Hitoshi Oshima
Corporate Auditor: Tetsuo Iwasa
Auditors: KPMG AZSA & Co.

LOCATIONS

HQ: Kirin Holdings Company, Limited
  10-1 Shinkawa 2-chome, Chuo-ku
  Tokyo 104-8288, Japan
Phone: 81-3-5541-5321   **Fax:** 81-3-5540-3547
Web: www.kirinholdings.co.jp

2009 Sales

	% of total
Japan	77
Asia/Oceania	20
Other regions	3
Total	**100**

PRODUCTS/OPERATIONS

2009 Sales

	% of total
Alcoholic beverages	48
Food & soft drinks	32
Pharmaceuticals	9
Other	11
Total	**100**

Selected Products

Alcoholic beverages
  XXXX Gold (beer)
  Chateau Mercian
  Four Roses Bourbon Whiskey
  Kirin Chu-hi Hyoketsu (alcoholic fruit drink)
  Kirin Lager Beer
  Kirin Nodogoshi (no-malt beer)
  Mercian Bon Rouge
  Mercian Franzia Wine
  Red Horse (beer)
  San Miguel (beer)
  Steinlater (beer)
  Tanrei (happo-shu beer)
Food
  Big M (chocolate milk)
  PURA (milk)
  Tasmainian Heritage (cheese)
Soft drinks
  Beri (juice)
  Gogono-Kocha (tea)
  Kirin Alkali-Ion-no-Mizu (mineral water)
  Kirin Fire (coffee drink)
  Kirin Nuda (sparkling water)
  Nama-cha (tea)
  Volvic (mineral water)
Pharmaceuticals
  ESPO
  GRAN
  PHOSBLOCK Tablets
  Rocaltrol Injection
Other
  Agricultural products
  Commercial flower production
  Health and dietary supplements

COMPETITORS

Anheuser-Busch InBev
Asahi Breweries
Asia Pacific Breweries
Carlsberg
Chugai
Coca-Cola
Diageo
E. & J. Gallo
FEMSA
Fonterra
Foster's Group
Heineken
ITOCHU
Kokubu
LVMH
Meg Snow Brand Milk Co.
Mercian
Molson Coors
Nippon Beet Sugar
Novartis
Pabst
PepsiCo
Red Bull
SABMiller
Sapporo
Suntory Holdings
Taiwan Tobacco & Wine
Takara
Tsingtao
Yanjing

HISTORICAL FINANCIALS

Company Type: Public

Income Statement

FYE: December 31

	REVENUE ($ mil.)	NET INCOME ($ mil.)	NET PROFIT MARGIN	EMPLOYEES
12/09	24,701	533	2.2%	35,150
12/08	21,275	887	4.2%	36,554
12/07	12,467	594	4.8%	27,543
12/06	10,609	449	4.2%	23,332
12/05	13,860	436	3.1%	22,089
Annual Growth	**15.5%**	**5.2%**	**—**	**12.3%**

2009 Year-End Financials

Debt ratio: 63.7%
Return on equity: —
Cash ($ mil.): 1,361
Current ratio: 1.06
Long-term debt ($ mil.): 6,781

No. of shares (mil.): 953
Dividends
  Yield: 1.5%
  Payout: 44.6%
Market value ($ mil.): 15,399

Stock History

Pink Sheets: KNBWY

	STOCK PRICE ($) FY Close	P/E High/Low		PER SHARE ($) Earnings	Dividends	Book Value
12/09	16.15	30	17	0.56	0.25	11.16
12/08	13.01	—	—	0.00	0.13	11.42
12/07	14.61	—	—	0.00	—	8.65
12/06	15.71	—	—	0.00	—	7.74
12/05	11.67	28	19	0.45	—	—
Annual Growth	**8.5%**			**5.6%**	**92.3%**	**13.0%**

Koç Holding

In Turkey, Koç (pronounced "coach") class equals first class. Led by its energy businesses, Koç Holding is Turkey's dominant industrial conglomerate. The company's Tofas unit, an alliance with Fiat, is Turkey's champion carmaker; Koç's joint venture with Ford Motor sells imported Ford models. Other businesses include consumer goods such as large household appliances (Arçelik, teaming up with LG Electronics) and energy (distribution of liquefied petroleum gas). Subsidiaries engage in food production, construction, international trading, and hospitality and tourism. Koç also operates banking, securities brokerage, and insurance businesses. The Koç family, one of the wealthiest in Turkey, controls the company.

Koç is reaching far across the Bosporus while simultaneously refocusing its efforts in consumer goods, automotive, finance, and energy markets. Koç and Royal Dutch Shell together continue to drive a 51% stake in oil refiner TÜPRAS. TÜPRAS, the 8th largest refining company in Europe, controls 40% ownership in the fuel distribution company Opet Petrolcülük. Significant company moves in 2008 include selling its Otomotiv Lastikleri Tevzi (Oltas) to Germany's Continental AG. Oltas has distributed Continental tires and related products since 2003. The company's interest in supermarkets dwindled to less than 50% with the sale of its stake in Migros. Its sway, however, in the IT data processing business of KoçNet Haberleme Teknolojileri ve Iletiim Hizmetleri A. increased to almost 100%. The company picked up military aero and marine tech simulator Kaletron, an arm of Kale Group, too.

With a combined stake of over 70%, members of the Koç family direct the operations of Koç Holding. Former chairman of the board Rahmi Koç holds an honorary chairman position, and his oldest son, Mustafa Koç (a third-generation owner), takes the reins as chairman.

HISTORY

In 1917, 16-year-old Vehbi Koç and his father opened a small grocery store in Ankara, Turkey. With the fall of the Ottoman Empire after WWI, Turkey's capital was moved to Ankara, which was then only a village. The Koçs recognized an opportunity and expanded into construction and building supplies, winning a contract to repair the roof of the Turkish parliament building. By age 26, Koç was a millionaire.

Ford Motor made Koç its Turkish agent in 1928. In 1931 Mobil Oil and Koç entered an exclusive agreement to search for oil in Turkey. The company incorporated in 1938 as Koç Ticaret Corporation, the first Turkish joint stock company with an employee stock-ownership program.

Despite Turkey's neutrality in WWII, the fighting disrupted Koç's business. The nation became isolationist after the war and restricted foreign concerns to selling through local agents; Koç benefited by importing foreign products.

General Electric and Koç entered a joint venture in 1946 to build Turkey's first lightbulb factory. In 1955 Koç set up Arçelik, the first Turkish producer of refrigerators, washing machines, and water heaters; Türk Demir Döküm, the first Turkish producer of radiators and, later, auto castings; and Turkay, the country's first private

producer of matches. In 1959 Koç constructed Turkey's first truck assembly plant (Otosan).

Other firsts followed in the 1960s as the company leveraged its size and government influence to attract more ventures. These included a tire factory (with Uniroyal), a cable factory (with Siemens), production of electric motors and compressors (with GE), and the production of Anadol, the first car to be made entirely in Turkey (by Otosan, under license from Ford). In 1974 Koç expanded into retailing with the purchase of Migros, Turkey's largest chain of supermarkets.

The Turkish military imposed martial law in 1980 and restricted foreign exchange payments, forcing Koç to limit its operations. In 1986, a year after foreign companies were allowed to export products directly to Turkey, Koç and American Express started Koç-Amerikan Bank (which Koç bought out and renamed Koçbank in 1992). In the late 1980s Vehbi's only son, Rahmi, took over the company's leadership. Vehbi Koç died in 1996.

Auto sales fell sharply in 1996 as buyers awaited the country's entry into the European Union's customs union. In an effort to offset market risks, Koç forged a number of alliances in 1997. It participated in a British-Canadian-Turkish consortium that was building a large power plant in central Turkey.

Reflecting a greater willingness to open the company to foreign investors, Koç announced plans to offer $250 million in shares in a public offering in 1998, but it soon canceled the offering because of market volatility. A year later the company completed an auto plant in Samarkand, Uzbekistan, to build Otoyol-Iveco buses and trucks.

Koç entered into a joint venture — Koç Finansal Hizmetler — with Unicredito Italiano in 2002 in an effort to further consolidate its financial holdings.

EXECUTIVES

Honorary Chairman: Rahmi M. Koç, age 80
Chairman: Mustafa V. Koç, age 50
Vice Chairman: Ömer M. Koç, age 48
Vice Chairman: Temel K. Atay, age 69
Vice Chairman: Suna Kiraç, age 69
CEO and Director: Bülent Bulgurlu, age 63
President and CFO, Finance: Ahmet Ashabolu
President, Consumer Durables Group:
  Aka Gunduz Ozdemir
**President, Defense Industry and Other Automotive
  Group:** Kudret Onen
President, Food/Retailing and Tourism: Ömer Bozer
President, Automotive Group: Turgay Durak
President, Energy: Erol Memio∂lu, age 56
President, Foreign Trade and Tourism: Hasan Bengü,
  age 61
President, Strategic Planning: Tamer Ha ̧imo∂lu
President, Auditing: Ali Tank Uzun
**President, Corporate Communications and Information
  Technology Group; and Director:** Ali Y. Koç, age 43
Chief Legal Advisor: Kenan Yilmaz
Secretary General: Tahsin Saltik
Human Resources Director: Mert Bayram

LOCATIONS

HQ: Koç Holding A.S.
  Nakkastepe Azizbey Sok. No. 1, Kuzguncuk
  34674 Istanbul, Turkey
Phone: 90-216-531-0000   **Fax:** 90-216-531-0099
Web: www.koc.com.tr

PRODUCTS/OPERATIONS

2009 Sales

	% of total
Energy	55
Consumer durables	15
Automotive	13
Finance	12
Other	5
Total	**100**

Core Businesses

Automotive
Construction and mining
Durable goods
Food/Beverage/Tobacco
Energy
Financial services
Information technology
International trade
Marinas
New business development
Tourism and services

COMPETITORS

Adam Opel
Caterpillar
Electrolux
Hellenic Petroleum
Honda
International Power
Renault
Robert Bosch
Sabanci
Siemens AG
Yazicilar

HISTORICAL FINANCIALS

Company Type: Public

Income Statement

FYE: December 31

	REVENUE ($ mil.)	NET INCOME ($ mil.)	NET PROFIT MARGIN	EMPLOYEES
12/09	29,817	1,745	5.9%	71,221
12/08	36,522	1,692	4.6%	73,677
12/07	39,735	3,302	8.3%	84,687
12/06	36,200	411	1.1%	88,248
12/05	18,168	446	2.5%	81,926
Annual Growth	**13.2%**	**40.7%**	**—**	**(3.4%)**

2009 Year-End Financials

Debt ratio: —   Current ratio: —
Return on equity: 18.6%   Long-term debt ($ mil.): —
Cash ($ mil.): —

Net Income History   Istanbul: KCHOL

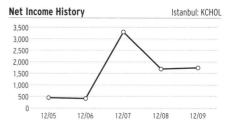

Komatsu Ltd.

Depsite a name that means "little pine tree," Komatsu produces an evergreen lineup of big equipment. The company is the world's #2 construction equipment maker, behind Caterpillar. Komatsu builds and sells building and mining equipment, from bulldozers and wheel loaders to dump trucks and debris crushers. Komatsu also produces industrial machinery, such as laser-cutting tools and sheet-metal presses. Other lines include generators, light armored vehicles, and diesel engines. Its engineering and construction arm supplies prefabricated structures, contracting, real estate sales, and leasing services. Subsidiaries, affiliates, and a distributor network drive global sales, with China as its fastest-growing market.

Amid a difficult global economy, Komatsu's performance has continued to decline. Year-over-year sales in 2009 and 2010 fell by almost 10% and 30%, respectively. However, revenues from China (the only region to sustain year-over-year improvement) grew by 24% in 2009 over 2008, and by more than 14% in 2010. Even with the increase, Komatsu's earnings during the same period plummeted by about 62% and 57%.

Komatsu has a diversified range of equipment and machines. Nonetheless, its business is dominated by construction, mining, and utility equipment markets, which represent about 85% of the company's sales. Market demand hinges largely upon infrastructure development projects, and as they dwindled in 2010 so too did revenues by more than 25% from the previous year.

Despite the downturn, the company managed to generate more than a 130% rise in cash flow from operating activities in 2010 over 2009. Komatsu's recessionary measures included reorganizing its hub plants for global production and consolidating sales and service networks. In Japan, North America, and Europe, the company trimmed, eliminated, and consolidated facilities to further curb operating expenses as well as balance inventory levels. (Four production bases remain in Japan, four in Europe, and one in the Americas.)

In the meantime, Komatsu is introducing products that feature lighter environmental impact. The Dantotsu line, for example, is touted as 25% more fuel-efficient with lower CO_2 emissions than previous models. The hybrid hydraulic excavator, Komatsu's flagship product, promises to scoop up sales in China and other strategic international sectors. The company is also expanding its hybrid electric forklift truck line, and aims to combine its production with building compact construction equipment lines.

Komatsu's future relies heavily on integrating information and communication technologies (ICT) with its products and parts. Its ICT focus led to the development of the Komatsu Machine Tracking System (KOMTRAX), now standard on its construction equipment. It also spurred introduction of the world's first Autonomous Haulage System (AHS); Codelco uses the remote-control system to run huge dump trucks at its copper mine in Chile. Komatsu's AHS is used at a mine in Australia, too. The company looks to further leverage other ICT applications to its portfolio.

HISTORY

Komatsu's roots reach back to the Takeuchi Mining Company, founded in Japan in 1894. The company grew during WWI, and in 1917 it created an in-house ironworks to make machine tools and mining equipment. The ironworks was separated in 1921 to create Komatsu Manufacturing.

The firm grew into one of Japan's major makers of machine tools and pumps by adding new products to its line. Komatsu introduced its first metal press in 1924 and in 1931 made Japan's first crawler-type farm tractor. Komatsu began making high-grade casting and specialty steel materials in 1935.

During WWII Komatsu made munitions and bulldozers for the Japanese Navy. After the war it began making construction machinery and industrial vehicles as Japan rebuilt its infrastructure. The company began building diesel engines in 1948. Komatsu continued to expand during the 1950s. In 1952 it began producing motor graders, which became its first construction equipment to be exported (to Argentina) in 1955.

During the 1960s Komatsu entered joint ventures with US manufacturers, including Cummins Engine (1961), Bucyrus Erie (1963), and International Harvester (now Navistar, 1965). Komatsu established its first overseas subsidiary, Komatsu Europe, in Belgium in 1967 and introduced the world's first radio-controlled bulldozer.

The company changed its name to Komatsu Limited in 1970. International expansion continued as subsidiaries were established in the US, Brazil, and Germany (1970), Singapore (1971), and Panama (1972). Komatsu began making bulldozers in Mexico (1976) and opened an Australian subsidiary (1978).

In the 1980s Komatsu pushed further into the US market, going head-to-head with Caterpillar. A strong dollar helped Komatsu undercut Caterpillar's prices by as much as 30%. In 1986 the company opened its first US factory in Chattanooga, Tennessee. In 1988 it merged American construction equipment-making operations with those of Dresser Industries, creating Komatsu Dresser.

Komatsu partnered with semiconductor giant Applied Materials in 1993 and entered the LAN market the next year with a print server and two types of hubs. The company expanded its construction equipment operations outside Japan in the mid-1990s, when it formed a joint venture in Vietnam and opened plants in China. Demand for construction equipment in Japan plunged soon after.

In 1997 Komatsu set up a joint venture with India's Larsen & Toubro to make hydraulic excavators. A semiconductor industry downturn prompted Komatsu to close some of its US silicon wafer operations in 1998.

Hammered by low demand for construction equipment in Japan (down nearly 80% over three years), Komatsu recorded its first loss in fiscal 1999 and closed plants. The company backed out of its joint venture with Applied Materials, selling its stake back to Applied Materials for $87 million in cash. Former GM manager Keith Sheldon was hired to overhaul the company's ailing global finances and prepare the company for listing on the New York Stock Exchange. In March 2000 the company sold its machine vision systems business to Cognex Corporation. Komatsu reached profitability in fiscal 2001 thanks to a new growth strategy focused on its construction and mining equipment businesses. Later the same year — as the economy swooned —

Komatsu announced that it expected losses and was cutting about 2,200 jobs in Japan.

Komatsu's reorganization plans launched during the last quarter of 2001 carried over through 2002 and 2003. The company implemented its new growth strategy for the construction and mining equipment business, reduced fixed costs, and restructured its electronics business. In 2003 the company showed an increase of 5.2% in consolidated net sales over the previous year. That year the company decided to dissolve its Komatsu Metal Ltd. subsidiary.

In 2005 the company sold a 75% stake in its US subsidiary Advanced Silicon Materials to Renewable Energy Corporation. Advanced Silicon Materials manufactured polycrystalline silicon for use in semiconductors.

EXECUTIVES

President, CEO, and Director: Kunio Noji, age 63
EVP and Representative Director: Yoshinori Komamura, age 62
Senior Executive Officer; VP, Construction and Mining Equipment Marketing Division; President, Product Support Division: Mamoru Hironaka
Senior Executive Officer; President, Defense Systems Division: Susumu Yamanaka
Senior Executive Officer; President, Development Division: Nobukazu Kotake
Senior Executive Officer and Director; President, Industrial Machinery: Yasuo Suzuki, age 62
Senior Executive Officer; President, Overseas Marketing, Construction and Mining Equipment Marketing Division: Taizo Kayata
Senior Executive Officer, Senmu; CFO, Supervising CSR, Corporate Communications and Investor Relations, and Director: Kenji Kinoshita, age 62
Senior Executive Officer and Director; President, Production Division Supervising Production and e-KOMATSU: Tetsuji Ohashi
Senior Executive Officer Supervising Compliance, Legal Affairs, Human Resources and Education and Safety and Health Care: Masakatsu Hioki
Senior Executive Officer, Senmu; Supervisor, Environment, Research and Design, Quality Assurance, and Director: Masao Fuchigami, age 61
Executive Officer and General Manager, Corporate Planning; President, Global Retail Finance Business: Mikio Fujitsuka
Auditors: KPMG AZSA & Co.

LOCATIONS

HQ: Komatsu Ltd.
2-3-6 Akasaka, Minato-ku
Tokyo 107-8414, Japan
Phone: 81-3-5561-2628   **Fax:** 81-3-3586-0374
US HQ: 1701 W. Golf Rd., Rolling Meadows, IL 60008
US Phone: 847-437-5800   **US Fax:** 847-437-5814
Web: www.komatsu.com

2010 Sales

	% of total
Asia/Pacific	
Japan	23
China	19
Other countries	21
Latin America	13
North America	10
Europe	6
Middle East & Africa	6
Commonwealth of Independent States (CIS)	2
Total	**100**

PRODUCTS/OPERATIONS

2010 Sales

	% of total
Construction, mining & utility equipment	89
Industrial machinery & others	11
Total	**100**

Products and Services

Construction and mining equipment
- Backhoe loaders
- Crawler dozers
- Crawler excavators
- Diesel engines and power generators
- Dump trucks
- Forest machines
- Hydraulic equipment
- Mini excavators
- Minimal swing radius excavators
- Mobile crushers/recyclers
- Motor graders
- Skid steer loaders
- Vibratory rollers
- Wheel excavators
- Wheel loaders

Industrial machinery, vehicles, and other
- Crankshaft millers
- Forging presses
- Forklift trucks
- Large presses
- Press brakes
- Recycling plants
- Shears
- Small and midsized presses

Electronics
- Excimer lasers
- Mobile tracking and communication terminals
- Network information terminals
- Semiconductor manufacturing-related thermoelectric devices
- Thermoelectric modules
- Vehicle controllers

COMPETITORS

Barloworld
Caterpillar
CLARK Material Handling
CNH Global
Coherent, Inc.
Comau
Cymer
Deere
Deere-Hitachi
Furukawa
Hitachi Construction Machinery
JLG Industries
John Deere Thibodaux
Kubota
Kuraki
Mahindra
Manitowoc
Metso Minerals
Mitsubishi Heavy Industries
Mitsubishi Materials
Mitsui
Nisshinbo
P & H Mining
RAG AG
Rasa Industries
Sumitomo
Terex
Toyota
Victor L. Phillips

HISTORICAL FINANCIALS

Company Type: Public

Income Statement

FYE: March 31

	REVENUE ($ mil.)	NET INCOME ($ mil.)	NET PROFIT MARGIN	EMPLOYEES
3/10	15,444	362	2.3%	43,458
3/09	20,782	810	3.9%	39,855
3/08	22,590	2,103	9.3%	39,267
3/07	16,063	1,397	8.7%	33,863
3/06	14,477	972	6.7%	34,597
Annual Growth	1.6%	(21.9%)	—	5.9%

2010 Year-End Financials

Debt ratio: 42.8%	No. of shares (mil.): 968
Return on equity: 4.2%	Dividends
Cash ($ mil.): 889	Yield: 0.8%
Current ratio: 1.62	Payout: 43.2%
Long-term debt ($ mil.): 3,851	Market value ($ mil.): 20,463

Stock History

Pink Sheets: KMTUY

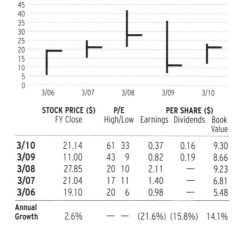

	STOCK PRICE ($) FY Close	P/E High/Low		PER SHARE ($) Earnings	Dividends	Book Value
3/10	21.14	61	33	0.37	0.16	9.30
3/09	11.00	43	9	0.82	0.19	8.66
3/08	27.85	20	10	2.11	—	9.23
3/07	21.04	17	11	1.40	—	6.81
3/06	19.10	20	6	0.98	—	5.48
Annual Growth	2.6%	—	—	(21.6%)	(15.8%)	14.1%

KPMG International

Businesses all over the world count on KPMG for accounting. KPMG is the smallest, yet one of the most geographically dispersed of accounting's Big Four firms, which also include Deloitte Touche Tohmatsu, Ernst & Young, and PricewaterhouseCoopers. KPMG, a cooperative that operates as an umbrella organization for its global network of member firms, has organized its structure into three operating regions: the Americas (which includes KPMG L.L.P.); Australia and Asia/Pacific; and Europe, the Middle East, South Asia, and Africa. Member firms' offerings include audit, tax, and advisory services. KPMG focuses on clients in such industries as financial services, consumer products, and government.

KPMG, which operates in more than 145 countries worldwide, is focusing its growth in the Middle East and the BRIC countries (Brazil, Russia, India, and China. Growth in those markets helped make up for losses elsewhere, which were a result of the global economic recession.

As the global economy stabilizes KMPG is looking for new opportunities. Increased spending on infrastructure has the company ramping up its advisory capabilities around the world. KPMG plans to tap its experience in building public-private partnerships in order to help finance future infrastructure projects. The company also is looking to meet an increased demand for risk management as businesses deal with new regulations and look to properly align themselves after the recession.

Another key issue KPMG is tackling is global accounting standards. The firm is a big proponent of International Financial Reporting Standards (IFRS). The set of global accounting practices have been adopted by more than 110 countries around the world, but KPMG would like to see that number grow. As countries make the shift, KPMG firms offer guidance and training.

HISTORY

Peat Marwick was founded in 1911, when William Peat, a London accountant, met James Marwick during an Atlantic crossing. University of Glasgow alumni Marwick and Roger Mitchell had formed Marwick, Mitchell & Company in New York in 1897. Peat and Marwick agreed to ally their firms temporarily, and in 1925 they merged as Peat, Marwick, Mitchell, & Copartners.

In 1947 William Black became senior partner, a position he held until 1965. He guided the firm's 1950 merger with Barrow, Wade, Guthrie, one of the US's oldest firms, and built its consulting practice. Peat Marwick restructured its international practice as PMM&Co. (International) in 1972 (renamed Peat Marwick International in 1978).

The next year several European accounting firms led by Klynveld Kraayenhoff (the Netherlands) and Deutsche Treuhand (Germany) began forming an international accounting federation. Needing an American member, the European firms encouraged the merger of two American firms founded around the turn of the century, Main Lafrentz and Hurdman Cranstoun. Main Hurdman & Cranstoun joined the Europeans to form Klynveld Main Goerdeler (KMG), named after two of the member firms and the chairman of Deutsche Treuhand, Reinhard Goerdeler. Other members were C. Jespersen (Denmark), Thorne Riddel (Canada), Thomson McLintok (UK), and Fides Revision (Switzerland).

Peat Marwick merged with KMG in 1987 to form Klynveld Peat Marwick Goerdeler (KPMG). KPMG lost 10% of its business as competing client companies departed. Professional staff departures followed in 1990 when, as part of a consolidation, the firm trimmed its partnership rolls.

In the 1990s the then-Big Six accounting firms all faced lawsuits arising from an evolving standard holding auditors responsible for the substance, rather than merely the form, of clients' accounts. KPMG was hit by suits stemming from its audits of defunct S&Ls and litigation relating to the bankruptcy of Orange County, California (settled for $75 million in 1998). Nevertheless, KPMG kept growing; it expanded its consulting division with the acquisition of banking consultancy Barefoot, Marrinan & Associates in 1996.

In 1997, after Price Waterhouse and Coopers & Lybrand announced their merger, KPMG and Ernst & Young announced one of their own. But they called it quits the next year, fearing that regulatory approval of the deal would be too onerous.

The creation of PricewaterhouseCoopers (PwC) and increasing competition in the consulting sides of all of the Big Five brought a realignment of loyalties in their national practices. KPMG Consulting's Belgian group moved to PwC and its French group to Computer Sciences Corporation. Andersen nearly wooed away KPMG's Canadian consulting group, but the plan was foiled by the ever-sullen Andersen Consulting group (now Accenture) and by KPMG's promises of more money. Against this background, KPMG sold 20% of its consulting operations to Cisco Systems for $1 billion. In addition to the cash infusion, the deal allowed KPMG to provide installation and system management to Cisco's customers.

Even while KPMG worked on the IPO of its consulting group (which took place in 2001), it continued to rail against the SEC as it called for relationships between consulting and auditing organizations to be severed. In 2002 KPMG sold its British and Dutch consultancy units to France's Atos Origin.

In 2003 the SEC charged US member firm KPMG L.L.P. and four partners with fraud in connection with alleged profit inflation at former client Xerox in the late 1990s. (In April 2005 the accounting firm paid almost $22.5 million, including a $10 million civil penalty, to settle the charges.)

KPMG exited various businesses around the globe during fiscal 2004, including full-scope legal services and certain advisory services, to focus on higher-demand services.

EXECUTIVES

Chairman: Timothy P. (Tim) Flynn, age 53
Deputy Chairman: John B. Harrison, age 53
COO: Brian Ambrose
Global Head, Insurance: Frank Ellenbuerger
Global Chair, Automotive: Dieter Becker
Global Vice Chair, Risk and Compliance: Larry Leva
Global Chair, Information, Communications and Entertainment: Gary Matuszak
Global Chair, Communications and Media: Sean Collins
Global Head, People, Performance, and Culture: Rachel Campbell
Global Head, Healthcare: Alan Downey
Global Head, Audit: Joachim Schindler
Global Head, Performance and Technology: Aidan Brennan
Global Head, Tax: Loughlin Hickey
Global Head, Markets: Neil D. Austin, age 58
Global Head, Advisory: Alan Buckle
Chairman, Americas Region; Chairman and CEO, KPMG LLP: John B. Veihmeyer, age 54
Chairman, Asia-Pacific and Chairman, China and Hong Kong: Carlson Tong, age 54
Chairman, EMA and Global Board Member: John Griffith-Jones
Chairman, High Growth Market Practice: Ian Gomes
Chairman, Global Financial Services Practice: Jeremy Anderson
Deputy Chairman and COO, KPMG LLP: Henry Keizer, age 53

LOCATIONS

HQ: KPMG International Cooperative
Burgemeester Rijnderslaan 20
1185 MC Amstelveen, The Netherlands
Phone: 31-20-656-6700 **Fax:** 31-20-656-6777
Web: www.kpmg.com

2009 Sales

	% of total
Europe, Middle East & Africa	54
Americas	31
Asia/Pacific	15
Total	**100**

PRODUCTS/OPERATIONS

2009 Sales

	% of total
Audit	50
Advisory	30
Tax	20
Total	**100**

2009 Sales by Industry

	% of total
Financial services	26
Industrial	25
Consumer	12
Infrastructure, Government & Healthcare	19
Information, Communication & Entertainment	18
Total	**100**

Selected Services

Audit services
  Attestation services
  Financial statement audit
Advisory services
  Audit support services
  Performance and technology
  Risk and compliance
  Transactions and restructuring
Tax services
  Corporate and business tax
  Global tax
  Global transfer pricing services
  Indirect tax
  International corporate tax
  International executive services
  Mergers and acquisitions

COMPETITORS

Bain & Company
Baker Tilly International
BDO International
Booz Allen
Deloitte
Ernst & Young Global
Grant Thornton International
H&R Block
Marsh & McLennan
McKinsey & Company
PricewaterhouseCoopers

HISTORICAL FINANCIALS

Company Type: Cooperative

Income Statement

FYE: September 30

	REVENUE ($ mil.)	NET INCOME ($ mil.)	NET PROFIT MARGIN	EMPLOYEES
9/09	20,110	—	—	140,235
9/08	22,690	—	—	136,896
9/07	19,810	—	—	123,322
9/06	16,880	—	—	112,795
9/05	15,690	—	—	103,621
Annual Growth	**6.4%**	**—**	**—**	**7.9%**

Revenue History

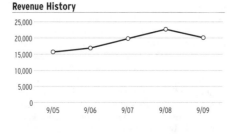

Koninklijke KPN

Koninklijke KPN, which is also known as Royal KPN, is the leading provider of telecommunications services in the Netherlands, where it has more than 5 million fixed-line phone customers. The company's core business, however, is KPN Mobile, which serves more than 31 million subscribers in the Netherlands, Germany, and Belgium. Through its ownership of several European ISPs, KPN also provides broadband Internet access to 2.5 million customers, and it offers business network services and data transport throughout Western Europe. Subsidiary Getronics provides a wide range of IT services to clients in Europe, Asia, the Middle East, and the Americas.

Up-and-down economic conditions and the company's sizable debt (due largely to paying high prices for advanced wireless phone licenses) have led KPN to sell many of its international holdings, including its stakes in US-based Infonet, Ireland's eircom, Czech phone company Cesk~Telecom, and Hungarian mobile phone operator Pannon GSM. It also sold KPN Belgium and its Belgian ISP, Planet Internet Belgium. The company in 2007 sold its international voice wholesale business, KPN Global Carrier Services, to US-based VoIP carrier iBasis. The deal gave KPN a 51% stake in iBasis. KPN sold its business and carrier services network operations in Belgium to Belgian mobile carrier Mobistar in 2010.

To expand its IP-based services, it acquired Dutch telecom firm Enertel from Greenfield Capital in a deal valued at €10 million. Other acquisitions by KPN included HubHop, a wireless Internet (Wi-Fi) services provider, and Freeler, a small ISP in the Netherlands. In 2008 the company bought 65% of Belgium-based Ortel Mobile from its founders to strengthen its position in the prepaid wireless services segment in the Netherlands, Germany, and Belgium. In late 2009 KPN bought out the minority shareholders of iBasis in a bid to strengthen its position in North America and the VoIP computer telephony market. It acquired the remaining 35% of Ortel that it did not already own in 2010.

Cost reduction efforts will include cutting up to 8,000 jobs through the year 2010 as the company refocuses on broadband Internet business for growth. Meanwhile, KPN aims to branch out from its traditional telecom activities and boost its competitiveness by consolidating its IT business into a new unit called KPN ICT Service.

HISTORY

Koninklijke KPN is a descendant of the Dutch PTT — a traditional European state-owned postal, telegraph, and telephone monopoly. The PTT traces its roots to the 1700s, when the Dutch provinces began taking over postal operations from the cities. Under Napoleonic rule in 1799, mail delivery was organized under one national service. In 1877 postal and telegraph services were assigned to the new ministry for water, commerce, and industry. The operation became an independent administration, called Postal Services and Telegraphy (P&T), in 1893.

The telephone made its Dutch debut in 1881 with Netherlands Bell Telephone, and several private operators and P&T soon entered the business. After building its first local phone exchange in 1911, P&T became the Staats Bedrijf der Posterijen, Telegraphie & Telephony (PTT) in 1928. In 1941 during the Nazi occupation, all independent phone operators were folded into PTT.

After WWII, business began to boom for PTT, which had fully automated its phone systems by 1962. Despite inflation and the government's practice of siphoning off PTT funds in the 1970s, the company stuck to a course of investment and new services. It launched a packet data network in 1982 and an analog mobile phone network in 1985.

Following years of debate, PTT became an independent corporation called PTT Nederland NV in 1989, but the state was its only shareholder. Momentum was building within Europe for liberalizing telecom services, and the door was opened to competition for some postal and telecom services. Fearing competition from the likes of British Telecom (now BT Group), PTT joined Sweden's Televerket (renamed Telia in 1993 and later TeliaSonera) to form Unisource, a global communications provider. Swisscom joined Unisource in 1993, and AT&T began working with the venture the next year.

Meanwhile, KPN launched a digital GSM (global system for mobile communications) mobile phone network in 1994, and Dutch mobile use began to take off. The company, now called Koninklijke PTT Nederland NV (or KPN; *Koninklijke* means "royal"), launched its long-awaited IPO that year; the state sold a 30% share. Also in 1995 the firm began offering Internet access.

KPN's mail delivery and logistics businesses were finally spun off in 1998 as TNT Post Group (KPN bought express carrier TNT in 1996). The company began to focus squarely on telecom and adopted the name Royal KPN. AT&T abandoned the unsuccessful Unisource venture that year, and the others decided to sell its assets. Wireless subsidiary KPN Mobile was formed in 1999 and took a 77% interest in German GSM operator E-Plus (BellSouth bought the remaining 23%, then sold it to KPN in 2002).

KPN announced it would take KPN Mobile public in 2001 and entered merger talks with Belgacom, Belgium's leading telecom company, but the companies could not come to terms.

Also in 2001 KPN raised $4.6 billion in a public offering that reduced the Dutch government's stake in the company to 35%. The next year the company dissolved KPN Qwest, its bankrupt joint venture formed in 1999 with US-based Qwest Communications, which operated a pan-European data communications network with connections to North America. The venture became another victim of the overdevelopment of broadband infrastructure and a general economic downturn in the telecom sector.

Also in 2002 KPN began searching for a buyer for its stake in the European wireless services joint venture with NTT DoCoMo and Hutchison Whampoa (formed in 2000). The next year the company sold its directory unit to private equity firm 3i Group and investment bank Veronis Suhler Stevenson Partners in a deal valued at $503 million. Also in 2003 the company sold its 16% stake in Ukrainian Mobile Communications for $55 million to Mobile Telesystems of Russia.

The company further strengthened its Dutch IT business in 2007 with the acquisition of Getronics for $1 billion. KPN announced late the next year that it would sell the public sector portion of Getronics, which provides IT services to the Dutch government and health care customers, to Total Specific Solutions.

EXECUTIVES

Chairman Supervisory Board:
Joseph B.M. (Jos) Streppel, age 60
Chairman Management Board and CEO:
A. J. (Ad) Scheepbouwer, age 66
Member Management Board and COO: Eelco Blok, age 53
Member Management Board and Managing Director, Netherlands: Baptiest Coopmans, age 45
CFO: Carla Smits-Nusteling, age 44
Managing Director, Consumer Segment: Marco Visser, age 47
Managing Director, KPN International: Carolien Nijhuis
Business Developments and Strategy Manager, Fixed Division: J. Wildeboer
Carrier Services Manager, Fixed Division:
Joost Farwerck, age 44
CEO, BASE: Libor Voncina
CEO, Getronics: Erik van der Meijden, age 50
CEO, E-Plus: Thorsten Dirks
Auditors: PricewaterhouseCoopers Accountants N.V.

LOCATIONS

HQ: Koninklijke KPN N.V.
Maanplein 55, Bldg. TP5
2516 CK The Hague, The Netherlands
Phone: 31-70-343-43-43   **Fax:** 31-70-446-05-93
US HQ: 20 2nd Ave., Burlington, MA 01803
US Phone: 781-505-7500   **US Fax:** 781-505-7300
Web: www.kpn.com

2009 Sales

	% of total
The Netherlands	70
Germany	23
Belgium	6
Other countries	1
Total	**100**

PRODUCTS/OPERATIONS

2009 Sales

	% of total
Mobile international	30
Consumer	29
Business	17
Getronics	15
Wholesale & operations	9
Total	**100**

COMPETITORS

Belgacom	TDC
BT	Tele2
COLT Group	Tele2 Netherlands
Deutsche Telekom	TeliaSonera
France Telecom	Vodafone
Magyar Telekom	Vodafone Libertel
Orange Business Services	

HISTORICAL FINANCIALS

Company Type: Public

Income Statement

FYE: December 31

	REVENUE ($ mil.)	NET INCOME ($ mil.)	NET PROFIT MARGIN	EMPLOYEES
12/09	19,278	3,122	16.2%	26,358
12/08	20,582	1,878	9.1%	40,288
12/07	18,593	3,904	21.0%	47,000
12/06	15,907	2,089	13.1%	28,368
12/05	14,136	1,702	12.0%	29,286
Annual Growth	**8.1%**	**16.4%**	**—**	**(2.6%)**

2009 Year-End Financials

Debt ratio: 325.7%
Return on equity: 58.0%
Cash ($ mil.): 3,855
Current ratio: 0.90
Long-term debt ($ mil.): 17,918
No. of shares (mil.): 1,618
Dividends
 Yield: 5.0%
 Payout: 44.5%
Market value ($ mil.): 27,458

Stock History

Pink Sheets: KKPNY

	STOCK PRICE ($) FY Close	P/E High/Low		PER SHARE ($) Earnings	Dividends	Book Value
12/09	16.97	9	7	1.91	0.85	3.40
12/08	14.63	15	13	1.07	0.79	3.25
Annual Growth	**16.0%**	**—**	**—**	**78.5%**	**7.6%**	**4.6%**

Kubota Corporation

Kubota has been the hand that turns the earth's soil for over a century. The diversified enterprise is Japan's largest maker of tractors and farm equipment, from rice transplanters to combine harvesters. It also leads in producing iron ductile pipe used in water-supply systems. Industrial castings (ductile tunnel segments) are part of Kubota's line, too, as well as PVC pipe, the engines for its agricultural and industrial movers, building materials (siding, cement roofing, and prefabricated houses), and, even vending machines for cigarettes and beverages. It has relatively recently entered into building water recycling and sewage-treatment plants.

Sales of agricultural machinery have dipped, in part due to the ripple effects of the 2007 reduction in subsidies that farmers receive from the Japanese government. Stiff competition is faced as well from majors Caterpillar, Deere, and Hitachi. Shoring up its bottom line in 2009, Kubota launched a trial program in central Japan for buying the rice and other produce from its client farmers, thereby ensuring a market for their harvest, and its own equipment. Simultaneously, the company is trimming prices for its large farm equipment, in the medium term, as production costs are squeezed.

The company looks to piggyback on growing local demand for farm machinery in China and Thailand, as well as an anticipated rise in exports to their bordering markets, namely Vietnam and India. Strengthening its manufacturing and marketing footprint, Kubota is doubling tractor production in 2010 at Thailand-based Siam Kubota Tractor Co., a joint venture with Siam Cement Group. Kubota plans to plow in more than 500 million yen to expand the plant's production capacity. Construction of a second facility and a research and development center in Thailand are also on the workbench. Responding to the Chinese government's ongoing push for agricultural mechanization, the company is preparing for a rise in demand for machinery in that country, too.

Holding even more potential, Kubota is keeping a close eye on sanitation and wastewater management opportunities, fueled by rising pollution and water shortages in Asia. Construction, too, in regions outside of Japan, has seen an uptick and consequently a rise in demand for Kubota's environmental waste lineup, along with its ductile iron pipes and construction machinery. Kubota teamed up in 2010 with Anhui Sanlian Pump Industry Co., a pump manufacturer in China's Anhui Province.

A downturn in the US and European construction market has had an adverse affect on Kubota's construction machinery, from small tractors and mowers to earthmovers. Given the global spotlight placed on shifting to biofuels, underpinned by corn production and large available crop land, Kubota is keeping its finger on the pulse of demand for farm equipment in the US and the former Soviet republics.

HISTORY

The son of a poor farmer and coppersmith, Gonshiro Oode left home in 1885 at age 14 and moved to Osaka to find work. He began as an apprentice at the Kuro Casting Shop, where he learned about metal casting. He saved his money and in 1890 opened Oode Casting.

Oode's shop grew rapidly, thanks to the industrialization of the Japanese economy and the expansion of the iron and steel industries. One of Oode's customers, Toshiro Kubota, took a liking to the hardworking young man, and in 1897 Kubota adopted him. Oode changed his own name to Kubota and also changed the name of his company to Kubota Iron Works.

Kubota made a number of technological breakthroughs in the early 1900s, including a new method of producing cast-iron pipe (developed in 1900). The company became the first to make the pipe in Japan, and it continued to grow as the country modernized its infrastructure.

Kubota began making steam engines, machine tools, and agricultural engines in 1917, and it also began exporting products to countries in Southeast Asia. In 1930 Kubota restructured and incorporated. It continued to add product lines, including agricultural and industrial motors.

Although WWII brought massive destruction to Japan, the peacetime that followed created plenty of work for Kubota's farm equipment and pipe operations as the country rebuilt. By 1960 the company was Japan's largest maker of farm equipment, ductile iron pipe, and cement roofing materials. That year Kubota introduced the first small agricultural tractor in Japan.

Over the next three decades, Kubota expanded its products and its geographic reach. The company created subsidiaries in Taiwan (1961), the US (1972), Iran (1973), France (1974), and Thailand (1977). It also made a major push into the US high-tech industry during the 1980s with the 44% purchase of supercomputer graphics company Ardent (1985). Two years later Kubota bought disk company Akashic Memories, and in 1989 it formed a joint venture with disk drive maker Maxtor to build optical storage products.

While loading up on high-tech operations, Kubota also expanded its lower-tech core businesses in the US. The company opened its first US manufacturing plant in 1989 in Georgia to make front-end loader attachments, and in 1990 it bought a 5% interest in Cummins Engine.

The next year Kubota took over the operations of struggling Stardent Computers; however, Kubota was unable to revive the graphic workstation business and dissolved its Kubota Graphics subsidiary in California in 1994.

In 1995 Kubota formed subsidiary Kubota Biotech to develop and sell biotechnological products such as biological insecticides. The next year Kubota launched a rice-cultivation machine for use in large fields.

In 1998 the company formed a joint venture in China to make cast-steel products, and the following year it established a subsidiary there to make combine harvesters.

With its sales decreasing in response to Japan's economic slowdown, in 2000 Kubota implemented a three-year cost-cutting strategy. It began cutting its workforce by about 13% and jettisoning unprofitable businesses.

Kubota moved on in 2007 to seal a new joint venture in India with two of Tata Group's metal companies, Tata Metaliks Limited and Metal One Corp. Another venture took root in Thailand with Siam Cement Public Co., to build tractors.

Management received new leadership in fall 2008. Daisuke Hatakake took the helm as chairman, and Yasua Masumoto as president.

EXECUTIVES

Chairman Kubota Corporation: Daisuke Hatakake, age 69
Vice Chairman: Moriya Hayashi, age 66
President & CEO Kubota Corporation and Director: Yasuo Masumoto, age 63
Director and President, Tractor: Satoshi Iida
Director and Managing Executive Officer; Corporate Planning & Control Dept. and Finance & Accounting Dept: Satoru Sakamoto, age 58
Managing Executive Officer; General Manager Social Infrastructure Consolidated Division, General Manager Material Division, General Manager Steel Castings Business Unit: Takeshi Torigoe, age 60
Managing Executive Officer; Personnel Dept., Secretary & Public Relations Dept., General Affairs Dept., Tokyo Administration: Masayoshi Kitaoka, age 60
Managing Executive Officer; General Manager R & D Headquarters Farm & Industrial Machinery Consolidated Division: Nobuyuki Toshikuni, age 59
Managing Executive Officer; General Manager Manufacturing Headquarters in Farm & Industrial Machinery Consolidated Division, General Manager Sakai Plant, Quality Assurance & Manufacturing Promotion Dept.: Morimitsu Katayama, age 62
Managing Executive Officer; Deputy General Manager Farm & Industrial Headquarters in Farm & Industrial Machinery Consolidated Division: Masatoshi Kimata, age 59
Managing Executive Office; General Manager Water Engineering & Solution Division, General Manager of Water & Sewage Engineering Business Unit, General Manager of Membrane Systems Business Unit, General Manager of Membrane Systems Business Coordination Dept., General Manager Tokyo Head Office: Hideki Iwabu, age 57
Managing Executive Officer; General Manager Construction Machinery Division, President of Kubota Construction Machinery Japan Co., Ltd.: Nobuyo Shioji, age 61
Executive Officer; President, Kubota Manufacturing of America Corporation: Takashi Yoshii, age 58
Auditors: Deloitte Touche Tohmatsu

LOCATIONS

HQ: Kubota Corporation
1-2-47, Shikitsu-higashi, Naniwa-ku
Osaka 556-8601, Japan
Phone: 81-6-6648-2111   **Fax:** 81-6-6648-3862
US HQ: 3401 Del Amo Blvd., Torrance, CA 90503
US Phone: 310-370-3370   **US Fax:** 310-370-2370
Web: www.kubota.co.jp

2010 Sales

	% of total
Asia/Pacific	
Japan	65
Other countries	12
North America	16
Europe	6
Other regions	1
Total	**100**

PRODUCTS/OPERATIONS

2010 Sales

	% of total
Farm & industrial machinery	66
Water & environment systems	24
Social infrastructure	7
Other	3
Total	**100**

Selected Products

Internal combustion machinery
  Ancillary tools and implements for agriculture
  Carriers
  Cleaning and vending machines for rice
  Combine harvesters
  Construction machinery
  Cooperative facilities for rice seedlings
  Dairy and stock raising facilities
  Engines
  Farm facilities
  Farm machinery
  Gardening facilities
  Gasoline and diesel engines for farming and industrial purposes
  Harvesters
  Implements and attachments for farm equipment
  Lawn and garden equipment
  Mini-excavators
  Multipurpose warehouse
  Outdoor power equipment
  Power tillers
  Reaper binders
  Rice driers
  Rice mill plants
  Rice transplanters
  Tillers
  Tractors
  Welders
  Wheel loaders

Pipes, valves, and industrial castings
  Cargo oil pipes
  Cast steel products
  Castings
  Castings for engines
  Castings for machinery
  Cast-iron soil pipes
  Ductile iron pipes
  Ductile tunnel segments
  Filament winding pipes
  G-columns
  G-piles
  Pipes
  Plastic valves
  Polyethylene pipes
  Polyvinyl chloride pipes and fittings
  Reformer tubes
  Rolls for steel mills
  Spiral welded steel pipes
  Suction roll shells for paper industry

Environmental engineering
  Amusement fountains
  Solid waste treatment plants
  Water- and sewage-treatment plants

Life environment and other
  Air-conditioning equipment
  CAD systems
  Cement siding materials
  Colored cement roofing materials
  Condominiums
  Crushing plants
  Dioxins decomposition systems
  Grinding mills

COMPETITORS

AGCO	IHI Corp.
Amerequip	Iseki & Company
Asahi/America	Isuzu
Caterpillar	J C Bamford Excavators
Chang-on	Japan Steel Works
CNH Global	Komatsu
Crane Co.	Lafarge
Deere	Marubeni-Komatsu
Fiat	Mitsubishi Steel Mfg.
Fuji Electric	Nippon Steel
Gradall Industries	Sekisui House
Hillco	Toro Company
Hitachi Construction Machinery	Toyota

HISTORICAL FINANCIALS

Company Type: Public

Income Statement

FYE: March 31

	REVENUE ($ mil.)	NET INCOME ($ mil.)	NET PROFIT MARGIN	EMPLOYEES
3/10	10,040	457	4.5%	24,778
3/09	11,384	494	4.3%	25,140
3/08	11,574	682	5.9%	24,464
3/07	9,571	649	6.8%	23,727
3/06	9,016	696	7.7%	23,049
Annual Growth	2.7%	(10.0%)	—	1.8%

2010 Year-End Financials

Debt ratio: 38.8%
Return on equity: 7.2%
Cash ($ mil.): 1,202
Current ratio: 1.86
Long-term debt ($ mil.): 2,625

No. of shares (mil.): 254
Dividends
Yield: 0.0%
Payout: —
Market value ($ mil.): 125

Stock History

NYSE: KUB

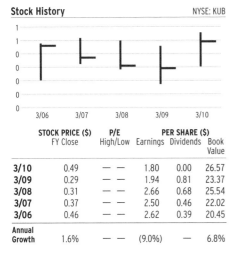

	STOCK PRICE ($) FY Close	P/E High/Low	PER SHARE ($) Earnings	Dividends	Book Value
3/10	0.49	— —	1.80	0.00	26.57
3/09	0.29	— —	1.94	0.81	23.37
3/08	0.31	— —	2.66	0.68	25.54
3/07	0.37	— —	2.50	0.46	22.02
3/06	0.46	— —	2.62	0.39	20.45
Annual Growth	1.6%	— —	(9.0%)	—	6.8%

Kyocera Corporation

Don't confuse Kyocera's ceramics with teacups and pottery. The company, which began producing technical ceramics nearly half a century ago, makes a wide range of components and fine ceramic products — including capacitors, fiber-optic connectors, photovoltaic solar cells, and semiconductors — primarily for customers in the electronics industry. Besides its ceramics and other electronic components, the company makes various types of finished electronics products, including wireless phones, office equipment such as photocopiers and fax machines, and digital and film cameras. Kyocera has about 190 subsidiaries and affiliates around the world; the company gets around 60% of sales outside Japan.

The global recession helped trim Kyocera's sales and drastically cut its profit margins. The company reduced its global workforce by more than 10% during the year. Global economic conditions are expected to lower demand for Kyocera's products in the near future. The company has made significant investments in its Chinese operations and could be adversely affected if the central government in the People's Republic makes unexpected changes in the business climate or its economic policy.

Kyocera and Japanese supermarket chain AEON partnered in 2009 to sell residential solar power generation systems. The company hopes to expand sales of the systems by capitalizing on AEON's nationwide retail network.

In 2008 Kyocera set plans to build a new solar cell plant in Yasu City, Shiga prefecture. The plant became the company's largest manufacturing facility in Japan when it was completed in 2010. Together with Kyocera's solar cell plant in Yohkaichi, the new facility will permit the company to double its annual output, from 300MW in 2008 to 1GW by the end of fiscal 2013.

Kyocera built a second solar photovoltaic module manufacturing facility in Tijuana, Mexico, responding to increased demand for alternative energy products. The company is one of the largest suppliers of solar cells and solar modules in the world, along with Q-Cells, Sharp, and Suntech Power.

In 2008 the company acquired the mobile phone business of SANYO Electric. The company will market both Kyocera and SANYO brand phones in Japan and other markets. In North America, Kyocera set up a subsidiary separate from Kyocera Wireless to assume the US-based SANYO business units, in order to maintain immediate continuity with its existing distribution network.

In 2007 Kyocera struck a mutual product supply agreement with Kennametal, a US-based manufacturer of cutting tools. The companies collaborate on marketing strategies and sell each other's complementary products on a worldwide basis. In 2008, however, Kyocera took the relationship to another level when it acquired Kennametal's On Time Machining (OTM) subsidiary. OTM supplies cutting tool products such as drills, mills, and counterbores. OTM's operations were folded into Kyocera's Industrial Ceramics division.

Tetsuo Kuba became president of Kyocera in 2009, succeeding Makoto Kawamura, who became the company's chairman.

HISTORY

Born to a poor Japanese family in 1932, Kazuo Inamori never quite fit the mold. He went to work for Shofu Industries (ceramic insulators) in the mid-1950s, but quit three years later and started Kyoto Ceramic KK with seven colleagues in 1959. Their first product was a ceramic insulator for cathode-ray tubes. In the late 1960s the company developed the ceramic package for integrated circuits (ICs) that has made it a world-class supplier.

Kyoto Ceramic started manufacturing in the US in 1971. A few years later the company began to diversify its interests when it ventured into artificial gemstones (Crescent Vert, 1977) and dental implants (New Medical, 1978). In 1979 Inamori bought control of failing Cybernet Electronics (Japanese citizens-band radio maker), using it to move Kyoto Ceramic into the production of copiers and stereos.

The company merged five subsidiaries in 1982, forming Kyocera Corporation. The 1983 acquisition of Yashica moved it into the production of cameras and other optical equipment. That year Kyocera ran into trouble. At the time, Nippon Telegraph and Telephone (NTT) was the only legal supplier of phones in Japan, and when Kyocera started marketing cordless phones without the required approval, the government forced it to recall the phones.

The government abolished NTT's monopoly in 1984, and Kyocera joined 24 other companies to form Daini-Denden ("second phone company") — now KDDI. In 1988 Inamori set up Kyocera regional offices in Asia, Europe, and the US. The company bought Elco (electronic connectors, US) in 1989 and AVX (multilayer ceramic capacitors, US) in 1990.

In order to diversify further, Kyocera entered into a series of alliances in the 1990s that included partnerships with Canon to produce video and electronic optical equipment, with Carl Zeiss (Germany) to make cameras and lenses, and with Cirrus Logic to make chips for a cordless phone project.

The company's Guangdong-based optical instrument joint venture began making cameras and lenses for the Chinese market in 1996. The next year Inamori went into partial retirement.

In 1999 Kyocera's product line grew even more diverse as it entered the health food market and began selling mushroom products in Japan. Kyocera purchased the wireless phone business of QUALCOMM in early 2000.

Expanding its operations in China, Kyocera in 2003 created a sales company, Kyocera (Tianjin) Sales and Trading Corporation, and established a subsidiary to make solar-power modules, Kyocera (Tianjin) Solar Energy Co., Ltd. Also that year the company made Kinseki Ltd., a manufacturer of artificial crystals and related products, a wholly owned subsidiary, later called Kyocera Kinseki Corporation.

In 2004 Japan Medical Materials Corporation was set up as a joint venture between Kyocera and Kobe Steel, with Kyocera taking a 77% equity interest.

In 2005 Kyocera Solar Europe was established in the Czech Republic to assemble solar modules. Also that year Kyocera Wireless outsourced production of its mobile handsets to Flextronics International, eliminating nearly 1,600 manufacturing jobs in Mexico and the US.

The following year Kyocera sold Kyocera Leasing to Diamond Lease (now Mitsubishi UFJ Lease & Finance).

EXECUTIVES

Chairman Emeritus: Kazuo Inamori, age 78
Chairman and Representative Director: Makoto Kawamura, age 61
President, Representative Director, and Executive Officer: Tetsuo Kuba, age 56
Director; Managing Executive Officer; General Manager Corporate Financial and Business Systems Administration: Shoichi Aoki, age 51
Director; Vice Chairman, Kyocera International: Rodney N. Lanthorne, age 65
Director; Managing Executive Officer; General Manager Corporate General Affairs Human Resources Group: Tsutomu Yamori, age 61
Director; Managing Executive Officer; Deputy General Manager Corporate Development: Yoshihiro Kano, age 57
Senior Executive Officer; Deputy General Manager Corporate Communication Equipment Group: Takenori Ugari
Executive Officer; Deputy General Manager Corporate Office of the Chief Executives: Michiaki Furuhashi
Executive Officer; General Manager International Division, Corporate Office of the Chief Executives: Kazumasa Umemura
Executive Officer; Deputy General Manager Corporate General Affairs Human Resources Group: Masaaki Itoh
Executive Officer; General Manager Corporate Mobile Product Development Division, Corporate Communication Equipment Group: Tsuyoshi Egami
Executive Officer; President, Kyocera America: Robert E. (Bob) Whisler

Executive Officer; President and Director, Kyocera International: John S. Rigby, age 54
Executive Officer; General Manager Marketing Division, Corporate New Business Division: Junichi Jinno
Managing Executive Officer; President and Director, Kyocera Communications: Eiichi Toriyama
President and CEO, Kyocera Mita America: Michael (Mike) Pietrunti
Auditors: ChuoAoyama PricewaterhouseCoopers

LOCATIONS

HQ: Kyocera Corporation
6 Takeda Tobadono-cho, Fushimi-ku
Kyoto 612-8501, Japan
Phone: 81-75-604-3500   **Fax:** 81-75-604-3501
US HQ: 8611 Balboa Ave., San Diego, CA 92123
US Phone: 858-576-2600   **US Fax:** 858-492-1456
Web: www.kyocera.com

2010 Sales

	% of total
Asia	
Japan	42
Other countries	16
US	18
Europe	18
Other regions	6
Total	**100**

PRODUCTS/OPERATIONS

2010 Sales

	% of total
Components	
Electronic devices	19
Applied ceramic products	15
Semiconductor parts	13
Fine ceramic parts	5
Equipment	
Telecommunications equipment	21
Information equipment	17
Other	12
Total	**100**

Selected Products

Electronic equipment
  Information equipment
    Copy machines
    Facsimile machines
    Page printers (Ecosys)
  Optical instruments
    Compact zoom cameras
    Digital cameras
    SLR cameras and lenses
  Telecommunications equipment
    Cellular handsets
    Personal Handyphone System (PHS) products (base stations handsets)
    Wireless local loop systems
Fine ceramics
  Applied Ceramic Products Group
    Cutting tools (Ceratip)
    Dental and orthopedic implants (Bioceram)
    Jewelry and applied ceramic products (Crescent Vert)
    Solar energy products
  Fine ceramic parts
    Ceramic substrates
    Fiber-optic network components
    OA equipment components
    Parts for semiconductor fabrication equipment
  Semiconductor parts
    Ceramic dual-in-line packages (Cerdips)
    Metalized products
    Multilayer packages
    Organic packages
Electronic devices
  Capacitors
  High-frequency modules
  Thin-film products
  Timing devices (TCXOs, VCOs)

COMPETITORS

Alps Electric	Oki Electric
Apple Inc.	Palm, Inc.
Canon	Panasonic Corp
Ericsson	Philips Electronics
FUJIFILM	Q-Cells
Fujitsu	Research In Motion
Hewlett-Packard	Ricoh Company
Hitachi	Saint-Gobain
Honeywell International	Samsung Electronics
Huawei Technologies	SANYO
IBIDEN	Seiko
IBM	Sharp Corp.
Konica Minolta	Shinko Electric
Lexmark	Sony
LG Electronics	Suntech Power
Molex	Tatung
Motorola	TDK
Murata Manufacturing	Toshiba
NEC	Tyco Electronics
NGK INSULATORS	UTStarcom
Nokia	Xerox
NTT	

HISTORICAL FINANCIALS

Company Type: Public

Income Statement

FYE: March 31

	REVENUE ($ mil.)	NET INCOME ($ mil.)	NET PROFIT MARGIN	EMPLOYEES
3/10	11,584	433	3.7%	63,876
3/09	11,601	303	2.6%	59,514
3/08	12,936	1,075	8.3%	66,496
3/07	10,900	904	8.3%	63,477
3/06	10,135	598	5.9%	61,468
Annual Growth	**3.4%**	**(7.8%)**	**—**	**1.0%**

2010 Year-End Financials

Debt ratio: 2.2%
Return on equity: 3.1%
Cash ($ mil.): 3,378
Current ratio: 3.58
Long-term debt ($ mil.): 314
No. of shares (mil.): 184
Dividends
  Yield: 0.0%
  Payout: —
Market value ($ mil.): 192

Stock History

NYSE: KYO

	STOCK PRICE ($) FY Close	P/E High/Low		PER SHARE ($) Earnings	Dividends	Book Value
3/10	1.05	—	—	2.36	0.00	79.08
3/09	0.69	1	—	1.62	0.00	74.14
3/08	0.85	—	—	5.70	0.00	79.27
3/07	0.80	—	—	4.79	0.94	70.06
3/06	0.75	—	—	3.16	0.86	60.25
Annual Growth	**8.8%**	**—**	**—**	**(7.0%)**	**—**	**7.0%**

Ladbrokes plc

Ladbrokes will take that bet — on anything from sports to politics to unique speculations. Ladbrokes makes odds online, over the phone, and at its more than 2,100 bookmaking shops in the UK, Ireland, and Belgium. The company's online gaming operations include a leading sportsbook that offers wagering on a host of international sporting events and boasts more than half a million users. It also operates one of Europe's top poker sites and a host of online casino games. In addition, Ladbrokes runs such poker events as Ladbrokes Poker Million.

The company has been focused on international expansion of its betting shop business. Ladbrokes acquired some 30 additional locations in Belgium during 2009. Also that year it entered the Madrid market through Sportium, a joint venture partnership with Spanish betting firm Cirsa. Sportium plans to operate 125 betting outlets by the end of 2010. Other areas of interest for Ladbrokes include China and Italy.

In 2010 the company tapped Richard Glynn to serve as CEO, replacing longtime chief executive Chris Bell. Glynn was previously head of telephone wagering rival Sporting Index. Bell, who joined the company in 1991 and was named CEO in 2006, stepped down amid criticism from shareholders over the lack of growth in the company's international online operations.

HISTORY

Ladbrokes traces its roots to the village of Ladbroke in central England, where Arthur Bendir, a local racehorse trainer, set up a partnership in 1886 to take bets on horse races. Although off-track betting was illegal, betting on credit was allowed for wealthier members of society. The partnership, Ladbroke and Co., moved to London in 1900 and established itself as a quality credit betting shop in the city's plush West End. Bendir sold the business in 1957 to the Stein family. In 1960 the government legalized cash betting and Ladbroke began to expand. Cyril Stein became chairman in 1966 and took the company public the next year as the Ladbroke Group. It had 109 off-track betting shops in operation; by 1971 it had 660.

Stein pushed to diversify the company into real estate and casinos during the 1970s, and in 1973 Ladbroke bought three hotels. In the late 1970s the company suffered a major setback when its casino ventures in London were closed down and it was found guilty of violating gaming laws. The firm abandoned the casino business in 1979. In 1984 the company bought the Belgian Le Tierce betting shop chain and broke into the US market in 1985 with the acquisition of the Detroit Race Course (sold 1998). In 1987 Ladbroke beat out competitors to buy the 91-hotel Hilton International chain from Allegis Corporation for more than $1 billion. The deal made Ladbroke one of the world's top hotel operators.

Stein retired as chairman in 1994 and was replaced by John Jackson. Peter George, who had been with the company since 1963, was appointed chief executive. That year the company re-entered the casino business, paying $75 million for three London casinos. Though Ladbroke's property and retail division suffered in the 1990s, the hotel chain continued to expand; by 1995 there were 160 in operation. In 1997 Ladbroke entered into a sales and marketing alliance with

US-based Hilton Hotels (now Hilton Worldwide) to promote the Hilton brand throughout the world. The next year Ladbroke acquired #3 betting shop operator Coral from leisure group Bass (which later split into Mitchells & Butlers and InterContinental Hotel Group). However, UK regulators later forced the company to sell the chain. (A venture capital company backed by Morgan Grenfell Private Equity bought it for about $655 million.)

With its $2 billion acquisition of Stakis in 1999, Ladbroke gained 55 hotels and 20 casinos in the UK and Ireland, as well as the LivingWell health club chain. Stakis' CEO, David Michels, became head of Hilton International. Ladbroke changed its name to Hilton Group that year. In 2000 Peter George resigned from the company and was replaced by Michels. That year Hilton Group sold its casino operations for $373 million to Gala Group. In 2001 the company bought the Scandic Hotels chain for about $885 million. Also that year Jackson retired as chairman and was replaced by Ian Robinson.

The company fully returned to its betting roots in 2006, selling its hospitality operations to Hilton Hotels (now Hilton Worldwide) for $5.7 billion and changing its name to Ladbrokes.

EXECUTIVES

Chairman: Peter Erskine, age 58
Chief Executive: Richard I. Glynn, age 46
Group Finance Director and Director; Managing Director, Belgian and Italian Businesses and Paddington Casino: Brian G. Wallace, age 55, $2,050,824 total compensation
Managing Director, Remote Betting and Gaming and Director: John P. O'Reilly, age 49, $2,943,175 total compensation
Managing Director, UK and Ireland Retail and Director: Richard J. Ames, age 40
Senior Independent Non-Executive Director: Nicholas M. H. Jones, age 63
Director Corporate Development: Christopher Palmer
Head Investor Relations: Kate Postans
Head Public Relations: Ciaran O'Brien
Auditors: Ernst & Young LLP

LOCATIONS

HQ: Ladbrokes plc
Imperial House, Imperial Dr., Rayners Lane, Harrow
London HA2 7JW, United Kingdom
Phone: 44-20-8868-8899   **Fax:** 44-20-8868-8767
Web: www.ladbrokesplc.com

PRODUCTS/OPERATIONS

2009 Sales

	% of total
UK retail OTC	45
UK retail machines	25
Online gaming	17
Ireland	8
Belgium	5
Telephone gaming	2
Total	**100**

COMPETITORS

365 Media	PartyGaming
888 Holdings	The Rank Group
Betfair	Sporting Index
Camelot Group	Sportingbet
Gala Coral Group	Victor Chandler
Genting Stanley	Webis Holdings
London Clubs	William Hill
Paddy Power	

HISTORICAL FINANCIALS

Company Type: Public

Income Statement

FYE: December 31

	REVENUE ($ mil.)	NET INCOME ($ mil.)	NET PROFIT MARGIN	EMPLOYEES
12/09	1,644	119	7.2%	15,700
12/08	1,666	291	17.4%	16,394
12/07	2,451	680	27.8%	15,607
12/06	1,855	1,209	65.1%	19,192
12/05	1,558	569	36.5%	50,991
Annual Growth	**1.4%**	**(32.4%)**	**—**	**(25.5%)**

2009 Year-End Financials

Debt ratio: —
Return on equity: —
Cash ($ mil.): 39
Current ratio: —
Long-term debt ($ mil.): —
No. of shares (mil.): 902
Dividends
 Yield: 10.7%
 Payout: —
Market value ($ mil.): 1,975

Stock History

Pink Sheets: LDBKY

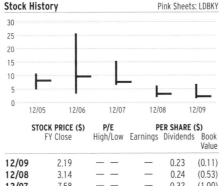

	STOCK PRICE ($) FY Close	P/E High/Low		PER SHARE ($) Earnings	Dividends	Book Value
12/09	2.19	—	—	—	0.23	(0.11)
12/08	3.14	—	—	—	0.24	(0.53)
12/07	7.58	—	—	—	0.32	(1.00)
12/06	9.62	—	—	—	0.26	(1.36)
12/05	8.13	—	—	—	0.20	4.95
Annual Growth	**(28.0%)**	**—**	**—**	**—**	**3.6%**	**—**

Lafarge S.A.

There's nothing abstract about Lafarge. The company is one of the world's top makers of cement, aggregates, concrete, and gypsum (alongside such heavyweights as Holcim and CEMEX). Cement accounts for about 60% of the building materials supplier's sales. Lafarge gypsum products (about 10% of sales) include wallboard, plasters, and insulation. The company has more than 2,000 plants operating around the world. Lafarge's growth strategy is to shift focus from Western Europe and North America to emerging markets such as Africa, the Middle East, Asia, Central Europe, and Latin America, which now account for more than half of sales.

Demand for building materials increased in emerging markets, while more established markets suffered during the economic downturn. As a result, sales for Lafarge went down. However, the company began growing itself in places such as the Middle East, Asia, Africa, Latin America, and other emerging regions, while making cuts in more familiar places like Europe.

Intent on maintaining a well-balanced geographic footprint (and spreading its risk) in the construction materials industry worldwide, Lafarge continues to seek both acquisition and joint venture opportunities abroad. Overall, Lafarge expects that construction growth in developing countries will far exceed the sector's growth in developed areas. On the downside, business in less established markets is typically more risky. But Lafarge is confident that those emerging markets will provide potential for solid growth. The company has been busy adding capacity in those markets.

Lafarge kicked off its growth into emerging markets with the 2008 acquisition of the cement producing unit of Orascom Construction Industries — a leader in the Middle East and Mediterranean Basin markets. Also that year Lafarge entered the Iraqi market, opening two cement plants, Bazian and Tasluja, in order to take advantage of the strong demand for building materials in the war-torn nation. The two plants have a total annual capacity of 5 million tons, and there are plans to renovate the plants and boost production. Lafarge continued its growth with other acquisitions in India and Algeria.

Meanwhile, Lafarge has been divesting some units in order to reduce debt. In 2009 Lafarge sold its asphalt and paving operations in Ontario, aggregate and concrete activities in Zurich, some assets of its asphalt, paving and concrete business in North America, and other units in Turkey and Chile.

In 2010 the company announced the sale of its minority stake in Portugal's Cimpor in exchange for a portion of Votorantim's assets in Brazil. It is also combining its Central European operations with construction firm STRABAG to create an Austrian joint venture. Lafarge will own 70% of the venture, which will have operations in Austria, the Czech Republic, Hungary, and Slovenia. By combining their activities the two companies hope to save costs and strengthen their investments.

Groupe Bruxelles Lambert holds nearly 30% of Lafarge.

HISTORY

Auguste Pavin de Lafarge started a small lime kiln along the Rhone river in 1831. By the turn of the century, the company's markets included the Americas and Asia, and in 1919 the company was incorporated as Chaux et Ciments du Lafarge et de Teil.

During the 1920s the company began producing portland cement, which could harden under water. It then capitalized on the Depression by buying failing cement companies.

The Lafarge family withdrew from the business in 1959, and the company began to grow through borrowing. That led to Lafarge's 1970 merger with Canada Cement, Canada's dominant cement maker. Lafarge's next big move in North America was the 1981 takeover of General Portland, a major US cement maker. The two companies, Lafarge Canada Cement and General Portland, were then merged, creating Lafarge Corporation.

Bertrand Collomb joined Lafarge in 1975 as chairman and CEO and became head of the company in 1989. Before his retirement in 2007, Collomb expanded the company's operations from 12 countries to more than 70.

Lafarge has grown through acquisitions, most notably the 1997 $3.7 billion purchase of Redland, a major UK roofing and aggregate company. Deals in 1999 included the acquisition of India-based Tisco's cement plants. That year the company also bought the remaining shares of Lafarge Braas GmbH, the holding company that houses its European roofing operations.

Lafarge's 2000 takeover bid for UK-based Blue Circle Industries failed, but it acquired a 23% stake in Blue Circle. In early 2001 Lafarge sold most of its specialty products business to Advent International and CVC Capital Partners for $747 million. Lafarge received a one-third stake in the new company being formed from the divisions, called MATERIS. Lafarge acquired the 77% of Blue Circle that it didn't already own for about $3.6 billion that July. The following year the company bought cement plants in Central Europe (Slovenia and Serbia-Montenegro).

In late 2002 the European Union fined Lafarge $248 million for its role in an alleged building materials price-fixing cartel. The next year Lafarge divested Lafarge Florida (part of Lafarge North America) and MATERIS (formerly part of its specialty products division).

The tsunami that struck Asia in December 2004 destroyed Lafarge's $220 million cement plant in Aceh, Indonesia, and killed about a third of the employees there. Lafarge had the only cement plant in the region. The facility was rebuilt in 2006.

Lafarge was formerly a high-flyer in the roofing industry but divested most of that business in 2007. Its roofing division was sold to private equity firm PAI Partners. Lafarge retained 35% ownership of the roofing business, which continues to use Lafarge brand names.

EXECUTIVES

Chairman and CEO: Bruno Lafont, age 54
Vice Chairman: Oscar Fanjul, age 60
CFO: Jean-Jacques Gauthier, age 51
EVP; President, Gypsum: Christian Herrault, age 59
EVP and Co-President, Cement: Guillaume Roux, age 51
EVP; Co-President, Cement: Isidoro Miranda, age 51
EVP; Co-President, Aggregates and Concrete: Gérard Kuperfarb, age 49
EVP; Co-President, Aggregates and Concrete: Thomas G. (Tom) Farrell, age 54
EVP Strategy, Business Development and Public Affairs: Jean Desazars de Montgailhard, age 58
EVP Organization and Human Resources: Eric C. Olsen, age 46
SVP Investor Relations: Jay Bachmann
Director Analysts Relations: Laurence LeGouguec
Director Institutional Investor Relations: Danièle Daouphars
Auditors: Deloitte & Associés

LOCATIONS

HQ: Lafarge S.A.
61, rue des Belles Feuilles
75782 Paris, France
Phone: 33-1-44-34-11-11   **Fax:** 33-1-44-34-12-00
US HQ: 12950 Worldgate Dr., Ste. 500
Herndon, VA 20170
US Phone: 703-480-3600   **US Fax:** 703-796-2215
Web: www.lafarge.com

2009 Sales

	% of total
Western Europe	29
Africa & the Middle East	25
North America	19
Asia	15
Central & Eastern Europe	7
Latin America	5
Total	**100**

PRODUCTS/OPERATIONS

2009 Sales

	% of total
Cement	60
Aggregates & concrete	32
Gypsum	8
Total	**100**

Selected Products

Cement
    Cements (marine, oil well, silica fume, slag, white)
    Hydraulic binders (road surfacing and natural lime)
    Masonry cements
Aggregates and Concrete
    Asphalt
    Crushed rock
    Gravel
    Industrial sand
    Precast concrete
    Ready-mix concrete
Gypsum
    Industrial plasters
    Plaster block
    Plasters
    Wallboard

COMPETITORS

Aggregate Industries
Boral
Cementos Portland Valderrivas
CEMEX
Ciments Français
CRH
Dyckerhoff
FLSmidth
Hanson Limited
HeidelbergCement
Holcim
Italcementi
Nippon Coke & Engineering
Saint-Gobain
Siam Cement
Sika
Sumitomo Osaka Cement
Taiheiyo Cement
Tarmac
Titan Cement
Uralita
USG
Vicat
Wienerberger

HISTORICAL FINANCIALS

Company Type: Public

Income Statement

FYE: December 31

	REVENUE ($ mil.)	NET INCOME ($ mil.)	NET PROFIT MARGIN	EMPLOYEES
12/09	22,765	1,499	6.6%	78,000
12/08	26,827	2,733	10.2%	83,438
12/07	25,926	3,173	12.2%	90,000
12/06	22,326	1,812	8.1%	71,000
12/05	18,975	1,692	8.9%	80,146
Annual Growth	**4.7%**	**(3.0%)**	**—**	**(0.7%)**

2009 Year-End Financials

Debt ratio: 91.6%
Return on equity: 7.6%
Cash ($ mil.): 3,182
Current ratio: 1.10
Long-term debt ($ mil.): 19,652

No. of shares (mil.): 286
Dividends
    Yield: 3.5%
    Payout: 72.3%
Market value ($ mil.): 23,734

Stock History

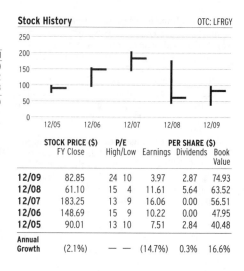

OTC: LFRGY

	STOCK PRICE ($) FY Close	P/E High/Low		PER SHARE ($) Earnings	Dividends	Book Value
12/09	82.85	24	10	3.97	2.87	74.93
12/08	61.10	15	4	11.61	5.64	63.52
12/07	183.25	13	9	16.06	0.00	56.51
12/06	148.69	15	9	10.22	0.00	47.95
12/05	90.01	13	10	7.51	2.84	40.48
Annual Growth	**(2.1%)**	**—**	**—**	**(14.7%)**	**0.3%**	**16.6%**

Lagardère SCA

Lagardère is shedding its missiles in favor of media. The company, whose primary holdings include media firm Lagardère Active (publisher of *ELLE* and *Premier*, and partial owner of French TV holding company Canal Plus France), has reduced its minority stake in #3 aerospace firm European Aeronautic Defence and Space Company (EADS) to about 12%. The company's other holdings include Lagardère Publishing (Hachette Livre book publishing, including subsidiaries Hachette UK and Hachette Book Group); Lagardère Services (press distribution and retail sales); and Lagardère Sports (sports broadcast rights marketing and management).

Lagardère has been busy making a few key acquisitions. In 2008 it boosted its Web presence with the acquisition of Doctissimo for an estimated €138 million ($205 million). Doctissimo is a publisher of five websites containing content for women based in France. The company bought Time Warner Book Group, the fifth biggest US book publisher, for $544 million in 2006 and renamed it Hachette Book Group. The move catapulted the company's position from the fifth- to the third-largest book publisher.

The company combined its Hachette Filipacchi Médias (print) with its Lagardère Active (radio, TV, and digital holdings) in 2006. Included in the Lagardère Active unit are mobile offerings (Cellfish Media); French Hachette Filipacchi Media (FHM) magazines such as French weekly *Paris Match*, as well as magazines in the UK (Hachette Filipacchi UK) and the US (Hachette Filipacchi Media U.S.); and a 20% stake in the French TV business Canal Plus France, which oversees pay TV service TPS, satellite TV provider CanalSat, and a stake in Canal Plus SA, among other things. (Canal Plus France was formed in 2007 when Vivendi's CANAL+ Groupe took control of TPS; Lagardère contributed to the $1 billion merger with its 34% stake in CanalSat.)

Lagardère set up a Sports division after acquiring Newsweb (sports-related Internet content provider) in 2006 and Sportfive (European football marketing and media rights) in 2007. The company also operates in the retail space through its stores; in 2008 Lagardère Services sold 80% of its stake in the Virgin Megastore group to Butler Capital Partners.

Also in 2008 the company formed Lagardère Entertainment, a subsidiary of Lagardère Active, to include the company's audiovisual production and distribution activities. The subsidiary is also responsbile for artist and audiovisual-rights management.

Chairman Arnaud Lagardère owns about 7% of the company (and controls some 11% of its votes) through Lagardère Capital & Management.

HISTORY

Jean-Luc Lagardère began his rise to industrial titan when he joined French aerospace contractor Dassault as an engineer in the 1950s. He was tapped to be president and CEO of military equipment manufacturer Mécanique Aviation TRAction (Matra) in 1963, where he pushed the firm to branch out into electronics, space systems, and automobiles during the 1970s. Lagardère turned his focus to the media world in 1981 when he joined with Filipacchi Médias to acquire control of venerable French publishing firm Hachette.

Started by schoolteacher Louis Hachette in 1826, the publishing firm first catered to the textbook market and later began producing general trade books and travel guides. It became involved in the newspaper business in the 1920s and launched fashion magazine *Elle* in 1945. A diversification strategy in the 1970s proved disastrous, however, leading to Lagardère's takeover.

The engineer-turned-entrepreneur launched international spinoffs of Hachette's magazines, including a successful US *Elle* in 1985 in partnership with media maven Rupert Murdoch. In the late 1980s Hachette invested in radio broadcasting, bought US magazine distributor Curtis Circulation, and acquired Spanish encyclopedia publisher Salvat. Meanwhile, Matra launched its Espace minivan in 1983 (marketed by Renault). In 1988 Hachette acquired encyclopedia publisher Grolier for $1.1 billion and later bought out Murdoch's share of *Elle*.

In 1990 Hachette bought a 25% stake in money-losing French TV network La Cinq. The station collapsed a year later, leaving Hachette with a $643 million write-off. To cover the huge debt, Lagardère merged Matra with Hachette in 1993 under the holding company that now bears his name. Its Matra division acquired British Aerospace's satellite division the next year and Hachette expanded its North American distribution business in 1995. Two years later Filipacchi Médias and Hachette Filipacchi Press merged to form Hachette Filipacchi Médias.

With French industry decreasing its reliance on defense business, Lagardère merged its Matra unit with France's state-owned aerospace firm, Aerospatiale, in 1999. Not long after, the new Aerospatiale Matra agreed to merge with Germany's DaimlerChrysler Aerospace and Spain's Construcciones Aeronauticas to form European Aeronautic Defence and Space Company (EADS). Completed the following year, the merger created the world's #3 aerospace company. (Lagardère retained a minority stake in the venture.)

Later in 2000 Lagardère sold Grolier to Scholastic Corp. for about $400 million and bought the rest of Hachette Filipacchi Médias from its minority shareholders. The same year Jean-Luc Lagardère escaped a 1988 fraud charge when a judge ruled that the time limit for prosecution had expired. To begin leveraging its media assets, the company created multimedia unit Lagardère Active in 2001.

The company bought most of the assets of Vivendi Universal Publishing (VUP) from media giant Vivendi for $1.2 billion in 2003. To get past antitrust authorities, Lagardère sold 60% of VUP, which it renamed Editis, to French firm Wendel Investissement. (Wendel ended up buying more of Editis in late 2004.)

Jean-Luc Lagardère died in 2003 of a rare neurological disease. Also that year the company exited the automotive design business with the sale of its Matra subsidiary.

In 2005 Lagardère decided to begin gradually reducing its holding in EADS to 7.5%. The company expected to complete the process in 2009.

Lagardère purchased Time Warner Book Group in 2006. Also that year Hachette Filipacchi Médias merged with Lagardère Active. In 2007 the company created a Sports division.

EXECUTIVES

Chairman and Co-Managing Partner; Chairman and CEO, Lagardère Media; Chairman, Lagardère Capital & Management and EADS: Arnaud Lagardère, age 49
VP and COO: Philippe Camus, age 62
Director and COO: Pierre Leroy, age 61
CFO: Dominique D'Hinnin, age 50
Chief Human Relations and Communications Officer: Thierry Funck-Brentano
Chairman and CEO, Lagardère Sports: Olivier Guiguet
Chairman and CEO, Lagardère Services: Jean-Louis Nachury
Chairman and CEO, Lagardère Publishing: Arnaud Nourry
Chairman and CEO, Lagardère Active: Didier Quillot
CEO, EADS: Louis Gallois, age 66
CEO, Airbus: Thomas (Tom) Enders, age 51
Chief International Affairs: Jean-Paul Gut, age 46
Corporate Secretary: Laure Rivière-Doumenc
Chief of Strategy and Development: Arnaud Molinié
Spokesperson and Chief of External Relations: Ramzi Khiroun
Auditors: Ernst & Young et Autres

LOCATIONS

HQ: Lagardère SCA
4 rue de Presbourg
75016 Paris, France
Phone: 33-1-40-69-16-00   **Fax:** 33-1-40-69-21-31
Web: www.lagardere.fr

2009 Sales

	% of total
Europe	
France	34
Other countries	44
US & Canada	13
Other regions	9
Total	**100**

PRODUCTS/OPERATIONS

2009 Sales

	% of total
Lagardère Services	43
Lagardère Publishing	29
Lagardère Active	22
Lagardère Sports	6
Total	**100**

Selected Operations

European Aeronautic Defence and Space Company (12%)
    Aeronautics
    Airbus
    Defense and civil systems
    Military transport aircraft
    Space systems
Lagardère Active
    Canal Plus France (20%)
    Doctissimo (websites)
    Hachette Filipacchi Médias (magazine publishing)
        Car & Driver
        Elle
        Entrevue
        Paris Match
        Premiere
Lagardère Publishing
    Hachette Livre (book publishing)
        Hachette Book Group
            Little, Brown Book Group
Lagardère Services
    Newspaper and magazine distribution
Lagardère Sports
    Newsweb (Internet content)
    Sportfive (European football marketing and media rights)

COMPETITORS

Advance Publications
Axel Springer
BAE SYSTEMS
Bauer Publishing (UK)
Bertelsmann
Boeing
Dawson Holdings
Disney
Hearst Corporation
Lockheed Martin
Meredith Corporation
Modern Times Group AB
Pearson plc
Textron

HISTORICAL FINANCIALS

Company Type: Public

Income Statement

	REVENUE ($ mil.)	NET INCOME ($ mil.)	NET PROFIT MARGIN	EMPLOYEES
12/09	11,880	235	2.0%	29,028
12/08	11,578	884	7.6%	29,393
12/07	12,632	830	6.6%	33,550
12/06	18,469	424	2.3%	30,487
12/05	15,411	831	5.4%	48,245
Annual Growth	**(6.3%)**	**(27.1%)**	**—**	**(11.9%)**

FYE: December 31

2009 Year-End Financials

Debt ratio: —
Return on equity: 3.9%
Cash ($ mil.): 1,095
Current ratio: 0.94
Long-term debt ($ mil.): —
No. of shares (mil.): 127
Dividends
  Yield: 4.6%
  Payout: 121.6%
Market value ($ mil.): 5,168

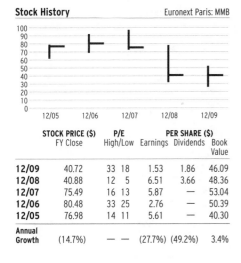

	STOCK PRICE ($) FY Close	P/E High/Low		PER SHARE ($) Earnings	Dividends	Book Value
12/09	40.72	33	18	1.53	1.86	46.09
12/08	40.88	12	5	6.51	3.66	48.36
12/07	75.49	16	13	5.87	—	53.04
12/06	80.48	33	25	2.76	—	50.39
12/05	76.98	14	11	5.61	—	40.30
Annual Growth	(14.7%)	—	—	(27.7%)	(49.2%)	3.4%

L'Air Liquide

Forget the outer planets, the earth has its own gaseous giant in the form of L'Air Liquide. Also known as Air Liquide, the company jockeys with Linde to be the world's largest industrial gas supplier. Its gases include argon, carbon dioxide, helium, hydrogen, nitrogen, and oxygen. Industrial gases are used by almost every major market in their production processes, while medical gases such as oxygen are used by hospitals and other health care providers. Air Liquide has more than a hundred subsidiaries in 75 countries, with a clear strength in Europe. The company operates in the US, its second-largest segment, through American Air Liquide. It also serves customers in Asia, Africa, and the Middle East.

With an established footprint in mature markets and production units all over the world, a key driver in the group's plan for long-term growth is seizing on opportunities to both acquire and build production facilities in emerging economies with a focus on five regions: China, India, Russia, Latin America, and the Middle East. Those regions open opportunities to reduce its overall cost base and to train and develop a new generation of personnel. In 2009 Air Liquide expanded its Middle Eastern operations with the acquisition of Saudi company Al Khafrah Industrial Gases. It also added new production units in the US, China, South Korea, and Malaysia.

New facilities are typically designed and built by Air Liquide's own global engineering and construction division. That division also offers design/build services to third-party customers in need of production facilities equipped with specialized technologies, such as adsorption, permeation, and cryogenics. In addition to engineering and construction, other services Air Liquide offers include gas cylinder rental and residual gas disposal for customers that deal in toxic, corrosive, or inflammable gases.

On the R&D side of its strategy, Air Liquide strives to improve gas production technology and develop new applications for gases. It maintains eight research centers in France, Germany, Japan, and the US focused on developing products that anticipate and meet evolving customer demands. The R&D group tackles three major project areas that Air Liquide believes are driving the world forward: a sustainable environment, high-tech communications, and health care. The teams study ways in which gases can enhance everything from photovoltaics and electronics to medical inhalation therapies. More than 60% of its R&D budget is dedicated to environmental work.

HISTORY

Just after the turn of the century, French chemist Georges Claude discovered a method for liquefying acetylene. He obtained financing from two acquaintances, Paul Delorme and Frederic Gallier, and L'Air Liquide (Air Liquide) was incorporated in 1902. Delorme became president of the company and served in that capacity until 1945.

After a few bumpy years, the company expanded, opening plants in Belgium and Brazil in 1906. Claude applied for a patent for neon tubes in 1907, and the company began producing oxygen in 1908. Before WWI Air Liquide had plants in Canada, Japan, Spain, and Sweden. Between the wars the company continued to expand, opening plants in Greece, Hong Kong, Malaysia, and Portugal. After WWII Claude was accused of collaborating with the Nazis on the development of the infamous V-1 and V-2 "buzz bombs." A French court sentenced him to life in prison, but he was released in 1950.

Despite sales declines in the 1960s, Paul Delorme's son Jean resisted the gas industry's trend toward diversification, choosing instead to sell the company's less profitable units. In 1969 the company opened for business in the US. Air Liquide's US operations grew and it had about a 14% market share in 1986. That year it acquired Texas-based Big Three Industries in a $1.6 billion deal, becoming the second-largest industrial gas producer in the US.

The recession of the early 1990s prompted cost-cutting and a restructuring that decentralized decision making to regional groups. Also, the company and the industry showed increased interest in small on-site production units specially designed for individual customers. In 1996 two large iron and steel contracts in Poland garnered a foothold there. In 1999 Air Liquide and Air Products and Chemicals agreed to jointly take over UK-based British Oxygen Corporation (BOC) in an $11.2 billion deal. Air Liquide had purchased BOC's operations in Belgium, the Netherlands, and Germany earlier that year.

In 2000 Air Liquide and Air Products and Chemicals shelved their plan to acquire BOC when it became clear that the deal could not gain approval by the US Federal Trade Commission because of antitrust concerns. The following year Air Liquide spurned acquisition offers by French utilities group Suez.

Air Liquide took advantage of the break-up of Messer Griesheim in 2004, buying a large portion of that company's operations — in Germany, the UK, and the US — for more than $3 billion. Analysts deemed the price a bit high, but Air Liquide wanted to act before rivals Praxair and Air Products and Chemicals jumped into the fray. Praxair was able to benefit from the Messer Griesheim firesale in any event. Late in the year Air Liquide sold some of its German assets to Praxair for about $650 million; the sale was mandated to satisfy antitrust and regulatory restrictions.

EXECUTIVES

Chairman and CEO: Benoît Potier, age 53
SEVP: Pierre Dufour, age 55
SVP Engineering, Construction, Research, and Technology: François Darchis, age 54
SVP: Jean-Pierre Duprieu, age 58
SVP Asia-Pacific: Jean-Marc de Royère, age 44
Group VP Finance and Operations Control: Fabienne Lecorvaisier, age 48
Group VP Large Industries World Business Line: Ron LaBarre, age 59
VP Americas: Michael J. (Mike) Graff, age 55
VP North-East Asia: Mok Kwong Weng
VP European Industrial Business: Guy Salzgeber, age 52
VP Human Resources: Augustin de Roubin, age 57
Investor Relations: Annie Fournier
Director External Relations: Corinne Estrade-Bordry
Auditors: Mazars & Guérard

LOCATIONS

HQ: L'Air Liquide S.A.
75, Quai d'Orsay
75321 Paris, France
Phone: 33-1-40-62-55-55
US HQ: 2700 Post Oak Blvd., Ste. 1800
Houston, TX 77056
US Phone: 713-624-8000
Web: www.airliquide.com

2009 Sales

	% of total
Europe	57
Americas	22
Asia/Pacific	19
Africa & Middle East	2
Total	**100**

PRODUCTS/OPERATIONS

2009 Sales

	% of total
Gas & services	85
Engineering & construction	8
Other	7
Total	**100**

2009 Sales by Business Line

	% of total
Industrial merchant	41
Large industries	32
Health care	18
Electronics	9
Total	**100**

Selected Products

Acetylene
Argon
Carbon dioxide
Carbon monoxide
Gas mixtures
Helium
Hydrogen
Liquid chemicals
Nitrogen
Oxygen
Silane
Synthesis gas

Selected Services

Dry ice blasting/cleaning
Engineering and construction
Gas cylinder rental and disposal
Gas safety audit and analysis
Gas safety training
On-site gas production

COMPETITORS

Air Products
Airgas
Iwatani International
The Linde Group
Messer Group
Praxair
Taiyo Nippon Sanso

HISTORICAL FINANCIALS

Company Type: Public

Income Statement

FYE: December 31

	REVENUE ($ mil.)	NET INCOME ($ mil.)	NET PROFIT MARGIN	EMPLOYEES
12/09	17,164	1,842	10.7%	5,124
12/08	18,469	1,793	9.7%	43,000
12/07	17,370	1,722	9.9%	40,000
12/06	14,445	1,414	9.8%	36,900
12/05	12,358	1,193	9.7%	35,900
Annual Growth	8.6%	11.5%	—	(38.5%)

2009 Year-End Financials

Debt ratio: —
Return on equity: 17.7%
Cash ($ mil.): 1,985
Current ratio: 1.19
Long-term debt ($ mil.): —

No. of shares (mil.): 283
Dividends
Yield: 2.7%
Payout: 51.0%
Market value ($ mil.): 33,668

Stock History

Pink Sheets: AIQUY

	STOCK PRICE ($) FY Close	P/E High/Low		PER SHARE ($) Earnings	Dividends	Book Value
12/09	119.00	19	12	6.31	3.22	39.27
12/08	92.25	24	13	6.17	—	34.16
12/07	149.82	9	4	29.23	—	32.92
12/06	118.67	5	4	23.27	—	29.31
12/05	96.22	5	4	19.77	—	24.82
Annual Growth	5.5%	—	—	(24.8%)	—	12.1%

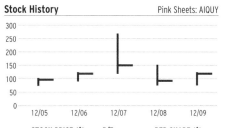

LEGO A/S

Toy blocks are the building blocks of success at LEGO. Keeping little hands busy worldwide for decades, LEGO Holding (dba LEGO Group) has made more than 200 billion of its interlocking toys. In a nod to kids' growing high-tech skills, the toymaker offers LEGO Mindstorms to build PC-programmable robots and BIONICLE sets that feature an evolving online story line. It makes its *Star Wars* and *Indiana Jones* toys under license with Lucasfilm. The group owns namesake retail outlets in the US and Europe and sells its products in more than 130 countries. Vice chairman Kjeld Kirk Kristiansen, grandson of the founder, is LEGO's majority shareholder.

Despite a downturn in the economy, LEGO has logged noteworthy revenue increases while its traditional-toy rivals saw sales slide. The company points to the success of its classic toy lines — LEGO City, LEGO Creator, LEGO Technic, and LEGO *Star Wars* — for the rise in revenue.

LEGO has been working to fine-tune its performance during the past few years. It has done so through product additions, such as the widely successful *Harry Potter* and *Star Wars* lines, as well as forming alliances with the NHL, the NBA, and NIKE.

And it's far from game over for LEGO's videogame business. The toy company in 2010 extended its licensing agreement with Warner Bros. Home Entertainment Group through 2016. Collectively, LEGO has sold nearly 50 million units of the games worldwide.

In a bid to make it to the big screen, LEGO launched its first full-length DVD movie in February 2010 under the *LEGO: The Adventures of Clutch Powers* title. The partnership with Universal Studios Home Entertainment is the first LEGO-based full-length direct-to-video motion picture produced. LEGO already produces television shows, educational materials, and merchandise including books, video games, and computer game software.

To streamline costs associated with production, LEGO phased out a production agreement it inked a few years ago with Flextronics. The strategy included moving production operations from Denmark, Switzerland, and the US to mostly lower-cost countries, such as the Czech Republic, Hungary, and Mexico.

LEGO's legal tussle with rival MEGA Brands (formerly Mega Bloks) continued after the Canadian Supreme Court issued its decision in 2005 giving LEGO the right to appeal the verdict of the Canadian Federal Court of Appeal. The original suit claimed Mega Bloks infringed upon LEGO's intellectual property by passing off its micro bricks as LEGO bricks. However, LEGO lost on its appeal later that year.

The word LEGO is derived from the Danish words for "play well," and children have been doing so with the company's familiar building blocks for years. To boot, LEGO toys were named the Toy of the Century by *FORTUNE* magazine.

HISTORY

Ole Kirk Christiansen opened a carpentry shop in 1916 in Denmark, and in 1932 began making carved wooden toys. Two years later Ole held a contest among his employees to name the company, from which came LEGO (a combination of two Danish words, "leg" and "godt," meaning "play well"). A fire destroyed the LEGO factory in 1942, but the company quickly resumed manufacturing.

The availability of quality plastic following WWII prompted the company to add plastic toys to its line. The predecessor to the common LEGO block was invented in 1949; called Automatic Binding Bricks, they fit on top of each other but did not snap together.

After hearing criticism that no company made a comprehensive toy system, in 1954 Ole's son Godfred assembled a list of 10 product criteria for LEGO's toys, including that they have lots of compatible components. Deciding that the Automatic Binding Bricks had the most potential, the firm launched the first LEGO playset in 1955. It introduced the "stud and tube" snap-together building block in 1958. LEGOs were soon one of the most popular toys in Europe. When a second fire in 1960 destroyed its warehouse for wooden toys, the company ceased production of wooden items in favor of plastics.

Luggage-maker Samsonite began manufacturing and distributing LEGOs in the US in 1961 under license. LEGO's first LEGOLAND park,

built from 42 million LEGO blocks, opened in Billund, Denmark, in 1968. (A UK park followed in 1996, a California park in 1999, and one in Germany in 2002.) By 1973, after relatively lackluster US sales, Samsonite opted not to renew its license, and the LEGO Company set up a sales and production facility in Connecticut. US sales increased tenfold by 1975.

Aiming for the preteen market, the company introduced the more-complex LEGO Technic model sets in 1977 and the popular LEGOLAND Space playset two years later. However, LEGO hit a bump when its patent for the LEGO brick expired in 1981 and a slew of knockoffs flooded the market.

The first LEGO Imagination Center opened in Minneapolis in 1992; the second followed in Walt Disney World five years later. Two years later Godfred died; his son, Kjeld, who changed the spelling of Christiansen to Kristiansen, succeeded him.

In the 1990s growth of the video game industry far outpaced the growth of the construction toys market, and LEGO suffered. With profits shrinking, in 1998 the company reversed its tradition of avoiding commercial tie-ins; it snapped together an agreement to produce building kits and figures based on the popular *Star Wars* movies and Walt Disney's Winnie the Pooh. However, those events came too late to prevent LEGO from suffering its first loss since the 1930s. The company began cutting up to 10% of its workers in 1999.

To build up its interactive, electronic, and educational toy development, LEGO bought smart toys developer Zowie Intertainment in 2000, marking the first time the company purchased another toymaker.

Facing record losses for 2003, LEGO announced significant changes to both its strategy and management structure. In October co-owner Kjeld Kirk Kristiansen resigned as the company's CEO, but remained on the board as vice chairman. Jørgen Vig Knudstorp, SVP of corporate affairs, was named as his replacement. Later that year the company changed its name from LEGO Company to LEGO Group. It also created LEGO Holding A/S to be parent of both the Danish and Swiss operations of the group.

It sold its LEGOLAND parks, which featured LEGO sculptures, rides, and exhibits, to the Blackstone Group in 2005.

EXECUTIVES

Chairman: Niels Jacobsen, age 53
Vice Chairman: Kjeld Kirk Kristiansen
CEO: Jørgen Vig Knudstorp
CFO: Sten Daugaard, age 53
EVP Corporate Center: Christian Iversen
EVP Community, Education, and Direct:
Lisbeth Valther Pallesen
EVP Markets and Products: Mads Nipper
EVP Global Supply Chain: Bali Padda
General Counsel and Director; Interim CEO, KIRKBI A/S: Poul Hartvig Nielsen
Manager Marketing, Hungary and Croatia: Tímea Gubás
Manager Marketing, Iberia: Joachim Schwidtal
Manager Marketing, Norway and Finland:
Johnny Skovlund
Manager Marketing, LEGO Russia: Olga Lombas
Marketing Coordinator, Denmark and Sweden:
Sanne Froberg
Manager Public Relations, UK and Ireland:
Melissa Wallace
Manager Brand, LEGO France: Olivia Lantigner
Director Marketing, LEGO Russia/Visegrad:
Marta Oziemska
Head Corporate Communications: Charlotte Simonsen
Auditors: PricewaterhouseCoopers

HQ: LEGO A/S
    Aastvej
    DK-7190 Billund, Denmark
Phone: 45-79-50-60-70
US HQ: 555 Taylor Rd., Enfield, CT 06083
US Phone: 860-763-3211   **US Fax:** 860-763-6680
Web: www.lego.com

PRODUCTS/OPERATIONS

Selected Products

Alpha Team
BIONICLE
CLIKITS (fashion design system for girls)
Discovery Kids
Dora the Explorer
Harry Potter
Knights Kingdom
LEGO BABY toys
LEGO Belville toys (for girls)
LEGO *Bob the Builder*
LEGO City
LEGO Creator sets
LEGO Designer
LEGO Duplo
LEGO Factory
LEGO Mindstorms
LEGO Quatro
LEGO Racers
LEGO Star Wars
LEGO Technic
Orient Expedition
Spiderman 2
Spybotics
Trains
X-Pod

COMPETITORS

Apple Inc.	Parc Paradisio
Discovery Toys	Playmobil
Disney	Simba Dickie Group
Hasbro	Smoby
Hershey Entertainment	Sony
JAKKS Pacific	Spin Master
K'NEX Industries	StarParks
Mattel	Toy Quest
MEGA Brands	VTech Holdings
Namco Bandai	

HISTORICAL FINANCIALS

Company Type: Private

Income Statement

FYE: December 31

	REVENUE ($ mil.)	NET INCOME ($ mil.)	NET PROFIT MARGIN	EMPLOYEES
12/09	2,246	260	11.6%	7,058
12/08	1,804	256	14.2%	5,388
12/07	1,585	203	12.8%	4,199
12/06	1,384	253	18.3%	4,922
12/05	1,117	80	7.2%	6,643
Annual Growth	19.1%	34.3%	—	1.5%

Net Income History

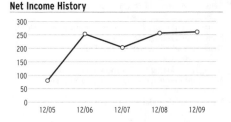

Lenovo Group

Lenovo may not be considered tech royalty, but it's definitely blue-blooded. The company was already the largest PC maker in the world's most populous country when it acquired IBM's PC operations for approximately $1.75 billion. It remains a leader in China, but the company now has a global presence. Lenovo's products include desktop and notebook PCs, workstations, servers, storage drives, and IT services. It also offers IT management software under the ThinkVantage name. Lenovo's principal facilities are in Beijing; Morrisville, North Carolina; and Singapore. It has research centers in China, Japan, and the US. Lenovo generates about half of its revenues in China and the greater Asia/Pacific region.

Citing a flagging economy, Lenovo announced a restructuring plan in 2009 that included a workforce reduction of 11%, executive pay cuts, and the consolidation of its China and the Asia/Pacific units. The company also initiated a management shakeup. Chairman Yang Yuanqing was tapped to replace William Amelio as CEO. Lenovo founder Liu Chuanzhi was named chairman. Amelio had spearheaded efforts to cut costs and build Lenovo into a global brand. Both Yang and Liu returned to positions they'd previously held. The management change may in part reflect a strategy shift for Lenovo. With corporate spending flagging, particularly in the US, the company plans to focus on China and other emerging markets, with an emphasis on consumers.

Not long after Yang took over as CEO, Lenovo realigned its corporate structure and product portfolio. The company created two new business units: Mature Markets and Emerging Markets. Its primary product lines now include the Think Product Group and the Idea Product Group. The Think unit is aimed primarily at the enterprise market, while its Idea unit is focused on consumers and small and midsized businesses.

Also in 2009 Lenovo acquired Seattle-based Switchbox Labs, a developer of consumer electronics. The company kept under wraps what Switchbox is developing and its product plans for the Switchbox technology.

Lenovo remains the leading PC maker in China, with nearly 30% market share, and it ranks fourth globally. Both at home and abroad the company faces stiff competition from market leaders Hewlett-Packard, Dell, and Acer.

Looking to focus on its core PC operations, Lenovo sold its mobile phone business, Lenovo Mobile Communications, to Hony Capital in 2008. Hony, the private equity arm of Legend Holdings, paid $100 million for the unit. A year later, Lenovo bought back the mobile communications business for about $200 million in cash and stock. The company cited the growth of the mobile Internet market and the increasing convergence between the PC and wireless handset sectors for the about-face in product strategy. Lenovo's move came as Dell introduced a mobile phone for the Chinese market.

Legend Holdings, which is controlled by the Chinese government, owns about 45% of Lenovo.

HISTORY

Liu Chuanzhi, an engineer at the Chinese Academy of Sciences who wrote industry research reports, established Legend Group Holdings Co. in 1984 in Beijing. Backed by a modest investment from the academy, Liu, who went on to become something of an entrepreneurial hero in China, and 10 other engineers were given a green light to form a retail business. They first bought and sold items ranging from TVs to roller skates, but later focused on distributing computer products and eventually moved into manufacturing PCs for AST Research. Legend introduced its first proprietary product, a Chinese character system for PCs, in 1985.

In 1988 the company formed Legend Holdings Limited, which was originally a Hong Kong-based PC distributor. The following year the parent company began designing and manufacturing motherboards and added systems integration services to its offerings. In 1990 China reduced import tariffs, a move that opened the trade door for companies such as IBM and Compaq. That year Legend Group Holdings began making its own brand of PCs.

Legend Holdings went public in 1994, and the following year began absorbing operations from its parent company, which retained approximately 60% ownership in the subsidiary. By 1996 it was tied with IBM for PC market share in China; it became the country's top brand the following year.

In 1998 parent company Legend Group Holdings transferred Beijing Legend Group to its Hong Kong-based subsidiary. The following year Microsoft, looking to extend its operating system dominance into China, teamed up with Legend Holdings to create set-top boxes. In 2000 the company partnered with Pacific Century CyberWorks to provide broadband Internet services. The following year Legend spun off its distribution business, Digital China, as a separate public company. In 2001 Yang Yuanqing was named CEO of the company.

In 2002 Legend Holdings changed its English company name to Legend Group Limited. The company launched a corporate brand, Lenovo, the following year, and in 2004 it officially adopted Lenovo as its English name. It also sold its non-telecom IT services business to AsiaInfo Holdings in 2004.

Lenovo acquired IBM's worldwide PC operations for approximately $1.75 billion in 2005. IBM executive Stephen Ward was named CEO of Lenovo at the time of the merger, but he was replaced by William Amelio before year's end. Amelio headed Dell's Asia/Pacific operations before joining Lenovo. In 2006 Lenovo launched a unit called Lenovo Services.

In 2007 Lenovo stopped using the IBM PC brand, to which it still held the rights, and began offering only Lenovo-branded machines. The next year it sponsored and supported the Olympic Summer Games in Beijing, providing more than 30,000 pieces of equipment and 600 engineers.

EXECUTIVES

Chairman: Liu Chuanzhi, age 66
Vice Chairman: Ma Xuezheng, age 57
CEO: Yang Yuanqing, age 46
SVP and CFO: Wong Wai Ming, age 52
SVP and CIO: Xiaoyan Wang, age 48
SVP and Chief Procurement Officer: Qiao Song, age 42
SVP and Chief Marketing Officer: David A. Roman
SVP Mature Markets: Milko Van Duijl, age 47
SVP Human Resources: Kenneth A. (Ken) DiPietro, age 51

SVP Emerging Markets: Chen Shaopeng, age 41
SVP and CTO: He (George) Zhiqiang, age 47
SVP; Acting CEO and President, Lenovo Mobile:
Lu Yan
SVP and General Counsel: Michael J. O'Neill, age 53
SVP Global Services: Peter Bartolotta
SVP E-Commerce and Chief Marketing Officer:
Deepak Advani, age 46
SVP Global Supply Chain: Gerry P. Smith, age 46
VP Investor Relations: Gary Ng
President and COO; Acting President, Latin America
Group: Rory Read, age 48
Company Secretary: Mok Fung Chu
Executive Director External Communications:
Raymond (Ray) Gorman
Auditors: PricewaterhouseCoopers

LOCATIONS

HQ: Lenovo Group Limited
23rd Fl., Lincoln House, Taikoo Place
979 King's Rd., Quarry Bay, Hong Kong
Phone: 2590-0228   **Fax:** 2516-5384
US HQ: 1009 Think Place, Morrisville, NC 27560
US Phone: 919-294-2500   **US Fax:** 877-411-1329
Web: www.lenovo.com

2010 Sales

	% of total
China	48
Mature Markets	37
Emerging Markets (excluding China)	15
Total	**100**

PRODUCTS/OPERATIONS

2010 Sales

	% of total
Notebook computers	63
Desktop computers	35
Other	2
Total	**100**

COMPETITORS

Acer
Apple Inc.
ASUSTeK
Dell
Digital China
Founder Holdings
Fujitsu
Great Wall Technology
Hedy Holding
Hewlett-Packard
Hitachi
IBM
Microsoft
NEC
Panasonic Corp
Positivo Informática
Samsung Electronics
Siemens AG
Sony
Toshiba
Wipro

HISTORICAL FINANCIALS

Company Type: Public

Income Statement

FYE: March 31

	REVENUE ($ mil.)	NET INCOME ($ mil.)	NET PROFIT MARGIN	EMPLOYEES
3/10	16,605	129	0.8%	22,205
3/09	14,901	(226)	—	22,511
3/08	16,352	485	3.0%	23,200
3/07	14,590	161	1.1%	25,100
3/06	13,344	28	0.2%	19,500
Annual Growth	**5.6%**	**46.9%**	**—**	**3.3%**

2010 Year-End Financials

Debt ratio: 12.5%	No. of shares (mil.): 9,791
Return on equity: 8.9%	Dividends
Cash ($ mil.): 2,439	Yield: 0.0%
Current ratio: 0.97	Payout: —
Long-term debt ($ mil.): 200	Market value ($ mil.): 52,480

Stock History

Pink Sheets: LNVGY

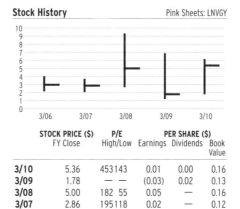

	STOCK PRICE ($) FY Close	P/E High/Low	PER SHARE ($) Earnings	Dividends	Book Value
3/10	5.36	453 143	0.01	0.00	0.16
3/09	1.78	— —	(0.03)	0.02	0.13
3/08	5.00	182 55	0.05	—	0.16
3/07	2.86	195 118	0.02	—	0.12
3/06	2.97	— 905	0.00	—	0.11
Annual Growth	**15.9%**	**— —**	**—**	**—**	**11.2%**

LG Corp.

LG Corp. is a major South Korean *chaebol* (family-run industrial group) that maintains core businesses in electronics, chemicals, and telecommunications. Also known as LG Group, it operates through a number of wholly owned, majority-owned, and minority-interest subsidiaries and affiliate companies in Korea and around the world. The most well known are probably LG Electronics and LG Chem; LG Corp. holds about a one-third ownership stake in each. Electronics is its largest segment in terms of revenue, but telecom represents the growth of its future business due to partnerships with Korea's three mobile operators. The company was founded in 1947 and 12 years later produced Korea's first radio.

LG Corp., named after founding companies Lucky and Goldstar, came into existence as a holding company in 2003. It was the first Korean corporation to introduce a holding company structure, in which investments and business divisions are separated.

Today, LG Electronics contributes substantially to LG Corp.'s overall business performance, posting its highest-ever revenue total in 2009 thanks to gains in foreign currency exchange and sales of core products, such as mobile handsets and digital TV sets. LCD panel manufacturer LG Display is also helping its parent produce solid performance results.

In addition to its better-known consumer products, the group's chemicals segment is a top maker of LCD polarizers, and it maintains a strong reputation for producing state-of-the-art batteries among global IT and automotive companies. In 2010, for instance, LG Chem broke ground on an electric vehicle battery manufacturing plant in Michigan. Once completed in 2013, the factory will supply power packs for some 600,000 electric vehicles or 200,000 hybrid vehicles per year, and it is expected to create

more than 500 jobs. The factory already has orders to fill from major carmakers, including a deal with General Motors to supply batteries for the Chevrolet Volt electric car.

Meanwhile, its telecommunications segment reorganized and simplified operations by combining three of its telecom affiliates (LG TeleCom, LG Dacom, and LG Powercom) into a single entity called LG U+ in 2010. The purpose behind merging these businesses is to create a more unified base for developing and providing cable and wireless telecom products and services geared at both businesses and consumers.

HISTORY

During WWII Koo In-Hwoi made tooth powder for Koreans to use in place of salt, then the common dentifrice. Koo founded the Lucky Chemical Company in 1947 to make facial creams and, later, detergent, shampoo, and Lucky Toothpaste. The enterprise soon became Korea's only plastics maker. Koo established a trading company in 1953.

Emulating Japanese exporters, Koo formed Goldstar Company in 1958 to make fans. The company became the first company in South Korea to make radios (1959), refrigerators (1965), TVs (1966), elevators and escalators (1968), and washing machines and air conditioners (1969). In 1967 Lucky collaborated with Caltex to build the Honam Oil Refinery, the first privately owned refinery in Korea. Both Lucky and Goldstar benefited from the *chaebol*'s cozy relationship with President Park Chung Hee's government (1962-79) and used plentiful loans from Korean banks to diversify into everything from energy and semiconductors to insurance. Lucky began petrochemical production in 1977 and later built the world's largest single-unit petrochemical plant in Saudi Arabia (1986).

During the 1970s and 1980s Goldstar expanded rapidly as it took advantage of cheap Korean labor to export private-label electronics items to its large retail customers abroad. In the late 1970s the group began investing heavily in semiconductor production, in part to fulfill its own chip requirements. Goldstar companies teamed with more technically accomplished partners, including AT&T, NEC, Hitachi, and Siemens, and set out to capture office-automation and higher-end consumer electronics markets with Goldstar-brand goods. In 1983 the *chaebol* became Lucky Goldstar.

Although electronics sales grew rapidly, Lucky Goldstar's inefficient organizational structure slowed progress, and in 1984 archrival Samsung finally outdid it. In the late 1980s Lucky Goldstar suffered from rising wage rates, labor unrest, and Korean currency appreciation. In 1989 the group created Goldstar Electron (LG Semicon Co.) and in 1990 business rebounded. Lucky Goldstar acquired 5% of US television maker Zenith in 1991.

In 1994 Lucky Goldstar signed an agreement with the government of the Sakha region in Russia to develop the Elga, the world's largest coal field. Lucky Goldstar became the LG Group in 1995, marking its new thrust: globalization. That year it acquired a controlling interest in troubled Zenith, by then the last TV manufacturer in the US.

The Asian contagion hit in 1997. LG Group announced that it would pull out of 90 business areas, but in 1998 it was one of several *chaebol* caught funneling money to ailing subsidiaries (the *chaebol* were collectively fined $93 million).

LG Group members went abroad in 1998 looking for new partners: Among other deals, LG Chemicals allied with top drugmakers such as SmithKline Beecham (now GlaxoSmithKline), Warner-Lambert (now Pfizer), and Merck; and British Telecommunications (now BT Group) bought a nearly 25% stake in LG Telecom.

Under government pressure to consolidate scattered businesses with those of other *chaebol*, LG Group in 1999 agreed to sell LG Semicon and began restructuring its operations. After lengthy negotiations, the Hyundai Group took control of the unit, which became Hyundai MicroElectronics. Electronics giant Philips paid $1.6 billion for a 50% stake in LG Electronics' LCD unit.

Looking for new markets, in 2001 LG's personal care products (detergents and diapers) unit LG Household & Healthcare launched operations in India.

In 2003 LG sold its DACOM IN, LG Cable, LG Caltex Gas, LG Nikko Copper, and Kukdong City Gas subsidiaries in an effort to divest its noncore operations. Also that year LG completed the restructuring of its operations into a traditional holding-company-type structure, with the new LG to be led by flagship companies LG Electronics and LG Chem. The following year saw GS Holdings splitting away from LG and taking with it LG-Caltex (now GS Caltex), LG Mart, LG Home Shopping, and GS Sports.

EXECUTIVES

Chairman and Co-CEO: Bon-Moo Koo, age 65
Vice Chairman and Co-CEO: Yu Sig Kang, age 61
President, COO, and Director: Juno Cho
EVP and Chief Procurement Officer, LG Electronics: Thomas K. (Tom) Linton
EVP and Chief Customer Officer, LG Electronics: Teddy B. B. Hwang
EVP and CFO, LG Electronics: David D. H. Jung
EVP and President and CEO, Air Conditioning Company, LG Electronics: Hwan Yong Nho, age 54
EVP, LG-DOW Polycarbonate: T. J. Wu
SVP and General Counsel: Jong Sang Lee
VP and Head Human Resources Team: Myung Kwan Lee
Vice Chairman and CEO, LG International; CEO, LG Electronics: Koo Bon-joon, age 59
Vice Chairman and CEO, LG Chem: Peter Bahnsuk Kim
CEO, LG N-Sys: Tae-Soo Chung
CEO, LG Telecom: Lee Sang-Cheol
CEO, Hi Business Logistics: Sang Gyu Choi
President, LG Economic Research Institute: Joo-Hyung Kim
President and CTO, LG Electronics: Woo Hyun Paik
President and CEO, LG Display: Young Soo Kwon
President, China, V-ENS: Woong-Pill Yang
President and CEO, LG Life Sciences: In Chull Kim
President and CEO, V-ENS: Woo-Jong Lee
President and CEO, Europe, LG Electronics: Jong-Eun (James) Kim
Auditors: Deloitte Anjin LLC

LOCATIONS

HQ: LG Corp.
LG Twin Towers, 20 Yeouido-dong
Yeongdeungpo-gu
Seoul 150-721, South Korea
Phone: 82-2-3773-5114 **Fax:** 82-2-3773-2292
Web: www.lg.co.kr

PRODUCTS/OPERATIONS

2009 Sales

	% of total
Electronics	42
Chemicals	37
Telecommunications	12
Services	9
Total	**100**

Selected Subsidiaries and Affiliates

Chemicals
  LG Chem
    LG DOW Polycarbonate
    SEETEC
  LG Household & Healthcare
    Coca-Cola Beverage Company
    Diamond Pure Water
  LG Hausys
  LG Life Sciences
  LG MMA
Electronics
  LG Electronics Inc.
    Hi Logistics
    Hiplaza
    LG Display
    LG Innotek Co., Ltd.
    System Air-Con Engineering
  Lusem
  Siltron
Telecommunications & Services
  G2R
    Alchemedia
    Bugs Com Ad
    G Outdoor
    HS Ad
    L. Best
    TAMS Media
    W Brand Connection
  LG CNS
    Biztech & Ektimo
    LG N-Sys
    Uccess Partners
    V-ENS
  LG Management Development Institute
  LG Solar Energy
  LG Sports
  LG U+
    AIN Teleservice
    CS Leader
    CS ONE Partner
    Dacom Crossing
    Dacom Multimedia Internet
  SERVEONE
    Konjiam Yewon

COMPETITORS

Akzo Nobel
AMD
BASF SE
Bayer AG
DuPont
Fujitsu
GE
Hewlett-Packard
Hitachi
IBM
ITOCHU
Marubeni
Motorola
Nokia
Panasonic Corp
Samsung Group
SANYO
Sharp Corp.
SK Group
Sony
Toshiba

HISTORICAL FINANCIALS

Company Type: Public

Income Statement

FYE: December 31

	REVENUE ($ mil.)	NET INCOME ($ mil.)	NET PROFIT MARGIN	EMPLOYEES
12/09	86,353	4,483	5.2%	186,000
12/08	71,276	2,344	3.3%	177,000
12/07	81,476	3,879	4.8%	160,000
12/06	66,017	640	1.0%	120,000
12/05	60,787	1,994	3.3%	—
Annual Growth	9.2%	22.4%	—	15.7%

Net Income History

Exchange: Korea

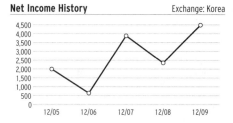

Lloyd's

Think of the Society of Lloyd's (dba Lloyd's of London) as a busy market where groups who have risks can meet up with groups who have money to insure risk. As the world's leading insurance exchange, Lloyd's regulates about 75 syndicates run by more than 40 managing agents. Customers include corporate underwriters and wealthy individuals transacting specialty property/casualty insurance business worth billions in premiums each year. Also part of the picture are Lloyd's brokers, who bring business to the market. Lloyd's is a top conduit for aviation and marine insurance, as well as its more specialized specialty insurance covering celebrity body parts or protecting against acts of terrorism.

The wealthy individuals it serves are called Names but their number has been dropping since the 1980s and is down to some 1,000.

Gross premiums written, for the entire Lloyd's market as a whole, totaled more than £16 billion in 2007.

Despite an overhaul, Lloyd's tradition of specialty lines has hampered its ability to compete against global insurance firms offering more comprehensive service. Encouraged by Lloyd's to consolidate, some syndicates, infused with capital from corporate-owned managing agencies that enables them to completely underwrite a contract, are turning into full-service insurance companies. Corporate underwriters, such as ACE Limited and Berkshire Hathaway's General Re, now account for most of Lloyd's capital backing, where Names once dominated.

While Lloyd's accepts risks in over 200 countries, North America, the UK, and Europe account for the lion's share of Lloyd's business. However, in 2008 Lloyd's announced it would actively seek more business in Asia and the Middle East to widen its range. At the same time, some Asian companies have entered into the market by buying up syndicate holders.

In another attempt to renew itself, Lloyd's is working to modernize its traditional accounting system and has shifted to a franchise system for managing agents. Lord Peter Levene, the former Mayor of London, assumed the chairman's post and has made many changes with hopes of keeping the Lloyd's market competitive.

HISTORY

In 1688 Edward Lloyd opened Lloyd's Coffee House near London's docks. Maritime insurance brokers and underwriters met at Lloyd's, which offered a comfortable venue for exchanging shipping information. The loose association of brokers began publishing shipping newspaper *Lloyd's List* in 1734 (sold 1996).

The coffeehouse attracted people who used insurance as a cover for gambling — members who "insured" the gender of the transvestite Chevalier d'Eon began Lloyd's tradition of specialty insurance.

In 1871 Parliament enacted the Lloyd's Act, which formed Lloyd's Corporation to oversee the activities of the underwriting syndicates (made up of Names with unlimited personal liability). In the 1880s the market began covering non-marine risks. By 1900 Lloyd's members wrote 50% of the world's non-life insurance. Prompt claims payment after the 1906 San Francisco earthquake boosted the market's image in the US. After WWI, Lloyd's members began writing automotive, credit, and aviation insurance.

In 1981 and 1982 a syndicate managed by Richard Outhwaite wrote contracts on the future liabilities of old insurance contracts with claims (many with environmental exposure) still pending.

During that decade Lloyd's attracted new Names: the merely well-off — highly paid people without great wealth — whose pledged assets were often overvalued in the 1980s boom. Exercising little oversight, Lloyd's let syndicates close their books on pending claims by reinsuring them repeatedly through new syndicates financed by neophyte Names.

The boom's end coincided with a rise in US environmental claims covered by insurance contracts such as those written by Outhwaite. When Names with reduced net worth balked at paying claims, Lloyd's faced disaster. From 1991 to 1994, the number of syndicates fell by half and premium rates increased. In 1993, with billions in claims and many Names refusing to pay or suing their syndicates for not disclosing the risks, Lloyd's imposed new underwriting and reporting rules, took control of most syndicates' back-office functions, and brought in capital by finally admitting corporate members (mostly foreign insurers).

Lloyd's reached a multibillion-pound settlement with most of its Names in 1996. It also required its active investors to help finance a new insurance company, Equitas, to cover old liabilities. In 1997 Lloyd's sought to increase the number of broker members. The next year, amid regulatory disagreements with Singapore's government and a faltering Asian economy, it called off plans to open an exchange branch there. In 1999 Lloyd's began cutting its operating costs. It also began bolstering its Central Fund with insurance rather than cash and admitted the captive insurer of pharmaceuticals powerhouse SmithKline Beecham (now GlaxoSmithKline) into its marketplace.

In 2000, as litigation dragged on over whether a recalcitrant group of Names owed Lloyd's more than £50 million for claims, the corporation continued to trim costs by selling property. That year the US became Lloyd's single largest market for the first time in the company's 300-year history.

After the insurer was hit hard by the attacks on the World Trade Center, resulting in £3.1 billion in losses, another first occurred: It issued an annual report to publicly document the heavy deficits.

The losses continued in 2005 with what the company said was the worst year for natural disasters on record. It paid out more than £3 billion but only showed a loss for the year of £103 million. The company then took steps to tighten its natural disaster underwriting guidelines.

EXECUTIVES

Chairman: Lord Peter Levene, age 67
CEO and Director: Richard Ward
Deputy Chairman, Lloyd's: Ewen H. Gilmour, age 56
Deputy Chairman, Lloyd's: Graham White
Deputy Chairman, Counsel: Bill Knight
Director Finance, Risk Management, and Operations: Luke Savage
Director and General Counsel: Sean McGovern
Director Franchise Performance: Rolf Tolle
Director Market Operations and North America: Sue Langley
Director International Markets and Business Development: Jose Ribeiro
CIO: Peter Hambling
Head, Risk Management: Olly Reeves
Head, Human Resources: Suzy Black
Head, Legal: Peter Spires
Head, Communications: Louise Shield
Head, Government Affairs: Alastair Evans
Head, International Market Access: Rosemary Beaver
Head, Market Risk and Reserving Unit and Lloyd's Actuary: Henry Johnson
Head, Market Finance: John Parry
Head, Market Relations: Sally Coryn
Head, Claims: Kent Chaplin
Head, Relationship Management: Bob Stevenson
Secretary to Council and Franchise Board: Gavin Steele
Manager Investor Relations: Christina Nallaiah
Auditors: Ernst & Young LLP

LOCATIONS

HQ: Society of Lloyd's
1 Lime St.
London EC3M 7HA, United Kingdom
Phone: 44-20-7327-1000   **Fax:** 44-20-7626-2389
US HQ: The Museum Office Bldg., 25 W. 53rd St., 14th Fl., New York, NY 10019
US Phone: 212-382-4060   **US Fax:** 212-382-4070
Web: www.lloyds.com

2009 Revenues

	% of total
Americas	
US & Canada	45
Other countries	6
Europe	
UK	20
Other countries	16
Central Asia & Asia/Pacific	9
Other regions	4
Total	**100**

PRODUCTS/OPERATIONS

2009 Revenues

	% of total
Reinsurance	36
Property	23
Casualty	20
Marine	7
Energy	6
Motor	5
Aviation	3
Total	**100**

COMPETITORS

Aon
AXA
General Re
Marsh & McLennan
Willis Group Holdings

HISTORICAL FINANCIALS

Company Type: Insurance society

Income Statement				FYE: December 31
	REVENUE ($ mil.)	NET INCOME ($ mil.)	NET PROFIT MARGIN	EMPLOYEES
12/09	563	228	40.4%	845
12/08	481	148	30.7%	806
12/07	858	328	38.3%	772
12/06	685	164	23.9%	761
12/05	254	(28)	—	603
Annual Growth	22.1%	—	—	8.8%

Net Income History

Lloyds Banking Group

Don't confuse Lloyds Banking Group with that *other* Lloyds. Unrelated to Lloyd's of London, Lloyds Banking Group was formed by the 2009 merger of UK banks Lloyds TSB and HBOS. Its retail banking services include deposit accounts, credit cards, loans, and wealth management. Lloyds Banking Group is also one of the nation's top home mortgage lenders. Other products include insurance and investment services through Scottish Widows, and wholesale and international banking for UK corporate clients and multinationals. Lloyds Banking Group, which operates under the brands Lloyds TSB, Halifax, and Bank of Scotland, has some 2,000 branches with representative offices in the Middle East, Asia, and the Americas.

The economic and financial crisis in 2008 and 2009 was a difficult time for Lloyds Banking Group. The UK government took a 40% stake in the company after bailing it out, along with seven other top banks, in 2008. Lloyds Banking group accepted some £17 billion ($25 billion) in taxpayer money. The government hoped the infusion of cash would loosen up credit markets and restore confidence in the financial system.

As part of a restructuring plan (and to repay the UK government), Lloyds Banking Group launched one of the largest-ever capital raisings in Europe, which included a £9 billion ($13 billion) debt exchange and a nearly £14 billion ($20 billion) rights issue. Lloyds Banking Group also announced plans to sell the 600 retail banking branches associated with the Lloyds TSB brand, along with a large part of its Cheltenham & Gloucester network in order to meet requirements set forth by regulators.

Around the same time of the government bailout, Lloyds TSB agreed to take over struggling HBOS, the UK's top mortgage lender. The controversial £12 billion ($22 billion) deal was announced after HBOS shares fell dramatically amid rising concerns surrounding the vitality of financial services companies worldwide.

Within weeks, though, Lloyds Banking Group revealed that HBOS had incurred some £11 billion ($18 billion) in losses, and shareholder unrest grew concerning the billions of pounds in toxic assets gained with the acquisition. The merger has meant drastic cost cuts and job losses, as the company has announced more than 17,700 job cuts across the UK since the beginning of 2009.

Needless to say, not everyone was happy with the HBOS merger. At Lloyds Banking Group's annual meeting in 2009, a large group of shareholders loudly criticized the company's board for the HBOS deal, demanding resignations and threatening lawsuits over the merger. In 2010 one group of disgruntled shareholders launched legal action in order to recoup up to £14 billion ($20 billion) that they claim they lost as a result of the merger.

Lloyds Banking Group has defended the merger, saying it helped improve the company's strategic position by improving its market position, brand recognition, and expanding its customer base. Although the deal brought short-term costs, company leaders are convinced that it is better positioned for future growth as the economy recovers.

After these turbulent few years, CEO Eric Daniels has announced that he will retire in 2011. The group is seeking his replacement.

HISTORY

In 1765 John Taylor and Sampson Lloyd II founded Taylors and Lloyds bank in Birmingham, England; five years later their sons opened a London agency. In 1852 the last Taylor involved with the bank died. In 1865 the bank converted to joint stock form and became Lloyds Banking Company Ltd. Over the next half century, it grew by merging with some 50 banks, becoming one of England's largest banks by the turn of the century.

Despite the post-WWI roller-coaster economy, the bank acquired Capital and Counties Bank (1918, bringing foreign connections); Fox, Fowler & Company (1921); and Cox & Company (1923). During both wars, deposits grew while lending dropped. After WWII, growth was hampered by high inflation.

Lloyds added branches and products in the 1960s. By 1971 it had branches in 43 countries. It moved into insurance (1972), home mortgages (1979), real estate agency services (1982), and merchant banking (1986).

In 1987 Latin American bank defaults pummeled Lloyds. Refocusing on domestic operations, the bank sold overseas subsidiaries (including Lloyds Bank Canada in 1990) and acquired 58% of life insurer Abbey Life (1988) and Cheltenham & Gloucester Building Society (1994). HSBC outbid Lloyds for Midland Bank in 1992; Lloyds bought TSB Group in 1995.

TSB Group evolved from the trustee savings banks (TSBs) formed in the 1800s. By 1860 there were 600 such banks, mainly in northern England and Scotland. During WWI many TSBs consolidated or closed. By WWII about 100 remained, and the mergers continued.

In the 1960s TSBs began offering checking accounts and trust services. Loans, credit cards, and other services came in 1973. In 1986 the four remaining TSBs (TSB Channel Islands, TSB England and Wales, TSB Northern Ireland, and TSB Scotland) agreed to merge and go public in order to gain equal footing with stock banks. TSB Group was born.

Flush with cash from its offering, TSB group defied the late 1980s recession to buy Target Group (life insurance, sold 1993), Hill Samuel (merchant banking), and other units; the purchases sent TSB sprawling.

As debt rose in the 1990s, TSB Group refocused on banking and insurance. TSB and Lloyds merged in 1995, linking their geographically complementary branch networks to fend off competition. In 1999 Lloyds TSB bailed out Abbey Life, which had nearly been bankrupted by the cost of settling pension mis-selling claims.

The bank in 2000 bought Scottish Widows to boost its fund management services. It sold the Abbey Life name and its new business to Zurich Financial Services' Allied Dunbar; Abbey Life continued to service existing business for Lloyds. Also that year, Lloyds TSB bought consumer and auto finance unit Chartered Trust from Standard Chartered.

In 2001 Lloyds TSB closed Bahamas-based subsidiary British Bank of Latin America because of alleged money-laundering links revealed in a US Senate report. Lloyds TSB's asset finance operations bought First National Vehicle Holdings and Abbey National Vehicle Finance from Abbey National plc in 2002.

The company sold its Abbey Life unit to Deutsche Bank for nearly $2 billion in 2007. (The life insurer had been closed to new business since 2000.)

EXECUTIVES

Chairman: Sir Winfried F. W. (Win) Bischoff, age 69
Deputy Chairman: Lord Alexander P. (Sandy) Leitch, age 62
Director, Group Finance: Tim J. W. Tookey, age 48
Group Executive Director, Wholesale: G. Truett Tate, age 60
Group Executive Director, UK Retail Banking: Helen A. Weir, age 48
Group Executive Director, Insurance and Investments: Archie G. Kane, age 58
Group Chief Executive and Director: J. Eric Daniels, age 59
Auditors: PricewaterhouseCoopers LLP

LOCATIONS

HQ: Lloyds Banking Group plc
25 Gresham St.
London EC2V 7HN, United Kingdom
Phone: 44-20-7626-1500   **Fax:** 44-20-7489-3484
Web: www.lloydsbankinggroup.com

PRODUCTS/OPERATIONS

2009 Sales

	% of total
Net trading income	42
Interest	20
Insurance premiums	20
Fees & commissions	6
Other	12
Total	**100**

Selected Brands

Bank of Scotland
Halifax
Lloyds TSB
Scottish Widows

COMPETITORS

Barclays	Northern Rock
Grupo Santander	Royal Bank of Scotland
HSBC	Standard Life Bank
Invesco	Woolwich

HISTORICAL FINANCIALS

Company Type: Public

Income Statement

FYE: December 31

	ASSETS ($ mil.)	NET INCOME ($ mil.)	INCOME AS % OF ASSETS	EMPLOYEES
12/09	1,636,006	4,502	0.3%	107,144
12/08	631,071	1,185	0.2%	120,826
12/07	703,434	6,548	0.9%	58,000
12/06	673,336	5,493	0.8%	62,630
12/05	534,007	4,298	0.8%	66,797
Annual Growth	32.3%	1.2%	—	12.5%

2009 Year-End Financials

Equity as % of assets: 4.2%
Return on assets: 0.4%
Return on equity: 10.9% ·
Long-term debt ($ mil.): 427,182
No. of shares (mil.): 17,019
Dividends
  Yield: 0.0%
  Payout: —
Market value ($ mil.): 88,629
Sales ($ mil.): 102,737

Stock History

NYSE: LYG

	STOCK PRICE ($) FY Close	P/E High/Low		PER SHARE ($) Earnings	Dividends	Book Value
12/09	5.21	28	7	0.48	0.00	4.05
12/08	10.87	68	12	0.80	1.94	0.80
12/07	73.33	21	16	4.51	2.74	1.42
12/06	86.60	23	17	3.78	2.71	1.28
12/05	56.73	22	18	2.97	2.28	1.03
Annual Growth	(45.0%)	—	—	(36.6%)	—	40.7%

Loblaw Companies

When grocery shopping in Canada, it's hard to escape the long arm of Loblaw. Loblaw Companies Ltd. is the market share leader among Canadian supermarket operators. Its corporate, franchised, and affiliated banners (22 in all) fly over more than 1,440 stores nationwide. Trade names include Loblaws, Atlantic SaveEasy, Extra Foods, Fortinos, No Frills, Provigo, Your Independent Grocer, T&T, and Zehrs Markets, to name a few. Its stores offer more than 8,000 private-label products, including its signature President's Choice brand, as well as traditional and organic grocery fare. Loblaw is also Canada's largest wholesale food distributor. Loblaw is a subsidiary of Canada's George Weston.

Loblaw is in year four of a five-year turnaround plan (dubbed Project Simplify) designed to transform it into a more efficient retailer and regain its financial footing for the long term. Initiatives include top management changes, simplifying its retail operations, information technology and supply chain initiatives (including delivering fresher goods to its stores), and expanding into ethnic foods, among many others. Problems at the company's Provigo subsidiary in Québec (acquired in 1998) have taken a heavy financial toll on Loblaw and contributed to the urgency to retool operations. Domestic competition from METRO Inc. and Sobeys, as well as poor operations at the Provigo stores, have hurt financial performance in recent years.

In 2008 the supermarket chain permanently cut prices on more than 1,000 grocery items at its Loblaws, Zerhs, Fortinos, and Your Independent Grocer banners in Ontario, its largest market. Overall, Loblaw has about a one-third share of Canada's grocery market. To stay at the top of Canada's food chain, Loblaw also has been building newer, bigger stores to replace older, smaller formats, and many of the company's large stores feature a pharmacy, photo shop, and financial services (some even include a fitness center).

Beyond groceries, Loblaw seeks to be a leading provider of drugstore, general merchandise, and financial products and services. In apparel, Loblaw has big plans for its "Joe Fresh Style" brand (launched in 2006). In a bid to become Canada's biggest "cheap chic" clothing brand, Loblaw has signed a deal to open an 8,000-sq.-ft. boutique on Toronto's trendy Queen Street West strip. It is also aggressively expanding its low-price Real Canadian Superstore format, which numbers about 110 stores.

George Weston controls Loblaw through its ownership of about 63% of Loblaw's common stock. In turn, Loblaw's former chairman W. Galen Weston owns more than 62% of George Weston.

HISTORY

Canadian Garfield Weston, CEO of a family business specializing in bakery goods, bought shares in Loblaw Groceterias, a Chicago-based food distributor, in the 1940s and 1950s. George Weston Limited controlled a majority interest by 1953 and incorporated the company as Loblaw Companies Limited three years later.

Over the next four decades, the Weston family transformed the distributor into an expansion vehicle through which George Weston acquired other food distributors and wholesalers across Canada and the midwestern US, at a rate of almost one a year into the 1960s. George Weston acquired National Grocers of Ontario in 1955, a stake in US-based retailer National Tea in 1956, British Columbia wholesaler Kelly Douglas & Co. in 1958, Maritime-based Atlantic Wholesalers in 1960, and Canadian supermarket chain Zehrmart in 1963.

Despite the restructuring of George Weston's operations in the 1970s, during which time many of its subsidiaries were consolidated, Garfield was persuaded by his son Galen not to sell Loblaw. When Garfield died in 1978, Galen became chairman of George Weston and Loblaw.

Loblaw went on a buying spree in 1982, acquiring Golden Dawn Foods, Star Supermarkets, and Wittington Leaseholds. It also acquired the remainder of National Tea.

After the Irish Republican Army tried to kidnap Galen in 1983, the Weston family started keeping a low public profile. Loblaw bought 26 St. Louis stores from Kroger in 1986.

Major union problems dogged the company in the 1980s and 1990s. In the early 1980s Loblaw attempted to gain union support for its super-

market expansion in Winnipeg, Canada, by matching the Manitoba Food and Commercial Workers Union's wage contract with competitor Safeway. In return, the company demanded a six-year, no-strike, no-lockout arrangement. Shortly after the deal was signed, employees of SuperValu accused the parent company of violating a number of contract agreements. Eventually the sides came to terms.

Labor unrest broke out again in 1993 in New Orleans when Loblaw engaged the United Food and Commercial Workers Union in a 34-week strike. The union finally conceded to Loblaw's original offer aimed at gaining parity in labor costs with other nonunionized food chains in the area.

In 1995 the company sold its 89 US supermarkets to St. Louis-based Schnuck Markets for around $354 million, and it sold its New Orleans stores, thereby divesting the last of its National Tea assets. By 1996 Loblaw no longer had any stores operating in the US, and it shifted its focus to Canadian expansion, adding about 50 new locations. Also that year a new labor agreement was signed, ending labor unrest and wage pressures from the company's heavily unionized workforce (79% of employees).

In 1997 Loblaw set its sights on conquering Quebec, where it had no significant presence, and strengthening Ontario. It began by opening its own stores, then took a giant leap forward in 1998 when it bought Montreal-based Provigo for $1.1 billion.

Richard Currie, Loblaw's president for 24 years and the man credited with molding the company into the multibillion-dollar company it has become, stepped down in late 2000; he was replaced by Loblaw veteran John Lederer.

In 2002 the company became the target of a $68 million class-action lawsuit following a hepatitis A health scare at one of its Toronto stores.

Allan Leighton, former CEO of Wal-Mart Europe, succeeded Lederer as president in 2006.

In 2007 Loblaw announced it was writing down its operations in the province to the tune of about $768 million tied to the Provigo stores. (The writedown led Loblaw to post its first annual loss in nearly 20 years.)

In September 2009 Loblaw acquired T&T Supermarket, Canada's largest retailer of Asian food, for $225 million CAD (about $206 million).

EXECUTIVES

Chairman: Galen G. Weston, age 37, $2,635,817 total compensation
Deputy Chairman and President: Allan L. Leighton, age 56, $4,504,375 total compensation
CFO: Sarah R. Davis
EVP Supply Chain, Distribution, and Information Technology: Peter K. McMahon, age 54, $2,773,378 total compensation
EVP and Chief Legal Officer; Director: Gordon A. M. Currie, age 51
EVP Market Lead Ontario Market: Roland Boudreau, age 60
EVP Real Estate and Special Projects, Loblaw Properties: S. Jane Marshall, age 54
EVP Operations: Arnu Misra
EVP Labor Relations: Roy R. Conliffe, age 59
EVP Quebec Market: Jocyanne Bourdeau, age 42
EVP Merchandising: Grant B. Froese, age 47
EVP Central Operations: Mark Butler, age 50
EVP Human Resources: Judy A. McCrie
EVP Fortinos and Fresh Food Development: Vince Scorniaenchi, age 49
EVP Marketing, Customer Relationship Management, and Loblaw Brands Limited: Calvin McDonald
EVP Grocery and No Frills National Merchandising: Garry Senecal

SVP, Secretary, and General Counsel: Robert A. Balcom, age 48
President, PC Bank: Barry K. Columb
Senior Manager Public Relations and Corporate Communication: Karen Gumbs
Senior Director Investor Relations: Kim Lee
Auditors: KPMG LLP

LOCATIONS

HQ: Loblaw Companies Limited
1 President's Choice Circle
Brampton, Ontario L6Y 5S5, Canada
Phone: 905-459-2500   **Fax:** 905-861-2206
Web: www.loblaw.com

2009 Stores

	No.
Ontario	508
Québec	428
British Columbia	104
Alberta	83
Nova Scotia	70
New Brunswick	62
Saskatchewan	62
Manitoba	52
Newfoundland & Labrador	52
Prince Edward Island	16
Yukon	3
Northwest Territories	2
Total	**1,442**

PRODUCTS/OPERATIONS

2009 Stores

	No.
Corporate	613
Franchised	416
Affiliated	413
Total	**1,442**

2009 Stores

	No.
No Frills	173
The Real Canadian Superstore	109
Maxi	91
Provigo	88
Extra Foods	85
Loblaws	76
Valu-mart	62
Atlantic Superstore	53
Your Independent Grocer	53
Atlantic SaveEasy	48
Zerhs Markets	43
SuperValu	22
Fortinos	20
Maxi & Cie	18
T&T Supermarket	18
Dominion (in Newfoundland & Labrador)	12
The Real Canadian Wholesale Club & other banners	471
Total	**1,442**

Selected Private-Label Brands

Blue Menu
Club Pack
Exact
G.R.E.E.N
Joe Fresh Style
LifeHome
Mini Chefs
no name
PC
PC Organics
President's Choice

COMPETITORS

7-Eleven	Katz Group
Canada Safeway	METRO
Canadian Tire	Sam's Club
Costco Wholesale Canada	Shoppers Drug Mart
Couche-Tard	Sobeys
H&M	Urban Outfitters
Jean Coutu	Wal-Mart Canada
Jim Pattison Group	Zara

HISTORICAL FINANCIALS

Company Type: Public

Income Statement

FYE: Saturday nearest December 31

	REVENUE ($ mil.)	NET INCOME ($ mil.)	NET PROFIT MARGIN	EMPLOYEES
12/09	29,287	625	2.1%	139,000
12/08	25,190	446	1.8%	139,000
12/07	29,922	336	1.1%	140,000
12/06	24,556	(188)	—	139,000
12/05	23,842	640	2.7%	119,000
Annual Growth	5.3%	(0.6%)	—	4.0%

2009 Year-End Financials

Debt ratio: 66.3%
Return on equity: 11.6%
Cash ($ mil.): 946
Current ratio: 1.20
Long-term debt ($ mil.): 3,966

No. of shares (mil.): 280
Dividends
  Yield: 2.5%
  Payout: 35.2%
Market value ($ mil.): 9,024

Stock History

Toronto: L

	STOCK PRICE ($) FY Close	P/E High/Low		PER SHARE ($) Earnings	Dividends	Book Value
12/09	32.28	16	12	2.27	0.80	21.39
12/08	28.60	18	13	1.63	0.69	17.06
12/07	34.59	46	26	1.22	0.86	20.20
12/06	41.83	—	—	(0.69)	0.72	16.69
12/05	48.34	28	19	2.32	0.72	18.06
Annual Growth	(9.6%)	—	—	(0.5%)	2.7%	4.3%

L'Oréal SA

L'Oréal's success is built on a strong foundation. The world's largest beauty products company, it creates makeup, perfume, and hair and skin care items. Its brands include L'Oréal and Maybelline (mass-market), Lancôme (upscale), and Redken and SoftSheen/Carson (retail and salon). L'Oréal, which owns Dallas-based SkinCeuticals, also conducts cosmetology and dermatology research. With more than 50% of sales generated outside of Europe, L'Oréal has focused on acquiring brands in those markets. L'Oréal also owns the UK-based natural cosmetics retailer The Body Shop International, which numbers some 2,550 stores worldwide. The firm's dermatology branch Galderma is a joint venture between L'Oréal and Nestlé.

In recent years, the firm has been expanding its professional division. To that end, in 2009 L'Oréal acquired three regional US distributors of professional products to salons: Idaho Barber and Beauty Supply, Maly's Midwest, and Marshall Salon Services. Also in the US, in April 2010 the firm agreed to acquire Essie Cosmetics, a maker of nail polish sold in salons and spas.

The French cosmetics giant is also expanding internationally. It tapped into the growing Turkish hair care market with its purchase of Canan in early 2008. (Founded in 1981, Canan generated about €26 million in 2006 and makes the Ipek brand, which is distributed in mass-market and retail outlets throughout Turkey.) L'Oréal has also enlisted the Indian actress Freida Pin (who appeared in *Slumdog Millionaire*) as a spokeswoman, hoping to gain traction in the Indian market. L'Oréal has set a target of increasing its customer base from 1.2 billion to 2.5 billion, with much of that growth coming from India and elsewhere outside Europe.

Consumer brands, such as GARNIER, L'Oréal, Maybelline, and Softsheen/Carson contribute more than half of the company's cosmetic sales. However, its well-known luxury brands, which are sold at department store cosmetic counters, perfumeries, and L'Oréal's own boutiques contribute about a quarter of cosmetics sales and continue to gain in popularity. To maintain its momentum in the luxury sector, L'Oreal in 2008 paid PPR more than $2 billion to acquire the rights to the Yves Saint Laurent, Boucheron, Stella McCartney, and Oscar de la Renta fragrance and cosmetics brands, among others.

Liliane Bettencourt, director and daughter of founder Eugène Schueller, is L'Oréal's primary stockholder. She and her family own 31% of the company's shares, while Nestlé owns 30%. The Bettencourts and Nestlé have been indirect owners of L'Oréal through the Gesparal SA holding company for some 30 years. (Gesparal was merged into L'Oréal in 2004.) In early 2009 both parties became able to sell their shares for the first time since 2004, which has led to speculation that Nestlé may attempt to take over L'Oréal. Further fueling suspicion has been a deepening estrangement between Bettencourt and her only daughter as well as a scandal that points to Bettencourt and her advisers for massive tax evasion and alleged illegal contributions to French President Nicolas Sarkozy.

HISTORY

Parisian Eugène Schueller, a chemist by trade, invented the first synthetic hair dye in 1907. Schueller quickly found a market for his products with local hairdressers and in 1909 established L'Oréal to pursue his growing hair products operation. The company's name came from its first hair color, Auréole (French for "aura of light").

L'Oréal expanded to include shampoos and soaps, all under the watchful direction of the energetic Schueller, who was known to taste hair creams to ensure that they were made up of the exact chemical composition that he required. In the 1920s the company began advertising on the radio (before its French competitors).

Demand for L'Oréal's products intensified after WWII. In 1953 the company formed licensee Cosmair to distribute its hair products to US beauty salons, and Cosmair soon offered L'Oréal's makeup and perfume as well. (Cosmair became L'Oréal USA in 2000.) When Schueller died in 1957, control of L'Oréal passed to right-hand man François Dalle. Dalle carried L'Oréal's hair care products into the consumer market and overseas and sold its soap units in 1961.

The company went public in 1963; Schueller's daughter, Liliane Bettencourt, retained a majority interest. Diversification came in 1965 with the acquisition of upscale French cosmetics maker Lancôme. L'Oréal entered the pharmaceuticals business in 1973 by purchasing Synthélabo. Bettencourt traded nearly half of her L'Oréal stock for a 3% stake in Swiss food producer Nestlé in 1974. L'Oréal purchased a minority stake in the publisher of French fashion magazine Marie Claire three years later.

During the 1980s L'Oréal vaulted from relative obscurity to become the world's #1 cosmetics company, largely through acquisitions. These included Warner Communications' cosmetics operations (Ralph Lauren and Gloria Vanderbilt brands, 1984), Helena Rubinstein (US beauty products, 1988), Laboratories Pharmaeutiques Goupil (1988), and its first major investment in Lanvin (1989). Englishman Lindsay Owen-Jones became CEO in 1988.

Chairman Jacques Correze died in 1991 during an investigation into his Nazi war activities. (He had served five years in prison.) In 1994 the company purchased control of Cosmair from Nestlé and Bettencourt. In 1995 L'Oréal became the #2 US cosmetics maker (behind Procter & Gamble, maker of Cover Girl and Max Factor) by buying #3 Maybelline for $508 million.

L'Oréal then added subsidiaries in Japan and China (1996) and in Romania and Slovenia (1997). In 2000 L'Oréal acquired Carson (an ethnic beauty products maker, now Soft Sheen/Carson Products), family-owned prestige cosmetics company Kiehl's Since 1851, and salon products maker Matrix Essentials (from Bristol-Myers Squibb).

Expanding aggressively into the Chinese market, L'Oréal acquired Chinese skin care brand Mininurse in late 2003; the next year it purchased Yue-Sai, a mass-market Chinese makeup and skin care brand, and its Shanghai manufacturing plant from Coty.

Chairman Lindsay Owen-Jones passed the CEO title to Jean-Paul Agon in 2006 after 18 years as chief executive. Owen-Jones began his career at L'Oréal in 1969; Agon joined L'Oréal in 1978. In June of 2006 L'Oréal acquired the UK's The Body Shop International for $1.14 billion.

In early 2008 L'Oréal's dermatology joint venture Galderma acquired CollaGenex Pharmaceuticals for about $420 million. Also that year it bought the 70% of Beauty Alliance it didn't already own. Beauty Alliance distributes beauty products to about 115,000 hair salons in the US.

EXECUTIVES

Chairman: Lindsay Owen-Jones, age 64
Vice Chairman: Jean-Pierre Meyers, age 61
CEO and Director: Jean-Paul Agon, age 54
EVP Administration and Finance: Christian Mulliez, age 49
EVP Human Resources: Geoff Skingsley, age 52
EVP Corporate Communications and External Affairs; CEO, L'Oréal Corporate Foundation: Béatrice Dautresme, age 64
General Manager, Active Cosmetics: Brigitte Liberman, age 53
Group General Manager, Financial Communications: Thierry Prevot
Managing Director, Latin America Zone and Africa, Middle East Zone: Alexandre Popoff, age 48
Managing Director, North America Zone; President and CEO, L'Oréal USA: Frédéric Rozé, age 49
President and CEO, L'Oréal USA: Laurent Attal
President, Luxury Products: Marc Menesguen, age 55
President, Consumer Products: Jean-Jacques Lebel, age 59
President, Professional Products Division: Nicolas Hiéronimus, age 46
Head, Investor Relations: Caroline Millot
Auditors: PricewaterhouseCoopers Audit

LOCATIONS

HQ: L'Oréal SA
41, rue Martre
92117 Clichy, France
Phone: 33-1-47-56-70-00   **Fax:** 33-1-47-56-86-42
US HQ: 575 5th Ave., New York, NY 10017
US Phone: 212-818-1500
Web: www.loreal.com

2009 Sales

	% of total
France	13
Rest of Europe	31
North America	24
Rest of world	32
Total	**100**

PRODUCTS/OPERATIONS

2009 Cosmetic Sales

	% of total
Consumer products	53
Luxury products	25
Professional products	15
Active cosmetics (dermo-cosmetic products)	7
Total	**100**

2009 Sales

	% of total
Cosmetics	93
The Body Shop	4
Dermatology	3
Total	**100**

Selected Operations

Consumer Products
 Gemey
 Laboratoires GARNIER
 L'Oréal Paris
 Maybelline
 SoftSheen Carson
Cosmetics
 Active Cosmetics
 La Roche-Posay
 Vichy
Luxury Products
 Biotherm
 Cacharel (fragrances only)
 Giorgio Armani (fragrances only)
 Guy Laroche (fragrances only)
 Helena Rubinstein
 Kiehl's
 Lancôme
 Paloma Picasso (fragrances only)
 Ralph Lauren (fragrances only)
 Shu Uemura
Pharmaceuticals and Dermatology
 Innéov Firmness
 RozexMetvix
 Tri-Luma
Professional Products
 Artec
 Inne
 Kérastase
 L'Oréal Professionnel
 Matrix
 Redken

Selected Subsidiaries

Carson/Soft Sheen Products
Galderma
L'Oréal USA
The Laboratoires Inneov
Sanofi-Synthélabo

COMPETITORS

Alberto-Culver
Alticor
Avon
Bath & Body Works
BeautiControl
Chanel
Clarins
Estée Lauder
Hoffmann-La Roche
Johnson & Johnson
LVMH
Mary Kay
Merle Norman
Modern Organic Products
Novartis
Nu Skin
Perrigo
Procter & Gamble
Puig
Revlon
Shiseido
Unilever
Yves Saint-Laurent Groupe

HISTORICAL FINANCIALS

Company Type: Public

Income Statement

FYE: December 31

	REVENUE ($ mil.)	NET INCOME ($ mil.)	NET PROFIT MARGIN	EMPLOYEES
12/09	25,042	2,569	10.3%	5,804
12/08	24,725	2,746	11.1%	67,500
12/07	25,114	3,909	15.6%	63,358
12/06	20,832	2,719	13.1%	60,851
12/05	17,211	2,336	13.6%	52,403
Annual Growth	**9.8%**	**2.4%**	**—**	**(42.3%)**

2009 Year-End Financials

Debt ratio: 20.2%
Return on equity: 14.2%
Cash ($ mil.): 1,681
Current ratio: 1.10
Long-term debt ($ mil.): 3,929
No. of shares (mil.): 586
Dividends
 Yield: 1.8%
 Payout: 46.8%
Market value ($ mil.): 65,526

Stock History

Pink Sheets: LRLCY

	STOCK PRICE ($) FY Close	P/E High/Low		PER SHARE ($) Earnings	Dividends	Book Value
12/09	111.79	26	15	4.40	2.06	33.24
12/08	87.81	29	16	4.65	1.95	28.44
12/07	144.22	23	17	6.45	—	34.20
12/06	100.13	25	19	4.42	—	32.91
12/05	74.37	22	17	3.71	—	29.61
Annual Growth	**10.7%**	**—**	**—**	**4.4%**	**5.6%**	**2.9%**

Lufthansa

Germany's air ambassador, Deutsche Lufthansa rivals the world's largest airline companies. Via its subsidiaries, the carrier operates more than 530 aircraft from hubs in Frankfurt, Munich, and Zurich. It flies passengers to some 250 destinations worldwide, not counting those served by code-sharing partners. (Code-sharing enables airlines to sell tickets on one another's flights and thus extend their networks.) Lufthansa's partners include fellow members of the Star Alliance, such as United Continental's United Airlines and Continental. The company's Lufthansa Cargo unit is a leading global airfreight carrier; Lufthansa also has interests in aircraft maintenance, catering, and information technology businesses.

In recent years Lufthansa has been growing its passenger airline portfolio which includes subsidiaries SWISS, Lufthansa CityLine, and British Midland Airways (bmi). Lufthansa holds a controlling stake in Eurowings, and a majority stake (over 90%) in Austrian Airlines through ÖLH Österreichische Luftverkehrs-Holding-GmbH, which is a joint venture between two of Lufthansa's subsidiaries.

Lufthansa is switching gears somewhat from acquisitions to buying planes, cutting costs and jobs, and integrating its new airline subsidiaries. As part of its Climb 2011 plan to reduce operational costs by $1.5 billion by 2011, the group trimmed jobs at Austrian, bmi, and Eurowings and is replacing smaller aircraft with larger planes for regional routes.

But as much as the business plan stresses cost cutting, the company plans to improve its product range, both in the air and on the ground, by refinement and innovation. Planned upgrades include improved seating, more luxury for first class, and an increased number of business and first class airport lounges with additional amenities, among other projects.

Passenger transportation accounts for about 65% of the company's sales, and Lufthansa hopes to grow in that area by building on one of its greatest strengths: its extensive international route network. The carrier views China, India, and Eastern Europe — places where it already has a foothold — as particularly promising expansion opportunities.

In 2009 Lufthansa bumped up its minority stake in Austrian Airlines to 95%, making Lufthansa the largest airline in Europe by sales and giving the carrier a foot in the door to Eastern Europe. Also in 2009 Lufthansa completed its acquisition of UK-based airline bmi. Lufthansa plans to get the financially troubled carrier back on its feet in order to compete with rival British Airways for additional traffic at London Heathrow, one of Europe's largest airports.

Lufthansa acquired a 45% stake in SN Airholding, parent of Brussels Airlines, in 2008 with the intention of buying the remaining 55%. Lufthansa's only airline investment outside of Europe is a 16% stake in US-based JetBlue Airways, which it purchased in 2008.

HISTORY

The Weimar government created Deutsche Luft Hansa (DLH) in 1926 by merging private German airlines Deutscher Aero Lloyd (founded 1919) and Junkers Luftverkehr (formed in 1921 by aircraft manufacturer Junkers Flugzeugwerke). DLH built what would become Europe's most comprehensive air route network by 1931. It served the USSR through Deruluft (formed 1921; dissolved 1941), an airline jointly owned by DLH and the Soviet government. In 1930 DLH and the Chinese government formed Eurasia Aviation Corporation to develop air transport in China.

DLH established the world's first transatlantic airmail service from Berlin to Buenos Aires in 1934 and went on to develop air transport throughout South America. The outbreak of WWII ended operations in Europe, and the Chinese government seized Eurasia Aviation in 1941. Klaus Bonhoeffer, head of DLH's legal department, led an unsuccessful coup against the Nazi leadership and was executed in 1945. Soon afterward all DLH operations ceased.

In 1954 the Allies allowed the recapitalization of Deutsche Lufthansa. The airline started with domestic routes, returned to London and Paris (1955), and then re-entered South America (1956). In 1958 it made its first nonstop flight between Germany and New York and initiated service to Tokyo and Cairo. Meanwhile, it started a charter airline with several partners in 1955. Lufthansa bought out its partners in 1959 and renamed the unit Condor two years later.

The carrier resumed service behind the Iron Curtain in 1966 with flights to Prague. The stable West German economy helped Lufthansa maintain profitability through most of the 1970s.

The reunification of Germany in 1990 ended Allied control over Berlin airspace, allowing Lufthansa, which had bought Pan Am's Berlin routes, to fly there under its own colors for the first time since the end of WWII. The company began seeking international partners in 1991, but that year European air travel suffered its first-ever slowdown, forcing Lufthansa into the red for the first time since 1973.

In 1997 the Star Alliance was formed, and Lufthansa signed a pact with Singapore Airlines. That year the German government sold its remaining 38% stake in Lufthansa. In 1998 Lufthansa and All Nippon Airways formed a codesharing alliance, and Condor was combined with Karstadt's tour company NUR Touristic to form C&N Touristic. (After buying UK-based travel operator Thomas Cook in 2000, C&N Touristic changed its name to Thomas Cook in 2001.)

In a plan to gain more access to London's Heathrow Airport, Lufthansa took a 20% stake in British Midland, which was admitted into the Star Alliance in 2000 along with Mexicana Airlines. In 2001 the airline bought the 52% of Texas-based Sky Chefs it did not already own and formed a new unit, LSG Sky Chefs International, to hold its catering operations.

Lufthansa said goodbye to its 24% stake in delivery firm DHL when it sold its share to Deutsche Post in 2002.

Swiss International Air Lines agreed to be acquired by Lufthansa in 2005. Although issues related to international air traffic rights delayed the completion of the transaction, Lufthansa took full ownership of the airline in 2007.

Lufthansa exited the leisure travel services business in 2006 by selling its 50% stake in leisure travel giant Thomas Cook AG to German retailer Karstadt Quelle, which owned the other half. In 2009 Lufthansa upped its stake in British Midland, the #2 carrier in that region (behind rival British Airways) to full ownership.

EXECUTIVES

Honorary Chairman, Supervisory Board:
Wolfgang Röller
Chairman, Supervisory Board: Jürgen Weber, age 69
Deputy Chairman, Supervisory Board: Frank Bsirske
Chairman, Executive Board and CEO:
Wolfgang Mayrhuber, age 63,
$3,142,625 total compensation
Deputy Chairman, Executive Board; Chairman and CEO, Lufthansa German Airlines: Christoph Franz, age 50, $744,967 total compensation
Member, Executive Board; Chief Officer, Group Airlines and Corporate Human Resources; Chairman, British Midland Airways: Stefan Lauer, age 55, $2,399,605 total compensation
Member, Executive Board; CFO and Head, Aviation Services; Chairman, LSG Lufthansa Service, Lufthansa Cargo, Lufthansa Technik:
Stephan Gemkow, age 50,
$2,373,974 total compensation
EVP, Operations, Lufthansa Passenger Airlines:
Jürgen Raps, age 59
EVP, Marketing and Sales, Lufthansa Passenger Airlines: Thierry Antinori
SVP and Head, Corporate Communications:
Klaus Walther
Chairman and CEO, Cargo: Carsten Spohr, age 43
CEO, Swiss International Air Lines: Harry Hohmeister, age 46
CEO, Lufthansa Technik: August-Wilhelm Henningsen, age 59
CEO, British Midland Airways:
Wolfgang Prock-Schauer, age 54
Chairman, LSG Lufthansa Service Holding:
Walter N. Gehl, age 57
Chairman, British Midland Airways: Nigel Turner
Chairman, Executive Board and CEO, Lufthansa Systems: Stefan Hansen, age 46
Director, Corporate Communications, The Americas:
Martin Riecken
Auditors: PwC Deutsche Revision AG

LOCATIONS

HQ: Deutsche Lufthansa AG
    Von-Gablenz-Straße 2-6
    D-50679 Cologne 21, Germany
Phone: 49-221-826-3992   **Fax:** 49-221-826-3646
Web: konzern.lufthansa.com/en

2009 Sales

	% of total
Europe	65
North America	16
Asia/Pacific	13
Middle East	3
Africa	2
Central & South America	1
Total	**100**

PRODUCTS/OPERATIONS

2009 Sales

	% of total
Passenger transportation	73
Maintenance, repair & overhaul	10
Logistics	9
Catering	7
Information technology services	1
Total	**100**

COMPETITORS

AAR Corp.	Deutsche Bahn
Aer Lingus	easyJet
Air Berlin	Gate Gourmet
Air France-KLM	Iberia
Alitalia	Japan Airlines
AMR Corp.	Qantas
Aviall	Ryanair
British Airways	TIMCO Aviation
Delta Air Lines	Virgin Atlantic Airways

HISTORICAL FINANCIALS

Company Type: Public

Income Statement

FYE: December 31

	REVENUE ($ mil.)	NET INCOME ($ mil.)	NET PROFIT MARGIN	EMPLOYEES
12/09	31,936	(143)	—	117,521
12/08	35,054	858	2.4%	108,123
12/07	33,000	2,591	7.9%	105,261
12/06	26,187	1,059	4.0%	93,541
12/05	21,394	537	2.5%	90,811
Annual Growth	**10.5%**	**—**	**—**	**6.7%**

2009 Year-End Financials

Debt ratio: —
Return on equity: —
Cash ($ mil.): 1,628
Current ratio: 0.99
Long-term debt ($ mil.): —

No. of shares (mil.): 458
Dividends
  Yield: 6.0%
  Payout: —
Market value ($ mil.): 7,712

Stock History

German: LHA

	STOCK PRICE ($) FY Close	P/E High/Low		PER SHARE ($) Earnings	Dividends	Book Value
12/09	16.84	—	—	(0.34)	1.00	19.41
12/08	15.77	14	7	1.83	—	21.30
12/07	26.82	6	5	5.30	—	—
12/06	27.51	—	—	—	—	13.32
12/05	14.82	—	—	—	—	11.20
Annual Growth	**3.2%**	**—**	**—**	**—**	**—**	**14.7%**

OAO LUKOIL

Most Russians look to LUKOIL for their oil and gas needs. Russia's #1 integrated oil company produces, refines, and sells oil and oil products; it accounts for 18% of Russia's crude oil production. In addition to power generation activities, LUKOIL has proved reserves of more than 19.3 billion barrels of oil equivalent, the majority of which is located in Russia. It has operations in 60 regions in Russia and 25 other countries, and owns seven refineries and 6,750 gas stations. LUKOIL president Vagit Alekperov controls about 20% of the company; Conoco-Phillips owns 20% but in 2010 announced it would sell its stake to raise cash. ING Bank Eurasia holds about 70% of LUKOIL's shares on behalf of other investors.

Consolidating its ownership position, in 2010 LUKOIL agreed to buy 7.6% of ConocoPhillips' holdings in LUKOIL for $3.4 billion. Conoco-Phillips' remaining shares will be sold to the public by the end of 2011.

The company explores for oil and gas in Azerbaijan, Colombia, Egypt, Iran, Kazakhstan, and other areas in the Middle East and Central Asia. It operates four refineries in Russia, one in Ukraine, one in Bulgaria, and one in Romania, and owns a gas stations network in Russia, the

Baltic states, Central and Eastern Europe, and the US.

LUKOIL, Russia's second-largest company behind natural gas monopoly Gazprom, is looking to transform itself from a top-heavy, bureaucratic enterprise into a decentralized, entrepreneurial company competing in free markets through joint ventures and strategic relationships. More than three-quarters of LUKOIL's sales are outside of Russia.

In 2009, seeking to grow its refining base in closer proximity to Western markets and its strategic partnership with TOTAL, LUKOIL acquired a 45% stake in the TRN Refinery in the Netherlands from TOTAL for about $600 million. In 2007 LUKOIL signed a strategic exploration and production agreement with Qatar Petroleum. The following year it began to re-engage in Iraq, where it had held oil concessions prior to the US-led invasion in 2003. It also acquired a retail network in Turkey in 2008 for $500 million.

In 2008 the company diversified its operations further, creating a power generation segment, which encompasses its own generators at well sites and a number of generating units in Bulgaria, Romania, and the Ukraine.

HISTORY

LUKOIL was formed from the combination of three major state-owned oil and gas exploration companies — Langepasneftegaz, Uraineftegaz, and Kogalymneftegaz — that traced their origins to the discovery of oil in western Siberia in 1964. More than 25 years later, after the Soviet Union broke up, the oil and gas sector was one of the first industries marked for privatization.

In 1992 the government called for Langepasneftegaz, Uraineftegaz, and Kogalymneftegaz to merge, and LUKOIL was created the next year. (The LUK of LUKOIL comes from the initials of the three companies.) Russian president Boris Yeltsin appointed Siberian oil veteran Vagit Alekperov as the company's first president. The Russian government also formed several other large integrated oil companies, including Yukos, Surgutneftegaz, Sidanco, and Sibneft.

LUKOIL went public on the fledgling Russian Trading System in 1994. The next year the company absorbed nine other enterprises, including oil exploration companies Astrakhanneft, Kaliningradmorneftegaz, and Permneft. That year LUKOIL became the first Russian oil company to set up an exploration and production trading arm. In 1996 LUKOIL acquired a 41% stake in *Izvestia*, Russia's major independent newspaper.

Chevron and LUKOIL, with seven other oil and gas companies and three governments, agreed in 1996 to build a 1,500-kilometer pipeline to link the Kazakhstan oil fields to world markets.

In 1997 LUKOIL became the first Russian corporation to sell bonds to international investors, and the government sold 15% of its stake in the company. That year LUKOIL's 50%-owned Nexus Fuels unit opened its first gas stations located in the parking lots of US grocery stores (the partnership dissolved and Nexus went bankrupt in 2000).

LUKOIL began a partnership with Conoco (later ConocoPhillips) in 1998 to develop oil and natural gas reserves in Russia's northern territories. LUKOIL also acquired 51% of Romania's Petrorel refinery. In 1999 it acquired

control of refineries in Bulgaria and Ukraine and in a petrochemical firm in Saratov. It also acquired oil company KomiTEK in one of Russia's largest mergers.

The government sold a 9% stake in LUKOIL to a Cyprus-based unit, Reforma Investments, held in part by LUKOIL's "boss of bosses," Vagit Alekperov (gained at the bargain price of $200 million). Critics cited the sale as Yeltsin's bid to gain Alekperov's political support.

The company announced the first major oil find in the Russian part of the Caspian Sea in 2000, and formed a joint venture (Caspian Oil Company) with fellow Russian energy giants Gazprom and Yukos to exploit resources in the Caspian. The next year LUKOIL acquired more than 1,300 gas stations on the East Coast of the US when it bought Getty Petroleum Marketing.

That year LUKOIL also acquired Bitech, a Canadian oil exploration and production firm with operations in the Republic of Komi in the Russian Federation. In 2002 the company sold its oil service business, a move that cut its overall workforce by some 20,000 and resulted in savings of $500 million annually.

With an appetite for expansion, the company upped its production with refinery acquisitions and invested heavily in new oil patches, such as the Caspian Sea. In 2005 LUKOIL acquired Finland-based Oy Teboil AB and Suomen Petrooli Oy, affiliated refined oil products companies, for an undisclosed amount. LUKOIL also acquired Nelson Resources, which had oil and gas interests in Western Kazakhstan, for about $2 billion.

The next year the company acquired Marathon Oil's assets in Khanty-Mansiysk Autonomous Region — Yugra of Western Siberia — for $787 million. LUKOIL also acquired 376 European gas stations from ConocoPhillips in 2006.

EXECUTIVES

Chairman: Valery Grayfer, age 80
President and Director: Vagit Y. Alekperov, age 59
First EVP Exploration and Production and Director: Ravil U. Maganov, age 55
First VP Economics and Finance: Sergei P. Kukura, age 56
First VP Refining, Marketing, and Distribution: Vladimir I. Nekrasov, age 52
VP and Head of Main Division of Treasury and Corporate Financing: Alexander K. Matytsyn, age 48
VP and Head of Main Division of Control and Internal Audit: Vagit S. Sharifov, age 64
VP and Head of Main Technical Division: Dzhevan K. Cheloyants, age 50
VP and Head of Main Division Oil and Gas Production and Infrastructure: Vladimir Mulyak, age 54
VP and Head of Main Division of Sales and Supplies: Valery Subbotin, age 35
VP and Head of Main Division of General Affairs, Corporate Security, and Communications: Anatoly A. Barkov, age 61
VP and Head of Main Division Strategic Development and Investment Analysis: Leonid A. Fedun, age 53
Chief Accountant: Lyubov Khoba, age 52
General Director, LUKOIL-Nizhnevolzhskneft: Yuri Kadzhoyan
General Director, LUKOIL-Volgogradneftegaz: Nikolay Nikolaev
Secretary and Head of the Board's Office: Evgueni Havkin, age 45
Head Human Resources, Main Division: Anatoly Moskalenko, age 50
Auditors: ZAO KPMG

LOCATIONS

HQ: OAO LUKOIL
11 Sretenski Blvd.
101 000 Moscow, Russia
Phone: 7-495-627-4444   **Fax:** 7-495-625-7016
Web: www.lukoil.com

PRODUCTS/OPERATIONS

2009 Sales

	% of total
Refined products	68
Crude oil	26
Petrochemicals	1
Gas & other	5
Total	**100**

COMPETITORS

Ashland Inc.
BP
Exxon Mobil
Gazprom Neft
Imperial Oil
Norsk Hydro ASA
Occidental Petroleum
PEMEX
PETROBRAS
Petróleos de Venezuela
Rosneft
Royal Dutch Shell
Surgutneftegas
Tatneft
TOTAL

HISTORICAL FINANCIALS

Company Type: Public

Income Statement

FYE: December 31

	REVENUE ($ mil.)	NET INCOME ($ mil.)	NET PROFIT MARGIN	EMPLOYEES
12/09	81,083	7,011	8.6%	143,400
12/08	107,680	9,144	8.5%	152,500
12/07	82,238	9,511	11.6%	150,000
12/06	68,109	7,484	11.0%	148,600
12/05	56,215	6,443	11.5%	145,400
Annual Growth	9.6%	2.1%	—	(0.3%)

2009 Year-End Financials

Debt ratio: 16.5%
Return on equity: 13.2%
Cash ($ mil.): 2,274
Current ratio: 1.84
Long-term debt ($ mil.): 9,265

No. of shares (mil.): 847
Dividends
  Yield: 0.7%
  Payout: 4.5%
Market value ($ mil.): 47,751

Stock History

Pink Sheets: LUKOY

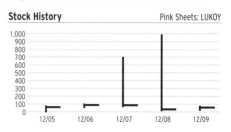

	STOCK PRICE ($) FY Close	P/E High/Low		PER SHARE ($) Earnings	Dividends	Book Value
12/09	56.40	8	3	8.28	0.37	66.13
12/08	33.10	90	2	10.88	1.31	59.46
12/07	84.30	60	6	11.48	0.35	48.68
12/06	86.70	10	6	9.04	1.03	38.86
12/05	59.15	9	1	7.79	—	31.66
Annual Growth	(1.2%)	—	—	1.5%	(28.9%)	20.2%

LVMH

LVMH Moët Hennessy Louis Vuitton is the world's largest luxury goods company, with brands that are bywords for the good life and everything showy. LVMH makes wines and spirits (Dom Pérignon, Moët & Chandon, Veuve Clicquot, and Hennessy), perfumes (Christian Dior, Guerlain, and Givenchy), cosmetics (Bliss, Fresh, and BeneFit), fashion and leather goods (Donna Karan, Givenchy, Kenzo, and Louis Vuitton), and watches and jewelry (TAG Heuer, Ebel, Chaumet, and Fred). LVMH's selective retail division includes Sephora cosmetics stores, Le Bon Marché Paris department stores, and 61% of DFS Group (duty-free shops). Chairman Bernard Arnault and his family, through Groupe Arnault, own about 47% of LVMH.

As sales of champagne, watches, perfumes, and other luxe items stumbled, even the world's largest purveyor of luxury goods wasn't immune to the global financial contagion. LVMH is taking a cautious approach in 2010, given the ongoing financial uncertainty caused by the financial crisis in Greece, concern about the fiscal health of other countries in Europe, and up-and-down stock market in the US. Still, it continues to invest in promising markets such as Brazil, China, the Middle East (Qatar and Bahrain), and Russia. China is a huge emerging market for luxury goods and a pillar of growth for the French company.

In early 2010 LVMH acquired a 40% stake in Dondup, an Italian apparel and denim brand for more than $43 million (or 30 million euros). Its plans are to expand Dondup's business internationally. Later in 2010 the company purchased a 70% stake in the Brazilian fragrance and cosmetics retailer Sack's. The acquisition, estimated to be worth R$250 million (US$145 million), is a move on LVMH's part to expand its Sephora beauty chain in Brazil, one of the fastest-growing beauty markets in the world. The self-serve cosmetics chain Sephora, with more than 1,000 stores in some 20 countries, has been a strong performer despite the recent economic malaise.

The company has been focusing on controlling as much of its distribution as possible. LVMH has more than 2,400 retail outlets (about 85% are outside of France). Nearly half are fashion and leather goods stores, led by Louis Vuitton, and also including Fendi boutiques, and hundreds of other shops under the Celine, Givenchy, Donna Karan, Thomas Pink, Pucci, and Marc Jacobs brands, among others. LVMH's namesake Louis Vuitton brand, as well as Fendi and Marc Jacobs, are proving resilient in Europe, despite the economic slowdown there, and posting strong revenue gains in Asia.

Striking out in a new direction, the luxury goods firm is venturing into the hotel business via a partnership with Egypt's Orascom Development Holding. Together the two plan to develop upmarket resorts in Egypt and Oman, with LVMH overseeing the design and running of the hotels, which are slated to open in 2012. With LVMH investing no capital in the hotel venture (it will be paid a management fee), the deal could prove less risky than its 2008 purchase of Dutch yacht maker Royal van Lent and the financial newspaper *Les Echos*.

HISTORY

Woodworker Louis Vuitton started his Paris career packing dresses for French Empress Eugenie. He later designed new types of luggage, and in 1854 he opened a store to sell his designs. In 1896 Vuitton introduced the LV monogram fabric that the company still uses. By 1900 Louis Vuitton had stores in the US and England, and by WWI Louis' son Georges had the world's largest retail store for travel goods.

Henry Racamier, a former steel executive who had married into the Vuitton family, took charge in 1977, repositioning the company's goods from esoteric status symbols to designer must-haves. Sales soared from $20 million to nearly $2.5 billion within a decade. Concerned about being a takeover target, Racamier merged Louis Vuitton in 1987 with Moët Hennessy (which made wines, spirits, and fragrances) and adopted the name LVMH Moët Hennessy Louis Vuitton.

Moët Hennessy had been formed through the 1971 merger of Moët et Chandon (the world's #1 champagne maker) and the Hennessy Cognac company (founded by Irish mercenary Richard Hennessy in 1765). Moët Hennessy acquired rights to Christian Dior fragrances in 1971.

Racamier tried to reverse the merger when disagreements with chairman Alain Chevalier arose. Racamier invited outside investor Bernard Arnault to increase his interest in the company. Arnault gained control of 43% of LVMH and became chairman in 1989. Chevalier stepped down, but Racamier fought for control for another 18 months and then set up Orcofi, a partner of cosmetics rival L'Oréal.

LVMH increased its fashion holdings with the purchases of the Givenchy Couture Group (1988), Christian Lacroix (1993), and Kenzo (1993). The company also acquired 55% of French media firm Desfosses International (1993), Celine fashions (1996), the Château d'Yquem winery (1996), and duty-free retailer DFS Group (1996). Next LVMH bought perfume chains Sephora (1997) and Marie-Jeanne Godard (1998). In 1998 LVMH integrated the Paris department store Le Bon Marché, which was controlled by Arnault.

LVMH accumulated a 34% stake in Italian luxury goods maker Gucci in early 1999 and planned to buy all of it. Fellow French conglomerate Pinault-Printemps-Redoute (PPR) later thwarted LVMH by purchasing 42% of Gucci.

Through its LV Capital unit, in 1999 LVMH began acquiring stakes in a host of luxury companies, including a joint venture with fashion company Prada to buy 51% of design house Fendi (LVMH bought Prada's 25.5% stake for $265 million in November 2001).

In 2001 LVMH bought Donna Karan International. The company sold its stake in Gucci to PPR for $806.5 million in October.

In 2004 LVMH won a landmark lawsuit against Morgan Stanley, alleging that the firm had used biased research in misstatements about the financial health of LVMH that caused damage to the company's image. The presiding Parisian court ordered Morgan Stanley to pay 100 million euros (about $38 million) in damages. Morgan Stanley appealed the ruling later that year.

In May 2007 LVMH acquired a 55% stake in Chinese distillery Wenjun for an undisclosed amount. (Jiannanchun, the distillery's previous owner, retained a 45% stake in Wenjun.)

In 2009 LVMH acquired 50% stakes in two French wine makers: privately held Cheval Blanc; and La Tour du Pin, owner of the Chateau Quinault l'Enclose estate.

EXECUTIVES

Chairman and CEO: Bernard Arnault, age 61
Vice Chairman: Pierre Godé, age 65
Vice Chairman: Antoine Bernheim, age 86
Group Managing Director and Board Member: Antonio (Toni) Belloni
General Secretary: Marc-Antoine Jamet
Member Executive Committee Finance: Jean-Jacques Guiony
Member Executive Board; CEO, Donna Karan and LVMH Inc.: Mark Weber, age 60
Member Executive Committee, Wines and Spirits: Christophe Navarre, age 52
Member Executive Committee, Fashion and Leather Goods; CEO, Louis Vuitton Malletier: Yves Carcelle
Member Executive Committee, Human Resources: Chantal Gaemperle
Member Executive Committee, Watches and Jewelry: Philippe Pascal
Member Executive Committee, Fashion: Pierre-Yves Roussel
Member Executive Committee, Investment Funds: Daniel Piette, age 65
Member Executive Committee, Development and Acquisitions, and Board Member: Nicolas Bazire, age 53
Member Executive Committee, Travel Retail; Chairman and CEO, DFS: Edward (Ed) Brennan
Advisor to the Chairman: Patrick Ouart
Acting CEO, Louis Vuitton North America: Geoffroy van Raemdonck
President and CEO, LVMH Perfumes and Cosmetics North America: Pamela Baxter
President and CEO, Moët Hennessy USA: Mark Cornell, age 43
Auditors: Deloitte & Associés

LOCATIONS

HQ: LVMH Moët Hennessy Louis Vuitton SA
22 avenue Montaigne
75008 Paris, France
Phone: 33-1-44-13-2222   **Fax:** 33-1-44-13-2119
US HQ: 19 E. 57th St., New York, NY 10022
US Phone: 212-931-2000   **US Fax:** 212-931-2903
Web: www.lvmh.com

2009 Sales

	% of total
Europe	
France	14
Other countries	21
Asia	
Japan	10
Other countries	23
US	23
Other regions	9
Total	**100**

PRODUCTS/OPERATIONS

2009 Sales

	% of total
Fashion & leather goods	37
Selective retailing	27
Perfumes & cosmetics	16
Wines & spirits	16
Watches & jewelry	4
Total	**100**

Selected Brands and Operations

Fashion and leather goods
  Berluti
  Celine
  Donna Karan
  Emilio Pucci
  Fendi
  Gabrielle Studio (Donna Karan label)
  Givenchy
  Kenzo
  Loewe
  Louis Vuitton
  Marc Jacobs
  Thomas Pink

Retailing
- DFS Group
- La Samaritaine
- Le Bon Marché
- Miami Cruiseline Services (duty-free shops)
- Sephora

Fragrances and cosmetics
- Aqua di Parma
- BeneFit
- Bliss
- Fresh
- Guerlain
- Kenzo Parfums
- Make Up For Ever
- Marc Jacobs Fragrances
- Parfums Christian Dior
- Parfums Givenchy

Spirits and wines
- 10 Cane
- Belvedere
- Canard-Duchêne
- Chandon Estates
- Château d'Yquem
- Dom Pérignon
- Hennessy
- Krug
- Mercier
- Moët & Chandon
- MountAdam
- Newton
- Ruinart
- Veuve Clicquot

Watches and jewelry
- Chaumet
- De Beers
- Ebel
- Fred
- Omas
- TAG Heuer
- Zenith

Media (Desfosses International Group)
- Investir
- La Tribune
- Les Echos
- Radio Classique

Other
- Royal van Lent (luxury yachts)

COMPETITORS

Armani
Avon
Bacardi
Brown-Forman
Calvin Klein
Chanel
Douglas Holding
E. & J. Gallo
Escada
Estée Lauder
Galeries Lafayette
Gianni Versace
Hermès
Hugo Boss
Inditex
Kirin Holdings Company
L'Oréal
MacAndrews & Forbes
Oscar de la Renta
Polo Ralph Lauren
PPR SA
Prada
Puig
Rémy Cointreau
Richemont
Shiseido
Swatch
Taittinger
Tiffany & Co.
Unilever
Vera Wang
Yves Saint-Laurent Groupe

HISTORICAL FINANCIALS

Company Type: Public

Income Statement

FYE: December 31

	REVENUE ($ mil.)	NET INCOME ($ mil.)	NET PROFIT MARGIN	EMPLOYEES
12/09	24,440	2,828	11.6%	77,302
12/08	24,234	3,267	13.5%	77,087
12/07	24,258	3,431	14.1%	71,885
12/06	20,193	2,850	14.1%	64,253
12/05	16,474	1,975	12.0%	61,088
Annual Growth	10.4%	9.4%	—	6.1%

2009 Year-End Financials

Debt ratio: —
Return on equity: 14.4%
Cash ($ mil.): 3,506
Current ratio: 1.81
Long-term debt ($ mil.): —
No. of shares (mil.): 490
Dividends
  Yield: 2.0%
  Payout: 43.2%
Market value ($ mil.): 55,042

Stock History

Euronext Paris: MC

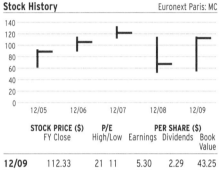

	STOCK PRICE ($) FY Close	P/E High/Low		PER SHARE ($) Earnings	Dividends	Book Value
12/09	112.33	21	11	5.30	2.29	43.25
12/08	67.33	19	9	6.00	0.49	37.10
12/07	121.70	21	18	6.21	—	34.82
12/06	105.48	22	17	5.20	—	28.55
12/05	88.88	25	17	3.60	—	22.86
Annual Growth	6.0%	—	—	10.2%	367.3%	17.3%

Magna International

Through its various subsidiaries and divisions, Magna International makes just about everything you might need to put together a motor vehicle. Magna Steyr, Magna's largest division, offers vehicle engineering and assembly. Magna's interior and exterior systems division (Decoma International) makes exterior trim, lighting, sealing systems, instrument and door panels, and sound insulation. Cosma International makes body and chassis systems. Magna Powertrain offers transaxles, transmission systems, and engine parts. Magna Mirrors makes automotive mirrors and driver assistance products.

In the midst of the industry downturn, which packed a double punch (decreased demand and the credit crisis) for the automotive industry, Magna continued to identify new areas of growth and to make investments. Taking heed of the market shift away from four-wheel-drive pick-up trucks and SUVs, Magna is focusing on developing a wide range of electric vehicle technologies and systems. To that end, the company opened a new hybrid- and electric-vehicle system development center in Michigan in 2010 to support its Magna E-Car Systems. That year Magna International partnered with semiconductor company

SEMIKRON to develop and produce power electronics for future vehicle applications. A year prior it acquired BluWav Systems, a developer and supplier of electric and energy management systems for electric vehicles. The company continues to work with Ford on developing a fully electric Ford vehicle that is scheduled for sale in 2011.

Magna International wants to take advantage of the burgeoning automobile market in Eastern Europe and Russia and continues to seek expansion opportunities in those regions by strengthening its ties to the GAZ Group, Russia's largest automaker. In 2010 it approved the appointment of its co-CEO to serve as chairman of GAZ.

With three Russia-based facilities already in operation, the company started construction on a stamping and assembly plant in St. Petersburg.

In 2010 its Magna Seating subsidiary partnered with Hollingsworth Logistics (a provider of industrial supply chain management) to create Chattanooga Seating Systems (CSS); Magna Seating will own 49% to Hollingsworth's 51%. The JV will provide for the engineering, manufacturing, and sequencing and delivery of complete seat systems for a midsize sedan that Volkswagen is building at its Tennessee assembly facility.

The company responded to crushing economic pressure on the auto industry by closing and/or consolidating Canadian, US, and European plants. Magna reduced its headcount by approximately 11,500, representing a 14% cutback between 2007 and 2009.

Chairman Frank Stronach and his daughter (former CEO) Belinda control Magna.

HISTORY

Magna International is rooted in a tool and die shop founded by Frank Stronach and friend Tony Czapka in Ontario, Canada, in 1957. Austrian-born Stronach immigrated to Canada in 1954. By the end of 1957, the business, called Multimatic, had 10 employees. Multimatic delved into car parts when it landed a contract in 1960 to make sun visor brackets for a General Motors division in Canada. As a hobby, Stronach bought his first racing horse the next year.

To go public, in 1969 Multimatic underwent a reverse merger with Magna Electronics, a publicly traded maker of components for aerospace, defense, and industrial markets. (Stronach retained control of the company.) Annual sales reached $10 million that year. The company expanded its automotive operations during the early 1970s by adding more stamped and electronic components. Magna was renamed Magna International in 1973.

With sales increasing steadily among its auto parts businesses, Magna sold its aerospace and defense business (now part of Heroux-Devtek) in 1981. The new Magna consisted of five distinct automotive divisions that made seat tracks, door latches, electronic components, and other auto parts. During the 1980s the company expanded by adding factories and product lines. It also capitalized on carmakers' penchants for outsourcing labor and bypassing unions. By 1987, when sales reached $1 billion, the company was producing systems for every area of the automobile. Stronach didn't spend all his time on cars, however. He had opened restaurants, tried various publishing ventures (which failed), and even made an unsuccessful run for a Canadian parliament seat in 1988.

Aggressive expansion during the 1980s eventually caught up with the company, and in 1989

Magna began to restructure, selling assets to pay off its debt. The company also was bailed out, in part, by two of its principal customers — General Motors and Chrysler. Having recovered somewhat, Magna began acquiring small auto parts companies in Europe in 1992.

Magna expanded its European presence with the purchase of Austria-based Steyr-Daimler-Puch in 1998, adding about $1 billion in annual sales. The deal steered Magna into the auto assembly business. Stronach also added Santa Anita Park to his holdings that year. In late 1999 the company's racetrack interests were spun off as Magna Entertainment, with Magna retaining a 78% stake. Stronach's horse, Red Bullet, won the 2000 Preakness.

Early in 2001 Stronach's daughter Belinda was named vice chairman and CEO. In 2002 Magna acquired rival automotive mirror maker Donnelly Corp. in a stock-and-debt deal worth $320 million. The company divested its stake in Magna Entertainment in 2003.

Early in 2004 Belinda Stronach stepped down as president, CEO, and director in order to make a bid for the leadership of Canada's new Conservative Party. Her father, Magna chairman Frank Stronach, assumed the role of interim president. Ms. Stronach's bid for the leadership of the Conservative Party was not successful. Mr. Stronach ran the company until 2005 when Magna adopted a co-CEO management structure with Donald Walker and Siegfried Wolf at the helm.

In May 2004 Magna and Daimler announced that Magna would buy 80% of Daimler's drivetrain manufacturing subsidiary New Venture Gear for about $435 million. In 2007 Magna bought out Daimler's stake.

In 2007 Russian conglomerate Basic Element, led by Russian aluminum magnate Oleg Deripaska, spent $1.54 billion to purchase 20% of Magna. The transaction gave Magna entry to the Russian market, but late in 2008 Deripaska's bank, BNP Paribas, made a margin call that forced the businessman to give up his shares.

EXECUTIVES

Chairman: Frank Stronach, age 76
Executive Vice Chairman: Belinda Stronach, age 43
Co-CEO and Director: Siegfried Wolf, age 52
Co-CEO and Director: Donald J. Walker, age 53
COO, Exteriors and Interiors: Tom Skudutis
EVP and CFO: Vincent J. Galifi
EVP and Chief Legal Officer: Jeffrey O. Palmer
EVP Corporate Development: Peter Koob
EVP; President, China, India, South East Asia, South America, and Africa: Herbert Demel, age 57
EVP Business Development: James J. Tobin Sr.
EVP, Magna Europe: Manfred Eibeck
EVP Global Human Resources: Marc J. Neeb
EVP: Alon Ossip
VP Investor Relations: Louis Tonelli
VP and Secretary: Bassem Shakeel
VP Finance: Patrick W.D. McCann
VP Special Projects: Joachim V. Hirsch
VP Taxation: David M. Williamson
VP Corporate Sales and Marketing: Gerd R. Brusius
VP Mergers and Acquisitions: Gary M. Cohn, age 49
Treasurer: Paul Brock
Auditors: Ernst & Young LLP

LOCATIONS

HQ: Magna International Inc.
  337 Magna Dr.
  Aurora, Ontario L4G 7K1, Canada
Phone: 905-726-2462   **Fax:** 905-726-7164
US HQ: 600 Wilshire Dr., Troy, MI 48084
US Phone: 248-729-2400   **US Fax:** 248-729-2410
Web: www.magnaint.com

2009 Sales

	% of total
Europe	49
North America	47
Other regions	4
Total	**100**

PRODUCTS/OPERATIONS

2009 Sales

	% of total
Exterior & interior systems	35
Body & chassis systems	20
Powertrain systems	14
Complete vehicle assembly	10
Tooling, engineering & other	9
Vision & electronic systems	8
Closure systems	4
Total	**100**

2009 Sales by Customer

	% of total
General Motors	18
BMW	16
Ford	15
Volkswagen	12
Fiat/Chrysler	11
Daimler	10
Other	18
Total	**100**

Selected Operations, Products, and Services

Cosma International Inc. — body and chassis systems
Decoma International — exterior and interior systems
Magna E-Car Systems
Magna Car Top Systems — roof systems
Magna Closures — closure systems
Magna Electronics — electronic systems
Magna Mirrors — vision systems
Magna Powertrain — powertrain systems
Magna Seating — seating systems
Magna Steyr — complete vehicle manufacturing and OEM engineering

COMPETITORS

A.G. Simpson
Aisin Seiki
AISIN World Corp.
American Axle & Manufacturing
ArvinMeritor
Benteler Automotive
BorgWarner
Calsonic Kansei
Commercial Vehicle
Dana Holding
Delphi Automotive
DENSO
Dura Automotive
Eaton
Faurecia
Ficosa
Gentex
GKN
Haldex
Hella
Johnson Controls
KUO
Lacks Enterprises
Lear Corp
Linamar Corp.
Plastic Omnium
Prodrive
Puradyn
Robert Bosch
Tenneco
Textron
Torotrak
Tower International
Toyota Auto Body
Trico Products
Valeo
Visteon
ZF Friedrichshafen

HISTORICAL FINANCIALS

Company Type: Public

Income Statement

FYE: December 31

	REVENUE ($ mil.)	NET INCOME ($ mil.)	NET PROFIT MARGIN	EMPLOYEES
12/09	17,367	(493)	—	72,500
12/08	23,704	71	0.3%	74,350
12/07	26,067	663	2.5%	83,900
12/06	24,180	528	2.2%	83,000
12/05	22,811	639	2.8%	82,000
Annual Growth	**(6.6%)**	**—**	**—**	**(3.0%)**

2009 Year-End Financials

Debt ratio: 1.6%
Return on equity: —
Cash ($ mil.): 1,334
Current ratio: 1.47
Long-term debt ($ mil.): 115
No. of shares (mil.): 242
Dividends
  Yield: 0.4%
  Payout: —
Market value ($ mil.): 6,126

Stock History

NYSE: MGA

	STOCK PRICE ($) FY Close	P/E High/Low		PER SHARE ($) Earnings	Dividends	Book Value
12/09	25.29	—	—	(2.20)	0.09	30.38
12/08	14.97	132	37	0.31	0.63	30.39
12/07	40.22	17	12	2.93	0.57	35.67
12/06	40.28	17	14	2.39	0.76	29.54
12/05	35.99	14	10	2.95	0.76	27.10
Annual Growth	**(8.4%)**	**—**	**—**	**—**	**(41.3%)**	**2.9%**

MAN SE

This venerable old MAN still shows all the right moves. For more than 250 years, MAN SE and its subsidiaries have manufactured transport- and energy-related equipment, from trucks and buses to diesel engines for ships. MAN Nutzfahrzeuge is one of Europe's largest truck and commercial vehicle makers, as well as a giant supplier of vehicle, boat, and power generation engines. MAN Diesel & Turbo makes a variety of compressors, expanders, and gas and steam turbines, as well as leads the world market for shipboard diesel engines and is second in stationary engines. It also provides parts and service. Volkswagen owns nearly 30% of MAN.

Management shake-ups have rattled MAN SE. CEO Hakan Samuelsson resigned unexpectedly in late 2009. Although the company has been the subject of an internal corruption probe, there were no allegations made against Samuelsson, who had served as CEO since 2005. Bribery charges were subsequently filed against former head of the MAN Turbo unit, Heinz Juergen Maus. Dr.-Ing. Georg Pachta-Reyhofen replaced Samuelsson. Pachta-Reyhofen previously served as head of MAN Diesel.

Beginning in 2010, MAN Diesel's operations merged with those of MAN Turbo AG to create

MAN Diesel & Turbo. Together, their products offer an impressive portfolio of large-bore diesel engines, compressors, and turbines. The merger also reduces the manufacturing and overhead costs of MAN's Power Engineering business by combining complementary operations, as well as helps to build and hold market positions. MAN Diesel engines are said to power the transport of more than 50% of the world's freight. Moreover, MAN Diesel ranks as the only provider of diesel engines for both marine propulsion and power plants. No lightweight, MAN Turbo is among the world's largest makers of thermal turbomachines. Its slate of products and services, from design to manufacture and assembly, fuels MAN SE's reach into more than 120 countries.

MAN's commercial vehicle business segment (MAN Nutzfahrzeuge and MAN Latin America), which accounts for about 70% of group revenues, is countering the weak economy by expanding into developing regions. In fall 2009 it acquired a 25% stake in China-based Sinotruk, a state-owned truck maker. MAN plans to produce a new series of heavy trucks; through the $800 million partnership, MAN will license engine, chassis, axles, and other technologies to Sinotruk, which will manufacture the series at its plants in China. In 2010 the Sinotruk-MAN partnership announced plans to debut a new truck brand for the China market in 2011. MAN also stepped up its efforts in Latin America. In 2009, it bought blue chip brand VW Truck & Bus, VW's vehicle manufacturing operations in Brazil. MAN increased its stake to 50% in an India-based joint venture with Force Motors Ltd., in 2008, as well.

Domestically, MAN raised its stake in EURO-Leasing GmbH to approximately 50% in 2009, snatching up majority control in the truck leasing company. EURO-Leasing operates a fleet of about 2,600 trailers and 8,000 semitrailers. At the same time, the company is streamlining noncore operations. MAN sold its 70% stake in industrial services group MAN Ferrostaal to International Petroleum Investment Co., a state-owned United Arab Emirates company.

HISTORY

MAN grew out of a company started by Carl August Reichenbach and Carl Buz, who leased an engineering plant in Augsburg, Germany, in 1844. Reichenbach, whose uncle had invented the flatbed printing press, began producing printing presses in 1845. On the same premises, Buz began manufacturing steam engines and industrial drive systems, and he soon added rotary printing presses, water turbines, pumps, and diesel engines. In 1898 the company took the name MAN (Maschinenfabrik Augsburg-Nurnberg) after merging with a German engineering company of the same name.

Another German heavy-industry company, Gutehoffnungshutte Aktienverein AG (GHH, with roots stretching to 1758), bought a majority interest in MAN in 1921. Through acquisitions and internal growth MAN emerged from the world wars as one of Germany's major heavy-industry companies, with added interests in commercial vehicles, shipbuilding, and plant construction. By 1955 MAN's commercial vehicles were a major division destined to dominate the company's sales; MAN moved the division's headquarters to Munich that year.

During the 1970s an overseas recession caused the sales of some operations to slump, although MAN's commercial vehicles and printing-equipment businesses held steady. When economic hardship reached Europe in the 1980s, MAN sought markets outside its home region, especially targeting Asia, the Middle East, and the US. Late in the decade the company dropped its less-profitable products (lifts, pumps, heavy cranes) and began licensing more of its technology and subcontracting out more work. MAN moved its corporate headquarters to Munich in 1985 and merged with GHH in 1986.

After a fast start in the 1990s, Europe's economy again faltered, taking a toll on the company's sales. MAN's profits slumped in fiscal 1994. It laid off about 10% of its workforce between 1993 and 1995. As the economy recovered, so did MAN, and by fiscal 1998, its stagnant profits had rebounded.

Early in 2000 MAN purchased truck makers ERF Holdings (UK) and STAR (Poland). Later that year MAN picked up ALSTOM's diesel engine business. MAN acquired the Neoplan bus-making business of Gottlob Auwarter GmbH in 2001, as well as the turbomachinery business of Switzerland's Sulzer. After discovering accounting irregularities that year, the company suspended the CEO (John Bryant) and CFO (Klaus Wagner) of the newly acquired ERF. In 2003 MAN sold its 51% stake in SMS AG.

In 2005 the MAN Group sold off its MAN Wolffkran subsidiary to private investors. The business sold and rented tower cranes, aka cherry pickers, for the building industry; the sale was part of the company's effort to pare down its operations to what are considered to be its core divisions.

In 2006 MAN sold MAN TAKRAF Fördertechnik to Germany's VTC Industrieholding. TAKRAF Fördertechnik, acquired by MAN in 1994, built equipment, systems, and complete facilities for open-pit mining, harbor and crane technology, and bulk cargo handling.

Also that year the company sold MAN Roland Druckmaschinen, its printing press business, to a new venture put together by Allianz Capital Partners for €624 million (about $790 million). MAN kept a 35% equity stake in the business following the transaction.

EXECUTIVES

Chairman of the Supervisory Board:
Ferdinand K. Piëch, age 72
Vice Chairman of the Supervisory Board:
Ekkehard D. Schulz, age 69
Vice Chairman of the Supervisory Board: Thomas Otto
**Interim CEO and Member of the Executive Board;
Chairman, Diesel:** Georg Pachta-Reyhofen, age 55
Member of the Executive Board; CEO, MAN Turbo AG:
Klaus Stahlmann
**Member of the Management Board; President, MAN
Latin America:** Antonio R. Cortes
Legal: Michael Fontaine
Chief Human Resources Officer: Jorg Schwitalla, age 49
Chief Compliance Officer: Olaf Schneider, age 38
Head, Investor Relations: Silke Glitza-Stamberger
Auditors: KPMG AG Wirtschaftsprüfungsgesellschaft

LOCATIONS

HQ: MAN SE
  Ungererstr. 69
  80805 Munich, Germany
Phone: 49-89-3609-80   **Fax:** 49-89-3609-8250
Web: www.man.de

2009 Sales

	% of total
Europe	
Germany	24
Other European Union	28
Other countries	6
America	20
Asia	16
Africa	5
Australia & Oceania	1
Total	**100**

PRODUCTS/OPERATIONS

2009 Sales

	% of total
Commercial vehicles	65
Diesel engines	20
Turbomachines	12
Other	3
Total	**100**

COMPETITORS

ALSTOM
ArvinMeritor
Baldwin Technology
China Yuchai
Cummins
Daimler
Dana Holding
DEUTZ
Dresser-Rand
Federal-Mogul
Fiat
GE Energy
GEA Group
Goss International
Hanjin Heavy Industries & Construction
Heidelberger Druckmaschinen
ITT Corp.
Kawasaki Heavy Industries
Koenig & Bauer
Mitsubishi Heavy Industries
Navistar International
PACCAR
Renault
Scania
Siemens AG
Sumitomo Heavy Industries
TUI
Voith
Volvo

HISTORICAL FINANCIALS

Company Type: Public

Income Statement

FYE: December 31

	REVENUE ($ mil.)	NET INCOME ($ mil.)	NET PROFIT MARGIN	EMPLOYEES
12/09	17,236	(370)	—	47,743
12/08	21,065	1,758	8.3%	51,321
12/07	22,826	1,790	7.8%	55,086
12/06	17,216	1,211	7.0%	50,290
12/05	13,476	547	4.1%	58,203
Annual Growth	**6.3%**	**—**	**—**	**(4.8%)**

2009 Year-End Financials

Debt ratio: —
Return on equity: —
Cash ($ mil.): 719
Current ratio: 1.23
Long-term debt ($ mil.): —

No. of shares (mil.): 147
Dividends
  Yield: 3.7%
  Payout: —
Market value ($ mil.): 11,469

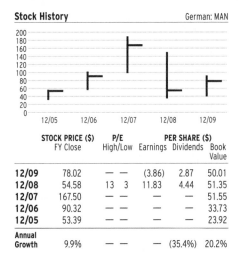
	STOCK PRICE ($) FY Close	P/E High/Low		PER SHARE ($) Earnings	Dividends	Book Value
12/09	78.02	—	—	(3.86)	2.87	50.01
12/08	54.58	13	3	11.83	4.44	51.35
12/07	167.50	—	—	—	—	51.55
12/06	90.32	—	—	—	—	33.73
12/05	53.39	—	—	—	—	23.92
Annual Growth	9.9%			—	(35.4%)	20.2%

Marks & Spencer

The sun never sets on Marks and Spencer (M&S). The British retail icon operates about 330 M&S department stores and some 340 Simply Food shops throughout the UK. Beyond Britain, it boasts more than 325 locations, mostly franchises, in about 40 countries, including China, India, Indonesia, and South Korea. Its department stores sell mid-priced apparel, food, and household items under the company's private label brands, including Autograph, Classic, per una, and Portfolio. About 90% of the company's sales are made in its home country, where it is the #1 provider of womenswear and lingerie.

The recession in the UK has put a damper on the revival that M&S enjoyed following the sale of its Brooks Brothers and Kings Super Markets businesses in the US. Indeed, after a 2008 holiday selling season that only Scrooge could love, M&S reported its worst sales figures in nearly a decade and closed 26 underperforming stores — mostly Simply Food locations — and eliminated some 1,230 jobs.

To ride out the recession, M&S in 2009 unveiled a new business strategy to boost sales. It's concentrating on increasing online sales and growing its international presence.

To that end, the firm opened some 30 stores overseas in 2009 and continued to build its business in Central and Eastern Europe. About half of the store openings were in the Czech Republic, Estonia, Greece, Poland, and Slovakia. In India M&S plans to open about 50 stores by 2015. M&S entered China in 2008 with a 40,000-square-foot store in Shanghai.

At home, the growth story for M&S is its food business, which helped to sustain the company while its apparel business struggled. Indeed, food now accounts for just over half of the company's sales. Of that, M&S's new "Eat Well" line of healthier foods accounts for about 30% of total food sales and some 1,300 products. The company has more than 300 small Simply Food outlets around the UK, located mainly on high streets or within railway stations and airports.

Its core womenswear business has been particularly hard hit in recent years, losing sales to rival ASDA's George clothing line. M&S has taken a number of steps to defend its UK apparel business. It has upgraded its women's Classic range and launched a petite line, and it has pared its menswear offering from eight brands to three (Autograph, Blue Harbour, and Collezione).

Marc Bolland, who had led rival Wm Morrison Supermarkets as its chief executive since 2006, joined M&S as its CEO in May 2010. He succeeded Stuart Rose.

HISTORY

Fleeing anti-Semitic persecution in Russian Poland, 19-year-old Michael Marks immigrated to England in 1882. Eventually settling in Leeds, Marks eked out a meager existence as a traveling peddler until he opened a small stall at the town market in 1884. Because he spoke little English, Marks laid out all of his merchandise and hung a sign that read, "Don't Ask the Price, It's a Penny," unaware at the time that self-service would eventually become the retailing standard. His methods were so successful that he had penny bazaars in five cities by 1890.

Finding himself unable to run the growing operation alone, Marks established an equal partnership with Englishman Tom Spencer, a cashier for a local distributor, forming Marks and Spencer in 1894. By the turn of the century, the company had 36 branches. Following the deaths of Spencer (1905) and Marks (1907), management of the company did not return to family hands until 1916, when Marks' 28-year-old son Simon became chairman.

Marks and Spencer broke with time-honored British retailing tradition in 1924 by eliminating wholesalers and establishing direct links with manufacturers. In 1926 the firm went public, and two years later it launched its now famous St Michael brand. The company turned its attention to pruning unprofitable departments to concentrate on goods that had a rapid turnover. In 1931 the Marks & Spencer stores (M&S) introduced a food department that sold produce and canned goods.

The company sustained severe losses during WWII, when bombing damaged approximately half of its stores. Marks and Spencer rebuilt, and in 1964 Simon's brother-in-law Israel Sieff became chairman. The company expanded to North America a decade later by buying three Canadian chains: Peoples (general merchandise, sold 1992), D'Allaird's (women's clothing, sold 1996), and Walker's (clothing shops, converted to M&S). Sieff's son Marcus Sieff became chairman in 1972. M&S opened its first store in Paris in 1975.

Derek Rayner replaced Marcus Sieff as chairman in 1984, becoming the first chairman hired from outside the Marks family since 1916. Under Rayner, Marks and Spencer moved into financial services by launching a charge card in 1985. The company purchased US-based Kings Super Markets and Brooks Brothers (upscale clothing stores) in 1988. Rayner retired in 1991, and CEO Richard Greenbury became chairman. During the 1990s M&S opened new stores in Germany, Hong Kong, Hungary, Spain, and Turkey.

Greenbury, the target of criticism that the company was too slow to expand or to embrace new ideas, was succeeded in 1999 as CEO by hand-picked heir Peter Salsbury. That year, continued poor sales led Marks and Spencer to cut 700 jobs, and close its 38 M&S stores in Canada. Chairman Luc Vandevelde took over as CEO in 2000 when Salsbury resigned.

Unhappy with the company's direction and its departure from older values, Marks and Spencer board members Sir David Sieff (the last remaining founder member), Sir Ralph Robins, and Sir Michael Perry left the board in 2001. Marks and Spencer sold Brooks Brothers to Retail Brand Alliance for $225 million (a loss from the $750 million the company paid for it in 1988) in 2001.

In 2002 Vandevelde — who is credited with masterminding the M&S turnaround — announced he would give up his role as CEO and hand the reins to managing director Roger Holmes. Vandevelde became the company's part-time chairman in 2003.

In May 2004 both Vandevelde and Holmes left M&S. Stuart Rose, formerly head of Arcadia, was named CEO; non-executive board member Paul Myners was named interim chairman of the company. In October M&S bought the Per Una brand from designer George Davies for about £126 million.

Lord Burns, a former chairman of Abbey National, took up the post of chairman in July 2006 after joining Marks and Spencer as deputy chairman in 2005. Burns was succeeded by CEO Rose in 2008. Rose stepped down as CEO in 2010 to make way for Marc Bolland, thus decoupling the roles of chairman and chief executive at the firm.

EXECUTIVES

Chairman: Sir Stuart A. Rose, age 61
Deputy Chairman: Sir David M. C. Michels, age 63
CEO: Marc J. (M. J.) Bolland, age 51
CFO: Alan Stewart, age 50
Executive Director Marketing: Steven (Steve) Sharp, age 59
Executive Director Clothing: Kate Bostock, age 53
Group Secretary, Head of Corporate Governance, and Director: Amanda Mellor
Director Food: John Dixon
Director Property and Store Development: Clem Constantine
Director Human Resources: Tanith Dodge
Director Retail: Steve Rowe
Director Store Marketing and Design: Nayna McIntosh, age 46
Director Information Technology and Logistics: Darrell Stein
Director GM Merchandising and Planning: Andrew Skinner, age 41
Director: Robert Swannell, age 59
Investor Relations: Majda Rainer
Auditors: PricewaterhouseCoopers LLP

LOCATIONS

HQ: Marks and Spencer Group plc
Waterside House, 35 N. Wharf Rd.
London W2 1NW, United Kingdom
Phone: 44-20-7935-4422   **Fax:** 44-845-303-0170
Web: www.marksandspencer.com

2010 Stores

	No.
UK	690
International	
Southern & Eastern Europe	160
Far East	74
Ireland & Channel Islands	30
Mediterranean & Islands	23
Middle East	23
Indian subcontinent	16
Bermuda	1
Total	**1,017**

2010 Sales

	% of total
UK	90
International	10
Total	**100**

PRODUCTS/OPERATIONS

2010 UK Stores

	No.
High Street	242
Simply Food (franchises)	194
Simply Food (wholly owned)	156
Major	42
Outlet	46
Premiere	10
Total	**690**

2010 Sales

	% of total
UK	
Food	46
General merchandise	44
International	
Retail	7
Wholesale	3
Total	**100**

COMPETITORS

Arcadia	J Sainsbury
ASDA	John Lewis
Benetton	Kingfisher
Berwin & Berwin	Littlewoods
Burberry	Mothercare
Carrefour	New Look
Co-operative Group	NEXT plc
Debenhams	Pret A Manger
Fortnum & Mason	Primark
Gap UK	Tesco
H&M	T.K. Maxx
Harrods	Topshop
Harvey Nichols	Zara
House of Fraser	

HISTORICAL FINANCIALS

Company Type: Public

Income Statement — FYE: Saturday nearest March 31

	REVENUE ($ mil.)	NET INCOME ($ mil.)	NET PROFIT MARGIN	EMPLOYEES
3/10	14,370	793	5.5%	76,267
3/09	12,876	722	5.6%	77,864
3/08	17,991	1,639	9.1%	75,389
3/07	16,896	1,298	7.7%	75,000
3/06	13,578	911	6.7%	65,000
Annual Growth	1.4%	(3.4%)	—	4.1%

2010 Year-End Financials

Debt ratio: —	No. of shares (mil.): 1,582
Return on equity: —	Dividends
Cash ($ mil.): 611	Yield: 4.1%
Current ratio: —	Payout: —
Long-term debt ($ mil.): —	Market value ($ mil.): 8,824

Stock History

Pink Sheets: MAKSY

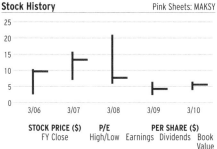

	STOCK PRICE ($) FY Close	P/E High/Low	PER SHARE ($) Earnings	PER SHARE ($) Dividends	PER SHARE ($) Book Value
3/10	5.58	— —	—	0.23	2.08
3/09	4.21	— —	—	0.32	1.89
3/08	7.72	— —	—	0.40	2.48
3/07	13.31	— —	—	0.30	2.05
3/06	9.69	— —	—	0.21	1.32
Annual Growth	(12.9%)	— —	—	2.3%	12.0%

Marubeni Corporation

Marubeni's name combines the Japanese words for "circle" and "red," and Marubeni hopes the comprehensive range of products manufactured and traded by its circle of operating units will keep the company out of the red. One of Japan's largest *sogo shosha* (general trading companies), Marubeni has 11 business divisions: Chemicals; Energy; Finance, Logistics & IT Business; Food; Forest Product; Lifestyle; Metals & Mineral Resources; Real Estate; Plant, Ship & Industrial Machinery; Power Projects & Infrastructure; and Transportation Machinery.

Marubeni has hundreds of operating companies in 70 countries, but it has been particularly active in Asia, where its diversity has enabled it to develop local industries and to help build utility and industrial infrastructures such as telephone systems, power plants, and water systems. The company has championed international expansion since the mid-1990s, but Japan's credit crunch and the Asian economic crisis have hurt the company's production and processing operations across Southeast Asia. Marubeni has been reducing debt, controlling operating costs, and investing in commodity trading, natural resources projects, and international power generation schemes.

Although Marubeni has investments worldwide, the rapidly growing Middle Eastern economies have been a major focus of interest. In 2009 the company completed the Laffan Refinery in Qatar, which began commercial operations that year. It also signed a $2 billion deal to build the Shuweihat S2 Independent Water and Power Producer project in the United Arab Emirates.

The company is also playing to its strengths. In 2008 to further boost its power plant division, a major revenue producer, Marubeni acquired US-based The PIC Group, Inc., an independent global provider of services and programs focused on power generation and other industrial facilities and services.

HISTORY

Marubeni's origins are closely linked to those of another leading Japanese trading company. ITOCHU founder Chubei Itoh set up Marubeni Shoten K. K. in 1858 as an outlet in Osaka for his textile trading business (originally C. Itoh & Co.). The symbol for the store was a circle (*maru*) drawn around the Japanese word for red (*beni*). As C. Itoh's global operations expanded, the Marubeni store served as headquarters.

Marubeni was split off from C. Itoh in 1921 to trade textiles, although it soon expanded its operations to include industrial and consumer goods. To mobilize for WWII, the Japanese government reunited Marubeni and C. Itoh in 1941, merging them with another trading company, Kishimoto, into a new entity, Sanko Kabushiki Kaisha. In 1944 Sanko, Daido Boeki, and Kureha Spinning were ordered to consolidate into a larger entity to be called the Daiken Co., but the war ended before all operations were fully integrated.

Spun off from Daiken in 1949, Marubeni began trading internationally. It opened a New York office in 1951 and diversified into food, metals, and machinery. During the Korean War, Marubeni benefited from the UN's use of Japan as a supply base.

In 1955 Marubeni merged with Iida & Company and changed its name to Marubeni-Iida. It received a government concession to supply silicon steel and iron sheets critical to the growing Japanese auto and appliance industries. The company expanded into engineering — building factories, aircraft, and a nuclear reactor for the Japan Atomic Energy Research Institute — and into petrochemicals, fertilizers, and rubber products.

Marubeni-Iida was behind the Fuyo *keiretsu* formed in the early 1960s. Fuyo (another word for Mt. Fuji) is a powerful assemblage of some 150 companies, including Canon, Hitachi, and Nissan, that form joint ventures and develop think tanks.

The firm became Marubeni Corp. in 1972, and a year later it bought Nanyo Bussan, another trading company. In 1973 Marubeni's image was tarnished by allegations that it had hoarded rice for sale on the Japanese black market.

In the 1990s Marubeni won several major construction contracts. Among them, Marubeni formed a venture in 1998 with John Laing and Turkey's Alarko Alsim to rebuild three airports in Uzbekistan.

Marubeni had begun offering Internet access in 1995, and two years later it launched an Internet-based long-distance telephone service. In 1999 the trading house formed two ventures with US firm Global Crossing, one to start operating Pacific Crossing One (the Japan-US cable) and another to lay a cable network in Japan.

That year Marubeni tied up with fellow trading company ITOCHU to integrate their steel processing subsidiaries in China to try to keep their Chinese businesses afloat. In 2000 ITOCHU and Marubeni formed an online steel trading joint venture with US-based e-commerce company MetalSite. The two companies also integrated their entire steel divisions in 2001, forming the Marubeni-Itochu Steel joint venture, among the largest steel companies in Japan.

Taking responsibility for the sharp downturn in Marubeni's financial performance, chairman Iwao Toriumi announced in 2001 that he would step down. The company launched a major restructuring effort the next year that was designed to give more autonomy to the managers of individual business units.

EXECUTIVES

Chairman: Nobuo Katsumata
President, CEO, and Director: Teruo Asada
SEVP and Director: Masaru Funai
SEVP and Director: Mamoru Sekiyama
Senior Managing Executive Officer; President and CEO, Marubeni America Corporation: Koichi Mochizuki
Managing Executive Officer and Director: Toshinori Umezawa
Managing Executive Officer and Director: Shinji Kawai
Managing Executive Officer: Mitsuru Akiyoshi
Managing Executive Officer: Norihiro Shimizu
Managing Executive Officer: Shigeru Yamazoe
Managing Executive Officer: Shigemasa Sonobe
Managing Executive Officer: Kenichi Hatta
Managing Executive Officer and Director: Hisashi Sunaoshi
Managing Executive Officer and Director: Fumiya Kokubu
Managing Executive Officer and Director: Takafumi Sakishima
Managing Executive Officer and Director: Michihiko Ota
CEO, CoActiv Capital Partners: Don Campbell
President, CoActiv Capital Partners Canada: Steve Klein
Auditors: Ernst & Young

HQ: Marubeni Corporation
4-2, Ohtemachi 1-chome, Chiyoda-ku
Tokyo 100-8088, Japan
Phone: 81-3-3282-2111 **Fax:** 81-3-3282-4241
US HQ: 375 Lexington Ave., New York, NY 10017
US Phone: 212-450-0100 **US Fax:** 212-450-0700
Web: www.marubeni.co.jp

PRODUCTS/OPERATIONS

2010 Sales

	% of total
Energy	24
Food	20
Metals & mineral resources	8
Chemicals	7
Forest products	7
Plant, ship & industrial machinery	7
Transportation machinery	5
Lifestyle	5
Power projects & infrastructure	4
Other	13
Total	**100**

COMPETITORS

ITOCHU	Samsung Group
Jardine Matheson	Seika
Kanematsu	Showa Denko
Largo Vista	Sime Darby
LG Group	Sojitz
Mitsubishi Corp.	Sojitz Corporation
Mitsubishi International	Sumikin Bussan
Mitsui	Sumitomo
Nissan Chemical	Sumitomo Heavy
Rio Tinto plc	Industries

HISTORICAL FINANCIALS

Company Type: Public

Income Statement
FYE: March 31

	REVENUE ($ mil.)	NET INCOME ($ mil.)	NET PROFIT MARGIN	EMPLOYEES
3/10	35,384	1,028	2.9%	5,679
3/09	41,140	1,143	2.8%	5,451
3/08	41,958	1,483	3.5%	3,856
3/07	31,042	1,013	3.3%	5,323
3/06	26,708	628	2.4%	3,562
Annual Growth	**7.3%**	**13.1%**	**—**	**12.4%**

2010 Year-End Financials

Debt ratio: 282.4%
Return on equity: 14.8%
Cash ($ mil.): 6,158
Current ratio: 1.40
Long-term debt ($ mil.): 22,706
No. of shares (mil.): 1,738
Dividends
Yield: 1.4%
Payout: 15.3%
Market value ($ mil.): 10,893

Stock History
Pink Sheets: MARUY

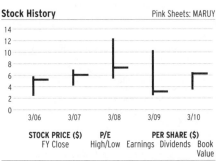

	STOCK PRICE ($) FY Close	P/E High/Low		PER SHARE ($) Earnings	Dividends	Book Value
3/10	6.27	11	6	0.59	0.09	4.63
3/09	3.14	15	4	0.66	0.03	3.35
3/08	7.31	14	7	0.86	—	4.52
3/07	6.07	12	8	0.58	—	3.64
3/06	5.24	16	8	0.34	—	3.25
Annual Growth	**4.6%**	**—**	**—**	**14.8%**	**200.0%**	**9.2%**

Mazda Motor

Mazda still has the Zoom-Zoom spirit, even as it jockeys for position alongside the top six automakers in Japan. Mazda — comprising Mazda USA, Europe, and China, along with Mazda in the 4As (Asia, Australia, Africa, Latin America) — makes SUVs, pickups, and commercial vehicles. Models sold in the US include sedans (Mazda3, Mazda6); sports cars (Miata, RX-8); and pickup trucks (B-Series). Mazda added SUVs and crossovers to its lineup with the Tribute, Mazda5, CX-7, and CX-9. Mazda sells its vehicles in some 140 countries. In late 2008 Ford Motor relinquished its control of Mazda by lowering its stake from about 33% to about 13%.

When cash-starved Ford lowered its stake in Mazda, a consortium of Hiroshima Bank, Panasonic (both Mazda business partners), and Mazda itself paid a combined sum of about $540 million to bring control of the company back to Japan. Ford and Mazda plan to continue their strategic alliance (AutoAlliance), even with two less Ford members on Mazda's board. AutoAlliance launched a new $500 million car plant at its AutoAlliance location in Thailand. Passenger cars Ford Fiesta and Mazda 2 will be manufactured at the new facility; the plant is expected to produce 275,000 units per year.

To reduce costs, Mazda executives took a 20% salary cut beginning in 2008. Additionally, the workforce was reduced and temporary workers' contracts were not renewed, and inventory adjustments were made to match demand.

China was the company's only market not to falter during the economic crisis of 2009. Early 2010 brought the news that Mazda is dissolving its three-way partnership with Ford and Chongqing Changan Automotive by the end of 2010. The JV will be divided into two entities: a 50/50 JV owned by Ford and Changan (Chang'an Ford), and a separate entity owned by Mazda and Changan (Chang'an Mazda). The three-way joint venture, known as Changan Ford Mazda Automobile Corporation, has been troubled at times with disagreements regarding production plans. Mazda believes the break-up will allow for more manufacturing freedom in China.

Following the independence from Ford, Takashi Yamanouchi took over as president and CEO of Mazda, assuming the responsibility of shoring up tumbling profits caused by an unstable yen and a decrease in demand. Former president Hisakazu Imaki continues serving as chairman, but plans to retire in the near future.

HISTORY

Ingiro Matsuda founded cork producer Toyo Cork Kogyo in Hiroshima in 1920. The company changed its name to Toyo Kogyo in 1927 and began making machine tools. Impressed by Ford trucks used in 1923 earthquake-relief efforts, Matsuda had the company make a three-wheel motorcycle/truck hybrid in 1931.

The second Sino-Japanese War forced Toyo Kogyo to make rifles and cut back on its truck production. Although the company built a prototype passenger car in 1940, the outbreak of WWII refocused it on weapons. The August 1945 bombing of Hiroshima killed more than 400 Toyo Kogyo workers, but the company persevered, producing 10 trucks that December. By 1949 it was turning out 800 per month.

The company launched the first Mazda, a two-seat minicar, in 1960. The next year Toyo Kogyo licensed Audi's new rotary engine technology. After releasing a string of models, the company became Japan's #3 automaker in 1964. Toyo Kogyo introduced the first Mazda powered by a rotary engine, Cosmo/110S, in 1967, followed by the Familia in 1968.

The company grew rapidly and began exporting to the US in 1970. However, recession, high gas prices, and concern over the inefficiency of rotary engines halted growth in the mid-1970s. Sumitomo Bank bailed out Toyo Kogyo. The company shifted emphasis back to piston engines but managed to launch the rotary engine RX-7 in 1978.

Ford's need for small-car expertise and Sumitomo's desire for a large partner for its client led to Ford's purchase of 25% of Toyo Kogyo in 1979. The company's early 1980s GLC/323 and 626 models were sold as Fords in Asia, Latin America, and the Middle East.

Toyo Kogyo changed its name to Mazda Motor Corporation in 1984. ("Mazda" is loosely derived from Matsuda's name, but the carmaker has never discouraged an association with the Zoroastrian god of light, Ahura Mazda.) The company opened a US plant in 1985, but a strong yen, expensive increases in production capacity, and a growing number of models led to increased overhead, soaring debt, and shrinking margins. Mazda launched the hot-selling Miata in 1989.

The company faced more problems with the early 1990s recession. In 1992 Mazda introduced a new 626 model. That year Mazda also sold half its interest in its Flat Rock, Michigan, plant to Ford. As the yen, development costs, and prices for its cars in the US all rose, sales in the US fell. In 1993 Mazda reorganized subsidiary Mazda of America by cutting staff.

Ford sank $481 million into Mazda in 1996, increasing its stake to 33%. That year the Ford-appointed former EVP of Mazda, Henry Wallace, became Mazda's president, making history as the first non-Japanese to head a major Japanese corporation. In 1997 Wallace resigned to become CFO of Ford's European operations, and former Ford executive James Miller replaced him. That year Mazda consolidated four US operations into Mazda North American Operations.

Restructuring continued in 1998 as Mazda consolidated some European operations and closed a plant in Thailand. In 1999 Mazda sold its credit division to Ford and its Naldec auto parts unit to Ford's Visteon unit. It announced plans to sell its stake in South Korean carmaker Kia Motors. Later in the year another American, Ford's Mark Fields, took over as president.

In 2000 Mazda recalled 30,000 of that year's MPV minivans to fix a powertrain control module and asked owners of all 2000 MPVs to bring in their vehicles for front-bumper reinforcement. Mazda also announced plans to close about 40% of its North American dealership outlets over the next three years.

In 2001 Mazda completed a program to assume direct control over distribution in some European markets including France, Italy, Spain, and the UK.

In 2007 Mazda opened a new vehicle assembly plant in Nanjing, China, and also began building a new passenger vehicle plant in Thailand.

To strengthen its sales in Japan, the company introduced the Mazda Advantage Loan in 2007 in cooperation with PRIMUS Financial Services. Mazda acquired a 40% stake in PRIMUS in March 2008 to strengthen its auto financing business.

EXECUTIVES

Chairman: Hisakazu Imaki
President, CEO, and Director: Takashi Yamanouchi
CFO and Director; Senior Managing Executive Officer, Corporate Planning, Product Profit Control, Financial Services and Cost Innovation: Kiyoshi Ozaki
Director and Senior Managing Executive Officer, Research and Development and Program Management; President, Mazda Engineering & Technology Co., Ltd.: Seita Kanai
Senior Managing Executive Officer, Corporate Planning, Product Strategy and Product Profit Control; Assistant to the Officer in charge of Cost Innovation: Akira Marumoto
Senior Managing Executive Officer, Global Marketing, Global Sales and Customer Service: Masazumi Wakayama
Senior Managing Executive Officer, Production, Business Logistics and IT Solution; Assistant to the Officer in charge of Cost Innovation; Assistant to the Officer in charge of Research and Development: Masamichi Kogai
Senior Managing Executive Officer, Research and Development Quality and Powertrain Development and Electric Drive System Development, and Director: Nobuhiro Hayama
Senior Managing Executive Officer, CSR, Environment and Corporate Communications, and Director: Yuji Harada
Managing Executive Officer; President and CEO, Mazda Motor of America (Mazda North American Operations): James J. (Jim) O'Sullivan
Executive Officer Global Marketing: Masahiro Moro
Auditors: KPMG AZSA & Co.

LOCATIONS

HQ: Mazda Motor Corporation
(Matsuda Jidosha Kabushiki Kaisha)
3-1, Shinchi, Fuchu-cho
Aki-gun, Hiroshima 730-8670, Japan
Phone: 81-82-282-1111 **Fax:** 81-82-287-5190
US HQ: 7755 Irvine Center Dr., Irvine, CA 92618
US Phone: 949-727-1990 **US Fax:** 949-752-2130
Web: www.mazda.com

2010 Sales

	% of total
Japan	41
North America	26
Europe	22
Other regions	11
Total	**100**

PRODUCTS/OPERATIONS

Selected Models

B-Series (pickup)
CX-7 (crossover SUV)
CX-9 (crossover SUV)
Mazda 2 (Demio)
Mazda 3 (Axela, hatchback sedan)
Mazda 5 (Premacy, minivan)
Mazda 6 (sport sedan)
Mazda 8 (MPV)
Mazda Biante (minivan)
MX-5 Miata (roadster)
RX-8 (sports car)
Tribute (SUV)

Selected Subsidiaries and Affiliates

AutoAlliance International, Inc.
Mazda Australia Pty. Ltd.
Mazda Motor Logistics Europe NV (Belgium)
Mazda Motor of America, Inc.

COMPETITORS

BMW	Kia Motors
Chrysler	Nissan
Daimler	Peugeot
Fiat	Renault
Ford Motor	Saab Automobile
Fuji Heavy Industries	Subaru of America
General Motors	Suzuki Motor
Honda	Toyota
Isuzu	Volkswagen

HISTORICAL FINANCIALS

Company Type: Public

Income Statement

FYE: March 31

	REVENUE ($ mil.)	NET INCOME ($ mil.)	NET PROFIT MARGIN	EMPLOYEES
3/10	23,345	59	0.3%	38,987
3/09	26,067	(735)	—	39,852
3/08	35,005	925	2.6%	39,364
3/07	27,552	626	2.3%	38,004
3/06	24,836	567	2.3%	36,626
Annual Growth	**(1.5%)**	**(43.3%)**	**—**	**1.6%**

2010 Year-End Financials

Debt ratio: —
Return on equity: 1.2%
Cash ($ mil.): 2,924
Current ratio: 1.33
Long-term debt ($ mil.): —
No. of shares (mil.): 1,770
Dividends
  Yield: 1.0%
  Payout: —
Market value ($ mil.): 5,023

Stock History

Tokyo: 7261

	STOCK PRICE ($) FY Close	P/E High/Low		PER SHARE ($) Earnings	Dividends	Book Value
3/10	2.84	—	—	(0.05)	0.03	3.10
3/09	1.69	—	—	0.00	0.03	2.40
3/08	3.56	11	5	0.66	—	3.14
3/07	5.53	16	11	0.44	—	2.27
3/06	6.08	15	7	0.40	—	1.91
Annual Growth	**(17.3%)**	**—**	**—**	**—**	**0.0%**	**12.8%**

METRO AG

A ride on this METRO could be a shopper's delight. The company is Germany's über retailer and ranks as the third-largest in the world (behind Wal-Mart Stores and Carrefour). METRO owns and operates more than 2,100 wholesale stores, supermarkets, hypermarkets, department stores, and the fast-growing Media Markt and Saturn consumer electronics chains. About half of its shops are in Germany, but METRO also has stores in some 35 other countries, including China, Egypt, India, the UK, and Vietnam. Store banners include METRO and Makro Cash & Carry wholesale outlets, Real hypermarkets, and Galeria Kaufhof department stores.

The global financial crisis derailed METRO's historically rapid store development plans in 2009. But while the company trimmed its store count at home, it continued to grow abroad, adding 80 stores in Eastern Europe, Asia, and Africa. For 2010 METRO has budgeted about €1.9 billion ($2.6 billion) for investment with plans to substantially increase new store openings. Its focus remains on Eastern Europe (especially Poland and Russia) and Asia. China is METRO's most promising new market. The company currently operates more than 40 Cash & Carry stores in more than 25 Chinese cities and plans to double the number of those stores by the end of the decade. In the near term, it plans to launch its Media Markt chain of consumer electronics stores in China in 2010. METRO's China push will pit it against US consumer eletronics giant Best Buy, which also has aggressive growth plans for the Chinese market. Elsewhere in Asia and Africa, METRO operates 30-plus stores in India, Japan, Morocco, Pakistan, and Vietnam. Egypt is also on the company's global itinerary, with the first Makro Cash & Carry store debuting in Cairo in June 2010.

More than 45% of the firm's revenues are earned from its METRO Cash & Carry and Makro wholesale outlets, which sell food and other grocery and non-grocery items to businesses and institutional customers. Consumer electronics accounts for some 30% of sales. With combined sales in excess of $27 billion and more than 800 stores in about 15 countries, Media Markt and Saturn are Europe's biggest electronics vendors.

In early 2010 the German retailer said that it hopes to sell its struggling Galeria Kaufhof chain of about 125 department stores throughout Germany. Potential buyers may include private equity firms.

METRO AG's largest shareholders are German conglomerate Franz Haniel and the Schmidt-Ruthenbeck and Beisheim families, which together control METRO with about 60% of the voting rights and are actively involved in the management of the company. To that end, Hans-Joachim Körber was succeeded as CEO of METRO by Eckhard Cordes, chief executive of Haniel. Under Cordes the company has been restructuring by selling poorly performing businesses. To that end, METRO in 2009 sold its AXXE restaurants and motels to Tank & Rast, which operates motorway services.

HISTORY

In 1964 Otto Beisheim founded METRO SB-Grossmarkte in the German town of Mulheim. A wholesale business serving commercial customers, it operated under the name METRO Cash & Carry. Three years later Beisheim received backing from the owners of Franz Haniel & Cie (an industrial company founded in 1756) and members of the Schmidt-Ruthenbeck family (also in wholesaling). This allowed METRO to expand rapidly in Germany and, in 1968, into the Netherlands under the name Makro Cash & Carry via a partnership with Steenkolen Handelsvereeniging (SHV). During the 1970s the company expanded its wholesaling operations within Europe and moved into retailing.

METRO's foray into retailing was aided during the next decade by the acquisition of department store chain Kaufhof AG. By the 1980s the rise of specialty stores had many department stores on the defensive, and Kaufhof's owners sold it to METRO and its investment partner, Union Bank of Switzerland.

As METRO's ownership interest in Kaufhof rose above 50%, the chain began converting some of its stores from department stores into fashion and sporting goods sellers. Kaufhof began acquiring a stake in computer manufacturer and retailer Vobis in 1989. In 1993 METRO, now operating as METRO Holding AG, acquired a majority interest in supermarket company Asko Deutsche Kaufhaus, which owned the Praktiker building materials chain. The reclusive Beisheim retired from active management the following year.

To cut costs and prepare for expansion into Asia, in 1996 METRO Holding merged its German retail holdings — Kaufhof; Asko; another grocery operation, Deutsche SB Kauf; and its German cash-and-carry operations — into one holding company, METRO AG.

In 1998 METRO bought the 196-store Makro self-service wholesale chain from Dutch-based SHV. METRO also added to its German food operations by acquiring the 94-store German Allkauf hypermarket chain and then by purchasing the 20-store Kriegbaum hypermarket chain.

Later that year METRO transferred its interests in noncore businesses, including office supply stores, footwear stores, discount stores, computer operations (including Vobis), and 25 unprofitable Kaufhof department stores to its Divaco (formerly Divag) unit. Divaco then sold 165 German Tip discount stores to Tengelmann Group.

Hans-Joachim Korber became METRO's CEO in 1999. In 2000 the company transferred 290 hypermarkets and department stores in Germany, Greece, Hungary, Luxembourg, and Turkey to a joint venture company (51% owned by Westdeutsche Landesbank) to raise cash for the expansion and remodeling of its wholesale outlets.

As part of its international expansion plan, in October 2003 METRO opened the first of two cash-and-carry distribution centers in Bangalore, India.

Gunther Hulse stepped down as chairman of METRO's supervisory board for personal reasons in June 2004. Hulse was succeeded by Theo Siegert, a member of the management board of Franz Haniel & Cie, a German wholesale drug distribution company.

METRO closed three of its Kaufhof stores in Germany in early 2005 amid slumping sales in its department store business. In late 2005 METRO took its DIY home improvement chain Praktiker Bau- und Heimwerkermärkte public.

In 2006 Theo Siegert stepped down as chairman of the supervisory board and was succeeded by Eckhard Cordes.

Continuing its global tour, METRO entered Kazakhstan and Egypt with Makro stores in those markets in 2009 and 2010, respectively.

EXECUTIVES

Chairman and CEO: Eckhard Cordes, age 60
CFO and CIO: Olaf Koch, age 40
Head of Corporate Relations:
Rainhardt von Leoprechting
Head of Corporate HR: Jurgen Pfister
Head of Investor Relations: Henning Gieseke
Head of Legal Affairs and Governance: Rolf Giebeler
Head of Sustainability Management: Marion Sollbach
Head of Strategic Quality Management:
Hans-Jürgen Matern
Head of Corporate Communications: René Beutner
Chairman, Galeria Kaufhof: Lorvo Mandac, age 60

CEO, Media-Saturn-Holding GmbH: Roland Weise
CEO, Media Markt: Michael Rook
CEO, METRO Cash & Carry Germany: John Rix
CEO, METRO Group Asset Management:
Michael Cesarz
CEO, Metro Cash and Carry (Asia/New Markets), Advertising: Frans W.H. Muller, age 49
CEO, Real, Import (MGB Hongkong), and Supply Chain Council of MGL METRO Group Logistics:
Joël Saveuse, age 57
Director: M. P. M. (Theo) de Raad, age 65
Auditors: KPMG Deutsche Treuhand-Gesellschaft AG

LOCATIONS

HQ: METRO AG
Schlüterstrasse 1
40235 Düsseldorf, Germany
Phone: 49-211-6886-0   **Fax:** 49-211-6886-2000
Web: www.metrogroup.de

2009 Stores

	No.
Western Europe	
Germany	1,017
Other countries	596
Eastern Europe	439
Asia & Africa	75
Total	**2,127**

2009 Sales

	% of total
Western Europe	
Germany	40
Other countries	32
Eastern Europe	24
Africa & Asia	4
Total	**100**

PRODUCTS/OPERATIONS

2009 Sales

	% of total
Cash & carry	47
Consumer electronics	30
Food retail	17
Department stores	5
Other	1
Total	**100**

2009 Stores

	No.
Media Markt & Saturn	818
METRO Cash & Carry	668
Real	441
Galeria Kaufhof	141
Other	59
Total	**2,127**

Selected Operations

Wholesale Stores
 Makro
 Metro Cash & Carry (wholesale stores)
Food
 Extra (supermarkets)
 Real (hypermarkets)
Nonfood Specialty Stores
 Media Markt (consumer electronics)
 Saturn (consumer electronics)
Department Store
 Galeria Kaufhof

Other Operations

Dinea Gastronomie (restaurants/catering)
METRO MGE Einkauf (purchasing)
METRO MGI Informatik (IT services)
METRO Real Estate Management (construction services)
METRO Werbegesellschaft (advertising)
METRO Online AG (Internet retailer)
MGB METRO Buying Group Hong Kong Ltd.
 (purchasing, Asia and non-European Union countries)

COMPETITORS

ALDI	Marktkauf
Best Buy	Maxeda
Carrefour	REWE
Casino Guichard	Royal Ahold
Delhaize	Tengelmann
Edeka Zentrale	Tesco
Lidl	Wal-Mart

HISTORICAL FINANCIALS

Company Type: Public

Income Statement

FYE: December 31

	REVENUE ($ mil.)	NET INCOME ($ mil.)	NET PROFIT MARGIN	EMPLOYEES
12/09	93,916	744	0.8%	286,091
12/08	95,784	789	0.8%	290,940
12/07	94,698	1,447	1.5%	281,455
12/06	79,002	1,574	2.0%	208,616
12/05	65,992	769	1.2%	246,875
Annual Growth	**9.2%**	**(0.8%)**	**—**	**3.8%**

2009 Year-End Financials

Debt ratio: —
Return on equity: 8.9%
Cash ($ mil.): 5,727
Current ratio: 0.82
Long-term debt ($ mil.): —
No. of shares (mil.): 327
Dividends
 Yield: 2.8%
 Payout: 100.6%
Market value ($ mil.): 19,938

Stock History

German: MEO

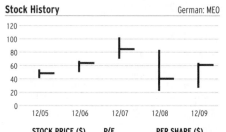

	STOCK PRICE ($) FY Close	P/E High/Low		PER SHARE ($) Earnings	Dividends	Book Value
12/09	61.01	37	17	1.68	1.69	26.28
12/08	40.27	47	14	1.73	1.66	25.10
12/07	84.55	27	19	3.71	—	28.17
12/06	63.74	15	12	4.26	—	23.54
12/05	48.32	27	22	1.93	—	18.51
Annual Growth	**6.0%**	**—**	**—**	**(3.4%)**	**1.8%**	**9.2%**

Michelin

The Michelin Man may look like a marshmallow, but what he's selling is tires. Behind that fluffy white figure is one of the world's top tire manufacturers, Compagnie Générale des Établissements Michelin, which produces more than 150 million tires annually for all kinds of vehicles. The majority of its sales are made from supplying replacement tires to the passenger car and truck markets. It is also a world leader in aircraft and earthmover tires. Michelin sells to both consumers and vehicle manufacturers. Included in its stable are brands recognized regionally (Kleber in Europe, Warrior in China) and worldwide (Michelin, BF Goodrich). The company also publishes about 10 million maps and travel guides per year.

The economic downturn, in the form of plummeting demand, hit home in 2009 as the company closed its 1,000-worker BF Goodrich plant in Opelika, Alabama. The decision to close the plant came from the company's desire to focus on the Michelin brand, which it says is more resilient than other brands. Europe was hit as well, with another 1,000 workers laid off in France, also part of a company-wide restructuring to focus on the best-selling brands.

In 2008 the company launched an initiative to reduce its resource consumption, emissions, and waste by 30% by 2013 (compared to 2005 numbers). Though it has seen a dip in income, by 2010 Michelin's cost-cutting measures and plans to improve efficiency were showing up as positive cash flow. Higher prices for its tires and lower materials costs also helped the bottom line.

Although its operations stretch worldwide, the company is banking on the Far East, a region that accounts for nearly one-third of the global tire market. India's truck market has grown to half the size of Europe's, and China is poised to surpass Japan as the third-largest market for automobiles (behind the US and Europe). China also boasts a 20% share of the global truck tire market. To take advantage of the burgeoning Asian market, Michelin increased its stake in South Korea-based Hankook Tires to about 10% in mid-2008. Other emerging markets include Eastern Europe and South America.

Despite high materials costs, the company also continues to do well in the developed markets of North America, Europe, and Japan by focusing on specialty tires including high-performance, winter, and 4x4. In these markets Michelin has experienced double-digit growth — margins that outperform market norms.

HISTORY

After toying with making rubber balls, Edouard Daubrée and Aristide Barbier formed a partnership in Clermont-Ferrand, France, in 1863 and entered the rubber business in earnest. Both men soon died, but Barbier in-law André Michelin, a successful businessman, took over the company in 1886. André recruited his brother, Edouard, a Parisian artist, to run the company, and in 1889 it was renamed Compagnie Générale des Établissements Michelin.

That year Edouard found that air-filled tires made bicycling more comfortable. But pneumatic tires were experimental and, because they were glued to the rims, required hours to change. In 1891 Edouard made a detachable bicycle tire that took only 15 minutes to change.

The Michelins promoted their tires by persuading cyclists to use them in long-distance races where punctures were likely. They demonstrated the applicability of such tires for cars in an auto race in 1895. In 1898 André commented that a stack of tires would look like a man if it had arms, a notion that led to the creation of Bibendum, the Michelin Man. André launched the *Michelin Guide* for auto tourists in 1900.

Expansion followed as Michelin opened a London office (1905) and began production in Italy (1906) and the US (in New Jersey in 1908). Innovations included detachable rims and spare tires (1906), tubeless tires (1930), treads (1934), and modern low-profile tires (1937). During the Depression, Michelin closed its US plant

and accepted a stake in Citroën, later converted into a minority stake in Peugeot, in lieu of payment for tires.

Michelin patented radial tires in 1946. Expansion was largely confined to Europe in the 1950s but, thanks to radials, increased worldwide in the 1960s. Sears began selling Michelin radials in 1966. Radials took hold during the 1970s, and Michelin returned to manufacturing in the US, opening a plant in South Carolina in 1975.

Expanding aggressively (Michelin opened or bought a plant every nine months from 1960 to 1990), the company went into the red when economic conditions dipped in the early 1980s and in 1990 and 1991. The company's $1.5 billion purchase of Uniroyal Goodrich in 1990 contributed to the latter losses but improved Michelin's position in the US, the world's largest auto market.

In response to the losses, Michelin attacked its bloated infrastructure and reinvented itself along nine product lines (according to tire/vehicle type plus travel, suspension, and primary product manufacturing). It also consolidated facilities and cut about 30,000 jobs. The company continued to focus on R&D, bringing out new high-performance tires such as its "green" tire designed to help cars save fuel.

Michelin bought a majority interest in a Polish tire maker in 1995, and the next year it bought 90% of Taurus, a Hungarian firm that produces most of that country's rubber. Michelin joined German competitor Continental in 1996 to make private-label tires for independent distributors. The next year Michelin introduced a run-flat tire — capable of traveling 50 miles after a puncture — for the automotive aftermarket. The company acquired Icollantas, a Colombian tire group with two factories in Bogotá and Cali, in 1998.

After leading the company for more than 40 years, patriarch François Michelin stepped down in 1999, leaving his youngest son, Edouard, in charge. Almost immediately, Edouard announced a restructuring that would cut 7,500 jobs in Europe, including almost 2,000 in France.

The European Commission fined Michelin nearly $20 million in 2001, claiming the company engaged in anticompetitive behavior by abusing its dominant position in Europe. Michelin announced a licensing agreement in 2004 for Toyo Tire to make, sell, and promote PAX system tires (run-flat tires).

Former co-managing partner Edouard Michelin, youngest son of patriarch François Michelin and the fourth generation of Michelins in the business, was killed in a boating accident in 2006.

EXECUTIVES

Chairman Supervisory Board:
Éric Bourdais de Charbonnière, age 70
Managing General Partner: Michel Rollier, age 66, $3,648,487 total compensation
Non-General Managing Partner, Group Executive Council and CFO: Jean-Dominique Senard, age 56, $935,833 total compensation
Group Executive Council, Managing Director Technology Center, and Non-General Managing Partner: Didier Miraton, age 52, $701,056 total compensation
Group Executive Council, Truck and Tires: Pete Selleck
Group Executive Council, Specialty Tires and Procurement: Bernard Vasdeboncoeur
Group Executive Council, Communication and Brands: Claire Dorland-Clauzel

Group Executive Council, Passenger Car and Light Truck; Racing: Florent Menegaux
Group Executive Council, Manufacturing Performance, Quality, and Supply Chain: Jean-Christophe Guérin
Group Executive Council, Marketing and Sales Performance Euromaster, TCI Maps and Guides, ViaMichelin, Michelin Lifestyle and Information Systems: Eric de Cromières
Group Executive Council, Human Resources, Organization: Jean-Michel Guillon
Investor Relations: Valérie Magloire
Auditors: PricewaterhouseCoopers Audit

LOCATIONS

HQ: Compagnie Générale des Établissements Michelin
23, place des Carmes-Déchaux
63040 Clermont-Ferrand, France
Phone: 33-4-73-32-20-00 **Fax:** 33-45-66-15-53
US HQ: 1 Parkway South, Greenville, SC 29615
US Phone: 864-458-5000 **US Fax:** 864-458-6359
Web: www.michelin.com

2009 Sales

	% of total
Europe	45
North America	34
Other regions	21
Total	**100**

PRODUCTS/OPERATIONS

2009 Sales

	% of total
Passenger car & light truck tires & related distribution	56
Truck tires & related distribution	30
Specialty business	14
Total	**100**

Selected Products and Services

Agricultural vehicle tires
Aircraft tires
Car tires
Construction vehicle tires
Engineering consulting for constructors and equipment manufacturers
Heavy-goods vehicle tires
Motorcycle, bicycle and scooter tires
Sports, leisure and work accessories
Travel maps and guides

Selected Brands

BF Goodrich
Euromaster
Kleber
Kormoran
Michelin
Riken
Taurus
Uniroyal
Warrior

COMPETITORS

Avalon Travel Publishing
Bridgestone
Continental AG
Cooper Tire & Rubber
Fieldens
Goodyear Tire & Rubber
Kumho Tire
Pirelli
Sime Darby
Sumitomo Rubber
Toyo Tire & Rubber
Watts Industrial Tyres
Yokohama Rubber

HISTORICAL FINANCIALS

Company Type: Public

Income Statement

FYE: December 31

	REVENUE ($ mil.)	NET INCOME ($ mil.)	NET PROFIT MARGIN	EMPLOYEES
12/09	21,221	149	0.7%	109,193
12/08	23,127	503	2.2%	117,565
12/07	24,827	1,136	4.6%	122,050
12/06	21,615	755	3.5%	115,755
12/05	18,463	1,053	5.7%	119,030
Annual Growth	3.5%	(38.7%)	—	(2.1%)

2009 Year-End Financials

Debt ratio: —
Return on equity: 2.0%
Cash ($ mil.): 1,764
Current ratio: 1.85
Long-term debt ($ mil.): —

No. of shares (mil.): 147
Dividends
  Yield: 1.9%
  Payout: 140.2%
Market value ($ mil.): 11,322

Stock History

Euronext Paris: ML

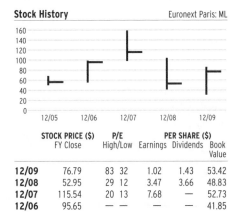

	STOCK PRICE ($) FY Close	P/E High/Low		PER SHARE ($) Earnings	Dividends	Book Value
12/09	76.79	83	32	1.02	1.43	53.42
12/08	52.95	29	12	3.47	3.66	48.83
12/07	115.54	20	13	7.68	—	52.73
12/06	95.65	—	—	—	—	41.85
12/05	56.23	—	—	—	—	36.24
Annual Growth	8.1%	—	—	(63.6%)	(60.9%)	10.2%

Mitsubishi Corporation

In Japanese *mitsubishi* means "three diamonds" and Mitsubishi Corporation is one of Japan's crown jewels. The *sogo shosha*, or trading company, operates through seven main business groups: living essentials (agricultural products, food and beverages, textiles, and construction materials); metals; machinery (power generation equipment, electrical systems, automobiles); energy (liquefied natural gas, crude oil); and chemicals (petrochemicals, fertilizers, plastics). Its other main business group is industrial finance, which handles banking, asset management, construction, and logistics. The company also has a business innovation unit, engaged in software, telecommunications, and environmental services.

Mitsubishi Corporation is part of the Mitsubishi *keiretsu*, a network of affiliated companies that has no official status as a group, but within which there is some cross-ownership and considerable business activity. Other affiliates include Mitsubishi Heavy Industries, The Bank of Tokyo-Mitsubishi, Mitsubishi Electric, Mitsubishi Motors, and Nikon.

Along with the rest of the Mitsubishi companies, Mitsubishi Corporation was hurt by Japan's persistent economic slump. The company restructured and reduced its workforce, and it divided the operations of its former information technology and electronics business among its other groups.

With Asian economies on the rise, however, Mitsubishi set about strengthening its financial position and devised a strategic growth plan that involves focusing on new operational initiatives, including new energy sources and the environment and financial services.

Energy plans include the development of biofuels, solar and wind energy technologies, and industrial emissions-reducing technologies. During 2007 the group began investing in energy-related assets as part of this strategy. It acquired nearly 40% of Encore Energy Pte., which in turn owns 51% of Medco Energy, an Indonesian oil and gas concern. The deal was valued at about $350 million and gave Mitsubishi a 20% stake in Medco. Mitsubishi was already working with Medco on an Indonesian gas plant, and the two companies plan to pursue further international energy partnerships. In 2009 Mitsubishi entered the solar energy business, buying 34% of a subsidiary of Spanish renewable energy firm Acciona SA.

On the financial front Mitsubishi is leveraging the group's financial assets and sheer size to facilitate the financing of its own, as well as other companies', growth efforts. The group is targeting real estate development, aircraft and other industrial leasing services, and it is considering strategic acquisitions of additional financial services assets.

HISTORY

Yataro Iwasaki's close ties to the Japanese government (along with subsidies and monopoly rights) ensured the success of his shipping and trading company, Mitsubishi. Founded in 1870, Mitsubishi diversified into mining (1873), banking (1885), and shipbuilding (1887); it began to withdraw from shipping in the 1880s. During the next decade it invested in Japanese railroads and property.

In 1918 the Mitsubishi *zaibatsu* (conglomerate) spun off its central management arm, Mitsubishi Trading (the forerunner of Mitsubishi Corporation). By WWII the group was a huge amalgam of divisions and public companies. During the war it made warplanes, ships, explosives, and beer.

The *zaibatsu* were dissolved by US occupation forces, and Mitsubishi was split into 139 entities. After the occupation, the Japanese government encouraged many of the former business groups to reunite around the old *zaibatsu* banks. In 1954 Mitsubishi Trading became the leader of the Mitsubishi Group and established Mitsubishi International (US), which became a leading exporter of US goods.

The 1964 merger of three Mitsubishi companies created Mitsubishi Heavy Industries, a top Japanese maker of ships, aircraft, plants, and heavy machinery. Mitsubishi Kasei, separated from Asahi Glass and Mitsubishi Rayon by a US fiat, became Japan's #1 chemical concern. Mitsubishi Electric emerged as one of the country's leading electrical equipment and electronics manufacturers. In 1971 Chrysler invested in Mitsubishi Motors, which began making cars for the US automaker. That year Mitsubishi Trading was renamed Mitsubishi Corp.

Through the 1980s Japan seemed economically invincible. Then its "bubble economy" burst. The group fell behind in electronics and autos in the US, consumer demand dried up at home, and Mitsubishi Bank was left with a heavy burden of bad loans. Group members, which traditionally provided materials, supplies, and sales outlets for each other, began loosening old *keiretsu* ties during Japan's recession of the 1990s.

In 1993 Chrysler sold its stock in Mitsubishi Motors, and two years later the companies severed production ties. This loss and declining demand in the US for Mitsubishi cars hurt auto sales.

Mitsubishi Bank merged with Bank of Tokyo in 1996 to form the biggest bank in the world, The Bank of Tokyo-Mitsubishi (BTM). In 1997 several Mitsubishi companies admitted paying off a corporate racketeer, setting off a wave of executive resignations. By 1999 BTM had tumbled from the top spot and was unable to keep the money freely flowing to fellow Mitsubishi members.

Hit hard by the Asian economic crisis, all the struggling Mitsubishi companies had to look outside of the *keiretsu* for help. In 2000 DaimlerChrysler acquired a controlling stake in Mitsubishi Motors for $2.1 billion.

Executives at Mitsubishi Motors were charged in 2001 after they allegedly kept the lid on thousands of reported defects in Mitsubishi cars instead of issuing recalls.

In 2006 Mitsubishi bolstered its automotive operations when it acquired shares in Isuzu from General Motors; Mitsubishi ended up with a 10% stake in Isuzu. Mitsubishi and Isuzu soon after formed a European joint venture to market light-duty trucks throughout the continent.

The following year Mitsubishi bought majority control of Nosan Corporation, a manufacturer of livestock feed. In late 2007 the company acquired the majority interest in Kentucky Fried Chicken Japan.

On the medical health care front, Mitsubishi shifted the focus of certain of its subsidiaries to providing services to hospitals and nursing facilities. It established the Trinity Healthcare Fund in 2007 to provide management support for the restructuring of hospitals and other medical institutions.

EXECUTIVES

Chairman: Yorihiko Kojima
President, CEO, and Director: Ken Kobayashi
SEVP, CFO, and Director: Ryoichi Ueda
SEVP; Group CEO, Living Essentials Group, and Director: Masahide Yano
SEVP; Group CEO, Business Service Group, and Director: Hideyuki Nabeshima
SEVP, Food, Agricultural Resources and Consumer Market Strategies, Customer Relations Management, Regional Strategy (Japan), and Director: Takeshi Inoue, age 64
SEVP, Resources and Energy Strategies, and Director: Hisanori Yoshimura
EVP; Group CEO, Global Environment Business Development Group: Nobuaki Kojima
EVP; Group CEO, Chemicals Group: Takahisa Miyauchi
EVP; Group CEO, Energy Business Group: Seiji Kato
EVP; Group CEO, Metals Group: Jun Kinukawa
EVP; Group CEO, Machinery Group Regional Development: Hajime Katsumura
EVP; Group CEO, Machinery Group: Osamu Komiya
EVP; Group CEO, Industrial Finance, Logistics and Development Group: Hideshi Takeuchi
EVP Corporate Administration, Legal and Human Resources, and Director: Tsuneo Iyobe
EVP Global Strategy, Regional Development, and Director: Hideto Nakahara
EVP; Chief Regional Officer, North America: Seiei Ono
Auditors: Deloitte Touche Tohmatsu

LOCATIONS

HQ: Mitsubishi Corporation
(Mitsubishi Shoji Kabushiki Kaisha)
3-1, Marunouchi 2-chome, Chiyoda-ku
Tokyo 100-8086, Japan
Phone: 81-3-3210-2121   **Fax:** 81-3-3210-8583
US HQ: 655 3rd Ave., New York, NY 10017
US Phone: 212-605-2000   **US Fax:** 212-605-2486
Web: www.mitsubishicorp.com

2010 Sales

	% of total
Japan	75
Australia	8
Thailand	7
Other countries	10
Total	**100**

PRODUCTS/OPERATIONS

2010 Sales

	% of total
Living Essentials	33
Energy	21
Chemicals	16
Metals	15
Machinery	13
Industrial Finance, Logistics & Development	2
Total	**100**

Selected Products and Services

Living Essentials
  Apparel
  Canned foods
  Ceramic materials
  Cigarettes
  Coffee beans, coffee and beverages
  Confections and snacks
  Contract food services
  Dairy foods and processed foods
  Fabrics
  Feedstuffs
  Fresh and frozen foods
  Grains and agricultural products
  Marine products
  Meat and livestock
  Mineral water
  Oils and fats
  Photosensitized materials
  Pulp, paper, and packaging materials
  Soft drinks
  Sweeteners
  Textile raw materials
  Textiles for industrial use
  Tires
  Wood, wood products, and construction materials

Energy
  Carbon materials and products
  Crude oil
  LNG
  LPG
  Orimulsion
  Petroleum products

Chemicals
  Fertilizers
  Fine and specialty chemicals
  Inorganic chemicals
  Petrochemicals
  Plastics

Metals
  Bullion and metals futures
  Fabricated steel structures
  Metallurgical and thermal coal
  Nonferrous metal products
  Nonferrous metals
  Nuclear fuel and components
  Precious metals
  Raw materials for steel
  Semifinished products
  Steel materials
  Specialty steel

Machinery
  Automobiles
  Commercial aviation
  Defense systems and equipment
  Electronics products
  Industrial, agricultural, construction, and other
    general machinery
  Plant and machinery for power generation, electricity,
    oil/gas/chemicals, steel/cement, and environmental
    protection
  Project development and construction
  Satellite communications
  Ships
  Space systems
  Transportation systems
Industrial Finance, Logistics and Development
  Commerce services
  Consumer services
  Financial services
  Logistics
Business Innovation
  Human care
  Information technology services
  Telecommunications systems and services

COMPETITORS

ITOCHU
Marubeni
Mitsui
Samsung Group
Sime Darby
Sumitomo

HISTORICAL FINANCIALS

Company Type: Public

Income Statement

FYE: March 31

	REVENUE ($ mil.)	NET INCOME ($ mil.)	NET PROFIT MARGIN	EMPLOYEES
3/10	48,994	3,125	6.4%	58,723
3/09	63,179	2,507	4.0%	60,095
3/08	60,736	3,679	6.1%	60,664
3/07	43,156	3,529	8.2%	55,867
3/06	41,058	2,978	7.3%	53,738
Annual Growth	**4.5%**	**1.2%**	**—**	**2.2%**

2010 Year-End Financials

Debt ratio: 109.6%
Return on equity: 11.1%
Cash ($ mil.): 11,796
Current ratio: 1.47
Long-term debt ($ mil.): 35,018

No. of shares (mil.): 1,697
Dividends
  Yield: 1.5%
  Payout: 21.8%
Market value ($ mil.): 44,847

Stock History

Pink Sheets: MSBHY

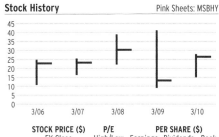

	STOCK PRICE ($) FY Close	P/E High/Low		PER SHARE ($) Earnings	Dividends	Book Value
3/10	26.43	15	9	1.79	0.39	18.83
3/09	13.21	18	4	2.31	0.16	14.44
3/08	30.31	14	8	2.80	—	17.05
3/07	23.20	12	8	2.08	—	14.75
3/06	22.80	14	6	1.75	—	11.93
Annual Growth	**3.8%**	**—**	**—**	**0.6%**	**143.8%**	**12.1%**

Mitsubishi UFJ Financial Group

Mitsubishi UFJ Financial Group (MUFG) is the largest banking group in Japan (surpassing Mizuho Financial and Sumitomo Mitsui Financial) and one of the largest in the world. The group provides retail banking, corporate banking, and trust services in more than 40 countries. Subsidiary The Bank of Tokyo-Mitsubishi UFJ operates about 700 branches across Japan and another 80 overseas. Mitsubishi UFJ Trust and Banking oversees some ¥28 trillion ($319 billion) in assets under management. Other holdings include investment bank Mitsubishi UFJ Securities and California-based Union Bank, which has more than 300 branches. MUFG was formed in the 2005 merger of Mitsubishi Tokyo Financial Group and UFJ Holdings.

The group also includes credit card company Mitsubishi UFJ NICOS and Mitsubishi UFJ Lease & Finance. MUFG has a modest goal — grow across all of its operating units. As customers shifted their focus from savings to investment, the company turned its sights towards growing customers' assets. The group also plans to grow its corporate investment banking and trust services both in Japan and throughout Asia.

In 2008 MUFG made headlines when it paid more than $9 billion for a 21% stake in Morgan Stanley, helping the investment bank avoid the fates of some of its peers. MUFG and Morgan Stanley combined their Japanese brokerage operations in 2010; to help fund that deal, MUFG announced a plan to raise more than $10 billion through a stock offering.

On a much smaller scale, Mitsubishi UFJ Trust and Banking has been expanding its reach by acquiring stakes in firms in other parts of the world. It became the first Japanese bank to acquire an interest in a Chinese asset manager when it bought out BNP Paribas Asset Management's 33% stake in a joint venture with Shenyin & Wanguo Securities. Mitsubishi UFJ Trust and Banking also bought a 10% stake in UK-based Aberdeen Asset Management.

As with most of its peers, MUFG was not immune to the global credit crisis that began in 2007. Its NICOS consumer lending subsidiary had a disappointing year due to the credit crunch. The unit sold its installment credit, car loan, and car leasing businesses to JACCS in 2008. In 2009 MUFG announced plans to close 50 branches and cut nearly 1,000 jobs as a part of a long-term restructuring plan. In addition, the bank planned to shut down some 200 ATMs and relocate another 1,000 employees.

MUFG is a member of the Mitsubishi group, a mélange of about 30 different companies — active in manufacturing, transportation, insurance, and other industries — that shared common ownership before World War II, but have been operated autonomously since.

HISTORY

Mitsubishi Bank emerged from the exchange office of the original Mitsubishi *zaibatsu* (industrial group) in 1885. It evolved into a full-service bank by 1895 and became independent in 1919, though its primary customers were Mitsubishi group companies. The bank survived WWII, but a US fiat dismantled the *zaibatsu* after the war.

Mitsubishi Bank reopened as Chiyoda Bank in 1948. After reopening offices in London and New York, the bank readopted the Mitsubishi name.

In the 1950s Mitsubishi Bank became the lead lender for the reconstituted Mitsubishi group (*keiretsu*). In the 1960s it followed its Mitsubishi partners overseas, helping finance Japan's growing international trade. In 1972 it acquired the Bank of California and began doing more business outside the group.

Japan's overinflated real estate market of the 1980s devastated many of the country's banks, including Nippon Trust Bank, of which Mitsubishi owned 5%. Japan's Ministry of Finance (MoF) urged Mitsubishi to bail Nippon out; as a reward for raising its stake in Nippon to 69% and assuming a mountain of unrecoverable loans, the MoF allowed Mitsubishi to begin issuing debt before other Japanese banks. In 1995 Mitsubishi Bank and Bank of Tokyo agreed to merge.

Bank of Tokyo (BOT) was established in 1880 as the Yokohama Specie Bank; the Iwasaki family, founders of the Mitsubishi group, served on its board. With links to the Imperial family, the bank was heavily influenced by government policy. With Japan isolated after the Sino-Japanese War, its international operations suffered greatly even before WWII. Completely dismantled after WWII, the bank was re-established in 1946 as the Bank of Tokyo, a commercial city bank bereft of its foreign exchange business. During the 1950s the government restored it as a foreign exchange specialist, but regulations limited its domestic business.

BOT evolved into an investment bank in the 1970s; its reputation as the leading foreign exchange bank brought in international clients and successful derivatives trading and overseas banking. By the time BOT and Mitsubishi Bank agreed to merge, BOT had 363 foreign offices (only 37 in Japan) with more foreign than Japanese employees.

The two banks merged in 1996 to form The Bank of Tokyo-Mitsubishi (BTM); Mitsubishi was the surviving entity. Their California banks merged to create Union Bank of California (UnionBanCal).

In 1998 Japanese banking regulators doled out nearly $240 billion to the industry to prop up failing banks and to strengthen healthier ones. Also that year BTM was fined for bribing MoF officials with entertainment gifts and posted a huge loss after writing off $8.4 billion in bad debt. Losses continued in 1999, and the bank responded by reorganizing operationally, cutting jobs and offices, and selling stock in UnionBanCal.

In 2000 BTM announced plans to form a financial group with Mitsubishi Trust Bank and Nippon Trust Bank. The following year the three banks unified and formed Mitsubishi Tokyo Financial Group. Before rolling into Mitsubishi Trust Financial Group, BTM paid back the money showered upon it by the Japanese government in 1998.

In 2005 Mitsubishi Tokyo Financial Group merged with UFJ Holdings, emerging (at that time) as the world's largest bank by assets. As a result of the merger, the group was renamed Mitsubishi UFJ Financial Group (MUFG).

The group spent the next few years taking advantage of its strength and size by increasing (or reacquiring) its stakes in various holdings. It bought the rest of UnionBanCal and Mitsubishi UFJ NICOS it didn't already own and acquired a stake in bulge-bracket firm Morgan Stanley.

EXECUTIVES

Chairman: Ryosuke Tamakoshi, age 63
President, CEO, and Director: Nobuo Kuroyanagi, age 68
Deputy President and Chief Compliance Officer: Kyota Omori, age 62
Deputy Chairman and Chief Audit Officer: Haruya Uehara, age 64
Senior Managing Director and CFO: Hiroshi Saito, age 59
Senior Managing Director and Chief Planning Officer: Nobushige Kamei, age 57
Senior Managing Director and Chief Risk Management Officer: Saburo Sano, age 61
Senior Managing Director: Toshihide Mizuno, age 60
President and CEO, Union Bank: Masashi Oka
CEO, HighMark Capital: Earle Malm
CEO Americas, Bank of Tokyo-Mitsubishi UFJ and Resident Managing Officer, Mitsubishi UFJ Financial Group: Masaaki (Masa) Tanaka, age 57
Auditors: Deloitte Touche Tohmatsu

LOCATIONS

HQ: Mitsubishi UFJ Financial Group, Inc.
4-5 Marunouchi 1-chome, Chiyoda-ku
Tokyo 100-8330, Japan
Phone: 81-3-3240-8111   **Fax:** 81-3-3240-8203
Web: www.mufg.jp

2010 Sales

	% of total
Asia/Oceania	
Japan	76
Other countries	7
Europe	12
US	4
Other regions	1
Total	**100**

PRODUCTS/OPERATIONS

2010 Sales

	% of total
Interest	
Loans, including fees	36
Investment securities	9
Trading account assets	6
Other	1
Noninterest	
Fees & commissions	22
Trading account profits	14
Other	12
Total	**100**

2010 Operating Profit

	% of total
Integrated Corporate Banking Business Group	
Domestic	26
Overseas	15
Global Markets	28
Integrated Retail Banking Business Group	27
Integrated Trust Assets Business Group	4
Total	**100**

COMPETITORS

Aozora Bank
BNP Paribas Bangkok
Chuo Mitsui Trust
Citigroup
HSBC
Ito-Yokado
Japan Post
Mizuho Financial
Mizuho Trust & Banking Ltd
ORIX
Resona
Shinsei Bank
Sony
Sumitomo Mitsui

HISTORICAL FINANCIALS

Company Type: Public

Income Statement

FYE: March 31

	ASSETS ($ mil.)	NET INCOME ($ mil.)	INCOME AS % OF ASSETS	EMPLOYEES
3/10	2,158,511	9,440	0.4%	115,300
3/09	1,988,981	(15,090)	—	122,100
3/08	1,911,928	(5,437)	—	78,300
3/07	1,583,253	4,943	0.3%	78,300
3/06	1,587,665	3,182	0.2%	80,000
Annual Growth	**8.0%**	**31.2%**	**—**	**9.6%**

2010 Year-End Financials

Equity as % of assets: 4.2%
Return on assets: 0.5%
Return on equity: 12.6%
Long-term debt ($ mil.): 152,784
No. of shares (mil.): 14,141
Dividends
  Yield: 0.0%
  Payout: —
Market value ($ mil.): 798
Sales ($ mil.): 56,231

Stock History

NYSE: MTU

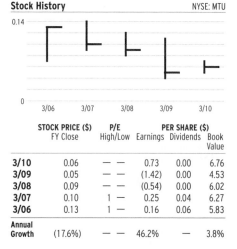

	STOCK PRICE ($) FY Close	P/E High/Low		PER SHARE ($) Earnings	Dividends	Book Value
3/10	0.06	—	—	0.73	0.00	6.76
3/09	0.05	—	—	(1.42)	0.00	4.53
3/08	0.09	—	—	(0.54)	0.00	6.02
3/07	0.10	1	—	0.25	0.04	6.27
3/06	0.13	1	—	0.16	0.06	5.83
Annual Growth	**(17.6%)**	**—**	**—**	**46.2%**	**—**	**3.8%**

Mitsui & Co.

Part of a network of companies that was founded by a samurai centuries ago, Mitsui & Co. now does battle in the marketplace. Mitsui & Co., a leading Japanese general trading firm, has more than 700 subsidiaries in a wide range of industries. The company has reorganized its business units into eight main classifications: chemicals, electronics and information, energy, foods, iron and steel, nonferrous metals, textiles, and machinery. Mitsui & Co. is part of Mitsui Group, one of Japan's largest *keiretsu* (companies loosely connected through cross-ownership).

Mitsui's energy sector, through its MOEX Offshore 2007 subsidiary, will likely see impairment losses on property, equipment, and mineral rights from its involvement with the massive oil rig fire and subsequent oil spill in the Gulf of Mexico during the summer of 2010. Though determining the exact cost of the incident and just who will pay for it may be at issue, Mitsui expects it may have some liability once the incident is sorted out.

Mitsui operates a joint venture with Posco, named Posco Terminal, which is responsible for the transportation, storage, and distribution of coal, iron ore, and ferroalloy. The company also owns a 15% stake in Valepar, a holding company that controls one-third of Brazilian iron ore producer Vale. (Vale is among the world's top three metals and minerals companies and attributes 5% of its production and reserves to Mitsui.) In Australia the company owns an almost-20% stake in Sims Metal Management, which also has significant North American operations.

To help pay down debt related to its purchase of Union Fenosa in 2009, Gas Natural sold power assets in Mexico to Mitsui and Tokyo Gas for $1.2 billion. Eyeing opportunities in the North American gas market, Mitsui in 2010 announced plans to invest $1.4 billion to develop a shale gas project in Pennsylvania with Anadarko Petroleum. It also teamed up with Penn West Energy Trust to form an $850-million natural-gas joint venture to develop an oil shale play in British Columbia.

Also in 2010 Mitsui teamed up with US fertilizer company Mosaic for a joint venture in a phosphorus ore development project in Peru. Mitsui will spend $275 million to acquire a 25% stake and voting rights in a subsidiary of Vale, while Mosaic will hold a 24% stake.

Mitsui entered the water infrastructure business in China in 2010 through a 50-50 joint venture with Singapore's Hyflux Ltd., a major provider of integrated water management services. Mitsui plans to do business with local governments and in areas with many industrial complexes by leveraging Hyflux's technological expertise and its own business network.

HISTORY

In the 17th century unemployed samurai (warrior nobleman) Sokubei Mitsui opened a sake and soy sauce brewery at the urging of his wife, Shuho. After parental encouragement, their youngest son, Hachirobei, went to Edo (now Tokyo) and opened a dry goods store in 1673. Breaking with Japanese retailing tradition, the store offered merchandise at fixed prices on a cash-and-carry basis.

Hachirobei in 1683 opened a currency exchange that evolved into Mitsui Bank. The bank became the Osaka government's official money changer in 1691 and was the first bank to offer money orders in Japan. Before his death in 1694, Hachirobei drafted a unique succession plan to hand down control of the company to every related family, not just the eldest son's side.

The shogun's government called upon Mitsui in the mid-1800s to help finance its war against rebels. The family hired Rizaemon Minomura, an outsider with influence in the government, to protect the company from increasing demands for money. Mitsui became the bank of the Meiji government after Minomura astutely switched support to the winning rebels. Government industrialization pushed Mitsui into textiles, paper goods, and machinery. Minomura emphasized foreign trade and banking, creating Mitsui Bussan (now Mitsui & Co.) and Mitsui Bank in 1876. In the late 1800s Mitsui Bussan profited from a Japanese military buildup, formed a shipping line to take on Mitsubishi's monopoly, and bought coal mines. The Mitsui family withdrew from Mitsui Bussan management in 1936, following attacks by right-wing terrorists who opposed its democratic leanings.

Mitsui prospered during the 1930s as Japan's military prepared for war. After the defeat, occupation forces disbanded Japan's *zaibatsu* industrial groups, slicing Mitsui into more than 200 separate entities. By 1950 more than two dozen leaders of the former Mitsui companies began gathering the Mitsui Group back together. Trading firm Mitsui & Co. was established in 1959. The oil crises of the 1970s stalled the oil-dependent Japanese economy, prompting Mitsui companies to expand operations overseas and move into industries such as technology and aluminum.

The mammoth Sakura Bank was formed in 1990 with the merger of Mitsui Bank and Taiyo Kobe Bank. Other major ventures were to follow: In 1992 Mitsui & Co. joined with Marathon and Royal Dutch Shell and others to search for oil and gas off Russia's Sakhalin Island; and Mitsui & Co. and other Japanese traders were enlisted by Oman in 1993 for a $9 billion liquefied natural gas transport venture.

In anticipation of deregulation in Japan's financial markets, four Mitsui Group firms' pension funds — Sakura Bank, Mitsui Marine & Fire Insurance, Mitsui Mutual Life Insurance, and Mitsui Trust and Banking — were linked in 1998. The next year Sakura Bank set aside old loyalties and agreed to merge with Sumitomo Bank, the Sumitomo *keiretsu's* main bank; the deal closed in 2001. The group's Mitsui Trust and Banking merged with Chuo Trust and Banking to form Chuo Mitsui Trust and Banking, part of Mitsui Trust Holdings.

Mitsui & Co. was implicated in bid-rigging and bribery scandals in 2002, and the company's chairman and CEO resigned. In 2003 the company moved into the German pesticide market by acquiring an 80% stake in Spiess-Urania Chemical, a subsidiary of Norddeutsche Affinerie.

In 2003 Mitsui acquired a 15% stake in Valepar, a holding company of Brazilian-based iron ore producer Companhia Vale do Rio Doce. Mitsui and International Power completed the acquisition of the 1,200 MW gas-fired Saltend Power plant in the UK from Calpine Corporation. In 2005 Mitsui acquired a stake in Gás Participações (Gaspart), a Brazil-based gas distribution company.

EXECUTIVES

Chairman: Shoei Utsuda, age 67
President, CEO, and Representative Director: Masami Iijima, age 60
EVP, CFO, Chief Compliance Officer, and Representative Director: Junichi Matsumoto, age 63
EVP; COO, Asia/Pacific Business Unit: Toshimasa Furukawa, age 61
Representative Director and Senior Executive Managing Officer: Takao Omae, age 60
Representative Director and Senior Executive Managing Officer; Director, Mitsui & Co. (Asia Pacific) Pte. Ltd: Norinao Iio, age 59
Representative Director and EVP; Director, Mitsui & Co., U.S.A.: Ken Abe, age 62
Representative Director and EVP; Director, Mitsui & Co. Europe Holdings PLC: Yoshiyuki Izawa, age 62
Senior Executive Managing Officer, CIO, Chief Privacy Officer, and Representative Director: Seiichi Tanaka, age 57
Senior Executive Managing Officer; COO, Americas Business Unit; President and CEO, Mitsui USA: Masaaki Fujita
Senior Executive Managing Officer; COO, Americas Business Unit: Koji Nakamura, age 62

Managing Officer; COO, IT Business Unit: Shuji Nakura
Managing Officer; COO, Foods and Retail Business Unit: Takashi Yamauchi
Managing Officer; COO, Foods & Retail Business Unit: Takashi Fukunaga
Managing Officer; COO, Financial Markets Business Unit: Mitsuhiko Kawai
Managing Officer; COO, Marine and Aerospace Business Unit: Masayoshi Komai
Managing Officer; COO, Mineral and Metal Resources Business Unit: Masayuki Kinoshita
Managing Officer; General Manager, Human Resources and General Affairs Division: Daisuke Saiga
Auditors: Deloitte Touche Tohmatsu

LOCATIONS

HQ: Mitsui & Co., Ltd.
(Mitsui Bussan Kabushiki Kaisha)
2-1, Ohtemachi 1-chome, Chiyoda-ku
Tokyo 100-0004, Japan
Phone: 81-3-3285-1111   **Fax:** 81-3-3285-9819
US HQ: 200 Park Ave., New York, NY 10166
US Phone: 212-878-4000   **US Fax:** 212-878-4800
Web: www.mitsui.co.jp

PRODUCTS/OPERATIONS

2010 Sales

	% of total
Energy	47
Minerals & metals	34
Machinery & infrastructure	10
Iron & steel	6
Chemical	2
Other	1
Total	**100**

COMPETITORS

ITOCHU
Kanematsu
Komatsu
Marubeni
Mitsubishi Corp.
Samsung Group
Sojitz
Sumitomo

HISTORICAL FINANCIALS

Company Type: Public

Income Statement

FYE: March 31

	REVENUE ($ mil.)	NET INCOME ($ mil.)	NET PROFIT MARGIN	EMPLOYEES
3/10	44,192	1,807	4.1%	41,454
3/09	56,897	1,826	3.2%	39,864
3/08	57,528	4,111	7.1%	42,621
3/07	41,435	2,560	6.2%	41,761
3/06	35,302	1,736	4.9%	40,993
Annual Growth	**5.8%**	**1.0%**	**—**	**0.3%**

2010 Year-End Financials

Debt ratio: 130.5%   No. of shares (mil.): 91
Return on equity: 8.3%   Dividends
Cash ($ mil.): 15,275   Yield: 0.0%
Current ratio: 1.79   Payout: —
Long-term debt ($ mil.): 31,391   Market value ($ mil.): 330

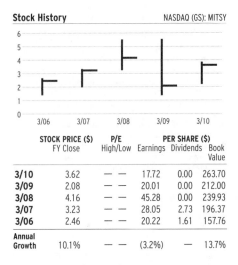

	STOCK PRICE ($) FY Close	P/E High/Low	PER SHARE ($) Earnings	Dividends	Book Value
3/10	3.62	— —	17.72	0.00	263.70
3/09	2.08	— —	20.01	0.00	212.00
3/08	4.16	— —	45.28	0.00	239.93
3/07	3.23	— —	28.05	2.73	196.37
3/06	2.46	— —	20.22	1.61	157.76
Annual Growth	10.1%	— —	(3.2%)	—	13.7%

Mizuho Financial

Mizuho means "golden ears of rice" in Japanese, but in the banking world it means the first bank with a trillion dollars in assets. Since surpassed by the likes of HSBC and Citigroup, Mizuho Financial Group is the parent of Mizuho Bank (retail banking), Mizuho Corporate Bank (commercial financial services), Mizuho Securities (investment and brokerage services), and Mizuho Trust & Banking. All told, the company has approximately 800 branches, sub-branches, and agencies in Japan and elsewhere. Mizuho Financial Group was formed in 1999 by the merger of The Dai-Ichi Kangyo Bank, Fuji Bank, and Industrial Bank of Japan (IBJ).

Mizuho is structured into three primary business segments. Its global corporate group provides securities and investment services to large companies around the world; it is expanding these operations internationally, in part through alliances. Mizuho's global retail group provides retail banking, mortgages, and other services to individuals and small to midsized companies. Finally, the global asset and wealth management division provides trust and investment services to wealthy individuals and other investors.

To build its brokerage business, Mizuho in 2009 merged its Mizuho Securities and Shinko Securities units to more effectively compete with the larger Nomura Holdings and Daiwa Securities. The combined company is seeking to expand in Asia as well as grow its overseas revenues by opening branches in South Korea, Vietnam, and Taiwan.

HISTORY

Of the three banks that combined to form Mizuho Holdings, Industrial Bank of Japan (IBJ) is the youngest, founded in 1902. Fuji Bank started in 1880, and Dai-Ichi Kangyo's roots reach back to 1872.

By the late 1990s Japanese banks faced the challenges of a fossilized banking system, chained together by the *keiretsu* cross-shareholding system that hindered companies' agility in the marketplace. Other economic stresses included the Asian financial crisis, which left banks holding thousands of bad loans. In 1997 the Big Bang of banking reform was supposed to free lending institutions to restructure for greater competition, with presumably sounder business models. The industry's reliance on government-sponsored bailouts underscored the need for change.

IBJ, Dai-Ichi Kangyo Bank, and Fuji Bank (none of them excessively chummy within their respective *keiretsu*) saw an opportunity to consolidate, strengthen their business through combined forces, and streamline their operations by closing redundant branches, agencies, and divisions.

Mizuho Holdings was formed in 1999 and placed atop the three banks as their new parent company. While Mizuho's $1.3 trillion in assets made it the largest bank in the world at the time, its copious debts weren't to be ignored either (though the bank waived the nearly $1 billion in debt of troubled retailer Sogo in 2001).

Also in 2001 other Japanese banks followed the lead of IBJ, Dai-Ichi Kangyo, and Fuji by joining with peers in the quest for size. Sumitomo Bank and Sakura Bank merged to form Sumitomo Mitsui Financial Group; and Sanwa Bank, Tokai Bank, and Toyo Trust and Banking combined to create UFJ Holdings.

Initially, the CEOs of the three banks that comprised Mizuho were tapped as co-CEOs of the company, but they resigned in 2002 after the banks' consolidation was marred by PR gaffes and computer glitches that caused customers to be double-billed, created a logjam of money transfers, and crashed thousands of ATMs. Terunobu Maeda was named the sole CEO of Mizuho later that year.

The company aggressively expanded in 2006 and 2007. During that period it opened offices on almost every continent, expanding its empire from Brazil to Russia, and China to Belgium. It achieved financial holding company status in the US in 2006, which allows it to engage in investment banking operations there.

Mizuho Asset Management, the result of the merger of Dai-ichi Kangyo Asset Management and Fuji Investment Management, debuted in 2007.

Also in 2007, at likely the worst possible time, the corporate bank created a division to invest in alternative investments such as collateralized debt obligations. Shortly afterward, the subprime market crashed, devaluing these risky investments.

EXECUTIVES

Chairman, President, CEO, and Head Human Resources: Takashi Tsukamoto, age 60
Managing Executive Officer, Credit Department, Mizuho Bank: Makio Tanehashi
Managing Director and Managing Executive Officer, Information and Technology and System Group, Operations Group, Customer Satisfaction Group, Mizuho Bank: Tadayuki Hagiwara
Managing Executive Officer, Head Strategic Planning, Information Technology Systems and Operations, Chief Strategy Officer, CIO, and General Manager, Group Strategic Planning: Daisaku Abe, age 53
Managing Executive Officer, Credit Department, Mizuho Bank: Kimiharu Mayama
Managing Executive Officer, Business Coordination and Development Group, Mizuho Bank: Masahiko Furutani
Managing Executive Officer, Strategic Planning Group, and Information and Technology and System Group, Mizuho Bank: Masatoshi Yano
Managing Executive Officer, Head Risk Management and Compliance, Chief Risk Officer, Chief Compliance Officer, and Director: Takeo Nakano, age 54
Managing Executive Officer, Head Internal Audit, and Chief Auditor: Hajime Saito

Managing Executive Officer and General Manager, Consulting Division, Mizuho Bank: Kouji Kawakubo
Managing Executive Officer, Personal Banking Group, Mizuho Bank: Toshitsugu Okabe
Managing Executive Officer, Trading and ALM Group, Mizuho Bank: Junichi Kato
Director; President and CEO, Mizuho Bank: Satoru Nishibori, age 57
Director; President and CEO, Mizuho Corporate Bank: Yasuhiro Sato, age 58
Chairman, Mizuho Corporate Bank: Hiroshi Saito, age 66
Chairman, Mizuho Bank: Seiji Sugiyama, age 63
Auditors: Ernst & Young ShinNihon

LOCATIONS

HQ: Mizuho Financial Group, Inc.
  5-1, Marunouchi 2-chome, Chiyoda-ku
  Tokyo 100-0004, Japan
Phone: 81-3-5224-1111   **Fax:** 81-3-5224-1059
US HQ: 1251 Avenue of the Americas
  New York, NY 10020
US Phone: 212-282-3000
Web: www.mizuho-fg.co.jp

PRODUCTS/OPERATIONS

Selected Subsidiaries

Mizuho Bank, Ltd.
Mizuho Corporate Bank (China), Ltd.
Mizuho Corporate Bank, Ltd.
Mizuho Factors, Limited
Mizuho Investors Securities Co., Ltd. (67%)
Mizuho Securities Co., Ltd. (90%)
Mizuho Trust & Banking Co., Ltd. (75%)
Mizuho Trust & Banking Co. (USA)

COMPETITORS

Bank of China
Bank of Yokohama
Barclays
BNP Paribas Bangkok
Chiba Bank
Chuo Mitsui Trust
Citigroup
Deutsche Bank
HSBC
Mitsubishi UFJ Financial Group
Resona
Shinsei Bank
Shizuoka Bank
Sumitomo Mitsui
UBS

HISTORICAL FINANCIALS

Company Type: Public

Income Statement

	ASSETS ($ mil.)	NET INCOME ($ mil.)	INCOME AS % OF ASSETS	EMPLOYEES
				FYE: March 31
3/10	1,708,296	10,785	0.6%	57,014
3/09	1,594,099	(10,880)	—	69,179
3/08	1,516,835	2,292	0.2%	49,114
3/07	1,253,159	5,305	0.4%	47,449
3/06	1,240,692	9,256	0.7%	45,758
Annual Growth	8.3%	3.9%	—	5.7%

2010 Year-End Financials

Equity as % of assets: 1.5%   Dividends
Return on assets: 0.7%   Yield: —
Return on equity: 85.7%   Payout: —
Long-term debt ($ mil.): 107,883 Market value ($ mil.): 458
No. of shares (mil.): 10,767   Sales ($ mil.): 31,966

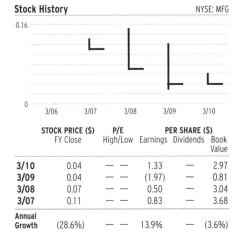

	STOCK PRICE ($) FY Close	P/E High/Low	PER SHARE ($) Earnings	Dividends	Book Value
3/10	0.04	— —	1.33	—	2.97
3/09	0.04	— —	(1.97)	—	0.81
3/08	0.07	— —	0.50	—	3.04
3/07	0.11	— —	0.83	—	3.68
Annual Growth	(28.6%)	— —	13.9%	—	(3.6%)

MOL Magyar Olaj-és Gázipari

The downstream operations of MOL Magyar Olaj-és Gázipari Rt. (Hungarian Oil and Gas Company, or MOL) have moved it up to become Hungary's biggest company and one of Central Europe's top refiners. MOL's refineries produce 90,400 barrels of oil equivalent per day, and it operates 1,000 gas stations in Croatia, the Czech Republic, Hungary, Italy, Poland, Romania, Slovakia, Slovenia, and the Ukraine. It plans to have 1,500 gas stations by 2010. Other activities include exploration and production in Hungary, Russia, and other areas of Central and Eastern Europe. In 2007 the company had proved and probable reserves of 434.2 million barrels of oil equivalent.

In addition to expanding its refining and marketing operations across Central Europe, the company has restructured its exploration and production activities to focus on the development of oil fields in Russia.

In 2007 MOL acquired two refining and marketing companies — IES in Italy and Tifon in Croatia. Also that year MOL announced plans to merge with Austria's OMV, though those plans were abandoned the next year due to regulatory concerns from the European Commission. In 2009 OMV sold its 21% stake in MOL to Russian oil company Surgutneftegas. Eyeing new areas of exploration, that year MOL also acquired a 10% stake in Pearl Petroleum, giving it access to gas-condensate fields in Iraq.

HISTORY

The oil refining industry in Hungary dates to the 1880s, when refineries were opened in Fiume (1882) and Budapest (1883). By 1913 Hungary had 28 plants.

Following Hungary's defeat in WWI, the country's refining industry fell into decline, as new national boundaries placed most of its former oil refineries and oil-producing regions outside its borders. By 1921 Hungary had only six operational refineries.

British and American investors set up the European Gas and Electric Company (EUROGASCO) in the US in 1931 to acquire oil and gas concessions in Central Europe and to build power plants. By 1937 EUROGASCO (controlled by Standard Oil of New Jersey) was producing oil. A year later Standard Oil set up the Hungarian-American Oil Industry Shareholding Co. (MAORT) to develop the fields, and in 1940 MAORT's production was meeting all of Hungary's oil needs.

During WWII, MAORT requisitioned all oil assets. The oil industry boomed as Hungary served as a major supplier for the German war machine. But by 1944, with German armies in retreat from the Eastern Front, much of Hungary's oil machinery and plants were dismantled. The remaining plants suffered heavy bombing from Allied forces or had equipment confiscated by Russian and Romanian troops.

After the war the Hungarian Soviet Crude Oil Co. began rebuilding Hungary's oil industry and started drilling on the Great Hungarian Plain in 1946. MAORT also ramped up oil production in the Trans-Danubian fields. In 1949, following charges of sabotage against MAORT managers, MAORT was nationalized and broken up into five national companies, which re-merged in 1952 with Hungarian Soviet Oil Co. (successor to Hungarian Soviet Crude Oil Co.).

In 1957 all operations of the Hungarian crude oil industry were consolidated under Crude Oil Trust, which took over the gas industry by 1960. That year the company was renamed National Crude Oil and Gas Trust (OKGT), and the focus of exploration soon shifted from Trans-Danubian fields to the Great Plain. By 1970 the Great Plain accounted for 67% of oil production and 96% of natural gas production.

Hungary began allowing foreign gasoline distributors to compete in domestic markets during the 1980s. Moving toward privatization, the Hungarian government founded MOL in 1991 as the successor to OKGT, which comprised nine oil and gas enterprises. In 1993 the socialist government sold 8% of MOL to the public. By 1998 the government had sold all but 25% of MOL.

During the 1990s the company also expanded in Central Europe. With Austria's OMV in 1994 it began building a 120-km pipeline linking Austria and Hungary, which gave it access to natural gas from Western Europe for the first time. MOL also opened up service stations in neighboring countries, beginning with one in Romania in 1996. By 2000 the company was operating about 80 stations in Romania, 18 in Slovakia, three in Ukraine, and two in Slovenia, in addition to its 330 stations in Hungary. MOL also acquired about 20% of chemical processor TVK in 1999 and upped the stake to nearly 33% by 2000. That year MOL also acquired 36% of Slovnaft, Slovakia's only oil refiner and its major retailer.

In 2003 MOL concluded a long-term crude oil supply agreement with Russian oil giant YUKOS.

The company agreed in 2004 to sell its gas businesses to E.ON Ruhrgas for about $1 billion. (After much scrutiny by Hungarian and EU regulators, the deal was completed in 2006.)

In 2005 MOL acquired the Romanian subsidiary of Royal Dutch Shell, including the purchase of 59 Shell filling stations. Royal Dutch Shell also sold MOL its Romania-based lubricants, aviation, and commercial businesses.

EXECUTIVES

Chairman and CEO: Zsolt Hernádi, age 48
Vice Chairman: Sándor Csányi, age 55
Group CEO and Director; Chairman, TVK: György Mosonyi, age 61
CFO and Director: József Molnár, age 54
Corporate Counsel: Pál Kara, age 38
EVP Corporate Centre: József Simola, age 42
EVP Refining and Marketing Division: Ferenc Horváth, age 47
EVP Exploration and Production; President, INA: Zoltán Áldott, age 42
EVP Retail: László Piry, age 43
EVP Strategy and Business Development: Lajos Alács, age 47
SVP Petrochemicals; CEO, TVK: Árpád Olvasó, age 51
Managing Director, Lubes Division: Ferenc Dénes, age 57
Managing Director, Natural Gas Transmission Division: János Zsuga
Managing Director, Health, Safety and Environmental Protection Division: Bela Cseh
Communications Director: Dora Somlyai, age 37
Director Investor Relations: Richárd Benke
Auditors: Ernst & Young Kft

LOCATIONS

HQ: MOL Magyar Olaj-és Gázipari Nyrt.
Október huszonharmadika u.18
H-1117 Budapest, Hungary
Phone: 36-1-464-1395   **Fax:** 36-1-464-1335
Web: www.mol.hu

PRODUCTS/OPERATIONS

2009 Sales

	% of total
Refining & marketing	74
Petrochemicals	9
Exploration & production	9
Gas & power	7
Other	1
Total	**100**

COMPETITORS

BG Group	OMV
BP	PKN ORLEN
CEPSA	Repsol YPF
Eni	Royal Dutch Shell
Hellenic Petroleum	TOTAL
Norsk Hydro ASA	

HISTORICAL FINANCIALS

Company Type: Public

Income Statement				FYE: December 31
	REVENUE ($ mil.)	NET INCOME ($ mil.)	NET PROFIT MARGIN	EMPLOYEES
12/09	16,959	550	3.2%	34,090
12/08	18,665	746	4.0%	17,213
12/07	15,001	1,518	10.1%	15,058
12/06	15,158	1,770	11.7%	13,861
12/05	11,505	1,162	10.1%	14,660
Annual Growth	10.2%	(17.1%)	—	23.5%

Net Income History
Budapest: MOL

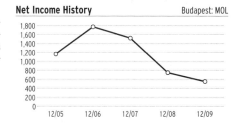

Munich Re Group

Some companies live with risk . . . Münchener Rückversicherungs-Gesellschaft (Munich Re), on the other hand, *thrives* on risk. Reinsurance coverage (insurance for insurers) includes fire, life, motor, and liability policies on both a facultative (individual risk) and treaty (categorized risk) basis. The company also provides direct insurance including life, health, and property coverage through Germany-based ERGO and other subsidiaries, and it provides asset management services through MEAG Munich ERGO. Through Munich Re America, Munich Re enjoys greater access to the US market. As one of the world's largest reinsurance and risk management firms, the company operates in some 160 countries.

Europe is Munich Re's biggest market and the company is expanding through acquisitions there, including purchases in the UK and Austrian markets. Though reinsurance is its largest operating segment, the company hopes to continue the growth of its traditional insurance segment in the core German market and other European markets, focusing on personal lines. In addition, the company is pursuing growth in Asian insurance markets.

Munich Re has also been realigning its US operations to boost its property/casualty insurance operations in that market. To further this strategy, in 2008 the company acquired US specialty property/casualty insurance provider The Midland Company for $1.3 billion; Midland's American Modern Insurance Group subsidiaries became part of the Munich Re America organization. Munich Re also bought Aon subsidiary Sterling Life Insurance for $352 million to expand its life and health insurance provisions in the US; Sterling Life was placed within the Munich Re America HealthCare division.

In 2009 Munich Re purchased HSB Group and its Hartford Steam Boiler Inspection and Insurance subsidiary, which is a specialty underwriter that provides reinsurance and insurance policies on steam boilers and mechanical and electrical equipment, from American International Group for $739 million. The acquisition expanded Munich Re's niche insurance and risk management offerings in North America.

Billionaire investment mogul Warren Buffet, who controls a number of insurance and reinsurance players through Berkshire Hathaway, has taken notice of Munich Re's successes. Buffet increased his stake in the company to 10% in 2010, but the activist investor has not indicated an intent to taking further control of the firm.

HISTORY

Investors Carl Thieme and Theodor Cramer-Klett founded Munich Re in 1880. Within a month Munich Re opened offices in Hamburg, Berlin, Vienna, and St. Petersburg, establishing treaties with German and Danish insurers. In 1888 Munich Re went public; two years later, it opened an office in London and helped finance the creation of Allianz, which would soon come to dominate the German insurance industry. In 1892 the firm opened a branch in the US (it incurred severe losses from the 1906 San Francisco earthquake).

WWI interrupted Munich Re's UK and US operations. The company recovered after 1918, only to be hobbled again by the Great Depression. In 1933 Munich Re executive Kurt Schmitt became minister of economic affairs for the Nazis. Objecting to the evolving policies of National Socialism, he left after a year, returning to Munich Re, where he became chief executive in 1938.

Hitler's ignition of WWII wasn't quite the boom Munich Re needed; its international business was again disrupted. After the war, the Allies further limited overseas operations. Because of his involvement with the Nazi government, Schmitt was replaced by Eberhard von Reininghaus in 1945. The division of Germany further hampered the company's recovery.

Jump-started by the Marshall Plan in 1950, the West German *Wirtschaftswunder* (economic miracle) kicked into high gear, as the devastated country rebuilt. Relaxation of occupation-era trading limits also helped as the company rebuilt its foreign business. By 1969, Munich Re's sales topped DM 2 billion. Amid the global oil crisis and a rash of terrorist acts in Germany, the firm reported its first-ever reinsurance loss in 1977.

German reunification in 1990 provided new markets for Munich Re, but advantages from new business in the East were wiped out by claims arising from that year's harsh winter.

In 1992 an investigation by the German Federal Cartel Office prompted a realignment in the insurance business — Allianz ceded its controlling interests in three life insurers (Hamburg-Mannheimer Versicherungs, Karlsruher Lebensversicherung, and Berlinische Lebensversicherung) to Munich Re, bringing it into direct insurance. Munich Re took over Deutsche Krankenversicherung (DKV) in 1996. Also that year Munich Re acquired American Re.

During the 1990s reinsurance sales dwindled as competition increased — forcing lower premiums — and alternatives to insurance and reinsurance became more common. Munich Re looked to direct insurance, particularly individual property/casualty and life insurance, to compensate. In 1997 it merged Hamburg-Mannheimer and DKV with another insurer, Victoria AG, to form ERGO Versicherungsgruppe. Within a year, ERGO's insurance income accounted for half of all revenues.

Munich Re and ERGO launched asset management firm MEAG Munich ERGO Asset-Management in 1999. That year Munich Re experienced its worst year ever after natural disasters hit its reinsurance business hard. To recoup its losses, the firm expanded both its reinsurance and primary insurance operations in Europe, North and South America, and Asia. Also in 2000, Munich Re bought CNA Financial's life reinsurance operations.

As one of the companies hit hardest financially by the World Trade Center tragedy, Munich Re paid out some $2 billion in claims. In 2003 Allianz and Munich Re terminated their cooperation agreement, as their shareholdings in each other fell to under 15%. (The two companies gradually sold off nearly all of their ownership interests in following years.)

In 2005 Munich Re took a nearly 75% hit on its profit margin due to re-investment in its American Re subsidiary, whose internal reserves required a $1.6 billion injection for expected claims

related to asbestos and environmental claims on policies mostly written between 1997 and 2002.

The company expanded in the European market in 2007 when it bought British underwriting management group Bell & Clements Group in an effort to bolster its bottom line with profit-making basic services. It also purchased MSP Underwriting, UK parent of Lloyd's Syndicate 318 manager Beaufort Underwriting Agency.

EXECUTIVES

Chairman, Supervisory Board: Hans-Jürgen Schinzler, age 70
Deputy Chairman, Supervisory Board: Hans-Peter Claußen
Chairman, Board of Management: Nikolaus von Bomhard, age 54, $4,664,731 total compensation
Member Board of Management Board, Chairman, Reinsurance Committee: Torsten Jeworrek, age 49, $3,209,263 total compensation
Member Board of Management, Life: Joachim Wenning, age 45, $1,270,672 total compensation
Member Board of Management, Europe and Latin America: Georg Daschner, age 61, $3,037,940 total compensation
Member Board of Management, Group Controlling, Corporate Finance Mergers and Acquisitions, Integrated Risk Management, Group Legal, Compliance, Group Taxation, and Investor and Rating Agency Relations: Jörg Schneider, age 52, $3,330,275 total compensation
Member Board of Management, Services, Germany, Asia/Pacific, and Africa: Ludger Arnoldussen, age 48, $2,152,571 total compensation
Member Board of Management, Health and Human Resources and Labor Relations Director: Wolfgang Strassl, age 53, $2,128,026 total compensation
Member Board of Management, Special and Financial Risks, Reinsurance Investments, and Central Procurement: Thomas Blunck, $2,251,205 total compensation
Member Board of Management, Global Clients and North America: Peter Röder, age 50, $1,996,848 total compensation
Head Group Communications: Christian Lawrence
Auditors: KPMG Bayerische Treuhandgesellschaft AG

LOCATIONS

HQ: Münchener Rückversicherungs-Gesellschaft Aktiengesellschaft
Königinstrasse 107
D-80802 Munich, Germany
Phone: 49-89-38-91-0   **Fax:** 49-89-38-91-98-88
US HQ: 555 College Rd. East, Princeton, NJ 08543
US Phone: 609-243-4200   **US Fax:** 609-243-8181
Web: www.munichre.com

2009 Written Premiums

	% of total
Europe	64
North America	25
Asia & Australasia	7
Latin America	2
Africa, Near & Middle East	2
Total	**100**

PRODUCTS/OPERATIONS

2009 Sales

	% of total
Reinsurance	
Property/casualty	62
Life & health	24
Insurance	13
Asset management	1
Total	**100**

Selected Subsidiaries

Reinsurance
  Great Lakes Reinsurance (UK) Plc
  The Midland Company (US, includes specialty
    insurance)
  Munich American Reassurance Company (US)
  Munich Reinsurance America, Inc. (US)
    American Modern Insurance Group
    HSB Group, Inc. (includes specialty insurance)
    Munich Re America HealthCare (includes health
      insurance)
  Munich Reinsurance Company of Africa Ltd (South
    Africa)
  Munich Reinsurance Company of Australasia Ltd
    (Australia)
  Munich Reinsurance Company of Canada
  Munich Re Underwriting (UK, Watkins Syndicate)
  New Reinsurance Company (Switzerland)
  Temple Insurance Company (Canada)
Direct insurance
  Bank Austria Creditanstalt Versicherung AG
  Deutsche Krankenversicherung (DKV)
  Deutscher Automobil Schultz
  ERGO Versicherungsgruppe AG
Asset management
  MEAG MUNICH ERGO AssetManagement GmbH

COMPETITORS

ACE Limited
AEGON
AIG
Allianz
Allstate
AXA
Bâloise-Holding
Berkshire Hathaway
Everest Re
General Re
Hannover Re
Helvetia Group
ING
Manulife Financial
MetLife
Nippon Life Insurance
OdysseyRe
PartnerRe
Prudential plc
Reinsurance Group of America
RenaissanceRe
Swiss Re
Transamerica Reinsurance
Transatlantic Holdings
XL Group plc

HISTORICAL FINANCIALS

Company Type: Public

Income Statement

FYE: December 31

	ASSETS ($ mil.)	NET INCOME ($ mil.)	INCOME AS % OF ASSETS	EMPLOYEES
12/09	320,194	3,675	1.1%	47,249
12/08	303,630	2,154	0.7%	44,209
12/07	315,359	5,795	1.8%	38,634
12/06	284,803	4,665	1.6%	37,210
12/05	258,934	3,249	1.3%	37,953
Annual Growth	5.5%	3.1%	—	5.6%

2009 Year-End Financials

Equity as % of assets: —
Return on assets: 1.2%
Return on equity: —
Long-term debt ($ mil.): —
No. of shares (mil.): 188

Dividends
  Yield: 5.1%
  Payout: 42.5%
Market value ($ mil.): 29,353
Sales ($ mil.): 85,394

Stock History

German: MUV2

	STOCK PRICE ($) FY Close	P/E High/Low		PER SHARE ($) Earnings	Dividends	Book Value
12/09	155.75	9	6	18.56	7.88	169.41
12/08	156.45	18	10	10.54	—	156.80
12/07	195.67	8	6	26.35	—	194.91
12/06	172.06	9	6	19.95	—	181.62
12/05	135.46	10	7	13.86	—	154.91
Annual Growth	3.6%	—	—	7.6%	—	2.3%

National Australia Bank

National Australia Bank (NAB) is one of Australia's Big Four banks (along with ANZ, Westpac, and Commonwealth Bank of Australia). It operates in Australia, New Zealand, Asia, the UK, and the US through subsidiaries that provide banking, wealth management, and investment banking services. NAB has more than 800 branches in Australia and (through Bank of New Zealand) another 200 in New Zealand. Subsidiaries Clydesdale Bank and Yorkshire Bank operate some 350 offices in the UK. NAB offers debt, risk management, and investment products for institutional clients. To establish a foothold in the US, NAB acquired Great Western Bancorporation for $A836 million ($798 million) in 2008.

One of Australia's largest agricultural lenders, NAB cushioned itself against losses from a widespread drought in 2006 and 2007 by its diversification abroad. The Great Western purchase, which added branches in five midwestern states and Arizona, fit in with this strategy while adding to its agribusiness portfolio. In 2008 the group established a formal agreement of cooperation with the state-owned Agricultural Development Bank of China; through the agreement, the companies will explore possible business and training opportunities.

The company has made other expansion moves in Asia. It took a 20% stake in Chinese property trust Union Trust and Investment in 2008. The deal made NAB the first foreign bank to buy into a Chinese trust firm. In 2009 NAB expanded its asset management business in Asia when it acquired Hong Kong-based Calibre Asset Management.

In 2009 NAB built up its offerings for high-networth customers. It bought the Australian life and pensions business of British insurance giant Aviva for $A825 million ($650 million), increasing its position in the life insurance market. It also agreed to acquire a majority stake in Goldman Sachs' Australia and New Zealand wealth management operations. Goldman Sachs will retain ownership of about 20% of the unit, which operates under the JBWere brand.

Also in 2009 NAB entered a bid for AXA Asia Pacific. The move upstaged a bid from rival AMP. NAB seemed to have won the bidding war when it reached a $A13 billion ($12 billion) deal with AXA in 2010, but regulators blocked the offer and NAB subsequently scrapped its bid.

With roots going back to the 1830s, subsidiary Clydesdale Bank is one of Scotland's largest banks and the third-largest clearing bank. It operates in the south of England (and north England and the Midlands through Yorkshire Bank).

HISTORY

Formed in 1858 in Melbourne, National Bank of Australasia (NBA) just missed the peak of the Victoria gold rush. The bank expanded across the territory and was one of the first to lend to farmers and ranchers using land deeds as security. In the late 1870s drought imperiled Victoria. Seeking greener pastures, NBA entered New South Wales in 1885, then headed into Western Australia. Economic instability continued; in 1893 the bank experienced its first panic and was shuttered for eight weeks. NBA reopened only to close a quarter of its branches between 1893 and 1896.

During the Australian commonwealth's early years, Western Australia was the bank's salvation as the economies in Victoria and South Australia stagnated. NBA helped fund Australia's WWI efforts through public loans. A postwar consolidation wave in banking swept up NBA, which made acquisitions in 1918 and 1922.

Overdue farm and ranch loans weakened the bank during the Depression. As WWII raged, the Commonwealth Bank (established in 1912) took greater control of Australia's banks. With competition among banks primarily limited to branch growth, NBA acquired Queensland National Bank in 1948 and Ballarat Banking Co. in 1955. The bank diversified into consumer finance through acquisition. In the 1960s Australia experienced an economic boom as immigration and industrialization grew. The boom went bust in the 1970s as the world sunk into recession. Still under the Commonwealth Bank's tight control, the banks watched business that had once been theirs lost to building societies, merchant banks, and credit unions.

The 1980s brought banking deregulation. To vie with foreign banks entering Australia, NBA in 1981 merged with Commercial Banking Co. of Sydney and became the National Commercial Banking Corp. of Australia in 1982. (It took its present name in 1984.) Throughout the 1980s the bank diversified and moved into the US and Japan. It invested in property and made loans to foreign countries. All too quickly, though, property values sank and countries defaulted on loans.

To fight recession, NAB looked abroad for opportunities. In 1987 it bought Clydesdale Bank, Northern Bank, and National Irish Bank from Midland Bank Group (now part of HSBC Holdings). Three years later, NAB bought Yorkshire Bank, then turned the four banks around by linking them and tightening loan operations. In 1992 it bought the troubled Bank of New Zealand, again tightening loan operations. Three years later NAB claimed Michigan National in the US.

After the mid-1990s economic recovery, NAB bought HomeSide to try to adapt the US mortgage firm's efficient operations for all its banks.

In 2000 the Australian Competition and Consumer Commission (ACCC) accused NAB of credit card transaction price-fixing; the bank faced a possible fine of nearly $6 million, but the ACCC dropped the litigation the following year.

Also in 2001 NAB sold US-based Michigan National Bank to ABN AMRO and sold mortgage lender HomeSide International to Washington Mutual the following year. In fiscal year 2002 the bank cut some 2,000 jobs, mostly in back-office operations.

During fiscal year 2003 the company booked pre-tax losses of some $360 million due to unauthorized trading in the company's foreign currency options department. By the end of March 2004, chairman Charles Allen, chief executive Frank Cicutto, and the heads of global markets and foreign exchange had resigned. Three more executives and at least five traders were fired.

NAB sold its Irish banks — National Irish Bank and Northern Bank — to Danske Bank in 2005. It retained its UK banks, Yorkshire Bank (England) and Clydesdale Bank (Scotland).

In 2006 NAB sold its Custom Fleet vehicle leasing division to GE Capital, as well as its Asian life insurance and wealth management operations. The downsizing was part of the company's move to streamline operations.

EXECUTIVES

Chairman: Michael A. Chaney, age 60
CEO, Managing Director, and Director:
 Cameron A. Clyne
Deputy Group CEO and Director: Michael J. Ullmer, age 58
Group Executive Business Banking: Joseph Healy
Group Executive Personal Banking: Lisa Gray
Group Executive Wholesale Banking: Rick Sawers
Group Executive Group Governance and Company Secretary: Michaela J. Healey, age 42
Group Executive New Zealand, Asia and the United States; Managing Director and CEO, BNZ:
 Andrew Thorburn
Chief Executive Group Business Services:
 Gavin R. Slater
Group Chief Risk Officer: Bruce Munro
Director Finance and Director: Mark A. Joiner
Secretary and General Counsel Corporate:
 Nathan Butler
General Manager Public Affairs, Research and Media:
 George Wright
Head Corporate Affairs, Business, Private & Wealth:
 Stacey Mitchell
Head Corporate Affairs, NAB Personal Banking:
 Luisa Ford
CEO, MLC: Stephen (Steve) Tucker
CEO, United Kingdom: Lynne M. Peacock, age 56
Auditors: Ernst & Young

LOCATIONS

HQ: National Australia Bank Limited
 800 Bourke St.
 Docklands, Victoria 3008, Australia
Phone: 61-3-8641-9083 **Fax:** 61-3-8641-4927
Web: www.nabgroup.com

2010 Sales

	% of total
Interest income	78
Life insurance income	12
Other	10
Total	**100**

PRODUCTS/OPERATIONS

Selected Subsidiaries

Calibre Asset Management
Great Western Bancorporation
nabCapital (formerly Institutional Markets & Services)
National Australia Group Europe Limited
 Clydesdale Bank PLC
  Yorkshire Bank Home Loans Limited
  Yorkshire Bank Investments Limited
 National Australia Group Europe Services Limited
National Australia Group (NZ) Limited
 Bank of New Zealand
  BNZ International Funding Limited
National Australia Trustees Limited
National Wealth Management Holdings Limited
MLC Limited
 National Wealth Management International Holdings Limited

COMPETITORS

Australia and New Zealand Banking
Barclays
Commonwealth Bank of Australia
HSBC
Lloyds Banking Group
Northern Rock (Asset Management)
Royal Bank of Scotland
Westpac Banking

HISTORICAL FINANCIALS

Company Type: Public

Income Statement

FYE: September 30

	ASSETS ($ mil.)	NET INCOME ($ mil.)	INCOME AS % OF ASSETS	EMPLOYEES
9/10	665,236	4,097	0.6%	—
9/09	570,851	2,259	0.4%	38,953
9/08	538,969	2,550	0.5%	39,729
9/07	501,056	4,945	1.0%	38,822
9/06	361,941	3,838	1.1%	38,433
Annual Growth	**16.4%**	**1.6%**	**—**	**0.4%**

2010 Year-End Financials

Equity as % of assets: 5.7%
Return on assets: 0.7%
Return on equity: 11.6%
Long-term debt ($ mil.): —
No. of shares (mil.): 2,133
Dividends
 Yield: 5.8%
 Payout: 77.3%
Market value ($ mil.): 52,426
Sales ($ mil.): 33,532

Stock History

Pink Sheets: NABZY

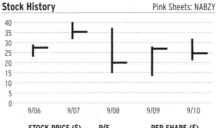

	STOCK PRICE ($) FY Close	P/E High/Low		PER SHARE ($) Earnings	Dividends	Book Value
9/10	24.57	17	12	1.85	1.43	17.70
9/09	26.84	26	13	1.07	1.48	15.47
9/08	19.91	17	7	2.14	1.58	12.61
9/07	35.24	17	13	2.38	1.52	12.30
9/06	27.40	15	12	1.95	1.24	9.73
Annual Growth	**(2.7%)**	**—**	**—**	**(1.3%)**	**3.6%**	**16.1%**

National Grid

It's not gridlock but a lock on the Grid that is a good thing for National Grid. It is the sole owner and operator of the electricity transmission system in England and Wales. It transmits electricity through about 4,500 miles of overhead and underground lines to distribution utilities serving more than 52 million people. National Grid also operates the UK natural gas transmission and distribution system (serving 11 million homes and businesses) through its National Grid Gas subsidiary. However, it is the company's Northeastern US gas distribution and power generation, transmission, and distribution operations, led by National Grid USA, that bring in the bulk of the company's revenues.

In the US the company distributes power to about 3.3 million customers in Massachusetts, New Hampshire, New York, and Rhode Island, and natural gas to 3.4 million clients in those states. It also manages the electricity distribution network in Long Island.

The company's long-term strategy is to focus on large-scale power and gas systems in the UK and the US and to better integrate its various operations. In 2010 a National Grid and TenneT joint venture began laying the first section of a high-voltage cable that will link the power grids in the UK and the Netherlands, bolstering power supply in both countries. The project, due for completion in 2011, will help the companies meet environmental goals by facilitating power flows from low-carbon generation plants.

With an eye on meeting ambitious European Union goals for carbon emission reductions, in 2009 National Grid released a report that by 2020 half of the UK's heating needs could be provided by biogas (converted from sewage and injected into the national gas distribution system), compensating for a decline in North Sea gas supply. In 2010 the company had one renewable gas plant under development in the US and two in the UK.

National Grid dramatically boosted its North American assets in 2007 by acquiring gas distributor KeySpan for more than $7 billion. To comply with federal regulations connected to the KeySpan deal, in 2008 National Grid sold its 2,480-MW Ravenswood Generating Station in New York City to TransCanada for $2.9 billion.

To raise cash and narrow its operational focus, the company has jettisoned a number of non-core operations. National Grid has sold its stakes in the alternative telecommunications network industry. The company has also sold its telecom interests in Chile, Argentina, and Poland, and it has written off its 33% stake in bankrupt UK telecommunications firm Energis, which uses fiber-optic cable strung along National Grid's power lines. National Grid has also sold former Lattice Group subsidiary 186k (fiber-optic networking) to Hutchison Whampoa, and has exited its telecom venture in Brazil. It also sold its electricity interconnector linking Australia to the island state of Tasmania.

HISTORY

The National Grid Company was formed in 1990 as part of the privatization of the electricity industry in England and Wales. Until then, the Central Electricity Generating Board (CEGB), a state monopoly responsible for power generation in England and Wales, owned the national power grid (transmission system) and sold power to 12 area boards, the regional authorities that distributed electricity to customers.

The Electricity Act of 1989 paved the way for competition; in 1990 the CEGB was split into The National Grid Company and three power-generating firms: National Power, PowerGen, and Nuclear Electric. The 12 area boards transferred their assets to 12 regional companies, which jointly owned National Grid. The company, keeping its monopoly status, was charged to develop and operate an efficient, coordinated, and economical transmission system and to facilitate competition among power producers.

The company moved outside the UK when it invested in Citelec in 1993. An international consortium, Citelec controlled Transener, the surviving transmission system after Argentina privatized its electric utilities.

Also in 1993 National Grid set up Energis as a telecommunications firm to provide service to businesses. Piggybacking its fiber-optic lines on National Grid's transmission network, Energis introduced national services in 1994, and by 1996 it had won several major customers, including the BBC and Microsoft.

In 1995 National Grid went public as The National Grid Group. It also secured concessions to build transmission lines in Pakistan, but in 1997 a new Pakistani government put the project on hold. That year it also upped its stake in Citelec from 15% to 41%, which increased its control over the development of Argentina's transmission system. With partner CINergy Global, it also acquired 80% of the Power Division of Zambia Consolidated Copper Mines in 1997, and it was chosen as a joint venture partner by India's Karnataka Electricity Board to build a transmission line in that state.

The company sold 26% of Energis in 1997; in 1998 it announced plans to sell the rest of Energis and launch a new company under the National Grid banner to set up telecom firms overseas. That year it laid plans to enter the US by agreeing to acquire New England Electric System (NEES). (The $3.2 billion purchase closed in 2000.)

In 1999 the company cut its stake in Energis to 46% and announced plans to shop for more US energy holdings. A deal was struck to purchase New York Utility Niagara Mohawk Holdings the following year. (The deal was completed in 2002.) Also in 2000 and 2001 the company continued to slim its stake in Energis (33%).

National Grid sold some noncore businesses in 2001, including UK metering company Datum Services and US energy marketer Allenergy, and pulled out of the transmission project in India. It also agreed to manage the Alliance Regional Transmission Organization (RTO) in the US. In 2002 National Grid sold Niagara Mohawk's 50% interest in Canadian Niagara Power to Canadian utility Fortis.

The firm changed its name to National Grid Transco in 2002 upon completion of its acquisition of Lattice Group in a $21.5 billion deal.

In 2005 National Grid Transco sold four of its regional gas distribution networks; the North England network was acquired by a consortium that includes United Utilities and Cheung Kong Infrastructure; the South of England and Scotland networks were sold to Scottish and Southern Energy, Borealis Infrastructure, and Ontario Teachers' Pension Plan; and the Wales & West distribution network was purchased by a consortium managed by Macquarie Bank Limited. The company dropped Transco from its name in 2005.

EXECUTIVES

Chairman: Sir John Parker, age 67
CEO and Director: Steven J. (Steve) Holliday, age 53, $4,471,900 total compensation
Executive Director, Gas Distribution and Board Member: Mark Fairbairn, age 51, $1,971,335 total compensation
Executive Director, Electricity Distribution and Generation and Board Member: Thomas B. (Tom) King, age 48, $3,112,427 total compensation
Executive Director, Transmission and Board Member: Nick Winser, age 49, $1,776,933 total compensation
Group Company Secretary, General Counsel, and Director: Helen M. Mahy, age 49
Finance Director and Board Member: Andrew R. J. Bonfield, age 47
Global Director Human Resources: Mike Westcott
Global Director Strategy and Business Development: Alison Wood
CIO: David W. Lister
Construction Operations Engineer: Kevin Wood
Corporate Press Officer: Gemma Stokes
Director Corporate Affairs: George Mayhew
Director Investor Relations, U.S.: George Laskaris
Director Investor Relations: David Rees
Auditors: PricewaterhouseCoopers LLP

LOCATIONS

HQ: National Grid plc
1-3 Strand
London WC2N 5EH, United Kingdom
Phone: 44-20-7004-3000   **Fax:** 44-20-7004-3004
US HQ: 25 Research Dr., Westborough, MA 01582
US Phone: 508-389-2000   **US Fax:** 508-389-2605
Web: www.nationalgrid.com

2010 Sales

	% of total
US	61
UK	39
Total	**100**

PRODUCTS/OPERATIONS

2010 Sales

	% of total
Gas distribution	37
Electricity distribution & generation	31
Transmission	27
Other	5
Total	**100**

COMPETITORS

CE Electric UK
Central Networks
Con Edison
Enterprise Group
HomeServe
IBERDROLA
Northeast Utilities
Northern Electric
Northern Ireland Electricity
Scottish and Southern Energy

HISTORICAL FINANCIALS

Company Type: Public

Income Statement

FYE: March 31

	REVENUE ($ mil.)	NET INCOME ($ mil.)	NET PROFIT MARGIN	EMPLOYEES
3/10	21,106	2,093	9.9%	28,000
3/09	22,200	1,346	6.1%	27,373
3/08	22,779	6,379	28.0%	27,600
3/07	17,270	2,747	15.9%	19,712
3/06	16,008	6,704	41.9%	20,529
Annual Growth	**7.2%**	**(25.3%)**	**—**	**8.1%**

2010 Year-End Financials

Debt ratio: 531.5%
Return on equity: 35.0%
Cash ($ mil.): 1,085
Current ratio: 0.77
Long-term debt ($ mil.): 33,629

No. of shares (mil.): 523
Dividends
Yield: 3.7%
Payout: 63.8%
Market value ($ mil.): 38,450

Stock History

NYSE: NGG

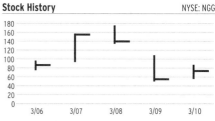

	STOCK PRICE ($) FY Close	P/E High/Low		Earnings	PER SHARE ($) Dividends	Book Value
3/10	73.46	20	14	4.20	2.68	12.09
3/09	54.90	39	19	2.71	2.35	10.78
3/08	139.45	14	11	12.14	2.96	20.43
3/07	155.05	31	19	5.01	2.62	15.50
3/06	86.42	8	7	11.75	—	11.62
Annual Growth	**(4.0%)**	**—**	**—**	**(22.7%)**	**0.8%**	**1.0%**

NEC Corporation

NEC makes a name for itself in Networking, Electronics, and Computers. The Japanese tech giant provides a broad range of IT products and services through five primary business groups. IT Services offers consulting, integration, and support services. Personal Solutions oversees PCs, peripherals, mobile handsets, and Internet service. Carrier Network supplies infrastructure equipment for telecom carriers. The Platform business supplies network systems such as servers, supercomputers, storage equipment, and IP telephony systems, while the Social Infrastructure segment provides broadcasting systems, satellites, and CCTV surveillance systems. NEC generates most of its sales in Japan.

In early 2010 the company refocused its corporate strategy to offer cloud computing services, expand its global business, and create new businesses. NEC is investing in technology to revamp its core IT system into a cloud service platform and develop systems for customers to provide their own cloud computing services.

As for its global business, it plans to expand newly acquired subsidiaries Sphere Communications (now NEC Sphere) and NetCracker. NEC also has partnerships with Alcatel-Lucent, EMC, and Philips to develop products specifically aimed at markets outside Japan.

Before creating new businesses, NEC had to divest some old ones. It spun off its Electron Devices segment when it merged NEC Electronics with Renesas Technology to form Renesas Electronics. The merging of NEC Electronics and Renesas created one of the largest chip makers in Japan, rivaling Toshiba Semiconductor. Facing intense competition in the mobile handset sector, particularly outside Japan, NEC decided to concentrate on domestic sales. It merged its mobile handset business with CASIO COMPUTER and Hitachi's joint venture, Casio Hitachi Mobile Communications Co., Ltd., to form NEC CASIO Mobile Communications.

NEC has suffered declining revenues since the onset of the global economic recession that began in late 2008. However, the company earned a net profit by reducing its operating costs, mostly by reducing headcount of outsourced engineers and administrative expenses.

Under the Personal Solutions segment, NEC is the leading provider of PCs in its home market. The division also oversees BIGLOBE, one of Japan's largest Internet service providers. Carrier Network provides enterprise and carrier-grade communications networking equipment, including 3G base stations, satellite systems, broadcasting transmitters and studio equipment, IP telephony systems, and microwave wireless access systems. Telecom companies are a large segment of NEC's customers.

Kaoru Yano stepped down as president of NEC in 2010 but retained his position as chairman. SVP Nobuhiro Endo, who has been with the company since 1981, was promoted to president.

HISTORY

A group of Japanese investors, led by Kunihiko Iwadare, formed Nippon Electric Company (NEC) in a joint venture with Western Electric (US) in 1899. Starting as an importer of telephone equipment, NEC soon became a maker and a major supplier to Japan's Communications Ministry. Western Electric sold its stake in NEC in 1925. The company became affiliated with the Sumitomo *keiretsu* (industrial group) in the 1930s and went public in 1949.

After Nippon Telegraph and Telephone (NTT) was formed in 1952, NEC became one of its four leading suppliers. The post-WWII need to repair Japan's telephone systems and the country's continuing economic recovery resulted in strong demand from NTT for NEC's products. In the 1950s and 1960s NTT business represented over 50% of sales, even though NEC had expanded overseas, diversified into home appliances, and formed a computer alliance with Honeywell (US). ITT (US), which had begun acquiring shares in the company decades earlier and owned as much as 59% of NEC, sold its stake in the 1960s.

In the 1970s Honeywell's lagging position in computers hurt NEC; the company recovered through in-house development efforts and a mainframe venture with Toshiba. In 1977 CEO Koji Kobayashi articulated his revolutionary vision of NEC's future as an integrator of computers and communications through semiconductor technology.

NEC invested heavily in R&D and expansion, becoming the world's largest semiconductor maker in 1985. Despite its proprietary operating system, NEC garnered over 50% of the Japanese computer market in the 1980s. NEC entered into a mainframe computer partnership with Honeywell and France's Groupe Bull in 1987.

By the early 1990s NEC had lost its status as the world's largest semiconductor maker to Intel. NEC bought 20% of US computer maker Packard Bell in 1995. The following year NEC merged most of its PC business outside Japan with that company, creating Packard Bell NEC.

NEC took control of Packard Bell NEC in 1998, upping its stake to 53%. A sluggish Japanese economy and slumping memory prices contributed to NEC's drop in income for fiscal 1998. A defense contract scandal involving overbilling and improper hiring by an NEC unit forced the resignation of chairman Tadahiro Sekimoto and, later, president Hisashi Kaneko.

New president Koji Nishigaki, the first at NEC without an engineering background, led a sweeping reorganization to cut 10% of the company's workforce — 15,000 employees — over three years. He revamped NEC operations around Internet application hardware, software, and services. In 1998 NEC formed a rare pact with a Japanese rival, allying with Hitachi to consolidate memory chip operations. NEC folded up its Packard Bell NEC division in 1999, imposing layoffs of about 80% of its staff, divesting it from the US retail market, and excising the historic Packard Bell brand name in that region.

In 2000 the company launched an aggressive spending program in a move to lead the broadband mobile networking market.

Nishigaki became vice chairman in 2004, and Akinobu Kanasugi was named president. Kanasugi held the post just two years, until poor health forced him to turn the reins over to SVP Kaoru Yano.

Early in 2005 the company dissolved its monitor joint venture with Mitsubishi and took full ownership of the unit (NEC Display Solutions). The next year it sold its European PC operations, Packard Bell, to Lap Shun "John" Hui, a co-founder of eMachines.

The company joined with Sumitomo Electric Industries in 2008 to acquire fiber-optic submarine cable manufacturer OCC Holdings.

EXECUTIVES

Chairman: Kaoru Yano, age 66
President and Director: Nobuhiro Endo, age 56
SEVP and Director: Toshimitsu Iwanami, age 61
SEVP and Director: Yukihiro Fujiyoshi, age 61
EVP and Director: Takao Ono, age 62
EVP and Director: Junji Yasui, age 59
SVP and Director: Toshiyuki Mineno, age 59
SVP and Director: Takuji Tomiyama, age 60
SVP and Director: Takemitsu Kunio, age 55
SVP and Director: Manabu Kinoshita, age 56
SVP: Takayuki Okada
SVP: Takashi Niino
SVP: Kuniaki Okada
SVP: Masato Yamamoto
SVP: Fujio Okada
SVP: Masaki Fukui
SVP: Tadashi Higashino
SVP: Minoru Terao
Corporate Auditor: Konosuke Kashima, age 64
Auditors: Ernst & Young ShinNihon

LOCATIONS

HQ: NEC Corporation
(Nippon Denki Kabushiki Kaisha)
5-7-1 Shiba, Minato-ku
Tokyo 108-8001, Japan
Phone: 81-3-3454-1111   **Fax:** 81-3-3798-1510
US HQ: 6535 N. State Hwy. 161, Irving, TX 75039
US Phone: 214-262-2000   **US Fax:** 214-262-2586
Web: www.nec.com

2010 Sales

	% of total
Japan	80
Rest of Asia	9
US	6
Europe	5
Total	**100**

PRODUCTS/OPERATIONS

2010 Sales

	% of total
IT Services	24
Personal Solutions	21
Carrier Networks	18
Platform Business	10
Social Infrastructure	9
Other (batteries, lighting, LCD panels)	18
Total	**100**

Selected Products

IT Services
Consulting
Maintenance
Outsourcing
Support
Systems integration
Personal Solutions
Internet service (NEC BIGLOBE)
Mobile handsets
Peripherals (floppy and optical drives, monitors, printers, projectors)
Personal computers
Carrier Network
Access Networking systems (broadband and mobile, microwave communication systems)
Backbone networking systems (SDH systems, WDM systems, routers/switching systems)
Network control platform systems
Network infrastructure (fixed-line and mobile communication systems)
Network service delivery platform systems
Platform Business Systems
Enterprise computing (workstations, servers, storage systems, mainframes, supercomputers)
Enterprise network systems (IP telephony, routers/switching systems, wireless LAN)
Networking equipment (enterprise, carrier)
Software (application, middleware, operating systems)
Storage products
Social Infrastructure
Aerospace and defense systems
Broadcasting systems and video equipment
Control systems
Fire and disaster prevention systems
Transportation and public systems

COMPETITORS

Acer	Lexmark
Alcatel-Lucent	Micron Technology
AMD	Microsoft
Apple Inc.	Mitsubishi Electric
Avaya	Motorola
Canon	Nokia
CASIO COMPUTER	Nortel Networks
Cisco Systems	NTT DATA
Citizen	Oki Electric
CSK	Panasonic Corp
Dell	Philips Electronics
Emerson Electric	Research In Motion
Epson	Ricoh Company
Ericsson	Samsung Electronics
FUJIFILM	Sharp Corp.
Fujitsu	Siemens AG
Harris Corp.	Sony
Hewlett-Packard	Sony Ericsson Mobile
Hitachi	STMicroelectronics
Huawei Technologies	Texas Instruments
IBM	Toshiba
Intel	Unisys
Kyocera	UTStarcom
Lenovo	ZTE

HISTORICAL FINANCIALS

Company Type: Public

Income Statement

FYE: March 31

	REVENUE ($ mil.)	NET INCOME ($ mil.)	NET PROFIT MARGIN	EMPLOYEES
3/10	38,655	123	0.3%	142,358
3/09	43,332	(3,049)	—	143,327
3/08	46,499	228	0.5%	152,922
3/07	39,473	77	0.2%	154,786
3/06	41,041	144	0.4%	154,180
Annual Growth	(1.5%)	(3.8%)	—	(2.0%)

2010 Year-End Financials

Debt ratio: 55.4%
Return on equity: —
Cash ($ mil.): 3,566
Current ratio: 1.29
Long-term debt ($ mil.): 4,726

No. of shares (mil.): 2,599
Dividends
 Yield: 1.3%
 Payout: 80.0%
Market value ($ mil.): 7,877

Stock History

Pink Sheets: NIPNF

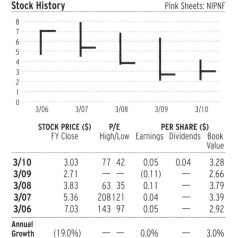

	STOCK PRICE ($) FY Close	P/E High/Low		PER SHARE ($) Earnings	Dividends	Book Value
3/10	3.03	77	42	0.05	0.04	3.28
3/09	2.71	—	—	(0.11)	—	2.66
3/08	3.83	63	35	0.11	—	3.79
3/07	5.36	208	121	0.04	—	3.39
3/06	7.03	143	97	0.05	—	2.92
Annual Growth	(19.0%)	—	—	—	0.0%	3.0%

Nestlé S.A.

With instant coffee, baby formula, and bottled water in the mix, Nestlé crunches more than just chocolate. The world's #1 food company in terms of sales, Nestlé is also the world leader in coffee (Nescafé). It also makes coffee for the home-brewing system, Nespresso. The company is one of the world's top bottled water makers, one of the biggest frozen pizza makers, and a big player in the pet food business (Purina). Its most well-known global food brands include Buitoni, Maggi, Milkmaid, Carnation, and Kit Kat. The company owns Gerber Products and Jenny Craig. In addition to its own products, Nestlé also owns approximately 30% of cosmetics giant L'Oréal.

In early 2010 the company acquired Kraft Foods' frozen pizza business in the US and Canada. Costing $3.7 billion, the purchase added the DiGiorno, Tombstone, California Pizza Kitchen, Jack's, and Delissio brands to Nestlé's product list. With only a minor presence up until then in the US and Canadian frozen pizza business, the purchase catapulted Nestlé into the leading position in the two countries.

During 2008 it saw a decline in the growth of its bottled water sales. In addition to a consumer trend toward buying "down market" brands, Nestlé attributed the decline to "the somewhat emotional debate about the perceived environmental issues around the category," meaning more and more people are turning away from bottled water due to the use and disposal problems of plastic water bottles.

As part of its strategy to concentrate on what it does best — sell food — Nestlé completed the divestment of one of its main nonfood operations, Alcon (ophthalmic drugs, contact-lens solutions, and equipment for ocular surgery), in 2010 for $28.3 billion.

Adding to its already impressive stable of #1 rankings in the food and beverage sector, Nestlé's $5.5 billion cash purchase of Gerber from Novartis in 2008 made Nestlé the world's largest baby food company. In addition, coupling the Novartis medical nutrition and Jenny Craig acquisitions with that of Gerber made Nestlé's Nutrition division into a world player in the nutrition, health, and wellness sectors. The company has announced that in 2011 it will create a new business unit, Nestlé Health Science, to develop products to treat conditions such as diabetes, obesity, and cardiovascular disease.

In 2008 Peter Brabeck-Letmathe stepped down as CEO; he remained in an active role as board chairman. Paul Bulcke, former head of Zone Americas for Nestlé, replaced Brabeck-Letmathe as CEO.

HISTORY

Henri Nestlé purchased a factory in Vevey, Switzerland, in 1843 that made products ranging from nut oils to rum. In 1867 he developed a powder made from cow's milk and wheat flour as a substitute for mother's milk. A year earlier Americans Charles and George Page had founded the Anglo-Swiss Condensed Milk Company in Cham, Switzerland, using Gail Borden's milk-canning technology.

In 1875 Nestlé sold his eponymous company, then doing business in 16 countries. When Anglo-Swiss launched a milk-based infant food in 1878, Nestlé's new owners responded by introducing a condensed-milk product. In 1905, a year after Nestlé began selling chocolate, the companies ended their rivalry by merging under the Nestlé name.

Hampered by limited milk supplies during WWI, the company expanded into regions less affected by the war, such as the US. In 1929 it acquired Cailler, the first company to mass-produce chocolate bars, and Swiss General, inventor of milk chocolate.

An investment in a Brazilian condensed-milk factory during the 1920s paid an unexpected dividend when Brazilian coffee growers suggested the company develop a water-soluble "coffee cube." Released in 1938, Nescafé instant coffee quickly became popular.

Other new products included Nestlé's Crunch bar (1938), Quik drink mix (1948), and Taster's Choice instant coffee (1966). Nestlé expanded during the 1970s with acquisitions such as Beringer Brothers wines (sold in 1995), Stouffer's, and Libby's.

Moving beyond foods in 1974, Nestlé acquired a 49% stake in Gesparal, a holding company that controls the French cosmetics company L'Oréal. It acquired pharmaceutical firm Alcon Laboratories three years later.

Helmut Maucher was named chairman and CEO in 1981. He began beefing up Nestlé's global presence. Boycotters had long accused Nestlé of harming children in developing countries through the unethical promotion of infant formula, and Maucher acknowledged the ongoing boycott by meeting with the critics and setting up a commission to police adherence to World Health Organization guidelines.

Nestlé bought Carnation in 1985. Maucher doubled the company's chocolate business in 1988 with the purchase of UK chocolate maker Rowntree (Kit Kat). Also in the 1980s Nestlé acquired Buitoni pastas.

The company expanded in the 1990s with the purchases of Butterfinger and Baby Ruth candies, Source Perrier water, Alpo pet food, and Ortega Mexican foods. Company veteran Peter Brabeck-Letmathe succeeded Maucher as CEO in 1997.

In 2001 it bought Ralston Purina for $10.3 billion, making it the world's largest pet food maker. In 2002 Nestlé acquired German ice-cream maker Schoeller Holding Group, as well as US food company Chef America, maker of Hot Pockets and Lean Pockets. Nestlé and Cadbury Schweppes made a joint $10.5 billion bid for The Hershey Company in 2002 but Hershey called the sale off later that year.

In 2004 CEO Peter Brabeck-Letmathe announced he was considering reducing the number of outside directorships that he held because of increased demands as the leader of Nestlé. Long-time chairman Rainer Gut retired in 2005 and Brabeck-Letmathe replaced him.

In 2006 Nestlé bought the Australian breakfast cereal, snack, and soup operations of Uncle Tobys from Burns Philp for $670 million. The cereal portion was integrated into Cereal Partners Worldwide. Hedging its bets, considering its food products (candy bars, ice cream) are on the opposite end of the waistline wars, Nestlé acquired Jenny Craig for $600 million in 2006.

In 2007 the company purchased the medical-nutrition business of Novartis for €1.88 billion ($2.5 billion). Brands in the acquisition included Boost and Resource nutritional supplements, and Optifast dieting products.

EXECUTIVES

Chairman: Peter Brabeck-Letmathe, age 65,
 $7,089,483 total compensation
First Vice Chairman: Andreas N. Koopmann, age 59
Second Vice Chairman: Rolf Hänggi, age 66
CEO: Paul Bulcke, age 55,
 $9,496,785 total compensation
**EVP Finance and Control, Global Nestlé Business
 Services, Legal, Intellectual Property, and Tax:**
 James Singh, age 63
**EVP, CTO, and Head Innovation, Technology, and
 Research and Development:** Werner J. Bauer, age 59
EVP Asia, Oceania, Africa, and Middle East:
 Frits van Dijk, age 63
EVP US, Canada, Latin America, and Caribbean:
 Luis Cantarell, age 57
EVP; Chairman and CEO, Nestlé Waters: John J. Harris,
 age 59
**EVP Pharmaceutical and Cosmetic Products; Liaison
 with L'Oréal, Human Resources:**
 Francisco Castañer Basco, age 65
**EVP Strategic Business Units, Marketing, Sales, and
 Nespresso:** Petraea Heynike, age 63
EVP Operations, Global Business Excellence (GLOBE):
 José Lopez, age 57
EVP Europe: Laurent Freixe
**Deputy EVP Human Resources and Centre
 Administration:** Jean-Marc Duvoisin, age 50
Corporate Secretary: Yves P. Bloch
Director Corporate Communications: Rudolf Ramsauer
Head Investor Relations: Roddy Child-Villiers
Chairman and CEO, Nestlé USA: Brad Alford
Auditors: KPMG Klynveld Peat Marwick Goerdeler SA

LOCATIONS

HQ: Nestlé S.A.
 Avenue Nestlé 55
 CH-1800 Vevey, Vaud, Switzerland
Phone: 41-21-924-1111 **Fax:** 41-21-924-4800
Web: www.nestle.com

PRODUCTS/OPERATIONS

2009 Sales

	% of total
Milk products & ice cream	20
Powdered & liquid beverages	18
Prepared dishes & cooking aids	18
Confectionery	12
Pet care	12
Nutrition	10
Water	9
Pharmaceutical products	1
Total	**100**

Selected Products and Brands

Bouillons, soups, seasonings, pasta, and sauces
 Buitoni
 Maggi
 Thomy
 Winiary
Chocolate, confectionery, and biscuits
 Aero
 Butterfinger
 Cailler
 Crunch
 Galak/Milkybar
 Kit Kat
 Nestlé
 Smarties
Coffee
 Bonka
 Nescafé
 Nespresso
 Ricoré, Ricoffy
 Taster's Choice

Frozen foods (prepared dishes, pizzas)
 Buitoni
 California Pizza Kitchen (licensed)
 Delissio (Canada only)
 Hot Pockets
 Lean Cuisine
 Stouffer's
 Tombstone
Healthcare and nutrition
 Clinutren
 Modulen
 Nutren
 Peptamen
Ice cream
 Chipwich
 Dreyer's
 Drumstick/Extrême
 Edy's
 Eskimo Pie
 Häagen-Dazs
Infant food and nutrition
 Cérélac
 Gerber
 Good Start
 Lactogen
 Neslac
 Nestogen
 Nestum
Performance nutrition
 PowerBar
 Pria
Petcare
 Alpo
 Cat Chow
 Dog Chow
 Fancy Feast
 Felix
 Gourmet
 Pro Plan
 Purina Friskies
 Purina ONE
 Tidy Cats
Refrigerated products (cold meat products, dough,
 pasta, pizzas, sauces)
 Buitoni
 Nestlé
 Toll House
Shelf-stable products
 Carnation
 Coffee-Mate
 Milkmaid
 Nestlé Omega
 Svelty
Water
 Arrowhead
 Deer Park
 Ice Mountain
 Levissima
 Nestlé Aquarel
 Nestlé Pure Life
 Nestlé Vera
 Ozarka
 Perrier
 Poland Spring
 S.Pellegrino
 San Bernardo
 Vittel
 Zephyrhills

COMPETITORS

Abbott Labs	Kent Gida
Associated British Foods	Kerry Group
Atkins Nutritionals	Kraft Foods
Bally Total Fitness	Lindt & Sprüngli
Barilla	Mars, Incorporated
Beech-Nut	maxingvest
Campbell Soup	Medifast
Coca-Cola	NutriSystem
ConAgra	PepsiCo
Danone	Procter & Gamble
Danone Water	Revlon
Dean Foods	Russell Stover
Dreyer's	Sara Lee
eDiets.com	Slim-Fast
Ferrara Pan Candy	Smucker
Fit America	Starbucks
General Mills	Suntory Holdings
GNC	Tata Global Beverages
Goya	United Biscuits
Heinz	Weight Watchers
Hershey	International
HMG	Wimm-Bill-Dann
Indofood	World's Finest Chocolate
Kellogg	

HISTORICAL FINANCIALS

Company Type: Public

Income Statement

FYE: December 31

	REVENUE ($ mil.)	NET INCOME ($ mil.)	NET PROFIT MARGIN	EMPLOYEES
12/09	103,679	10,046	9.7%	278,000
12/08	104,061	17,079	16.4%	283,000
12/07	95,463	10,103	10.6%	276,000
12/06	80,716	8,074	10.0%	265,000
12/05	69,208	5,792	8.4%	250,000
Annual Growth	**10.6%**	**14.8%**	**—**	**2.7%**

2009 Year-End Financials

Debt ratio: 18.3%
Return on equity: 21.1%
Cash ($ mil.): 2,634
Current ratio: 1.10
Long-term debt ($ mil.): 8,638

No. of shares (mil.): 3,465
Dividends
 Yield: 2.9%
 Payout: 48.6%
Market value ($ mil.): 161,401

Stock History

Pink Sheets: NSRGY

	STOCK PRICE ($) FY Close	P/E High/Low		PER SHARE ($) Earnings	Dividends	Book Value
12/09	46.58	17	10	2.80	1.36	13.60
12/08	37.59	27	17	1.83	0.74	13.87
12/07	40.65	1	—	61.27	0.59	13.34
12/06	29.18	2	1	19.31	0.48	12.06
12/05	22.72	2	1	15.49	0.61	10.93
Annual Growth	**19.7%**	**—**	**—**	**(34.8%)**	**22.2%**	**5.6%**

Nikon Corporation

Nikon's focus extends far wider than most consumers would believe. Though well-known for its cameras, lenses, and other consumer optical products, Nikon vies with national rival Canon and Netherlands-based ASML Holding to be the world's top producer of photolithography steppers, which is the crucial equipment used to etch circuitry onto semiconductor wafers and LCD panels. The company also makes a range of other products, including eyewear, surveying instruments, microscopes, industrial equipment, and electronic imaging equipment. Founded in 1917, Nikon is part of the huge Mitsubishi *keiretsu*, a group of businesses linked by cross-ownership.

Nikon eliminated more than 1,000 jobs in early 2010 as it reorganized to adjust to the sluggish semiconductor and LCD markets. To that end, by October 2009 it cut from four to two the number of Nikon subsidiaries that make semiconductor and LCD displays and streamlined its sales and service operations in Japan and abroad. Nikon hopes to realize about ¥20 billion (nearly $225 million) in fixed-cost savings by 2012 as a result of the cuts. The measures to right-size its operations come amid the global economic slowdown and declining demand for its goods, especially digital cameras and components used in LCD TVs.

Facing tougher market conditions, Nikon saw its leadership change in mid-2010. Executive vice president Makoto Kimura was named president, succeeding Michio Kariya, who remained chairman. Kimura, lauded for his deep understanding of both technology and business, aims to reshape Nikon's corporate culture and place the camera maker on a new direction for steady earnings growth.

Nikon hopes to recapture consumers' interest by pooling its effort to create next-generation products. The company is setting aside some ¥160 billion (about $1.8 billion) for capital investments and ¥220 billion (about $2.5 billion) for research and development by 2011. One channel for investment is Nikon's instruments business, which includes digital cameras and exposure meters. In the field of microscopy, Nikon in late 2009 signed a licensing agreement with Harvard University that granted it the rights to use the Stochastic Optical Reconstruction Microscopy (STORM) technology in the creation of a super resolution microscope.

The company is also extending its brand to a more youthful audience. Men in their 40s and 50s constitute Nikon's average customer demographic, but the firm hopes to bolster its appeal to teenagers and twenty-somethings. To achieve this, Nikon broadcasts content on the Nintendo Wii's Wiinoma video-on-demand service channel, which is available to console owners in Japan. Nikon's programs explain the technical aspects of digital cameras and photolithography systems.

The range of Nikon's products offers a snapshot of the optical world. Its cameras have caught images from every manned space flight since Apollo 13. Its microscopes are used in schools and cell biology research laboratories, and its eye examination equipment and prescription glasses and sunglasses are fixtures in opticians' offices worldwide.

HISTORY

Lensmaker Nippon Kogaku KK formed in 1917 with the merger of three large Japanese optical glassmakers. Nippon Kogaku started selling binoculars in 1921; the company introduced its first microscope four years later.

In 1932 the company adopted the brand name Nikkor for its lenses, which were attached to other manufacturers' cameras. By WWII the company had diversified into cameras, microscopes, binoculars, surveying equipment, measuring instruments, and eyeglass lenses. During this time the Japanese government bought nearly all of the company's products. Nippon Kogaku began using the Nikon brand name on its cameras in 1946.

The company introduced its first commercially available pocket camera in the early 1950s, but few of Nikon's cameras made it out of Japan. The world would not begin to appreciate the quality of Nikon's products until photojournalists began using them in the Korean War.

Continuing a European expansion in the 1960s, the company opened subsidiaries in Switzerland (1961) and the Netherlands (1968). The company, in conjunction with undersea explorer Jacques Cousteau and a partner, introduced an underwater camera system in 1963. The 1970s were years of further development: The company introduced high-precision coordinate measuring instruments (1971) and sunglasses (1972), among other products. During the late 1970s Canon passed Minolta and Nikon as the world's top seller of cameras, setting off a battle that has seesawed ever since.

In 1980 the company developed its first stepper system for the semiconductor industry. By 1984 Nikon controlled 53% of the Japanese stepper market. Nippon Kogaku changed its name in 1988 to Nikon Corporation.

The company further broadened its geographic scope in the early 1990s, opening subsidiaries in South Korea (1990), Thailand (1990), Hungary (1991), Italy (1993), and Singapore (1995). When demand for chips dropped in the early 1990s, so did Nikon's sales, and the company lost money in fiscal 1993 and fiscal 1994. It restructured its unprofitable camera division, cutting staff by a third to save cash.

In 1997 Shoichiro Yoshida, a Nikon designer since the 1950s who became a proponent of the company's stepper business, was named president, replacing Shigeo Ono, who became chairman. A slumping Asian market and declining prices for chips caused demand for steppers to fall and left the company with slack earnings for fiscal 1998 and 1999. Rebounds in the markets for digital cameras and semiconductor equipment led Nikon back into the black in 2000.

In 2001 the company expanded its semiconductor equipment offerings by entering the market for chemical mechanical polishing (CMP) equipment. In June of that year Ono retired as chairman; Yoshida replaced him. In 2005 Yoshida stepped down, and EVP Michio Kariya became chairman.

EXECUTIVES

Chairman: Michio Kariya
President and Director: Makoto Kimura
EVP, CFO, and Director: Ichiro Terato
VP, Business Administration Center: Tsuneyoshi Kon
President, Customized Products Division, Business Administration Center: Yoshimichi Kawai
President, Center Glass Division, Core Technology, and Director: Kyoichi Suwa
President, Intellectual Property, Precision Equipment Company, and Director: Kazuo Ushida
President and General Manager Sales Division, Instruments Company, and Director: Toshiyuki Masai
President and CEO, Nikon, Inc.: Yasuyuki Okamoto
Managing Director, Nikon Hong Kong Ltd.: Nobuyoshi Gokyu
General Manager, Financing and Accounting, and Director: Norio Hashizume
General Manager, Information Systems Headquarters: Kenichi Kanazawa
General Manager, Development Headquarters, Imaging Company: Kazuyuki Kazami
General Manager, Production Headquarters, Precision Equipment Company: Teruo Hashimoto
Head, Manufacturing Reform Project; Chairman, Sendai Nikon Corporation and Nikon Co. Ltd.: Masaaki Okajima
Auditors: Deloitte Touche Tohmatsu

LOCATIONS

HQ: Nikon Corporation
Fuji Bldg., 2-3 Marunouchi 3-chome, Chiyoda-ku
Tokyo 100-8331, Japan
Phone: 81-3-3214-5311   **Fax:** 81-3-3216-1454
US HQ: 1300 Walt Whitman Rd., Melville, NY 11747
US Phone: 631-547-4200   **US Fax:** 631-547-4025
Web: www.nikon.com

2010 Sales

	% of total
Asia/Oceania	
Japan	24
Other countries	18
North America	33
Europe	25
Total	**100**

PRODUCTS/OPERATIONS

2010 Sales

	% of total
Imaging products	72
Precision equipment	19
Instruments	6
Other	3
Total	**100**

Selected Products

Imaging products
  Camera lenses
  Compact cameras
  Digital cameras
  Film scanners
  Single-lens reflex (SLR) cameras
Precision equipment
  Semiconductor and liquid crystal display (LCD) steppers
Instruments
  Biological and industrial microscopes
  Inspection equipment
  Measuring instruments
  Medical imaging systems
  Ophthalmic instruments
Other
  Binoculars
  Eyeglasses
  Sunglasses
  Surveying instruments
  Telescopes

COMPETITORS

ASML
Canon
Carl Zeiss
Eastman Kodak
FSI International
FUJIFILM
Olympus
Ultratech

HISTORICAL FINANCIALS

Company Type: Public

Income Statement

FYE: March 31

	REVENUE ($ mil.)	NET INCOME ($ mil.)	NET PROFIT MARGIN	EMPLOYEES
3/10	8,474	(111)	—	26,125
3/09	9,043	288	3.2%	23,759
3/08	9,626	760	7.9%	25,342
3/07	6,981	465	6.7%	22,705
3/06	6,217	246	4.0%	18,725
Annual Growth	8.0%	—	—	8.7%

2010 Year-End Financials

Debt ratio: —
Return on equity: —
Cash ($ mil.): 1,162
Current ratio: 1.62
Long-term debt ($ mil.): —

No. of shares (mil.): 396
Dividends
  Yield: 0.4%
  Payout: —
Market value ($ mil.): 8,728

Stock History

Tokyo: 77310

	STOCK PRICE ($) FY Close	P/E High/Low		PER SHARE ($) Earnings	Dividends	Book Value
3/10	22.02	—	—	(0.34)	0.08	10.13
3/09	11.37	20	5	1.86	0.06	9.83
3/08	26.74	24	13	1.83	—	9.99
3/07	21.08	—	—	—	—	7.45
3/06	17.95	—	—	—	—	5.22
Annual Growth	5.2%	—	—	—	33.3%	18.0%

Nintendo Co.

Nintendo wants everyone — from little Marios to seasoned Donkey Kongs — to play, especially if the game's on its Nintendo DS device or Wii console. One of the Big Three in the videogame business, Nintendo's Wii, Game Boy, and GameCube do battle with Microsoft's Xbox and Sony's PlayStation for the hearts and dollars of devoted gamers. Indeed, Nintendo is the market-leading game maker, but its rivals aren't sitting still. Nintendo's been busy pumping out products as it works to attract multi-generational users. They include its videogame players Nintendo DS (2004), Game Boy Micro (2005), DS Lite (2006), and the popular Wii, pronounced "we," videogame system (2006) that quickly became a top seller.

Nintendo (which, loosely translated, means "leave luck to heaven") continues to launch Wii hardware, software, and accessories. Since the debut of its Wii hardware, the firm has sold more than 50 million units. Wii software, such as "Mario Kart Wii" and "Wii Sports," are seeing brisk sales. The company boasts more than 90 titles that have sold 1 million-plus since their launch. Overall, the Wii is boosting net sales in Nintendo's electronic entertainment products

division. While Nintendo expands its Wii software portfolio in 2010, it's also developing and expanding the system's "channel" features, such as the ability to create caricatures, surf the Web, and view weather forecasts and news. Nintendo moved away from its core market of young male gamers with its launch of Wii Fit. It's chasing after women and older gamers for the first time.

Nintendo's Wii game console follows its competitors' offerings — Microsoft's Xbox 360 and Sony's PlayStation 3. Unlike those two offerings, Wii is a game console first and foremost and not a digital entertainment hub. The company hopes that its Wii system, priced at about half of what Sony's Playstation 3 sells for, depending on features, will woo game players and make gaming a family activity.

The company plans concentrate its efforts on its games, in contrast to competitors Sony and Microsoft, which are developing increasingly complex multimedia systems. The introduction of the Nintendo DS system was a competitive move designed to counter the launch of Sony's PlayStation Portable (PSP). The company has launched Nintendo Wi-Fi Connection, a free service that allows DS system players to play other users simply by connecting to a wireless network.

Nintendo once ruled the golden age of the video game industry until more powerful machines introduced by SEGA (in 1989) and Sony (in 1994) pared down its kingdom (SEGA has since stopped making console systems). Microsoft entered the gaming hardware market in 2001, leaving Nintendo with a shrinking piece of the pie.

Nintendo owns a majority stake in the Seattle Mariners baseball team, which it purchased for $125 million in 1992.

HISTORY

Nintendo Co. was founded in 1889 as the Marufuku Company to make and sell *hanafuda*, Japanese game cards. In 1907 the company began producing Western playing cards. It became the Nintendo Playing Card Company in 1951 and began making theme cards under a licensing agreement with Disney in 1959.

During the 1950s and 1960s Hiroshi Yamauchi took the company public and diversified into new areas (including a "love hotel"). The company took its current name in 1963. Nintendo began making toys at the start of the 1970s and entered the budding field of video games toward the end of the decade by licensing Magnavox's Pong technology. Then it moved into arcade games. Nintendo established its US subsidiary, Nintendo of America, in 1980; its first hit was *Donkey Kong* ("silly monkey") and its next was *Super Mario Bros.* (named after Nintendo of America's warehouse landlord).

The company released Famicom, a technologically advanced home video game system, in Japan in 1983. With its high-quality sound and graphics, Famicom was a smash, selling 15.2 million consoles and more than 183 million game cartridges in Japan alone. Meanwhile, in 1983 and 1984, the US home game market crashed, sending pioneer Atari up in flames. Nintendo persevered, successfully launching Famicom in the US in 1986 as the Nintendo Entertainment System (NES).

To prevent a barrage of independently produced, low-quality software (which had contributed to Atari's demise), Nintendo established

stringent licensing policies for its software developers. Licensees were required to have approval of every game design, buy the blank cartridges from the company, agree not to make the game for any of Nintendo's competitors, and pay Nintendo royalties for the honor of developing a game.

As the market became saturated, Nintendo sought new products, releasing Game Boy in 1989 and the Super Family Computer game system (Super NES in the US) in 1991. The company broke with tradition in 1994 by making design alliances with companies like Silicon Graphics. After creating a 32-bit product in 1995, Nintendo launched the much-touted N64 game system in 1996. It also teamed with Microsoft and Nomura Research Institute on a satellite-delivered Internet system for Japan. Price wars between the top contenders continued in the US and Japan.

In 1998 Nintendo released Pokémon, which involves trading and training virtual monsters (it had been popular in Japan since 1996), in the US. The company also launched the video game *The Legend of Zelda: Ocarina of Time*, which sold 2.5 million units in about six weeks.

The company bought a 3% stake in convenience store operator LAWSON in early 2000 in hopes of using its online operations to sell video games. Nintendo also teamed with advertising agency Dentsu to form ND Cube, a joint company that develops game software for mobile phones and portable machines.

In 2001 Nintendo launched its long-awaited GameCube console system (which retailed at $100 less than its console rivals, Sony's PlayStation 2 and Microsoft's XBox); the system debuted in North America in November. In addition, the company came out with Game Boy Advance, its newest handheld model with a bigger screen and faster chip.

In 2003 the company cut its royalty rates (charged to outside game developers), in an effort to enhance its video game titles portfolio. Later in the year Nintendo bought a stake (about 3%) in game developer and toy maker Bandai, a move expected to solidify cooperation between the two companies in marketing game software.

EXECUTIVES

President and Director: Satoru Iwata
Director; Chairman and CEO, Nintendo of America: Tatsumi Kimishima
Director; General Manager, General Affairs Division and General Affairs Department: Koji Yoshida
Director; General Manager, Personnel Division and Department: Kaoru Takemura
Director; General Manager, Acting Manufacturing Division: Takao Ohta
Director; General Manager, Tokyo Branch Office Marketing Division and Administration Department: Kazuo Kawahara
Senior Managing Director; General Manager, Integrated Research and Development Division: Genyo Takeda
Senior Managing Director; General Manager, Entertainment Analysis and Development Division: Shigeru Miyamoto
Senior Managing Director; General Manager, Corporate Analysis and Administration Division: Yoshihiro Mori
Senior Managing Director; General Manager, Marketing Division: Shinji Hatano
Senior Managing Director; General Manager, Manufacturing Division: Nobuo Nagai
Managing Director; General Manager, Finance and Information Systems Division and Finance Department: Masaharu Matsumoto
Managing Director; International Division: Eiichi Suzuki
Auditors: Kyoto Audit Corporation

LOCATIONS

HQ: Nintendo Co., Ltd.
11-1 Kamitoba Hokotate-cho, Minami-ku
Kyoto 601-8501, Japan
Phone: 81-75-662-9614   **Fax:** 81-75-662-9540
US HQ: 4600 150th Ave. NE, Redmond, WA 98052
US Phone: 425-882-2040   **US Fax:** 425-882-3585
Web: www.nintendo.co.jp

2009 Sales

	% of total
Japan	51
Americas	24
Europe	23
Other regions	2
Total	**100**

PRODUCTS/OPERATIONS

Game Consoles and Hardware

Game Boy
Game Boy Advance
Game Boy Player
GameCube
Nintendo DS
Nintendo DS Lite
Super Nintendo Entertainment System (Super NES)
Wavebird
Wii

Selected Games

Donkey Kong series
Mario Kart series
Pokémon series
Star Wars Episode I Racer
Spider-Man series
Super Mario series
Yoshi series
Zelda series

COMPETITORS

Atari
Editis
Electronic Arts
LeapFrog
Lucasfilm Entertainment
Microsoft
Namco Bandai
SEGA
Sony
Take-Two

HISTORICAL FINANCIALS

Company Type: Public

Income Statement

FYE: March 31

	REVENUE ($ mil.)	NET INCOME ($ mil.)	NET PROFIT MARGIN	EMPLOYEES
3/09	18,899	2,869	15.2%	4,306
3/08	16,843	2,592	15.4%	—
3/07	8,200	1,479	18.0%	3,150
3/06	4,332	837	19.3%	3,150
3/05	4,803	815	17.0%	—
Annual Growth	**40.8%**	**37.0%**	**—**	**11.0%**

2009 Year-End Financials

Debt ratio: 0.9%
Return on equity: 22.7%
Cash ($ mil.): 7,773
Current ratio: 3.05
Long-term debt ($ mil.): 119

No. of shares (mil.): 1,133
Dividends
   Yield: 0.0%
   Payout: —
Market value ($ mil.): 425

HOOVER'S HANDBOOK OF WORLD BUSINESS 2011

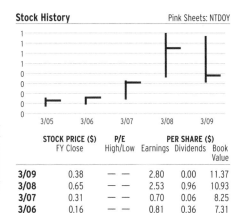

Stock History

Pink Sheets: NTDOY

	STOCK PRICE ($) FY Close	P/E High/Low	Earnings	Dividends	Book Value
3/09	0.38	— —	2.80	0.00	11.37
3/08	0.65	— —	2.53	0.96	10.93
3/07	0.31	— —	0.70	0.06	8.25
3/06	0.16	— —	0.81	0.36	7.31
3/05	0.13	— —	0.77	0.13	7.58
Annual Growth	**30.8%**	**— —**	**38.1%**	**—**	**10.7%**

Nippon Life Insurance

Nippon Life Insurance, also known as Nissay, is Japan's largest life insurer. The company, which has some 12 million policyholders in Japan, uses a door-to-door sales corps to peddle its traditional insurance products, including individual and group life and annuity policies. Nippon Life also sells through agencies and partnerships with financial institutions such as banks. In addition to its life insurance products, the company administers defined contribution pension plans and medical coverage plans and provides asset management services. Through its Nissay Dowa General Insurance affiliate, the company sells auto and other property/casualty insurance.

Nippon Life, along with its competitors in Japan, is faced with several market challenges, including a declining population (meaning a smaller customer pool), an aging population (meaning more payouts on claims), and an uneven economic recovery (which translates to cutbacks in personal expenditures).

To combat some of these problems, Nippon Life has been broadening its sales channels beyond its traditional field sales force to include an agency network and partnerships with financial services firms. (Deregulation has allowed sales of some insurance products at banks.) It has also been adding more medical coverage products to appeal to older consumers and is expanding its international operations, particularly in China, Thailand, and the US. Nippon Life is also investing in information technology system improvements to enhance customer service.

Other Nippon Life subsidiaries and affiliates are involved in real estate investment, mortgage lending, and investment advisory, among other financial services activities. The company made a $1.2 billion real estate investment in 2009 when it purchased the Japan headquarters of ailing US insurer AIG.

HISTORY

Nippon Life, known as Nissay, was a product of the modernization that began after US Commodore Matthew Perry opened Japan's ports to foreigners in 1854. Industry and trade were Japan's first focus, but financial infrastructure soon followed. The country's first insurer (Meiji Mutual) opened in 1881. In 1889 Osaka banker Sukesaburo Hirose founded Nippon Life as a stock company. It grew and opened branches in Tokyo (1890) and Kyushu (1895).

In the 20th century, the company developed a direct sales force and began lending directly to businesses. Lending remained the backbone of its asset strategy through most of the century. The insurance market in Japan grew quickly until the late 1920s but had already slowed by the eve of the Depression.

After WWII the company reorganized as a mutual and began mobilizing an army of women to build its sales of installment-premium, basic life policies. In 1962 the company began automating its systems and established operations in the US (1972) and the UK (1981).

As interest rates rose in the wake of oil price hikes in the 1970s, the company began offering term life and annuities and slowly moved to diversify its asset holdings from mostly government bonds (whose yields declined as rates rose) to stocks. This movement accelerated in the 1980s, as the businesses that traditionally borrowed from Nippon Life turned directly to capital markets to raise money through debt issues. Seeking to replace its shrinking lending business, the company began investing in US real estate and businesses whose values rose in the mid-1980s. The company reached its zenith in 1987; it owned about 3% of all the stocks on the Tokyo Exchange, held more real estate than Mitsubishi's real estate units, and had bought 13% of US brokerage Shearson Lehman from American Express.

By the end of the year, thanks to the US stock market crash, the value of the Shearson investment had fallen 40%. But the company felt confident enough of its importance as the world's largest insurance company (by assets) to crow its intentions to strong-arm Japan's Ministry of Finance into letting it diversify into trust and securities operations.

Then its bubble burst. In 1989 real estate crashed, and the stock market lost more than half its value. Japan's economy failed to improve, and Nippon Life was left struggling with nonperforming loans and assets whose value had declined. The company suffered further from policy cancellations and from the Ministry of Finance's focus on buoying banks. In 1997 the ministry asked Nippon Life to convert its subordinated debt from Nippon Credit Bank (now Aozora Bank) to stock. That year Nippon Life formed an alliance with Marsh & McLennan's Putnam Investments subsidiary to help manage its assets; the relationship deepened in 1998 when they began developing investment trust products.

The next year Nippon Life faced a shareholder lawsuit over its involvement in the collapse of Nippon Credit Bank; the company claims the Ministry of Finance tricked it into bailing out the bank, even though it was beyond rescue. In 2001 the company merged its Nissay General subsidiary with Dowa Fire & Marine, creating nonlife insurer Nissay Dowa.

In 2003 joint venture Nissay-SVA Life Insurance was formed with consumer electronics manufacturer SVA (Group) Ltd.

EXECUTIVES

Chairman: Ikuo Uno, age 75
Vice Chairman: Mitsuhiro Ishibashi, age 68
President: Kunie Okamoto, age 66
EVP and Director: Eitaro Waki, age 65
Director; General Manager, Corporate and Worksite Sales Headquarters: Taeko Yazaki
Director; General Manager, Sendai Branch; General Manager, Tohoku Corporate Relations Management Dept.: Takashi Motoyama
Director; General Manager, Personnel Dept.: Yoshinori Terajima
Director; General Manager, Policy Management Dept.: Satoru Naito
Director; General Manager, Sales Manager Business Planning Office: Toshifumi Terada
Director; General Manager, Europe; Deputy Chief, International Planning and Operations Dept.; General Manager, London Representative Office: Tetsuya Miyagawa
Director; General Manager, Business Process and Information Systems Planning Dept.: Masami Kuroda
Director; General Manager, Corporate Marketing Planning Dept.: Jyunichi Noro
Director; General Manager, Agency Marketing Headquarters: Yasuomi Matsuyama
Director; Deputy Chief, Auditing Dept.: Makoto Yanagihara
Director; General Manager, Secretarial Dept.; General Manager, Public Affairs Dept.: Kazuo Kobayashi
Senior Managing Director and Director; General Manager, Tokai Regional Headquarters; General Manager, Head Office Tokai Corporate Marketing Dept.: Sadao Kato, age 61
President and CEO, Nippon Life Benefits: Toshihiro Nakashima
Auditors: Tohmatsu & Co.

LOCATIONS

HQ: Nippon Life Insurance Company
(Nippon Seimei Hoken Kabushiki Kaisha)
3-5-12, Imabashi, Chuo-ku
Osaka 541-8501, Japan
Phone: 81-6-6209-5525   **Fax:** 81-3-5533-5282
US HQ: 521 5th Ave., New York, NY 10175
US Phone: 212-682-3000   **US Fax:** 212-286-0938
Web: www.nissay.co.jp

PRODUCTS/OPERATIONS

2009 Sales

	% of total
Premiums	76
Investment income	19
Other	5
Total	**100**

COMPETITORS

AIG
Allianz
Asahi Mutual Life
AXA
AXA Life Insurance
Daido Life
Dai-ichi Mutual Life
Fukoku Mutual
Gibraltar Life Insurance
The Hartford
ING
Meiji Yasuda Life
MetLife
Mitsui Life
Sompo Japan Insurance
Sumitomo Life
Taiyo Life
Tokio Marine

HISTORICAL FINANCIALS

Company Type: Mutual company

Income Statement   FYE: March 31

	ASSETS ($ mil.)	NET INCOME ($ mil.)	INCOME AS % OF ASSETS	EMPLOYEES
3/10	526,998	2,629	0.5%	67,438
3/09	472,808	1,563	0.3%	66,074
3/08	487,306	2,604	0.5%	63,802
3/07	442,317	2,590	0.6%	62,757
3/06	432,269	1,745	0.4%	66,437
Annual Growth	**5.1%**	**10.8%**	**—**	**0.4%**

2010 Year-End Financials

Equity as % of assets: —   Long-term debt ($ mil.): —
Return on assets: 0.5%   Sales ($ mil.): 72,170
Return on equity: —

Net Income History

Nippon Steel

When it comes to steel, Nippon Steel rates as Japan's heavy lifter. The company, the world's second-largest steelmaker after ArcelorMittal, manufactures pig iron and ingots, steel bars, plates, sheets, pipes, and tubes, as well as specialty, processed, and fabricated steel products. Nippon Steel's annual crude steel output is roughly 31 million tons. The company's operations include engineering, construction, chemicals, nonferrous metals, ceramics, electricity supply, information and communications, and urban development (theme parks and condominiums). Nippon Steel also provides energy, finance, and insurance services.

The company has experienced steady growth in its overall business due to an increase in exports primarily to East Asia and more specifically, China. The rising demand for steel has brought its own challenges, such as bottlenecked production, that Nippon Steel plans to resolve by improving its integrated production process.

Part of the strategy calls for alliances with other major steelmakers, including one with POSCO, where Nippon Steel has transferred its direct-melting gasification technology. Nippon Steel has also formed an alliance with Kobe Steel to acquire equity stakes in East Asia United Steel, which will share semi-finished products. Nippon Steel and Sumitomo Metal Industries integrated their building products units (structural steel sheet) and civil engineering materials operations, creating two new joint ventures. The companies are majority-owned by Nippon Steel, with Sumitomo taking 25% and 15% stakes, respectively.

Nippon Steel and Ternium agreed to form a joint venture in Monterrey, Mexico, in 2010 to manufacture and sell hot-dip galvanized and galvannealed steel sheets to serve the Mexican automobile market. Production at the $350 million Tenigal SRL de CV facility is set to begin in 2013.

The company again joined up with Sumitomo Metal Industries in 2009 when the two companies agreed to form a joint venture that will combine their arc-welded stainless steel pipe and tube operations. Sumitomo will own 60% of the JV. The operations that make up the new company, which will be called Sumikin & Nippon Steel Stainless Steel Pipe Co., achieved sales of more than $250 million in 2008.

HISTORY

As Japan prepared for war, the government in 1934 merged Yawata Works, its largest steel producer, and other Japanese steelmakers into one giant company — Japan Iron & Steel. During postwar occupation, Japan Iron & Steel was ordered to dissolve. Yawata Iron & Steel and Fuji Iron & Steel emerged from the dissolution, and with Western assistance the Japanese steel industry recovered from the war years. In the late 1960s Fuji Steel bought Tokai Iron & Steel (1967), and Yawata Steel took over Yawata Steel Tube Company (1968).

Yawata and Fuji merged in 1970 and became Nippon Steel, the world's largest steelmaker. In the 1970s the Japanese steel industry was criticized in the US; American competitors complained that Japan was "dumping" low-cost exports. Meanwhile, Nippon Steel aggressively courted China.

The company diversified in the mid-1980s to wean itself from dependence on steel. It created a New Materials unit in 1984, retraining "redundant" steelworkers to make silicon wafers and forming an Electronics Division in 1986. Nippon Steel began joint ventures with IBM Japan (small computers and software), Hitachi (office workstations), and C. Itoh (information systems for small and midsized companies) in 1988 as increased steel demand for construction and cars in Japan's "bubble economy" took the company to new heights.

In an atmosphere of economic optimism, the company spent more than four times the expected expense to build an amusement park capable of competing with Tokyo Disneyland. The company plowed ahead, spending some $230 million on the park. Space World amusement park opened on the island of Kyushu in 1990. The company's bubble burst that year. (The theme park declared bankruptcy in May 2005, and was sold to Kamori Kanko later that year.)

In response, Nippon Steel cut costs and intensified its diversification efforts by targeting electronics, information and telecommunications, new materials, and chemicals markets. Seeking to remake its steel operations, the company began a drastic, phased restructuring in 1993 that included a step most Japanese companies try to avoid — cutting personnel. A semiconductor division was organized that year as part of the company's diversification strategy.

Upgrading its steel operations, Nippon Steel and partner Mitsubishi in 1996 introduced the world's first mass-production method for making hot-rolled steel sheet directly from smelted stainless steel. Profits were hurt that year by a loss-making project in the information and communications segment and by a steep decline in computer memory-chip prices.

The company began operation of a Chinese steelmaking joint venture, Guangzhou Pacific Tinplate, in 1997. The next year its Singapore-based joint venture with Hitachi, Ltd., began mass-producing computer memory chips in hopes of stemming semiconductor losses. But falling prices convinced Nippon Steel to get out of the memory chip business and in 1999 it sold its semiconductor subsidiary to South Korea's United Microelectronics.

That year the US imposed antidumping duties on the company's steel products. The next year Nippon Steel agreed to form a strategic alliance with South Korea-based Pohang Iron and Steel (POSCO), at that time the world's #1 steel maker.

In 2001 Nippon Steel formed a cooperative alliance — focused on automotive sheet products — with French steel giant Usinor (now a part of ArcelorMittal). At the end of the year, Nippon Steel decided to form an alliance with Kobe Steel to pare down costs and share in distribution and production facilities. In 2002 the company continued its series of comprehensive alliances by forming alliances with Japanese steelmaker Nippon Metal Industry to exchange its semi-finished stainless steel technologies and with POSCO to build environment-related businesses.

In 2004 Nippon Steel formed a joint venture with Baoshan Iron & Steel and Arcelor to manufacture high-grade automotive steel sheets.

Nippon Steel moved into the South American market in 2006, forming alliances with steelmaker Usiminas and iron miner CVRD. The next year it created a JV with Baosteel and Arcelor-Mittal that produces automotive steel sheets.

EXECUTIVES

Chairman: Akio Mimura, age 69
President and Board Member: Shoji Muneoka, age 63
EVP and Board Member: Hiroshi Shima, age 62
EVP and Board Member: Kiichiroh Masuda, age 62
EVP and Board Member: Hideaki Sekizawa, age 64
EVP and Board Member: Tetsuo Imakubo, age 63
EVP and Board Member: Bun'yu Futamura, age 62
Managing Director Corporate Planning, Accounting, and Finance, and Board Member: Shinichi Taniguchi, age 60
Managing Director and Director Steel Research Laboratories: Yasuo Takeda, age 60
Managing Director; General Manager, Shanghai-Baoshan Cold-Rolled and Coated Sheet Products Project: Yuki Iriyama, age 62
Managing Director and Board Member: Yasuo Hamamoto, age 59
Managing Director, Director Flat Products and Bar and Wire Rod Divisions, and Board Member: Kohzoh Uchida, age 61
Managing Director; General Superintendent, Kimitsu Works: Keisuke Kuroki, age 60
Managing Director; General Manager Personnel and Labor Relations, and Board Member: Kizo Hirayama, age 61
Director and General Manager Technical Administration and Planning: Hiroshi Kimura
Director Environment and Process Technology: Ikuya Yamamoto
Director and General Manager General Administration: Kosei Shindo
Director and General Manager Sales Administration and Planning Division: Masaru Kiuchi
Director and General Manager Corporate Planning: Katsuhiko Ota
President, Nippon Steel Engineering Co.: Makoto Haya, age 64
President, NS Solutions Corporation: Mitsuo Kitagawa, age 63
Auditors: KPMG AZSA & Co.

LOCATIONS

HQ: Nippon Steel Corporation
(Shin Nippon Seitetsu Kabushiki Kaisha)
Marunouchi Park Bldg., 2-6-1
Marunouchi, Chiyoda Ward
Tokyo 100-8071, Japan
Phone: 81-3-6867-4111 **Fax:** 81-3-6867-5607
US HQ: 780 3rd Ave., 34th Fl., New York, NY 10017
US Phone: 212-486-7150 **US Fax:** 212-593-3049
Web: www.nsc.co.jp/en

PRODUCTS/OPERATIONS

2010 Sales

	% of total
Steelmaking & Steel Fabrication	78
Engineering & Construction	9
Chemicals	5
Systems Solutions	4
Urban Development	2
New Materials	2
Total	**100**

Selected Products and Services

Steelmaking and Steel Fabrication
 Fabricated and processed steels
 Pig iron and ingots
 Pipes and tubes
 Plates and sheets
 Sections
 Specialty sheets
Engineering and Construction
 Building construction
 Civil engineering
 Marine construction
 Plant and machinery
 Technical cooperation
Chemicals
 Aluminum products
 Ammonium sulfate
 Cement
 Ceramic products
 Coal tar
 Coke
 Ferrite
 Metallic foils
 Slag products
System Solutions
 Communications services
 Computers and equipment
 Data processing
 Systems development and integration
Urban Development
 Condominiums
 Theme parks
New Materials
 Semiconductor bonding wire
 Silicon wafers
 Titanium products
 Transformers
Other operations
 Services
  Energy services
  Financial services
  Insurance services
 Transportation
  Loading and unloading
  Marine and land transportation
  Warehousing

COMPETITORS

ArcelorMittal	Mitsubishi Corp.
BlueScope Steel	POSCO
Corus Group	ThyssenKrupp Steel
JFE Holdings	United States Steel
Kobe Steel	Vale
Marubeni	Yamato Kogyo

HISTORICAL FINANCIALS

Company Type: Public

Income Statement

FYE: March 31

	REVENUE ($ mil.)	NET INCOME ($ mil.)	NET PROFIT MARGIN	EMPLOYEES
3/10	37,626	(118)	—	52,205
3/09	49,029	2,160	4.4%	50,077
3/08	48,613	3,575	7.4%	15,083
3/07	36,499	2,979	8.2%	14,346
3/06	33,227	2,925	8.8%	15,212
Annual Growth	**3.2%**	**—**	**—**	**36.1%**

2010 Year-End Financials

Debt ratio: —
Return on equity: —
Cash ($ mil.): 844
Current ratio: 1.20
Long-term debt ($ mil.): —
No. of shares (mil.): 6,806
Dividends
 Yield: 0.4%
 Payout: 3.8%
Market value ($ mil.): 26,948

Stock History

Pink Sheets: NISTY

	STOCK PRICE ($) FY Close	P/E High/Low		PER SHARE ($) Earnings	Dividends	Book Value
3/10	3.96	17	12	0.26	0.01	2.92
3/09	2.70	30	10	0.24	0.10	2.52
3/08	5.09	18	8	0.54	—	2.82
3/07	7.02	17	7	0.46	—	2.36
3/06	3.88	9	5	0.43	—	2.10
Annual Growth	**0.5%**	**—**	**—**	**(11.8%)**	**(90.0%)**	**8.7%**

Nippon Telegraph and Telephone

Nippon Telegraph and Telephone (NTT) has executed an AT&T-style breakup into two local carriers and a long-distance provider — but unlike Ma Bell's gang, this family is sticking together. One of the world's largest telecom companies, NTT is a holding company for regional local phone companies NTT East and NTT West, which enjoy de facto monopolies in their markets; and long-distance carrier NTT Communications, which faces growing competition. NTT also operates a leading ISP and it owns a controlling stake in Japan's dominant cellular carrier, NTT DoCoMo. It provides IT services through majority-owned NTT DATA. NTT also has holdings throughout the Pacific Rim and in the US. The company is 34%-owned by the state.

Nippon Telegraph and Telephone does business principally in Japan. The company also operates or has investments in operations throughout the Pacific Rim — including in Australia, Hong Kong, Malaysia, the Philippines, Singapore, and Taiwan — as well as in Europe, Latin America, and the US.

The company in 2010 acquired a 70% stake in Singapore-based Emerio GlobeSoft as part of an effort to give a boost to its technology services business. Active primarily in the Asia/Pacific region, Emerio specializes in custom software development and support, IT network support, and business process outsourcing services such as account processing.

Previous acquisitions included the purchase of mobile phone application developer Panasonic Mobile Communications from parent Panasonic Corporation (formerly Matsushita Electric) in 2008.

NTT's international holdings include Hong Kong's HKNet, a minority stake in Philippine Long Distance Telephone, and Australia-based Davnet Telecommunications (Davtel), which it has renamed NTT Australia. In the US, NTT owns Web-hosting company Verio.

Combined sales from data transport, Internet services, and mobile phone operations have eclipsed conventional wireline voice revenue; in contrast to the high-growth cellular market, NTT's number of fixed-line subscribers is on the decline.

HISTORY

In 1889 the Japanese Ministry of Communications began telephone service, operated as a monopoly after 1900. In 1952 the ministry formed Nippon Telegraph and Telephone Public Corporation (NTT). Regulated by the Ministry of Posts and Telecommunications, NTT was charged with rebuilding Japan's war-ravaged phone system. Another company, Kokusai Denshin Denwa (now KDD), was created in 1953 to handle international phone service.

Japanese authorities cast NTT in the image of AT&T but prohibited it from manufacturing to encourage competition among equipment suppliers. Nonetheless, NTT bought most equipment from favored Japanese vendors. By the late 1970s NTT was a large bureaucracy, perceived as inefficient and corrupt. NTT's president quipped that the only equipment the firm would buy overseas was telephone poles and mops, but in 1981 NTT was forced to allow US companies to bid. The phone firm spent heavily in the 1980s, installing a nationwide fiber-optic network and high-speed ISDN lines.

In 1985 Japan privatized NTT as a precursor to deregulation. At its IPO, NTT became the world's most valuable public company. NTT International was established to provide overseas telecom engineering, and NTT Data Communications Systems, Japan's largest systems integrator, was formed in 1988.

As Japan's stock market bubble burst in 1990, NTT chose AT&T, Motorola, and Ericsson to develop a digital mobile phone system and the next year formed NTT Mobile Communications Network (NTT DoCoMo) as its mobile carrier. Following the deregulation of Japan's cellular market, NTT launched its Personal Handyphone Service (PHS) in 1995.

The Japanese government unveiled a plan to break up NTT in 1996, a year before the World Trade Organization spearheaded a historic agreement to open international telecom markets. Meanwhile, the government forced NTT to allow rivals to connect to its new, all-digital systems. Overseas NTT made its first significant investment in the US by buying a 12.5% stake in local carrier Teligent (later reduced).

In 1998 tiny Tokyo Telecommunications Net (a Tokyo Electric Power affiliate) offered discount phone rates, spurring NTT to do the same. NTT spun off DoCoMo in the world's largest IPO at the time.

NTT lost its 1999 bidding war with the UK's Cable and Wireless for International Digital Communications. That year NTT split into three carriers, two near-monopoly regional local phone providers — NTT East and NTT West — and a long-distance and international carrier called NTT Communications. Unlike AT&T's breakup in 1984, this split featured a holding company — the new NTT — that owns the three carriers. Criticized for continuing to promote last-generation ISDN as the key to high-speed Internet access, NTT in 1999 began to test higher-speed digital subscriber line (DSL) service and planned to cut 21,000 jobs at NTT West and NTT East over three years.

The company pressed forward with international investments, taking a 49% stake in HKNet of Hong Kong and a 49% stake in Davnet Telecommunications, a subsidiary of Australia's Davnet Limited (both were later increased to 100%). In 2000 the Japanese government said it would sell another 6% of NTT. That year NTT paid $5.5 billion for the 90% of US Web-hosting firm Verio that it didn't already own.

EXECUTIVES

Chairman: Norio Wada, age 70
President, CEO, and Board Member: Satoshi Miura, age 66
SEVP Business Strategy, CFO, Director Strategic Business Development Division, and Board Member: Hiroo Unoura, age 61
SEVP Risk Management and International Standardization, Chief Compliance Officer, and Board Member: Kaoru Kanazawa, age 65
SEVP, CTO, CIO, and Board Member: Noritaka Uji, age 61
EVP, Director Technology Planning Department and Next Generation Network Office, and Board Member: Yasuyoshi Katayama, age 58
SVP, Director General Affairs Department and Internal Control Office, and Board Member: Tetsuya Shouji
SVP, Director Research and Development Planning Department, and Board Member: Hiromichi Shinohara
SVP, Director Finance and Accounting Department, and Board Member; President, NTT Capital UK: Toshio Kobayashi, age 58
SVP, Director Corporate Strategy Planning Department, and Board Member; President, NTT Investment Partners: Hiroki Watanabe, age 57
President and CEO, Europe and Europe Online: Masaaki Moribayashi
President and CEO, Verio: Kiyoshi Maeda
President, NTT West: Shinichi Otake, age 62
President, DATA: Kazuhiro (Kaz) Nishihata
President, NTT East: Tsutomu Ebe, age 62
President, NTT Communications: Hiromi Wasai, age 64
President, NTT DoCoMo: Ryuji Yamada, age 62
President and CEO, America: Kazuhiro Gomi
Auditors: KPMG AZSA & Co.

LOCATIONS

HQ: Nippon Telegraph and Telephone Corporation (Nippon Denshin Denwa Kabushiki Kaisha)
3-1, Otemachi 2-chome, Chiyoda-ku
Tokyo 100-8116, Japan
Phone: 81-3-5205-5581   **Fax:** 81-3-5205-5589
US HQ: 101 Park Ave., 41st Fl., New York, NY 10178
US Phone: 212-661-0810   **US Fax:** 212-661-1078
Web: www.ntt.co.jp

PRODUCTS/OPERATIONS

2010 Sales

	% of total
Mobile	37
Regional	33
Long distance & international	11
Data	9
Other	10
Total	**100**

COMPETITORS

AT&T
BT
Cable & Wireless
Deutsche Telekom
Fujitsu
Internet Initiative Japan
Jupiter Telecommunications
Kansai Electric
KDDI
Pacnet
SOFTBANK MOBILE
Telstra
Tokyo Electric

HISTORICAL FINANCIALS

Company Type: Public

Income Statement

FYE: March 31

	REVENUE ($ mil.)	NET INCOME ($ mil.)	NET PROFIT MARGIN	EMPLOYEES
3/10	109,837	5,311	4.8%	195,000
3/09	107,069	5,537	5.2%	196,300
3/08	107,067	6,367	5.9%	193,800
3/07	91,350	4,049	4.4%	199,733
3/06	92,138	4,277	4.6%	199,113
Annual Growth	**4.5%**	**5.6%**	**—**	**(0.5%)**

2010 Year-End Financials

Debt ratio: 43.9%
Return on equity: 6.7%
Cash ($ mil.): 9,829
Current ratio: 1.18
Long-term debt ($ mil.): 36,870

No. of shares (mil.): 2,646
Dividends
    Yield: 0.0%
    Payout: —
Market value ($ mil.): 600

Stock History

NYSE: NTT

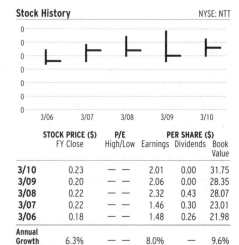

	STOCK PRICE ($) FY Close	P/E High/Low	Earnings	Dividends	Book Value
3/10	0.23	— —	2.01	0.00	31.75
3/09	0.20	— —	2.06	0.00	28.35
3/08	0.22	— —	2.32	0.43	28.07
3/07	0.22	— —	1.46	0.30	23.01
3/06	0.18	— —	1.48	0.26	21.98
Annual Growth	**6.3%**	**— —**	**8.0%**	**—**	**9.6%**

Nissan Motor Co.

Nissan Motor, one of Japan's leading auto makers, wants to get big by going small. Through its small-car initiative, the company primarily produces low-cost and fuel-efficient small cars with standard comfort, safety, style, and performance. Nissan's models include Maxima and Sentra cars, and Altima and Infiniti upscale sedans, as well as pickups, SUVs, and sports cars. It is also one of the world's largest manufacturers of forklifts. Renault holds a 44% stake in Nissan Motor, constituting the Renault-Nissan Alliance, which is largely focused on manufacturing all-electric vehicles. Nissan primarily manufactures in China, Japan, Mexico, Spain, the UK, and the US.

Like other automakers, Nissan hit a downturn in sales in 2008 and 2009. The company posted its first loss in a decade, followed by a modest uptick in 2009. Results were driven primarily by the global economic downturn and credit crisis, and Nissan's determined recovery initiative. The crisis came as Nissan was enjoying one of the car industry's most dramatic turnarounds in recent memory. Nissan's CEO Carlos Ghosn (also Renault's CEO) was heralded as a "turnaround artist" for pulling Nissan from the salvage yard in 1999 and resurrecting it from a wrecking ball of debt that totaled billions. Shortly thereafter, the Renault-Nissan alliance was born.

Under Ghosn's watchful guidance, the partnership capitalized on the synergies between the two companies, with each experiencing reciprocal benefits — Renault adopted Nissan's production system, and Nissan adopted Renault's management practices. The Alliance supports shared technologies, platforms, and even production facilities — all of which give these companies a competitive edge in the marketplace by allowing them to save on production, purchasing, and related costs. With these best practices in place, the company was able to immediately respond to the industry's turbulence by implementing cost-cutting measures and focusing on two growth areas: the global entry market (small cars) and zero-emissions vehicles.

The partnership allows Nissan to tackle projects such as an all-electric vehicle (EV) that it otherwise could not afford on its own. Through the Alliance, Nissan and Renault have invested billions in research, development, and production of vehicles with batteries. Shifting into high gear, the Alliance is creating infrastructure to ensure its electric vehicles can be powered once they are produced. It partnered with German power utility RWE to set up an electric vehicle charging network in Germany, which aims to get an estimated 1,000 charging stations up and running.

Nissan plans to launch its first EV — the Nissan Leaf — in the US and Japan, with full-scale production and marketing scheduled to begin in 2012. Its affiliate Automotive Energy Supply Corporation is producing a laminated lithium-ion battery developed by Nissan for use in its vehicles — the company's competitors are ordering the batteries, as well. Nissan formed a joint venture with Sumitomo in late summer 2010 to recycle and resell expensive lithium-ion batteries. Nissan holds 51% of the JV known as 4R Energy Corp. Nissan continues to develop flex-fuel, fuel cell, and other hybrid vehicles, alongside its traditional combustion engine offerings.

Geographically, Nissan aims to increase its presence in emerging markets such as Brazil, Russia, India, and China. The Alliance, which is principally represented by Nissan in China, created a joint venture known as Dongfeng Nissan with local carmaker Dongfeng Motor. Nissan and Dongfeng will introduce Qichen, a low-priced automobile that will only be available in China, in 2012. It will be marketed to low-wage consumers in China's interior regions. The Alliance is also making concerted steps to expand in India, where it has built a new plant in Chennai and is developing a super-low-cost vehicle with Indian motorcycle maker Bajaj.

On the Western front, the Alliance joined with Daimler in early 2010 to develop a new generation of small cars, including electric versions. Nissan-Renault and Daimler have a reciprocal agreement: Nissan-Renault will provide transmissions for certain of Daimler's Mercedes-Benz models and in return Daimler will provide Nissan with engines for its Infiniti luxury model car. The companies will take equity shares in each other, as well.

HISTORY

In 1911 US-trained Masujiro Hashimoto established Tokyo-based Kwaishinsha Motor Car Works to repair, import, and manufacture cars. Kwaishinsha made its first car, sporting its DAT ("fast rabbit" in Japanese) logo, in 1913. Renamed DAT Motors in 1925 and suffering from a strong domestic preference for American cars, the company consolidated with ailing Jitsuyo Motors in 1926. DAT introduced the son of DAT in 1931 — the Datsun minicar ("son" means "damage or loss" in Japanese, hence the spelling change).

Tobata Casting (cast iron and auto parts) bought Datsun's production facilities in 1933. Tobata's Yoshisuke Aikawa believed there was a niche for small cars, and the car operations were spun off as Nissan Motors that year.

During WWII the Japanese government limited Nissan's production to trucks and airplane engines; Nissan survived postwar occupation, in part, due to business with the US Army. The company went public in 1951 and signed a licensing agreement the next year with Austin Motor (UK), which put it back in the car business. A 40% import tax allowed Nissan to compete in Japan even though it had higher costs than those of foreign carmakers.

Nissan entered the US market in 1958 with the model 211, using the Datsun name; it established Nissan Motor Corporation in Los Angeles in 1960. Exports rose as factory automation led to higher quality and lower costs. In the 1970s Nissan expanded exports of fuel-efficient cars such as the Datsun B210. The company became the leading US car importer in 1975.

The company's name change in the US from Datsun to Nissan during the 1980s confused customers and took six years to complete. In 1986 Nissan became the first major Japanese carmaker to build its products in Europe. It launched its high-end Infiniti line in the US in 1989.

Nissan and Japanese telecom firm DDI Corporation set up cellular phone operations in 1992. Japan's recession resulted in a $450 million loss the next year. The company cut costs in 1993 and sold $200 million in real-estate holdings in 1994.

Nissan suffered its fourth straight year of losses, posting an $834 million loss for 1996. Fiscal 1997 brought profits for Nissan — its first

since 1992 — in part the result of cost-cutting moves, sales to countries with currencies stronger than the yen, and the launching of new models. In 1998 Nissan made plans to cut production in Japan by 15% over five years, and it received an $827 million loan from the government-owned Japan Development Bank to restructure its debt.

Suffering under an estimated $30 billion in debt in 1999, Nissan invited major carmakers to buy into the company. Renault took a 37% stake and a 15% stake (later increased to 23%) in affiliate Nissan Diesel Motor for $5.4 billion. The stake gave Renault veto power and enabled it to install its chief cost-cutter, Carlos Ghosn, as chief operating officer. Ghosn began plans to slash the number of suppliers, close five plants, and cut its workforce by 14% by 2002.

In 2000 Nissan sold its stake in Fuji Heavy Industries. That year Ghosn became president of Nissan; Nissan's former president, Yoshikazu Hanawa, remained as CEO and chairman. Nissan also announced that it was developing a full-sized truck for the US market. Late in the year the company announced plans to build a $930 million manufacturing plant in the US.

Ghosn was named CEO (in addition to president) in 2001. Later in 2001 Nissan announced it would take a 15% stake in Renault while the French carmaker would increase its stake in Nissan to 44%. These steps, along with the French government's decision to reduce its interest in Renault from 44% to 25%, were aimed at further strengthening the bond between the two companies. In 2002 Nissan and Renault completed their planned equity swap.

In 2006 Nissan sold its remaining 6% stake in Nissan Diesel Motor to AB Volvo.

EXECUTIVES

Chairman, President, and CEO: Carlos Ghosn, age 56
COO; External and Government Affairs, Intellectual Asset Management Design, Brand Management, Corporate Governance and Global Internal Audit and Director: Toshiyuki Shiga
EVP Research and Development and Total Customer Satisfaction Function and Director: Mitsuhiko (Mike) Yamashita
EVP Manufacturing and SCM and Director: Hidetoshi Imazu
EVP Americas Operations: Carlos Tavares
EVP Purchasing and Pacific Operations and Director: Hiroto Saikawa, age 56
EVP Europe, Africa, Middle East, India and New Project and Director: Colin Dodge
SVP and CFO, Control, Budget, and Accounting: Joseph G. (Joe) Peter, age 47
SVP Office of CEO: Greg Kelly
SVP External and Government Affairs and Intellectual Asset Management: Hitoshi Kawaguchi
SVP Technology Development Division: Minoru Shinohara
SVP Global Marketing and Sales, Global Aftersales and Conversion Business: Junichi Endo
SVP Japan Marketing and Sales: Takao Katagiri
SVP Corporate Administration, Alliance Coordination Office, Security Office, Legal Department, and Supply Chain: Philippe Klein, age 53
SVP Production Engineering Division: Shigeaki Kato
SVP Purchasing: Yasuhiro Yamauchi
SVP Powertrain Engineering Division: Yo Usuba
SVP Sales and Marketing, Nissan North America: Brian Carolin
SVP Design and Brand Management and Director: Shiro Nakamura
Auditors: Ernst & Young ShinNihon

LOCATIONS

HQ: Nissan Motor Co., Ltd.
(Nissan Jidosha Kabushiki Kaisha)
1-1, Takashima 1-chome, Nishi-ku, Yokohama-shi
Kanagawa 220-8686, Japan
Phone: 81-45-523-5523
US HQ: 1 Nissan Way, Franklin, TN 37067
US Phone: 615-725-1000   **US Fax:** 615-725-3343
Web: www.nissan-global.com

2009 Sales

	% of total
North America	30
China	22
Japan	18
Europe	15
Other regions	15
Total	**100**

PRODUCTS/OPERATIONS

2009 Sales

	% of total
Automotive	99
Sales financing	1
Total	**100**

Selected Products

Forklift
  Electric rider
  IC cushion tire
  IC pneumatic tire
  Manual pallet
  Narrow aisle
  Pallet trucks
  Tow tractor
  Walkie stackers
Infiniti
  EX35 Journey
  FX50
  G37 convertible
  G37 coupe
  G37 sedan
  M37
  QX56 2WD
Nissan
  370 Z Coupe
  Altima
  Altima coupe
  Altima hybrid
  Armada
  Cube
  Frontier
  GT-R
  Maxima
  Murano
  Pathfinder
  Rogue
  Sentra
  Titan
  Versa
  Xterra

COMPETITORS

BMW	Isuzu
Chrysler	Kia Motors
CLARK Material Handling	Mazda
Crown Equipment	Mitsubishi Motors
Daihatsu	NACCO Industries
Daimler	Peugeot
Deere	Saab Automobile
Fiat	Suzuki Motor
Ford Motor	Tata Motors
Fuji Heavy Industries	Toyota
General Motors	Volkswagen
Honda	Volvo
Hyundai Motor	Volvo Car Corp.

HISTORICAL FINANCIALS

Company Type: Public

Income Statement   FYE: March 31

	REVENUE ($ mil.)	NET INCOME ($ mil.)	NET PROFIT MARGIN	EMPLOYEES
3/09	86,724	(2,402)	—	160,422
3/08	108,504	4,835	4.5%	180,535
3/07	88,872	3,912	4.4%	186,336
3/06	80,876	4,444	5.5%	183,356
3/05	79,953	4,776	6.0%	183,607
Annual Growth	**2.1%**	**—**	**—**	**(3.3%)**

2009 Year-End Financials

Debt ratio: 67.5%
Return on equity: —
Cash ($ mil.): 6,504
Current ratio: 1.32
Long-term debt ($ mil.): 24,678

No. of shares (mil.): 2,039
Dividends
  Yield: 0.0%
  Payout: —
Market value ($ mil.): 152

Stock History   Pink Sheets: NSANY

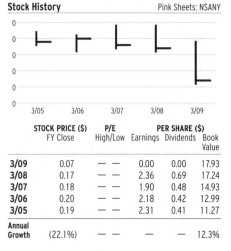

	STOCK PRICE ($) FY Close	P/E High/Low		Earnings	PER SHARE ($) Dividends	Book Value
3/09	0.07	—	—	0.00	0.00	17.93
3/08	0.17	—	—	2.36	0.69	17.24
3/07	0.18	—	—	1.90	0.48	14.93
3/06	0.20	—	—	2.18	0.42	12.99
3/05	0.19	—	—	2.31	0.41	11.27
Annual Growth	**(22.1%)**	**—**	**—**	**—**	**—**	**12.3%**

Nokia Corporation

Wireless wizard Nokia continues to cast a spell on the mobile phone market. The company is the world's #1 maker of cell phones, ahead of such rivals as Motorola and Samsung. Nokia is also aiming for the top of the mobile Internet market. Its business is divided primarily into four divisions: devices (mobile device manufacturing); services (multimedia Internet services); market and solutions (R&D, sales, and distribution); and NAVTEQ (digital map data and content). Nokia's wireless network products business is operated in partnership with Munich-based Siemens as Nokia Siemens Networks; the joint venture is the #3 player in the wireless networking equipment market, behind Ericsson and Alcatel-Lucent.

Nokia's historically robust mobile phone unit has claimed about 40% of the global cell phone market by offering a broad selection of products across a range of market niches (and continents).

Early in 2010 the company acquired geographic data and mapping software maker MetaCarta as part of its ongoing investment in technology to support location-based mobile services for wireless phones. That year Nokia also acquired Novarra, a developer of a browser and service platform for mobile devices. Nokia uses the Novarra software on its Series 40 platform,

and other handset manufacturers employ Novarra's mobile software products, as well. It later bought US-based mobile application tracking and reporting service provider Motally to further enhance the wireless Web-browsing functionality of its mobile devices.

In mid-2010 Nokia agreed to sell its wireless modem business to Renesas Electronics for about $200 million; the deal includes the transfer of more than 1,000 employees to Renesas and plans for the two companies to cooperate in developing high-speed modem technology. The sale of the business is part of Nokia's strategy to focus on its core handset business, which is facing increased competition from Apple's iPhone and other smartphone makers.

Also that year the company hired Stephen Elop, former leader of Microsoft's core business software division, as its CEO, replacing Olli-Pekka Kallasvuo, who remained chairman of Nokia Siemens Networks. The change in leadership comes as Nokia finds itself losing ground in the US against manufacturers of smartphones featuring Google's Android operating system, such as Samsung and Motorola, as well as Apple with its iPhone. The company is still the global leader in wireless handset market share, but its performance in the US has been lackluster. Elop, a Canada native, is the first person from outside of Finland to lead Nokia.

HISTORY

Nokia got its start in 1865 when engineer Fredrik Idestam established a mill to manufacture pulp and paper on the Nokia River in Finland. Although Nokia flourished within Finland, the company was not well known to the rest of the world until it attempted to become a regional conglomerate in the early 1960s. French computer firm Machines Bull selected Nokia as its Finnish agent in 1962, and Nokia began researching radio transmission technology. In 1967, with the encouragement of Finland's government, Nokia merged with Finnish Rubber Works (a maker of tires and rubber footwear, formed in 1898) and Finnish Cable Works (a cable and electronics manufacturer formed in 1912) to form Nokia Corporation.

The oil crisis of 1973 created severe inflation and a large trade deficit for Finland. Nokia reassessed its heavy reliance on Soviet trade and shifted its focus to consumer and business electronics. Nokia's basic industries — paper, chemicals, electricity, and machinery — were modernized and expanded into robotics, fiber optics, and high-grade tissues.

The company acquired a 51% interest in the state-owned Finnish telecom company in 1981 and named it Telenokia. The next year Nokia designed and installed (in Finland) the first European digital telephone system. Also in 1982 Nokia acquired interests in Salora, Scandinavia's largest maker of color televisions, and Luxor, the Swedish state-owned electronics and computer firm.

Nokia acquired control of Sahkoliikkeiden, Finland's largest electrical wholesaler, in 1986. It then created the largest information technology (IT) group in Scandinavia, Nokia Data, by purchasing Ericsson's Data Division in 1988. Sales soared, but profits plunged because of stiff price competition in consumer electronics.

To raise cash, the company sold Nokia Data to IT services company ICL in 1991 and bought UK mobile phone maker Technophone, which had been #2 in Europe, after Nokia. Under the leadership of Jorma Ollila (appointed CEO in 1992 and chairman in 1999), Nokia intensified its focus on telecommunications and sold its non-core power (1994), televisions, and tire and cable machinery (1995) units.

It also began selling digital phones at the end of 1993. The company expected to sell 400,000; it shipped 20 million in 1995. The company rode the phones' success to a billion-dollar profit in 1997.

Nokia sold more than 40 million mobile phones in 1998 to surpass Motorola and became the world's #1 mobile phone company. Extending its push into Internet capability, Nokia that year bought several small companies that develop e-commerce and telephony technologies. In 1999 Nokia penned deals to put its wireless application protocol (WAP) software into Hewlett-Packard's and IBM's network servers.

Although Nokia was leaps and bounds ahead of its rivals with digital phones and dominated the European global system for mobile communications (GSM) market, it lagged in the US market, where many big carriers adopted QUALCOMM's CDMA standard. Nokia in 2000 began to cover the bases for the third generation by offering products to bridge the gap between generations.

In 2001 Nokia added Internet security appliances to its product line-up with the acquisition of Ramp Networks. Nokia formed a subsidiary, Vertu, in 2002 to sell "luxury" mobile phones and accessories made of precious metals.

In an effort to jumpstart slowing handset sales as the cell phone market in the West and Japan flirted with saturation, Nokia in 2003 teamed with other phone makers and wireless service providers to develop a common global standard for 3G phone software. After inking several new deals in Europe and Asia, Nokia was a supplier to half of the world's commercial 3G networks by the end of 2003.

In 2008 Nokia acquired Montreal-based messaging software developer OZ Communications and subscriber network database specialist Apertio. Nokia ended 2008 by acquiring the 52% in UK-based mobile software licensing company Symbian that it did not already own for about $410 million in cash.

EXECUTIVES

Chairman: Jorma Ollila, age 60,
$580,492 total compensation
Vice Chairman: Dame Marjorie M. Scardino, age 63,
$220,785 total compensation
President and CEO: Stephen A. Elop, age 46
CTO: Richard L. (Rich) Green, age 54
EVP and CFO: Timo Ihamuotila, age 44,
$2,230,878 total compensation
EVP Devices: Kai Öistämö, age 46,
$2,861,561 total compensation
EVP Mobile Phones: Mary T. McDowell, age 46,
$2,513,622 total compensation
EVP Human Resources: Juha Äkräs, age 45
EVP Corporate Relations and Responsibility: Esko Aho,
age 56
EVP and General Manager Markets: Niklas Savander,
age 48
EVP Solutions: Alberto Torres, age 45
EVP Services: Tero Ojanperä, age 44
SVP Corporate Communications: Arja Suominen
SVP Marketing, Go-To-Market Operations:
Charmaine Eggberry
SVP Sales, Great China, Japan, and Korea; President, Nokia China: Colin Giles
VP North American Sales: Ian G. A. Laing, age 50
VP and Head, Treasury and Investor Relations:
Kristian Pullola
CEO Nokia Siemens Networks: Rajeev Suri, age 42
President and CEO NAVTEQ: Judson C. Green, age 58
President, Nokia, North America: Mark Louison
Director, Corporate Development Communications:
Mark Durrant
Auditors: PricewaterhouseCoopers Oy

LOCATIONS

HQ: Nokia Corporation
Keilalahdentie 2-4
Fl-02150 Espoo, Finland
Phone: 358-7-1800-8000 **Fax:** 358-7-1803-4003
US HQ: 102 Corporate Park Dr., White Plains, NY 10604
US Phone: 914-368-0400 **US Fax:** 914-368-0501
Web: www.nokia.com

2009 Sales

	% of total
Europe	36
Asia/Pacific	22
China	16
Middle East & Africa	14
Latin America	7
North America	5
Total	**100**

2009 Sales by Customer Location

	% of total
China	15
India	7
UK	5
Germany	4
Russia	4
US	4
Indonesia	3
Finland	1
Other countries	57
Total	**100**

PRODUCTS/OPERATIONS

2009 Sales

	% of total
Devices & services	68
Nokia Siemens Networks	30
NAVTEQ	2
Total	**100**

Selected Operations

Mobile phones
　Analog mobile cellular phones
　Digital mobile cellular phones
　Handheld telephone/personal organizers
　Phone accessories (batteries, cases, chargers)
Networks
　Base station site products
　Corporate network products
　　Base stations
　　Messaging platforms
　　Wireless local-area network (LAN) systems
　　Wireless access systems
　Fault-tolerant network routers
　Fixed network switching systems
　Internet protocol (IP) network switching systems
　Microwave radios
　Mobile radio systems
　Network, messaging, and multimedia services and software
　Radio base station controllers
　Radio network controllers
　Wireless network nodes, gateways, switches, and servers
Multimedia (services for advanced mobile devices)
　Convergence products
　Enhancements
　Entertainment
　Imaging
Enterprise solutions
　Business-optimized mobile services

COMPETITORS

Accenture
Alcatel-Lucent
Apple Inc.
Cisco Systems
Ericsson
Fujitsu
Garmin
HP Enterprise Business
HTC Corporation
Huawei Technologies
IBM
Kyocera
LG Group
Microsoft
Motorola
NEC
Oki Electric
Palm, Inc.
Panasonic Mobile Communications
QUALCOMM
Research In Motion
Samsung Electronics
SANYO
Sony Ericsson Mobile
Tellabs
TomTom
ZTE

HISTORICAL FINANCIALS

Company Type: Public

Income Statement

FYE: December 31

	REVENUE ($ mil.)	NET INCOME ($ mil.)	NET PROFIT MARGIN	EMPLOYEES
12/09	58,738	1,277	2.2%	123,553
12/08	71,751	5,643	7.9%	125,829
12/07	75,062	10,592	14.1%	100,534
12/06	54,298	5,686	10.5%	68,483
12/05	40,628	4,297	10.6%	58,874
Annual Growth	**9.7%**	**(26.2%)**	**—**	**20.4%**

2009 Year-End Financials

Debt ratio: 33.9%
Return on equity: 6.6%
Cash ($ mil.): 1,637
Current ratio: 1.55
Long-term debt ($ mil.): 6,352
No. of shares (mil.): 3,745
Dividends
　Yield: 3.2%
　Payout: 173.5%
Market value ($ mil.): 68,969

Stock History

NYSE: NOK

	STOCK PRICE ($) FY Close	P/E High/Low		PER SHARE ($) Earnings	Dividends	Book Value
12/09	18.42	69	35	0.34	0.59	5.01
12/08	21.99	37	12	1.48	0.71	5.37
12/07	56.51	23	10	2.69	0.61	5.80
12/06	26.81	22	17	1.39	0.49	4.22
12/05	21.67	23	17	0.98	0.40	3.86
Annual Growth	**(4.0%)**	**—**	**—**	**(23.3%)**	**10.2%**	**6.8%**

Nomura Holdings

Nomura Holdings is the parent company of Nomura Securities, Japan's leading investment bank and brokerage house. The company performs trading, equity and bond underwriting, research, and mergers and acquisitions (M&A) advisory services. It also makes private equity and venture capital investments. Nomura's largest segment is domestic retail, which provides investment consulting and brokerage services to consumers in its home market. The firm has operations in more than 30 countries. Nomura Securities International is the company's US trading and investment banking unit.

Subsidiary Nomura Asset Management is Japan's largest asset management company with some ¥20 trillion (about $224 billion) in assets under management. Other divisions include Nomura Trust & Banking, big-ticket financing firm Nomura Babcock & Brown, and the Nomura Institute of Capital Markets Research.

The global financial crisis has impacted Nomura, which reported steep declines in 2008 and 2009. The company lost some ¥208 billion ($2 billion) in 2009 alone on trading and equity investments. The US subprime mortgage bust further hurt the group, which lost money on mortgage-backed securities.

In response, Nomura has cut operating costs and fine-tuned its offerings. It acquired brokerage firm Instinet in 2007, allowing it to participate in electronic trading. The following year, the company boosted its global investment banking capabilities by acquiring parts of the fallen bulge-bracket firm Lehman Brothers, including operations in Asia, Europe, and the Middle East, as well as the India-based back office operations. (In its post-acquisition transition, the company laid off some 11% of its UK workforce, or about 1,000 employees in its London office.) In an effort to boost its domestic asset management business, Nomura agreed to buy NikkoCiti Trust and Banking from Citigroup in 2009. The company also exited the US residential mortgage-backed securities business entirely.

The Lehman Brothers acquisition helped boost Nomura's profile in European equities and fixed-income trading. Adding on to that purchase, Nomura announced plans to buy London-based Tricorn Partners — a move that will further complement its UK corporate finance advisory business.

Nomura's Asset Management subsidiary agreed in 2009 to buy a 35% stake in LIC Mutual Fund Asset Management Company of India. The deal will give Nomura a larger foothold in the Indian market and strengthen its credentials as an international asset manager.

In efforts to boost its commodities business, Nomura agreed to buy Nexen Energy Marketing London Limited (NEML) in 2010.

HISTORY

Tokushichi Nomura started a currency exchange, Nomura Shoten, in Osaka in 1872 and began trading stock. His son, Tokushichi II, took over and in 1910 formed Nomura's first syndicate to underwrite part of a government bond issue. It established the Osaka Nomura Bank in 1918. The bond department became independent in 1925 and became Nomura Securities. The company opened a New York office in 1927, entering stock brokerage in 1938.

The firm rebuilt and expanded retail operations after WWII. It encouraged stock market investing by promoting "million ryo savings chests" — small boxes in which people saved cash (ryo was an old form of currency). When savings reached 5,000 yen, savers could buy into investment trusts. Nomura distributed more than a million chests in 10 years.

Nomura followed clients overseas in the 1960s, helped underwrite a US issue of Sony stock, and opened a London office. It became Japan's leading securities firm after a 1965 stock market crash decimated rival Yamaichi Securities. The firm grew rapidly in the 1970s, ushering investment capital in and out of Japan and competing with banks by issuing corporate debt securities.

As the Japanese economy soared in the 1980s, the company opened Nomura Bank International in London (1986) and bought 20% of US mergers and acquisitions advisor Wasserstein Perella (1988, sold 2001).

Then the Japanese economic bubble burst. Nomura's stock toppled 70% from its 1987 peak and underwriting plummeted. In 1991 and 1992, amid revelations that Nomura and other brokerages had reimbursed favored clients' trading losses, the firm was accused of manipulating stock in companies owned by Japanese racketeers. Nomura's chairman and president — both named Tabuchi — resigned, admitting no wrongdoing.

Junichi Ujiie became president after the payoff scandal; he restructured operations to prepare for Japan's financial deregulation. Nomura invested in pub chain Inntrepreneur and William Hill, a UK betting chain. It also created an entertainment lending unit to lend against future royalties or syndication fees, and spun off a minority stake in its high-risk US real estate business, which ceased lending altogether the next year.

In 1998 Nomura was dealt a double blow when Asian economies collapsed and Russia defaulted on its debts. Incurring substantial losses, the firm refocused on its domestic market and reduced overseas operations.

In 1999 Nomura bailed out ailing property subsidiary Nomura Finance, which had been crippled by the sinking Japanese real estate market. It also invested heavily in UK real estate and bought 40% of the Czech beer market with South African Breweries.

The next year the firm agreed to buy the business services arm of Welsh utilities firm Hyder; it also bought 114,000 flats in Germany with local government authorities, its first European deal outside the UK. Also in 2000 Nomura sold its assets in pachinko parlors and "love" hotels, Japanese cultural traditions with less-than-sparkling reputations. British authorities that year fined Nomura traders in relation to charges of trying to rig Australia's stock market in 1996.

The company converted to a holding company structure in 2001 and, months later, made its debut on the NYSE. It made two big deals in the UK that year, buying hotel chain Le Méridien and becoming the nation's largest pub owner via the purchase of some 1,000 locations from Bass. In 2002 the company decided to sell the network of more than 4,100 pubs to a consortium of private investors for some $3 billion.

In 2007 Nomura acquired global agency brokerage Instinet. The deal allowed the company to begin offering electronic trading services. In 2008 Japanese regulators chose a consortium led by Nomura to take control of troubled Ashikaga Bank from the government; Nomura's private equity arm took a stake of about 45% in Ashikaga.

EXECUTIVES

Chairman: Junichi Ujiie, age 65
President, CEO, and Director; President, CEO, and Director, Nomura Securities Co., Ltd.: Kenichi Watanabe, age 57
Deputy President, COO, and Director, Nomura Holdings and Nomura Securities; Chairman and CEO, Wholesale: Takumi Shibata, age 57
Executive Managing Director and CFO; Executive Managing Director Nomura Securities Co., Ltd.: Masafumi Nakada, age 52
Executive Managing Director and Head of Corporate; Executive Managing Director, Nomura Securities Co., Ltd.; Director, Nomura Asset Management Co., Ltd.: Noriaki Nagai, age 52
Executive Managing Director and Global Markets CEO; EVP, Nomura Securities Co., Ltd.: Akira Maruyama, age 53
Executive Managing Director and Domestic Retail CEO; Deputy President, Nomura Securities Co., Ltd.: Hitoshi Tada, age 55
Executive Managing Director and Investment Banking CEO; EVP, Nomura Securities Co., Ltd.: Hiromi Yamaji, age 55
Executive Managing Director, Group Compliance Head, Head Global Operations, and CIO; Senior Corporate Managing Director, Nomura Securities Co., Ltd.: Hiroshi Tanaka, age 54
Executive Managing Director and Head of Communications: Toshio Hirota, age 53
Executive Managing Director and Asset Management CEO; Director, President, and CEO, Nomura Asset Management Co., Ltd.: Atsushi Yoshikawa, age 56
Executive Managing Director and Merchant Banking CEO; Director and President, Nomura Principal Finance Co., Ltd; Senior Managing Director, Nomura Securities Co., Ltd.: Soichi Nagamatsu, age 59
Senior Corporate Managing Director and Global Markets Deputy CEO; Senior Corporate Managing Director, Nomura Securities: Hiromasa Yamazaki
Senior Corporate Managing Director Global Research; Senior Corporate Managing Director, Nomura Securities Co., Ltd.: Hideyuki Takahashi
Chief Risk Officer and Senior Managing Director: David Benson
President and CEO, Nomura Holding America: Naoki Matsuba
Auditors: Ernst & Young ShinNihon

LOCATIONS

HQ: Nomura Holdings, Inc.
1-9-1, Nihonbashi, Chuo-ku
Tokyo 103-8645, Japan
Phone: 81-3-5255-1000
US HQ: 2 World Financial Center, Bldg. B
New York, NY 10281
US Phone: 212-667-9300   **US Fax:** 212-667-1058
Web: www.nomura.com

PRODUCTS/OPERATIONS

2010 Sales

	% of total
Net gain on trading	31
Commissions	29
Interest & dividends	17
Asset management & portfolio service fees	10
Fees from investment banking	9
Other	4
Total	**100**

COMPETITORS

Bank of America
Barclays
Boom Securities
Daiwa Securities Group
Deutsche Bank
Goldman Sachs
HSBC
Nikko Cordial
UBS Investment Bank

HISTORICAL FINANCIALS
Company Type: Public

Income Statement
FYE: March 31

	REVENUE ($ mil.)	NET INCOME ($ mil.)	NET PROFIT MARGIN	EMPLOYEES
3/10	14,637	731	5.0%	26,374
3/09	6,831	(7,280)	—	25,626
3/08	16,000	(681)	—	18,027
3/07	17,632	1,499	8.5%	16,145
3/06	15,316	2,599	17.0%	14,668
Annual Growth	(1.1%)	(27.2%)	—	15.8%

2010 Year-End Financials
Debt ratio: 338.5%
Return on equity: 3.8%
Cash ($ mil.): 14,588
Current ratio: —
Long-term debt ($ mil.): 77,663
No. of shares (mil.): 3,599
Dividends
Yield: 0.0%
Payout: —
Market value ($ mil.): 285

Stock History
NYSE: NMR

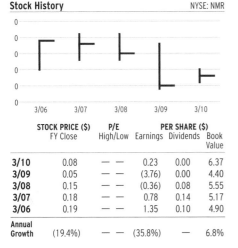

	STOCK PRICE ($) FY Close	P/E High/Low	Earnings	Dividends	Book Value
			PER SHARE ($)		
3/10	0.08	— —	0.23	0.00	6.37
3/09	0.05	— —	(3.76)	0.00	4.40
3/08	0.15	— —	(0.36)	0.08	5.55
3/07	0.18	— —	0.78	0.14	5.17
3/06	0.19	— —	1.35	0.10	4.90
Annual Growth	(19.4%)	— —	(35.8%)	—	6.8%

Norsk Hydro

Like the aluminum products it manufactures and sells, Norwegian industrial giant Norsk Hydro is both nimble and flexible. The company focuses almost exclusively on aluminum production, though it still has a toehold in renewable energy. Its operations include cast house products, building systems, extruded and rolled products, and automotive and transport products, distributed throughout Asia, Europe, and North and South America. Norsk Hydro ranks among the world's top five producers, along with Rio Tinto Alcan, RUSAL, and Alcoa. In a major deal to expand its operations in South America, Norsk Hydro agreed in 2010 to acquire the Brazilian bauxite mining and alumina refining units of Vale SA for $5 billion.

When completed, the Vale deal would give Norsk Hydro control of the world's third-largest bauxite mine and the world's biggest alumina refinery, which would supply the company with enough raw materials to operate for decades. Norsk Hydro agreed to pay Vale $1.1 billion in cash and a 22% stake in Norsk Hydro for its assets. The Norwegian government is backing the deal and has agreed to reduce its stake in Norsk Hydro by about 20%.

In 2009 Svein Richard Brandtzæg took over as chief executive. He had been in charge of Hydro's Aluminum Products unit previously. Eivind Reiten resigned after eight years in charge of the company.

Though Norsk Hydro combined its energy operations with Norwegian state-owned Statoil several years ago, it continues to own and operate 17 hydroelectric power stations in Norway.

HISTORY

Norwegian entrepreneurs Sam Eyde and Kristian Birkeland began Norsk Hydro-Elektrisk Kvaelstofaktieselskap (Norwegian Hydro-Electric Nitrogen Corp.) in 1905. The company used electricity generated from waterfalls to extract nitrogen from the air to produce fertilizer.

After WWII the Norwegian government seized German holdings in Norsk Hydro and took a 48% stake in the company. It grew to be the largest chemical firm in Scandinavia. In 1965, when Norway granted licenses for offshore petroleum exploration, the company formed partnerships with foreign companies. These included Phillips Petroleum, which spurred the North Sea boom in 1969 when its drilling rig Ocean Viking struck oil in the giant Ekofisk field, and Elf Aquitaine, which oversaw the Frigg discovery in 1971. The Norwegian state increased its share of Norsk Hydro to 51% in 1972.

The company also branched out with hydroelectric-powered aluminum processing at its Karmoy Works (1967) and with a fish-farming subsidiary, Mowi (1969). During much of the 1970s, it focused on oil and gas development, which added to the treasury and helped finance growth, often through acquisitions.

Norsk Hydro pushed into the European fertilizer market by buying Dutch company NSM in 1979; during the 1980s it acquired interests in fertilizer operations in France, Sweden, and the UK. In petrochemicals it expanded by buying two British PVC makers. Norsk Hydro-controlled Hydro Aluminum merged with ASV, another Norwegian aluminum company, in 1986, and the company consolidated its aluminum holdings two years later.

Hydro served as operator in the Oseberg field, which began production in 1988 and grew rapidly to become a major source of oil and gas. In 1990 it bought 330 Danish gasoline stations from UNO-X; in 1992 it purchased Mobil Oil's Norwegian marketing and distribution system. Two years later Norsk Hydro merged its oil and marketing operations in Norway and Denmark with Texaco's.

A weak world economy and increased competition limited its revenues in 1992 and 1993. The company countered slumping sales by selling noncore subsidiaries, including pharmaceutical unit Hydro Pharma (1992) and chocolate maker Freia Marabou (1993).

Norsk Hydro expanded further during the early 1990s, acquiring fertilizer plants in Germany, the UK, and the US, as well as W. R. Grace's ammonia plants in Trinidad and Tobago. The firm acquired Fisons' NPK fertilizer business in 1994. The company agreed to an asset swap with Petro-Canada in 1996, becoming a partner in oil and gas fields off the east coast of Canada. That year Norsk Hydro bought UNO-X's Swedish gas station operations.

The Norwegian government's stake in Norsk Hydro was reduced from 51% to about 45% in 1999 when the company and state-owned Statoil made a deal to take over Saga Petroleum, Norway's leading independent oil producer, to keep it out of foreign hands.

In light of major losses in 1999 by Hydro Agri, the company made plans in 2000 to close several European nitrogen fertilizer operations. However, it agreed to modernize and expand its Hydro Aluminum Sunndal facility, to make it the largest aluminum plant in Europe. That year the company also sold Saga UK (North Sea assets) to Conoco, and its fish-farming unit to Dutch company Nutreco.

In 2001 the company acquired a stake in Soquimich, an industrial minerals company in Chile, and majority control of Slovakian aluminum producer Slovalco.

The new decade brought with it a new focus; the company began to make aluminum and oil and energy its primary business lines. Toward that end Norsk Hydro bought VAW Aluminum from E.On AG for $2.8 billion in a deal that enabled it to expand its product base in Europe and the US, especially to key customers in the automobile industry. It then sold its flexible packaging unit to Alcan for about $545 million in 2003. Furthering the same goal, the company announced in 2003 and then followed through on a spinoff of its agrochemical unit the following year. The resultant company is called Yara International.

EXECUTIVES

Chairperson: Terje Vareberg, age 61
Deputy Chairperson: Bente Rathe, age 56
President and CEO: Svein R. Brandtzæg, age 52
CFO: Jørgen C. Arentz Rostrup, age 43
CIO: Stig Heggelund
Chief Communication Officer: Inger Sethov
EVP Primary Metal: Hilde M. Aasheim, age 52
EVP Legal and Corporate Social Responsibility: Odd I. Biller, age 61
EVP Rolled Products: Oliver Bell
EVP Aluminium Products: Svein Richard Brandtzæg, age 52
EVP Projects: Tom Røtjer, age 57
EVP Extrusion: Johnny Undeli
EVP Human Resources and Organizational Development: Anne Harris, age 49
EVP Energy: Arvid Moss, age 52
EVP Metal Markets: Kjetil Ebbesberg
Head Investor Relations: Stefan Solberg
Auditors: Deloitte AS

LOCATIONS

HQ: Norsk Hydro ASA
Drammensveien 260
N-0283 Oslo, Norway
Phone: 47-22-53-81-00 **Fax:** 47-22-53-27-25
Web: www.hydro.com

2009 Sales

	% of total
European Union	
Germany	19
UK	7
France	7
Italy	7
Other	23
Non-EU	
Switzerland	8
Other	4
US	9
Other regions	16
Total	**100**

2009 Sales

	% of total
Metal markets	33
Primary metals	25
Extruded products	19
Rolled products	18
Energy	5
Total	**100**

Selected Operations

Aluminum products
   Hydro aluminum automotive
   Hydro aluminum extrusion
   Hydro aluminum rolled products and wire rod

Aluminum metal

Energy
   Hydroelectric power stations

COMPETITORS

Alcoa
BHP Billiton
Chinalco
Rio Tinto Alcan
RUSAL

HISTORICAL FINANCIALS

Company Type: Public

Income Statement

FYE: December 31

	REVENUE ($ mil.)	NET INCOME ($ mil.)	NET PROFIT MARGIN	EMPLOYEES
12/09	11,601	72	0.6%	19,249
12/08	12,554	(498)	—	22,634
12/07	17,401	3,433	19.7%	24,692
12/06	31,396	2,783	8.9%	33,605
12/05	25,750	2,324	9.0%	32,765
Annual Growth	**(18.1%)**	**(58.1%)**	**—**	**(12.5%)**

2009 Year-End Financials

Debt ratio: 4.8%
Return on equity: —
Cash ($ mil.): 443
Current ratio: 1.85
Long-term debt ($ mil.): 384

No. of shares (mil.): 1,205
Dividends
   Yield: —
   Payout: —
Market value ($ mil.): 10,100

Stock History

Pink Sheets: NHYDY

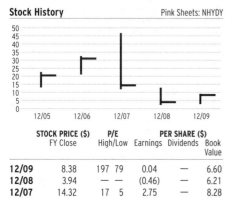

	STOCK PRICE ($) FY Close	P/E High/Low		PER SHARE ($) Earnings	Dividends	Book Value
12/09	8.38	197	79	0.04	—	6.60
12/08	3.94	—	—	(0.46)	—	6.21
12/07	14.32	17	5	2.75	—	8.28
12/06	31.00	14	10	2.24	—	12.81
12/05	20.43	12	7	1.84	—	11.72
Annual Growth	**(20.0%)**	**—**	**—**	**(61.6%)**	**—**	**(13.4%)**

Novartis AG

Although it's based in neutral Switzerland, Novartis has been aggressive in attacking illnesses on four fronts: pharmaceuticals, generics, vaccines and diagnostics, and consumer health. Its largest division, Pharmaceuticals, develops and manufactures prescription drugs for blood pressure, cancer, and other ailments. Novartis' Sandoz subsidiary produces generic drugs and active pharmaceutical ingredients, while the Vaccine and Diagnostics segment makes vaccines and blood-screening tools. The Consumer Health unit includes OTC medications such as Benefiber, Excedrin, and Theraflu, along with CIBA Vision's contact lenses and eye care products and Animal Health's companion and agricultural animal care products.

Making a bold move in the eye-care market, Novartis has also purchased a majority stake (about 77%) in consumer health, pharmaceutical, and surgical equipment maker Alcon from Nestlé for some $39 billion. The deal was kicked off with Novartis' purchase of a 25% stake in Alcon for $10.4 billion in mid-2008. Then, in 2010 Novartis exercised its option to buy Nestlé's remaining 52% stake in Alcon for $28.3 billion. Novartis hopes to eventually make Alcon a wholly owned subsidiary by purchasing the remaining shares (representing a 23% stake) from minority holders.

Novartis' blockbuster prescription drugs include high blood pressure treatment Diovan, leukemia drug Gleevec/Glivec, and Zometa, an intravenous treatment for bone tumors caused by prostate, lung, and breast cancers. Other well-performing products include Femara, used to treat postmenopausal women with early and advanced breast cancer, and Lucentis, a treatment for age-related macular degeneration.

Like most large drugmakers, Novartis is facing increasing pressure to develop new blockbusters in the face of patent expiration and rising levels of generic competition. Several of its former best sellers, including Famvir (antiviral), Lotrel (high blood pressure), and Trileptal (epilepsy treatment), are experiencing dwindling sales due to launches of generic versions.

To ward off competitive pressures, Novartis maintains a healthy drug pipeline with about 150 candidates in clinical development stages. R&D programs are focused on core therapeutic areas including cardiology, metabolism, oncology, neurology, respiratory, ophthalmic, and infectious disease. In the US market, recently launched products include Femara for breast cancer, which received FDA approval in 2009, and schizophrenia treatment Fanapt, which was approved in 2010.

Novartis is counting on the launch of its new drug for multiple sclerosis, Gilenya, to be a big revenue earner in the coming years. Gilenya is the US market's first oral treatment for MS.

To avoid losing too much of its business to generics, Novartis makes its own generic drugs through the Sandoz segment. Novartis has grown the Sandoz business through acquisitions, and in 2009 completed a $1.3 billion deal to acquire the specialty generic injectables arm of Austrian-based Ebewe Pharma.

In early 2010 Daniel Vasella stepped down as CEO after holding the job for 14 years, but remained chairman. Joe Jimenez moved from his position as head of the company's pharmaceutical division to become CEO.

HISTORY

Johann Geigy began selling spices and natural dyes in Basel, Switzerland, in 1758. A century later the Geigy family began producing synthetic dyes. About that time Alexander Clavel also entered the synthetic dye trade in Basel, forming the Gesellschaft fur Chemische Industrie Basel (Ciba). Ciba was Switzerland's #1 chemical firm at century's end.

After WWI, Ciba, Geigy, and Sandoz (a Basel synthetic dye maker founded in 1886) formed the Basel AG cartel to compete with German rival I.G. Farben. Basel used its profits to diversify into pharmaceuticals and other chemicals and to gain a foothold in the US. In 1929 Basel merged with German and, later, French and British counterparts, but WWII shattered the so-called Quadrapartite Cartel in 1939, leaving only Basel AG intact.

Basel scientist Paul Muller won a Nobel Prize in 1948 for inventing DDT. Basel AG voluntarily dissolved itself back into its component parts in 1951.

Ciba, Geigy, and Sandoz continued to diversify. Finding new markets in agricultural chemicals, Geigy had passed Ciba in sales by 1967. That year Sandoz bought the Wander group of companies (dietetic products). Ciba and Geigy merged in 1970 and began a series of US acquisitions, including Funk Seeds in 1974. Sandoz bought Minneapolis-based Northrup, King & Co. (1976) and Dutch seed company Zaadunie (1980).

Ciba-Geigy and US biotech company Chiron started a joint venture in 1986 to produce and market genetically engineered vaccines (Ciba-Geigy acquired 50% of Chiron in 1994). Sandoz also bought shares in US biotechnology companies, including Genetic Therapy and SyStemix, in 1991. It bought Gerber (founded 1927) in 1994.

Ciba-Geigy and Sandoz rejoined to form Novartis in 1996. To win approval for the merger, Sandoz (whose Daniel Vasella became CEO of the new company) sold its corn herbicide and US animal health businesses. Chairman Alex Krauer, who had overseen the formation of Novartis, stepped down in 1998, leaving the post to Vasella.

In 2000 Novartis spun off its crop protection and seed units. The firm's joint venture with BioTransplant successfully cloned genetically altered pigs whose organs would be more suitable for human transplants in 2001.

Novartis' consumer health business got a Boost, literally, when it purchased Mead Johnson's adult nutrition business in 2004. The buy included brands such as Boost nutritional drinks, and feeding tube products Isocal and Ultracal. That same year the company purchased the US and Canadian consumer products division of Bristol-Myers Squibb, which brought headache remedy Excedrin, cold and flu treatment Comtrex, and Keri moisturizers into the company's consumer products stable.

In 2005 the firm acquired Hexal AG, one of Germany's top generics makers, and a controlling stake in Hexal's sister firm Eon Labs, a US generics manufacturer.

In 2006 Novartis acquired NeuTec Pharma, a UK-based biopharmaceutical company with two drug candidates that target otherwise drug-resistant "superbugs." That same year, Novartis spent $5.1 billion to acquire struggling vaccine and biopharmaceuticals products maker Chiron.

Novartis sold off the last of its non-health care businesses in 2007, when Nestlé purchased Novartis' medical nutrition business for $2.5 billion and its Gerber baby products business for $5.5 billion.

EXECUTIVES

Chairman: Daniel L. Vasella, age 55,
$17,325,266 total compensation
Vice Chairman: Hans-Jörg Rudloff, age 69
Vice Chairman: Ulrich Lehner, age 63
CEO: Joseph (Joe) Jimenez Jr., age 50,
$7,447,284 total compensation
CFO: Jonathan R. (Jon) Symonds, age 50
**Group Head Quality Assurance and Technical
Operations:** Andreas Rummelt, age 53,
$39,168,495 total compensation
General Counsel: Thomas Werlen, age 44,
$1,989,837 total compensation
Head Human Resources: Juergen Brokatzky-Geiger,
age 57, $2,617,279 total compensation
Head Group Country Management and External Affairs:
Kim Stratton
**Head Parmaceuticals, North America; President,
Novartis Pharmaceuticals Corporation:**
Andre (Andy) Wyss
Head Novartis Group Quality: Juan Andres
Head Corporate Communications: Sheldon Jones
Corporate Secretary: Monika Matti
Public Relations, US: Pamela (Pam) McKinlay
Secretary to Executive Committee: Bruno Heynen
President, Novartis Institutes for BioMedical Research:
Mark C. Fishman, age 58,
$6,848,281 total compensation
**CEO, Consumer Health Division; Head, Novartis
Animal Health Business Unit:** George Gunn, age 59
CEO, Vaccines and Diagnostics Division:
Andrin Oswald
CEO, Sandoz Division: Jeffrey (Jeff) George, age 36
CEO, Novartis Pharmaceuticals: David R. Epstein,
age 48
Auditors: PricewaterhouseCoopers AG

LOCATIONS

HQ: Novartis AG
Lichtstrasse 35
CH-4056 Basel, Switzerland
Phone: 41-61-324-1111 **Fax:** 41-61-324-8001
US HQ: 608 5th Ave., New York, NY 10020
US Phone: 212-307-1122 **US Fax:** 212-246-0185
Web: www.novartis.com

2009 Sales

	% of total
US	32
Germany	9
Japan	8
France	5
UK	3
Switzerland	2
Other	41
Total	**100**

PRODUCTS/OPERATIONS

2009 Sales

	% of total
Pharmaceuticals	65
Sandoz	17
Consumer Health	13
Vaccines & Diagnostics	5
Total	**100**

2009 Pharmaceutical Sales

	% of total
Oncology	32
Cardiovascular & metabolism	31
Neuroscience & ophthalmics	17
Immunology & infectious disease	11
Respiratory	4
Other pharmaceutical products	5
Total	**100**

Selected Products

Pharmaceuticals
  Aclasta (osteoporosis)
  Clozaril (schizophrenia)
  Comtan/Stalevo (Parkinson's disease)
  Diovan (hypertension)
  Elidel (eczema)
  Exelon (Alzheimer's disease)
  Exforge (hypertension)
  Exjade (iron chelator)
  Extavia (multiple sclerosis)
  Famvir (antiviral for herpes)
  Fanapt (schizophrenia)
  Femara (advanced breast cancer)
  Focalin (ADHD)
  Foradil (asthma)
  Gleevec/ Glivec (leukemia and gastrointestinal tumor
    treatment)
  Lescol (cholesterol)
  Lotrel (hypertension)
  Lucentis (age-related macular degeneration)
  Miacalcic (osteoporosis)
  Myfortic (transplant)
  Neoral/Sandimmun (transplant rejection preventative)
  Ritalin (attention deficit hyperactivity disorder)
  Sandostatin LAR (cancer)
  Tekturna/Rasilez (blood pressure)
  Tegretol (epilepsy, acute mania, and bipolar affective
    disorders)
  Trileptal (epilepsy)
  Visudyne (wet age-related macular degeneration)
  Voltaren (antirheumatic)
  Xolair (asthma)
  Zometa (cancer complications)
Sandoz generic pharmaceuticals
  Acetylcysteine (respiratory)
  Amoxicillin (antibiotic)
  Fentanyl (pain)
  Omeprazole (heartburn)
  Simvastatin (cholesterol)
  Tacrolimus (transplant)
  Tiamulin (statin)
  Vancomycin (antibiotic)
Consumer Health
  Animal health
    Agita (fly control)
    Atopica (atopic dermatitis management)
    Deramaxx (pain relief for dogs and cats)
    Sentinel (flea control for dogs)
  CIBA Vision
    AQuify Multi-Purpose Solution (aka Solocare,
      contact lens cleaning solution)
    Cibasoft (contact lenses)
    Clear Care (aka Aosept, contact lens cleaning
      system)
    Focus (contact lenses)
    FreshLook (tinted contact lenses)
    Night & Day (continual wear contact lenses)
  OTC
    Benefiber (fiber supplements)
    Excedrin (systemic analgesic)
    Nicotinell (or Habitrol, smoking cessation patch)
    Prevacid (heartburn)
    Theraflu (flu treatment)
    Triaminic (cough and cold remedy)
Vaccines and diagnostics
  Flu vaccines (Agrippal, Begrivac, Fluad, Fluvirin,
    Optaflu)
  HIV and hepatitis vaccines (Procleix)
  Meningitis vaccines (Menjugate)
  Pediatric vaccines (Polioral, Quinvaxem)
  Traveling vaccines (Encepur, Ixiaro, Rabipur)

COMPETITORS

Abbott Labs
Allergan
Amgen
AstraZeneca
Bausch & Lomb
Baxter International
Bayer AG
Biogen Idec
Bristol-Myers Squibb
Dr. Reddy's
Eli Lilly
Essilor International
Genzyme
GlaxoSmithKline
Johnson & Johnson
Merck
Novo Nordisk
Perrigo
Pfizer
Ranbaxy Laboratories
Roche Holding
Sanofi-Aventis
Teva Pharmaceuticals

HISTORICAL FINANCIALS

Company Type: Public

Income Statement

FYE: December 31

	REVENUE ($ mil.)	NET INCOME ($ mil.)	NET PROFIT MARGIN	EMPLOYEES
12/09	45,103	8,454	18.7%	99,834
12/08	42,584	8,195	19.2%	96,717
12/07	38,072	11,946	31.4%	98,200
12/06	36,031	7,175	19.9%	100,735
12/05	32,212	6,130	19.0%	90,924
Annual Growth	**8.8%**	**8.4%**	**—**	**2.4%**

2009 Year-End Financials

Debt ratio: 15.1%
Return on equity: 15.7%
Cash ($ mil.): 2,894
Current ratio: 1.73
Long-term debt ($ mil.): 8,675

No. of shares (mil.): 2,290
Dividends
  Yield: 3.1%
  Payout: 46.3%
Market value ($ mil.): 124,623

Stock History

NYSE: NVS

	STOCK PRICE ($) FY Close	P/E High/Low		PER SHARE ($) Earnings	Dividends	Book Value
12/09	54.43	15	9	3.69	1.71	25.06
12/08	49.76	17	12	3.59	1.54	21.96
12/07	54.31	12	10	5.13	1.10	21.50
12/06	57.44	20	17	3.04	0.89	17.96
12/05	52.48	21	17	2.62	0.86	14.41
Annual Growth	**0.9%**	**—**	**—**	**8.9%**	**18.7%**	**14.8%**

Novo Nordisk

Novo Nordisk gives diabetics the tools to stick it to their disease. One of the world's leading producers of insulin, Novo Nordisk also makes insulin analogues, injection devices, and diabetes education materials. Its products include analogues Levemir and NovoLog (which mimic natural insulin regulation more closely than human insulin) and the FlexPen, a pre-filled insulin injection tool. In addition to its diabetes portfolio, the firm has products in the areas of hemostasis management (blood clotting), human growth hormone, and hormone replacement therapy. The not-for-profit Novo Nordisk Foundation, through its Novo A/S subsidiary, controls the voting power in Novo Nordisk.

Novo Nordisk's non-diabetic biopharmaceuticals include Activelle (hormone replacement), NovoSeven (a hemophilia treatment), and Norditropin (human growth hormone).

Novo Nordisk is growing on the strength of its insulin product lines, as well as burgeoning sales of NovoSeven and human growth hormone. In particular, increased demand for prefilled cartridges and insulin analogues, or modern insulins, is contributing to strong results. Modern insulins imitate the body's own physiological processes of regulating insulin more successfully and thus are said to better regulate glucose and produce fewer complications.

In early 2010 the company's diabetes drug Victoza was approved in the US and Japan as a once-daily injection to control blood sugar levels. Since it is the only once-daily drug of its kind on the US market, Novo Nordisk is banking on the modern insulin to become one its lead products.

As with most biopharmaceutical enterprises, Novo Nordisk engages in alliances with medical institutions and other drug companies to further its research and marketing activities. In 2009 it bought some technology assets from its former partner, the now-defunct Neose Technologies; the two companies had been working together on hemophilia therapies using Neose's GlycoPEGylation technology. Up until 2010 the company owned about one-third of ZymoGenetics, a Seattle-based biotechnology company; however, it sold its stake to Bristol-Myers Squibb after owning about one-quarter of the company since 1988.

The company's pipeline includes candidates in areas such as inflammation and obesity. It is also developing additional treatments for hemophilia and type 2 diabetes.

In 2008 the company halted development on its AERx inhaled insulin product, believing that the product could not provide significant benefits over existing therapies. The decision came soon after Pfizer's much-publicized failure with Exubera, its own inhaled insulin, which had not sold well. Novo Nordisk had been working on AERx with drug delivery specialist Aradigm.

HISTORY

Novo Nordisk was formed by the 1989 merger of Danish insulin producers Novo and Nordisk.

Soon after Canadian researchers extracted insulin from the pancreases of cattle, Danish researcher August Krogh (winner of the 1920 Nobel Prize in physiology) and physician Marie Krogh, his wife, teamed up with H. C. Hagedorn, also a physician, to found Nordisk Insulinlaboratorium. One of their lab workers was an inventor named Harald Pedersen, and in 1923 Nordisk hired Pedersen's brother, Thorvald, to analyze chemicals. The relationship was unsuccessful, however, and the brothers left the company.

The Pedersens decided to produce insulin themselves and set up operations in their basement in 1924. Harald also designed a syringe that patients could use for their own insulin injections. Within a decade their firm, Novo Terapeutisk Laboratorium, was selling its product in 40 countries.

Meanwhile, Nordisk introduced a slow-acting insulin in 1936. NPH insulin, launched in the US in 1950, soon became the leading longer-acting insulin. Nordisk later became a major maker of human growth hormone.

During WWII Novo produced its first enzyme, trypsin, used to soften leather. It began producing penicillin in 1947 and during the 1950s developed Heparin, a trypsin-based drug used to treat blood clots. The company unveiled more industrial enzymes in the 1960s.

In 1981 Novo began selling its insulin in the US through a joint venture with E. R. Squibb (now part of Bristol-Myers Squibb). The next year Novo was the first to produce human insulin (actually a modified form of pig insulin), and in 1983 Nordisk introduced the Nordisk Infuser, a pump that constantly released small quantities of insulin. Two years later Novo debuted the NovoPen, a refillable injector that looked like a fountain pen.

Novo was the world's #2 insulin maker (and the world's largest maker of industrial enzymes) when it merged with #3, Nordisk, in 1989. By combining their research and market share, they were better able to compete globally with then-#1 Eli Lilly. After the merger, Novo Nordisk introduced the NovoLet, the world's first prefilled, disposable insulin syringe.

Novo Nordisk introduced drugs for depression (Seroxat, 1992), epilepsy (Gabitril, 1995), and hemophilia (NovoSeven, 1995). The company entered a joint marketing alliance with Johnson & Johnson subsidiary LifeScan, the world's #1 maker of blood glucose monitors, in 1995. It also began working with Rhône-Poulenc Rorer on estrogen replacement therapies.

Eli Lilly raised a new challenge in 1996 with the FDA approval of Humalog (the US's first new insulin product in 14 years), which is absorbed faster, giving users more flexibility in their injection schedule. (Novo Nordisk's own fast-acting insulin product, NovoLog, received FDA approval four years later.) A 1998 marketing pact with Schering-Plough signaled Novo Nordisk's desire to boost sales of its diabetes drugs in the US, where Eli Lilly has historically dominated.

In 2000 Novo Nordisk split its health care and enzymes businesses; the split left Novo Nordisk with all the health care operations, while a new company, Novozymes, was formed to carry out the enzyme business. It bought out the remaining shares in its Brazilian subsidiary, Biobrás, in 2001. The following year the company spun off its US-based biotechnology firm, ZymoGenetics, though it retained a significant minority stake in the company.

Novo Nordisk divested its 29% stake in Ferrosan, a Danish consumer health care and medical devices company, in 2005.

Biopharmaceuticals
  NovoSeven (recombinant hemophilia therapy)
  Norditropin (human growth hormone)
  Activelle (hormone replacement therapy)
  Vagifem (hormone replacement therapy)

COMPETITORS

Alkermes
Amylin Pharmaceuticals
Animas
Baxter International
Becton, Dickinson
Biogen Idec
Eli Lilly
Genentech
GlaxoSmithKline
MannKind
MDRNA
Medtronic
Merck Serono
Novartis
Ortho-McNeil Pharmaceutical
Pfizer
Sanofi-Aventis
Talecris
Wockhardt

HISTORICAL FINANCIALS

Company Type: Public

Income Statement

FYE: December 31

	REVENUE ($ mil.)	NET INCOME ($ mil.)	NET PROFIT MARGIN	EMPLOYEES
12/09	9,838	2,074	21.1%	29,000
12/08	8,658	1,833	21.2%	26,600
12/07	8,246	1,680	20.4%	26,000
12/06	6,858	1,142	16.7%	23,000
12/05	5,357	931	17.4%	22,000
Annual Growth	16.4%	22.2%	—	7.2%

2009 Year-End Financials

Debt ratio: 2.7%
Return on equity: 31.5%
Cash ($ mil.): 2,176
Current ratio: 2.44
Long-term debt ($ mil.): 187

No. of shares (mil.): 600
Dividends
  Yield: 6.9%
  Payout: 24.5%
Market value ($ mil.): 7,379

Stock History

NYSE: NVO

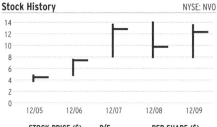

	STOCK PRICE ($) FY Close	P/E High/Low		PER SHARE ($) Earnings	Dividends	Book Value
12/09	12.30	4	2	3.43	0.84	11.47
12/08	9.73	5	3	2.94	0.60	10.45
12/07	12.80	5	3	2.64	0.99	10.57
12/06	7.40	4	3	1.77	0.75	8.89
12/05	4.46	3	3	1.41	0.38	7.31
Annual Growth	28.9%	—	—	24.9%	21.9%	11.9%

NTT DoCoMo

The Japanese yen for mobility means business for NTT DoCoMo. The mobile phone carrier is one of the world's largest wireless network operators in terms of subscribers, behind global leader Vodafone. NTT DoCoMo has about 54 million subscribers to its FOMA-branded wireless voice network while about 47 million customers subscribe to its i-mode mobile Internet services. The company also sells wireless telephone handsets under the DoCoMo brand and it provides emergency satellite communications services primarily for maritime use. NTT DoCoMo is the wireless spinoff of Japan's leading telecommunications carrier Nippon Telegraph and Telephone (NTT); NTT owns 66% of NTT DoCoMo.

DoCoMo means "anywhere" and NTT DoCoMo is everywhere in the Japanese market for mobile communication services. However, faced with a mature market and stiff competition at home, NTT DoCoMo has renewed its efforts to tap into growth markets abroad, particularly in the Asia/Pacific region.

Its largest purchase in this overseas push was the 2009 acquisition of about one-quarter of India-based Tata Teleservices for about $2.7 billion. The company hopes to tap into the burgeoning Indian market through this alliance with the telecommunications arm of the Tata Group. Also that year, NTT DoCoMo bought a 35% stake in US multimedia software maker PacketVideo to bolster its internal efforts to develop applications for mobile video services. It acquired the rest of the company from parent NextWave Wireless for about $115 million late the next year.

NTT DoCoMo in 2008 bought stakes in operators in Bangladesh (TM International, 30%) and the Philippines (PLDT, 20%). Additionally, the company has i-mode network technology licensing agreements with about a dozen GSM network operators in Europe, including Russia and Greece, as well as in the Asia/Pacific region.

NTT DoCoMo's efforts to garner higher subscription fees from its existing customer base in Japan and improve retention have included an increase in the variety of mobile services it offers, the introduction of cell phones offering a broader set of features (e-mail, music playback, and gaming), and ongoing investments in its network infrastructure to enable bandwidth-hungry streaming content such as video programming.

HISTORY

Formed in 1952 by the Japanese Ministry of Communications to rebuild Japan's war-ravaged phone system, Nippon Telegraph and Telephone (NTT) enjoyed a monopoly on phone services for more than four decades.

NTT first went into mobile communications with a maritime phone service in 1959, and in 1968 the company began offering paging services. Other telecommunications services followed: car phone service (1979), in-flight phone service (1986), and mobile phone service (1987).

In 1991 NTT established a subsidiary to adopt these wireless segments; it launched operations in 1992 as NTT Mobile Communications Network under the leadership of NTT executive Kouji Ohboshi. The firm quickly took on the DoCoMo nickname. The year closed with slightly more than a million analog mobile phone users in Japan — a market DoCoMo shared with upstart telecom companies DDI and IDO (later bought by DDI). Paging service was more popular, and DoCoMo won more than 3 million customers.

DoCoMo in 1993 launched digital mobile phone service based on a scheme called PDC (personal digital cellular) — a system incompatible with the digital standards that would take root in Europe and the US. Liberalization of the cellular phone market in 1994 triggered unexpected growth: Customers who previously had to lease mobile phones from the network operators could now buy them at retail stores. Further competition emerged in 1995 with the launch of personal handyphone services, or PHS (parent company NTT was among the companies providing PHS), but DoCoMo's subscriber count passed 3.5 million mobile phone users — about half the market.

DoCoMo's pager business peaked in 1996 before commencing a long-term decline; the mobile phone market, where DoCoMo had more than 8 million subscribers, overtook it. The company launched a satellite-based mobile phone system that year to serve customers beyond the range of cell sites, reaching ships and mountainous regions.

Financial crises rocked the Pacific Rim in 1997, and Japan's Fair Trade Commission rocked NTT by ordering it to cut its 95% ownership of DoCoMo. Customers continued to flock to mobile phones despite economic turmoil, and DoCoMo passed the 15-million-subscriber mark. In 1998 DoCoMo gave hope to Japan's low-flying market when it left the nest: Its mammoth IPO raised more than $18 billion.

Meanwhile, DDI (now KDDI) had become the first Japanese carrier to launch a digital mobile phone network based on CDMA (code division multiple access) technology. Though DoCoMo still used PDC, it redoubled its efforts to help develop and standardize a next-generation, wideband version of CDMA.

In 1999 DoCoMo took over NTT's unprofitable PHS unit and rolled out a high-speed data service over the PHS network. That year it acquired a 19% stake in the telecom unit of Hong Kong's Hutchison Whampoa, but failed expectations led the company to sell its stake in Hutchison 3G UK to Hutchison Whampoa in 2005 for €120 million.

In 2000 the company adopted NTT DoCoMo as its corporate name. To promote its new data services, NTT DoCoMo launched a joint venture in Japan with Microsoft (Mobimagic). It took the i-mode service international in 2001 when the company teamed up with Telecom Italia Mobile to introduce the 3G service in Europe.

The company staked its claim in the US, too, by paying $9.8 billion for a 16% stake in AT&T Wireless in 2001. NTT DoCoMo sold its stake following the 2004 takeover of AT&T Wireless by rival Cingular Wireless (now AT&T Mobility) in a deal valued at $41 billion.

After the number of paging service subscribers fell to less than 300,000 from a high of 6.5 million (in 1996), NTT DoCoMo ended the service in early 2007. It additionally dissolved allucher, a marketing and consulting services provider to mobile phone users, and its animation-related Web portal management and marketing business known as Hive. Meanwhile, NTT DoCoMo also discontinued its Personal Handyphone Service (PHS) and its CITYPHONE digital mobile service in 2008.

EXECUTIVES

President, CEO, and Board Member: Ryuji Yamada, age 62
SEVP Multimedia Services and Technology and Board Member: Kiyoyuki Tsujimura, age 60
SEVP Global Business and Board Member: Masatoshi Suzuki, age 58
SEVP and Board Member: Hiroshi Matsui, age 64
EVP, CFO, Managing Director Accounts and Finance, and Board Member: Kazuto Tsubouchi, age 58
EVP and Deputy Managing Director Corporate Marketing: Haruhide Nakayama
EVP, Managing Director Research and Development, and Board Member: Mitsunobu Komori, age 58
EVP and Managing Director, Kansai Regional Office: Shozo Nishimura
EVP and Managing Director, Tokai Regional Office: Toru Kobayashi
EVP, Managing Director Corporate Strategy and Planning, and Board Member: Kaoru Kato, age 59
EVP Consumer Sales and Director: Bunya Kumagai, age 58
EVP and Managing Director Corporate Marketing: Akio Oshima
SVP, Managing Director Human Resources Management, and Board Member: Takashi Tanaka, age 55
SVP and Managing Director Information Systems: Seiji Nishikawa
SVP, Managing Director Public Relations, and Deputy Managing Director Mobile Society Research Institute: Yoshikiyo Sakai
SVP and Managing Director Consumer Services: Hiroyasu Asami
SVP and Managing Director Research and Development Strategy: Seizo Onoe
Head Investor Relations: Osamu Hirokado
Auditors: KPMG AZSA & Co.

LOCATIONS

HQ: NTT DoCoMo, Inc.
Sanno Park Tower, 11-1 Nagatacho-2-chome
Chiyoda-ku
Tokyo 100-6150, Japan
Phone: 81-3-5156-1338   **Fax:** 81-3-5156-0271
Web: www.nttdocomo.com

PRODUCTS/OPERATIONS

2010 Sales

	% of total
Wireless services	
Cellular	
Voice	44
Packet communications	37
Other	6
Equipment sales	13
Total	**100**

Selected Services

Cellular
i-mode (wireless Internet access)
In-flight telephone
Mobile multimedia
Satellite mobile communications
Third-generation (3G) wireless (W-CDMA)
World Call (direct international calling)

COMPETITORS

BT
China Mobile
EMOBILE
Hutchison Telecommunications
KDDI
Optus
SK Telecom
SOFTBANK MOBILE
Telstra
Vodafone

HISTORICAL FINANCIALS

Company Type: Public

Income Statement

FYE: March 31

	REVENUE ($ mil.)	NET INCOME ($ mil.)	NET PROFIT MARGIN	EMPLOYEES
3/10	46,220	5,338	11.5%	22,297
3/09	45,721	4,850	10.6%	21,831
3/08	47,303	4,931	10.4%	22,100
3/07	40,800	3,897	9.6%	21,591
3/06	40,715	5,215	12.8%	21,646
Annual Growth	**3.2%**	**0.6%**	**—**	**0.7%**

2010 Year-End Financials

Debt ratio: 9.3%
Return on equity: 11.3%
Cash ($ mil.): 3,859
Current ratio: 1.73
Long-term debt ($ mil.): 4,634

No. of shares (mil.): 4,161
Dividends
  Yield: 0.0%
  Payout: —
Market value ($ mil.): 682

Stock History

NYSE: DCM

	STOCK PRICE ($) FY Close	P/E High/Low	PER SHARE ($) Earnings	Dividends	Book Value
3/10	0.16	— —	1.28	0.00	12.02
3/09	0.14	— —	1.15	0.00	10.73
3/08	0.15	— —	1.15	0.00	10.32
3/07	0.16	— —	0.88	0.17	8.52
3/06	0.13	— —	1.15	0.35	8.32
Annual Growth	**5.3%**	**— —**	**2.7%**	**—**	**9.6%**

Oki Electric Industry

Oki Electric Industry is plugged into a variety of products. The company's core businesses include computer peripherals and telecommunications equipment. It sells printers, facsimile machines, and related accessories through its Oki Data subsidiary. Oki's telecom products include communications servers, broadband networking equipment, and VoIP software for carriers, as well as IP communications, contact center, and videoconferencing products for the enterprise market. Other Oki products include security products, such as iris recognition systems and facial recognition software.

In order to combat a slumping telecommunications market and worldwide downturn in information technology spending, Oki Electric has realigned its operations. Its restructuring efforts include a shift away from hardware sales to broader service offerings such as network design, installation, and maintenance.

In 2008 the company sold its Oki Semiconductor unit to ROHM. It also formed a new US-based subsidiary, OKI Electric America, to handle marketing and sales of its office and telecom products.

HISTORY

Engineer Kibataro Oki founded Meikosha in Tokyo in 1881 to produce telephones (only five years after they were invented). Meikosha was soon producing telegraphs, bells, and medical equipment. Its main factory adopted the name Oki Electric Plant in 1889, and the marketing division began operating under the name Oki & Company in 1896.

In 1907, a year after the founder's death, the Oki groups were united as a limited partnership. Divided again in 1912, they were recombined in 1917 as Oki Electric Co. Oki continued to expand its product line to include automatic switching equipment (1926) and electric clocks (1929).

The manufacturer produced communications equipment for the Japanese military during WWII, but after the war it started working on the teleprinter and added consumer goods such as portable stoves. The company adopted its present name, Oki Electric Industry Company, in 1949.

Oki entered the semiconductor and computer industries in the 1950s, joining Fujitsu, Hitachi, Mitsubishi, Nippon Electric Co., and Toshiba as one of Japan's Big Six electronics makers by 1960. It then began developing overseas businesses, particularly in Latin America, where it built communications networks in Honduras (1962) and Bolivia (1966) and radio networks in Brazil (1971).

In 1970 Oki formed a computer software unit. The company was a major telecommunications equipment supplier for the Japanese government until the mid-1970s, when the government increased its purchases from other companies.

Oki started building PCs in 1981. It consolidated its US operations as Oki America in 1984. A new financial crisis followed in the mid-1980s when the bottom fell out of the semiconductor market — Oki's earnings plummeted into the red in 1986. However, by the end of the decade Oki had become a major provider of automated teller machines (ATMs) and bank computer systems; growth in the Japanese financial industry sparked a ninefold increase in Oki's sales in 1989. In 1994 Oki established subsidiary Oki Data Corp. to handle printer and fax machine operations.

Plunging memory prices and higher taxes stymied Oki's recovery in fiscal 1998, so the company halted mass random-access memory (RAM) production and closed an assembly and testing facility. Oki shifted its semiconductor focus to large-scale integrated circuits, and placed more emphasis on its information systems segment, which had seen increasing sales.

Further battered by a weak Asian economy, Oki restructured in 1999. That year the company bought Toshiba's ATM operations. It also launched an access control system that uses a person's iris for identification and payment services.

In 2000 Oki announced plans to establish (along with NTT Data, NTT DoCoMo, Microsoft and others) Payment First Corporation, an Internet payment company.

Responding to poor market conditions, Oki announced in 2001 that it would reduce its workforce by about 10% over two years. The company also sold its automotive electronics division to Keihin Corporation.

Oki acquired the driver chip business for large TFT-LCDs from Texas Instruments Japan in early 2005. TFT-LCD drive chips are used in notebook computers, monitors, and TVs.

EXECUTIVES

President, CEO, and Director: Katsumasa Shinozuka
SEVP and Board Member: Naoki Sato
SVP, Managing Director, and Director:
Hideichi Kawasaki
SVP, Managing Director, and Director:
Keiichi Fukumura
SVP, Managing Director, and Director: Yutaka Asai
SVP, Managing Director, and Director:
Masayoshi Matsushita
SVP, Managing Director, and Director: Masao Miyashita
SVP, Managing Director, and Director:
Hironori Kitabayashi
SVP and Director: Hiroshi Enomoto
SVP and Director: Masasuke Kishi
Executive Director and Director: Hideto Morizono
Executive and Director: Kazuhiro Iritani
Director: Harushige Sugimoto
Director: Minoru Morio
Auditors: Ernst & Young ShinNihon

LOCATIONS

HQ: Oki Electric Industry Company, Limited
(Oki Denki Kogyo Kabushiki Kaisha)
3-16-11, Nishi-Shimbashi, Minato-ku
Tokyo 105-8460, Japan
Phone: 81-3-5403-1211   **Fax:** 81-3-5445-6380
US HQ: 2000 Bishops Gate Blvd., Mt. Laurel, NJ 08054
US Phone: 856-235-2600   **US Fax:** 856-222-5320
Web: www.oki.com

PRODUCTS/OPERATIONS

2010 Sales

	% of total
Info-Telecom systems	62
Printers	33
Other	5
Total	**100**

COMPETITORS

Canon	Mitsubishi Electric
CASIO COMPUTER	NCR
Cisco Systems	NEC
Dell	NTT DATA
Diebold	Panasonic Corp
Epson	Ricoh Company
Fuji Xerox	Samsung Group
Fujitsu	SANYO
Hewlett-Packard	Sharp Corp.
Hitachi	Siemens AG
IBM	Sony
Konica Minolta	Wincor Nixdorf
Kyocera	Xerox
Lexmark	

HISTORICAL FINANCIALS

Company Type: Public

Income Statement

FYE: March 31

	REVENUE ($ mil.)	NET INCOME ($ mil.)	NET PROFIT MARGIN	EMPLOYEES
3/10	4,789	78	1.6%	18,111
3/09	5,609	(463)	—	17,415
3/08	7,248	6	0.1%	22,640
3/07	6,098	(309)	—	21,380
3/06	5,789	43	0.7%	21,175
Annual Growth	(4.6%)	16.2%	—	(3.8%)

2010 Year-End Financials

Debt ratio: —
Return on equity: 13.0%
Cash ($ mil.): 624
Current ratio: 1.17
Long-term debt ($ mil.): —

No. of shares (mil.): 683
Dividends
  Yield: —
  Payout: —
Market value ($ mil.): 575

Stock History

Tokyo: 67030

	STOCK PRICE ($) FY Close	P/E High/Low		PER SHARE ($) Earnings	Dividends	Book Value
3/10	0.84	22	13	0.06	—	0.91
3/09	0.65	—	—	0.00	—	0.85
3/08	1.93	345	192	0.01	—	1.40
3/07	1.93	—	—	—	—	1.36
3/06	3.20	—	—	—	—	1.67
Annual Growth	(28.4%)	—	—	144.9%	—	(14.0%)

OMV

Oil and chemicals group OMV is Austria's largest industrial company. A leading oil and gas company in Central and Eastern Europe, it explores for natural gas and crude oil; refines crude oil; and imports, transports, and stores gas. OMV has proved reserves of 1.2 billion barrels of oil equivalent; it produces about 317,000 barrels of oil equivalent per day and sells 13 billion cubic feet of gas annually. The bulk of OMV's sales comes from refining and marketing, with the company operating five refineries and more than 2,430 gas stations in 13 countries. OMV's largest shareholders are Austrian state holding company ÖIAG (32%) and the International Petroleum Investment Company (IPIC) of Abu Dhabi (20%).

OMV's primary sources for oil and gas are Austria and Romania; however, it also has major field developments in Kazakhstan, Libya, New Zealand, Pakistan, Tunisia, and Yemen.

Its natural gas network, serving about 90% of Austria's natural gas demand, draws gas supplies from Russia, Norway, and Germany, as well as from domestic reserves. Austria's gas market, now dominated by OMV, is slated for full competition, and OMV is among state-controlled companies set for full privatization. In 2006 Russian energy giant Gazprom signed long-term contracts for gas deliveries with OMV.

After plans to merge with Hungary's MOL went south in 2008, OMV the next year sold its 21% stake in it to Russian oil company Surgutneftegas for €1.4 billion ($1.85 billion). Also in 2009, in keeping with its focus on retail markets in the Danube region, southeastern Europe, and the Black Sea region, OMV sold sell subsidiary OMV Italia; San Marco Petroli acquired the network of about 100 gas stations in the northern-Italian region of Triveneto.

OMV has been disposing of some of its heating oil operations. In 2008 it disposed of its Bayern GmbH, and it plans to sell its OMV Wärme VertriebsgmbH by the end of 2010. At that point, the sale of heating oil to private clients will be handled by partners, but OMV will continue to service corporate customers.

Eyeing new areas of exploration, that year OMV also acquired a 10% stake in Pearl Petroleum, giving it access to gas-condensate fields in Iraq.

HISTORY

Oil exploration began in Austria in the 1920s, largely as joint ventures with foreign firms such as Shell and Socony-Vacuum. Full-scale production did not get underway until 1938, when the Anschluss (the absorption of Austria by Germany) paved the way for Germany to exploit Austria's natural resources to fuel its growing war machine. In the division of spoils following WWII, Russia gained control of Austria's oil reserves.

The Russian-administered oil assets were transferred to the new Austrian government in 1955, which authorized the company Österreichische Mineralölverwaltung (ÖMG) in 1956 to control state oil assets. ÖMG, state-controlled by the Austrian Mineral Oil Administration, set about building a major refinery in 1960 and acquiring marketing companies Martha and ÖROP in 1965.

In 1968 ÖMG became the first Western company to sign a natural gas supply contract with Russia. In 1974 the firm commissioned the Trans-Austria Gas Pipeline, which enabled the supply of natural gas to Italy. That year ÖMG changed its named to ÖMV Aktiengesellschaft (ÖMV became OMV in 1995 for international markets).

During the 1970s OMV expanded its crude supply arrangements, tapping supplies from Iran, Iraq, Libya, and other Middle Eastern countries. It moved into oil and gas exploration in the mid-1980s, forming OMV Libya (acquiring 25% of Occidental's Libyan production) and OMV UK.

With Austria moving toward increasing privatization, in 1987 about 15% of OMV's shares were sold to the public. The government sold another 10% two years later. In 1989 OMV acquired PCD Polymere. With the aim of merging state-owned oil and chemical activities, OMV acquired Chemie Linz in 1990. The company also opened its first OMV-branded service station that year. In 1994 OMV reorganized itself as an integrated oil and gas group based in Central Europe, with international exploration and production activities, and with other operations in the chemical and petrochemical sectors.

In 1995 OMV acquired TOTAL-AUSTRIA, expanding its service stations by 59. The company introduced OMV lubricants to the Greek market in 1996. It also expanded its OMV service station network in Hungary to 66 stations after acquiring 31 Q8 (Kuwait) sites. In 1997 the Stroh Company's retail network in Austria was merged into OMV.

Expanding its retail network even farther, OMV acquired BP's retail network in the Czech Republic, Slovakia, and Hungary in 1998. It also sold its stake in Chemie Linz and acquired a 25% stake in major European polyolefin producer Borealis, which in turn acquired PCD Polymere. In 1999 the company pushed its retail network into Bulgaria and Romania. That year OMV also acquired Australian company Cultus Petroleum.

OMV and Shell agreed to develop North Sea fields together in 2000. That year OMV also formed a joint venture with Italy's Edison International to explore in Vietnam and acquired more than 9% of Hungarian rival MOL. It upped that stake to 10% in 2001.

In 2002 OMV opened its first gas station in Serbia and Montenegro. It also increased its German gas station count from 79 to 151 with the purchase of 32 units from Royal Dutch Shell and 40 stations from Martin GmbH & Co.

In 2003 the company acquired Preussag Energie's exploration and production assets for $320 million. That year the company moved into Bosnia-Herzegovina, opening nine gas stations.

During 2004 the company bought up 51% of Romania's Petrom, making it the top oil and gas producer in Central Europe. As part of the deal, OMV chose to divest itself of its quarter-chunk of Rompetrol.

In a major consolidation move, in 2006 OMV agreed to buy Austrian power firm Verbund for $17 billion, but the move was rebuffed by government regulators. The next year the company announced plans to merge with Hungary's energy powerhouse MOL, but those plans were called off, as well, due to European Commission regulatory concerns in 2008.

EXECUTIVES

Chairman: Peter Michaelis, age 64
Chairman, Supervisory Board: Rainer Wieltsch, age 66
Deputy Chairwoman, Supervisory Board:
Alyazia Ali Saleh Al Kuwaiti, age 35
Chairman Executive Board and CEO:
Wolfgang Ruttenstorfer, age 60
Deputy Chairman Executive Board and Head Refining and Marketing: Gerhard Roiss, age 58
Deputy Chairman: Khadem Abdulla Al Qubaisi, age 39
Deputy Chairman: Wolfgang C. G. Berndt, age 67
CFO: David C. Davies, age 55
Head Exploration and Production: Helmut Langanger, age 60
Head Investor Relations: Angelika Altendorfer-Zwerenz
Spokesperson: Sven Pusswald

LOCATIONS

HQ: OMV Aktiengesellschaft
Trabrennstraße 6-8
1020 Vienna, Austria
Phone: 43-1-40-440-0   **Fax:** 43-1-40-440-27900
Web: www.omv.com

2009 Sales

	% of total
Europe	
Central & Eastern Europe	
Austria	34
Germany	20
Romania	18
Other countries	15
Other countries	5
Other regions	8
Total	**100**

PRODUCTS/OPERATIONS

2009 Sales

	% of total
Refining & marketing	65
Exploration & production	18
Gas & power	15
Corporate & other	2
Total	**100**

COMPETITORS

BP
Eni
Exxon Mobil
Hellenic Petroleum
MOL
PKN ORLEN
Royal Dutch Shell
Unipetrol

HISTORICAL FINANCIALS

Company Type: Public

Income Statement

FYE: December 31

	REVENUE ($ mil.)	NET INCOME ($ mil.)	NET PROFIT MARGIN	EMPLOYEES
12/09	25,679	1,028	4.0%	34,676
12/08	36,002	2,155	6.0%	41,282
12/07	29,500	2,712	9.2%	33,665
12/06	25,028	1,824	7.3%	40,993
12/05	18,451	1,488	8.1%	49,919
Annual Growth	**8.6%**	**(8.8%)**	**—**	**(8.7%)**

2009 Year-End Financials

Debt ratio: —
Return on equity: 7.5%
Cash ($ mil.): 967
Current ratio: 1.19
Long-term debt ($ mil.): —
No. of shares (mil.): 299
Dividends
Yield: 3.3%
Payout: 52.2%
Market value ($ mil.): 13,146

Stock History

Pink Sheets: OMVKY

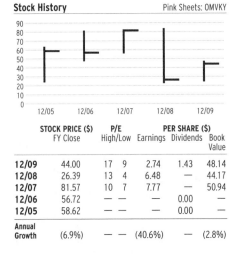

	STOCK PRICE ($) FY Close	P/E High/Low		PER SHARE ($) Earnings	Dividends	Book Value
12/09	44.00	17	9	2.74	1.43	48.14
12/08	26.39	13	4	6.48	—	44.17
12/07	81.57	10	7	7.77	—	50.94
12/06	56.72	—	—	—	0.00	—
12/05	58.62	—	—	—	0.00	—
Annual Growth	**(6.9%)**	**—**	**—**	**(40.6%)**	**—**	**(2.8%)**

PKN ORLEN

Crudely moving into the private market, Polski Koncern Naftowy ORLEN is the largest refiner and distributor of oil in Poland. The company owns a total of seven refineries (including three in the Czech Republic and one in Lithuania) and has some 2,700 retail sites in the Czech Republic, Germany, Lithuania, and Poland. PKN ORLEN owns an 85% stake in chemical maker Anwil, has holdings in several other Polish companies, and controls Czech refiner and retailer UNIPETROL. Two former state monopolies, Petrochemia Plock (Poland's largest refinery) and Centrala Produktow Naftowych (Poland's #1 petroleum distributor), merged in 1999 to create PKN ORLEN. The Polish government still owns 10% of the company.

The company also manufactures liquefied propane-butane gas (LPG) for use at industrial plants and for heating public buildings. Other PKN ORLEN products include polyvinyl chloride plastics used in foils, containers, bottles, cable insulation, and auto parts; nitric fertilizers; asphalts for construction of roads, airports, and sports facilities; and basic industrial and engine oils.

Its Eko subsidiary burns hazardous waste, while its ORLEN Transport division handles the distribution of fuel to its gas stations. Its Solino

holdings (70%) produce salt and brine and use salt caverns for underground storage of petroleum and fuels.

In 2007 PKN ORLEN's Unipetrol sold Czech company Kaucuk to Poland's Dwory for $195 million.

HISTORY

The merger between Petrochemia Plock, Poland's largest refiner and petrochemicals maker, and CPN (Centrala Produktow Naftowych), the nation's largest motor fuel distributor, created Polski Koncern Naftowy (PKN) in 1999.

Poland's oil industry stretches back to the late 1800s, when five refineries were built in the nation's southern region. The Polish Oil Monopoly was formed in 1944 to oversee the country's oil distribution operations; it assumed the CPN name a year later.

While the rest of the world increasingly turned to oil as an energy source after WWII, Poland continued to rely on coal, and its oil industry grew slowly. CPN was split into 17 regional branches in 1955. The branches controlled local operations, and the head office in Warsaw handled pricing and purchasing.

In the late 1950s the Soviet Union began building the Friendship pipeline to deliver crude oil to East Germany and Poland. The Polish government responded by forming Petrochemia to develop a refinery next to the pipeline in the city of Plock.

The Petrochemia refinery began producing refined products in 1964; four years later it started processing crude oil to make fuels, lubricants, and bitumen. The refinery also began making products such as detergents and plastics from processed refinery gases and other hydrocarbons. It added petrochemicals in 1970.

Because of the oil industry's slow growth in Poland, the country managed to avoid some of the impact of the 1970s energy crisis. (Even as late as 1995, oil accounted for only 17% of Poland's energy consumption.) But it was forced to pay higher prices for Russian crude. In 1975 the government decided to expand its refining operations and created a second major refiner, Rafineria Gdanska, to focus on motor oils.

Locked behind the Iron Curtain, Poland was not able to build its oil operations until the early 1990s. In 1992 Petrochemia began expanding its refinery facilities to reach a production capacity of 820,000 barrels per day within 10 years.

After Communism's demise, the Polish government started planning the privatization of its oil operations. After several plans were adopted and discarded in the early 1990s, the government finally decided in 1996 to split CPN up among the nation's refineries. Holding company Nafta Polska was formed that year to own 75% stakes in Poland's refineries and in CPN and carry out the privatization process.

In 1997 CPN was stripped of its fuel depots and rail transport operations, which were placed under the Nafta Polska umbrella. Displeased with the plan to carve up CPN, the distributor's management rallied against the government's plan. The Polish government gave in and went back to the drawing board.

A successful plan was formed in 1998, namely to merge Petrochemia and CPN. The companies were combined in 1999, and 30% of the new PKN was floated on the Warsaw and London stock exchanges. The next year the government spun off an additional 42% stake and the company added ORLEN to its name (combining the

Polish words for eagle and energy). Also in 2000 the government began preparing to float Refineria Gdanska. PKN hoped to get a piece of its regional rival, but the state left PKN out of the bidding to encourage competition.

PKN acquired some 494 gas stations in Germany from BP, who sold them to meet German antitrust regulations for its merger with Veba Oel, in late 2002. In 2004 PKN purchased 63% of UNIPETROL; the European Commission's Competition Directorate granted approval of the purchase in mid-2005.

EXECUTIVES

Chairman, Supervisory Board: Maciej Mataczynski
President, Management Board: Dariusz J. Krawiec
VP and CFO: Slawomir R. Jedrzejczyk, age 41
Member, Management Board, Petrochemical Operations: Marek Serafin, age 42
Member, Management Board, Refinery Operations: Krystian Pater, age 46
Member, Management Board, Sales: Wojciech R. Kotlarek, age 49
Auditors: KPMG Audyt. Sp. z o.o.

LOCATIONS

HQ: Polski Koncern Naftowy ORLEN Spolka Akcyjna
ul. Chemików 7
09-411 Plock, Poland
Phone: 48-24-365-00-00   **Fax:** 48-24-365-40-40
Web: www.orlen.pl

2009 Sales

	% of total
Poland	46
Germany	18
Czech Republic	12
Baltic States	8
Other	16
Total	**100**

PRODUCTS/OPERATIONS

2009 Sales

	% of total
Refining	54
Retail	33
Petrochemicals	13
Total	**100**

COMPETITORS

BP
Exxon Mobil
LUKOIL
MOL
OMV
Royal Dutch Shell
Statoil
TOTAL

HISTORICAL FINANCIALS

Company Type: Public

Income Statement

FYE: December 31

	REVENUE ($ mil.)	NET INCOME ($ mil.)	NET PROFIT MARGIN	EMPLOYEES
12/09	23,707	457	1.9%	22,535
12/08	26,745	(842)	—	22,955
12/07	25,823	977	3.8%	22,927
12/06	18,167	682	3.8%	24,113
12/05	12,679	1,409	11.1%	21,825
Annual Growth	**16.9%**	**(24.6%)**	**—**	**0.8%**

2009 Year-End Financials

Debt ratio: —	No. of shares (mil.): 428
Return on equity: 6.3%	Dividends
Cash ($ mil.): 1,026	Yield: 0.0%
Current ratio: —	Payout: —
Long-term debt ($ mil.): —	Market value ($ mil.): 14,521

Stock History

Pink Sheets: PSKNY

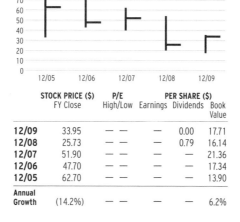

	STOCK PRICE ($) FY Close	P/E High/Low		PER SHARE ($) Earnings	Dividends	Book Value
12/09	33.95	—	—	—	0.00	17.71
12/08	25.73	—	—	—	0.79	16.14
12/07	51.90	—	—	—	—	21.36
12/06	47.70	—	—	—	—	17.34
12/05	62.70	—	—	—	—	13.90
Annual Growth	**(14.2%)**	**—**	**—**	**—**	**—**	**6.2%**

Otto Group

Otto has the mail-order business in the bag. The world's largest mail-order group sells merchandise in Germany and about 20 countries in Europe, North America, and Asia through more than 600 print catalogs, the Internet, and some 650 OTTO shops. The company sells products from apparel to appliances to sporting goods. Otto also owns a majority stake in the Crate & Barrel housewares chain. The group's two other businesses — financial services (EOS) and logistics and travel services (Otto Freizeit und Touristik Group), together contribute about 12% of sales. Overall, Otto operates more than 120 companies. The family of chairman Michael Otto owns the majority of the company.

Otto's core business is multichannel retail, which accounts for nearly 90% of the group's total sales. The company operates more than 340 bricks-and-mortar stores, and some 50 online shops, and boasts more than 1,900 catalog titles. Already a giant in catalogs, Otto is actively expanding its e-commerce operations. The group aims to make 20% of its retail sales online by 2010.

Looking to capitalize on the woes of a compatriot and competitor, Otto has been eyeing its insolvent rival Arcandor AG's Primondo home shopping business and its Karstadt chain of sporting goods stores. Indeed, the company has won conditional approval from the European Union to buy the Russian business and trademark rights of Quelle, Primondo's insolvent mail-order business. Otto, which already rings up about €200 million ($275 million) in Russia, has offered to divest some trademarks to address competition concerns.

Otto's Hermes Logistik unit supports Otto's own retail businesses and those of other clients. The company also operates the Mondial Relay (France) and Parcelnet (UK) courier and fulfillment services.

Otto Freizeit und Touristik Group provides travel services through more than 400 Reiseland and Travel Overland travel agencies and travel portals in Germany.

On the financial services front, EOS is a leading provider to financial services in Europe. The group also operates Hanseatic Bank in partnership with France's Société Général, to which it sold a 75% stake in 2005.

Otto has grown largely through its acquisitions and diversification tactics (entering non-mail-order businesses). The firm derives more than 50% of its sales in Germany, and customers there can get same-day delivery of many of Otto's wares.

HISTORY

East German refugee Werner Otto founded Otto Versand (German for "dispatch") in Hamburg, West Germany, in 1949. It distributed its first catalog in 1950; 300 hand-bound copies offered only shoes, but in 28 styles. Instead of being required to pay upon delivery, customers received bills with their orders; this was new for mail orders. By 1956 the firm employed 500 people; by 1958 the catalog had expanded to 200 pages, offering low-cost women's fashions and other products to 200,000 potential customers.

In 1963 Otto Versand began taking phone orders. Its catalog grew to 800 pages and 1 million copies by 1967. The following year it published the Post Shop Magazine, its first special-interest catalog, which targeted fashion-conscious youth. In 1969 Otto Versand formed Hanseatic Bank to offer customers monthly payment plans; three years later it formed the Hermes Express Package delivery service.

The firm began a shopping spree in the 1970s by investing in mail-order companies 3 Suisses International (France, 1974), Heinrich Heine (luxury clothes and household goods, West Germany, 1974) and Hanau (West Germany, 1979).

Werner's son Michael succeeded him as chairman in 1981, and in 1982 he led the acquisition of low-cost women's apparel firm Spiegel. Michael immediately revamped Spiegel into an upscale retailer. The ownership of Spiegel was restructured in 1984, but the Otto family remained in control of the US company.

Throughout the 1980s the firm continued investing in European companies (entering the UK in 1986 and Austria in 1988) and began Otto-Sumisho in Japan (a joint venture, 1986). Its combined catalog circulation reached 200 million in 1987.

Otto Versand launched 24-hour delivery service in 1990; that year it expanded to the Polish market by forming joint venture Otto-Epoka. In 1991 it began 24-hour phone sales and acquired a majority stake in Grattan (the UK's fourth-largest mail-order firm). Acquisitions continued during the early and mid-1990s, including Margareta (Hungary), Postalmarket (Italy's largest mail-order firm), and Otto-Burlingtons (Germany-India joint venture).

Otto Versand acquired a majority stake in Reiseland's 60 travel agencies in 1993 and bought two UK collection agencies in 1994. In 1994 it became Germany's first mail-order firm to offer an interactive CD-ROM catalog.

The firm bought a majority stake in US housewares retailer Crate & Barrel in 1998 and bought German computer wholesaler Actebis Holding. It then formed Zara Deutschland, a joint venture in Germany (with Spain's Inditex), to sell clothing in a new chain of outlets. Otto Versand added to its travel business (about 140 locations) in 1998 with the purchase of 25 offices from American Express Germany. It closed Postalmarket that year because of problems with the Italian postal service.

In 1999 Otto Versand acquired the Freemans catalog business (nearly $900 million in 1998 sales) from the UK's Sears PLC. The deal nearly doubled the company's UK mail-order market share, from 8% to 15%. In late 1999 the firm formed a joint venture with Harrods to sell fancy English goods online.

In early 2000 Otto Versand set up a joint venture with America Online and Deutsche Bank 24 to offer online banking, Internet service, and PCs. In October 2001 the company entered into a joint venture with US Internet travel service provider Travelocity.com to form Travelocity Europe.

In 2003 Otto Versand changed its name to Otto GmbH & Co KG.

In 2005 Otto sold its longstanding controlling interest in US catalog company Spiegel as well as a 75% stake in Hanseatic Bank to French banking giant Société Général.

In mid-2007 the company sold its information technology distribution subsidiary, Actebis Holding, to German equity investment firm Arques.

EXECUTIVES

Supervisory Board Chairman: Michael Otto, age 67
Executive Board Chairman and CEO, Otto Group: Hans-Otto Schrader, age 53
Executive Board Vice Chairman, Otto Group; Executive Board Member, Marketing, Sales, E-Commerce, OTTO: Rainer Hillebrand, age 53
Deputy Chairman: Uwe Rost
CFO, Otto Group and Group IT: Juergen Schulte-Laggenbeck
Chief Human Resources Officer, Otto Group; Executive Board Member Human Resources and Controlling, OTTO: Alexander Birken
Executive Board Member, Group Services: Hanjo Schneider, age 48
Executive Board Member, Group Retail: Timm Homann
Executive Board Member, Human Resources and Controlling, Otto Group: Winfried Zimmermann
Executive Board Member, Merchandising OTTO: Michael Heller
Executive Board Chairman, Baur Versand (GmbH & Co. KG): Marc Opelt
Executive Board Chairman, KG EOS Holding GmbH & Co: Hans-Werner Scherer, age 55
Executive Board Chairman, SCHWAB VERSAND GmbH: Rolf Schäfer, age 63
Executive Board Chairman, Otto Freizeit und Touristik: Gunther Holzschuh, age 57
VP Corporate Communications: Thomas Voigt
VP Corporate Responsibility: Johannes Merck
CEO, Crate & Barrel Holdings, Inc.: Barbara A. Turf, age 65
Auditors: KPMG AG

LOCATIONS

HQ: Otto (GmbH & Co KG)
Wandsbeker Strasse 3-7
22172 Hamburg, Germany
Phone: 49-40-64-61-0   **Fax:** 49-40-64-61-8571
Web: www.ottogroup.com

2010 Sales

	% of total
Europe	
Germany	57
France	14
Other countries	16
North America	10
Asia	3
Total	**100**

PRODUCTS/OPERATIONS

2010 Sales

	% of total
Multichannel retail	88
Services	8
Financial services	4
Total	**100**

Selected Operations

3 Suisses International Group (multichannel retail)
ALBA MODA GmbH (multichannel retail)
Crate & Barrel (multichannel retail)
EOS Group (financial services)
Frankonia (multichannel retail)
Grattan (multichannel retail)
Handelsgesellshaft Heinrich Heine GmbH (multichannel retail)
Hanseatic Bank GmbH (consumer loans)
Hermes Logistik Group (logistics services)
Mondial Relay (logistics services)
myToys.de Gmbh (multichannel retail)
Otto Freizeit und Touristik Group (tourism services)
Parcelnet (logistics services)
Reiseland (travel agencies)
Witt (multichannel retail)

COMPETITORS

Amazon.com	L.L. Bean
American Express	Macy's
Arcandor	Maxeda
Bed Bath & Beyond	METRO AG
Deutsche Post	Orchard Brands
Direct Marketing	Pier 1 Imports
Fast Retailing	PPR SA
Hammacher Schlemmer	Provell
Hanover Direct	Schickedanz
J. C. Penney	TAKKT AG
Lands' End	TUI
Littlewoods	Williams-Sonoma

HISTORICAL FINANCIALS

Company Type: Private

Income Statement

FYE: Last day in February

	REVENUE ($ mil.)	NET INCOME ($ mil.)	NET PROFIT MARGIN	EMPLOYEES
2/10	14,705	273	1.9%	47,952
2/09	13,696	408	3.0%	49,539
2/08	18,503	341	1.8%	52,668
2/07	20,138	386	1.9%	53,051
2/06	17,272	228	1.3%	55,116
Annual Growth	(3.9%)	4.6%	—	(3.4%)

2010 Year-End Financials

Debt ratio: 74.8%   Current ratio: —
Return on equity: —   Long-term debt ($ mil.): 2,122
Cash ($ mil.): —

Net Income History

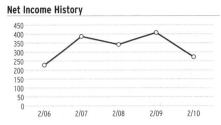

Panasonic Corporation

Panasonic Corporation (formerly Matsushita Electric Industrial) is one of the world's top consumer electronics makers. It changed its name after more than 70 years to match its recognizable brands: Panasonic, Quasar, Technics, and others. Its Digital AVC Networks unit makes TVs, VCRs, CD and DVD players, PCs, cell phones, and fax machines. Panasonic also sells components (batteries, electric motors), home appliances (washing machines, vacuum cleaners), and factory-automation equipment (industrial robots). It owns and operates Panasonic Corporation of North America and added SANYO Electric to its portfolio in late 2009.

Panasonic purchased a controlling stake in SANYO Electric in December 2009 in a deal worth more than 400 billion yen or $4.6 billion. The move made it Japan's second-largest electronics company after Sony and gave the manufacturer the keys to the growing hybrid car battery market. SANYO Electric is the world's largest maker of rechargeable batteries and is developing lithium-ion batteries with automaker Volkswagen. The deal positions both firms as leaders in green energy.

Panasonic, along with other Japanese consumer electronics makers, is struggling to make money on products like TVs, VCRs, and DVD players. To compensate, the company has been looking to greener pastures — namely the future of green energy — to fuel its growth. SANYO Electric fits neatly into this strategy.

The company also sold a 60% stake in its mobile phone software subsidiary, Panasonic Mobile Communications, to NTT Data in mid-2008.

The fast-growing flat-screen television market has become a focus for the company; with its PDP (plasma display panel) and liquid crystal display (LCD) products, the company's Panasonic brand has been a top PDP manufacturer in recent years. To meet the increasing demand for PDPs, Panasonic Corporation expanded production to full capacity at its third domestic plant in Amagasaki in 2007. It strengthened its partnership with Hitachi in May 2007, as well, with an agreement to supply each other with PDPs. It is also building an LCD plant with electronics partner Hitachi (a joint venture 92%-owned by Panasonic called IPS Alpha Technology), giving Panasonic Corporation an increased supply of LCD panels for its TVs.

China is becoming a more important manufacturing center for Panasonic Corporation. The company is shifting its low-end product manufacturing to China (due primarily to lower production costs), with more expensive products being made in Japan and Southeast Asia. However, the company is planning to build a large manufacturing plant in China. The plant, which will produce home appliances, will primarily serve the Chinese market. In India, where Panasonic operates a handful of companies, the firm is consolidating its operations there under Panasonic India Pvt. Ltd.

HISTORY

Grade school dropout Konosuke Matsushita took $50 in 1918 and went into business making electric plugs (with his brother-in-law, Toshio Iue, founder of SANYO). His mission, to help people by making high-quality, low-priced conveniences while providing his employees with good working conditions, earned him the sobriquet, "god of business management." Matsushita Electric Industrial grew by developing inexpensive lamps, batteries, radios, and motors in the 1920s and 1930s.

During WWII the Japanese government ordered the firm to build wood-laminate products for the military. Postwar occupation forces prevented Matsushita from working at his firm for four years. Thanks to unions' efforts, he rejoined his namesake company shortly before it entered a joint venture with Dutch manufacturer Philips in 1952. The following year it moved into consumer goods, making televisions, refrigerators, and washing machines and later expanding into high-performance audio products. Matsushita bought a majority stake in Victor Company of Japan (JVC, originally established by RCA Victor) in 1954. Its 1959 New York subsidiary opening began Matsushita's drive overseas.

Sold under the National, Panasonic, and Technics names, the firm's products were usually not cutting-edge but were attractively priced. Under Masaharu Matsushita, the founder's son-in-law who became president in 1961, the company became Japan's largest home appliance maker, introducing air conditioners, microwave ovens, stereo components, and VCRs in the 1960s and 1970s. JVC developed the VHS format for VCRs, which beat out Sony's Betamax format.

Matsushita built much of its sales growth on new industrial and commercial customers in the 1980s. The company expanded its semiconductor, office and factory automation, auto electronics, audio-visual, housing, and air-conditioning product offerings that decade. Konosuke died in 1989.

The next year Matsushita joined the Japanese stampede for US acquisitions, buying Universal Studios' then-owner, MCA. In 1993 Yoichi Morishita was named president and the company acquired Philips' stake in their joint venture. Two years later, when cultural incompatibility depressed MCA's performance, Matsushita sold 80% of the company (now Universal) to liquor mogul Seagram, resulting in a fiscal 1996 loss. That year Matsushita pushed the technology envelope, introducing the first DVD player.

In fiscal years 1998 and 1999 the company's income dropped, partly due to a slow domestic economy. A lagging market led Matsushita to close its North American semiconductor operations in late 1998.

In 2000 Yoichi Morishita became chairman and Kunio Nakamura took the reins as president of Matsushita. The next year the company began making chips for cell phones, digital cameras, and digital TVs. In 2002 Matsushita announced plans to turn around its financial slump by cutting 13,000 local jobs (through early retirement) and trimming directors' salaries.

In early 2004 Matsushita acquired affiliate Matsushita Electric Works (MEW), a company in which it previously held a 32% share. MEW, which makes lighting, security systems, and kitchen and bathroom fittings, was spun off from Matsushita in 1935. The acquisition makes Matsushita the largest Japanese electronic and electrical equipment manufacturer.

In June 2006 senior managing director Fumio Ohtsubo was named president, succeeding Kunio Nakamura, who became chairman of the company's board of directors.

In a rather large shift to leverage the strength of its Panasonic brand name, Matsushita in October 2008 changed the name of its company to Panasonic Corporation.

EXECUTIVES

Chairman: Kunio Nakamura, age 71
Honorary Chairman: Masaharu Matsushita, age 98
Vice Chairman: Masayuki Matsushita, age 65
President and Board Member: Fumio Ohtsubo, age 65
Managing Director Accounting, Finance, and Information Systems and Board Member: Makoto Uenoyama, age 57
Managing Director Personnel, General Affairs, Social Relations, and e-Work Promotion Office and Board Member: Masatoshi Harada, age 55
Managing Director and Board Member; President, Home Appliances Company in Charge of Lighting: Kazunori Takami, age 56
Managing Director Industrial Sales and Board Member: Yoshihiko (Yoshi) Yamada, age 59
Board Member; President, System Networks Company and Panasonic System Networks Co., Ltd.: Takashi Toyama, age 55
Managing Executive Officer; President, Automotive Systems Company: Kazuhiro Tsuga
Managing Executive Officer; President, Panasonic Electronic Devices: Toshiaki Kobayashi
Managing Executive Officer and Representative in Kansai Corporate Risk Management and Corporate Information Security: Yutaka Takehana
Managing Executive Officer and Director Corporate Management Division for Asia and Oceania; Managing Director, Panasonic Asia Pacific Pte. Ltd.: Ikuo Miyamoto
Managing Executive Officer Corporate Communications, Advertising, Corporate Citizenship, and CSR Office: Takumi Kajisha
Executive Officer; President, Energy Company: Naoto Noguchi
Executive Officer; President, Lighting Company: Yoshio Ito
Executive Officer; General Manager Corporate Finance and Investor Relations Group in Charge of Financial Operations Center: Hideaki Kawai
Executive Officer; Director, Corporate Management Division for North America; Chairman and CEO, North America: Joseph M. (Joe) Taylor
Auditors: KPMG AZSA & Co.

LOCATIONS

HQ: Panasonic Corporation
(Panasonikku Kabushiki Kaisha)
1006 Oaza Kadoma
Kadoma, Osaka 571-8501, Japan
Phone: 81-6-6908-1121   **Fax:** 81-6-6908-2351
US HQ: 1 Panasonic Way, Secaucus, NJ 07094
US Phone: 201-348-7000   **US Fax:** 201-348-7016
Web: panasonic.net

2010 Sales

	% of total
Japan	54
Asia & China	23
Americas	12
Europe	11
Total	**100**

PRODUCTS/OPERATIONS

2010 Sales

	% of total
Digital AVC Networks	39
PEW & PanaHome	19
Home appliances	13
Components & devices	12
SANYO	5
Other	12
Total	**100**

Selected Segments and Products

AVC Networks
  Camcorders
  Computer drives (CD-ROM, DVD-ROM/RAM)
  Computers (PCs)
  Digital cameras
  DVD players and recorders
  Fax machines
  Printers
  Telephones
  TVs (color, LCD, plasma display)
  VCRs
PEW and PanaHome
  Automation controls
  Beauty and personal care products
  Condominiums
  Electronic and plastic materials
  Health-enhancing products
  Home amenity and security systems
  Home remodeling
  Interior furnishings
  Medical and nursing care facilities
  Rental apartment housing
  Residential real estate
Home appliances
  Air conditioners and purifiers
  Dishwashers
  Dryers
  Fans
  Refrigerators
  Vacuum cleaners
  Water heaters
  Washing machines
Components and devices
  Batteries (dry, rechargeable)
  Displays (CRTs, LCDs, PDPs)
  Electric motors
  General components (capacitors, resistors, printed circuit boards)
  Magnetic recording heads
  Semiconductors

Selected Brands

National
Panasonic
Quasar
Technics
Victor

COMPETITORS

A123 Systems
Apple Inc.
BSH Bosch und Siemens Hausgeräte
BYD
Canon
Dell
Eastman Kodak
Electrolux
Fujitsu Technology Solutions
GE Appliances & Lighting
Haier Group
Hewlett-Packard
IBM
Intel
Konica Minolta
LG Electronics
Motorola
NEC
Nokia
Olympus
Philips Electronics
Procter & Gamble
Samsung Electronics
Sharp Corp.
Sony
Technicolor
Toshiba
Truly International
Tyco Electronics
Whirlpool
Yuasa Battery Thailand

HISTORICAL FINANCIALS

Company Type: Public

Income Statement

FYE: March 31

	REVENUE ($ mil.)	NET INCOME ($ mil.)	NET PROFIT MARGIN	EMPLOYEES
3/10	80,025	(1,116)	—	384,586
3/09	79,822	(3,895)	—	292,250
3/08	90,908	2,826	3.1%	305,828
3/07	77,445	1,846	2.4%	328,645
3/06	75,831	1,317	1.7%	334,402
Annual Growth	1.4%	—	—	3.6%

2010 Year-End Financials

Debt ratio: 36.8%
Return on equity: —
Cash ($ mil.): 11,974
Current ratio: 1.35
Long-term debt ($ mil.): 11,100

No. of shares (mil.): 2,070
Dividends
  Yield: 0.0%
  Payout: —
Market value ($ mil.): 342

Stock History

NYSE: PC

	STOCK PRICE ($) FY Close	P/E High/Low	PER SHARE ($) Earnings	Dividends	Book Value
3/10	0.17	— —	0.00	0.00	14.55
3/09	0.11	— —	(1.87)	0.26	13.82
3/08	0.22	— —	1.34	0.35	18.12
3/07	0.17	— —	0.84	0.25	16.09
3/06	0.19	— —	0.59	0.17	15.60
Annual Growth	(2.7%)	— —	—	—	(1.7%)

Pearson plc

There's nothing fishy about information from Pearson, home of salmon-colored newspaper *The Financial Times*. The media giant operates through three main business groups: Pearson Education, Penguin Group, and FT Group. Pearson Education is the world's top educational publisher of textbooks and related material. Pearson provides financial information and business news through FT Group, which includes *The Financial Times* (known locally as the "Pink 'Un"), related website FT.com, and the 50%-owned *The Economist*. Penguin Group publishes fiction, nonfiction, and reference titles through imprints such as Putnam and Viking.

Under CEO Marjorie Scardino, Pearson has shed many of its non-media assets — which once included The Tussaud Group's wax museums — and is focusing on its desire to become a leading education company. In 2008 Pearson took steps to accomplish this goal with the significant purchases of Harcourt Assessment (testing) and Harcourt Education (textbooks), both representing major additions to its education holdings. Further plans to bolster education include investing in content, building up technology and services offerings, growing in international markets, and improving efficiency. In the services

arena, in 2010 Pearson agreed to pay about $80 million for school improvement services provider America's Choice.

At its FT unit the company merged the *Financial Times'* print and online divisions. In 2010 FT Group acquired Medley Global Advisors, a provider of macroeconomic intelligence to hedge funds and banks. FT made the purchase in order to grow its investments in premium services, therefore reducing its reliance on advertising. Pearson has denied that it will sell off the FT Group amid previous speculation. However, in 2008 the company sold its 50% stake in the *Financial Times'* German edition, *FT Deutschland*, to Gruner + Jahr.

In another significant move toward shedding noncore assets, in 2010 Pearson sold its stake in Interactive Data Corporation to private equity firms Silver Lake and Warburg Pincus for some $2 billion. The company plans to use the proceeds of the disposal for additional acquisitions to complement its education businesses.

One of the most famous brands in book publishing, Penguin is facing challenges along with the rest of the consumer publishing market. Penguin is focused on increasing its digital content. *New York Times* US bestsellers from the imprint in 2009 include Kathryn Stockett's *The Help* and Janice Y.K. Lee's *The Piano Teacher*.

In order to reduce its reliance on its core US and UK markets, Pearson is increasing its investments in emerging markets. New products include FT Group's *Pharmawire* and *Debtwire* in the Asia/Pacific region and *dealReporter* in emerging markets in Europe, the Middle East, and Africa. And in 2010 Pearson purchased English training business the Wall Street Institute from The Carlyle Group for $92 million.

HISTORY

In 1844 Samuel Pearson became a partner in a small Yorkshire building firm. When he retired in 1879 his grandson Weetman took over, moving the company to London in 1884. The business enjoyed extraordinary success — building the first tunnel under New York's Hudson River and installing Mexico City's drainage system. By the 1890s the company (incorporated as S. Pearson & Son in 1897) was the world's #1 contractor.

In the 1920s the company bought newspapers and engaged in oil exploration. Weetman died in 1927, and so did the construction business. His heirs then bought into several unrelated businesses. Pearson bought control of *The Financial Times* newspaper in 1957, a deal that also brought it 50% of *The Economist* (*The Financial Times* had acquired half of *The Economist* in 1928). The company later added stakes in vintner Chateau Latour (1963, sold 1988) and publisher Longman (1968). The firm went public in 1969.

During the 1970s Pearson bought Penguin Books (1971) and Madame Tussaud's (1978). In 1989 it added Addison-Wesley (educational publisher, US) and Les Echos (financial newspaper publisher, France).

Concentrating on media interests, the company bought Thames Television in 1993 and Grundy Worldwide (game shows and soap operas) in 1995. It acquired HarperCollins Educational Publishing from News Corp. in 1996, as well as US publisher Putnam Berkley from MCA, gaining such authors as Tom Clancy and Amy Tan. By the mid-1990s, however, Pearson's holdings still lacked focus, and earnings were depressed. Marjorie Scardino, a Texan who had been

CEO of The Economist Group since 1992, replaced Frank Barlow in 1997, becoming the first woman to lead a major UK company. She rounded out Pearson's TV holdings with the purchase of All American Communications that year.

In 1998 Pearson bought Simon & Schuster's reference and educational publishing divisions from Viacom (now CBS Corporation) for $4.6 billion and sold Tussaud's amusement business.

As part of a long-term plan to build *The Financial Times* brand online, Pearson bought 60% of Data Broadcasting Corporation (now called Interactive Data Corporation) in 2000. Pearson bought troubled UK publisher Dorling Kindersley for nearly $500 million and later combined the firm with its Penguin unit.

Later in 2000 Pearson combined its TV operations with CLT-Ufa, co-owned by German media company Bertelsmann and Audiofina, into a new publicly traded broadcasting firm called RTL Group. Pearson took a 22% stake in RTL. In 2001 Pearson formed a joint venture with an arm of Chinese state television to produce programming for a Chinese audience. In late 2001 Pearson sold its stake in RTL to Bertelsmann. Spain's Telefónica divested its 5% stake in the company in late 2004.

As a result of shareholders pressuring Scardino to focus more on the company's overperforming education unit, the company acquired professional testing unit Promissor from Houghton Mifflin in 2006. The company sold its Pearson Government Solutions unit in 2006 to Veritas Capital for some $560 million.

In 2007 Pearson bolstered its US assessment and international textbook holdings with the purchases of exam-testing company Harcourt Assessment and textbook publisher Harcourt Education Ltd. from Reed Elsevier for $950 million. Later in 2007 Pearson sold its French newspaper *Les Echos* to French luxury goods conglomerate LVMH for €240 million.

The company in 2008 sold its Data Management business, which manufactured scanners, printed forms, and provided support services for customers in education and in commercial and government organizations, to M&F Worldwide.

EXECUTIVES

Chairman: Glen R. Moreno, age 67
Chief Executive and Director:
 Dame Marjorie M. Scardino, age 63
CFO and Director: Robin Freestone, age 51
EVP: Steve Dowling
Chairman and CEO, Penguin Group: John C. Makinson, age 55
Director; Chief Executive, Pearson North America Education: William T. (Will) Ethridge, age 58
Director Global Communications: Luke Swanson, age 40
Director; Chief Executive, Financial Times Group: Rona A. Fairhead, age 48
Government Relations: Jeff Taylor
Investor Relations: Simon Mays-Smith
Head Corporate Communications and Media Relations: Charles Goldsmith
Auditors: PricewaterhouseCoopers LLP

LOCATIONS

HQ: Pearson plc
  80 Strand
  London WC2R ORL, United Kingdom
Phone: 44-20-7010-2000   **Fax:** 44-20-7010-6060
US HQ: 1330 Avenue of the Americas
  New York, NY 10019
US Phone: 212-641-2400   **US Fax:** 212-641-2500
Web: www.pearson.com

2009 Sales

	% of total
North America	65
Europe	22
Asia/Pacific	9
Other regions	4
Total	**100**

PRODUCTS/OPERATIONS

2009 Sales

	% of total
Education	
North American	44
International	18
Professional	5
Penguin	18
Financial Times Group	
Interactive Data	9
FT Publishing	6
Total	**100**

Selected Education Holdings

International
North American
Professional
   Addison Wesley Professional, Prentice Hall PTR, Cisco
     Press (for IT professionals)
   Peachpit Press and New Riders Press (graphics and
     design professionals)
   Pearson VUE (professional testing business)
   Prentice Hall Financial Times (business education
     market)
   Que/ Sams (consumer and professional imprint)

Selected Financial Times Group Holdings

FT Publishing
   The Economist Group (50%)
   The Financial Times
   FT.com (financial news)
   FTSE International (50%, with London Stock
     Exchange; market indices)

Selected Penguin Holdings

Avery
Berkley Books
Dorling Kindersley
Dutton
Frederick Warne
Hamish Hamilton
Ladybird
Michael Joseph
Penguin
Penguin Business
Penguin Classics
Penguin Reference
Plume
Puffin
Viking

COMPETITORS

Bloomberg L.P.
Bloomsbury
Cengage Learning
Crain Communications
Daily Mail
Dow Jones
Editis
Educational Development
Forbes
Hachette Book Group
HarperCollins
Houghton Mifflin Harcourt
McGraw-Hill
PLATO Learning
Random House
Reed Elsevier Group
Scholastic
Telekurs
Thomson Reuters
Wolters Kluwer

HISTORICAL FINANCIALS

Company Type: Public

Income Statement
FYE: December 31

	REVENUE ($ mil.)	NET INCOME ($ mil.)	NET PROFIT MARGIN	EMPLOYEES
12/09	8,957	736	8.2%	37,164
12/08	7,050	428	6.1%	33,680
12/07	8,286	565	6.8%	32,692
12/06	8,107	874	10.8%	34,341
12/05	7,061	1,110	15.7%	32,203
Annual Growth	**6.1%**	**(9.8%)**	**—**	**3.6%**

2009 Year-End Financials

Debt ratio: 44.5%
Return on equity: 10.6%
Cash ($ mil.): 1,194
Current ratio: 1.85
Long-term debt ($ mil.): 3,080
No. of shares (mil.): 811
Dividends
Yield: 2.4%
Payout: 64.7%
Market value ($ mil.): 18,543

Stock History
NYSE: PSO

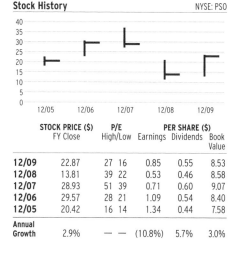

	STOCK PRICE ($) FY Close	P/E High/Low		PER SHARE ($) Earnings	Dividends	Book Value
12/09	22.87	27	16	0.85	0.55	8.53
12/08	13.81	39	22	0.53	0.46	8.58
12/07	28.93	51	39	0.71	0.60	9.07
12/06	29.57	28	21	1.09	0.54	8.40
12/05	20.42	16	14	1.34	0.44	7.58
Annual Growth	**2.9%**	**—**	**—**	**(10.8%)**	**5.7%**	**3.0%**

Pernod Ricard

Pernod Ricard, one of the world's largest producers of spirits, wants to be the absolute top global brand of vodka and premium Scotch whisky. The company's iconic brands include Absolut Vodka and Chivas Regal Scotch Whisky. Pernod Ricard also sells libations ranging from anise drinks and liqueurs (Pernod) to clear spirits (Beefeater and Seagram's gin). In addition, Pernod offers Jameson Irish whisky, Martell cognac, the liqueur Kahlúa, and Jacob's Creek and other wines. It added the coveted Absolut vodka brand to its holdings in 2008 when it acquired Sweden's V&S Group. Pernod Ricard was created in 1975 by the merger of Ricard and Pernod.

The company beat out US-based Fortune Brands with its $8 billion bid for the V&S Group during the Swedish government's auction of the maker of Absolut vodka. The iconic and highly profitable brand filled out the company's premium vodka line. Selling some 5 million cases of Absolut a year in the US, the acquisition also bolstered Pernod's US sales. V&S, for which Pernod also assumed $546 million in debt, continues to be based in Sweden. After the acquisition, Pernod pulled out of Maxxium Worldwide, a distribution operation that V&S had belonged

to, along with Beam Global Spirits & Wine, Rémy-Cointreau, and The Edrington Group.

To satisfy regulatory authorities with regard to its acquisition of V&S, Pernod sold its Wild Turkey brand to Campari for €437 million ($575 million) in 2009. Included in the Wild Turkey deal was American Honey liqueur.

In recent years Pernod Ricard has been streamlining its brand portfolio and focusing on the premium liquor market. Most recently, in 2010 it agreed to sell its Lindauer and several other minor New Zealand wine brands to Australia's Lion Nathan and Indevin. Other recent divestments include the sale of its Renault cognac brand to Finnish beverage distributor for the Nordic and Baltic countries, Altia Corp., and Ambrosio Velasco (a Spanish winemaker and owner of the Pacharán Zoco brand) to Spanish liquor company Diego Samora. In addition, the company sold its subsidiary Domecq Bodegas to a consortium of buyers.

The Ricard family controls about 20% of the company's voting rights.

HISTORY

Henri-Louis Pernod inherited Pernod Fils, an absinthe distillery, from his father-in-law in 1805 and immediately moved it to Pontarlier, France, to avoid stiff French import taxes. Demand for absinthe, a potent liqueur, spread quickly, and by the 1870s the liqueur was the toast of Paris. It was even featured in Impressionist paintings, and rumor has it that Vincent Van Gogh's psychosis might have been caused by it.

In the late 1800s serious competition for the absinthe market emerged from distiller Pernod Avignon, run by Jules Pernod (no relation to Henri-Louis). In 1906 Switzerland banned absinthe and France followed suit in 1915. In 1926 Henri-Louis joined with another anise distiller, Aristide Hemard, and formed Etablissements Hemard et Pernod Fils. Jules joined them in 1928. The resulting company was named Pernod.

Four years later the ban on pastis was lifted by the French government, and Paul Ricard, who made pastis illegally beforehand, began selling it openly. The licorice-flavored drink became popular in France. His company, Ricard, became a successful spirits maker and went public in 1962. Ricard acquired the Biscuit cognac brand in 1966.

Pernod and Ricard merged in 1975 to form Pernod Ricard. The company's operations included Campbell (scotch), SEGM (spirits exporter), and JFA Pampryl (fruit juice). In 1976 the group acquired CDC (Cinzano, Dubonnet). Two years later Patrick Ricard, son of Paul, became chairman and CEO.

Expanding through acquisitions in the 1980s, Pernod Ricard bought US-based Austin Nichols (Wild Turkey) from du Ligget Group in 1980 and acquired control of both Sias-MPA (fruit preparations) in 1982 and Compagnie Francaise des Produits Orangina (soft drinks) in 1984. The next year the firm added Ramazzotti (spirits, Italy) and IGM (distribution, Germany) to its mix, and in 1988 it bought Irish Distillers (whiskey), Yoo-Hoo Industries (US), and BWG (distribution, Ireland; sold in 2002). Australia's Orlando Wyndham Wines was added to the company's wine list in 1989 and merged with Pernod Ricard's Wyndham Estate winery the following year.

The group also acquired Spain's Larios gin, the Czech Republic's Becherovka liqueurs, and Italcanditi, a fruit preparations firm. Pernod Ricard added Mexican distillery Tequila Viuda de

Romero (Real Hacienda tequila) to its liquor cabinet in January 2000.

Pernod Ricard later teamed up with liquor giant Diageo to bid on Seagram's spirits and wine business. Their collective bid of $8.2 billion (with Pernod Ricard paying $3.2 billion) was accepted in December 2000, with Pernod Ricard agreeing to acquire such brands as Chivas Regal, Glenlivet, and Glen Grant (which was sold to Campari in 2006).

In 2001 the company sold its soft-drink business in Continental Europe, North America, and Australia to Cadbury Schweppes for about $640 million to help finance the Seagram's deal. After months of delay, the company finalized its deal to buy a part of Seagram's drinks business from Vivendi Universal after finally gaining FTC approval in December 2001.

By 2005 Pernod was back in a shopping mood. To help allay anti-competitive concerns, Pernod Ricard enlisted the help of Fortune Brands for its friendly bid for rival distiller Allied Domecq. As part of the deal, Fortune Brands ended up with Pernod Ricard's Larios gin, as well as several brands from Allied Domecq (including Canadian Club whisky, Clos du Bois wine, Courvoisier cognac, Maker's Mark bourbon, and Sauza tequila). Pernod Ricard paid about $14 billion for its former chief competitor Allied Domecq. Fortune Brands anted up about $5 billion for its part of the acquisition.

Pernod became the owner of Dunkin' Donuts and Baskin-Robbins ice cream operations as a result of the Allied Domecq buyout; in 2006 it sold both companies to a consortium of buyers that included Bain Capital, Carlyle Group, and Thomas H. Lee Partners. Pernod Ricard also sold its Bushmills Irish whisky to competitor Diageo, and its Braemar, Glen Grant, and Old Smuggler brands to Campari.

In 2008 the company sold off 14 labels, including wine brands Farmingham, Canei, La Ina, and Rio Viejo, and Spanish brandy brands Carlos I, Carlos III, and Filipe II. The next year it sold the Tia Maria coffee liqueur to Illva Saronno for €125 million ($177 million) in cash.

EXECUTIVES

Chairman: Patrick Ricard, age 65
CEO and Director: Pierre Pringuet, age 60
Managing Director Finance: Gilles Bogaert
Managing Director Swiss: Francisco de la Vega, age 55
Managing Director Brands: Thierry Billot, age 55
Managing Director Human Resources: Bruno Rain
Chief Marketing Officer: Martin Riley, age 55
SVP Spirits: Marty Crane
VP Communications: Olivier Cavil, age 37
VP Brand Security: Stephen N. Fisher
VP Financial Communications and Investor Relations: Denis Fiévet
VP and General Counsel: Ian FitzSimons
VP Information Systems: Jean Chavinier
Chairman and CEO, Premium Wine Brands: Jean-Christophe Coutures, age 43
Chairman and CEO, The Absolut Company: Philippe Guettat, age 46
Chairman and CEO, Pernod Ricard Americas: Philippe A. X. Dréano, age 52
Chairman and CEO, Pernod Ricard Asia: Pierre Coppéré, age 56
Director; Chairman and CEO, Pernod: César Giron, age 47
Auditors: Deloitte & Associés

LOCATIONS

HQ: Pernod Ricard SA
  12, place des États-Unis
  75783 Paris, France
Phone: 33-1-41-00-41-00 **Fax:** 33-1-41-00-41-41
US HQ: 100 Manhattanville Rd., Purchase, NY 10577
US Phone: 914-848-4800
Web: www.pernod-ricard.com

2010 Sales

	% of total
Europe	
France	9
Other	36
Americas	28
Asia & other	27
Total	**100**

PRODUCTS/OPERATIONS

Selected Strategic Brands

Absolut
Ballentine's
Beefeater
Chevas Regal
The Glenlivet
Havana Club
Jacob's Creek
Jameson
Kahlúa
Malibu
Martell
Montana
Mumm
Perrier-Jouët
Plymouth
Ricard
Royal Salute

COMPETITORS

Bacardi
Beam Global Spirits & Wine
Brown-Forman
Campari
Constellation Brands
Diageo
E. & J. Gallo
Fortune Brands
Foster's Americas
LVMH
Rémy Cointreau
UB Group

HISTORICAL FINANCIALS

Company Type: Public

Income Statement

FYE: June 30

	REVENUE ($ mil.)	NET INCOME ($ mil.)	NET PROFIT MARGIN	EMPLOYEES
6/10	8,643	1,194	13.8%	18,177
6/09	10,118	1,357	13.4%	18,975
6/08	10,403	1,372	13.2%	19,300
6/07	8,681	1,153	13.3%	17,684
6/06	7,612	841	11.0%	17,600
Annual Growth	**3.2%**	**9.2%**	**—**	**0.8%**

2010 Year-End Financials

Debt ratio: —
Return on equity: 10.9%
Cash ($ mil.): 856
Current ratio: 1.49
Long-term debt ($ mil.): —

No. of shares (mil.): 264
Dividends
  Yield: 1.0%
  Payout: 16.9%
Market value ($ mil.): 20,635

Stock History

Euronext Paris: RI

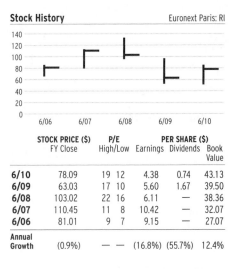

	STOCK PRICE ($) FY Close	P/E High/Low		Earnings	PER SHARE ($) Dividends	Book Value
6/10	78.09	19	12	4.38	0.74	43.13
6/09	63.03	17	10	5.60	1.67	39.50
6/08	103.02	22	16	6.11	—	38.36
6/07	110.45	11	8	10.42	—	32.07
6/06	81.01	9	7	9.15	—	27.07
Annual Growth	**(0.9%)**	**—**	**—**	**(16.8%)**	**(55.7%)**	**12.4%**

PETROBRAS

PETRÓLEO BRASILEIRO (PETROBRAS) isn't brash, but it is Brazil's top company and has operations in 24 countries. It explores for oil and gas and produces, refines, purchases, and transports oil and gas products. The company has proved reserves of about 14.1 billion barrels of oil equivalent and operates 16 refineries, an extensive pipeline network, and more than 8,000 gas stations. Petrobras Distribuidora is Brazil's top retailer of oil products and fuel alcohol. Petrobras Energía Participaciones is a leading Argentine oil firm. Other units produce electricity (through 10 power plants), petrochemicals, and natural gas. Brazil's government owns 56% of PETROBRAS.

Petrobras Internacional, also known as Braspetro, conducts exploration worldwide, including in Angola, Kazakhstan, Nigeria, the UK, the US, and across Latin America.

Although most of PETROBRAS' wells are onshore, the bulk of its production comes from offshore operations; the company is recognized as a leader in offshore drilling technology and deepwater wells. In 2009 it was operating more than 110 production platforms. It has made some major finds that have boosted the country's long-term oil assets. In 2007 PETROBRAS announced a major offshore oil discovery in the Tupi that could boost Brazil's oil reserves by 40%. In 2008 it reported it had discovered a major natural gas field near the Tupi find. The company plans to triple production outside Brazil to 300,000 barrels per day.

PETROBRAS is also a major ethanol producer, and plans to invest a further $2.8 billion in biofuels between 2009 and 2013 to help ensure Brazil's fuel independence.

To boost its natural gas operations, PETROBRAS is investing $2 billion to build a pipeline from gas fields in Bolivia to Brazil.

The company has also restructured the Brazilian petrochemical industry to make it more efficient. Its actions have included the purchase of the petrochemical assets of the Ipiranga Group in 2007 and Suzano Petroquímica, a leader in Latin American polypropylene resin production, in 2008.

HISTORY

"O petróleo é nosso!"

"The oil is ours!" proclaimed the Brazilian nationalists' slogan in 1953, and President Getúlio Vargas approved a bill creating a state-run monopoly on petroleum discovery, development, refining, and transport. The same year that PETRÓLEO BRASILEIRO (PETROBRAS) was created, a team led by American geologist Walter Link reported that the prospects of finding petroleum in Brazil were slim. The report outraged Brazilian nationalists, who saw it as a plov for foreign exploitation. PETROBRAS proved it could find oil, but Brazil continued to import crude oil and petroleum products. By 1973 the company produced about 10% of the nation's needs.

When oil prices soared during the Arab embargo, the government, instead of encouraging exploration for domestic oil, pushed PETROBRAS into a program to promote alcohol fuels. The company was forced to raise gasoline prices to make the more costly gasohol attractive to consumers. During the 1979 oil crunch the price of gasohol was fixed at 65% of gasoline. But during the oil glut of the mid-1980s, PETROBRAS' cost of making gasohol was twice what it cost to buy gasoline — in other words, PETROBRAS lost money.

PETROBRAS soon began overseas exploration. In 1980 it found an oil field in Iraq, an important trading partner during the 1980s. The company also drilled in Angola and, through a 1987 agreement with Texaco, in the Gulf of Mexico.

In the mid-1980s PETROBRAS began production in the deepwater Campos basin off the coast of Rio de Janeiro state. Discoveries there in 1988, in the Marlim and Albacora fields, more than tripled its oil reserves. It plunged deep into the thick Amazon jungle in 1986 to explore for oil, and by 1990 Amazon wells were making a significant contribution to total production. That year, to ease dependence on imports, PETROBRAS launched a five-year, $16.9 billion plan to boost crude oil production. It also began selling its mining and trading assets.

Before the invasion of Kuwait, Brazil relied heavily on Iraq, trading weapons for oil. After the invasion spawned increases in crude prices, PETROBRAS raised pump prices but, yielding to the government's anti-inflation program, still did not raise them enough to cover costs. It lost $13 million a day.

The company sold 26% of Petrobras Distribuidora to the public in 1993 and privatized several of its petrochemical and fertilizer subsidiaries. A 1994 presidential order, bent on stabilizing Brazil's 40%-per-month inflation, cut the prices of oil products. In 1995 the government loosened its grip on the oil and gas industry and allowed foreign companies to enter the Brazilian market. In the wake of this reform, PETROBRAS teamed up with a Japanese consortium to build Brazil's largest oil refinery.

In 1997 PETROBRAS appealed a $4 billion judgment from a 1992 shareholder lawsuit; the suit alleged PETROBRAS had undervalued shares during the privatization of the loss-making Petroquisa affiliate. (The appeal was granted in 1999.)

As part of an effort to boost oil production, PETROBRAS also began to raise money abroad in 1999. The next year PETROBRAS and Spanish oil giant Repsol YPF agreed to swap oil and gas assets in Argentina and Brazil in a deal worth more than $1 billion.

In 2000 the company announced plans to change its corporate name to PETROBRAX, but fierce political and popular reaction forced the company to abort this plan in 2001. In an even greater public relations disaster that year, one of PETROBRAS' giant rigs sank off of Brazil and 10 workers were killed. In 2001 PETROBRAS announced that it was going to spend as much as $3 billion to buy an oil company in order to increase its production in the Gulf of Mexico.

In 2002 the company expressed an interest in buying Argentina's major oil company (YPF) from Spanish/Argentine energy giant Repsol YPF. That year PETROBRAS bought control (59%) of Argentine energy company Perez Companc in a deal valued at $1 billion. PETROBRAS also reported its first oil find in Argentina in 2002.

In 2006 the company acquired a 50% stake in a deepwater block in Equatorial Guinea from a private group for an undisclosed sum.

EXECUTIVES

Chairman: Guido Mantega, age 61
CEO and Director: José S. Gabrielli de Azevedo, age 61
CFO and Chief Investor Relations Officer:
Almir G. Barbassa, age 63
Chief Gas and Energy Officer:
Maria das Graças Silva Foster, age 57
Chief International Officer: Jorge L. Zelada, age 53
Chief Audit Officer, Petrobras International Finance:
Gerson L. Gonçalves, age 57
Chief Downstream Officer: Paulo R. Costa, age 56
Chief Exploration and Production Officer:
Guilherme de Oliveira Estrella, age 68
Chief Services Officer: Renato de Souza Duque, age 55
Chief Commercial Officer, Petrobras International Finance: Guilhermes P.G. França, age 51
General Counsel; Chief Legal Officer, Petrobras International Finance: Nilton A. de Almeida Maia, age 53
Executive Manager Corporate Finance; Chairman and CEO, Petrobras International Finance:
Daniel Lima de Oliveira, age 58
General Manager Corporate Accounting; Chief Accounting Officer, Petrobras International Finance:
Mariângela M. Tizatto, age 50
Auditors: Ernst & Young Auditores Independentes S/C

LOCATIONS

HQ: PETRÓLEO BRASILEIRO S.A. — PETROBRAS
Avenida República do Chile 65, Sala 2202-A
20031-912 Rio de Janeiro, Brazil
Phone: 55-21-3224-1510   **Fax:** 55-21-2262-3678
US HQ: 570 Lexington Ave., 43rd Fl.
New York, NY 10022
US Phone: 212-829-1517   **US Fax:** 212-832-5300
Web: www.petrobras.com.br

2009 Sales

	% of total
Brazil	28
Other countries	72
Total	**100**

PRODUCTS/OPERATIONS

2009 Sales

	% of total
Refining, transportation & marketing	47
Exploration & production	24
Distribution	19
Other	10
Total	**100**

Selected Subsidiaries

Downstream Participações S.A. (asset exchanges between Petrobras and Repsol-YPF)
Petrobras Comercializadora de Energia Ltda
Petrobras Distribuidora SA (BR; distribution and marketing of petroleum products, fuel alcohol, and natural gas)
Petrobras Energía Participaciones (59%; oil and gas, Argentina)
Petrobras Gás SA (Gaspetro, management of the Brazil-Bolivia pipeline and other natural gas assets)
Petrobras Internacional SA (Braspetro; overseas exploration and production, marketing, and services)
Petrobras International Finance Company PIFCO (oil imports)
Petrobras Negócios Eletrônicos S.A.
Petrobras Química SA (Petroquisa, petrochemicals)
Petrobras Transporte SA (Transpetro, oil and gas transportation and storage)

COMPETITORS

Ashland Inc.	Marathon Oil
BHP Billiton	Norsk Hydro ASA
BP	Occidental Petroleum
Chevron	PEMEX
Devon Energy	Petróleos de Venezuela
Eni	Royal Dutch Shell
Exxon Mobil	Sunoco
Imperial Oil	TOTAL
Koch Industries, Inc.	

HISTORICAL FINANCIALS

Company Type: Public

Income Statement

FYE: December 31

	REVENUE ($ mil.)	NET INCOME ($ mil.)	NET PROFIT MARGIN	EMPLOYEES
12/09	91,869	15,504	16.9%	76,919
12/08	118,257	18,879	16.0%	74,240
12/07	87,735	13,138	15.0%	68,931
12/06	72,347	12,826	17.7%	62,266
12/05	56,324	10,186	18.1%	53,904
Annual Growth	**13.0%**	**11.1%**	**—**	**9.3%**

2009 Year-End Financials

Debt ratio: 61.2%
Return on equity: 22.2%
Cash ($ mil.): 16,169
Current ratio: 1.38
Long-term debt ($ mil.): 48,352

No. of shares (mil.): 6,428
Dividends
  Yield: 0.0%
  Payout: 0.6%
Market value ($ mil.): 306,499

Stock History

NYSE: PBR

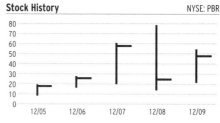

	STOCK PRICE ($) FY Close	P/E High/Low		PER SHARE ($) Earnings	Dividends	Book Value
12/09	47.68	15	6	3.54	0.02	14.63
12/08	24.49	18	3	4.30	0.25	9.63
12/07	57.62	40	14	1.50	0.72	10.14
12/06	25.75	9	6	2.92	1.67	6.89
12/05	17.82	8	4	2.36	1.01	5.12
Annual Growth	**27.9%**	**—**	**—**	**10.7%**	**(62.5%)**	**30.0%**

Petróleos de Venezuela

American motorists rely on Petróleos de Venezuela S.A. (PDVSA), one of the top exporters of oil to the US. The state-owned company is a global oil giant. It has proved reserves of more than 78 billion barrels of oil — the most outside the Middle East — and about 4.7 trillion cu. meters of natural gas. PDVSA's exploration and production take place in Venezuela, but the company also has refining and marketing operations in the Caribbean, Europe, and the US. Subsidiary CITGO Petroleum supplies gasoline to some 8,000 US retail outlets. PDVSA also makes Orimulsión, a heavy fuel alternative made from bitumen.

Outside Venezuela, the company refines, markets, and transports petroleum products in Belgium, the Caribbean, Germany, Sweden, the UK, and the US. On the domestic front, PDVSA's BITOR subsidiary mines Venezuela's extensive bitumen reserves, turning the tarlike ooze into Orimulsión, a patented fuel marketed as an alternative to coal for electric generating plants.

In a move that requires massive foreign investment, PDVSA is expanding its production of petrochemicals, gas, and Orimulsión. In 2009 PDVSA and Vietnam-based state oil company Petrovietnam formed a joint venture (PetroMacareo, 60% owned by PDVSA) to refine Venezuelan crude oil. It also signed deals with Portugal, Iran, Belarus, and Russia, securing additional international help in upgrading Venezuela's aging oil and expensive Orimulsión infrastructure.

However, investors will step carefully: Venezuelan President Hugo Chávez's tightening state control over the oil company's operations has led to major commercial instability for foreign firms. As part of a nationalization drive, in 2007 the company took control of 32 oil fields run by private, including foreign, enterprises.

HISTORY

Invited by dictator Juan Vicente Gómez, Royal Dutch Shell looked for oil in Venezuela just before WWI. After the war US companies plunged in. Standard Oil of Indiana began Creole Petroleum in 1920 to explore in Venezuela, selling the company in 1928 to Standard of New Jersey.

When the Venezuelan government threatened to nationalize its oil industry in 1938, the foreign oil companies agreed to pay more taxes and royalties. But in 1945 Venezuela set a pattern for the rest of the world's oil-rich nations when it decreed it was a 50% partner in all oil operations. Venezuela was pivotal to OPEC's creation in 1960, and the next year the government created the Venezuelan Petroleum Corporation (CVP), which was granted the nation's unassigned petroleum reserves. By the early 1970s CVP produced about 2% of the nation's oil.

President Carlos Andrés Pérez nationalized oil holdings in 1975, paying only $1 billion for foreign-owned oil assets and creating Petróleos de Venezuela S.A. (PDVSA) to hold the properties. Venezuela formed stand-alone PDVSA subsidiaries: Shell operations became Maraven, Creole became Lagoven, and smaller companies combined into Corpoven. (All units were merged into PDVSA in 1998.)

Free of debt and buoyed by high crude prices in the late 1970s and early 1980s, PDVSA formed ventures (Ruhr Oel) with Germany's Veba Oel and Sweden's Nynas Petroleum. In the US,

PDVSA bought 50% of CITGO, the former refining and marketing arm of Cities Service Co., from Southland in 1986 (and the rest in 1990). PDVSA also bought a 50% stake in a Unocal refinery in 1989 to create joint venture UNO-VEN.

After the 1991 Gulf War, Venezuela increased its own production despite OPEC oil quotas. The next year PDVSA opened some marginal fields to foreign investment for the first time since the industry's 1975 nationalization.

Venezuelan President Rafael Caldera named Luis Giusti president of the company in 1994, and the next year Venezuela's oil industry was opened to foreign investment. In 1996 PDVSA began building a $1.5 billion plastics plant with Mobil (later Exxon Mobil). PDVSA and Unocal finally ended UNO-VEN the next year when UNO-VEN CEO David Tippeconnic took over as head of CITGO.

The rush for Venezuelan oil rights was on by 1997; one week's worth of bidding brought in $2 billion from top international oil companies. Meanwhile, PDVSA searched for facilities to refine the heavy crude, striking deals with Phillips Petroleum (later renamed ConocoPhillips) in 1997 and Amerada Hess (later renamed Hess Corporation) in 1998.

PDVSA's profits took a hit in 1998 when oil prices fell to record lows. Concerns arose about the firm's direction that year after populist Hugo Chávez was elected as Venezuela's president. Chávez and his allies sought to retain state control over PDVSA's resources and keep a closer check on foreign partners.

In 1999 PDVSA, suffering from a devastated domestic economy, decided to expand its downstream operations globally. As part of that plan, it formed a Houston-based crude and products marketing firm, PDVSA Trading.

Tightening his control of the company, in 2000 Chávez appointed army generals to head up both PDVSA (Guaicaipuro Lameda) and CITGO (Oswaldo Contreras Maza). The appointments followed a management shake-up and an oil workers' strike.

In 2001 PDVSA with other oil partners announced that it had secured $1.1 billion in funding to develop an extra-heavy crude production project in the Hamaca region of the Orinoco basin.

In 2002 Chávez replaced Lameda as PDVSA's top executive with banker Gastón Parra. However, growing management discontent with Chávez's board of directors led to a major strike and a serious disruption of the company's oil production.

The strike spread into other industries and led to violence and a revolt by some military leaders. Pedro Carmona, president of Venezuela's top business association, was appointed to lead a civilian junta in the run-up to national elections. But Chávez refused to step down, and within a few days loyalist troops brought him back to power. In a move to make peace with PDVSA managers, Chávez removed Parra and other controversial appointees from the company's board. He then announced that he would appoint Alí Rodríguez, the former oil minister and head of OPEC, to take over the reins at PDVSA.

However, continued political turmoil led to another major strike in 2002. In 2003 the government threatened to split the company in two as a way to break the striking managers' hold and restore full production. The strike led to a third of the workforce being laid off that year.

Energy and mines minister Rafael Ramírez became PDVSA's president in November 2004.

EXECUTIVES

President, CEO, and Director: Rafael Ramírez Carreño
VP Exploration and Production: Eulogio Del Pino
VP Refining, Commerce, and Supply; President, PDV Marina; Director: Asdrúbal Chávez
Financial Executive Director: Nicolás Veracierta
Internal Finance Director; Board Member: Eudomario Carruyo
Internal Director, Production and Services: Ricardo Coronado
Internal Gas Director: Carlos Vallejo
Internal Director, Planning and Control: Fadi Kabboul
Director and External Manager: Iván Orellana
Manager Industrial Safety: Ángel E. Ortiz
Manager National Communications: Alfredo Cárquez
Managing Internal Director: Jesús Villanueva
Manager Production and Logistics and Internal Director: Luis Pulido
Managing Internal Director: Dester Rodríguez
Manager Prevention and Control: Wilmer Barrientos Fernández
Managing Internal Director Research and Development: Hercilio Rivas
Regional Manager, Cuba: Luis Gómez Gil
Auditors: KPMG Alcaraz Cabrera Vázquez

LOCATIONS

HQ: Petróleos de Venezuela S.A.
Edificio Petróleos de Venezuela, Avenida Libertador
La Campiña, Apartado 169
Caracas 1050-A, Venezuela
Phone: 58-212-708-4111   **Fax:** 58-212-708-4661
Web: www.pdvsa.com

2009 Sales

	% of total
Venezuela	56
US	33
Other countries	11
Total	**100**

PRODUCTS/OPERATIONS

Selected Subsidiaries and Affiliates

Bitúmenes Orinoco, SA (BITOR, bitumen and Orimulsión)
Carbozulia, SA (coal)
CIED
CITGO Petroleum Corp. (refining, marketing, and petrochemicals; US)
CVP
Deltaven
Intevep, SA (research and support)
Palmaven, SA (agricultural assistance and conservation projects)
PDV Marina
PDVSA Gas
PDVSA Petróleo
PDVSA Trading (crude oil and products marketing, US)
Pequiven, SA (petrochemicals)

COMPETITORS

BHP Billiton	Nigerian National
BP	Petroleum
Chevron	NIOC
ConocoPhillips	Norsk Hydro ASA
Devon Energy	Occidental Petroleum
Eni	PEMEX
Exxon Mobil	PETROBRAS
Harvest Natural Resources	Qatar Petroleum
Imperial Oil	Royal Dutch Shell
Koch Industries, Inc.	Saudi Aramco
Marathon Oil	Sunoco
	TOTAL

HISTORICAL FINANCIALS

Company Type: Government-owned

Income Statement

FYE: December 31

	REVENUE ($ mil.)	NET INCOME ($ mil.)	NET PROFIT MARGIN	EMPLOYEES
12/09	75	5	6.0%	102,750
12/08	126	9	7.4%	98,113
12/07	96	6	6.5%	77,292
12/06	99	6	5.5%	68,106
12/05	86	7	7.6%	59,678
Annual Growth	(3.3%)	(8.8%)	—	14.5%

2009 Year-End Financials

Debt ratio: —
Return on equity: —
Cash ($ mil.): —
Current ratio: —
Long-term debt ($ mil.): 18

Net Income History

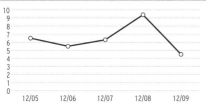

Petróleos Mexicanos

Petróleos Mexicanos (PEMEX) not only fuels Mexico's automobile engines, the state-owned oil company also fuels the nation's economy, accounting for some one-third of the Mexican government's revenues and about 7% of its export earnings. The integrated company's operations, spread throughout Mexico, range from exploration and production to refining and petrochemicals. PEMEX's P.M.I. Comercio Internacional subsidiary manages the company's trading operations outside the country. In 2009 PEMEX reported estimated proved reserves of 14 billion barrels of oil equivalent. That year PEMEX produced about 3.8 million barrels of oil equivalent per day.

PEMEX's refining operations (with a capacity of more than 1.5 million barrels of crude per day) convert crude oil into gasoline, jet fuel, diesel, fuel oil, asphalts, and lubricants. PEMEX's Gas and Basic Petrochemicals unit processes natural gas and natural gas liquids and ships and sells natural gas and liquefied petroleum gas throughout Mexico. It also produces several basic petrochemical feedstocks.

Long recognized as the tangible expression of Mexican nationalism, PEMEX has faced popular opposition in its bid to follow other Latin American state oil companies and privatize some operations. PEMEX is, however, working to become more responsive to market conditions.

Between 2005 and 2009 the company discovered 20 crude oil fields and 49 natural gas fields, bringing its total number of producing fields to about 400. In 2009 PEMEX announced a major reorganization aimed at improving operational efficiency and harnessing the latest technology to expand its reserves and increase production, both of which had been static or falling over the previous five years.

Like other oil majors, PEMEX suffered financially in 2009 as the global recession weakened oil demand and prices, resulting in the company posting decreased revenues and a net income figure only slightly better than in 2008.

HISTORY

Histories of precolonial Mexico recount the nation's first oil business: Natives along the Tampico coast gathered asphalt from naturally occurring deposits and traded with the Aztecs.

As the 20th century began, Americans Edward Doheny and Charles Canfield struck oil near Tampico. Their success was eclipsed in 1910 by a nearby well drilled by British engineer Weetman Pearson, leader of the firm that became Pearson PLC.

President Porfirio Díaz had welcomed foreign ownership of Mexican resources, but revolution ousted Díaz, and the 1917 Constitution proclaimed that natural resources belonged to the nation. Without enforcing legislation, however, foreign oil companies continued business as usual until a 1925 act limited their concessions. During a bitter labor dispute in 1938, President Lázaro Cárdenas expropriated foreign oil holdings — the first nationalization of oil holdings by a non-Communist state. Subsequent legislation created Petróleos Mexicanos (PEMEX).

Without foreign capital and expertise, the new state-owned company struggled, and Mexico had to import petroleum in the early 1970s. But for many Mexicans, PEMEX remained a symbol of national identity and economic independence. That faith was rewarded in 1972 when a major oil discovery made PEMEX one of the world's top oil producers again. Ample domestic oil supplies and high world prices during the Iranian upheaval in the late 1970s fueled a boom and a government borrowing spree in Mexico. Between 1982 and 1985 PEMEX contributed more than 50% of government revenues.

When oil prices collapsed in 1985, Mexico cut investment in exploration, and production dropped. To decrease its reliance on oil, Mexico began lowering trade barriers and encouraging manufacturing, even allowing some foreign ownership of petrochemical processing.

Elected in 1988, President Carlos Salinas de Gortari began to reform PEMEX. Labor's grip on the company was loosened in 1989 when a union leader was arrested and jailed after a gun battle. In 1992, after a PEMEX pipeline explosion killed more than 200 people in Guadalajara, four of its executives and several local officials were sent to prison, amid public cries for company reform.

President Ernesto Zedillo appointed Adrián Lajous Vargas head of PEMEX in 1994. Under the professorial Lajous, PEMEX began to adopt modern business practices (such as trimming its bloated payroll), look for more reserves, and improve its refining capability. Lajous tried to sell some petrochemical assets in 1995, but had to modify the scheme the next year after massive public protests by the country's nationalists. Still, PEMEX began selling off natural gas production, distribution, and storage networks to private companies.

Though oil prices were dropping, in 1998 Mexico finally upped PEMEX's investment budget and PEMEX dramatically increased exploration and production. In spite of 2000's looming national election (elections traditionally had caused bureaucrats to keep a low profile to protect their jobs), Lajous again fanned the flames of the opposition: In 1998 he signed a major deal to sell Mexican crude to Exxon's Texas refinery, and in 1999 a four-year-old PEMEX/Shell joint venture announced it would expand its US refinery.

In 1999 Lajous resigned and was replaced by Rogelio Montemayor, a former governor. The next year Vicente Fox was elected as Mexico's new president, the country's first non-Institutional Revolutionary Party (PRI) leader in seven decades. He announced plans to replace PEMEX's politician-staffed board with professionals — Montemayor was among the casualties — and modernize the company, but he ruled out privatizing PEMEX as politically unfeasible.

Fox appointed Raúl Muñoz, formerly with Dupont Mexico, in 2003 to lead PEMEX. Muñoz, however, was engulfed in a scandal involving the misuse of funds and forced to resign the following year. His replacement, Luis Ramírez, lasted until the next national election, when incoming President Felipe Calderón appointed Jesús Reyes.

Reyes was replaced by Juan José Suárez Coppel in 2009.

EXECUTIVES

Chairman: Georgina Y. Kessel Martínez, age 60
Director General and CEO: Juan J. Suárez Coppel
CFO: Esteban Levin Balcells, age 38
Chief of Staff: Mariano Ruiz-Funes Macedo, age 52
Chief Staff, General Direction:
Homero Niño de Rivera Vela
Corporate Director Operations:
Carlos R. Murrieta Cummings
Corporate Director, Engineering and Project Development: Jorge J. Borja Navarrete, age 67
Director General, Pemex Gas and Basic Petrochemicals: Roberto Ramírez Soberón, age 60
Director General, Pemex Exploration and Production:
Carlos A. Morales Gil, age 56
Director General, Pemex Petrochemicals:
Rafael Beverido Lomelín, age 68
Director General, Pemex Refining:
José A. Ceballos Soberanis, age 67
Director General, International Commerce:
Rosendo Zambrano Fernández
Deputy Director Finance and Treasury:
Mauricio Alazraki Pfeffer, age 45
Deputy Director Corporate Services:
Ignacio López Rodríguez, age 39
General Counsel: José N. García Reza, age 45
Secretary: Alejandro Fleming Kauffman
Executive Coordinator to General Direction:
Roberto Ortega Lomelín, age 60
Technical Secretary of Director General:
Raoul Capdevielle Orozco, age 67
Acting Corporate Director Management:
Marco A. Murillo Soberanis, age 51
Auditors: KPMG Cárdenas Dosal, S.C.

LOCATIONS

HQ: Petróleos Mexicanos
Avenida Marina Nacional 329, Colonia Huasteca
11311 México, D.F., Mexico
Phone: 52-55-1944-2500   **Fax:** 52-55-1944-9378
Web: www.pemex.com

2009 Sales

	% of total
Mexico	55
Other countries	44
Services income	1
Total	**100**

Peugeot S.A.

PRODUCTS/OPERATIONS

2009 Sales

	% of total
Exploration & production	52
Refining	34
Gas & basic petrochemicals	11
Petrochemicals	3
Total	**100**

Selected Subsidiaries

PEMEX Exploración y Producción (petroleum and natural gas exploration and production)
PEMEX Gas y Petroquímica Básica (natural gas, liquids from natural gas, and ethane processing)
PEMEX Petroquímica (petrochemical production)
PEMEX Refinación (refining and marketing)
P.M.I. Comercio Internacional (international trading)

COMPETITORS

Ashland Inc.
BHP Billiton
BP
Chevron
Devon Energy
Eni
Exxon Mobil
Imperial Oil
Koch Industries, Inc.
Marathon Oil
Norsk Hydro ASA
Occidental Petroleum
PETROBRAS
Petróleos de Venezuela
Royal Dutch Shell
Sunoco
TOTAL

HISTORICAL FINANCIALS

Company Type: Government-owned

Income Statement

FYE: December 31

	REVENUE ($ mil.)	NET INCOME ($ mil.)	NET PROFIT MARGIN	EMPLOYEES
12/09	83,586	(7,260)	—	145,146
12/08	96,442	(8,133)	—	143,421
12/07	104,004	(1,676)	—	141,146
12/06	104,645	4,182	4.0%	141,275
12/05	87,279	(7,079)	—	139,171
Annual Growth	(1.1%)	—	—	1.1%

2009 Year-End Financials

Debt ratio: —
Return on equity: —
Cash ($ mil.): —
Current ratio: —
Long-term debt ($ mil.): 40,589

Net Income History

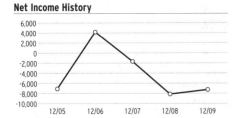

Peugeot S.A.

Peugeot S.A. enjoys its space under L'Arc de Triomphe, besting rival Renault to claim the top spot in the battle for auto sales in France. Peugeot makes cars and light commercial vehicles under the Peugeot and Citroën brands. France's best-selling auto brand, Peugeot is among the top manufacturers in European passenger car and commercial vehicle sales. Also part of Peugeot's automotive division are Faurecia (auto parts), GEFCO (transportation and logistics), and Banque PSA Finance (financial services for dealers and customers). Other group products include motorbikes, scooters, and light-armored vehicles. Peugeot makes most of its sales in Europe. The Peugeot family controls more than 45% of the voting stock.

With an almost 14% market share in Europe, Peugeot was the first to offer an all-electric vehicle in France; the company launched the Peugeot iOn and EX1 and Citroën C-Zero in 2010. It will premier its hybrid diesel engines in 2011. The company focuses on efficiently building almost all of its vehicles on one of three basic platforms. This keeps the new models rolling out, while keeping development and production costs under control.

Some of those new models included the Citroën C3 Picasso and the Peugeot 3008, which were released in Europe in 2009. Peugeot manufactures its cars at 15 production centers, as well as 16 powertrain and casting plants. The car company does not perform as an island unto itself, rather it maintains partnerships with Renault, Fiat, Ford, BMW, Toyota, and Mitsubishi, and is engaged in five industrial joint ventures. Along with its peripheral interests in auto parts, transportation and logistics, and financial services, the company is expanding its tailored mobility services through Mu by Peugeot for its electric vehicles. The program allows customers to swap their electric model cars for a gasoline- or diesel-powered vehicle for longer trips. Mu not only extends Peugeot's existing services, but also promotes its new electric vehicle.

But technology and design were not enough to keep Peugeot from experiencing many of the same industry problems as its European and North American peers in regard to the economic downturn and credit crisis that plagued automotive manufacturers in 2009. The company was additionally affected by stagnant European markets, high materials costs, compliance costs associated with the new Euro IV environmental standards, and intense competition from Asian rivals. In 2009 Peugeot and rival Renault were each offered a €3 billion state loan by the French government, if they vowed not to lay off more French workers or to close plants.

In addition to contending with the global downturn in the automotive industry during 2009, Peugeot had to deal with acrimony in the boardroom. The supervisory board ousted Christian Streiff, chairman of the management board, after two years in the post. The board designated Philippe Varin, CEO of Corus, to succeed Streiff.

Management is in agreement, however, to keep Peugeot focused on expanding its market share in South America, Russia, and in China. In China in 2010 Peugeot and Dongfeng Motor's joint venture Dongfeng Peugeot Citroën Automobile agreed to build a third plant in Wuhan to introduce 12 new passenger car models under the Peugeot and Citroën brands.

HISTORY

In 1810 brothers Frédéric and Jean-Pierre Peugeot made a foundry out of the family textile mill in the Alsace region of France and invented the cold-roll process for producing spring steel. Bicycle production began in 1885 at the behest of avid cyclist Armand Peugeot, Jean-Pierre's grandson.

Armand turned to automobiles and built Peugeot's first car, a steam-powered three-wheeler, in 1889. A gas-fueled Peugeot tied for first place in the 1894 Paris-Rouen Trials, the earliest auto race on record. That year the budding carmaker built the first station wagon, followed in 1905 by the first compact, the 600-pound "Le Bébé."

Peugeot built factories in France, including one in Sochaux (1912) that remains the company's main plant. It made the first diesel passenger car in 1922. The 1929 introduction of the reliable 201 model was followed by innovations such as synchromesh gears in 1936. The company suffered heavy damage in WWII, but quickly bounced back and began expanding overseas after the war.

In 1954 CEO Roland Peugeot rebuffed a board proposal calling for global expansion that would place the company in competition with US automakers. By 1976 the French government persuaded Peugeot to merge with Citroën.

André Citroën founded his company in 1915, and in 1919 it became the first in Europe to mass-produce cars. Citroën hit the skids during the Depression and in 1934 handed Michelin a large block of stock in lieu of payment for tires. Citroën never fully recovered, though by 1976 the company's line ranged from the 2CV minicar (discontinued in 1990) to limousines.

In 1978 Peugeot bought Chrysler's aging European plants and withering nameplates, including Simca (France) and Rootes (UK). Peugeot changed the nameplates to Talbot but sales continued to slide. It lost nearly $1.2 billion from 1980 to 1984.

Jacques Calvet took over as CEO in 1984. He cut 30,000 jobs and spent heavily on modernization. Aided by the strong launch of the 205 superminicar, Peugeot returned to profitability in 1985, and by 1989 had halved its production break-even point. In the 1980s Peugeot inked production deals with Renault (industrial vehicles, motors, gearboxes) and Fiat (light trucks).

Peugeot withdrew from the US in 1991 after five years of declining sales. A year later Renault and Peugeot developed electric cars and set up servicing centers throughout France. Citing an economic slump in 1993, Peugeot suffered its first loss ($239 million) since 1985.

Peugeot and rival Renault together introduced a V6 engine in 1996. Jean Martin Folz replaced Calvet as managing board chairman in 1997. In an effort to capitalize on the growing South American car market, the company purchased more than 80% of Argentina's Sevel, and built a plant in Brazil.

In 2001 Peugeot announced that it was building an engine plant in Brazil and agreed to produce a subcompact car for the European market with Toyota. The following year Peugeot formed an alliance with BMW to develop and build a line of small diesel engines for use in vehicles made by both companies.

In 2005 Peugeot achieved a major milestone when, for the first time, it sold more than 1 million units outside its traditional market of Western Europe. Christian Streiff replaced Folz as managing board chairman in 2007.

EXECUTIVES

Chairman Supervisory Board: Thierry Peugeot, age 53
Vice Chairman Supervisory Board: Jean-Louis Silvant, age 72
Vice Chairman Supervisory Board: Jean-Philippe Peugeot
Chairman Managing Board: Philippe Varin, age 58
Member Managing Board Finance and Strategic Development: Frédéric Saint-Geours, age 60
Member Managing Board Automobile Programmes and Strategy: Grégoire Olivier, age 49
Member Managing Board Manufacturing and Components: Guillaume Faury, age 42
EVP Purchasing: Jean-Christophe Quémard
EVP and Corporate Secretary: Jean-Claude Hanus
EVP Human Resources: Denis Martin
SVP Corporate Communications: Liliane Lacourt
SVP China: Claude Vajsman
SVP Executive Development: Bernd Schantz, age 59
SVP Latin America: Vincent Rambaud
Director Peugeot and Citroën Retails: Christophe Bergerand, age 46
Director French Sales, Peugeot: Olivier Veyrier, age 52
Corporate Communications: Cécile Durand
Auditors: PricewaterhouseCoopers

LOCATIONS

HQ: Peugeot S.A.
75, avenue de la Grande-Armée
75116 Paris, France
Phone: 33-1-40-66-55-11   **Fax:** 33-1-40-66-54-14
Web: www.psa-peugeot-citroen.com

PRODUCTS/OPERATIONS

2009 Sales

	% of total
Automobile division	73
Faurecia	18
GEFCO	6
Banque PSA Finance	3
Total	**100**

2009 Unit Sales

	Units	% of total
Peugeot brand	1,842,000	58
Citroën brand	1,346,000	42
Total	**3,188,000**	**100**

Selected Subsidiaries

Automobiles Citroën
Automobiles Peugeot
Banque PSA Finance
Faurecia (71%, automotive components)
GEFCO (logistics and transportation services)

COMPETITORS

BMW
Chrysler
CRCAM IDF CCI
Daimler
Fiat
Ford Motor
General Motors
Honda
Isuzu
Kia Motors
Mazda
Nissan
Norbert Dentressangle
Piaggio & Co.
Renault
Saab Automobile
Suzuki Motor
Toyota
Volkswagen
Volvo Car Corp.
Yamaha Motor

HISTORICAL FINANCIALS

Company Type: Public

Income Statement

FYE: December 31

	REVENUE ($ mil.)	NET INCOME ($ mil.)	NET PROFIT MARGIN	EMPLOYEES
12/09	69,391	(1,826)	—	186,220
12/08	76,615	(705)	—	201,690
12/07	89,216	1,216	1.4%	207,800
12/06	74,665	83	0.1%	211,700
12/05	66,637	1,173	1.8%	208,500
Annual Growth	**1.0%**	**—**	**—**	**(2.8%)**

2009 Year-End Financials

Debt ratio: —
Return on equity: —
Cash ($ mil.): 12,923
Current ratio: 1.12
Long-term debt ($ mil.): —

No. of shares (mil.): 234
Dividends
Yield: 0.0%
Payout: —
Market value ($ mil.): 7,938

Stock History

Pink Sheets: PEUGY

	STOCK PRICE ($) FY Close	P/E High/Low		PER SHARE ($) Earnings	Dividends	Book Value
12/09	33.92	—	—	(7.34)	0.00	76.22
12/08	17.13	—	—	(2.13)	1.86	79.15
12/07	76.32	17	12	5.68	—	89.58
12/06	66.23	71	51	1.02	—	77.08
12/05	57.68	13	10	5.28	—	70.15
Annual Growth	**(12.4%)**	**—**	**—**	**—**	**—**	**2.1%**

Philips Electronics

Royal Philips Electronics has its royal fingers in lots of different pies. It makes consumer electronics, including TVs, VCRs, DVD players, and fax machines. But it also makes light bulbs (#1 worldwide), electric shavers and other personal care appliances, as well as medical systems and silicon systems solutions. Consumer electronics account for the largest portion of the company's sales. Philips has been dumping noncore businesses — such as its stakes in TSMC, LG Display, and music giant PolyGram — while acquiring and forming joint ventures in its primary lines of business, including medical-equipment development, energy-efficient lighting, and lifestyle products.

Continuing to focus on its core businesses, the company in 2009 sold its nearly 15% stake in LG Display for about €630 million (about $900 million). LG Display, originally a joint venture with LG Electronics, was formed when the two firms merged their LCD businesses. In 2008 Philips also unloaded the final shares in Taiwan Semiconductor Manufacturing Company, one of the largest contract semiconductor manufacturers in the world. Philips sold majority control of its chip unit (renamed NXP Semiconductors) to

a consortium of private equity firms for €3.4 billion (nearly $5 billion) two years earlier. (Philips still owns a 20% stake in NXP.)

The divestitures were outshined in 2008 by two of the largest acquisitions in Philips' history, however. That year it purchased Respironics, a leading medical alert system in North America, for about €3 billion. Respironics also develops medical devices for people suffering from sleep apnea and other respiratory disorders. The purchase strengthened the company's home health care business. Philips' other significant 2008 acquisition involved Genlyte Group, which it bought for nearly $3 billion. Continuing to invest in this bright spot of its business, Philips in 2010 purchased specialized lighting company Burton Medical Products Corporation to boost its health care facility lighting.

The downturn in the global economy has hurt Philips' consumer electronics business, which includes TVs and MP3 players. In response to the losses, the company in 2009 announced the cut of about 6,000 jobs across all sectors.

Beefing up its health care information technology holdings, Philips in 2008 acquired VISICU, which develops remote patient-monitoring systems, for about €300 million (about $430 million) and cardiac data monitoring company TOMCAT Systems. In 2010 it took over the Chinese company Shanghai Apex Electronics Technology (Apex). Apex is a manufacturer of ultrasound transducers, which improve the image quality of ultrasound systems.

HISTORY

Gerard Philips (later joined by brother Anton) founded Philips & Co. in the Dutch city of Eindhoven in 1891. Surviving an industry shakeout, Philips prospered as a result of Gerard's engineering and Anton's foreign sales efforts. The company had become Europe's #3 light bulb maker by 1900. It adopted the name Philips Gloeilampenfabrieken (light bulb factory) in 1912.

The Netherlands' neutrality during WWI allowed Philips to expand and integrate into glass manufacturing (1915) and X-ray and radio tubes (1918). The company set up its first foreign sales office in Belgium in 1919; it started building plants abroad in the 1930s to avoid trade barriers and tariffs.

During WWII Philips created US and British trusts to hold majority interests in North American Philips (NAP) and in Philips' British operations. Following the war, the company established hundreds of subsidiaries worldwide. It repurchased its British businesses in 1955; NAP operated independently until it was reacquired in 1987.

The company started marketing televisions and appliances in the 1950s. Philips introduced audiocassette, VCR, and laser disc technology in the 1960s but had limited success with computers and office equipment. Despite its development of new technologies, in the 1970s Philips was unable to maintain market share against an onslaught of inexpensive goods from Japan. Meanwhile, NAP acquired Magnavox (consumer electronics, US) in 1974. NAP also purchased GTE Television in 1981 and Westinghouse's lighting business in 1983. In 1986 it provided $60 million in seed money to start Taiwan Semiconductor Manufacturing with the Taiwanese government.

Philips' successful PolyGram unit (formed in 1972) went public in 1989 and bought record companies Island (UK) that year and A&M (US) the next. In 1991 the company changed its name to Royal Philips Electronics.

Ill-timed product introductions contributed to huge losses in the early 1990s. Philips cut some 60,000 jobs and sold money-losing businesses, including its computer business. Cor Boonstra, a former Sara Lee executive, was named chairman and president in 1996. Philips sold its cellular communications business in 1996 to AT&T and merged its systems integration unit with BSO/Origin to form Origin B.V. Continuing to focus on core businesses, it sold its 75% stake in PolyGram to Seagram in 1998.

In 1999 Philips bought VLSI for nearly $1 billion. In 2000 Philips divested its 24% stake ($3.8 billion) in semiconductor equipment maker ASML Holding. In 2001 Boonstra retired and COO Gerard Kleisterlee became chairman and president. That same year Philips completed its acquisition of the Healthcare Solutions Group of Agilent Technologies for $1.7 billion.

Since 2001, Philips has cut more than 35,000 jobs; the reductions are the result of support staff job eliminations and the sale of noncore businesses (Communication, Security, and Imaging unit to Robert Bosch; contract manufacturing services to Jabil Circuit; health care products group to Platinum Equity Holdings).

Frits Philips, son of founder Anton Philips and the last member of the Philips family to manage the company (he retired in 1977), died in 2005 at the age of 100. (He had been instrumental in the development of the audiocassette and the compact disc.) In 2007 Kleisterlee was appointed to serve another four-year term as president and CEO.

In March 2008 Philips completed the acquisition of respiratory products firm Respironics. The $5.1 billion purchase of the Pennsylvania-based company increased Philips' presence in the home health care solutions market, a new line of business for the Dutch conglomerate.

Philips paid €170 million ($241.5 million) to acquire the Italian espresso machine maker Saeco International Group in 2009. Following the purchase, Saeco became part of the domestic appliances unit of the Philips Consumer Lifestyle business.

EXECUTIVES

Chairman, Supervisory Board: Jan-Michiel Hessels, age 68
Vice Chairman, Supervisory Board: John M. Thompson
Chairman Management Board, President and CEO: Gerard Kleisterlee, age 64
Member Group Management Committee and CTO: Rick Harwig, age 60
Member Group Management Committee, Chief Legal Officer, and Company Secretary: Eric Coutinho, age 59
Member Group Management Committee, Chief Strategy Officer, and Group Controller: Gerard Ruizendaal, age 51
Member Group Management Committee, CIO, and Global Head Purchasing: Maarten de Vries
Member Group Management Committee and Global Head Human Resources Management: Hayko Kroese, age 54
EVP and CFO: Pierre-Jean Sivignon, age 53
EVP; CEO, Philips Lighting: Rudy S. Provoost, age 51
EVP; CEO, Philips Healthcare: Stephen H. (Steve) Rusckowski, age 53
EVP; CEO, Greater China: Patrick S. Kung
EVP: Gottfried Dutiné, age 58
SVP and General Manager, Global Business Unit Hospitality: Paul Peeters, age 46
Head Investor Relations: Stewart McCrone
Director Corporate Communications: David L. Wolf
CEO, Philips Consumer Lifestyle: Pieter Nota, age 46
Auditors: KPMG Accountants N.V.

LOCATIONS

HQ: Royal Philips Electronics N.V.
(Koninklijke Philips Electronics N.V.)
Breitner Center, Amstelplein 2
1096 BC Amsterdam, The Netherlands
Phone: 31-40-27-91111   **Fax:** 31-40-27-44947
Web: www.philips.com

2009 Sales

	% of total
Mature markets	60
Emerging markets	40
Total	**100**

PRODUCTS/OPERATIONS

2009 Sales

	% of total
Consumer lifestyle	37
Health care	34
Lighting	29
Total	**100**

Selected Products

Consumer electronics
  Audio
  Consumer communications
  Display
  Licenses
  Peripherals and accessories
  Video
Medical systems
  Asset management services
  Cardiac and monitoring systems
  Computed tomography
  Customer financing
  Dictation and speech recognition systems
  Document management services
  Magnetic resonance
  Medical IT
  Nuclear medicine
  Personal health care
  Sleep and respiratory products
  Ultrasound
  X-ray
Lighting
  Automotive and special lighting
  Lamps
  Lighting electronics
  Luminaires
Domestic appliances and personal care
  Espresso machines
  Food and beverage
  Home environment care
  Oral health care
  Shaving and beauty
Miscellaneous
  Corporate investments
  Navigation technology
  Optical storage
  Shared services
  Technology and design

COMPETITORS

BSH Bosch und Siemens Hausgeräte	Pioneer Corporation
Covidien	ResMed
De'Longhi	Samsung Group
Fujitsu	SANYO
GE	Sharp Corp.
GE India	Siemens AG
Harman International	Siemens Corp.
Invacare	Sony
LG Electronics	Spectrum Brands
Mitsubishi Electric	Technicolor
OSRAM	Texas Instruments
Panasonic Corp	Toshiba

HISTORICAL FINANCIALS

Company Type: Public

Income Statement

FYE: December 31

	REVENUE ($ mil.)	NET INCOME ($ mil.)	NET PROFIT MARGIN	EMPLOYEES
12/09	66,469	608	0.9%	115,924
12/08	37,190	(262)	—	121,000
12/07	39,390	6,128	15.6%	123,801
12/06	35,621	7,109	20.0%	121,732
12/05	36,117	3,409	9.4%	159,226
Annual Growth	**16.5%**	**(35.0%)**	**—**	**(7.6%)**

2009 Year-End Financials

Debt ratio: 24.9%
Return on equity: 2.8%
Cash ($ mil.): 6,286
Current ratio: 1.48
Long-term debt ($ mil.): 5,217
No. of shares (mil.): 927
Dividends
  Yield: 2.0%
  Payout: 130.3%
Market value ($ mil.): 39,100

Stock History

NYSE: PHG

	STOCK PRICE ($) FY Close	P/E High/Low		PER SHARE ($) Earnings	Dividends	Book Value
12/09	42.19	66	30	0.66	0.86	22.57
12/08	28.01	—	—	(0.27)	0.97	24.71
12/07	62.92	12	9	5.59	0.89	34.40
12/06	49.58	8	6	6.00	0.58	32.77
12/05	36.83	14	10	2.71	0.47	21.37
Annual Growth	**3.5%**		**— —**	**(29.8%)**	**16.3%**	**1.4%**

Pirelli & C.

What do cars and buildings have in common? Pirelli can make them both go. The company's main activity is tires (or tyres, as the company spells it), with real estate second, followed by a smattering of other offerings including broadband access, renewable energy, and R&D. Pirelli makes tires for cars, industrial and commercial vehicles, motorcycles, and farm machinery at about 25 plants located in a dozen countries. Its real estate sector invests in European real estate companies and provides financing services and real estate management. The company is also known for its stylish media campaigns; its famous calendar has revved more than a few motors. Giovanni Battista Pirelli formed the company in 1872.

Flat tire sales for the first quarter in 2008 led Pirelli to map out a plan for global expansion through joint ventures and acquisitions. The company purchased real estate firms in Germany and Poland and launched operations in Romania. The tire business opened a tire steel-cord plant in Romania with joint venture partner Continental AG and a radial truck tire operation in China, and signed a tire joint venture agreement with the Russian government for a Russian plant to serve it and its former fellow Soviet Union nations. Pirelli has also created a new Italian R&D facility, and is eyeing Russia and India as its next stops.

To focus on its core tire business, Pirelli divested its more than 56% stake in Pirelli & C. Real Estate (Pirelli RE) in fall 2010. Once the spinoff occurred, Pirelli RE's name changed to Prelios. Pirelli also agreed to sell its Pirelli Broadband unit to Switzerland-based Advanced Digital Broadcast Holdings (ADB) in late 2010 for a reported €30 million ($42 million). In March 2009 Pirelli sold its stake in Submarine Networks (submarine telecom systems) to Alcatel-Lucent, the parent company of Submarine Networks. It made about €56 million (about $75 million) on the deal.

The company's Pirelli Ambiente unit announced plans in 2010 to join with GWM Renewable Energy on a solar energy project in Italy. With 7 megawatts (MW) already in operation, the new venture plans to increase the output to about 100 MW.

In March 2009 Pirelli sold its stake in Submarine Networks (submarine telecom systems) to Alcatel-Lucent, the parent company of Submarine Networks.

Members of the company's controlling shareholder pact own about 46% of Pirelli. The pact includes Camfin, Mediobanca, Edizione Holding (parent company of the Benetton Group), Fondiaria-SAI, Allianz, Assicurazioni Generali, and Intesa Sanpaolo.

HISTORY

After fighting for Italian unification with Garibaldi in the 1860s, Giovanni Battista Pirelli observed that France, not Italy, was providing rubber tubes for an Italian ship salvage attempt. The young patriot reacted by founding Pirelli & Co. in Milan, Italy, in 1872 to manufacture rubber products. In 1879 Pirelli began making insulated cables for the rapidly growing telegraph industry, and by 1890 he was making bicycle tires. Pirelli introduced his first air-filled automobile tire in 1899.

Foreign expansion began when Pirelli opened cable factories in Spain (1902), the UK (1914), and Argentina (1917). The company set up Societe Internationale Pirelli (SIP) in Switzerland in 1937 and consolidated all non-Italian operations within it. After WWII the group expanded along with the growth in worldwide auto sales. Pirelli began production in Turkey and Greece in 1962, and six years later it set up cable plants in Peru.

Pirelli's first radial tires (early 1970s) backfired when they wore out too quickly. In 1971 the company swapped stock with tire maker Dunlop (UK). Although the firms engaged in joint research and development (R&D), they never consolidated production.

Pirelli S.p.A., the Italian operating company, and SIP became holding companies in 1982 by transferring their operating units into jointly owned Pirelli Societe Generale (Switzerland). That year Pirelli started producing fiber-optic cables. Heavy spending on R&D and new equipment bolstered the newly unified tire business, and the 1986 purchase of Metzeler Kautscuk (Germany) made Pirelli one of the world's largest motorcycle tire manufacturers.

Pirelli S.p.A. became an operating company in 1988 when it bought SIP's Pirelli Societe Generale holdings. It launched a hostile bid for Firestone through Pirelli Tyre, but was outbid by Bridgestone. Pirelli settled for the much smaller Armstrong Tire. In 1989 Pirelli sold nearly 24% of Pirelli Tyre to the public.

In 1990 Pirelli proposed an unusually complex and convoluted merger with Continental AG (Germany) designed to leave Pirelli in control. Continental declined, but negotiations continued throughout 1991 until Continental terminated the talks after learning of Pirelli's deteriorating financial condition.

Pirelli became a top power-cable maker with operations in more than 20 countries in 1998 by acquiring Germany-based Siemens' power cable unit in a $277 million deal.

In 1999 Pirelli agreed to ally with Cooper Tire and Rubber, including an arrangement whereby Cooper would distribute and sell Pirelli tires for passenger cars and light trucks in the US, Canada, and Mexico. In return, Pirelli agreed to sell Cooper tires in South America.

In 2000 Pirelli sold its terrestrial optical systems business to Cisco Systems for about $2.15 billion. Also in 2000 the company sold its fiber-optic telecommunications business to Corning for about $3.6 billion.

In 2001 the company separated energy cables and systems from its telecom business to focus on new growth. In a surprise July announcement, Pirelli announced that it and the Benetton family had agreed to buy the 23% controlling stake in Olivetti — controlled by Roberto Colaninno, the CEO of both Olivetti and Telecom Italia. Pirelli sold its enameled wire holdings in late 2002 to Investitori Associati, an Italy-based investment group. After merging its operating company (Pirelli SpA) and holding company (Pirelli & C. SpA) in 2003, the company changed its name to Pirelli & C. SpA.

Pirelli's two cable divisions were sold in 2005. They included energy (low-, medium-, and high-voltage power cables and building wire products) and telecommunications (cable assemblies and hardware and fiber-optics). The company sold the divisions to Goldman Sachs in a deal worth about $1.6 billion (€1.3 billion) including debt, and they are now known as Prysmian Cables & Systems. Pirelli still has some tech-related operations through Pirelli Broadband Solutions and Pirelli Labs.

EXECUTIVES

Chairman and CEO; Interim CEO, Pirelli Broadband Solutions: Marco Tronchetti Provera, age 62
Deputy Chairman: Alberto Pirelli
Deputy Chairman: Carlo Alessandro Puri Negri, age 57
Finance Director: Francesco Tanzi, age 45
Product Director, Pirelli Tyre: Maurizio Boiocchi
Director Institutional and Cultural Affairs:
  Antonio Calabrò, age 60
Director Internal Audit: Maurizio Bonzi, age 49
Director Media Communications: Maurizio Abet, age 41
Director Industrial Property: Pier Giovanni Giannesi
Director Image and Brand Extension; CEO, PZero Moda: Andrea Imperiali, age 46
Head People Development: Donatella de Vita
Head Human Resources: Fabrizio Rutschmann
Head Investor Relations: Valeria Leone, age 49
Head Pirelli S.A. Brasile:
  Giancarlo Rocco di Torrepadula
Secretary: Anna Chiara Svelto

CEO, Pirelli Tire North America: Mauro Pessi
CEO, Pirelli & C. Real Estate: Giulio Malfatto, age 54
CEO, Pirelli Eco Technology:
  Raffaele Bruno Tronchetti Provera, age 69
CEO, Pirelli & C. Ambiente: Giorgio Bruno
CEO and Managing Director, Pirelli Tyre and Parts:
  Francesco Gori, age 58
Corporate Social Responsibility Manager:
  Eleonora Giada Pessina
Assistant to Chairman and General Counsel:
  Francesco Chiappetta, age 50
Auditors: Reconta Ernst & Young S.p.A.

LOCATIONS

HQ: Pirelli & C. S.p.A.
  Viale Piero e Alberto Pirelli n. 25
  20126 Milan, Italy
Phone: 39-02-64421   **Fax:** 39-02-6442-2670
US HQ: 100 Pirelli Dr., Rome, GA 30161
US Phone: 706-368-5800   **US Fax:** 706-368-5832
Web: www.pirelli.com

2009 Sales

	% of total
Europe	
Italy	9
Other countries	33
Central & South America	34
Asia/Pacific & Africa	16
North America	8
Total	**100**

PRODUCTS/OPERATIONS

2009 Sales

	% of total
Tires	89
Real estate	6
Broadband	3
Other	2
Total	**100**

COMPETITORS

Bayerische Immobilien
Bridgestone
Bridgestone Bandag
Continental AG
Falken Tire
Goodyear Tire & Rubber
Kumho Tire
Marangoni
Michelin
Nexity International
Sime Darby
Sumitomo Rubber
Watts Industrial Tyres

HISTORICAL FINANCIALS

Company Type: Public

Income Statement

FYE: December 31

	REVENUE ($ mil.)	NET INCOME ($ mil.)	NET PROFIT MARGIN	EMPLOYEES
12/09	6,395	(32)	—	29,565
12/08	6,569	(582)	—	31,056
12/07	9,618	476	5.0%	30,780
12/06	6,387	(1,384)	—	28,617
12/05	5,399	473	8.8%	26,827
Annual Growth	**4.3%**	**—**	**—**	**2.5%**

2009 Year-End Financials

Debt ratio: —	No. of shares (mil.): 475
Return on equity: —	Dividends
Cash ($ mil.): 906	Yield: 0.0%
Current ratio: 1.22	Payout: —
Long-term debt ($ mil.): —	Market value ($ mil.): 3,147

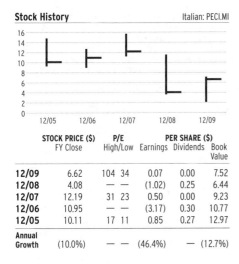

	STOCK PRICE ($)	P/E		PER SHARE ($)		
	FY Close	High/Low		Earnings	Dividends	Book Value
12/09	6.62	104	34	0.07	0.00	7.52
12/08	4.08	—	—	(1.02)	0.25	6.44
12/07	12.19	31	23	0.50	0.00	9.23
12/06	10.95	—	—	(3.17)	0.30	10.77
12/05	10.11	17	11	0.85	0.27	12.97
Annual Growth	(10.0%)	—	—	(46.4%)	—	(12.7%)

POSCO

POSCO has steeled itself for any set of business conditions. The company makes hot- and cold-rolled steel products (plate steel, stainless steel, electrical steel, and wire rods), which it sells to the auto and shipbuilding industries. It produces more than 30 million tons of steel a year, making it the world's #3 steelmaker behind the combined ArcelorMittal and Nippon Steel. Subsidiaries include POSCO Engineering & Construction (which builds steel plants, steel-related infrastructure, and energy facilities) and POSDATA (systems integration). The South Korean government privatized its stake in POSCO in 2001, ending the company's 30-year steel-making monopoly.

Unfortunately for POSCO, South Korea has little native iron ore, and the company has had to look elsewhere for its raw materials. It purchases iron ore and coal from Australia, Brazil, Canada, China, India, and Russia from the likes of Vale, Rio Tinto, and BHP Billiton. To that end, POSCO has developed about 18 joint ventures, including six in China and others in Australia, Africa, and the Americas.

China and India are major sources of ore for POSCO. China is POSCO's largest export market. South Korea represents around two-thirds of total sales, a figure that gives POSCO a one-third share of the country's steel production rate. In 2009 the company boosted its stake in stainless steel maker Taihan ST Co. to 85% to consolidate its domestic market share.

In 2010 POSCO acquired a majority stake in Daewoo International Corporation. Daewoo shareholders voted to put the company's depressed shares up for sale after the South Korean government gave its approval for the deal early in 2010. POSCO named its former CFO, Lee Dong-hee, as vice chair and CEO of Daewoo after the deal closed.

POSCO's hot- and cold-rolled products segments account for about two-thirds of sales. Hot-rolled products are used in the construction of automobile chassis, buildings and bridges, industrial pipes and tanks, and railway rolling stocks. The company's cold-rolled products such as cold-rolled coils and galvanized cold-rolled products are used in the automotive industry to manufacture car body panels and for other uses like household goods, electrical appliances, and engineering and metal parts.

Geographically expanding its operations, POSCO formed an alliance with long-time rival Nippon Steel, whereby each has taken a small stake in the other; it has formed a joint venture with Steel Authority of India, and plans to establish agreements with other steelmakers in China and Europe. It also intends to diversify into the energy distribution business, bioscience, and other emerging high-tech areas.

HISTORY

After the Korean War, South Korea, the US, and its allies wanted to rebuild South Korea's infrastructure as quickly as possible. Steel was given a high priority, and before long about 15 companies were making various steel products. Quality was a problem, though, as the companies used dated production processes.

With the backing of South Korean president Chung Hee Park, momentum for a large steel plant grew in the late 1960s. In 1967 the South Korean government and Korean International Steel Associates (KISA) — a consortium of seven Western steelmakers — signed an agreement that called for the completion of an integrated mill by 1972. Pohang Iron & Steel Co. (POSCO), the operating company, was incorporated in 1968. Efforts to raise the necessary capital failed, however, and KISA was dissolved in 1969.

Undaunted, the South Koreans turned to the Japanese, who arranged loans covering most of the mill's costs and the early phases of planning and construction. The Japanese also transferred the technology needed to run such a plant. Slow and deliberate planning resulted in a plant far away from Seoul (part of a plan to locate industries throughout the country) and a design that lent itself to future expansion. The first stage, including a blast furnace and two steel converters, was completed in 1973. By the time the fourth stage of construction began in 1979, the Koreans had gained enough confidence to take over many of the tasks. When the last stage was completed in 1981, the plant had an annual capacity of 8.5 million tons.

To ensure steel of acceptable quality, POSCO focused first on plain high-carbon steel for general construction, rather than on specialized (and difficult to produce) varieties. The company gradually broadened its specialized offerings.

In 1985 POSCO began construction on a second integrated steel plant located in Kwangyang. That plant was also built in four stages; its annual production capacity, when it was completed in 1992, was 11.4 million tons. By 1987 POSCO was exporting almost 3 million tons of steel a year and using its knowledge to assist in plant construction projects in other countries.

By the mid-1990s POSCO was exporting 6 million tons of steel annually. The South Korean government sold a 5% stake in POSCO to the public in 1998 and vowed to open up the primary steelmaking industry to competition. However, facing a severe downturn in steel demand that year because of sluggishness in Asian and domestic markets, the company canceled two projects in China and suspended two in Indonesia. In 1999 POSCO merged its two subsidiaries, Pohang Coated Steel and Pohang Steel Industries, to create Pohang Steel Co. The South Korean government continued selling off its 13% stake in 1999.

In 2000 POSCO sold its 51% stake in telecommunications company Shinsegi Telecom to SK Telecom in exchange for cash and a 6.5% stake in SK Telecom. It also formed a strategic alliance — exploration of joint ventures, shared research, and joint procurement — with Nippon Steel, the world's #1 steelmaker. The deal also calls for each to take increased equity stakes (2% or 3%) in the other. After about 30 years of government control, the South Korean government sold its remaining shares of POSCO in 2001.

In 2002 Chairman Yoo was indicted for influencing POSCO subsidiaries and contractors to buy inflated shares of Tiger Pools International (South Korea's sole sports lottery business) for Kim Hong-Gul, the third son of South Korean President Kim Dae-Jung. That same year Pohang Iron & Steel Co. officially changed its company name to POSCO to try and strengthen brand recognition.

In 2003 Yoo resigned ahead of the company's shareholder meeting amid his possible involvement in illegal stock transactions.

The company invested in its Mexican operations in 2006, announcing a joint venture coil processing facility with Daewoo International.

EXECUTIVES

CEO and Director: Chung Joon-Yang, age 62
President, Chief Financial and Planning Officer, and Director: Choi Jong-Tae, age 60
SEVP and Chief Staff Officer: Park Han-Yong, age 59
SEVP Raw Materials Procurement: Kwon Young-Tae, age 60
SEVP; Head of Stainless Steel Business Division: Oh Chang-Kwan, age 57
SEVP Corporate Communication: Kim Sang-Young, age 58
SEVP; Head of Carbon Steel Business Division: Kim Jin-Il, age 57
EVP and CTO: Cho Noi-Ha, age 57
EVP Stainless Steel Raw Materials Procurement: Jang Young-Ik, age 56
EVP; General Superintendent, Gwangyang Works: Kim Joon-Sik, age 56
EVP and Head of Growth and Investment Division: Yoon Yong-Won, age 58
EVP Stainless Steel Business Division: Yoo Kwang-Jae, age 58
EVP; General Superintendent, Pohang Works: Cho Bong-Rae, age 57
EVP and Chief Marketing Officer: Shin Jung-Suk, age 57
EVP Corporate Strategy and Green Development Project and Chief Risk Management Officer: Park Ki-Hong, age 52
EVP; General Superintendent, Technical Research Laboratories: Choo Wung-Yong, age 57
SVP Human Resources and Innovation: Kim Yeung-Gyu, age 55
SVP Finance: Lee Young-Hoon, age 50
Auditors: Samil Pricewaterhousecoopers

LOCATIONS

HQ: POSCO
POSCO Center 892, Daechi-dong, Gangnam-gu
Seoul 135-777, South Korea
Phone: 82-2-3457-0114 **Fax:** 82-2-3457-0114
US HQ: 2 Executive Dr., Ste. 805, Fort Lee, NJ 07024
US Phone: 201-585-3060 **US Fax:** 201-585-6001
Web: www.posco.co.kr

	% of total
Asia/Pacific	
Korea	61
China	14
Japan	4
Other Asia	8
North America	2
Other regions	11
Total	**100**

PRODUCTS/OPERATIONS

2009 Sales

	% of total
Steel	77
Engineering & Construction	11
Trading	8
Other	4
Total	**100**

COMPETITORS

ArcelorMittal
Baosteel
Bechtel
Fluor
Hitachi
Hyundai Steel
JFE Holdings
Kobe Steel
Mitsubishi Steel Mfg.
Nippon Steel
Samsung Group
Severstal
Tata Steel
ThyssenKrupp Steel
United States Steel

HISTORICAL FINANCIALS

Company Type: Public

Income Statement

FYE: December 31

	REVENUE ($ mil.)	NET INCOME ($ mil.)	NET PROFIT MARGIN	EMPLOYEES
12/09	31,614	2,761	8.7%	29,811
12/08	32,977	3,437	10.4%	28,543
12/07	33,766	3,802	11.3%	28,543
12/06	27,496	3,526	12.8%	28,297
12/05	25,790	3,933	15.3%	28,853
Annual Growth	5.2%	(8.5%)	—	0.8%

2009 Year-End Financials

Debt ratio: 26.6%	No. of shares (mil.): 349
Return on equity: 11.4%	Dividends
Cash ($ mil.): 1,884	Yield: 0.0%
Current ratio: 2.22	Payout: —
Long-term debt ($ mil.): 7,060	Market value ($ mil.): 39

Stock History

NYSE: PKX

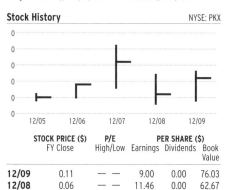

	STOCK PRICE ($) FY Close	P/E High/Low	PER SHARE ($) Earnings	Dividends	Book Value
12/09	0.11	— —	9.00	0.00	76.03
12/08	0.06	— —	11.46	0.00	62.67
12/07	0.16	— —	12.51	2.20	75.00
12/06	0.09	— —	11.20	1.73	66.85
12/05	0.05	— —	12.41	1.66	54.77
Annual Growth	21.8%	— —	(7.7%)	—	8.5%

PPR SA

PPR has transformed itself from a conglomerate to the world's third-largest luxury group (behind LVMH and Richemont). PPR's stable of global luxury brands includes a 99% stake in Italian luxury goods company Gucci Group, and luxury brands Alexander McQueen, Balenciaga, Boucheron, Bottega Veneta, Stella McCartney, and Yves Saint Laurent, among others. The group's other activities include the multichannel merchant Redcats, Fnac music and book stores, the Conforama chain of household furniture and appliance stores, and the German athletic shoemaker PUMA. PPR is run by François-Henri Pinault, the son of its founder François Pinault.

The global recession has hurt retailers and PPR is no exception. However, the group's Gucci brand turned in a relatively strong performance, outpacing PPR's other luxury brands (including Bottega Veneta and Yves Saint Laurent), as well as PPR's consumer retail businesses. PPR credits Gucci's success to taking the brand further upscale.

Looking to further increase its exposure to its core luxury business, PPR in December 2009 sold its controlling stake in CFAO to the public. The €806 million ($1.2 billion) in proceeds from the offering of the African car distributor went to Discodis, a wholly owned subsidiary of PPR. Following the IPO of CFAO, book-and-music retailer Fnac is considered its next likely target for disposal. Fnac has about 80 stores in France and more than 60 in seven other European countries. A leading retailer in France, Fnac stores sell books, CDs and DVDs, personal computers, software, computer games, cameras, and audio and video equipment. Conforama is France's #1 furniture and household appliances retailer with about 160 stores in France and more than 55 in about a half a dozen other countries in Europe.

The international catalog-and-Internet retailer Redcats Group operates more than 60 e-commerce sites and includes the La Redoute and the Redcats USA businesses, a multichannel retailer focused on plus-size apparel, and home and leisure goods. Redcats USA also operates about 480 AVENUE plus-size apparel retail stores in some three dozen US states.

On the luxury side of the group, PPR's Paris jewelry house, Boucheron, is expanding in China where it already operates two stores. Under the terms of the deal with its partner Peace Mark Group, the jewelry chain will open 10 more stores in China over the next five years.

PPR inked a deal with L'Oréal in 2008 to acquire the rights to the Yves Saint Laurent and Boucheron fragrance and cosmetics brands, among others. Valued at more than $2 billion, the agreement allows L'Oréal to expand its portfolio of luxury labels.

Self-made billionaire François Pinault has a cache of prestigious businesses, including auction house Christie's. His investment firm, Artémis, controls PPR with about 55% of the voting rights.

HISTORY

Sixteen-year-old François Pinault left school in 1952 to join the family timber business. He took over the firm when his father died in 1963; that year the company was renamed Pinault Group. Pinault diversified the company into

wood importing and retailing, eventually building a flourishing enterprise. In 1973 Pinault began to show his talent for the art of the deal. Sensing the demand for timber was peaking, he sold 80% of the business, buying it back two years later at an 85% discount.

During the 1970s Pinault bought struggling timber businesses and turned them around. (He was helped, in part, by a policy of the French government that subsidized purchases of failing companies in order to preserve jobs.) Pinault purchased bankrupt wood panel manufacturer Isoroy in 1986 for a token fee. In 1987 he bought ailing paper company Chapelle Darblay, selling it three years later at a 40% profit. By 1988, when it filed to go public on the Paris exchange, Pinault Group was a vertically integrated timber manufacturing, trading, and distribution company.

Pinault began to diversify outside the timber industry in the 1990s. It acquired electrical equipment distributor CFAO (Compagnie Française de l'Afrique Occidentale) in 1990, the Conforama furniture chain in 1991, and Au Printemps (owner of Printemps stores and 54% of catalog company Redoute) in 1992. The firm then became the Pinault-Printemps Group. The purchase of Au Printemps left the company heavily in debt, and it sold some of its noncore assets during the early 1990s.

In 1993 Pinault-Printemps bought a majority stake in Groupelec and merged it with electrical equipment subsidiary CDME, forming Rexel. In 1994 the company completed its acquisition of Redoute. After renaming itself Pinault-Printemps-Redoute (PPR), it bought a majority stake in French book and music retailer Fnac (buying the rest in 1995). In 1995 Rexel head Serge Weinberg took over the company after CEO Pierre Blayau ran afoul of Pinault over strategy.

In 1999 PPR sparked a string of legal battles between it and LVMH when it purchased 42% of luxury goods maker Gucci. (The move thwarted LVMH's efforts to take over Gucci by diluting LVMH's stake in the firm.) In early 2000 PPR bought France's largest computer retailer, Surcouf.

In March 2001 a Dutch court granted a request by LVMH and ordered an investigation into the legality of the alliance of PPR and Gucci. In a deal to end years of litigation, PPR purchased LVMH's stake in Gucci for $806.5 million in October 2001, increasing its ownership to 53.2%.

The company sold Yves Saint Laurent's haute couture division to French dressmaking company SLPB Prestige Services in 2002. In 2003 PPR increased its stake in Gucci to 67.58%.

In 2005 François-Henri Pinault, the son of the company's founder, joined the company as its new CEO, succeeding Serge Weinberg. That year the company changed its name to PPR from Pinault-Printemps-Redoute.

In August 2006, as part of its strategy to focus on its luxury business, PPR sold its Paris-based department store chain Printemps to Italy's La Rinascente for about $1.3 billion.

To secure a foothold in the international premium footwear market, PPR increased its nearly 30% stake in PUMA in July 2007 to more than 60%. The deal, valued at more than $7 billion, placed the German athletic shoemaker in PPR's brand portfolio alongside its luxury holdings.

In a bid to increase its presence in the luxury watch business, PPR in 2008 acquired a 23% stake in the Swiss watchmaking company Sowind Group, the maker of high-end Girard-Perregaux and JeanRichard watches.

EXECUTIVES

Chairman and CEO: François-Henri Pinault, age 48
Deputy CEO and CFO: Jean-François Palus, age 47
SVP Human Resources: Phillippe Decressac
SVP Corporate, Social, and Environmental Responsibility: Laurent Claquin, age 38
Chairman and CEO, Conforama: Thierry Guibert, age 39
Chairman and CEO, Puma: Jochen Zeitz, age 46
Chairman and CEO, Redcats Group and Chairman, La Redoute: Jean-Michel Noir, age 42
Chairman and CEO, CFAO: Alain Viry
Chairman and CEO, Fnac: Christophe Cuvillier
Chairman, President, and CEO, Gucci Group: Robert Polet, age 54
Director Communications: Claude Chirac, age 47
Press Contact: Charlotte Judet
Auditors: Deloitte & Associés

LOCATIONS

HQ: PPR SA
 10, Avenue Hoche
 75381 Paris, France
Phone: 33-1-45-64-61-00   **Fax:** 33-1-44-90-62-25
Web: www.ppr.com

2009 Sales

	% of total
Europe	
France	43
Other countries	28
Americas	16
Asia	12
Africa	1
Total	**100**

PRODUCTS/OPERATIONS

2009 Sales

	% of total
Fnac	26
Gucci Group	21
Redcats	20
Conforama	18
Puma	15
Total	**100**

Selected Company-Owned Luxury Brands

Alexander McQueen
Balenciaga
Bottega Veneta
Boucheron
Gucci
Sergio Rossi
Stella McCartney
Yves Saint Laurent

Selected Operations

Luxury Goods
 Gucci Group N.V. (99.39%, leather goods and apparel)
 PUMA (athletic footwear)
Retail
 Conforama (furniture and appliances; Croatia, France, Italy, Luxembourg, Portugal, Spain, and Switzerland)
 Fnac (electronics, books, music; Belgium, Brazil, France, Italy, Monaco, Portugal, Spain, Switzerland, and Taiwan)
 Redcats Group (catalogs, including Brylane, Daxon, Ellos, and Redoute)

COMPETITORS

adidas
Amazon.com
ASICS
Auchan
Burberry
C&A
Carrefour
Casino Guichard
Chanel
Christian Dior
Gianni Versace
IKEA
K-Swiss
LVMH
METRO AG
New Balance
NIKE
Otto Group
Prada
Richemont
Saucony
Virgin Group
Vivarte

HISTORICAL FINANCIALS

Company Type: Public

Income Statement

FYE: December 31

	REVENUE ($ mil.)	NET INCOME ($ mil.)	NET PROFIT MARGIN	EMPLOYEES
12/09	23,683	1,496	6.3%	73,000
12/08	28,474	1,469	5.2%	88,000
12/07	29,086	1,533	5.3%	93,000
12/06	23,656	966	4.1%	78,453
12/05	21,040	679	3.2%	84,316
Annual Growth	**3.0%**	**21.8%**	**—**	**(3.5%)**

2009 Year-End Financials

Debt ratio: —
Return on equity: 10.3%
Cash ($ mil.): 1,354
Current ratio: 0.90
Long-term debt ($ mil.): —
No. of shares (mil.): 127
Dividends
 Yield: 3.9%
 Payout: 42.4%
Market value ($ mil.): 15,288

Stock History

Euronext Paris: PP

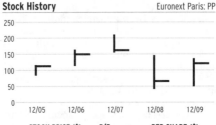

	STOCK PRICE ($) FY Close	P/E High	P/E Low	PER SHARE ($) Earnings	PER SHARE ($) Dividends	PER SHARE ($) Book Value
12/09	120.73	12	5	11.16	4.73	125.11
12/08	65.68	14	4	10.33	2.58	105.01
12/07	161.91	20	15	10.55	—	107.15
12/06	149.34	22	16	7.43	—	93.47
12/05	112.69	22	17	5.20	—	74.68
Annual Growth	**1.7%**	**—**	**—**	**21.0%**	**83.3%**	**13.8%**

Pricewaterhouse-Coopers

Not merely the firm with the longest one-word name, PricewaterhouseCoopers (PwC) is also one of the world's largest accounting networks. PwC was formed when Price Waterhouse merged with Coopers & Lybrand in 1998, bypassing then-leader Andersen. With some 770 offices in more than 150 countries, the accountancy provides clients with services in three business lines: assurance (including financial and regulatory reporting), tax, and advisory.

PwC's member firms are locally owned and operated. The largest geographic segment is western Europe (accounting for more than 40% of all gross revenues), followed by the North America/Caribbean region. Other regions, in descending order of revenues, are Asia, Australasia/Pacific Islands, Central and Eastern Europe, Middle East and Africa, and South and Central America. PricewaterhouseCoopers International oversees the strategic growth and development activities for the network and provides support services to the member firms.

In 2009 PwC acquired several units of management consultant firm BearingPoint, which months earlier had entered bankruptcy and begun selling itself off. It bought BearingPoint's Japanese operations, adding some 1,500 professionals and establishing itself as an advisory services leader there. The firm also acquired most of BearingPoint's North American commercial services business and offices in China and India.

The accounting business received a boost from the implementation of such regulatory and financial reporting rules as the International Financial Reporting Standards (IFRS) and the Sarbanes-Oxley Act. More recently, the industry faced criticism for the practice of mark-to-market accounting, which many say contributed to the global economic crisis in 2008. PwC stands behind the practice as the best accounting method of complex financial instruments.

In 2009 Samuel DiPiazza retired as CEO. Dennis Nally, previously a senior partner of the US firm, was elected PwC's global chairman.

HISTORY

In 1850 Samuel Price founded an accounting firm in London and in 1865 took on partner Edwin Waterhouse. The firm and the industry grew rapidly, thanks to the growth of stock exchanges that required uniform financial statements from listees. By the late 1800s Price Waterhouse (PW) had become the world's best-known accounting firm.

US offices were opened in the 1890s, and in 1902 United States Steel chose the firm as its auditor. PW benefited from tough audit requirements instituted after the 1929 stock market crash. In 1935 the firm was given the prestigious job of handling Academy Awards balloting. It started a management consulting service in 1946. But PW's dominance slipped in the 1960s, as it gained a reputation as the most traditional and formal of the major firms.

Coopers & Lybrand, the product of a 1957 transatlantic merger, wrote the book on auditing. Lybrand, Ross Bros. & Montgomery was formed in 1898 by William Lybrand, Edward Ross, Adam Ross, and Robert Montgomery. In

1912 Montgomery wrote Montgomery's Auditing, which became the bible of accounting.

Cooper Brothers was founded in 1854 in London by William Cooper, eldest son of a Quaker banker. In 1957 Lybrand joined up to form Coopers & Lybrand. During the 1960s the firm expanded into employee benefits and internal control consulting, building its technology capabilities in the 1970s as it studied ways to automate the audit process.

Coopers & Lybrand lost market share as mergers reduced the Big Eight accounting firms to the Big Six. After the savings and loan debacle of the 1980s, investors and the government wanted accounting firms held liable not only for the form of audited financial statements but for their veracity. In 1992 the firm paid $95 million to settle claims of defrauded investors in MiniScribe, a failed disk-drive maker. Other hefty payments followed, including a $108 million settlement relating to the late Robert Maxwell's defunct media empire.

In 1998 Price Waterhouse and Coopers & Lybrand combined PW's strength in the media, entertainment, and utility industries, and Coopers & Lybrand's focus on telecommunications and mining. But the merger brought some expensive legal baggage involving Coopers & Lybrand's performance of audits related to a bid-rigging scheme involving former Arizona governor Fife Symington.

Further growth plans fell through in 1999 when merger talks between PwC and Grant Thornton International failed. The year 2000 began on a sour note: An SEC conflict-of-interest probe turned up more than 8,000 alleged violations, most involving PwC partners owning stock in their firm's audit clients.

The SEC grew ever more shrill in its denunciation of potential conflicts of interest arising from auditing companies the firm hoped to recruit or retain as consulting clients. PwC saw the writing on the wall and in 2000 began making plans to split the two operations. As part of this move, the company downsized and reorganized many of its operations.

The following year PwC paid $55 million to shareholders of MicroStrategy Inc., who charged that the audit firm defrauded them by approving the client firm's inflated earnings and revenues figures.

The separation of PwC's auditing and consulting functions finally became a reality in 2002, when IBM bought the consulting business. (The acquisition took the place of a planned spinoff.)

In 2003 former client AMERCO (parent of U-Haul) sued PwC for $2.5 billion, claiming negligence and fraud in relation to a series of events that led to AMERCO restating its results. The suit was settled for more than $50 million the following year.

PwC endured a two-month suspension in Japan in 2006 after three partners of its firm there were implicated in a fraud investigation involving a PwC client, Kanebo. To distance itself from the scandal, PwC's existing Japanese firm was renamed and a second firm was launched.

In 2007 US arm PricewaterhouseCoopers agreed to pay $225 million to settle a class-action lawsuit related to the Tyco International financial scandal. The suit asserted that the auditors should have uncovered a $5.8 billion overstatement of earnings during the four years ending in 2002. The fraud sent Tyco top executives to prison.

EXECUTIVES

Chairman: Dennis M. Nally, age 57
Global Leader Operations: Paul Boorman
Global Strategy and Transformation Leader: Christopher (Chris) Kelkar
Global Leader for Risk and Quality: Pierre Coll
Global Leader, Advisory Services: Juan Pujadas
Global Assurance Leader: Donald A. McGovern Jr.
Global and US Human Capital Leader: Dennis J. Finn
Global Leader, Tax; Managing Partner, PricewaterhouseCoopers, UK: Richard Collier-Keywood
Global Leader Clients and Markets: Donald V. Almeida
Global Leader Public Policy and Regulation: Peter L. Wyman
Global General Counsel: Javier H. Rubinstein
Director Global Public Relations: Mike Davies
Chairman and Senior Partner US: Robert E. (Bob) Moritz
Chair, Global Board, Los Angeles: Brad Oltmanns
Chairman, Regional Asia Board: Silas S.S. Yang
Chairman India: Gautam Banerjee
Chairman and Senior Partner, United Kingdom: Ian Powell
US PR Leader: Jonathan Stoner

LOCATIONS

HQ: PricewaterhouseCoopers International Limited
300 Madison Ave., New York, NY 10017
Phone: 646-471-4000   **Fax:** 813-286-6000
Web: www.pwcglobal.com

PRODUCTS/OPERATIONS

2009 Sales

	% of total
Assurance	50
Tax	27
Advisory	23
Total	**100**

2009 Sales by Industry

	% of total
Industrial products	22
Banking & capital markets	13
Asset management	12
Retail & consumer	10
Energy, utilities & mining	9
Technology	6
Insurance	5
Entertainment & media	4
Government	4
Professional services	4
Pharmaceuticals	3
Automotive	3
Information & communications	3
Health care	2
Total	**100**

Selected Products and Services

Audit and assurance
  Actuarial services
  Assistance on capital market transactions
  Corporate reporting improvement
  Financial accounting
  Financial statement audit
  IFRS reporting
  Independent controls and systems process assurance
  Internal audit
  Regulatory compliance and reporting
  Sarbanes-Oxley compliance
  Sustainability reporting
Crisis management
  Business recovery services
  Dispute analysis and investigations

Human resources
  Change and program effectiveness
  HR management
  International assignments
  Reward
Performance improvement
  Financial effectiveness
  Governance, risk, and compliance
  IT effectiveness
Tax
  Compliance
  EU direct tax
  International assignments
  International tax structuring
  Mergers and acquisitions
  Transfer pricing
Transactions
  Accounting valuations
  Advice on fundraising
  Bid support and bid defense services
  Commercial and market due diligence
  Economics
  Financial due diligence
  Independent expert opinions
  Mergers and acquisitions advisory
  Modeling and business planning
  Post deal services
  Private equity advisory
  Privatization advice
  Project finance
  Public company advisory
  Structuring services
  Tax valuations
  Valuation consulting

COMPETITORS

Bain & Company
Baker Tilly International
BDO International
Booz Allen
Boston Consulting
Deloitte
Ernst & Young Global
Grant Thornton International
H&R Block
KPMG
Marsh & McLennan
McKinsey & Company

HISTORICAL FINANCIALS

Company Type: Partnership

Income Statement

FYE: June 30

	REVENUE ($ mil.)	NET INCOME ($ mil.)	NET PROFIT MARGIN	EMPLOYEES
6/09	26,171	—	—	163,545
6/08	28,185	—	—	155,693
6/07	25,150	—	—	146,767
6/06	21,986	—	—	142,162
6/05	18,998	—	—	130,203
Annual Growth	**8.3%**	**—**	**—**	**5.9%**

Revenue History

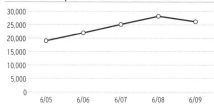

Prudential plc

When it comes to life insurance, a little prudence goes a long way. Working through its subsidiaries, Prudential is the UK's largest life insurer and the largest European insurer operating in Asia. In addition to insurance, Prudential UK's products include pensions, annuities, investment bonds, and fund management. Other businesses include UK fund manager M&G. In Asia, the company sells life insurance, savings, and investment products through its Prudential Corporation Asia unit. In the US, Prudential owns Jackson National Life Insurance, which offers annuities and life insurance. Prudential plc was formed in 1848 to offer life insurance and loans to the middle class.

A key part of Prudential's growth strategy and differentiation from its competitors is its presence in Asia, which it considers the engine of its growth. Prudential has about 30 businesses that are spread over 13 Asian countries. In China, for example, it quickly established bases in 10 cities by working with China's CITIC Group. In India it works through a joint venture with ICICI Bank.

The company expanded its operations in Singapore when it agreed to acquire United Overseas Bank's life insurance unit in early 2010 for 428 million Singapore dollars ($307 million). Along with becoming owner of UOB Life Assurance Ltd., Prudential also entered into an agreement through which UOB will sell Prudential's life, accident, and health insurance policies for 12 years at the bank's more than 400 branches in Singapore, Indonesia, and Thailand, giving Prudential a greater presence in all of those markets. Prudential has operations in about a dozen Asian countries.

Prudential made a splashy bid on AIG's Hong Kong-based American International Assurance (AIA) business in 2010. The $35.5 billion deal ($25 billion in cash, $8.5 billion in securities, and $2 billion in stock) would have made Prudential the largest life insurer in Hong Kong and allowed AIG to pay off a chunk of its debt to the US government. However, Prudential's shareholders were not impressed and raised a ruckus over the deal. To appease them, Prudential attempted to reduce its offer to $30 billion — which AIG coolly refused — and then simply withdrew its entire offer.

Another strategic area of focus is retirement savings in the US. Its Jackson National Life Insurance takes advantage of the fact that the US has the largest market for retirement-related financial products. Prudential intends to place particular emphasis on variable annuity products. It also looks to diversify its earnings and offerings by making bolt-on acquisitions when opportunities emerge.

After helping oversee the shift in focus that brought the company growth in Asia and stability during the 2008 economic downturn, CEO Mark Tucker stepped down at the end of September 2009. The company chose CFO Tidjane Thiam to replace him. Thiam, a native of Ivory Coast, became the first black CEO of a FTSE 100 company.

HISTORY

Actually, prudence almost killed Prudential before it ever got started. Founded in 1848 as Prudential Mutual Assurance Investment and Loan Association, the firm initially insured middle-class customers. The Dickensian conditions of the working poor made them too risky for insurers. Unfortunately the company found few takers of the right sort, and by 1852 Prudential was in peril.

Two events saved Prudential: The House of Commons pressed for insurance coverage for all classes, and Prudential's own agents pushed for change. The company expanded into industrial insurance, a modest coverage for the working poor. In 1864, to quell criticism of the insurance industry, Prudential brought in independent auditors to confirm its soundness. This soon became a marketing tool and business took off. The Pru, as it came to be known, became the leading industrial insurer by the 1880s. It covered half the country's population by 1905. The firm's salesmen were known for making personal visits to customers (the "Man from the Pru" became a ubiquitous icon in the 1940s and was revived in 1997).

During the two world wars, Prudential boosted its reputation by honoring the policies of war victims when it could have legally denied them. Between wars the company added fire and accident insurance in Europe.

The 1980s were volatile for insurance companies, especially in the wake of Britain's financial deregulation in 1986. Therefore, in 1982, under the direction of CEO Brian Corby, the Pru reorganized product lines and in 1985 entered the real estate business. In 1986 it entered the US market by buying US-based Jackson National Life Insurance.

Prudential, which had considered selling Mercantile and General Reinsurance in the early 1990s (purchased in 1969), sold the reinsurer back to Swiss Re in 1996. It also formed Prudential Bank and created an Asian emerging-market investment fund that year.

Insurance regulators reprimanded the company for mis-selling financial products in 1997. In 1998 Jackson National bought a California savings and loan, enabling it to sell investment products in the US. Also that year the Pru sold its Australian and New Zealand businesses, and Prudential Bank launched its pioneering Internet bank Egg Banking.

In 1999 Prudential bought investment manager M&G Group. The company then changed its name to Prudential plc and began talks with the Prudential Insurance Company of America to resolve confusion of their similar names as they expanded into new markets. Also in 1999 the Pru joined forces with the Bank of China to offer pension and asset management in Hong Kong.

The company announced plans in 2000 to sell a chunk of its institutional fund management business as well as its traditional balanced pension business to Deutsche Bank. That year the company spun off 20% of Egg (it sold the rest in 2007).

Entering the Japanese life insurance market, Prudential bought Orico Life in 2001. Prudential's hopes of capturing the lucrative annuities market by acquiring American General were dashed that year as American General instead embraced American International Group, leaving the Pru with a $600 million break-up fee. To consolidate operations, the firm sold its general insurance business in 2001 to Swiss insurer Winterthur (a subsidiary of Credit Suisse).

In early 2006 Prudential rejected a takeover offer from larger rival Aviva valued at nearly $30 billion.

HISTORICAL FINANCIALS

Company Type: Public

Income Statement

	ASSETS ($ mil.)	NET INCOME ($ mil.)	INCOME AS % OF ASSETS	EMPLOYEES
12/09	362,721	1,078	0.3%	27,389
12/08	311,954	(566)	—	29,683
12/07	438,675	2,046	0.5%	29,172
12/06	423,990	1,713	0.4%	34,789
12/05	356,771	1,308	0.4%	31,661
Annual Growth	0.4%	(4.7%)	—	(3.6%)

FYE: December 31

2009 Year-End Financials

Equity as % of assets: 2.8%
Return on assets: 0.3%
Return on equity: 12.5%
Long-term debt ($ mil.): 11,831
No. of shares (mil.): 1,270

Dividends
Yield: 2.0%
Payout: 74.4%
Market value ($ mil.): 41,228
Sales ($ mil.): 76,603

Stock History

NYSE: PUK

	STOCK PRICE ($) FY Close	P/E High/Low		PER SHARE ($) Earnings	Dividends	Book Value
12/09	32.47	40	10	0.86	0.64	7.87
12/08	18.31	—	—	(0.46)	0.53	5.77
12/07	57.17	41	29	1.66	0.69	9.75
12/06	54.30	39	27	1.42	0.65	8.46
12/05	32.86	31	26	1.09	0.54	7.04
Annual Growth	(0.3%)	—	—	(5.8%)	4.3%	2.8%

Publicis Groupe

Advertising is *la joie de vivre* for Publicis. One of the world's largest advertising and media services conglomerates, the company provides a wide range of corporate communication and media services, including creative advertising, media and campaign planning, marketing, and public relations. Its flagship advertising networks include Leo Burnett, Fallon Worldwide, Digitas, Razorfish, and Saatchi & Saatchi; Publicis' Starcom MediaVest and ZenithOptimedia units are among the world's largest media planning enterprises. The company serves such big names as Cadbury, Coca-Cola, General Mills, Hewlett-Packard, and Procter & Gamble.

Publicis is the leading provider of advertising and marketing services in Europe and ranks behind only conglomerates Omnicom and WPP in worldwide revenue. Its media services operations rank behind WPP's Mindshare and Mediaedge:cia in total worldwide billings. In addition, its Specialized Agencies and Marketing Services division provides marketing and communications services through a number of agencies, including Arc Worldwide (relationship marketing); Burrell Communications and Bromley Commu-nications (multicultural advertising); and Manning, Selvage & Lee and Kekst and Company (public relations).

Like its competitors, Publicis uses acquisitions to strengthen its position in key areas, and lately the company has been focused on expanding its digital marketing capabilities. In 2007, Publicis hit the ground running when it bought US-based Digitas for $1.3 billion. Digitas owns offices in Boston, Chicago, Detroit, and New York and brought such high-tech clients as AT&T Mobility, IBM, and Hewlett-Packard to Publicis' portfolio. A few months later, Publicis acquired Business Interactif, an interactive marketing agency based in France.

About that same time, Publicis also snatched up Communication Central Group (CCG), one of the largest interactive marketing agencies in China. CCG was later rebranded as Digitas Greater China. In late 2008, Publicis acquired the search marketing business of DoubleClick's Performics operations. Also in 2008, Leo Burnett's Asia/Pacific network got a boost when Publicis acquired W&K Communications, an agency specializing in advertising, promotion, television production, and media buying services, and owning a presence in Beijing and Guangzhou, China. W&K was later renamed Leo Burnett W&K Beijing Advertising Co.

In addition to China, the company is looking to expand into India; it plans to either open additional offices in the country or use it as an outsourcing post to serve other parts of the company. Overall Publicis sees Brazil, China, India, Mexico, Russia, and Turkey as emerging markets ripe for growth. In late 2010, Publicis announced it was acquiring a 49% stake in the Talent Group, a Brazil-based advertising firm.

As the digital arena continues to reign supreme in the advertising industry, Publicis made another strong move to beef up these operations in 2009, when it acquired interactive ad agency Razorfish from Microsoft.

Publicis' Healthcare Communications Group segment got a boost in 2010 through the acquisition of Resolute Communications Ltd, a public relations and consulting agency focusing on the health care sector.

HISTORY

In 1926 Marcel Bleustein, then 19 years old, started France's first advertising agency, which he called Publicis (a takeoff on "publicity" and "six"). He launched his own radio station, Radio Cite, after the French government banned all advertising on state-run stations, and by 1939 he had expanded into film distribution and movie theaters. With the outbreak of WWII, Bleustein fled to London to serve with the Free French Forces.

Having adopted the name Bleustein-Blanchet, he returned to France following the liberation and revived his advertising business. In 1958 he bought the former Hotel Astoria on the Champs-Elysées and opened the first Le Drugstore. The original structure burned in a 1972 fire, and legend has it that Bleustein-Blanchet tapped Maurice Lévy to lead the company after he found Lévy salvaging records amid the ruins.

To expand its business, Publicis formed an alliance — Chicago-based Foote, Cone & Belding Communications (FCB) — in 1988. The partnership soured five years later, however, when Publicis acquired France's Groupe FCA. (FCB claimed the acquisition was a breach of contract and countered by establishing a new holding company for itself, True North Communications.) Bleustein-Blanchet died in 1996, and his daughter, Elisabeth Badinter, was named chair of the supervisory board.

In 1997 Publicis and True North divided their joint network, Publicis Communications, with True North getting the European offices and Publicis getting Africa, Asia, and Argentina. Later that year Publicis attempted a $700 million hostile bid for the 81.5% of True North it didn't already own to stop True North's acquisition of Bozell, Jacobs, Kenyon & Eckhardt. The bid failed, and Publicis' stake in True North was reduced to 11%. (True North was later acquired by Interpublic Group in 2001.)

In 1998 Lévy helped soothe a bitter feud among the descendants of Marcel Bleustein: Elisabeth Badinter had battled with her sister Michele Bleustein-Blanchet over Bleustein-Blanchet's desire to sell her stake in Publicis' holding company. Lévy's solution allowed Bleustein-Blanchet to sell her shares and left Badinter with control of the company.

Continuing its US expansion, in 1999 Publicis bought a 49% stake in Burrell Communications Group (one of the largest African-American-owned ad agencies in the US).

In 2000 the company bought advertising outfit Fallon McElligott (now Fallon Worldwide), marketing firm Frankel & Co., and media buyer DeWitt Media (which was merged into Optimedia). Publicis capped off the year by acquiring Saatchi & Saatchi for about $1.9 billion. Along with the deal, it inherited Saatchi's 50% of media buying unit Zenith Media (jointly owned by Cordiant Communications). In 2001 it merged Optimedia and Zenith, with Publicis owning 75% of the new business.

2002 was a big year for Publicis and the ad industry in general; the decision to acquire Bcom3 catapulted the company into the really big leagues and created a distinct size difference between the top four advertising conglomerates and everyone else.

From 2002 to 2005, the company worked on integrating Bcom3 and Saatchi & Saatchi into its operational infrastructure.

In order to generate better synergy between its two leading agency networks (Saatchi & Saatchi and Fallon Worldwide), Publicis created a new mini structure called SSF Group in mid-2007.

EXECUTIVES

Chairman, Supervisory Board: Elisabeth Badinter, age 66
Vice Chairman, Supervisory Board: Sophie Dulac, age 52
Chairman, Management Board, and CEO: Maurice Lévy, age 67
COO: Jean-Yves Naouri, age 48
Member, Management Board, EVP, and CFO: Jean-Michel Etienne, age 55
Member Management Board; CEO, Saatchi & Saatchi Worldwide: Kevin J. Roberts, age 60
President and COO, Dentsu Inc.; Member, Supervisory Board: Tatsuyoshi Takashima
Head, Real Estate; Member, Supervisory Board: Henri-Calixte Suaudeau, age 74
SVP Internal Audit, Human Resources, Communication, and Sustainable Development: Mathias Emmerich, age 47
SVP Mergers and Acquisitions and Legal Departments: Isabelle Simon
Chairman and CEO, Leo Burnett Worldwide: Thomas (Tom) Bernardin
Executive Chairman, PublicisLive: John Rossant

President, Publicis Consultants, France; Acting
 President, Publicis Events France: Fabrice Fries
President, Europe, MS&L Group: Anders Kempe
President, Americas, MS&L Group: Jim Tsokanos
CEO, Re:sources Worldwide: Daniele Bessis
CEO, VivaKi: Jack Klues, age 55
CEO, Emotion: Isabelle Chovet
CEO and Chief Creative Officer, Kaplan Thaler Group:
 Linda Kaplan, age 59
CEO, Public Relations and Events Management
 Activities: Olivier Fleurot, age 55
Director External Communications: Peggy Nahmany,
 age 41
Director Investor Relations: Martine Hue
Auditors: Ernst & Young et Autres

LOCATIONS

HQ: Publicis Groupe S.A.
 133, Avenue des Champs-Elysées
 75008 Paris, France
Phone: 33-1-4443-7000   Fax: 33-1-4443-7525
US HQ: 950 6th Ave., New York, NY 10001
US Phone: 212-279-5550   US Fax: 212-279-5560
Web: www.publicisgroupe.com

2009 Sales

	% of total
North America	46
Europe	35
Asia/Pacific	11
Latin America	5
Africa & Middle East	3
Total	**100**

PRODUCTS/OPERATIONS

2009 Sales

	% of total
SAMS (Specialized Agencies & Marketing Services)	44
Traditional advertising	35
Media	21
Total	**100**

Selected Operations and Agencies

Specialized Agencies and Marketing Services Group
 (SAMS)
 Arc Worldwide (relationship marketing and
  promotional campaigns)
 Bromley Communications (49%, multicultural
  advertising, US)
 Digitas Inc. (digital communications and marketing
  services, US)
 Kekst and Company (public relations, US)
 Lápiz (multicultural marketing, US)
 Manning, Selvage & Lee (public relations, US)
 Medicus Group (health care marketing, US)
 Nelson Communications (health care marketing, US)
 Publicis Dialog (sales promotion and direct marketing)
 Razorfish (digital communications and marketing
  services, US)
 Rowland Companies (public relations, US)
Advertising
 Bartle Bogle Hegarty (49%)
 Beacon Communications (66%, Japan)
 Fallon Worldwide (US)
 Kaplan Thaler Group (US)
 Leo Burnett (US)
 Publicis Worldwide
 Saatchi & Saatchi (US)
Media Services
 Denuo
 Médias & Régies Europe
 Starcom MediaVest Group (US)
 ZenithOptimedia (UK)

COMPETITORS

Aegis Group	Interpublic Group
Dentsu	Omnicom
Hakuhodo	WPP
Havas	

HISTORICAL FINANCIALS

Company Type: Public

Income Statement

FYE: December 31

	REVENUE ($ mil.)	NET INCOME ($ mil.)	NET PROFIT MARGIN	EMPLOYEES
12/09	6,484	578	8.9%	45,000
12/08	6,630	674	10.2%	44,727
12/07	6,875	701	10.2%	43,808
12/06	5,792	585	10.1%	39,939
12/05	4,904	459	9.4%	38,610
Annual Growth	**7.2%**	**5.9%**	**—**	**3.9%**

2009 Year-End Financials

Debt ratio: 63.8%   No. of shares (mil.): 179
Return on equity: —   Dividends
Cash ($ mil.): 2,264   Yield: 2.1%
Current ratio: 0.98   Payout: 31.6%
Long-term debt ($ mil.): 2,574   Market value ($ mil.): 7,306

Stock History

Pink Sheets: PUBGY

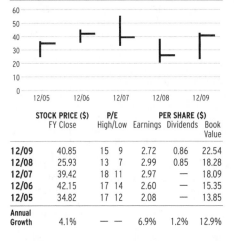

	STOCK PRICE ($) FY Close	P/E High/Low		PER SHARE ($) Earnings	Dividends	Book Value
12/09	40.85	15	9	2.72	0.86	22.54
12/08	25.93	13	7	2.99	0.85	18.28
12/07	39.42	18	11	2.97	—	18.09
12/06	42.15	17	14	2.60	—	15.35
12/05	34.82	17	12	2.08	—	13.85
Annual Growth	**4.1%**	**—**	**—**	**6.9%**	**1.2%**	**12.9%**

Qantas Airways

Qantas Airways, Australia's #1 airline, flies to
about 60 destinations at home and another 100
(including some served by code-sharing partners) in about 40 countries. (Code-sharing enables carriers to sell tickets on one another's
flights and thus extend their networks.) Qantas
owns regional carrier QantasLink and low-fare
carrier Jetstar, both of which operate in Australia
and the Asia/Pacific region. Overall, the Qantas
fleet includes about 230 aircraft. The company
also owns a 58% stake in Jetset Travelworld, a
leading Australian travel agency. Qantas is part
of the Oneworld alliance, which is led by British
Airways and American Airlines.

Qantas sold its DPAX air freight unit to Toll
Holdings, a transport and logistics group, in
mid-2010. DPAX is one of the largest independent express air freight operators in Asia.

In 2008 Qantas and British Airways (BA) began
merger talks, but an agreement could not be
reached. The combination would have resulted
in an $8 billion company owning about 500 air-
craft. However, BA disagreed with Qantas owning more than 50% of the combined firm.
(Australian law states that Qantas has to remain
majority-owned by Australian investors with its
head office residing in Australia.)

Like other airlines, Qantas has been hit hard
by high fuel costs and low consumer demand.
Since 2008 the company has eliminated some
3,250 jobs, abandoned plans to hire 1,200 positions, cut unprofitable traffic routes, and reduced its aircraft fleet by about 10%.

Focusing its efforts on expanding its network,
Qantas formed a code-sharing agreement in
early 2009 with Etihad Airways, sharing passengers on routes from Australia to Europe via the
Middle East. Qantas opened up non-stop service
in 2008 to Buenos Aires, the carrier's first foray
into South America. Qantas also increased
flights on its high-growth routes to the US,
China, Hong Kong, and South Africa.

However, Qantas has sustained heavy losses
on trans-Pacific routes because of increased
competition and a drop in traffic on routes between Australia and the US.

Losses on international routes would be hurting Qantas more if not for good returns on its fre-
quent flyer program and from Jetstar. The budget
carrier has flourished in the midst of the global
economic recession that has made consumers
wary of buying full-price airlines tickets.

In 2010 Jetstar announced an alliance with
low-cost, Malaysia-based carrier AirAsia. Besides
bolstering Jetstar's operations in Southeast Asia,
the partnership is expected to save Qantas hundreds of millions of dollars through joint purchasing of supplies and services.

To battle competition from Virgin Blue in the
Pacific region, Jetstar will launch flights from
Australia to Fiji in 2010. Qantas owns a 46%
stake in Air Pacific, Fiji's national airline but announced in 2009 plans to sell its stake as the airline has been hemorrhaging profits.

Qantas went through a leadership change in
2008 following the retirement CEO Geoff Dixon.
He was succeeded by Jetstar CEO Alan Joyce.

HISTORY

Ex-WWI pilots Wilmot Hudson Fysh and Paul
McGinness and stockman Fergus McMaster
founded Queensland and Northern Territory
Aerial Services (Qantas) in 1920 to provide an air
link between Darwin in the Northern Territory
and the railheads in Queensland. In 1922 Qantas began carrying airmail over a 577-mile route
between Charleville and Cloncurry, and by 1930
it covered northeastern Australia with air
routes. Qantas moved its headquarters to Sydney in 1938.

Qantas and Imperial Airways (predecessor of
British Airways, or BA) formed Qantas Empire
Airways in 1934 to fly the last leg of a London-to-
Australia mail route (Singapore to Brisbane). Qantas bought the British share of Qantas Empire in
1947 (when Qantas made its first Sydney-London
flight) and was subsequently nationalized.

By 1950 the airline served most major cities
in the Pacific Rim. Qantas inaugurated a route
to Johannesburg (1952) and opened the Southern Cross route, previously operated by British
Commonwealth Pacific Airlines, to San Francisco and Vancouver via Honolulu (1953).

In 1958 Qantas offered the first complete
round-the-world service. (Pan Am had started a
similar service in 1957 but was barred by the US
government from crossing North America.) It
bought 29% of Malayan Airways in 1959 and
added several European destinations in the 1960s,
including Frankfurt (1966) and Amsterdam
(1967). Founder Fysh retired as chairman in 1966,
and the airline took its present name in 1967.

Tourism in Australia boomed in the 1970s. Competition from foreign (especially US) airlines initially hurt Qantas, contributing to a $4 million loss in 1971 (its second since 1924). But in 1973 annual boardings jumped 28%. Qantas' Aussie passengers flew some 4,217 miles per journey — the longest average trip of any airline.

In 1987 Qantas bought a stake in Fiji's Air Pacific. Later acquisitions included Australia-Asia Airlines (1989) and 20% of Air New Zealand (1990; sold 1997). Qantas enjoyed record profits in 1989, but a strike by domestic pilots paralyzed Australia's tourist industry that year.

The Australian airline industry was deregulated in the early 1990s, and Qantas formed regional carrier Airlink in 1991. The next year it merged with Australia Airlines, and in 1993 the Australian government sold BA a 25% stake in Qantas. Still, the airlines' 1994 attempt to set prices and services together was rejected by Australian authorities.

Because Australian privatizations had deluged the stock exchange with issues, Qantas delayed its IPO until 1995. Also that year Qantas and BA got approval for a joint service agreement that allowed them to operate some facilities together.

The carrier began code-sharing with American Airlines in 1995; three years later Qantas joined the Oneworld global marketing alliance, led by American and BA. The airline expanded its code-sharing with affiliate Air Pacific in 2000, even as it braced for competition at home from Virgin Atlantic's new Australian low-fare carrier.

In 2002 Qantas began negotiations to acquire a stake in Air New Zealand, but Qantas' offer to acquire a 23% stake in the smaller airline was rejected in 2003 by regulators.

A proposed purchase of Qantas by an investment group led by Macquarie Bank and TPG failed to win shareholder approval in 2007. The airline's board agreed to the investment group's $9.1 billion offer in December 2006, but several institutional shareholders opposed the deal.

In mid-2008 Qantas acquired a 58% stake in Jetset Travelworld Limited, one of Australia's largest travel agency franchises.

EXECUTIVES

Chairman: Leigh Clifford, age 63
CEO and Director: Alan Joyce, age 44
CFO: Gareth Evans
SEVP The Americas and Pacific: Wally R. Mariani
Group Executive Government and Corporate Affairs: David Epstein
Group Executive, Qantas Commercial: Rob Gurney
Group Executive, Qantas Airlines Operations: Lyell Strambi
Group Executive People: Jon Scriven
Chief Risk Officer: Rob Kella
General Counsel: Brett Johnson
Company Secretary: Cassandra Hamlin
Executive Manager Engineering: Chris Nassenstein
Executive Manager, QantasLink: Narendra Kumar Saranam
Executive Manager, Corporate Services and Technology: David Hall
Executive Manager Qantas Customer and Marketing: Lesley Grant
Group CEO, Jetstar: Bruce Buchanan
CEO, Qantas Loyalty: Simon Hickey
Auditors: KPMG

LOCATIONS

HQ: Qantas Airways Limited
Qantas Centre, Level 9, Bldg. A, 203 Coward St. Mascot, New South Wales 2020, Australia
Phone: 61-2-9691-3636   **Fax:** 61-2-9691-3339
US HQ: 6080 Center Dr., Ste. 400
Los Angeles, CA 90045
US Phone: 310-726-1400
Web: www.qantas.com.au

PRODUCTS/OPERATIONS

2010 Sales

	% of total
Passenger	79
Freight	6
Other	15
Total	**100**

2010 Sales

	% of total
Qantas	70
Jetstar	15
Qantas Frequent Flyer	7
Qantas Freight	7
Jetset Travelworld Group	1
Total	**100**

COMPETITORS

Air France-KLM
Air New Zealand
All Nippon Airways
American Express
Carlson Wagonlit
Cathay Pacific
China Eastern Airlines
China Southern Airlines
Delta Air Lines
Lufthansa
SAS
Singapore Airlines
Thomas Cook
TUI
United Continental
Virgin Blue

HISTORICAL FINANCIALS

Company Type: Public

Income Statement

FYE: June 30

	REVENUE ($ mil.)	NET INCOME ($ mil.)	NET PROFIT MARGIN	EMPLOYEES
6/10	11,793	99	0.8%	32,490
6/09	11,707	99	0.8%	33,030
6/08	15,552	931	6.0%	33,670
6/07	12,870	611	4.7%	34,267
6/06	9,961	350	3.5%	34,832
Annual Growth	**4.3%**	**(27.0%)**	**—**	**(1.7%)**

2010 Year-End Financials

Debt ratio: —	No. of shares (mil.): 2,265
Return on equity: 2.0%	Dividends
Cash ($ mil.): 3,172	Yield: 0.0%
Current ratio: 0.93	Payout: —
Long-term debt ($ mil.): —	Market value ($ mil.): 4,267

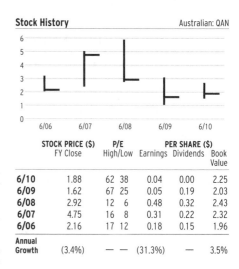

Stock History   Australian: QAN

	STOCK PRICE ($) FY Close	P/E High/Low		PER SHARE ($) Earnings	Dividends	Book Value
6/10	1.88	62	38	0.04	0.00	2.25
6/09	1.62	67	25	0.05	0.19	2.03
6/08	2.92	12	6	0.48	0.32	2.43
6/07	4.75	16	8	0.31	0.22	2.32
6/06	2.16	17	12	0.18	0.15	1.96
Annual Growth	**(3.4%)**	**—**	**—**	**(31.3%)**	**—**	**3.5%**

Rabobank Group

Rabobank Group has its roots deep in Dutch soil. Founded as a cooperative of Dutch agricultural banks in the late 1800s, the company has some 150 member banks that have more than 1,000 branches in the Netherlands and dozens of subsidiaries around the world that focus on the food, agribusiness, and financial industries. The cooperative's wholesale and international retail banking arm, Rabobank International, has offices in some 30 countries. Other global activities include trade and commodity finance. Rabobank Group also owns US agribusiness lender Rabo AgriFinance, California-based Rabobank, N.A., and Swiss private bank Sarasin. Rabobank Group is owned by its member banks.

While Rabobank has to vie with competitors such as ING Groep in most areas of domestic banking, it has a near-stranglehold on the agricultural loan market in the Netherlands. Other significant operations include mortgage lending, asset management, leasing, insurance, real estate services, and lending to small and mid-sized domestic business customers. Rabobank Group also owns retail banks ACCBank in Ireland and Poland's BGZ Bank.

Subsidiary Rabo Development supports the group's international expansion by investing in financial institutions in developing nations. Through the development program, it takes significant minority stakes in retail and rural banks and provides management and administrative support. In 2008 Rabobank acquired a 40% stake in Paraguay's Banco Regional and a 35% stake in Banque Populaire du Rwanda. The Rabo Development initiative has invested in about a half-dozen banks in Africa, as well as China.

Despite the global economic turmoil (or perhaps because of it), Rabobank increased its loan portfolio in 2009 while credit markets remained tight. It was able to expand its lending activities thanks to one of the most sterling credit ratings in the financial services industry, and by maintaining its laser-like focus on lending to the relatively stable food and agribusiness sectors.

HISTORY

Dutch Rabobank Group sprang from a German idea, actually. Friedrich Raiffeisen founded a banking cooperative in Heddesdorf, Germany, in 1864 that catered to farmers' needs, provided assistance to members, and reinvested profits in the bank. Not much later, the cooperative banking model crossed the border to the Netherlands. In 1897 a farmer-owned cooperative called the Boerenleenbank opened in the town of Geldorp. Other Boerenleenbanks sprouted soon after.

Southern farmers created the Cooperatieve Vereeniging van Raiffeisen-Banken en Landbouwvereenigingen in Utrecht in 1898. This organization centralized the administration of the local banks. Farmers in the north followed suit and formed the Cooperatieve Centrale Boerenleenbank. A move to merge the two organizations failed because of traditional north-south rivalries in the country.

Farmer-owned cooperative banks continued to spread until there were over 1,200 such locally operating banks by the 1920s. After WWII, cooperative banks slowly entered the urban markets of the Netherlands.

The Dutch banking industry restructured in the 1950s, allowing banks to offer multiple services. In the next decade the banks in both of the centralized organizations started to offer insurance products and commercial accounts.

In the early 1970s Cooperatieve Vereeniging van Raiffeisen-Banken en Landbouwvereenigingen and Cooperatieve Centrale Boerenleenbank announced plans to merge. The new entity, Rabobank (Cooperatieve Centrale Raiffeisen-Boerenleenbank), boasted 1,500 independent banks in its network in 1972. By the late 1970s Rabobank changed its membership requirements to allow nonmembers to hold private accounts.

With the unified European market just around the corner, the bank found itself torn between the need to compete and to stay loyal to its original customers' needs. Rabobank expanded its food and agricultural sector services. It entered new international markets and acquired foreign agribusiness banks.

In 1986 it began to offer mutual funds and stock brokerage services. The next year commercial loans outweighed loans for agriculture. In the 1990s Rabobank sowed the seeds of diversification with the acquisitions of insurer Interpolis; durable equipment leaser and financier De Lage Landen; asset manager Robeco; and venture capital firm Gilde Investment Management.

Rabobank's expansion of its business lines, however, didn't guarantee its survival in the predatory banking world of the European common market. Insiders and analysts pined for a suitable partner. Rabobank, a bit wary of noncooperative banks, sought joint ventures rather than mergers.

Rabobank bought the remaining shares of fund management subsidiary Robeco in 2000 with an eye toward expanding that division. In 2001 Robeco bought US-based Harbor Capital Advisors from glass container producer Owens-Illinois. The next year Rabobank purchased VIB Corp, owner of Valley Independent Bank, which it later renamed Rabobank N.A.

The bank's hopes for extending roots into Midwestern US soil were dashed in 2004. Omaha-based, government-sponsored Farm Credit Services of America backed out of a sale agreement, citing unexpected costs and protests from farming groups. In a effort to make reparations, Farm Credit agreed to pay Rabobank $10 million.

In 2005 the company expanded its offerings in Africa through its acquisition (as the head of a financing consortium) of a 49% interest in Tanzania's National Microfinance Bank, which offers savings products and micro-loans to the southeast African country's predominantly rural population.

That year it cemented its ownership of health insurance firm Eureko when it merged its Interpolis insurance unit into Eureko subsidiary Achmea. The deal bumped Rabobank's stake in Eureko from 5% to 37%.

Undeterred by the failure of the Farm Credit deal, Rabobank embarked on an acquisition spree in 2006. That year, it bought US lender Central Coast Bancorp, acquired a 10% stake in Hangzhou Cooperative Bank of China, and bought Athlon Holding through its lease financing subsidiary De Lage Landen. In 2007, Rabobank N.A. acquired Mid-State Bancshares for $851 million. The group also invested in Indonesian banks Bank Haga and Bank Hagakita (which were merged into PT Rabobank International Indonesia in 2008), giving Rabobank access to small and midsized businesses in that region, and purchased a controlling stake in Swiss company Bank Sarasin.

EXECUTIVES

Chairman, Supervisory Board: Lense Koopmans, age 67
Deputy Chairman, Supervisory Board: A. J. A. M. (Antoon) Vermeer, age 60
Chairman, Executive Board: Pieter W. (Piet) Moerland, age 61
Member, Executive Board; Vice Chairman, Rabobank International: Sipko N. Schat, age 50
Member, Executive Board and CFO: Albertus (Bert) Bruggink, age 46
Member, Executive Board: Piet (Piet) van Schijndel, age 59
Member, Executive Board: Berry Marttin, age 45
Member, Exectuive Board: Gerlinde Silvis, age 50
Senior Managing Director, Rabobank International: Ralf Dekker
Senior Managing Director, Legal and Tax Affairs: Jan van Veenendaal
Director Human Resources: Bert Ferwerda, age 50
Secretary: Sjoerd E. Eisma, age 61
Global Head, Renewable Energy and Infrastructure Finance: Marcel Gerritsen
Managing Director, Renewable Energy and Infrastructure Finance, Americas: Thomas Emmons
Secretary Investor Relations: Ellen Cobet
Manager, Rural and Retail: Harry de Roo
Chairman, Schretlen & Co: Gerbert Mos
Chairman, Robeco Groep: D. P. M. Verbeek
Chairman, FGH Bank and Acting Chairman Rabo Bouwfonds: P. C. Keur
Chairman, Rabo Real Estate Group: Hans van der Linden
Auditors: Ernst & Young Accountants LLP

LOCATIONS

HQ: Rabobank Group
Croeselaan 18
3521 CB Utrecht, The Netherlands
Phone: 31-30-216-0000   **Fax:** 31-30-216-1916
US HQ: 245 Park Ave., 37th Fl., New York, NY 10167
US Phone: 212-916-7800
Web: www.rabobank.com

PRODUCTS/OPERATIONS

2009 Sales

	% of total
Interest	82
Fees & commissions	12
Other	6
Total	**100**

Selected Subsidiaries and Affiliates

ACCBank (Ireland)
Athlon (leasing)
Bank BGZ (Poland)
Bank Sarasin (private bank, Switzerland)
De Lage Landen (leasing)
Freo (leasing)
Obvion (mortgage broker, 70%)
Orbay (asset manager)
Rabo Real Vastgoedgroep (property development)
Rabobank Nederland
Robeco (asset manager)
Schretlen & Co (private bank)

COMPETITORS

BNG	DZ BANK
BNP Paribas	Grupo Santander
BNP Paribas Fortis	HSBC
Crédit Agricole	ING
Deutsche Bank	Société Générale

HISTORICAL FINANCIALS

Company Type: Cooperative

Income Statement

FYE: December 31

	ASSETS ($ mil.)	NET INCOME ($ mil.)	INCOME AS % OF ASSETS	EMPLOYEES
12/09	870,953	3,279	0.4%	59,939
12/08	862,783	3,882	0.4%	60,568
12/07	839,723	3,918	0.5%	54,737
12/06	734,131	3,094	0.4%	47,876
12/05	599,533	2,467	0.4%	50,533
Annual Growth	**9.8%**	**7.4%**	**—**	**4.4%**

2009 Year-End Financials

Equity as % of assets: —
Return on assets: 0.4%
Return on equity: —
Long-term debt ($ mil.): 246
Sales ($ mil.): 34,759

Net Income History

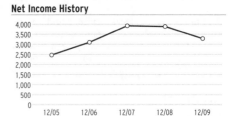

Rallye S.A.

Retail giant Rallye musters its businesses around not just the French flag, but around flags worldwide. Rallye's Casino Guichard-Perrachon subsidiary operates about 10,000 hypermarkets, supermarkets, and convenience stores in Europe (mostly France), Asia/Pacific, and Latin America. It also has a foothold in the sporting goods and athletic shoe department with Groupe Go Sport, which runs about 400 shops. In addition to retailing, the company is active in real estate development, banking, and a variety of investment vehicles. Foncière Euris controls about 60% of Rallye.

Rallye's Casino subsidiary is a leading supermarket chain in France and operates in about 10 countries worldwide. Store banners include Casino, Franprix, Géant, Leader Price, and Monoprix. Casino is the #1 convenience store operator in France with stores under the Petit Casino, Spar, and Vival names. Casino has grown by purchasing stakes in supermarket, hypermarket, and convenience store companies with international locations. It plans to continue expanding globally, focusing on South America and Asia/Pacific.

While Rallye exited the footwear retail business in the US with its sale of The Athlete's Foot, the company plans to continue to expand Groupe Go Sport in Europe. The retailer was formed when Rallye merged two subsidiaries: Go Sport (France's #2 sporting goods retailer) with about 150 stores and Courir (France's #1 sports and leisure footwear retailer) with more than 200.

Rallye has increased its e-commerce activities through its majority stake of Cdiscount.com, a French online retailer of CDs, videos, and more. Cdiscount belongs to the non-food group, which also includes Mercialys (retail real estate development), Casino Cafeteria (corporate cafeterias), and Banque Casino (consumer lending).

In order to strengthen its financial flexibility, the company plans to significantly reduce its debt. To this end, Rallye looks to dispose of commercial real estate and private equity investments valued at more than $1 billion by the end of 2010. Its supermarket group anticipates saving about $200 million in 2009 by making store operations more efficient and lowering supply chain and overhead costs.

HISTORY

Rallye has its roots in Casino Guichard-Perrachon, which was formed after Geoffroy Guichard took over his father-in-law's general store in 1892.

In the early 1920s the company, which would later become a Rallye holding, opened factories to produce items that included food and soap. In 1924 Rallye was formed as a food retailer. Also that year a food distribution group that would become an important acquisition for Rallye in the 1990s, Genty, was founded (renamed Genty Cathiard in 1959).

By WWII Casino had 215 branches. During the war Casino's troubles included 70 stores leveled and 450 damaged in bomb attacks.

The firm launched its first supermarket (Grenoble) in 1960 and its first cafeteria in 1967. It expanded its Géant hypermarkets (Marseille) in 1970 and formed Casino USA in 1976.

Rallye entered sporting goods in 1981 through the purchase of France's 11-unit Athletic Attic chain and the acquisition of a minority stake of US sports footwear and apparel retailer The Athlete's Foot Group. Rallye then acquired majority control of Athlete's Foot in 1984.

Rallye's sales reached $4.4 billion in 1989. The next year it acquired the food distribution group Genty Cathiard, which included retail units Go Sport (sporting goods) and Courir (sports footwear). The acquisition moved Rallye from #8 to #5 in French supermarket groups.

By 1991 Rallye operated 51 hypermarkets and 227 supermarkets. That year Euris, headed by Jean-Charles Naouri, bought a stake in Rallye, which had heavy debt after borrowing funds to acquire Genty Cathiard. Rallye traded its food retail operations (close to 300 hypermarkets and supermarkets) with food giant Casino in exchange for a 30% stake in Casino in 1992.

Rallye merged with subsidiary Genty Cathiard in 1993, when the company went public. Also in 1993 Rallye began a major restructuring for Go Sport that lasted until 1996.

French supermarket chain Promodès made a hostile takeover attempt on Casino and Rallye in 1997, which would have made Promodès France's largest retailer. Rallye (which still had 30% of Casino and about 40% of voting rights) made a friendly counter bid; Promodès backed out and Rallye took control of Casino. By 1998 The Athlete's Foot Group had grown to more than 260 US outlets (company-owned) and more than 400 franchises (about 180 in the US).

Franchises were also located in 38 countries, including Australia, Canada, France, and Hong Kong. Go Sport operated 80 outlets in France and six in Belgium, and there were more than 100 Courir stores (France) by the beginning of 1998. Rallye spun off nearly 20% of Courir in 1999.

Casino expanded its international markets in 1999 by acquiring stakes in food retailing companies in countries that included Brazil, Colombia, Thailand, and Venezuela. Go Sport grew in 1999 by launching new stores in France, Belgium, and Poland — a new market.

In 2000 Casino bought a 51% stake in French online CD retailer Cdiscount.com. Although Rallye as a whole nearly doubled its net profit in 2000, Athlete's Foot suffered a loss of almost $29 million that year and began a three-year restructuring plan that included the closure of 84 unprofitable stores. Conversely, 100 new Athlete's Foot franchises opened in 2001, including the first stores in Mexico and Hungary.

In 2002 Casino acquired a nearly 40% stake in Laurus, a leading retailer in the Netherlands. In December 2003 Rallye sold its interest in The Athlete's Foot (TAF) to the chain's managers in a management-led buyout for an undisclosed sum. Accounting for less than 1% of Rallye's sales, TAF had closed nearly 100 branches since 2001 but was still unprofitable.

François de Montaudouin resigned as managing director of Rallye in January 2004 and was succeeded by chairman Jean-Charles Naouri.

In 2005 the company held an initial public offering for its shopping center real estate development company, Mercialys.

EXECUTIVES

Chairman, President, and CEO: Jean-Charles Naouri, age 61
Deputy Managing Director, Finance: Didier Carlier, age 58
Executive Director: Jacques Dumas, age 58
Auditors: KPMG Audit

LOCATIONS

HQ: Rallye S.A.
83, rue du Faubourg-Saint-Honoré
75008 Paris, France
Phone: 33-1-44-71-13-73   **Fax:** 33-1-44-71-13-70
Web: www.rallye.fr

2009 Sales

	% of total
France	67
Latin America	24
Asia	6
Rest of world	3
Total	**100**

PRODUCTS/OPERATIONS

2009 Sales

	% of total
Food & general retailing	97
Sporting & goods retailing	3
Total	**100**

COMPETITORS

ALDI	METRO AG
Auchan	PPR SA
Carrefour	Primisteres Reynoird
E.Leclerc	Royal Ahold
Galeries Lafayette	Tesco
Guyenne et Gascogne	Wal-Mart
ITM Entreprises	

HISTORICAL FINANCIALS

Company Type: Public

Income Statement

FYE: December 31

	REVENUE ($ mil.)	NET INCOME ($ mil.)	NET PROFIT MARGIN	EMPLOYEES
12/09	39,382	966	2.5%	36
12/08	41,507	390	0.9%	178,327
12/07	38,503	2,229	5.8%	165,975
12/06	30,715	194	0.6%	152,953
12/05	25,012	5	0.0%	147,520
Annual Growth	**12.0%**	**278.6%**	**—**	**(87.5%)**

2009 Year-End Financials

Debt ratio: —
Return on equity: 16.0%
Cash ($ mil.): 4,741
Current ratio: 0.99
Long-term debt ($ mil.): —
No. of shares (mil.): 42
Dividends
  Yield: 7.5%
  Payout: 74.9%
Market value ($ mil.): 1,487

Stock History

Euronext Paris: RAL

	STOCK PRICE ($) FY Close	P/E High/Low		PER SHARE ($) Earnings	Dividends	Book Value
12/09	35.11	11	5	3.50	2.62	235.41
12/08	22.69	—	—	(2.89)	2.58	50.21
12/07	71.39	8	5	10.82	0.00	67.48
12/06	54.13	—	—	0.00	0.00	45.85
12/05	42.98	—	—	—	1.99	38.05
Annual Growth	**(4.9%)**	**—**	**—**	**(43.1%)**	**7.1%**	**57.7%**

Reckitt Benckiser

With a cart full of products, Reckitt Benckiser (rhymes with "freezer") wants to clean up. Among the top household and personal care products makers worldwide, the company makes a variety of consumer products, including air fresheners (Air Wick), household cleaners (Lysol, Easy-Off), laundry products (Woolite), furniture polishes (Old English), dishwashing detergents (Electrasol), and anti-acne (Clearasil). It also makes over-the-counter pharmaceuticals (Gaviscon) and offers products for hair removal, denture cleaning, and pest control (d-Con). Reckitt Benckiser also butters its bread with French's mustard.

In its biggest acquisition since Reckitt Benckiser was formed in 1999, the company in

2010 agreed to acquire health care product company SSL International for about $3.8 billion. The takeover of the maker of Durex condoms and Scholl foot care products outside the US adds both of these well-known brands to Reckitt Benckiser's health and personal care division; it also makes Reckitt Benckiser the world's largest condom manufacturer. More broadly, the acquisition is an example of the consumer goods firms' move into the OTC (over-the-counter) medical products sector, which has traditionally been dominated by pharmaceutical and medical supply companies.

The pending SSL deal follows two other major acquisitions: the 2008 purchase of Adams Respiratory Therapeutics for more than $2 billion. Adams, known as Adams Laboratories, was a specialty pharmaceutical company that made over-the-counter products, including its best-selling Mucinex brand cold remedy. In 2006 it bought Boots Healthcare International in a deal valued at about £1.9 billion that added Nurofen (analgesic), Strepsils (cold remedies), and Clearasil (anti-acne) to its stable of non-prescription products. It also bought former Boots brands — Clearasil, Strepsils, and Sweetez — in India.

However, focusing on the health care side of its business has come with some hurdles. The press drew attention to the company through a broadcast by the BBC's *Newsnight* program that investigated the methods the company has used to retain its Gaviscon market share. The program accused Reckitt Benckiser of attempting to delay the introduction of a generic product that competed with its Gaviscon power brand. The company refutes the allegations but nevertheless has weathered negative press.

HISTORY

Reckitt & Colman's roots can be traced to Jeremiah Colman, who bought a flour mill near Norwich, England, in 1804. In 1823 his nephew James joined the company, and their business was incorporated as J. and J. Colman. Jeremiah died in 1851 and James' son, also named Jeremiah, became a partner, taking over the operations when his father died in 1854. The company moved to Carrow that year.

Colman worked to make the Carrow facilities as self-sufficient and waste-free as possible. The factory had its own foundry, print shop, paper mill (to make containers), and fire brigade. By-products from the milling process were sold to farmers for cattle feed and fertilizer. The company continued to expand, adding wheat flour and using the leftover starch from milling operations to make laundry bluing.

In 1903 the mill acquired Keen, Robinson & Co., a manufacturer of spices. J. and J. Colman got a lock on British mustard sales in 1912 when it acquired its only major competitor, Joseph Farrow & Company. A year later it joined another rival, starch maker Reckitt & Sons, in a joint venture in South America. The joint venture between Colman and Reckitt was a success, and in 1921 they pooled their overseas operations.

The two companies created Reckitt & Colman Ltd. in 1938 to manage their operations, although each company maintained a separate listing on the London Stock Exchange. In 1954 they formally merged into a single entity.

Reckitt & Colman formed its US subsidiary in 1977, and during the 1980s it made a number of acquisitions (Airwick air fresheners, Gold Seal bath products) to expand its presence in the US.

In 1990 the firm picked up such brands as Black Flag (insecticide), Woolite (fabric care), and Easy-Off (oven cleaner) when it bought Boyle-Midway from American Home Products.

The company gained the Lysol brand in 1994 when it bought L&F Household from Eastman Kodak. To help finance the $1.6 billion deal, Reckitt & Colman sold its flagship Colman Mustard unit to Unilever. Its French's operations in the US (mustard, Worcestershire sauce) were its only remaining food business.

Michael Colman, the last active family member, stepped down as chairman in 1995. In 1996 Reckitt & Colman sold its US personal products unit.

In 1998 Reckitt & Colman bought certain cleaning products brands, including Spray'n Wash and Glass Plus, from S.C. Johnson & Son for about $160 million. CEO Vernon Sankey resigned in 1999, and Michael Turrell became the acting chief executive.

Johann A. Benckiser founded Benckiser in 1823 in the Netherlands to make industrial chemicals. The company launched Calgon Water Softener in 1956 and released Calgonit automatic dishwashing detergent in 1964. From 1982 to 1992 a number of acquisitions expanded the company's market in Central Europe and North America. By 1999 Benckiser's products were sold in 45 countries, including Eastern Europe, Asia, and the Middle East.

In 2000 Reckitt Benckiser announced plans to unload 75 brands to focus on more growth-oriented brands. As part of an effort to expand its presence in the Asia/Pacific region, it bought Korean household products maker Oxy Co. (Oxy Clean fabric treatment) in 2001.

In 2002 the company won FDA approval to market Subutex and Suboxone in the US. Both are drugs for the treatment of opiate dependence. They are available in 24 other countries.

In 2006 Reckitt Benckiser completed the previously announced acquisition of Boots Healthcare International (BHI) from Boots Group (now Alliance Boots) for about about £1.9 billion. BHI is a leading UK maker of drugs such as Nurofen (ibuprofen) and Strepsils (sore throat remedy).

The company added to its lineup in 2008 when it acquired Adams Respiratory Therapeutics, known for its Mucinex brand.

EXECUTIVES

Chairman: Adrian D. P. Bellamy, age 68
Deputy Chairman: Peter Harf, age 64
CEO and Director: Bart Becht, age 53
CFO and Director: Colin Day, age 55
EVP Category Development: Rakesh Kapoor, age 51
EVP Supply Chain: Amedeo Fasano, age 48
EVP Developing Markets: Freddy Caspers, age 47
EVP North America and Australia: Rob de Groot, age 43
EVP Europe: Salvatore Caizzone, age 45
SVP Human Resources: Simon Nash, age 48
Company Secretary: Elizabeth (Liz) Richardson
Director Investor Relations: Joanna Speed
Auditors: PricewaterhouseCoopers LLP

LOCATIONS

HQ: Reckitt Benckiser Group plc
103-105 Bath Rd.
Slough SL1 3UH, England
Phone: 44-1753-217-800   **Fax:** 44-1753-217-899
Web: www.rb.com

2009 Sales

	% of total
Europe	45
North America & Australia	28
Developing markets	19
Pharmaceuticals	8
Total	**100**

PRODUCTS/OPERATIONS

2009 Sales

	% of total
Health & personal care	27
Fabric care	20
Surface care	17
Home care	13
Dishwashing	11
Pharmaceuticals	8
Food	3
Other household	1
Total	**100**

Selected Brands

Fabric care
Ava
Calgon
Cherie
Colon
Dosia
Napisan
Oxy Clean
Resolve
Spray'n Wash
Vanish

Surface care
Brasso
Dettox
Easy Off
Harpic
Lime-A-Way
Lysol
Old English
Home Care

Air care
Airwick
d-Con
Haze
Mortein
Pest Control
Wizard

Dishwashing
Calgonit
Electrasol
Finish
Jet-Dry

Health and personal care
Dettol
Disprin
Gaviscon
Immac
Kukident
Lemsip
Steradent
Veet

COMPETITORS

Alliance Boots	Heinz
Alticor	Henkel
Blyth	Johnson & Johnson
Chattem	Kraft Foods
Church & Dwight	McBride plc
Clorox	Procter & Gamble
Colgate-Palmolive	Sara Lee
ConAgra	S.C. Johnson
Del Monte Foods	Unilever
GlaxoSmithKline	

HISTORICAL FINANCIALS

Company Type: Public

Income Statement

FYE: December 31

	REVENUE ($ mil.)	NET INCOME ($ mil.)	NET PROFIT MARGIN	EMPLOYEES
12/09	12,347	2,258	18.3%	24,900
12/08	9,499	1,621	17.1%	24,300
12/07	10,519	1,873	17.8%	23,400
12/06	9,638	1,320	13.7%	21,900
12/05	7,190	1,151	16.0%	20,300
Annual Growth	14.5%	18.4%	—	5.2%

2009 Year-End Financials

Debt ratio: —
Return on equity: 40.5%
Cash ($ mil.): 559
Current ratio: —
Long-term debt ($ mil.): —

No. of shares (mil.): 720
Dividends
  Yield: 2.7%
  Payout: —
Market value ($ mil.): 38,478

Stock History

London: RB

	STOCK PRICE ($) FY Close	P/E High/Low	PER SHARE ($) Earnings	Dividends	Book Value
12/09	53.45	— —	—	1.45	8.88
12/08	37.31	— —	—	0.00	6.62
12/07	58.17	— —	—	1.00	6.61
12/06	45.70	— —	—	0.81	5.08
12/05	33.03	— —	—	0.62	4.44
Annual Growth	12.8%	— —	—	23.7%	19.0%

Reed Elsevier Group

Finding legal, business, or scientific information is a cinch thanks to Reed Elsevier Group. The firm's legal publishing operations fall under the LexisNexis brand, offering online, CD-ROM, and hard copy legal, corporate, and government information. Its Elsevier unit publishes scientific, technical, and medical information. Reed Elsevier also publishes business-to-business titles worldwide through Reed Business Information, and organizes international exhibitions through Reed Exhibitions. Revenues come from subscriptions, circulation sales, advertising, and exhibition fees. Reed Elsevier PLC and Reed Elsevier NV each own 50% of Reed Elsevier Group.

Looking to expand its risk management and business services operations, in 2008 Reed Elsevier acquired credit risk firm ChoicePoint for $4.1 billion, including the assumption of $600 million in debt. The information collection giant was absorbed by LexisNexis (the company's largest revenue generator), giving the subsidiary new products for fraud prevention and credential verification. Also in 2008 Reed Elsevier appointed Ian Smith as the company's new CEO. Smith resigned in 2009, however,

after only eight months on the job. He was replaced by Erik Engstrom. Though no specific reason was given for the change in leadership, one likely cause is that the global recession has taken its toll on the company's business.

Profits at the company's underperforming Reed Business Information have dropped, and Reed Elsevier had been looking to retool the trade magazine unit. It had previously planned to sell the division in order to reduce its reliance on advertiser-funded media and pay down debt that was incurred as a result of the ChoicePoint purchase. However, those plans were scrapped due to unfavorable market conditions, and in 2009 the company instead began selling off several US titles, including *Broadcasting & Cable*, *Multichannel News*, and *This Week In Consumer Electronics*. Cuts at RBI continued in 2010 with the sale of more US titles, such as *Interior Design* and *Furniture Today*.

Things are looking a bit brighter at the company's Elsevier unit, which publishes journals (both print and electronic) and books, and offer information though databases and software. In 2009 subscriptions increased slightly, and online sales grew in medical reference, clinical decision-making, and nursing areas. Its Reed Exhibition business, however, is not fairing as well: Sales of exhibition space at conferences, like Midem and Mipcom, were down, resulting in a drop in revenue for the year.

HISTORY

Newsprint manufacturer Albert E. Reed & Co. was named after its founder in 1894. It went public in 1903. For the next 50 years, Reed grew by buying UK pulp and paper mills. Reed began making packaging materials in the 1930s and added building products in 1954. The company expanded into New Zealand (1955), Australia (1960), and Norway (1962).

Chairman Sir Don Ryder radically altered the company in the 1960s and 1970s, leading Reed into other paper-related products and into the wallpaper, paint, and interior-decorating and do-it-yourself markets. Reed bought International Publishing, Mirror Group Newspapers, and 29% of Cahners Publishing in 1970 (buying the remaining 71% in 1977). By 1978 Ryder's strategy proved flawed. Coordinating so many companies was difficult, and, strapped for cash, Reed dumped most of its Australian businesses.

The company sold the Mirror Group to Robert Maxwell in 1984 and divested the remainder of its nonpaper and nonpublishing companies by 1987 to focus on publishing. It bought Octopus Publishing (1987), the UK's TV Times (1989), News Corp.'s Travel Information Group (1989), and Martindale-Hubbell (1990).

Reed International merged its operations with those of Elsevier, the world's leading scholarly journal publisher, in 1993. Five Rotterdam booksellers and publishers founded Elsevier in 1880. It took its name from a famous Dutch family publishing company, which had operated from the late 16th century to the early 18th century.

Elsevier entered the scientific publishing market in the 1930s, and following WWII diversified into trade journals and consumer manuals. The company made its first US acquisition, Congressional Information Service, in 1979. The company fended off a takeover bid by Maxwell in 1988 by planning a merger with UK publisher Pearson; Maxwell was thwarted, the merger ultimately failed, and Elsevier later sold its Pearson

stock. Elsevier bought Maxwell's Pergamon Press in 1991.

Reed and Elsevier were both listed on the NYSE in 1994. Reed Elsevier built its US presence that year with its purchase of Mead's LexisNexis online service. The company acquired Tolley, a UK tax and legal publisher, and a 50% interest in Shepard's, a US legal citation service in 1996. Reed Elsevier sold IPC Magazines (now IPC Media) for $1.4 billion in 1998 to an investment group led by venture capitalists Cinven. Later that year the company bought Matthew Bender and the remaining 50% of Shepard's from Times Mirror.

Crispin Davis, the former head of Aegis Group, became CEO in 1999. The firm reorganized Cahners that year, laying off several hundred employees and consolidating magazine operations. It also boosted its scientific publishing profile by unveiling Web-based scientific information service ScienceDirect. Reed Elsevier purchased educational publisher Harcourt General in 2001 to boost its market share in the US. The company had to sell some of Harcourt's businesses (including the higher education and corporate training operations) to the former Thomson Corporation (now Thomson Reuters) in order to ease antitrust concerns.

In 2002 the company also changed its name to Reed Elsevier Group plc.

The company next began boosting its units with acquisitions: risk-management information provider Seisint for $775 million through its LexisNexis unit (2004) and the medical publishing business of MediMedia for nearly $340 million (2005). Its Elsevier unit acquired IT publisher Syngress in late 2006.

After years of disappointing sales in its education division, the company sold its Harcourt businesses, along with other education assets, in 2007. Houghton Mifflin acquired the Harcourt Education, Harcourt Trade, and Greenwood-Heinemann divisions for some $4 billion. In a separate deal, Reed Elsevier sold its international textbook publisher Harcourt Education Ltd. and the US-based testing company Harcourt Assessment to international education and information company Pearson for $950 million.

EXECUTIVES

Chairman: Anthony J. (Tony) Habgood, age 63
CEO and Director; CEO, Reed Elsevier PLC, Reed Elsevier NV, Elsevier Division: Erik Engstrom, age 46, $2,948,498 total compensation
CFO and Director: Mark H. Armour, age 55, $2,450,558 total compensation
Director; CEO, LexisNexis Division: Andrew (Andy) Prozes, age 64, $2,900,021 total compensation
CEO, Elsevier Health Sciences: Michael Hansen
CEO, Reed Business Information: Keith Jones
Chairman and CEO, Reed Exhibitions: Michael (Mike) Rusbridge
Chief Strategy Officer: Julian Ashworth
General Counsel and Company Secretary: Stephen J. (Steve) Cowden
Group Treasurer: Paul Richardson
Director Corporate Finance and Investor Relations Contact: Sybella Stanley
Director Human Resources: Ian Fraser, age 47
Director Global Government Affairs; Vice Chairman and Head Global Academic and Customer Relations, Elsevier: Youngsuk (Y.S.) Chi
Director Corporate Relations: Patrick Kerr
Manager Corporate Finance and Investor Relations Contact: James Statham
VP and Treasurer, Reed Elsevier Inc., and Investor Relations Contact, US: Kenneth (Ken) Fogarty
Auditors: Deloitte & Touche

LOCATIONS

HQ: Reed Elsevier Group plc
1-3 Strand
London WC2N 5JR, England
Phone: 44-20-7930-7077 **Fax:** 44-20-7166-5799
US HQ: 125 Park Ave., 23rd Fl., New York, NY 10017
US Phone: 212-309-8100 **US Fax:** 212-309-8187
Web: www.reedelsevier.com

2009 Sales

	% of total
North America	55
Europe	
UK	8
The Netherlands	4
Other Europe	19
Other regions	14
Total	**100**

PRODUCTS/OPERATIONS

2009 Sales

	% of total
LexisNexis	42
Elsevier	33
Reed Business Information	14
Reed Exhibitions	11
Total	**100**

2009 Sales

	% of total
Subscriptions	45
Circulation	28
Advertising	10
Exhibition	10
Other	7
Total	**100**

Selected Operations

Legal, corporate, and government information
    LexisNexis

Scientific and medical publishing
    Elsevier
        Elsevier Health Sciences
        Elsevier Science & Technology

Trade exhibitions and conferences
    Reed Exhibitions

COMPETITORS

Advance Publications
Dow Jones
IHS
Informa
John Wiley
McGraw-Hill
Nielsen Holdings
Pearson plc
Penton Media
Thomson Reuters
United Business Media
Verlagsgruppe Georg von Holtzbrinck
Wolters Kluwer

HISTORICAL FINANCIALS

Company Type: Joint venture

Income Statement				FYE: December 31
	REVENUE ($ mil.)	NET INCOME ($ mil.)	NET PROFIT MARGIN	EMPLOYEES
12/09	9,669	629	6.5%	33,300
12/08	7,720	695	9.0%	32,800
12/07	9,151	2,402	26.2%	31,500
12/06	10,570	1,224	11.6%	36,800
12/05	8,888	798	9.0%	36,500
Annual Growth	2.1%	(5.8%)	—	(2.3%)

2009 Year-End Financials

Debt ratio: 229.0%   Current ratio: —
Return on equity: —   Long-term debt ($ mil.): 6,415
Cash ($ mil.): —

Net Income History

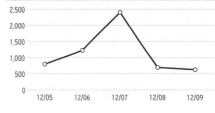

Renault

In Renault's road race against rival Peugeot Citroën to be France's dominant automaker, second place will have to *deux*. Renault manufactures and markets vehicles under three brands: Renault, Dacia, and Renault Samsung Motors (Renault holds an 80% stake to Samsung Group's 20%). Renault's small to midsize range vehicles include brands such as Clio, Laguna, Mégane, Modus, Logan, Espace, Twingo, and Scénic; light commercial vehicles include Kangoo Express, Trafic, and Master. Renault holds a 93% stake in Automobile Dacia (Romania's leading automaker), and a 44% stake in Nissan Motor, which is known as the Renault-Nissan Alliance.

Renault ceased being French-centric over a decade ago when it entered into an alliance with Japanese automaker Nissan. France may remain the industrial heart of Renault, but its cars are now produced in 18 different countries, with more than 20 of its manufacturing plants located beyond its borders. The synergies between Renault and Nissan have produced a reciprocal benefit — Renault has adopted a better production system with Nissan's support, and Nissan has embraced better cost-control measures practiced by Renault. The alliance gives both companies a competitive edge over other automakers through shared technologies and platforms.

The alliance also allows Renault and Nissan to tackle projects such as electric vehicles, the cost of which would be prohibitive if each company had to bear it separately. The Renault-Nissan Alliance is making a tandem expansion into emerging countries such as Russia, India, and Brazil; together, the companies can grow on a bigger scale and expand at a faster rate.

In an attempt to get a larger piece of the growing car market in India, Renault has announced plans to introduce six new models in that country between 2001 and 2013. To get a larger chunk of the rapidly growing Russian car market, Renault-Nissan forged an alliance with Russian carmaker AvtoVAZ in 2008.

Renault-Nissan entered yet another collaborative agreement in 2010 when it joined up with Daimler to give Toyota and Volkswagen a run for their money. Renault will provide its small-car technology to Daimler for use in certain of its models. As part of the deal, Renault and Nissan will each take a 1.55% share in Daimler, while Daimler will hold a 3.1% stake in each of them.

Serving as president, chairman, and CEO of both Renault and Nissan, Carlos Ghosn — nicknamed "Le Cost Killer" based on his talent for

turning red ink black — has pulled both companies' feet out of the fire.

Amid the economic crisis, Renault won a government package in early 2009 that includes a five-year, €7.5 billion ($9.8 billion) low-interest loan under the condition that it would not lay off any more employees, at least through the first year, or close factories.

The French government holds about a 15% stake in Renault.

HISTORY

In the Paris suburb of Billancourt in 1898, 21-year-old Louis Renault assembled a motorized vehicle with a transmission box of his own design. Louis and his brothers, Marcel and Fernand, established Renault Freres and produced the world's first sedan in 1899. Marcel died in a racing accident (1903) and Fernand left the business (1908), leaving Louis in sole possession of the company. He renamed it La Société Louis Renault in 1908.

In 1914 a fleet of 600 Paris taxis shuttled French troops to fight the Germans in the Battle of the Marne. Renault also built light tanks and airplane engines. Between world wars Renault expanded into trucks, tractors, and aircraft engines. Renault sustained heavy damage in WWII, but Louis Renault operated the remaining Paris facilities for the Germans during their occupation of France. After the liberation of Paris, he was accused of collaboration and died in prison while awaiting trial in 1944. The de Gaulle government nationalized Renault in 1945 and gave the company its present name.

Worldwide economic growth aided Renault's postwar comeback. The company achieved its greatest success in high-volume, low-cost cars such as the 4 CV in the late 1940s and 1950s, the Renault 4 in the 1960s and 1970s, and the Renault 5 in the 1970s and 1980s.

In 1979 Renault acquired 46% of American Motors Corporation (AMC). In the early 1980s AMC fared poorly, and Renault suffered from a worldwide slump in auto sales, an aging product line, and stiff competition from Japanese carmakers. Decreasing sales, an unwieldy bureaucracy, and above-average wages contributed to a $1.5 billion loss in 1984.

Georges Besse took over Renault in 1985 and trimmed employment by 20,000. When Besse was assassinated by terrorists in 1986, Raymond Levy assumed his role and continued his policies, laying off 30,000 more workers and selling AMC to Chrysler (1987).

Renault and Volvo agreed to extensive cross-ownership and cooperation in 1990. In 1994 Renault swapped its 25% stake in Volvo's car division for the latter's 45% stake in Renault's troubled truck unit. (Volvo sold its remaining 11% stake in 1997.)

The French government reduced its share of the company from 80% to 52% in 1995 and to 44% the following year. In 1997 it shut down a Belgian plant that employed more than 3,000 workers and fired a similar number of employees in France. In 1999 Renault paid $5.4 billion for a 37% stake in Nissan.

Early in 2000 Renault sold its Mack truck unit to AB Volvo in exchange for a 15% stake in the Swedish truck maker.

In 2001 Renault announced plans to further strengthen ties with Nissan, increasing its stake in Nissan to 44% while granting Nissan a 15% stake in Renault. The French Finance Ministry also announced that it would reduce the French government's stake in Renault from 44% to 25% through a future public offering. The two deals were completed in 2002. In 2003 the French government further reduced its stake in Renault from 25% to about 15%.

In 2005 Carlos Ghosn was appointed as CEO; he also remained as CEO with Nissan. Ghosn had been Renault's chief cost cutter since 1999. Ghosn made public his plans to revamp Renault by slashing the number of suppliers, close five plants, and cut its workforce by 14%.

In 2006 Renault called an emergency board meeting to consider a proposal by billionaire General Motors investor Kirk Kerkorian. Kerkorian suggested GM, Renault, and Nissan form a three-way global automotive alliance. In the midst of the 2006 Paris Auto Show the parties announced there would be no three-way alliance.

EXECUTIVES

Chairman and CEO: Carlos Ghosn, age 56
Honorary President: Louis Schweitzer, age 68
COO; Leader, Europe Management Committee: Patrick Pélata, age 54
EVP and CFO; Chairman and CEO, RCI Banque: Dominique Thormann, age 56
EVP and Leader Asia Africa Management Committee: Katsumi Nakamura, age 57
EVP Engineering and Quality: Odile Desforges, age 60
EVP Sales and Marketing; Leader of the Europe Region Management Committee; President, Renault Retail Group: Jérôme Stoll, age 56
EVP Plan, Product Planning, and Programs: Philippe Klein, age 53
EVP Manufacturing and Logistics: Michel Gornet, age 63
SVP Global Marketing: Stephen Norman, age 56
SVP Group Human Resources: Gérard Leclercq, age 61
SVP Vehicle Engineering: Nadine Leclair, age 53
SVP Corporate Design: Laurens G. van den Acker, age 45
SVP Quality: Jean-Pierre Vallaude, age 58
SVP Communications: Marie-Françoise Damesin, age 53
SVP Global Supply Chain: Michel Faivre-Duboz, age 59
SVP Legal Department and Public Affairs: Christian Husson, age 60
Corporate Secretary General: Laurence Dors, age 54
Expert Fellow: Christian Deleplace
Auditors: Deloitte & Associés

LOCATIONS

HQ: Renault
13-15 quai Le Gallo
92513 Boulogne-Billancourt, France
Phone: 33-1-76-84-04-04
Web: www.renault.com

2009 Sales

	% of total
Europe	78
Americas	8
Euromed (Algeria, Morocco, Romania, Turkey)	7
Asia & Africa	7
Total	**100**

PRODUCTS/OPERATIONS

2009 Sales

	% of total
Automobiles	96
Sales financing	4
Total	**100**

Selected Products

Automobiles
  Clio
  Duster
  Espace
  Fluence
  Kangoo
  Koleos
  Laguna
  Logan
  Master
  Mégane (Coupé, Grand Tour, Renault Sport, Coupé-Cabriolet, GT)
  Modus
  Safrane
  Sandero
  Scenic
  Symbol/Thalia
  Trafic
  Twingo
  Wind
Light Commercial Vehicles
  Master
  New Kangoo Express
  Trafic

COMPETITORS

BMW	Mahindra
Chrysler	Mazda
Daimler	Peugeot
Fiat	Saab Automobile
Ford Motor	Suzuki Motor
General Motors	Tata Motors
Honda	Toyota
Isuzu	Volkswagen
Kia Motors	Volvo Car Corp.

HISTORICAL FINANCIALS

Company Type: Public

Income Statement

FYE: December 31

	REVENUE ($ mil.)	NET INCOME ($ mil.)	NET PROFIT MARGIN	EMPLOYEES
12/09	48,316	(4,397)	—	121,422
12/08	53,266	844	1.6%	129,068
12/07	59,880	4,024	6.7%	130,179
12/06	54,788	3,883	7.1%	128,893
12/05	48,957	4,089	8.4%	126,584
Annual Growth	**(0.3%)**	**—**	**—**	**(1.0%)**

2009 Year-End Financials

Debt ratio: —	No. of shares (mil.): 285
Return on equity: —	Dividends
Cash ($ mil.): 11,499	Yield: 0.0%
Current ratio: 0.95	Payout: —
Long-term debt ($ mil.): —	Market value ($ mil.): 14,783

Stock History

Euronext Paris: RNO

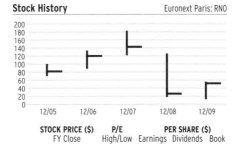

	STOCK PRICE ($) FY Close	P/E High/Low		PER SHARE ($) Earnings	Dividends	Book Value
12/09	51.88	—	—	(17.38)	0.00	82.85
12/08	26.15	40	6	3.13	1.69	93.78
12/07	142.79	12	8	14.97	—	111.46
12/06	120.06	9	6	14.55	—	95.93
12/05	81.60	6	5	15.49	—	79.79
Annual Growth	**(10.7%)**	**—**	**—**	**—**	**—**	**0.9%**

Repsol YPF

The sun shines on Repsol YPF, Spain's largest oil company. A fully integrated oil and gas company, it operates in Latin America, the Middle East, and North Africa. The firm controls YPF, Argentina's #1 oil company, and has operations in about 30 other countries. Repsol YPF operates five refineries in Spain and one in Peru and produces chemicals, plastics, and polymers. It sells gas under the brands Campsa, Petronor, and Repsol at more than 6,000 service stations in Europe and Latin America. It is one of Spain's largest sellers of liquefied petroleum gas and liquefied natural gas. In 2008 Repsol YPF reported estimated proved reserves of 2.2 billion barrels of oil equivalent.

Repsol YPF plans to invest more than €21 billion (more than $26 billion) over the next few years in its operations, particularly in exploration and production, including its Spanish refineries, which will receive an investment of about €4 billion (more than $4 billion).

To meet growing demand, in 2008 the company announced plans to double its Cartagena (Spain) refinery production capacity from 100,000 barrels of oil per day to 220,000 barrels of oil per day. That year Repsol YPF sold its retail fuel operations in Brazil, Chile, and Ecuador as part of its strategy of divesting non-core assets.

The company acquired its current name and expanded its reserves significantly with the purchase of YPF, Argentina's leading oil company. To comply with its agreement with Argentina's government to divest 11% of the company's refining and marketing assets in Argentina, Repsol YPF slashed 700 of its stations and a refinery in a $1 billion asset swap with Brazil's Petrobras.

HISTORY

Repsol YPF, officially created as Repsol in 1987, is actually the result of efforts that began as early as the 1920s to organize Spain's fragmented energy industry.

Following an era of dependency on foreign investment prior to and during Francisco Franco's dictatorship (1939-75), Spain began reorganizing its energy industry. In 1979 it set up the Instituto Nacional de Hidrocarburos, which in 1981 incorporated all public-sector firms involved in gas and oil under one government agency.

Repsol was formed six years later to provide central management to a Spanish oil company that could compete in the unified European market. The government chose the name Repsol, after a well-known brand of Spanish lubricant products. The firm was charged with pursuing a global strategy to bring together all levels of the industry.

In 1989 Repsol offered 26% of the firm on the Madrid and New York stock exchanges, raising more than $1 billion. That year Repsol increased its marine fleet with the purchase of the Naviera Vizcaina shipping company and bought Carless Refining & Marketing, a UK business with a chain of 500 service stations operating mainly under the Anglo brand. Although Spain was opening its doors to foreign investment, the Spanish government maintained control over the country's energy industry, including a tightly guarded distribution network under state-controlled Campsa. Campsa oversaw a marketing/logistics system of pipelines, storage terminals, and sales outlets.

The European Community demanded that Spain open its markets to other EC members, forcing Campsa in 1991 to divide its 3,800 gasoline stations among its four major shareholders: Cepsa (Spain's largest private refiner), Petromed, Ertoil, and Repsol. Repsol gained 66% of the logistical network and use of the Campsa brand name.

Repsol and Spanish bank La Caixa merged their interests in natural gas in 1992 to create Gas Natural, a new gas distributor. That year the Spanish government began reducing its majority holding, and by 1996 its stake had dwindled to 10%. (It sold its remaining stock in 1997.)

Expanding its South American operations, Repsol acquired control of Argentinian oil company Astra CAPSA and a Peruvian oil refinery in 1996. That year Repsol purchased a 30% stake in the Tin Fouye Tabankort field in Algeria.

In 1999 Repsol paid $2 billion for a 15% stake in giant oil company YPF, which was auctioned off by Argentina's government. After acquiring another 83% of YPF for $13.2 billion, Repsol changed its name to Repsol YPF. To help pay down debt incurred in the acquisition, Repsol YPF sold its UK North Sea oil and gas operations to US independent Kerr-McGee for $555 million in 2000. That year the company (as part of its commitment to Argentina's government after acquiring YPF) agreed to swap some of its Argentine refining and marketing assets for Brazilian oil and gas operations owned by Petrobras.

In 2002 Repsol YPF sold oil and gas assets in Indonesia to CNOOC for about $585 million.

Former chairman of Spain's top gas supplier Gas Natural S.A., Antonio Brufau, replaced Alfonso Cortina de Alcocer as chairman of Repsol in 2004.

In 2006 the company acquired BP's 28% stake in the Shenzi field in the Gulf of Mexico. The next year Repsol YPF began selling minority stakes in YPF to generate cash to support the Argentine company's growth.

EXECUTIVES

Chairman and CEO: Antonio Brufau Niubó, age 62
First Vice Chairman: Luis Fernando del Rivero Asensio, age 61
Second Vice Chairman: Isidre Fainé Casas, age 67
Vice Chairman Repsol Foundation:
Enrique Locutura Rupérez
COO: Miguel Martínez San Martín
CFO: Fernando Ramírez Mazarredo
General Counsel, Secretary, and Director:
Luis Suárez de Lezo Mantilla, age 59
Executive Managing Director, Upstream:
Nemesio Fernández-Cuesta Luca de Tena
Executive Managing Director, Downstream:
Pedro Fernández Frial
Executive Managing Director, YPF: Antonio Gomis Sáez
Executive Managing Director HR and Organization:
Cristina Sanz Mendiola
Executive Director La Caixa: Jaume Giró Ribas
Head Exploration and Production, Brazil: Javier Moro
Director Communication Services and Country Coordination: Manuel Hermógenes Rollano
Corporate Director Communications:
Begoña Elices García
Auditors: Deloitte SL

LOCATIONS

HQ: Repsol YPF, S.A.
Paseo de la Castellana, 278-280
28046 Madrid, Spain
Phone: 34-91-348-81-00   **Fax:** 34-91-314-28-21
Web: www.repsol.com

PRODUCTS/OPERATIONS

2009 Sales

	% of total
Downstream	65
YPF	17
Gas Natural SDG	10
Upstream	6
LNG	2
Total	**100**

COMPETITORS

Anadarko Petroleum
Apco Oil and Gas International
BHP Billiton
BP
Devon Energy
Endesa S.A.
Eni
Exxon Mobil
IBERDROLA
Imperial Oil
Koch Industries, Inc.
Marathon Oil
Murphy Oil
Noble Energy
Norsk Hydro ASA
Occidental Petroleum
PEMEX
PETROBRAS
Petrobras Argentina
Petróleos de Venezuela
Pioneer Natural Resources
RasGas
Royal Dutch Shell
TOTAL

HISTORICAL FINANCIALS

Company Type: Public

Income Statement

FYE: December 31

	REVENUE ($ mil.)	NET INCOME ($ mil.)	NET PROFIT MARGIN	EMPLOYEES
12/09	70,273	2,500	3.6%	41,014
12/08	85,944	3,999	4.7%	36,302
12/07	76,591	4,686	6.1%	36,700
12/06	67,811	4,125	6.1%	36,931
12/05	57,065	3,708	6.5%	35,909
Annual Growth	**5.3%**	**(9.4%)**	**—**	**3.4%**

2009 Year-End Financials

Debt ratio: 77.2%
Return on equity: 8.8%
Cash ($ mil.): 3,308
Current ratio: 1.23
Long-term debt ($ mil.): 22,087
No. of shares (mil.): 1,221
Dividends
  Yield: 4.9%
  Payout: 101.1%
Market value ($ mil.): 46,648

Stock History

NYSE: REP

	STOCK PRICE ($) FY Close	P/E High/Low		PER SHARE ($) Earnings	Dividends	Book Value
12/09	38.21	22	11	1.85	1.87	23.42
12/08	30.32	20	7	3.14	0.56	23.21
12/07	52.44	16	12	3.84	0.43	22.29
12/06	45.52	14	10	3.38	0.77	18.85
12/05	34.83	13	9	3.03	0.30	15.83
Annual Growth	**2.3%**	**—**	**—**	**(11.6%)**	**58.0%**	**10.3%**

Ricoh Company

Ricoh may be best known for its imaging equipment, but the company is more than just another copycat. One of the world's leading manufacturers of copiers and supplies, Ricoh also makes fax machines, scanners, and printers. Other products from the company, which has more than 250 subsidiaries and affiliates worldwide, include digital cameras, servers, software for its products, semiconductors, printed circuit boards, thermal paper labels, and optical data storage drives. Ricoh is represented in the US and across the Americas by its Ricoh Americas subsidiary and distributes and services office equipment through IKON Office Solutions.

The company acquired IKON (through Ricoh Americas) for about $1.6 billion in 2008. The purchase significantly expanded Ricoh's international operations, particularly in North America and Europe, and broadened its customer base in the corporate and government markets.

Ricoh continues to develop its networked imaging and connectivity products, which include laser printers, copiers, and document management software and systems. In 2011 it will expand into a new product division, digital projectors.

Although printers and office equipment are Ricoh's biggest moneymakers, the company has moved beyond its core products into related services, including systems customization, integration, managed services, and IT service. Services allow the company to continue to earn revenue from customers well after the equipment is purchased. Ideally, it wants to offer facility management services that operate centralized printing centers and IT consulting services. For the consumer market, in 2009 it launched a beta version of an online storage service called quanp, short for "quantum paper." The service, which includes a Windows-based client program that enables visual search tools, lets users upload, store, and access digital photos and other content.

To further streamline its global operations, Ricoh consolidated seven sales companies and its corporate marketing group into one subsidiary, called Ricoh Japan Corporation, in 2010. It also took complete control of InfoPrint Solutions, a manufacturer and distributor of high-volume production printers, which began as a joint venture with IBM. In India, it spent about $1 million to open more offices and grow its South Asia business. Ricoh leases its equipment through a separate publicly traded company in Japan named Ricoh Leasing Co., Ltd.

HISTORY

Ricoh began in 1936 as the Riken Kankoshi Company, making photographic paper. With founder Kiyoshi Ichimura at the helm, the company soon became the leader in Japan's sensitized paper market. It changed its name to Riken Optical Company in 1938 and started making cameras. Two years later it produced its first camera under the Ricoh brand.

By 1954 Ricoh cameras were Japan's #1 seller and also popular abroad. The next year it entered the office machine market with its compact mimeograph machine. Ricoh followed that in 1960 with an offset duplicator.

Ricoh built its business in the 1960s with a range of office machines, including reproduction and data processing equipment and retrieval systems. The company began establishing operations overseas, including US subsidiary Ricoh Industries U.S.A. in 1962. The US unit started marketing cameras but found greener pastures in the copier industry, where Ricoh's products were sold under the Pitney Bowes and Savin brand names. It changed its name to Ricoh Company in 1963. Two years later Ricoh entered the emerging field of office computers and introduced an electrostatic copier. In 1968 Ichimura died, and Mikio Tatebayashi took over as president for the next eight years.

During the 1970s Ricoh debuted the first high-speed fax machine and began consolidating its network outside Japan. In 1973 it established a second US subsidiary — Ricoh Electronics — to assemble copier supplies and parts, becoming the first Japanese company to produce copiers in the US. It released a plain-paper copier in 1975, followed the next year by a daisy wheel printer and its first word processor. Tatebayashi died in 1976 and was replaced by Takeshi Ouye as president. Subsidiary Rapicom was established in 1978 in Japan to develop fax products.

Throughout the 1970s Savin and Pitney Bowes continued to brand and sell Ricoh-made products in the US, but in the early 1980s Ricoh started marketing products under its own name. It introduced a PC and its first laser printer in 1983. By the next year Ricoh had 7% of the US copier market. Other products introduced in the 1980s included a color copier, minicomputers developed with AT&T, and (in Japan) a digital copier that could also be used as an input/output station for electronic filing systems. Ricoh's overseas sales continued to grow in the late 1980s and for a while exceeded its domestic sales. In 1983 Ouye turned over leadership of the company to Hiroshi Hamada.

Ricoh founded Tailien Optical (Shenzhen) Co. Ltd. in 1992 to make compact camera parts. As the 1990s progressed, the company increasingly pushed products based on digital technologies.

Ricoh won licensing fees from Samsung Electronics in a 1995 dispute over fax machine patents. Seeking to boost international sales, it bought Savin in the US and Gestetner Holdings (later renamed NRG Group) in Europe that year. The next year Hamada was named chairman and CEO; Masamitsu Sakurai became president.

The company's push during the mid-1990s to increase overseas sales paid off. Amid an Asian economic crisis, Ricoh's overall sales remained relatively stable, while sales of its copiers outside Japan increased 20% and 9% for 1998 and 1999, respectively.

In 2000 the company reorganized its US operations and consolidated its European distribution centers. Early the following year Ricoh boosted its push into the US market with its acquisition of office equipment supplier Lanier Worldwide for about $250 million. Despite shaky world economic conditions, in fiscal 2002 Ricoh saw growth in sales and profits, with strong overseas sales making up for slightly lowered revenues from Japan.

Ricoh augmented its printer business by acquiring Hitachi Printing Solutions in 2004. Two years later Shiro Kondo became president and CEO of Ricoh, and Hamada stepped up to the chairmanship. In 2007 the company's Ricoh Europe subsidiary acquired the European operations of Danka Business Systems. The purchase included 16 companies in 12 countries.

EXECUTIVES

Chairman: Masamitsu Sakurai, age 68
President, CEO, and Director: Shiro Kondo, age 61
Deputy President and Director: Katsumi (Kirk) Yoshida, age 64
Deputy President and Director: Koichi Endo, age 66
EVP, CFO, CIO, Chief Strategy Officer, and Director; General Manager, CRGP, Global Marketing Support Division, and Trade Affairs and Export and Import Administration Division: Zenji Miura, age 60
EVP, CTO, and Director; President, Ricoh Innovation: Kiyoshi Sakai, age 64
EVP, Chief Human Resources Officer, and Director; General Manager, Personnel Division: Takashi Nakamura, age 64
EVP, Chief Marketing Officer, and Director: Masayuki Matsumoto
EVP and Director; General Manager, Global Marketing Group: Kazunori Azuma, age 61
EVP and CFO, Americas: Martin Brodigan, age 48
SVP; President, Ricoh Leasing: Sadahiro Arikawa, age 61
SVP; General Manager, Corporate Technology Development Group; Chairman, Ricoh Software Research Center: Hiroshi Kobayashi, age 62
SVP; General Manager, Production Business Group: Kenichi Kanemaru, age 57
SVP; General Manager, Research and Development Group: Terumoto Nonaka, age 62
SVP; General Manager, Marketing Group: Kenji Hatanaka, age 64
SVP; General Manager, Americas Marketing Group: Kazuo (Kevin) Togashi, age 60
SVP; General Manager, Office Business Planning Center: Norio Tanaka, age 62
Chairman and CEO, Americas: Matthew J. (Matt) Espe, age 51
Auditors: KPMG AZSA & Co.

LOCATIONS

HQ: Ricoh Company, Ltd.
8-13-1 Ginza, Chuo-ku
Tokyo 104-8222, Japan
Phone: 81-3-6278-5254   **Fax:** 81-3-3543-9329
US HQ: 5 Dedrick Place, West Caldwell, NJ 07006
US Phone: 973-882-2000   **US Fax:** 973-882-2506
Web: www.ricoh.com

2010 Sales

	$ mil.	% of total
Japan	13,693	50
Americas	6,021	22
Europe	4,979	18
Other countries	2,645	10
Adjustments	(5,586)	—
Total	**21,752**	**100**

PRODUCTS/OPERATIONS

2010 Sales

	$ mil.	% of total
Imaging & Solutions		
Imaging solutions	16,303	75
Network system solutions	2,947	14
Industrial products	1,093	5
Other	1,337	6
Adjustments	72	—
Total	**21,752**	**100**

Selected Products

Imaging & Solutions
Imaging Solutions
Diazo copiers
Digital duplicators
Digital monochrome and color copiers
Fax machines
Imaging supplies and consumables
Wide-format copiers
Printing systems (laser, multifunction)
Scanners
Network System Solutions
Document management software
Networking and applications software
Network systems
Personal computers
Servers
Services and support
Industrial
Electronic components
Measuring equipment
Optical equipment
Semiconductor devices
Thermal media
Other
Digital cameras and other photographic equipment
Financing and logistics services
Optical disks

COMPETITORS

3M
Brother Industries
Canon
CASIO COMPUTER
Dell
Eastman Kodak
Epson
Fuji Xerox
FUJIFILM
Hewlett-Packard
Hitachi
Konica Minolta
Kyocera Mita
Lexmark
NEC
Nikon
Océ
Oki Electric
Olympus
Panasonic Corp
SANYO
Sharp Corp.
Toshiba
Xerox

HISTORICAL FINANCIALS

Company Type: Public

Income Statement

FYE: March 31

	REVENUE ($ mil.)	NET INCOME ($ mil.)	NET PROFIT MARGIN	EMPLOYEES
3/10	21,752	301	1.4%	108,525
3/09	21,501	67	0.3%	110,000
3/08	22,254	1,067	4.8%	83,456
3/07	17,564	949	5.4%	81,939
3/06	16,428	833	5.1%	76,150
Annual Growth	**7.3%**	**(22.5%)**	**—**	**9.3%**

2010 Year-End Financials

Debt ratio: 52.9%   No. of shares (mil.): 726
Return on equity: 2.9%   Dividends
Cash ($ mil.): 2,612   Yield: 2.1%
Current ratio: 1.73   Payout: 85.0%
Long-term debt ($ mil.): 5,553   Market value ($ mil.): 11,428

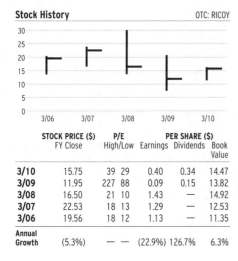

	STOCK PRICE ($)	P/E	PER SHARE ($)		
	FY Close	High/Low	Earnings	Dividends	Book Value
3/10	15.75	39 29	0.40	0.34	14.47
3/09	11.95	227 88	0.09	0.15	13.82
3/08	16.50	21 10	1.43	—	14.92
3/07	22.53	18 13	1.29	—	12.53
3/06	19.56	18 12	1.13	—	11.35
Annual Growth	(5.3%)	— —	(22.9%)	126.7%	6.3%

Rio Tinto

Rio Tinto is on the lookout for pay dirt. Rio Tinto Limited, one of the world's largest mining operations (along with BHP Billiton and Vale), is the Australian half of dual-listed sister companies, with Rio Tinto plc taking up residence in London. Although each company trades separately, the two Rio Tintos operate as one business. Rio Tinto mines iron, copper, uranium, industrial minerals (borax, salt, talc), gold, and diamonds. It also produces aluminum products through Rio Tinto Alcan. The company sells globally, but the majority of its operations are located in Australia and North America.

By focusing on large-scale, long-life mining operations, Rio Tinto has tried to weather commodity prices that have dipped and risen over several years. Like its rivals, the company continues to seek acquisitions as it cuts costs and improves productivity. Rio Tinto's tight-fisted operating style, while providing exceptional margins for its industry, has drawn the ire of unions, which have been critical of the company's employment and environmental records.

In 2007 Rio Tinto made a successful $38 billion offer to buy Alcan, then the world's #3 aluminum producer. That came not long after Alcoa, #2 in the world, had offered $33 billion. The deal combined Rio Tinto's own aluminum operations with Alcan's to form the new world leader, Rio Tinto Alcan, based in Canada.

After that acquisition, Rio Tinto announced a major divestment program. In early 2008 it sold stakes in two North American properties to Hecla Mining and Barrick Gold. The properties had been a part of Kennecott Minerals and netted Rio Tinto about $2.5 billion. Later that year the company spun off most of its North American coal operations into a company called Cloud Peak Energy.

A further step in the divestment plan was taken in early 2009 when the company sold its undeveloped potash assets and a Brazilian iron ore mine to Vale for about $1.5 billion.

The company's most significant deals, though, have been the ones that didn't happen. In 2008 BHP Billiton approached Rio Tinto with an offer to buy its Anglo-Australian rival at a price that valued the company at nearly $150 billion. The combination would have created the world's largest minerals company and one of the largest companies of any sort in terms of market cap.

In an effort to obstruct BHP Billiton's takeover bid for Rio Tinto, in 2008 Alcoa and Aluminum Corporation of China (Chinalco) acquired 14% of Rio Tinto for $14 billion. Early the next year Chinalco stepped in with an offer to assist Rio Tinto out of a portion of its debt. The complicated arrangement would have given Rio Tinto $19.5 billion. Chinalco's stake in Rio Tinto would have been raised to 19% and the Chinese company would have had the right to name two members to Rio Tinto's Board.

However, the transaction — never popular with domestic investors — fell through.

HISTORY

Rio Tinto Limited began life as the Zinc Corporation in 1905 to recover zinc from the tailings of the silver and lead mines around Australia's mineral-rich Broken Hill area. The company expanded steadily, extending its operations into a wide range of mining and metallurgical activities, primarily in Australia. By 1914 it had changed its name to Consolidated Zinc Corporation. The company discovered the world's largest deposit of bauxite (1955) and formed Hamersley Holdings with Kaiser Steel (1962) to mine iron ore.

Rio Tinto plc (UK) began with mining operations in Spain in 1873. It sold most of its Spanish holdings in 1954 and branched out to Australia, Africa, and Canada. In 1962 Rio Tinto and Australia's Consolidated Zinc merged to form RTZ. The companies merged their Australian interests as a partially owned subsidiary, CRA (from Conzinc Riotinto of Australia).

In 1968 RTZ bought U.S. Borax, which was built on one of the earth's few massive boron deposits. (The use of boron in cleansers was widespread in the late 19th century.) A 1927 discovery in the Mojave Desert led to development of a large boron mine. Until its Turkish mine was nationalized, RTZ controlled the world's boron supply. It sold U.S. Borax's consumer products operations in 1988.

RTZ opened a large copper mine at Bougainville in Papua New Guinea in 1969. Subsidiary CRA discovered diamonds in Western Australia's Argyle region three years later. CRA then opened Australia's largest thermal-coal development at Blair Athol in 1984.

RTZ bought Kennecott Corporation in 1989 and expanded its copper operations. Kennecott had been formed by Stephen Birch and named for Robert Kennicott (a typo altered the spelling of the company's name); it had begun mining at Bingham Canyon, Utah, in 1904. Kennicott had died in Alaska while trying to establish an intercontinental telegraph line. Backed by J.P. Morgan and the Guggenheims, Birch also built a railroad to haul the ore. Kennecott merged its mine and railroad operations in 1915. Kennecott consolidated its hold on Chile's Braden copper mine (1925) and on the Utah Copper Company (1936) and other US mines. When copper prices slumped, British Petroleum's Standard Oil of Ohio subsidiary bought Kennecott (1981). In 1989 RTZ purchased British Petroleum's US mineral operations, including Kennecott.

By the 1990s RTZ and CRA (by then 49%-owned by RTZ) were increasingly competing for mining rights to recently opened areas of Asia and Latin America. RTZ sold the last of its non-mining holdings (building products group) in 1993. In 1995 RTZ brought CRA into its operations. Through Kennecott, RTZ purchased US coal mine operators Nerco, Cordero Mining Company, and Colowyo Coal Company. Also in 1995 the company acquired 13% of Freeport-McMoRan Copper & Gold (sold in 2004).

The RTZ and CRA company names were changed to Rio Tinto plc and Rio Tinto Limited, respectively, in 1997. In 1999 Rio Tinto bought 80% of Kestrel (coal, Australia) and increased its ownership of Blair Athol from 57% to 71%.

In 2000 CEO Leon Davis retired; his position passed to energy group executive Leigh Clifford. Davis accepted a position as non-executive deputy chairman (he retired from the board in 2005).

In 2001 Rio Tinto increased its holdings in Queensland Alumina, Coal & Allied Industries, and Palabora Mining, and it began developing the Hail Creek Coal Project in Australia, which is based on one of the largest coking coal deposits in the world. In 2003 Rio Tinto sold its 25% stake in Minera Alumbrera (Argentina) and Peak Gold Mine (Australia) to Wheaton River Minerals.

Tom Albanese succeeded Clifford in 2007.

EXECUTIVES

Chairman: Jan P. du Plessis, age 55
CEO and Board Member: Tom Albanese, age 51, $2,003,000 total compensation
Finance Director and Board Member: Guy R. Elliot, age 53, $1,433,000 total compensation
Global Head Legal: Debra A. Valentine, age 55, $1,415,000 total compensation
Global Head Human Resources: Hugo Bague, age 48, $1,448,000 total compensation
Global Head Secretarial Services and Company Secretary: Ben Mathews, age 42
Group Executive Technology and Innovation: Grant Thorne, age 59, $956,000 total compensation
Group Executive, Business Support and Operations: Bret Clayton, age 47, $1,331,000 total compensation
Chief Executive, Technology and Innovation: Preston Chiaro, age 56, $1,428,000 total compensation
Chief Executive, Iron Ore: Sam Walsh, age 59, $1,359,000 total compensation
Chief Executive, Aluminum: Oscar Y. L. Groeneveld, age 54
Chief Executive, Copper: Andrew Harding, age 43
Chief Executive, Energy: Doug Ritchie, age 53
Chief Executive, Diamonds: Keith Johnson
CEO, Rio Tinto Alcan: Jacynthe Côté, age 51
Managing Director; President, Simandou: David Smith
Global Practice Leader, Media Relations: Christina Mills
Auditors: PricewaterhouseCoopers

LOCATIONS

HQ: Rio Tinto Limited
120 Collins St., Level 33
Melbourne 3000, Australia
Phone: 61-3-9283-3333   **Fax:** 61-3-9283-3707
Web: www.riotinto.com

2009 Sales

	% of total
China	24
North America	23
Europe (except UK)	14
Japan	14
Other Asia	13
Australia	3
UK	3
Other	6
Total	**100**

PRODUCTS/OPERATIONS

2009 Sales

	% of total
Iron Ore	29
Aluminum	27
Energy	15
Copper	14
Diamonds & Minerals	6
Other	9
Total	**100**

Selected Holdings

Aluminum
  Bell Bay
  Boyne Island (59%, smelting)
  Queensland Alumina Ltd. (80%)
  Tiwai Point (79%, New Zealand)
  Weipa (Australia)

Iron Ore
  Hamersley Iron Pty. Ltd.
    Channar (60%)
    Marandoo
    Nammuldi
  Iron Ore Co. of Canada (59%)
  Robe River Iron Associates (53%)

Energy & Minerals
  Coal
    Bengalla (30%, Australia)
    Blair Athol Coal (71%)
    Hail Creek Coal (82%)
    Hunter Valley Operations (76%)
    Kestrel (80%)
    Mt Thorley (61%)
    Warkworth (42%)
  Rio Tinto Industrial Minerals
    Rio Tinto Iron & Titanium (titanium dioxide,
      Canada/South Africa)
    Rio Tinto Minerals (boron, salt, and talc;
      Argentina/Australia/US)

Copper & Diamonds
  Copper
    Escondida (30%, Chile)
    Grasberg (40%, Indonesia)
    Kennecott Utah Copper (US)
    Northparkes (80%)
    Palabora (58%, South Africa)
  Diamonds
    Argyle Diamond Mines
    Diavik (60%, Canada)

Gold
  Barneys Canyon (US)
  Bingham Canyon (US)
  Escondida (30%, Chile)
  Rawhide (51%, US)

COMPETITORS

Alcoa
ALROSA
Anglo American
AngloGold Ashanti
ASARCO
Barrick Gold
BHP Billiton
Cliffs Natural Resources
Codelco
CONSOL Energy
Fortescue Metals
Freeport-McMoRan
Glencore
Goldcorp
Grupo México
ITOCHU
Kaiser Aluminum
Marubeni
Newmont Mining
Norsk Hydro ASA
Recylex
RUSAL
Southern Copper
Teck
Vale

HISTORICAL FINANCIALS

Company Type: Public

Income Statement

FYE: December 31

	REVENUE ($ mil.)	NET INCOME ($ mil.)	NET PROFIT MARGIN	EMPLOYEES
12/09	41,825	5,335	12.8%	101,994
12/08	54,264	4,609	8.5%	74,734
12/07	29,700	7,312	24.6%	51,677
12/06	22,465	7,438	33.1%	31,854
12/05	19,033	5,215	27.4%	32,000
Annual Growth	**21.8%**	**0.6%**	**—**	**33.6%**

2009 Year-End Financials

Debt ratio: 50.5%
Return on equity: 16.6%
Cash ($ mil.): 4,233
Current ratio: 2.07
Long-term debt ($ mil.): 22,155
No. of shares (mil.): 1,214
Dividends
  Yield: 1.1%
  Payout: 29.8%
Market value ($ mil.): 90,891

Stock History

Australian: RIO

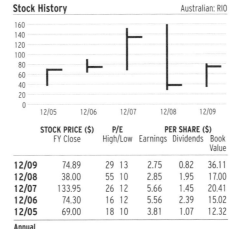

	STOCK PRICE ($) FY Close	P/E High/Low	PER SHARE ($) Earnings	Dividends	Book Value
12/09	74.89	29 13	2.75	0.82	36.11
12/08	38.00	55 10	2.85	1.95	17.00
12/07	133.95	26 12	5.66	1.45	20.41
12/06	74.30	16 12	5.56	2.39	15.02
12/05	69.00	18 10	3.81	1.07	12.32
Annual Growth	**2.1%**	**— —**	**(7.8%)**	**(6.4%)**	**30.9%**

Robert Bosch

Robert Bosch has spent more than a century establishing a name for really "boss" automobile and industrial equipment, as well as consumer goods and building systems. An industry leader, Bosch operates through 300 subsidiaries in 60 countries; its core lines include automotive systems, from diesel or hybrid drive to steering, starter motors and generators, electronics, and brakes. Subsidiary Bosch Rexroth makes electric, hydraulic, and pneumatic machinery for industrial use. Bosch Security makes various protection systems. Bosch also makes photovoltaic and wind-turbine components, heat pumps for buildings, and home appliances, through Bosch-Siemens Hausgerate.

The economic recession and financial credit crisis, coupled with weakened automotive and industrial demand (representing collectively 60% of Bosch revenues) have hurt revenues. Bosch has struggled to stay in the German public's favor by avoiding cuts in headcount, as it worked to shore up net earnings. As a result, the company is clear about extending its reach into the Asia/Pacific region. Bosch is equally intent upon expanding its portfolio of energy efficient, resource conserving products.

The company established a joint venture with DEUTZ AG (engines) and Eberspaecher GmbH (exhaust treatment technology and heating systems) to develop exhaust after-treatment systems for construction and agricultural machinery, as well as commercial vehicles. The JV is initially targeting sales to the United Arab Emirates, where urbanization has been accompanied by rising emissions.

A partnership with Samsung SDI called SB LiMotive (formed to compete in the lithium-ion auto battery market) is proving to be a positive investment, too. The joint venture scored its first contract in 2009 — a 10-year deal to supply lithium-ion batteries for trucks and buses to parts maker Delphi for use in hybrid commercial vehicles, starting in 2012.

Seeing the future of green technologies, Bosch acquired approximately 69% control of Aleo Solar AG, a module manufacturer late in 2009, along with Johanna Solar Technology GmbH earlier in the year. In 2008, it bought a majority stake in ersol Solar Energy, a German manufacturer of wafer-based mono- and polycrystalline silicon solar cells and thin-film solar modules.

Complementing its capabilities in sensors and micro-systems technology, Bosch acquired a majority stake in Health Hero Network, which develops software and equipment to monitor patients with chronic health conditions. Bosch Security Systems also snagged Canada's Extreme CCTV Inc.

Bosch is unique, not only in that it is large, with ties to almost every automobile enterprise in the world, but that a charitable foundation, Robert Bosch Stiftung, holds 92% of shares in the company. More than 90% of voting rights are held by Robert Bosch Industrietreuhand, an industrial trust.

HISTORY

Self-taught electrical engineer Robert Bosch opened a Stuttgart workshop in 1886 and the following year produced the world's first alternator for a stationary engine. In 1897 his company built the first automobile alternator. Later electrical automotive product launches included spark plugs (1902), starters (1912), and regulators (1913). Bosch believed in treating employees well and shortened their workday to eight hours (extraordinary for 1906).

US operations begun in 1909 were confiscated during WWI as part of a trade embargo against Germany. Bosch survived the German depression of the 1920s, introduced power tools (1928) and appliances (1933), and bought Blaupunkt (car radios, 1933). Industrial and military demand for the company's products continued from the 1930s until WWII. Bosch died in 1942 and left 90% of his company to charity.

Bosch suffered severe damage in WWII, and its US operations were again confiscated. It rebuilt after the war and enjoyed growing demand for its appliances and automotive products as postwar incomes increased worldwide. In 1963 Hans Merkle took the helm. Believing fuel efficiency and pollution control would be important issues in the future, Bosch invested heavily to develop automotive components that would raise gas mileage and lower emissions. The company made the world's first electronic fuel-injection (EFI) system in 1967. Also that year Bosch and Siemens (West Germany) formed Bosch-Siemens Hausgerate to make home appliances.

The oil crisis of the 1970s increased awareness of fuel efficiency and benefited sales of EFI systems. Buying a plant in Charleston, South Carolina, Bosch re-entered the US in 1974 to make fuel-injection systems. It introduced the first antilock braking system in 1978.

A 1984 strike against Bosch in Germany disrupted automobile production throughout Europe. In the late 1980s the company developed technology for multiplexing (employing one wire to replace many by using semiconductor controllers) in automobiles, established it as an industry standard, and licensed it to chip makers Intel (US), Philips (the Netherlands), and Motorola (US). Throughout the 1980s and into the 1990s, Bosch acquired various telecommunications companies.

In 1993 Bosch's sales dropped for the first time since 1967. In response, the company cut its workforce. In 1996 Bosch bought Emerson's half of joint venture S-B Power Tool Co., which makes Bosch, Dremel, and Skil brand tools. Further consolidating its position as a world leader in braking systems, Bosch also purchased AlliedSignal's struggling light-vehicle braking unit. The company sold its private mobile radio business to Motorola in 1997.

In 1998 the company's Bosch-Siemens Hausgerate joint venture opened a plant in the US and bought Masco's Thermador unit (cooktops, ovens, and ranges). In 1999 Bosch sold its US-based telecom unit to a joint venture of Motorola and Cisco Systems. The next year UK-based General Electric Company (now Marconi) bought the German operations of Bosch's telecom unit.

Early in 2000 the company sold its mobile-phone business to Siemens AG. That year the company's joint venture with Siemens bought Rexroth AG (Atecs Mannesmann AG's automation and packaging technology group) for about $9.2 billion. The new division was named Bosch Rexroth AG. In 2001 Bosch bought out Siemens' stake in Bosch Rexroth and consolidated its operations as a wholly owned subsidiary.

In 2006 Robert Bosch purchased Telex Communications for $420 million. Telex is a provider of audio, wireless, communications, and safety equipment with applications in large public places, including stadiums and airports.

EXECUTIVES

Chairman Supervisory Council: Hermann Scholl, age 75
Deputy Chairman Supervisory Council: Alfred Löckle
Chairman Management Board: Franz Fehrenbach, age 61
Deputy Chairman Management Board: Seigfried Dais, age 62
Member Management Board; Chairman, Automotive Group: Bernd Bohr, age 54
President, Solar Energy: Holger von Hebel, age 45
President, Diesel Systems: Gerhard Turner
President, Chassis Systems Brakes: Gerhard Steiger
President, Starter Motors and Generators: Ulrich Kirschner
President, Security Systems: Gert van Iperen
President, Power Tools: Stefan Hartung
President, Automotive Electronics: Christoph Kuebel
President, Drive and Control Technology: Albert Hieronimus
President, Car Multimedia: Uwe Thomas
President, Thermotechnology: Uwe Glock
President, Packaging Technology: Friedbert Klefenz
President, Electrical Drives: Udo Wolz
President, Chassis Systems Control: Werner Struth
President, Automotive Aftermarket: Robert Hanser
VP Corporate Communications: Uta-Micaela Dürig
Head Media Relations and Public Relations: Henrik Hannemann
Auditors: PwC Deutsche Revision AG

LOCATIONS

HQ: Robert Bosch GmbH
Postfach 106050
D-70049 Stuttgart, Germany
Phone: 49-711-811-0   **Fax:** 49-711-811-6630
US HQ: 2800 S. 25th Ave., Broadview, IL 60155
US Phone: 708-865-5200   **US Fax:** 708-865-6430
Web: www.bosch.com

2009 Sales

	% of total
Europe	62
Americas	18
Asia/Pacific	20
Total	**100**

PRODUCTS/OPERATIONS

2009 Sales

	% of total
Automotive technology	57
Consumer goods & building technology	30
Industrial technology	13
Total	**100**

Selected Divisions and Products

Automotive Technology
  Car multimedia
  Chassis systems brakes
  Chassis systmes control
  Diesel systems
  Electrical drives
  Gasoline systems
  Starter motors and generators
  Steering systems
Consumer Goods and Building Technology
  Household appliances
  Power tools
  Security systems
  Thermotechnology (gas-fired hot water heating systems)
Industrial Technology
  Drive and control technology
  Packaging technology
  Solar energy

COMPETITORS

BorgWarner
Dana Holding
Delphi Automotive
DENSO
Eaton
Electrolux
Emerson Electric
Federal-Mogul
GE
Honeywell International
Ingersoll-Rand
Johnson Controls
Magna International
Pioneer Corporation
Prestolite Electric
Senior plc
Snap-on
Stanley Black and Decker
Tenneco
Trane Inc.
Valeo
Visteon
Whirlpool

HISTORICAL FINANCIALS

Company Type: Private

Income Statement

FYE: December 31

	REVENUE ($ mil.)	NET INCOME ($ mil.)	NET PROFIT MARGIN	EMPLOYEES
12/09	54,711	(1,740)	—	270,687
12/08	63,607	524	0.8%	281,717
12/07	68,178	4,195	6.2%	271,265
12/06	57,632	2,863	5.0%	258,000
12/05	49,102	2,902	5.9%	249,000
Annual Growth	**2.7%**	**—**	**—**	**2.1%**

Net Income History

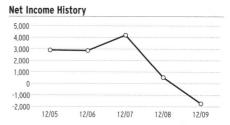

Roche Holding

Roche is on a roll. The company operates two segments, pharmaceuticals and diagnostics, and sells its products in some 180 countries. Roche's prescription drugs include cancer therapies MabThera/Rituxan and Avastin, anemia treatment NeoRecormon/Epogin, hepatitis drug Pegasys, transplant drug CellCept, macular degeneration therapy Lucentis, and Tamiflu, which is used to prevent and treat influenza, including pandemic strains. The company markets many of its bestsellers through subsidiary Genentech and affiliate Chugai Pharmaceutical. Roche's diagnostics arm offers advanced DNA tests, diabetes monitoring supplies, and point-of-care diagnostics used in a variety of health care settings.

To narrow its focus on pharmaceuticals and diagnostics, Roche has steadily dropped noncore operations over the last decade, including its consumer health and vitamin business, its fine chemicals business, and its fragrance and flavors business. In order to expand its pharmaceutical product offerings and stave off revenue losses from patent expirations and other competitive pressures, the company conducts widespread research and development programs. It also pursues growth in key therapeutic areas through acquisitions and partnerships.

Subsidiary Genentech is one of the world's largest biotech companies, and in 2009 Roche took control of the unit to ensure its future role in the biopharmaceuticals market. Roche completed a $46.8 billion tender offer to acquire the 44% of Genentech that it did not already own.

In another move to secure its global presence, in 2008 Roche upped its stake in Japan's Chugai Pharmaceutical from 50.1% to about 60%.

The company also invests heavily in internal R&D programs to expand its pipeline of future traditional small-molecule and biotechnology drug candidates. The bulk of Roche's research and development efforts are aimed at cardiovascular, metabolic, viral, oncology, inflammatory, autoimmune, and central nervous system disorders. The company has about 110 drugs in development, including efforts to expand indications for existing drugs. New products approved for marketing include Actemra/RoActemra, a rheumatoid arthritis medicine launched in the US in 2010 and in the EU in 2009.

In response to the fears over pandemic flu strains, Roche has ramped up its production of Tamiflu by increasing capacity at its own facilities and by forming international manufacturing partnerships.

Roche has agreed to acquire private US research firm Mirus Bio, which is developing RNAi (Ribonucleic Acid interference) technologies, for $125 million. The Mirus Bio purchase will fit in nicely with Roche's existing RNAi partnership with Alnylam Pharmaceuticals.

Not one to neglect its smaller divisions, Roche has been aggressively adding to its diagnostic testing stable through acquisitions as well. One major acquisition came with the $3.4 billion purchase of Ventana Medical Systems, a diagnostic firm focusing on cancers, in 2008. The purchase expanded the company's operations into tissue-based diagnostics.

Descendants of the founding Hoffmann and Oeri families own about half of the company. Fellow druggernaut Novartis owns 33%.

HISTORY

Fritz Hoffmann-La Roche, backed by family wealth, began making pharmaceuticals in a lab in Basel, Switzerland, in 1894. At the time, drug compounds were mixed at pharmacies and lacked uniformity. Hoffmann was not a chemist, but saw the potential for mass-produced, standardized, branded drugs.

By WWI, Hoffman had become successful, selling Thiocal (cough medicine), Digalen (digitalis extract), and other products on four continents. During the war, the Bolsheviks seized the firm's St. Petersburg, Russia, facility, and its Warsaw plant was almost destroyed. Devastated, Hoffmann sold company shares outside the family in 1919 and died in 1920.

As WWII loomed, Roche divided its holdings between F. Hoffman-La Roche and Sapac, which held many of Roche's foreign operations. US operations became more important during the war. Roche synthesized vitamins C, A, and E (eventually becoming the world's top vitamin maker) and built plants and research centers worldwide.

Roche continued to develop such successful products as tranquilizers Librium (1960) and Valium (1963) — the world's best-selling prescription drug prior to anti-ulcer successors Tagamet (SmithKline Beecham, now part of GlaxoSmithKline) and Prilosec (AstraZeneca). Roche made its first fragrance and flavor buy, Givaudan, in 1963.

In the 1970s, after several governments accused it of price-gouging on Librium and Valium, Roche agreed to price restraints. The company was fined for vitamin price-fixing in 1976. It was also rapped that year for its slow response to an Italian factory dioxin leak that killed thousands of animals and forced hundreds of families to evacuate.

Roche became one of the first drugmakers to sell another's products when it agreed to sell Glaxo's Zantac ulcer treatment in the US in 1982. The move let Roche maintain its large US sales force at the time when Valium went off patent, decimating the company's drug sales.

Roche acquired a product pipeline when it bought a majority stake in genetic engineering firm Genentech in 1990. In 1994 it bought the struggling Syntex, solidifying its position in North America. The company gained Aleve and other products in 1996 when it bought out its joint venture with Procter & Gamble.

In its biggest acquisition ever, Roche bought Corange in 1998 for $10.2 billion. In 1999 Roche announced it had located the gene that causes osteoarthritis.

Also in 1999 Roche agreed to a record-setting fine to end a US Justice Department investigation into Roche's role in an alleged vitamin price-fixing cartel; in 2000 it agreed to pay out again (to 22 states) to settle a lawsuit regarding the cartel. A related European Union probe the following year also found Roche guilty and levied heavy fines against the firm.

In 2000 two long-time Roche leaders, chairman Fritz Gerber and CFO Henri Meier, retired. The next year rival Swiss pharmaceuticals firm Novartis bought a 20% stake in Roche. In 2005 Roche sold its consumer health business, which included vitamins, the analgesic Aleve, and antacid Rennie, to Bayer HealthCare.

In 2006 Roche received approval for the application of its cancer drug MabThera (known as Rituxan in the US) in treating rheumatoid arthritis throughout the EU. It also put its postmenopausal osteoporosis treatment Boniva out on the EU and US markets at that time.

EXECUTIVES

Chairman: Franz B. Humer, age 64
Vice Chairman: André Hoffman, age 52
Vice Chairman: Bruno Gehrig, age 63
CEO Roche Group: Severin Schwan, age 42
COO, Pharma Division and Member Corporate Executive Committee: Pascal Soriot, age 51
CFO and Deputy Head Corporate Executive Committee: Erich Hunziker, age 57
Chief Compliance Officer: Urs Jaisli, age 54
Head Pharma Partnering and Member of the Enlarged Executive Committee: Daniel (Dan) Zabrowski, age 51
COO, Diagnostics Division and Member of the Executive Committee: Daniel O'Day, age 46
Head Business Area Roche Diabetes Care and Member of the Enlarged Corporate Executive Committee: Burkhard G. Piper, age 48
Head Group Communications and Member of the Enlarged Corporate Executive Committee: Stephan Feldhaus
Member of the Enlarged Corporate Executive Committee; Chairman, President, and CEO, Chugai: Osamu Nagayama, age 62
Member of the Enlarged Executive Committee; Head Roche Pharma Research and Early Development: Jean-Jacques Garaud, age 55
Head Human Resources: Silvia Ayyoubi, age 56
General Counsel: Gottlieb A. Keller, age 55
Head CEO Office and Secretary to the Corporate Executive Committee: Per-Olof Attinger, age 49
Secretary to the Corporate Executive Committee: René Kissling, age 44
Leader Investor Relations: Karl Mahler
Head Media Relations: Alexander Klauser
CEO, Genentech: Ian T. Clark, age 50
Auditors: KPMG Klynveld Peat Marwick Goerdeler SA

LOCATIONS

HQ: Roche Holding Ltd
    Grenzacherstrasse 124
    CH-4070 Basel, Switzerland
Phone: 41-61-688-11-11   **Fax:** 41-61-691-93-91
US HQ: 340 Kingsland St., Nutley, NJ 07110
US Phone: 973-235-5000   **US Fax:** 973-235-7605
Web: www.roche.com

2009 Sales

	% of total
Europe	37
North America	37
Asia	17
Latin America	6
Africa, Australia & Oceania	3
Total	**100**

PRODUCTS/OPERATIONS

2009 Sales

	% of total
Pharmaceuticals	
Oncology	42
Virology	12
Inflammatory, autoimmune & transplantation	6
Metabolic & bone	5
Renal anemia	3
Other	11
Diagnostics	21
Total	**100**

Selected Products

Top Selling
Activase/TNKase (cardiovascular)
Avastin (colorectal cancer, non-small cell lung cancer, breast cancer, kidney cancer)
Bonviva/Boniva (osteoporosis)
CellCept (transplantation)
Herceptin (HER2-positive breast cancer)
Lucentis (wet age-related macular degeneration)
MabThera/Rituxan (non-Hodgkin's lymphoma, rheumatoid arthritis, chronic lymphocytic leukemia)
Madopar (Parkinson's disease, restless leg syndrome)
NeoRecormon/Epogen (anemia, oncology)
Neutrogin (neutropenia associated with chemotherapy)
Nutropin (growth hormone deficiency)
Pegasys (hepatitis B and C)
Pulmozyme (cystic fibrosis)
Rocephin (bacterial infections)
Tamiflu (treatment and prevention of influenza)
Tarceva (advanced non-small cell lung cancer, advanced pancreatic cancer)
Valcyte/Cymevene (cytomegalovirus infection)
Xeloda (colorectal cancer, breast cancer, colon cancer)
Xenical (weight loss, weight control)
Xolair (asthma)

Other Products
Actemra/RoActemra (rheumatoid arthritis)
Anaprox (pain, fever, and inflammation)
Fuzeon (HIV)
Invirase (HIV)
Kytril (nausea and vomiting induced by chemotherapy or radiation therapy)
Mircera (predialysis)
Roferon-A (hepatitis C, hairy cell leukemia, AIDS-related Kaposi's sarcoma)
Valium (anxiety disorders)

COMPETITORS

Abbott Labs
Amgen
Astellas
AstraZeneca
Bayer AG
Becton, Dickinson
Biogen Idec
Bristol-Myers Squibb
Eli Lilly
Gilead Sciences
GlaxoSmithKline
Johnson & Johnson
Merck
Novartis
Pfizer
Sanofi-Aventis
Siemens Healthcare Diagnostics
Takeda Pharmaceutical

HISTORICAL FINANCIALS

Company Type: Public

Income Statement

	REVENUE ($ mil.)	NET INCOME ($ mil.)	NET PROFIT MARGIN	EMPLOYEES
12/09	49,279	7,499	15.2%	81,507
12/08	45,356	8,492	18.7%	67,695
12/07	42,939	8,664	20.2%	78,604
12/06	35,667	6,460	18.1%	74,372
12/05	26,985	5,114	19.0%	48,972
Annual Growth	16.2%	10.0%	—	13.6%

FYE: December 31

2009 Year-End Financials

Debt ratio: 490.7%
Return on equity: 30.5%
Cash ($ mil.): 2,353
Current ratio: 1.74
Long-term debt ($ mil.): 34,820

No. of shares (mil.): 863
Dividends
Yield: 0.0%
Payout: —
Market value ($ mil.): 150,410

Stock History

Pink Sheets: RHHBY

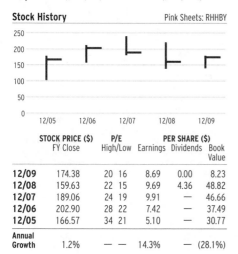

	STOCK PRICE ($) FY Close	P/E High/Low	PER SHARE ($) Earnings	Dividends	Book Value
12/09	174.38	20 16	8.69	0.00	8.23
12/08	159.63	22 15	9.69	4.36	48.82
12/07	189.06	24 19	9.91	—	46.66
12/06	202.90	28 22	7.42	—	37.49
12/05	166.57	34 21	5.10	—	30.77
Annual Growth	1.2%	— —	14.3%	—	(28.1%)

Rogers Communications

Canada calls on Rogers Communications. Its Rogers Wireless subsidiary is Canada's #1 mobile phone outfit with about 8 million subscribers across the country; services are sold under the Rogers Wireless and Fido brands. As the nation's #1 cable TV operator, the company also serves some 2.3 million viewers throughout eastern Canada through subsidiary Rogers Cable. Its cable unit also oversees the company's Internet and nationwide traditional and computer telephony services. Rogers Media oversees broadcasting and publishing operations and it holds the company's stake in Rogers Blue Jays Baseball Partnership, with interests in the Toronto Blue Jays major league baseball team and Rogers Centre sports complex.

Rogers' wireless business has grown to make up more than half of the company's sales ahead of its shrinking cable unit. Rogers Wireless provides mobile broadband data services such as Web access and streaming media in addition to standard voice and messaging services.

Rogers Cable provides broadband Internet access to about 1.6 million customers and, through its Rogers Home Phone division, it serves about 1 million callers with voice-over-cable and traditional home phone services. Rogers also offers a video-on-demand service under the Rogers on Demand brand. The cable unit also operates its retail arm, Rogers Retail. Formed in 2007, the retail unit sells Rogers-branded wireless and home entertainment products and services (cell phones, wireless plans, DVDs, and video games among others) from more than 400 stores.

Late in 2009 the company bought equity stakes in Quebec-based rival COGECO Inc. and its subsidiary Cogeco Cable to strengthen its position in the cable market. Rogers increased its 20% stake in COGECO to about one-third, and it took a nearly 20% stake of the cable subsidiary.

In 2010 Rogers agreed to acquire Atria Networks, an Ontario-based fiber-optic communications network operator, for $425 million in cash. The deal will add more than 1,000 clients to Rogers' list and increase the company's capacity to deliver datacentric network services to other business customers in the region.

Rogers Media owns more than 50 radio and TV broadcast stations. It also publishes 70 consumer magazines, trade publications, and directories. The subsidiary also owns a regional sports network (Rogers Sportsnet), a home shopping network (The Shopping Channel), 50% of HDTV producer and distributor Dome Productions, and numerous Internet holdings.

Founder, CEO, and company majority owner Ted Rogers died in December 2008. The company's president and COO, Nadir Mohamed, was named as his successor the following year.

HISTORY

Edward Rogers, at age 21, transmitted Canada's first radio signal across the Atlantic in 1921. He invented the first alternating current (AC) radio tube in 1925, which revolutionized the home-receiver industry.

Son of a wealthy businessman, Rogers founded Rogers Majestic in Toronto in the mid-1920s to make his radio tubes. He also established several radio stations, including CFRB ("Canada's First Rogers Batteryless"), which later commanded the country's largest audience.

In 1931 Rogers won the first experimental license to broadcast TV, but his businesses were sold when he died in 1939. His son Ted Rogers Jr. was only five at the time, but even as a youngster he showed business acumen, buying up shares of Standard Broadcasting. In his twenties he bought CHFI, a Toronto radio station that pioneered FM broadcasting.

Rogers moved into cable TV and in 1967 was awarded licenses for Toronto, Brampton, and Leamington. Rogers Cable TV expanded when it bought Canadian Cablevision (1979) and Premier Cablevision (1980). With the takeover of UA-Columbia Cablevision in 1981, Rogers became Canada's largest cable operator.

The firm also began pushing cellular phone service through subsidiary Rogers Cantel in 1985. (The carrier won a license for nationwide coverage in 1992.) In 1986 all of Rogers' holdings were combined to form Rogers Communications.

Rogers acquired a stake in telecom company Unitel in 1989. When it received permission to sell long-distance in 1992, Unitel geared up to take on monopoly Bell Canada. However, the venture wasn't successful, and Rogers walked away from its 32% stake in 1995.

Meanwhile, in 1994 Rogers acquired rival cable TV and publishing firm Maclean-Hunter. The next year it acquired Shaw Communications' Vancouver cable system and began providing Internet access. Rogers sold its 62% stake in Toronto Sun Publishing to management in 1996.

Expenses related to cable network upgrades and Cantel's development created operating losses for several years. To raise cash, in 1998 Rogers sold subsidiary Rogers Telecom to local phone startup MetroNet Communications and sold its home-security unit to Protection One.

In 1999 Microsoft paid $400 million for a 9% stake in the company; Rogers agreed to use Microsoft set-top box software and offer Microsoft's Web services to its customers. Also in 1999 AT&T and British Telecommunications (now BT Group) together bought a 33% stake in Cantel; Rogers' stake fell to 51%.

The next year Rogers agreed to buy Quebec cable operator Videotron. But media firm Quebecor, backed by pension fund manager Caisse, weighed in with a rival bid, and Rogers collected a breakup fee of about $160 million when Videotron terminated the companies' deal. Soon thereafter, the company announced the creation of Rogers Telecom (reusing the name), a unit set up to enter the telephone market.

Also in 2000 Rogers purchased an 80% stake in the Toronto Blue Jays baseball team for $112 million (it later acquired the remaining 20%). The next year Rogers gained another 75,000 cable subscribers with the acquisition of Cable Atlantic.

In 2001 AT&T Wireless bought out British Telecom's stake in Rogers Wireless, raising their ownership to a third. Rogers Communications bought AT&T Wireless' stake in Rogers Wireless in 2004 and in early 2005 bought the rest of the shares it did not already own. Later that year the firm made another major purchase, this time the acquisition of Call-Net Enterprises, owner of Sprint Canada. Rogers expanded its media holdings in 2007 with the acquisition of five TV stations from CTVglobemedia.

EXECUTIVES

Chairman: Alan D. Horn, age 58
President, CEO, and Director: Nadir H. Mohamed, age 53
EVP Regulatory and Vice Chairman: Philip B. (Phil) Lind, age 64
EVP Finance and CFO: William W. (Bill) Linton
EVP Network and CTO: Robert F. (Bob) Berner
EVP and COO, Rogers Cable: Michael A. Adams, age 48
EVP Emerging Business and Corporate Development and Deputy Chairman: Edward S. Rogers
EVP and Chief Marketing Officer: John Boynton
EVP Sales, Distribution, and Service: James S. (Jim) Lovie
EVP Information Technology and CIO: Jerry D. Brace
SVP Human Resources and Chief Human Resources Officer: Kevin P. Pennington
SVP Strategy and Development and Director: Melinda M. Rogers
SVP, General Counsel, and Secretary: David P. Miller
VP Investor Relations: Bruce M. Mann
VP Corporate Communications and Corporate Affairs: Terrie L. Tweddle
President, Rogers Retail, Rogers Cable Inc.: Charles W. (Chuck) van der Lee, age 57
President, Rogers Sportsnet, Rogers Media: Douglas Beeforth
President and CEO, Rogers Media: Keith Pelley, age 46
President and CEO, Publishing, Rogers Media: Brian Segal
President and CEO, Toronto Blue Jays and Rogers Centre: Paul M. Beeston, age 64
President, Communications: Robert W. (Rob) Bruce
Auditors: KPMG LLP

LOCATIONS

HQ: Rogers Communications Inc.
333 Bloor St. East, 10th Fl.
Toronto, Ontario M4W 1G9, Canada
Phone: 416-935-7777 **Fax:** 416-935-3597
Web: www.rogers.com

PRODUCTS/OPERATIONS

2009 Sales

	% of total
Wireless	55
Cable operations	33
Media	12
Total	**100**

2009 Wireless Sales

	% of total
Postpaid voice	70
Data	20
Equipment	6
Prepaid voice	4
Total	**100**

2009 Cable Sales

	% of total
Core cable	45
Internet	20
Home phone	13
Business solutions	12
Retail	10
Total	**100**

2009 Media Sales

	% of total
Television	33
Publishing	19
The Shopping Channel	18
Radio	16
Sports Entertainment	14
Total	**100**

Selected Operations

Wireless Communications
　Cellular service
　Data service
　Digital PCS
Cable and Telephone
　Cable television
　Broadband Internet access
　Dial-up Internet access
　Local access
　Long-distance
　Teleconferencing
Media
　Radio
　TV broadcasting
　Televised shopping
　Publishing

COMPETITORS

Astral Media	Glentel
Axia NetMedia	Manitoba Telecom Services
BCE	MTS Allstream
Bell Aliant	Quebecor
Bell Mobility	SaskTel
CanWest Global	Shaw Broadcast Services
Communications	Shaw Communications
CBC	Sprint Nextel
COGECO	Telemedia
Cogeco Cable	Tele-Metropole
Corus Entertainment	TELUS
CTVglobemedia	Transcontinental Inc.
Fundy Communications	Vonage

HISTORICAL FINANCIALS

Company Type: Public

Income Statement

FYE: December 31

	REVENUE ($ mil.)	NET INCOME ($ mil.)	NET PROFIT MARGIN	EMPLOYEES
12/09	11,179	1,408	12.6%	28,985
12/08	9,270	819	8.8%	29,200
12/07	10,308	648	6.3%	24,400
12/06	7,578	533	7.0%	22,500
12/05	6,417	(38)	—	21,000
Annual Growth	**14.9%**	**—**	**—**	**8.4%**

2009 Year-End Financials

Debt ratio: 198.1%
Return on equity: 35.5%
Cash ($ mil.): 365
Current ratio: 0.82
Long-term debt ($ mil.): 8,064

No. of shares (mil.): 566
Dividends
　Yield: 3.7%
　Payout: 48.9%
Market value ($ mil.): 16,708

Stock History

NYSE: RCI

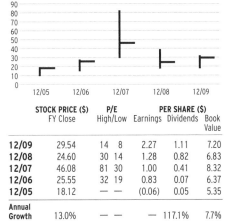

	STOCK PRICE ($) FY Close	P/E High/Low		PER SHARE ($) Earnings	Dividends	Book Value
12/09	29.54	14	8	2.27	1.11	7.20
12/08	24.60	30	14	1.28	0.82	6.83
12/07	46.08	81	30	1.00	0.41	8.32
12/06	25.55	32	19	0.83	0.07	6.37
12/05	18.12	—	—	(0.06)	0.05	5.35
Annual Growth	**13.0%**	**—**	**—**	**—**	**117.1%**	**7.7%**

Rolls-Royce Group

Rolls-Royce doesn't make luxury cars — BMW owns those operations — but it *can* provide serious horsepower. The company is the world's #2 aircraft engine maker behind General Electric division GE Aviation. Rolls-Royce's civil and defense aerospace business makes both commercial and military engines for a broad customer base, including more than 650 airlines, 4,000 corporate and utility aircraft and helicopter operators, and 160 armed forces around the world. It also supplies power generation systems to the oil and gas industry and is one of the world's largest makers of marine propulsion systems. German carmaker BMW owns about 9% of Rolls-Royce Group.

Rolls-Royce's Europe and North American markets have traditionally accounted for the lion share of revenue, but that is slowly changing as the company builds its clientele in Asia, South America, and the Middle East. Additionally, the company has seen a marked increase in revenue derived from services.

In 2009 the company focused on developing four advanced manufacturing research centers in the US, the UK, and Singapore. Rolls-Royce invested £300 million (more than $450 million)

in its UK factories as part of its almost £2 billion (over $3 billion) capital replacement plan to be carried out over a period of 10 years.

Rolls-Royce engines power some 30 types of civil aircraft, from small executive jets to large passenger aircraft. On the defense side, Rolls-Royce has an approximate quarter market share of the world's military engine manufacturing. Its portfolio covers all major sectors — combat, helicopters, unmanned and tactical aircraft, training, and transport. With the US government approving funding, the company moves ahead in collaboration with General Electric to develop the F136 engine for the F-35 Joint Strike Fighter.

The company's marine business also boasts an extensive range, from ship design to power systems and controls. It is benefitting from defense contracts in the US and the UK, where its engines power US Marine Corps and Royal Navy ships. Rolls-Royce's merchant marine operations are headquartered in Shanghai, taking strategic advantage of its proximity to the shipbuilding centers of China, Japan, and Korea. In 2010 subsidiary Rolls-Royce Marine bought Norwegian engineering firm ODIM ASA. The purchase adds automated handling systems for seismic and offshore drilling vessels.

In the energy market, Rolls-Royce's global position as a leading supplier of power and compression equipment, such as industrial gas turbines, to the oil and gas industry also helps to keep its portfolio balanced and diverse. The company established a civil nuclear business unit in 2009. Its nuclear market was strengthened further by Rolls-Royce's agreement with electric service provider EDF Energy to enter into a joint venture, with EDF Energy giving support to the UK facility.

Although Rolls-Royce shares its name with the luxury car, the two parted ways when the British government split them in 1971.

HISTORY

In 1906 automobile and aviation enthusiast Charles Rolls and engineer Henry Royce unveiled the Silver Ghost, an automobile that earned Rolls-Royce a reputation as maker of the best car in the world.

A year after Rolls' 1910 death in a biplane crash, Royce suffered a breakdown. From his home Royce continued to design Rolls-Royce engines such as the Eagle, its first aircraft engine, in 1914, and other engines used to power airplanes during WWI — but management of the company fell to Claude Johnson, who remained chief executive until 1926.

Although the company returned to primarily making cars after WWI, its engines were used in several history-making flights and, in 1931, set world speed records for land, sea, and air. Rolls-Royce bought the Bentley Motor Company that year. In 1933 it introduced the Merlin engine, which powered the Spitfire, Hurricane, and Mustang fighters of WWII. Rolls-Royce began designing a jet engine in 1938 and over the years it pioneered the turboprop engine, turbofan, and vertical takeoff engine.

Realizing that it had to break into the lucrative US airliner market to stay alive, Rolls-Royce bought its main British competitor, Bristol-Siddley Engines, in 1966. With Bristol-Siddley came its contract to build the engine for the Anglo-French Concorde in 1976 and a US presence. Lockheed ordered the company's RB211 engine for its TriStar in 1968, but Rolls-Royce underestimated the project's technical and financial challenges and entered bankruptcy in 1971. The British government stepped in and nationalized the aerospace division and sold the auto group. The RB211 entered service on the TriStar in 1972 and on the Boeing 747 in 1977.

Rolls-Royce was reprivatized in 1987. In a diversification effort two years later, the company bought mining, marine, and power plant specialist Northern Engineering Industries. In the early 1990s the aerospace market was hurt by military spending cutbacks and a recession; the company cut over 18,000 jobs.

A joint venture with BMW launched the BR710 engine for Gulfstream and Canadair's long-range business jets in 1990. The company bought Allison Engine in 1995. Rolls-Royce sold Parsons Power Generation Systems to Siemens in 1997. In 1998 the British government approved a repayable investment of about $335 million in the company to develop a new model of Trent aircraft engines.

Rolls-Royce pumped up its gas and oil equipment business in 1999 by buying the rotating compression equipment unit of Cooper Cameron, and it became one of the world leaders in marine propulsion by acquiring Vickers. The company then took full control of its aircraft-engine joint venture with BMW; in return BMW received a 10% stake in Rolls.

Early in 2001 the company cut about 11% of its workforce in response to the worldwide crisis in the commercial jet business.

In 2002 the company announced that it had inked a 10-year, $2 billion deal to supply engines to Gulfstream Aerospace. That year Rolls-Royce sold its Vickers Defence Systems unit, which made tanks and armored vehicles, to Alvis Plc. In 2003 Sir Ralph Robins, who had been executive chairman for more than a decade, retired from his post.

Early in 2004 Rolls-Royce and GE Aircraft Engines were picked to supply engines for Boeing's upcoming 787 Dreamliner.

EXECUTIVES

Chairman: Sir Simon Robertson, age 68
Chief Executive and Board Member: Sir John Rose, age 57, $2,157,730 total compensation
COO and Board Member: Mike J. Terrett, age 51, $1,792,677 total compensation
Finance Director and Board Member: Andrew B. Shilston, age 54, $1,399,207 total compensation
Director Engineering and Technology and Board Member: Colin P. Smith, age 54, $1,133,744 total compensation
Board Member; President and CEO, North America: James M. Guyette, age 64, $1,140,423 total compensation
Board Member: John F. Rishton, age 52
Deputy Chief Operating Officer; President, Gas Turbine Supply Chain: Alain Michaelis, age 43
Chief Procurement Officer: Mike Orris
Chief Scientific Officer: Paul Stein
Company Secretary and General Counsel: Tim Rayner
Director Manufacturing: Mike Lloyd
Director Human Resources: Tom F. R. Brown
Director Corporate Affairs: Peter Morgan
Director Global Corporate Development: Miles A. Cowdry
Head Corporate Communications: Josh Rosenstock
President and CEO, Optimized Systems and Solutions: Paul Inman
President, Defence Aerospace: Daniel G. (Dan) Korte, age 49
President, Gas Turbine Services: Tony Wood
President, Marine: John Paterson
President, Rolls-Royce Nuclear: Lawrie Haynes
President, Civil Aerospace: Mark King
Auditors: KPMG Audit Plc

LOCATIONS

HQ: Rolls-Royce Group plc
65 Buckingham Gate
London SW1E 6AT, United Kingdom
Phone: 44-20-7222-9020
US HQ: 1875 Explorer St., Ste. 200, Reston, VA 20190
US Phone: 703-834-1700   **US Fax:** 703-709-6086
Web: www.rolls-royce.com

2009 Sales

	% of total
Europe	
UK	14
Other countries	22
North America	
US	28
Canada	3
Asia	27
Australasia	2
Africa	1
Other regions	3
Total	**100**

PRODUCTS/OPERATIONS

2009 Sales

	% of total
Civil aerospace	44
Marine	26
Defense aerospace	20
Energy	10
Total	**100**

Selected Products and Services

Aircraft engines
Automation and control equipment
Diesel and gas turbine engines
Electric propulsion systems
Engine support services
Fuel cells
Generators
Offshore drilling equipment
Overhaul and repair services
Technical publications
Training

Selected Subsidiaries

Civil aerospace
Optimized Systems and Solutions Limited (OSyS) (advanced controls and predictive data management)
Rolls-Royce Leasing Limited (engine leasing)
Rolls-Royce Total Care Services Limited (aftermarket support services)
Corporate
Rolls-Royce International Limited (international support and commercial information services)
Rolls-Royce Power Engineering plc (power generation and marine systems)
Energy
Rolls-Royce Fuel Cell Systems Limited (fuel cell system development)
Rolls-Royce Power Development Limited (project development)
Tidal Generation Limited (development of tidal generation systems)
Marine
ODIM ASA (offshore drilling, naval, and power generation equipment)
Rolls-Royce Marine Electrical Systems Limited (marine electrical systems)
Rolls-Royce Marine Power Operations Limited (nuclear submarine propulsion systems)
Rolls-Royce Power Engineering plc (energy and marine systems)

COMPETITORS

Emerson Electric	McDermott
GE Aviation	Pratt & Whitney
GE Honda Aero Engines	SAFRAN
Honeywell Aerospace	Siemens AG
IHI Corp.	Volvo
Kawasaki Heavy Industries	

HISTORICAL FINANCIALS

Company Type: Public

Income Statement

FYE: December 31

	REVENUE ($ mil.)	NET INCOME ($ mil.)	NET PROFIT MARGIN	EMPLOYEES
12/09	16,585	3,537	21.3%	38,500
12/08	13,144	(1,947)	—	39,000
12/07	14,843	1,198	8.1%	38,600
12/06	14,013	1,947	13.9%	37,300
12/05	11,360	726	6.4%	36,200
Annual Growth	**9.9%**	**48.6%**	**—**	**1.6%**

2009 Year-End Financials

Debt ratio: 47.3%
Return on equity: 73.1%
Cash ($ mil.): 4,717
Current ratio: 1.49
Long-term debt ($ mil.): 2,846

No. of shares (mil.): 1,854
Dividends
  Yield: 3.0%
  Payout: 12.1%
Market value ($ mil.): 14,276

Stock History

Pink Sheets: RYCEY

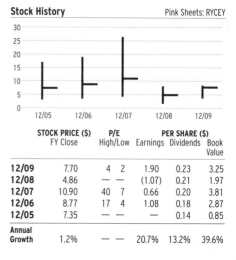

	STOCK PRICE ($) FY Close	P/E High	P/E Low	PER SHARE ($) Earnings	PER SHARE ($) Dividends	PER SHARE ($) Book Value
12/09	7.70	4	2	1.90	0.23	3.25
12/08	4.86	—	—	(1.07)	0.21	1.97
12/07	10.90	40	7	0.66	0.20	3.81
12/06	8.77	17	4	1.08	0.18	2.87
12/05	7.35	—	—	—	0.14	0.85
Annual Growth	**1.2%**	**—**	**—**	**20.7%**	**13.2%**	**39.6%**

Royal Ahold

A tattered prince of global food retailing, Royal Ahold owns or has an interest in more than 5,200 supermarkets and specialty stores in Europe and the US. While its status as one of the world's largest grocery retailers has been greatly diminished, it still ranks as a leading supermarket operator along the East Coast of the US under names, including Giant Food and Stop & Shop, which account for about 60% of its total sales. Royal Ahold also operates Albert Heijn (the #1 food retailer in The Netherlands), as well as stores in Portugal, the Baltic states, the Czech Republic, and Slovakia. Other interests include the US online grocery service Peapod and a majority stake in Scandinavian food seller ICA AB.

Ahold in February 2010 acquired 25 Ukrop's Super Market stores, inventory, equipment, and leases, in a $140 million transaction. The Ukrop's chain became part of Ahold USA's Giant-Carlisle division, which already boasts Virginia-based Martin's supermarkets. Buying Ukrop's is part of Ahold's strategy shift to expand its holdings in the US and specifically in Virginia.

A slew of asset sales since 2003 have transformed Royal Ahold from a multinational company into a smaller, more focused business. Most recently, Ahold sold its majority stake in

Schuitema, a Dutch retailer and food distributor, to CVC Capital Partners in mid-2008 in return for cash and the transfer of 50-plus Schuitema stores to Ahold.

In the Netherlands, the company owns or franchises more than 1,890 stores, including some 835 Albert Heijn supermarkets, about 540 Gall & Gall liquor stores, and 500-plus Etos health and beauty care stores.

Ahold's other European holdings include Albert supermarkets and Hypernova stores in Central Europe, and a 60% share in the #1 Swedish grocery chain ICA AB, which operates more than 2,300 retailer-owned and company-owned stores in Sweden, Norway, and the Baltic states.

HISTORY

Albert Heijn and his wife took over his father's grocery store in Ootzaan, Netherlands, in 1887. By the end of WWI, the company had 50 Albert Heijn grocery stores in Holland, and at WWII's end it had almost 250 stores. In 1948 the company went public.

It opened its first self-service store in 1952 and its first supermarket in 1955. Growing into the #1 grocer in the Netherlands, Albert Heijn opened liquor and cosmetic stores in 1973. (It changed its name to Ahold that year to better reflect its range of businesses.) Ahold expanded outside the Netherlands in 1976 when it founded supermarket chain Cadadia in Spain (sold 1985).

Ahold entered the US in 1977 by purchasing BI-LO and furthered its expansion in 1981 by adding Pennsylvania-based Giant Food Stores. In 1987, in honor of its 100th anniversary, Ahold was granted the title Koninklijke (Dutch for "royal"). In 1988 it bought a majority stake in Dutch food wholesaler Schuitema.

The company added New York-based TOPS Markets in 1991. That year Royal Ahold founded food retailer and distributor Euronova (now called Ahold Czech Republic), and in 1992 it acquired 49% of Portuguese food retailer Jerónimo Martins Retail. In 1993 Cees van der Hoeven was promoted to chief executive and Royal Ahold was listed on the NYSE.

Other acquisitions included New England grocery giant The Stop & Shop Companies in 1996.

Royal Ahold acquired 50% of Sweden's top food seller, ICA AB, in 1999. In 2000 Royal Ahold acquired Spanish food retailer Kampio, and #2 and #4 foodservice distributors U.S. Foodservice and PYA/Monarch. In 2001 Royal Ahold bought Alliant Exchange, parent of Alliant Foodservice, which distributes food to more than 100,000 customers, and Bruno's Supermarkets, which operates more than 180 stores in the Southeast.

In February 2003 CEO Cees van der Hoeven and CFO Michiel Meurs resigned following an announcement that the grocery giant would restate its financial results by at least $500 million because of accounting irregularities at U.S. Foodservice. In May 2003 IKEA veteran Anders Moberg became acting CEO. Soon after, Ahold said it would restate earnings downward by $880 million because of the accounting scandal at U.S. Foodservice. Adding to its woes, in July the public prosecutor in Amsterdam launched a criminal investigation into possible falsification of accounts by the company.

In October 2003 Royal Ahold published its long-awaited 2002 results, revealing a $1.27 billion loss, which the retailer attributed to special charges related to overstated profits at U.S. Foodservice. In 2004 Karel Vuursteen resigned as

chairman of the supervisory board for personal reasons and was succeeded by René Dahan. Also that year Ahold reached a settlement with the Dutch public prosecutor in which the company agreed to pay €8 million. In return, the Dutch prosecutor agreed not to undertake proceedings against Royal Ahold. In October the company reached a settlement with the US Securities and Exchange Commission that imposed no fines on Royal Ahold due, in part, to its "extensive co-operation" with the investigation.

In 2005 the grocery giant sold its BI-LO and Bruno's chains in the southeastern US to an affiliate of Lone Star Funds. That year the company settled a US class action lawsuit by paying $1.1 billion to shareholders who purchased stock between July 3, 1999, and February 23, 2003; just before the 2003 accounting scandal broke. It also reached an agreement to settle litigation with the Dutch Shareholders' Association.

The grocery chain also sold 13 large Hypernova hypermarkets in Poland to Carrefour and a local operator in early 2005. The company also moved its corporate headquarters from Zaandam to Amsterdam later in the year.

More than three years after teetering on the brink of bankruptcy as a result of one of Europe's largest financial scandals, a Dutch court found former CEO Cees van der Hoeven and former CFO Michael Meurs guilty of fraud. They were accused of improperly booking sales from four subsidiaries in Scandinavia, Argentina and Brazil. Both were fined and given suspended sentences. Former executive board member Jan Andreae, who headed Ahold's European operations, was sentenced to four months in jail, suspended for two years, and fined.

CEO Anders Moberg left the company in July 2007. Also in July, U.S. Foodservice was finally sold to a consortium of Clayton, Dubilier & Rice and Kohlberg Kravis Roberts & Co. for about $7.1 billion. In November John Rishton, Ahold's CFO who had been serving as interim chief executive since Moberg's departure, was named to the post permanently.

EXECUTIVES

Chairman: René Dahan, age 69
Vice Chairman: Tom de Swaan, age 63
President and CEO: John F. Rishton, age 52, $4,236,128 total compensation
EVP; COO Europe; President and CEO, Ahold Nederland: A. Dick Boer, age 53, $2,649,674 total compensation
EVP; COO USA: Lawrence S. (Larry) Benjamin, age 54, $2,346,818 total compensation
EVP and CFO: Kimberly A. Ross, age 45, $2,129,755 total compensation
EVP and Chief Corporate Governance Counsel: Lodewijk Hijmans van den Bergh, age 47
SVP Corporate Communications: Kerry Underhill
VP Corporate Communications: Jochem van de Laarschot
VP Investor Relations: Henk Jan ten Brinke
President and CEO, Albert and Hypernova: Jan Van Dam, age 38
President and CEO, Peapod: Andrew B. Parkinson
Division President, Giant Food Stores: Rick Herring
Division President, Giant-Landover: Robin S. Michel
Division President, Stop & Shop New England: Mark McGowan
Division President, Stop & Shop Metro New York: Ron Onorato
General Manager, Albert Heijn: Sander van der Laan, age 41
General Manager, Gall & Gall: Peter Zoutendijk
Auditors: Deloitte Accountants B.V.

LOCATIONS

HQ: Royal Ahold N.V.
(Koninklijke Ahold N.V.)
Piet Heinkade 167 – 173
1019 GM Amsterdam, The Netherlands
Phone: 31-20-509-51-00 **Fax:** 31-20-509-51-10
US HQ: 1385 Hancock St., Quincy Center Plaza
Quincy, MA 02169
US Phone: 781-380-8000 **US Fax:** 617-770-8190
Web: www.ahold.com

2009 Sales

	% of total
US	59
Europe	
The Netherlands	35
Other countries	6
Total	**100**

2009 Stores

	No.
Europe	2,196
US	713
Total	**2,909**

PRODUCTS/OPERATIONS

2009 Sales

	% of total
Stop & Shop/Giant-Landover	46
Albert Heijn	35
Giant-Carlisle	13
Albert/Hypernova	6
Total	**100**

2009 Stores

	No.
Albert Heijn, Etos, Gall & Gall	1,892
Stop & Shop/Giant-Landover	561
Albert/Hypernova	304
Giant-Carlisle	152
Total	**2,909**

Selected Operations

Retail
  Europe
    Albert (supermarkets, Czech Republic and Slovakia)
    Albert Heijn (supermarkets)
    Etos (health and beauty stores)
    Feira Nova (hypermarkets, Portugal)
    Gall & Gall (liquor stores)
    Hypernova (hypermarkets, Slovakia)
    ICA AB (60%, supermarkets, Scandinavia)
    Jerónimo Martins (49%, supermarkets and hypermarkets, Portugal)
    Pingo Doce (supermarkets, Portugal)
  US
    Giant-Carlisle (supermarkets)
    Giant-Landover (supermarkets)
    Stop & Shop (supermarkets)
    Peapod (online grocery shopping, US)

COMPETITORS

A&P
ALDI
Carrefour
Delhaize
Golub
Kooperativa Förbundet
Kroger
Lidl
METRO AG
NorgesGruppen
Safeway
Shaw's
Tesco
Wal-Mart

HISTORICAL FINANCIALS

Company Type: Public

Income Statement

FYE: Sunday nearest December 31

	REVENUE ($ mil.)	NET INCOME ($ mil.)	NET PROFIT MARGIN	EMPLOYEES
12/09	40,022	1,281	3.2%	206,000
12/08	36,255	1,521	4.2%	202,275
12/07	41,437	4,335	10.5%	118,715
12/06	59,200	1,207	2.0%	164,078
12/05	52,697	188	0.4%	167,801
Annual Growth	(6.6%)	61.5%	—	5.3%

2009 Year-End Financials

Debt ratio: 32.2%
Return on equity: —
Cash ($ mil.): 3,852
Current ratio: 1.27
Long-term debt ($ mil.): 2,512

No. of shares (mil.): 1,181
Dividends
  Yield: 1.1%
  Payout: 18.9%
Market value ($ mil.): 22,431

Stock History

Pink Sheets: AHONY

	STOCK PRICE ($) FY Close	P/E High/Low	PER SHARE ($) Earnings	Dividends	Book Value
12/09	18.99	19 14	1.06	0.20	6.60
12/08	17.34	17 9	1.25	0.18	5.58
12/07	20.31	9 6	2.96	0.00	4.75
12/06	17.45	19 13	0.94	0.00	5.81
12/05	11.15	103 75	0.13	0.00	5.33
Annual Growth	14.2%	— —	69.0%	—	5.5%

Royal Bank of Canada

Royal Bank of Canada reigns as Canada's banking monarch. Canada's largest bank, also known as RBC Financial Group, has five segments: Canadian banking (including business and retail banking and investment), wealth management (asset management and trust services for wealthy clients), insurance (active in Canada and the US), international banking, and capital markets. In addition to more than 1,100 domestic locations, the bank has about 125 offices in the Caribbean and operations in some 50 countries. Its US operations include RBC Bank (USA) in the Southeast, RBC Dominion Securities, and RBC Wealth Management.

In 2008 Royal Bank of Canada agreed to buy back some $850 million in auction-rate securities and pay the New York State Attorney General a nearly $10 million fine. Auction-rate securities were sold to investors as a low-risk investment, but as the economy worsened in 2007 and 2008, banks canceled the regular auctions, rendering the securities worthless. Customers and regulators claimed that banks continued to sell them the securities even though they knew the investments had become very high risk.

Other RBC subsidiaries include Canadian discount brokerage RBC Action Direct and RBC Insurance, active in Canada and the US. In 2007 the company bought the electronic brokerage business of New York boutique Carlin Financial Group (now RBC Carlin), which serves professional traders.

The following year, its Voyageur Asset Management unit (now RBC Global Asset Management) acquired Access Capital Strategies, which invests in debt securities that invest in low-income housing and other community development assets. RBC Global hopes to capture the small but growing ethical investor demographic.

The company then acquired Houston-based energy advisory firm Richardson Barr (now RBC Richardson Barr), strengthening RBC's energy exploration and production practice. RBC Capital Markets acquired Ferris, Baker Watts, the largest retail brokerage and investment bank based in the Baltimore/Washington, DC, area.

RBC Bank has been purchasing community banks in Alabama, Georgia, and Florida, the latest being Alabama National BanCorporation in 2008, and it continues to seek out bargains in the battered US financial services industry, particularly in banking and wealth management.

Beyond North America, RBC provides foreign exchange services and import/export services for Canadian and multinational clients. The bank has set out to become a leader in wealth management, acquiring and adding services to attract high-net-worth clients (and the fees it can charge them for handling their assets). To that end, it acquired UK private bank Abacus Financial Services Group. In 2008 RBC bought the Jersey-based Mourant Limited and its offshore law firm. The deal also added to RBC's international reach by establishing a presence in Dubai and the Cayman Islands.

HISTORY

Royal Bank of Canada (RBC) has looked south of the border ever since its 1864 creation as Merchants Bank in Halifax, Nova Scotia, a port city bustling with trade spawned by the US Civil War. After incorporating in 1869 as Merchants Bank of Halifax, the bank added branches in eastern Canada. Merchants opened a branch in Bermuda in 1882. Gold strikes in Canada and Alaska in the late 1890s pushed it into western Canada.

Merchants opened offices in New York and Cuba in 1899 and changed its name to Royal Bank of Canada in 1901. RBC moved into new Montreal headquarters in 1907 and grew by purchasing such banks as Union Bank of Canada (1925). In 1928 it moved into the 42-story Royal Bank Building, then the tallest in the British Empire.

The bank faltered during the Depression but recovered during WWII. After the war RBC financed the expanding minerals and oil and gas industries. When Castro took power in Cuba, RBC tried to operate its branches under communist rule but sold out to Banco Nacional de Cuba in 1960.

RBC opened offices in the UK in 1979 and in West Germany, Puerto Rico, and the Bahamas in 1980. As Canada's banking rules relaxed, RBC bought Dominion Securities in 1987. The US Federal Reserve approved RBC's brokerage arm for participation in stock underwriting in 1991.

In 1992 the bank faced a $650 million loss after backing the Reichmann family's Olympia & York property development company, which failed under the weight of its UK projects. The next year an ever-diversifying RBC bought Royal

Trustco, Canada's #2 trust company, and Voyageur Travel Insurance, its largest retail travel insurer. A management shakeup in late 1994 ended with bank president John Cleghorn taking control of the company.

In 1995 RBC listed on the New York Stock Exchange and the next year joined with Heller Financial (an affiliate of Japan's Fuji Bank) to finance trade between Canada and Mexico. It began offering PC home banking in 1996 and Internet banking in 1997. That year RBC became one of the world's largest securities-custody service providers with its acquisition of The Bank of Nova Scotia's institutional and pension custody operations.

The company and Bank of Montreal agreed to merge in 1998, but Canadian regulators, fearing the concentration of banking power seen in the US, rejected the merger. In response, the bank trimmed its workforce and orchestrated a sale-leaseback of its property portfolio (1999).

In the late 1990s RBC grew its online presence by purchasing the Internet banking operations of Security First Network Bank (now Security First Technologies, 1998), the online trading division of Bull & Bear Group (1999), and 20% of AOL Canada (1999). It also bought several trust and fiduciary services businesses from Ernst & Young.

In 2000 it acquired US mortgage bank Prism Financial and the Canadian retail credit card business of BANK ONE. RBC also sold its commercial credit portfolio to U.S. Bancorp. The company agreed to pay a substantial fine after institutional asset management subsidiary RT Capital Management came under scrutiny from the Ontario Securities Commission for alleged involvement in illegal pension-fund stock manipulation. RBC ended up selling RT Capital to UBS AG the following year.

Also in 2001 RBC made another US purchase: North Carolina's Centura Banks (now RBC Centura Banks). It sold Bull & Bear Securities to JB Oxford Holdings of Los Angeles.

It sold Houston-based home lender RBC Mortgage to New Century Financial in 2005.

EXECUTIVES

Chairman: David P. O'Brien, age 68
President, CEO, and Director: Gordon M. Nixon, age 52
Chief Administrative Officer and CFO: Janice R. Fukakusa
Chief Risk Officer: Morten Friis
EVP Global Services; CEO, RBC Dexia Investor Services: José Placido
VP and Secretary: Carol J. McNamara
Group Head Wealth Management and President and CEO, RBC Asset Management: M. George Lewis
Group Head Canadian Banking: David I. (Dave) McKay, age 46
Group Head Strategy, Treasury, and Corporate Services: Barbara G. Stymiest
Group Head International Banking and Insurance; Chairman and CEO, RBC Bank (USA): W. James (Jim) Westlake
Co-Group Head Capital Markets; Chairman and Co-CEO, RBC Capital Markets: Doug McGregor, age 54
Co-Group Head Capital Markets; President and Co-CEO, RBC Capital Markets: Mark Standish, age 49
Managing Director and Head European Structured Interest Rate Sales: Bertrand Fitoussi
Managing Director Rates Trading Europe, RBC Capital: Diego Megia
Head RBC Wealth Management Strategy: Brenda Vince
President, RBC Asset Management: Doug Coulter
President, Phillips Hager & North: Damon Williams
CEO, RBC Global Asset Management: John Montalbano
Auditors: Deloitte & Touche LLP

LOCATIONS

HQ: Royal Bank of Canada
200 Bay St., Royal Bank Plaza
Toronto, Ontario M5J 2J5, Canada
Phone: 416-974-5151   **Fax:** 416-955-7800
US HQ: 1 Liberty Plaza, New York, NY 10006
US Phone: 212-858-7100   **US Fax:** 212-428-2329
Web: www.rbc.com

PRODUCTS/OPERATIONS

2009 Sales

	% of total
Interest	
Loans	35
Securities	15
Other	3
Noninterest	
Insurance premiums, investment & fee income	15
Trading revenue	7
Investment management & custodial fees	4
Service charges	4
Securities brokerage commissions	3
Mutual fund revenue	3
Underwriting & other advisory fees	3
Other	8
Total	**100**

COMPETITORS

AGF Investments
Bank of America
Barclays
BMO Financial Group
Caisse de dépôt et placement du Québec
Caisses centrale Desjardins
Canadian Western Bank
Central 1 Credit Union
CI Financial
CIBC
Citigroup
Deutsche Bank
Dundee Corp.
Goldman Sachs
Great-West Lifeco
Guardian Capital Group
HSBC
HSBC Bank Canada
JPMorgan Chase
Kleinwort Benson (Channel Islands)
Knightswood Financial
Laurentian Bank
National Bank of Canada
Nomura Securities
Power Financial
Safety First Savings & Mortgage
Scotiabank
Sprott Resource Lending
TD Bank
UBS
Vancity

HISTORICAL FINANCIALS

Company Type: Public

Income Statement

FYE: October 31

	ASSETS ($ mil.)	NET INCOME ($ mil.)	INCOME AS % OF ASSETS	EMPLOYEES
10/09	610,777	3,598	0.6%	80,000
10/08	598,631	3,767	0.6%	80,000
10/07	628,863	5,753	0.9%	70,000
10/06	478,754	4,217	0.9%	60,858
10/05	398,858	2,878	0.7%	60,000
Annual Growth	**11.2%**	**5.7%**	**—**	**7.5%**

2009 Year-End Financials

Equity as % of assets: 4.9%
Return on assets: 0.6%
Return on equity: 13.5%
Long-term debt ($ mil.): 6,025
No. of shares (mil.): 1,424
Dividends
Yield: 4.0%
Payout: 77.9%
Market value ($ mil.): 66,913
Sales ($ mil.): 35,568

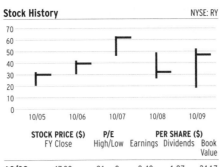

	STOCK PRICE ($) FY Close	P/E High/Low		PER SHARE ($) Earnings	Dividends	Book Value
10/09	47.00	21	8	2.40	1.87	24.17
10/08	32.03	17	10	2.80	1.65	17.87
10/07	61.97	14	11	4.39	1.90	17.98
10/06	39.59	13	10	3.20	1.27	14.04
10/05	30.03	14	10	2.18	1.00	11.84
Annual Growth	**11.8%**	**—**	**—**	**2.4%**	**16.9%**	**19.5%**

Royal Bank of Scotland

If you have overdraft protection for your checking account, you can thank The Royal Bank of Scotland (RBS), which introduced the service in 1728. Today, RBS is one of Europe's largest banking groups. Through subsidiaries Royal Bank of Scotland and National Westminster Bank, it has the UK's largest bank network of more than 2,000 branches. RBS offers private banking and insurance products through Coutts Group and Adam & Company. Other divisions include Ulster Bank, which operates in Ireland and Northern Ireland; Citizens Financial, which operates as Citizens Bank and Charter One in the US; and US transaction processor RBS Lynk. After a series of bailouts in 2008 and 2009, the UK government owns 84% of RBS.

The group was crippled by both the global financial crisis and its ambitious international expansion, primarily its disastrous 2007 investment in Dutch bank ABN AMRO. In late 2008 the UK took a 60% stake in RBS, but the bank still ended up reporting an annual loss of some £28 billion ($41 billion) — the largest loss in British corporate history. The government has since stepped in twice more to help RBS manage its debt and interest payments.

The government intervened with the contingency that RBS make significant efforts to get back on solid ground. Towards that end, the group is cutting costs and selling operations to refocus on its core banking business. It is selling its insurance businesses, several retail branches, and its interest in RBS Sempra Commodities. It has agreed to sell more than 300 branches and offices to Banco Santander for an estimated £1.65 billion ($2.6 billion). RBS is also selling noncore asset management units to Aberdeen Asset Management for a gain of £84.7 million ($135 million). In 2010 RBS sold its factoring and invoice financing unit to GE Capital and its payment services unit Global Merchant Services to Advent International and Bain Capital. Other divisions are simply being run down and closed.

RBS is also scaling back on the international growth that weakened the group during the economic fallout. In 2009 the group sold its 4% stake in Bank of China for some £1.6 billion ($2.4 billion); it also sold most of its operations in Southeast Asia to Australia and New Zealand Banking Group for about $550 million. RBS divested units in Argentina, Colombia, Chile, the United Arab Emirates, Kazakhstan, and Pakistan — all assets gained as part of its ABN AMRO transaction.

Also as part of the government rescue, RBS went through a management shakeup. Fred Goodwin, the architect of the bank's international expansion, was removed as CEO. He was replaced by Stephen Hester, formerly the CEO of British Land Company. Johnny Cameron, chairman of the group's global banking and markets segment (which lost the group's most money in 2008) was also ousted, and chairman Tom McKillop retired early.

HISTORY

Royal Bank of Scotland was founded in 1727, but its roots go back to the Darien Company, a merchant expedition that was established to set up a Scottish trading colony in Panama. The Darien expedition ended disastrously in 1699. In 1707 England voted to compensate Scottish creditors for the colony's failure (in part because England had promised support, then reneged, contributing to the collapse), and a small industry sprang up around paying creditors and loaning them money. In 1727 the Equivalent Company, the combined entity of these organizations, was granted a banking charter and became Royal Bank of Scotland.

Indicative of the bank's foresight and savvy, Royal Bank of Scotland introduced overdraft protection in 1728.

In 1826 the Parliament voted to take away Scottish banks' right to issue banknotes for less than five pounds, which would have required banks to use gold or silver. Few banks had such reserves, and the move sparked an outcry. Novelist Sir Walter Scott's *The Letters of Malachi Malagrowther*, which defended the Scottish one-pound note, helped shoot down the proposal.

RBS expanded throughout Scotland over the next 50 years. It opened a London branch in 1874; it didn't establish a branch outside London until it bought Williams Deacon's Bank, which had a branch network in North England. RBS continued to use the Williams Deacon's name, as it did with Glyn, Mills & Co., which it purchased in 1939.

In 1968 RBS took on its modern persona as a public company when it merged with National Commercial Bank. The company moved overseas during the 1970s, establishing offices in Hong Kong and major US cities.

RBS spent the next 20 years trying to achieve another merger of the same scale as National Commercial. In 1981 the bank was wooed by Standard Chartered Bank and Hongkong and Shanghai Bank (now part of HSBC Holdings), but British regulators denied both suitors.

The bank moved into telephone operations in 1985, when it set up Direct Line for selling car insurance. In 1988 RBS bought New England bank Citizens Financial. In 1989 the company entered into an alliance with Banco Santander (now Santander Central Hispano), Spain's largest banking group. The alliance created a cross-pollination of ideas and strategies that boosted both banks' operations. The first fruit of the alliance came in 1991 with the launch of Interbank On-line Systems (IBOS), which connected several European banks and allowed for instantaneous money transfers.

In the 1990s RBS was linked with a variety of partners. It even made a bid for the much larger bank Barclays, in a move regarded as cheeky, but was rebuffed. In 2000 RBS acquired NatWest after a prolonged takeover battle with rival Bank of Scotland (now part of HBOS plc). Royal Bank also sold the assets of NatWest's Equity Partners unit and launched NatWest Private Banking to target wealthy investors.

In 2004 RBS made several acquisitions to boost its US presence: It paid about $360 million for the credit card business of Connecticut-based People's Bank and bought payments processor Lynk Systems (now RBS Lynk), while Citizens Financial bought Cleveland-based bank Charter One Financial.

In 2007 RBS led the consortium that acquired the Dutch bank for €71 billion in a deal that was called the largest ever in the banking industry. The buyers carved ABN AMRO into pieces; RBS took the global wholesale and international retail operations in Asia, Eastern Europe, and the Middle East. The ambitious takeover preceded the global economic crisis, though, and RBS was among the hardest hit financial groups.

The troubled company made several moves to try and raise capital. Early in 2008 the company announced a £12 billion rights issue. RBS also tried but failed to find a buyer for its insurance arm. However, other assets were divested that year. The company sold rolling stock leasing firm Angel Trains to Babcock & Brown and others, and it sold its joint venture Tesco Personal Finance back to supermarket giant Tesco. The efforts proved inadequate, though. The government took a controlling stake in the group in 2008, the same year that RBS reported the largest corporate loss in British history.

EXECUTIVES

Chairman: Sir Philip Hampton, age 56, $1,114,820 total compensation
Group Chief Executive and Director: Stephen A. M. Hester, age 49, $1,775,837 total compensation
CFO and Director: Bruce W. Van Saun, age 53, $1,114,820 total compensation
Chief Administration Officer: Ron Teerlink, age 49
Global Head Markets: Peter Nielsen
Group Secretary: Aileen Taylor
Group General Counsel: Chris Campbell
Group Treasurer: John Cummins
Group Chief Economist and Head Communications: Andrew McLaughlin
Head Human Resources: Neil Roden
Head Investor Relations: Richard O'Connor
Head Strategy and Corporate Finance: Jennifer Hill
Head Group Corporate Affairs: Andrew Wilson, age 38
Co-Head, Global Banks and Markets, Americas; Head, Fixed Income Trading for Americas: Michael Lyublinsky
Co-Head, Global Banking and Markets, Americas; Head, North America Corporate Coverage and Advisory: Bob McKillip
CEO, Global Banking and Markets: John Hourican, age 39
CEO, RBS Insurance: Paul Geddes, age 40
CEO, Wealth Management: John Baines
CEO, Americas; Chairman and CEO, Citizens Financial Group: Ellen Alemany, age 54
Auditors: Deloitte & Touche LLP

LOCATIONS

HQ: The Royal Bank of Scotland Group plc
   36 St. Andrew Sq.
   Edinburgh EH2 2YB, United Kingdom
Phone: 44-131-556-8555   **Fax:** 44-131-557-6140
US HQ: 1 Citizens Plaza, Providence, RI 02903
US Phone: 401-456-7000   **US Fax:** 401-456-7819
Web: www.rbs.com

PRODUCTS/OPERATIONS

2009 Sales

	% of total
Interest	
Loans & advances to customers	48
Debt securities	8
Loans & advances to banks	1
Noninterest	
Fees & commissions	17
Net insurance premium income	9
Gain on redemption of own debt	7
Other	10
Total	**100**

Selected Subsidiaries

Citizens Financial Group, Inc. (banking, US)
Coutts & Co (private banking)
National Westminster Bank Plc
RBS Insurance Group Limited
The Royal Bank of Scotland plc
Ulster Bank Limited (Northern Ireland)

COMPETITORS

AIB
Alliance & Leicester
Bank of America
Bank of Ireland
Barclays
Citigroup
HSBC
ING Direct UK
Irish Life
JPMorgan Chase
Lloyds Banking Group
PNC Financial
Standard Chartered
Standard Life

HISTORICAL FINANCIALS

Company Type: Public

Income Statement

FYE: December 31

	ASSETS ($ mil.)	NET INCOME ($ mil.)	INCOME AS % OF ASSETS	EMPLOYEES
12/09	2,701,824	(3,700)	—	201,700
12/08	3,475,911	(49,748)	—	199,000
12/07	3,794,006	15,396	0.4%	226,400
12/06	1,706,438	12,145	0.7%	135,000
12/05	1,336,453	9,276	0.7%	137,000
Annual Growth	**19.2%**	**—**	**—**	**10.2%**

2009 Year-End Financials

Equity as % of assets: 4.6%
Return on assets: —
Return on equity: —
Long-term debt ($ mil.): 486,093
No. of shares (mil.): 2,898
Dividends
Yield: 0.0%
Payout: —
Market value ($ mil.): 43,344
Sales ($ mil.): 89,221

Stock History

NYSE: RBS

	STOCK PRICE ($) FY Close	P/E High/Low		PER SHARE ($) Earnings	Dividends	Book Value
12/09	14.95	—	—	(2.04)	0.00	42.71
12/08	21.96	—	—	(42.17)	16.15	29.40
12/07	348.62	15	11	29.49	—	36.53
Annual Growth	**(79.3%)**	**—**	**—**	**—**	**—**	**8.1%**

Royal Dutch Shell

Royal Dutch Shell sits on an oil and gas throne that is only slightly lower than that of #1 oil company Exxon Mobil. The company has worldwide proved reserves of 14.1 billion barrels of oil equivalent. Most of the oil giant's crude is produced in Nigeria, Oman, the UK, and the US. Royal Dutch Shell is also investing heavily in the Athabasca Oil Sands Project, which converts oil sands in Alberta to synthetic crude oil. The company operates 44,000 gas stations (the world's largest retail fuel network) in more than 80 countries. Royal Dutch Shell also produces refined products and chemicals at 35 refineries, transports natural gas, trades gas and electricity, and develops renewable energy sources.

While committed to developing clean energy, in 2009 Royal Dutch Shell announced that it would focus on clean oil production technology (such as carbon sequestration) and biofuels, which are more in line with its core oil and gas competencies, rather than on wind power and solar energy. In 2010 the company formed a $12 billion joint venture with Brazil's Cosan to ramp up ethanol production.

Boosting its oil business, that year Royal Dutch Shell announced its gas-to-liquids plant and liquefied natural gas project in Qatar, which is due to come onstream in 2011. The two projects will deliver 350,000 barrels of oil equivalent per day, or 10% of the company's total production, and make Qatar a core region for Royal Dutch Shell's future growth. It followed this up with the announcement in 2010 to form a $3 billion joint venture with PetroChina to acquire Arrow Energy, which has major natural gas assets in Northern Australia.

Expanding its unconventional natural gas resources, in 2010 the company spent $4.7 billion to acquire East Resources, which holds 1 million acres of Marcellus Shale, one of the fastest-growing shale plays in the US.

In 2009 the company made significant oil discoveries in the deepwater eastern Gulf of Mexico at West Boreas, Vito and the Cardamom Deep, and in 2010 at the Appomattox prospect in the Mississippi Canyon block. The finds expand Shell Oil's long-term development plans in the area.

In response to the BP oil rig disaster in the Gulf of Mexico, the company joined forces with Exxon Mobil, Chevron, and ConocoPhillips to form a $1 billion rapid-response joint venture that will be able to better manage and contain future deepwater spills.

Former CFO Peter Voser, also a director, was named company CEO in 2009. While Royal Dutch Shell's long-term prospects look solid, the global recession, low commodity prices, and a slump in demand for oil and gas led to significantly lower revenues in 2009.

As part of its strategy of selling noncore downstream assets to raise cash, in 2010 Royal Dutch Shell agreed to sell its Finnish and Swedish operations (including a refinery in Gothenburg and 565 gas stations) to Finland-based St1 for $640 million.

HISTORY

In 1870 Marcus Samuel inherited an interest in his father's London trading company, which imported seashells from the Far East. He expanded the business and, after securing a contract for Russian oil, began selling kerosene in the Far East.

Standard Oil underpriced competitors to defend its Asian markets. Samuel secretly prepared his response and in 1892 unveiled the first of a fleet of tankers. Rejecting Standard's acquisition overtures, Samuel created "Shell" Transport and Trading in 1897.

Meanwhile, a Dutchman, Aeilko Zijlker, struck oil in Sumatra and formed Royal Dutch Petroleum in 1890 to exploit the oil field. Young Henri Deterding joined the firm in 1896 and established a sales force in the Far East.

Deterding became Royal Dutch's head in 1900 amid the battle for the Asian market. In 1903 Deterding, Samuel, and the Rothschilds (a French banking family) created Asiatic Petroleum, a marketing alliance. With Shell's non-Asian business eroding, Deterding engineered a merger between Royal Dutch and Shell in 1907. Royal Dutch shareholders got 60% control; "Shell" Transport and Trading, 40%.

After the 1911 Standard Oil breakup, Deterding entered the US, building refineries and buying producers. Shell products were available in every state by 1929. Royal Dutch/Shell joined the 1928 "As Is" cartel that fixed prices for most of two decades.

The post-WWII Royal Dutch/Shell profited from worldwide growth in oil consumption. It acquired 100% of Shell Oil, its US arm, in 1985, but shareholders sued, maintaining Shell Oil's assets had been undervalued in the deal. They were awarded $110 million in 1990.

Management's slow response to two 1995 controversies — environmentalists' outrage over the planned sinking of an oil platform and human rights activists' criticism of Royal Dutch/Shell's role in Nigeria — spurred a major shakeup. It began moving away from its decentralized structure and adopted a new policy of corporate openness.

In 1996 Royal Dutch/Shell and Exxon (now Exxon Mobil) formed a worldwide petroleum additives venture. Shell Oil joined Texaco (now part of Chevron) in 1998 to form Equilon Enterprises, combining US refining and marketing operations in the West and Midwest. Similarly, Shell Oil, Texaco, and Saudi Arabia's Aramco combined downstream operations on the US's East and Gulf coasts as Motiva Enterprises.

In 1999 Royal Dutch/Shell and the UK's BG plc acquired a controlling stake in Comgas, a unit of Companhia Energética de São Paulo and the largest natural gas distributor in Brazil, for about $1 billion. In 2000 the company sold its coal business to UK-based mining giant Anglo American for more than $850 million.

In 2002, in connection with Chevron's acquisition of Texaco, Royal Dutch/Shell acquired ChevronTexaco's (now Chevron) stakes in the underperforming US marketing joint ventures Equilon and Motiva. That year the company, through its US Shell Oil unit, acquired Pennzoil-Quaker State for $1.8 billion. Also that year Royal Dutch/Shell acquired Enterprise Oil for $5 billion, plus debt. In addition, it purchased RWE's 50% stake in German refining and marketing joint venture Shell & DEA Oil (for $1.35 billion).

In 2004 the company reported that it had overestimated its reserves by 24%. The bad news resulted in the ouster of the chairman and CFO.

Revelations of overestimated oil reserves in 2004 prompted a push for greater transparency in the company's organizational structure. This led to the 2005 merger of former publicly traded owners Royal Dutch Petroleum and The "Shell" Transport and Trading Company into Royal Dutch Shell.

Searching for new oil assets, in 2006 the company acquired a large swath of oil sands acreage in Alberta, Canada. Further boosting its oil sands business, in 2007 the company acquired the 22% of Shell Canada that it did not already own.

In 2008 Royal Dutch Shell expanded its exploration assets in Alaska by acquiring 275 lease blocks in the Chukchi Sea for $2.1 billion.

EXECUTIVES

Chairman: Jorma Ollila, age 60
Deputy Chairman: Lord John O. Kerr of Kinlochard, age 68
CEO and Board Member: Peter R. Voser, age 52, $4,524,612 total compensation
CFO and Board Member: Simon Henry, age 49, $1,532,091 total compensation
Executive Director Upstream International and Board Member: Malcolm Brinded, age 57, $3,803,713 total compensation
Chief Human Resources and Corporate Officer: Hugh Mitchell, age 53
Downstream Director: Mark Williams, age 59
Company Secretary: Michiel Brandjes, age 55
EVP Russia and Caspian Region: Charles Watson
EVP Upstream Australia: Ann Pickard
EVP Shell Canada: John Abbott
EVP Americas Shell Gas & Power: Curtis R. Frasier
SVP, General Counsel, and Corporate Secretary, Shell Oil Company: Bill Lowrey
Chairman, Shell Companies in Australia: Russell R. Caplan, age 63
Chairman and Managing Director, Shell Petroleum Development Company Nigeria; VP Production, Africa: Mutiu Sunmonu
Chairman, Shell U.K. Limited: James Smith
President; Director Upstream Americas, Shell Oil Company; Chairman, Shell Canada: Marvin E. Odum, age 52
President, Shell Energy North America (US): Mark Quartermain
Auditors: PricewaterhouseCoopers LLP

LOCATIONS

HQ: Royal Dutch Shell plc
Carel van Bylandtlaan 30
2596 HR The Hague, The Netherlands
Phone: 31-70-377-9111
Web: www.shell.com

2009 Sales

	$ mil.	% of total
Eastern Hemisphere		
Europe	103,424	37
Africa, Asia, Australia/Oceania	80,398	29
Western Hemisphere		
US	60,721	22
Other countries	33,645	12
Adjustments	6,941	—
Total	**285,129**	**100**

PRODUCTS/OPERATIONS

2009 Sales

	$ mil.	% of total
Downstream	250,104	90
Upstream	27,996	10
Corporate & other	88	—
Adjustments	6,941	—
Total	**285,129**	**100**

COMPETITORS

7-Eleven
Ashland Inc.
BHP Billiton
BP
Chevron
ConocoPhillips
Dow Chemical
DuPont
Eastman Chemical
Eni
Exxon Mobil
FEC Resources
Hess Corporation
Huntsman International
Imperial Oil
Koch Industries, Inc.
Marathon Oil
Norsk Hydro ASA
Occidental Petroleum
PEMEX
PETROBRAS
PetroKazakhstan
Petróleos de Venezuela
Repsol YPF
Sinopec Shanghai Petrochemical
Sunoco
TOTAL

HISTORICAL FINANCIALS

Company Type: Public

Income Statement				FYE: December 31
	REVENUE ($ mil.)	NET INCOME ($ mil.)	NET PROFIT MARGIN	EMPLOYEES
12/09	285,129	12,518	4.4%	101,000
12/08	458,361	26,277	5.7%	102,000
12/07	355,782	31,331	8.8%	104,000
12/06	318,845	25,442	8.0%	108,000
12/05	306,731	25,311	8.3%	109,000
Annual Growth	(1.8%)	(16.1%)	—	(1.9%)

2009 Year-End Financials

Debt ratio: 22.6%
Return on equity: 9.5%
Cash ($ mil.): 9,719
Current ratio: 1.14
Long-term debt ($ mil.): 30,862
No. of shares (mil.): 3,121
Dividends
Yield: 5.5%
Payout: 81.4%
Market value ($ mil.): 187,587

Stock History

NYSE: RDS.A

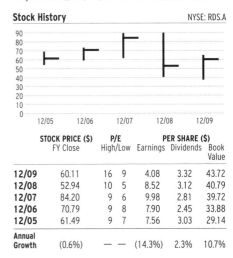

	STOCK PRICE ($) FY Close	P/E High/Low		PER SHARE ($) Earnings	Dividends	Book Value
12/09	60.11	16	9	4.08	3.32	43.72
12/08	52.94	10	5	8.52	3.12	40.79
12/07	84.20	9	6	9.98	2.81	39.72
12/06	70.79	9	8	7.90	2.45	33.88
12/05	61.49	9	7	7.56	3.03	29.14
Annual Growth	(0.6%)	—	—	(14.3%)	2.3%	10.7%

RWE

RWE doesn't stand for Runs With Electricity, but it could. Through its subsidiaries, the energy conglomerate provides electricity and gas to residential and business customers, primarily in Central and Western Europe. RWE is one of Germany's top two electricity suppliers (along with E.ON); it also owns major UK-based utilities, and German-based electricity and gas supplier RWE npower. RWE owns oil and gas exploration and production unit RWE-DEA; other businesses include companies engaged in gas transportation and storage, power generation (including wind), energy trading, information technology, and coal mining. In 2008 RWE served 14 million electricity customers, and 6 million gas customers.

The company discovered that its international acquisitions of water utilities in the early 2000s left it overextended, and RWE decided to sell its water assets in order to save cash and streamline its operations around its core power businesses. In 2006 the company sold its Thames Water unit to Kemble Water Limited, a consortium led by Macquarie Bank's European Infrastructure Funds. It spun off its American Water unit in 2008, and is looking to sell its minority holding in that company in 2010.

As Germany's old industrial controls continue to tumble like Berlin's famous wall in the face of European Union-wide deregulation, RWE is doing its best to cope with the chaos of a new order by restructuring its regional energy businesses. The company's former German utility unit, RWE Energie, lost its regional monopoly status because of deregulation, and RWE has responded by splitting its domestic power generation, distribution, and supply operations into new units. RWE has also responded by acquiring utilities and energy services companies in the Czech Republic, Hungary, Poland, and Slovakia, and by targeting expansion in Europe. It is also boosting its renewable energy initiatives.

In 2008 RWE agreed to sell its gas distribution network in Germany within two years in order to settle an antitrust case regarding its gas supply network.

After being outmaneuvered by EDF in its plan to grow its Pan-European power footprint by acquiring British Energy, RWE in 2009 acquired Dutch power utility Essent for $10.7 billion. It also agreed to form a joint venture with E.ON to develop 6,000 MW of nuclear power capacity in the UK.

In a move to reduce its dependency on the wholesale gas markets, in 2009 RWE agreed to buy 70% of the Breagh North Sea gas field for about $350 million.

HISTORY

Founded at the end of the 19th century, RWE mirrored the industrialization of Germany in its growth. It was formed as Rheinisch-Westfälisches Elektrizitätswerk in 1898 by Erich Zweigert, the mayor of Essen, and Hugo Stinnes, an industrialist from Mulheim, to provide electricity to Essen and surrounding areas. The company began supplying power in 1900.

Stinnes persuaded other cities — Gelsenkirchen and Mulheim — to buy shares in RWE in 1905. In 1908 RWE and rival Vereinigte Elektrizitätswerk Westfalen (VEW) agreed to divide up the territories that each would supply.

Germany's coal shortages, caused by WWI, prompted RWE to expand its coal operations, and it bought Rheinische Aktiengesellschaft für Braunkohlenbergbau, a coal producer, in 1932. RWE also built a power line network, completed in 1930, to connect populous northern Germany with the south. By 1939, as WWII began, the company had plants throughout most of western Germany. However, the war destroyed much of its infrastructure, and RWE had to rebuild.

The company continued to rely on coal for most of its fuel needs in the 1950s, but in 1961 RWE and Bayern Atomkraft sponsored the construction of a demonstration nuclear reactor, the first of several such projects, at Gundremmingen. The Gundremmingen plant was shut down in 1977, and to replace it RWE built two 1,300-MW reactors that began operation in 1984.

RWE began to diversify, and in 1988 it acquired Texaco's German petroleum and petrochemical unit, which became RWE-DEA. By 1990 RWE's operations also included waste management and construction. RWE reorganized, creating RWE Aktiengesellschaft as a holding company for group operations.

RWE-DEA acquired the US's Vista Chemical in 1991, and RWE's Rheinbraun mining unit bought a 50% stake in Consolidation Coal from DuPont. (The mining venture went public in 1999 as CONSOL Energy.) RWE led a consortium that acquired major stakes in three Hungarian power companies in 1995.

Hoping to play a role in Germany's telecommunications market, RWE teamed with VEBA in 1997 to form the o.tel.o joint venture, and RWE and VEBA gained control of large German mobile phone operator E-Plus. The nation's telecom market was deregulated in 1998, but Mannesmann and former monopoly Deutsche Telekom proved to be formidable competitors. In 1999 RWE and VEBA sold o.tel.o's fixed-line business (along with the o.tel.o brand name) and cable-TV unit Tele Columbus. The next year the companies sold their joint stake in E-Plus.

Faced with deregulating German electricity markets, RWE Energie had begun restructuring as soon as the market opened up in 1998. It agreed to buy fellow German power company VEW in a $20 billion deal that closed in 2000. RWE also joined with insurance giant Allianz and France's Vivendi in a successful bid for a 49.9% stake in state-owned water distributor Berliner Wasserbetriebe (Vivendi later spurned an RWE offer to buy its energy businesses).

After taking advantage of deregulating markets in Germany, RWE moved to pick up other European utilities: It acquired UK-based Thames Water (later renamed RWE Thames Water) in 2000 and bought a majority stake in Dutch gas supplier Intergas the next year. In 2002 the company issued an exchange offer to acquire UK electricity supplier Innogy (later renamed RWE npower) for a total of about $4.4 billion in cash and $3 billion in assumed debt. It also completed a $3.7 billion purchase of Czech Republic gas supplier Transgas.

In a move to further streamline operations, RWE sold its 50% stake in refinery and service station subsidiary Shell & DEA Oil to Deutsche Shell and Shell Petroleum. To do battle in an increasingly competitive utility industry, RWE is acquiring stakes in other European utilities. In 2003 RWE also acquired North American utility American Water Works, which was combined with the US operations of RWE Thames Water, for $4.6 billion in cash and $4 billion in assumed debt.

EXECUTIVES

Chairman: Manfred Schneider, age 71
Deputy Chairman: Frank Bsirske
President, CEO, and Member Executive Board;
 Chairman, Amprion: Jürgen Großmann, age 58
COO International and Member Executive Board: Ulrich Jobs, age 57
COO National and Member Executive Board: Rolf Martin Schmitz, age 53
CFO and Member Executive Board: Rolf Pohlig, age 57
Chief Strategy Officer and Member Executive Board: Leonhard Birnbaum, age 43
Member Executive Board: Alwin Fitting, age 57
VP Investor Relations: Stephan Lowis
Manager Investor Relations, UK, USA, Australia, and Canada: Gunhild Grieve
Auditors: PricewaterhouseCoopers AG

LOCATIONS

HQ: RWE Aktiengesellschaft
 Opernplatz 1
 45128 Essen, Germany
Phone: 49-201-12-15025   **Fax:** 49-201-12-15265
Web: www.rwe.com

2009 Sales

	% of total
Europe	
Germany	62
Other countries	20
UK	18
Total	**100**

PRODUCTS/OPERATIONS

2009 Sales

	% of total
Geographic Divisions	
Germany	
Sales & distribution	27
Power generation	13
UK	9
Central & Eastern Europe	7
Netherlands & Belgium	2
Operating Divisions	
Trading & gas midstream	31
Gas & oil upstream	2
Renewables	1
Other	9
Total	**100**

Selected Divisions and Subsidiaries

RWE Energy (German and continental European downstream energy operations)
RWE npower (formerly RWE Innogy, electricity and gas supply, UK)
RWE Supply & Trading (power, gas, coal, and oil trading)
RWE-DEA AG (oil and gas exploration, production, and storage)
RWE Power (upstream energy operations)

COMPETITORS

BP
Centrica
Electricité de France
Endesa S.A.
Enel
E.ON
Exxon Mobil
Royal Dutch Shell
Vattenfall

HISTORICAL FINANCIALS

Company Type: Public

Income Statement

	REVENUE ($ mil.)	NET INCOME ($ mil.)	NET PROFIT MARGIN	EMPLOYEES
12/09	66,201	5,491	8.3%	70,726
12/08	68,995	4,054	5.9%	66,000
12/07	62,566	4,244	6.8%	63,439
12/06	58,387	5,294	9.1%	68,534
12/05	49,526	3,064	6.2%	85,928
Annual Growth	7.5%	15.7%	—	(4.8%)

FYE: December 31

2009 Year-End Financials

Debt ratio: 133.0%
Return on equity: 31.7%
Cash ($ mil.): 4,406
Current ratio: 1.08
Long-term debt ($ mil.): 24,392

No. of shares (mil.): 523
Dividends
Yield: 6.6%
Payout: 67.2%
Market value ($ mil.): 50,980

Stock History

Pink Sheets: RWEOY

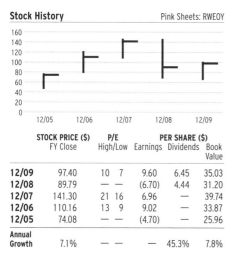

	STOCK PRICE ($) FY Close	P/E High/Low		PER SHARE ($) Earnings	Dividends	Book Value
12/09	97.40	10	7	9.60	6.45	35.03
12/08	89.79	—	—	(6.70)	4.44	31.20
12/07	141.30	21	16	6.96	—	39.74
12/06	110.16	13	9	9.02	—	33.87
12/05	74.08	—	—	(4.70)	—	25.96
Annual Growth	7.1%	—	—	—	45.3%	7.8%

SABMiller

Thanks to this outfit, beer drinkers in every time zone can enjoy Miller Time. SABMiller is one of the world's largest brewers, offering 200 international, national, and local beer brands in 75 countries across the globe. Its brands include Castle Lager, the top beer in Africa, and Grolsch, Miller, and Peroni, just to name a few. In Latin and South America it owns Bavaria and Cervecería Nacional; in the US the company owns 58% of MillerCoors, a joint venture with Molson Coors. In addition to brewing, SABMiller is one of the world's largest bottlers of Coca-Cola products. The Altria Group owns about 27% of SABMiller; Columbia-based Santo Domingo Group owns approximately 14%.

The company continues to build its brewing business through targeted acquisitions, international partnerships, and brand development worldwide. It also leverages its operational infrastructure to sell not only beer but water and soft drinks. To that end, it added the leading water company in Uganda, Rwenzori, in 2010 as part of a strategy to build a total beverage business (beer, soft drinks, and bottled water) in its home country of Africa. In addition to African acquisitions, it is building a malt facility in Uganda, and is planning to open four new breweries in Africa.

Turing from beer to soda, through a direct agreement with The Coca-Cola Company, SABMiller bottles soft drinks for 20 African countries, including its home country of South Africa; it covers another 18 through an alliance with South African beer maker Castel.

In Central and South America, SABMiller provides libations for six countries — Colombia, Ecuador, El Salvador, Honduras, Panama, and Peru. The company is the #1 brewer by market share in each of these countries. In addition it bottles Coke products in El Salvador and Honduras; it also bottles Pepsi products in Panama for PepsiCo International.

Turning to Europe, in 2008 it acquired Dutch brewer Royal Grolsch for about $1.2 billion. SAB has operations in 10 European countries: the Czech Republic, Hungary, Italy, the Netherlands, Poland, Romania, Russia, Slovakia, Spain (the Canary Islands), and Ukraine.

The company's business in the US, where it competes with giant Anheuser-Busch (now part of the world's #1 brewer, Anheuser-Busch InBev), had been relatively stagnant. SABMiller formed MillerCoors with Molson Coors in 2008, adding the popular domestic labels Miller and Coors, as well as imports including Molson Canadian and Pilsner Urquell, and craft brews such as Leinenkugel's and Blue Moon to its US offerings. It is now the second-largest brewer in the US, with a 30% market share.

In China, SABMiller produces the popular Snow beer brand through a joint venture with China Resources Enterprise — called Snow Breweries (CR Snow). (SABMiller owns 49%, China Resources owns 51%.) In a bid to better compete with Tsingtao and build a national presence in China's still-fragmented beer industry, Snow Breweries in 2009 acquired Amber Breweries, which is based in the high-beer-consumption province of Shandong, for about $42 million in 2009.

HISTORY

British sailor Frederick Mead purchased the Castle Brewery in Johannesburg in 1892, about 15 years after gold was discovered in South Africa. Mead took his brewing operation public as South African Breweries (SAB) in 1895. The company launched its flagship Castle Lager three years later and survived the Anglo-Boer War (1899-1902) as South Africa's fastest-growing non-industrial firm. Mead died in 1915.

The brewer acquired the Grand Hotel in Cape Town in 1921 and a stake in Schweppes (carbonated drinks) in 1925. In the late 1940s SAB began an extensive expansion program involving its breweries, small hotels, and pubs. In 1951 it acquired the Hotel Victoria in Johannesburg. An increase in beer taxes during the 1950s led SAB to start producing liquors. With beer demand slackening, South Africa's three largest brewers — SAB, Ohlsson's, and United Breweries — merged in 1956. The new company, which took the SAB name, controlled about 90% of the beer market. Beer taxes continued to pressure sales, and in 1960 SAB acquired control of Stellenbosch Farmers' Winery to extend its product range. In 1962 the restriction prohibiting alcohol consumption by blacks was lifted, opening an enormous market. SAB continued to extend its range of beer brands during the 1960s by adding licenses to brew Amstel and Carling Black Label.

Further diversifying, SAB formed Barsab (an investment venture with Thomas Barlow & Sons) in 1966. The company launched its hotel

division, Southern Sun Hotels, three years later by merging its hotels with those owned by the Sol Kerzner family. The Barsab venture was dissolved in 1973, leaving SAB with furniture and footwear businesses. The following year it acquired the South African bottling business of Pepsi (converted to Coca-Cola in 1977). The company added the beer interests of the Rembrandt Group and a 49% stake in Appletiser, a fruit drinks company, in 1979. (It gained control of it in 1982.)

SAB moved into apparel retailing with its purchase of the Scotts Stores (1981) and Edgars (1982). After forming a joint venture with Ceres Fruit Juices (1986), SAB made a number of investments in South Africa, including Lion Match Company (1987), Da Gama Textiles (1989), and Plate Glass (1992).

In the 1990s the company expanded internationally. It acquired stakes in breweries in Hungary (1993), Tanzania and China (1994), and Poland and Romania (1996). Graham Mackay (now CEO) became managing director in 1996.

The company moved its main listing to the London Stock Exchange in 1999. It then bought controlling interests in Czech brewers Pilsner Urquell and Radegast to become the largest brewer in Central Europe, and sold its 68% interest in Plate Glass to Dibelco. Bevcon (a consortium of three South African companies) sold its 27% interest in SAB in 1999.

The continuing woes of the South African economy in 2000 fueled SAB's desire to continue expanding its international base. In 2001 SAB announced its China Resources Breweries Ltd joint venture in the Sichuan province of China.

In 2002 SAB bought Miller Brewing from Philip Morris (now Altria Group) for $5.6 billion, making it the world's second-largest brewer at the time. SAB then changed its name to SABMiller plc.

SABMiller has invested heavily in China Resources Breweries, with whom it partnered to purchase the Chinese brewing assets of Lion Nathan Limited in 2004.

In 2005 SABMiller acquired almost 97% of Bavaria S.A., the second-largest brewer in South America. Bavaria's brands include Águila, Atlas, Cristal, and Pilsener.

EXECUTIVES

Chairman: Meyer Kahn, age 70
CEO and Director: E.A. G. (Graham) Mackay, age 60, $5,643,995 total compensation
CFO and Director: Malcolm I. Wyman, age 63, $2,881,371 total compensation
Group Company Secretary and General Counsel: John Davidson, age 51
Group Treasurer: David Mallac
Global Purchasing: Dieter Schulze
Director Marketing: Nick Fell, age 56
Director Corporate Affairs: Sue Clark, age 46
Director Human Resources and Supply Chain: Tony van Kralingen, age 52
SVP Investor Relations: Gary Leibowitz
SVP Industry Affairs: Mike Short
CEO, MillerCoors: W. Leo Kiely III, age 63
President, Ursus Breweries: Gary Whitlie
Managing Director, Royal Grolsch: Rob Snel, age 60
Managing Director and Chairman, SAB South Africa: Norman J. Adami, age 55
Managing Director, SABMiller Asia: Ari Mervis, age 46
Managing Director, SABMiller Europe: Alan Clark, age 50
President, SABMiller Latin America: Barry Smith, age 60
President and Chief Commercial Officer, MillerCoors; CEO Miller Brewing: Tom Long, age 51
Auditors: PricewaterhouseCoopers LLP

LOCATIONS

HQ: SABMiller plc
  1 Stanhope Gate
  London W1K 1AF, United Kingdom
Phone: 44-20-7659-0100   **Fax:** 44-20-7659-0111
US HQ: MillerCoors, 3939 W. Highland Blvd.
  Milwaukee, WI 53201
US Phone: 414-931-2000
Web: www.sabmiller.com

2010 Sales

	% of total
Africa	
South Africa	19
Other countries	10
Latin America	23
Europe	22
North America	20
Asia	6
Total	**100**

2010 Brewing Operations

	No. of breweries
Africa	
South Africa	7
Other countries	30
Europe	22
Latin America	17
Asia	12
North America	8
Total	**96**

PRODUCTS/OPERATIONS

Selected Brands

Beer
  North America (Miller Brewing Company and
    MillerCoors LLC joint venture)
    Blue Moon
    Coors Banquet
    Coors Light
    Henry Weinhard's
    Icehouse
    Keystone Light
    Killian's
    Leinenkugel's
    MGD 64
    Mickey's
    Miller Chill
    Miller Genuine Draft
    Miller High Life
    Miller Lite
    Milwaukee's Best
    Molson Canadian
    Olde English 800
    Sparks
    Steel Reserve
Soft drinks and juice
  Appletiser (South Africa)
  Coca-cola (licensed, El Salvador, Honduras, Angola;
    South Africa and 20 other African markets)
  Club (Ghana)
  Malta Vigor (Panama)
  Pepsi (licensed, Panama)
  Tropical (Honduras)
Water
  Ambo (Ethiopia)
  Rwenzori (Uganda)
  Voltic (Ghana, Nigeria)

COMPETITORS

AmBev
Andina
Anheuser-Busch InBev
Asahi Breweries
Asia Pacific Breweries
Boston Beer
Brau Union
Carlsberg A/S
Coca-Cola
Danone Water
Diageo
E. & J. Gallo
FEMSA
FEMSA Cerveza
Foster's Group
Fuller's
Grupo Modelo
Heineken
Kingway Brewery
Kirin Holdings Company
Lion Nathan
Nestlé Waters
Pabst
PepsiCo
Quinsa
San Miguel Corporation
Sapporo
Suntory Holdings
Tsingtao
UB Group

HISTORICAL FINANCIALS

Company Type: Public

Income Statement

FYE: March 31

	REVENUE ($ mil.)	NET INCOME ($ mil.)	NET PROFIT MARGIN	EMPLOYEES
3/10	18,020	1,910	10.6%	70,131
3/09	18,980	2,157	11.4%	68,635
3/08	21,680	2,288	10.6%	69,116
3/07	18,813	1,883	10.0%	66,949
3/06	15,307	1,674	10.9%	53,772
Annual Growth	**4.2%**	**3.4%**	**—**	**6.9%**

2010 Year-End Financials

Debt ratio: 39.2%
Return on equity: 10.8%
Cash ($ mil.): 779
Current ratio: 0.65
Long-term debt ($ mil.): 7,809
No. of shares (mil.): 2,126
Dividends
  Yield: 3.3%
  Payout: 52.5%
Market value ($ mil.): 41,072

Stock History

Pink Sheets: SBMRY

	STOCK PRICE ($) FY Close	P/E High	P/E Low	PER SHARE ($) Earnings	PER SHARE ($) Dividends	PER SHARE ($) Book Value
3/10	19.32	21	8	1.22	0.64	9.37
3/09	10.37	11	6	1.25	0.58	7.23
3/08	11.04	25	5	1.34	0.52	8.25
3/07	11.15	20	4	1.10	0.45	6.78
3/06	11.36	17	5	1.04	0.38	6.14
Annual Growth	**14.2%**	**—**	**—**	**4.1%**	**13.9%**	**11.1%**

Saint-Gobain

One of the world's largest materials groups, Compagnie de Saint-Gobain is in a glass by itself. The mega-group develops, manufactures, and distributes a wide variety of products for construction, transportation, industrial, food storage, and solar energy use. Saint-Gobain operates in four primary sectors: Building Distribution, Construction Products (insulation, roofing, and other products), Innovative Materials (Flat Glass and High-Performance Materials such as mineral ceramics, performance polymers, and glass fabrics), and Packaging (glass bottles). It owns notable brands including Gyproc, Dahl International, and CertainTeed. Saint-Gobain dates to the 1660s, when it made mirrors for the Palace of Versailles.

The group operates in more than 60 nations around the world. It has worked to expand its international presence, particularly its presence in emerging markets in Asia, Latin America, Africa and the Middle East, and Eastern Europe. Another key strategy is developing more sustainability technologies to take advantage of increasing interest in environmental issues.

In another deal, Saint-Gobain has agreed to sell its advanced ceramics unit to US specialty manufacturer CoorsTek for $245 million. To weather the financial crisis, the group has cut costs and worked to improve operating efficiencies. It did not, however, cut its research and development budget.

In 2009 the group established Saint-Gobain Solar, a unit dedicated to solar-related products including photovoltaic panels and solar heating systems. It plans to expand that business by more than ten-fold within five years; to that end, Saint-Gobain acquired the 70% of Luxembourg-based solar roof tiles maker Solarwood Technology it didn't already own in 2010.

French holding company Wendel Investissement is Saint-Gobain's largest shareholder with a stake of 18%. Wendel also has three seats on the company's board of directors.

HISTORY

Originally called Dunoyer, Saint-Gobain (named after the factory location) was founded in 1665 by order of the Sun King, Louis XIV, who needed mirrors to adorn his palaces. Because Venice had the monopoly on glass, Louis lured Venetian artisans to Paris. Some were poisoned by Italian assassins, but enough remained to teach Parisians their secrets. Saint-Gobain glass decorates the Palace of Versailles' Hall of Mirrors.

With its decreed glass monopoly in France, the company grew steadily until the French Revolution interrupted its prosperity. By the early 1800s, however, Saint-Gobain was shining again. It set up a sales office in New York in 1830 and its first foreign subsidiary in Germany in 1857. Under chemist Joseph Gay-Lussac's direction, Saint-Gobain began dabbling in chemicals in the mid-1800s.

Expanding to Italy (1889) and Spain (1904), the firm was Europe's leading glassmaker by 1913. Saint-Gobain pioneered the production of tempered security glass in the 1920s; it diversified into glass fiber in the 1930s.

Pilkington, a UK competitor, developed a glassmaking method in 1959 that obviated the need for polishing and therefore slashed production costs. Saint-Gobain refit its factories to use the Pilkington method to keep its 50% EC market share. In 1968 the shareholding Suez Group forced Saint-Gobain to merge with Pont-à-Mousson (now Saint-Gobain Canalización), then the world's leading iron pipe maker. The merger led to a much-needed restructuring that included selling Saint-Gobain's chemical interests.

The company acquired a majority interest in US building-material maker CertainTeed in 1976. In 1982 it was forced to divest some of its interests when it was nationalized by France's new socialist government. Despite nationalization the company grew steadily during the 1980s, investing in Compagnie Générale des Eaux, the world's largest drinking-water distributor. In 1986, after a change in France's political climate, Saint-Gobain became the first company to be reprivatized. Three years later it purchased Générale Française de Céramique (clay tile) and a controlling interest in Vetri (glass containers, Italy).

Saint-Gobain bought Norton (the world's leader in abrasives) and UK glassmaker Solaglas in 1990. With the 1991 purchases of German glassmakers GIAG and Oberland, Saint-Gobain became the world's #1 glass manufacturer within a year.

After the recession of the early 1990s, Saint-Gobain sold its paper and packaging interests to Jefferson Smurfit in 1994, raising more than $1 billion for acquisitions. With Ball Corporation, it formed a glass container joint venture, Ball-Foster Glass, in 1995; the next year it bought Ball's stake. Acquisitions in 1997 included industrial ceramics firms in Germany and France and UK abrasives maker Unicorn International. In 1998 Saint-Gobain bought Bird Corp. (roofing materials, US) and CALMAR (plastic pump sprayers, US).

In 2000 Saint-Gobain acquired Meyer International (a UK building materials supplier), Raab Karcher (a German building materials distributor), and US-based polymer specialist Chemfab. In 2002 Saint-Gobain acquired the 25% of France-based Lapeyre (doors, windows, cabinetry) stock it didn't own.

In 2005 the company made a hostile $6.5 billion bid for UK drywall/plasterboard maker BPB after friendly overtures were rejected. BPB rejected Saint-Gobain's initial offer as too low. Saint-Gobain came back with a sweetened $6.68 billion bid, which BPB accepted.

Also that year the company formed a joint venture with Owens Corning to merge their reinforcements and composites businesses. Owens Corning bought out Saint-Gobain's 40% stake in the venture for $640 million in 2007.

Saint-Gobain acquired HeidelbergCement's industrial mortars division Maxit in 2007. The deal made Saint-Gobain the top producer in Germany and Scandinavia and strengthened its position in the rest of Europe.

In 2007 it sold 80% of its specialty bottle maker Desjonqueres to two investment funds, Sagard and Cognetas. It planned to sell its packaging operations but halted those plans when the global financial markets crashed.

Saint-Gobain bought a 44% stake in Japanese insulation maker MAG in 2008. Later that year Saint-Gobain was fined nearly £900 million ($1.1 billion) by the European Union for alleged price fixing; it was one of the largest fines ever levied against a single firm. Also in 2008 French holding company Wendel Investissement became Saint-Gobain's largest shareholder with a stake of approximately 20%. Wendel gained two board seats and a third seat in 2009.

EXECUTIVES

Honorary Chairman: Jean-Louis Beffa, age 69
Chairman and CEO: Pierre-André de Chalendar, age 52
CFO: Laurent Guillot, age 41
SVP; President, Innovative Materials Sector (Flat Glass and High-Performance Materials): Jean-Pierre Floris, age 62
SVP; President, Building Distribution Sector: Benoît Bazin, age 41
SVP International Development; General Delegate, Brazil, Argentina, and Chile: Jean-Claude Breffort, age 62
SVP and Director Audit and Internal Control: Jean-François Phelizon, age 64
SVP; Director, Construction Products Sector: Claude Imauven, age 53
SVP; President, Packaging Sector: Jérôme Fessard, age 56
SVP Human Resources: Claire Pedini, age 45
VP Communications: Sophie Chevallon
VP Corporate Planning: David Molho
VP Marketing: Gérard Aspar
VP Research and Innovation: Didier Roux
VP Development and Recruitment: Valerie Gervais
Corporate Secretary: Bernard Field, age 64
General Delegate, North America: Gilles Colas
Director; COO, Saint-Gobain Eurocoustic: Bernard Cusenier, age 63
Auditors: PricewaterhouseCoopers Audit

LOCATIONS

HQ: Compagnie de Saint-Gobain
Les Miroirs, 18 Avenue d'Alsace
92400 Courbevoie, France
Phone: 33-1-47-62-30-00   **Fax:** 33-1-47-78-45-03
US HQ: 750 E. Swedesford Rd., Valley Forge, PA 19482
US Phone: 610-341-7000   **US Fax:** 610-341-7777
Web: www.saint-gobain.com

2009 Sales

	% of total
Western Europe	
France	29
Other countries	42
Asia & emerging countries	16
North America	13
Total	**100**

PRODUCTS/OPERATIONS

2009 Sales by Segment

	% of total
Building distribution	45
Construction products	
Exterior	14
Interior	12
Innovative materials	
Flat glass	12
High-performance materials	8
Packaging & other	9
Total	**100**

Selected Segments and Products

Construction products
  Exterior fittings
    Asphalt roofing shingles
    Siding
    Vinyl fences
  Gypsum
    Ceiling tiles
    EPS insulation
    Plaster
    Plasterboard
  Industrial mortars
    Flooring screed
    Interior rendering
    Masonry mortar
    Tile adhesive and grouting
    Wall rendering products
  Insulation
    Glass wool
    Insulating foam
    Metal frames
    Rock wool
    Soundproof ceilings
  Pipe
    Complete piping systems
    Ductile cast iron and steel manhole covers
Flat glass
  Construction glass
  Furniture glass
  Automotive glazing
  Photovoltaic systems
  Solar heating systems
  Specialty glass
    Fireproof glass
    Nuclear safety glass
High-performance materials
  Abrasives
    Bonded abrasives
    Superabrasives
    Thin grinding wheels
  Ceramics
    Advanced ceramics
    Crystals
    Diesel particulate filters
    Grains and powders
  Performance plastics
    Bearings and seals
    Films, foams, and coated fabrics
    Fluid control systems
  Textiles
    Glass fiber yarn
    Reinforcement fabrics for construction and manufacturing
Packaging
  Glass bottles and jars

COMPETITORS

Anchor Glass
Asahi Glass
Ball Corp.
CRH
DuPont
Georgia-Pacific
Gerresheimer Glas
Guardian Industries
Johns Manville
Knauf Insulation
Kubota
Kyocera
Lafarge
Nippon Electric Glass
Nitto Boseki
Owens-Illinois
PPG Industries
Rexam
RHI
Royal Group
SCHOTT
Wolseley

HISTORICAL FINANCIALS

Company Type: Public

Income Statement
FYE: December 31

	REVENUE ($ mil.)	NET INCOME ($ mil.)	NET PROFIT MARGIN	EMPLOYEES
12/09	53,425	286	0.5%	198,713
12/08	60,674	1,909	3.1%	209,175
12/07	63,577	2,177	3.4%	205,730
12/06	54,703	2,153	3.9%	206,940
12/05	41,423	1,491	3.6%	199,630
Annual Growth	6.6%	(33.8%)	—	(0.1%)

2009 Year-End Financials

Debt ratio: —
Return on equity: 1.3%
Cash ($ mil.): 4,464
Current ratio: —
Long-term debt ($ mil.): —

No. of shares (mil.): 513
Dividends
  Yield: 2.2%
  Payout: —
Market value ($ mil.): 31,099

Stock History
Euronext Paris: SGO

	STOCK PRICE ($) FY Close	P/E High/Low		PER SHARE ($) Earnings	Dividends	Book Value
12/09	60.63	—	—	—	1.36	44.69
12/08	48.62	—	—	—	2.35	39.24
12/07	128.74	—	—	—	—	43.58
12/06	124.64	—	—	—	—	37.14
12/05	86.45	—	—	—	—	28.33
Annual Growth	(8.5%)	—	—	—	(42.1%)	12.1%

Samsung Group

Samsung Group has reason to sing. The *chaebol* (family-controlled conglomerate) has surpassed its former archrival, the erstwhile Hyundai Group, to become the #1 business group in South Korea. Samsung's flagship unit is Samsung Electronics, which is one of the world's top makers of DRAMs and other memory chips, as well as a global heavyweight in all sorts of electronic gear, including LCD panels, DVD players, and wireless phones. Other affiliated companies include credit-card unit Samsung Card, Samsung Life Insurance, Samsung SDS (IT services), Samsung Securities, and trading arm Samsung C&T Corporation.

Samsung C&T also has an engineering and construction division that handles building and civil infrastructure projects, including airports, bridges, roads, subways, and harbors. Samsung also has operations in chemicals and shipbuilding. Samsung Petrochemical Company is a leading producer of purified terephthalic acid (PTA), a raw material used to make polyester fiber. Samsung Heavy Industries (SHI) builds oil tankers, container ships, liquefied natural gas (LNG) carriers, and passenger ships, along with ship automation systems.

In 2007 Samsung was implicated in a wide-ranging bribery scandal. A former top attorney for the conglomerate alleged that the group bribed not only government officials to protect its business interests, but also made regular payoffs to prosecutors, judges, and members of the media. Samsung denied the accusations, calling them "malicious and unfounded."

A government inquiry into the allegations led to the indictment of chairman and CEO Lee Kun-Hee on tax evasion and criminal breach of trust charges in 2008. He was not indicted on any bribery charges. The special prosecutor took note of Samsung's crucial role in the South Korean economy — the group is the country's largest conglomerate and accounts for one-fifth of South Korea's exports — in declining to jail Lee or the other nine Samsung executives who were indicted on similar charges. Lee pleaded not guilty to the charges as his trial began.

The breach of trust charges stemmed from allegations that Lee directed Samsung subsidiaries to sell stock to his son, Jae-Yong, at below-market prices to allow his heir to take greater control of Samsung enterprises.

In a statement, Samsung formally apologized "for causing concerns," and promised to undertake reforms of its corporate policies as a result.

Shortly after the indictment, Lee Kun-Hee resigned as chairman and CEO of Samsung Group, and his son, Lee Jae-Yong, resigned from his post with Samsung Electronics to take another position with the group but outside of South Korea.

After a brief trial, Lee Kun-Hee was convicted in 2008 of tax evasion charges but acquitted on the breach of trust charges. The court suspended a sentence of three years on the conviction, keeping the billionaire industrialist out of prison. Lee Kun-Hee was fined $109 million for evading taxes, however.

At the end of 2009 Lee Kun-Hee was pardoned by Lee Myung-Bak, the president of South Korea, and in 2010 he returned to the Samsung *chaebol* as chairman of Samsung Electronics.

HISTORY

In 1936 Japan-educated Lee Byung-Chull began operating a rice mill in Korea, then under Japanese rule. By 1938 Lee had begun trading in dried fish and had incorporated as Samsung (Korean for "three stars"). WWII left Korea fairly unscathed, and by war's end Samsung had transportation and real-estate adjuncts.

The Korean War, however, destroyed nearly all of Samsung's assets. Left with a brewery and an import business for UN personnel, Lee reconstructed Samsung in South Korea. In 1953 he formed the highly profitable Cheil Sugar Company, the country's only sugar refiner at the time. Textile, banking, and insurance ventures followed.

A 1961 political coup brought Park Chung Hee to power in South Korea. Lee, wealthy and tied to the former government, was accused of illegal profiteering. A 1966 smuggling case involving one of Lee's sons led to another scandal, but charges were dropped when Lee gave the government an immense fertilizer plant. Despite the political change, Samsung still grew, diversifying into paper products, department stores, and publishing.

In 1969, with help from SANYO, Lee established Samsung Electronics, which benefited from the government's export drive and low wage rates. By disassembling Western-designed electronics, Samsung Electronics figured out how to produce inexpensive black-and-white TVs

and, later, color TVs, VCRs, and microwave ovens. It manufactured these products under private labels for corporations including General Electric and Sears. In concert with the government's industrialization push, the *chaebol* also began making ships (1974), petrochemicals (1977), and aircraft engines (1977). By the 1980s Samsung was exporting electronics under its own name.

When Lee died in 1987, his son Lee Kun-Hee assumed control. After years of importing technology and spending freely on R&D, in 1990 Samsung became a world leader in chip production. Encouraged by the government, Samsung agreed to cooperate with fellow *chaebol* Goldstar (now LG Group) to obtain foreign technology to develop LCDs. In 1994 Lee, a longtime car lover, announced plans to form Samsung Motors.

In 1996 Lee was caught in a corruption scandal and got a two-year suspended sentence for bribery. The next year Asian financial markets crashed. To lessen its debt, the group sold Samsung Heavy Industries' construction-equipment business to Sweden's Volvo and sold Samsung Electronics' power-device unit to Fairchild Semiconductor. Also in 1998 the South Korean government fined several *chaebol*, including Samsung, a collective $93 million for illegally funneling money to weaker subsidiaries.

News surfaced in July 2005 that Samsung Group had attempted to acquire Kia Motors in 1997. Conversations between a Samsung official and the former head of a daily newspaper were allegedly intercepted and recorded by the country's National Intelligence Service. The group apologized over the conversation, which also allegedly centered on illegal political donations during the 1997 presidential election.

The group broke ground on its largest overseas facility yet in early 2006 — a mobile phone production and research base in Tianjin, China.

In 2008 Lee Kun-Hee's son and heir apparent, Lee Jae-Yong, transferred to China from South Korea — to hone his management skills, in the official version, and to escape the spotlight of the South Korean media, in unofficial reports.

EXECUTIVES

Chairman and CEO: Choi Gee-sung
Vice Chairman: Lee Sang-Dae
Vice Chairman: Kim Jing-Wan
CTO and Director; Vice Chairman and CEO, Samsung Electronics: Yoon-Woo Lee, age 64
EVP, European Operations: Shin Sang-Heung
EVP, North American Operations; President and CEO, Samsung Electronics America: Choi Chang-Soo
EVP, South East Operations: Shin Jung-Soo
SVP Middle East and African Operations: Bae Yong-Tae
Chief Public Relations Officer: Yoon Soon-Bong
President and CEO, LCD Division, Device Solution Unit, Samsung Electronics: Jang Won-Gi
President and CEO, Samsung Venture Investment Corp.: Choi Woi-Hong
President and CEO, Samsung Fine Chemicals: Bae Ho-Won
President and CEO, Samsung Total Petrochemicals: Yoo Suk-Ryul
President and CEO, Samsung Everland: Choi Joo-Hyeon
President and CEO, Cheil Industries: Hwang Baek
President, Samsung Card: Choi Doh-Seok, age 61
Director; President, Digital Media and Communication: Gee-Sung Choi, age 59
Head Corporate Auditing Team and Director; President, Samsung Electronics: Ju-Hwa Yoon

LOCATIONS

HQ: Samsung Group
Samsung Electronics Bldg.
1320-10 Seocho-2-dong, Seocho-gu
Seoul 137-857, South Korea
Phone: 82-2-2255-0114
US HQ: 105 Challenger Rd., Ridgefield Park, NJ 07660
US Phone: 201-229-4000   **US Fax:** 201-229-4029
Web: www.samsung.com

PRODUCTS/OPERATIONS

Selected Operations

Chemicals
Samsung Fine Chemicals Co., Ltd.
Samsung Petrochemical Co., Ltd.

Electronics
Samsung Corning Precision Glass Co., Ltd. (TV picture-tube glass)
Samsung Electro-Mechanics Co., Ltd. (electronic components)
Samsung Electronics Co., Ltd. (semiconductors, consumer electronics)
Samsung Mobile Display Co., Ltd. (flat panel displays)
Samsung Networks Inc. (calling cards, data communications, Internet telephony, telephone services)
Samsung SDI Co. Ltd. (displays, lithium-ion batteries, corporate research and development)
Samsung SDS Co., Ltd. (systems integration, telecommunications)
Samsung Techwin Co., Ltd. (aircraft engines, cameras, optical instruments, semiconductor manufacturing equipment)

Financial and Insurance
Samsung Card Co., Ltd. (loans, cash advances, financing)
Samsung Fire & Marine Insurance Co., Ltd.
Samsung Investment Trust Management Co., Ltd.
Samsung Life Insurance Co., Ltd.
Samsung Securities Co., Ltd.
Samsung Venture Investment Co., Ltd.

Other
Cheil Worldwide Inc. (advertising)
Cheil Industries Inc. (textiles)
S1 Corporation (security systems)
Samsung C&T Corporation (general trading)
Samsung Engineering Co., Ltd.
Samsung Everland Inc. (amusement parks)
Samsung Heavy Industries Co., Ltd. (machinery, vehicles)
Samsung Lions (pro baseball team)
Samsung Medical Center (hospital)
The Shilla Hotels & Resorts Co., Ltd.

COMPETITORS

ABB	Ningbo Bird
Acer	Nokia
Apple Inc.	Nortel Networks
BenQ	Northrop Grumman
Daewoo International	OCI Company
DuPont	Oki Electric
Electrolux	Panasonic Corp
Epson	Panasonic Electric Works
Ericsson	Philips Electronics
Fujitsu	SANYO
Haier	Sharp Corp.
Hitachi	Siemens AG
Hyundai Corporation	SK Group
IBM	Sony
ITOCHU	Ssangyong
Kyobo Life Insurance	Tatung
LG Group	TDK
Marubeni	telent
Micron Technology	Tokio Marine
Mitsui	Toshiba
Motorola	ZTE
NEC	

HISTORICAL FINANCIALS

Company Type: Group

Income Statement				FYE: December 31
	REVENUE ($ mil.)	NET INCOME ($ mil.)	NET PROFIT MARGIN	EMPLOYEES
12/09	119,229	8,123	6.8%	277,000
12/08	150,999	4,653	3.1%	276,000
12/07	172,853	8,462	4.9%	263,000
12/06	161,479	8,433	5.2%	254,000
12/05	141,421	9,483	6.7%	229,000
Annual Growth	(4.2%)	(3.8%)	—	4.9%

2009 Year-End Financials

Debt ratio: 5.3%
Return on equity: —
Cash ($ mil.): —
Current ratio: —
Long-term debt ($ mil.): 3,041

Net Income History

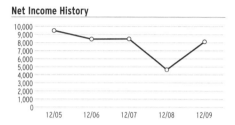

San Miguel

Filipinos filling out grocery lists turn to San Miguel Corporation (SMC). It is the largest beverage and food firm in the Philippines, selling an array of products. Grab one of its Red Horse brewskies and listen up. Its Purefoods unit manufactures just about every food product one's tummy could want — from burger patties to the cheese and condiments to put on the patties, from butter to put on the bun to ice cream and coffee for dessert, Purefoods makes it. SMC also has real estate, packaging, and agribusiness subsidiaries. The conglomerate is in the process of shedding various operations as part of an effort to diversify into heavy industry, banking, infrastructure, telecommunications, and energy.

As part of its strategy to diversify, in early 2009 the company acquired a controlling stake (50.1%) in the country's biggest oil refiner, Petron Corporation. Petron distributes products (including lubrication, grease, asphalt, and specialty products) through a network of bulk plants and more than 1,200 service stations. San Miguel intends to acquire 100% of Petron. SMC also owns a minority share in Manila Electric (Meralco) and the Philippines' Bank of Commerce. It is in the process of acquiring cell phone wholesaler, Express Telecommunications, as well as a stake in a tollway project in the Philippines.

Speading itself farther afield, in 2008 SMC formed a joint venture — Liberty Telecommunications Holdings — with Qatar Telecom (QTel) in order to investigate opportunities in the wireless broadband, mobile and mobile broadband businesses in the Philippines. (QTEL already has operations in the Asian arena, having recently completed the acquisition of a large mobile operator in Indonesia.)

On the sell-off side of its diversification strategy, in 2009 it sold 48% of its San Miguel Brew-

ery to Japan's Kirin for about $1.2 billion. In 2007 it sold its 65% stake in Coca-Cola Bottlers Philippines to The Coca-Cola Company, which had previously owned 35% of the Philippine bottler. The deal was worth $590 million. SMC also sold National Foods, a leading supplier of milk, cheese, and other dairy products in Australia, to Kirin Holdings for about $2.6 billion in 2007. SMC plans to divest itself of its packaging and food businesses as well.

It had planned to sell a minority stake in subsidiary San Miguel Pure Foods but scrapped any sale in 2010 when it was unable to reach an agreement with bidders as to the percentage of Pure Foods to be sold. The final bidders (a consortium made up of the Campos family, which owns food conglomerate NutriAsia, and Century Pacific Group of Companies), with which the company had been in negotiations for more than a year, wanted to acquire 100% ownership of Pure Foods, but San Miguel was insistent upon retaining a majority ownership. The nixing of the Pure Foods sale was a setback in San Miguel's diversification plan.

Top Frontier Investment owns 28% of the company; The San Miguel Corporation Retirement Plan owns some 27%; and ASC Investors owns about 5%.

HISTORY

Don Enrique Barretto y de Ycaza opened La Fabrica de Cerveza de San Miguel, a brewery, in Manila in 1890. By 1900 the European-styled beers of San Miguel were outselling imported brands five to one. The company became a corporation in 1913. By WWI the brewery was selling beer in Hong Kong, Shanghai, and Guam.

Andres Soriano y Roxas joined San Miguel in 1918 and in the 1920s established the Royal Soft Drinks Plant (1922), the Magnolia Ice Cream Plant (1925), and the first non-US national Coca-Cola bottling and distribution franchise (1927). After WWII, the company added additional facilities and factories as it modernized and expanded.

In the 1960s the firm changed its name to San Miguel Corporation (SMC). After the death of Andres in 1964, his son Andres Soriano Jr. became president. He decentralized operations into product segments. SMC continued to diversify in the 1970s.

A family feud erupted in 1983 when members of the controlling Soriano and Zobel families engaged in a proxy battle. Realizing he couldn't win the proxy fight, Enrique Zobel sold all of his shares (about 20% of SMC) to Eduardo Cojuangco, a Ferdinand Marcos ally and president of United Coconut Planters Bank. Upon Soriano's death in 1984, Cojuangco became chairman.

Cojuangco's estranged cousin Corazon Aquino won the 1986 national election, and her government claimed assets associated with Marcos and his followers, including Cojuangco's share of SMC. Cojuangco left the country with Marcos, and Andres Soriano III became CEO. Cojuangco returned to the Philippines in 1989 to reclaim his share of the company. In mid-1998, immediately following Cojuangco-backed Joseph Estrada's election as president of the Philippines, Andres Soriano III stepped down, and Cojuangco returned to SMC's helm.

SMC sold Coca-Cola Bottlers Philippines to Sydney-based Coca-Cola Amatil (CCA) in 1995 in exchange for a 25% stake in CCA. Four years later SMC flirted with plans to sell its interest in CCA, and then went on a buying binge. SMC and a company it majority owns, La Tondeña

Distillers, jointly bought Filipino juice maker Sugarland. SMC then bought Australian brewer J. Boag & Son in 2000.

Estrada announced the government's plan to sell a 27% stake in SMC, but those plans were altered dramatically after Estrada's ouster in early 2001. His successor, President Gloria Arroyo, said the government would seize 47% of the company's shares controlled by United Coconut Planters Bank (27%) and Cojuangco (20%).

Meanwhile, company expansion continued. San Miguel agreed to buy the Philippines' largest processed-meat maker, Pure Foods. The company bought 65% of bottler Coca-Coca Philippines from CCA in July, giving up its stake in CCA as part of the deal. In 2001 SMC then acquired 83% of rival RFM's Cosmos Bottling, the Philippines' #2 soft drink company, further consolidating its domestic beverage dominance. The company transferred its 49% stake in Sugarland to La Tondeña Distillers, which then became the sole owner of the juice maker.

In 2002 Japanese brewer Kirin paid $530 million for 15% of San Miguel. Following an announced expansion plan into Asia, San Miguel purchased a Thailand industrial complex for $20 million in September 2003 and Thai Amarit Brewery in April 2004. SMC snapped up a majority stake in Singapore-based ice-cream producer King's Creameries the following year and acquired control of Australia's National Foods for $1.45 billion.

EXECUTIVES

Chairman and CEO:
Eduardo M. (Danding) Cojuangco Jr., age 74
President and COO: Ramon S. Ang, age 56
CFO and Treasurer: Ferdinand K. Constantino, age 58
Corporate Secretary and General Counsel:
Francis H. Jardeleza, age 60
SVP, San Miguel Brewery: M. L. Menlou B. Bibonia
SVP, Group Audit: Veneranda M. Tomas
SVP Finance: Eduardo Sergio G. Edeza
VP, Corporate Sales: Roberto T. Ongsiako
VP Corporate Finance: Bella O. Navarra
Head Technology Center: Lubin B. Nepomuceno
Head Human Resources: David S. Santos
President, Ginebra San Miguel: Gerardo C. Payumo, age 52
President, San Miguel Pure Foods Company:
Francisco S. Alejo III, age 61
Auditors: Manabat Sanagustin & Co.

LOCATIONS

HQ: San Miguel Corporation
40 San Miguel Ave.
Mandaluyong, Metro Manila 1550, Philippines
Phone: 63-2-632-3000   **Fax:** 63-2-632-3099
Web: www.sanmiguel.com.ph

PRODUCTS/OPERATIONS

2009 Sales

	% of total
Beverages	46
Food	43
Packaging	11
Total	**100**

COMPETITORS

Amcor	First Pacific
Anheuser-Busch InBev	Fonterra
Asahi Breweries	Heineken
Asia Brewery	Indofood
Ayala	International Paper
Ball Corp.	JG Summit Holdings
Banco de Oro	Kraft International
Cargill	Metro Pacific
Coca-Cola	Nestlé
Dairy Farm International	PepsiCo
Danone	SABMiller
Del Monte Pacific	Tsingtao
Diageo	Tyson Foods

HISTORICAL FINANCIALS

Company Type: Public

Income Statement

FYE: December 31

	REVENUE ($ mil.)	NET INCOME ($ mil.)	NET PROFIT MARGIN	EMPLOYEES
12/09	3,753	1,306	34.8%	14,593
12/08	3,524	421	12.0%	15,344
12/07	3,743	202	5.4%	15,252
12/06	5,080	215	4.2%	27,349
12/05	4,270	169	4.0%	26,495
Annual Growth	**(3.2%)**	**66.7%**	**—**	**(13.9%)**

2009 Year-End Financials

Debt ratio: 34.4%
Return on equity: —
Cash ($ mil.): 4,511
Current ratio: 3.17
Long-term debt ($ mil.): 1,548

No. of shares (mil.): 2,291
Dividends
Yield: 53.9%
Payout: 41.5%
Market value ($ mil.): 728

Stock History

Pink Sheets: SMGBY

	STOCK PRICE ($) FY Close	P/E High/Low		PER SHARE ($) Earnings	Dividends	Book Value
12/09	0.32	1	—	0.41	0.17	2.01
12/08	0.18	3	2	0.09	0.11	1.37
12/07	0.34	7	4	0.07	0.26	1.42
12/06	0.31	5	4	0.07	0.16	1.16
12/05	0.31	6	4	0.06	0.07	1.13
Annual Growth	**0.8%**	**—**	**—**	**61.7%**	**24.8%**	**15.4%**

Sanofi-Aventis

Sanofi-Aventis is out to make all the world's creatures a little healthier. The company develops and manufactures prescription and over-the-counter drugs and vaccines for mankind and man's best friend. Sanofi-Aventis' pharmaceutical division is its biggest revenue generator with top sellers that include blood thinners Plavix and Lovenox, cancer drug Taxotere, and insulin brand Lantus. And most US consumers will recognize at least one of the brands produced by subsidiary Chattem (Gold Bond, Icy Hot, and Selsun Blue, to name a few). For the quadrupeds

among us, Sanofi-Aventis operates Merial, one of the world's largest animal health companies. Vaccines are produced through the Sanofi Pasteur subsidiary.

Sanofi-Aventis has worked hard to diversify its operations in the wake of and ahead of patent expirations for some of its biggest sellers. Its allergy blockbuster Allegra and sleep aid Ambien have both lost their patent protection in recent years (as has Lovenox), clearing the way for generic competition.

One area in which the company has been particularly focused on growing is the worldwide OTC market. In late 2009 it shelled out nearly $2 billion to acquire Chattem, which not only gave it a hefty line of well-known consumer products, but also increased Sanofi-Aventis' presence in the US.

Sanofi-Aventis decided it too would take advantage of patent expirations by growing its generics business; especially in the European generics market where it maintains the Winthrop brand. In 2009 it completed a nearly $3 billion takeover bid to acquire the remaining shares of Czech generics maker Zentiva, in which it already held a 25% stake. Sanofi-Aventis became sizeable in South America when it agreed to buy top Brazilian generic drug manufacturer Medley for $663 million in 2009.

In 2010 Sanofi-Aventis took its plan to reduce its reliance on prescription drugs one step further by entering the market for medical devices. The company has joined forces with medical equipment maker Agamatrix to develop blood sugar monitoring devices for diabetes patients.

In 2009 Sanofi-Aventis began cutting back on its pipeline of drug candidates in an effort to save on R&D costs. Late in 2009 Sanofi-Aventis announced plans to cut 1,700 US pharmaceutical jobs or 25% of its American drug operations, ahead of patent expirations. In 2010 Sanofi-Aventis formed a major outsourcing agreement with contract research organization Covance.

Sanofi-Aventis also has animal health operations through its Merial subsidiary, which was formerly a joint venture with Merck. The company announced a new joint venture, combining Merial with Merck's animal health business, Intervet, to create one of the largest animal health companies in the world.

French oil company TOTAL and beauty products firm L'Oréal, both companies important to the firm's convoluted history of mergers and alliances, own significant stakes in Sanofi-Aventis. TOTAL, which controls about 14% of the company's voting rights, is the parent company of Elf Aquitaine, itself the founder of Sanofi-Aventis' predecessor company Sanofi. L'Oréal, which controls some 15%, was once a majority owner of drugmaker Synthélabo, which merged with Sanofi in 1999.

HISTORY

The Sanofi group got its start in 1973 when French oil conglomerate Elf Aquitaine merged several health care, cosmetics, and animal nutrition companies into one subsidiary. In 1977 Sanofi set up a Japanese subsidiary, through which it developed joint ventures with Japan's Meiji Seika Kaisha and Taisha Pharmaceutical firms. In 1979 Elf spun off Sanofi, although it retained ownership of more than half of the company. Almost from its founding Sanofi grew through acquisitions and alliances. During the 1980s it used a massive war chest to buy stakes and set up joint ventures, such as one with American Home Products (now Wyeth) in 1982.

The company bought *couturier et parfumier* Nina Ricci in 1988; such well-known fragrances as L'Air du Temps put it among the industry's top perfume houses. But Sanofi overreached the next two years and was outbid by American Home Products for AH Robins (the drug firm bankrupted by lawsuits over deaths from its Dalkon Shield IUD) and by Rhône-Poulenc (now part of Aventis) for Rorer. A chastened Sanofi and Kodak subsidiary Sterling Drug in 1991 entered into an alliance that didn't involve an exchange of cash.

In 1993 Sanofi bought the perfume business of fashion designer Yves Saint-Laurent. Sanofi began divesting such noncore businesses as veterinarian and biotech operations in 1995. After suffering a loss in its perfume and beauty division in 1996, it sold Nina Ricci. The rest of its beauty division was sold in 1999 in preparation for the Synthélabo merger.

Synthélabo was founded in 1970 when drug firms Laboratoires Dausse and Laboratoires Robert et Carriere merged. In 1973 it became a 53%-owned subsidiary of L'Oréal. In 1980 drug firm Metabio-Jouillie became a part of Synthélabo, making it the #3 drug company in France.

Throughout the 1980s Synthélabo acquired, merged, and formed joint ventures, including some in Japan with Mitsubishi Chemical, Fujisawa Pharmaceutical (1985), and Tanabe Seiyaku (1987). The company continued its acquisitive ways in the 1990s, buying several French rivals.

In 1997 Synthélabo bought Pharmacia & Upjohn's German generic drug subsidiary Sanorania Pharma. As Synthélabo and Sanofi merged in 1999, the new company's concentration on pharmaceuticals dictated several changes, including the sale of the company's interests in joint venture Pasteur Sanofi Diagnostics, as well as its beauty division, home to such well-known perfume lines as Yves Saint Laurent.

But the merger wasn't without its problems: Former Synthélabo CEO Hervé Guérin was ousted as vice-chairman and COO of Sanofi-Synthélabo after he and chairman Jean-François Dehecq butted heads. In 2002 the company boosted its pipeline by entering into an alliance with Immuno-Designed Molecules, a biotechnology firm focusing on cancer drugs.

Sanofi-Synthélabo acquired Aventis in 2004.

The company received EU approval in 2006 for the use of its weight-loss drug rimonabant, sold under the brand name Acomplia. However, in 2008 Sanofi-Aventis suspended marketing efforts for Acomplia due to reports of psychiatric side effects; the company canceled all clinical trials for the drug later that year.

In 2010 the company again decided to boost its treatments for leukemia and certain blood disorders by agreeing to buy privately held TargeGen in a deal that could be worth up to $560 million with milestone payments.

EXECUTIVES

Chairman: Serge Weinberg, age 59
CEO and Director: Christopher A. (Chris) Viehbacher, age 50
EVP and CFO: Jérôme Contamine, age 52
EVP Research and Development: Marc Cluzel, age 54
SVP Pharmaceutical Operations Europe and Canada (excluding France and Germany): Belén Garijo, age 51
SVP Pharmaceutical Operations, United States and Canada: Gregory Irace, age 51
SVP Pharmaceutical Operations, Intercontinental: Antoine Ortoli, age 56

SVP Pharmaceutical Operations, Asia/Pacific and Japan: Olivier Charmeil, age 47
SVP Industrial Development and Innovation: Jean-Philippe Santoni, age 55
SVP Legal Affairs and General Counsel: Karen Linehan, age 51
SVP Human Resources: Roberto Pucci, age 46
SVP and Chief Medical Officer: Jean-Pierre Lehner, age 62
SVP Communications: Laure Thibaud, age 51
SVP Discovery Research: Jean-Marc Herbert
SVP Corporate Social Responsibility: Gilles Lhernould, age 54
SVP Audit and Internal Control Assessment: Marie-Hélène Laimay, age 51
SVP Global Oncology: Debasish Roychowdhury, age 48
SVP Pharmaceutical Customer Solutions: Jean-François Brin, age 45
SVP Corporate Affairs: Philippe Peyre, age 59
SVP Vaccines: Wayne F. Pisano, age 55
VP Media Relations and Corporate Communications: Jean-Marc Podvin
VP Investor Relations: Sébastien Martel
President, Global Operations: Hanspeter Spek, age 60
Auditors: PricewaterhouseCoopers Audit

LOCATIONS

HQ: Sanofi-Aventis
174 avenue de France
75013 Paris, France
Phone: 33-1-53-77-40-00   **Fax:** 33-1-53-77-43-03
Web: www.sanofi-aventis.com

2009 Sales

	% of total
Europe	41
US	32
Other regions	27
Total	**100**

PRODUCTS/OPERATIONS

2009 Sales

	% of total
Pharmaceuticals	88
Vaccines	12
Total	**100**

2009 Pharmaceutical Sales

	% of total sales
Lantus	11
Lovenox	10
Plavix	9
Taxotere	7
Aprovel	4
Eloxatin	3
Other pharmaceuticals	56
Total	**100**

COMPETITORS

Abbott Diabetes Care	Medtronic Limited
Abbott Labs	Merck
Amgen	Novartis
Apotex	Novo Nordisk
AstraZeneca	Pfizer
Bayer AG	Procter & Gamble
Bayer Diabetes Care	Roche Diagnostics
Boehringer Ingelheim	Roche Holding
Bristol-Myers Squibb	Sandoz International
Eli Lilly	GmbH
GlaxoSmithKline	Sunovion
Insulet Corporation	Teva Pharmaceuticals
Johnson & Johnson	Watson Pharmaceuticals
LifeScan	

HISTORICAL FINANCIALS

Company Type: Public

Income Statement

FYE: December 31

	REVENUE ($ mil.)	NET INCOME ($ mil.)	NET PROFIT MARGIN	EMPLOYEES
12/09	44,070	8,156	18.5%	104,867
12/08	40,618	6,050	14.9%	98,213
12/07	42,938	7,738	18.0%	99,495
12/06	38,939	5,290	13.6%	100,289
12/05	33,881	2,683	7.9%	97,181
Annual Growth	**6.8%**	**32.0%**	**—**	**1.9%**

2009 Year-End Financials

Debt ratio: 12.4%
Return on equity: 12.3%
Cash ($ mil.): 6,725
Current ratio: 1.60
Long-term debt ($ mil.): 8,543
No. of shares (mil.): 2,622
Dividends
  Yield: 2.8%
  Payout: 54.0%
Market value ($ mil.): 147,551

Stock History

NYSE: SNY

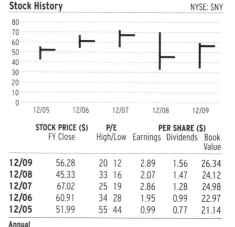

	STOCK PRICE ($) FY Close	P/E High/Low		PER SHARE ($) Earnings	Dividends	Book Value
12/09	56.28	20	12	2.89	1.56	26.34
12/08	45.33	33	16	2.07	1.47	24.12
12/07	67.02	25	19	2.86	1.28	24.98
12/06	60.91	34	28	1.95	0.99	22.97
12/05	51.99	55	44	0.99	0.77	21.14
Annual Growth	**2.0%**	**—**	**—**	**30.7%**	**19.3%**	**5.7%**

SAP AG

SAP's plans to dominate the software world are very enterprising. The company is the leading provider of enterprise resource planning (ERP) software used to integrate back-office functions such as distribution, accounting, human resources, and manufacturing. More than 97,000 companies in some 120 countries use its software. SAP has leveraged its prominent position in the ERP market to expand into related fields, including business intelligence, CRM software, database products, and mobile infrastructure tools. As part of that strategic push, the company acquired business intelligence software provider Business Objects for $6.8 billion in 2008 and bought Sybase for about $5.8 billion in 2010.

SAP's acquisition of Business Objects expanded its product line and bolstered its business intelligence offerings, but was also a response in part to competitive pressure from Oracle, Microsoft, Hewlett-Packard, and IBM. The Sybase purchase added both database products and tools for transmitting and managing data to smartphones and other mobile devices; it also increased SAP's competition with Oracle, which has been particularly aggressive in encroaching on SAP's territory in recent years.

The replacement of former CEO Léo Apotheker in February 2010 by co-CEOs Bill McDermott and Jim Hagemann Snabe had led to speculation that SAP might become more active on the acquisition front. The SAP board declined to renew Apotheker's contract amid growing shareholder unease that rivals (Oracle in particular) were stealing too much of SAP's market share.

SAP has historically eschewed pursuing acquisitions and has instead methodically transitioned towards incorporating Web-based capabilities into its product lines, as well as tailoring its offerings for various industries (including financial services and retail), and expanding its products for small and midsized businesses. The company's huge installed base of customers provides a steady stream of recurring licensing and service revenues and profits. When it has relied on acquisitions the deals have typically been smaller, select purchases, such as the 2009 purchase of France-based Highdeal, a developer of transaction automation and service provisioning applications.

Like many large software providers, SAP is working towards making much of its software available as hosted, on-demand applications as more and more customers move from traditional client/server installed software to distributed software in cloud-computing environments. It has enhanced its service offerings (with an emphasis on expanding its services for large enterprise clients) and focused on key industries such as banking, retail, utilities, and the public sector.

Three of SAP's founders — Hasso Plattner, Dietmar Hopp, and Klaus Tschira — collectively control about 28% of the company.

HISTORY

Former IBM software engineers Hasso Plattner, Hans-Werner Hector, Dietmar Hopp, Claus Wellenreuther, and Klaus Tschira started SAP in 1972 when the project they were working on for IBM was moved to another unit.

While rival software firms made many products to automate the various parts of a company's operations, these engineers decided to make a single system that would tie a corporation together. In 1973 they launched an instantaneous accounting transaction processing program called R/1. By 1979 they had adapted the program to create R/2, mainframe software that linked external databases and communication systems.

The company went public in 1988. That year Plattner began a project to create software for the computer network market. In 1992, as sales of its R/2 mainframe software lagged, SAP introduced its R/3 software.

In 1996 Hector decided to sell holdings amounting to about 10% of SAP's stock, a move that possibly undermined hostile-takeover barriers; he left the company after a dispute with Hopp.

In 1998 SAP listed its stock on the NYSE. In 1999 the company expanded on the Internet, unveiling a Web-based exchange (mySAP.com) supporting online transactions and other services. The company's longstanding resistance to employee stock options weakened in 2000 when SAP approved an option program to offset the loss of more than 200 key US managers in an 18-month period. Later that year SAP launched a US subsidiary (SAP Markets) and increased its minority stake in software maker Commerce One. In 2001 SAP acquired enterprise portal software provider Top Tier Software, renaming it SAP Portals. It also invested additional money

in Commerce One, raising its ownership stake to about 20%. The company reabsorbed its SAP Portals and SAP Markets subsidiaries in 2002, integrating their offerings into its mySAP product family.

The next year SAP announced it was acquiring the public stake in SAP SI as part of a plan to fold that company into its services operations. Following Oracle's acquisition of ERP rival PeopleSoft, SAP acquired TomorrowNow, a PeopleSoft support firm, in an effort to lure customers away from Oracle.

In 2005 SAP agreed to acquire retail software specialist Retek, but it was eventually outbid by Oracle. Later in the year SAP acquired point-of-sale software provider Triversity, as well as KhiMetrics, a developer of pricing and forecasting software for the retail market.

EXECUTIVES

Chairman: Hasso Plattner, age 66
Deputy Chairman: Lars Lamadé, age 38
Co-CEO; CEO, Business Solutions & Technology: Jim Hagemann Snabe, $1,040,300 total compensation
Co-CEO; President and CEO, Global Field Operations: William R. (Bill) McDermott, age 48, $1,168,900 total compensation
COO: Gerhard Oswald, age 56, $4,415,487 total compensation
CFO: Werner Brandt, age 56, $2,335,677 total compensation
CTO: Vishal Sikka
COO, SAP North America: Steven M. (Steve) Winter
Interim Chief Communications Officer: Jen Roach
SVP and Chief Customer Officer: Jeff Harvey
SVP and General Manager, Central Region, SAP North America: Maj. Paul Carreiro
SVP Operations and Communications: Rick Knowles
SVP and General Manager, East Region, SAP North America: Gregory (Greg) McStravick
President, SAP Asia/Pacific and Japan: Steve Watts
President, SAP China: Hera K. Siu
President, SAP North America; CEO, SAP America: Robert Enslin
Head Global Human Resources and Director Labor Relations: Angelika Dammann
Head Investor Relations: Stefan Gruber
Auditors: KPMG AG

LOCATIONS

HQ: SAP AG
Dietmar-Hopp-Allee 16
69190 Walldorf, Germany
Phone: 49-6227-74-7474   **Fax:** 49-6227-75-7575
US HQ: 3999 West Chester Pike
Newtown Square, PA 19073
US Phone: 610-661-1000
Web: www.sap.com

2009 Sales

	% of total
Americas	
US	25
Other Americas	8
EMEA	
Germany	19
Other EMEA	34
Asia/Pacific	
Japan	5
Other Asia/Pacific	9
Total	**100**

PRODUCTS/OPERATIONS

2009 Sales

	% of total
Software & related services	77
Professional services & other	23
Total	**100**

2009 Sales

	% of total
Service Industries	23
Discrete Industries	20
Process Industries	19
Consumer Industries	19
Public Services	10
Financial Services	9
Total	**100**

Selected Software

SAP Business All-in-One
SAP Business ByDesign
SAP Business One
SAP Business Suite

Selected Services

Application hosting
Business consulting
Custom development
Financing
Implementation
Maintenance
Training

COMPETITORS

BMC Software
CA, Inc.
CDC Software
Epicor Software
Hewlett-Packard
IBM
Lawson Software
Microsoft
Oracle
salesforce.com

HISTORICAL FINANCIALS

Company Type: Public

Income Statement

FYE: December 31

	REVENUE ($ mil.)	NET INCOME ($ mil.)	NET PROFIT MARGIN	EMPLOYEES
12/09	15,295	2,505	16.4%	47,578
12/08	16,322	2,636	16.2%	51,536
12/07	15,058	2,822	18.7%	58,610
12/06	12,414	2,471	19.9%	39,355
12/05	10,115	1,778	17.6%	34,550
Annual Growth	**10.9%**	**8.9%**	**—**	**8.3%**

2009 Year-End Financials

Debt ratio: —
Return on equity: 22.4%
Cash ($ mil.): 2,700
Current ratio: 1.54
Long-term debt ($ mil.): —

No. of shares (mil.): 1,188
Dividends
  Yield: 0.8%
  Payout: 24.2%
Market value ($ mil.): 79,678

Stock History

NYSE: SAP

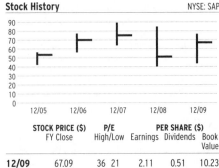

	STOCK PRICE ($) FY Close	P/E High/Low		PER SHARE ($) Earnings	PER SHARE ($) Dividends	PER SHARE ($) Book Value
12/09	67.09	36	21	2.11	0.51	10.23
12/08	51.05	38	19	2.21	0.71	8.59
12/07	75.14	38	28	2.34	0.68	8.05
12/06	70.05	38	28	2.01	0.45	6.82
12/05	53.38	39	30	1.42	0.34	5.79
Annual Growth	**5.9%**	**—**	**—**	**10.4%**	**10.7%**	**15.3%**

SAS AB

Airline group SAS carries passengers throughout Scandinavia — and well beyond. Most of the company's sales come from its Scandinavian Airlines operations, which include units operating in Denmark, Norway, and Sweden, as well as Scandinavian Airlines International, which serves destinations in Europe, North America, and Asia. SAS and its associated carriers serve more than 175 destinations with a fleet of about 260 aircraft. SAS extends its reach as a member of the global Star Alliance, a marketing and code-sharing partnership led by United Continental's United Airlines and Lufthansa. (Code-sharing allows carriers to sell tickets on one another's flights and thus offer potential passengers more destinations.)

Carriers outside the Scandinavian Airlines system generate about 10% of SAS sales and have become increasingly important contributors to the parent company's revenue mix. Subsidiaries include Widerøe, a Norway-based regional airline; Finnish carrier Blue1; and Estonian Air. SAS's aviation services businesses, which account for about 25% of sales, include ground-handling and aircraft maintenance units, as well as freight hauler SAS Cargo.

The SAS growth strategy calls for the company to focus on its core markets in Northern Europe, and toward that end, in 2009 it sold its majority stake in Spanair, Spain's #2 carrier (behind Iberia), to an assortment of Spanish investors. (It still owns about 20% of Spanair.) In addition, SAS plans to divest its 49% stake in Estonian Air. SAS agreed in 2009 to sell its 20% stake in fellow Star Alliance member bmi to Lufthansa, which already owned 80% of the UK carrier.

A difficult financial environment brought about by unexpectedly high fuel prices followed by a plunge in travel demand has led SAS to join many of its peers in reducing flight capacity, grounding aircraft and cutting jobs. The company has also considered seeking outside investment, and Lufthansa has been reported to be considering a bid; Air France-KLM is also a candidate. In August 2009 the carrier announced it would slash up to 1,500 more jobs, bringing its total of jobs cut to about 9,000 — some 40% of the SAS workforce. In an effort to raise funds and streamline its operations, SAS sold its 20% stake in regional airline Skyways Holding in late 2010; Largus Holding now owns 100% of Skyways.

Its involvement in an air-cargo price-fixing scheme damaged SAS's image and bottom line. In June 2008 SAS Cargo Group paid a $54 million criminal fine to the US government for its part in the antitrust conspiracy.

The Swedish government owns 21% of SAS while the government of Norway owns 15% and the government of Denmark owns 14%.

HISTORY

The national airlines of Sweden (ABA), Norway (DNL), and Denmark (DDL) first met in 1938 to negotiate joint service to New York. The plan was delayed by WWII but kept alive in Sweden, where banker Marcus Wallenberg founded Svensk Interkontinental Luftrafik (SILA), a private airline that in 1943 replaced ABA as Sweden's international carrier. With SILA's financial backing, the yet-to-be-formed Scandinavian Airlines System (SAS) obtained the necessary landing concessions to open a Stockholm-New York air route in 1945. SAS was formed in 1946.

After opening service to South America (1946), Southeast Asia (1949), and Africa (1953), SAS inaugurated the world's first commercial polar route in 1954. It formed charter airline Scanair in 1961 and Danish domestic carrier Danair, through a joint venture, in 1971.

Deregulation of US airlines (1978) signaled the demise of nationally protected airlines. SAS seemed ill-equipped to adapt and reported its first loss in 18 years in 1980. Jan Carlzon, former head of Swedish airline Linjeflyg, became SAS's president in 1981. By targeting businessmen as the airline's most stable market and substituting an economy-rate business class for first-class service on European flights, Carlzon turned SAS's losses into profits by the end of 1982.

The company bought about 25% of Airlines of Britain Holdings in 1988, gaining a foothold at London's Heathrow Airport. Another purchase that year brought SAS nearly 10% of Continental Airlines Holdings. In 1989 the airline signed agreements that provided route coordination and hub-sharing with Swissair, Finnair, LanChile, and Canadian Airlines International.

SAS tried in the early 1990s to merge with KLM, Swissair, and Austrian Airlines to create a new international carrier, but that effort failed in 1993, leading to the replacement of Carlzon. New CEO Jan Stenberg consolidated the group, shed noncore businesses, and cut 15,000 jobs. By late 1994 SAS had sold SAS Service Partner (catering, its largest nonairline unit), Diners Club Nordic, and most of the SAS Leisure Group. By spinning off its 42% stake in LanChile and creating a new Latvian airline with Baltic International, SAS focused its air routes in Scandinavia, Western Europe, and the Baltic region.

The SAS trading subsidiary was folded into the airline unit in 1994. In 1997 the company joined UAL's United Airlines, Lufthansa, VARIG, and others to form the Star Alliance. In 1998 SAS acquired Finland's Air Botnia (later renamed Blue1).

SAS boosted its cargo services in 2000 when it partnered with giants Lufthansa Cargo and Singapore Airlines to harmonize their cargo handling and information technology services.

The SAS consortium was restructured into a single publicly traded company, SAS AB, in 2001. That year SAS and Danish carrier Maersk Air were fined by the European Commission for agreeing not to compete on certain Scandinavian routes. SAS EVP Vagn Sørensen accepted responsibility for the illegal agreement and resigned. A month later SAS's board of directors also resigned, and a new board was elected at an extraordinary shareholders' meeting held later that year. At that time Jørgen Lindegaard took over the CEO position.

Also in 2001 a Scandinavian Airlines flight crashed while attempting to take off from Milan's Linate airport, killing all 110 on board. The following year SAS joined with Deutsche Lufthansa and Singapore Airlines to form WOW, a global cargo alliance.

To focus on its core airline operations, SAS sold a 25% interest in its Rezidor hotel business to Carlson Hotels Worldwide in 2005. (By 2007 SAS had sold the remainder of its stake in the hotel unit.)

Lindegaard stepped down in 2006 after five years at the helm. Mats Jansson, the CEO for Swedish food importer and retailer Axel Johnson AB, took over as president and CEO. Jansson stepped down in October 2010, and Rickard Gustafson was named to replace him beginning in early 2010. In the meantime, John Dueholm is serving as acting CEO.

EXECUTIVES

Chairman: Fritz H. Schur, age 58
Vice Chairman: Jacob Wallenberg, age 54
Acting President and Acting CEO: John S. Dueholm, age 59
COO SAS Scandinavian Airlines: Peter Möller
Deputy President and CFO: Mats Lönnqvist, age 56
Deputy President, EVP Human Resources and Corporate Communications and Strategy, SAS Scandinavian Airlines: Henriette Fenger Ellekrog, age 44
CIO: Mats Fagerlund
Chief Commercial Officer, SAS Scandinavian Airlines: Robin Kamark
EVP, SAS Individual Holdings: Benny Zakrisson, age 50
SVP and General Counsel: Mats Lönnkvist, age 55
VP Sales, Asia Pacific and EMEA: David Hughes
VP Corporate Communications: Bertil Ternert
CEO SAS Cargo: Leif Rasmussen
CEO Widerøe: Lars Kobberstad
CEO Blue1: Stefan Wentjärvi
Account Manager: Tomas Linden
Director Media Relations: Elisabeth Manzi
Auditors: Deloitte & Touche AB

LOCATIONS

HQ: SAS AB
Frösundaviks Allé 1, Solna
SE-195 87 Stockholm, Sweden
Phone: 46-8-797-00-00
Web: www.sasgroup.net

2009 Traffic Revenue

	% of total
Europe	41
Domestic	33
Intercontinental	16
Intra-Scandinavian	10
Total	**100**

PRODUCTS/OPERATIONS

2009 Sales

	% of total
Traffic revenue	
Passenger revenue	73
Charter	5
Mail & freight	2
Other	4
Other operating revenue	
Ground handling services	3
Terminal & forwarding services	2
Technical maintenance	1
In-flight sales	1
Sales commissions & charges	1
Other	8
Total	**100**

COMPETITORS

Aer Lingus
Air Berlin
Air France-KLM
Alitalia
AMR Corp.
A.P. Møller – Mærsk
British Airways
Delta Air Lines
easyJet
Finnair
Iberia
Ryanair
Servisair
Virgin Atlantic Airways

HISTORICAL FINANCIALS

Company Type: Public

Income Statement			FYE: December 31
	REVENUE ($ mil.)	NET INCOME ($ mil.)	NET PROFIT MARGIN	EMPLOYEES
---	---	---	---	---
12/09	6,248	410	6.6%	18,786
12/08	6,852	552	8.1%	23,082
12/07	8,162	100	1.2%	26,538
12/06	7,317	674	9.2%	26,554
12/05	6,971	22	0.3%	32,363
Annual Growth	(2.7%)	108.0%	—	(12.7%)

2009 Year-End Financials

Debt ratio: —
Return on equity: 30.3%
Cash ($ mil.): 69
Current ratio: 0.71
Long-term debt ($ mil.): —

No. of shares (mil.): 329
Dividends
  Yield: —
  Payout: —
Market value ($ mil.): 5,533

Stock History

OMX Stockholm: SAS

	STOCK PRICE ($) FY Close	P/E High/Low	PER SHARE ($) Earnings	Dividends	Book Value
12/09	16.82	36 2	6.02	—	4.82
12/08	146.45	— —	(147.29)	—	3.40
12/07	388.94	— —	—	—	8.13
12/06	509.92	— —	—	—	7.26
12/05	393.76	— —	—	—	4.39
Annual Growth	(54.5%)	— —	—	—	2.3%

Saudi Arabian Oil

State-owned Saudi Arabian Oil Co. (Saudi Aramco) is the king of oil. It is the world's #1 oil producer, supplying more than 10% of the world's oil demand. In 2009 the company reported proved oil reserves of about 260 billion barrels; it also owns 275 trillion cu. ft. of natural gas reserves (the fourth largest in the world). It has a production capacity of 12 million barrels a day, operates refineries, markets oil internationally, and distributes it domestically. Saudi Aramco owns a fleet of oil tankers and invests in refineries, marketing, and distribution ventures in other countries, including China, Japan, South Korea, and the US.

Saudi Aramco harnesses the know-how of oil partners in other countries to develop its reserves, as well as to enhance its oil production, storage, marketing, and distribution capabilities. For example, Motiva Enterprises (its 50-50 joint venture with Royal Dutch Shell's Shell Oil) operates three US refineries and markets its gasoline at Shell-branded gas stations. A planned $7 billion expansion of Motiva's refinery in Port Arthur, Texas, will make it the largest in the US and one of the biggest in the world.

Another joint venture is Petro Rabigh, an integrated refining/petrochemical facility built in Saudi Arabia. Petro Rabigh went public in early 2008; Saudi Aramco and Sumitomo Chemical each own 38% of the company. In 2008 the company teamed up with TOTAL to form the Jubail Refining and Petrochemical Company. The JVs are building two new refineries in Saudi Arabia with a combined capacity of 800,000 barrels per day. In 2009 Saudi Aramco began exporting ultra-low sulfur diesel fuels through a joint-venture with Royal Dutch Shell.

In 2009 the company boosted its overall production capacity by 2 million barrels per day (an amount larger than the oil output of several major oil producing countries).

Saudi Aramco dates back to 1933 when Saudi Arabia opened up a large area for exploration by Standard Oil of California (now Chevron).

EXECUTIVES

Chairman; Minister of Petroleum and Mineral Resources: Ali I. Al-Naimi
President, CEO, and Director: Khalid A. Al-Falih
SVP Exploration and Producing and Director: Amin H. Nasser
SVP Finance: Abdullatif A. Al-Othman
SVP Refining, Marketing, and International: Khalid G. Al-Buainain, age 51
SVP Operations, Saudi Aramco: Abdulrahman F. Al-Wuhaib
SVP Engineering and Project Management and Director: Salim S. Al-Aydh
SVP Industrial Relations and Director: Abdulaziz F. Al-Khayyal
VP, Petrochemical Project: Abdulaziz Al-Judaimi
General Counsel: David B. Kultgen
Executive Director, Business Development: Motassim Ma'ashouq

LOCATIONS

HQ: Saudi Arabian Oil Co.
P.O. Box 5000
Dhahran 31311, Saudi Arabia
Phone: 966-3-872-0115   **Fax:** 966-3-873-8190
US HQ: 9009 West Loop S., Houston, TX 77096
US Phone: 713-432-4000
Web: www.saudiaramco.com

PRODUCTS/OPERATIONS

Selected Subsidiaries and Affiliates

Aramco Associated Company (US)
Aramco Gulf Operations Company Limited
Aramco Overseas Company B.V. (the Netherlands)
Aramco Training Services Company (US)
Jubail Refining and Petrochemical Company
Petro Rabigh Company
Saudi Refining Inc. (US)
  Motiva Enterprises LLC (50%, US)
Saudi Petroleum Ltd. (Singapore/Japan)
Saudi Petroleum International, Inc. (US)
Saudi Petroleum Overseas Ltd. (UK)
Vela International Marine Limited

COMPETITORS

BP
Chevron
Exxon Mobil
NIOC
PEMEX
PETROBRAS
Petróleos de Venezuela
Qatar Petroleum
Royal Dutch Shell
TOTAL

HISTORICAL FINANCIALS

Company Type: Government-owned

Income Statement			FYE: December 31
	REVENUE ($ mil.)	NET INCOME ($ mil.)	NET PROFIT MARGIN	EMPLOYEES
---	---	---	---	---
12/08	233,300	—	—	54,441
12/07	162,300	—	—	52,093
12/06	168,000	—	—	51,356
12/05	150,000	—	—	51,843
12/04	116,000	—	—	—
Annual Growth	19.1%	—	—	1.6%

Revenue History

Schneider Electric

If you're building something and are hungry for power, this company could help. Schneider Electric is one of the world's largest manufacturers of equipment for electrical power distribution and for industrial control and automation. The company helps power generators distribute electricity; designs automation systems for the automobile and water treatment industries; builds smart electric networks and utility management systems for energy, water treatment, oil and gas, and marine applications; and manages electric power in residential, industrial, and commercial buildings. With operations in more than 100 countries, Schneider Electric gets more than half of its sales outside Europe.

Schneider's brands include Merlin Gerin and Square D (electrical distribution products), as well as Télémécanique (automation and control). The company's electrical lineup and scope of business continues to mount through acquisition of add-on businesses, ones that complement and expand existing operations. It is also growing geographically through acquisitions, particularly in high-growth emerging economies including China, India, Russia, and Brazil.

Schneider rang in 2010 by agreeing to acquire Cimac, a Dubai-based control and system integrator. The acquisition would increase the company's geographic footprint in the Gulf countries. It next agreed to purchase Australia's Scada Group for A$200 million (about €140 million or around $191 million). With operations in North America and the UK in addition to "Oz," Scada makes telemetry products for customers in electric power generation, oil and gas production, and water/wastewater treatment.

Schneider Electric was selected by AREVA, along with ALSTOM, to purchase AREVA's power transmission and distribution business (moving electricity long distances to homes and businesses). General Electric and Toshiba were ousted as potential buyers in favor of the two French companies, which promised not to lay off workers and to offer positions to AREVA employees in their respective geographic areas. ALSTOM and Schneider completed the acquisition agreement with AREVA in 2010.

In 2008 Schneider acquired Xantrex Technology for about $500 million to strengthen its product portfolio in power inverters for solar and wind energy products. Earlier that year the company purchased Wessen, a Russia-based maker of switches, sockets, and other wiring devices that complements Schneider's existing wiring portfolio.

In 2007 Schneider bought video security systems specialist Pelco for about $1.5 billion, adding to its Building Automation business. Earlier that year Schneider acquired American Power Conversion (APC) for about $6.1 billion in cash, widening the company's portfolio in uninterruptible power supply systems.

Other Schneider operations include Kavlico (sensors and transducers) and Dinel (optoelectronic sensors and amplifiers). In 2003 the company acquired TAC Limited (building automation and security controls), but it was not until 2009 that Schneider fully integrated TAC into its company structure as Schneider Electric Buildings Business. Schneider sells its products to the construction, electric power, industrial, and infrastructure markets.

HISTORY

Schneider Electric's predecessor was founded in 1782 to make industrial equipment. After the upheavals of the French Revolution and the Napoleonic Wars, the firm came under the control of brothers Adolphe and Eugene Schneider in 1836. Within two years they had built the first French locomotive (the country's first rail line had opened in 1832).

Schneider became one of France's most important heavy-industry companies, branching into a variety of machinery and steel operations. However, the country's industrial development continued to trail that of Britain and Germany due to recurrent political strife, including the revolution of 1848 and the Franco-Prussian War. France also possessed fewer coal and iron deposits.

During WWI Schneider was a key part of France's war effort. It entered the electrical contracting business in 1929 and fought off nationalization attempts in the mid-1930s.

The blitzkrieg of 1939 brought much of France under Nazi occupation, and the Schneider factories that were not destroyed were commandeered by the Germans. The company rebuilt after the war, aided by the French government. It was restructured as a holding company, and its operating units were split into three subsidiaries: civil and electrical engineering, industrial manufacturing, and construction. Charles Schneider, the last family member to lead the company, died in 1950.

In 1963 Schneider concluded an alliance with the Empain Group of Belgium, and by 1969, three years after Schneider went public, the two companies merged to become Empain-Schneider. It was a period when the company made numerous noncore acquisitions, entering such fields as ski equipment, fashion, publishing, and travel.

Schneider began reorganizing in 1980. The effort entered its final phase in 1993 with a major recapitalization that saw the merger of its former parent company, Société Parisienne d'Entreprises et de Participations, with Schneider SA and the issue of new stock to existing stockholders. It also streamlined operations. Merlin Gerin

(acquired 1975) and Télémécanique (1988) became Schneider Electric in Europe, and their North American operations were merged into Square D after its acquisition in 1991.

Schneider's 1994 takeover of two Belgian subsidiaries led Belgium's government to charge then-CEO Didier Pineau-Valencienne with fraud in the valuation of the stock. (A Belgian newsmagazine reported in 1997 that the government turned down an offer to settle out of court.)

In 1996 Schneider established the Schneider Electric (China) Investment Co. in Beijing, China's first totally French-owned firm. In 1999 Schneider agreed to pay $1.1 billion for Lexel, a joint venture owned by Finland's Ahlstrom and Denmark's NKT Holding, to broaden its electrical equipment offerings for the household. That year the company changed its name to Schneider Electric.

In 2004 Schneider acquired the Kavlico sensor business of Solectron and the US-based Andover Controls (building automation and security controls) from Balfour Beatty. Schneider in 2006 acquired the Asian and US operations of Invensys Building Systems. Also in 2006 Schneider bought the Napac subsidiary of L'Air Liquide. The French firm makes remote management products for the infrastructure market.

EXECUTIVES

Chairman: Henri Lachman, age 71
Vice Chairman: Léo Apotheker, age 57
President and CEO: Jean-Pascal Tricoire, age 47
CIO: Hervé Coureil, age 40
Chief Marketing Officer: Aaron L. Davis, age 44
Secretary: Philippe Bougon
EVP IT Business: Laurent Vernerey, age 50
EVP Industry Business: Clemens Blum
EVP Finances: Emmauel Babeau
EVP Global Supply Chain: Hal Grant, age 50
EVP Power, North America and Buildings Businesses: Christopher B. (Chris) Curtis, age 53
EVP Custom Sensors and Technologies Business: Eric Pilaud, age 53
EVP Power Asia/Pacific Business: Eric Rondelat, age 44
EVP Industry Business: Michel Crochon, age 59
EVP Customers and Alliances: Christian Wiest, age 60
EVP Global Human Resources: Karen Ferguson, age 45
EVP Strategy and Innovation: Philippe Delorme, age 39
EVP Power Global and EMEAS Business: Julio Rodriguez, age 46
Head Investor Relations: Carina Ho
President, Power, Buildings, and Energy, US: Jeff Drees
Director Institutional Press and Public Relations: Véronique Roquet Montegon
Auditors: Ernst & Young et Autres

LOCATIONS

HQ: Schneider Electric SA
35 rue Joseph Monier
92500 Rueil-Malmaison, France
Phone: 33-41-29-70-00   **Fax:** 33-41-29-71-00
US HQ: 1415 S. Roselle Rd., Palatine, IL 60067
US Phone: 847-397-2600   **US Fax:** 847-925-7500
Web: www.schneider-electric.com

2009 Sales

	% of total
Europe	41
North America	27
Asia-Pacific	21
Other	11
Total	**100**

PRODUCTS/OPERATIONS

2009 Sales

	% of total
Buildings	31
Industry	25
Datacenters & networks	18
Energy & infrastructure	16
Residential	10
Total	**100**

Selected Operations and Products

Custom Sensors & Technologies (sensors, motors, actuators, encoders, motion control products)
Dinel (optoelectronic amplifiers and sensors)
Kavlico (sensors)
Merlin Gerin (circuit breakers, panelboards, and remote installation management equipment)
Square D (electrical distribution and industrial control equipment, US)
TAC (building automation and security products)
Télémécanique (industrial automation products and systems)

COMPETITORS

ABB
Alcatel-Lucent
ALSTOM
Bechtel
Beghelli
Bharat Heavy Electricals
Checkpoint Systems
Danaher
Eaton
Electricité de France
EMCOR
Emerson Electric
Endress + Hauser
Finmeccanica
Fluor
GE
GE Security
Itron
Johnson Controls
Legrand
Measurement Specialties
Mitsubishi Electric
Nissin Electric
Rockwell Automation
Roper Industries
Sentry Technology
Siemens AG
Technology Research Corp.
Transtector
Vicon Industries
Woodhead Industries

HISTORICAL FINANCIALS

Company Type: Public

Income Statement

FYE: December 31

	REVENUE ($ mil.)	NET INCOME ($ mil.)	NET PROFIT MARGIN	EMPLOYEES
12/09	22,635	1,281	5.7%	116,065
12/08	25,809	2,429	9.4%	113,904
12/07	25,477	2,387	9.4%	120,000
12/06	18,114	1,777	9.8%	105,000
12/05	13,831	1,219	8.8%	—
Annual Growth	**13.1%**	**1.2%**	**—**	**3.4%**

2009 Year-End Financials

Debt ratio: —
Return on equity: 7.9%
Cash ($ mil.): 5,033
Current ratio: 1.58
Long-term debt ($ mil.): —
No. of shares (mil.): 263
Dividends
  Yield: 4.2%
  Payout: 97.8%
Market value ($ mil.): 29,989

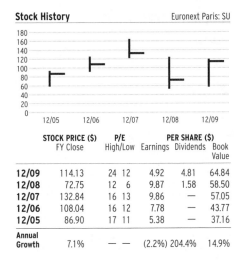

	STOCK PRICE ($) FY Close	P/E High/Low		PER SHARE ($) Earnings	Dividends	Book Value
12/09	114.13	24	12	4.92	4.81	64.84
12/08	72.75	12	6	9.87	1.58	58.50
12/07	132.84	16	13	9.86	—	57.05
12/06	108.04	16	12	7.78	—	43.77
12/05	86.90	17	11	5.38	—	37.16
Annual Growth	7.1%	—	—	(2.2%)	204.4%	14.9%

Securitas AB

Securitas profits from the lack of *caritas* in human nature. Securitas is one of the world's top security services firms, providing security guards to banks, retailers, large corporations, small businesses, and residential customers in more than 40 countries, mainly in North America and Europe. Securitas' purchase of US security firms Pinkerton's and Burns International Services gave it a dominant position in the US security-guard services market. Securitas primarily operates through three divisions: Security Services North America, Security Services Europe, and Mobile and Monitoring (alarm systems).

In addition to guarding, the company provides specialized consulting and investigation services through its Pinkerton subsidiary, which operates as part of Security Services North America. The company's Mobile and Monitoring services include alarm systems monitoring and mobile security officers who attend to multiple customers within a specified geographical area.

The acquisitive company has been busy expanding in Europe and Latin America, snapping up smaller firms at a rapid pace in order to increase its market share on a global level. To that end, the company added UK-based Nikaro, a security provider that operates a fleet of some 750 vehicles and about 1,200 security guards, in 2010. Later that year it agreed to acquire Reliance Security Group, a UK-based security company that also provides building maintenance, catering, cleaning, grounds maintenance, and reception services. Securitas also snapped up a 75% stake in security guard company Guardian Security in Montenegro in mid-2010, giving it a foothold in southeastern Europe.

In 2009 Securitas acquired the security services company World Wide Security in Chile; the security services company Vigilan in Argentina; security services company MKB Tactical in South Africa; and the security services company Interlabora in Spain. On the Asian front, Securitas picked up ESC and SSA Guarding Company in Thailand for 27 million kronor (about $4 million) in the latter part of 2010.

HISTORY

Securitas established its first outpost in 1934, in Helsingborg, Sweden, when Erik Philip-Sörensen bought Hälsingborgs Nattvakt and renamed it Securitas. Erik was following in the footsteps of his father, who in 1901 had established a small Danish guard company as part of the ISS Group of security companies. Securitas was housed within ISS as well.

Sörensen spent the next two decades establishing and acquiring more Swedish firms and adding them to the Securitas family. He also added to his own family two sons, Sven and Jörgen, who would figure into Securitas' future. Jörgen began establishing new branches in Belgium and the UK in the late 1950s. The companies were combined into one company, Group 4, in 1968.

In 1974, two years after the Securitas name was finally branded onto all of the firm's security companies, the elder Sörensen retired. Sven and Jörgen bid against ISS for control of the company and won. Seven years later they divided the company equally: Sven took half of the Securitas operations in Sweden, and Jörgen assumed control of the international businesses (which became Group 4 Securitas). In 1983 Sven sold Securitas. Jörgen bought back some of the Swedish operations, but by 1985 the rest of the company had ended up in the hands of Swedish investment firm Investment AB Latour (now chaired by Gustaf Douglas, also vice chairman of Securitas).

The new owners trimmed away all companies that weren't directly related to guard services and alarm systems. Securitas then began an acquisition rampage in 1988 with the purchase of Swedish lock manufacturer Assa. Not content with the lovely lakes and mountains of Sweden, Securitas bought companies in Denmark, Norway, and Portugal and set up new operations in Hungary.

Securitas went public in 1991 and soon bought US lock maker Arrow; it also began cutting a wider swath through Europe. With its 1992 purchase of security firm Protectas, Securitas gained operations in Austria, France, Germany, and Switzerland; it bought more firms in Spain in 1992 and in Finland the next year. To streamline further, Securitas merged its lock manufacturing operations with those of Finland's Metra, creating Assa-Abloy. It spun off the new company in 1994 but retained a 45% stake. Securitas made more acquisition raids in Estonia, Poland, and the UK in 1996.

In 1997 Securitas created Securitas Direct to handle its domestic and small-scale alarms business; the division quickly became active throughout Scandinavia, as well as in France, Spain, and Switzerland. That year the company made more acquisitions in France and Sweden. In 1998 Securitas made two significant purchases: Raab Karcher Sicherheit, the market leader in industrial guarding services in Germany; and Proteg, France's security market leader (Securitas sold Proteg's fire protection divisions to Williams PLC in 1999).

The granddaddy of acquisitions was still to come. In early 1999 Securitas bought 150-year-old US security firm Pinkerton's in a bid to create the largest security firm in the world. Securitas took over Pinkerton's operations in the Czech Republic, Germany, Portugal, and the UK. The next year Securitas made several US acquisitions, including the purchase of Burns International Services for $650 million.

In 2001 the company became the second-largest cash-handling services provider in the US when it bought the remaining 51% of Loomis, Fargo & Co. (Securitas had previously acquired 49% of Loomis as part of the Burns deal).

In 2003 it acquired Lincoln Security, a security-guard service provider operating in California, Nevada, and Oregon. It also acquired Armored Motor Services of America. Later that year Securitas expanded its Security Services Europe offerings through the acquisition of Spanish-based Ebro Vigilancia & Seguridad and Netherlands-based VNV. The company acquired UK security alarm firm Bell Group in 2004 as a platform for Securitas Systems' UK and Ireland business.

In 2006 Securitas spun off two of its divisions into independent specialized security companies: Securitas Direct AB and Securitas Systems AB (which was renamed Niscayah Group). It also announced plans to spin off its Loomis cash-handling operations (which it eventually did in 2008). The divestitures mark the company's shift to focus exclusively on its security guard operations.

The company's 2007 purchases included Chubb Van den Enden Bewaking & Facilitair Beheer (the Netherlands) and Protection Service (France), as well as shares of security firms in Romania and Columbia.

EXECUTIVES

Chairman: Melker Schörling, age 63, $1,100,000 total compensation
Vice Chairman: Carl Douglas, age 45, $93,380 total compensation
President, CEO, and Director: Alf Göransson, age 53, $2,553,245 total compensation
SVP Corporate Finance: Kim Svensson, age 43
SVP Finance: Jan Lindström, age 44
SVP Corporate Communications and Public Affairs: Gisela Lindstrand, age 48
SVP and Chief Legal Counsel: Bengt Gustafson, age 61
President, Aviation: Marc Pissens, age 59
President, Monitoring: Lucien Meeus, age 63
President, Mobile Division: Erik-Jan Jansen
President, Mobile Services: Morten Rønning, age 50
President, Security Services Europe: Bart Adam, age 45
President, Security Services North America: Santiago Galaz, age 51
Head Investor Relations: Micaela Sjökvist
Auditors: PricewaterhouseCoopers AB

LOCATIONS

HQ: Securitas AB
Lindhagensplan 70
SE-102 28 Stockholm, Sweden
Phone: 46-10-470-30-00   **Fax:** 46-10-470-31-21
US HQ: 2 Campus Dr., Parsippany, NJ 07054
US Phone: 973-267-5300   **US Fax:** 973-397-2681
Web: www.securitasgroup.com

2009 Sales

	% of total
US	34
France	11
Spain	10
Sweden	6
Other countries	39
Total	**100**

PRODUCTS/OPERATIONS

2009 Sales

	% of total
Security services Europe	50
Security services North America	38
Mobile & monitoring	10
Other	2
Total	**100**

Seiko Epson

Seiko Epson makes its mark on paper and glass. A top printer manufacturer, the company produces dot matrix, ink jet, laser, and thermal printers, as well as printer components. Its product portfolio also includes projectors, scanners, and PCs; electronic devices and components, including semiconductors and LCDs; and precision products, such as lenses and factory automation equipment. Also referred to as simply Epson, the company is a manufacturing arm of Seiko Group. Other Seiko Group companies include Seiko Holdings and Seiko Instruments. Seiko Epson gets more than half of its sales in the Asia/Pacific region.

With facilities in more than 40 countries, the company markets its products worldwide. It has regional headquarters in China, the Netherlands, Singapore, and the US.

Seiko Epson's IT products — including printers, scanners, projectors, and PCs (marketed in Japan) — account for about two-thirds of its sales. The company develops its printing and imaging products to keep up with industry trends, including the move from black-and-white to color, as well as improved networking capabilities. It targets both the office and consumer markets with its printers and projectors.

The company's electronic devices segment (about a quarter of sales) encompasses LCDs and semiconductors. Seiko Epson offers displays through its Epson Imaging Devices subsidiary, which produces displays for mobile phones, automobiles, and industrial applications. The company's semiconductor products include application-specific ICs, controllers, LCD drivers, and microcomputers. Its Epson Toyocom subsidiary develops quartz optical, sensing, and timing devices. In 2010 Seiko Epson transferred assets relating to small and midsized TFT LCDs to Sony. Such LCDs are used in small electronics, such as wireless phones and cameras.

Although watches and precision products constitute the company's smallest segment (about 5% of sales), Seiko Epson has no plans to wind down its oldest business. The skills gleaned from watchmaking, including miniaturization and precision timing, have given rise to some of the company's other lines, including LCDs and semiconductors. Other precision products include contact lenses and factory automation robotics.

HISTORY

In 1881, 21-year-old Kitaro Hattori, who had begun working in the jewelry trade at age 13, opened a Tokyo watch shop and called it K. Hattori & Co. In 1892 Hattori started a factory in Seikosha to manufacture wall clocks and, later, watches and alarm clocks. K. Hattori & Co. went public in 1917. In 1924 it began using the Seiko brand on its timepieces. Kitaro's son Ganzo formed Daini Seikosha Co., precursor of Seiko Instruments, in 1937.

The company formed Daiwa Kogyo Ltd., a maker of mechanical watches, in 1942. In 1959 Daiwa Kogyo merged with the Suwa plant of Daini Seikosha to form Suwa Seikosha. Shinshu Seiki (renamed Epson in 1982) was established in 1961.

A big break came for Shinshu Seiki in 1964, when it developed crystal chronometers and printing timers for the Tokyo Olympics' official

timekeepers. It was the first time a precision timepiece and a printer had been combined. In 1968 Shinshu Seiki debuted the EP-101, the first commercially successful miniature printer, which was used primarily with calculators.

During the late 1960s Suwa Seikosha entered the semiconductor field when it began developing LSI devices (large-scale integrated circuits) for its watches. The company introduced the world's first quartz watch in 1969 and the first quartz digital watch in 1973. It soon expanded into LCD technology.

Shinshu Seiki established the Epson brand and formed its US affiliate, Epson America, in 1975. With the advent of the PC in the 1970s, Shinshu Seiki also began working on computer printers. It released its first dot matrix model in 1978.

In 1982 Shinshu Seiki changed its name to Epson. Three years later Epson and Suwa Seikosha merged to form Seiko Epson.

In 1990 the company established Epson Europe in the Netherlands. Seiko Epson unveiled digital cameras in 1996. In 1998 the company established a regional headquarters in China.

With profit margins from its printers shrinking, in 2000 the company consolidated its printer operations in China, Indonesia, and Singapore, and expanded its LCD products line. The following year Seiko Epson formed a joint venture with IBM to produce logic chips for cell phones, handheld computers, and other devices.

Seiko Epson made its debut on the Tokyo Stock Exchange in 2003. In 2004 Seiko Epson combined its LCD manufacturing operations with those of SANYO Electric to form Sanyo Epson Imaging Devices Corporation. (It acquired Sanyo's stake in the venture two years later, forming its Epson Imaging Devices subsidiary.) Seiko Epson merged its quartz device operations with Toyo Communications to form Epson Toyocom in 2005.

EXECUTIVES

Chairman: Seiji Hanaoka
Vice Chairman: Yasuo Hattori
President and Board Member: Minoru Usui
Managing Director; President, Epson Toyocom: Torao Yajima
COO, Semiconductor Operations Divisions; President, Tohoku Epson Corporation: Ryuhei Miyagawa
COO, Business Products Operations Division: Kiyofumi Koike
COO, Watch Operations Division: Akio Mori
COO, Imaging Products Operations and Director: Tadaaki Hagata
Deputy COO, Imaging and Information Operations Division; Senior General Manager, Imaging and Information Planning and Design General Control Department: Koichi Endo
Deputy COO, Imaging Products Operations Division, and General Administrative Manager, Imaging Products Business Management General Center: Noriyuki Hama
Deputy General Administrative Manager, Corporate Research and Development Division: Yoneharu Fukushima
General Administrative Manager, Intellectual Property Division: Masataka Kamiyanagi
Deputy General Administrative Manager, Global Sales and Marketing Planning Division: Noboru Ushijima
Senior Managing Director and Board Member: Masayuki Morozumi
Managing Director and Board Member: Kenji Kubota
Managing Director and Board Member: Seiichi Hirano
Managing Director and Board Member: Toru Oguchi
President, Epson America: John Lang
President, Epson Imaging Devices: Shuji Aruga
Vice-Chairman, Epson (China) Co., Ltd.: Kazuki Ito
Auditors: ChuoAoyama PricewaterhouseCoopers

HISTORICAL FINANCIALS
Company Type: Public

Income Statement
FYE: December 31

	REVENUE ($ mil.)	NET INCOME ($ mil.)	NET PROFIT MARGIN	EMPLOYEES
12/09	8,717	295	3.4%	211,459
12/08	7,286	299	4.1%	221,475
12/07	9,826	82	0.8%	250,000
12/06	8,830	124	1.4%	215,000
12/05	7,310	341	4.7%	217,000
Annual Growth	4.5%	(3.6%)	—	(0.6%)

2009 Year-End Financials
Debt ratio: —
Return on equity: 25.4%
Cash ($ mil.): 347
Current ratio: 1.05
Long-term debt ($ mil.): —
No. of shares (mil.): 365
Dividends
  Yield: 4.1%
  Payout: 49.4%
Market value ($ mil.): 3,557

Stock History
OMX Stockholm: SECUB

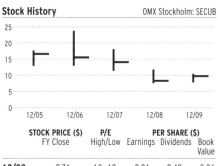

	STOCK PRICE ($) FY Close	P/E High/Low	PER SHARE ($) Earnings	Dividends	Book Value
12/09	9.74	13 10	0.81	0.40	3.36
12/08	8.28	14 10	0.82	0.40	3.00
12/07	14.06	— —	—	—	3.77
12/06	15.50	— —	—	—	3.84
12/05	16.58	— —	—	—	5.01
Annual Growth	(12.5%)	— —	(1.2%)	0.0%	(9.5%)

LOCATIONS

HQ: Seiko Epson Corporation
3-3-5 Owa
Suwa, Nagano 392-8502, Japan
Phone: 81-266-52-3131 **Fax:** 81-266-53-4844
US HQ: 3840 Kilroy Airport Way, Long Beach, CA 90806
US Phone: 562-981-3840 **US Fax:** 562-290-5220
Web: global.epson.com

2010 Sales

	% of total
Asia/Pacific	
Japan	41
Oceania & other countries	17
Europe	21
Americas	21
Total	**100**

PRODUCTS/OPERATIONS

2010 Sales

	% of total
Information-related equipment	72
Electronic devices	24
Precision products	3
Other	1
Total	**100**

Selected Products

Information-related equipment
　Printers
　Personal computers
　Projectors
　Scanners
Electronic devices
　Crystal devices
　LCDs
　Semiconductors
Precision products
　Factory automation
　Optical devices
　Watches

COMPETITORS

Acer	Lexmark
Advantest	LSI Corp.
AMD	NEC
Bausch & Lomb	NVIDIA
Brother Industries	Océ
Canon	Oki Electric
CASIO COMPUTER	Panasonic Corp
Citizen	Ricoh Company
Dell	Samsung Group
Eastman Kodak	SANYO
Fujitsu	Sharp Corp.
Hewlett-Packard	Sony
Himax	Swatch
Hitachi	Tokyo Electron
IBM	Toshiba
InFocus	Toshiba TEC
Intel	Xerox
Konica Minolta	Yamaha
Kyocera	Zebra Technologies

HISTORICAL FINANCIALS

Company Type: Public

Income Statement

FYE: March 31

	REVENUE ($ mil.)	NET INCOME ($ mil.)	NET PROFIT MARGIN	EMPLOYEES
3/10	10,630	(55)	—	77,936
3/09	11,538	(169)	—	72,326
3/08	13,574	305	2.2%	88,925
3/07	12,014	(60)	—	87,626
3/06	13,178	(152)	—	90,701
Annual Growth	**(5.2%)**	**—**	**—**	**(3.7%)**

2010 Year-End Financials

Debt ratio: —	No. of shares (mil.): 196
Return on equity: —	Dividends
Cash ($ mil.): 2,083	Yield: 0.6%
Current ratio: 1.81	Payout: 9.3%
Long-term debt ($ mil.): —	Market value ($ mil.): 3,076

Stock History

Tokyo: 6724

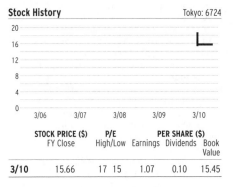

	STOCK PRICE ($) FY Close	P/E High/Low	PER SHARE ($) Earnings	Dividends	Book Value
3/10	15.66	17 15	1.07	0.10	15.45

Sharp Corporation

Sharp's business is pointed at the electronics market. Best known for its consumer electronics, the company is also a leading maker of electronic components and computer hardware and peripherals. Its flagship components business makes LCDs (used in everything from airplane cockpits to PCs to pinball machines), flash memory, integrated circuits, and laser diodes used in optical data drives. Sharp also makes PCs, printers, and cell phones; consumer audio and video products, such as Blu-ray disc players and LCD TVs; and a variety of appliances, such as air cleaning systems and steam ovens. The company is one of the world's largest manufacturers of photovoltaic solar cells.

The company sees solar energy as key to its future, likening solar cell plants to the oil fields of the 21st century. In Japan, which makes up close to half to the company's sales, government assistance with installation costs has increased demand for solar cells. The company is working to further its solar ambitions in Japan by adding solar power generation capacity to facilities where the company plans to produce its next generation thin-film solar cells and other products. Sharp also collaborates with companies such as Enel S.p.A., an electric power producer in Italy, to increase solar cell production by operating small solar power generation ventures.

In 2010 Sharp agreed to pay $305 million in cash for California-based Recurrent Energy, a solar project developer and power generation company. Recurrent has a strong development pipeline of projects with customers that include Southern California Edison and the Sacramento Municipal Utility District, as well as joint development projects in Europe and the Middle East.

Sharp also targets such products as LCD TVs, phone handsets, and home networking gear for growth. On the components side, the company sees demand for advanced LCDs increasing as new handheld devices come into the mainstream. Sharp shifted the focus of its television business from traditional cathode ray tube-based

TVs to flat-panel LCD TVs. It is expanding its line of LED devices and components, which are touted as being highly energy efficient, even as it works to develop products using those components including LED backlit TVs.

In 2008 Sharp and Sony agreed to form a joint venture — Sharp Display Products Corporation — to operate an LCD panel plant in Sakai City. The plant will make LCD panels and modules for LCD TVs for both companies. Sharp owns 66% of the JV, with Sony owning 34%.

The company is teaming up with rival Pioneer to work together on developing consumer electronics products, such as car navigation systems, displays, DVD players, and home networking equipment. As part of the cooperative agreement, Sharp made an equity investment in Pioneer, taking a stake of 14% and becoming Pioneer's biggest shareholder. (Pioneer now holds 9%.)

In 2008 Sharp pleaded guilty to fixing prices on LCD panels under charges brought by the US Department of Justice and agreed to pay a fine of $120 million. Federal prosecutors and antitrust regulators previously investigated alleged price fixing in the semiconductor industry, with mixed results. They found multiple violations in the DRAM business, but none in the markets for graphics processing chips and cards and for static RAMs.

HISTORY

Tokuji Hayakawa got started in manufacturing in 1912 when he established Hayakawa Electric Industry to make a type of belt buckle he had designed. Three years later he invented the first mechanical pencil, named the Ever-Sharp, which was a commercial success. After an earthquake leveled much of Tokyo in 1923, including Hayakawa's business, he moved to Osaka and sold the rights to his pencil to finance a new factory. He introduced Japan's first crystal radio sets in 1925 and four years later debuted a vacuum tube radio.

Following WWII, Hayakawa Electric developed an experimental TV, which it began mass-producing in 1953. The company was ready with color TVs when Japan initiated color broadcasts in 1960. Hayakawa Electric grew tremendously during the 1960s, introducing microwave ovens (1962), solar cells (1963), the first electronic all-transistor-diode calculator (1964), and the first gallium arsenide LED (1969). The firm opened a US office in 1962.

In 1970 the company began to make its own semiconductor devices and changed its name to Sharp Corporation, a nod to the name of its first product. It began mass production of LCDs in 1973. Sharp later introduced the first electronic calculator with an LCD (1973), solar-powered calculators (1976), and a credit card-sized calculator (1979).

The company began producing VCRs in the early 1980s, and in 1984 Sharp introduced its first color copier. That year the firm introduced a fax machine and began concentrating its marketing efforts on small businesses (while its competitors were scrambling for large corporate accounts). Haruo Tsuji became president in 1986. He restructured the company and concentrated research on LCDs. Sharp blitzed the market with a new line of creative products in the late 1980s, including a high-definition LCD color TV (1987) and a notebook-sized PC (1988).

Sharp introduced a cordless pocket telephone in 1992 that operated continuously for over five hours, as well as a low-cost high-definition television (HDTV). That year the company announced strategic alliances with Apple to build the Newton personal digital assistant (which flopped) and with Shanghai Radio and Television to make air conditioners, fax machines, copiers, and printers (Shanghai Sharp Electronics began production in 1994).

Katsuhiko Machida became president in 1998 as the company attempted to pump younger blood into its veins; Tsuji became company adviser. A downturn in the global economy and competitive pricing in the LCD business again put Sharp's profits under pressure in 2001. The company reduced its workforce and simplified its organizational structure.

Also in 2001 Sharp introduced its AQUOS flat-panel TV, which became a popular model among consumers; it had made 10 million AQUOS TVs by mid-2006. Sharp launched an online music distribution service, Any Music, in 2004. Sharp and Sony Ericsson started working together on a 3G FOMA mobile phone for the Japanese market that year.

In 2006 Sharp recalled 28,000 battery packs made by Sony for laptop computers in the Japanese market because the lithium-ion batteries were at risk of overheating and catching fire.

Katsuhiko Machida was promoted to chairman in 2007. Succeeding him as president was Mikio Katayama, a corporate director since 2003, who had joined Sharp in 1981.

EXECUTIVES

Chairman and CEO: Katsuhiko Machida, age 67
President and COO: Mikio Katayama, age 52
Senior Executive Managing Officer and CTO; Group General Manager, Intellectual Property Group: Kenji Ohta, age 62
EVP and Director; Chief Officer, General Administration and Solar Business, and Group General Manager, Global Brand Strategy Group: Toshishige Hamano, age 64
EVP Audio-Visual Systems Business and Director: Masafumi Matsumoto, age 61
EVP, Chief Legal Affairs Officer, and Director; Group General Manager, Tokyo Branch: Toshio Adachi, age 62
EVP Electronic Components and Devices Business and Director; Group General Manager, Sales and Marketing Group, Electronic Components and Devices: Yoshiaki Ibuchi, age 63
Group General Manager, Business Solutions Group: Fujikazu Nakayama
Group General Manager, Production Technology Development Group: Toshihiko Hirobe, age 54
Group General Manager, Liquid Crystal Display Production Group: Taimi Oketani
Group General Manager, Electronic Components and Devices Group: Miyoshi Yamauchi
Group General Manager, Corporate Research and Development Group: Shigeaki Mizushima, age 55
Group General Manager, Human Resources Group and Director: Nobuyuki Taniguchi, age 52
Group General Manager, Corporate Sales Group: Kazutaka Ihori
General Manager, North and South America; Chairman and CEO, Sharp Electronics: Kozo Takahashi
Auditors: KPMG AZSA & Co.

LOCATIONS

HQ: Sharp Corporation
22-22 Nagaike-cho, Abeno-ku
Osaka 545-8522, Japan
Phone: 81-6-6621-1221   **Fax:** 81-6-6625-0918
US HQ: Sharp Plaza, Mahwah, NJ 07495
US Phone: 201-529-8200   **US Fax:** 201-529-8425
Web: www.sharp.co.jp

2009 Sales

	% of total
Asia	
Japan	46
China	14
Americas	17
Europe	16
Other regions	7
Total	**100**

PRODUCTS/OPERATIONS

2009 Sales

	% of total
Consumer/information products	
Audiovisual & communications equipment	46
Information equipment	12
Health & environmental equipment	8
Electronic components	
Liquid crystal displays (LCDs)	20
Solar cells	6
Other electronic devices	8
Total	**100**

Selected Products

Consumer/information products
  Audiovisual and communication equipment
    Audio amplifiers
    Blu-ray disc players
    Digital cameras
    High-definition televisions
    Liquid crystal display DVD televisions
    Liquid crystal display televisions
    Liquid crystal display video projectors
    Mobile phones
    Video cameras
  Information equipment
    Calculators
    Digital copiers
    Fax machines
    Mobile business tools
    Personal computers
    Printers
  Home appliances
    Air cleaning systems
    Superheated steam ovens
Electronic components
  Flash memory
  Integrated circuits
  Laser diodes and other optoelectronic devices
  Radio-frequency components
  Satellite broadcasting components
  Solar cells and other photovoltaic devices

COMPETITORS

AU Optronics	Motorola
Avago Technologies	NEC
BP Solar	Oki Electric
Canon	Palm, Inc.
CASIO COMPUTER	Panasonic Corp
Dell	Philips Electronics
Eastman Kodak	Pioneer Corporation
Electrolux	Q-Cells
Epson	Ricoh Company
Ericsson	Samsung Electronics
First Solar	SANYO
Fuji Xerox	Siemens AG
FUJIFILM	SolarWorld
Fujitsu	Sony
GE	SunPower
Hewlett-Packard	Suntech Power
Hitachi	Tatung
IBM	TCL
Konica Minolta	Toshiba
Kyocera	TPV Technology
Lexmark	Victor Company of Japan
LG Electronics	Xerox
Mitsubishi Electric	Yingli

HISTORICAL FINANCIALS

Company Type: Public

Income Statement

FYE: March 31

	REVENUE ($ mil.)	NET INCOME ($ mil.)	NET PROFIT MARGIN	EMPLOYEES
3/09	29,267	(1,293)	—	54,700
3/08	34,420	1,027	3.0%	53,708
3/07	26,536	869	3.3%	48,927
3/06	23,792	754	3.2%	46,872
3/05	23,687	717	3.0%	46,751
Annual Growth	**5.4%**	**—**	**—**	**4.0%**

2009 Year-End Financials

Debt ratio: 40.8%
Return on equity: —
Cash ($ mil.): 3,262
Current ratio: 1.09
Long-term debt ($ mil.): 4,360
No. of shares (mil.): 1,100
Dividends
  Yield: 0.9%
  Payout: —
Market value ($ mil.): 8,778

Stock History

Pink Sheets: SHCAY

	STOCK PRICE ($) FY Close	P/E High/Low		Earnings	PER SHARE ($) Dividends	Book Value
3/09	7.98	—	—	0.00	0.07	9.71
3/08	17.06	28	19	0.88	—	11.27
3/07	19.26	26	17	0.76	—	9.12
3/06	17.74	—	—	0.00	—	8.49
3/05	15.13	30	21	0.65	—	8.51
Annual Growth	**(14.8%)**	**—**	**—**	**—**	**—**	**3.3%**

Shiseido Company

Since your face is a veritable canvas, Shiseido wants to be the paint. As the largest cosmetics manufacturer in Japan, Shiseido makes and markets makeup and skin care products for men and women. It also manufactures toiletries, sun care products, fragrances, professional salon hair care products, and pharmaceuticals. Its 20-plus brands include namesake Shiseido, Elixir Superieur, Maquillage, and Integrate brands, which are sold in department stores, as well as in chain, general merchandise, and drugstores. Other interests include specialty fragrance, and hair and skin care salons.

With a presence in some 70 overseas markets, Shiseido continues to grow outside Japan. (The firm's international business has grown to account for 38% of sales in fiscal 2009, up from about a quarter of sales in 2005.) In its effort to gain a foothold in the US cosmetics market, in 2010 the company paid $1.7 billion for San Francisco-based Bare Escentuals, manufacturer of mineral-based makeup. The purchase made Bare Escentuals a separate division under Shiseido Americas Corporation and retained the company's CEO Leslie Blodgett. While Bare Escentuals benefitted from increased access to the

Asian cosmetics market, Shiseido boosted its presence in the US, where Bare Escentuals generates more than 85% of its sales.

To specifically target the Chinese market, Shiseido launched a cosmetics brand named Urara in 2006. Sales in China doubled from 2004 to 2006 and the company sees vast potential in the marketplace. Shiseido plans to maintain strong growth in China by enhancing its selection of makeup products. Helping with its Southeast Asia expansion goal, the company opened a new plant in Vietnam in early 2010, its 15th globally.

The company is also working to strengthen its base in Asia and has formed a Russian subsidiary — Shiseido (Rus) LLC — to sell its products in Moscow and Saint Petersburg, which account for the majority of cosmetic sales in Russia. It is also eyeing the north African market with shops in Egypt (at a duty-free shop in the Cairo airport) and Morocco's Casablanca. South Africa is also on the firm's radar. In Europe, the Japanese cosmetics maker aims to compete against French rival L'Oréal and others following the opening of a sales subsidiary in Switzerland (called Shiseido SA) in early 2010.

The firm also has an Institute of Beauty Sciences, which researches the relationship between "cosmetic behavior" and psychology.

HISTORY

Arinobu Fukuhara, former head pharmacist for the Japanese navy, established Japan's first modern drugstore, Shiseido Pharmacy, in 1872. Attracted by the store's Western-style products and format, the customers were the nobility and the rich. Shiseido manufactured Japan's first toothpaste in 1888 and introduced its first cosmetics product (Eudermine, a skin lotion) in 1897. Fukuhara opened the country's first soda fountain in 1902, later adding ice cream, a rarity in Japan at that time.

Arinobu's third son, Shinzo, created Shiseido's first extensive makeup lines, introducing flesh-toned face powder in 1906, hair tonic in 1915, shaded face powder in 1917 (in hues from white to purple), and a fragrance line and cold cream in 1918. Under Shinzo's influence, cosmetics replaced drugs as Shiseido's mainstay.

Shiseido began franchise operations in 1923 and business boomed. The firm went public that year; in 1927 Shinzo became Shiseido's first president. In 1937 the company began issuing its Hanatsubaki ("Camellia") magazine (a cultural magazine featuring fashion, travel, arts, and literary commentaries), which is still issued on a monthy basis. During WWII the company couldn't make cosmetics, only medicines, and many of Shiseido's factories were destroyed. This led to near-bankruptcy in 1945, but Shiseido rebounded the next year, thanks to nail enamel.

In 1951 it introduced its de Luxe high-end cosmetics line, and by 1956 it had become the #1 Japanese cosmetics firm. With moves into Taiwan, Singapore, Hong Kong, and Hawaii in the late 1950s and early 1960s, Shiseido began overseas operations. It steadily expanded its international business by setting up subsidiaries across the world, including one in New York City in 1965, and in Italy in 1968.

In the 1970s Shiseido failed at marketing its products in the US, and at home its market share was slipping. Seen as being out of touch with the young, it was also hampered by strict product development laws that caused delays in getting products to market. In the mid-1980s it developed a successful US marketing strategy that included selling exclusive product lines in high-end department stores such as Macy's; it also made several acquisitions, including Zotos (hair products, US, 1988).

The firm's first prescription-only drug, an ophthalmological treatment used in certain types of cataract surgery and cornea transplants, was launched in 1993. In 1996 it announced a biological compound that retards skin aging by preventing oxidization. The company bought the Helene Curtis salon hair care business in the US and Canada from Unilever that year. In 1997 Shiseido bought Helene Curtis Japan salon hair operations and a New Jersey factory, which more than doubled its North American production.

Also in 1997 Akira Gemma (a Shiseido veteran of nearly four decades) became CEO, and the company expanded into Croatia, the Czech Republic, Hungary, and Vietnam. It bought the professional salon products business of the US's Lamaur Corporation in 1998.

Shiseido opened a New York City flagship store in 1998 and began selling cosmetics in Russia in 1999. It also began selling soap, shampoo, and baby powder in 1999 under the wildly popular Hello Kitty name, licensed from Japanese media firm Sanrio. In 2000 Shiseido bought the Sea Breeze line of facial products from Bristol-Myers Squibb. In 2001 Morio Ikeda took over from Gemma as president and CEO; Gemma was named chairman.

In 2002 Shiseido, together with Limited Brands, introduced a new retail beauty company called aura science. In the fall of 2003 the introduction of two new fragrances under the brand name FCUK (French Connection United Kingdom) by Shiseido's Zirh International subsidiary was met with vocal protest from some consumers.

Shiseido reorganized its operations in China in 2004. As Shinzo Maeda replaced Ikeda as chief executive in mid-2005, he made plans to continue Shiseido's makeover begun by Ikeda in 2001.

Shiseido Malaysia Sdn. Bhd., a joint venture, was formed in early 2005 through a partnership with Warisan TC Holdings Berhad. Since 1977 a division of Warisan, Tung Pao Sdn. Bhd., has distributed Shiseido brands in Malaysia.

EXECUTIVES

President, CEO, and Director: Shinzo Maeda, age 59
Corporate Senior Executive Officer Research, Development, Production, Technical Affairs and Logistics, and Director: Masaaki Komatsu
Corporate Senior Executive Officer and Director; President and CEO, Shiseido Business Solutions Co.: Yasuhiko Harada
Corporate Senior Executive Officer, Domestic Cosmetics Business Sales; President and Representative Director, Shiseido Sales Co.: Toshimitsu Kobayashi
Corporate Executive Officer Advertising Creation and Beauty Solutions, and Domestic Non-Shiseido Brand Business: Kiyoshi Kawasaki
Corporate Executive Officer, Chief Officer International Business, and Director: Carsten Fischer
Corporate Officer, Healthcare Business and Frontier Sciences Business and Chief Officer of Healthcare Business Division; President and Representative Director, Shiseido Beauty Foods Co.: Toshio Yoneyama
Corporate Officer Technical Planning and Technical Affairs, and General Manager Quality Management Department: Tsunehiko Iwai
Corporate Officer General Affairs, Legal Affairs, and Executive Affairs, and General Manager General Affairs Department: Takafumi Uchida
Corporate Officer Business Strategy and Marketing, Domestic Cosmetics Business, and Director: Tatsuomi Takamori

Corporate Officer Personnel and General Manager Personnel Department: Mitsuo Takashige
Corporate Officer, General Manager Corporate Planning Department, and Director: Hisayuki Suekawa
Chief Officer Professional Business Operations Division: Kozo Hanada
President and CEO, Shiseido Cosmetics America Ltd.: Heidi Manheimer, age 47
Chairman and CEO, Shiseido Americas: Shoji Takahashi
Auditors: KPMG AZSA & Co.

LOCATIONS

HQ: Shiseido Company, Limited
5-5, Ginza 7-chome, Chuo-ku
Tokyo 104-0061, Japan
Phone: 81-3-3572-5111   **Fax:** 81-3-3289-1235
US HQ: 900 3rd Ave., New York, NY 10022
US Phone: 212-805-2300   **US Fax:** 212-688-0109
Web: www.shiseido.co.jp

2010 Sales

	% of total
Japan	63
Asia/Oceania	17
Europe	13
Americas	7
Total	**100**

PRODUCTS/OPERATIONS

2010 Sales

	% of total
Domestic cosmetics	61
Overseas cosmetics	36
Other	3
Total	**100**

COMPETITORS

Alberto-Culver
Alticor
Avon
Bath & Body Works
Beiersdorf
Body Shop
Chanel
Colgate-Palmolive
Estée Lauder
Henkel
Inter Parfums
Kao
L'Oréal
Mary Kay
Procter & Gamble
Revlon
Shu Uemura
Unilever
Yves Saint-Laurent Groupe

HISTORICAL FINANCIALS

Company Type: Public

Income Statement				FYE: March 31
	REVENUE ($ mil.)	NET INCOME ($ mil.)	NET PROFIT MARGIN	EMPLOYEES
3/10	6,950	414	6.0%	28,968
3/09	7,095	199	2.8%	28,810
3/08	7,286	357	4.9%	28,793
3/07	5,893	215	3.6%	27,460
3/06	5,707	123	2.2%	25,781
Annual Growth	5.0%	35.5%	—	3.0%

2010 Year-End Financials

Debt ratio: —
Return on equity: 11.1%
Cash ($ mil.): 756
Current ratio: 1.22
Long-term debt ($ mil.): —
No. of shares (mil.): 398
Dividends
Yield: 2.3%
Payout: 56.0%
Market value ($ mil.): 8,711

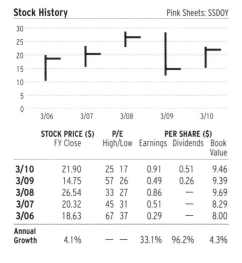

	STOCK PRICE ($) FY Close	P/E High/Low		PER SHARE ($) Earnings	Dividends	Book Value
3/10	21.90	25	17	0.91	0.51	9.46
3/09	14.75	57	26	0.49	0.26	9.39
3/08	26.54	33	27	0.86	—	9.69
3/07	20.32	45	31	0.51	—	8.29
3/06	18.63	67	37	0.29	—	8.00
Annual Growth	4.1%	—	—	33.1%	96.2%	4.3%

Siemens

In a seemingly complicated world, Siemens, one of the largest electronics and industrial engineering firms in the galaxy, has streamlined its primary business divisions to include Industry, Energy, and Healthcare. Its operations encompass automation and controls; building technologies; motors and drives; lighting; transportation; power generation, transmission, and distribution; heating and ventilation; financial products and services; security products; and diagnostic and imaging systems. Its energy-related products range from oil and gas conversion to wind farms.

The company competes with industry rivals by developing new technology at over 175 research and development facilities throughout the world; additionally, it operates corporate technology departments in Germany, the US, China, and India.

Given the success of its wind power business expansion, the company is focusing on expanding its know-how in solar thermal power plants. It increased its stake in Archimede Solar Energy (ASE) from 28% to 45% in 2010 and is aiming to combine its technology in steam turbine generators with ASE's production of solar receivers to enhance plant efficiency and reduce solar power production costs. In the fall of 2009 the company further strengthened its position in renewable energy markets by acquiring Solel Solar Systems, an Israeli solar power manufacturer, for more than $400 million. The company created a $3.5 billion joint venture with Shanghai Electric Group in 2010 to research and develop steam and gas turbines.

Since 2006 Siemens has been under a cloud of corruption charges. After cooperating with various investigations by the SEC, the US Department of Justice, and other prosecutors and regulators around the world as a result of the corruption cases, Siemens settled the claims in late 2008. The company agreed to pay record-setting fines of $1.6 billion to American and European authorities (including $450 million to the Justice Department, $350 million to the SEC, and $540 million to German prosecutors). Siemens pleaded guilty to US federal charges that it violated a law banning the use of corrupt practices in foreign business dealings, but it avoided pleading guilty to bribery charges, allowing it to remain a potential government contractor in the US and elsewhere.

HISTORY

Electrical engineer Werner von Siemens and craftsman Johann Halske formed Siemens & Halske in 1847. The firm's first major project linked Berlin and Frankfurt with the first long-distance telegraph system in Europe (1848). In 1870 it completed a 6,600-mile telegraph line from London to Calcutta, India, and in 1874 it made the first transatlantic cable, linking Ireland to the US.

Siemens & Halske's history of firsts includes Europe's first electric power transmission system (1876), the world's first electrified railway (1879), and one of the first elevators (1880). In 1896 it patented the world's first X-ray tube and completed the first European subway, in Budapest, Hungary.

By the next century it had formed light-bulb cartel OSRAM with German rivals AEG and Auer (1919) and created a venture with Furukawa Electric called Fuji Electric (1923). It developed radios and traffic lights in the 1920s and began producing electron microscopes in 1939.

Siemens & Halske played a critical role in Germany's war effort in WWII and suffered heavy losses. During the 1950s it recovered by developing data processing equipment, silicates for semiconductors, and the first implantable pacemaker. It moved into the nuclear industry in 1959 when its first reactor went into service at Munich-Garching. In 1966 the company reincorporated as Siemens AG. It formed joint ventures with Bosch (BSH Bosch und Siemens Hausgeräte, appliances, 1967) and AEG (Kraftwerk Union, nuclear power, 1969), among others. AEG dropped out of Kraftwerk Union (now Siemens Power Generation) in 1977.

In 1981 Karlheinz Kaske became the first CEO from outside the von Siemens family. Under his lead the firm entered joint ventures with Philips, Intel, and Advanced Micro Devices. In 1988 and 1989 it made several buys, including Bendix Electronics (US), and was a willing buyer when IBM wanted to unload Rolm (then the #1 maker of PBXs). It had acquired all of Rolm's businesses by 1992. That year Heinrich von Pierer replaced Kaske as CEO.

Siemens and German computer maker Nixdorf combined computer businesses to form Siemens Nixdorf Informationssysteme (SNI) in 1990. In 1998 Siemens sold its defense electronics operations to British Aerospace and Daimler-Benz and bought CBS's power generation business (formerly Westinghouse Electric). In 1999 it spun off its semiconductor operations into Infineon Technologies.

In 2000 BSH paid $9.2 billion for the engineering and automotive parts unit Atecs Mannesmann. Siemens shares began trading on the New York Stock Exchange in 2001. The slump in the telecommunications industry hurt Siemens that year, and the company cut 9,700 jobs; in 2002 it announced an additional 6,500 jobs to be cut from its telecom unit.

In 2005 Klaus Kleinfeld, who had headed Siemens' US operations, was named CEO; von Pierer became chairman of the company's supervisory board. The company exited the auto parts market when it sold its VDO Automotive unit to Continental for $16.7 billion in 2007.

The company grew its Healthcare division with major acquisitions. It purchased Diagnostic Products Corporation (DPC), a maker of immunodiagnostic systems, for about $1.9 billion in 2006. On the heels of the DPC buy, the company acquired the diagnostics division of Bayer for more than $5 billion. In 2007 the company purchased Dade Behring Holdings, a provider of diagnostic testing kits, for $7 billion.

Siemens attracted unwanted attention in 2006 when it was accused of making improper payments to secure contracts in Eastern Europe and the Middle East; embezzlement and tax evasion were also among the charges levied against the company. Siemens, which was involved in a number of bribery cases prior to 2006, uncovered more than $500 million worth of suspicious transactions made over a seven-year period with its own probe. The investigation led to the arrest of several Siemens managers, and in 2007 Heinrich von Pierer, the chairman of Siemens' supervisory board who served as the company's CEO from 1992 to 2005, announced his resignation. German authorities later filed civil proceedings against von Pierer seeking damages. Siemens' CEO, Klaus Kleinfeld, then stepped down. Peter Löscher, a veteran of General Electric and Merck, succeeded Kleinfeld.

EXECUTIVES

Chairman: Gerhard Cromme, age 66,
$547,661 total compensation
First Deputy Chairman: Berthold Huber, age 60,
$218,850 total compensation
Second Deputy Chairman: Josef Ackermann, age 62,
$185,504 total compensation
President, CEO, and Member Managing Board:
Peter Löscher, age 53, $6,672,119 total compensation
EVP, CFO, Head Corporate Finance and Controlling, and Member Managing Board: Joe Kaeser, age 53,
$2,646,438 total compensation
EVP, Head Corporate Technology, and Member Managing Board; CEO, Healthcare Sector; Vice Chairman, Supervisory Board, BSH Bosch und Siemens Hausgeräte: Hermann Requardt, age 55,
$2,591,400 total compensation
EVP, General Counsel, Head Corporate Legal and Compliance, and Member Managing Board; Chairman, Siemens Corporation: Peter Y. Solmssen, age 55,
$2,505,010 total compensation
EVP and Member Managing Board; CEO, Energy Sector: Wolfgang Dehen, age 56,
$3,031,458 total compensation
EVP, Head of Supply Chain Management, Chief Sustainability Officer, and Member Managing Board: Barbara Kux, age 56, $2,526,897 total compensation
EVP, Director Labor, and Member Managing Board: Siegfried Russwurm, age 47,
$2,462,872 total compensation
Chief Counsel Compliance: Klaus Moosmayer
Chief Audit Officer: Hans Winters, age 40
Chief Compliance Officer: Josef Winter
President and CEO, Siemens Financial Services: Roland W. Chalons-Browne, age 53
President and CEO, Siemens Energy & Automation: Dennis Sadlowski
President and CEO, Siemens Energy; CEO, Energy Sector Service Division: Randy H. Zwirn
President and CEO, Siemens Corporation: Eric Spiegel
Head Corporate Human Resources: Brigitte Ederer, age 54
Head Corporate Communications and Government Affairs: Stephan Heimbach
Head Corporate Information Technology: Norbert Kleinjohann
Managing Director and Head Business Administration, Siemens Financial Services: Peter Moritz
Auditors: Ernst & Young Wirtschaftsprüfungsgesellschaft

LOCATIONS

HQ: Siemens Aktiengesellschaft
Wittelsbacherplatz 2
D-80333 Munich, Germany
Phone: 49-89-636-00   **Fax:** 49-89-636-34242
US HQ: 527 Madison Ave., New York, NY 10022
US Phone: 212-258-4000   **US Fax:** 212-767-0580
Web: www.siemens.com

2009 Sales

	% of total
Europe, CIS, Africa, Middle East	
Germany	15
Other countries	41
Americas	
US	21
Other countries	7
Asia, Australia	
China	7
India	2
Other countries	7
Total	**100**

PRODUCTS/OPERATIONS

2009 Sales

	% of total
Energy	44
Industry	36
Health Care	19
Other	1
Total	**100**

Selected Operations

Industry
    Building technology (heating and ventilation, security,
        fire safety systems)
    Industry automation (manufacturing and process
        automation)
    Industry solutions (systems integration for industrial
        plants)
    Mobility (transportation systems)
    Motion control (converters, drives, motors, numerical
        control systems)
    OSRAM (light-emitting diodes, light bulbs)
Energy
    Fossil power generation (gas and steam turbines and
        generators, power plants)
    Oil and gas (extraction, conversion, and transportation
        systems)
    Power distribution (powergrid automation, switch
        gear, components)
    Power transmission (high-voltage equipment)
    Renewable energy (wind energy)
    Service rotating equipment (power plant services and
        operation)
Health care
    Diagnostics (immune diagnostics, molecular analysis)
    Imaging and IT (imaging systems and networking)
    Workflow and solutions (health care systems and
        services)
Other
    BSH Bosch und Siemens Hausgeräte (equity
        investment)
    Financial services (cross-sector)
    IT solutions and services (cross-sector)
    Nokia Siemens networks (equity investment)
    Real estate (cross-sector)

COMPETITORS

ABB
Abbott Labs
Accenture
Affiliated Computer Services
Alcatel-Lucent
ALSTOM
AREVA
Avaya
Baldor Electric
Beckman Coulter
Bombardier
BP Solar
Capgemini
Cerner
Computer Sciences Corp.
Danfoss Turbocor
Danieli
Dassault
Dresser-Rand
Eaton
Emerson Electric
FANUC
Gamesa
GE
GN ReSound
Hitachi
Hologic
Honeywell International
HP Enterprise Services
Huawei Technologies
IBM
Johnson Controls
MAN
McKesson
Mitsubishi Electric
Mitsubishi Heavy Industries
NEC
Nichia
Nortel Networks
OSRAM
Philips Electronics
Philips Healthcare
REpower Systems
Roche Diagnostics
Rockwell Automation
SAP
Schneider Electric
Société Générale
Sonova
Toshiba
Tyco
United Technologies
Varian Medical Systems
Veolia Environnement
Vestas Wind Systems

HISTORICAL FINANCIALS

Company Type: Public

Income Statement			FYE: September 30
	REVENUE ($ mil.)	**NET INCOME** ($ mil.)	**NET PROFIT MARGIN**	**EMPLOYEES**
9/09	111,834	3,643	3.3%	405,000
9/08	111,989	8,291	7.4%	427,000
9/07	103,706	5,449	5.3%	398,000
9/06	110,872	3,852	3.5%	475,000
9/05	90,569	2,699	3.0%	461,000
Annual Growth	**5.4%**	**7.8%**	**—**	**(3.2%)**

2009 Year-End Financials

Debt ratio: 71.1%
Return on equity: 9.4%
Cash ($ mil.): 14,822
Current ratio: 1.19
Long-term debt ($ mil.): 27,633

No. of shares (mil.): 870
Dividends
    Yield: 1.3%
    Payout: 45.3%
Market value ($ mil.): 117,975

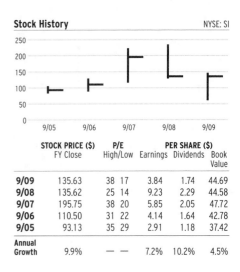

	STOCK PRICE ($) FY Close	P/E High/Low		PER SHARE ($) Earnings	Dividends	Book Value
9/09	135.63	38	17	3.84	1.74	44.69
9/08	135.62	25	14	9.23	2.29	44.58
9/07	195.75	38	20	5.85	2.05	47.72
9/06	110.50	31	22	4.14	1.64	42.78
9/05	93.13	35	29	2.91	1.18	37.42
Annual Growth	**9.9%**	**—**	**—**	**7.2%**	**10.2%**	**4.5%**

Sime Darby Berhad

Malaysia's oldest and largest conglomerate, Sime Darby began in rubber and stretched out from there. With operations in more than 20 countries throughout Asia, Australasia, and Europe, its core business activities include oil palm and rubber plantations in Indonesia and Malaysia; production of edible oils; tire manufacturing; automobile sales (BMW, Ford, Hyundai, Land Rover) and heavy equipment (Caterpillar); residential and commercial property development; and oil and gas exploration and the construction and operation of power plants. The general trading arm distributes products, such as advanced composite materials, auto parts, and sealants. It also has stakes in hotels, hypermarkets, and medical facilities.

In recent years, the multinational company has been expanding its plantation operations in Indonesia and beyond, as well as its auto assembly business. To that end, Sime Darby Plantation has acquired a 63-year concession in Liberia to develop 220,000 hectares of land into oil palm and rubber estates. On the auto front, Sime Darby announced it would assemble the Hyundai Getz, a compact car, at a Malaysian plant. It also acquired Special Brand, an importer and distributor of vehicles, in December 2005.

Sime Darby's industrial division is active in mining in Australasia and is in the oil and gas business in Singapore. It is increasing its exposure to China, particularly in the mining sector, where it hopes to capitalize on that country's rapid urbanization and demand for natural resources. China is Sime Darby's third-largest market (after Malaysia and Australasia), accounting for more than 15% of sales. It operates cargo ports, water treatment plants, and also sells cars there. In August 2009 Sime Darby acquired Ramunia Holdings, an oil and gas services provider based in Malaysia, for about $160 million in cash. The purchase included Ramunia's nearly 200 acres of land currently under lease.

With his employment contract due to expire in late 2010, CEO Ahmad Zubir Murshid stepped down in May and took a leave of absence. His exit from the executive suite comes as the conglomerate was preparing to take a $300 million hit to its second-half earnings because of losses in its energy division, which generates some 10% of its revenue. Following news of Zubir's departure, Sime Darby in mid-2010 named Mohammad Bakke Salleh, chief executive of state-run Felda Global Ventures Holdings, as its acting president and CEO.

HISTORY

William Sime, a 37-year-old Scottish adventurer, convinced Henry Darby, a wealthy 50-year-old English banker, that money could be made in rubber, a product that had just been introduced to Malaya from Brazil. Together they established Sime, Darby & Co., Ltd., in 1910 to manage about 500 acres of rubber estates in the jungles of Malacca, Malaya. To overcome local hostility to their venture, the pair maintained close links with the Chinese business community.

Riding a rubber boom, Sime, Darby became a managing agent for other plantations before moving into general trading. In 1915 it set up a branch office in Singapore and formed a London office for marketing. To clear jungle and meet growing demand for rubber, in 1929 Sime, Darby bought Sarawak Trading, which held a franchise for Caterpillar earth-moving equipment. In 1936 Sime, Darby moved its headquarters to Singapore.

In 1958 Sime Darby Holdings Ltd. was incorporated in England as successor to Sime, Darby & Co., Ltd. When demand for rubber softened in the 1960s, it was one of the first plantations to diversify into palm oil and cocoa production. It acquired the Seafield Estate and Consolidated Plantations in the 1970s, becoming a dominant force in Malaysian plantations while it started processing crops into finished products. Success of the switch to oil palms allowed the conglomerate's autocratic British CEO, Denis Pinder, to gobble up numerous firms. In 1973 allegations appeared in newspapers about improprieties at "Slime Darby." Pinder ended up in Changi prison on misdemeanor charges. The mysterious death of Sime Darby's outside auditor, found stabbed in his bathtub, was ruled a suicide.

After Pinder's successor upset Malaysians by investing in unsuccessful European ventures, Pernas (the Malaysian government trading corporation) bought Sime Darby shares on the London Stock Exchange and demanded an Asian majority be placed on the board. Outmaneuvered, the British lost control of Sime Darby in 1976. The only man acceptable as chairman to both Asian and British board members was Tun Tan Siew Sin, a former Malaysian finance minister and son of Tun Tan Cheng Lock, one of Malaysia's founding fathers. The firm, reincorporated in Malaysia as Sime Darby Berhad in 1978, moved its head office to Kuala Lumpur in 1979.

Sime Darby acquired the tire-making operations of B.F. Goodrich Philippines in 1981 and the Apple Computer (now Apple Inc.) franchise for southeast Asia in 1982. It bought an interest in United Estates, a Malaysian property development firm, two years later. In 1989 Sime Darby bought Dur-A-Vend, a UK condom wholesaler marketing a product called Jiffy with the slogan "Do it in a Jiffy." Sime Darby moved into tourism in 1991, acquiring Sandestin Resorts in Florida.

Expanding its financial portfolio in 1996, Sime Darby acquired control of United Malayan Banking (breaking it up into Sime Bank and SimeSecurities). The next year it consolidated its travel-related holdings into its Sime Wings unit. Hurt by regional financial turmoil, Sime Darby

in 1999 sold Sime Bank and SimeSecurities to Malaysian financier Tan Sri Rashid Hussain.

In 1999 it divested Sandestin Resorts, LEC Refrigeration, and its 7% stake in British chemical firm Elements. Despite its streamlining, the firm could not resist picking up power generation assets as the power industry restructured. In 2000 it increased its stake in Port Dickson Power to 60%. Sime Darby also sold its insurance operations that year.

The company in late 2007 purchased the plantation giants Golden Hope Plantations Berhad, and Kumpulan Guthrie Berhad, and merged them with its own plantation operation to form Sime Darby Plantation, the world's largest palm oil producer.

In 2009 Sime Darby's Plantation Division succeeded in deciphering and sequencing the palm oil genome. Also that year, the group acquired Ramunia Holdings Berhad, an oil and gas services provider based in Malaysia.

EXECUTIVES

Chairman: Tun Musa Hitam, age 75
Deputy Chairman:
Tun Dato' Seri Ahmad Sarji bin Abdul Hamid, age 71
Acting President and CEO: Bakke Salleh, age 56
Group COO: Dato' Abdul Wahab Maskan, age 59
Group CFO: Tong Poh Keow, age 54
EVP Group Corporate Services: Dato' Sekhar Krishnan
EVP Group Human Resources:
Mohamed Ishak Abdul Hamid
EVP Property Division: Dato' Tunku Putra Badlishah
EVP Energy and Utilities Division: Hisham Hamdan
EVP Motors Division: Dato' Lawrence Lee
EVP Industrial Division: Scott W. Cameron
EVP China Operations: Dato' Louis Lu De Sheng
Acting EVP Plantation: Franki A. Dass
SVP and Head of Group Corporate Assurance:
Nik Muhammad Hanafi Nik Abdullah
Director Special Projects: Dato' Ir. Jauhari Hamidi
Group Secretary: Norzilah Megawati Abdul Rahman
Auditors: PricewaterhouseCoopers

LOCATIONS

HQ: Sime Darby Berhad
Wisma Sime Darby, 19th Fl., Jalan Raja Laut
50350 Kuala Lumpur, Malaysia
Phone: 60-3-2691-4122   **Fax:** 60-3-2698-7398
Web: www.simedarby.com

2009 Sales

	% of total
Malaysia	31
Australasia	20
China	16
Singapore	11
Europe	6
Other countries in South East Asia	6
Indonesia	5
Other	5
Total	**100**

PRODUCTS/OPERATIONS

2009 Sales

	% of total
Plantation	34
Industrial	25
Motors	24
Energy & utilities	10
Property	5
Healthcare & other	2
Total	**100**

COMPETITORS

Anglo-Eastern Plantations	Jardine Matheson
Ansell	Joy Global
Bridgestone	Komatsu
Cummins	Marubeni
Daimler	Michelin
General Motors	MMC Corporation
Goodyear Tire & Rubber	New Britain Palm
Hopewell Holdings	Swire Pacific
HSBC	Wilmar
Hutchison Whampoa	Yokohama Rubber
Inoue Rubber (Thailand)	

HISTORICAL FINANCIALS

Company Type: Public

Income Statement

FYE: June 30

	REVENUE ($ mil.)	NET INCOME ($ mil.)	NET PROFIT MARGIN	EMPLOYEES
6/09	8,761	661	7.5%	100,000
6/08	10,448	1,152	11.0%	100,000
6/07	5,995	462	7.7%	30,000
6/06	5,474	304	5.6%	28,770
6/05	4,906	211	4.3%	24,916
Annual Growth	**15.6%**	**33.1%**	**—**	**41.5%**

2009 Year-End Financials

Debt ratio: 9.1%   Current ratio: —
Return on equity: —   Long-term debt ($ mil.): 569
Cash ($ mil.): —

Net Income History

Malaysia: SIME

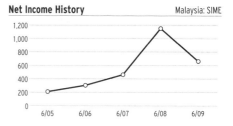

Singapore Airlines

For people in Singapore, traveling very far means traveling by air, and that means Singapore Airlines (SIA). The carrier flies to about 65 cities in about 35 countries, primarily in the Asia/Pacific region but also in Europe and North America. It boasts a fleet of about 100 aircraft. SIA extends its network via code-sharing with fellow members of the Star Alliance marketing partnership including Lufthansa and United Airlines. (Code-sharing allows airlines to sell tickets on one another's flights and thus offer service to additional destinations.) The government of Singapore, through Temasek Holdings, owns about 55% of SIA.

Besides its main passenger transportation business, SIA units include regional carrier SilkAir and SIA Cargo, which operates about a dozen freighters. In addition, SIA owns a 49% stake in UK-based Virgin Atlantic Airways. Airline operations account for some 95% of SIA's sales. The company also owns SIA Engineering, which offers aircraft maintenance and repair.

The airline industry took a nosedive when fuel prices surged to all-time highs in 2008 followed by a credit crisis and global recession, which caused travel and cargo demand to plummet.

Though SIA adheres to a conservative fuel-hedging strategy, the airline lost millions in 2009 on its pre-purchased contracts. (Fuel-hedging is when airlines lock in a pre-determined price for future jet fuel purchases.)

SIA reacted to the economic downturn by reducing overall capacity by about 10% and slimming down its operating fleet (especially to make way for new, more fuel-efficient aircraft). SIA also implemented some no-pay leave in April and May 2009 for employees and trimmed salaries to pull down operating costs. The measures have helped SIA navigate the recession as well as improving revenues from SilkAir and SIA Cargo.

In 2009 SIA divested its 81% stake in Singapore Airport Terminal Services (SATS), which provides catering, security, and cargo handling to SIA and other airlines, by distributing shares of SATS to it shareholders.

To continue growth on long-haul flights, SIA is adding aircraft to its fleet including Airbus A380s. (Singapore Airlines made history in 2007 by offering the first commercial flight with the A380, the world's largest passenger plane.) SIA is using its A380s to fly to cities including London, Paris, Hong Kong, Sydney, Melbourne, Tokyo, and Zurich. The carrier also added A330s to its fleet for medium-haul and regional routes.

SIA is increasing the frequency of service on high-demand routes, particularly in Southeast Asia, where it faces brisk competition. It also has added destinations in southern Europe, the Middle East, and Malaysia. In addition, SIA hopes to take advantage of China's boom in air traffic.

HISTORY

Singapore Airlines (SIA) was formed as Malayan Airways in 1937 but did not begin scheduled service until 1947, when the Mansfield & Co. shipping line used it to link Singapore with other Malayan cities. The airline added service to Vietnam, Sumatra, and Java by 1951 and opened routes to Borneo, Brunei, Burma, and Thailand by 1958.

Meanwhile, British Overseas Airways Corporation (BOAC, predecessor of British Airways) bought 10% of Malayan in 1948 and raised its stake to 30% in 1959. Australia's Qantas Airways also took a 30% stake in Malayan that year. In 1963 the governments of Singapore, Malaya, Sarawak, and Sabah merged to form Malaysia, inspiring Malayan to change its name to Malaysian Airways. Singapore seceded from the federation in 1965 but joined Malaysia to buy control of the airline from BOAC and Qantas in 1966, changing the name to Malaysia-Singapore Airlines.

The carrier extended service to Bombay, London, Melbourne, and Rome in 1971 and then to Athens, Frankfurt, Osaka, and Zurich in 1972. That year managerial disagreements led Malaysia and Singapore to dissolve the company to form two separate national airlines: The domestic network went to the Malaysian Airline System, and international routes went to SIA. Joe Pillay of Singapore's ministry of finance became SIA's first chairman. The government owned 82%, and employees held 17%.

SIA initiated such now well-known amenities as free drinks, hot towels, and headsets in 1972, thereby gaining a reputation for outstanding service. By 1974 it served 25 cities worldwide. It added flights to Auckland and Paris in 1976, Tehran and Copenhagen in 1977, and San Francisco, its first US destination, in 1978.

In 1985 the government reduced its stake in SIA to 63%. The company joined Cathay Pacific and Thai International in 1988 to form Abacus, a computer reservation system for Asia/Pacific carriers. The next year SIA bought stakes in Delta Air Lines and Swissair; the three created a route network reaching 82 countries. In 1995 SIA ordered 77 Boeing 777s for delivery between 1997 and 2004.

The US and Singapore governments signed an "open skies" agreement in 1997 (the first between the US and an Asian nation), allowing unlimited flights between the two countries, but SIA canceled its alliance with Delta and Swissair in favor of one with Germany's Lufthansa.

A December 1997 crash of a new SilkAir 737 killed all 104 people on board; investigators speculated that the crash was an act of suicide by the pilot. (Two years later SIA agreed to pay settlements of up to $195,000 to each family.) The Asian financial crisis added to the airline's woes, but SIA was able to cut costs when the government reduced contributions to the national pension plan and the Singapore airport lowered landing fees.

In 1999 SIA implemented code-sharing with SAS, and soon announced it would join SAS in the global Star Alliance marketing network. SIA bought a 49% stake in UK carrier Virgin Atlantic for some $960 million, acquired 25% of Air New Zealand (reduced to 7% in 2001), and joined the Star Alliance in 2000. Also that year 82 passengers died when a Singapore Airlines flight crashed into debris on an out-of-service runway.

In the airline industry downturn that followed the September 11, 2001, attacks on the US, SIA was forced to tighten its belt. By the next year, however, nearly all of the service that the carrier had suspended had been restored.

The airline trimmed its schedule and cut jobs in 2003 because of decreased demand for air travel to Asia, which stemmed in part from fears of the SARS virus. SIA sold its remaining stake in Air New Zealand in 2004.

EXECUTIVES

Chairman: Stephen C. Y. Lee, age 63
CEO and Director: Chew Choon Seng, age 63
SEVP Operations and Planning: Bey Soo Khiang
EVP Marketing and the Regions; Chairman, SilkAir: Goh Choon Phong, age 47
EVP Human Resources and Planning: Ng Chin Hwee
SVP Corporate Services: Teoh Tee Hooi
SVP Cabin Crew: Tan Pee Teck
SVP Flight Operations: Gerard Y. B. Hock
SVP Europe: Thoeng Tjhoen Onn
SVP Finance: Chan Hon Chew
SVP Product and Services: Yap Kim Wah
SVP Southeast Asia: Teh Ping Choon
SVP Human Resources: Loh Meng See
SVP Commercial Technology: Tan Chik Quee
SVP North Asia: Ng Kian Wah
SVP Engineering: Mervyn Sirisena
Regional VP, South West Pacific: Paul W. L. Tan
Regional VP, Americas: Lim Wee Kok
CEO, SilkAir: Chin Yau Seng, age 38
President and CEO, SIA Engineering: William S. K. Tan
President and CEO, Singapore Airport Terminal Services: Clement H. Y. Woon
Company Secretary: Ethel M. L. Tan
Auditors: Ernst & Young LLP

LOCATIONS

HQ: Singapore Airlines Limited
Airline House, 25 Airline Rd.
819829, Singapore
Phone: 65-6541-4885 **Fax:** 65-6542-9605
Web: www.singaporeair.com

2010 Airline Operations Revenue

	% of total
East Asia	35
Europe	14
Southwest Pacific	12
Americas	6
West Asia & Africa	5
Non-scheduled services & other	28
Total	**100**

PRODUCTS/OPERATIONS

2010 Revenue

	% of total
Airline operations	76
Cargo operations	18
Airport terminal services & food operations	3
Engineering services	3
Total	**100**

COMPETITORS

Air France-KLM
AMR Corp.
British Airways
Cathay Pacific
China Airlines
China Eastern Airlines
China Southern Airlines
Delta Air Lines
Garuda Indonesia
Japan Airlines
Korean Air
Malaysian Airlines
Qantas

HISTORICAL FINANCIALS

Company Type: Public

Income Statement

FYE: March 31

	REVENUE ($ mil.)	NET INCOME ($ mil.)	NET PROFIT MARGIN	EMPLOYEES
3/10	9,082	200	2.2%	20,962
3/09	10,519	754	7.2%	31,834
3/08	11,564	1,547	13.4%	30,088
3/07	9,555	1,452	15.2%	29,125
3/06	8,245	809	9.8%	28,558
Annual Growth	**2.4%**	**(29.5%)**	**—**	**(7.4%)**

2010 Year-End Financials

Debt ratio: —
Return on equity: 2.1%
Cash ($ mil.): 3,196
Current ratio: 1.45
Long-term debt ($ mil.): —
No. of shares (mil.): 1,192
Dividends
Yield: 1.3%
Payout: 107.7%
Market value ($ mil.): 13,081

Stock History

Singapore: SIA

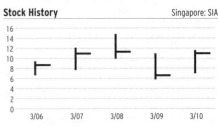

	STOCK PRICE ($) FY Close	P/E High/Low		PER SHARE ($) Earnings	Dividends	Book Value
3/10	10.98	89	56	0.13	0.14	8.25
3/09	6.58	18	10	0.59	0.13	7.69
3/08	11.29	12	8	1.20	—	9.19
3/07	10.94	11	7	1.13	—	8.35
3/06	8.65	15	11	0.63	—	6.99
Annual Growth	**6.1%**	**—**	**—**	**(32.6%)**	**7.7%**	**4.2%**

Sinopec Shanghai Petrochemical

China's own entry into the world of giant chemical companies, Sinopec Shanghai Petrochemical Company is one of that country's largest producers of ethylene, a crucial ingredient in the manufacture of synthetic fibers and plastics. It also makes petroleum-based fuels and oils and other intermediate petrochemicals, such as benzene. The company operates primarily within China; most of its revenues are from eastern China. Though it was founded as a maker of synthetic fibers, that segment is Shanghai Petrochemical's smallest now; petroleum products account for almost half of sales. China Petroleum & Chemical (Sinopec), which is controlled by the Chinese government, owns about 55% of Shanghai Petrochemical.

The company's petroleum products segment includes gasoline, jet fuel, and other refined products. The next largest product grouping is petrochemicals such as ethylene, propylene, and aromatics (benzene, toluene, and butadiene). These chemicals are then used in the manufacture of not only the company's synthetic fiber but also the polyethylene and polypropylene plastics and resins.

Founded in 1972 as a synthetic fibers manufacturing complex, the company has gone through three subsequent major expansions, the last of which came at the turn of this century and brought Shanghai Petrochemical into a true globally competitive state.

Wang Zhiqing was named president of Shanghai Petrochemical in 2010. He replaced Rong Daoguang, who resigned as president but remained the company's chairman.

HISTORY

The Mao-inspired Cultural Revolution of the 1960s restored the aging leader's political grip, but it also caused immense economic disruptions in China, including a virtual shutdown of foreign trade. In the early 1970s party reformists led by Zhou Enlai and Deng Xiaoping advocated improved contact with the outside world and the restoration of foreign trade, giving the Chinese economy access to much-needed technology. In 1972, the year President Nixon's visit to China restored Sino-US ties, China began contracting for plant and equipment imports, especially in the petrochemical areas of chemical fertilizers for agriculture and artificial fibers for industrial use. That year Shanghai Petrochemical Company was founded as China's first large petrochemical enterprise, using imported equipment and technology.

Under Sinopec's control, Shanghai Petrochemical fit squarely into the government's Four Modernizations policy (agriculture, industry, technology, and defense). Other factors in the firm's growth were the booming economies of the coastal cities in the east and south, made possible by economic liberalization policies that encouraged foreign investment. The Guangdong province in the south led the way as Hong Kong enterprise migrated there in the 1980s in

search of lower wages and overhead. The expansion of industrial output there and in other provinces resulted in greatly increased demand for petrochemicals.

Emboldened by growth and further reforms in the oil industry, Sinopec restructured Shanghai Petrochemical in 1993 and listed it on the Hong Kong and New York stock markets. (It was the first Chinese company listed on the New York Stock Exchange.) The company formed a joint venture with US-based agribusiness giant Continental Grain in 1995 to build a liquid petroleum gas plant and teamed up with British Petroleum (now BP) to build an acrylonitrile plant. The company entered a joint venture with Union Carbide (purchased by Dow Chemical) in 1996 to build a polymer emulsion plant in China. Shanghai Petrochemical increased its market share for acrylics with its 1997 purchase of the Zhejiang Acrylic Fibre Plant, then a producer of about 40% of China's total acrylic-fiber output. Annual production grew to 130,000 tons by 1999.

Three broad-reaching events have hammered the company's profits: the Asian economic crisis, the decrease of Sinopec's subsidy on crude oil, and a global oversupply of petrochemicals. In 1997 Shanghai Petrochemical's product-mix adjustments, combined with cost cutting, offset some of the increased crude costs and lower prices. The company announced in 1998 that the Chinese government planned to crack down on the smuggling of foreign petrochemicals and help the domestic market. The firm remains vulnerable to policy changes, however. Additionally, consolidation of the Chinese petrochemical industry could translate into lost jobs. The company continued to modernize its facilities and increase its capacity in 2000 when it moved to upgrade operations in order to become a world-class production base for petrochemicals and derivatives.

EXECUTIVES

Chairman: Rong Guangdao, age 54
Vice Chairman: Du Chongjun, age 55
President: Wang Zhiqing, age 48
CFO: Ye Guohua
VP and Director: Li Honggen, age 54
VP and Director: Shi Wei, age 50
VP: Tang Chengjian, age 54
VP: Zhang Jianping, age 47
Secretary, General Counsel and Director:
  Zhang Jingming, age 52
Independent Supervisor: Liu Xiangdong, age 58
Independent Supervisor: Yin Yongli, age 70
Supervisor: Wang Yanjun, age 49
Supervisor: Zhang Chenghua, age 54
Auditors: KPMG

LOCATIONS

HQ: Sinopec Shanghai Petrochemical Company Limited
  (Sinopec Shanghai Shiyou Huagong Gufen Youxien Gongsi)
  48 Jinyi Rd., Jinshan District
  Shanghai 200640, China
Phone: 86-21-5794-3143   **Fax:** 86-21-5794-0050
Web: www.spc.com.cn

2009 Sales

	% of total
Eastern China	93
Other parts of China	7
Total	**100**

PRODUCTS/OPERATIONS

2009 Sales

	% of total
Petroleum products	40
Resins & plastics	26
Intermediate petrochemicals	18
Synthetic fibers	6
Other	10
Total	**100**

Selected Products

Petroleum Products
  Diesel
  Gasoline
  Jet oil
  Residual oil
Resins and Plastics
  LDPE film and pellets
  Polyester chips
  PP pellets
  PVA
Intermediate Petrochemicals
  Benzene
  Butadiene
  Ethylene
  Ethylene glycol
  Ethylene oxide
Synthetic Fibers
  Acrylic staple
  Acrylic top
  Polyester filament-POY
  Polyester staple
  PP fiber
  PVA fiber

COMPETITORS

BASF SE
CNOOC
DuPont
ExxonMobil Chemical
Formosa Plastics
Marubeni
PetroChina
Shell Chemicals

HISTORICAL FINANCIALS

Company Type: Public

Income Statement			FYE: December 31	
	REVENUE ($ mil.)	NET INCOME ($ mil.)	NET PROFIT MARGIN	EMPLOYEES
12/09	7,558	242	3.2%	17,131
12/08	8,994	(910)	—	17,597
12/07	7,416	223	3.0%	19,252
12/06	6,379	108	1.7%	22,922
12/05	5,599	229	4.1%	25,481
Annual Growth	7.8%	1.4%	—	(9.4%)

2009 Year-End Financials

Debt ratio: 2.0%
Return on equity: 11.6%
Cash ($ mil.): 18
Current ratio: 0.63
Long-term debt ($ mil.): 45
No. of shares (mil.): 72
Dividends
  Yield: 0.0%
  Payout: —
Market value ($ mil.): 412

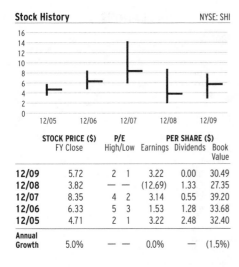

	STOCK PRICE ($)	P/E		PER SHARE ($)		
	FY Close	High/Low		Earnings	Dividends	Book Value
12/09	5.72	2	1	3.22	0.00	30.49
12/08	3.82	—	—	(12.69)	1.33	27.35
12/07	8.35	4	2	3.14	0.55	39.20
12/06	6.33	5	3	1.53	1.28	33.68
12/05	4.71	2	1	3.22	2.48	32.40
Annual Growth	5.0%	—	—	0.0%	—	(1.5%)

Skanska AB

Skanska lays out a healthy smorgasbord of construction services. Scandinavia's largest construction and property development group, Skanska provides building, financing, development, and management services for commercial, residential, and civic projects in Europe, the US, and Latin America. Its areas of expertise include office buildings, industrial plants, single- and multifamily residences, hospitals, bridges, and highways. Its US divisions include Skanska USA Civil and Skanska USA Building. The group has completed work for clients such as Boeing, IKEA, Volvo, and PETROBRAS.

Skanska's largest single market is the US, where it ranks among the largest construction companies. The group has participated in such US projects as the $1 billion renovation of the United Nations headquarters, the $1 billion Meadowlands football stadium in New Jersey, and the $2.2 billion Croton Water Filtration Plant in the Bronx. The latter is Skanska's largest US project ever.

The company's largest segment by far is its construction business. Its construction units are active in Skandinavia, Central Europe, the UK, the US, and Latin America. Skanska's development segments (residential, commercial, and infrastructure) are primarily active in Europe. The company participates in public-private-partnership projects including highways, hospitals, utilities, and public schools.

Like all construction firms, Skanska took a hit in the building downturn, especially in its residential and infrastructure development arms. It responded by cutting costs and curtailing new investments, instead focusing on completing and selling existing developments and securing new contracts. The strategy helped Skanska weather the economic recession relatively unscathed. The group is now hoping to see an increase in infrastructure projects as a result of various government stimulus packages (particularly in the US). Skanska has also begun offering commercial development services in the US.

Another area of focus for the group is green construction. The company delivered Europe's first Green Building-certified project in the Czech Republic. In the US, Skanska redesigned and retrofitted the 32nd floor of the Empire State Building (where Skanska USA is now housed) in a LEED Platinum-certified project. The company has also built an apartment building in Sweden offering solar energy panels as part of its sustainable urban living program.

HISTORY

In 1887 Rudolf Fredrik Berg, a young engineer, founded Aktiebolaget Skånska Cementgjuteriet, initially devoted to manufacturing decorative concrete fittings for churches and public buildings. The company soon diversified its services by making construction components and performing construction work. Skanska received its first order from abroad within 10 years.

Great Britain's National Telephone bought 62 miles of hollow concrete blocks used for holding phone cables, which represented Skanska's further expansion in the building materials market and its first foray into the telecom arena. The company then began producing concrete pipes in 1902 at a St. Petersburg factory in Russia. The pipes replaced the old wooden sewers used throughout the Russian empire.

Skanska reached a milestone in 1927 when it constructed Sweden's first asphalt-paved road. It garnered another record in 1943, constructing what was then the world's longest concrete arch-span bridge, Sweden's 264-meter-long Sando Bridge. Until the 1960s, the Sando stood as the longest such bridge in the world.

Achieving a breakthrough in construction technology, Skanska in 1952 developed its Allbetong method, which allowed off-site production of some prefabricated components. By the mid-1950s, Skanska had become a major player in international markets.

Listed on the Stockholm Stock Exchange A-list in 1965, Skanska entered markets in the Middle East and Africa in the late 1960s and moved into Poland and the Soviet Union during the 1970s. In 1974 Skanska completed the 750-room Forum hotel in Warsaw, its first turnkey-hotel project outside Sweden.

To reflect its global presence, the company dropped its original name in 1984 and became simply Skanska AB. In 1994 Skanska, already entrenched in the New York area, doubled its US presence by buying Atlanta-based Beers Construction, one of the largest construction companies in the Southeast.

In 1995 a Skanska-led consortium was awarded a contract to build the 10-mile-long Oresund Link between Sweden and Denmark, the first fixed road and rail connections between the Scandinavia peninsula and the rest of Europe (completed 2000).

At the beginning of 1999, Skanska acquired Argentine construction company SADE, firmly establishing the company's presence in Latin America. By year's end, in alliance with US firm MasTec, Skanska obtained a $1.4 billion contract to construct a fiber-optic network for US telecom company RCN.

In 2000 the company bought Norwegian company Kvaerner's construction unit and the US-based construction management companies Barclay White and Baugh Enterprises. In 2001 the company's US-based group began projects related to the reconstruction of Ground Zero in New York City.

Skanska's success in the US may have prompted the company to look there for leadership. In 2002 the group selected Stuart Graham, who had been president of Skanska USA, as its new president and CEO, replacing Claes Björk. Graham had been with Skanska since it acquired Sordoni Construction in 1990. Also in 2002 Skanska gained a nationwide footprint in US infrastructure by acquiring California-based civil engineering firm Yeager Construction, which it merged with Skanska USA Civil.

In 2003 the Swedish competition authority imposed fines on 11 companies that it alleged had participated in an illegal cartel to inflate asphalt contract prices. Skanska and rival NCC received the stiffest penalties, but Skanska countered that only one of its employees had confessed to price-fixing and that the company had cooperated fully with authorities.

In 2005 Skanska completed the Cooper River Bridge in South Carolina, the longest cable-stayed bridge in North America. The following year it bought UK transportation and utilities contractor McNicholas plc.

Stuart Graham stepped down as CEO in 2008. Johan Karlström, formerly president of Skanska USA Building, was named Graham's successor.

EXECUTIVES

Chairman: Sverker Martin-Löf, age 67, $158,455 total compensation
President, CEO, and Director: Johan Karlström, age 53, $2,837,078 total compensation
EVP and CFO: Hans Biörck, age 59
EVP Skanska Norway, Skanska Finland, Skanska Sweden, Skanska Commercial Development Nordic, and Skanska Commercial Development Europe: Claes Larsson, age 45
EVP Skanska Czech Republic and Skanska Poland: Roman Wieczorek
EVP Skanska Infrastructure Development, Skanska UK, and Sustainability and Green Construction: Mats Williamson
EVP Residential Development Nordic and IT: Tor Krusell, age 46
EVP Communications: Karin Lepasoon, age 42
EVP: Michael (Mike) McNally, age 55
SVP Human Resources: Veronica Rörsgård, age 36
SVP Investor Relations: Pontus Winqvist
SVP Legal Affairs: Einar Lundgren
SVP Information Technology: Magnus Norrström
SVP Corporate Finance: Staffan Schéle
SVP Sustainability and Green Construction: Noel Morrin
SVP Risk Management: Thomas Alm, age 61
President, Skanska USA Building: William (Bill) Flemming
President, Skanska USA Civil: Richard (Rich) Cavallaro
Auditors: KPMG Bohlins AB

LOCATIONS

HQ: Skanska AB
Råsundavägen 2
SE-169 83 Solna, Sweden
Phone: 46-10-488-0000   **Fax:** 46-8755-1256
Web: www.skanska.com

2009 Sales

	% of total
Europe	
Sweden	19
Other Nordic countries	14
Other countries	29
US	33
Other regions	5
Total	**100**

PRODUCTS/OPERATIONS

2009 Sales

	% of total
Construction	92
Residential development	5
Commercial development	3
Total	**100**

COMPETITORS

Bechtel
Bilfinger Berger
Bouygues
Bovis Lend Lease
Colas
EIFFAGE
Fluor
Foster Wheeler
HOCHTIEF
Jacobs Engineering
NCC
Parsons Corporation
Peter Kiewit Sons'
Technip
Uhde
VINCI

HISTORICAL FINANCIALS

Company Type: Public

Income Statement
FYE: December 31

	REVENUE ($ mil.)	NET INCOME ($ mil.)	NET PROFIT MARGIN	EMPLOYEES
12/09	19,029	505	2.7%	51,660
12/08	18,505	407	2.2%	56,482
12/07	21,678	640	3.0%	57,857
12/06	18,326	530	2.9%	—
12/05	15,588	487	3.1%	53,806
Annual Growth	5.1%	0.9%	—	(1.0%)

2009 Year-End Financials

Debt ratio: —
Return on equity: 19.0%
Cash ($ mil.): 1,309
Current ratio: 1.19
Long-term debt ($ mil.): —

No. of shares (mil.): 423
Dividends
  Yield: 4.3%
  Payout: 60.3%
Market value ($ mil.): 7,156

Stock History
OMX Stockholm: SKAB

	STOCK PRICE ($) FY Close	P/E High/Low		PER SHARE ($) Earnings	Dividends	Book Value
12/09	16.91	14	7	1.21	0.73	6.73
12/08	9.98	17	7	0.96	—	5.81
12/07	19.06	—	—	—	—	7.57
12/06	19.70	—	—	—	—	6.62
12/05	15.20	—	—	—	—	5.48
Annual Growth	2.7%	—	—	26.0%	—	5.3%

SNCF

France's state-owned railway company, Société Nationale des Chemins de Fer Français (SNCF), is still blazing a trail as the nation's primary provider of local and long-distance passenger and freight service. Overall, the SNCF network covers 120 countries, spanning more than 32,000 km (almost 20,000 miles) of track and about 3,000 stations. SNCF's Eurostar joint venture shuttles passengers between Paris and London via the Channel Tunnel ("Chunnel"), and high-speed train operator Thalys links Paris with other European capitals. SNCF's high-speed TGV passenger trains travel at up to 350 mph.

With the addition of the Gares & Connexions (manages and develops train stations in France) unit in 2009, SNCF now operates five main divisions. Other divisions include SNCF Geodis (freight transport and logistics), SNCF Voyages (long-distance, high-speed passenger transport), SNCF's Proximités (commuter travel), and SNCF Infra, which engineers and maintains rail infrastructure.

SNCF acquired a majority stake in liligo.com, one of the leading travel search engines in France, in late 2010. The addition of liligo strengthens SNCFs' desire to develop its consumer-oriented online services both in France and across Europe.

The boost in its Proximités division requires more in-service train cars to handle the increase in commuters. In early 2010 SNCF ordered 80 train cars from Canada-based Bombardier, with an option for an additional 50. The contract is valued at as much as €8 billion (almost $12 billion). Bombardier will build the trains in France for a scheduled shipment in mid-2013.

Along with its primary rail operations, SNCF owns stakes in dozens of other passenger and freight transportation companies. Holdings managed by the rail company's main investment arm, SNCF-Participations, include a stake in Keolis (45%), a French bus operator that also has operations in Algeria, Australia, Canada, and Germany. SNCF also holds a 95% share in Geodis, one of France's largest transport and logistics groups, and owns Seafrance, a ferry operator.

To be a major player in Europe's increasingly deregulated road and rail transport network, SNCF is forging cross-border alliances: Transnational ventures have included working with Deutsche Bahn to design a European high-speed rail system, operating a bus and rail joint venture with UK-based Go-Ahead Group, and entering into a joint venture with UK's FirstGroup to operate TransPennine Expressway in northern England. Adding steam to its European expansion, in September 2009 SNCF and Channel Tunnel operator Groupe Eurotunnel bought rail freight company Veolia Cargo from Veolia Transportation (itself owned by Veolia Environnement). SNCF will take over Veolia Cargo's operations in Germany, Italy, and the Netherlands, and Eurotunnel will take over Veolia's France operations.

HISTORY

France's first railway line, opened in 1827, was used to haul coal from Saint-Etienne to the port of Andrezieux. Four years later the first steam locomotives and passenger service were introduced between Saint-Etienne and Lyon. Paris opened its first rail line in 1837. Although the early railway companies were under private ownership, the state controlled the network of rail lines through licensing. Under Napoleon III's Second Empire (1852–1870), the government encouraged an expansion of railway lines that linked Paris to every major town and city in France. By 1870 the main routes of France's modern railway system had been laid; by 1914 the network system had grown to nearly 40,000 km.

After the devastation of WWI, railway companies invested heavily in rebuilding. Burdened by debt, the rail network was forced to seek government intervention for its survival. In 1938 the government set up Société Nationale des Chemins de Fer Français to unify the five largest railway systems: Compagnie de l'Est, Compagnie du Midi, Compagnie du Nord, Compagnie du Paris-Lyon-Méditerranée, and Compagnie du Paris-Orléans.

Although WWII destroyed the French railway system for a second time, the massive rebuilding enabled postwar French governments to adopt modern innovations. In 1950 SNCF began a systemwide electrification of its tracks; a decade later 7,600 km of its major lines were powered by electricity.

SNCF also pioneered the development of fast trains. Following an overhaul of SNCF in the early 1970s, the company continued to develop high-speed trains to stay competitive with airlines. In 1981 the company's TGV (*train à grande vitesse*) hit a record speed of 380 kph (236 mph). TGVs entered commercial service that year. By 1987 some 43 cities were connected to Paris by TGVs.

To add to its European logistics and freight services, SNCF acquired 20% of Spanish trucking firm TRANSFESA in 1993. In 1995 it launched Eurostar, a London-Paris service using the newly opened Channel Tunnel. Partners in the joint venture were Belgian National Railroads (Société Nationale des Chemins de Fer Belges) and European Passenger Services, the British Rail unit later spun off as Eurostar (UK). That year SNCF saw its operations disrupted by a nationwide rail strike that lasted three weeks.

Diversifying further, SNCF also entered telecommunications in 1996 and set up a communications network to lease spare capacity. That year the company's chairman resigned following charges of corruption related to his tenure at an oil company. SNCF, also plagued by debts and strikes, decided to get back on track. It began restructuring and appointed former Aerospatiale chief Louis Gallois to head the company. In 1997 it shifted most of its debt load to Réseau Ferré de France, which was created to manage France's rail infrastructure.

In 1999 SNCF acquired Via-GTI, France's largest privately owned public transport company, which was in a joint venture with UK transport group Go-Ahead to operate the Thameslink train franchise. That year SNCF acquired Swiss rolling stock group Ermewa; it also sold its hotel interests to Accor but formed an alliance with the hotelier to offer discount lodging.

SNCF and German railway Deutsche Bahn agreed in 2000 to collaborate on developing a new generation of high-speed trains.

SNCF's rail operations were hampered by labor unrest in 2003, capped by a strike in May and June of that year. After a decade at SNCF, Gallois left the company in 2006 to serve as co-CEO of defense group EADS.

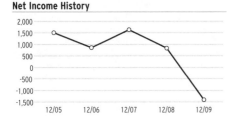
Société Générale

Société Générale wants to be top brass in the French banking industry. The bank (familiarly known as SocGen) commands a three-pronged campaign, with operations in global investment management (including SG Private Banking and majority-owned online brokerage Boursorama); retail banking and specialized financial services, including finance, leasing, and insurance; and corporate and investment banking, focusing on European capital markets, derivatives, and structured finance. In the US, the company controls asset manager The TCW Group. SocGen has about 3,000 branches in France (including its Crédit du Nord division), and some 5,300 locations worldwide.

SocGen, which has retail banking operations in some 40 countries, has worked to boost its international franchise, both through organic growth and through acquisition. Key markets for the retail banking sector include Central and Eastern Europe, the Mediterranean, Africa, and Asia. The company has spent years building up its portfolio in banks in those regions, including majority stakes in Russia's Rosbank in 2008 and in Macedonia's Ohridska Banka and Bauritanian Bank Banque in 2007.

Additionally, SocGen is building its consumer credit operations through acquisitions and expansions in France, Germany, Italy, Poland, and Russia. It expanded its leasing capabilities in Scandinavia as well as asset management operations in India, Japan, and South Korea through acquisitions and alliances. In all, SocGen operates in about 80 countries around the world.

In 2009 SocGen announced an agreement to merge its asset management business with that of fellow French banking giant Crédit Agricole. The combined firm will have more than E590 billion ($800 billion) of assets under management. SocGen will own about 25% of the joint venture, while Crédit Agricole will hold the other 75%. The year before, SocGen merged the brokerage activities of subsidiary Fimat with Crédit Agricole Corporate and Investment Bank (formerly Calyon), creating a joint venture named Newedge.

In 2008 SocGen uncovered fraud by one of its traders in one of the world's largest-ever instances of trading fraud. Soon after, the company began raising funds to help cover the estimated $7.1 billion cost of the fraud and also initiated legal proceedings against the (now former) employee. The Banking Commission of France fined the company $6.3 billion for breaches in internal controls.

Additionally, chairman and then-CEO Daniel Bouton and co-CEO Philippe Citerne each gave up a half-year's salary to compensate for the company's losses. Although Bouton's offers to resign amidst the firestorm were twice rejected by SocGen's board of directors, he eventually did step down. CFO Frédéric Oudéa succeeded him in both positions. Didier Alix and Séverin Cabannes replaced Citerne as deputy CEOs.

HISTORY

In 1864 French steel magnate Joseph Schneider, along with a group of Parisian bankers, incorporated Société Générale pour Favoriser le Développement du Commerce et de l'Industrie en France. The bank, which for obvious reasons came to be known as Société Générale, had the duty "to encourage the development of trade and industry in France." It took deposits from the public and offered lines of credit to companies. The bank also helped organize businesses and invested in them.

By the 1890s Société Générale's branches placed shares with the public and issued private, unsecured loans in France and Russia.

The bank counted 14,000 shareholders in 1895, and 18 years later the number had boomed to 122,000. The bank continued its brisk growth through the first decades of the 20th century, opening more than 1,400 branches by 1933.

Although Société Générale managed to move into Africa and America in the 1930s, the Depression and WWII forced the bank to reduce its size and close branches at home.

After WWII, the bank was nationalized by the French government to help rebuild the war-ravaged country. Société Générale (already active in New York) was well-positioned to distribute the US-sponsored postwar reconstruction initiative, aka the Marshall Plan. For 30 years the bank grew steadily under state control.

The 1960s were a boom time for French exports. The decade brought Société Générale greater expansion, both geographically (Europe, Latin America) and economically, thanks to the specialization of credit, investment banking, finance leasing for companies, and home mortgages for retail customers. The bank also began dealing in Eurocurrencies (money deposited outside the investing company or government's home country).

In 1973 a new law in France allowed the bank to sell up to 25% of its shares to its staff and a limited circle of institutional investors.

A year later, amid the oil crisis, low-quality Eurocurrency market loans came back to haunt Société Générale. In one case the bank had unwisely lent Eurodollars to the United States National Bank of San Diego, which failed and cost Société Générale $7.5 million.

In 1975 the bank launched Agrifan, an export-based food products trading company, to great success. Agrifan was followed by two more companies specializing in food-industry equipment and medical supplies.

Conservatives regained power in the French government in 1986. The next year Société Générale was officially privatized.

In 1998 the bank extended the reach of its financial services by acquiring Barr Devlin, a US-based investment banker and adviser, and Yamaichi Capital Management in Japan.

The next year Société Générale undertook a friendly merger with fellow French banking gargantuan, Paribas, only to have Banque Nationale de Paris swoop in and steal the prize to form BNP Paribas.

Société Générale had to satisfy itself with a piecemeal expansion. By 2000 it had hammered out an ambitious strategic alliance with Spain-based Santander Central Hispano. The French bank also snapped up 30% of Italian insurer Società Assicuratrice Industriale's Banca SAI subsidiary, giving it access to SAI's 3 million customers. The buying spree continued into 2001, with Société Générale acquiring Deutsche Bank's leasing and vehicle-fleet businesses, Gefa and ALD. The bank then bought a controlling stake in LA-based fund manager TCW Group.

SocGen sold its South American retail banking unit, Banco Société Générale Argentina, to Argentine banking group Banco Banex in 2005. The following year, SocGen spun off US-based investment bank Cowen Group.

EXECUTIVES

Chairman and CEO: Frédéric Oudéa, age 47
Vice Chairman: Anthony B. Wyand, age 66
Group CFO: Didier Valet, age 42
Deputy CEO Corporate and Investment Banking:
  Séverin Cabannes, age 52
CEO Corporate and Investment Banking Asia/Pacific:
  Hikaru Ogata
CEO Corporate and Investment Banking:
  Michel Péretié, age 56
Group Chief Risk Officer: Benoît Ottenwaelter, age 56
Global Head Securities Services: Alain Closier, age 58
Global Head Private Banking: Daniel Truchi, age 59
Head Group Strategy: Philippe Heim, age 42
Head Investor Relations: Hans van Beeck
Head Group Communication: Caroline Guillaumin
Head Specialized Financial Services: Didier Hauguel,
  age 50
Head International Retail Banking: Jean-Louis Mattei,
  age 63
Head Global Investment Management and Services:
  Jacques Ripoll, age 44
Head Payment Services: Yannick Chagnon, age 62
Head Group Human Resources:
  Anne Marion-Bouchacourt, age 52
Head Group Information Systems: Maurice Kouby
Head Group Resources: Françoise Mercadal-Delasalles,
  age 47
**Corporate Secretary and Chief Legal and Compliance
  Officer:** Patrick Suet, age 56
**CEO, SG Corporate and Investment Banking,
  Americas:** Diony Lebot
Senior Advisor, Chairman and CEO: Didier Alix, age 64
**Chairman and CEO, SOGECAP and Head Insurance
  Business Line:** Philippe Perret
Auditors: Ernst & Young Audit

LOCATIONS

HQ: Société Générale
  29, boulevard Haussmann
  75009 Paris, France
Phone: 33-1-42-14-20-00
Web: www.societegenerale.com

PRODUCTS/OPERATIONS

2009 Sales

	% of total
Interest & similar income	50
Fees & dividends	17
Net gains on financial transactions	2
Other	31
Total	**100**

Selected Subsidiaries and Affiliates

Ald International SAS & Co (specialist financing,
  Germany)
Banque de Polynésie (72%)
Boursorama SA (56%, brokerage)
Crédit du Nord
Eléaparts (real estate management)
Fiditalia SPA (specialist financing, Italy)
Fontanor (specialist financing)
Généfim (real estate)
Généfimmo (real estate)
Généfinance (portfolio management)
Génégis I (real estate management)
Génévalmy (real estate management)
Géniki (54%, Greece)
Géninfo (portfolio management)
Inora Life (insurance, Ireland)
Komercni Banka (60%, Czech Republic)
Linden SAS (specialist financing)
SG Asia (Hong Kong) Ltd. (financial company)

SG Asset Management Singapore Ltd. (financial
  company)
SG de Banques au Sénégal (59%)
SG Calédonienne de Banque (90%)
SG Financial Services Holding
SG Hambros Limited (Holding) (bank, UK)
SKB Banka (99.7%, Slovenia)
Société Générale Algérie (bank)
Société Générale de Banques au Cameroun (58%)
Société Générale Marocaine de Banques (53%, Morocco)
Soge Périval IV (real estate management)
Sogéfontenay (real estate management)
Valminvest (real estate management)

COMPETITORS

BBVA
BNP Paribas
Caisse des Dépôts et Consignations
CIC
CRCAM IDF CCI
Crédit Agricole
Crédit Foncier de France
Credit Suisse
Deutsche Bank
HSBC France
Natixis
Union Financière de France

HISTORICAL FINANCIALS

Company Type: Public

Income Statement

FYE: December 31

	ASSETS ($ mil.)	NET INCOME ($ mil.)	INCOME AS % OF ASSETS	EMPLOYEES
12/09	1,467,168	1,588	0.1%	160,144
12/08	1,592,739	3,909	0.2%	163,000
12/07	1,577,527	2,361	0.1%	151,000
12/06	1,262,360	7,632	0.6%	119,779
12/05	1,004,780	5,833	0.6%	103,555
Annual Growth	**9.9%**	**(27.8%)**	**—**	**11.5%**

2009 Year-End Financials

Equity as % of assets: 4.6%
Return on assets: 0.1%
Return on equity: 2.5%
Long-term debt ($ mil.): —
No. of shares (mil.): 711
Dividends
  Yield: 2.5%
  Payout: 268.8%
Market value ($ mil.): 49,860
Sales ($ mil.): 14,468

Stock History

Pink Sheets: SCGLY

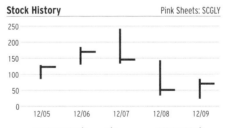

	STOCK PRICE ($) FY Close	P/E High/Low		PER SHARE ($) Earnings	Dividends	Book Value
12/09	70.16	127	41	0.64	1.72	94.45
12/08	50.74	30	8	4.74	1.71	81.09
12/07	145.62	83	47	2.88	—	64.77
12/06	169.66	11	8	16.04	—	53.93
12/05	123.05	10	7	12.78	—	39.24
Annual Growth	**(13.1%)**	**—**	**—**	**(52.7%)**	**0.6%**	**24.6%**

Sodexo

This company has a lot of mouths to feed. Formerly Sodexho Alliance, Sodexo is the world's #2 contract foodservice provider (after Compass Group), with operations in about 80 countries. Its subsidiaries offer corporate foodservice and hospitality services, vending services, and food-services for educational institutions and other public-sector clients. Other operations include event concessions, health care foodservices, and such outsourced on-site service solutions as cleaning, groundskeeping, and laundry. Its US-based subsidiary, Sodexho, Inc., is one of the largest contract foodservice providers in North America. The company has some 33,900 service sites worldwide.

In addition to its core foodservice and facilities management services, Sodexo is a leading provider of voucher cards in Europe and Latin America used to buy groceries, clothing, and other basic necessities. The company operates voucher systems for both employers that use the cards as a form of employee benefits, as well as for government welfare programs. Vouchers include restaurant, gift, and childcare passes.

The company won the contract for organizing the 2010 Winter Olympics in Vancouver. During 2009 it increased its contract obligations with France's Ministry of Justice to deliver service solutions to 27 additional prisons. It also won the Microsoft Europe contract and renewed its contract with Procter & Gamble, for which Sodexo provides a wide range of services at 38 sites in 13 European countries. It also signed a 30-year contract to design, construct, and manage a military training center for The Defense Training Review in the UK. In addition, Sodexo made acquisitions in high-growth markets in 2009, including Zehnacker, a facilities management services provider in Germany, RKHS in India, and Comfort Keepers in the US.

During 2008 it signed contracts to provide services to GlaxoSmithKline in Canada and Société Générale in France.

The company changed its name in 2008 to Sodexo, dropping both the word "Alliance" and the "h," as part of a global rebranding effort. The name change was intended to raise the company's profile and recognition by focusing on the singular name (that it also hopes is easier to spell and pronounce without the extra letter).

Chairman Pierre Bellon and his family own about 38% of the company.

HISTORY

The Bellon family had been luxury ship hospitality specialists since the turn of the century, 60 years before Pierre Bellon founded Sodexho in 1966. By 1971 Bellon had his first contract outside France to provide foodservice to a Brussels hospital. Sodexho continued to expand its services into the late 1970s, entering remote site management in Africa and the Middle East in 1975 and starting its service vouchers segment in Belgium and Germany in 1978.

Sodexho jumped the pond in 1980, expanding its businesses into North and South America. The company went public on the Paris Bourse exchange in 1983. Two years later it bought Seiler, a Boston vending machine company-turned-restaurateur. Sodexho then bought San Francisco's Food Dimensions in 1987. After beefing up its American operations with four other

US acquisitions, the company merged Food Dimensions and Seiler in 1989. Sodexho's US river cruise company, Spirit Cruises — an echo of the Bellon family's original calling — was also included in the merger. The merged US companies were renamed Sodexho USA in 1993.

The 1990s proved an era of growth and acquisitions for Sodexho. The company expanded into Japan, Africa, Russia, and five Eastern European countries in 1993. The company acquired a 20% stake in Corrections Corporation of America the following year and virtually doubled its size with the acquisition of the UK's Gardner Merchant in 1995. The largest catering company in that region, Gardner Merchant had holdings that spanned Australia, Asia, northern Europe, the UK, and the US — generally markets where Sodexho did not have a strong presence. That year the company also acquired Partena, a Swedish security and care company, from Volvo's Fortos.

Gardner Merchant's US business was officially merged with Sodexho USA in 1996 to make it the #4 foodservice company in the US. Also that year Sodexho acquired Brazilian service voucher company Cardapio. After a year of legal wrangling, Sodexho also lost a fight for control of Accor's Eurest France to rival caterer Compass Group and sold off its minority interest. The next year Sodexho acquired 49% of Universal Ogden Services, renamed Universal Services, an American remote site manager. To signify its efforts to maintain the individuality of the companies it acquires, Sodexho changed its name to Sodexho Alliance in 1997.

Marriott International merged its foodservice branch with Sodexho's North American foodservice operations in 1998. With a 48% stake, Sodexho Alliance became the largest shareholder; former Marriott International stockholders took the rest, with the Marriott family controlling 9%. Before the merger, Sodexho USA was less than one-fourth the size of Marriott International's foodservice division. Sodexho acquired GR Servicios Hoteleros in 1999, thereby becoming the largest caterer in Spain.

In 2001 its initial $900 million bid to buy the 52% of Sodexho Marriott Services it didn't already own was rebuffed by its subsidiary's shareholders. Sodexho Alliance made a better offer (about $1.1 billion) and finally reached an agreement to purchase the rest of Sodexho Marriott Services. The deal was completed later that year and Sodexho Marriott Services changed its name to Sodexho, Inc. Also that year the company agreed to pay some $470 million for French rival Sogeres and US-based food management firm Wood Dining.

In 2002 the company announced it had detected accounting and management errors in its UK operations, causing the value of its stock to fall by nearly one-third. In addition, the company replaced its UK management team because of poor performance there.

Admitting no wrongdoing, Sodexho settled an $80 million race-bias lawsuit just before it was to go to trial in 2005. The suit, brought by the African-American employees of its American subsidiary, Sodexho, Inc., charged that African-Americans were routinely passed over for promotions and were segregated within the company. Sodexho also agreed to increase company diversity through promotion incentives, monitoring, and training.

In 2005 Bellon stepped down as company CEO but remained chairman. He was replaced by Sodexho veteran Michel Landel.

EXECUTIVES

Chairman: Pierre Bellon, age 77
Vice Chairman: Remí Baudin, age 79
Group CEO and Director: Michel Landel, age 58
Group COO; President and CEO, Sodexo North America, Food and Facilities Management Services: George Chavel
Group COO; CEO, Europe, Food and Facilities Management Services: Philip Jansen, age 43
Group COO; CEO, Service Vouchers and Cards, and CEO, South America, Food and Facilities Management Services: Pierre Henry, age 58
Group COO; CEO, Remote Sites and Asia/Australia, Food Management Services: Nicholas Japy, age 54
Group EVP and Chief Marketing Officer, Offer Marketing, Supply Chain and Sustainable Development: Damien Verdier, age 53
Group EVP and Group CFO: Siân Herbert-Jones, age 50
Group EVP and Chief Human Resources Officer: Elisabeth Carpentier, age 56
Group SVP and Chief Strategy Officer Strategy, Innovation, Brand and Communications: Roberto Cirillo
Group SVP Communications and Sustainable Development: Clodine Pincemin, age 58
President, School Services Division: Stephen Dunmore
President, Sodexo Canada: Dean Johnson
President and COO, Education Market: Lorna Donatone
CEO, France and Morocco: Michel Franceschi
Chief Executive, UK and Ireland: Yann Coléou
Investor Relations: Pierre Benaich
Communications Manager, Corporate Communications and Sustainable Development: Grégory Takahashi
Auditors: PricewaterhouseCoopers

LOCATIONS

HQ: Sodexo
255, quai de la Bataille de Stalingrad
92130 Issy-les-Moulineaux, France
Phone: 33-1-30-85-75-00   **Fax:** 33-1-30-43-09-58
US HQ: 9801 Washingtonian Blvd.
Gaithersburg, MD 20878
US Phone: 301-987-4000   **US Fax:** 301-987-4439
Web: www.sodexo.com

2009 Sales

	% of total
North America	39
Continental Europe	36
UK & Ireland	9
Rest of the world	16
Total	**100**

PRODUCTS/OPERATIONS

2009 Sales

	% of total
On-site service solutions	95
Motivation solutions	5
Total	**100**

Selected Operations

On-site service solutions
  Corporate hospitality and foodservices
  Event concessions
  Facilities management and support
  Institutional foodservices
  Healthcare catering and foodservices
  Leisure and hospitality services
  Vending services
Motivation solutions (service vouchers and cards)

Selected On-Site Service Solution Sectors

Corporate
Defense
Education
Health care
Justice
Remote sites
Seniors

COMPETITORS

Accor	Elior
ARAMARK	Healthcare Services
Autogrill	ISS A/S
Cintas	SSP
Compass Group	SSP America
Davis Service	UniFirst
Delaware North	

HISTORICAL FINANCIALS

Company Type: Public

Income Statement

FYE: August 31

	REVENUE ($ mil.)	NET INCOME ($ mil.)	NET PROFIT MARGIN	EMPLOYEES
8/09	20,991	603	2.9%	379,749
8/08	19,965	582	2.9%	355,044
8/07	18,264	495	2.7%	342,380
8/06	16,419	427	2.6%	332,096
8/05	14,266	207	1.4%	324,446
Annual Growth	**10.1%**	**30.7%**	**—**	**4.0%**

2009 Year-End Financials

Debt ratio: —
Return on equity: 18.7%
Cash ($ mil.): 1,721
Current ratio: 0.95
Long-term debt ($ mil.): —
No. of shares (mil.): 155
Dividends
  Yield: 3.2%
  Payout: 50.3%
Market value ($ mil.): 8,883

Stock History

Pink Sheets: SDXAY

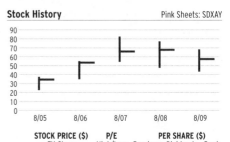

	STOCK PRICE ($) FY Close	P/E High/Low		PER SHARE ($) Earnings	Dividends	Book Value
8/09	57.45	19	12	3.62	1.82	21.41
8/08	67.85	21	14	3.55	1.69	20.35
8/07	66.01	27	19	2.99	—	20.09
8/06	53.38	21	14	2.63	—	17.89
8/05	34.44	30	19	1.22	—	16.88
Annual Growth	**13.6%**	**—**	**—**	**31.2%**	**7.7%**	**6.1%**

SOFTBANK CORP.

SOFTBANK's investment strategy is anything but soft. Under the leadership of founder, chairman, and CEO Masayoshi Son (sometimes referred to as the Bill Gates of Japan), the company makes investments in a variety of ventures. Its portfolio holdings span the mobile and fixed-line telecommunications, Internet commerce and content, technology services, marketing, and broadband infrastructure sectors, and more. The company also invests venture capital in Internet-related concerns in Asia and the US. Interests in SOFTBANK MOBILE, SOFTBANK TELECOM, and Yahoo Japan, along with its minority stake in Yahoo!, comprise the bedrock of SOFTBANK's holdings.

Despite its soft spot for all things technological, SOFTBANK also shops outside the wired world: The company acquired the Fukuoka Daiei Hawks (now the Fukuoka Softbank Hawks), a professional baseball team, in 2005.

Masayoshi Son owns 30% of SOFTBANK, which has stakes in more than 60 companies.

HISTORY

Ethnic Korean Masayoshi Son grew up in Japan using the name Yasumoto to conform with the Japanese policy of assimilation. In the early 1970s, the 16-year-old came to the US and began using his Korean name. Son entered the University of California at Berkeley and, while there, invented the prototype for the Sharp Wizard handheld organizer.

Bankrolled by the nearly $1 million that Sharp paid him for his patent, Son returned to Japan and founded software distributor SOFTBANK in 1981. The company got its first big break when it inked a distribution agreement with Joshin Denki, one of Japan's largest consumer electronics retailers, that year. Son used this agreement to gain exclusive distribution rights for much of the software he distributed.

SOFTBANK went public in 1994. That year, as part of an evolving plan to control digital data delivery, Son bought the trade show division of Ziff-Davis Publishing, augmenting it in 1995 with the purchase of COMDEX, the trade show operations of the Interface Group. The next year SOFTBANK bought the rest of Ziff-Davis. It also bought 80% of Kingston Technology (sold 1999) and a stake in Yahoo! — which laid the cornerstone for its Internet empire.

SOFTBANK accelerated its Internet investment pace in 1997, taking stakes in dozens of Web companies. That year it filed suit against Yell Publishing, a Japanese firm that published a book accusing SOFTBANK of issuing phony financial statements, among other improprieties.

In 1998 the firm moved into financial services, entering a joint venture with E*TRADE to offer online stock trading in Japan. SOFTBANK also took Ziff-Davis public (it retained a majority stake).

Internal changes marked 1999 when SOFTBANK merged with MAC, Son's private asset management company, and transformed itself into a holding company focused on Internet-related companies. It teamed with the National Association of Securities Dealers to create a Japanese version of the Nasdaq stock market (launched in 2000; closed in 2002). SOFTBANK also partnered with Microsoft and Tokyo Electric Power to launch SpeedNet, a Japanese Internet service provider.

In 2000 the nearly decimated Ziff-Davis announced it would transform its online arm, ZDNet, from a tracking stock into a stand-alone company and adopt the ZDNet name; later CNET Networks (now a part of CBS Interactive) bought both companies instead. That year SOFTBANK formed venture capital funds focusing on areas such as Latin America, Japan, Europe, the UK, and emerging markets.

The company reorganized in 2000 and placed most of its non-Japan-based holdings under a new unit called SOFTBANK Global Ventures. Sharpening its focus on Internet investments, SOFTBANK sold its stake in antivirus software maker Trend Micro. Branching into banking, SOFTBANK headed a consortium that paid $932 million for Japan's failed Nippon Credit Bank. SOFTBANK's share of the bank (renamed Aozora) stood at nearly 49%. The firm's stock price tumbled in 2000, and it considered taking several holding companies public.

In 2001 Cisco bought a nearly 2% stake in SOFTBANK in exchange for the firm's 12% stake in the hardware company's Japanese unit. The company also sold its SOFTBANK Forums Japan, an Internet trade show company, to MediaLive International. In 2002 Nasdaq Japan announced its plans to close, after two loss-making years. SOFTBANK owned 43%.

In an attempt to create a larger domestic market for its e-commerce and Internet companies, SOFTBANK moved aggressively into the broadband market, providing asymmetric digital subscriber line (ADSL) services.

EXECUTIVES

Chairman, President, and CEO: Masayoshi Son, age 53
Director; President and Director, SOFTBANK Holdings: Ronald D. (Ron) Fisher, age 62
Director; President and CEO, Yahoo! Japan: Masahiro Inoue, age 53
Corporate Auditor: Mitsuo Sano, age 53
Auditors: ChuoAoyama PricewaterhouseCoopers

LOCATIONS

HQ: SOFTBANK CORP.
1-9-1 Higashi Shinbashi, Minato-ku
Tokyo 105-7303, Japan
Phone: 81-3-6889-2000   **Fax:** 81-3-5543-0431
Web: www.softbank.co.jp

PRODUCTS/OPERATIONS

2010 Sales

	% of total
Mobile communications	60
Fixed-line telecommunications	12
Internet culture	9
e-Commerce	9
Broadband infrastructure	7
Other	3
Total	**100**

Selected Investments

All About, Inc. (online marketplace, 35%)
Firstserver, Inc. (Internet services, 65%)
G-cluster Global Corporation (online game services, 56%)
Japan Cyber Educational Institute (online university, 77%)
MySpace Japan K.K. (50%)
Odds Park Corp. (horse racing information)
SOFTBANK Capital Partners LP (venture capital, 3%)
SOFTBANK MOBILE Corp.
SOFTBANK Ranger Venture Investment Partnership (venture capital)
TV Bank Corporation (video content)
Yahoo Japan Corporation (41%)

COMPETITORS

3i Group
Accel Partners
Alloy Ventures
Benchmark Capital
Hummer Winblad
Internet Capital
JAFCO
Kleiner Perkins
Safeguard Scientifics
Sequoia Capital
Trinity Ventures

HISTORICAL FINANCIALS

Company Type: Public

Income Statement

FYE: March 31

	REVENUE ($ mil.)	NET INCOME ($ mil.)	NET PROFIT MARGIN	EMPLOYEES
3/10	29,795	1,043	3.5%	21,885
3/09	26,043	444	1.7%	21,048
3/08	28,548	1,094	3.8%	19,040
3/07	661	245	37.0%	17,804
3/06	9,660	490	5.1%	14,182
Annual Growth	32.5%	20.8%	—	11.5%

2010 Year-End Financials

Debt ratio: 415.0%
Return on equity: 23.4%
Cash ($ mil.): 7,419
Current ratio: —
Long-term debt ($ mil.): 21,086
No. of shares (mil.): 1,082
Dividends
 Yield: 0.2%
 Payout: 5.4%
Market value ($ mil.): 26,890

Stock History

Tokyo: 99840

	STOCK PRICE ($) FY Close	P/E High/Low	PER SHARE ($) Earnings	Dividends	Book Value
3/10	24.84	29 17	0.93	0.05	4.69
3/09	12.91	56 16	0.40	0.03	3.56
3/08	18.20	30 17	0.97	0.03	3.57
3/07	25.71	135 71	0.23	—	2.24
3/06	29.35	103 24	0.43	—	1.91
Annual Growth	(4.1%)	— —	21.3%	29.1%	25.2%

Sojitz Corporation

Sojitz Corporation is trading in all kinds of places. The company's 500 subsidiaries trade in a wide array of businesses, ranging from steel and automobile parts to apparel, making it one of the largest trading houses in Japan. Sojitz's other major businesses include aerospace, foods, oil and gas, chemicals and plastics, retail property development, and construction materials. The rest of Asia and North America (through its Sojitz Corporation of America unit) are major contributors to its overseas trading operations. Sojitz was formed by the 2003 merger of two Japanese trading powerhouses, Nissho Iwai and Nichimen Corporation.

As part of its cost restructuring to reduce debt, Sojitz went on a tear to sell off its low-performing business divisions and additional real estate holdings. The company then reorganized into five business units: machinery and aerospace, energy and mineral resources, chemicals and plastics, real estate development and forest products, and consumer lifestyle business.

It also formed a subsidiary in China to enter key businesses such as the automotive, ball bearing, textiles, and plastics industries. In 2009 it transferred its domestic foodstuffs business to a wholly owned subsidiary called Sojitz Foods Corporation.

HISTORY

The Nissho and Iwai companies got their acts together as Nissho Iwai in 1968, but each company dates back to the middle of the 19th century. In 1863, Bunsuke Iwai opened a shop in Osaka to sell imported goods such as glass, oil products, silk, and wine. The Meiji government, which came to power in 1868, encouraged modernization and industrialization, a climate in which Iwai's business flourished. In 1877 Iwajiro Suzuki established a similar trading concern, Suzuki & Co., that eventually became Nissho.

After cotton spinning machines were introduced in Japan in the 1890s, both Iwai and Suzuki imported cotton. Iwai began to trade directly with British trader William Duff & Son (an innovation in Japan, where the middleman, or *shokan*, played the paramount role in international trade). Iwai became the primary agent for Yawata Steel Works in 1901 and was incorporated in 1912. Meanwhile, Suzuki, solely engaged in the import trade, emerged as one of the top sugar brokers in the world and established an office in London.

To protect itself from foreign competition, Iwai established a number of companies to produce goods in Japan, including Nippon Steel Plate (1914) and Tokuyama Soda (1918). Stagnation after WWI forced Suzuki to restructure. In 1928 the company sold many of its assets to trading giant Mitsui and reorganized the rest under a new name, Nissho Co.

Both Iwai and Nissho subsequently grew as they helped fuel Japan's military expansion in Asia in the 1930s. But Japan's defeat in WWII devastated the companies. When the occupation forces broke up Mitsui and other larger trading conglomerates, both companies took advantage of the situation to move into new business areas. In 1949 Nissho established Nissho Chemical Industry, Nissho Fuel, and Nijko Shoji (a trading concern). It also opened its US operations, Nissho American Corp., in 1952.

Poor management by the Iwai family led the company into financial trouble in the 1960s and prompted the Japanese government to instruct the profitable Nissho to merge with Iwai in 1968.

In 1979 Nissho Iwai was accused of funneling kickbacks from US aircraft makers to Japanese politicians. The scandal led to arrests, the resignation of the company's chairman, and the suicide of another executive. Nissho Iwai exited the aircraft marketing business in 1980.

Despite Japan's recession in the 1990s, Nissho Iwai managed to make some significant investments. In 1991 the company teamed up with the Russian government to develop a Siberian oil refinery. A year later Nissho acquired a stake in courier DHL International, and in 1995 it set up a unit to process steel plates in Vietnam.

However, in the late 1990s rough economic conditions caught up with the firm. It dissolved its NI Finance unit (domestic financing) in 1998 after its disastrous performance. The large trading firm, or *sogo shosha*, also began a major restructuring effort to get back on track.

In 1999 Nissho Iwai sold its headquarters, its 5% stake in DHL International, and its stake in a Japanese ISP, Nifty. CEO Masatake Kusamichi resigned. He was replaced by Shiro Yasutake, who took charge of the firm's restructuring. In 2000, the company's ITX Corp. acquired five IT-related affiliates of Nichimen Corp.

As part of the group's streamlining efforts, in 2001 Nissho Iwai spun off its nonferrous marketing unit (Alconix) and agreed to merge the group's LNG operations with Sumitomo's LNG

business. The next year Hidetoshi Nishimura replaced Yasutake as CEO.

In 2003 Nissho Iwai merged with the smaller Nichimen Corp. to form Nissho Iwai-Nichimen Holdings. Hidetoshi Nishimura, president and CEO of Nissho Iwai, and Toru Hambayashi, president of Nichimen, became co-CEOs of the new holding company. Former board member Akio Dobashi took over the reins as president and sole CEO early in 2004; in April he moved over to the chairman's seat and Yutaka Kase assumed the president and CEO titles. In June the company changed its name from Nissho Iwai-Nichimen Holdings to Sojitz Holdings Corporation. As part of its ongoing reorganization in 2005, the company renamed itself yet again when it merged the holding company into Sojitz Corporation.

EXECUTIVES

Chairman: Akio Dobashi
Vice Chairman: Masaki Hashikawa
President and CEO: Yutaka Kase
EVP, CFO, and Director: Yoji Sato
EVP and Director: Hiroyuki Tanabe
Senior Managing Executive Officers and CIO: Shinichi Taniguchi
SVP and General Manager Energy and Mineral Resources Unit: Masahiro Komiyama
SVP Chemicals and Plastics Division: Michifumi Watanabe
SVP and General Manager Risk Management: Yoshio Mogi
SVP and General Manager Energy and Mineral Resources, The Americas Energy Unit: Satoshi Mizui
SVP Machinery and Aerospace Division and Senior General Manager Information and Industrial Machinery Unit: Yoshihisa Suzuki
SVP Real Estate Development and Forest Products: Masaru Ogawa
SVP Consumer Lifestyle Business Division and Senior General Manager Textiles and General Merchandise Unit: Masao Goto
SVP Consumer Lifestyle Business Division and Senior General Manager Foods Unit: Takashi Ikeda
SVP and General Manager Machinery and Aerospace, Automotive Unit: Tatsunobu Sako
SVP Machinery and Aerospace: Michiharu Katsura
SVP Real Estate Development and Forest Products Division: Takahiro Toyoda
President, Consumer Lifestyle Business: Keisuke Ishihara
President and CEO, Americas: Jun Matsumoto
President, Machinery and Aerospace: Kazunori Teraoka
President, Energy and Mineral Resources: Hiroshi Kanematsu
President, Real Estate Development and Forest Products: Masao Ichishi
President, Chemicals and Plastics: Joji Suzuki
Human Resources and General Affairs: Masayuki Hanai
Auditors: KPMG AZSA & Co.

LOCATIONS

HQ: Sojitz Corporation
1-20 Akasaka 6-chome, Minato-ku
Tokyo 107-8655, Japan
Phone: 81-3-5520-5000　　**Fax:** 81-3-5520-2390
US HQ: 1211 Avenue of the Americas, 44th Fl.
New York, NY 10036
US Phone: 212-704-6500　　**US Fax:** 212-704-6543
Web: www.sojitz.com

2010 Sales

	% of total
Asia & Oceania	
Japan	83
Other countries	10
Europe	3
North America	2
Other regions	2
Total	**100**

PRODUCTS/OPERATIONS

2010 Sales

	% of total
Energy & Mineral Resources	26
Consumer Lifestyle Business	23
Machinery & Aerospace	21
Chemicals & Plastics	12
Overseas subsidiaries	11
Real Estate Development & Forest Products	5
Other	2
Total	**100**

COMPETITORS

Chori
ITOCHU
Kanematsu
Marubeni
Mitsubishi Corp.
Mitsui
Sekisui House
Sumitomo
Toyota Tsusho
Xstrata

HISTORICAL FINANCIALS

Company Type: Public

Income Statement

FYE: March 31

	REVENUE ($ mil.)	NET INCOME ($ mil.)	NET PROFIT MARGIN	EMPLOYEES
3/10	41,474	39	0.1%	17,331
3/09	53,103	195	0.4%	17,524
3/08	58,120	631	1.1%	18,440
3/07	44,271	499	1.1%	18,844
3/06	42,292	372	0.9%	17,213
Annual Growth	(0.5%)	(43.1%)	—	0.2%

2010 Year-End Financials

Debt ratio: —
Return on equity: 1.4%
Cash ($ mil.): 4,916
Current ratio: 1.53
Long-term debt ($ mil.): —
No. of shares (mil.): 1,233
Dividends
　Yield: 2.6%
　Payout: 62.5%
Market value ($ mil.): 2,408

Stock History

Tokyo: 27680

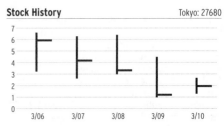

	STOCK PRICE ($) FY Close	P/E High/Low		PER SHARE ($) Earnings	Dividends	Book Value
3/10	1.95	34	18	0.08	0.05	3.08
3/09	1.20	28	7	0.16	0.05	2.66
3/08	3.32	12	6	0.51	—	3.89
3/07	4.17	14	6	0.44	—	3.36
3/06	5.92	8	4	0.85	—	2.94
Annual Growth	(24.2%)	—	—	(44.6%)	0.0%	1.2%

Sony Corporation

Many eyes and hands are on Sony — or, more likely, on its high-profit consumer electronics products and gaming systems. The company makes a host of other items, including digital and video cameras, Walkman stereos, and semiconductors. Sony, one of the world's top media conglomerates, boasts entertainment assets such as music (Sony Music Entertainment), motion pictures (Sony Pictures Entertainment and Sony Digital Production), DVDs (Sony Pictures Home Entertainment), and TV programming (Sony Pictures Television). Under the direction of Sir Howard Stringer, the firm's first non-Japanese leader, Sony's realigning its business and shedding some longtime traditions in its effort to right the Sony mother ship.

The rising Yen and global economic crisis that hit manufacturers hard beginning in late 2008 sidelined Sony for the short term. In response, Sony has undertaken a major restructuring to improve its profitability. It has been selling off some facilities — most recently a factory in Western Japan that makes small liquid crystal display (LCD) panels used in mobile phones and digital cameras to Kyocera Corp.

The firm's admitted missteps (such as snubbing the move from analog to digital and not embracing the LCD display format for flat panels) have it limping in certain areas of its business. As a result, agile upstart companies have stolen market share from the behemoth. Also, the company has lost market share to Apple in music players, and it fights a continued battle with Microsoft and Nintendo for top player among game console sales globally.

Sony continues to rely on its bread-and-butter business — electronics — which represents some 65% of its revenue. Sony entered into an agreement with Sharp in 2009 to form a joint venture company — called Sharp Display Products (SDP) — to make and sell large LCD panels and modules. Sony strengthened its position as a small and midsized LCD supplier by acquiring the assets of Seiko Epson's LCD business in 2010. The transaction gives Sony a bigger stake in thin-film transistor display technology, which offers improved picture quality.

Sony's PlayStation 3 leverages the company's gaming expertise and competes with Microsoft's Xbox 360 and Nintendo's Wii system. The company is focused on building its network services. Like the Xbox 360, the PlayStation 3 is more of a multimedia entertainment hub than a video game system; its computing power allows users to play a game, chat online, and listen to music all at the same time.

To combat losses in a weakening music industry, Sony merged its music division with BMG. The company (called Sony BMG Music Entertainment, a 50-50 joint venture) was the #2 player (after Universal Music). Bertelsmann, part owner in BMG, sold its stake in the BMG joint venture to Sony in October 2008 in a $1.2 billion deal, following speculation that Bertelsmann was looking to exit the music business. Sony renamed the entity Sony Music Entertainment and made it a wholly owned subsidiary of Sony Corporation of America. As part of the deal, Bertelsmann received selected European music catalog assets from the Sony BMG joint venture that generated some $20 million in 2007 revenue.

Sony led a consortium of companies (including cable company Comcast and several investment firms) that bought movie studio MGM in 2005; the acquisition has allowed Sony to license and distribute MGM's sizeable film library (4,000 films and over 10,000 television episodes). To take the network concept into another dimension, Sony formed a joint venture with Discovery Communications and IMAX to develop a 3D TV network. The companies hope to introduce the network to cable and satellite customers by 2011.

HISTORY

Akio Morita, Masaru Ibuka, and Tamon Maeda (Ibuka's father-in-law) started Tokyo Telecommunications Engineering in 1946 with funding from Morita's father's sake business. The company produced the first Japanese tape recorder in 1950. Three years later Morita paid Western Electric (US) $25,000 for transistor technology licenses, which sparked a consumer electronics revolution in Japan. His firm launched one of the first transistor radios in 1955, followed by the first Sony-trademarked product, a pocket-sized radio, in 1957. The next year the company changed its name to Sony (from "sonus," Latin for "sound," and "sonny," meaning "little man"). It beat the competition to newly emerging markets for transistor TVs (1959) and solid-state videotape recorders (1961).

Sony launched the first home video recorder (1964) and the first solid-state condenser microphone (1965). Its 1968 introduction of the Trinitron color TV tube began another decade of explosive growth. Sony bet wrong on its Betamax VCR (1976), which lost to rival Matsushita's VHS as the industry standard. However, 1979 brought another success, the Walkman personal stereo.

Pressured by adverse currency rates and competition worldwide, Sony used its technology to diversify beyond consumer electronics and began to move production to other countries. In the 1980s it introduced Japan's first 32-bit workstation and became a major producer of computer chips and floppy disk drives. The purchases of CBS Records in 1988 ($2 billion) and Columbia Pictures in 1989 (a $4.9 billion deal, which included TriStar Pictures) made Sony a major force in the rapidly growing entertainment industry.

The firm manufactured Apple's PowerBook, but its portable CD player, Data Discman, was successful only in Japan (1991). In the early 1990s Sony joined Nintendo to create a new kind of game console, combining Sony's CD-ROM drive with the graphic capabilities of a workstation. Although Nintendo pulled out in 1992, Sony released PlayStation in Japan (1994) and in the US (1995) to great success.

In 1999 Nobuyuki Idei became CEO, and the company introduced a Walkman with the capability to download music from the Internet.

In early 2001 Sony started an online bank with Japan's Sakura Bank and JP Morgan Chase. In the course of the fiscal year ending March 2002, Sony laid off about 13,700 employees, primarily in its electronics and music businesses.

Sony unveiled the Vaio Pocket in 2004, a portable music player designed to compete with Apple's iPod; Vaio Pocket debuted in the US later that year.

To manage its financial units (Sony Life Insurance Company, Sony Assurance, and Sony Bank), it created Sony Financial Holdings in 2004. The company announced in 2005 that Idei would be succeeded by foreigner Howard Stringer, who had been in charge of Sony's entertainment unit.

In 2005 Sony sold its minority stake in music club Columbia House to BMG Direct, a subsidiary of Germany's Bertelsmann. In December 2005 the company spun off Sony Communication Network, the subsidiary that operates So-Net Internet service (which has nearly 3 million subscribers), through an IPO.

In June 2006 Sony created a holding company for its Japanese-based retail operations (Sony Plaza, Sony Family Club, B&C Laboratories, CP Cosmetics, Maxim's de Paris, and Lifeneo) and sold 51% of the holding company to investment firm Nikko Principal Investments Japan.

EXECUTIVES

Chairman, President, and CEO; Chairman and CEO, Sony Corporation of America: Sir Howard Stringer, age 68
Vice Chairman: Ryoji Chubachi, age 63
EVP; President, Networked Products and Services Group; President and Group CEO, Sony Computer Entertainment; Chairman, Sony Computer Entertainment America: Kazuo (Kaz) Hirai, age 49
EVP; Head Global Sales and Marketing, Sony Ericsson Mobile Communications: Kristian Tear
EVP and eCFO: Masaru Kato
EVP; President, Semiconductor Business Group; Deputy President, Consumer Products and Devices Group: Tadashi (Tan) Saito
EVP, Sony Financial Holdings: Katsumi Ihara, age 60
EVP, Human Resources and Corporate Workplace Solutions: Kunitaka Fujita
EVP, China: Akira Kubota
EVP, Intellectual Property and Disc Manufacturing: Keiji Kimura, age 58
EVP and General Counsel, Sony Corporation and Sony Corporation of America: Nicole Seligman, age 53
Executive Deputy President; President, Consumer Products and Devices Group: Hiroshi Yoshioka, age 57
SVP and Chief Transformation Officer: George Bailey
SVP, Global Sales and Marketing: Kiyoshi Shikano
SVP, Corporate Communications and Corporate Social Responsibility: Shiro Kambe
CEO, Sony Music Entertainment: Rolf Schmidt-Holz
President, Sony Marketing: Nobuki Kurita
President and CEO, Sony Computer Entertainment America: Jack Tretton
Chairman and CEO, Sony Pictures Entertainment: Michael M. Lynton
President and COO, Sony Electronics: Phil Molyneux
Auditors: ChuoAoyama PricewaterhouseCoopers

LOCATIONS

HQ: Sony Corporation
   7-1, Konan, 1-chome, Minato-ku
   Tokyo 108-0075, Japan
Phone: 81-3-6748-2111   **Fax:** 81-3-6748-2244
US HQ: 550 Madison Ave., New York, NY 10022
US Phone: 212-833-6722   **US Fax:** 212-833-6938
Web: www.sony.net

2010 Sales

	% of total
Japan	29
Europe	23
US	22
Other regions	26
Total	**100**

PRODUCTS/OPERATIONS

2010 Sales

	% of total
Consumer products & devices	41
Networked products & services	21
Financial services	12
Pictures	10
Music	7
B2B & disc manufacturing	5
Other	4
Total	**100**

2010 Consumer Products and Devices Sales

	% of total
Televisions	34
Digital imaging	23
Audio & video	17
Components	16
Semiconductors	10
Total	**100**

2010 Networked Products and Services Sales

	% of total
Game	56
PC & other	44
Total	**100**

Selected Products

Electronics
  Video
  TVs and monitors
  Information and communication
  Audio
  Semiconductors
Games (hardware and software)
Pictures
Financial services
Music

COMPETITORS

Apple Inc.
Bertelsmann
Dell
Disney
Eastman Kodak
Fujitsu
Hewlett-Packard
IBM
Intel
Kyocera
LG Electronics
Microsoft
Motorola
Nintendo
Nokia
Panasonic Corp
Philips Electronics
Pioneer Corporation
Samsung Group
SANYO
Sharp Corp.
Technicolor
Universal Studios
Victor Company of Japan

HISTORICAL FINANCIALS

Company Type: Public

Income Statement

FYE: March 31

	REVENUE ($ mil.)	NET INCOME ($ mil.)	NET PROFIT MARGIN	EMPLOYEES
3/10	77,825	(440)	—	167,900
3/09	79,457	(1,017)	—	171,300
3/08	88,928	3,703	4.2%	180,500
3/07	70,537	1,074	1.5%	163,000
3/06	63,734	1,054	1.7%	158,500
Annual Growth	**5.1%**	**—**	**—**	**1.5%**

2010 Year-End Financials

Debt ratio: 31.2%
Return on equity: —
Cash ($ mil.): 12,855
Current ratio: 1.02
Long-term debt ($ mil.): 9,970
No. of shares (mil.): 1,005
Dividends
  Yield: 0.0%
  Payout: —
Market value ($ mil.): 415

Stock History

NYSE: SNE

	STOCK PRICE ($) FY Close	P/E High/Low	PER SHARE ($)		
			Earnings	Dividends	Book Value
3/10	0.41	— —	(0.44)	0.00	31.85
3/09	0.21	— —	(1.01)	0.23	30.33
3/08	0.40	— —	3.54	0.13	34.58
3/07	0.43	— —	1.02	0.21	28.53
3/06	0.39	— —	0.99	0.22	27.19
Annual Growth	**1.3%**	**— —**	**—**	**—**	**4.0%**

Statoil ASA

The status of Statoil (formerly StatoilHydro) is that it is Norway's oil and gas exploration, production, transport, refining, and marketing giant. Statoil operates in 40 countries, focusing its upstream activities on the Norwegian continental shelf, the North Sea, the Caspian Sea, Western Africa, the US, and Venezuela. It has proved reserves of 6 billion barrels of oil equivalent. In 2007 Statoil acquired the oil and gas operations of Norsk Hydro in a $30 billion deal and became StatoilHydro. The Norwegian government owns 62.5% of Statoil (which reclamed its original name in 2009).

To generate cash to invest in its core exploration and production assets, in 2010 Statoil announced plans to spin off its retail network of about 2,300 gas stations (including a chain of 200 automated outlets) in eight north European countries. Statoil will retain at least 50% of the unit following the spin off. It also agreed to sell a 40% stake in its Peregrino oil field (offshore Brazil) to Sinochem for $3 billion.

The company manages the state's direct financial interest (known as SDFI) in oil and gas partnerships active on the Norwegian continental shelf. It also owns the world's largest offshore gas platform, the Aasgard B off Norway's west coast. In addition, Statoil supplies electricity in Norway and Sweden.

Statoil is not only Norway's largest oil and gas group, it is also one of the largest international exploration and production companies. It has developed new oil and gas assets (based on its success in the Norwegian Continental Shelf) in four focus areas: deepwater, harsh environment, gas value chains, and heavy oil.

Expanding its upstream, midstream, and downstream assets, in 2007 the company acquired up to $4.2 billion of subsea equipment from Aver Kvaerner, Canada's North American Oil Sands Corporation for $1.96 billion, and 274 gas stations in Scandinavia from ConocoPhillips.

In 2008 the company paid about $1.8 billion to acquire holdings in heavy-oil and deep-water projects in Brazil and the Gulf of Mexico from Anadarko Petroleum. That year Statoil got the go-ahead from the EU Commission to acquire

ConocoPhillips' Jet gas station chain in Norway, Sweden, and Denmark. It also teamed up with Chesapeake Energy to jointly explore unconventional gas opportunities around the world, including in the Marcellus Shale play in the US.

Expanding its footprint, in 2009 the company bought a crude oil terminal in the Bahamas (and a 50% interest in a related tugboat business) from World Point Terminals for $263.2 million.

It increased its footprint in Alaska (where it is the fourth largest explorer) by acquiring a 25% stake in 50 ConocoPhillips oil leases located in the Chukchi Sea.

HISTORY

To exert greater control over exploration and production of the Norwegian continental shelf (NCS), the government of Norway set up Den norske stats oljeselskap (Statoil) in 1972.

A decade earlier three geologists had visited Norway on behalf of Phillips Petroleum (later renamed ConocoPhillips) to apply for sole rights to explore on the NCS. The government initially refused drilling rights to foreign companies, and in 1963 Norway claimed sovereignty over the NCS. Two years later the government began allowing exploration. Phillips' major discovery in the Ekofisk field in 1969 prompted Norway to set up its own oil company. After Statoil's formation in 1972, the company garnered funds to expand through taxation of multinationals, production limits, leasing contracts, and other measures.

In 1974 a giant discovery was made in the North Sea's Statfjord field, and Statoil was given a 50% stake. A year later Statoil began exploring for oil and gas, exporting oil, and commissioning its first subsea oil pipeline, the Norpipe, which extended to the UK. In 1986 Statoil's gas pipeline system, the Statpipe, began transporting gas from the North Sea to the mainland.

Moving into retailing, Statoil acquired Esso's service stations and other downstream operations in Sweden and Denmark in 1985 and 1986. The next year, cost overruns stemming from the extension of Statoil's Mongstad oil refinery led to the ousting of the company's first president, Arve Johnsen, and many of his deputies. Harald Norvik was appointed CEO in 1988.

In 1990 Statoil and BP teamed up to develop international operations, and in 1992 Statoil acquired BP's service stations in Ireland. Statoil and Neste Chemicals (later part of Industri Kapital) formed the Borealis petrochemicals group in 1994.

The company in 1995 acquired Aran Energy, moving into exploration of offshore Ireland and the UK. Statoil brought its field projects in China and Azerbaijan onstream in 1997. That year Statoil spun off its shipping operations as Navion, partly owned by Norway's Rasmussen group. It also contracted with Kvaerner to build a giant offshore gas platform for the Aasgard field in the Norwegian Sea.

The Aasgard field project resulted in cost overruns in 1999, again leading to a Statoil board shakeup and CEO resignation. Norvik, who had advocated partial privatization of Statoil, was replaced by Olav Fjell, former head of Norway's Postbanken (who resigned in 2003). That year Statoil helped Norsk Hydro take over rival Saga in return for some of Saga's assets.

As part of a major restructuring in 2000, Statoil sold most assets of US unit Statoil Energy. Political opposition that year postponed Statoil's plans for partial privatization, but the government proceeded with an IPO in 2001, raising about $3 billion.

In 2002 Statoil sold its oil and gas assets in the Danish North Sea to Dong, the Danish state oil company, for about $120 million. That year the company also acquired the Polish unit of Sweden's Preem Petroleum, which owned 79 gas stations in Poland.

In 2003 Statoil sold its Navion unit to shipping group Teekay for about $800 million. That year it also acquired two Algerian natural gas projects from BP for $740 million. A bribery scandal involving an Iranian oil contract forced the resignation of the chairman, CEO, and another top executive in 2003.

Statoil sold its 50% stake in petrochemicals venture Borealis in 2005.

In 2006 the company acquired three oil prospects in the Gulf of Mexico from Plains Exploration & Production for $700 million. It also acquired offshore assets in the Gulf of Mexico from Anadarko Petroleum for $901 million.

EXECUTIVES

Chairman: Svein Rennemo, age 62
Deputy Chairman: Marit Arnstad, age 47
President and CEO: Helge Lund, age 47, $1,775,239 total compensation
CFO: Eldar Sætre, age 54
EVP International Exploration and Production: Peter Mellbye, age 60, $1,032,462 total compensation
EVP Technology and New Energy: Margareth Øvrum, age 52, $775,822 total compensation
EVP Projects and Procurement: Gunnar Myrebøe, age 60, $632,984 total compensation
EVP Corporate Staff and Services: Helga Nes, age 53, $509,978 total compensation
EVP Manufacturing and Marketing: Jon Arnt Jacobsen, age 52, $741,136 total compensation
EVP Exploration and Production, Norway: Øystein Michelsen, age 53, $705,241 total compensation
EVP and Chief of Staff: Tove Stuhr Sjøblom
EVP Natural Gas: Rune Bjørnson, age 50
EVP Development and Production, North America: Bill Maloney
SVP Trading and Operations, Natural Gas: Torgrim Reitan
SVP Global Exploration: Tim Dodson, age 50
SVP Corporate Human Resources: Jens R. Jenssen, age 56
SVP Investor Relations: Lars Troen Sørensen
President, StatoilHydro Brazil: Kjetil Hove
President Canada: Lars C. Bacher
Auditors: Ernst & Young AS

LOCATIONS

HQ: Statoil ASA
Forusbeen 50
N-4035 Stavanger, Norway
Phone: 47-51-99-00-00　　**Fax:** 47-51-99-00-50
US HQ: 1055 Washington Blvd., 7th Fl.
Stamford, CT 06901
US Phone: 203-978-6900　　**US Fax:** 203-978-6952
Web: www.statoil.com

2009 Sales

	% of total
Norway	78
US	9
Sweden	4
Denmark	4
Other countries	5
Total	**100**

PRODUCTS/OPERATIONS

2009 Sales

	% of total
Manufacturing & marketing	54
Exploration & production	31
Natural gas	15
Total	**100**

COMPETITORS

BP
Exxon Mobil
OMV
Royal Dutch Shell
TOTAL

HISTORICAL FINANCIALS

Company Type: Public

Income Statement				FYE: December 31
	REVENUE ($ mil.)	NET INCOME ($ mil.)	NET PROFIT MARGIN	EMPLOYEES
12/09	80,101	3,152	3.9%	29,000
12/08	93,535	6,169	6.6%	29,500
12/07	96,421	8,133	8.4%	29,500
12/06	68,024	6,499	9.6%	25,435
12/05	58,135	4,542	7.8%	25,644
Annual Growth	**8.3%**	**(8.7%)**	**—**	**3.1%**

2009 Year-End Financials

Debt ratio: 48.4%
Return on equity: 9.7%
Cash ($ mil.): 4,255
Current ratio: 1.04
Long-term debt ($ mil.): 16,515

No. of shares (mil.): 3,184
Dividends
Yield: 17.5%
Payout: 75.8%
Market value ($ mil.): 13,649

Stock History

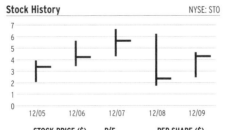

NYSE: STO

	STOCK PRICE ($) FY Close	P/E High/Low		PER SHARE ($) Earnings	Dividends	Book Value
12/09	4.29	5	3	0.99	0.75	10.72
12/08	2.36	3	1	1.92	0.59	9.59
12/07	5.63	3	2	2.55	0.75	10.27
12/06	4.22	2	1	3.01	0.54	6.14
12/05	3.38	2	1	2.09	0.49	4.95
Annual Growth	**6.1%**	**—**	**—**	**(17.0%)**	**11.2%**	**21.3%**

STMicroelectronics

STMicroelectronics (ST) is one of the world's largest and most respected semiconductor companies; it competes with Texas Instruments to be the top maker of analog chips. ST makes many types of discrete devices (such as transistors and diodes) and integrated circuits (ICs), including microcontrollers, memory chips, and application-specific ICs. It sells to manufacturers in the telecommunications, computer, consumer electronics, industrial, and automotive markets. Clients include Alcatel-Lucent, Bosch, Hewlett-Packard, and Nokia. STMicroelectronics gets most of its sales outside of Europe.

ST focuses on intensive product development, especially in close concert with key long-term strategic allies such as Alcatel-Lucent, Nokia, and Seagate Technology. The company also expanded its product range through a series of small, complementary acquisitions.

In 2010 ST formed a joint venture with Sharp and Enel Green Power (a unit of Italian utility giant Enel S.p.A.). The three companies will team up to build a thin-film solar cell production plant in the Catania province of Italy. Solar cells produced at the plant, which is scheduled to begin operations in 2011 with an initial capacity of 160 MW, will be marketed throughout Europe and in the Mediterranean region by Sharp and Enel Green Power.

The highly cyclical semiconductor industry was in one of its down periods during 2009, resulting from the global recession and lower sales of consumer electronics. Competition within the industry remains intense, as the big global players scrapped for market share during the downturn. Following the decision to sell its flash memory business, ST opted to close three plants — a 6-inch (150mm) wafer fabrication facility (fab) in Texas; an 8-inch (200mm) fab in Arizona; and a chip packaging and testing facility in Morocco. Production was shifted from those plants to other facilities around the world or to contractors over a transition period of two to three years. The three facilities employed about 4,000 people in all.

To strengthen its position in SoC design and in the market for digital TV chips, ST in 2008 acquired Genesis Microchip for around $336 million in cash. Genesis was among the leading vendors of video chips for flat-panel displays and digital TVs. Genesis became part of ST's Home Entertainment & Displays Group.

ST formed a joint venture in 2008 with archrival NXP. The two European chip makers combined their wireless semiconductor operations into a JV with 7,500-plus employees. ST got 80% of the JV company, ST-NXP Wireless, and paid $1.55 billion to NXP as part of the transaction.

Just weeks after completing the JV with NXP, ST agreed to merge Ericsson Mobile Platforms with ST-NXP Wireless into a wireless technology joint venture. The 50-50 joint venture between Ericsson and ST encompasses two companies, a development and marketing company with about 7,000 employees and a platform design company with around 1,000 employees. NXP sold its 20% stake in ST-NXP Wireless to ST as the transaction closed in 2009. Ericsson paid $1.1 billion to take a 50% stake in ST-NXP Wireless, which was renamed ST-Ericsson.

The French and Italian governments own more than 27% of STMicroelectronics.

HISTORY

SGS-THOMSON was formed through the 1987 merger of SGS Microelettronica, a state-owned Italian chip maker, and the nonmilitary electronics arm of Thomson-CSF (now Thales). Included in the deal were two US operations: SGS Semiconductor in Phoenix and Texas-based Thomson Components-Mostek (acquired by Thomson in 1986 from United Technologies).

Microelettronica was part of Finmeccanica, formed in 1948 as the engineering subsidiary of the (now liquidated) Italian state industrial holding company IRI.

Thomson SA got its start shortly before the turn of the century, when a group of French businessmen acquired patents from General Electric predecessor Thomson-Houston Electric and created Compagnie Française Thomson-Houston to produce power generation equipment.

Both Thomson and Microelettronica were struggling at the time of their merger. Pasquale Pistorio, a Motorola veteran who became head of SGS in 1980, was named president of the company. To jump-start the organization, he closed and sold factories, trimmed management, and shifted jobs to the Mediterranean and Asia.

SGS-THOMSON lost $300 million in its first two years of operation, made a small profit in 1989, then stumbled again as recession spread across Europe. To secure the company's market presence, Pistorio began making acquisitions and forging alliances with major chip buyers such as Alcatel (now Alcatel-Lucent), Hewlett-Packard, and Sony. By 1993 SGS-THOMSON had become the world's #1 maker of erasable programmable read-only memories (EPROMs). Profits soared to $160 million, and the company bought Tag Semiconductors, a maker of low-cost chips, from US conglomerate Raytheon. SGS-THOMSON went public in 1994.

Thomson sold off its stake in the company in 1997 and SGS-THOMSON changed its name to STMicroelectronics (ST) in 1998. The company formed development deals with Philips Electronics (for advanced chip manufacturing processes) in 1997 and with Mitsubishi (for flash memory chips) in 1998.

In 1999 ST bought Adaptec's Peripheral Technology Solutions group, which made chips for disk drives; Vision Group, a developer of image sensors; and Arithmos, a maker of ICs for digital displays. In 2000 ST acquired the Canada-based semiconductor fabrication operations of Nortel Networks for about $100 million. The deal included a six-year supply agreement worth at least $2 billion. The following year, though, ST announced that a sluggish chip industry would lead it to close the former Nortel fab as part of an overall reduction in its capital spending; ST later closed a fab in California as well.

In 2002 the company announced that it planned to sell its small PC graphics chip business. Later that year ST bought Alcatel Microelectronics from French telecom giant Alcatel for about $345 million. In a related transaction, ST resold Alcatel's mixed-signal chip business to AMI Semiconductor (the operating unit of AMIS Holdings, now part of ON Semiconductor). In 2004 the company spun off UPEK, a supplier of fingerprint scanners and other biometric authentication equipment.

Pistorio retired in 2005; company veteran Carlo Bozotti was designated as his successor. That year ST decided to exit the DSL chip business, a market it entered when it acquired Alcatel Microelectronics.

EXECUTIVES

Chairman: Antonino Turicchi, age 44
Vice Chairman: Gérald Arbola, age 62
President and CEO: Carlo Bozotti, age 58, $2,467,891 total compensation
COO: Alain Dutheil, age 65
EVP and CFO: Carlo Ferro, age 49
EVP and CTO: Jean-Marc Chery, age 50
EVP and General Manager, Sales and Marketing, Europe, Middle East, and Africa: Andrea Cuomo, age 56
EVP and General Manager, Front-End Manufacturing: Orio Bellezza, age 51
EVP, Infrastructure and Services: Otto Kosgalwies, age 54
EVP, Central Packaging and Test Manufacturing: Jeffrey See, age 65
EVP and General Manager, Industrial Multisegment Sector: Carmelo Papa, age 61
EVP and Chief Administrative Officer: Tjerk Hooghiemstra, age 53
EVP, Quality, Education, and Sustainable Development: Georges Auguste, age 61
EVP and General Manager, Home Entertainment and Displays Group: Philippe Lambinet, age 53
Group VP Corporate Media and Public Relations: Maria Grazia Prestini
VP and Chief Compliance Officer: Alisia Grenville, age 43
VP and General Counsel: Pierre Ollivier, age 55
VP Human Resources: Patrice Chastagner, age 63
VP Communication; President, STMicroelectronics Foundation: Carlo E. Ottaviani, age 67
Director Investor Relations: Celine Berthier
Senior Public Relations Manager Americas Region: Kristine Rizzo
Auditors: PricewaterhouseCoopers SA

LOCATIONS

HQ: STMicroelectronics N.V.
39, Chemin du Champ des Filles, Plan-Les-Ouates
1228 Geneva, Switzerland
Phone: 41-22-929-29-29 **Fax:** 41-22-929-29-88
US HQ: 1310 Electronics Dr., Carrollton, TX 75006
US Phone: 972-466-6000 **US Fax:** 972-466-8387
Web: www.st.com

2009 Sales

	$ mil.	% of total
Singapore	4,697	55
Netherlands	1,553	18
US	798	9
Japan	300	4
France	139	2
Italy	121	1
Other countries	902	11
Total	**8,510**	**100**

PRODUCTS/OPERATIONS

2009 Sales

	$ mil.	% of total
Automotive, consumer, computer & communication infrastructure	3,198	38
Industrial & multisegment sector	2,641	31
Wireless	2,585	30
Other	86	1
Total	**8,510**	**100**

COMPETITORS

Analog Devices
Atmel
Avago Technologies
Broadcom
Cypress Semiconductor
Fairchild Semiconductor
Freescale Semiconductor
Fujitsu Semiconductor
Himax
IBM Microelectronics
Infineon Technologies
Intel
International Rectifier
Intersil
Linear Technology
LSI Corp.
Marvell Technology
Maxim Integrated Products
MediaTek
Microchip Technology
National Semiconductor
NVIDIA
NXP Semiconductors
ON Semiconductor
QUALCOMM
Renesas Electronics
RF Micro Devices
ROHM
Samsung Electronics
SanDisk
Sharp Corp.
Spansion
Texas Instruments
Toshiba Semiconductor
Trident Microsystems
TSMC
Vishay Intertechnology

HISTORICAL FINANCIALS

Company Type: Public

Income Statement

	REVENUE ($ mil.)	NET INCOME ($ mil.)	NET PROFIT MARGIN	EMPLOYEES
12/09	8,510	(1,131)	—	51,560
12/08	9,842	(786)	—	51,810
12/07	10,001	(477)	—	52,180
12/06	9,854	782	7.9%	51,770
12/05	8,882	266	3.0%	50,000
Annual Growth	**(1.1%)**	**—**		**0.8%**

FYE: December 31

2009 Year-End Financials

Debt ratio: 32.4%
Return on equity: —
Cash ($ mil.): 1,588
Current ratio: 2.78
Long-term debt ($ mil.): 2,316

No. of shares (mil.): 882
Dividends
  Yield: 2.5%
  Payout: —
Market value ($ mil.): 8,172

Stock History

NYSE: STM

	STOCK PRICE ($) FY Close	P/E High/Low	Earnings	Dividends	Book Value
12/09	9.27	— —	(1.29)	0.23	8.11
12/08	6.65	— —	(0.88)	0.23	9.25
12/07	14.30	— —	(0.53)	0.30	10.86
12/06	18.40	24 18	0.83	0.12	11.06
12/05	18.00	68 48	0.29	0.12	9.62
Annual Growth	**(15.3%)**	**— —**	**—**	**17.7%**	**(4.2%)**

Stora Enso Oyj

Stora Enso Oyj's roots reach back more than 700 years. The forest products company is among the largest producers of newsprint and sawn softwood timber in Europe. It plays a major role in meeting the needs of publishers, advertisers, office suppliers, and packagers of consumer and industrial goods for a range of paper products, from magazine paper to newsprint and book paper, fine papers, and container board. Stora Enso's wood-based lines serve construction, interior decorator, and biofuel industries.

Stora Enso is carving out an expanded geographic presence; its direction looks to court new customers as well as reduce raw material costs. In 2009 the company teamed up with Arauco, one of the largest forestry enterprises in Latin America. The 50-50 venture acquired a majority stake in the Uruguayan operations of Spanish pulp producer Grupo ENCE, securing low-cost pulp — a critical raw material in its operations. In Brazil, Stora Enso partners with Fibria to control Veracei Celulose, a producer of eucalyptus pulp that is undergirded by a fiber base of 234,000 hectares of land. Stora Enso also ties up with Arauco to operate a coated magazine paper mill.

In another developing region, China, the company is wooing paper and paperboard demand through joint ventures with Chinese companies Shandong Haiti Paper and Gaofeng Forest. Stora Enso launched eucalyptus plantations in southern China with an eye toward developing an integrated pulp and paper, or board facility.

Stora Enso's international moves are part of a group-wide reorganization brought on by a slew of issues, including a sustained increase in production costs, overcapacity in publication paper and fine paper, along with growing competition over demand eroded by the global economic recession. In mid-2010 the company sold its Kotka Mill division — laminating paper, special coated magazine paper, and sawmill businesses — to private equity firm OpenGate Capital.

Other restructuring efforts in 2009, 2008, and 2007 pushed the closure of mills in Finland, the Netherlands, Germany, and Sweden, representing a total reduction in capacity of more than a million tons of paper and board, and approximately 900,000 tons of pulp.

In a more dramatic move, Stora Enso dropped Stora Enso North America (SENA), one of its strongest subsidiaries, to rival NewPage for about $1.7 billion and an equity stake of nearly 20% in the combined entity. In addition, the company sold off its fine paper retail business, Papyrus, to Altor Fund II for about $980 million.

Foundation Asset Management controls nearly 27% of Stora Enso's voting rights. The Finnish State holds 25% of the voting rights, while the Social Insurance Institution of Finland controls another 10%.

HISTORY

Stora Enso's ancestors were mining Kopperberg Mountain in Sweden as long ago as 1288. The mountain housed a copper mine that Swedish nobles and German merchants managed as a cooperative. By the 17th century King Karl IX instituted German mining methods to increase production. Copper became Sweden's largest export, at one point accounting for 60% of the country's gross national product.

Copper production slowed after two cave-ins in 1655 and 1687, and exploitation of the region's timber and iron ore resources began. By the early 1800s the company was producing pig and bar iron. In 1862 all of the company's activities were combined to form Stora Kopparbergs Bergslag. The role of copper became less important as the company consolidated its iron works and ventured into forest products. The firm reorganized as a limited liability company in 1888.

By 1915 Stora Kopparbergs had firmly established pulp and paper mills, as well as iron and steel works concentrated along the Dalalven River Basin. The company's activities revolved around these facilities for the next 60 years.

During the 1960s Stora Kopparbergs was hurt by low bulk commodity prices and increased competition. The company, feeling the crunch of the oil crisis, sold its holdings in steel and mining between 1976 and 1978. With its purchase of Billerud (forestry), the company became Sweden's largest industrial concern in 1984. Stora Kopparbergs shortened its name to Stora, meaning "great" or "large" in Swedish, to commemorate the event.

Stora went on a shopping spree in the late 1980s and early 1990s to compete with its giant US rivals. At home it bought Papyrus and Swedish Match; abroad it acquired Feldmuhle Nobel of Germany and France's Les Paperteies de la Chapelle-Darblay. In 1998 Stora established operations in China through a joint venture. The company also merged with Finnish forest products company Enso Gutzeit Oyj to form Stora Enso Oyj that year.

Hans Gutzeit founded a sawmill in 1872 on the Finnish island of Kotka. The company constructed a pulp mill to use waste wood from the Kotka sawmill, and in 1912 it purchased rival sawmill Enso Trasliperi Aktiebolaget to increase its access to hydropower. Gutzeit's Norwegian shareholders sold the company to the new Finnish state in 1919. In 1924 the company was renamed Enso-Gutzeit.

In the 1950s and 1960s the company added a paper mill, a box factory, bleaching plants, and pulp mills. It entered Canada through a 50% stake in Eurocan Pulp & Paper in 1970. (It obtained full ownership in 1979.) Enso-Gutzeit took part in a 1980s Finnish consolidation trend by buying rival A. Ahlstrom Oy's pulp and paper mills. The company merged with Veitsiluoto in 1996 to form Enso Oy. Two years later Enso Oy merged with Stora to form Stora Enso.

Stora Enso bought US-based Consolidated Papers (now Stora Enso North America) for $4.9 billion in 2000. The acquisition moved Stora Enso past International Paper as the world's #1 paper and board producer.

Labor disputes shut down all of the company's paper mills in Finland in 2005, overshadowing reported sales and profit improvements. The labor disputes stemmed from disagreements over plant shutdowns for mid-summer and Christmas holidays, as well as outsourcing. Strikes by workers were followed by lockouts (one lasting more than a month) by employers, which temporarily crippled the country's paper industry and affected the chemical and transportation sectors as well. Stora Enso then announced plans to eliminate about 2,000 jobs and close five plants in Europe and the US.

In 2005 Stora Enso bought German paper wholesaler Schneidersöhne Group for €450 million. In 2006 it sold its pulp subsidiary Celulose Beira Industrial (aka Celbi) to Portugal-based Altri for nearly $550 million.

EXECUTIVES

Chairman: Gunnar Brock, age 60
Vice Chairman: Juha Rantanen, age 57
CEO: Jouko Karvinen, age 53
Deputy CEO, Strategy, Purchasing, and IT: Hannu Ryöppönen, age 58
CFO: Markus Rauramo, age 42
EVP Newsprint and Book Paper; Country Manager, Finland: Juha Vanhainen, age 48
EVP Fine Paper: Aulis Ansaharju, age 59
EVP Magazine Paper: Hannu Alalauri, age 51
EVP Wood Products: Hannu Kasurinen, age 47
EVP Wood Supply, Pulp Supply, HR, Sustainability and Latin America; Country Manager, Sweden: Elisabet Salander Björklund, age 52
EVP Consumer Board, Market Services, and Asia Pacific: Mats Nordlander, age 49
EVP Industrial Packaging and Russia: Veli-Jussi Potka, age 50
EVP Technology and Investments, Country Manager, Germany: Bernd Rettig, age 53
SVP Investor Relations: Ulla Paajanen-Sainio
SVP Group Human Resources Services: Gerda Platzer
Head Sustainability: Eija Pitkänen
Head Group Communications: Lauri Peltola
Auditors: Deloitte & Touche Oy

LOCATIONS

HQ: Stora Enso Oyj
Kanavaranta 1
FI-00101 Helsinki, Finland
Phone: 358-20-46-131   **Fax:** 358-20-46-214-71
Web: www.storaenso.com

2009 Sales

	% of total
Europe	
Germany	18
Sweden	9
Finland	7
UK	7
France	7
Netherlands	5
Spain	4
Poland	3
Italy	3
Austria	3
Russia	2
Denmark	2
Belgium	2
Baltic States	1
Czech Republic	1
Other countries	7
Asia/Pacific	
China & Hong Kong	3
Japan	2
Australia & New Zealand	1
Other countries	3
Middle East	2
Africa	3
Americas	
Brazil	2
US	1
Other countries	1
Other regions	1
Total	**100**

PRODUCTS/OPERATIONS

2009 Sales

	% of total
Consumer board	21
Fine paper	20
Magazine paper	19
Newsprint & book paper	15
Wood products	14
Industrial packaging	9
Other	2
Total	**100**

Selected Products

Book paper
Business forms
Cartonboards
Coreboards and tubes
Corrugated boxes
Digital papers
Directory paper
Document papers
Envelope papers
Fluff pulp
Foodservice boards
Graphic board
Graphic paper
Kraft papers
Laminated papers
Liquid packaging boards
Magazine paper
Newsprint
Paper-grade pulp
Sawn boards
Scholastic paper

COMPETITORS

Amcor
Iggesund Paperboard
International Paper
Metsäliitto
Myllykoski Paper
NewPage
Norske Skog
OfficeMax
Sappi
Smurfit-Stone Container
UPM-Kymmene
Wausau Paper
Weyerhaeuser

HISTORICAL FINANCIALS

Company Type: Public

Income Statement

FYE: December 31

	REVENUE ($ mil.)	NET INCOME ($ mil.)	NET PROFIT MARGIN	EMPLOYEES
12/09	13,068	(1,259)	—	28,696
12/08	15,545	(951)	—	33,815
12/07	19,685	(313)	—	37,997
12/06	19,254	772	4.0%	43,887
12/05	15,618	(154)	—	46,664
Annual Growth	(4.4%)	—	—	(11.4%)

2009 Year-End Financials

Debt ratio: 55.3%
Return on equity: —
Cash ($ mil.): 1,276
Current ratio: 1.43
Long-term debt ($ mil.): 4,154

No. of shares (mil.): 789
Dividends
Yield: 4.1%
Payout: —
Market value ($ mil.): 5,516

Stock History

Pink Sheets: SEOAY

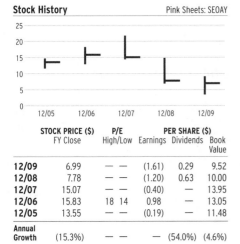

	STOCK PRICE ($) FY Close	P/E High/Low	PER SHARE ($) Earnings	Dividends	Book Value
12/09	6.99	— —	(1.61)	0.29	9.52
12/08	7.78	— —	(1.20)	0.63	10.00
12/07	15.07	— —	(0.40)	—	13.95
12/06	15.83	18 14	0.98	—	13.05
12/05	13.55	— —	(0.19)	—	11.48
Annual Growth	(15.3%)	— —	—	(54.0%)	(4.6%)

Suzuki Motor

Suzuki Motor Corporation is a leading Japanese carmaker and the world's #3 motorcycle manufacturer behind Honda and Yamaha. Suzuki's passenger car models include the Alto, Grand Vitara, Swift, Splash, and SX4. Its motorcycle products include cruiser, motocross, off-road, scooter, street, and touring models, as well as ATVs. Suzuki Motor's non-vehicle products include outboard motors for boats and motorized wheelchairs. The company, via a global network, serves more than 190 countries. It builds its lineup on its own and through numerous subsidiaries and joint ventures overseas.

A key part of the Japanese car maker's global operating strategy, however, is its presence in Asia. Suzuki subsidiary Maruti Suzuki India is India's largest passenger car company. Suzuki is expanding its vehicle lineup in China through Suzuki China, which imports and sells Japanese-made cars. The company imports and exports Suzuki-brand vehicles through Suzuki Automobile (Thailand), a joint venture with Siam International Corp. Demand in Vietnam, the Philippines, and Malaysia has continued to grow modestly, too.

Despite these inroads, the global economic recession's impact plus unfavorable currency exchange rates drove down Suzuki's sales. Amid the crisis, cuts to operating expenses coupled with a small uptick in Asian sales buoyed a passable increase in earnings.

Partnerships are particularly vital to Suzuki's future. The company brokered a tie-up with German giant Volkswagen AG in early 2010. VW picked up an approximate 20% stake in Suzuki, creating one of the world's largest auto alliances. VW's entry into China widens the door for Suzuki to China's growing car market. Suzuki is also looking to build upon VW's experience in green technology, including building gasoline-electric hybrids, electric vehicles, and more fuel-efficient gasoline engines. The new alliance follows the decision by Suzuki and General Motors in late 2009 to terminate CAMI Automotive, a car assembly joint venture based in Canada. Their 10-year venture included collaboration on various technologies, such as hybrid vehicles.

Elsewhere, Suzuki partners with other carmakers in specific product lines. The company holds a mutual OEM vehicle supply agreement with Nissan Motor in domestic and international markets, as well as vehicle supply agreements with Mazda Motor, Fiat Group, and Adam Opel, and a diesel engine license from Fiat Powertrain.

Suzuki is also moving ahead with a slew of product introductions, including the Kizashi sedan and Wagon R (in India), a continuously variable transmission on its Palette mini vehicle, and a few cell-powered scooters. The latter launch aims to regain Suzuki's momentum with motorcycle users, largely served in overseas markets. The business has suffered slumping sales and operating losses. Although managing to maintain a profit, Suzuki's marine and power products have been hurt by double-digit declines in sales as well, largely due to weak demand for outboard motors, attributed to the economic downturn.

HISTORY

In 1909 Michio Suzuki started Suzuki Loom Works in Hamamatsu, Japan. The company went public in 1920 and continued producing weaving equipment until the onset of WWII, when it began to make war-related products.

Suzuki began developing inexpensive motor vehicles in 1947, and in 1952 it introduced a 36cc engine to motorize bicycles. The company changed its name to Suzuki Motor and launched its first motorcycle in 1954. Suzuki's entry into the minicar market came in 1955 with the Suzulight, followed by the Suzumoped (1958), a delivery van (1959), and the Suzulight Carry FB small truck (1961).

Suzuki's triumph in the 1962 50cc-class Isle of Man TT motorcycle race started a string of racing successes that brought international prominence to the Suzuki name. The company established its first overseas plant in Thailand in 1967.

In the 1970s Suzuki met market demand for motorcycles with large engines. Meanwhile, a mid-1970s recession and falling demand for low-powered cars in Japan led the minicar industry there to produce two-thirds fewer minicars in 1974 than in 1970. Suzuki responded by pushing overseas, beginning auto exports, and expanding foreign distribution. In 1975 it started producing motorcycles in Taiwan, Thailand, and Indonesia.

Suzuki boosted capacity internationally throughout the 1980s through joint ventures. Motorcycle sales in Japan peaked in 1982, then tapered off, but enjoyed a modest rebound in the late 1980s. In 1988 the company agreed to handle distribution of Peugeot cars in Japan.

Suzuki and General Motors began their long-standing relationship in 1981 when GM bought a small stake in Suzuki. The company began producing Swift subcompacts in 1983 and sold them through GM as the Chevy Sprint and, later, the Geo Metro. In 1986 Suzuki and GM of Canada jointly formed CAMI Automotive to produce vehicles, including Sprints, Metros, and Geo Trackers (Suzuki Sidekicks), in Ontario; production began in 1989.

Although sales via GM increased through 1990, US efforts with the Suzuki nameplate faltered shortly after Suzuki formed its US subsidiary in Brea, California, in 1986. A 1988 *Consumer Reports* claim that the company's Samurai SUV was prone to rolling over devastated US sales. The next year Suzuki's top US executives quit, apparently questioning the company's commitment to the US market.

Suzuki expanded a licensing agreement with a Chinese government partner in 1993, becoming the first Japanese company to take an equity stake in a Chinese carmaking venture. In a case that was later overturned, a woman was awarded $90 million from Suzuki after being paralyzed in a Samurai rollover in 1990. The company sued Consumers Union, publisher of *Consumer Reports*, in 1996, charging it had intended to fix the results in the 1988 Samurai testing.

GM raised its 3% stake in Suzuki to 10% in 1998. The company teamed up with GM and Fuji Heavy Industries (Subaru) in 2000 to develop compact cars for the European market. It was also announced that GM would spend about $600 million to double its stake in Suzuki to 20%. In 2001 Suzuki announced that it had agreed to cooperate with Kawasaki in the development of new motorcycles, scooters, and ATVs.

GM sold almost all of its 20% stake in Suzuki in early 2006 to raise cash for its own beleaguered operations. GM divested the remaining 3% stake in late 2008 for about $230 million as it endured a dire cash crisis.

EXECUTIVES

Chairman and CEO: Osamu Suzuki
General Manager, Finance Department: Yuichi Miyazaki
Senior Managing Officer and Director: Naoki Aizawa
Senior Managing Officer and Director: Eiji Mochizuki
Senior Managing Officer and Director: Minoru Tamura
Senior Managing Officer and Director: Toyokazu Sugimoto
Senior Managing Officer and Director: Osamu Honda
Senior Managing Officer and Director: Takao Hirosawa
Senior Managing Officer and Director: Toshihiro Suzuki
Senior Managing Officer and Director: Masanori Atsumi
Senior Managing Officer and Director: Shinzo Nakanishi
Senior Managing Officer and Director: Takashi Nakayama
Auditors: Seimei Audit Corporation

LOCATIONS

HQ: Suzuki Motor Corporation
300 Takatsuka-Cho, Minami-ku
Hamamatsu City, Shizuoka 432-8611, Japan
Phone: 81-53-440-2061   **Fax:** 81-53-440-2776
US HQ: 3251 E. Imperial Hwy., Brea, CA 92821
US Phone: 714-996-7040   **US Fax:** 714-524-8499
Web: www.globalsuzuki.com

2010 Sales

	% of total
Asia	
Japan	39
Other countries	31
Europe	18
North America	5
Other regions	7
Total	**100**

PRODUCTS/OPERATIONS

2010 Sales

	% of total
Automobiles	86
Motorcycles	11
Other products	3
Total	**100**

Selected Products

Automobiles
 Alto/CELERIO
 APV
 Grand Vitara SUV
 Jimny
 Kizashi sport sedan
 Splash
 Swift
 SX4 Crossover, Sport, SportBack
Motorcycles/ATV
 Cruiser
 Dual purpose
 Motocross
 Offroad
 Scooter
 Sport Enduro Tourer
 Street
 Supersport
Outboard motors
 Carburetor series (4-stroke)
 Electronic fuel injection series (4-stroke)
 Kerosene Outboards (2-stroke)

COMPETITORS

Bajaj Auto
BMW
Brunswick Corp.
Chrysler
Daimler
Ducati
Ek Chor China Motorcycle
Ford Motor
General Motors
Harley-Davidson
Honda
Hyundai Motor
Kawasaki Heavy Industries
Mahindra
Mazda
Nissan
Piaggio & Co.
Polaris Industries
Renault
Tata Motors
Toyota
Triumph Motorcycles
Volkswagen
Yamaha Motor

HISTORICAL FINANCIALS

Company Type: Public

Income Statement

	REVENUE ($ mil.)	NET INCOME ($ mil.)	NET PROFIT MARGIN	EMPLOYEES
				FYE: March 31
3/10	26,636	326	1.2%	51,503
3/09	30,887	282	0.9%	50,241
3/08	35,273	808	2.3%	50,241
3/07	26,841	636	2.4%	45,510
3/06	23,361	561	2.4%	40,798
Annual Growth	**3.3%**	**(12.7%)**	**—**	**6.0%**

2010 Year-End Financials

Debt ratio: —
Return on equity: 3.9%
Cash ($ mil.): 1,590
Current ratio: 1.58
Long-term debt ($ mil.): —
No. of shares (mil.): 451
Dividends
 Yield: 0.5%
 Payout: 20.0%
Market value ($ mil.): 10,038

Stock History

Tokyo: 72690

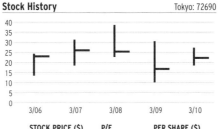

	STOCK PRICE ($) FY Close	P/E High/Low		PER SHARE ($) Earnings	Dividends	Book Value
3/10	22.26	45	32	0.60	0.12	22.77
3/09	16.74	54	19	0.55	0.08	14.57
3/08	25.33	24	15	1.57	—	17.38
3/07	25.96	24	15	1.28	—	16.10
3/06	23.01	23	13	1.04	—	11.63
Annual Growth	**(0.8%)**	**—**	**—**	**(12.8%)**	**50.0%**	**18.3%**

The Swatch Group

Swatch is worth watching. The Swatch Group (formerly Société Suisse de Microélectronique & d'Horlogerie) is the world's second-largest watchmaker (after Citizen Watch). Its 20 or so brands range from low-priced, collectible Swatch and Flik Flak to premium-priced Blancpain, Breguet, and Omega brands. Swatch watches are sold at some 15,000 retailers worldwide, plus at more than 500 Swatch stores, more than 1,000 shop-in-shops, and some 140 kiosks. The company supplies nearly all the components for its own watches and is a supplier to other watchmakers. Its Dress Your Body subsidiary designs and makes jewelry for the Swatch Group brands.

A products portfolio that spans different price points has worked well for Swatch, particularly during the economic downturn. While it caters to the upscale market with its Breguet and Omega brands, the watchmaker peddles its Swatch-brand watches at much lower price tags. Diversifying has allowed the company to ride out a recession more easily than some of its high-end rivals.

Swatch controls about a fourth of the worldwide watch market. The company, which has more than 100 subsidiaries and affiliated units, also makes watch components and private-label watches. In addition, it makes semiconductors, quartz oscillators, and industrial lasers, among other items, for industries such as telecommunications and medical electronics. The company's EM-Microelectronic subsidiary is the leading producer of radio frequency identification (RFID) technology that is taking hold in the retail industry. Swatch also provides timing and scoring services at major sporting events, such as the Olympic Games.

Inking deals in recent years has fueled growth for Swatch. Building its luxury watch business, Swatch Group in late 2007 formed a new company to make watches under the iconic Tiffany & Co. brand name. The Tiffany Watch Co., based in Switzerland, is authorized to use the Tiffany name and trademarks. The watch collection, which debuted at Baselworld in 2009, ranges from about £2,000 to £5,000 (or between $3,000 and $8,000). The watches are distributed through the Swatch retail network and through Tiffany stores. Swatch also acquired 270-year-old Jaquet Droz (luxury watches). The artistic watch brand enables Swatch to merge technology and tradition.

Swatch has likewise been disposing of assets in order to focus on its core operations. In early 2010 the company sold the assets of its Microcomponents Ltd of Switzerland and Zhuhai SMH Watchmaking Co. subsidiaries, which produce stepper motors and clocks for automobile instrument panels, to Singapore's Juken Technology. The deal was worth some S$6 million and included the units' manufacturing centers in China and Switzerland.

The company has been striking deals with retailers to further its products. Swatch formed a retail partnership in 2006 with Tourneau, the world's largest watch store, to open watch stores in high-end outlet malls across the US. In 2008 it took a significant stake in luxury goods retailer Rivoli Group, based in Dubai.

As of 2009, a group (known as the Hayek Pool) headed by then-chairman Nicolas Hayek (who died in mid-2010) controlled 41% of The Swatch Group's shares.

HISTORY

The Swatch Group was first established when watchmakers ASUAG and SSIH were merged in 1983. ASUAG was founded in 1931 in Switzerland to make watches. By the late 1970s ASUAG had acquired some 100 family-owned companies, many of which were operating independently and inefficiently. When it merged with SSIH, ASUAG owned the Longines and Rado brands and made watch components.

Watchmaker SSIH was formed in 1930 with the merger of brands Tissot and Omega (which traced its history to 1848). SSIH and other Swiss watchmakers were struggling by the late 1970s. The market was flooded with cheaper watches made in Japan and Hong Kong that used quartz technology (a technology invented — but ignored — by the Swiss). SSIH had licensed out its prestigious Omega brand to other manufacturers in various countries, hurting that brand's reputation.

With both ASUAG and SSIH on the verge of bankruptcy, Swiss banks named Nicolas Hayek (then the CEO of consulting firm Hayek Engineering) to advise the companies on their futures. He recommended that ASUAG and SSIH merge and then mass-produce a low-cost watch and sell it globally at a set price. The two companies merged in 1983, forming SMH (Société Suisse de Microélectronique & d'Horlogerie); its headquarters were ASUAG's in Biel, Switzerland.

SMH had sales of about $1.1 billion with losses of some $124 million in 1983. That year it introduced the Swatch watch amid some resistance and objections that the watch would ruin the Swiss image of makers of high-quality, premium-priced watches. But Swatch watches became fashion statements and pop-culture icons in the 1980s and Hayek, who spearheaded the turnaround, became a Swiss business hero. Hayek and a group of investors bought a controlling 51% stake of SMH, and he became CEO in 1985.

In 1992 the company bought Blancpain (luxury watches) and Frederic Piguet (luxury watch components). By 1993 SMH had expanded into semiconductor chips, pagers, and telephones. The next year it formed a joint venture (19%-owned by SMH) called Micro Compact Car (MCC) with Daimler-Benz to make a battery- and gasoline-powered Swatchmobile.

Because of difficulty in translating its name into other languages, the company changed its name in 1998 to The Swatch Group. That year it also sold its 19% stake in MCC to Daimler-Benz. In 1999 Swatch bought Groupe Horloger Breguet, a manufacturer of mechanical timepieces since 1775, and Swiss watch case maker Favre & Perret. In 2000 the growing company pocketed German luxury watchmaker Glashütter, among others. Acquisitions in 2001 included two Greek companies, Aliki Perri and Alikonia. Swatch bought Swiss watch dial maker Rubattel & Weyermann in 2002. Later that year Hayek retired as CEO, but remained chairman; his son Nicolas became CEO.

In 2004 Swatch unveiled the Paparazzi, a watch it made in collaboration with MSN Direct (a division of Microsoft) which can link to updated international news, weather forecasts, and lottery results. All that, and it tells the time.

In October 2006 the company acquired watch dial maker MOM Le Prélet SA of Switzerland.

Founder and chairman Nicolas Hayek died unexpectedly of heart failure in June 2010. He was succeeded by his daughter, vice chairman Nayla Hayek.

EXECUTIVES

Chairwoman: Nayla Hayek
Vice Chairman: Peter Gross
President Executive Management Board and Director: Nicolas G. (Nick) Hayek Jr.
Member Executive Group Management Board, EM Microelectronic, Micro Crystal, Renata, Microcomponents, Oscilloquartz, and Lasag: Mougahed Darwish
Member Executive Management Board, Tissot, Certina, Mido, Brazil, and Switzerland: Françoise Thiébaud
Member Executive Management Board and President, Japan and Korea: Arlette-Elsa Emch
Member Executive Management Board, Blancpain, Middle East, Central and South America: Marc A. Hayek
Member Executive Management Board and President, France, Les Boutiques, Italy, Spain, and Flik Flak: Florence Ollivier-Lamarque
Member Executive Management Board, Legal, Licences, Strategic Projects, Real Estate (except Engineering), Patents (ICB), Swatch Group Greece, Swatch Group Poland: Hanspeter Rentsch
Member Extended Group Management Board Finance, Reporting, and Investor Relations: Thierry Kenel
Corporate Treasurer: Thomas Dürr
Company Secretary: Roland Bloch
Head Media Relations: Beatrice Howald
Auditors: PricewaterhouseCoopers Ltd.

LOCATIONS

HQ: The Swatch Group SA
Seevorstadt 6
CH-2501 Biel, Bern, Switzerland
Phone: 41-32-343-68-11 **Fax:** 41-32-343-69-11
US HQ: 1200 Harbor Blvd., Weehawken, NJ 07086
US Phone: 201-271-1400 **US Fax:** 201-558-5042
Web: www.swatchgroup.com

2009 Sales

	% of total
Europe	45
Asia	44
America	8
Oceania	2
Africa	1
Total	**100**

PRODUCTS/OPERATIONS

2009 Sales

	% of total
Watches & jewelry	82
Watch production	11
Electronic systems	7
Total	**100**

Selected Products and Brands

Watches
  Basic Range
    Flik Flak
    Swatch
  High Range
    Longines
    Rado
  Middle Range
    Calvin Klein
    Certina
    Hamilton
    Mido
    Pierre Balmain
    Tissot
  Prestige
    Blancpain
    Breguet
    Glashüte Original/Union
    Jaquet-Droz
    Léon Hatot
    Omega
    Paparazzi
  Private Label
    Endura

Jewelry
  Dress Your Body
Retailing
  Les Boutiques

Selected Electronic Systems Operations

EM Microelectronic-Marin SA (microelectronics)
Lasag AG (lasers for industrial applications)
Omega Electronics SA (sports timing equipment, information displays system)
Oscilloquartz SA (high-stability frequency sources)

COMPETITORS

Armitron
Benetton
Bulgari
CASIO COMPUTER
Citizen
Fossil, Inc.
Guess?
Hermès
LVMH
Movado Group
Richemont
Rolex
Seiko
Tiffany & Co.
Timex

HISTORICAL FINANCIALS

Company Type: Public

Income Statement

	REVENUE ($ mil.)	NET INCOME ($ mil.)	NET PROFIT MARGIN	EMPLOYEES
12/09	4,954	735	14.8%	23,562
12/08	5,375	793	14.8%	24,270
12/07	5,011	901	18.0%	23,577
12/06	3,951	680	17.2%	21,268
12/05	3,262	472	14.5%	20,650
Annual Growth	**11.0%**	**11.7%**	**—**	**3.4%**

FYE: December 31

2009 Year-End Financials

Debt ratio: —
Return on equity: 13.5%
Cash ($ mil.): 1,058
Current ratio: 4.36
Long-term debt ($ mil.): —
No. of shares (mil.): —
Dividends
  Yield: 1.7%
  Payout: 29.8%
Market value ($ mil.): —

Stock History

Swiss: UHR

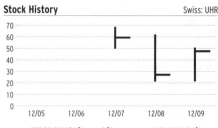

	STOCK PRICE ($) FY Close	P/E High/Low		PER SHARE ($) Earnings	Dividends	Book Value
12/09	47.59	18	8	2.75	0.82	—
12/08	26.98	21	8	2.89	0.80	—
12/07	59.34	21	16	3.18	—	—
Annual Growth	**(10.4%)**	**—**	**—**	**(7.0%)**	**2.5%**	**—**

Taiwan Semiconductor

If you're absolutely fabless, this is the company for you. Taiwan Semiconductor Manufacturing Company (TSMC) is the first and largest dedicated silicon foundry (contract semiconductor manufacturer) in the world, with 10 plants in Asia and one in the US. TSMC makes chips for hundreds of manufacturers, such as Freescale Semiconductor and NXP (which outsource to TSMC to boost capacity), and fabless semiconductor companies, such as Broadcom and NVIDIA.

Foundries aim to save clients the costs and time associated with building wafer fabrication plants (fabs) of their own, which becomes ever more important as the price tags for state-of-the-art fabs climb into the billions of dollars. Their services are especially vital for fabless companies whose entire business model is predicated on outsourcing all manufacturing.

In November 2009 TSMC won a legal battle against rival Semiconductor Manufacturing International Corp. (SMIC) when SMIC was found guilty of stealing trade secrets from TSMC related to its manufacturing processes. The dispute has been going on since 2003, when TSMC filed suit against SMIC for patent infringement; though SMIC disputed the allegations, it agreed to a settlement in 2005 that included a $175 million fine and the rights to use TSMC patents. The following year TSMC filed another suit, alleging that SMIC violated the terms of the agreement by continuing to steal trade secrets. TSMC is receiving $200 million, as well as an unknown amount of stock and warrants, in damages.

TSMC expanded production capacity by consolidating ownership of former joint ventures; it also continues to pace the semiconductor industry by remaining on the cutting edge of chip-making processes. In December 2009 it agreed to acquire a 20% stake (for $193 million) in Motech Industries, a solar-cell manufacturer. The acquisition will make TSMC the largest shareholder in Motech, and will expand its presence in energy-savings industries.

While continuing to build on TSMC's well-established reputation for technological leadership, founder and chairman Morris Chang — a chip industry legend — focused on delivering the best service in the industry (for example) by serving more of clients' needs via the Internet. The company also backed up its bet on a surge in chip manufacturing in mainland China by establishing operations there.

TSMC's biggest challenge isn't competitive or technological — it's dealing with the effects of the global recession, which affects sales of its customers. When those chip companies lose business, they place fewer and smaller orders with TSMC.

Philips, one of TSMC's initial investors, sold its remaining shares in the company in 2008 as part of a planned, phased divestiture. The government of Taiwan has an equity stake of approximately 6%.

HISTORY

Morris Chang learned early to adapt to rapid change. The future founder and chairman of Taiwan Semiconductor Manufacturing Company (TSMC) lived in six cities before age 18, as his family fled the ravages of the Sino-Japanese War and WWII in China. Chang immigrated to the US to attend MIT and Stanford, where he ultimately earned a Ph.D. in electrical engineering.

In 25 years at Texas Instruments (TI), Chang worked his way up from the ranks of technical management into the executive suite. In 1983 he resigned from TI to become CEO of General Instrument (acquired in 2000 by Motorola), but in 1985 the Taiwanese government recruited him to head its Industrial Technology Research Institute (ITRI). He remained chairman of ITRI from 1988 to 1994.

Working from his position at ITRI, Chang became chairman of contract electronics manufacturer United Microelectronics Corporation (UMC) in 1987. Also that year he founded TSMC as the world's first dedicated contract semiconductor manufacturer — the first silicon foundry. Chang's pioneering role in the foundry industry has earned him many accolades, including the first-ever Robert N. Noyce Medal of the Institute of Electrical and Electronics Engineers and the first-ever Exemplary Leadership award (subsequently named in his honor) of the Fabless Semiconductor Association (now the Global Semiconductor Alliance). Known for his analytical mind, Chang was once ranked among the top 1,000 players of contract bridge in the world.

Throughout the 1990s TSMC continued to be among industry leaders both in production capacity and in deployment of cutting-edge technology. The company opened its first US office in 1992 and its first European office in 1993. During the early 1990s it opened a series of fabs in the Hsinchu industrial zone in northwestern Taiwan. In 1997 TSMC broke ground on the first of a series of fabs in the Tainan industrial zone in southern Taiwan, and in 1998 it opened its first office in Japan. The following year TSMC and Philips began construction on their Systems on Silicon Manufacturing Company (SSMC) foundry joint venture in Singapore.

TSMC made a series of acquisitions in 2000 as it enjoyed a string of record sales months: It bought out Acer's majority share in their Taiwan-based joint venture, it bought out three minority partners in the US-based WaferTech joint venture, and it acquired outright Taiwan's #3 chip foundry, Worldwide Semiconductor Manufacturing.

Despite a broad industry downturn, in 2001 the company continued its rollout of cutting-edge manufacturing processes for 300mm silicon wafers and for 0.13-micron chip circuitry designs. The company weathered a dismal 2001 — by consensus the worst year in the chip industry's history — better than its smaller rivals, and by 2002 TSMC began efforts to expand its manufacturing reach into mainland China, where it established an office.

In 2003 TSMC filed a lawsuit against Semiconductor Manufacturing International Corp. (SMIC), its up-and-coming rival on the Chinese mainland, alleging patent infringement and misappropriation of trade secrets. The competitors reached a legal settlement in 2005, with SMIC agreeing to pay $175 million to TSMC.

Morris Chang stepped aside as CEO in 2005, while remaining chairman. Rick Tsai, who was TSMC's president and COO, was promoted to CEO. F. C. Tseng, previously the company's deputy CEO, became vice chairman. Chang returned to the CEO position when Tsai left the company in 2009.

The TSMC-SMIC legal dispute flared up again in 2006, as TSMC filed suit against its mainland competitor and claimed that SMIC breached the 2005 settlement agreement. SMIC denied the allegations and filed a countersuit against TSMC.

EXECUTIVES

Chairman and CEO: Morris Chang, age 78
Vice Chairman: F. C. Tseng
SVP Operations: Mark Liu
SVP Business Development: Che-Chai (C. C.) Wei
SVP Information Technology, CIO, and Information Technology/Material Management and Risk Management Officer: Stephen T. (Steve) Tso
VP, CFO, and Spokesperson: Lora Ho
VP Human Resources: Peng-Heng Chang
VP Mainstream Technology Business: M. C. Tzeng
VP; President North America: Rick Cassidy, age 58
VP Research and Development: Wei-Jen Lo
VP Design and Technology Platform: Fu-Chieh Hsu
VP Quality and Reliability: N. S. Tsai
VP and General Counsel: Richard (Dick) Thurston
VP Research and Development: Jack Sun
VP Advanced Technology Business: Y. P. Chin
VP Worldwide Sales and Marketing: Jason C.S. Chen
President, TSMC Japan: Makoto Onodera
President, TSMC Europe: Maria Marced
Director; President, New Business Development Organization: Rick Tsai
Head Investor Relations: Elizabeth Sun
Auditors: Deloitte & Touche

LOCATIONS

HQ: Taiwan Semiconductor Manufacturing
Company Limited
(Taiwan Jiti Dianlu Zhizao Gufeng Youxian Gongsi)
8 Li-Hsin Rd. 6, Hsinchu Science Park
Hsinchu 300, Taiwan
Phone: 886-3-563-6688   **Fax:** 886-3-563-7000
US HQ: 2585 Junction Ave., San Jose, CA 95134
US Phone: 408-382-8000   **US Fax:** 408-382-8008
Web: www.tsmc.com.tw

2009 Sales

	% of total
US	56
Asia/Pacific	
Taiwan	13
Other countries	21
Europe	10
Total	**100**

PRODUCTS/OPERATIONS

2009 Sales

	% of total
Wafer fabrication	88
Photomask manufacturing	6
Other	6
Total	**100**

2009 Sales by Customer

	% of total
Fabless semiconductor & systems companies	80
Integrated device manufacturers	20
Total	**100**

Selected Services

Semiconductor photomasks (circuit pattern guides)
Design
Manufacturing

Semiconductor wafers (integrated circuits and other semiconductor devices)
Computer-aided design
Manufacturing
Packaging
Testing

HISTORICAL FINANCIALS

Company Type: Public

Income Statement				FYE: December 31
	REVENUE ($ mil.)	NET INCOME ($ mil.)	NET PROFIT MARGIN	EMPLOYEES
12/09	9,174	2,768	30.2%	24,466
12/08	10,169	3,050	30.0%	22,843
12/07	9,922	3,358	33.8%	23,020
12/06	9,737	3,847	39.5%	22,246
12/05	8,104	2,845	35.1%	21,496
Annual Growth	3.1%	(0.7%)	—	3.3%

2009 Year-End Financials

Debt ratio: 2.3%
Return on equity: 18.5%
Cash ($ mil.): 5,313
Current ratio: 3.28
Long-term debt ($ mil.): 353
No. of shares (mil.): 5,181
Dividends
Yield: 104.4%
Payout: 69.8%
Market value ($ mil.): 1,839

Stock History

NYSE: TSM

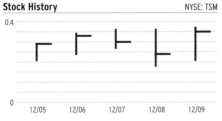

	STOCK PRICE ($) FY Close	P/E High/Low	PER SHARE ($) Earnings	Dividends	Book Value
12/09	0.35	1 —	0.53	0.37	2.96
12/08	0.24	1 —	0.58	0.36	2.81
12/07	0.30	1 —	0.70	0.45	2.89
12/06	0.33	— —	0.74	0.38	3.01
12/05	0.29	1 —	0.55	0.29	2.61
Annual Growth	4.8%	— —	(0.9%)	6.3%	3.2%

Tata Group

India's largest industrial conglomerate, Tata Group runs more than 90 companies with activities ranging from manufacturing and chemicals to consumer products and business services. Its Tata Steel unit is India's largest private steelmaker. Automaker Tata Motors made big news with its ultracheap Nano car and its acquisitions of Land Rover and Jaguar from Ford in 2008. Tata Power is the largest private power utility in India; Tata Communications provides international telephone network services; Tata Consultancy Services provides outsourced business services; and Tata Tea is one of the world's top tea producers and owner of the venerable Tetley brand. Tata Group is managed through holding company Tata Sons.

The Tata family owns about 3% of Tata Sons. Much of the rest is held by charitable trusts established by the family; more than 60% of Tata Sons' profits are channeled into philanthropic trusts. Tata Sons generally holds only minority stakes in the group's companies but maintains control with the support of other investors, including state-owned financial institutions.

Under the guidance of Ratan Tata, who took over as Tata Sons' chairman in the 1990s, the company has diversified geographically, so as not to be completely dependent on the Indian economy. Tata Steel acquired Corus Group for £6.2 billion ($11.3 billion) in 2007, a move that created the sixth-largest steel company in the world. Tata Motors made an even bigger splash with the acquisitions of Land Rover and Jaguar. In 2009, Tata Tea joined with the European Bank for Reconstruction and Development to buy a 51% stake in Grand, a Russian coffee and tea distributor.

The luxury nameplates and broadening business lines are part of Tata's overseas expansion plans. At home, the company made the news with its debut of the Tata Nano, a barebones automobile for the Indian market priced about Rs115,000 ($2,400). Tata hopes the car will garner the scooter and three-wheel market share.

HISTORY

Jamsetji Tata, a Parsi (Zoroastrian) from Bombay, started a textile trading company in 1868. He began in textile manufacturing, then embarked on a mission to industrialize India. Before his death in 1904 Tata had built the Taj Mahal Hotel in Bombay and set in motion plans to create a hydroelectric power plant, a forum for technical education and research in India, and a steel mill to supply rapidly expanding railroads.

Jamsetji's son Dorabji carried on. Dorabji found a jungle site for the steel mill, renamed the area Jamshedpur after his father, and in 1907 established Tata Iron and Steel Company (Tisco). Three years later Tata Hydro-Electric Power went on line. By 1911 Jamsetji's plans were realized when the Indian Institute of Science opened.

The British chairman of the Railway Board promised "to eat every pound of steel rail" Tata made. Tata shipped 1,500 miles of rail to British troops in Mesopotamia during WWI.

Six years after Dorabji's death in 1932, J. R. D. Tata, the son of Dorabji's cousin, took over the family empire. India's first licensed pilot, J. R. D. had started Tata Airlines, later nationalized as Air India. He founded Tata Chemicals in 1939. After WWII and Indian independence, the government built a state-owned steel industry but allowed Tata's mills to operate through a grandfather clause. Inefficient government operations led to high fixed prices for steel, and Tata profited.

Tata Engineering & Locomotive Co. (Telco), founded in 1945 to make steam locomotives, entered truck production in 1954 by collaborating with Daimler-Benz (now Daimler AG). With help from Swiss firm Volkart Brothers, the company also started the Voltas manufacturing conglomerate. In 1962 Tata joined James Finlay of Scotland to create Tata-Finlay, now Tata Tea.

For a long time India's socialist government and unwieldy bureaucracy hampered Tata. The group was reluctant to pay bribes for licenses to enter new fields, and red tape and trade restrictions discouraged expansion abroad. A 1970 antitrust law ended the "managing agency" system, in which Tata Sons had held interests in subsidiaries and Tata Industries managed them for a fee; the subsidiaries became independently managed.

J. R. D. Tata retired as chairman in 1991, and his nephew Ratan Tata took control of the holding company. In 1994 Tata formed a major alliance with Daimler-Benz to assemble cars. A Tata IBM joint venture in 1997 launched the first computer operating system in Hindi, India's national language. (Tata sold its IBM stake in 1999.) Not every new venture flew, though. In 1998 Tata dropped a proposal to start an Indian airline that hadn't won government approval after three years.

In 2000 Tata Tea bought UK tea bag maker Tetley, an acquisition that made Tata the world's largest tea producer. The following year Tata joined with insurance giant AIG to create joint ventures Tata AIG General Insurance and Tata AIG Life Insurance. Also in 2001, Tata and Singapore Airlines jointly bid for a 40% stake in Air India, but Singapore Airlines later withdrew and the deal fell through.

In 2002 the group acquired a 45% stake in telecom giant Videsh Sanchar Nigam (VSNL) from the Indian government. Tata Coffee signed an agreement to supply Starbucks with premium coffee beans starting in 2004. Early the next year the group bought Singapore's National Steel, which boosted Tata's capacity by 2 million tons and greatly enhanced its position in the Asia/Pacific region.

The group boosted its consumer products operations in 2006 with the acquisitions of the Eight O'Clock coffee brand and a 30% stake in health products maker Energy Brands.

In 2006 the group agreed to make investments in Bangladesh totaling about $3 billion (including a steel plant, urea factory, and coal-powered energy plants), but it abandoned that plan two years later when it failed to get a government guarantee for a natural gas supply.

Tata Motors and Brazilian truck chassis manufacturer Marcopolo formed a joint venture to make buses and coaches for India and other countries. The unit then joined with Fiat to build cars for the Indian and export markets. In 2007 Tata Power acquired a 30% stake in the coal subsidiaries of Indonesian mining company Bumi Resources. The deal gives it a guaranteed coal supply for the construction of the Mundra Ultra Mega Power Project, one of a series of ambitious government-planned plants.

In 2008 Tata Group merged its VSNL, VSNL International, and Teleglobe subsidiaries to form Tata Communications.

EXECUTIVES

Chairman: Ratan N. Tata, age 72
Member, Group Executive Office and Group Corporate Centre; Executive Director, Tata Sons: Arunkumar R. (Arun) Gandhi
Member, Group Executive Office and Group Corporate Centre, and Finance Director; Finance Director, Tata Sons: Ishaat Hussain, age 63
Member, Group Executive Office and Group Corporate Centre: R. Gopalakrishnan
Member, Group Executive Office and Group Corporate Centre; Executive Director, Tata Sons: Alan Rosling
Member, Group Executive Office and Group Corporate Centre; Managing Director, Tata Industries: Kishor A. Chaukar, age 62
Member, Group Corporate Centre; Chairman Tata Coffee and Asian Coffee; Vice Chairman, Tata Tea and Indian Hotels: R. K. Krishna Kumar
Member, Group Corporate Centre; Chairman, Tata Refractories and TRF; Director, Tata Sons, Tata Industries, Tata Motors, and Tata International: Jamshed J. (JJ) Irani, age 74
Member, Group Corporate Centre; Vice Chairman, Tata Sons and Tata Investment Corporation: Noshir A. Soonawala
Managing Director and CEO, CMC: R. Ramanan
Managing Director, Tata Steel: Hemant M. Nerurkar, age 61
Managing Director, Tata Limited: Anwar Hasan
Chief Representative North America, Tata Sons: David Good
Group Chief Representative, Tata Sons, China: James Zhan
VP Group Publications and Media: Christabelle Noronha
Auditors: A.F. Ferguson & Co.

LOCATIONS

HQ: Tata Group of Companies
Bombay House, 24 Homi Mody St.
Mumbai 400 001, India
Phone: 91-22-6665-8282   **Fax:** 91-22-6665-8160
US HQ: 1700 N. Moore St., Ste. 1005,
Arlington, VA 22209
US Phone: 703-243-9787   **US Fax:** 703-243-9791
Web: www.tata.com

PRODUCTS/OPERATIONS

Selected Subsidiaries and Affiliates

Chemicals
  Advinus Therapeutics
  General Chemical Industrial Products (US)
Consumer products
  Alliance Coffee Limited
  Tata Tea
    Eight O'Clock Coffee
    Watawala Plantations
  Westland (formerly EastWest Books and Westland Books)
Energy
  Tata Power
    Coastal Gujarat Power
    North Delhi Power
Engineering
  Hispano Carrocera, S.A. (Spain)
  Jaguar Land Rover (UK)
  TAL Manufacturing Solutions
  Voltas
    Metrovol FZE
    Voice Antilles NV
Information systems and communications
  Tata Communications
  Tata Consultancy Services
    AP Online
    CMC
    Diligenta (UK)
    Financial Network Services (HK) (Hong Kong)
    Swedish Indian IT Resources AB
    Syscrom SA (Chile)
    Tata Consultancy Services Do Brasil SA
    Tata Consultancy Services Luxembourg SA Capellen
    Tata Infotech (Singapore) Pte
    TCS Financial Network Services (Indonesia)
  Tatanet

Materials
  Tata Advanced Materials
  Tata Steel
    Corus (UK)
    Jamshedpur Injection Powder
    Tata BlueScope Steel (50%)
    Tata Ryerson
    Tata Steel KZN
Services
  Indian Hotels Company
    Roots Corporation
  Tata Asset Management
  Tata Industrial Services

COMPETITORS

Crompton Greaves
Essar Group
GE
Hindustan Unilever
RPG Enterprises
Wipro

HISTORICAL FINANCIALS

Company Type: Group

Income Statement

FYE: March 31

	REVENUE ($ mil.)	NET INCOME ($ mil.)	NET PROFIT MARGIN	EMPLOYEES
3/09	70,800	1,700	2.4%	357,000

Tate & Lyle

Consumers looking for a sugar rush from Tate & Lyle — recently one of the world's largest makers of white and raw cane sugar — will have to look elsewhere. Headquartered in London, Tate & Lyle makes sugar by-products such as molasses used in animal feed, citric acid, and starches used in foodstuffs. The company remains a top supplier of sucralose, the no-calorie sweetener sold in some 50 countries worldwide under the brand name SPLENDA. Serving multiple sectors, Tate & Lyle's customers include manufacturers in the food, beverage, pharmaceutical, cosmetic, industrial, and animal-feed industries.

Javed Ahmed, who replaced Iain Ferguson as CEO in 2009, is steering the company in a new direction. Under Ahmed's leadership, Tate & Lyle is focused on growing its Specialty Food Ingredients business, while selling assets of its sugar and bulk ingredients businesses to fund that growth. To that end, the company sold its sugar-refining operation in Europe to American Sugar Refining (ASR) for about £211 million ($318 million) in 2010. The sale included cane sugar refineries in the UK and Portugal, a syrup factory in London, and associated sugar and syrup brands. (Previously, Tate & Lyle sold its Canadian sugar business [Redpath] to ASR.) Also, the company has announced plans to sell the remaining businesses within its sugar division, principally molasses and Vietnamese sugar. The firm is planning to sell its entire 75% stake in a sugar joint venture in Vietnam.

The company uses grains, wheat, and corn to make ethanol (used as an alternative fuel), citric acids (used in foods and beverages), starches

(used in foodstuffs and packaging), and sweeteners (corn syrup, fructose, and others used in beverages, baked goods, and pharmaceuticals).

One of Tate & Lyle's major European non-sugar holdings is German ingredients maker G. C. Hahn. In addition to its headquarters in Germany, Hahn, which makes dairy stabilizer systems, has production facilities in the US, the UK, and Australia. In the US, Tate & Lyle has significant wet corn milling operations, processing about 2% of the US's annual corn crop.

In addition, the company has a 50-50 joint venture with chemical giant DuPont named DuPont Tate & Lyle Bio Products that produces 1,3-propanediol (under the brand name Bio-PDO) from renewable resources (corn sugar). Bio-PDO is a biodegradable ingredient that can be used in place of glycols in cosmetics and liquid detergents and in industrial products such as antifreeze and plastics.

HISTORY

Henry Tate founded Henry Tate & Sons in 1869 and the next year began building a sugar refinery in Liverpool. Tate was noted for his philanthropy, and in 1896 he provided the money to found the Tate Gallery. When he died three years later, he left the business to his sons. In 1903 William Henry Tate took the company public, although only 17 investors, primarily family members, put up money for the company.

Abram Lyle founded his sugar company in 1881 when he bought Odam's and Plaistow Wharves, on the River Thames, to build a sugar refinery. While Tate focused on sugar cubes, Lyle concentrated on a sugary concoction called Golden Syrup.

WWI saw an interruption in raw beet sugar imports from Germany and Austria, and in 1918 the two companies began discussing a merger. Although they combined, creating Tate & Lyle in 1921, they kept separate sales organizations into the 1940s. Seeking new sources of sugar, Tate & Lyle began investing abroad. In 1937 it created the West Indies Sugar Company and built a processing plant in Jamaica.

Although WWII brought sugar rationing (1940) and both of Tate & Lyle's London factories were severely damaged by bombs, there was great demand for the company's inexpensive syrup. Following the war, a movement to nationalize Tate & Lyle failed. In the 1950s Tate & Lyle expanded, buying Rhodesian Sugar Refineries (1953, now ZSR) and Canada & Dominion Sugar Company (1959, later Redpath Industries). It added United Molasses in 1965.

Tate & Lyle acquired the only other independent British cane refiner, Manbre and Garton, in 1976. That year it entered the US market when it bought Refined Sugars. The company added Portuguese sugar refiner Alcântara in 1983; US beet refiner Great Western Sugar Company in 1985; and Staley Continental (now A E Staley Manufacturing), a major producer of high-fructose corn syrup, in 1988. It sold Staley's food service business to SYSCO that year and bought Amstar Sugar Corporation (which became Domino Sugar). Tate & Lyle launched Splenda Sucralose, a low-calorie sweetener, in 1992 in cooperation with Johnson & Johnson. The company began investing millions in emerging markets in 1990 through acquisitions and joint ventures, including Mexico's Occidente in 1995. Larry Pillard became CEO in 1996. Sucralose was approved for use in the US in 1998.

In 2001 Tate & Lyle sold off the Domino brand to a group of investors led by Flo-Sun, Inc., chairman Alfonso Fanjul and his brother, J. Pepe Fanjul. In 2004 Tate & Lyle became the sole manufacturer of the SPLENDA brand of sucralose, when it renegotiated its alliance with McNeil Nutritionals. That same year Tate & Lyle formed a joint venture with DuPont to make an ingredient made from renewable sources such as corn to replace petrochemicals in the manufacture of clothing, plastics, and textiles.

In the largest food antitrust class-action suit in US history, parent Tate & Lyle paid $100 million in 2004 to settle a lawsuit concerning sweeteners used by Coke and Pepsi. The suit alleged that Tate & Lyle conspired to fix prices of high-fructose corn syrup.

In 2005 the company acquired Italian ingredients maker Cesalpinia Foods; in 2006 it acquired Netherlands-based biodegradable-plastic company Hycail BV and US specialty-food-ingredient operation Custom Continental Ingredients. Archer-Daniels-Midland sold its 6% share of Tate & Lyle in 2005.

To reduce the impact of exposure to the volatile raw material and commodity markets, in 2007 Tate & Lyle sold its 49% holding in Mexican cane sugar business, Occidente, to E D & F Man Holdings. Also that year it sold its Canadian sugar business (Redpath) to American Sugar Refining for £131 million ($269 million).

In 2008 the company sold its international sugar-trading and -marketing division to Bunge Limited. It disposed of its European starch business, selling operations in France, Belgium, Spain, Italy, and the UK to Tereos for approximately $440 million as well.

EXECUTIVES

Chairman: Sir Peter Gershon, age 62
Chief Executive and Director: Javed Ahmed, age 50, $1,388,219 total compensation
Group Finance Director and Board Member: Timothy (Tim) Lodge, $1,054,308 total compensation
EVP Human Resources: Rob Luijten
EVP, Company Secretary, and General Counsel: Robert (Rob) Gibber, age 47
VP Sales and Marketing, Tate & Lyle Food Ingredients, Europe: James Blunt
VP Marketing, SPLENDA, Sucralose: Dave Tuchler
President, Innovation and Commercial Development: Karl Kramer
President, Speciality Food Ingredients: Olivier Rigaud
President, Global Research and Development: Robert (Bob) Fisher
President, Sugars: Ian Bacon, age 52
President, Bulk Ingredients: Matthew (Matt) Wineinger, age 44
Research Scientist: Annette Evans
Director Investor and Media Relations: Chris McLeish
Director Corporate Communications: Rowan Adams
Manager Marketing Communications, Americas: Pashen Black
Auditors: PricewaterhouseCoopers LLP

LOCATIONS

HQ: Tate & Lyle PLC
Sugar Quay, Lower Thames St.
London EC3R 6DQ, United Kingdom
Phone: 44-20-7626-6525   **Fax:** 44-20-7623-5213
US HQ: 2200 E. Eldorado St., Decatur, IL 62525
US Phone: 217-421-4230   **US Fax:** 217-421-2881
Web: www.tate-lyle.co.uk

2010 Sales

	% of total
US	47
Europe	
UK	14
Other European countries	22
Other	17
Total	**100**

PRODUCTS/OPERATIONS

2010 Sales

	% of total
Primary products	71
Value-added products	29
Total	**100**

2010 Sales

	% of total
Goods & services	91
Joint ventures	9
Total	**100**

2010 Sales

	% of total
Food & industrial ingredients	67
Sugars	28
Sucralose	5
Total	**100**

Selected Products and Brands

Animal feed
   Corn gluten feed
   Corn gluten meal
   Molasses
Food and beverage
   Glucose
   High fructose corn syrup
   KRYSTAR (crystalline fructose)
   PROMITOR (dietary fibers)
   SPLENDA (sucralose sweetener)
   STA-Lite (polydextrose)
Value-added starches
   FREEZIST
   Merigel
   Resistamyl
   STA-Slim
   TENDERJEL
Industrial
   Citric acid
   Ethanol
   ETHYLEX (paper starch)
   Pearl starches
   STA-LOK (catonic starches)
   STADEX (dextrin)
   STARPOL (water-soluble polymers)
   StaZan X (industrial zanthan gums)
   Susterra (industrial-grade plastic)
Personal care and pharmaceuticals
   SPLENDA (sucralose sweetener)
   Zernea (cosmetics ingredients)

COMPETITORS

ADM
Ag Processing Inc.
Akzo Nobel
Amalgamated Sugar
American Crystal Sugar
Associated British Foods
C&H Sugar
Cargill
Casco
Connell Company
Corn Products International
CSM
Cumberland Packing
Danisco A/S
Eurosugar
Florida Crystals
Greencore
Holly Sugar
Imperial Sugar
Kerry Group
M. A. Patout
Merisant
Michigan Sugar Company
Nordzucker
NutraSweet
Onex
Penford
PPB Group
Roquette Frères
Sterling Sugars
Südzucker
Sugar Cane Growers Cooperative of Florida
Tereos
Tongaat Hulett
U.S. Sugar
Western Sugar Cooperative

HISTORICAL FINANCIALS

Company Type: Public

Income Statement

FYE: March 31

	REVENUE ($ mil.)	NET INCOME ($ mil.)	NET PROFIT MARGIN	EMPLOYEES
3/10	5,283	23	0.4%	5,625
3/09	5,049	92	1.8%	5,718
3/08	5,717	387	6.8%	6,488
3/07	6,345	421	6.6%	9,194
3/06	6,034	(52)	—	9,349
Annual Growth	(3.3%)	—	—	(11.9%)

2010 Year-End Financials

Debt ratio: —
Return on equity: 1.7%
Cash ($ mil.): 759
Current ratio: —
Long-term debt ($ mil.): —

No. of shares (mil.): 459
Dividends
  Yield: 5.0%
  Payout: —
Market value ($ mil.): 3,143

Stock History

Pink Sheets: TATYY

	STOCK PRICE ($) FY Close	P/E High/Low		PER SHARE ($) Earnings	Dividends	Book Value
3/10	6.84	—	—	—	0.35	2.80
3/09	3.70	—	—	—	0.33	3.13
3/08	10.77	—	—	—	0.43	4.13
3/07	11.31	—	—	—	0.40	4.26
3/06	9.94	—	—	—	0.34	3.56
Annual Growth	(8.9%)	—	—	—	0.7%	(5.8%)

TDK Corporation

While TDK may be best known for blank audiotapes and CDs, the company actually records most of its sales from the sale of manufactured electronic materials and components. The company, which pioneered the use of the magnetic substance ferrite in the 1930s, is a major supplier of such products as ferrite magnets, transformer and inductor cores, and multilayer chip capacitors. Other components include voltage-controlled oscillators, noise reduction filters, and magnetic recording heads used inside computer disk drives.

In 2008 the company acquired EPCOS, a leading rival in passive components, for about €1.2 billion ($1.9 billion). While TDK and EPCOS both make similar products — capacitors, inductors, sensors, and high-frequency components — they compete in different areas. EPCOS specializes in customizing products for individual customer needs, particularly for the automotive and telecommunications markets. TDK has a strong position in commodity products, and sells to the consumer electronics, computer, wireless, and automotive industries.

TDK carved out its passive components business, which was combined with EPCOS to form a new company, TDK-EPC Corporation. TDK-EPC operates as a wholly owned subsidiary of TDK. The business groups TDK is transferring to TDK-EPC include capacitors, magnetics, network devices, sensors and actuators, and electronic components sales and marketing.

TDK is slowing production and streamlining operations to deal with lagging demand for equipment such as video equipment and mobile phones in the struggling global economy. In addition, the company is focusing on the development of materials and process technologies to grow its product manufacturing businesses.

Consistently looking overseas for expansion of its business, the company gets much of its sales from the Asia/Pacific region, aside from Japan. Like many manufacturers, TDK has set up operations in China to take advantage of lower production costs and to gain access to the world's largest consumer market.

In 2009 TDK and Fujitsu terminated their hard disk drive (HDD) joint venture, with TDK acquiring the entire operation. Fujitsu is withdrawing from the HDD business.

In 2007 TDK sold its worldwide recording media business to Imation for about $261 million, with TDK becoming a significant shareholder in Imation, 3M's recording media spinoff. Under the deal, Imation received rights to the TDK brand name for recording media products, including magnetic tape, optical media, flash memory-based media, and accessories.

HISTORY

Kanzo Saito, who had previously raised rabbits for their fur, took out a patent in 1935 on ferrite, a type of ceramic made mainly from iron oxide that held promise for electronics applications. (Japan's Yogoru Kato is credited with inventing the material.) Saito founded Tokyo Denkikagaku Kogyo K.K. (TDK) to pioneer the mass production of ferrite and output rose quickly as developers found countless new uses for the substance. Saito handed over the presidency of the company in 1946 to Teiichi Yamazaki, who expanded TDK's portfolio into products such as magnetic recording tape (1952).

The company's global thrust began when it opened a Los Angeles office in 1959. Two years later it was listing shares on the Tokyo Stock Exchange. TDK branched into cassette tapes in 1966 and electromagnetic wave absorbers in 1968, the year the company opened its first overseas manufacturing center in Taiwan.

During the 1970s TDK launched operations in Australia, Europe, and South America. It began listing its shares on the New York Stock Exchange in 1982. That year the company also introduced a solar battery. In 1983 TDK officially changed its name to TDK Corporation.

In 1987 Hiroshi Sato was appointed president of the company. TDK bought integrated circuit maker Silicon Systems in 1989 (sold in 1996 to Texas Instruments) as Sato began to modernize the company's offerings and organization. With a conservative management style, he'd often wait to see how other companies fared in new markets before committing TDK, prompting the industry to label him the "gambler who follows someone else." During his tenure, Sato gave the company solid footholds in niches such as optical disks, high-density heads, and cellular phone components.

To reverse falling profits in 1992, Sato made plans to eliminate managers by playing on the Japanese sense of honor — he asked them to accept pay cuts and work on standby at home until their retirement, expecting that they would simply resign. Sato was forced to scuttle the plan amid international outcries and depleted morale.

In 1994 it began producing high-end magnetic heads in China, but poor demand and a weakened yen hurt sales and profits. Meanwhile, TDK had become the global leader in magnetic tape manufacturing. In 1998 Sato and Yamazaki retired; Hajime Sawabe was tapped as president and CEO.

TDK, like other high-tech firms, suffered the ravages of the deep slump in the electronics market during the early 21st century. Sales of components fell off as manufacturers reacted to weak demand for PCs, mobile phones, and other electronics gear.

Competitive pricing in the CD-R market led to losses for TDK's recording media business in 2001, prompting it to close many of its manufacturing plants and outsource its blank tape and CD manufacturing. Meanwhile, price pressures from competitors in China and Taiwan, especially in the recordable media sector, added to TDK's woes and contributed to losses in 2002.

In 2005 TDK sold its semiconductor business in order to focus on core product lines. It continued to make capacitors, ferrite cores, inductors, and high-frequency components.

Hajime Sawabe was named chairman and CEO in 2006, while EVP Takehiro Kamigama was promoted to president and COO.

In 2007 TDK acquired a 74% equity stake in Magnecomp Precision Technology (MPT), which makes suspension assemblies for hard disk drive magnetic heads, for $123 million. The business was purchased from Magnecomp International Ltd., a Singapore-based company.

Adding to its hard-disk drive (HDD) business in a period of consolidation among vendors in that market, in 2007 TDK purchased the HDD heads business of Alps Electric for about $315 million.

EXECUTIVES

Chairman: Hajime Sawabe, age 68
President, CEO, and Director: Takehiro Kamigama, age 52
EVP, CFO, and Director: Seiji Enami, age 63
SVP and Director: Shinichi Araya, age 58
SVP: Raymond Leung, age 53
SVP: Kenichiro Fujihara, age 61
SVP: Takeo Suzuki, age 66
SVP: Shiro Nomi, age 61
Corporate Officer: Masataka Kajiya
Corporate Officer: Junji Yoneyama, age 55
Corporate Officer: Atsuo Kobayashi, age 50
Corporate Officer: Hiroyuki Uemura
Corporate Officer: Takeshi Nomura, age 58
Corporate Officer: Shinya Yoshihara, age 55
Corporate Officer: Seiji Osaka
Corporate Officer: Takaya Ishigaki, age 57
Corporate Officer: Robin Zeng
Corporate Communications: Kazutoshi Kogure
Auditors: KPMG AZSA & Co.

LOCATIONS

HQ: TDK Corporation
1-13-1 Nihonbashi, Chuo-ku
Tokyo 103-8272, Japan
Phone: 81-3-5201-7102   **Fax:** 81-3-5201-7114
US HQ: 901 Franklin Ave., Garden City, NY 11530
US Phone: 516-535-2600   **US Fax:** 516-294-8318
Web: www.tdk.co.jp

2009 Sales

	% of total
Japan	28
Europe	10
Americas	8
Asia & other regions	54
Total	**100**

PRODUCTS/OPERATIONS

2009 Sales

	% of total
Electronic materials & components	
Recording devices	34
Electronic devices	23
Electronic materials	20
Others	20
Recording media	3
Total	**100**

Selected Products

Data Storage
  Magnetic heads (hard disk drives)
  Thermal printing heads

Electronic Components
  Anechoic chambers
  Capacitors
  Converters
  Cores and magnets
    Ferrite
    Metal
    Rubber and plastic
  Electrodes
  Ferrite electromagnetic wave absorbers
  Inductors and coils
  Noise filters
  Optical isolators
  Oscillators
  Power supplies
  PTC/NTC thermistors
  Sensors
  Transformers
  Uninterruptible power systems (UPS)
  Varistors

Other
  Factory automation systems
  MPEG-4 based streaming server software
  Organic EL displays
  Solar cells

HISTORICAL FINANCIALS

Company Type: Public

Income Statement

FYE: March 31

	REVENUE ($ mil.)	NET INCOME ($ mil.)	NET PROFIT MARGIN	EMPLOYEES
3/09	7,477	(649)	—	66,429
3/08	8,684	716	8.2%	60,212
3/07	7,318	595	8.1%	51,614
3/06	6,821	378	5.5%	53,923
3/05	6,133	310	5.1%	37,115
Annual Growth	5.1%	—	—	15.7%

2009 Year-End Financials

Debt ratio: 37.9%
Return on equity: —
Cash ($ mil.): 1,703
Current ratio: 2.41
Long-term debt ($ mil.): 2,159

No. of shares (mil.): 130
Dividends
Yield: 0.0%
Payout: —
Market value ($ mil.): 50

Stock History

Pink Sheets: TTDKF

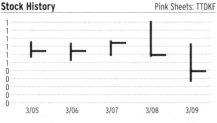

	STOCK PRICE ($) FY Close	P/E High/Low	PER SHARE ($) Earnings	Dividends	Book Value
3/09	0.39	— —	(5.03)	0.00	43.96
3/08	0.59	— —	5.55	1.24	55.43
3/07	0.74	— —	4.49	0.86	49.96
3/06	0.64	— —	2.83	0.68	46.50
3/05	0.64	— —	2.35	0.56	45.97
Annual Growth	(11.6%)	— —	—	—	(1.1%)

Telecom Italia

Telecom Italia's wireline unit is Italy's #1 telephone operator, with some 16 million fixed access lines. Broadband connections total nearly 9 million and its domestic wireless business also leads with about 32 million subscribers. While Telecom Italia does most of its business domestically, Europe and Latin America are key international markets. Its wireline holdings provide broadband network services in France, Germany, and the Netherlands, as well as wholesale network access in Europe and South America. Its TIM Brasil subsidiary is a leader in the Brazilian wireless market. Through Olivetti, Telecom Italia also provides office peripherals such as ink-jet printer heads, largely for the banking industry.

The company's Telecom Italia Media unit includes leading ISP Nuova Tin.it. Its media business also encompasses MTV Italia, La7 Televisioni, and TM News, which distributes Associated Press news and other content to media and corporate subscribers. Telecom Italia is trying to realize increased wireless service and advertising revenue from its mobile business with the introduction in 2008 of MTV Mobile wireless content for cell phone users. In 2009 Telecom Italia Mobile became the first Italian carrier to sell a wireless phone, the HTC Dream, based on the Android mobile device software from Google; it also carries the Apple iPhone.

The company is disposing of noncore assets in order to better focus on its domestic business, as well as the Brazilian market. As part of this, the company sold its German broadband unit, Hansenet, to Telefonica for €900 million in 2010.

Like many global companies, Telecom Italia has to deal with the continuing credit crisis and financial uncertainty, especially when it comes to the company's net financial debt of €34 billion (about $50 billion). Shaky market conditions could make it difficult for Telecom Italia to refinance its debt on an ongoing basis. The former state-owned monopoly also faces increased competition in its home market for fixed-line and mobile voice communications and for broadband connections.

An investment group made up primarily of Italian financial backers, including investment bank Mediobanca, and led by Madrid-based telecom giant Telefónica, took control of Telecom Italia in 2007. The holding company, known as Telco SpA, spent $5.58 billion to acquire about one-quarter of Telecom Italia. Telefónica owns 42% of Telco SpA.

HISTORY

After gaining political power in Italy, Benito Mussolini began a program of nationalization, focusing first on three major banks and their equity portfolios. Included were three local phone companies that became the core of Societa Finanziaria Telefonica (STET), created in 1933 to handle Italy's phone services under the state's industrial holding company, Istituto per La Ricostruzione Industriale (IRI).

Germany and Italy grew closer in the years leading up to WWII, and Italian equipment makers entered a venture with Siemens to make phone equipment. STET came through the war with most of its infrastructure intact and a monopoly on phone service in Italy. Siemens' properties, along with those of other equipment makers, were taken over by another company,

TETI, which was nationalized and put under STET's control in 1958. This expanded STET's monopoly to include equipment manufacturing.

Italy's industries were increasingly nationalized under IRI. Companies within the IRI family forged alliances with each other and with independent companies, which frequently were absorbed into STET.

STET's scope expanded during the 1960s and 1970s to include satellite and data communications, but its monopoly was undermined by new technologies such as faxes, PCs, and teleconferencing. In the technology race among equipment makers, STET fell behind. And in a satellite communications era, STET's status as a necessary long-distance carrier was threatened. Despite these pressures, change did not come easily to STET. State monopolies maintained popular support, not only on nationalistic grounds but also because of labor's strong anticompetitive stance.

Anticipating privatization, however, IRI reorganized STET in 1994 and poured new capital into the company. Its mobile phone business was spun off as Telecom Italia Mobile (TIM) in 1995.

To end political feuding, the government abruptly replaced the heads of STET and Telecom Italia in 1997. Telecom Italia was merged with STET, which took the Telecom Italia name and was privatized that year. Berardino Libonati became chairman, and Franco Bernabe, formerly CEO of oil company ENI, took the helm as CEO.

Erstwhile rival Olivetti launched a hostile takeover bid for Telecom Italia in 1999. Though Telecom Italia tried to fend off the smaller firm with various maneuvers, including a proposed merger with Deutsche Telekom, Olivetti gained 55% of Telecom Italia. Olivetti CEO Roberto Colaninno took over as chairman and CEO.

That year Telecom Italia sold 50% of Stream, its pay-TV unit, to an investor group led by News Corp. And in a venture with Lockheed Martin and TRW, Telecom Italia planned to develop a $3.5 billion global broadband satellite system called Astrolink.

In 2001 Colaninno and several other Telecom Italia officials were named as suspects in an investigation of whether the company had violated accounting, conflict-of-interest, and share-manipulation laws. Colaninno was replaced when tire maker Pirelli and Edizione Holding, the parent company of the Benetton Group, acquired a 23% stake in Olivetti.

Telecom Italia teamed up with Rupert Murdoch's News Corp. to develop the Stream pay TV joint venture, renamed Sky Italia in 2002. In 2003 the company sold its nearly 62% stake in directories unit SEAT Pagine Gialle to an investor group for $3.55 billion.

Once the subsidiary, Telecom Italia became the parent company after the 2003 merger with former parent Olivetti. The reorganization simplified a corporate structure that was, at best, confusing: Olivetti, through its Tecnost unit, had acquired a controlling 55% stake in Telecom Italia in 1999. Two years later, tire maker Pirelli and the Benetton family teamed up to take control of Olivetti. Olivetti's largest shareholder was Olimpia, a company owned by Pirelli and the Benetton Group, among others.

After spurning an offer from AT&T to buy the company, Telecom Italia named Pasquale Pistorio chairman in 2007, replacing Guido Rossi, who had held the position for only seven months. Telefónica subsequently won control of the company. Later that year, Pistorio was replaced by Gabriele Galateri as chairman; Galateri was nominated by another top shareholder, Mediobanca.

EXECUTIVES

Chairman: Gabriele Galateri di Genola, age 63
CEO and Director: Franco Bernabé, age 62
Head Administration, Finance, Control, and International Business: Andrea Mangoni
Head Strategy and Innovation: Cesare Sironi
Head Domestic Legal Affairs and Board Secretary: Antonino Cusimano, age 46
Head Audit and Compliance Services: Frederico M. D'Andrea
Head National Wholesale Services: Riccardo Delleani, age 50
Head Domestic Market Operations: Marco Patuano, age 46
Head External Relations: Carlo Fornaro, age 50
Head Human Resources, Organization, and Industrial Relations: Antonio Migliardi, age 51
Head Information Technology: Giovanni P. Chiarelli
Head Security: Damiano Toselli, age 57
Head Purchasing: Stefano Ciurli, age 48
Head Disposals; EVP of Telecom Italia Media and Head of the Media Business Unit: Giovanni Stella, age 62
Head Quality of Service: Paolo D'Andrea
Head International Operations: Francesco Armato
Chief Regulatory Officer: Alessandro Talotta
Manager Public Affairs Department: Paolo Annunziato
CEO Assistant: Franco R. Brescia
Auditors: Reconta Ernst & Young S.p.A.

LOCATIONS

HQ: Telecom Italia S.p.A.
Piazza degli Affari 2
20123 Milan, Italy
Phone: 39-02-85-95-1
Web: www.telecomitalia.it

2009 Sales

	% of total
Italy	80
Latin America	19
Other regions	1
Total	**100**

PRODUCTS/OPERATIONS

2009 Sales

	% of total
Domestic	80
Brazil mobile	18
Olivetti	1
Media	1
Total	**100**

Selected Subsidiaries and Affiliates

Wireline
BBNed N.V. (96%, telecommunications services, The Netherlands)
HanseNet Telekommunikation GmbH (broadband network operator, Germany)
Liberty Surf Group
Loquendo S.p.A.
Matrix S.p.A. (Internet services)
Nuova Tin.it S.r.l. (Internet services)
Path. Net S.p.A. (99.9%, networking systems and telecommunications)
Telecontact Center S.p.A.
Telecom Italia Deutschland GmbH (Germany)
Telecom Italia Sparkle Group (development of international services for heavy users such as fixed-line operators, ISPs, and international companies)
Telecom Italia Sparkle S.p.A.
Latin American Nautilus Group
Med-1 Group
Mediterranean Nautilus Group
Pan European Backbone
Telecom Italia San Marino S.p.A. (formerly Intelcom San Marino)
Telecom Italia Sparkle France S.A.S.
Telecom Italia Sparkle of North America Inc. (US)
Telecom Italia Sparkle Singapore
Telefonia Mobile Sammarinese S.p.A. (San Marino)
Thinx S.r.l.
TIM Group

Mobile
TIM Brasil Group
TIM Celular S.A.
Blah! S.A.
CRC — Centro de relacionamento com clientes Ltda
TIM Participações Group
TIM Nordeste Telecomunicações S.A.
TIM Sul S.A.
TIM Italia
Olivetti Group
Olivetti S.p.A. (formerly Olivetti Tecnost)
Olivetti I-Jet S.p.A.
Olivetti International B.V. (The Netherlands)
Wirelab S.p.A. (10%)
Media
Telecom Italia Media S.p.A.
Holding Media e Comunicazione S.p.A. (TV licenses for La7 and MTV Italia)
TIM News

COMPETITORS

América Móvil	Ricoh Company
BT	SFR
Cable & Wireless	Swisscom
Canon	Tele2
Deutsche Telekom	Telefónica
FastWeb	Tiscali
France Telecom	Vivo Participações
Hewlett-Packard	Vodafone Omnitel
Hutchison Whampoa	Wind Telecomunicazioni
IBM	Xerox
KPN	

HISTORICAL FINANCIALS

Company Type: Public

Income Statement				FYE: December 31
	REVENUE ($ mil.)	NET INCOME ($ mil.)	NET PROFIT MARGIN	EMPLOYEES
12/09	39,334	2,287	5.8%	73,589
12/08	43,010	3,122	7.3%	77,825
12/07	46,056	3,614	7.8%	83,429
12/06	42,098	3,980	9.5%	83,209
12/05	36,358	3,821	10.5%	85,484
Annual Growth	**2.0%**	**(12.0%)**	**—**	**(3.7%)**

2009 Year-End Financials

Debt ratio: 130.3%
Return on equity: 6.2%
Cash ($ mil.): 7,888
Current ratio: 0.92
Long-term debt ($ mil.): 48,456
No. of shares (mil.): 1,322
Dividends
Yield: 2.3%
Payout: 44.3%
Market value ($ mil.): 29,232

Stock History

NYSE: TI

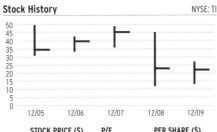

	STOCK PRICE ($) FY Close	P/E High/Low		PER SHARE ($) Earnings	Dividends	Book Value
12/09	22.11	23	12	1.15	0.51	28.14
12/08	22.90	29	8	1.55	0.83	27.86
12/07	45.39	27	21	1.77	1.50	28.86
12/06	39.75	20	16	2.11	1.33	25.99
12/05	34.59	24	16	2.01	0.95	23.07
Annual Growth	**(10.6%)**	**—**	**—**	**(13.0%)**	**(14.4%)**	**5.1%**

Telefónica, S.A.

Telefónica calls Spain home, but customers in 25 countries call home with Telefónica. The company provides fixed and mobile telecommunications services across Europe and Latin America. Its fixed-line portfolio includes traditional voice, Internet access, cable and satellite television, enterprise networking and hosting, and wholesale services. Its mobile business encompasses voice, messaging, and corporate infrastructure services. Telefónica's domestic unit has about 24 million mobile users, 6 million Internet and data access subscribers, and more than half a million pay TV users. Through Telefónica de España, the company is the leading fixed-line operator in Spain with about 15 million lines in service.

The company maintains a huge presence in Latin America, with major operations in Argentina, Brazil, Chile, Colombia, Mexico, Peru, and Venezuela. Telefónica has increased its holdings in Brazil and Chile in recent years.

Telefónica bought California-based communications software developer JAJAH for €145 million in cash in 2010 in order to enhance its ability to offer computer telephony services to customers regardless of their location. JAJAH specializes in applications that allow interoperability between wired and wireless IP-based communications systems.

The company also bought broadband service provider Hansenet from Telecom Italia. The deal added about 2 million high-speed Internet customers to Telefónica's books and gave it a better foothold in Germany where its O2 unit struggles to gain ground on rivals Vodafone and United Internet, not to mention incumbent provider Deutsche Telekom.

Telefónica owns a 42% stake in Telco S.p.A., a holding company that controls a quarter of Telecom Italia.

HISTORY

When a 1923 military coup brought General Miguel Primo de Rivera to power in Spain, the government-run phone system was in shambles. More than half of the country's 90,000 lines did not work. With little cash in the government coffers, Primo de Rivera sought foreign assistance.

Supported by National City Bank (now Citigroup), US-based ITT bought three private Spanish phone companies, later combining them to form Compañía Telefónica Nacional de España. The ITT unit gained the state phone concession in 1924, and the government agreed not to reclaim the system for 20 years. But when Franco came to power in 1939, he froze Telefónica's assets. ITT tried to sell the company to German buyers in 1941 but backed out when the US State Department objected. The Spanish government nationalized Telefónica in 1945, keeping 41% of its shares.

Long-distance service was introduced in 1960, satellite communications in 1967, and international service in 1971. Still, when Spain entered the European Union (EU) in 1986, Telefónica was unprepared for the increase in demand for services, and complaints rose.

The firm purchased a minority stake in Compañía de Teléfonos de Chile in 1990, and a Telefónica-led consortium won a bid to manage the southern half of ENTEL, Argentina's former state phone system. The company acquired a majority stake in Peru's telecom monopoly in 1994 and a year later joined Unisource, a European telecom consortium.

The Spanish government at first defied the EU's directive to break up its telecom monopoly. But in 1994 the government announced it would meet the EU's 1998 deadline for opening telecom markets; in exchange Telefónica won permission to begin new businesses when competition arrived.

Flamboyant former investment banker Juan Villalonga took over as chairman in 1996. The boyhood friend of Spain's prime minister began expanding Telefónica's presence in Latin America with several acquisitions in 1997. They included 35% of Brazil's Companhia Riograndense de Telecomunicações (CRT); a large stake in Multicanal, Argentina's #1 cable company (sold in 1998 to Grupo Clarin); and 35% of satellite TV service Vía Digital.

Also in 1997 Telefónica broke off with Unisource and allied with British Telecom (now BT Group) and MCI (now WorldCom), only to have the alliance break up when MCI agreed to be bought by WorldCom (1998). Meanwhile, the Spanish government had finished divesting its interest in the company in 1997 (retaining a golden share), and competition came to Spain the next year. The company revamped its corporate structure, cut 10,000 jobs, and became Telefónica S.A. It also won fixed-line phone company Telesp and a cellular company in Brazil's auction of the former national phone company, Telebras.

In 1999 Telefónica sold to the public a part of its Internet unit, Terra Networks (formerly Telefónica Interactiva).

To expand its multimedia offerings, Telefónica bought Netherlands-based independent TV producer Endemol for $5.3 billion in 2000 and formed Telefónica Media (it agreed to sell the stake back to a consortium including the company's founder, John de Mol, in 2007 for $3.65 billion). After dropping out of the UK wireless license auction, the company teamed up with Finland's Sonera (later acquired by Telia) to win a license in the German auction. But when merger talks with Dutch telecom carrier KPN broke down, Villalonga resigned over disagreements on the direction of the company.

In 2001 Telefónica combined its Brazilian mobile telephone holdings with those of Portugal Telecom to form market leader Brasilcel. Telefónica then spent $2.7 billion in Mexico in 2001 and 2002 to buy four wireless operators and a 65%-stake in a fifth (Pegaso PCS) to achieve #2 in that market.

The company acquired the assets of BellSouth Latin America Group, which had holdings in 10 South and Central American countries, in a $5.8 billion deal in 2005.

The company sold its stake in phone directory business Telefónica Publicidad e Información (TPI) to Yell Group in 2006. Also that year, Telefónica purchased the remaining 7% stake of its Telefónica Móviles wireless arm that it did not already own and integrated those operations. The company's 2006 acquisition of UK-based mobile phone operator O2 for more than $31 billion gave Telefónica a strong presence in the UK and Germany. The Spanish operator previously had no operations in those regions.

The company, in partnership with a coalition of Italian financial backers, bought a stake in Telecom Italia for about $5.58 billion in mid-2007. Telefónica also sold its 75% stake in Dutch TV producer Endemol for $3.65 billion in 2007.

EXECUTIVES

Chairman and CEO: Cesareo Alierta (César) Izuel, age 65
Vice-Chairman: Isidre Fainé Casas, age 67
Vice-Chairman: Vitalino M. Nafría Aznar, age 60
COO: Julio Linares López
CFO and General Manager, Finance and Corporate Development: Santiago Fernández Valbuena, age 52
Secretary and Head, Legal Board: Ramiro Sánchez de Lerín García-Ovies
General Manager, Telefónica España: Guillermo P. Ansaldo, age 45
General Manager, Internal Audit: Calixto Ríos Pérez, age 64
Director Affiliates and Industrial Alliances; Chairman, O2 Czech Republic: Jaime Smith Basterra, age 44
Director; General Manager, Telefónica Latinoamérica: José M. Álvarez-Pallete López, age 46
Technical General Secretary to the Chairman: Luis Abril Pérez, age 61
Chairman and CEO, Telefónica O2 Europe: Matthew Key, age 47
Auditors: Ernst & Young, S.L.

LOCATIONS

HQ: Telefónica, S.A.
  Gran Vía 28
  28013 Madrid, Spain
Phone: 34-91-584-0306   **Fax:** 34-91-584-9347
Web: www.telefonica.com

2009 Sales

	% of total
Telefónica Latin America	40
Telefónica Spain	35
Telefónica Europe	24
Other	1
Total	**100**

COMPETITORS

América Móvil
Brasil Telecom
BT
Cableuropa
Carphone Warehouse
COLT Group
France Telecom
Hutchison Telecommunications
Jazztel
KPN
Orange España
Portugal Telecom
Telecom Italia
Telemar Norte Leste
TeliaSonera
Telmex
Virgin Mobile
Vodafone
Vodafone España

HISTORICAL FINANCIALS

Company Type: Public

Income Statement

FYE: December 31

	REVENUE ($ mil.)	NET INCOME ($ mil.)	NET PROFIT MARGIN	EMPLOYEES
12/09	83,665	11,145	13.3%	257,426
12/08	84,304	11,031	13.1%	257,035
12/07	82,976	13,093	15.8%	248,487
12/06	69,853	8,230	11.8%	232,996
12/05	45,014	5,283	11.7%	207,641
Annual Growth	**16.8%**	**20.5%**	**—**	**5.5%**

2009 Year-End Financials

Debt ratio: 224.8%	No. of shares (mil.): 1,521
Return on equity: 40.2%	Dividends
Cash ($ mil.): 13,061	Yield: 3.4%
Current ratio: 0.88	Payout: 55.9%
Long-term debt ($ mil.): 70,020	Market value ($ mil.): 182,105

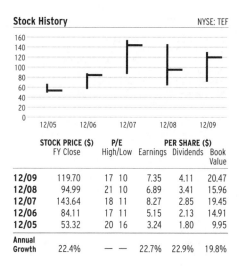

	STOCK PRICE ($) FY Close	P/E High/Low		PER SHARE ($) Earnings	Dividends	Book Value
12/09	119.70	17	10	7.35	4.11	20.47
12/08	94.99	21	10	6.89	3.41	15.96
12/07	143.64	18	11	8.27	2.85	19.45
12/06	84.11	17	11	5.15	2.13	14.91
12/05	53.32	20	16	3.24	1.80	9.95
Annual Growth	**22.4%**	**—**	**—**	**22.7%**	**22.9%**	**19.8%**

Teléfonos de México

Teléfonos de México (Telmex) is one of Mexico's top providers of fixed-line telecommunications services with about 18 million lines in service. The company also offers services for managing corporate networks, Internet access services, information network management, telephone and computer equipment sales, and interconnection services to other telecommunications carriers. Mexican billionaire Carlos Slim Helú raised his stake in Telmex from 71% to 93% in 2010 as part of a broader restructuring of his Latin American telecom holdings that brought the operations of Telmex, Telmex Internacional (Telint), and Carso Global Telecom under the ownership and control of his mobile phone company América Móvil.

Enacted to better withstand mounting competition in the region, the $21 billion deal resulted in the acquisition of domestic fixed line business Telmex and regional operator Telint through Carso Global Telecom by América Móvil. The move came as Telmex, which has an 80% share of the fixed-line and Internet market in Mexico, faces growing pressure from media and cable television companies including Televisa, which offer bundled TV, phone, and Internet services.

Hoping to boost its operational effectiveness, in 2008 the company spun off all communications operations outside of Mexico as well as its telephone directory business into a new company. The restructuring divided Telmex in two with all international operations under the management of a new holding company that was named Telmex Internacional.

Telmex was originally formed in 1947 by LM Ericsson and taken over by the Mexican government in 1972, which sold its shares in the company in 1990-91.

HISTORY

Mexican Telephone and Telegraph, backed by investors allied with AT&T Corp., received a government concession to operate in Mexico City in 1903. Two years later a Swedish consortium led by equipment maker Ericsson also won a concession, and it became Empresa de Teléfonos Ericsson in 1909.

In 1915 Mexican Telephone and Telegraph was nationalized. The company languished after WWI, but the Ericsson enterprise thrived. In 1925 International Telephone and Telegraph (ITT), led by telecom pioneer Sosthenes Behn, won the concession to operate Mexican Telephone and Telegraph. ITT expanded operations nationwide and linked to AT&T's system in the US. In 1932 ITT won control of Ericsson.

Teléfonos de México (Telmex) was created to buy the ITT and Ericsson subsidiaries in Mexico in 1947. Private investors bought Telmex in 1953, but it remained under close state regulation until the government bought 51% of the voting shares in 1972. Phone service grew slowly, and the government continually raised the long-distance tax until it accounted for half of Telmex's revenues. By the 1980s the government was using Telmex funds for unrelated programs.

The 1985 earthquakes heavily damaged Telmex's facilities, and it was forced to modernize and expand in the rebuilding stage. To improve the inefficient enterprise, President Carlos Salinas announced in 1989 that Telmex would be privatized. The following year a consortium that included Grupo Carso, SBC Communications (now known as AT&T Inc.), and France Telecom won voting control of Telmex. (France Telecom sold its stake in 2000.)

Telmex bought a 49% stake in Empresas Cablevision's Mexican cable business in 1995, and the next year it teamed with Sprint to offer business telecom services in the US and Mexico. After long-distance competition began in 1997, Telmex surrendered about a quarter of its market share. Many customers, angered over years of unexplained hang-ups and incorrect billings, switched providers. Also that year Telmex and Sprint formed another venture to resell long-distance service to Mexican-Americans. However, the venture had to gain approval from the FCC, and regulators insisted that Telmex lower the high termination fees charged to US long-distance providers. Telmex agreed to do so, and the venture won approval in 1998. Telmex also invested in former US ISP Prodigy in 1998.

Meanwhile, Telmex maintained a de facto monopoly over local service until 1999 when MAXCOM, backed by Grupo Radio Centro, entered the market. Telmex gained strength in other communications arenas, receiving additional radio spectrum for mobile and PCS wireless services, joining SBC to buy Cellular Communications of Puerto Rico, and buying Miami-based Topp Telecom (prepaid cellular service) and Dallas-based CommSouth (prepaid local service). It bought out Sprint's share of their joint venture and took a 1% stake ($100 million) in Williams Communications Group (now WilTel Communications), the US-based fiber-optic firm. It also began managing Guatemalan phone company TELGUA and the next year acquired a controlling stake.

Also in 2000 Telmex and Microsoft introduced T1msn, a Spanish-language Internet portal (T1msn acquired the Spanish-language portal Yupi in 2001). Telmex also formed a joint venture with Bell Canada International and SBC to expand operations in South America.

Telmex's 2004 acquisition of AT&T Latin America expanded its operations in Argentina, Brazil, Chile, Colombia, and Peru. The company also acquired long-distance carrier Chilesat. Through additional purchases made in 2004 and 2005, Telmex also took control of Brazilian telecom provider Embratel by buying the stake formerly held by MCI in a deal valued at $400 million. In

a separate deal, the company sold its stake in MCI to Verizon Communications for $1.1 billion.

As part of its plan to expand its television business, the company bought Colombian cable providers TV Cable and Cable Pacífico in late 2006. It further boosted its pay-TV holdings with the acquisition of Chile-based ZAP Television Satelital in 2007. Telmex also continued its South American expansion in 2007 with the purchase of Peruvian cable TV operator Boga Comunicaciones.

EXECUTIVES

Co-Chairman: Carlos Slim Domit, age 43
Co-Chairman: Jaime Chico Pardo, age 60
Vice Chairman: Juan A. Pérez Simón, age 69
CEO and Director: Héctor Slim Seade, age 47
CFO: Adolfo Cerezo Pérez
Director, Mass Market: Patrick Slim Domit
Director, Residential Market:
 Andrés R. Vázquez del Mercado Benshimol
Director, Human Resources: Jaime Pérez Gómez
Director, Operational Support:
 Maria del Consuelo Gómez Colin
Director, Legal: Sergio F. Medina Noriega
Director, Corporate Market: Isidoro Ambe Attar
Director, Technical and Long Distance:
 Eduardo Gómez Chibli
Director, Strategic Alliances, Communication, and
 Institutional Relations: Arturo Elías Ayub
Director, Regulation and Legal Affairs:
 Javier Mondragón Alarcón
Division Director, Northwest: José A. Reynoso del Valle
Division Director, Central: Miguel Macias Viveros
Division Director, North: Raymundo Velasco Paulín
Division Director, South: Hiram Ontiveros Medrano
Division Director, Metro: Oscar L. Aguilar Ramírez
Dean of Inttelmex: Javier Elguea Solís
Auditors: Mancera, S.C.

LOCATIONS

HQ: Teléfonos de México, S.A.B. de C.V.
 Parque Vía 198, Colonia Cuauhtémoc
 06599 México, D.F., Mexico
Phone: 52-55-5703-3990   **Fax:** 52-55-5545-5550
Web: www.telmex.com.mx

PRODUCTS/OPERATIONS

2009 Sales

	% of total
Local service	55
Long distance	19
Other	26
Total	**100**

Selected Services

Calling cards
Internet access
Local fixed-line access
National and international fixed-line long distance
Network engineering
Pay phones
Telephone directories
Wireless data networking

COMPETITORS

Alestra
Avantel
Axtel
Iusacell
Maxcom
NextiraOne Europe
Quepasa Corporation
Televisa

HISTORICAL FINANCIALS

Company Type: Public

Income Statement

FYE: December 31

	REVENUE ($ mil.)	NET INCOME ($ mil.)	NET PROFIT MARGIN	EMPLOYEES
12/09	9,134	1,570	17.2%	52,946
12/08	9,006	1,464	16.3%	54,317
12/07	12,024	3,263	27.1%	56,796
12/06	16,102	2,626	16.3%	76,394
12/05	15,018	2,597	17.3%	75,484
Annual Growth	(11.7%)	(11.8%)	—	(8.5%)

2009 Year-End Financials

Debt ratio: 227.8%
Return on equity: 54.2%
Cash ($ mil.): 1,103
Current ratio: 1.39
Long-term debt ($ mil.): 6,689

No. of shares (mil.): 910
Dividends
Yield: 52.1%
Payout: 38.8%
Market value ($ mil.): 1,157

Stock History

NYSE: TMX

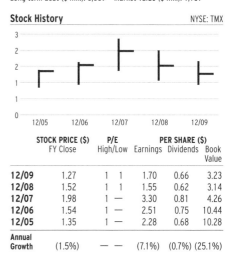

	STOCK PRICE ($) FY Close	P/E High/Low		PER SHARE ($) Earnings	Dividends	Book Value
12/09	1.27	1	1	1.70	0.66	3.23
12/08	1.52	1	1	1.55	0.62	3.14
12/07	1.98	1	—	3.30	0.81	4.26
12/06	1.54	1	—	2.51	0.75	10.44
12/05	1.35	1	—	2.28	0.68	10.28
Annual Growth	(1.5%)	—	—	(7.1%)	(0.7%)	(25.1%)

Telenor ASA

Telenor dominates the Norwegian telecommunications market with millions of mobile, fixed-line telephone, and Internet accounts. It also offers cable television in Norway and satellite television in Nordic countries through subsidiary Telenor Broadcast. The company serves about 3 million mobile phone users in Norway through Telenor Mobil. Its businesses in Denmark and Sweden each contribute about 2 million subscribers. Outside of the Nordic region, Telenor operates in Eastern Europe (including Russia, Ukraine, and Hungary) and in Asia (primarily Thailand). With about 170 million mobile subscribers overall, through subsidiaries and affiliated companies, Telenor is among the largest global wireless carriers.

The company does business in Eastern Europe through a 36% stake in VimpelCom, one of Russia's largest mobile operators. In 2010 Telenor combined its Russian operations with a 56% share of Ukrainian wireless operator Kyivstar to create a new restructured wireless carrier in the region. Telenor's partner in the deal was Altimo (the telecom unit of financial and industrial conglomerate Alfa Group), a company that also held large stakes in VimpelCom and Kyivstar. The merger ended a five-year dispute over governance of shared holdings in the region. The combined business in Eastern Europe became known as VimpelCom Ltd. and boasts about 90 million subscribers, spanning eight former Soviet bloc countries and parts of Southeast Asia. Altimo controls 44% of VimpelCom.

The company's other efforts to gain ground in developing markets included the more than $1 billion acquisition of Indian carrier (and partner) Unitech Wireless in 2009. The deal put Telenor in control of about two-thirds of the company, which was rebranded as Uninor, and gave it significant access to the Indian wireless market (one the world's largest) where Bharti Airtel and Vodafone Essar lead the industry.

The company's other international mobile holdings include Total Access Communication (Thailand), Pannon (Hungary), Promonte (Montenegro), Grameenphone (Bangladesh), Telenor Serbia, Telenor Pakistan, Telenor Sweden, and Telenor Danmark.

Telenor Broadcast serves about 3 million households in the Nordic region with satellite, cable, and broadband connections through subsidiary Canal Digital Group. It offers transmission and encryption services to broadcasters through Telenor Satellite Broadcasting, Norkring, and Conax.

The Norwegian government, through the Ministry of Trade and Industry, owns about 54% of Telenor.

HISTORY

Telecommunications arrived in Norway in 1855 when the first telegraph line was opened and the Norwegian Telegraph Administration was created. By 1880 telephone systems were being installed, followed by the first automatic phone exchange (1918), Telex services (1946), and a transmitter network for television, which debuted in 1960. Mobile phone service was introduced in 1966 but it was not until 1969 that the agency's name was changed to Norwegian Telecommunications Administration.

Norway had progressed to its first computer-controlled phone exchange by the mid 1970s and in 1976 launched a national satellite system (NORSAT) that linked North Sea oil explorers with Norway's mainland. It opened the world's first fully automated coastal earth station in 1982 to carry maritime traffic as part of the INMARSAT system and a year later automated its last manually operated phone exchange. (Telenor held a stake in INMARSAT until it sold it in 2006.)

In the mid-1980s the national carrier became known as Norwegian Telecom (Televerket). In 1984 it introduced an upgraded mobile phone system and a numeric paging system (alphanumeric paging followed in 1991). The first digital phone exchanges arrived in 1986 and two years later Televerket was reorganized into three units: the national operator (Televerket), a sales subsidiary (TBK), and a state regulatory agency for equipment approval (STF).

The company in 1990 organized its mobile services under a single division (Tele-mobil), which a year later became a limited company. Two years later data transmission was opened to competition and the resale of surplus leased line capacity was allowed.

In 1993 Televerket reorganized under the name Norwegian Telecom Group. A year later it became a state-owned company and in 1995 was renamed Telenor. That year it teamed up with British Telecommunications (now BT Group) and Tele Danmark (now TDC) to create the

Swedish telecom competitor Telenordia (Telenor and BT became 50-50 owners in 2000).

Telenor in 1997 took a 10% stake in VIAG Interkom, a joint venture with BT and Germany's VIAG to operate both a mobile and fixed line network in Germany (BT bought Telenor's stake in 2000). That year the Norwegian telecom network was completely digitized and Telenor introduced its Internet unit, Telenor Nextel.

Telenor expanded its Internet activities in Europe, as deregulation of Norway's telecom market in 1998 increased competition there. The next year Telenor's plans to merge with Swedish telecom Telia fell through; Telia later merged with Sonera of Finland to form TeliaSonera. In 2000 Telenor changed the name of its installation and services unit to Bravida and spun it off. Telenor also acquired 54% of Danish mobile operator Sonofon. That year Norway's government sold about 20% of Telenor in a public offering.

The carrier beefed up its satellite operations in 2001, buying Lockheed Martin's COMSAT Mobile Communications. It also took full ownership of Telenordia, the Swedish fixed-line venture it held with BT, and it took full ownership of Hungarian mobile phone operator Pannon GSM. The company sold Telenor Media, its directory-publishing unit, to US-based private equity firm Texas Pacific Group for about $670 million.

Telenor sold Russian telecom subsidiaries Comincom and Combellga to Golden Telecom in 2003 in exchange for a nearly 21% stake in that firm. In 2004 Telenor acquired the Norwegian operation of Italian ISP Tiscali. The next year the company acquired Denmark's third-largest broadband provider, Cybercity, and Sweden's second-largest broadband provider, Bredbandsbolaget (B2 Bredband).

Hoping to boost its market share in Denmark, Telenor acquired Tele2 Denmark from Tele2 in 2007. Meanwhile, the company strengthened its position in the Nordic markets with the acquisitions of smaller rivals Spray Telecom (Sweden) and Talkmore (Norway).

EXECUTIVES

Chairman: Harald Norvik, age 63
Vice Chairman: John Giverholt, age 53
President and CEO: Jon F. Baksaas, age 56
EVP and CFO: Richard Olav Aa
EVP; Head Group Business Development and Research: Morten K. Sørby, age 51
EVP; Head Asia Operations: Sigve Brekke
EVP; Head Operations, Central and Eastern Europe: Jan E. Thygesen, age 59
EVP and Head Communications and Corporate Responsibility: Hilde M. Tonne
EVP; Head Mobile and Fixed Network Operations, Sweden and Denmark: Ragnar H. Korsæth
Interim EVP and Interim Head People and Organization: Ingvald Fergestad
SVP Corporate Communications: Pål Kvalheim
CEO, Telenor Sweden: Lars-Åke Norling
CEO, Telenor Connexion: Per Simonsen, age 46
CEO, Promonte: Christopher Laska
CEO, AeroMobile: Pål Bjørdal
CEO, Pannon: Anders Jensen
CEO, Grameenphone: Oddvar Hesjedal
CEO, DiGi Malaysia: Henrik Clausen
CEO, Telenor Pakistan: Jon Eddy, age 44
CEO, Telenor Denmark: Jon Erik Haug
Head Investor Relations: Marianne Moe
Auditors: Ernst & Young AS

LOCATIONS

HQ: Telenor ASA
Snarøyveien 30
N-1331 Fornebu, Norway
Phone: 47-678-90-000   **Fax:** 47-678-90-000
Web: www.telenor.com

2009 Sales

	% of total
Europe	
Norway	35
Sweden	12
Other countries	20
Asia	
Thailand	12
Other countries	20
Other regions	1
Total	**100**

PRODUCTS/OPERATIONS

2009 Sales

	% of total
Services	
Mobile telephony	64
Wireline	13
Satellite & TV distribution	9
IT & software	7
Other	4
Customer equipment	3
Total	**100**

COMPETITORS

Bharti Airtel
BT
CELCOM
Computer Sciences Corp.
Deutsche Telekom
France Telecom
Hutchison Telecommunications
Mahanagar Telephone Nigam
Maxis
Modern Times Group AB
Pakistan Telecom
Reliance Communications
Tata Teleservices
TDC
Tele2
TeleComputing
TeliaSonera
TietoEnator
Vodafone Essar

HISTORICAL FINANCIALS

Company Type: Public

Income Statement

FYE: December 31

	REVENUE ($ mil.)	NET INCOME ($ mil.)	NET PROFIT MARGIN	EMPLOYEES
12/09	16,806	1,739	10.3%	40,300
12/08	13,772	2,099	15.2%	38,800
12/07	17,061	3,543	20.8%	35,800
12/06	9,322	1,146	12.3%	35,600
12/05	10,188	1,349	13.2%	27,600
Annual Growth	**13.3%**	**6.5%**	**—**	**9.9%**

2009 Year-End Financials

Debt ratio: 44.3%
Return on equity: 14.2%
Cash ($ mil.): 1,976
Current ratio: 0.79
Long-term debt ($ mil.): 5,796
No. of shares (mil.): 553
Dividends
 Yield: 0.0%
 Payout: —
Market value ($ mil.): 3,975

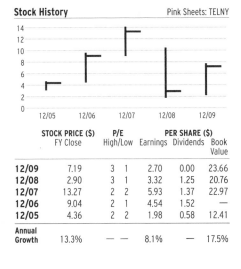

	STOCK PRICE ($) FY Close	P/E High/Low		PER SHARE ($) Earnings	Dividends	Book Value
12/09	7.19	3	1	2.70	0.00	23.66
12/08	2.90	3	1	3.32	1.25	20.76
12/07	13.27	2	2	5.93	1.37	22.97
12/06	9.04	2	1	4.54	1.52	—
12/05	4.36	2	2	1.98	0.58	12.41
Annual Growth	13.3%	—	—	8.1%	—	17.5%

Grupo Televisa

With its television, radio, film, Internet, and publishing interests, Grupo Televisa is *número uno* in the Latin media world. The company is Mexico's #1 TV broadcaster with four networks boasting about 260 affiliate stations (almost 220 of which are company-owned). It also has a 51% stake in cable joint venture Cablevisión and a 60% stake in Innova's Sky direct-to-home digital satellite television system. The company's publishing unit, Editorial Televisa, is a leading producer of Spanish-language magazines. Televisa also has operations in radio through Radiópolis (a 50%-owned joint venture with Grupo Prisa), film and TV production and distribution, and sports and entertainment.

With the company already dominating Mexican broadcast television, Televisa has been focused on diversifying its holdings through investments in cable TV systems, telecommunications, and alternative media outlets. It owns nearly 60% of Cablemás, Mexico's #2 cable system, in addition to its stakes in Cablevisión and Sky. The company has also agreed to acquire a 30% stake in Nextel Mexico, a regional subsidiary of US-based wireless communications company NII Holdings. In addition, its Televisa Interactive Media has a growing portfolio of online destinations including Spanish-language Internet portal Esmas.com and social networking site Gyggs.

Televisa continues to be a leading source of Spanish-language programming outside of Mexico as well. Most importantly it produces and sells shows to Univision Communications, the leading Hispanic media company in the US. In 2010 Televisa announced it would invest $1.2 billion in Univision. The deal gives Televisa a 5% stake and marks the end of hostilities between the two companies that centered on programming distribution rights and royalty payments. The disputes erupted into lawsuits after Univision was taken private by Broadcast Media Partners, a group of private equity firms led by Texas Pacific Group and Thomas H. Lee Partners. On the heels of the new peace with Univision, the Spanish-language media giants agreed to extend their distribution arrangement until 2020. Televisa will also give 50% of its TuTv venture with Univision to the US broadcaster.

The Televisa has also partnered with Telemundo (owned by NBC Universal) to broadcast shows produced by the #2 US-based Spanish-language broadcaster. The partnership, which launched in 2008, marked the first time Televisa has acquired programming from a foreign producer.

Mexican media mogul and CEO Emilio Azcárraga Jean controls Televisa through a trust.

HISTORY

Credited with launching the Golden Age of Mexican cinema in the 1940s via his Churrubusco Studios, Emilio Azcárraga Vidaurreta was a radio pioneer who also owned one of Mexico's first TV channels. He joined fellow TV channel owners Rómulo O'Farrill (a newspaper publisher) and Guillermo Camarena (an inventor) to form one network, Telesistema Mexicana, in 1954. When Azcárraga Vidaurreta died in 1972, his son Emilio Azcárraga Milmo took the reins of the company, dubbed it Grupo Televisa, and began his long stint as chairman. His aggressive style earned him the nickname "El Tigre" (The Tiger).

Azcárraga Milmo saw Mexican television as an escape for the nation's middle and lower classes. He nurtured stars for soap operas (called *telenovelas*) and variety shows and insisted upon the actors' loyalty in return. Grupo Televisa started producing feature films for markets in Mexico and abroad in 1978. It also ran cable TV and music recording businesses and a regional TV network that it bought in 1982. The company used its news programs to support Mexico's Institutional Revolutionary Party (PRI).

A 1990 attempt to start a sports newspaper in the US (*The National*) met with failure (it closed after a year, leaving the company with heavy debts). Azcárraga Milmo bought out the other principal investors in 1990 and reorganized Televisa into a holding company, taking it public in 1991. The company launched its Skytel paging service in Mexico in 1992 and bought a minority stake in US-based Univision Communications. The Mexican government privatized the Televisión Azteca network in 1993, giving Televisa its first taste of competition in the TV broadcast market.

Televisa joined Brazil's Organizações Globo and TCI (later AT&T Broadband) in 1995 to develop direct-to-home (DTH) satellite television. (News Corporation joined the venture, later called Sky, in 1997.) The company also pared its staff by 12% and divested some of its lesser operations, including the sale of 49% of its cable TV businesses to telephone giant Teléfonos de México (Telmex).

A month before his death in 1997, Azcárraga Milmo installed his 29-year-old son, Emilio Azcárraga Jean, as president and CEO of the company. The company sold half of its stake in Univision the next year and slashed more jobs. Holding company Grupo Televicentro sold a 9% stake in Televisa in 2000 and used the proceeds to pay off debt. It also sold its newspaper, *Ovaciones*, in 2000. Later that year Televisa consolidated its ownership of publishing unit Editorial Televisa.

A plan to merge its radio stations with those of Grupo Acir was foiled when Mexican competition authorities ruled against it. But the next year the company was able to strike a deal to sell 50% of its radio station subsidiary to Grupo Prisa. Also that year the company eliminated 730 jobs in response to falling advertising revenue.

It again increased its stake in Univision from 6% to 15%. (It sold all its holdings in the US Hispanic broadcaster in 2007.) The company agreed to form a television production company in a joint venture with Endemol in 2001.

In 2002 Televisa sold its Fonovisa Records regional music label to Univision for $210 million.

EXECUTIVES

Chairman, President, and CEO:
Emilio Fernando Azcárraga Jean, age 42
CFO: Salvi R. Folch Viadero, age 43
EVP and Director: Alfonso de Angoitia Noriega, age 48
EVP and Director: Bernardo Gómez Martínez, age 43
Corporate VP Sales and Marketing:
Alejandro Jesus Quintero Iñíguez, age 60
VP Technical Operations and Services, and Television Production: Maximiliano Arteaga Carlebach, age 67
VP and Corporate Controller:
Jorge A. Lutteroth Echegoyen, age 57
VP Production: Jorge Eduardo Murguía Orozco, age 60
VP Legal and General Counsel:
Joaquín Balcarcel Santa Cruz, age 41
VP Newscasts: Leopoldo G. González Blanco, age 51
VP Televisa Regional: Félix José Araujo Ramírez, age 59
CEO, Sistema Radiópolis:
Francisco Javier Mérida Guzmán, age 43
CEO, Corporación Novavision:
Alexandre Moreira Penna, age 55
CEO, Cablevisión: Jean Paul Broc Haro, age 48
CEO, Televisa Publishing and Interactive Media:
Eduardo Michelsen Delgado, age 39
President Television and Contents, and Director:
José A. Bastón Patiño, age 42
Director Investor Relations: Carlos Madrazo Villaseñor
Media Relations: Manuel Compeán
Auditors: PricewaterhouseCoopers

LOCATIONS

HQ: Grupo Televisa, S.A.B.
Avenida Vasco de Quiroga, No. 2000, Colonia Santa Fe, Delegación Álvaro Obregón
01210 México, D.F., Mexico
Phone: 52-55-5261-2000   **Fax:** 52-55-5261-2494
Web: www.televisa.com

PRODUCTS/OPERATIONS

2009 Sales

	% of total
Television	
TV broadcasting	40
Programming	6
Pay-TV channels	5
Cable & telecom	
Sky	19
Other	17
Publishing	6
Other businesses	7
Total	**100**

Selected Operations

Television
  Broadcast TV channels
    Channel 2
    Channel 4
    Channel 5
    Channel 9
  Pay-TV channels
    American Network
    Bandamax
    Canal de las Estrellas Latinoamérica
    Canal de Telenovelas
    Cinema Golden Choice Latinoamérica
    De Película
    Ritmoson Latino
    Telehit
Cable and telecommunications
  Cablemás (58%, cable TV services)
  Cablevisión (51%, cable TV services)
  Innova (Sky, 59%, direct satellite broadcasting)
  TuTv (Spanish-language cable channels, US)

Magazine publishing
  Caras
  Cinemania
  Conozca Más
  Furia Musical
  Gente y la Actualidad
  National Geographic Traveler
  TV y Novelas
  Vanidades
Other businesses
  Feature film production
  Gaming (bingo and sports books)
  Radiópolis (50%, radio broadcasting)
  Sports
    América (soccer team, Mexico City)
    Estadio Azteca (sports stadium, Mexico City)
  Televisa Interactive Media (online content)

COMPETITORS

CIE
Cisneros Group
MVS
Radio Center Group
Satmex
Telemundo Communications
TV Azteca
Univision

HISTORICAL FINANCIALS

Company Type: Public

Income Statement

FYE: December 31

	REVENUE ($ mil.)	NET INCOME ($ mil.)	NET PROFIT MARGIN	EMPLOYEES
12/09	4,015	461	11.5%	24,362
12/08	3,481	566	16.3%	22,528
12/07	3,805	826	21.7%	17,777
12/06	3,513	795	22.6%	16,200
12/05	3,023	617	20.4%	15,100
Annual Growth	7.4%	(7.1%)	—	12.7%

2009 Year-End Financials

Debt ratio: 113.0%
Return on equity: 15.4%
Cash ($ mil.): 2,296
Current ratio: 2.13
Long-term debt ($ mil.): 3,309

No. of shares (mil.): 557
Dividends
Yield: 73.7%
Payout: 130.0%
Market value ($ mil.): 886

Stock History

NYSE: TV

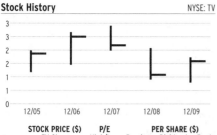

	STOCK PRICE ($) FY Close	P/E High/Low		PER SHARE ($) Earnings	Dividends	Book Value
12/09	1.59	2	1	0.90	1.17	5.26
12/08	1.08	2	1	0.85	0.26	5.48
12/07	2.18	2	2	1.29	0.16	6.09
12/06	2.50	2	1	1.36	0.16	5.83
12/05	1.87	6	3	0.35	0.16	4.85
Annual Growth	(4.0%)	—	—	26.6%	64.4%	2.0%

TeliaSonera AB

An expert at cold calling, TeliaSonera offers telecommunications services primarily in the chilly Nordic regions where it is a leading telecom company. It provides wireless phone services to about 135 million subscribers in Denmark, Finland, Norway, and Sweden. With more than 2.6 million Internet customers, TeliaSonera is also the leading ISP in the Baltic and Nordic regions. Additionally, the company provides television services over Internet connections to some 867,000 subscribers. Other TeliaSonera activities include the sale of telecom equipment and the provision of wholesale network capacity to other carriers.

The company's sales of fixed voice lines continue to fall as more customers migrate to mobile and Internet protocol-based services. In addition to a growing wireless segment, TeliaSonera has experienced growth in broadband sales in most regions, particularly its core markets of Sweden and Finland.

While firmly rooted in the Nordic region, the company has expanded further into the European continent by offering wholesale carrier services to other operators over its fiber-optic network. Its network backbone connects Europe, the Americas, and Asia.

TeliaSonera's Baltic holdings include mobile subsidiaries in the markets of Azerbaijan, Georgia, Kazakhstan, and Moldova. It also has a stake in Russian mobile operator MegaFon. In 2008 TeliaSonera expanded into Cambodia and Nepal. All told, the company has investments in about 30 countries.

TeliaSonera is also using acquisitions to spur expansion. In 2009 TeliaSonera also acquired the remaining shares it did not already own of Estonian carrier AS Eesti Telekom and it raised its stake in the Lithuanian firm TEO LT. Also that year the company acquired the Norwegian broadband and VoIP business of rival Tele2 through subsidiary NextGenTel in a bid to build its assets in Norway.

Also in 2009 the company launched fourth-generation (4G) data services in Oslo and Stockholm, using the Long Term Evolution (LTE) industry standard. TeliaSonera implemented LTE equipment from Ericsson for Stockholm and LTE equipment made by Huawei Technologies for Oslo, along with 4G data modems supplied by Samsung Electronics. TeliaSonera holds nationwide 4G licenses for Finland, Norway, and Sweden. While the 4G service launch is historic, most people won't be making use of the service for some time to come.

The Kingdom of Sweden owns about 37% of TeliaSonera; the Republic of Finland owns nearly 14%.

HISTORY

Telia's wires go back to 1853 when the Swedish government created Kongl. Elektriska Telegraf-Verket to operate a telegraph line linking Stockholm and Uppsala. The next year it opened a line that reached the main European continent; the company became Telegrafverket in 1860.

Just a year after the telephone was invented in 1876, the firm installed its first phone line. The 1880s saw private phone companies sprout up in Sweden's larger cities, and by 1900 Telegrafverket had installed some 62,000 telephones.

Even though Sweden was open to telecom competition, the company became a de facto monopoly in 1918 when it bought the country's largest exchange, Stockholms Allmanna Telefon. In 1921 Telegrafverket began laying its first long-distance cable.

Telegrafverket began automating its phone systems in the 1930s. After WWII, the company entered a major growth period: More than 110,000 telephone users were connected in 1947 alone. Also in the mid-1940s, Telegrafverket launched one of the world's first mobile phone networks (closed radio).

Renamed Televerket, the firm continued to grow rapidly in the 1960s and 1970s and introduced data communications services in 1965. It teamed up with equipment maker Ericsson in 1970 to form Ellemtel, an R&D concern that developed the first all-digital public switching system. (Ellemtel ceased operations in 1999.) Televerket began moving into satellite services in 1970, when INTELSAT installed an earth station in the Nordic region. In the early 1980s it rolled out several new services, including cable TV, cellular, and international packet switching.

Meanwhile, the company began losing its monopoly status in the 1980s and lost its government funding in 1984. Fearing competition from giants such as AT&T and British Telecom (now BT Group), the company in 1991 joined the Netherlands' Royal KPN to form Unisource, a global telecommunications provider; Swisscom joined the group two years later. Sweden's telecom deregulation was completed in 1993, and the firm became Telia. That year it ventured into the Baltic states.

AT&T teamed up with Unisource in 1994 to provide services to multinationals. In 1995 Telia began providing Internet access and announced it was installing an overlay Internet protocol (IP) backbone. Moving into the Americas in 1997, Telia led a consortium that secured rights to offer cellular service in Brazil.

Unisource never took off, and after AT&T jumped ship in 1998, Telia and its partners began divesting the venture's assets.

In 2000 the Swedish government floated 30% of Telia. In 2002 Telia acquired Nordic region competitor Sonera and the two companies were combined to form TeliaSonera. As a condition of the merger, the group was required to sell Telia Mobile Finland that year as well.

In 2004 the group acquired the Danish operations of Orange, the wireless unit of France Telecom. The acquisition improved TeliaSonera's market position in Denmark, moving it from fourth- to third-largest mobile operator. In 2004 it sold its Sonera Zed unit, an aggregator and reseller of digital content to mobile phone users, to Spanish interactive media group Wisdom Entertainment. It also unloaded its stake in satellite company Eutelsat.

TeliaSonera expanded its holdings in Norway in 2006 when it acquired an 82% stake in NextGenTel Holding, the country's #2 broadband provider, and 33% of retail holding company ComHouse. That year TeliaSonera also purchased the shares it did not already own of wireless services firm Päämies, which operated via a network of retail shops throughout Finland. Acquisitions in 2007 included Cygate, a Nordic provider of managed IP services, and mobile carrier debitel Denmark. TeliaSonera bought the remaining two-thirds of ComHouse in 2008.

France Telecom offered to acquire TeliaSonera for nearly $42 billion in 2008; TeliaSonera ultimately rejected the bid.

EXECUTIVES

Chairman: Anders Narvinger, age 62
Vice Chairman: Timo Peltola, age 64
President and CEO: Lars Nyberg, age 59,
$29,091,211 total compensation
EVP and CFO: Per-Arne Blomquist, age 48,
$4,297,200 total compensation
SVP and Head Group Communications:
Cecilia Edström, age 44
SVP and Head Group Human Resources:
Karin Eliasson, age 59
**SVP and Head Head of Sales Division Business
Services, Sweden and Finland:** Sverker Hannervall,
age 50
SVP and CIO: Ake Södermark, age 55
SVP, General Counsel, and Head Group Legal Affairs:
Jan H. Ahrnell, age 51
VP Corporate Communications: Jacob Broberg
VP Investor Relations: Andreas Ekström, age 35
President, Broadband Services: Anders Gylder, age 50
President, Mobility: Håkan Dahlström, age 48
President, Eurasia: Tero E. Kivisaari, age 38
Auditors: PricewaterhouseCoopers AB

LOCATIONS

HQ: TeliaSonera AB
Stureplan8
SE-106 63 Stockholm, Sweden
Phone: 46-8-504-550-00   **Fax:** 46-8-504-550-01
US HQ: 2201 Cooperative Way, Ste. 302
Herndon, VA 20171
US Phone: 703-546-4000   **US Fax:** 703-546-4125
Web: www.teliasonera.com

2009 Sales

	% of total
Sweden	33
Finland	17
Norway	9
Other countries	41
Total	**100**

PRODUCTS/OPERATIONS

2009 Sales

	% of total
Mobility services	44
Broadband services	39
Eurasia	12
Other	5
Total	**100**

2009 Sales

	% of total
Mobile communications	54
Fixed communications	38
Equipment sales, financial services, managed services & other	8
Total	**100**

COMPETITORS

BT
Cable & Wireless
COLT Group
Deutsche Telekom
Elisa Corporation
France Telecom
Global Crossing
Hi3G Denmark
Invitel
KPN
Level 3 Communications
Liberty Global
Mobile TeleSystems
Orange Business Services
Rostelecom
TDC
Tele2
Telefónica
Telenor
Vivo Participações
Vodafone

HISTORICAL FINANCIALS

Company Type: Public

Income Statement — FYE: December 31

	REVENUE ($ mil.)	NET INCOME ($ mil.)	NET PROFIT MARGIN	EMPLOYEES
12/09	15,184	2,960	19.5%	29,734
12/08	13,342	2,762	20.7%	30,037
12/07	15,049	3,171	21.1%	31,292
12/06	13,286	2,813	21.2%	28,528
12/05	11,010	1,720	15.6%	28,175
Annual Growth	**8.4%**	**14.5%**	**—**	**1.4%**

2009 Year-End Financials

Debt ratio: —
Return on equity: —
Cash ($ mil.): 3,128
Current ratio: 1.30
Long-term debt ($ mil.): —
No. of shares (mil.): 4,490
Dividends
Yield: 3.5%
Payout: 43.1%
Market value ($ mil.): 32,387

Stock History

OMX Stockholm: TLSN

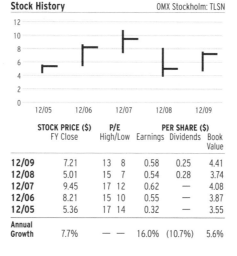

	STOCK PRICE ($) FY Close	P/E High/Low		Earnings	Dividends	Book Value
12/09	7.21	13	8	0.58	0.25	4.41
12/08	5.01	15	7	0.54	0.28	3.74
12/07	9.45	17	12	0.62	—	4.08
12/06	8.21	15	10	0.55	—	3.87
12/05	5.36	17	14	0.32	—	3.55
Annual Growth	**7.7%**	**—**	**—**	**16.0%**	**(10.7%)**	**5.6%**

Telstra Corporation

As Australia's #1 telecommunications carrier, Telstra provides fixed-line services to about 9 million access lines, and it serves 10 million mobile phone customers. It is also the country's leading ISP, through BigPond, with more than 3 million broadband subscribers. Telstra's largest market is consumer and residential customers, but its business and government segment comes in a close second. It also provides wholesale network services to other communications companies, while its Sensis telephone directory unit specializes in print, online, and wireless advertising. Telstra owns half of pay television operator FOXTEL, while News Corp. and Consolidated Media Holdings each own 25% of FOXTEL.

Telstra was delivered a blow by the Australian government in 2008 when it was shut out of an auction to bid on the construction of a A$43 billion nationwide broadband network. Telstra's proposal did not include plans for how the network would benefit small and midsized businesses as required by the government.

Subsequent negotiations between Telstra and the government (also a shareholder in the company) during 2009 and 2010 became entangled in broader legislation related to changes to federal telecommunications regulations. The government has asserted that Telstra should break up into two businesses in order to increase competition in the industry for the benefit of the consumer. If Telstra will not do so voluntarily, the government has said that it should be barred from bidding on the wireless spectrum licenses it needs for its mobile business.

The restructuring would divide the company into separate wholesale and retail businesses and make Telstra's landline telephone business part of the nationwide network. The company would also have to sell its cable network and its stake in FOXTEL. Telstra is opposing the legislation.

Telstra is trying to turn around underperforming units, such as its fixed-line services and directories businesses, which saw sales slip for the year. As part of Telstra's broader strategy of focusing on core telecom services business lines, the company sold its IT services business, KAZ Group, to Fujitsu for A$200 million in 2009. Also that year, David Thodey took over as company CEO following the departure of Sol Trujillo.

The company's Telstra International unit oversees the company's operations in Australasia from facilities in Hong Kong, Singapore, and in New Zealand (through TelstraClear). Its 50-50 joint venture with PCCW, known as REACH, is Asia's largest international carrier of voice, private line, and Internet protocol data services.

The company expanded its interests in China in 2010 when it bought mobile news and entertainment content provider LMobile.

HISTORY

When Australia gained independence in 1901, telecommunications were assigned to the new state-owned Postmaster-General's Department (PMG). Engineer H. P. Brown, who had managed the UK's telegraph and telephone system, became head of PMG in 1923. He set up research labs that year, oversaw the first overseas call to London in 1930, and streamlined operations until his reign ended in 1939.

During WWII Australia quickly expanded its communications infrastructure to assist the Allied Front in the South Pacific. Following the war, the government formed the Overseas Telecommunications Commission (OTC) in 1946 to handle international operations independent of PMG.

Even as new technology connected the continent and boosted the productivity of PMG, its postal operations steadily recorded losses during the postwar era. In 1974 a Royal Commission recommended that postal and telecom services be split. Australian Telecommunications Commission (Telecom Australia) was launched in 1975 (OTC retained overseas services); it turned a profit in its first year.

Looking to connect residents in the outback, the firm signed Japan's Nippon Electric (now NEC) in 1981 to set up a digital radio transmission system; by the next decade it connected some 50,000 outback users. Also in 1981 Telecom Australia took a 25% stake in government-owned satellite operator AUSSAT and launched nationwide paging and mobile phone service in Melbourne and Sydney.

Renamed Australian Telecommunications in 1989, the carrier got its first whiff of competition as others were allowed to provide phone equipment. Two years later Optus Communications began competing with Telecom Australia;

for the privilege, it was forced to buy the unsuccessful AUSSAT. Long-distance competition began in 1991 followed by mobile phone competition in 1992. In response, Telecom Australia merged with OTC to become Australian and Overseas Telecommunications Corporation (AOTC). AT&T's Frank Blount became CEO.

AOTC became Telstra Corporation in 1993 and launched a digital wireless GSM-based network. It joined with Rupert Murdoch's News Corp. to form pay TV operator Foxtel in 1995.

That year Telstra teamed with Microsoft to create ISP On Australia. Microsoft dropped out in 1996, but Telstra kept the service (Big Pond) and its portal (renamed Telstra.com in 1999). The government fully deregulated telecommunications and sold a third of Telstra to the public in 1997. In 1999 Telstra posted an Australian record-setting profit, former Optus CEO Ziggy Switkowski succeeded Blount, and the government floated an additional 17% stake.

In 2004 the company acquired Australia-based Trading Post Group for nearly $484 million, bolstering advertising and publishing operations. Telstra also bought technology services provider Kaz Group that year for $252 million.

Former chairman Bob Mansfield resigned after conflicts with the board of directors over the proposed acquisition of publisher John Fairfax Holdings. Late the same year CEO Ziggy Switkowski was sacked by the board after holding the position for six years, during which time the company's share price dropped considerably. The company hired former Orange SA CEO Sol Trujillo to take his place in 2005. That year, Trujillo outlined a plan to reduce the company's payroll by 12,000 positions.

In 2006 the company bought competitor New World Mobile Holdings and merged it with the operations of subsidiary Hong Kong CSL to create CSL New World. Also that year the company acquired a controlling stake in China-based real estate listings website SouFun. The Australian comonwealth reduced its majority stake in Telstra from 52% to 18% in 2007.

The company moved to boost ad revenue in China in 2008 with the acquisition of controlling interests in Chinese Web content providers Norstar Media and Autohome/PCPop.

EXECUTIVES

Chairman: Catherine B. Livingstone, age 54
CEO and Board Member: David Thodey, age 55, $2,818,994 total compensation
Acting COO: Michael Rocca, $2,036,494 total compensation
CFO, Group Managing Director Finance and Administration, and Board Member: John Stanhope, age 59, $2,463,911 total compensation
Chief Marketing Officer: Kate McKenzie, $1,130,492 total compensatio
CIO and Group Managing Director Information Technology: John McInerney
Group General Counsel: Will Irving
Group Managing Director Media Services; CEO, Sensis: Bruce J. Akhurst, age 50, $2,607,299 total compensation
Group Managing Director Enterprise and Government: Nerida Caesar, $296,392 total compensation
Group Managing Director Telstra International: Tarek A. Robbiati
Group Managing Director Consumer and Channels: Gordon S. Ballantyne

Acting Group Managing Director Wireless, Data, Applications, and Services: Philip Jones
Group Managing Director Country Wide: Brett Riley
Group Managing Director Public Policy and Communications: David Quilty
Group Managing Director Customer Satisfaction, Simplification, Productivity, and Head Program Office: Robert A. Nason
Group Managing Director Wholesale: Paul Geason
Group Managing Director Human Resources: Andrea Grant
Company Secretary: Carmel Mulhern
Director Investor Relations: Ben Spincer
Auditors: Ernst & Young

LOCATIONS

HQ: Telstra Corporation Limited
Level 41, 242 Exhibition St.
Melbourne 3000, Australia
Phone: 61-8-8308-1721
Web: www.telstra.com.au

2010 Sales

	% of total
Australia	92
Other countries	8
Total	**100**

PRODUCTS/OPERATIONS

2010 Sales

	% of total
Fixed-line	
Standard telephone	23
Internet	9
Other	9
Mobile	29
Directories & advertising	9
IP & data access	7
International	6
Other	8
Total	**100**

2010 Sales by Market

	% of total
Consumer	41
Enterprise & government	17
Business	15
Wholesale	9
Directories & advertising	9
Other	9
Total	**100**

Selected Services

Advertising and directory services
Audio, video, and Internet conferencing
Broadband ISP
Cable TV
Data transmission
E-mail
Enhanced fax products and services
Freecall (toll-free 1-800 phone service)
Information technology (IT) services
Internet access
Mobile phone service
Prepaid telephony
Satellite transmission

COMPETITORS

Global Crossing
Hutchison Telecommunications Australia
Optus
Pacnet
PowerTel
Telecom Corporation of New Zealand

HISTORICAL FINANCIALS

Company Type: Public

Income Statement

FYE: June 30

	REVENUE ($ mil.)	NET INCOME ($ mil.)	NET PROFIT MARGIN	EMPLOYEES
6/10	21,432	3,374	15.7%	45,220
6/09	20,607	3,279	15.9%	43,181
6/08	24,014	3,564	14.8%	46,649
6/07	20,333	2,779	13.7%	47,840
6/06	16,861	2,322	13.8%	49,443
Annual Growth	**6.2%**	**9.8%**	**—**	**(2.2%)**

2010 Year-End Financials

Debt ratio: —
Return on equity: —
Cash ($ mil.): 1,658
Current ratio: 0.83
Long-term debt ($ mil.): —

No. of shares (mil.): —
Dividends
  Yield: 8.6%
  Payout: 88.9%
Market value ($ mil.): —

Stock History

Australian: TLS

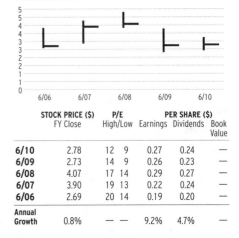

	STOCK PRICE ($) FY Close	P/E High/Low		PER SHARE ($) Earnings	Dividends	Book Value
6/10	2.78	12	9	0.27	0.24	—
6/09	2.73	14	9	0.26	0.23	—
6/08	4.07	17	14	0.29	0.27	—
6/07	3.90	19	13	0.22	0.24	—
6/06	2.69	20	14	0.19	0.20	—
Annual Growth	**0.8%**	**—**	**—**	**9.2%**	**4.7%**	**—**

Tengelmann

Americans know Tengelmann Group best through its stake in A&P (Great Atlantic & Pacific Tea Company) supermarkets. But the 430-odd A&P stores are only a tiny part of Tengelmann, a big European food and general merchandise retailer. Its four retail divisions operate more than 4,500 supermarkets, do-it-yourself and general merchandise stores, and the Plus Online business in Germany and 15 other European countries. Banners include: Kaiser's and Tengelmann (supermarkets) in Germany; OBI (DIY supply stores) in Germany and a dozen other European countries; and KiK (discount apparel and general merchandise shops) in Germany and four other countries. The family-run firm is led by CEO Karl-Erivan Haub.

Tengelmann Group is losing its appetite for food retailing in Germany and the US. The on-going poor performance at A&P has for years been a source of frustration for Tengelmann — A&P's biggest shareholder — and it appears to have had enough. Indeed, in August 2010 CEO Haub announced that A&P will eventually be combined with another retailer. Haub, who said Tengelmann plans to hold a stake in the combined company, did not say what company A&P will ultimately be merged with.

In Germany, which accounts for about two-thirds of Tengelmann Group's sales, the company is restructuring by moving away from food and focusing instead on its better performing OBI and KiK divisions. To that end, it sold its Plus chain of more than 2,000 discount food stores in Germany to rival Edeka in late 2008. (It also sold all of its Plus stores in eight other European countries to local rivals.) The company's shrinking Kaiser's Tengelmann supermarket unit operates about 660 stores in Berlin, Munich, and the lower Rhine region, after exiting other German markets.

Beyond food, Tengelmann's OBI chain of some 330 DIY stores is enjoying more success and leads the German market. (OBI has about another 200 locations in a dozen other countries in Europe.) KiK operates more than 2,400 stores in Germany and has another 450 additional locations in Austria, Slovakia, Slovenia, and the Czech Republic. Tengelmann recently announced plans to almost double the number of KiK stores in Europe in the next five years.

Its TREI Real Estate unit has commercial retail holdings in about half a dozen countries in Europe. Tengelmann plans to expand its real estate holdings in Eastern Europe by developing and leasing specialty stores there. Also, in 2010 it acquired a stake in the Woolworth variety store chain in Germany, which has been in administration since 2009.

Tengelmann's other holdings include: a 30% stake in TEDI, a 1-Euro discount shop with more than 940 branches throughout Germany; and a 15% share in the 4,000-store Netto discount chain in Germany.

HISTORY

William and Louise (Scholl) Schmitz founded Wilh. Schmitz Scholl in Mülheim, Germany, in 1867, importing goods and processing coffee. In 1893 the Schmitzes' sons opened their first retail store, selling groceries, sweets, coffee, tea, and cocoa. The family called the store Tengelmann, after employee Emil Tengelmann, to avoid the social stigma then attached to grocers in Germany.

The company rebuilt after WWII left many of its stores in ruins. The man who would guide the company through much of its growth was still a youngster at the time. In 1952 Erivan Haub, the great-grandson of William and Louise Schmitz, was 20 when he was sent to the US for three years to learn the ropes at supermarkets in California and Illinois. He saw that US grocery stores, unlike most in Germany, let consumers serve themselves. Haub passed this practice along to his relatives, and Tengelmann Group opened its first self-serve stores in Germany soon afterward. Haub developed a fondness for the US during this trip that has not faded: His children were born in America to give them citizenship; St. Joseph's University in Philadelphia named its business school after Haub to recognize the family's contributions.

Haub took over as head of the company in 1969 after his uncle's death. First on his shopping list was acquisitions. He bought Kaiser's Kaffee-Geschaft, a troubled German supermarket chain, two years later, then converted some of the stores into the discount Plus format. Tengelmann adopted the role of rescuer again in 1979 when it agreed to buy more than half of the troubled US supermarket chain Great Atlantic & Pacific Tea Company (A&P). Haub turned the grocer around by focusing on acquisitions and revamping older store formats.

International expansion marked the tone of Tengelmann in the 1990s. Using its Plus discount chain as a vehicle, Tengelmann branched into East Germany, Hungary, Poland, and other countries once part of the communist bloc. Germany, with its stiff competition and strict laws limiting acquisitions and requiring shops to close early on weeknights, paled in comparison as a growth opportunity to the hungry environments in the East.

Tengelmann enraged Holocaust survivors in 1991 when it proposed building a Kaiser's supermarket on part of the Ravensbrück Nazi concentration camp site, where approximately 92,000 women and children had been killed. The company canceled its plans after worldwide protests, although the local community, in need of jobs, had supported the idea.

Heavy competition among German retailers hammered profits in 1995. Haub announced plans to cut costs and restructure the company. The changes included modifying the Plus store format from discounter to neighborhood convenience store; Haub continued to back new deep-discount chain Ledi. The youngest Haub son, Christian, was promoted to CEO of A&P in 1998.

In the midst of a restructuring, in 2000 the company announced it would sell or close at least 600 of the poorly performing Tengelmann and Kaiser's stores.

After 33 years as the sole managing partner of the Tengelmann Group, Erivan Haub turned the management of the company over to his sons Karl-Erivan and Christian in 2002.

In 2005 The Kd Kaiser's drugstore chain was sold to Dirk Rossmann. It also sold its profitable A&P Canada division to METRO INC and disposed of its 22 Interfruct Cash & Carry stores in Hungary and Slovenia. The company entered the Romanian market late in the year with the opening of 18 Plus discount stores there.

In 2008 Tengelmann sold its 34-store Plus Hellas chain in Greece to Delhaize. That year it sold a 70% stake in its 2,765 Plus stores in Germany to rival Edeka.

EXECUTIVES

Chairman, Holding Management Board; CEO, Europe: Karl-Erivan W. Haub
CFO: Jens-Jürgen Böckel, age 67
CEO and Managing Partner, KiK: Stefan Heinig
CEO, Obi: Sergio Giroldi
Chairman, President, and CEO, The Great Atlantic and Pacific Tea Company, Inc. (A&P): Christian W. E. Haub
Executive Director, Human Resource Department; Chairman and CEO, Kaiser's Tengelmann: Bernd Ahlers
Divisional Manager, National Quality Management, Consumer Protection and Organic Farming, Kaiser's Tengelmann AG: Paul Daum
Director Trading, Kaiser's Tengelmann AG: Raimund Luig
Head, Public Relations Department: Sieglinde Schuchardt
Public Relations: Jutta Meister
Auditors: KPMG Deutsche Treuhand-Gesellschaft AG

LOCATIONS

HQ: Tengelmann Warenhandelsgesellschaft KG
Wissollstraße 5-43
45478 Mülheim an der Ruhr, Germany
Phone: 49-208-5806-0   **Fax:** 49-208-5806-6401
Web: www.tengelmann.de

2009 Sales

	% of total
Germany	66
Rest of Europe	34
Total	**100**

2009 Stores

	No.
Germany	3,427
Rest of Europe	1,092
Total	**4,519**

PRODUCTS/OPERATIONS

Selected Store Operations

Kaiser's (supermarkets)
KiK (discount clothing stores)
Obi (do-it-yourself supply, hardware, and appliance retailer)
Tengelmann (supermarkets)
The Great Atlantic & Pacific Tea Company (41%, grocery store chain)

COMPETITORS

Acme Markets
ALDI
Carrefour
Casino Guichard
D'Agostino Supermarkets
Delhaize
Edeka Zentrale
H&M
Home Depot
Inditex
ITM Entreprises
Kingfisher
Kings Super Markets
Lidl
Marktkauf
Maxeda
METRO AG
Otto GmbH & Co KG
Praktiker
REWE
SPAR Handels
Stop & Shop
Tesco
Village Super Market
Wal-Mart

HISTORICAL FINANCIALS

Company Type: Private

Income Statement

	REVENUE ($ mil.)	NET INCOME ($ mil.)	NET PROFIT MARGIN	EMPLOYEES
12/09	16,253	—	—	84,516
12/08*	12,360	—	—	83,655
4/08	37,725	—	—	116,447
4/07	33,465	—	—	151,753
4/06	32,454	—	—	150,880
Annual Growth	**(15.9%)**	**—**	**—**	**(13.5%)**

FYE: December 31

*Fiscal year change

Revenue History

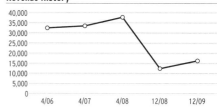

Tesco PLC

Tesco is proof of the good a little dressing up can do. The world's fourth-largest grocery retailer, Tesco runs about 4,800 stores in the UK (where it's the #1 retailer), and more than a dozen other countries in Europe, Asia, and the US (under the Fresh & Easy banner). Built on the "pile it high, sell it cheap" creed of founder Sir Jack Cohen, Tesco abandoned its discount format, with its down-market image, for a variety of dressier mid-market formats. Its operations include supermarket, convenience, and gasoline retailing (Tesco Express), small urban stores (Tesco Metro), superstores (Tesco Extra), and financial services (Tesco Personal Finance). Tesco.com is Britain's leading Internet delivery service.

Tesco's formula for growth is to diversify into new countries, new products, and new services. It has moved beyond groceries and far beyond the UK in recent years to become a global retailer of general merchandise, as well as food. It has also expanded into services. To that end, Tesco bought out its joint venture partner — Royal Bank of Scotland — in Tesco Personal Finance (TPF) for about $1.9 billion in July 2008. The purchase is part of Tesco's strategy to expand into the service sector, which is outpacing food in terms of growth.

Tesco is also looking to gain market share in the telecommunications business. The company operates a joint venture alongside O2 in the mobile phones business that boasts some 2 million customers. Beginning in mid-2009 Tesco began dueling with Carphone Warehouse (and its US partner Best Buy) for market share by opening in-store phone shops, eventually rolling out the service to all of its Tesco Extra locations within three years.

Tesco is expanding faster away from home. In China, one of the world's hottest retail markets, Tesco operates more than 80 hypermarkets, about a dozen convenience stores, and several Lifespace shopping malls. The company's strategy is to invest £2 billion ($3.1 billion) to build 80 five-story Lifespace malls, which also house movie theaters and restaurants, and to add about 20 hypermarkets by about 2015. The UK-based firm has also opened its first cash and carry store in India via a franchise agreement with the retail arm of India's Tata Group.

While historically it has relied on organic international growth, typically via joint ventures and store-by-store openings, Tesco stepped out of that norm with a major acquisition of a chain of hypermarkets in South Korea from E-Land Group for about $2 billion in 2008.

Since the 2007 launch in the US of a new convenience store chain called Fresh & Easy Neighborhood Market, the chain has grown to number about 145 shops in Arizona, Nevada, and Southern California. However, plans to grow the store count to 200 locations have been postponed due to the recession, which has hit Fresh & Easy's market area especially hard.

Chief executive Terry Leahy has announced that he will retire in March 2011 after 14 years at Tesco's helm. Philip Clarke, who currently leads the retailer's international operations in Asia and Europe, has been tapped to replace him.

Warren Buffett, American billionaire and chairman and CEO of US investment firm Berkshire Hathaway, owns about 3% of Tesco.

HISTORY

With WWI behind him, in 1919 Jack Cohen invested his serviceman's gratuity in a grocery stall in London's East End. He introduced his first private-label product, Tesco Tea, in 1924 — the name was the combination of the initials of his tea supplier (T. E. Stockwell) and the first two letters of Cohen's last name. By the late 1920s Cohen had several stalls, and in 1929 he opened his first store, under the Tesco name, in Edgeware, London.

Cohen founded Tesco Stores Limited in 1932. During the rest of the decade, the company added more than 100 stores, mainly in London. Cohen visited the US in 1935, studying its self-service supermarkets, and returned to England with a plan of using a similar "pile it high and sell it cheap" format. Delayed by WWII, Tesco opened its first American-styled store in 1947 and went public that year as Tesco Stores Holdings. By 1950 the company ran 20 self-service stores.

Tesco grew primarily through acquisitions during the 1950s and 1960s, adding about 600 stores. By the early 1970s, however, competition and a recession battered Tesco. Managing director Ian MacLaurin initiated radical changes, including abandoning trading stamps and, to shed its down-market image, refurbishing stores with a more upscale decor. A price-slashing initiative in 1977 dramatically increased Tesco's market share within a year. Because cheap brands were best-sellers, Tesco began creating its own private-label brands. The company also started closing unprofitable stores while opening superstores, some with gas stations.

In 1979, the year Sir Jack Cohen died, Tesco entered Ireland by buying Three Guys (abandoning the effort in 1986). In 1983 the company became Tesco, and two years later it named MacLaurin as chairman. By 1991 Tesco was the UK's largest independent gasoline retailer.

Looking for new opportunities, in 1992 Tesco introduced small urban stores called Tesco Metro and the next year began expanding outside England, acquiring stores in France and Scotland. In 1994 it acquired an initial 51% stake in Global, a 43-store grocery chain in Hungary.

Tesco returned to Ireland in 1997 by acquiring 109 Associated British Food stores. It also named John Gardiner as chairman (replacing the retiring MacLaurin) and Terry Leahy as CEO.

In March 2002 Tesco acquired the travel company First Class Leisure and renamed the business Tesco Freetime. In January 2003 Tesco completed the acquisition of the British convenience store chain T&S Stores for £519 million.

In April 2004 David Reid became non-executive chairman, replacing Gardiner, who retired from Tesco. In mid-2005 Tesco opened its first Kipa store in Turkey since it acquired the Turkish chain in 2003.

In 2006 the company bought 27 small stores from Edeka in the Czech Republic. In December Tesco increased its stake in China's Ting Hsin Holding Corp. to 90% from 50% in a deal valued at about $352 million. (Tesco entered China in 2004, paying approximately $275 million for 50% in Ting Hsin's subsidiary Ting Cao.)

In the year ended February 2007, Tesco increased its international selling space by 25%. In early November the British retailer opened its first US store: a Fresh & Easy Neighborhood Market in Hemet, California (outside Los Angeles).

In August 2008 Tesco bought the UK operation of Handleman, a leading UK-based distributor and store merchandiser of books, music, computer games, and other products.

EXECUTIVES

Chairman: David E. Reid, age 63, $1,264,704 total compensation
Deputy Chairman: Patrick Cescau, age 61
Chief Executive and Director: Sir Terence P. (Terry) Leahy, age 54, $8,492,940 total compensation
Group Finance Director and Board Member: Laurie McIlwee, age 47, $2,550,577 total compensation
International and IT Director and Board Member: Philip (Phil) Clarke, age 49, $5,045,738 total compensation
Director Commercial and Marketing and Board Member: Richard W. P. Brasher, age 48, $4,717,288 total compensation
Board Member; CEO, Retail Services and Director Group Strategy: Andrew T. Higginson, age 52, $5,404,688 total compensation
Board Member; Director Retail and Logistics: David T. Potts, age 53, $5,058,815 total compensation
Board Member; President and CEO, Fresh & Easy Neighborhood Market: Tim J. R. Mason, age 52, $8,376,033 total compensation
Board Member; Corporate and Legal Affairs Director: Lucy Neville-Rolfe, age 57, $3,150,012 total compensation
Board Member; Company Secretary: Jonathan Lloyd, age 43
CEO, Tesco.com and Tesco Direct: Laura Wade-Gery, age 44
CEO, Tesco Personal Finance Limited (Tesco Bank): Benny Higgins, age 49
CEO, Tesco Mobile and Tesco Telecoms: Lance Batchelor
CEO, Tesco Ireland: Gordon Fryett, age 56
CEO, Central Europe and Turkey: Trevor Masters
Director Investor Relations: Steve Webb, age 49
Auditors: PricewaterhouseCoopers LLP

LOCATIONS

HQ: Tesco PLC
New Tesco House, Delamare Road
Cheshunt, Hertfordshire EN8 9SL, United Kingdom
Phone: 44-1992-632-222
Web: www.tescoplc.com

2010 Sales

	% of total
Europe	
UK	68
Other countries	16
Asia	15
US	1
Total	**100**

2010 Stores

	No.
UK	2,482
Thailand	663
Poland	336
South Korea	305
Hungary	176
US	145
Japan	142
Czech Republic	136
Ireland	119
Turkey	105
China	88
Slovakia	81
Malaysia	32
Total	**4,810**

PRODUCTS/OPERATIONS

Selected Subsidiaries and Joint Ventures

C Two-Network Co. Ltd. (Japan)
Dobbies Garden Centres PLC (Scotland)
Ek-Chai Distribution System Co. Ltd. (99%, Lotus stores, Thailand)
Hymall (90%, China)
Tesco Global Aruhazak (99%, Kaposvar and Tesco stores, Hungary)
One Stop Stores Ltd. (One Stop convenience stores, England and Wales)

Samsung Tesco. Co. Limited (94%, Homeplus stores, South Korea)
Tesco Ireland Limited (Tesco stores)
Tesco Kipa (93%, hypermarkets, Turkey)
Tesco Mobile Ltd. (50%, telecommunications, England)
Tesco Personal Finance Group Limited (50%, credit cards, savings accounts, loans, online banking, insurance)
Tesco Polska Sp. Z o.o. (Czestochowa stores, Poland)
Tesco Stores CR a.s. (Czech Republic)
Tesco Stores SR a.s. (Slovakia)

COMPETITORS

7-Eleven	Matalan
ALDI	METRO AG
Alliance Boots	Musgrave Retail Partners
ASDA	Netto Foodstores
BP	NEXT plc
Carphone Warehouse	Primark
Carrefour	Royal Dutch Shell
Co-operative Group	SPAR Handels
Dunnes Stores	Stater Bros.
Exxon Mobil	T.K. Maxx
First Quench	Virgin Money
The Gap	Vons
Iceland Foods	Waitrose
J Sainsbury	Wal-Mart
John Lewis	Wm Morrison
Lidl	Supermarkets
Marks & Spencer	Wyevale Garden

HISTORICAL FINANCIALS

Company Type: Public

Income Statement

FYE: Last Saturday in February

	REVENUE ($ mil.)	NET INCOME ($ mil.)	NET PROFIT MARGIN	EMPLOYEES
2/10	86,685	3,545	4.1%	472,094
2/09	76,842	3,041	4.0%	468,508
2/08	93,844	4,214	4.5%	444,000
2/07	83,743	3,716	4.4%	413,061
2/06	68,701	2,734	4.0%	237,024
Annual Growth	6.0%	6.7%	—	18.8%

2010 Year-End Financials

Debt ratio: —
Return on equity: 17.4%
Cash ($ mil.): 4,294
Current ratio: —
Long-term debt ($ mil.): —

No. of shares (mil.): 2,662
Dividends
 Yield: 1.9%
 Payout: —
Market value ($ mil.): 77,883

Stock History

Pink Sheets: TSCDY

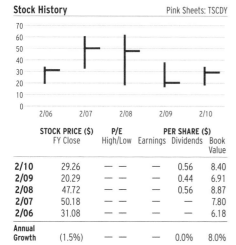

	STOCK PRICE ($) FY Close	P/E High/Low		PER SHARE ($) Earnings	Dividends	Book Value
2/10	29.26	—	—	—	0.56	8.40
2/09	20.29	—	—	—	0.44	6.91
2/08	47.72	—	—	—	0.56	8.87
2/07	50.18	—	—	—	—	7.80
2/06	31.08	—	—	—	—	6.18
Annual Growth	(1.5%)	—	—	—	0.0%	8.0%

Teva Pharmaceuticals

The backbone of Teva Pharmaceutical Industries is its world-leading generic pharmaceuticals business. Through subsidiary Teva Pharmaceuticals USA, the company makes generic versions of hundreds of brand-name antibiotics, heart drugs, heartburn medications, and more. Teva's US generic products include equivalents of such blockbusters as antidepressant Prozac and osteoporosis drug Fosamax. The company, Israel's top drugmaker, also develops and manufactures proprietary drugs, including multiple sclerosis treatment Copaxone, Parkinson's disease treatment Azilect, and a portfolio of women's health treatments. Its active pharmaceutical ingredients division makes drug components for Teva and other manufacturers.

In 2008 Teva acquired US rival generic drugmaker Barr Pharmaceuticals for $7.5 billion. The purchase also helped boost Teva's position in key European countries and gave it a strong position in the branded and generic contraceptive market. The company completed another large-scale acquisition in 2010, when it acquired private German-based generics producer ratiopharm, which markets a full range of therapeutic drugs in over 25 countries around the globe, from the controlling Merckle family for about $5 billion.

Teva had already been working to expand in the European generics market for several years, establishing outposts by acquiring drug manufacturers in Germany, Hungary, the Netherlands, and the UK. To further its generics operations in Spain, Teva acquired Bentley Pharmaceuticals in 2008, while the Barr purchase gave it entry into Russia and Croatia. Additional expansion efforts include a joint venture with Kowa Company in Japan, and investments in Brazil, India, Colombia, and Turkey.

To enhance its position in the targeted growth area of generic biotech drugs, the company acquired US private biotechnology company CoGenesys, a former unit of Human Geonome Sciences, in 2008 for $400 million. In 2009 it moved to increase its biotech portfolio again by forming a joint venture with Swiss active pharmaceutical ingredient firm Lonza to produce generic biosimilars. Lonza is already set up to produce biosimilars, also called follow-on biologics (FOBs). Teva sees an opportunity to get into a high risk, high potential reward part of the industry before the field gets crowded.

Although the company's main money-making business is generics, its branded line, Teva (Hebrew for nature), is continuing to develop other proprietary drugs: Its pipeline includes products for neurological disorders, autoimmune diseases, and oncology, targeting such ailments as Alzheimer's disease, Crohn's disease, and lupus. The firm has developed a line of respiratory products as well. Teva uses its access to Israel's academic community to target potential projects.

In 2009 the company launched about 20 new generic versions of popular drugs including schizophrenia treatment Risperdal and Topamax, a treatment for epilepsy. One of Teva's keys to success is its strategy of filing patent challenges on branded products, thus attempting to gain a "first-to-market" advantage with its generic equivalents. It also achieves its early market strategy by entering marketing alliances with branded pharmaceutical makers, including Savient Pharmaceuticals, Valeant Pharmaceuticals (formerly Biovail), and Impax Laboratories.

HISTORY

Teva traces its origins to Salomon, Levin and Elstein Ltd., a drug distribution firm based in Jerusalem, which, at the time, was a Jewish section of British-controlled Palestine.

Ironically, in the 1930s the company benefited from the emigration of Jewish people, many of whom were scientists, seeking to escape the Nazi regime in Germany, which at the time was the global leader in drug development. The company went public in 1951.

In 1968 Eli Hurvitz was appointed to Teva's board of directors, and scripted much of the company's growth. In 1970 Teva merged with Assia Chemical Laboratories (Hurvitz's old employer) and another company to form Teva Pharmaceutical Industries.

Ten years later Teva sold a 20% stake of itself to Koor Industries in exchange for Koor subsidiary Ikapharm, Teva's closest competitor. (Koor later launched a takeover bid, but the Founders Group, Teva's controlling shareholders, foiled the attempt.)

In 1985 Teva moved into the US. It formed a joint venture with W. R. Grace called TAG Pharmaceuticals (Teva bought out W. R. Grace's portion in 1991). In 1985 TAG bought Lemmon Co. The purchased company was famous — or infamous — for its tranquilizer Quaalude, which had gained notoriety as the recreational drug of choice for many young people. Lemmon, which ceased production of Quaalude prior to Teva's purchase, became the acquirer's generic manufacturing division.

Teva bought Abic, Israel's #2 drugmaker, in a complex 1988 transaction that gave Canadian investor and Seagram's heir Charles Bronfman a stake in the company. British publisher Robert Maxwell also bought a substantial stake in Teva. (Following Maxwell's mysterious death in 1993, his estate sold his stake.)

In the 1990s Teva turned its attention to Europe, buying companies in France, Italy, the UK, and Hungary. In 1996 the company bought US firm Biocraft Laboratories, merging it with Lemmon and forming Teva Pharmaceuticals USA.

That year Copaxone received FDA approval. In 1998 the company reorganized after officials realized that it had to evolve from being a collection of disparate operating entities to a more centralized operation. It also divested several operations — including its Russian joint venture, its yeast and alcohol fermentation business, and some of its German operations — in order to concentrate on pharmaceuticals.

The company has remained acquisitive, acquiring generics firms Copley Pharmaceuticals and Novapharm in 1999 and 2000, respectively, and bought Bayer's French generic operations in 2002.

The company acquired rival generics manufacturer IVAX Corporation in January 2006.

EXECUTIVES

Chairman: Phillip Frost, age 73
Vice Chairman: Prof Moshe Many, age 81
President and CEO: Shlomo Yanai, age 57
CFO: Eyal Desheh, age 57
EVP and Global Head of Quality:
 Frances M. (Fran) Sakers
Chief Research and Development Officer:
 Ben-Zion Weiner, age 65
Group VP Global Generic Resources: Jacob Winter, age 58
Group VP Global Branded Products:
 Prof Yitzhak Peterburg, age 58

Group VP, Teva Generics System: Aharon (Arik) Yaari, age 58
Corporate VP, Chief Legal Officer, and Company Secretary: Richard S. Egosi, age 47
Corporate VP Business Development: Prof Itzhak Krinsky, age 57
Corporate VP Human Resources: Isaac (Ika) Abravanel, age 55
VP Product Portfolio Management: Shosh Neumann, age 53
VP Corporate Communications: Yossi Koren
VP and CTO: Rodney Kasan, age 67
VP Strategic Business Planning and New Ventures: Aharon Schwartz, age 67
VP Global Generic Research and Development: Christopher Pelloni, age 58
VP Global Innovative Research and Development: Irit Pinchasi, age 57
President and CEO, Teva Europe: Gerard W. M. Van Odijk, age 52
President and CEO, Teva North America and President and CEO, Teva USA: William S. (Bill) Marth, age 55
Director Corporate Communications: Ayala Miller
Senior Director Investor Relations: Elana Holzman
Auditors: Kesselman & Kesselman

LOCATIONS

HQ: Teva Pharmaceutical Industries Limited (Teva Ta'asiyot Farmatsevtiyot Be'am)
5 Basel St.
Petah Tikva 49131, Israel
Phone: 972-3-926-7267   **Fax:** 972-3-923-4050
Web: www.tevapharm.com

2009 Sales

	$ mil.	% of total
North America	8,585	62
Europe	3,271	24
Other regions	2,043	14
Total	**13,899**	**100**

PRODUCTS/OPERATIONS

2009 Sales

	% of total
Generic pharmaceuticals	67
Branded pharmaceuticals	19
Active pharmaceutical ingredients	4
Other	10
Total	**100**

2009 Sales by Therapeutic Category

	% of total
Anticancer & autoimmune	22
Central nervous system	16
Cardiovascular	11
Gastrointestinal & metabolism	10
Genito urinary system & sex hormones	10
Respiratory	8
Anti-infectives (including antibiotics)	6
Musculoskeletal	3
Other	14
Total	**100**

Selected Generic Products

Acetaminophen and codeine (Tylenol)
Amoxicillin (Amoxil)
Bromatapp (Dimetapp)
Carbamazepine (Tegretol)
Cephalexin (Keflex)
Cimetidine (Tagamet)
Ciprofloxacin (Cipro)
Clemastine fumarate (Tavist)
Clotrimazole (Lotrimin)
Diclofenac extended release (Voltaren XR)
Diltiazem HCl (Cardizem)
Fluconazole Injection (Diflucan)
Fluoxetine (Prozac)
Ketoconazole cream (Nizoral Cream)
Lovastatin (Mevacor)
Metronidazole (Flagyl)
Sotalol hydrochloride (Betapace)
Sulfamethoxazole and Trimethoprim (Bactrim)
Tizanidine (Zanaflex)
Tramadol hydrochloride (Ultram/Ultracet)

COMPETITORS

Abbott Labs
AstraZeneca
Bayer HealthCare Pharmaceuticals
Biogen Idec
Bio-Rad Labs
Boehringer Ingelheim
Bristol-Myers Squibb
Dr. Reddy's
Forest Labs
GlaxoSmithKline
Johnson & Johnson
King Pharmaceuticals
Merck
Mylan
Novartis
Perrigo
Pfizer
Ranbaxy Laboratories
Sandoz International GmbH
Sanofi-Aventis
Taro
Watson Pharmaceuticals
Wockhardt

HISTORICAL FINANCIALS

Company Type: Public

Income Statement

FYE: December 31

	REVENUE ($ mil.)	NET INCOME ($ mil.)	NET PROFIT MARGIN	EMPLOYEES
12/09	13,899	2,000	14.4%	35,089
12/08	11,085	635	5.7%	38,307
12/07	9,408	1,952	20.7%	27,912
12/06	8,408	546	6.5%	26,700
12/05	5,250	1,072	20.4%	14,700
Annual Growth	**27.6%**	**16.9%**	**—**	**24.3%**

2009 Year-End Financials

Debt ratio: 22.4%
Return on equity: 11.3%
Cash ($ mil.): 1,995
Current ratio: 1.60
Long-term debt ($ mil.): 4,311

No. of shares (mil.): 936
Dividends
Yield: 0.9%
Payout: 21.5%
Market value ($ mil.): 52,584

Stock History

NASDAQ (GS): TEVA

	STOCK PRICE ($) FY Close	P/E High/Low		PER SHARE ($) Earnings	Dividends	Book Value
12/09	56.18	25	18	2.23	0.48	20.54
12/08	42.57	64	46	0.78	0.41	17.41
12/07	46.48	20	14	2.38	0.33	14.66
12/06	31.08	65	42	0.69	0.25	11.90
12/05	43.01	29	17	1.59	0.22	6.46
Annual Growth	**6.9%**	**—**	**—**	**8.8%**	**21.5%**	**33.6%**

Thomson Reuters

Financial information is king and Thomson Reuters Corporation holds the crown. The financial data powerhouse was created as the result of the $16 billion cash and stock purchase of news service Reuters by niche information provider The Thomson Corporation. The combined entity is the leader in financial data, with approximately 34% of the market share. (Information service Bloomberg is a close second with 33% of the market.) Thomson Reuters provides electronic information and services to businesses and professionals worldwide, serving the legal, financial services, tax and accounting, health care and science, and media markets.

The acquisition of Reuters in 2008 significantly expanded the geographic reach of the business, with the former Thomson having earned most of its revenue from the US, while the majority of Reuters' revenue came from Europe. Tom Glocer, former CEO of Reuters, was named head of Thomson Reuters and has been overseeing the integration. His first order in the consolidation was to cut some 1,500 jobs.

Thomson Reuters is organized into two units, the Markets division and the Professional division. The company's Markets division consists of Sales & Trading, Investment & Advisory, Enterprise, and Media businesses, and includes established brands and products such as Reuters, Omgeo, Lipper, Tradeweb, First Call, Datastream, and Thomson ONE. The company's Professional division includes non-financial business segments devoted to Legal, Tax & Accounting, and Healthcare & Science. Professional operations include Thomson Reuters, Legal; Elite (business management software); Thomson Scientific (technical information and applications); Thomson Tax & Accounting (tax and accounting information, software, and services); and Baker Robbins & Company (technology consulting).

As part of an effort to expand its content offerings, the company acquired some 30 companies in 2009. Within the Markets division, it bolstered its editorial operations with the purchase of Breakingviews, a financial commentary website managed by Reuters. It also acquired Hugin Group, a provider of regulatory and news distribution services, from NYSE Euronext.

In 2010 it expanded the Legal division with the acquisition of Round Table Group, a provider of expert witness consulting services to litigators, and Complinet, a provider of compliance information solutions. Also that year Thomson Reuters acquired Discovery Logic, a provider of customizable analytics solutions for scientific research.

After the combination of Thomson and Reuters, the Thomson family, through its Woodbridge investment firm, took a 53% economic and voting interest in Thomson Reuters. Former Reuters shareholders have a 24% stake in the company, while former Thomson shareholders own 23%.

The company was previously owned through a complex dual listing, and had additionally traded on the London Stock Exchange and Nasdaq through the Thomson Reuters PLC entity. In 2009 it unified its ownership structure in order to simplify trading. As a result, the company ceased to be listed on the London Stock Exchange and Nasdaq.

HISTORY

The Thomson Corporation was established when Roy Thomson started a radio station in Ontario in 1930. He next began purchasing town newspapers, venturing outside Ontario in 1949 and into the US in 1952.

The Thomson newspaper empire grew rapidly, and the company next entered into a North Sea oil drilling venture. Oil accounted for the bulk of Thomson's profits by 1976, when Thomson died, and the company used its oil earnings to expand and diversify its publishing interests.

Purchases included American Banker and Bond Buyer (financial publications, 1983), Gale Research (library reference materials, 1985), and several online information providers. Thomson then completed the sale of its oil and gas holdings. In 1991 it bought Maxwell's Macmillan Professional and Business Reference Publishing. It bought law and textbook publisher West Publishing in 1996. Continuing its selective divestment of newspapers, the company sold 43 daily papers in the US and Canada in 1996. In 2000 Thomson announced it would sell its newspapers to focus on the Internet.

Other Thomson purchases included a pair of tax and law publishing units from UK's Pearson; Knight-Ridder's Technimetrics financial information unit; Sylvan Learning Systems' Prometric division, which provided computer-based testing services; and Wave Technologies International, a provider of multimedia instructional products. Thomson also bought the online data services division of Dialog, and it acquired rival financial data provider Primark for $1 billion. In 2001 the company bought the higher education and corporate training businesses of Harcourt General (which later became Harcourt Education) from Reed Elsevier Group plc (formerly Reed Elsevier plc), and acquired business content provider NewsEdge.

Thomson started trading on the New York Stock Exchange in mid-2002. Later that year it beefed up its Internet education group with the purchase of certain e-learning assets from McGraw Hill. In 2003 the company purchased Elite Information Group, a maker of law firm practice software, for more than $100 million. (The software firm later dropped the "Information Group" portion of its name to become simply Elite.)

In 2006 Thomson purchased Solucient LLC, a provider of data and advanced analytics to hospitals and health systems; Quantitative Analytics, Inc., a provider of financial database integration and analysis solutions; and LiveNote Technologies, a provider of transcript and evidence management software to litigators and court reporters. Kenneth Thomson died at the age of 82 that year.

The following year Thomson exited the educational information market when it sold Thomson Learning to investment groups Apax Partners and OMERS Capital for $7.7 billion. Thomson cited a lack of growth potential as its primary rationale for selling Thomson Learning (now called Cengage Learning). It used the proceeds of the sale to help acquire Reuters in 2008 in a $16.2 billion deal that created the largest player in the field of financial data.

Later in 2008 Thomson Reuters sold Dialog to ProQuest Information and Learning. At the end of the year it acquired financial software firm Paisley. In 2009 it unified its dual-listed ownership structure in order to simplify trading.

EXECUTIVES

Chairman: David K. R. Thomson, age 52
Deputy Chairman: W. Geoffrey (Geoff) Beattie, age 50
Deputy Chairman: Niall FitzGerald, age 65
CEO and Director: Thomas H. (Tom) Glocer, age 50
EVP and CFO: Robert D. (Bob) Daleo, age 60
EVP and CTO: James Powell
EVP and Global Chief Marketing Officer: Gustav Carlson
EVP and Chief Human Resources Officer: Stephen G. Dando, age 48
EVP and General Counsel: Deirdre Stanley, age 45
EVP: Jonathan S. Newpol
Chief Medical Officer: Raymond J. (Ray) Fabius, age 56
Global Head Business Operations: Alisa Bowen, age 37
SVP Investor Relations: Frank J. Golden
SVP and CIO: Kelli Crane
CEO, Markets Division: Devin N. Wenig, age 43
CEO, Reuters Foundation: Monique Villa
CEO, Professional Division: James C. (Jim) Smith
CEO, Scientific: Vin Caraher
CEO, Tax and Accounting: Roy M. Martin Jr.
CEO, Healthcare and Science: Mike Boswood
CEO, Legal: Peter Warwick
Auditors: PricewaterhouseCoopers LLP

LOCATIONS

HQ: Thomson Reuters Corporation
3 Times Square, New York, NY 10036
Phone: 646-223-4000
Web: www.thomsonreuters.com

2009 Sales

	$ mil.	% of total
Americas	7,699	59
Europe, Middle East & Africa	3,948	30
Asia/Pacific	1,350	11
Total	**12,997**	**100**

PRODUCTS/OPERATIONS

2009 Sales

	$ mil.	% of total
Markets	7,535	58
Professional		
Legal	3586	28
Tax & Accounting	1006	8
Healthcare & Science	878	6
Adjustments	(8)	—
Total	**12,997**	**100**

Selected Offerings

Markets
Reuters (business newswire service)
Thomson Financial (content, analytical applications, and transaction platforms to financial professionals)
Thomson ONE (flagship financial product)
Professional
Legal
West (legal, regulatory, and compliance information)
FindLaw (legal directory)
Elite (law firm management software)
Tax and Accounting
Thomson Tax & Accounting (tax and accounting information, software, and services)
Healthcare and Science
Baker Robbins & Company (technology consulting)
PDR (Physicians Desk Reference)
Solucient (databases and analytics)
Thomson Scientific (technical information and applications)

COMPETITORS

Agence France-Presse	MarketWatch
Associated Press	Pearson plc
Bloomberg L.P.	Reed Elsevier Group
D&B	Track Data
Dow Jones	United Business Media
FactSet	UPI
Forbes	Wolters Kluwer
IHS	

HISTORICAL FINANCIALS

Company Type: Public

Income Statement

FYE: December 31

	REVENUE ($ mil.)	NET INCOME ($ mil.)	NET PROFIT MARGIN	EMPLOYEES
12/09	12,997	867	6.7%	55,000
12/08	11,707	1,405	12.0%	53,700
12/07	7,296	4,004	54.9%	40,000
12/06	6,641	1,120	16.9%	32,375
12/05	8,703	934	10.7%	40,500
Annual Growth	**10.5%**	**(1.8%)**	**—**	**8.0%**

2009 Year-End Financials

Debt ratio: 35.4%
Return on equity: —
Cash ($ mil.): 1,111
Current ratio: 0.78
Long-term debt ($ mil.): 6,821
No. of shares (mil.): 832
Dividends
  Yield: 3.5%
  Payout: 110.9%
Market value ($ mil.): 26,841

Stock History

NYSE: TRI

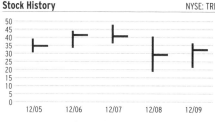

	STOCK PRICE ($) FY Close	P/E High/Low		PER SHARE ($) Earnings	Dividends	Book Value
12/09	32.25	36	22	1.01	1.12	23.15
12/08	29.15	22	11	1.81	1.08	24.18
12/07	40.75	8	6	6.20	0.98	16.31
12/06	41.44	25	20	1.73	0.88	12.59
12/05	34.60	27	22	1.42	0.79	11.97
Annual Growth	**(1.7%)**	**—**	**—**	**(8.2%)**	**9.1%**	**17.9%**

ThyssenKrupp

How do you say "giant engineering and steel company" in German? Try ThyssenKrupp and pronounce it "TISS-in." The company is one of the world's largest steel producers and operates worldwide in two business areas: Materials and Technologies. The first is composed of the company's steel (carbon and stainless steel) and materials services businesses. ThyssenKrupp's Technologies sector consists of its elevators unit and the marine systems, components technology (for the auto and engineering markets), and plant technology (construction and environmental services) segments. Although its combined interests range from elevators to shipbuilding, the company has historically relied on the cyclical steel market.

Amid the global economic crisis, the company began to implement a reorganization of its business structure in 2009, bringing its operations together within the Materials and Technologies divisions and then further dividing them into eight business segments. Its subsidiary holding companies — that is, ThyssenKrupp Elevator, ThyssenKrupp Steel, and so forth — will be absorbed into the parent company, and ThyssenKrupp will become a more centralized entity.

As part of the restructuring process, Thyssen-Krupp divested its scaffolding unit (Safway Services) and industrial services subsidiary (ThyssenKrupp Industrieservice). The businesses together had sales of about €800 million ($1.2 million US). The hope with all of the restructuring is to provide ThyssenKrupp with better balance so that it won't have to rely so heavily on that cyclical steel market.

In 2010 ThyssenKrupp sold its Hamburg-based mega-yacht and shipbuilding operations to Abu Dhabi MAR Group. ThyssenKrupp is exiting the civil shipbuilding business to focus on constructing military vessels. ThyssenKrupp also sold its interest in Hellenic Shipyards to Abu Dhabi MAR, following problems related to the Greek government's financial problems.

The company is constructing a steel-slab facility in Brazil in partnership with Vale, which will be the sole supplier of iron ore to the plant. Vale increased its ownership in the subsidiary running the plant from 10% to just more than 25% with a €965 ($1.4 billion US) investment in mid-2009. The facility is expected to start production in 2010.

ThyssenKrupp is a product of the 1999 merger of Thyssen AG and Fried. Krupp AG Hoesch-Krupp. The Krupp Foundation owns 25% of the company.

HISTORY

Formed separately in the 1800s, both Thyssen and Krupp flourished in their early years under family control. Friedrich Krupp opened his steel factory in 1811. He died in 1826 and left the nearly bankrupt factory in the hands of his 14-year-old son Alfred, who turned the business around. At the first World's Fair in 1851, Alfred unveiled a steel cannon far superior to earlier bronze models. Twenty years later August Thyssen founded a puddling and rolling mill near Mulheim. He bought small factories and mines, and by WWI he ran Germany's largest iron and steel company. During the world wars the resources of both companies were turned toward military efforts.

Post-WWII years were tough for both companies. Thyssen was split up by the Allies, and when it began production again in 1953, it consisted of one steel plant. In the Krupp camp, Alfred's great-grandson Alfried was convicted in 1948 of using slave labor during WWII. Released from prison in 1951, Alfried rebuilt Krupp. After near ruin following WWII, both companies emerged and enjoyed a resurgence, along with the German economy, in which they prospered and expanded during the 1950s.

By the 1980s Thyssen's businesses included ships, locomotives, offshore oil rigs, specialty steel, and metals trading and distribution. Krupp continued to grow, and in 1992 it took over engineering and steelmaking concern Hoesch AG. (Eberhard Hoesch had begun making railroad tracks in the 1820s. The company grew and expanded into infrastructure and building products.)

The new Fried. Krupp AG Hoesch-Krupp bought Italian specialty steelmaker Acciai Speciali Terni, chemical-plant builder Uhde, and South African shipper J.H. Bachmann. Its automotive division formed a joint venture in Brazil and added production sites in China, Mexico, Romania, and the US. In 1997 Thyssen expanded in North America with its $675 million acquisition of Giddings & Lewis (machine tools, US) and the

purchase of Copper & Brass Sales (metals processing and distributing).

Krupp attempted a hostile takeover of Thyssen in 1997. The takeover failed, but the companies soon agreed to merge their steel operations to form Thyssen Krupp Stahl. Bigger plans were in the works, and in 1998 the two companies agreed to merge. That year Thyssen sold its Plusnet fixed-line phone business to Esprit Telecom Group.

In 1999 Krupp's automotive division (Krupp Hoesch Automotive) bought Cummins' Atlas Crankshaft subsidiary. Thyssen also bought US-based Dover's elevator business for $1.1 billion. Krupp and Thyssen completed their merger in 1999. The company planned to spin off its steel operations, but held off due to its success in 2000. To speed corporate decision-making, the company made plans to scrap its dual-management structure in 2001.

Early in 2001 ThyssenKrupp agreed to buy 51% of Fiat unit Magneti Marelli's suspension-systems and shock-absorbers business. It also had the option of buying the remainder after 2004. In 2002 the company formed alliances with NKK and Kawasaki Steel to share its steel sheet making technologies while expanding its business with Japanese automotive makers in Europe. ThyssenKrupp's joint venture with Chinese steelmaker ANSC Angang New Steel, known as TAGAL, began producing galvanized coil of which about 80% will be used in China's burgeoning automotive industry.

In 2004 ThyssenKrupp sold its residential real estate unit for around $2.8 billion to a consortium of real estate funds operated by Morgan Stanley and Corpus-Immobiliengruppe. It divested the automotive segment of the capital goods unit in 2006, selling it off in pieces.

EXECUTIVES

Chairman Emeritus: Berthold Beitz, age 66
Chairman: Gerhard Cromme, age 66
Chairman, Executive Board: Ekkehard D. Schulz, age 69
Vice Chairman, Executive Board: Heinrich Hiesinger, age 50
Member Executive Board, Controlling, Accounting, and Financial Reporting, Corporate Finance, Investor Relations, Mergers and Acquisitions, Taxes and Customs, Materials Management, and Business Services: Alan Hippe, age 43
Member Executive Board, Technologies; CEO, Elevator Technology: Olaf Berlien, age 47
Member Executive Board, Materials; CEO, Steel Europe and Steel Americas: Edwin Eichler, age 52
Member Executive Board, Human Resources Information Management: Ralph Labonte, age 56
Corporate Center Communications, Strategy and Technology: Stefan Ettwig
Head Investor Relations: Claus Ehrenbeck
Auditors: KPMG Deutsche Treuhand-Gesellschaft AG

LOCATIONS

HQ: ThyssenKrupp AG
August-Thyssen-Strasse 1
40211 Düsseldorf, Germany
Phone: 49-211-824-0   **Fax:** 49-211-824-360-00
US HQ: 3155 W. Big Beaver Rd., Troy, MI 48007
US Phone: 248-643-3929   **US Fax:** 248-643-3518
Web: www.thyssenkrupp.com

2009 Sales

	% of total
European Union	62
Americas	20
Asia/Pacific	10
Other regions	8
Total	**100**

PRODUCTS/OPERATIONS

2009 Sales

	% of total
Services	28
Technologies	25
Steel	24
Elevator	13
Stainless	10
Total	**100**

COMPETITORS

Acerinox	Magna International
ArcelorMittal	MAN
Bechtel	Marubeni
Corus Group	Nippon Steel
Descours & Cabaud	POSCO
GEA Group	Qingdao Iron and Steel
Ingersoll-Rand	Schindler Holding
ITOCHU	Sumitomo Metal Industries
JFE Holdings	United States Steel
Kobe Steel	United Technologies

HISTORICAL FINANCIALS

Company Type: Public

Income Statement

FYE: September 30

	REVENUE ($ mil.)	NET INCOME ($ mil.)	NET PROFIT MARGIN	EMPLOYEES
9/09	59,181	(2,733)	—	187,495
9/08	77,174	3,288	4.3%	199,374
9/07	73,853	3,001	—	191,350
9/06	59,783	2,162	3.6%	187,586
9/05	50,658	1,232	2.4%	185,932
Annual Growth	**4.0%**	—	—	**0.2%**

*Fiscal year change

2009 Year-End Financials

Debt ratio: —
Return on equity: —
Cash ($ mil.): 3,976
Current ratio: 1.27
Long-term debt ($ mil.): —

No. of shares (mil.): 464
Dividends
 Yield: 11.0%
 Payout: —
Market value ($ mil.): 15,943

Stock History

German: TKA

	STOCK PRICE ($) FY Close	P/E High/Low		PER SHARE ($) Earnings	Dividends	Book Value
9/09	34.33	—	—	(5.85)	3.79	36.10
9/08	30.38	10	4	6.63	—	34.24
9/07	91.41	—	—	—	—	32.18
9/06	33.71	9	5	4.11	—	23.26
9/05	20.92	9	7	2.47	—	22.75
Annual Growth	**0.5%**	—	—	—	—	**11.6%**

Tokio Marine

Thoroughly modern Tokio Marine Holdings might have old roots, but it still knows how to learn new tricks. Japan's oldest property/casualty insurance company, the firm has one of the largest insurance sales networks in Japan and has expanded its insurance operations to about 40 additional countries in Asia, Europe, and North America. Through Tokio Marine & Nichido Fire (TMNF), Nisshin Fire, Philadelphia Insurance Companies, Kiln, and other subsidiaries, Tokio Marine Holdings provides marine, property/casualty, personal accident, fire, auto, and life insurance as well as reinsurance. It also offers asset management, pension plans, and other services.

Acquisitions and ventures overseas have been a main part of the company's strategy for growth as it aspires to become a top player in the global insurance industry. Tokio Marine is especially seeking growth in the European and North American markets. Its TMNF subsidiary acquired UK firm Kiln, a top Lloyd's of London property/casualty insurer, and its subsidiaries in 2008 for about $900 million.

To expand its niche property/casualty offerings in the US, the company spent $4.7 billion to acquire Philadelphia Insurance Companies (then named Philadelphia Consolidated Holding) later that year. Philadelphia Insurance Companies specializes in non-standard and specialty property/casualty and professional liability insurance. Previous acquisitions expanded Tokio Marine's operations in Singapore, Malaysia, and the domestic Japanese market.

Tokio Marine partnered with Alinma Bank in 2010 to establish an insurance firm in Saudi Arabia, a largely untapped market for the company. The two companies will hold equal stakes in the new company, which will sell life and nonlife insurance products as well as "takaful," a type of insurance tailored to conform with Islamic law. Other potential countries targeted for growth efforts include China and India.

The company changed its name from Millea Holdings to Tokio Marine Holdings in 2008. The move aimed to align the company's operations with the main insurance subsidiary, Tokio Marine & Nichido Samuel, which was created through the merger of Tokio Marine and Fire (Japan's oldest insurer founded in 1879) and Nichido Fire and Marine in 2002.

HISTORY

After the US forced Japan to open to trade in 1854, Western marine insurers began operating there. In 1878 Japan's government organized backers for a Japanese marine insurance firm. Tokio Marine and Fire Insurance was founded the next year.

Tokio grew quickly, insuring trading companies like Mitsubishi and Mitsui; it soon had offices in London, Paris, and New York. Increased competition in the 1890s forced it to curtail its foreign operations and begin using brokers in most other countries.

Victory in the Russo-Japanese War of 1904-05 buoyed the country, but the economy slowed as it demobilized. Businesses responded by forming cooperative groups known as *zaibatsu*. Tokio Marine and Fire was allied with the Mitsubishi group.

Before WWI, Tokio expanded by adding fire, personal accident, theft, and auto insurance, and it continued to buy foreign sales brokers. Japan's insurance industry consolidated in the 1920s, and the company bought up smaller competitors. The 1923 Tokyo earthquake hit the industry hard, but Tokio's new fire insurance operations had little exposure.

Most of Tokio's foreign operations were seized during WWII. In 1944 Tokio merged with Mitsubishi Marine Insurance and Meiji Fire Insurance. Business grew in WWII, but wartime destruction left Tokio with nothing to insure and no money to pay claims.

After the war Tokio slowly recovered and resumed overseas operations. Although the US had dismantled the *zaibatsu* during occupation, Tokio allied once again with Mitsubishi when Japan's government rebuilt most of the old groups as *keiretsu*.

During the 1950s and 1960s, the company grew its personal lines, adding homeowners coverage. Domestic business slowed during the 1970s and 1980s, and Tokio boosted operations overseas. It added commercial property/casualty insurer Houston General Insurance (a US company sold in 1997), Tokio Reinsurance, and interests in insurance and investment management firms.

In the 1980s the firm invested heavily in real estate through *jusen* (mortgage companies). Japan's overheated real estate market collapsed in the early 1990s, dumping masses of nonperforming assets on *jusen* and their investors (the country's major banks and insurers, including Tokio).

Deregulation began in 1996, and economic recession soon followed. In 1998 Tokio joined other members of the Mitsubishi group, including Bank of Tokyo-Mitsubishi and Meiji Life Insurance, to form investment banking, pension, and trust joint ventures. The firm also formed its own investment trust and allied with such foreign financial companies as BANK ONE and United Asset Management to develop new investment products. Brokerage firm Charles Schwab Tokio Marine Securities, a joint venture, was launched in 1999. That year Tokio consolidated its foreign reinsurance operations into Tokio Marine Global Re in Dublin, Ireland, and kicked off a business push that included reorganizing its agent force and planning for online sales.

Millea Holdings was created in 2002 as the holding company for the merger between Tokio Marine and Fire and Nichido Fire and Marine. The two were combined and renamed Tokio Marine & Nichido Fire Insurance, a subsidiary of Millea Holdings.

The company's 2005 acquisition of Real Seguros allowed the company to bring its life insurance products to Brazil (renamed Tokio Marine Seguradora). In 2006 Millea acquired Nisshin Fire and Marine Insurance Company as a separately operated subsidiary. In 2007 the firm purchased Asia General Holdings and its life insurance subsidiaries, which operated in Singapore and Malaysia. It also purchased Japanese fire insurance provider Nihon Kousei Kyousaikai.

In 2008 Millea Holdings changed its name to Tokio Marine Holdings to reflect the positive brand recognition associated with the Tokio Marine name.

EXECUTIVES

Chairman: Kunio Ishihara, age 67
President and Board Member: Shuzo Sumi
Board Member; President, Nisshin Fire:
 Hiroshi Miyajima, age 60
EVP and Board Member: Toshiro Yagi
EVP and Board Member: Daisaku Honda, age 61
Senior Managing Director: Shin-Ichiro Okada
Senior Managing Director: Hiroshi Amemiya, age 60
Managing Director: Hiroshi Endo
Auditors: ChuoAoyama PricewaterhouseCoopers

LOCATIONS

HQ: Tokio Marine Holdings, Inc.
   (Tokyo Kaijo Horudingusu Kabushiki Kaisha)
   Tokio Marine Nichido Building Shinkan, 1-2-1
   Marunouchi, Chiyoda-ku
   Tokyo 100-0005, Japan
Phone: 81-3-6212-3333
Web: www.tokiomarinehd.com/en

2010 Sales

	% of total
Japan	85
Americas	9
Other regions	6
Total	**100**

PRODUCTS/OPERATIONS

2010 Sales

	% of total
Property/casualty	76
Life	23
Other	1
Total	**100**

COMPETITORS

AIG	Hiscox
Allianz	ING
Aviva	Markel
Brit Insurance	MS&AD Holdings
Chubb Corp	Nippon Life Insurance
Daido Life	NKSJ Holdings
Dai-ichi Mutual Life	Prudential plc
Equity Insurance	Sumitomo Life
Fuji Fire and Marine	Travelers Companies
HCC Insurance	Zurich Financial Services

HISTORICAL FINANCIALS

Company Type: Public

Income Statement

FYE: March 31

	ASSETS ($ mil.)	NET INCOME ($ mil.)	INCOME AS % OF ASSETS	EMPLOYEES
3/10	186,264	1,385	0.7%	29,578
3/09	156,726	238	0.2%	28,063
3/08	174,060	1,095	0.6%	24,959
3/07	146,154	789	0.5%	23,280
3/06	131,980	1,335	1.0%	19,761
Annual Growth	**9.0%**	**0.9%**	**—**	**10.6%**

2010 Year-End Financials

Equity as % of assets: —
Return on assets: 0.8%
Return on equity: —

Long-term debt ($ mil.): —
Sales ($ mil.): 38,522

Net Income History

Tokyo: 8766

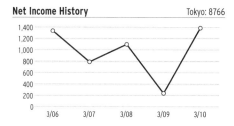

Tokyo Electric

Japan Inc. would grind to a halt without Tokyo Electric Power Company (TEPCO), which supplies power to a population of 44 million customers in Tokyo, Yokohama, and the rest of the Kanto region. One of the world's largest electric utilities, TEPCO's 190 power plants have the generating capacity of approximately 64,000 MW, primarily produced by thermal, nuclear, and hydroelectric power sources. Through interests in telecom businesses, the company offers telephony and Internet services; it also has international consulting and power generation operations. Other businesses include construction, real estate, and transportation companies. It also invests in independent power producers in other countries.

Although public confidence has been shaken by a rash of accidents within Japan's nuclear industry, the company promotes the use of nuclear power as an Earth-friendly energy source. However, the company has struggled to restore its credibility after the Japanese government shut down TEPCO's 17 nuclear reactors due to safety concerns, prompted by the company's admittance of falsifying safety data to cover up faults at several of its nuclear facilities in 2002. In 2009 it reopened the Kashiwazaki-Kariwa Nuclear Power Station, which was closed in 2007 due to a major earthquake in the region.

TEPCO has diversified its operations in the face of deregulation. The company's liberalization of the retail electric power market has resulted in about 60% of TEPCO's revenues coming from retail sales. The company also owns a majority stake in telecommunications firm POWEREDCOM, which offers data communications services through TEPCO and other Japanese utilities' fiber-optic networks. POWEREDCOM has absorbed local and long-distance phone company Tokyo Telecommunication Network (TTNet).

The company is also developing new green energy sources, such as wind and solar. In 2009 the company agreed to build a major solar project in Kawasaki City, Kanagawa, to serve about 5,900 households. In 2010 it teamed up with Toyota Tsusho to fund wind power company Eurus Energy Holdings.

HISTORY

The Tokyo Electric Power Company (TEPCO) descended from Tokyo Electric Light, which was formed in 1883. In 1887 the company switched on Japan's first power plant, a 25-KW fossil fuel generator. Fossil fuels were the main source of electricity in Japan until 1912, when long-distance transmission techniques became more efficient, making hydroelectric power cheaper.

In 1938 Japan nationalized electric utilities, despite strong objections from Yasuzaemon Matsunaga, a leader in Japan's utility industry and former president of the Japan Electric Association. After WWII Matsunaga championed public ownership of Japan's power companies, which helped in 1951 to establish the current system of 10 regional companies, each with a service monopoly. Tokyo Electric Power was the largest. That year it was listed on the Tokyo Stock Exchange and was regulated by the Ministry of International Trade and Industry. (The ministry has regulated electric utilities since 1965.)

Fossil fuel plants made a comeback in Japan in the postwar era because they could be built more economically than hydroelectric plants. When the OPEC oil embargo of the 1970s demonstrated Japan's dependence on foreign oil, TEPCO increased its use of liquefied natural gas (LNG) and nuclear energy sources. (It brought its first nuke online in 1971.) In 1977 it formed the Energy Conservation Center to promote conservation and related legislation.

To further reduce its oil dependence TEPCO joined other US and Japanese firms in building a coal gasification plant in California's Mojave Desert in 1982. Two years later TEPCO announced it would begin building its first coal-burning generator since the oil crisis. It established Tokyo Telecommunication Network (TTNet), a partnership to provide telecommunications services, in 1986 and TEPCO Cable TV in 1989.

As part of its interest in alternative energy systems, TEPCO established a global environment department in 1990 to conduct R&D on energy and the environment. Its environmental program has included reforestation and fuel cell research.

Liberalization in 1995 allowed Japan's electric utilities to buy power from independent power producers; TEPCO quickly lined up 10 suppliers. The company proceeded with energy experimentation in 1996, trying a 6,000-KW sodium-sulfur battery at a Yokohama transformer station. The next year the company announced that it would become the first electric utility to sell liquefied natural gas as part of its energy mix, and finished building the world's largest nuclear plant.

To gain experience in deregulating markets, TEPCO invested in US power generating company Orion Power in 1999. (It agreed to sell its 5% stake to Reliant Energy in 2001.) At home the firm joined Microsoft and SOFTBANK to form SpeedNet, which provides Internet access over TTNet's network. In 2000 TEPCO got its first taste of deregulation when large customers (accounting for about a third of the market) began choosing their electricity suppliers. Also in 2000 TEPCO joined a group of nine Japanese electric companies to create POWEREDCOM.

In 2001 TEPCO joined up with Sumitomo and Electricité de France to build Vietnam's first independent power plant.

To raise cash, in 2006 Mirant sold its power plants in the Philippines to TEPCO and Marubeni for $3.4 billion.

EXECUTIVES

Chairman: Tsunehisa Katsumata
President and Director: Masataka Shimizu
EVP and Director; General Manager, Nuclear Power Plant Siting Division: Ichiro Takekuro
EVP and Director; General Manager, Power Network Division: Takashi Fujimoto
EVP, General Manager, Marketing and Sales, and Director: Shigeru Kimura
EVP, General Manager, Engineering Research and Development, and Director: Hiroyuki Ino
EVP and Director; Deputy General Manager, Nuclear Power Plant Siting Division: Norio Tsuzumi
EVP and Director: Susumu Shirakawa
Managing Director and Deputy General Manager, Power Network Division: Hiroshi Yamaguchi
Managing Director and General Manager, Business Development Division: Makio Fujiwara
Managing Director; Deputy General Manager, Nuclear Power Plant Siting Division: Sakae Muto
Auditors: Ernst & Young ShinNihon

LOCATIONS

HQ: Tokyo Electric Power Company
(Tokyo Denryoku Kabushiki Kaisha)
1-1-3 Uchisaiwai-cho, Chiyoda-ku
Tokyo 100-8560, Japan
Phone: 81-3-4216-1111   **Fax:** 81-3-4216-2539
US HQ: 1901 L St. NW, Ste. 720, Washington, DC 20036
US Phone: 202-457-0790   **US Fax:** 202-457-0810
Web: www.tepco.co.jp

PRODUCTS/OPERATIONS

2010 Sales

	% of total
Electricity	89
Energy & environment	7
Living environment & lifestyle-related	2
Information & telecommunications	2
Total	**100**

Selected Subsidiaries

TEPCO CABLE TELEVISION Inc. (85%, cable television)
TEPCO SYSTEMS CORPORATION (information software and services)
Toden Kogyo Co., Ltd. (facilities construction and maintenance)
Toden Real Estate Co., Inc. (property management)
Tokyo Densetsu Service Co., Ltd. (facilities construction and maintenance)
Tokyo Electric Power Environmental Engineering Company, Incorporated (facilities construction and maintenance)
Tokyo Electric Power Services Company, Limited (facilities construction and maintenance)

COMPETITORS

Chubu Electric Power
Chugoku Electric Power
Hokkaido Electric Power
Hokuriku Electric Power
Internet Initiative Japan
Jinpan International
Kansai Electric
KDDI
Korea Electric Power
Kyushu Electric Power
NTT
Osaka Gas
Shikoku Electric
Tohoku Electric Power
Tokyo Gas

HISTORICAL FINANCIALS

Company Type: Public

Income Statement

FYE: March 31

	REVENUE ($ mil.)	NET INCOME ($ mil.)	NET PROFIT MARGIN	EMPLOYEES
3/10	54,115	1,328	2.5%	52,452
3/09	60,518	(869)	—	5,126
3/08	55,183	(1,512)	—	52,319
3/07	44,821	2,530	5.6%	52,584
3/06	41,632	2,640	6.3%	51,560
Annual Growth	6.8%	(15.8%)	—	0.4%

2010 Year-End Financials

Debt ratio: —
Return on equity: 5.2%
Cash ($ mil.): 1,944
Current ratio: 0.51
Long-term debt ($ mil.): —
No. of shares (mil.): 1,349
Dividends
  Yield: 2.3%
  Payout: 57.0%
Market value ($ mil.): 36,264

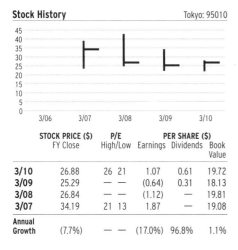

	STOCK PRICE ($) FY Close	P/E High/Low		PER SHARE ($) Earnings	Dividends	Book Value
3/10	26.88	26	21	1.07	0.61	19.72
3/09	25.29	—	—	(0.64)	0.31	18.13
3/08	26.84	—	—	(1.12)	—	19.81
3/07	34.19	21	13	1.87	—	19.08
Annual Growth	(7.7%)	—	—	(17.0%)	96.8%	1.1%

Tokyo Electron

Tokyo Electron Limited (TEL) is the one of the world's largest manufacturers of semiconductor production equipment. TEL's chip-making systems include chemical vapor deposition, thermal processing, etching, cleaning, and probing equipment. The company also makes flat-panel display (FPD) production equipment, and distributes other companies' chip-making equipment, computer systems, networking products, and software in Japan. Subsidiary Tokyo Electron Device distributes chips, boards, and software made by companies including AMD, Microsoft, and Texas Instruments. Chip production equipment accounts for about three-quarters of TEL's sales, and customers outside Japan account for about 60% of total sales.

The global recession is driving down sales of digital home appliances, mobile phones, and PCs, creating a downturn in the semiconductor industry, which is severely impacting suppliers of semiconductor equipment. TEL postponed construction of a new plant it planned to build in Miyagi prefecture, waiting for market conditions to improve before restarting the project.

TEL expanded its cooperative development relationship with ASML Holding, the world's largest vendor of microlithography equipment. The companies, which don't compete with each other, cooperatively evaluated their complementary products, and stepped up a program that puts their most advanced equipment at each other's disposal.

Looking to unlock the potential of the Asian solar market, TEL turned to OC Oerlikon, a maker of thin-film silicon photovoltaic (PV) production equipment. The global suppliers sealed a strategic cooperation agreement that joins the Swiss company's PV technology with the Japanese sales and customer support network, and semiconductor know-how.

HISTORY

Frustrated by the unreliable semiconductor production equipment their employer, Nissho Trading Co. (now Sojitz), was importing from the US, Tokuo Kubo and Toshio Kodada quit their jobs at Nissho in 1963 and founded Tokyo Electron Laboratories (TEL). Tokyo Broadcasting System provided some initial backing.

At first about half of the company's sales came from importing US semiconductor equipment. The other half came from exporting Japanese electronics, such as car radios. In 1968 TEL and US-based diffusion furnace maker Thermco Systems (later acquired by Allegheny International) formed TEL-Thermco Engineering Co. TEL followed with other joint ventures, paying royalties to manufacture other companies' products in Japan.

The company's US unit, TEL America (now Tokyo Electron America), was established in 1972. In 1978 Tokyo Electron Laboratories was renamed Tokyo Electron Limited (also TEL).

TEL went public in 1980. In 1981 the company formed a joint venture with GenRad (later acquired by Teradyne) to make test systems in the US. In 1988 TEL acquired Thermco's stake in their joint venture.

The company began a major international expansion in 1993, setting up shop in South Korea. In the following years it expanded into Germany, Italy, the UK, and Taiwan. In 1996 TEL managing director Tetsuro Higashi was named president. (He later became chairman and CEO.)

In 1997 TEL delivered the first of its 300mm wafer production equipment. The next year the company acquired the semiconductor equipment division (now part of Tokyo Electron Arizona) of Sony's Material Research Corp. Also in 1998 TEL formed Tokyo Electron EE Limited to refurbish and upgrade semiconductor manufacturing equipment.

The company formed its French subsidiary in 1999. That year TEL and AlliedSignal (now Honeywell International) formed a joint venture to develop chip-making equipment. Also in 1999 rival Tegal won a permanent injunction against TEL to stop US sales of some of TEL's wafer etching equipment; legal wrangling over patent issues continued between the two companies through 2000.

In 2000 TEL acquired US-based Supercritical Systems, a maker of semiconductor cleaning devices. The next year the company bought Timbre Technologies, a US-based maker of metrology tools used in chip production, for $138 million.

In 2002 the company expanded its reach into China when it opened a support office there. TEL finally prevailed over Tegal in the long-running patent infringement case, with the US Court of Appeals for the Federal Circuit finding for the Japanese company.

That same year TEL agreed with Dainippon Screen and Ebara on forming a joint venture to develop an electron-beam lithography system, using technology from Toshiba. The company also became involved in the Albany NanoTech project, supporting advanced semiconductor R&D in cooperation with researchers at the University at Albany, in the state capital of New York.

Kiyoshi Sato was promoted to president and CEO in 2003, succeeding Tetsuro Higashi, who became chairman. The company marked its 40th anniversary. TEL and Nikon agreed on joint development of liquid immersion exposure systems for semiconductor manufacturing. The company consolidated its service and support division as Tokyo Electron BP Ltd. that year. TEL also began working with ASML Holding on linking their respective production tools.

Continuing the trend of cooperative relations with other vendors of semiconductor manufacturing equipment, TEL partnered with Mattson Technology in 2004. Later in the year it created a new American holding company, Tokyo Electron US Holdings, to oversee such subsidiaries as Tokyo Electron America, Tokyo Electron Massachusetts, TEL Technology Center America, and Tokyo Electron Arizona.

TEL made management changes at the outset of 2005, following a series of restructuring moves for the corporation. Tetsuro Higashi reclaimed the CEO's post, while Kiyoshi Sato remained as president and COO. TEL's Cleaning Systems product line was renamed Surface Preparation Systems. The company's Manufacturing division became the Manufacturing and IT division.

The company went through a sweeping reorganization in 2006, with the semiconductor production equipment division divided into four product-specific divisions. A new Sales & Services division was created, organized on a customer basis. Later in the year the company created TEL Venture Capital, a firm that will make seed and early-stage investments in promising technology ventures, emulating similar investment firms established by competitors Applied Materials and Novellus Systems.

EXECUTIVES

Chairman and CEO: Tetsuro (Terry) Higashi
Vice Chairman and President, SPE Investor Relations, Legal, and Intellectual Property/Strategic Alliance: Tetsuo (Tom) Tsuneishi
Vice Chairman and President, FPD/PVE: Kiyoshi (Ken) Sato
President and Director: Hiroshi Takenaka
EVP and General Manager, FPD/PVE Division: Mitsuru Onozato
EVP and General Manager, Manufacturing, and Director: Hirofumi Kitayama
EVP, General Manager, SPE Business Strategy, and Director: Kenji Washino
EVP and General Manager, SPE Division, and Director: Hikaru Ito
SVP and General Manager, Development Division: Masami Akimoto
SVP and General Manager, Corporate Strategic Planning and Human Resources Development: Hiroki Takebuchi
SVP and General Manager, Corporate Administration Division and Compliance/Internal Control, and Director: Takashi Nakamura
SVP and General Manager, PVE Business Unit and FPD/PVE Division: Takashi Ito
Auditors: KPMG AZSA & Co.

LOCATIONS

HQ: Tokyo Electron Limited
Akasaka Biz Tower, 3-1 Akasaka 5-chome, Minato-ku
Tokyo 107-6325, Japan
Phone: 81-3-5561-7000   **Fax:** 81-3-5561-7400
US HQ: 2400 Grove Blvd., Austin, TX 78741
US Phone: 512-424-1000   **US Fax:** 512-424-1001
Web: www.tel.com

2010 Sales

	% of total
Japan	39
Taiwan	22
US	13
South Korea	13
Other countries	13
Total	**100**

PRODUCTS/OPERATIONS

2010 Sales

	% of total
Industrial electronic equipment	
Semiconductor production	63
Flat-panel display & photovoltaic cell production	17
Electronic components & computer networks	20
Total	**100**

Selected Products

Production Equipment
  Liquid crystal displays
    Coater/developers
    Plasma etcher/ashers
  Semiconductors
    Carrierless cleaners
    Coater/developers
    Metal chemical vapor deposition (CVD) systems
    Oxidation/diffusion furnaces and LP-CVD systems
    Plasma etchers
    Scrubbers
    Spin-on dielectric coaters
    Wafer probers
    Wafer-level burn-in and test systems
Distributed Products
  Data management software
  Film metrology tools
  Lithography process management software
  Semiconductor manufacturing yield management
    software
  Semiconductors and board-level products
  Storage area network (SAN) equipment
  Wafer inspection systems

COMPETITORS

AIXTRON
Amtech Systems
Applied Materials
ASM International
Aviza Technology
Dainippon Screen
EG Systems
FEI
FSI International
Future Electronics
Hitachi
Hitachi Kokusai Electric
Intevac
Lam Research
Mattson Technology
Novellus
Semitool
Tegal
Tokyo Seimitsu
ULVAC
Veeco Instruments

HISTORICAL FINANCIALS

Company Type: Public

Income Statement

FYE: March 31

	REVENUE ($ mil.)	NET INCOME ($ mil.)	NET PROFIT MARGIN	EMPLOYEES
3/10	4,516	14	0.3%	10,068
3/09	5,223	78	1.5%	10,391
3/08	9,125	1,070	11.7%	10,429
3/07	7,228	774	10.7%	9,528
3/06	5,730	408	7.1%	8,950
Annual Growth	**(5.8%)**	**(57.0%)**	**—**	**3.0%**

2010 Year-End Financials

Debt ratio: —
Return on equity: 0.3%
Cash ($ mil.): 614
Current ratio: 4.64
Long-term debt ($ mil.): —
No. of shares (mil.): 179
Dividends
  Yield: 0.2%
  Payout: —
Market value ($ mil.): 11,972

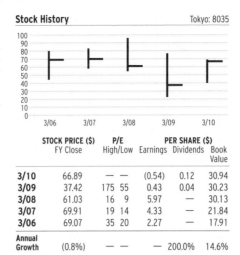

	STOCK PRICE ($) FY Close	P/E High/Low		PER SHARE ($) Earnings	Dividends	Book Value
3/10	66.89	—	—	(0.54)	0.12	30.94
3/09	37.42	175	55	0.43	0.04	30.23
3/08	61.03	16	9	5.97	—	30.13
3/07	69.91	19	14	4.33	—	21.84
3/06	69.07	35	20	2.27	—	17.91
Annual Growth	**(0.8%)**	**—**	**—**	**—**	**200.0%**	**14.6%**

Tomkins plc

Tomkins companies make and distribute automotive products, industrial power systems, plumbing components, valves, and construction products, while also designing integrated circuits for automotive and industrial customers. In the US, Tomkins' brand divisions include Gates (automotive belts and hoses) and Selkirk (chimneys and venting pipe products). The multinational conglomerate gets nearly 10% of its sales from the Detroit Three — Chrysler, Ford Motor, and General Motors. Tomkins makes more than half of its sales in the US. Canada-based Onex and the Canada Pension Plan Investment Board (CPPIB) acquired Tomkins in the latter part of 2010 for $5 billion.

The transaction, which was split fairly equally between Onex and CPPIB, included the assumption of Tomkins' debt. Investment firm Onex and CPPIB began research into the potential takeover bid for Tompkins earlier in 2010. Gains made by the Canadian dollar against the British pound made the addition of the UK conglomerate attractive.

Tomkins will continue to emphasize its engineering services operations. To that end, the company acquired Hydrolink, a fluid engineering services provider to the oil and gas and marine sectors with customer in the Middle East. The company has also made steps to increase its presence in filtration as evidenced by the acquisition of Koch filter in early 2010 for a reported $35.5 million. The Koch purchase, coupled with the acquisition of Trion in 2008, gives Tomkins a sizable share of the non-residential replacement air filter market. In a related field, Tomkins acquired the remaining 40% stake in Rolastar, an India-based ducting manufacturer. On the other side of the coin, Tomkins exited the window and door market in late 2009 when Philips Doors and Windows ceased operations due to the dramatic downturn in the residential construction market.

Toward the second goal, Tomkins in 2009 made headway by investing in new plants and equipment in its targeted growth regions of Asia and Eastern Europe while shuttering older, less efficient plants. In China, Tomkins is winning more automotive business from local carmakers like Chery Automobile and Brilliance China Automotive Holdings.

HISTORY

Tomkins was founded in 1925 as the F. H. Tomkins Buckle Company, a maker of buckles and fasteners. Tomkins continued to develop within this niche market for the next six decades. In 1983 Gregory Hutchings acquired a 23% stake in the company. Hutchings, who at age 24 had started his own construction business, had won a reputation as a go-getter when he caught the eye of Lords Hanson and White; he was hired by the Hanson Group in 1980 as its chief acquisition scout. In 1984 Hutchings became Tomkins' CEO and set about acquiring manufacturing companies in the UK and the US.

The company acquired Ferraris Piston Service (auto components) and Hayter (a garden tool manufacturer) that year, followed by Pegler-Hattersley (plumbing fixtures) in 1986, Smith & Wesson (guns) in 1987, and Murray Ohio (lawn mowers and bicycles) the next year. In 1992 the company acquired Rank Hovis McDougall, a leading UK baker and food manufacturer.

Tomkins made only eight major purchases between 1983 and 1993, as Hutchings worked to put his acquisitions on a sound financial footing, upgrading plants and equipment and giving each company the autonomy to become efficient.

In 1994 Tomkins bought Outdoor Products and Dynamark Plastics from Noma Industries of Canada: Outdoor Products complemented the Murray Ohio operations, and injection molder Dynamark Plastics fit into Tomkins' industrial products portfolio.

Two years later the company acquired Gates, a US maker of automotive belts and hoses, with operations in 15 countries; the move gave Tomkins access to new markets in Latin America and Southeast Asia. That year Tomkins acquired the hose operations of Nationwide Rubber Enterprises, making Gates the leading manufacturer of curved hose in Australia. In 1997 Tomkins acquired US firm Stant, a leading maker of windshield wipers, fuel tank caps, and other auto accessories, to further complement Gates' product lines.

Besides acquisitions, Tomkins regularly disposed of companies that no longer fit its strategic plan. It sold Inchbrook Printers in 1996 and Ferraris Piston Service, the first business purchased by Tomkins under Hutchings' leadership, in 1997. In a symbolic break with its past, Tomkins sold F. H. Tomkins Buckle in 1998.

That year Tomkins made another automotive equipment acquisition when it bought US-based Schrader-Bridgeport; it also bought Martine Spécialités, a supplier of frozen patisserie products. In 1999 the company acquired ACD Tridon, a Canadian manufacturer of automotive parts.

In 2000 Smith & Wesson settled more than a dozen lawsuits with US cities attempting to collect damages for handgun violence cases. Breaking rank with other handgun makers, the company agreed to install child-safety locks on its guns and ensure that gun sellers conduct background checks.

Tomkins moved to exit the food manufacturing business in 2000, selling Red Wing and agreeing to sell the European operations of Ranks Hovis McDougall. Hutchings resigned that year in the midst of an investigation of his spending practices (including his use of corporate jets and the presence of Hutchings' wife and housekeeper on the company payroll), and chairman David Newlands took over. That year the company sold its bicycle, snow blower, and mowing machinery businesses (Hayter and Murray). In 2001 Tomkins sold Smith & Wesson to Smith & Wesson Holding Corporation (formerly Saf-T-Hammer), a manufacturer of gun safety equipment, for $15 million.

In 2002 Tomkins sold its Gates Consumer and Industrial (GCI) division to the Rutland Fund for about $35 million in cash. GCI's products included carpet padding and accessories, diving suits, and commercial rubber compounds. Also that year Jim Nicol took over as CEO. The following year Tomkins sold its Milliken Valve subsidiary to the Henry Pratt Company for $7.3 million in cash.

In 2006 Tomkins acquired chimney and vent pipe manufacturer Selkirk, L.L.C. Selkirk became a subsidiary within Tomkins' Air Systems Components business. The following year, to fuel organic growth, Tomkins acquired the 40% of Schrader Engineered Products (valves and fittings) it did not already own.

EXECUTIVES

Non-Executive Chairman: David B. Newlands, age 63, $590,435 total compensation
CEO and Director: James (Jim) Nicol, age 56, $5,068,105 total compensation
CFO and Director: John W. Zimmerman, age 46, $2,414,061 total compensation
COO, Building Products: Terry J. O'Halloran, age 62
EVP Corporate Development: David J. (D.J.) Carroll, age 52
VP Human Resources: Mildred P. Woryk, age 50
President, Industrial and Automotive: Alan J. Power, age 47
Company Secretary: Denise P. Burton, age 51
General Counsel: George S. Pappayliou, age 55
Auditors: Deloitte LLP

LOCATIONS

HQ: Tomkins plc
East Putney House, 84 Upper Richmond Rd.
London SW15 2ST, United Kingdom
Phone: 44-20-8871-4544   **Fax:** 44-20-8877-9700
Web: www.tomkins.co.uk

2009 Sales

	$ mil.	% of total
US	2,172.9	52
Europe		
UK	297.0	7
Other countries	603.5	14
Other regions	1,106.7	27
Total	**4,180.1**	**100**

PRODUCTS/OPERATIONS

2009 Sales

	$ mil.	% of total
Industrial & Automotive		
Power Transmission	1,763.4	42
Fluid Power	588.7	14
Fluid Systems	313.6	8
Other	463.4	11
Building Products		
Air Systems Components	874.2	21
Other	140.3	3
Door & windows	36.5	1
Total	**4,180.1**	**100**

2009 Sales by End Market

	% of total
Industrial	28
Automotive Original Equipment	23
Automotive Aftermarket	23
Non-Residential Construction	16
Residential Construction	8
Other	2
Total	**100**

COMPETITORS

Applied Industrial Technologies
BorgWarner
Bridgestone
Commercial Vehicle
Continental AG
Continental International
Drew Industries
Goodyear Tire & Rubber
Hayden Automotive
IBM Microelectronics
Invensys
Koninklijke Econosto
LSI Corp.
Mark IV
Precision Castparts
Simpson Manufacturing
Sloan Valve
SmarTire Systems
STMicroelectronics
Tenneco
Texas Instruments
United Technologies
Uponor
US Motor Works
Velan
YKK
ZF Friedrichshafen

HISTORICAL FINANCIALS

Company Type: Private

Income Statement

FYE: Saturday nearest December 31

	REVENUE ($ mil.)	NET INCOME ($ mil.)	NET PROFIT MARGIN	EMPLOYEES
12/09	4,180	6	0.1%	26,797
12/08	5,516	(46)	—	20,994
12/07	5,840	292	5.0%	35,894
12/06	5,419	252	4.6%	38,299
12/05	5,776	313	5.4%	37,324
Annual Growth	**(7.8%)**	**(62.8%)**	**—**	**(7.9%)**

2009 Year-End Financials

Debt ratio: 45.0%
Return on equity: 0.4%
Cash ($ mil.): 445
Current ratio: 2.28
Long-term debt ($ mil.): 691

Net Income History

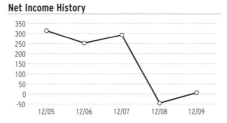

Toronto-Dominion Bank

The Toronto-Dominion Bank wants to score financial TDs at home and abroad. Also known as TD Bank or TD Financial Group, and one of Canada's largest banks, it provides retail banking services under the TD Canada Trust banner, including checking and savings accounts, loans, credit cards, and mortgages, through more than 1,100 branches. TD also offers financial and advisory services to businesses. Other operations include TD Insurance, TD Asset Management (mutual funds), and TD Securities (investment banking, equities, and foreign exchange). US subsidiary TD Bank, N.A., formed by the 2008 merger of TD Banknorth and Commerce Bancorp, has about 1,300 branches in about a dozen eastern states.

The $8.5 billion acquisition and subsequent merger of Commerce Bancorp added some 450 branches along the eastern seaboard to TD Bank's US network and exemplified the company's expansion plans. It has been looking for new ways to increase earnings outside of its core business of retail banking in Canada — a mature market with limited growth potential and several large competitors — and because of Canada's ban on bank mergers, has had to expand to the south. In 2010 TD Bank, N.A. added more than 60 branches in Florida by acquiring three failed banks that had been seized by regulators. It later bought The South Financial Group to further expand in the Sunshine State and establish a presence in the Carolinas; that deal added about 70 locations.

TD sold the US operations of online discount brokerage TD Waterhouse to Ameritrade (now TD AMERITRADE) in early 2006. (TD Waterhouse continues to operate in Canada.) As part of the deal, TD acquired a 40% stake in TD AMERITRADE; it upped its stake to 45% in 2009, and bought the operations of online broker thinkorswim Group in Canada. Also that year TD upped its stake in Luxembourg-based Internaxx to 75%, which should help it expand its online brokerage business in Europe.

On the other side of the ledger, TD sold fund of funds manager TD Capital Private Equity Investors (now Northleaf Capital Partners) to the unit's management team in 2009. The move was designed to allow TD to focus on its core business operations.

HISTORY

The Bank of Toronto was established in 1855 by flour traders who wanted their own banking facilities. Its growth encouraged another group of businessmen to found the Dominion Bank in 1869. Dominion emphasized commercial banking and invested heavily in railways and construction.

As the new nation expanded westward, both banks established branch networks. They helped fund Canada's primary industries — dairy, mining, oil, pulp, and textiles. True to its pioneering spirit, a Bank of Toronto official claimed to be the first to have set up a branch office with the help of aviation (in Manitoba in the 1920s).

The demand for agricultural products and commodities dropped after WWI, but production continued full throttle, creating a world grain glut that helped trigger the stock market crash of 1929. Both the Bank of Toronto and Dominion Bank contracted during the 1930s. After growing during and subsequent to WWII, The

Bank of Toronto and Dominion Bank decided to increase their capital base, merging into a 450-branch bank in 1955.

In the 1970s TD Bank opened offices in Bangkok, Beirut, and Frankfurt, among other cities abroad. During the 1980s it was active in making loans to less-developed countries. After the deregulation of the Canadian securities industry in 1987, then-CEO Richard Thomson reduced international lending and began focusing on brokerage activities. The strategy paid off when several Latin American countries fell behind on their loans in the late 1980s.

As the North American economy slowed in the early 1990s, TD Bank's nonperforming loans increased and, with it, its loan loss reserves. The bank still made acquisitions, including Central Guaranty Trust (1993) and Lancaster Financial Holdings (1995, investment banking). It worked to build its financial services, expanding its range of service offerings and geographic coverage and buying New York-based Waterhouse Investor Services (1996); 97% of Australia-based Pont Securities (1997); and California-based Kennedy, Cabot & Co. (1997). In 1998 the bank sold its payroll services to Ceridian, and its Waterhouse Securities unit bought US discount brokerage Jack White & Co.

That year the government nixed TD Bank's merger with Canadian Imperial on the same day it voided the Royal Bank of Canada/Bank of Montreal deal. The banks believed the consolidation was necessary to stave off foreign banks' encroachment into Canada, but the government had domestic antitrust concerns: Though Canada has one-tenth the population of the US, its five top banks all ranked in the top 15 in North America.

In 1999 TD Bank bought Trimark Financial's retail trust banking business and spun off part of Waterhouse Investor Services, which would become part of TD Waterhouse Group. That year the bank ramped up its focus on Internet banking.

Not giving up on acquisition-fueled growth, in 2000 the company bought CT Financial Services (now TD Canada Trust) from British American Tobacco. As a condition for government approval, TD Bank had to sell its MasterCard credit portfolio (sold to Citibank Canada) and a dozen southern Ontario branches (to Bank of Montreal).

The company's plans to hitch a ride on the Wal-Mart gravy train derailed in 2001. Arrangements to open bank branches in some US-based Wal-Mart stores were squelched by regulators enforcing the banking and commerce barrier. TD Bank later closed all of its existing branches (more than 100 in all) inside Canadian Wal-Marts as part of a broader restructuring.

TD Bank suffered its first-ever annual loss during fiscal year 2002. Write-downs on loans to telecommunications, technology, and energy firms contributed mightily to the dismal results.

Frustrated by limited growth opportunities at home, in 2005 TD Bank ventured south of the border with its purchase of a stake in Banknorth. TD Bank paid about $4.8 billion in cash and stock for its original 51% stake (it bought the rest in 2007). Additionally, in 2006 the company assumed about a 40% ownership in TD AMERITRADE as part of the sale of TD Waterhouse.

EXECUTIVES

Chairman: John M. Thompson
Director: Brian M. Levitt, age 63
President, CEO, and Director: W. Edmund (Ed) Clark, age 62
Group Head Finance and CFO: Colleen M. Johnston

Group Head Corporate Operations: Mike Pedersen
Group Head Wholesale Banking; Chairman, President, and CEO, TD Securities: Robert E. (Bob) Dorrance, age 54
Group Head Wealth Management; Chairman and CEO, TD Waterhouse Canada: William H. (Bill) Hatanaka
Group Head Canadian Banking, Canadian Personal and Commercial Banking; President and CEO, TD Canada Trust: Timothy D. (Tim) Hockey, age 46
Group Head Insurance and Global Development, Canadian Personal and Commercial Banking; Deputy Chair, TD Canada Trust: Bernard T. (Bernie) Dorval, age 56
Chief Economist: Craig Alexander
EVP and Chief Marketing Officer: Dominic J. Mercuri
EVP and CIO: Kevin Kessinger
EVP Legal and Compliance and General Counsel: Christopher A. Montague
EVP, TD Asset Management: Brian Murdock
EVP Human Resources and Corporate and Public Affairs: Teri L. Currie
EVP Corporate Development, Group Strategy, and Treasury and Balance Sheet Management: Riaz E. Ahmed
EVP Direct Channels and Distribution Strategy: Brian J. Haier
EVP and Chief Risk Officer: Mark R. Chauvin
Chairman and EVP, TD Insurance: Alain P. Thibault
Auditors: Ernst & Young LLP

LOCATIONS

HQ: The Toronto-Dominion Bank
Toronto-Dominion Centre, 55 King St. West
Toronto, Ontario M5K 1A2, Canada
Phone: 416-982-8222 **Fax:** 416-982-5671
US HQ: 31 W. 52nd St., New York, NY 10019
US Phone: 212-827-7000 **US Fax:** 212-827-7248
Web: www.td.com

PRODUCTS/OPERATIONS

2009 Sales

	% of total
Interest	
Loans	53
Securities	18
Deposits with banks	2
Noninterest	
Investments & securities services	9
Service charges	5
Insurance, net of claims	4
Card services	3
Trading income	3
Credit fees	2
Other	1
Total	**100**

Selected Canadian Subsidiaries

CT Financial Assurance Company
First National Bank of Canada
Meloche Monnex Inc.
  Security National Insurance Company
    Primmum Insurance Company
    TD Direct Insurance Inc.
    TD General Insurance Company
    TD Home and Auto Insurance Company
TD Asset Finance Corp.
TD Asset Management Inc.
  TD Waterhouse Private Investment Counsel Inc.
TD Capital Funds Management Ltd.
TD Capital Group Limited
TD Capital Trust
TD Investment Services Inc.
TD Life Insurance Company
TD Mortgage Corporation
  The Canada Trust Company
  TD Pacific Mortgage Corporation
TD Mortgage Investment Corporation
TD Nordique Investments Inc.
TD Parellel Private Equity Investors Ltd.
TD Securities Inc.
TD Timberlane Investments Limited
  TD McMurray Investments Limited
  TD Redpath Investments Limited
  TD Riverside Investments Limited

TD Vermillion Holdings
  TD Financial International
  Canada Trustco International
    TD Reinsurance (Barbados)
  Toronto Dominion International
TD Waterhouse Canada Inc.
  thinkorswim Canada
Truscan Property Corporation
VFC Inc.

Selected US Subsidiaries

TD Discount Brokerage Acquisition
TD Discount Brokerage Hedging
TD Discount Brokerage Holdings
Toronto Dominion Holdings (U.S.A.)
  TD Equity Options,
  TD USA Insurance.
  Toronto Dominion Capital (U.S.A.).
  Toronto Dominion Investments.

COMPETITORS

Bank of America
Berkshire Hills Bancorp
BMO Financial Group
Caisses centrale Desjardins
Charles Schwab
CI Financial
CIBC
E*TRADE Financial
Edward Jones
FMR
KeyCorp
Laurentian Bank
Morgan Stanley
National Bank of Canada
RBC Financial Group
Scotiabank
Sovereign Bank

HISTORICAL FINANCIALS

Company Type: Public

Income Statement

FYE: October 31

	ASSETS ($ mil.)	NET INCOME ($ mil.)	INCOME AS % OF ASSETS	EMPLOYEES
10/09	519,607	2,909	0.6%	65,930
10/08	465,778	3,170	0.7%	58,792
10/07	442,175	4,187	0.9%	51,163
10/06	350,440	4,106	1.2%	51,147
10/05	310,246	1,894	0.6%	50,991
Annual Growth	**13.8%**	**11.3%**	**—**	**6.6%**

2009 Year-End Financials

Equity as % of assets: 6.3%
Return on assets: 0.6%
Return on equity: 10.1%
Long-term debt ($ mil.): 11,547
No. of shares (mil.): 875

Dividends
  Yield: 4.3%
  Payout: 70.4%
Market value ($ mil.): 46,726
Sales ($ mil.): 23,705

Stock History

NYSE: TD

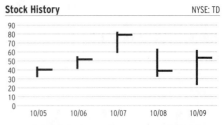

	STOCK PRICE ($) FY Close	P/E High/Low		PER SHARE ($) Earnings	Dividends	Book Value
10/09	53.38	19	7	3.24	2.28	41.25
10/08	38.90	15	8	4.03	1.95	29.92
10/07	78.98	14	10	5.74	2.24	25.61
10/06	51.67	10	7	5.65	1.60	20.00
10/05	40.19	16	12	2.72	1.32	15.40
Annual Growth	**7.4%**	**—**	**—**	**4.5%**	**14.6%**	**27.9%**

Toshiba Corporation

Toshiba products play an active role, be it in computing, controlling, powering, or communicating — transporting, cooking, playing, or even elevating. The company's portfolio includes personal and professional computers (notebook PCs, servers), telecommunications and medical equipment (mobile phones, X-ray machines), industrial machinery (power plant reactors, elevators), consumer appliances (microwaves, DVD players), electronic components (electron tubes, batteries), and semiconductors. Its portfolio also includes air traffic control and railway transportation systems.

In 2009 Toshiba named Norio Sasaki, a veteran of the company's power generation business, to succeed Atsutoshi Nishida as CEO. Sasaki was handpicked by Nishida, who became chairman of the company. Sasaki's appointment came soon after the company announced its biggest ever annual loss.

The company announced in mid-2010 that it would combine its wireless handset business with that of archrival Fujitsu to create the largest cell phone maker in Japan in hopes of better competing with market leader Nokia and a number of key players from Asia and North America; Fujitsu will own a controlling stake in the new company.

Toshiba acquired the hard-disk drive business of Fujitsu in 2009. In addition to augmenting Toshiba's consumer product-oriented disk drive line, the purchase moved the company into the enterprise disk drive business.

Toshiba, which holds a 67% stake in Westinghouse Electric, shares ownership with The Shaw Group (20%) and IHI (3%). The remaining 10% is held by Kazatomprom, a state-owned uranium supplier based in Kazakhstan, which acquired the stake from Toshiba for $540 million in 2007. In 2009 Toshiba, along with Tokyo Electric Power Company and the Japan Bank for International Cooperation, invested in Canadian uranium producer Uranium One.

Toshiba has used partnerships (often with competitors) to fuel product development and reduce costs. The company has worked with rivals such as Fujitsu and NEC on semiconductor development. In 2007 Toshiba formed a partnership with Sharp that will see the LCD specialist buy 50% of its system LSI chips from Toshiba; for its part, Toshiba will purchase approximately 40% of its LCD panels from Sharp by 2010.

In mid-2010 Toshiba announced plans for a JV with China-based consumer electronics maker TCL Corporation. Toshiba will own 49% of the venture, which will be called Toshiba Visual Products (China) Co. TCL will own the other 51%, and will sell Toshiba-brand TVs and other products in China, as well as contract-manufacture TVs for the JV.

HISTORY

Two Japanese electrical equipment manufacturers came together in 1939 to create Toshiba. Tanaka Seizo-sha, Japan's first telegraph equipment manufacturer, was founded in 1875 by Hisashige Tanaka, the so-called Edison of Japan. In the 1890s the company started making heavier electrical equipment such as transformers and electric motors, adopting the name Shibaura Seisakusho Works in 1893. Seisakusho went on to pioneer the production of hydroelectric generators (1894) and X-ray tubes (1915) in Japan.

The other half of Toshiba, Hakunetsusha & Company, was founded by Ichisuke Fujioka and Shoichi Miyoshi as Japan's first incandescent lamp maker (1890). Renamed Tokyo Electric Company (1899), the company developed the coiled filament lightbulb (1921), Japan's first radio receiver and cathode-ray tube (1924), and the internally frosted glass lightbulb (1925). In 1939 it merged with Shibaura Seisakusho to form Tokyo Shibaura Electric Company (Toshiba).

Toshiba was the first company in Japan to make fluorescent lamps (1940), radar systems (1942), broadcasting equipment (1952), and digital computers (1954). Production of black-and-white televisions began in 1949. Even so, through the 1970s the company was considered an also-ran, trailing other Japanese business groups, known as *keiretsu*, partly because of its bureaucratic management style.

Electrical engineer Shoichi Saba became president in 1980. Saba invested heavily in Toshiba's information and communications segments. The company became the first in the world to produce the powerful one-megabit DRAM chip (1985). That year it unveiled its first laptop PC. In the meantime Saba (named chairman, 1986) pushed Toshiba into joint ventures to exchange technology with companies such as Siemens and Motorola.

But in 1987 Toshiba incurred the wrath of the US government. A subsidiary sold submarine sound-deadening equipment to the USSR, resulting in threats of US sanctions and a precipitous decline in its stock price and in US sales. Chairman Saba and president Sugichiro Watari resigned in shame.

In 1996 the company appointed marketing and multimedia specialist Taizo Nishimuro as president, breaking its tradition of filling the position with an engineer from its heavy electrical operations.

In 1998 the company looked to boost earnings by cutting its workforce and allying with other manufacturers such as GE and Fujitsu in development deals. But continued semiconductor price declines, and sluggish demand in Japan, caused the company to record its first annual loss in more than two decades.

Nishimuro made plans to cut 5,000 jobs, and streamlined Toshiba's 15 divisions to eight in-house companies. Toshiba in 1999 agreed to take a $1 billion charge to settle a class-action lawsuit alleging some manufacturers supplied potentially corrupt disk drives in its portable computers — even though no Toshiba customer complaints were filed.

In 2000 Nishimuro stepped down as CEO. SVP Tadashi Okamura assumed the post. Nishimuro filled the vacant chairman's seat. Toshiba announced another restructuring effort in 2001, which included plans to reduce its workforce, shift manufacturing to overseas plants, and withdraw from unprofitable businesses.

In 2005 Atsutoshi Nishida, an executive that led the company's PC operations, succeeded Okamura as CEO.

The company acknowledged a setback for its consumer electronics business in 2008, when it announced the discontinuation of HD-DVD development. Toshiba was the primary backer of the HD-DVD format for high-definition DVD players and recorders — a market where it battled with Sony, the primary backer of the Blu-ray format, for support among manufacturers, media companies, and consumers.

EXECUTIVES

Chairman: Atsutoshi Nishida, age 66
President, CEO, and Director: Norio Sasaki, age 61
SEVP and Director: Masashi Muromachi, age 60
EVP, CFO, and Director: Fumio Muraoka, age 62
EVP and Director: Kazuo Tanigawa
EVP and Director: Masao Namiki, age 61
EVP: Ichiro Tai
EVP: Yoshihiro Maeda
EVP, Toshiba Semiconductor: Koji Iwama
SVP: Toshiharu Watanabe
SVP: Hidejiro Shimomitsu
SVP: Toshinori Moriyasu
SVP: Shozo Saito
SVP: Yoshihide Fujii
SVP: Hideo Kitamura
SVP: Hisao Tanaka
Chairman and CEO, Toshiba America:
 Masahiko (Masa) Fukakushi
**Chairman and CEO, Toshiba America Business
 Solutions:** Masahiro Yamada
**President and CEO, Toshiba America Consumer
 Products:** Atsushi Murasawa
President and CEO, Toshiba Medical Systems:
 Satoshi Tsunakawa, age 55
**President and CEO, Toshiba America Information
 Systems:** Mark A. Simons
Managing Director, Australia: Mark Whittard
Auditors: Ernst & Young

LOCATIONS

HQ: Toshiba Corporation
 1-1, Shibaura 1-chome, Minato-ku
 Tokyo 105-8001, Japan
Phone: 81-3-3457-4511   **Fax:** 81-3-3456-1631
US HQ: 1251 Avenue of the Americas, Ste. 4110
 New York, NY 10020
US Phone: 212-596-0600   **US Fax:** 212-593-3875
Web: www.toshiba.co.jp

2010 Sales

	% of total
Asia/Pacific	
Japan	45
Other countries	21
North America	18
Europe	13
Other regions	3
Total	**100**

PRODUCTS/OPERATIONS

2010 Sales

	% of total
Digital products	34
Social infrastructure	34
Electronic devices	19
Home appliances	8
Other	5
Total	**100**

Selected Products

Digital products
 Digital Media Network Company
  Digital cameras
  Digital tuners
  DVD players and recorders
  Hard disk drives
  Industrial and surveillance cameras
  Optical disk drives
  Projectors
  Televisions
 Mobile Communications Company
  Mobile phones
 Personal Computer & Network Company
  Handheld computers
  Notebook computers
  Servers

Social infrastructure
  Industrial and Power Systems & Services Company
    Boiling water reactor plants
    Building energy management systems
    Control and measurement system devices
    Industrial computers
    Nuclear fuel reprocessing plants
    Power generating equipment (hydroelectric, thermal, geothermal)
    Railway station service systems
    Superconducting magnets
    Transportation management systems
    Water supply and sewage monitoring systems
  Social Network & Infrastructure Systems Company
    Air traffic control and navigation aid systems
    Automatic letter processing systems
    Banknote processing machines
    Broadcasting systems
    Face recognition security systems
Electronic devices
  Semiconductor Company
    LSI systems
    Memory
    Microprocessors
Home appliances
  Air conditioners
  Batteries
  Lighting
  Microwaves
  Refrigerators
  Washing machines

COMPETITORS

ABB
Acer
Alcatel-Lucent
ALSTOM
Apple Inc.
AREVA
Canon
CASIO COMPUTER
Dell
Electrolux
Emerson Electric
Ericsson
FUJIFILM
Fujitsu
GE
Hewlett-Packard
Hitachi
IBM
Ingersoll-Rand
Intel
KONE
Kyocera
Lenovo
Mitsubishi Electric
Motorola
NEC
Nokia
NTT DATA
Oki Electric
Panasonic Corp
Philips Electronics
Pioneer Corporation
Ricoh Company
Samsung Electronics
Schindler Holding
Seagate Technology
Seiko
Sharp Corp.
Siemens AG
Sony
Sony Ericsson Mobile
Spansion
STMicroelectronics
Texas Instruments
Unisys
Western Digital
Xerox

HISTORICAL FINANCIALS
Company Type: Public

Income Statement
FYE: March 31

	REVENUE ($ mil.)	NET INCOME ($ mil.)	NET PROFIT MARGIN	EMPLOYEES
3/10	69,853	(57)	—	204,000
3/09	70,210	(3,531)	—	199,000
3/08	79,922	1,283	1.6%	198,000
3/07	60,375	1,166	1.9%	191,000
3/06	54,529	665	1.2%	172,000
Annual Growth	6.4%	—	—	4.4%

2010 Year-End Financials

Debt ratio: 120.5%
Return on equity: —
Cash ($ mil.): 2,885
Current ratio: 1.11
Long-term debt ($ mil.): 10,367

No. of shares (mil.): 4,238
Dividends
Yield: 0.0%
Payout: —
Market value ($ mil.): 22,083

Stock History
Pink Sheets: TOSBF

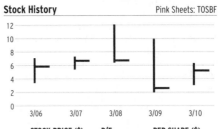

	STOCK PRICE ($) FY Close	P/E High/Low		PER SHARE ($) Earnings	Dividends	Book Value
3/10	5.21	—	—	(0.05)	0.00	2.03
3/09	2.61	—	—	(1.09)	0.05	1.09
3/08	6.71	32	18	0.37	—	2.43
3/07	6.68	21	17	0.33	—	2.22
3/06	5.82	36	19	0.19	—	2.01
Annual Growth	(2.7%)	—	—	—	—	0.2%

TOTAL S.A.

TOTAL does it all. One of the world's largest integrated oil companies, it explores for, develops, and produces crude oil and natural gas; refines and markets oil; and trades and transports both crude and finished products. Operating in more than 130 countries, the company has reserves of 10.5 billion barrels of oil equivalent. It has interests in 25 refineries (and directly operates 12) and about 16,500 gas stations, primarily under the TOTAL and Elf brands, mostly in Europe and Africa. TOTAL's chemical units produce petrochemicals, monomers, polymers, and specialty chemicals such as adhesives, inks, paints, resins, and rubbers. It also has interests in LNG production, coal mining, and power generation.

With an eye to restructuring as a pure integrated oil business, in 2007 TOTAL announced plans to sell its then-18% stake in pharmaceutical manufacturer Sanofi-Aventis. By mid-2009 the stake had fallen below 10%; TOTAL has made a point to divest the stake slowly and deliberately.

In 2010, in order to cut costs, TOTAL announced plans to merge its Italian retail operations with ERG's to create TotalERG, the #3 gas station network in Italy, with 3,400 outlets. It also agreed to sell two noncore oil fields in the Norwegian sector to BP for $991 million.

The company has announced plans to invest heavily in refinery expansion in Jubail, Saudi Arabia, and in Port Arthur, Texas. Other long-term growth initiatives include teaming up with Gazprom and Statoil to develop the vast Shtokman gas field in the Barents Sea. (Ownership breakdown for the project is as follows: Gazprom has 51%, TOTAL 25%, StatoilHydro 24%.) It also announced plans to invest $1.5 billion in a petrochemical project in Arzew, Algeria, which it will develop with Algeria's Sonatrach.

In 2008 it paid $470 million to buy Canada's Synenco Energy, whose principal asset is a 60% stake in the Northern Lights oil sands project in the Athabasca region. Sinopec owns the remaining stake in the project. Again looking to expand its Canadian oil sands assets, in 2009 TOTAL made a $617 million bid to acquire UTS Energy. That bid failed, but TOTAL came back in 2010 with a $1.4 billion offer that led to an acquisition agreement for UTS. Following the acquisition, it absorbed UTS's 20% stake in the Fort Hills oil sands project into its Canadian exploration and production unit and spun off the rump of UTS as a new oil sands explorer, SilverBirch Energy.

In the US in early 2010, in a further expansion, TOTAL also acquired 25% of Chesapeake Energy's Barnett Shale properties, forming a $2.25 billion joint venture with that company.

HISTORY

A French consortium formed the Compagnie Française des Pétroles (CFP) in 1924 to develop an oil industry for the country. Lacking reserves within its borders, France had a 24% stake in the Turkish Petroleum Company (TPC), acquired from Germany in 1920 as part of the spoils from WWI. When oil was discovered in Iraq in 1927, the TPC partners (CFP; Anglo-Persian Oil, later BP; Royal Dutch Shell; and a consortium of five US oil companies) became major players in the oil game.

In 1929 France acquired a 25% stake in CFP (raised to 35% in 1931) but ensured the company's independence from government control. CFP began establishing refining and transporting capabilities, and by the start of WWII it was a vertically integrated petroleum company.

With France's occupation by Germany during WWII, CFP was effectively blocked from further expansion, and its stake in Iraq Petroleum (formerly the TPC) was held by its partners until the end of the war. In 1948, over French protests, the US partners ended the "Red Line" agreement, a pact that limited members' competition in that Middle Eastern region.

After WWII, CFP diversified its sources for crude, opening a supply in 1947 from the Venezuelan company Pantepec and making several major discoveries in colonial Algeria in 1956. It also began supplying crude to Japan, South Korea, and Taiwan in the 1950s. To market its products in North Africa and France and other European areas, it introduced the brand name TOTAL in 1954. It began making petrochemicals in 1956.

Algeria in 1971 became North Africa's first major oil-producing country to nationalize its petroleum industry. This was not as dire a blow to CFP as it could have been; by that time the company got only about 20% of its supplies from Algeria. Exploration had paid off, with discoveries in Indonesia in the 1960s and the North Sea in the early 1970s.

CFP joined Elf Aquitaine in 1980 to buy Rhône-Poulenc's petrochemical segment. Ten years later it purchased state-owned Orkem's coating business (inks, resins, paints, and adhesives).

In 1985 the company had adopted its brand name as part of its new name, TOTAL Compagnie Française des Pétroles, shortened in 1991 to TOTAL. The firm was listed on the NYSE that year. The French government began reducing its stake in TOTAL in 1992 (ultimately to less than 1%). The company expanded reserves with stakes in fields in Argentina, the Caspian Sea, and Colombia.

In 1995, the year Thierry Desmarest became CEO, TOTAL contracted to develop two large oil and gas fields in Iran, despite US pressure not to do business there. The next year TOTAL led a consortium (including Russia's Gazprom and Malaysia's Petronas) in a $2 billion investment in Iran's gas sector, just days after selling its 55% stake in its North American arm, Total Petroleum, to Ultramar Diamond Shamrock — insulating TOTAL from the threat of US sanctions.

TOTAL bought Belgium's Petrofina, an integrated oil and gas company, for $11 billion in 1999 and became TOTAL FINA. Within days the new TOTAL FINA launched a $43 billion hostile bid for rival Elf Aquitaine. Elf made a counterbid, but TOTAL FINA wound up acquiring 95% of Elf in 2000 for $48.7 billion and became TOTAL FINA ELF. The new company gained control of the remainder of Elf later that year.

In 2001 an explosion in a TOTAL FINA ELF subsidiary's petrochemical and fertilizer plant in southern France killed 29 people and injured 2,500. In 2003 a number of former Elf executives and state officials were named in a corruption scandal that implicated the former French oil giant in influence peddling and bribery in the early 1990s. TOTAL FINA ELF was renamed TOTAL S.A. in 2003.

In 2006 the company spun off its Arkema unit, which produces chlorochemicals, intermediates, and performance polymers.

EXECUTIVES

Chairman: Thierry Desmarest, age 64, $3,045,994 total compensation
CEO and Director: Christophe de Margerie, age 59, $2,673,771 total compensation
CFO: Patrick de La Chevardière, age 53
Chief Administrative Officer: Jean-Jacques Guilbaud, age 57
General Secretary, Total Refining and Marketing: Bertrand Deroubaix, age 54
General Counsel: Peter Herbel
Group Treasurer: Jérôme Schmitt, age 44
EVP Sustainable Development and Environment: Manoelle Lepoutre
SVP Overseas, Downstream: Alain Champeaux
SVP Trading and Shipping: Pierre Barbé
SVP Human Resources: François Viaud
SVP Geosciences, Exploration and Production: Marc Blaizot, age 56
SVP Scientific Development: Jean-François Minster
SVP Industrial Safety: Jean-Marc Jaubert
SVP Exploration and Production, Africa: Jacques Marraud des Grottes, age 57
SVP Strategy, Business Development and Research and Development, Exploration and Production.: Patrick Pouyanné
VP Corporate Communications: Yves-Marie Dalibard
President, Exploration and Production: Yves-Louis Darricarrére, age 59
President, Chemicals: François Cornélis, age 61
President, Refining and Marketing: Michel Bénézit, age 55
President, Gas and Power: Philippe Boisseau
Auditors: KPMG Audit

LOCATIONS

HQ: TOTAL S.A.
 2 place Jean Miller, La Défense 6
 92078 Courbevoie, France
Phone: 33-1-47-44-45-46 **Fax:** 33-1-47-44-58-24
US HQ: 1201 Louisiana, Ste. 1800, Houston, TX 77002
US Phone: 713-483-5000
Web: www.total.com

2009 Sales

	% of total
Europe	
France	25
Other countries	46
Africa	7
North America	7
Other regions	15
Total	**100**

PRODUCTS/OPERATIONS

2009 Sales

	% of total
Downstream	77
Upstream	12
Chemicals	11
Total	**100**

COMPETITORS

Akzo Nobel
Ashland Inc.
BASF SE
BHP Billiton
BP
Chevron
ConocoPhillips
DuPont
Eni
Exxon Mobil
Imperial Oil
MOL
Norsk Hydro ASA
Occidental Petroleum
Pakistan State Oil
PEMEX
PETROBRAS
Petróleos de Venezuela
Royal Dutch Shell
Statoil
Toreador Resources

HISTORICAL FINANCIALS

Company Type: Public

Income Statement

FYE: December 31

	REVENUE ($ mil.)	NET INCOME ($ mil.)	NET PROFIT MARGIN	EMPLOYEES
12/09	160,738	12,106	7.5%	96,387
12/08	225,987	14,927	6.6%	96,959
12/07	201,150	19,378	9.6%	96,442
12/06	175,209	15,539	8.9%	95,070
12/05	170,121	14,584	8.6%	112,877
Annual Growth	**(1.4%)**	**(4.5%)**	**—**	**(3.9%)**

2009 Year-End Financials

Debt ratio: 37.0%
Return on equity: 16.8%
Cash ($ mil.): 16,714
Current ratio: 1.45
Long-term debt ($ mil.): 27,857
No. of shares (mil.): 2,349
Dividends
 Yield: 3.5%
 Payout: 59.4%
Market value ($ mil.): 215,581

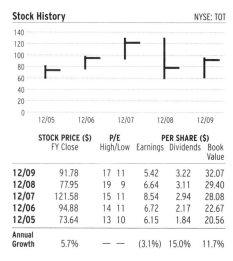

Stock History					NYSE: TOT

	STOCK PRICE ($) FY Close	P/E High/Low	PER SHARE ($) Earnings	Dividends	Book Value
12/09	91.78	17 11	5.42	3.22	32.07
12/08	77.95	19 9	6.64	3.11	29.40
12/07	121.58	15 11	8.54	2.94	28.08
12/06	94.88	14 11	6.72	2.17	22.67
12/05	73.64	13 10	6.15	1.84	20.56
Annual Growth	**5.7%**	**— —**	**(3.1%)**	**15.0%**	**11.7%**

Toyota Motor

Toyota Motor, the world's largest automotive manufacturer (overtaking GM in 2008), designs and manufactures a diverse product line-up that ranges from subcompacts to luxury and sports vehicles to SUVs, trucks, minivans, and buses. Its vehicles are produced either with combustion or hybrid engines, as with the Prius. Toyota's subsidiaries also manufacture vehicles: Daihatsu Motor produces mini-vehicles, while Hino Motors produces trucks and buses. Additionally, Toyota makes automotive parts for its own use and for sale to others. Popular models include the Camry, Corolla, Land Cruiser, and luxury Lexus line, as well as the Tundra truck.

Toyota's reputation for safety and quality, fundamental to its rise in the global auto industry, has been damaged by a series of recalls. Toyota recalled more than 8 million (5 million in the US) vehicles worldwide for defective gas pedals, faulty floor mats, and problems with braking software. While denying that software glitches were at fault, Toyota has acknowledged that it needs to respond faster to customer complaints. It has set up a central quality committee, hired chief quality officers for key regions such as North America, and plans to set up additional quality control training facilities — in China, Europe, North America, and Southeast Asia — modeled after its training center in Japan.

Amid these efforts, the company suspended US sales of eight models tapped for the safety recall. It halted production of the subject models, including the top-selling Camry, at US and Canadian plants. The recalls are the largest for Toyota in the US, and the suspension of sales and production resulting from vehicle defects topped the industry's charts.

The bulk of the recalls occurred on the heels of the global automotive industry downturn, which was driven by the twin factors of the credit crisis and the widespread recession.

In early 2010 the company sold off Toyota Financial Services Securities Corp. (the brokerage unit of its financial arm, Toyota Financial Services Corp.) to Tokai Tokyo Financial Holdings.

Additionally, the California-based NUMMI (New United Motor Manufacturing Inc.) joint venture with GM fell apart when GM pulled out in mid-2009. Toyota moved production at NUMMI to other plants in Canada and Texas; it dismissed nearly 5,000 workers and shuttered the plant in the spring of 2010.

The doors weren't closed for long. Luxury electric-car maker Tesla (based in California) purchased the NUUMI plant within a month, and Toyota invested $50 million in Tesla's stock at the closing of Tesla's IPO in mid-2010. The two companies will cooperate on the development of electric parts, production systems, and vehicles.

Like its competitors, Toyota is beefing up its Chinese operations by joining forces with local automotive players. With its partner China FAW Group Corporation, Toyota builds Land Cruisers and Corollas in country.

India is also generating a lot of interest in the automotive industry. Reacting to India-based Tata Motors' inexpensive Nano model, Toyota announced plans to build and market similar vehicles in that country, as well. To that end, the company is investing in the construction of a manufacturing plant near Bangalore.

HISTORY

In 1926 Sakichi Toyoda founded Toyoda Automatic Loom Works. In 1930 he sold the rights to the loom he invented and gave the proceeds to his son Kiichiro Toyoda to begin an automotive business. Kiichiro opened an auto shop within the loom works in 1933. When protectionist legislation (1936) improved prospects for Japanese automakers, Kiichiro split off the car department, took it public (1937), and changed its name to Toyota.

During WWII the company made military trucks, but financial problems after the war caused Toyota to reorganize in 1950. Its postwar commitment to R&D paid off with the launch of the four-wheel-drive Land Cruiser (1951); full-sized Crown (1955); and the small Corona (1957).

Toyota Motor Sales, U.S.A., debuted the Toyopet Crown in the US in 1957, but it proved underpowered for the US market. Toyota had better luck with the Corona in 1965 and with the Corolla (which became the best-selling car of all time) in 1968. By 1970 Toyota was the world's fourth-largest carmaker.

Toyota expanded rapidly in the US. During the 1970s the oil crisis caused demand for fuel-efficient cars, and Toyota was there to grab market share from US makers. In 1975 Toyota displaced Volkswagen as the US's #1 auto importer. Toyota began auto production in the US in 1984 through NUMMI, its joint venture with GM. The Lexus line was launched in the US in 1989.

Because of European restrictions on Japanese auto imports until the year 2000, Toyota's European expansion slowed. Toyota responded in 1992 by agreeing to distribute cars in Japan for Volkswagen and also by establishing an engine plant (later moved to full auto production) in the UK. The sport utility vehicle (SUV) mania of the 1990s spurred Toyota's introduction of luxury minivans and light trucks. Hiroshi Okuda, a 40-year veteran with Toyota and the first person from outside the Toyoda family to run the firm, succeeded Tatsuro Toyoda as president in 1995.

In 1997 Toyota introduced the Prius, a hybrid electric- and gas-powered car. The next year it boosted its stake in affiliate Daihatsu (minivehicles) to about 51%. Okuda became chairman in 1999, replacing Shoichiro Toyoda, and Fujio Cho became president (now chairman).

In 2000 Toyota bought a 5% stake in Yamaha (the world's #2 motorcycle maker) and raised its stake in truck maker Hino Motors from about 20% to around 34%.

International developments included Toyota's agreement with the Chinese government to produce passenger cars for sale in China built by joint venture Tianjin Toyota Motor Corp. Early in 2001 Toyota opened a new plant in France. Later that year Toyota also increased its stake in Hino Motors to 50%. In 2004 Toyota forged a joint venture agreement with Guangzhou Automobile Group to build engines in China. In mid-2005 Toyota established 14 Lexus dealerships in China. The company began joint car production in Europe with PSA Peugeot Citroën in 2005.

Also in 2005 Toyota bought just under 9% of General Motors' 20% stake in Fuji Heavy Industries — the Japanese maker of Subaru passenger vehicles. The two companies began production of Toyota Camrys at Fuji Heavy Industry's underutilized Subaru of Indiana plant in 2007.

Akio Toyoda, grandson of Toyota's founder, was promoted to president of the company in 2009.

The company revenues fell more than 20% in 2009, and it posted its first net loss since 1950.

EXECUTIVES

Chairman: Fujio Cho, age 73
Vice Chairman: Katsuaki Watanabe, age 68
Vice Chairman: Kazuo Okamoto, age 66
President and Representative Director: Akio Toyoda, age 54
EVP and Representative Director: Takeshi Uchiyamada, age 64
EVP and Representative Director: Shinichi Sasaki, age 63
EVP and Representative Director: Satoshi Ozawa, age 61
EVP and Representative Director: Atsushi (Art) Niimi, age 63
EVP and Representative Director:
Yukitoshi (Yuki) Funo, age 63
EVP and Representative Director: Yoichiro Ichimaru, age 62
Senior Managing Director; Chief Officer of the Purchasing Group: Yasumori Ihara, age 58
Senior Managing Director; President and COO, Toyota Motor Engineering & Manufacturing North America: Tetsuo Agata, age 57
Senior Managing Director; Chief Officer of the China Operations Group: Akira Sasaki, age 62
Senior Managing Director; Chief Officer, Business Development Group; Chief Officer, IT and ITS Group: Nobuyori Kodaira, age 61
Senior Managing Director; Chief Officer, Government and Public Affairs Group: Mamoru Furuhashi, age 60
Senior Managing Director; Chief Officer Production Engineering Group; Chief Officer Manufacturing Group: Takahiro Iwase, age 58
Director; President and COO, Toyota Motor North America; Chairman and CEO, Toyota Motors Sales, U.S.A.: Yoshimi Inaba, age 64
Auditors: PricewaterhouseCoopers Aarata

LOCATIONS

HQ: Toyota Motor Corporation
(Toyota Jidosha Kabushiki Kaisha)
1, Toyota-cho
Toyota, Aichi 471-8571, Japan
Phone: 81-565-28-2121   **Fax:** 81-565-23-5800
US HQ: 601 Lexington Ave., 49th Fl.
New York, NY 10023
US Phone: 212-223-0303   **US Fax:** 212-759-7670
Web: www.toyota.co.jp

2010 Sales

	% of total
Asia	
Japan	38
Other countries	13
North America	30
Europe	11
Other	8
Total	**100**

2010 Unit Sales

	No.	% of total
Asia		
Japan	2,162,418	30
Other countries	979,651	13
North America	2,097,374	29
Europe	858,390	12
Other regions	1,139,329	16
Total	**7,237,162**	**100**

PRODUCTS/OPERATIONS

2010 Sales

	% of total
Automotive	89
Financial services	6
Other	5
Total	**100**

Selected Products

Vehicles
  4Runner
  Allion (sold in Japan)
  Alphard (minivan sold in Japan)
  Aurus (hybrid)
  Avalon
  Camry (also hybrid)
  Corolla
  Corolla Rumion
  Crown
  FJ Cruiser
  Highlander (also hybrid)
  Land Cruiser
  Lexus
    GX
    LS600h (hybrid)
    LX (SUV)
    RX
    SC
  Mark X (sold in Japan)
  Matrix
  Premio (sold in Japan)
  Prius (hybrid)
  RAV4
  Scion
  Sequoia
  Sienna (minivan)
  Tacoma (truck)
  Tundra (truck)
  Vanguard
  Vellfire (minivan)
  Venza
  Wish (minivan sold in Japan)
  Yaris (marketed in Japan as the Vitz)
Other products
  Factory automation equipment
  Forklifts and other industrial vehicles
  Housing products

Selected Investments

Daihatsu Motor (51%, motor vehicles)
Hino Motors Ltd. (50%, trucks)

HISTORICAL FINANCIALS

Company Type: Public

Income Statement

FYE: March 31

	REVENUE ($ mil.)	NET INCOME ($ mil.)	NET PROFIT MARGIN	EMPLOYEES
3/10	204,443	2,260	1.1%	320,590
3/09	211,024	(4,491)	—	320,808
3/08	263,028	17,187	6.5%	316,121
3/07	203,219	13,951	6.9%	299,394
3/06	179,732	11,723	6.5%	285,977
Annual Growth	3.3%	(33.7%)	—	2.9%

2010 Year-End Financials

Debt ratio: 67.7%
Return on equity: 2.1%
Cash ($ mil.): 24,364
Current ratio: 1.22
Long-term debt ($ mil.): 75,682

No. of shares (mil.): 1,568
Dividends
  Yield: 0.0%
  Payout: —
Market value ($ mil.): 1,360

Stock History

NYSE: TM

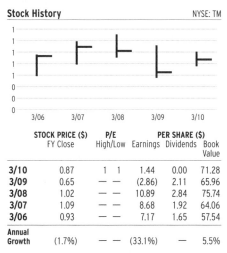

	STOCK PRICE ($) FY Close	P/E High/Low		PER SHARE ($) Earnings	Dividends	Book Value
3/10	0.87	1	1	1.44	0.00	71.28
3/09	0.65	—	—	(2.86)	2.11	65.96
3/08	1.02	—	—	10.89	2.84	75.74
3/07	1.09	—	—	8.68	1.92	64.06
3/06	0.93	—	—	7.17	1.65	57.54
Annual Growth	(1.7%)	—	—	(33.1%)	—	5.5%

Transocean Ltd.

Like an NFL tight end, offshore drilling contractor Transocean dreams of going deep but doesn't mind eating a little mud. Transocean specializes in deepwater drilling and it isn't afraid of harsh environments. The company operates in the world's major offshore oil-producing regions, including Africa, Asia, Brazil, Canada, India, the Middle East, the Gulf of Mexico, and the North Sea. It has a fleet of 138 mobile offshore drilling units (70 semisubmersibles and drillships, 65 jackup rigs, and three other rigs). Transocean's other operations include management of third-party drilling services. Major customers include BP and Chevron.

In 2010 the company was caught up in a major disaster (along with rig leaseholder BP) when one of its Gulf of Mexico deepwater rigs caught fire and sank, taking 11 lives, and spewing millions of gallons of oil from the sea floor.

As oil majors continue to drill in deeper waters, Transocean operates new rigs and is adding upgrades to existing ones to keep up with demand. It has five ultra-deepwater drillships able to drill in water depths of 12,000 feet. In 2009 the company had 10 Ultra-Deepwater Floaters (semisubmersibles and drillships) under construction or contracted for construction.

In a major expansion, in 2007 it acquired GlobalSantaFe for almost $18 billion. The acquisition made Transocean the world's largest offshore contract drilling company, expanding its fleet and strengthening its position in various global markets.

In 2007 Chevron also awarded the company's semisubmersible rig, the *Transocean Richardson*, a three-year contract for exploration and appraisal drilling offshore. That year Anadarko Petroleum contracted ultra-deepwater drillship *Discoverer Spirit* for three years.

In 2008 the company won a five-year contract for drillship work from Reliance Industries valued at more than $900 million. It also agreed to sell two semisubmersible rigs to drilling company Northern Offshore Ltd. for $750 million.

HISTORY

Transocean's predecessors include Forex, SEDCO, and The Offshore Company. Forex was founded in France in 1942 to perform land drilling in France, North Africa, and the Middle East. Oil services firm Schlumberger bought 50% of the firm in 1959. In 1964 Forex and Languedocienne created offshore drilling venture Neptune. By the time Schlumberger bought the rest of Forex in 1972, Forex had absorbed Neptune's operations.

Originally named Southeastern Drilling, SEDCO was created in 1947 by Bill Clements (later a Texas governor) to drill in shallow marsh waters in the US; it pushed into deeper waters in the 1960s. SEDCO received bad publicity in 1979 when a rig it leased to PEMEX exploded off Mexico's coast, causing the worst oil spill in history at the time. Schlumberger bought SEDCO in 1984 and combined it with Forex to form Sedco Forex Drilling in 1985.

In 1953 pipeline firm Southern Natural Gas Co. (SNG) acquired DeLong-McDermott, a contract drilling joint venture formed by DeLong Engineering and marine construction firm J. Ray McDermott. The new firm was called The Offshore Company. (McDermott sold its stake in

Offshore when it began to compete with McDermott's own operations.)

Offshore pioneered the use of jackup rigs in the Gulf of Mexico during the 1950s. It also introduced a patented system that allowed a drilling barge to be lowered and elevated for relocation. By 1963 Offshore was one of the first drillers operating in the North Sea; it went public in 1967.

During the 1970s SNG (incorporated as Southern Natural Industries in 1973) expanded its offshore drilling and exploration business. Offshore drilled its first deepwater well, off Southeast Asia, in 1976. Two years later Offshore became a wholly owned subsidiary of SNG. By the 1980s Offshore had one of the largest offshore drilling fleets in the US.

SNG's name was changed to Sonat in 1982, and Offshore became Sonat Offshore Drilling. That year it began building the industry's first fourth-generation semisubmersible rig. The company had 24 rigs by 1984 and set a deepwater record in 1987 by drilling more than 7,500 feet.

In the mid-1980s the oil industry lost speed, and Sonat focused on its gas operations. After two years of losses, Sonat Offshore was again profitable in 1990. However, its parent decided to spin off Sonat Offshore in 1993, retaining a 40% stake. (Sonat sold this stake in 1995.)

The oil industry began to recover in 1994. Two years later Sonat Offshore set another deepwater record by drilling at more than 7,600 feet and began building a drillship that could work at depths of 10,000 feet. Late that year it acquired Norwegian firm Transocean and became Transocean Offshore.

The new company's first year was filled with problems, including a fire on a semisubmersible conversion project (*Transocean Marianas*) and a strike by Norwegian offshore workers. But the firm won contracts from Chevron and Unocal for two new ultra-deepwater drillships. In 1999 Transocean Offshore merged with Sedco Forex, which had been spun off by Schlumberger, in a $3.2 billion deal that formed Transocean Sedco Forex.

As part of its merger, in 2000 Transocean Sedco Forex sold its coiled tubing drilling services unit, Transocean Petroleum Technology, to Schlumberger for $25 million. Later that year Transocean Sedco Forex agreed to buy R&B Falcon in an $8.8 billion deal that included the assumption of $3 billion in debt; the transaction closed in 2001.

The company also announced plans in 2001 to dispose of its turnkey operations and its Venezuelan land and barge drilling business to focus on its core activities, but subsequently backed away from that plan.

Transocean Sedco Forex changed its corporate name in 2002 to Transocean Inc. Later that year Michael Talbert replaced Victor Grijalva as chairman and Robert Long was appointed president and CEO of the company.

In 2003 Transocean acquired the remaining 50% stake in the Deepwater Pathfinder drillship from ConocoPhillips, the former joint venture partner of the vessel.

The next year the company spun off TODCO, a Gulf of Mexico shallow- and inland-water business segment it acquired in the R&B Falcon deal.

In 2006 Transocean secured an $862 million contract to build a drillship for Chevron.

EXECUTIVES

Chairman: Robert E. (Bob) Rose, age 70
Vice Chairman: J. Michael Talbert, age 63
President and CEO: Steven L. Newman, age 45,
  $2,392,364 total compensation
EVP Asset and Performance: Arnaud A. Y. Bobillier,
  age 54
EVP Global Business: Ihab Toma
SVP and CFO: Ricardo H. Rosa
SVP Europe and Africa: David A. Tonnel
**SVP, General Counsel, and Assistant Corporate
  Secretary:** Eric B. Brown, age 58,
  $1,908,554 total compensation
SVP Human Resources and Information Technology:
  Sherry Richard, age 53
VP and CIO: John L. Truschinger
VP Quality, Health, Safety, and Environment:
  Adrian P. Rose
VP and Controller: John H. Briscoe, age 52
VP and Treasurer: Ramon (Ray) Yi, age 55
VP Human Resources: Ian M. Clark
VP Marketing: Terry B. Bonno
VP Investor Relations and Communications:
  Gregory S. (Greg) Panagos
VP Engineering and Technical Services: N. Pharr Smith
Corporate Secretary and Associate General Counsel:
  Philippe A. Huber
Director Corporate Communications: Guy A. Cantwell
Auditors: Ernst & Young LLP

LOCATIONS

HQ: Transocean Ltd.
  Chemin de Blandonnet 10
  CH-1214 Vernier, Genève, Switzerland
Phone: 41-22-930-9000
US HQ: 4 Greenway Plaza, Houston, TX 77046
US Phone: 713-232-7500   **US Fax:** 713-232-7027
Web: www.deepwater.com

2009 Sales

	$ mil.	% of total
US	2,239	19
UK	1,563	14
India	1,084	9
Other countries	6,670	58
Total	**11,556**	**100**

PRODUCTS/OPERATIONS

2009 Sales

	$ mil.	% of total
Contract drilling	10,607	92
Contract drilling intangible revenues	281	2
Other	668	6
Total	**11,556**	**100**

Selected Subsidiaries

Caspian Sea Ventures International Ltd. (British Virgin
  Islands)
Global Offshore Drilling Limited (Nigeria)
GlobalSantaFe (Africa) Inc. (Cayman Islands)
GlobalSantaFe (Labuan) Inc. (Malaysia)
GlobalSantaFe U.S. Holdings Inc.
Hellerup Finance International Ltd. (Ireland)
International Chandlers, Inc.
PT Hitek Nusantara Offshore Drilling (80%, Indonesia)
R&B Falcon Drilling Co.
R&B Falcon Offshore Limited, LLC
R&B Falcon (UK) Ltd.
SDS Offshore Ltd. (UK)
Sedco Forex Corporation

Sedco Forex International, Inc. (Panama)
Sedco Forex Technical Services, Inc. (Panama)
Sonat Offshore S.A. (Panama)
Target Drilling Services Ltd. (UK)
Transhav AS (Norway)
Transnor Rig Ltd. (UK)
Transocean Alaskan Ventures Inc.
Transocean Brasil Ltda.
Transocean Drilling (U.S.A.) Inc. (formerly Wilrig
  (U.S.A.) Inc.)
Transocean Services AS (Norway)
Transocean Sino Ltd. (UK)
Triton Holdings Limited (British Virgin Islands)
Triton Industries, Inc. (Panama)

COMPETITORS

Atwood Oceanics
Diamond Offshore
Ensco
Helmerich & Payne
John Wood Group
Nabors Well Services
Noble
Parker Drilling
Pride International
Rowan Companies
Saipem

HISTORICAL FINANCIALS

Company Type: Public

Income Statement

FYE: December 31

	REVENUE ($ mil.)	NET INCOME ($ mil.)	NET PROFIT MARGIN	EMPLOYEES
12/09	11,556	3,181	27.5%	19,300
12/08	12,674	4,202	33.2%	21,600
12/07	6,377	3,131	49.1%	21,100
12/06	3,882	1,385	35.7%	10,700
12/05	2,892	716	24.7%	11,600
Annual Growth	**41.4%**	**45.2%**	**—**	**13.6%**

2009 Year-End Financials

Debt ratio: 47.9%
Return on equity: 17.2%
Cash ($ mil.): 1,130
Current ratio: 1.24
Long-term debt ($ mil.): 9,849

No. of shares (mil.): 319
Dividends
Yield: 0.0%
Payout: —
Market value ($ mil.): 26,415

Stock History

NYSE: RIG

	STOCK PRICE ($) FY Close	P/E High	P/E Low	PER SHARE ($) Earnings	PER SHARE ($) Dividends	PER SHARE ($) Book Value
12/09	82.80	10	5	9.84	0.00	64.42
12/08	47.25	12	3	13.09	0.00	51.80
12/07	143.15	11	5	14.14	0.00	39.39
12/06	80.89	21	15	4.28	0.00	21.43
12/05	69.69	33	19	2.13	0.00	25.02
Annual Growth	**4.4%**	**—**	**—**	**46.6%**	**—**	**26.7%**

TUI AG

TUI has the European travel business cornered. Through its tourism umbrella of companies, TUI holds a 51% stake in TUI Travel, which sells leisure travel packages and provides other travel services under some 200 brands in more than 20 countries. TUI Travel owns about 3,500 retail travel stores across Europe and operates a fleet of more than 150 aircraft. TUI's tourism segment also includes hotels and resorts (more than 240 hotels, including brands such as Riu, Grupotel, Robinson, Magic Life, and Grecotel) and cruise operations. The company narrowed its focus to travel services in 2009, selling its container shipping operations and reducing its stake in Hapag-Lloyd, a former subsidiary, to about 40%.

Albert Ballin Holding, a German consortium led by logistics magnate Klaus-Michael Kühne and the Hamburg municipal government, in early 2009 acquired Hapag-Lloyd for some $3.3 billion in cash and $2.7 billion in assumed debt. As part of the deal, TUI acquired its minority stake in Hapag-Lloyd from the consortium for about $950 million. TUI's investments in its container transportation business, most notably the 2005 purchase of Canada-based CP Ships for almost $2 billion, made Hapag-Lloyd one of the world's largest container carriers. Yet the enlarged Hapag-Lloyd did not perform as well as TUI had hoped, and the sale of its primary container operations came amid pressure from shareholders, who had seen their stock's performance trail that of a major German index since TUI acquired CP Ships.

Under pressure from the global economic downturn, the company has seen its revenues plummet in recent years (from a peak of $32 billion in 2007 to $19 billion in 2009, a 40% drop), largely a result of consumers curbing their travel spending and the disposal of Hapag-Lloyd. Its bottom line also fell into the red in 2008 but made a recovery in 2009, rising above $580 million. To maintain profitability, TUI plans to continue streamlining its operations (which may include refinancing ships and hotels, selling non-core real estate), a move expected to generate more than $600 million in cash by 2012.

Hapag-Lloyd's cruise business (Hapag-Lloyd Kreuzfahrten) was not divested along with its container shipping unit and represents another potential growth area for TUI. In 2009 the company entered the German market for premium cruises with the launch of its TUI Cruises segment. TUI Cruises is the result of a joint venture between TUI and Royal Caribbean Cruises. Its first vessel was christened *Mein Schiff*, which translates as "My Ship."

HISTORY

What became TUI was founded in Berlin in 1923 as Preussische Bergwerks-und Hutten-Aktiengesellschaft (Prussian Mine and Foundry Company) to operate former state-owned mining companies, saltworks, and smelters. Despite outmoded equipment and a war-shattered economy, the company prospered. So in 1929 the Prussian parliament combined Preussag with Hibernia and Preussischen Elektrizitats to form the state-run VEBA group, hoping to stimulate foreign investment.

Operating as part of VEBA didn't work out as well as Preussag had hoped, and WWII left the company a shell of its former self. In 1952, as restrictions on steel production were lifted and industry rebounded, Preussag relocated to Hanover. After taking steps to reestablish itself, Preussag made a public offering in 1959; VEBA kept about 22%.

A worldwide steel glut that lasted through the 1960s forced Preussag to diversify. Acquisitions included railroad tank car and transport agent VTG and shipbuilding and chemical companies. The company also formed oil exploration unit Preussag Energie in 1968. In 1969 VEBA sold its remaining stake in Preussag to Westdeusche Landesbank (WestLB).

When the 1970s oil crisis drove up steel costs, Preussag began international ventures to counter falling revenues at home. But the 1980s brought PR disasters. The European Commission fined Preussag and five other zinc producers for antitrust violations in 1984.

In 1989 Preussag reorganized into a holding company with four independent units: coal, oil, natural gas, and plant construction. But it was about to take a sharp business turn. Michael Frenzel, who had managed WestLB's industry holdings, became CEO in 1994 in the midst of another steel recession. Frenzel was determined to shift Preussag away from its rusting past and toward services and technology. In 1997 it acquired container shipping and travel firm Hapag-Lloyd, which had a 30% stake in Touristik Union International (TUI). By the end of 1998, the acquisitions of the rest of TUI, First Reisebuero Management, and a 25% stake in the UK's Thomas Cook (raised to 50.1% in 1999) had made Preussag Europe's top tourism group.

As part of its restructuring, Preussag traded its plant engineering units and half of its shipbuilding unit (HDW) to Babcock Borsig for a 33% stake in that company in 1999. Preussag then made plans to transfer another 25% of HDW to Sweden's Celsius in a deal (along with Babcock Borsig) to merge Celsius' Kockums submarine shipyards with HDW. That year Hapag-Lloyd and TUI were merged into Hapag Touristik Union (renamed TUI Group in 2000); VTG merged with Lehnkering, a 126-year-old freight forwarding group, becoming VTG-Lehnkering.

Preussag also acquired a stake in French package tour leader Nouvelles Frontières and sold a metals trading unit, W. & O. Bergmann, to Enron. By 2002 the company had sold off most of its non-tourism operations, changed its name to TUI, and restructured its business to concentrate on travel-related businesses.

In 2004 TUI Travel Solutions GmbH sold 50% of its stake in TQ3 Travel Solutions to Navigant International. (It sold the rest of TQ3 to Navigant two years later.) WestLB surrendered its majority shareholding of TUI in 2004, freeing up 90% of the company's shares for free float.

In 2005 the company purchased Canada-based CP Ships for almost $2 billion, making Hapag-Lloyd one of the world's largest container carriers. Two years later, TUI expanded its travel business by buying First Choice Holidays and combining the UK-based company with its existing tourism operations to form TUI Travel, a publicly traded company in which TUI held a controlling stake. Around the same time, the company decided to shed its container shipping operations and focus solely on its tourism and travel services businesses.

To this end, in March 2009 TUI sold Hapag-Lloyd to a German consortium but retained a 43% stake in the company.

EXECUTIVES

Chairman: Dietmar Kuhnt, age 72
Deputy Chairman: Petra Gerstenkorn, age 56
CEO: Michael Frenzel, age 63
Executive Director Finance: Rainer Feuerhake, age 66
Executive Director Tourism; CEO, First Choice Holidays and TUI Travel: Peter Long, age 58
Executive Director Human Resources and Legal Affairs: Peter Engelen, age 54
Director Hotels and Resorts Sector: Karl J. Pojer
Head Media Relations and Deputy Head Group Communications: Robin Zimmermann
Head Investor Relations: Björn Beroleit
Controller: Horst Baier, age 53
CEO, TUI Cruises: Richard J. Vogel
Auditors: PricewaterhouseCoopers AG Wirtschaftsprufungsgesellschaft

LOCATIONS

HQ: TUI AG
Karl-Wiechert-Allee 4
D-30625 Hannover, Germany
Phone: 49-511-566-00   **Fax:** 49-511-566-1901
Web: www.tui-group.com

2009 Sales

	% of total
Europe	
Germany	25
Other countries	63
North & South America	8
Other regions	4
Total	**100**

PRODUCTS/OPERATIONS

2009 Sales

	% of total
Tourism	
TUI Travel	89
TUI Hotels & Resorts	2
Cruises	1
Container shipping (discontinued operation)	8
Total	**100**

COMPETITORS

Accor
American Express
Carlson Wagonlit
Carnival Corporation
Club Med
Kuoni Travel
REWE
Royal Caribbean Cruises
Thomas Cook
Travelport

HISTORICAL FINANCIALS

Company Type: Public

Income Statement

FYE: September 30

	REVENUE ($ mil.)	NET INCOME ($ mil.)	NET PROFIT MARGIN	EMPLOYEES
9/09*	19,118	584	3.1%	69,536
12/08	26,378	(200)	—	70,200
12/07	32,184	258	0.8%	68,521
12/06	27,065	(1,175)	—	53,930
12/05	21,556	542	2.5%	61,559
Annual Growth	**(3.0%)**	**1.9%**	**—**	**3.1%**

*Fiscal year change

2009 Year-End Financials

Debt ratio: —
Return on equity: 18.8%
Cash ($ mil.): 2,118
Current ratio: 0.72
Long-term debt ($ mil.): —
No. of shares (mil.): 251
Dividends
  Yield: —
  Payout: —
Market value ($ mil.): 2,586

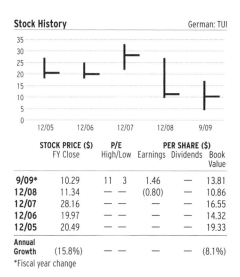

Stock History

German: TUI

	STOCK PRICE ($) FY Close	P/E High/Low		PER SHARE ($) Earnings	Dividends	Book Value
9/09*	10.29	11	3	1.46	—	13.81
12/08	11.34	—	—	(0.80)	—	10.86
12/07	28.16	—	—	—	—	16.55
12/06	19.97	—	—	—	—	14.32
12/05	20.49	—	—	—	—	19.33
Annual Growth	**(15.8%)**	**—**	**—**	**—**	**—**	**(8.1%)**

*Fiscal year change

UBS AG

If you be wealthy then UBS is for you. UBS is one of the world's largest private banks with operations in more than 40 countries. UBS also provides asset management and investment banking, as well as traditional banking services in its home country of Switzerland. The group includes four primary segments: Wealth Management & Swiss Bank, Wealth Management Americas, UBS Investment Bank, and Global Asset Management. Investment management clients include ultra-wealthy individuals, corporations, and institutional investors. Asset classes offered include internal and external mutual bonds, money markets, stocks, and bonds. Investment banking options include securities underwriting, advisory, and foreign exchange.

UBS suffered severe losses in 2007 and 2008 related to investments in the US subprime mortgage market. It was one of Europe's hardest-hit financial institutions, and in late 2008 UBS received government bailout funds to the tune of CHF 68 billion ($60 billion).

In 2009 the company restructured to separate its struggling divisions into four autonomous units. UBS cut costs as well, including cutting some 12,500 jobs (it cut 6,000 jobs the previous year). In 2008 it sold $15 billion in distressed mortgage assets to BlackRock, shut down its municipal bond business, and sold its 3.4 billion shares in Bank of China. It also sold UBS Fiduciary Trust to Wilmington Trust, its mortgage servicing business to Impac Mortgage, and its Canadian energy business to JPMorgan Chase.

The company ran into more trouble in 2009. To settle claims that it helped American clients avoid paying taxes to the US government, the company paid a $780 million fine and turned over once-secret banking client records. It has also exited the US cross-border banking business. Some UBS account-holders countered by suing the company in Swiss court.

The turmoil was the final straw for CEO Rohrer, who was replaced in 2009 by Oswald Grübel, the former CEO of rival Credit Suisse. Grübel retired from Credit Suisse in 2007 and was credited with turning that company around after a period of poor performance. UBS continued to clear out its top management that year and brought in former Swiss finance minister Kaspar Villiger as its chairman. Shortly after Grübel took office he announced the sale of UBS Pactual, the company's Brazilian unit. However, UBS wasn't away from Brazil for long. It returned to the globally important market in 2010 when it bought brokerage Link Investimentos.

HISTORY

Businessmen in Winterthur, Switzerland, formed the Bank of Winterthur in 1862 to serve trading interests, finance railroads, and operate a warehouse. In 1912 the bank merged with the Bank of Toggenburg (formed in 1863) to create Schweizerische Bankgesellschaft — Union Bank of Switzerland (UBS).

It expanded in Switzerland, buying smaller banks and adding branches. After growing in the post-WWI era, it was hit hard by the Depression. UBS benefited from Switzerland's neutrality in WWII, gaining deposits from both Jews and Nazis. In 1946 the bank opened an office in New York. Expansion in Switzerland continued after the war with the purchase of Eidgenossische Bank of Zurich.

UBS continued its acquisitions in the 1950s; by 1962 it had 81 branches. Other purchases included Interhandel, a cash-rich Swiss financial concern (1967), and four savings banks (1968). In 1967 it opened a full-service office in London, and during the 1970s established several securities underwriting subsidiaries abroad.

International financial markets became supercharged in the 1980s, and UBS resolved to catch up with its domestic peers in international operations. As London prepared for financial deregulation in 1986, UBS bought brokerage house Phillips & Drew.

The firm's UK brokerage business was hit hard by the 1987 US stock market crash; over the next two years losses continued, prompting an overhaul of the London operations. Then its US operations were jarred by the collapse of the junk bond market in 1990. The next year UBS set up offices in Paris, Singapore, and Hong Kong and took over Chase Manhattan's New York money management unit.

Meanwhile, the firm continued to expand within Switzerland, buying five more banks to boost market share and fill in gaps in its branch network. These buys left UBS with overlapping operations and a bloated infrastructure when recession hit. Falling real estate values left the bank with a heavy load of nonperforming loans. In 1994 profits plummeted. Stockholder Martin Ebner, unhappy with the performance of president Robert Studer, tried to gain control of UBS; failing that, he sought to have Studer charged with criminal fraud. In 1996 he almost thwarted Studer's election to the chairmanship.

That year, after rebuffing Credit Suisse Group's merger bid, UBS began a draconian reorganization, cutting domestic branches and writing down billions of francs in bad loans, leading to UBS' first loss ever (with another the next year). In 1998 the company merged with Swiss Bank Corp., then cut 23% of its staff. Later that year the bank lost $1.6 billion in the stumbling Long-Term Capital Management hedge fund, prompting chairman Mathis Cabiallavetta to resign.

As UBS struggled to swallow Swiss Bank in 1999, it retreated from riskier markets, began selling some $2 billion in real estate, and sold

its 25% stake in Swiss Life/Rentenanstalt. In 2000 UBS bought US broker Paine Webber.

The bank came under computer attack in 2002 when a disgruntled PaineWebber employee set off a "logic bomb" in UBS's computer system. Despite the deletion of 1,000 files across the company network and $3 million in damages, UBS and its stock price weathered the attack.

UBS's 2006 acquisition of #2 Brazilian investment bank Banco Pactual for about $2.6 billion gave it a foothold in the volatile yet growing Brazilian private equity market. It also bought the private client services business of Piper Jaffray Companies for $875 million and KeyCorp's McDonald Investments.

The company suffered severe losses related to its investments in the US subprime mortgage market in 2007 and 2008, spurring the government to provide bailout funds. UBS ended up writing down around $40 billion and closing its Dillon Read Capital Management operations.

EXECUTIVES

Chairman: Kaspar Villiger, age 69,
$651,809 total compensation
Vice Chairman: Michel Demaré, age 54
Group CEO: Oswald J. Grübel, age 66
Group COO; CEO, Corporate Center: Ulrich Körner, age 48
Group CFO: John Cryan, age 49
Co-CEO, UBS Investment Bank: Carsten Kengeter, age 43, $12,707,547 total compensation
Co-CEO, UBS Investment Bank:
Alexander Wilmot-Sitwell, age 49
Regional COO, Americas: Diane Frimmel
Group Chief Risk Officer: Philip J. Lofts
Group Treasurer: Stephan Keller
Group General Counsel: Markus U. Diethelm, age 52
Head Global Real Estate, Global Asset Management:
Paul W. Marcuse
Head Investment Management, Wealth Management and Swiss Bank: Michael Strobaek
Head Wealth Management, Europe: Jakob Stott, age 55
Head Banking Products and Wealth Services:
Bernhard Buchs
Head Group Controlling and Accounting:
Peter Thurneysen
Head Human Resources: John F. Bradley, age 49
Global Head Investor Relations: Caroline Stewart
Chief Communication Officer: Michael Willi
Secretary: Luzius Cameron
Chairman, UBS France and UBS Monaco, Wealth Management and Swiss Bank: Niklaus Pfau
President, UBS Investment Bank; Chairman and CEO, UBS Group Americas: Robert Wolf, age 48
Auditors: Ernst & Young Ltd.

LOCATIONS

HQ: UBS AG
Bahnhofstrasse 45
CH-8098 Zurich, Switzerland
Phone: 41-44-234-1111   **Fax:** 41-44-239-9111
US HQ: 1285 Avenue of the Americas
New York, NY 10019
US Phone: 212-713-3000   **US Fax:** 212-713-6211
Web: www.ubs.com

2009 Sales

	% of total
Europe	
Switzerland	45
Other countries	5
US	35
Asia/Pacific	14
Other countries	1
Total	**100**

PRODUCTS/OPERATIONS

2009 Sales

	% of total
Interest	56
Net fees & commissions	43
Other	1
Total	**100**

2009 Assets

	% of total
Cash & equivalents	10
Reverse repurchase agreements	9
Trading portfolio	17
Positive replacement values	31
Loans	23
Other	10
Total	**100**

2009 Sales by Segment

	% of total
Wealth Management & Swiss Bank	59
Investment Bank	31
Wealth Management Americas	10
Total	**100**

COMPETITORS

Bank of America	JPMorgan Chase
Barclays	Julius Baer
CIBC	Mitsubishi UFJ Financial
Citigroup	Group
Coutts Group	Mizuho Financial
Credit Suisse	Morgan Stanley
Deutsche Bank (Hungary)	RBC Financial Group
Goldman Sachs	UniCredit
HSBC	Wells Fargo Advisors

HISTORICAL FINANCIALS

Company Type: Public

Income Statement

FYE: December 31

	ASSETS ($ mil.)	NET INCOME ($ mil.)	INCOME AS % OF ASSETS	EMPLOYEES
12/09	1,291,474	(2,047)	—	65,233
12/08	1,894,004	(19,586)	—	79,166
12/07	2,014,914	(3,887)	—	85,208
12/06	1,967,772	10,064	0.5%	78,986
12/05	1,570,424	10,694	0.7%	69,569
Annual Growth	(4.8%)	—	—	(1.6%)

2009 Year-End Financials

Equity as % of assets: 3.1%	Dividends
Return on assets: —	Yield: 0.0%
Return on equity: —	Payout: —
Long-term debt ($ mil.): 126,545	Market value ($ mil.): 56,723
No. of shares (mil.): 3,796	Sales ($ mil.): 39,932

Stock History

NYSE: UBS

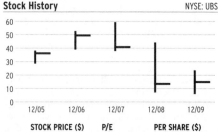

	STOCK PRICE ($) FY Close	P/E High/Low		PER SHARE ($) Earnings	Dividends	Book Value
12/09	14.94	—	—	(0.72)	0.00	10.41
12/08	13.54	—	—	(7.15)	0.00	8.12
12/07	40.83	—	—	(2.02)	1.96	8.31
12/06	49.46	11	8	4.88	1.28	10.75
12/05	36.15	8	6	4.85	0.75	8.90
Annual Growth	(19.8%)	—	—	—	—	4.0%

UniCredit

Give credit where credit is due: UniCredit is a giant among Europe's banking giants. Also known as UniCredito Italiano, the company and its units have some 10,000 financial services branches in some 50 countries around the world. UniCredit's retail banking operations are led by HVB in Germany, Bank Austria (that country's top bank), and UniCredit Banca in Italy. The company owns several units in Central and Eastern Europe, too, including Yapi Kredi in Turkey and Bank Pekao in Poland. (It is the largest foreign bank in the region.) UniCredit also has corporate banking, asset management, investment banking, private banking, and related businesses.

UniCredit has established itself as a global presence over the course of the past several years, as former CEO Alessandro Profumo ushered in a series of mergers and acquisitions. Among those deals were the company's $18 billion acquisition of HVB and Bank Austria in 2005 (one of the largest cross-border banking deals ever seen in Europe) and the nearly $30 billion purchase of Italian bank Capitalia in 2007. Also under his tenure, the company partnered with Koç Holding to take a majority stake in Yapi Kredi (2002) and acquired a 92%-stake in Kazakhstan's ATF Bank (2007). It also made investments in Bosnia, Hungary, Russia, and Serbia.

The HVB acquisition made UniCredit a powerhouse in Germany and Austria and brought the company sizeable holdings in Central and Eastern Europe, while the Capitalia acquistion strengthened its position at home. After years of expansion, though, UniCredit was one of the harder-hit banks in the financial crisis as loan losses soared in its newer markets.

After 13 years at the helm, Profumo was pushed out as CEO in 2010. Not only had he lost favor for his aggressive and risky expansion into Eastern Europe, but he was also called to task for his role in Libya's acquisition of a 7.6% stake in UniCredit. (That development brought much-needed capital but made investors nervous about outside ownership and influence.) Deputy CEO Federico Ghizzoni, a long-time veteran of the bank, was named Profumo's successor.

UniCredit is the product of the mergers of several Italian banks, including Banca CRT, Cariverona Banca, Cassamarca, and Rolo Banca 1473, some of which had roots in Renaissance-era lenders. The bank's corporate structure includes six divisions: retail banking, corporate banking, markets and investment banking, Central Eastern Europe, Poland, and private banking and asset management.

HISTORY

UniCredito Italiano's ancestor Banca di Genova was formed in 1870, just after Italy unified. Within a year the bank was in a South American banking venture, Banco de Italia y Rio de la Plata. A banking crisis beginning in the late 1880s threatened the company, which was saved and reorganized with the aid of German banking interests. The changes gave the bank — which was renamed Credito Italiano — an advantage over home-grown rivals and pointed it in the direction of German-style universal banking, including making direct investments in Italy's late-blooming industrial sector.

In the early 20th century, Credito Italiano joined other banks in foreign ventures in Albania, Brazil, and China, and opened offices in London and New York.

After the 1929 crash, Credito Italiano acquired several failed banks. But Credito Italiano itself was none too healthy: Government attempts in the 1920s to peg the lira to the pound led to industrial stagnation, leaving the bank holding highly illiquid industrial investments, and by the early 1930s it was essentially an industrial holding company.

Credito Italiano's existence was threatened when the Depression hit in earnest. To save the bank and its peers, Mussolini established the Istituto per la Ricostruzione Industriale (IRI) in 1933 as a "temporary" Resolution Trust-style holding company (IRI was finally liquidated in 2000) to take over the industrial assets of Credito Italiano and several other banks. IRI was instantly a major shareholder in Credito Italiano. IRI-held banks were designated "banks of national interest" three years later and were allowed to provide only short-term commercial banking services, a limit that remained in effect for more than 50 years.

In 1946, to fill the need for long-term industrial credit to rebuild war-torn Italy, Credito Italiano joined with Banca Commerciale Italiana (now part of IntesaBci) and Banco di Roma to form Mediobanca.

Credito Italiano went public in 1969 (IRI sold its interest in the bank in 1993). As a bank of national interest, Credito Italiano was called upon to help bail out several of the country's industrial groups in 1979 (it did so reluctantly).

Changing laws allowed the company to expand its branch network in 1980, and in 1982 IRI allowed Credito Italiano to raise capital (although it was still obliged to prop up struggling state industries). But the 1987 US stock market crash caused Credito Italiano's earnings to plunge 33%. Two years later it bought a stake in Banca Nazionale dell'Agricoltura, then Italy's largest private bank.

In 1995 the company joined forces with Rolo Banca 1473 (named for the year its progenitor was founded) to form Credito Italiano Group. Two years later, Alessandro Profumo became CEO. He would usher in more than a decade of rapid and agressive expansion.

Credito Italiano merged in 1998 with UniCredito, a collection of several northern Italian banks. One, Cassa di Risparmio di Verona Vicenza Belluno e Ancona (Cariverona) began in 1501 as a pawnshop operated by monks.

Foreshadowing the bank's shift to an Internet growth strategy (announced after talks with Spain's Banco Bilbao Vizcaya Argentaria fell through) UniCredito in 1999 announced plans for an electronic stock market, to include after-hours trading. It also continued to boost holdings in Eastern European banks. In 2000 the company entered into securities brokerage and mutual fund administration with its purchase of US-based Pioneer Investment Management.

In 2001 UniCredito bought 10% of the Pirelli/Benetton-owned holding company formed to control Italian telecommunications company Olivetti. The bank acquired HVB and Bank Austria in 2005 in an $18 billion cross-border deal, one of the largest such deals ever seen in Europe. The bank strengthened its hold at home in 2007 with the nearly $30 billion purchase of Italian bank Capitalia. Antitrust authorities ordered UniCredit to sell its stake in Assicurazioni Generali following the Capitalia transaction.

EXECUTIVES

Chairman: Dieter Rampl, age 63
Vice Chairman: Vincenzo C. Buonaura, age 64
Vice Chairman: Fabrizio Palenzona, age 57
Vice Chairman: Farhat O. Bengdara, age 45
Deputy Vice Chairman: Luigi Castelletti, age 55
CEO: Federico Ghizzoni, age 55
CFO: Marina Natale
Deputy CEO and Head, GBS Strategic Business Area: Paolo Fiorentino, age 54
Deputy CEO and Head, CIB and PB Strategic Business Area: Sergio P. Ermotti, age 50
Deputy CEO and Head, Retail Strategic Business Area: Roberto Nicastro, age 45
Chief Risk Officer: Karl Guha, age 46
Global Head, Equity Capital Markets: Christian Steffens
Head, Retail Italy Network Division; CEO, UniCredit Banca: Gabriele Piccini, age 54
Head, Financing and Advisory: Vittorio Ogliengo, age 52
Head Compliance and Corporate Affairs: Farugue Nadine Farida
Head, Human Resources: Salvatore (Rino) Piazzolla, age 57
Head, Strategy and Marketing: Francesco Giordano, age 43
Head, Institutional and Regulatory Strategic Advisory: Carmine Lamanda, age 69
Head, Media Relations and Executive Communications: Marcello Berni
Secretary: Lorenzo Lampiano
General Counsel and Group Compliance Officer: Nadine Faruque, age 49
Auditors: KPMG S.p.A.

LOCATIONS

HQ: UniCredit S.p.A.
Piazza Cordusio
20123 Milan, Italy
Phone: 39-02-88-621   **Fax:** 39-02-8862-8503
US HQ: 150 E 42nd St., New York, NY 10017
US Phone: 212-546-9600   **US Fax:** 212-826-8623
Web: www.unicredit.it

2009 Sales by Region

	% of total
Italy	40
Central & Eastern Europe	24
Germany	18
Austria	8
Other	10
Total	**100**

PRODUCTS/OPERATIONS

2009 Sales

	% of total
Interest	75
Fees & commissions	20
Financial assets & liabilities held for trading	3
Other	2
Total	**100**

COMPETITORS

ABN AMRO Group
Antonveneta
Banca Popolare di Milano
Banco Popolare
BNP Paribas
Credit Suisse
Deutsche Bank
Intesa Sanpaolo
UBS

HISTORICAL FINANCIALS

Company Type: Public

Income Statement

FYE: December 31

	ASSETS ($ mil.)	NET INCOME ($ mil.)	INCOME AS % OF ASSETS	EMPLOYEES
12/09	1,331,098	2,916	0.2%	165,062
12/08	1,473,790	6,384	0.4%	174,519
12/07	1,503,926	9,830	0.7%	177,571
12/06	1,086,159	8,085	0.7%	142,406
12/05	932,044	3,235	0.3%	132,917
Annual Growth	9.3%	(2.6%)	—	5.6%

2009 Year-End Financials

Equity as % of assets: 6.2%
Return on assets: 0.2%
Return on equity: 3.6%
Long-term debt ($ mil.): —
No. of shares (mil.): 13,347

Dividends
Yield: 0.0%
Payout: —
Market value ($ mil.): 44,809
Sales ($ mil.): 63,610

Stock History

Pink Sheets: UNCFF

	STOCK PRICE ($) FY Close	P/E High/Low		PER SHARE ($) Earnings	Dividends	Book Value
12/09	3.36	28	6	0.14	0.00	6.23
12/08	2.08	19	5	0.36	0.31	5.85
12/07	7.07	14	9	0.67	0.30	5.07
12/06	7.41	13	11	0.59	0.25	3.56
12/05	5.83	16	11	0.37	0.21	3.47
Annual Growth	(12.9%)	—	—	(21.6%)	—	15.7%

Unilever

One is a lonely number, unless you're Unilever. A top maker of packaged consumer goods worldwide, Unilever products are sold in more than 170 countries throughout Africa, Asia, Latin America, the Middle East, North America, and Western Europe. The company's offerings span several categories, including savory, dressings, and spreads; ice cream and beverages; personal care; and home care. Unilever's vast portfolio includes 11 brands that ring up more than $1 billion each annually. The best sellers include Hellmann's (mayonnaise), Knorr (soups), Lipton (tea), Dove and Lux (soaps), and Sure and Degree (antiperspirants). Unilever is the operating arm of Netherlands-based Unilever N.V. and UK-based Unilever PLC.

After divesting the majority of its Western European frozen foods business to private equity firm Permira in 2006 for more than $2.2 billion, in 2010 Unilever sold its Shedd's Country Crock line of chilled side dishes to Hormel Foods. (It retained ownership of Shedd's spreads and trademarks, however.) The company has agreed to sell its remaining Italian frozen foods business to the UK's Birds Eye Iglo Group for €805 million (about $1 billion). On the plus side, Unilever upped its stake in Israeli ice-cream maker

Strauss Ice Cream to 90% (from 50%) and has agreed to acquire a Danish ice cream maker from a Norway-based dairy group, both in 2010.

While food products account for more than 50% of Unilever's sales, personal care products and other high-growth industries are key to its growth strategy. To that end, in fall 2010 the company agreed to acquire the maker of Alberto VO5 hair care products, Alberto-Culver, for $3.7 billion in cash. The purchase would vault Unilever to #1 status as the world's leader in hair conditioning, #2 in shampoo, and third place in hair styling.

Previously, Unilever bought salon hair care products maker TIGI in 2009. The purchase, valued at more than $410 million, included TIGI's hair-styling academies and added the Bed Head, Catwalk, and S-factor brands, among others, to Unilever's offering of hair care products. Unilever has also announced plans to acquire the personal care and European laundry business of Sara Lee. The approximately €1.3 billion ($1.5 billion) purchase includes more than 90 brands (Sanex, Radox, and Duschdas).

Unilever in 2008 sold its North American laundry portfolio of brands, sold in the US, Canada, and Puerto Rico, to Vestar Capital Partners for $1.45 billion. Included in the transaction were Snuggle, All, Wisk, Surf, and Sunlight fabric-cleaning brands, as well as Unilever's manufacturing plant in Baltimore.

HISTORY

After sharpening his sales skills in the family wholesale grocery business, Englishman William Lever formed a new company in 1885 with his brother James. Lever Brothers introduced Sunlight, the world's first packaged, branded laundry soap. Sunlight was a success in Britain, and within 15 years Lever Brothers was selling soap worldwide. Between 1906 and 1915 the company grew mostly through acquisitions. Needing vegetable oil to make soap, the company established plantations and trading companies worldwide. During WWI Lever began using its vegetable oil to make margarine.

Rival Dutch butter makers Jurgens and Van den Berghs were pioneers in margarine production. In 1927 they created the Margarine Union, a cartel that owned the European market. The Margarine Union and Lever Brothers merged in 1930, but for tax reasons formed two separate entities: Unilever PLC in London and Unilever N.V. in Rotterdam, the Netherlands.

Despite the Depression and WWII, Unilever expanded, acquiring US companies Thomas J. Lipton (1937) and Pepsodent (1944). Unilever benefited from the postwar boom in Europe, the increasing use of margarine, new detergent technologies, and the growing use of personal care products.

Although product development fueled some growth, acquisitions (at one time running at the rate of one per week) played a major role in shaping Unilever. These included Birds Eye Foods in the UK (1957) and, in the US, Good Humor (1961), Lawry's Foods (1979), Ragu (1986), Chesebrough-Ponds (1987), Calvin Klein Cosmetics (1989, now Unilever Cosmetics International), Fabergé/Elizabeth Arden (1989), and Breyers ice cream (1993).

In 1995 Unilever began cutting its global workforce by 7,500. The following year it bought hair care and deodorant maker Helene Curtis. Unilever shed its specialty chemicals operations in 1997.

In 2000 the company bought US weight-management firm Slim-Fast Foods for $2.3 billion and ice-cream maker Ben & Jerry's. As part of its previously announced brand-reduction strategy, Unilever also that year sold its European bakery supplies business to CSM. Later that same year the company bought Bestfoods for $24 billion, which would result in putting Bestfoods' US baking business (Entenmann's, Oroweat bread) up for sale. George Weston's offer of $1.77 billion won the bidding war for Bestfoods' US baking business.

In 2001 Unilever sold its Elizabeth Arden fragrance and skin care business to French Fragrances. Also in 2001 it sold its North American seafood businesses (the Gorton's brand in the US and BlueWater in Canada) to seafood conglomerate Nippon Suisan Kaisha.

In 2002 Unilever sold its retail dry cleaning and laundry-related business to ZOOTS-The Cleaner Cleaner, and its institutional and industrial cleaning business, DiverseyLever, to Johnson Wax Professional. It also sold 19 of its North American food brands (including Argo and Kingsford cornstarches, Mazola corn oil, Karo corn syrup, and Henri's salad dressings) to a subsidiary of Associated British Foods plc.

Unilever exited the fragrance business when it sold its Unilever Cosmetics International unit to Coty in 2005 for about $800 million. Also that year, Antony Burgmans became chairman and Patrick Cescau took the title of CEO. Burgmans later stepped down and Michael Treschow, chairman of Ericsson, took over. Treschow is the first outsider to hold the position at the company. (Cescau retired in 2008 after 35 years at Unilever and outsider Paul Polman from Nestlé USA and P&G took over as CEO.)

In mid-2006 Unilever sold the majority of its Western European frozen foods business to private-equity firm Permira for more than $2.2 billion. The transaction included the Iglo and Birds Eye brands in Austria, Belgium, France, Germany, Greece, Ireland, the Netherlands, Portugal, and the UK.

EXECUTIVES

Chairman: Michael Treschow, age 67
Vice Chairman: Jeroen van der Veer, age 62
CEO and Director: Paul Polman, age 53
CFO and Director: Jean-Marc Huët, age 40
Chief Human Resources Officer: Sandy Ogg, age 56
Chief Security Officer: Adam Mallalieu
Chief Research and Development Officer:
Prof Geneviève B. Berger, age 55
Chief Supply Chain Officer: Pier Luigi Sigismondi, age 44
Chief Legal Officer and Secretary: Tonia Lovell, age 41
Chief Marketing and Communications Officer:
Keith Weed, age 48
Group Controller and SVP Finance Categories:
Howard Green
Group Treasurer: Pascal Visée, age 48
Group Secretary: Sven Dumoulin
EVP, UK and Ireland: Amanda Sourry
EVP, North America: Eugenio Minvielle, age 46
EVP, Laundry Care: Randy Quinn
EVP, Southeast Asia and Australasia: Jan Zijderveld
SVP Communications and Sustainability: Gavin Neath
President, Global Foods, Home, and Personal Care:
Michael B. (Mike) Polk, age 49
President, Unilever Mexico: Guilherme Loureiro
President, Americas: David (Dave) Lewis, age 45
Auditors: PricewaterhouseCoopers Accountants N.V.

HQ: Unilever
Unilever House, 100 Victoria Embankment
London EC4Y 0YD, United Kingdom
Phone: 44-20-7822-5252   **Fax:** 44-20-7822-5951
HQ: Unilever N.V.
Weena 455
3000 DK Rotterdam, The Netherlands
Phone: 31-10-217-4000   **Fax:** 31-10-217-4798
US HQ: 700 Sylvan Ave., Englewood Cliffs, NJ 07632
US Phone: 201-894-4000
Web: www.unilever.com

2009 Sales

	% of total
Asia Africa CEE	38
The Americas	32
Western Europe	30
Total	**100**

PRODUCTS/OPERATIONS

2009 Sales

	% of total
Savory, dressings & spreads	33
Personal care	30
Ice cream & beverages	20
Home care & other	17
Total	**100**

Selected Brands

Culinary (Calvé, Colmans, Hellman's, Knorr, Lipton Cup-a-Soup, Ragu, Skippy)
Carb options (low-carb Ragu, Wish-Bone, Skippy, Lipton)
Deodorants (Axe, Brut, Degree, Dove, Rexona)
Hair care (Organics, Suave, SunSilk, ThermaSilk, TIGI)
Household care (Domestos, Sunlight)
Ice cream (Ben & Jerry's, Breyers, Good-Humor, Klondike, Magnum, Popsicle, Solero)
Laundry (Ala, Cif, Comfort, Omo, Surf)
Personal wash (Dove, Lever 2000, Lux, Pond's, Q-tips, Vaseline)
Salad dressing (Wish-Bone)
Spreads, oils, and other cooking products (Becel, Bertolli, Country Crock, I Can't Believe It's Not Butter!, Promise, Rama)
Tea-based beverages (Lipton)
Toothpaste (Close Up, Signal)
Weight management (Slim-Fast)

COMPETITORS

Alberto-Culver	Kraft Foods
Alticor	L'Oréal
Atkins Nutritionals	LVMH
Avon	Mars, Incorporated
Beiersdorf	McBride plc
Campbell Soup	Meda Pharmaceuticals
Church & Dwight	Nestlé
Clorox	PepsiCo
Coca-Cola	Procter & Gamble
Colgate-Palmolive	Reckitt Benckiser
ConAgra	Revlon
Dairy Farmers of America	Sara Lee International
Danone	Household and Body Care
Del Monte Foods	S.C. Johnson
The Dial Corporation	Shiseido
Estée Lauder	smart balance
General Mills	Tata Group
Johnson & Johnson	Uniq
Kao	

HISTORICAL FINANCIALS

Company Type: Group

Income Statement

FYE: December 31

	REVENUE ($ mil.)	NET INCOME ($ mil.)	NET PROFIT MARGIN	EMPLOYEES
12/09	57,074	5,296	9.3%	163,000
12/08	57,117	7,449	13.0%	174,000
12/07	59,151	6,088	10.3%	175,000
12/06	52,300	6,260	12.0%	179,000
12/05	46,984	4,460	9.5%	206,000
Annual Growth	**5.0%**	**4.4%**	**—**	**(5.7%)**

2009 Year-End Financials

Debt ratio: 63.8%
Return on equity: —
Cash ($ mil.): —
Current ratio: —
Long-term debt ($ mil.): 11,024

Net Income History

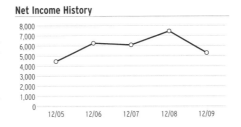

Vale S.A.

Vale has more than one iron in the fire. Iron ore and pellets account for more than half of Vale's sales, and the company accounts for a third of the world's ocean-shipped iron ore. Vale also mines for bauxite, nickel, kaolin, and potash. Other products include steel, copper, and aluminum. It has holdings in hydroelectric power generation and in rail and shipping businesses, mainly to support its mining activities in Brazil. The company is the world's #1 iron ore miner and among the top three overall, having grown dramatically with the 2006 acquisition of Vale Limited (formerly Vale Inco). In 2010 Vale announced that it planned to spin off its fertilizer division with an IPO in the first half of 2011.

The spin-off, in the form of new company Vale Fertilizantes, will control all of Vale's fertilizer assets. The move is an attempt to bring value to Vale at a time when the global fertilizer sector is seen as outperforming other commodities. It is expected that Vale Fertilizantes will be an exchange-listed company.

Vale spent much of 2010 acquiring fertilizer companies and forming ventures. Mitsui teamed up with US fertilizer company Mosaic in 2010 for a joint venture, investing in a Vale phosphorus ore development project in Peru. Mitsui will spend $275 million to acquire a 25% stake and voting rights in a Vale subsidiary, while Mosaic will hold a 24% stake. The project is located in northwestern Peru's Piura province. Vale also completed a $4.7 billion deal for Brazil's Fosfertil and US-based agribusiness Bunge Co.

In 2010 Vale agreed to sell its Brazilian aluminum operations to Norwegian aluminum producer Norsk Hydro for $5 billion. Norsk Hydro agreed to pay Vale $1.1 billion in cash and a 22% stake in Norsk Hydro, which when the deal closes would control the world's third-largest bauxite mine and the world's biggest alumina refinery. Vale said it was selling the assets because its presence in the primary aluminum metal industry is small, and has little growth potential due to the lack of access to low-cost sources of power generation in Brazil.

As a part of its drive to become the world's biggest mining company, Vale announced plans to invest up to $20 billion in acquisitions in 2011, and as much as $100 billion through 2015. The majority of the funds would go to secure iron ore, with most of that being spent in Brazil.

Remaining active in the mining sector, Vale is developing a copper mine in Zambia in a $400 million joint venture with African Rainbow Minerals. The Konkola North project is expected to begin production in 2013. In 2010 Vale acquired a 51% stake in Guinea iron-ore mining firm BSG Resources for $2.5 billion.

Vale also bought Rio Tinto's potash assets and a Brazilian iron mine from the Anglo-Australian giant in 2009 for about $1.5 billion.

Toward the end of 2007, the company — then called Companhia Vale do Rio Doce — decided that it wanted a new brand identity and so ditched its longtime nickname, CVRD, in favor of Vale. Two years later it changed its name legally, dropping the more formal Companhia Vale do Rio Doce.

Investment group Valepar controls a third of Vale. The Brazilian government holds limited veto power on any permanent company changes.

HISTORY

During the 1890s, as land reforms opened the way for foreign investments in Brazil, the mineral-rich state of Minas Gerais caught the attention of mining companies from Europe and the US. British engineers founded the Itabira Iron Ore Company and took over the Doce River Valley's Vitória-Minas Railroad. After Brazil's revolution (1930), Itabira was split up. One of the new companies, Itabira Mineração, began shipping iron ore in 1940.

A 1942 agreement, prompted by the outbreak of WWII, established iron export regulations from Brazil to the US and the UK. Later that year the Companhia Vale do Rio Doce (CVRD) was formed, with the Brazilian government owning 80%. The new company received the assets of Itabira, including Brazil's "iron mountain," Caué Peak. By the end of the 1940s, 80% of Brazil's iron ore exports were mined by CVRD. During the 1950s CVRD invested in land holdings and shipping operations. The company set up a shipping and logistics subsidiary in 1962.

CVRD teamed up with US Steel in 1970 to mine iron ore at Carajás in Amazonian Brazil; two years later the site was found to hold the world's largest iron ore reserves (18 billion tons). By 1975 CVRD had become the world's largest iron ore exporter. A year later the company finished doubling the tracks of the Vitória-Minas Railroad. It also set up a manganese mining company (Urucum Mineração) and an alumina production facility (Alumina do Norte do Brasil, or Alunorte).

To support its Carajás mining operations, CVRD added the Estrada de Ferro de Carajás railway (finished 1985) and a hydroelectric project. In all, the giant Carajás project involved investments from the US, Japan, France, the European Economic Community, and the World Bank. (The Carajás area, like many mining sites in Brazil, has been the site of intense controversy because it attracts subsistence miners, including children, who work under dangerous circumstances.) By the late 1980s the company had become a major supplier of pelletized iron, used as feed for steel mill blast furnaces.

In 1992 CVRD expanded into the production of chemicals (Rio Capim Química, now Pará Pigmentos SA). The company acquired stakes in two steel mills — Siderúrgica de Tubarão and Aço Minas Gerais SA — in 1993. In 1996 it invested in gold finds in Pará state. CVRD was privatized in 1997.

The company listed ADR shares on the NYSE in 2000. Acquisitions that year included Brazilian iron ore companies SOCOIMEX and SAMITRI (73%). CVRD sold its 50% stake in pulp and paper group Bahia Sul, to Suzano for $320 million in 2001. It also sold its 51% share of pulp maker Cenibra and its share of steelmaker Companhia Siderúrgica Nacional (CSN).

In 2002 the Brazilian Treasury and the National Social and Economic Bank (BNDES) sold 33% of CVRD's shares, further privatizing the company. CVRD disposed of its last gold mine (Fazenda Brasileiro) in 2003.

Under pressure from increasing globalization, Vale had been forced to trim some of its operations (including its stake in CSN) to focus on mining and bulk transport. Those asset sales helped fund Vale's win over Australian mining giant BHP Billiton, the world's #2 iron ore producer, in a battle for Brazil's iron miner Caemi Mineração e Metalurgia, #4 worldwide. (From 2001 through 2006 the company picked up stakes in Caemi until it owned it fully.)

EXECUTIVES

Chairman: Sérgio Ricardo Silva Rosa, age 50
Vice Chairman: Mário da Silveira Teixeira Jr., age 64
President and CEO: Roger Agnelli, age 51
CFO: Guilherme Perboyre Cavalcanti
Executive Officer, Fertilizers: Mário Alves Barbosa Neto
Executive Officer, Integrated Operations, Logistics, Project Management, and Sustainability: Eduardo de Salles Bartolomeo, age 46
Executive Officer, Non-Ferrous Minerals and Basic Metals Operations; President and CEO, Vale Inco: Tito Botelho Martins Jr., age 47
Executive Officer, Ferrous Minerals, Marketing, Sales, and Strategy: José Carlos Martins, age 60
Executive Officer, Human Resources and Corporate Services: Carla Grasso, age 48
Press Manager: Mônica Ferreira
Auditors: PricewaterhouseCoopers Auditores Independentes

LOCATIONS

HQ: Vale S.A.
Avenida Graça Aranha, 26
20030-900 Rio de Janeiro, Brazil
Phone: 55-21-3814-4477   **Fax:** 55-21-3814-4040
Web: www.vale.com.br

2009 Sales

	$ mil.	% of total
Asia		
China	9,003	38
Japan	2,412	10
Other countries	2,218	9
Americas		
Brazil	3,655	15
US	832	3
Other countries	1,252	6
Europe	4,036	17
Middle East/Africa/Oceania	531	2
Adjustments	(628)	—
Total	**23,311**	**100**

PRODUCTS/OPERATIONS

2009 Sales

	$ mil.	% of total
Ferrous minerals	14,475	62
Non-ferrous minerals	7,265	22
Aluminum	2,050	9
Logistic services	1,104	5
Other products	825	3
Adjustments	(2,408)	—
Total	**23,311**	**100**

COMPETITORS

AHMSA
Alcoa
Anglo American
BHP Billiton
BHP Billiton Plc
Cliffs Natural Resources
Exxaro
Freeport-McMoRan
Kumba Iron Ore
Norilsk Nickel
Rio Tinto Limited
Rio Tinto plc
Teck
Xstrata

HISTORICAL FINANCIALS

Company Type: Public

Income Statement

FYE: December 31

	REVENUE ($ mil.)	NET INCOME ($ mil.)	NET PROFIT MARGIN	EMPLOYEES
12/09	23,311	5,349	22.9%	60,036
12/08	37,426	13,218	35.3%	62,490
12/07	32,242	11,825	36.7%	57,043
12/06	19,651	6,528	33.2%	52,646
12/05	14,549	4,470	30.7%	38,560
Annual Growth	**12.5%**	**4.6%**	**—**	**11.7%**

2009 Year-End Financials

Debt ratio: 43.7%
Return on equity: 13.4%
Cash ($ mil.): 7,293
Current ratio: 2.32
Long-term debt ($ mil.): 20,650

No. of shares (mil.): 5,257
Dividends
  Yield: 1.6%
  Payout: 46.4%
Market value ($ mil.): 152,611

Stock History

NYSE: VALE

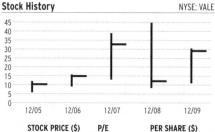

	STOCK PRICE ($) FY Close	P/E High/Low		PER SHARE ($) Earnings	Dividends	Book Value
12/09	29.03	31	12	0.97	0.45	10.83
12/08	12.11	17	3	2.58	0.32	8.10
12/07	32.67	16	6	2.41	0.34	6.33
12/06	14.87	11	7	1.35	0.26	3.74
12/05	10.28	11	6	1.05	0.28	1.96
Annual Growth	**29.6%**	**—**	**—**	**(2.0%)**	**12.6%**	**53.4%**

Veolia Environnement

Voila! Veolia Environnement holds water — as well as waste management, energy, and transportation — operations. The company's Veolia Eau unit, which provides water and wastewater services to more than 80 million people in more than 60 countries, is the world's largest water company, ahead of SUEZ Environnement. Veolia Environmental Services, one of the world's leading waste management companies, serves more than 70 million people a year. Majority-owned energy unit Dalkia (Veolia Energy Services) operates global cogeneration facilities and heating and cooling systems, and Veolia Transport (formerly Connex) is a top European provider of bus, light-rail, and rail transport and operates in about 30 countries.

In 2008 more than 70% of the company's revenues was generated through contracts with local public authorities.

Veolia Environnement is strategically targeting expansion in its core European markets, and in new markets in Eastern and Central Europe, and in Asia (especially in China). To generate cash, in 2010 Veolia Environnement sold US waste-to-energy contractor Montenay International (which held its North American waste-to-energy assets) to Covanta Holding for $450 million. Marking a push for more green energy projects in Europe, that year the company opened France's largest biomass-fueled boiler plant, serving a district heating system in Val d'Oise.

Later in 2009 the company named Antoine Frérot as CEO. He had been in charge of Veolia's water division previously.

Veolia Environnement was formed from the water, waste, energy, and transport businesses of the former Vivendi group. (The name Veolia is derived from Aeolus, the keeper of the winds in Greek mythology). The group spun off Veolia Environnement (then called Vivendi Environnement), sold a minority stake to the public, and renamed itself Vivendi Universal in 2000 (and Vivendi in 2006).

HISTORY

What is now Veolia Environnement originated in 1853 as Compagnie Générale des Eaux in Paris. The company irrigated farmlands and subsequently supplied water. By 1860 Paris had granted the company a 50-year contract to provide the city's water. In 1880 it moved beyond France to provide water in Venice, Italy. Operations in Turkey (Istanbul) and Portugal (Oporto) followed.

Compagnie Générale des Eaux extended its water network in 1924, and by WWII it supplied half of all urban households in France. After the war the company expanded into household waste collection (1953) and operation of household waste incineration and compost plants (1967). Wastewater treatment activities began in 1972.

In the next decade Compagnie Générale des Eaux dove into diversification. It increased its holding in energy-conversion systems operator Compagnie Générale de Chauffe to 100% (making it France's leading energy company) in 1980. That year it merged its wastewater treatment subsidiaries to create Omnium de Traitement et de Valorisation (OTV). Its waste operations were further augmented through the takeover of Compagnie Générale d'Entreprises Automobiles

(CGEA), a transport and waste management firm. The company also ventured into telecommunications, pay-TV, and construction (it gained a controlling stake in builder SGE in 1988 but disposed of its interest in the firm, later known as VINCI, in 2000).

CGEA bid for and won control of several former British Rail lines in 1996 when the UK's railway system was privatized. Operating under the name Connex, the company began to run trains throughout southeastern England, the UK's largest commuting area.

In 1998 CGEA changed its name to Vivendi. The group (which came to include mobile phone provider Cegetel and a stake in the Havas media company) transferred the Compagnie Générale des Eaux name to its water business. Vivendi also organized its Compagnie Générale de Chauffe and Sithe Energies (now a part of Dynergy) subsidiaries into a single energy division, named Dalkia. In 1999 Sithe Energies bought 23 thermal power plants from US utility GPU (later FirstEnergy) and became the leading independent power producer in the northeastern US.

Vivendi continued its charge into the US that year. The group acquired waste services company Superior Services (then the US's fourth-biggest solid waste company). Its purchase of USFilter transformed Vivendi into the world's largest water company and marked the biggest acquisition of a US firm by a French company.

The ever-evolving Vivendi transformed into a global media company and renamed itself Vivendi Universal in 2000. It bought Seagram and French pay-TV provider CANAL+ and spun off its water, waste management, transportation, and energy operations (Vivendi Environnement) after turning down German utility RWE's $28 million offer to buy the business.

Vivendi Environnement's waste operations grew after snapping up operations in Brazil, Hong Kong, and Mexico from Waste Management. In 2001 the company merged its Dalkia energy operations with the energy services operations of Electricité de France (EDF).

In 2002 Vivendi Universal reduced its stake in Vivendi Environnement from 63% to about 20%; the next year Vivendi Environnement changed its name to Veolia Environnement. Vivendi finally divested all of its interest in Veolia in the middle of 2006.

In 2007 the company acquired Thermal North America, Inc., the largest portfolio of district heating and cooling networks in the US.

EXECUTIVES

Chairman; CEO, EDF: Henri Proglio, age 61
Vice Chairman: Louis Schweitzer, age 68
CEO and Director: Antoine Frérot, age 52
CFO: Pierre-François Riolacci, age 43
SEVP Public Entities and European Affairs:
Jean-Pierre Frémont
EVP and COO; Head, Waste Management Division:
Denis Gasquet, age 56
EVP; CEO, Veolia Water Solutions and Technologies:
Jean-Michel Herrewyn, age 49
EVP Industrial Markets: Stéphane Caine
EVP and Head, Energy Services Division; CEO, Dalkia:
Olivier Barbaroux, age 54
EVP; CEO Transport: Cyrille du Peloux, age 56
SVP Human Resources: Véronique Rouzaud, age 51
SVP and Secretary General: Olivier Orsini
Director Research and Innovation: Philippe Martin
General Secretary; Chairman and CEO, Veolia Environnement Services-Ré: Alain Tchernonog, age 66
Auditors: Salustro Reydel

LOCATIONS

HQ: Veolia Environnement SA
36-38, avenue Kléber
75116 Paris, France
Phone: 33-1-71-75-00-00　**Fax:** 33-1-71-75-10-45
US HQ: 14950 Heathrow Forest, Ste. 200
Houston, TX 77032
US Phone: 800-522-4774
Web: www.veoliaenvironnement.com

2009 Sales

	% of total
Europe	
France	40
Other countries	35
North America	9
Asia/Pacific	8
Other regions	8
Total	**100**

PRODUCTS/OPERATIONS

2009 Sales

	% of total
Water	36
Environmental services	26
Energy services	21
Transportation	17
Total	**100**

Selected Operations

Water
　Veolia Eau — Compagnie Générale des Eaux
　Veolia Water S.A.
Environmental Services
　Veolia Environmental Services North America Corp.
Energy
　Dalkia (66%)
Transport
　Veolia Transportation, Inc.

COMPETITORS

Alpheus	Severn Trent
American States Water	Shanks
AWG Plc	SNCF
Bouygues	Stagecoach
Electricité de France	SUEZ Environnement
Electricité de Strasbourg	Thames Water
Elyo	ThermoEnergy
Kelda	United Utilities
Northumbrian Water	Vattenfall
Pennon	Waste Management
RWE	Waste Recycling
SABESP	Welsh Water

HISTORICAL FINANCIALS

Company Type: Public

Income Statement

FYE: December 31

	REVENUE ($ mil.)	NET INCOME ($ mil.)	NET PROFIT MARGIN	EMPLOYEES
12/09	49,519	1,207	2.4%	95,789
12/08	51,228	573	1.1%	336,013
12/07	47,968	1,364	2.8%	319,502
12/06	37,792	1,002	2.7%	298,498
12/05	29,998	740	2.5%	271,153
Annual Growth	**13.3%**	**13.0%**	**—**	**(22.9%)**

2009 Year-End Financials

Debt ratio: 236.5%　　　　No. of shares (mil.): 497
Return on equity: 11.7%　 Dividends
Cash ($ mil.): 8,047　　　　Yield: 3.6%
Current ratio: 1.15　　　　 Payout: 96.1%
Long-term debt ($ mil.): 25,292　Market value ($ mil.): 23,440

Stock History 　　　　　　　　　　NYSE: VE

	STOCK PRICE ($) FY Close	P/E High/Low		PER SHARE ($) Earnings	Dividends	Book Value
12/09	47.12	32	15	1.78	1.71	21.50
12/08	44.70	107	24	1.24	1.71	19.92
12/07	133.91	45	31	3.14	1.55	22.50
12/06	99.29	40	24	2.52	1.12	11.58
12/05	53.65	29	21	1.88	0.85	9.08
Annual Growth	**(3.2%)**	**—**	**—**	**(1.4%)**	**19.1%**	**24.0%**

VINCI

Veni, vidi, vici . . . VINCI. Through its VINCI Construction division, this company conquers the world as one of the largest building, civil engineering, and maintenance contractors. VINCI operates in four main sectors: concessions, energy, roads, and construction. VINCI Energies is a leader in electrical engineering and information technology. Roadworks and urban transport infrastructure is handled by Eurovia, which operates some 300 quarries that provide building materials. VINCI Concessions builds and operates parking garages, toll roads, and airports, while VINCI Park manages parking facilities in about a dozen countries. VINCI is active in some 100 countries.

VINCI has an aggressive growth strategy as it continues to increase revenues and grow organically and through acquisitions. As a whole, VINCI is expanding in regions with economic growth such as central and eastern Europe and the Middle East. The company also sees opportunities in North America where aging infrastructure needs to be replaced. The company strengthened its position in the UK in 2008 when it bought British construction and facilities management firm Taylor Woodrow from Taylor Wimpey. In 2009 VINCI Construction acquired the troubled UK builder Haymills Group as that company teetered on the brink of collapse.

In 2010 VINCI boosted its cooperation with the Qatar-owned investment company Qatari Diar, when it bought technology services firm Cegelec in exchange for a stake in VINCI. Qatari Diar now is VINCI's largest shareholder after employee savings funds, owning between 5% and 8% of the company. The partnership will provide joint venture opportunities in the Middle East and beyond. Later that year the two partners announced plans for a parking lot joint venture, which will run lots in Qatar. The two already are working on a proposed €2.2 billion ($3 billion) bridge that would link Qatar and Bahrain.

VINCI's Eurovia subsidiary has been investing heavily in the raw materials used for road building. It has bought several European gravel quarry operations and road construction companies over the last several years. In 2010 it bought about 100 quarries from Tarmac.

In 2008 Eurovia branched out from the road to the rails when it acquired rail infrastructure firm Vossloh Infrastructure Services (now ETF-Eurovia Travaux Ferroviaires) from Vossloh. The division specializes in rail track maintenance and installation.

Not to be left out of the growth spurt, VINCI Park has been busy making acquisitions in the US, Canada, and Europe in efforts to make it one of the largest parking operators in the world. VINCI Park (and subsidiaries such as LAZ Parking in the US) manages more than a million on-street and off-street parking spaces in Europe, North America, and Asia.

VINCI merged the functions of its chairman and CEO in 2010. CEO Xavier Huillard took over as chairman and CEO, while Chairman Yves-Thibault de Silguy became vice-chairman and senior director.

HISTORY

VINCI's origins lie with French conglomerate Vivendi (now Vivendi Universal), which was founded in 1853 as Compagnie Générale des Eaux. Its mission was to irrigate French farmland and supply water to towns. The company won contracts to serve Lyons (1853), Nantes (1854), Paris (1860), and Venice (1880). Générale des Eaux moved into construction in 1972, building an office tower (and later hotels and houses) in Paris. The company also entered communications in the 1980s.

In 1988 Générale des Eaux acquired control of construction and civil engineering giant Société Générale d'Entreprises. SGE subsidiaries included Campenon Bernard SGE (part of Générale des Eaux since 1981), Sogea, Freyssinet, Cochery Bourdin Chaussé, Saunier Duval, Tunzini, Lefort Francheteau, and Wanner. SGE traces its construction roots to 1910. It became a subsidiary of Générale d'Electricité in 1966. Glassmaker Saint-Gobain acquired control of SGE in 1984. Under Générale des Eaux, SGE enhanced its European profile through acquisitions, including British builder Norwest Holst (1989), German road builder VBU (1991), and German pipe and duct maker MLTU (1992).

Générale des Eaux acquired publisher Havas in 1998 and took the name Vivendi — representing vivacity and mobility. Its purchase of USFilter in 1999 made Vivendi the world's largest water company. Vivendi's SGE unit (renamed VINCI) agreed to acquire the construction arm of rival conglomerate Suez's GTM unit in 2000.

Groupe GTM traces its roots to Société Lyonnaise des Eaux et de L'Eclairage, a leading French water utility. Formed in 1880, Lyonnaise des Eaux built up its French and international operations to include water distribution, as well as gas and electricity production and distribution. A century later the company had diversified into such businesses as heating (Cofreth), waste management (Sita), and communications, acquiring a stake in Lyonnaise Communications (now Lyonnaise Câble) in 1986.

In 1990 Lyonnaise des Eaux acquired construction firm Dumez, whose subsidiary GTM-Entrepose was France's largest car park manager. Four years later Dumez-GTM was formed to consolidate the construction and civil engineering businesses of Dumez and GTM-Entrepose. In 1997 Lyonnaise des Eaux and Compagnie de

Suez merged to create a leading provider of private infrastructure services, Suez Lyonnaise des Eaux (which shortened its name to SUEZ in 2001). Compagnie Universal du Canal Maritime de Suez, the builder of the Suez Canal, was founded in 1858 and became Financière de Suez in 1958. In 1967 Financière de Suez acquired control of Lyonnaise des Eaux.

SGE changed its name to VINCI in 2000. That year, as part of their strategy to rationalize operations and focus on core businesses, Vivendi and SUEZ agreed to a friendly takeover of GTM by VINCI. SUEZ emerged as the combined company's largest shareholder, but by the next year both SUEZ and Vivendi Universal had exited most of VINCI's capital, leaving no core stockholder.

VINCI expanded its concessions holdings in 2002 by hooking up with construction group Eiffage to grab a 17% stake in Europe's second-largest toll road operator, ASF, which was floated that year by the French government.

In 2006 chairman Antoine Zacharias resigned after an attempt to oust CEO Xavier Huillard failed. He was replaced by Yves-Thibault de Silguy, formerly of SUEZ.

In 2007 VINCI's top French construction businesses, Sogea Construction and GTM Construction, merged to create VINCI Construction France, its domestic construction giant.

EXECUTIVES

Chairman: Yves-Thibault de Silguy, age 61
CEO and Director; Chairman and CEO, VINCI Concessions: Xavier Huillard, age 56
EVP and CFO: Christian Labeyrie, age 53
EVP Contracting; Chairman, VINCI Construction: Richard Francioli, age 50
VP Business Development: Jean-Luc Pommier, age 57
VP Human Resources and Sustainable Development: Franck Mougin, age 51
Director Legal Affairs: Patrick Richard
Director Corporate Communication: Pierre Duprat
Chairman and CEO, Eurovia: Jacques Tavernier, age 59
Chairman and CEO, Escota: Philippe E. Daussy
Chairman, VINCI Autoroutes: Pierre Coppey, age 46
Chairman, VINCI Immobilier: Olivier de la Roussière
Chairman, VINCI Construction Grand Projects: Pierre Berger
Chairman and CEO, VINCI Energies: Jean-Yves Le Brouster, age 62
Chairman, VINCI Park: Denis Grand
Chairman, VINCI PLC: John Stanion
Chairman, VINCI Construction Filiales Internationales: Sébastien Morant
CEO, Entrepose Contracting: Dominique Bouvier
CEO and Director, Solétanche Freyssinet: Bruno Dupety
CEO, Autoroutes du Sud de la France: Pierre Anjolras
Director; Chairman, Solétanche Freyssinet: Jean-Pierre Lamoure
Auditors: Salustro Reydel

LOCATIONS

HQ: VINCI
1 cours Ferdinand-de-Lesseps
92851 Rueil-Malmaison, France
Phone: 33-1-47-16-35-00   **Fax:** 33-1-47-51-91-02
Web: www.vinci.com

PRODUCTS/OPERATIONS

2009 Sales

	% of total
Construction	45
Roads	25
Concessions/park	17
Energy	13
Total	**100**

Selected Subsidiaries

VINCI Construction
　CFE (46.8%; Benelux)
　　DEME (50%; dredging)
　VINCI Construction France
　VINCI PLC (UK)
　VINCI Construction Filiales Internationales (Germany, Central Europe, overseas France, Africa)
　VINCI Construction Grands Projets
　Freyssinet (specialized civil engineering)
VINCI Concessions
VINCI Park
Eurovia
VINCI Energies
　Actemium (industry solutions)
　Axians (voice-data-image communication)
　Citéos (urban lighting)
　Graniou (telecommunications infrastructure)
　Omexom (high-voltage power transmission)
　Opteor (maintenance)

COMPETITORS

Atlantia	HOCHTIEF
Bechtel	Louis Berger
Bilfinger Berger	Parsons Corporation
Bouygues	Schneider Electric
Bovis Lend Lease	Skanska
EIFFAGE	WS Atkins
FCC Barcelona	

HISTORICAL FINANCIALS

Company Type: Public

Income Statement

FYE: December 31

	REVENUE ($ mil.)	NET INCOME ($ mil.)	NET PROFIT MARGIN	EMPLOYEES
12/09	46,810	2,434	5.2%	161,746
12/08	48,129	2,395	5.0%	163,494
12/07	45,132	2,330	5.2%	158,000
12/06	33,819	1,676	5.0%	142,500
12/05	25,726	1,188	4.6%	142,000
Annual Growth	**16.1%**	**19.6%**	**—**	**3.3%**

2009 Year-End Financials

Debt ratio: —　　　　　　　　No. of shares (mil.): 550
Return on equity: 18.1%　　　Dividends
Cash ($ mil.): 7,964　　　　　　Yield: 4.1%
Current ratio: 0.91　　　　　　Payout: 50.4%
Long-term debt ($ mil.): —　　Market value ($ mil.): 31,095

Stock History

Euronext Paris: DG

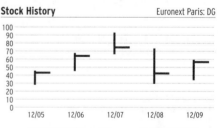

	STOCK PRICE ($) FY Close	P/E High/Low		PER SHARE ($) Earnings	Dividends	Book Value
12/09	56.57	13	8	4.60	2.32	27.22
12/08	42.28	15	7	4.65	2.14	21.59
12/07	74.55	21	15	4.45	—	20.42
12/06	63.85	—	—	—	—	21.28
12/05	43.02	8	6	5.28	—	10.01
Annual Growth	**7.1%**	**—**	**—**	**(3.4%)**	**8.4%**	**28.4%**

Virgin Group

Led by adventurous founder, chairman, and owner Sir Richard Branson, holding company Virgin Group gets around. The group's travel-related operations, led by 51%-owned Virgin Atlantic Airways, are among its biggest breadwinners. The airline flies to 30 destinations around the world with a fleet of about 40 aircraft. Virgin Atlantic is complemented by its Australian low-fare cousin, Virgin Blue, which operates a fleet of about 80 aircraft. Virgin Group also operates rail franchises in the UK and sells tour packages. Besides travel and leisure, the group's major operating areas include beverages, financial services, and telecom (Virgin Media). Virgin, with offices in about 30 countries, was established in 1970.

Branson has made Virgin one of the most recognizable brands in the world by plastering it on everything from balloon flights to wine, representing more than 200 branded companies overall. Rather than maintaining full ownership of the companies, Branson typically has entered new businesses via partnerships with other investors or by licensing the Virgin brand.

Virgin Group's latest airline venture, V Australia, is the international arm of Virgin Blue with flights to New Zealand and throughout the South Pacific islands. V Australia gives Qantas a run for its money on the Australia-US routes. The airline took wing in 2009 with service from Sydney to Los Angeles, quickly followed by service from Brisbane and Melbourne to the "city of angels." A year later it launched to South Africa, just in time for FIFA World Cup action.

Virgin Group also flies Virgin America, a luxury low-fare carrier that operates out of San Francisco. The US airline licenses the Virgin brand and borrows heavily from the Virgin marketing playbook; Virgin Group is limited by US law to a minority stake in the carrier. Its destinations include 10 major US cities as well as service to Toronto.

The group continues to look for new growth opportunities to balance against the airline industry's ups and downs. Emerging Virgin projects include stem-cell storage, alternative energy, and other things that strike Sir Richard's fancy. Virgin's space tourism division got off the ground in 2010 when a Scaled Composites test rocket took flight. The company launched into another new space that year when it formed Virgin Healthcare with the purchase of 75% of Assura Group's Assura Medicals, a British health care provider with about 30 general practitioner clinics in the UK.

HISTORY

Always one to revel in competition, Richard Branson got his start in the business world at the age of 17, dropping out of boarding school to pursue his magazine, *Student,* in 1968. Two years later he was on to a new challenge when he started Virgin — a mail-order record company named for his lack of experience at such things. After a postal strike in 1971 put a damper on that enterprise, Branson opened the first Virgin record store. Continued success led to a recording studio and record label that went on to sign several popular British rock bands in the 1970s, including the Sex Pistols, Genesis, and the Rolling Stones.

With his entertainment businesses flourishing in the early 1980s, Branson sought a new adventure and found it in the airline industry, another business he knew very little about. Virgin Atlantic Airways took off in 1984 with one plane and one transatlantic route. Growing steadily, Virgin Atlantic became one of the world's most profitable airlines in the 1980s. The company added Virgin Holidays (tours) to its travel group in 1985.

Branson collected all his businesses (except the travel operations) into a new company called Virgin Group and took it public in 1986. Despite the enterprise's continued growth and profits, the market slashed its value after the crash of 1987, and a frustrated Branson bought it all back the following year. Virgin sold its smaller UK record stores in 1988 to focus on the development of its Megastores concept. It also entered the hotel business that year.

Virgin started Britain's first national commercial rock radio station in 1992. Branson sold the Virgin Music Group (a decision he still regrets) to THORN EMI that year for about $1 billion. He used the proceeds to build Virgin Atlantic. By the early 1990s the airline had added to its fleet and had new routes, including flights to Asia. It also took on British Airways and won a libel suit in 1993.

The company debuted Virgin Cola in 1994 and bought 25% of the Our Price record store chain with WH Smith (it purchased the rest in 1998). Virgin acquired MGM Cinemas (the UK's largest theater operator) and introduced its financial services business in 1995. Meanwhile, it added dozens of new Megastores around the world in the mid-1990s. Virgin got back into the recording business in 1996 when it launched the V2 record label. It also bought low-fare Euro Belgian Airlines (renamed Virgin Express).

Virgin looked to keep itself on the right track in 1997 when it got into the rail business. Realizing that the right track might be the Internet, Branson has pushed the group toward the age of e-commerce and online services with Virgin.com. Mobile phone sales (at its existing retail locations) entered the company's cornucopia in 1999. Late that year Virgin agreed to sell its cinema chain to Vivendi (later Vivendi Universal), raising funds for other online and retail ventures. It launched a major Australian airline (Virgin Blue) in 2000.

In 2000 the company sold 49% of Virgin Atlantic to Singapore Airlines. Virgin agreed to sell Virgin Sun (package holidays) to rival travel firm First Choice Holidays in 2001. Also that year the company sold its 16 French Megastores, as well as some international rights to the Virgin brand, to France's Lagardère. Virgin Mobile in 2002 began offering prepaid wireless service in the US in conjunction with Sprint PCS.

In 2006 UK cable operator NTL bought Virgin Mobile, which continued to operate under the Virgin brand. NTL subsequently changed its name to Virgin Media; Virgin Group retains a minority stake.

In order to focus more attention on its core business of transportation and renewable energy, Virgin in 2007 sold off its Virgin Entertainment Group operations, which operated the Virgin Megastores chain. Virgin sold the segment to Related Companies and Vornado Realty Trust.

EXECUTIVES

Chairman: Sir Richard Branson, age 60
Non-Executive Chairman: Peter Norris, age 54
CEO, Virgin Games: Simon Burridge
CEO, The Carbon War Room: Jigar Shah
CEO, Virgin Atlantic: Steve Ridgway
CEO and Managing Director, Virgin Blue:
 John Borghetti, age 54
CEO, Virgin Money: Asheesh Advani
CEO, Virgin Limited Edition, London: Jon Brown
Executive Director, Brand and Marketing:
 Ashley Stockwell
Commercial Director: Patrick McCall, age 44
Auditors: KPMG

LOCATIONS

HQ: Virgin Group Ltd.
 The School House, 50 Brook Green
 London W6 7RR, United Kingdom
Phone: 44-207-313-2000
Web: www.virgin.com

PRODUCTS/OPERATIONS

Selected Operations

Lifestyle
 Virgin Active
 Virgin Books
 Virgin Drinks
 Virgin Games
 Virgin Health Bank
 Virgin Life Care
 Virgin Spa
Media and Mobile
 Virgin 1
 Virgin Connect
 Virgin Media
 Virgin Mobile
Money
 Virgin Money
 Virgin Money Giving
Music
 V Festivals
 Virgin Megastore
 Virgin Radio International
People and Planet
 Virgin Earth Challenge
 Virgin Green Fund
 Virgin Unite
Travel
 Blue Holidays
 Virgin America
 Virgin Atlantic
 Virgin Blue
 Virgin Galactic
 Virgin Holidays
 Virgin Holidays Cruises
 Virgin Holidays Hip Hotels
 Virgin Limited Edition
 Virgin Limobike
 Virgin Limousines
 Virgin Trains
 Virgin Vacations

COMPETITORS

Accor	News Corp.
Air France-KLM	Pearson plc
AMR Corp.	PepsiCo
AT&T	Qantas
British Airways	The Rank Group
BT	RTL Group
Coca-Cola	Sony
Disney	Starwood Hotels & Resorts
EMI Group plc	Time Warner
HMV	United Continental
Japan Airlines	Verizon
Lufthansa	Vivendi
Marriott	Vodafone

Income Statement				FYE: March 31
	REVENUE ($ mil.)	NET INCOME ($ mil.)	NET PROFIT MARGIN	EMPLOYEES
3/09	18,000	—	—	50,000
3/08	23,000	—	—	50,000
3/07	20,000	—	—	50,000
Annual Growth	(5.1%)	—	—	0.0%

Revenue History

Vivendi

Vivendi is the bright sun at the center of a solar system of market-leading media and telecommunications holdings. The company's telecom holdings include a controlling stake in SFR, as well as a majority stake in fixed-line operator Neuf Cegetel. Vivendi also owns a controlling stake in Maroc Telecom, the largest telecom company in Morocco. Vivendi's media assets include Universal Music Group, the leading global music publishing and recording company, and Activision Blizzard, which develops, publishes, and distributes video games. Vivendi also owns CANAL+, the top pay-television provider in France and a leading producer and distributor of pay-TV and films.

Vivendi agreed to sell its 20% stake in NBC Universal to NBC Universal's majority owner General Electric for $5.8 billion in 2009. General Electric pushed for the acquisition to facilitate the proposed sale of a controlling 51% interest in NBC Universal to Philadelphia-based cable operator Comcast.

Looking to better compete with global games leader Electronic Arts, Vivendi acquired US-based video game developer Activision in 2008. It combined Activision with its Vivendi Games subsidiary to form Activision Blizzard. The move brings together a variety of leading game titles under a single brand, including *World of Warcraft*, *Guitar Hero*, and *Call of Duty*.

Also that year Vivendi merged SFR and Neuf Cegetel into one company under the SFR brand; the combined entity is Europe's largest alternative telecommunications operator.

Vivendi is also looking to international markets for growth. It acquired 51% of Brazilian telephone company GVT Holding for $4.1 billion in 2009 amid protests from GVT's other suitor, Telefónica. Vivendi bought essentially all of the remaining shares the following year.

HISTORY

Authorized by an imperial decree, Compagnie Générale des Eaux was founded in 1853 by investors such as the Rothschild family and Napoleon III's half-brother to irrigate French farmland and supply water to towns. It won contracts to serve Lyons (1853), Nantes (1854), Paris (1860), and Venice (1880).

After WWI Générale des Eaux created water engineering firm Société Auxiliaire de Distribution d'Eau (Sade, 1918) and extended its water distribution network to several areas of France. By 1953 the company had added trash collection to its services. In the 1960s it began managing district heating networks and waste incineration/composting plants. The company moved into construction in 1972. By the time Guy Dujouany became chairman in 1976, water distribution accounted for less than half of the company's sales.

Dujouany began an expansion drive. In 1980 Générale des Eaux became France's #1 private energy management firm when it bought Générale de Chauffe. Also that year it expanded its wastewater and waste management businesses and moved into transportation, buying Compagnie Générale d'Entreprises Automobiles (CGEA). The company also entered communications in the 1980s: it took a 15% stake in pay-TV provider CANAL+ (1983) and it created mobile phone unit Société Francaise de Radiotelephonie (SFR, 1987).

Générale des Eaux took its water services global in the 1990s. Dujouany stepped down in 1996 and was succeeded by Jean-Marie Messier, who immediately dumped some businesses. In 1997 the company launched telecom provider Cegetel and increased its stake in publisher Havas to 30%. In 1998 the firm bought the rest of Havas, increased its ownership in CANAL+, and took the name Vivendi to represent "vivacity" and "mobility."

Its purchase of USFilter in 1999 made Vivendi the world's largest water company. In 2000 Vivendi brought its environmental services businesses together under the Vivendi Environnement umbrella and sold a minority stake in the new company to the public.

Later that year, in a $34 billion deal that set the stage for Vivendi's transformation into a global conglomerate, the company bought Seagram and the portion of CANAL+ that it didn't already own. The combined company became Vivendi Universal (VU). VU sold Seagram's liquor business for $8.1 billion to Diageo and Pernod Ricard, which split up the various Seagram's brands between them.

In 2001 the company struck the biggest deal in its history by agreeing to buy the entertainment assets of USA Networks (now named InterActiveCorp). VU combined Universal Studios with the USA business — which included film and TV production and cable channels — into a new company called Vivendi Universal Entertainment (VUE).

But in 2002 VU posted a roughly $25 billion loss, the largest one-year loss in French corporate history, and Messier's reputation took on some tarnish. He was forced to resign. He was replaced by Jean-René Fourtou, the former vice chairman of drug maker Aventis (now Sanofi-Aventis).

Adding insult to injury, the US SEC accused Messier and other executives, including finance director Guillaume Hannezo, of accounting irregularities. Messier was fined $1 million, barred from being an officer or director of a public US company for 10 years, and denied a $25 million "golden parachute" deal. He was later fined €1 million by France's market regulators for inaccurate financial reporting. VU shareholders also filed a lawsuit against the former managers demanding that they pay $54 million toward a US civil fine and legal costs.

To give the company some breathing room, Fourtou reduced VU's stake in Vivendi Environnement (and sold the rest in 2006). In 2002 VU completely exited the publishing business by selling Vivendi Universal Publishing (now named Editis) to Lagardère for $1.2 billion, and Houghton Mifflin to Thomas H. Lee and Bain Capital for $1.6 billion.

In 2004 VU saw its Hollywood aspirations fade to black. A prominent part of Fourtou's debt reduction plan was the sale of 86%-owned VUE, with the exception of Universal Music Group, to GE, the parent company to NBC TV network. In the deal that included Universal Studios, cable TV channels, and theme parks, and created NBC Universal, VU received $3.8 billion in cash and retained a 19% stake in the new company.

In 2005 Fourtou stepped down as CEO, replaced by former COO Jean-Bernard Lévy. Fourtou became chairman of the supervisory board. To concentrate on its core businesses, Vivendi sold the non-French assets of CANAL+ Group.

Citing a desire to further reduce costs, the company in 2006 ended its listing on the New York Stock Exchange. It also dropped Universal from its name — and became simply Vivendi.

EXECUTIVES

Chairman Supervisory Board: Jean-René Fourtou, age 71
Vice Chairman Supervisory Board: Henri Lachmann, age 72
Chairman Management Board; Chairman, Activision Blizzard and GVT: Jean-Bernard Lévy, age 55
CFO and Member Management Board: Philippe G. H. Capron, age 52
Member Management Board; Chairman Executive Board, CANAL+ Group: Bertrand Meheut, age 59
Member Management Board; Co-CEO, Universal Music Group: Lucian Grainge, age 49
Member Management Board; Chairman and Co-CEO, Universal Music Group: Douglas P. (Doug) Morris, age 71
Member Management Board; Chairman Management Board, Maroc Telecom: Abdeslam Ahizoune, age 55
Member Management Board; Chairman and CEO, SFR Cegetel: Frank Esser, age 52
SEVP Human Resources: Stéphane Roussel, age 48
SEVP Strategy and Development: Régis Turrini, age 51
SEVP Communications and Sustainable Development: Simon Gillham, age 53
EVP, General Counsel, and Secretary Supervisory and Management Boards: Jean-François Dubos, age 65
EVP Innovation; Deputy CFO; Chairman, Vivendi Mobile Entertainment: Sandrine Dufour, age 39
President and CEO, Activision Blizzard: Robert A. (Bobby) Kotick, age 47
Auditors: RSM Salustro Reydel

LOCATIONS

HQ: Vivendi
42 avenue de Friedland
75380 Paris, France
Phone: 33-1-71-71-10-00   **Fax:** 33-1-71-71-10-01
US HQ: 800 Third Ave., New York, NY 10022
US Phone: 212-572-7000
Web: www.vivendi.com

2009 Sales

	% of total
Europe	
France	63
Other countries	11
US	11
Morocco	8
Other countries	7
Total	**100**

PRODUCTS/OPERATIONS

2009 Sales

	% of total
SFR	46
Canal+ Group	17
Universal Music Group	16
Activision Blizzard	11
Maroc Telecom	10
Total	**100**

Selected Subsidiaries and Affiliates

CANAL+ Group
Universal Music Group
SFR
Neuf Cegetel
Maroc Telecom S.A.

COMPETITORS

Bouygues
CompleTel
Eidos
Electronic Arts
EMI Group plc
France Telecom
ITV
Lucasfilm Entertainment
Orange
Sony Music
Take-Two
Tele2
THQ
Tiscali
Virgin Group
Warner Music

HISTORICAL FINANCIALS

Company Type: Public

Income Statement

FYE: December 31

	REVENUE ($ mil.)	NET INCOME ($ mil.)	NET PROFIT MARGIN	EMPLOYEES
12/09	38,886	2,990	7.7%	48,284
12/08	35,790	5,214	14.6%	44,243
12/07	31,877	5,548	17.4%	37,223
12/06	26,444	6,851	25.9%	37,014
12/05	23,075	5,052	21.9%	34,031
Annual Growth	13.9%	(12.3%)	—	9.1%

2009 Year-End Financials

Debt ratio: 37.9%
Return on equity: 9.4%
Cash ($ mil.): 4,795
Current ratio: 0.64
Long-term debt ($ mil.): 11,974

No. of shares (mil.): 1,229
Dividends
Yield: 6.7%
Payout: 65.5%
Market value ($ mil.): 36,634

Stock History

Euronext Paris: VIV

	STOCK PRICE ($) FY Close	P/E High/Low		PER SHARE ($) Earnings	Dividends	Book Value
12/09	29.80	11	8	3.07	2.01	25.67
12/08	32.79	14	7	3.14	3.66	25.94
12/07	46.19	15	12	3.31	—	24.36
12/06	39.06	9	7	4.58	—	21.37
12/05	31.34	10	8	3.22	—	20.82
Annual Growth	(1.3%)	—	—	(1.2%)	(45.1%)	5.4%

Vodafone

Customers have voted with their phones to make Vodafone Group one of the world's top wireless phone services carriers with about 300 million customers in more than 20 countries. In terms of subscribers, Vodafone trails only China Mobile. The company does most of its business in Europe, where it is a leader in the wireless markets of the UK and Germany. It also provides data, broadband Internet, and fixed-line phone services; in Germany, these services are overseen by subsidiary Arcor. Vodafone increasingly serves callers in Asia, Africa, the Middle East, and the Pacific region through subsidiaries and joint ventures. In the US, the group holds a 45% stake in the leading US wireless provider Verizon Wireless.

Vodafone Group has grown rapidly through acquisitions which have helped it toward its goal of creating a pan-European wireless network consisting of far-flung affiliates united largely under the Vodafone brand. Besides being among the top mobile service providers in the UK, the group also supplies incumbent UK carrier BT Group with mobile network capacity. The group's extensive European wireless operations include subsidiaries and affiliates in the Czech Republic, France, the Netherlands, and Spain.

In 2008 CEO Arun Sarin resigned as Vodafone's CEO and was replaced by deputy CEO Vittorio Colao. The new chief has said that the company's plans include a continued expansion into Africa, Asia, and the Middle East through acquisitions and partnerships, while exiting noncore markets. The company's key areas for growth in terms of service segments are mobile data, broadband, and corporate accounts.

To this end, Vodafone in 2008 raised its stake in South Africa's largest wireless operator Vodacom from 50% to 65% and took a controlling stake in Ghana's third-largest mobile carrier. The company in 2009 combined its mobile operations in Australia with those of Hong Kong-based Hutchison Telecommunications. As part of the deal, Hutchison Telecommunications Australia paid $500 million to acquire Vodafone Australia and form a joint venture in which each company has a 50% stake. In 2010 Vodafone sold its 3% stake in China Mobile for about $6.7 billion.

Closer to home, Vodafone bought the remaining one-quarter of German fixed-line operator Arcor's shares that it did not already own from Deutsche Post and Deutsche Bahn for about €474 million in 2008. The transaction was part of the company's plan to focus on providing a more extensive range of bundled services to German subscribers.

HISTORY

Vodafone was formed in 1983 as a joint venture between Racal Electronics (a UK electronics firm) and Millicom (a US telecom company), and was granted one of two mobile phone licenses in the UK. It launched service in 1985 as a Racal subsidiary. Vodafone and Cellnet, the other licensee, were swamped with demand. In 1988 Racal offered 20% of Vodafone to the public; three years later the rest of the firm was spun off to become Vodafone Group.

Vodafone moved beyond the UK in the 1990s. By 1993 it had interests in mobile phone networks in Australia, Greece, Hong Kong, Malta, and Scandinavia.

For a time Vodafone and Cellnet, a joint venture of British Telecom (now BT Group) and Securicor, enjoyed a duopoly in the UK. Regulators elected not to impose price controls, and the pounds rolled in. But in 1993 a new wireless provider, One 2 One, launched a digital network in London. Vodafone countered that year with its own GSM (global system for mobile communications) digital network.

With increasing competition at home, Vodafone continued to expand in 1994. It launched or bought stakes in operations in Fiji, Germany, South Africa, and Uganda.

Digital service took on a larger role in Vodafone's UK business, and by 1997 some 85% of new subscribers were opting for digital GSM. In 1998 Vodafone sold its French service provider, Vodafone SA, and bought digital cellular carrier BellSouth New Zealand. It also expanded into Egypt by buying a minority stake in Misrfone, marking the largest British investment in Egypt since the Suez Canal.

In 1999 Vodafone prevailed in a brief bidding war with Bell Atlantic (now Verizon) to buy AirTouch Communications for about $60 billion. Vodafone's Chris Gent took over as CEO of the new company, Vodafone AirTouch. The prize for Vodafone: entry into the lucrative US market, plus the opportunity to consolidate minority interests in European wireless carriers.

Vodafone AirTouch moved to significantly boost its European footprint in 1999 by launching a $131 billion hostile takeover bid for Germany's Mannesmann. The company acquired Mannesmann for about $180 billion in stock in 2000 and agreed to sell the conglomerate's engineering operations and its UK mobile phone unit, Orange. (France Telecom bought Orange for $37.5 billion later that year.)

In 2000 Vodafone AirTouch expanded its US presence by combining its US wireless operations with those of Bell Atlantic and GTE to form Verizon Wireless. The company had failed to strengthen its presence in that market two years previously when it lost a bidding war with Cingular Wireless (now AT&T Mobility) over the acquisition of AT&T Wireless.

That year the company dropped AirTouch from its name and became Vodafone Group once again. It also continued its expansion push, investing in China Mobile (Hong Kong) and buying Irish mobile phone operator Eircell in a deal that was completed in 2001. That year Vodafone expanded its stakes in Japan Telecom Holdings and its J-Phone mobile phone operations by buying out rival BT Group; it also bought BT's remaining interest in Spain's Airtel.

Vodafone sold its 98%-owned Vodafone Japan unit in 2006 to SOFTBANK in a deal valued at nearly $16 billion. The group's acquisition activities in regions outside of Europe included the 2006 purchase of Telsim (formerly the #2 mobile service operator in Turkey) for about $4.6 billion. The next year Vodafone outbid several rivals to win control of one of India's largest telecom companies, Hutchison Essar, in a deal valued at about $9 billion. Also in 2007 the group bought fixed-line broadband Internet businesses in Italy and Spain from Sweden-based Tele2 for more than $1 billion.

Arun Sarin resigned as CEO in 2008. He was replaced by deputy CEO Vittorio Colao.

EXECUTIVES

Chairman: Sir John R. H. Bond, age 69, $1,006,471 total compensation
Deputy Chairman: John G. S. Buchanan, age 66, $269,901 total compensation
CEO: Vittorio A. Colao, age 48, $5,320,259 total compensation
CFO and Director: Andrew N. (Andy) Halford, age 51, $3,282,062 total compensation
CTO and Director: Stephen C. (Steve) Pusey, age 48, $1,308,000 total compensation
Group Chief Marketing Officer: Wendy Becker, age 44
Group General Counsel and Company Secretary: Rosemary Martin, age 50
Group Research and Development Director: Siavash M. Alamouti
Global Director Terminals: Patrick Chomet
Director Group Investor Relations: Richard C. Snow, age 43
Director Human Resources: Ronald Schellekens, age 46
Director Group Strategy and Business Development: Warren Finegold, age 53
Director Mobile Payments: Cenk Serdar, age 41
Director Group External Affairs: Matthew Kirk, age 49
Regional President, Americas: Terry D. Kramer, age 50
Auditors: Deloitte LLP

LOCATIONS

HQ: Vodafone Group Plc
Vodafone House, The Connection
Newbury, West Berkshire RG14 2FN
United Kingdom
Phone: 44-1635-33-251   **Fax:** 44-1635-45-713
Web: www.vodafone.com

2010 Sales

	% of total
Europe	67
Africa & Central Europe	18
Asia/Pacific & Middle East	15
Total	**100**

PRODUCTS/OPERATIONS

2010 Sales

	% of total
Voice	67
Messaging	11
Data	10
Fixed line	8
Other	4
Total	**100**

Selected Subsidiaries and Affiliates

Arcor AG & Co KG (fixed-line operator, Germany)
Cellco Partnership (Verizon Wireless, 45%, wireless network operator, US)
Polkomtel S.A. (Plus GSM, 24%, wireless network operator, Poland)
Safaricom Limited (40%, wireless network operator, Kenya)
Société Française du Radiotéléphone S.A. (SFR, 44%, wireless and fixed-line network operator, France)
Vodacom Group (Pty) Limited (50%, holding company, South Africa)
Vodafone Hutchison Australia Ltd. (50%, joint venture)
Vodafone Albania Sh. A. (99.9%, wireless network operator)
Vodafone Czech Repubilc a.s. (mobile network operator)
Vodafone D2 GmbH (wireless network operator, Germany)
Vodafone Egypt Telecommunications SAE (55%, wireless network operator)
Vodafone España, S.A. (wireless network operator, Spain)
Vodafone Fiji Limited (49%, wireless network operator)
Vodafone Hungary Mobile Telecommunications Limited, (wireless network operator, Hungary)
Vodafone Ireland Limited (formerly Eircell, wireless network operator)
Vodafone Libertel N.V. (wireless network operator, The Netherlands)
Vodafone Limited (wireless network operator, UK)
Vodafone Malta Limited (wireless network operator)

Vodafone Network Pty Limited (wireless network operator, Australia)
Vodafone New Zealand Limited (wireless network operator)
Vodafone Omnitel N.V. (77%, wireless network operator, Italy)
Vodafone-Panafon Hellenic Telecommunications Company S.A. (99.9%, telecommunications and wireless network operator, Greece)
Vodafone Portugal-Comunicações Pessoais, S.A. (wireless network operator)
Vodafone Romania S.A. (mobile network operator)
Vodafone Telekomunikasyon A.S. (mobile network operator, Turkey)

COMPETITORS

AT&T Mobility
Belgacom
China Mobile
Deutsche Telekom
Hutchison Whampoa
KPN
M1
NTT DoCoMo
Orange
Swisscom
Telefónica Europe
Telekom Austria
Telstra
Virgin Mobile Telecoms

HISTORICAL FINANCIALS

Company Type: Public

Income Statement

FYE: March 31

	REVENUE ($ mil.)	NET INCOME ($ mil.)	NET PROFIT MARGIN	EMPLOYEES
3/10	67,010	13,026	19.4%	84,990
3/09	58,281	4,376	7.5%	79,097
3/08	70,597	13,253	18.8%	72,000
3/07	61,417	(10,714)	—	66,000
3/06	51,247	(38,266)	—	60,000
Annual Growth	**6.9%**	**—**	**—**	**9.1%**

2010 Year-End Financials

Debt ratio: 32.6%
Return on equity: 10.1%
Cash ($ mil.): 6,665
Current ratio: 0.50
Long-term debt ($ mil.): 44,372

No. of shares (mil.): 5,266
Dividends
  Yield: 3.4%
  Payout: 47.8%
Market value ($ mil.): 184,971

Stock History

NASDAQ (GS): VOD

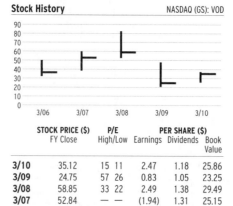

	STOCK PRICE ($) FY Close	P/E High/Low		PER SHARE ($) Earnings	Dividends	Book Value
3/10	35.12	15	11	2.47	1.18	25.86
3/09	24.75	57	26	0.83	1.05	23.25
3/08	58.85	33	22	2.49	1.38	29.49
3/07	52.84	—	—	(1.94)	1.31	25.15
3/06	36.39	—	—	(6.10)	0.87	28.32
Annual Growth	**(0.9%)**	**—**	**—**	**—**	**7.9%**	**(2.2%)**

Volkswagen

With cars named for climate patterns, insects, and small mammals, Volkswagen (VW) leads the Continent as Europe's #1 carmaker. Along with Golf (referring to the Gulf Stream) and the New Beetle, VW's annual production of 6 million cars, trucks, and vans includes such models as Passat (trade wind), Jetta (jet stream), Rabbit, and Fox. VW also owns a garage full of luxury carmakers — AUDI, Lamborghini, Bentley, and Bugatti. Other makes include SEAT (family cars, Spain) and SKODA (family cars, the Czech Republic). Late in 2009 VW acquired a 49.9% stake in Porsche for about €3.9 billion (about $5.79 billion) as the first step in combining the two into an integrated car company.

VW intends to put Porsche under its umbrella, but will preserve Porsche's brand autonomy. VW sees the combined group — which will include 10 distinct and separate brands, along with the Porsche Holding auto trading business currently held by the Porsche and Piëch families — as a way to become an industry leader in terms of global market presence, innovation, purchasing, and manufacturing. VW expects to complete the entire transaction by 2011.

Under the deal, the Porsche and Piëch families would remain the largest shareholders in the combined company; Qatar, a Gulf emirate, is expected to be its third-largest investor. The German state of Lower Saxony, which controls 20% of VW's voting stock, will retain the right to block important decisions.

In early 2010 VW completed a $2.5 billion deal for a nearly 20% stake in Suzuki Motor Corp. The tie-up gives VW greater access to markets in India and Southeast Asia, where Suzuki is established. Another attraction for VW is Suzuki's savvy in manufacturing cars inexpensively and profitably, something VW has been working on.

VW has responded to the economic turmoil by maintaining strict cost controls and reducing production in order to lower excess inventory. However, it is counting on growth in China, Brazil, India, and Russia — where sales continue to be strong — to offset difficult conditions in North America and Western Europe. The company continues to develop energy-efficient technologies and environmentally friendly versions of its popular brands.

VW operates more than 60 production plants in Europe, the Americas, Asia, and Africa. It holds 68% of the voting rights in Swedish truck maker Scania and about 30% of MAN. VW's substantial presence in the Chinese market stems from an early entrance into that country in 1984.

While the US automotive industry was hit particularly hard in 2008 and 2009, China, which became VW's largest market (even over Germany) in 2009, remained relatively strong, and was a mitigating factor for VW in its ability to steer through recessionary obstacles.

In 2009 VW sold VW Truck & Bus to MAN for nearly €1.2 billion in cash. The Brazilian subsidiary makes vehicles for the Latin American and South African markets.

HISTORY

Since the early 1920s auto engineer Ferdinand Porsche (whose son later founded the Porsche car company) had wanted to make a small car for the masses. He found no backers until he met Adolf Hitler in 1934. Hitler formed the Gesellschaft zur

Vorbereitung des Volkswagens (Company for the Development of People's Cars) in 1937 and built a factory in Wolfsburg, Germany.

No cars were delivered during WWII, as the company produced military vehicles using slave labor of Jews and Russian prisoners of war.

Following WWII British occupation forces oversaw the rebuilding of the bomb-damaged plant and initial production of the odd-looking "people's car" (1945). The British appointed Heinz Nordhoff to manage Volkswagen (1948) and then turned the company over to the German government (1949).

In the 1950s VW launched the Microbus and built foreign plants. Although US sales began slowly, by the end of the decade acceptance of the little car had increased. Advertising that coined the name "Beetle" helped carve VW's niche in the US. VW sold stock to the German public in 1960. In 1966 it purchased Auto Union (AUDI) from Daimler-Benz. The Beetle became a counterculture symbol in the 1960s, and US sales took off. By the time of Nordhoff's death in 1968, the Beetle had become the best-selling car in history.

In the 1970s the Beetle was discontinued in every country except Mexico. VW lost heavily during the model-changeover period.

VW agreed to several deals in the 1980s, including a car venture in China (1984), the purchase of 75% of SEAT (1986; it bought the rest in 1990), and the merger of its suddenly faltering Brazilian unit with Ford's ailing Argentine operations to form Autolatina (1987). In 1990 the company began building China's largest auto plant and acquired a 70% stake in Czech auto company Skoda. After suffering a $1.1 billion loss, the company put Ferdinand Piëch in the driver's seat in 1993. Under his leadership the company cut costs and boosted sales by resuscitating the SEAT and Skoda brands.

VW acquired Rolls-Royce Motor Cars, Vickers' Cosworth auto engines subsidiary, Italian sportscar maker Bugatti, and Italy's Automobili Lamborghini — all in 1998. Although less luxurious than VW's other pursuits, the New Beetle helped boost US sales that year. Also in 1998 VW established a $12 million fund to compensate the surviving 2,000 concentration-camp inmates forced to work as slave labor during WWII. However, the company was hit with a class-action lawsuit filed on behalf of Holocaust survivors anyway.

VW hoped to tap the market in China after getting approval in 1999 to sell a newly developed minicar there. That year it announced plans to invest $1 billion in its Mexico plant over the next five years.

Volkswagen expanded into heavy commercial vehicles in 2000 by purchasing a 34% stake in Swedish truck maker Scania (from holding company Investor). Anticipating China's entry into the World Trade Organization, Volkswagen announced in 2001 that it would invest $1.7 billion in China and the Asia/Pacific region over the next five years. Later in the year, 12,500 workers at the company's Mexico plant went on strike for 19 days over a pay dispute.

Former BMW head Bernd Pischetsrieder succeeded Piëch as CEO in 2002. The next year the final classic Beetle rolled off the VW assembly line in Mexico. Also in 2003 BMW took control of the Rolls-Royce brand from Volkswagen.

In 2006 Pischetsrieder stepped down and was replaced by AUDI chief Martin Winterkorn. The management shake-up was attributed to an internal power struggle between Pischetsrieder and supervisory board chairman Ferdinand Piëch, a grandson of Porsche founder Ferdinand Porsche.

EXECUTIVES

Chairman Supervisory Board: Ferdinand K. Piëch, age 72
Chairman Management Board: Martin Winterkorn, age 63
Chairman Management Board, Porsche AG: Matthias Müller, age 57
Chairman Volkswagen Financial Services: Frank Witter, age 51
EVP Group Sales and Marketing: Detlef Wittig, age 68
Member Management Board, Finance and Controlling; CFO, Porsche Automobil: Hans D. Pötsch, age 59
Member Management Board; Chairman Board of Management, Audi AG: Rupert Stadler, age 47
Member Management Board for the Volkswagen Brand, Development: Ulrich Hackenberg, age 60
Member Management Board for the Volkswagen Brand, Production and Logistics: Hubert Waltl
Member Management Board, Commercial Vehicles, Production: Thomas Ulbrich
Member Management Board, Group Production: Michael Macht, age 49
Member Management Board, Procurement: Francisco Javier Garcia Sanz, age 53
Member Management Board for the Volkswagen Brand, Components: Werner Neubauer, age 61
Member Management Board, Sales: Christian Klingler, age 41
Member Management Board, Human Resources and Director Labor: Horst G. Neumann, age 61
Member Management Board, Skoda Auto, Technical Development: Eckhard Scholz, age 46
President and CEO, Volkswagen Group of America: Jonathan Browning, age 51
President and CEO, Volkswagen Group China: Karl-Thomas Neumann, age 49
Group Head Investor Relations: Christine Ritz
Auditors: PricewaterhouseCoopers AG Wirtschaftsprufungsgesellschaft

LOCATIONS

HQ: Volkswagen AG
Brieffach 1849
38436 Wolfsburg, Germany
Phone: 49-5361-9-0   **Fax:** 49-5361-9-28282
US HQ: 3800 Hamlin Rd., Auburn Hills, MI 48326
US Phone: 248-754-5000   **US Fax:** 248-754-6405
Web: www.volkswagenag.com

2009 Sales

	% of total
Europe	54
Asia/Pacific	25
South America	13
North America	8
Total	**100**

PRODUCTS/OPERATIONS

2009 Sales

	% of total
Automotive	89
Financial services	11
Total	**100**

Selected Makes and Models

AUDI
A3
A4
A5
A6
A8
Q7
R8
TT Coupe
TT Roadster
Bentley
Arnage
Azure
Continental Flying Spur
Continental GT Coupe
Continental GTC
Mulsanne

Bugatti
EB 110
Veyron
Lamborghini
Gallardo
Gallardo Spyder
Gallardo Valentino Balboni
Murciélago
Scania
Buses
Engines
Trucks
SEAT
Alhambra
Altea
Altea XL
Cordoba
Exeo
Ibiza
Leon
Skoda
Fabia
Octavia
Roomster
Praktik
Superb
Yeti
Volkswagen Passenger Vehicles
Eos
Fox
Golf
New Beetle
New Beetle Cabriolet
Jetta
Passat
Phaeton
Polo
Scirocco
Sharan
Tiguan
Touareg
Touran

COMPETITORS

BMW
Chrysler
Daimler
Fiat
Ford Motor
Ford Motor Company Brasil
Fuji Heavy Industries
General Motors
Honda
Isuzu
Mazda
Nissan
Peugeot
Porsche Automobil Holding
Renault
Saab Automobile
Suzuki Motor
Toyota

HISTORICAL FINANCIALS

Company Type: Public

Income Statement

FYE: December 31

	REVENUE ($ mil.)	NET INCOME ($ mil.)	NET PROFIT MARGIN	EMPLOYEES
12/09	150,754	1,376	0.9%	368,500
12/08	160,412	6,699	4.2%	369,928
12/07	160,286	6,067	3.8%	329,305
12/06	138,362	3,628	2.6%	328,599
12/05	112,826	1,326	1.2%	344,902
Annual Growth	**7.5%**	**0.9%**	**—**	**1.7%**

2009 Year-End Financials

Debt ratio: 104.9%
Return on equity: 2.8%
Cash ($ mil.): 29,436
Current ratio: 1.12
Long-term debt ($ mil.): 53,018

No. of shares (mil.): 295
Dividends
Yield: 2.5%
Payout: 81.2%
Market value ($ mil.): 32,559

Stock History

German: VOW

	STOCK PRICE ($) FY Close	P/E High/Low		PER SHARE ($) Earnings	Dividends	Book Value
12/09	110.36	128	30	3.41	2.77	171.38
12/08	352.38	80	12	16.74	2.54	167.26
12/07	229.76	19	8	15.22	—	159.02
12/06	113.31	13	6	9.29	—	120.30
12/05	52.83	19	11	3.43	—	94.73
Annual Growth	20.2%	—	—	(0.1%)	9.1%	16.0%

AB Volvo

Despite the fact that the name "Volvo" conjures up more visions of soccer moms than of burly truck drivers, AB Volvo has parked its car business. The company is now a leading maker of trucks, buses, and construction equipment as well as marine (Volvo Penta), aircraft (Volvo Aero), and industrial engines. The company's most widely known business — auto making — was sold to US-based carmaker Ford Motor Company. Ford, in turn, sold the business in mid-2010 to Geely Automobile of China. Volvo is focusing on its remaining units, particularly trucks. Its other interests include full control of the famous Mack Trucks brand in North America and Renault Trucks in Europe.

With multiple segments operating all around the world, the challenge for Volvo has been finding the right product mix in the right market. Declining demand in traditionally strong markets, such as North America, Japan, and Western Europe, has spurred the company to bolster its bus, truck, and heavy equipment operations, and shed noncore operations with poor growth. The company began scaling back production in the second half of 2008 in order to reduce the effects of excess inventory on the business and shore up its product pricing. Workforce reductions in 2008 and 2009 accompanied the resizing.

Aiming to centralize its management resources more efficiently and economically, Volvo also merged its subsidiary UD Trucks Corporation (formerly Nissan Diesel Motor) with its Japanese subsidiary Volvo Nippon KK, a maker of large Volvo trucks, in 2010. As part of the move, Volvo Nippon's shares were acquired by the sister subsidiary.

The company angled for a piece of India's market by forming two joint ventures in 2008. It formed Volvo Bus Body Technologies with Indian manufacturer Jaico Automobiles, to build buses on the subcontinent. It also formed VE Commercial Vehicles, a joint venture with Indian car maker Eicher Motors, to make and sell trucks and buses for the Indian market.

In the meantime, the company decided that it would be more cost efficient to buy the products from a third party than to operate certain plants. Volvo sold its bus body manufacturing facility in Turku, Finland in 2008 to a group of private investors. The new owners continue to produce bus bodies for Volvo.

Scaling back on other operations, the company sold its Volvo Material Handling Equipment business in mid-2008 to Linamar Corporation's Skyjack division.

For Volvo Penta, the group's strategy is focused on innovation. While subject to similiar trends in global demand as the truck and heavy equipment segments, Volvo Penta increased its penetration of the commercial boat industry because of lagging leisure boat sales. Volvo Aero, on the other hand, has been trying to grow through partnerships. It has entered agreements with Pratt & Whitney to provide aircraft engine components for Mitsubishi's regional jet as well as Rolls-Royce to develop compressor cases for the Airbus A350 engines.

HISTORY

Swedish ball bearing maker SKF formed Volvo (Latin for "I roll") as a subsidiary in 1915. It began building cars in 1926, trucks in 1928, and bus chassis in 1932 in Gothenburg. Sweden's winters and icy roads made the company keenly attentive to engineering and safety. Volvo bought an engine maker in 1931. In 1935 Volvo became an independent company led by Assar Gabrielsson and Gustaf Larson.

Sweden's neutrality during WWII allowed Volvo to grow and move into component manufacturing and tractor production. Output in 1949 exceeded 100,000 units, 80% of which were sold in Sweden. The purchase of Bolinder-Munktell (farm machinery, diesel engines; Sweden; 1950) enhanced Volvo's position in the Swedish tractor market. Volvo introduced turbocharged diesel truck engines and windshield defrosters and washers in the 1950s. By 1956 car production had outstripped truck and bus output.

Aware that it was too small to compete in global markets, Volvo diversified (energy, industrial products, food, finance, and trading). Volvo increased its market share by purchasing several trucking and construction equipment companies that included White Motors' truck unit (US, 1981) and Leyland Bus (UK, 1986). In the 1980s Volvo acquired drug and biotechnology concern Pharmacia (now Pfizer) and Custos (investments, Sweden). The company consolidated its food and drug units with state-controlled holding company Procordia in 1990.

At that time, however, Volvo was facing stagnant sales. It embarked on the largest industrial undertaking in Swedish history, spending more than $2 billion to modernize plants and develop a series of high-performance family sedans, which it introduced in 1991. Still, high costs and persistent recession in Europe kept the company in the red during the early 1990s.

Adding to its troubles, there was public outcry against a planned merger with French automaker Renault. The plan was abandoned in 1993, and the company sold its drug and consumer product interests (which had landed back in Volvo's lap when the government divested Procordia in 1993).

In 1997 Volvo sold its 11% stake in Renault left over from the abandoned merger. The next year the company strengthened its line of excavators and its Far Eastern presence by buying Samsung Heavy Industries' construction equipment unit.

Anticipating a lower demand for cars, Volvo closed an assembly plant in Canada in 1998, and in 1999 it acquired a 13% stake (later upped to 25%) in rival truck maker Scania. To pay for its new focus on making heavy trucks, Volvo sold its auto brand and manufacturing operations in Sweden, Belgium, and the Netherlands to Ford Motor Company for $6.45 billion in 1999. Volvo then agreed to take a 20% stake in the truck and construction equipment operations of Japan's Mitsubishi Motors.

In 2000 Volvo boosted its stake in Scania to 46%. Volvo then turned to France's Renault, and bought the company's Mack truck unit in exchange for a 15% stake in Volvo.

Volvo's Renault Trucks subsidiary inked a technology transfer deal in 2002 with Chinese truckmaker Dongfeng Motors. In 2003 Volvo became the first Western truck manufacturer to produce vehicles under its own name in Russia. The following year Volvo opened a new truck factory in China with its partner China National Heavy Truck Corporation.

In 2006 the company negotiated with Nissan and the Chinese government to purchase Nissan's 50% stake in Dongfeng Motor Co., Ltd. — China's largest maker of commercial trucks. In 2007 it acquired Nissan Diesel Motor.

EXECUTIVES

Chairman: Louis Schweitzer, age 68
President, CEO, and Director: Leif Johansson, age 58
SVP and CFO: Mikael Bratt, age 42
SVP; President, Trucks Asia: Pär Östberg, age 48
SVP Technology; President, Volvo Powertrain: Peter Karlsten, age 52
SVP, Secretary, and General Counsel: Eva Persson, age 57
Vice Chairman, Mack Trucks: Paul L. Vikner, age 61
President and CEO, Volvo Construction Equipment North America: Göran Lindgren
President, Volvo Trucks: Staffan Jufors, age 58
President, Construction Equipment: Olof Persson, age 46
President, Aero: Staffan Zackrisson, age 57
President, Renault Trucks: Stefano Chmielewski, age 57
President, Volvo Business Services: Elisabeth Rocke, age 50
President, Volvo Penta: Göran Gummeson, age 63
President, Volvo Buses: Håkan Karlsson, age 48
President and CEO, North American Trucks; President and CEO, Mack Trucks: Dennis R. (Denny) Slagle, age 56
President, Volvo Group North America: Salvatore L. Mauro, age 50
Director Investor Relations: Anders Christensson
Director Corporate Communications, Volvo Group North America: Marjorie A. Meyers
Director Investor Relations: Patrik Stenberg
Auditors: PricewaterhouseCoopers AB

LOCATIONS

HQ: AB Volvo
AB Volvo
S-405 08 Götenburg, Sweden
Phone: 46-31-66-0000
US HQ: 570 Lexington Ave., 20th Fl.
New York, NY 10022
US Phone: 212-418-7400   **US Fax:** 212-418-7435
Web: www.volvogroup.com

2009 Sales

	% of total
Europe	45
Asia	21
North America	18
South America	8
Other regions	8
Total	**100**

PRODUCTS/OPERATIONS

2009 Sales

	% of total
Trucks	63
Construction equipment	16
Buses	8
Financial services	5
Volvo Penta	4
Volvo Aero	4
Total	**100**

Selected Products and Brand Names

Trucks
  Mack
  Renault
  Volvo
Construction Equipment
  Articulated haulers
  Backhoe loaders
  Excavators
  Motor graders
  Skid steer loaders
  Wheel loaders
Buses
  City buses
  Coaches
  Intercity buses
Volvo Penta
  Marine engines (luxury and work boats)
  Industrial engines (forklifts and construction equipment)
Financial Services
  Customer financing
  Insurance
Volvo Aero
  Aircraft engines
  Engine components

COMPETITORS

Caterpillar
Cummins
Cummins Westport
Daimler
Daimler Trucks North America
Deere
Fiat
Fuji Heavy Industries
General Motors
Hino Motors
Honda
Isuzu
MAN
Mitsubishi Motors
Navistar
Navistar International
Nissan
Oshkosh Truck
PACCAR
Penske
Rolls-Royce
Scania
Suzuki Motor
Terex
Toyota

HISTORICAL FINANCIALS

Company Type: Public

Income Statement

FYE: December 31

	REVENUE ($ mil.)	NET INCOME ($ mil.)	NET PROFIT MARGIN	EMPLOYEES
12/09	30,374	(2,047)	—	97,030
12/08	39,112	1,290	3.3%	101,380
12/07	44,580	2,347	5.3%	101,700
12/06	37,729	2,371	6.3%	83,190
12/05	30,250	1,641	5.4%	81,078
Annual Growth	**0.1%**	**—**	**—**	**4.6%**

2009 Year-End Financials

Debt ratio: 158.5%
Return on equity: —
Cash ($ mil.): 2,954
Current ratio: 1.17
Long-term debt ($ mil.): 14,637

No. of shares (mil.): 2,027
Dividends
  Yield: 3.3%
  Payout: —
Market value ($ mil.): 17,326

Stock History

Pink Sheets: VOLVY

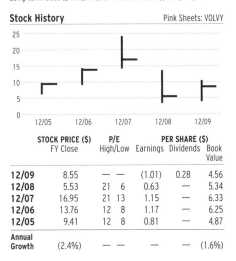

	STOCK PRICE ($) FY Close	P/E High/Low		PER SHARE ($) Earnings	Dividends	Book Value
12/09	8.55	—	—	(1.01)	0.28	4.56
12/08	5.53	21	6	0.63	—	5.34
12/07	16.95	21	13	1.15	—	6.33
12/06	13.76	12	8	1.17	—	6.25
12/05	9.41	12	8	0.81	—	4.87
Annual Growth	**(2.4%)**	**—**	**—**	**—**	**—**	**(1.6%)**

Wal-Mart de México

Just call it Wal-Mex. Wal-Mart de México is the numero uno retailer in Mexico, with some 2,000 stores and restaurants there and in five other countries in Central America. These include Bodega food and general merchandise discount stores and Superama supermarkets; Suburbia apparel stores; and some 360 Vips restaurants. It also runs about 250 Wal-Mart Supercenters and SAM'S CLUB warehouses and Banco Wal-Mart. Its stores are located throughout Mexico, although most are in and around Mexico City. Wal-Mart Stores grabbed a stake in the company in 1991 when it combined its Mexican stores with those of Cifra in a joint venture. Wal-Mart later acquired Cifra and renamed the business Wal-Mart de México in 2000.

Wal-Mart has shaken up Mexico's grocery and department store sectors since entering the country in the early 1990s. Now the country's largest supermarket operator and private employer, Wal-Mart de México operates more stores than any of its parent company's other international divisions and contributes more than a quarter of its international sales.

Fast-growing Wal-Mex opened about 20 stores in 2009, after adding 180 locations in more than 50 new cities the previous year. The

firm's recent growth has been fueled by newly acquired Wal-Mart Centroamerica from majority owner Wal-Mart and regional investors. Wal-Mart has identified similarities between its Central American and Mexican markets and, as the deal is structured, is consolidating Wal-Mart Centroamerica and Wal-Mex under Wal-Mex leadership. As a result of the deal, Wal-Mex upped its store count by about 520 locations and extended its reach into Guatemala, El Salvador, Nicaragua, Honduras, and Costa Rica.

Leading the enlarged organization is Scot Rank Crawford, who was named CEO of the company in 2010. He succeeded Eduardo Solorzano Morales, who resigned after five years in the chief executive's suite to become chairman.

HISTORY

Spanish-born Jerónimo Arango Arias studied art and literature at several American universities without graduating. In his twenties he wandered around Spain, Mexico, and the US. He struck upon an idea after seeing a crowd waiting in line at the E. J. Korvette discount department store in New York City. Jerónimo called his two brothers, Plácido and Manuel, and convinced them to join him in a new business venture.

Borrowing about $250,000 from their father, a Spanish immigrant to Mexico who had been successful in textiles, the three brothers opened their first Aurrerá Bolivar discount store in downtown Mexico City in 1958. Offering goods and clothing well below manufacturers' list prices, the store was an immediate hit with consumers but encountered hostility from competing Mexico City retailers. When local retailers threatened to boycott the Arangos' suppliers, the company turned to suppliers in Guadalajara and Monterrey.

In 1965 the Arango brothers formed a joint venture with Jewel Cos. of Chicago to open new Aurrerá stores. Jewel bought a 49% interest in the business a year later. Plácido and Manuel left the business with their portion of the money, but Jerónimo stayed as head of the company, taking it public in 1976.

By 1981 almost a third of Jewel's earnings came from its operations in Mexico. But the next year the peso crashed, obliterating its earnings there. American Stores took over Jewel in 1984, and Jerónimo bought back Jewel's stake in the company (which was renamed Cifra that year).

With the Mexican economy staggering from the peso devaluation, weak oil markets, and a huge debt crisis, Jerónimo was taking a major risk. Although no new stores were opened, none were closed. Employees were expected to work longer, and those who left were not replaced. With Mexico's middle class hit hard, Jerónimo emphasized the Bodega Aurrerá no-frills warehouses, which discounted all kinds of nonperishable merchandise, from canned chili to VCRs.

Cifra and Wal-Mart Stores formed a joint venture in 1991 to open Club Aurrerá membership clubs similar to SAM'S CLUB outlets. The two companies expanded the venture the next year to include the development of SAM'S CLUB and Wal-Mart Supercenters in Mexico.

Remodeling began on Cifra's stores in 1992. The work was completed two years later, and the company was poised to take advantage of Mexico's much-improved economy.

However, devaluation struck again late in 1994. The resulting contraction of credit and rise in prices hit Mexican consumers hard, and Cifra's 1995 sales declined 15%. But again it kept on as many employees as possible, transferring them to new stores that had been in development. Despite the hard times, Cifra opened 27 new stores (including 15 restaurants). The company was able to withstand the difficulties in part because it stayed debt-free.

Wal-Mart consolidated its joint venture into Cifra in 1997 in exchange for about 34% of that company; Wal-Mart later raised its stake to 51%. The cost-conscious companies combined the joint venture stores and Cifra's separate stores under one umbrella. Cifra opened 11 stores and eight restaurants that year.

Cifra opened nine stores and 17 restaurants in 1998; the next year it opened about 20 stores and nearly 25 restaurants. In early 2000 Cifra was renamed Wal-Mart de México. Shortly thereafter, Wal-Mart upped its stake in Wal-Mart de México to about 61%.

In November 2002 Eduardo Castro-Wright was promoted from COO to CEO of Wal-Mart de México, succeeding Cesareo Fernandez who retained the chairman's title.

In March 2003 Mexico's Federal Competition Commission closed an investigation of Wal-Mex's purchasing practices, citing a lack of evidence that the retailer violated competition laws. Overall in 2003, Wal-Mex entered nine new cities in Mexico and added 46 new outlets.

In 2005 Fernandez stepped down as chairman and was succeeded by Ernesto Vega. CEO Eduardo Castro-Wright left Wal-Mex to become COO of the Wal-Mart Stores Division in the US. He was succeeded by Eduardo Solorzano, formerly COO of Wal-Mex. Also that year Wal-Mex acquired the Mexican assets (29 hypermarkets) of French retailer Carrefour.

In 2006 Wal-Mex received a license from Mexico's Finance Ministry to organize and operate a bank there. In 2007 Banco Wal-Mart began operations with 16 branches in Mexico.

Wal-Mex inked a deal with Tobacco One in 2008 to distribute the tobacco firm's Rojo cigarette line in about 140 supercenters and some 60 Superama stores throughout Mexico.

EXECUTIVES

Chairman: Eduardo Solorzano Morales, age 53
President and CEO: Scot Rank Crawford, age 49
EVP, CFO, and Director: Rafael Matute Labrador, age 50
EVP Specialty Business: Gian Carlo Nucci Vidales, age 40
SVP, General Counsel, and Secretary:
José L. Rodríguezmacedo Rivera
SVP Real Estate Development: Xavier Ezeta González, age 44
SVP Corporate Affairs and People Division:
Raúl Argüelles Díaz González, age 46
SVP Bodega Aurrerá: Alberto Ebrard Casaubón, age 48
SVP Retail Development:
Simona Visztová Hromkovicova, age 42
SVP and Executive Officer, Banco Wal-Mart de México:
José M. Urquiza
SVP Sam's Club: Rodolfo Von Der Meden Alarcón, age 46
SVP Wal-Mart Supercenter and Superama:
Miguel Baltazar Rodríguez, age 57
SVP Real Estate: Xavier del Río Troncoso, age 62
VP Marketing: Laurence Pepping Valles, age 45
VP Administration: Roque Velasco Ruiz, age 48
VP Systems: María del Carmen Valencia Martínez, age 42
VP Distribution and Logistics: Mario Romero
VP People Division: Rubén Camarena Torres, age 53
VP Legal and Real Estate: Gerardo Cicero
Auditors: Mancera, S.C.

LOCATIONS

HQ: Wal-Mart de México, S.A.B. de C.V.
Blvd. Manuel Ávila Camacho 647, Colonia Periodista, Delegación Miguel Hidalgo 11220 México, D.F., Mexico
Phone: 52-55-5283-0100   **Fax:** 52-55-5387-9420
Web: www.walmartmexico.com.mx

PRODUCTS/OPERATIONS

2009 Stores

	No.
Bodega Aurrerá	684
VIPS Restaurants	366
Wal-Mart Supercenters	169
SAM'S CLUB	98
Suburbia	86
Superama	69
Total	**1,472**

2009 Sales

	% of total
Bodega Aurrerá	34
Wal-Mart Supercenters	28
SAM'S CLUB	27
Superama	5
Suburbia	4
Restaurants	2
Total	**100**

Selected Operations

Banco Wal-Mart de México
Bodega Aurrerá (large, limited-assortment discount warehouses)
Sam's Club (membership-only warehouse outlets)
Suburbia (apparel stores)
Superama (supermarkets)
Vips (restaurants)
Wal-Mart Supercenters (discount hypermarkets)

COMPETITORS

Banamex
Banorte
Chedraui
Comerci
Costco Wholesale
El Puerto de Liverpool
Financiero Santander
Gigante
Grupo Carso
H-E-B
Safeway
Sanborns
Sears Roebuck de México
Soriana

HISTORICAL FINANCIALS

Company Type: Public

Income Statement

FYE: December 31

	REVENUE ($ mil.)	NET INCOME ($ mil.)	NET PROFIT MARGIN	EMPLOYEES
12/09	20,660	1,289	6.2%	213,770
12/08	17,774	1,065	6.0%	170,014
12/07	20,597	1,303	6.3%	157,432
12/06	18,389	1,148	6.2%	141,704
12/05	15,314	879	5.7%	124,295
Annual Growth	**7.8%**	**10.1%**	**—**	**14.5%**

2009 Year-End Financials

Debt ratio: —   Current ratio: —
Return on equity: 21.9%   Long-term debt ($ mil.): —
Cash ($ mil.): —

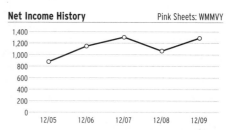

Wesfarmers Limited

Wesfarmers Limited first began growing its business by providing merchandise and services to farmers in Western Australia. The firm now is considered the country's largest retailer after its 2007 acquisition of food and liquor retailer Coles Group. It also has interests in far-ranging businesses, including general merchandise, home-improvement, and office products retailing; coal mining; gas processing and distribution; chemical and fertilizer production; building materials sales; distribution of maintenance, repair, and operating products and industrial and safety products; insurance; and rail transport. True to its heritage, Wesfarmers still provides agricultural merchandise and services.

Wesfarmers first floated on the public stock exchange (Sydney) in 1984. Although its beginnings were in agriculture, Wesfarmers now draws about 85% of its sales from its retail operations, which in addition to all the Coles Group stores include Bunnings home improvement and outdoor living products stores.

Wesfarmers, which was founded in 1914 as a farmers' co-operative, spent more than $18 billion in November 2007 to acquire Australian supermarket and liquor store operator Coles Group, together with its BI-LO, Coles, Coles Express, Liquor Land, Vintage Cellars, Target, Kmart, and Officeworks stores. The acquisition, which ranked as the largest takeover in Australia's history, gave Wesfarmers the designation as the country's top retailer. (Wesfarmers had already owned an 11% stake in Coles.) Soon after the deal was completed, Wesfarmers announced plans to overhaul the Coles operation in a five-year turnaround focused on the Coles supermarket chain. The turnaround process, which promised to be difficult enough, has been complicated by the global economic downturn and crisis in the credit markets.

As part of the reorganization, Coles Group sold its online pharmacy business — Pharmacy Direct — to RX Direct, whose directors and shareholders are all pharmacists. Coles is also shedding some supermarket and liquor stores as it attempts to improve its overall store network. While Coles is making some progress, the chain is still losing market share to archrival Woolworths.

Outside the retail arena, recent acquisitions include the purchase of the New Zealand-based packaging firm Expresspak in mid-2009. To strengthen its position in the foodservice industry, Wesfarmers Industrial acquired Expresspak, which specializes in paper and plastic food and beverage packaging, to add to its Packaging House business. As part of the deal, the firm operates independently under the Expresspak name but shares its resources with Wesfarmers subsidiary Packaging House, whose offerings are largely of the industrial sort (steel strapping, tape, film). The acquisition puts Packaging House, which provides hygiene, foodservice, cleaning and chemicals and industrial packaging, in a market-leading position in the foodservice packaging sector.

In April 2010 the company merged its Wesfarmers Chemicals & Fertilisers and Wesfarmers Energy divisions to form Wesfarmers Chemicals, Energy & Fertilisers, and also made other organizational and management changes in the industrial divisions.

The company has also undergone a change in leadership during the restructuring. In March 2009 Wesfarmers named Terry Bowen its financial director. He stepped into the role after it was vacated by Gene Tilbrook, who retired after logging more than 20 years with the firm.

EXECUTIVES

Chairman: Robert (Bob) Every, age 64
Managing Director: Richard J. Barr Goyder, age 47
Finance Director: Terry Bowen
Chief Human Resources Officer: Ben Lawrence
Chief Executive, Chemicals: Ian Hansen
Executive General Manager, Business Development: Tim Bult
Executive General Manager, Corporate Affairs: Mark Triffitt
Managing Director, Wesfarmers Insurance: Robert Scott
Managing Director, Wesfarmers Chemicals, Energy & Fertilizers: Tom O'Leary
Managing Director, Wesfarmers Resources: Stewart Butel
Managing Director, Coles: Ian McLeod, age 51
Managing Director, Home Improvement and Office Supplies: John Gillam
Managing Director, Target: Launa Inman
Managing Director, Kmart: Guy Russo
Managing Director, Wesfarmers Industrial and Safety: Olivier Chretien
Auditors: Ernst & Young

LOCATIONS

HQ: Wesfarmers Limited
    Level 11, Wesfarmers House, 40 The Esplanade
    Perth 6000, Australia
Phone: 61-8-9327-4211   **Fax:** 61-8-9327-4216
Web: www.wesfarmers.com.au

PRODUCTS/OPERATIONS

2010 Sales

	% of total
Coles	32
Home improvement & office supplies	27
Target	13
Kmart	7
Resources	6
Insurance	4
Industrial & safety	4
Chemicals & fertilizers	4
Energy	3
Total	**100**

COMPETITORS

ALDI
Australia and New Zealand Banking
Caltex Australia
Commonwealth Bank of Australia
Harvey Norman Holdings
Insurance Australia
Metcash
Woolworths Limited

HISTORICAL FINANCIALS

Company Type: Public

Income Statement

FYE: June 30

	REVENUE ($ mil.)	NET INCOME ($ mil.)	NET PROFIT MARGIN	EMPLOYEES
6/10	44,380	1,340	3.0%	200,000
6/09	41,034	1,235	3.0%	200,000
6/08	32,233	1,009	3.1%	200,000
6/07	8,245	667	8.1%	160,000
6/06	6,444	765	11.9%	30,000
Annual Growth	**62.0%**	**15.0%**	**—**	**60.7%**

2010 Year-End Financials

Debt ratio: —
Return on equity: 6.6%
Cash ($ mil.): 1,404
Current ratio: 1.23
Long-term debt ($ mil.): —
No. of shares (mil.): 1,005
Dividends
  Yield: 4.0%
  Payout: 84.5%
Market value ($ mil.): 24,660

Stock History

Australian: WES

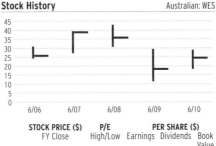

	STOCK PRICE ($) FY Close	P/E High/Low		PER SHARE ($) Earnings	Dividends	Book Value
6/10	24.53	25	16	1.16	0.98	21.04
6/09	18.22	23	9	1.28	1.49	19.41
6/08	35.83	26	19	1.64	0.64	18.72
6/07	38.81	24	17	1.64	2.04	2.96
6/06	25.79	16	13	1.90	1.44	2.41
Annual Growth	**(1.2%)**	**—**	**—**	**(11.6%)**	**(9.2%)**	**71.8%**

Westpac Banking

Westpac Banking keeps its pact to serve customers in Australia, New Zealand, and the neighboring Pacific islands. Its transforming deal to buy St.George Bank in 2008 catapulted Westpac from fourth to second among Australia's leading banks and it now has its sights set on becoming the largest financial services firm in the country. Westpac serves some 10 million customers through more than 1,400 branches. It offers consumer and business banking, investment services through its BT Financial Group, and corporate financial services through Westpac Institutional Bank. Its Westpac New Zealand arm reaches 1.2 million Kiwis. Westpac Banking was founded in 1817 as the Bank of New South Wales.

Throughout its history Westpac has been focused on growth. The acquisition of St.George (which continues to operate under that name) helped the company achieve monumental expansion. The combination sets Westpac and its St.George subsidiary behind only the National Australia Bank in terms of assets.

Earlier in 2008 Westpac bought the franchise distribution business from RAMS, which offers mortgage origination services. The deal did not include the company's mortgage book, but it helped provide Westpac with growth opportunities for its retail banking business.

JPMorgan Chase owns about 12% of Westpac.

HISTORY

Westpac proudly calls itself Australia's "First Bank." But when predecessor Bank of New South Wales was founded in 1817, some 90% of the eponymous colony's inhabitants were convicts or their relatives. (The penal colony was established just 30 years before the bank.) The British challenged the bank's charter, forcing it to become a joint-stock company.

New South Wales' parliament rechartered the company as a bank in 1850, amidst the country's first gold rushes. (Some bank branches consisted of tents in mining camps.) Heavy British investment and an influx of colonists kept the country growing. The bank's future partner, Commercial Bank of Australia, was founded in 1866 in Melbourne, in the neighboring colony of Victoria. More than half of the country's banks disappeared in a panic at the end of the century, when land speculation and a collapse in wool prices caused a depression.

Australia became a country with the onset of the 20th century, and its government formed Commonwealth Bank, a central bank. The Bank of New South Wales, now known as "The Wales," helped finance Australia's WWI efforts. Along with the rest of the world, the country and the bank rode up the Roaring '20s and down the Great Depression.

About 65% of the bank's male staff enlisted during WWII. Its New Guinea branches closed; others were hit by air raids. In 1947 the government moved to nationalize the prospering country's banks within the Commonwealth Bank, but the courts helped the banks fend off the attack on their independence.

The Bank of New South Wales moved into the newly opened savings banking market in 1956. The next year it bought into Australian Guarantee Corporation (it bought the rest in 1988).

The bank expanded abroad and diversified operations in the 1970s. Battered by a lagging, protectionist economy, Australia moved to deregulate banking in the 1980s. As foreign banks hustled in, Bank of New South Wales and Commercial Bank of Australia in 1982 made what was then the largest merger in Australia's history.

The new bank, known as Westpac (for its Western Pacific market area), began building its non-teller-based banking networks in the early 1980s. The company developed an extensive ATM network and established telephone and computerized banking. Later that decade it bought a stake in London gold dealer Johnson Matthey (1986) and all of William E. Pollock Government Securities (1987).

In 1992 Australia's wealthiest man, Kerry Packer, took a 10% share in troubled Westpac, gaining board seats for himself and friend "Chainsaw" Al Dunlap. Packer's power grab failed, and he sold the stake in 1993.

After buying itself into the equities market in the mid-1980s, Westpac sold its Ord Minnett brokerage division in 1993. The bank withdrew from Asia and expanded closer to home in the mid 1990s, buying Western Australia's Challenge Bank in 1995, Trust Bank of New Zealand in 1996, and Victoria's Bank of Melbourne in 1997.

In 1998 the bank agreed to merge its back-office operations with those of ANZ Banking Group, providing economies of scale while avoiding antitrust issues. The next year Westpac announced 3,000 job cuts, mainly through attrition, to ready itself for increased competition from changes in Australian law. Pacific operations caused waves in 2000: Westpac said it would pull out of Kiribati in response to government action, and a coup in Fiji prompted the bank to reduce employees' hours (a move that was criticized by the Fiji government). The next year, however, Westpac was strengthening ties to the Pacific market. It doubled its holdings in the Bank of Tonga (on the island of Tonga) and its share of Pacific Commercial Bank (on the island of Samoa).

In 2007 subsidiary Westpac Essential Services Trust formed a joint venture with another Australian firm to operate the Airport Link Company, a rail-to-airport passenger service in Sydney. The trust was established so investors could invest in public-private partnership (PPP) assets.

Westpac bought St.George Bank in 2008, making it Australia's #2 bank.

EXECUTIVES

Chairman: Ted Evans, age 67
Deputy Chairman: John S. Curtis, age 60
Managing Director and CEO: Gail P. Kelly, age 53
SVP and COO: Manuela Adl
CFO: Philip (Phil) Coffey, age 51
Chief Risk Officer: Greg Targett, age 53
Group Executive, People and Performance: Ilana Atlas, age 54
Group Executive, Technology: Bob McKinnon, age 55
Group Executive, Westpac Institutional Bank: Rob Whitfield, age 43
Group Executive, Retail and Business Banking: Peter Hanlon, age 54
Group Executive, Product and Operations: Peter Clare, age 46
Group Chief Transformation Officer: Brad Cooper, age 47
Secretary: Rebecca Farrell
Head, Investor Relations: Andrew Bowden
Head of Advice Sales, Financial Planning, and Advice: Chris Davies
Group Executive, Counsel and Secretariat: John Arthur
CEO, BT Financial Group: Rob Coombe, age 46
CEO, St.George Bank: Rob Chapman
CEO, Westpac New Zealand: George Frazis, age 45
Auditors: PricewaterhouseCoopers

LOCATIONS

HQ: Westpac Banking Corporation
    Level 20, 275 Kent St.
    Sydney 2000, Australia
Phone: 61-2-9293-9270   **Fax:** 61-2-8253-4128
US HQ: 575 5th Ave., 39th Fl., New York, NY 10017
US Phone: 212-551-1800   **US Fax:** 212-551-1999
Web: www.westpac.com.au

2009 Sales

	% of total
Australia	85
New Zealand	13
Other	2
Total	**100**

PRODUCTS/OPERATIONS

2009 Sales by Segment

	% of total
Westpac Retail & Business Banking	40
Westpac Institutional Bank	20
St.George Bank	19
New Zealand Banking	9
BT Financial Group Australia	5
Other	7
Total	**100**

COMPETITORS

Australia and New Zealand Banking
Barclays
Commonwealth Bank of Australia
Hang Seng Bank
HBOS Australia
HSBC
Macquarie Group
National Australia Bank

HISTORICAL FINANCIALS

Company Type: Public

Income Statement

FYE: September 30

	ASSETS ($ mil.)	NET INCOME ($ mil.)	INCOME AS % OF ASSETS	EMPLOYEES
9/10	599,605	6,154	1.0%	38,962
9/09	514,533	3,007	0.6%	37,032
9/08	361,928	3,177	0.9%	28,302
9/07	333,989	3,076	0.9%	28,018
9/06	223,499	2,291	1.0%	27,224
Annual Growth	**28.0%**	**28.0%**	**—**	**9.4%**

2010 Year-End Financials

Equity as % of assets: 6.2%
Return on assets: 1.1%
Return on equity: 18.3%
Long-term debt ($ mil.): 152,665
No. of shares (mil.): 595

Dividends
    Yield: 5.5%
    Payout: 59.4%
Market value ($ mil.): 64,843
Sales ($ mil.): 38,035

Stock History

NYSE: WBK

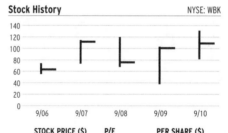

	STOCK PRICE ($) FY Close	P/E High/Low		PER SHARE ($) Earnings	Dividends	Book Value
9/10	108.91	13	8	10.04	5.96	62.20
9/09	100.74	19	7	5.38	5.68	50.77
9/08	75.90	14	8	8.21	5.52	24.68
9/07	111.63	14	9	8.22	5.43	23.82
9/06	63.12	12	9	6.19	3.96	17.78
Annual Growth	**14.6%**	**—**	**—**	**12.9%**	**10.8%**	**36.8%**

Wipro Limited

You might say this company has really cleaned up in the technology services business. Wipro is one of India's leading providers of system integration and outsourcing services, but it also manufactures a variety of consumer products, including hand soap. Operating in more than 30 countries, its Wipro Technologies arm offers software development and business process outsourcing (BPO) services, as well as consulting and product engineering. Its Wipro Infotech unit focuses on providing IT products and services to customers in India and the Asia/Pacific region. Wipro's consumer products include soaps and personal care products (led by the Santoor, Yardley, and Unza brands), commercial lighting, and office furniture.

Once highly diversified, Wipro has focused on expanding its technology services businesses, which accounted for about 90% of the company's revenues in 2009. This strategy has paid off as the company's IT operations have been instrumental in driving overall sales and profits steadily up. The company has benefited especially from the trend of cost-conscious companies, particularly in the US (which accounts for almost half of its business), looking to outsource their IT operations as they try to boost profits. However, a weakened US economy has Wipro looking to developing markets in Asia, Europe, and the Middle East for growth. To this end, the company opened a new Wipro Technologies office in South Korea in mid-2010.

The company added to its IT infrastructure services operations with the 2009 purchase of Citi Technology Services (renamed Wipro Technology Services) from Citigroup. The unit provides IT support services to Citi businesses worldwide.

Though consumer products account for a small percentage of its overall revenues, Wipro has maintained a competitive position in several product categories, including soaps and lighting. In 2009 the company bought personal care products maker Yardley's business in Asia, the Middle East, Australia, and west Africa for about $45 million from UK-based Lornamead Group. Wipro has said that it plans to continue building its consumer products business through further acquisitions and a steady focus on markets in Africa, Asia, and India.

In addition to technology and consumer products, Wipro manufactures hydraulic parts and equipment primarily for the automotive market through Wipro Infrastructure Engineering (formerly Wipro Fluid Power). It also provides support services for users of General Electric medical equipment through Wipro GE Healthcare, a joint venture 51% owned by GE.

Chairman Azim Premji owns about 80% of the company.

HISTORY

In 1947 M. H. Hasham Premji turned down an offer from the prime minister of Pakistan to migrate from India and become finance minister. Premji cited his loyalty to India as well as to his business, Western Indian Vegetable Products (Wipro), founded in 1946 to sell cooking oil. Wipro went public in 1947.

Like any proper Indian industrialist, Premji eventually diversified into other markets, including bath soap and hydraulic fluid. Instead of employing the customary tactic of courting Indian bureaucrats to help grow his business, Premji focused on customers. He kept costs low by branding generic products and selling directly to retailers instead of middlemen. When Premji died of a heart attack in 1966, he left behind a $2 million business.

Premji's 21-year-old son, Azim, who had only three months left in his engineering degree program at Stanford, returned home and took the reins in 1968. Although he had little idea how to run a business, he took a cue from his father's success and continued diversifying into new markets. India ordered computing giant IBM to leave the country in 1977 after a dispute over investment and intellectual property, opening the door for Wipro to tackle computer manufacturing and distribution. Instead of plucking away ex-IBM employees, Premji hired managers from a truck maker and a refrigeration company, who together helped turn Wipro computers into a leading national brand.

In 1980 Wipro began offering IT services in India. Three years later the company moved into software, offering branded products in the same market as US upstart Microsoft. Wipro entered the toilet soap and dot matrix printer markets in 1985.

It was in the late 1980s that Wipro finally discovered its growth business, software services (it abandoned software sales in 1990). The company's reputation as a software integrator was secured in 1989 when Wipro and General Electric, whose business model Premji admired and followed very carefully, formed Wipro GE Medical Systems as a joint venture. Possessing GE as a partner and long-term client over the next decade attracted scores of research and development contracts from blue-chip clients in the US (Cisco Systems), Japan (Hitachi), and Europe (Alcatel).

During the early 1990s Wipro began transitioning away from costly onsite software projects in the US to more profitable offshore development in India. It also entered the lighting business in 1992. With Taiwan-based Acer, Wipro formed a joint venture in 1995 to manufacture and sell computers and other peripherals in India. The company reorganized in 1999 into four companies, each run separately: software, hardware and systems, consumer care and lighting, and hydraulic fluid. Wipro Net was also formed to offer e-commerce implementation services. In 2000 Wipro listed on the New York Stock Exchange, gaining an international investment audience for what few shares Premji didn't already own. The move caused his personal wealth to soar.

In 2002 Wipro launched genetic data software division Healthcare and Life Sciences. Also that year the company bought Indian call center operator Spectramind for $90 million and American Management Systems' global energy practice for $24 million to form Wipro BPO Solutions. The following year, though, it reorganized its operations, folding Wipro BPO into its global IT services division, Wipro Technologies, along with the technology-oriented parts of its HealthSciences unit.

In an effort to strengthen its networking infrastructure services business, the company acquired US-based Infocrossing in 2007 for about $413 million. Looking to expand its consumer products presence in southeast Asia, the company in 2007 purchased Unza Holdings, a Singapore-based maker of cosmetics and toiletries, for about $246 million.

EXECUTIVES

Chairman, CEO, and Managing Director:
Azim H. Premji, age 64
CFO and Director: Suresh C. Senapaty, age 53
Chief Strategy Officer: Rishad Premji
Chief Sustainability Officer: Anurag Behar, age 41
Chief Quality Officer: Jagdish Ramaswamy, age 45
EVP Human Resources; President, Infrastructure Engineering Division: Pratik Kumar, age 44
Interim Head Mergers and Acquisitions:
Sridhar Srinivasan
Managing Director, Wipro GE Healthcare: V. Raja
Director; Co-CEO, IT Business: Suresh Vaswani, age 50
Director; Co-CEO, IT Business: Girish S. Paranjpe, age 52
President, Global Sales and Operations:
Martha H. Béjar
President, Wipro Consumer Care and Lighting:
Vineet Agrawal, age 48
President, Wipro Eco-Energy: T. K. Kurien, age 50
Chief Sales and Operations Officer, USA and Canada:
Sid Nair
Auditors: KPMG

LOCATIONS

HQ: Wipro Limited
Doddakannelli, Sarjapur Road
Bangalore, Karnataka 560 035, India
Phone: 91-80-2844-0011   **Fax:** 91-80-2844-0054
US HQ: 2 Tower Center Blvd., Ste. 2200
East Brunswick, NJ 08816
US Phone: 732-509-1500
Web: www.wipro.com

2010 Sales

	% of total
US	45
Europe	22
India	22
Other regions	11
Total	**100**

PRODUCTS/OPERATIONS

2010 Sales

	% of total
IT services	75
IT products	13
Consumer care & lighting	8
Others	4
Total	**100**

COMPETITORS

Accenture	Komatsu
Acer	Lenovo
BearingPoint	L'Oréal
Capgemini	MindTree
Cognizant Tech Solutions	Perot Systems
Computer Sciences Corp.	Philips Electronics
Convergys	Procter & Gamble
Dell	Redington Group
GE	Satyam
HCL Technologies	Sauer-Danfoss
Hewlett-Packard	Siemens Healthcare
Hindustan Unilever	Sony
Hitachi	Tata Consultancy
HP Enterprise Services	Tech Mahindra
Hyundai Motor	TeleTech
IBM	Toshiba
Infosys	Unilever
Ingram Micro	

HISTORICAL FINANCIALS

Company Type: Public

Income Statement

FYE: March 31

	REVENUE ($ mil.)	NET INCOME ($ mil.)	NET PROFIT MARGIN	EMPLOYEES
3/10	6,040	1,024	17.0%	108,000
3/09	4,880	660	13.5%	100,000
3/08	4,960	810	16.3%	90,000
3/07	3,469	676	19.5%	50,000
3/06	2,380	455	19.1%	53,700
Annual Growth	**26.2%**	**22.5%**	**—**	**19.1%**

2010 Year-End Financials

Debt ratio: 9.2%
Return on equity: 28.3%
Cash ($ mil.): 1,441
Current ratio: 1.90
Long-term debt ($ mil.): 402

No. of shares (mil.): 2,447
Dividends
   Yield: 17.3%
   Payout: 20.0%
Market value ($ mil.): 760

Stock History

NYSE: WIT

	STOCK PRICE ($) FY Close	P/E High/Low		PER SHARE ($) Earnings	Dividends	Book Value
3/10	0.31	1	—	0.25	0.05	1.78
3/09	0.08	1	—	0.27	0.05	1.18
3/08	0.17	1	—	0.33	0.05	1.33
3/07	0.22	1	1	0.28	0.14	0.96
3/06	0.20	1	1	0.19	0.03	0.72
Annual Growth	**11.6%**	**—**	**—**	**7.1%**	**13.6%**	**25.3%**

Wolseley plc

In business for more than 100 years, Wolseley went from shearing sheep in Australia to building some of the first automobiles in the UK to becoming the world's largest distributor of heating and plumbing supplies to professional contractors. The company distributes central heating equipment, fittings, lumber, pipes, underground drainage equipment, valves, and other building materials from about 4,400 outlets in more than 25 countries in North America and Europe. The company's customers include building contractors, plumbing and heating engineers, and industrial and mechanical contractors. Outside the UK, Wolseley subsidiaries include Ferguson Enterprises in the US, and Brossette, Manzardo, and WASCO in Europe.

The deteriorating housing markets in the US and UK, along with the global credit crisis, are pinching Wolseley's sales. Prior to the current slowdown, Wolseley had aggressively increased the number of outlets it operates from about 3,600 in 2004 to more than 5,300 in 2008. But in fiscal 2009 it trimmed about 900 locations from its outlet count.

In response to the slump in construction, the company is seeking to exit the building supply market in the US and Ireland and focus on its core heating and plumbing business in North America. To that end, in May 2009 Wolseley sold a majority stake in its former subsidiary, North Carolina-based Stock Building Supply, to The Gores Group, a private equity firm. (Wolseley retained a 49% share of the new joint venture.) Prior to the sale, Wolseley had made substantial cuts both at Ferguson and Stock Building Supply by cutting more than 7,000 jobs and closing some 270 branches. In early 2010 Wolseley sold its retail network in the Republic of Ireland and some stores in Northern Ireland to private investor WIBHM for about £25 million (nearly $40 million). The stores operated under the Brooks, Encon Ireland, Heat Merchants, and Tubs and Tiles banners. In addition, the firm is cutting hundreds of jobs elsewhere in Europe.

In North America (45% of sales) the group is bringing the business activities of Wolseley Canada under the management of Ferguson, the US's largest wholesale distributor of plumbing supplies, pipes, valves, and fittings, and a major distributor of heating, ventilation, and air conditioning (HVAC) equipment.

Leading the trimmed down company is Ian Meakins, who joined Wolseley as CEO in mid-2009. He succeeded Claude "Chip" Hornsby, who resigned from the position after three years.

HISTORY

In the late 1800s Irishman Frederick Wolseley immigrated to Australia, where he developed the world's first mechanical sheep shearer. In 1889 he formed Wolseley Sheep Shearing Machine Company. Herbert Austin, a young engineer who perfected Wolseley's machine, moved back to England and became manager of the company's Birmingham factory when the company relocated there in 1893.

In 1895 Austin, amazed by an automobile exhibition he attended in Paris, obtained an advance from the company to develop an automobile; it went into production in 1901. The car manufacturing operations were separated from the company's other machinery operations and soon were bought by Vickers. (Austin went out on his own in 1905 and began producing cars under his own name — the venerable Austin line.)

By the middle of the century, Wolseley Sheep Shearing had grown to include central heating and plumbing products distribution. In 1958 it joined with Geo. H. Hughes to form Wolseley-Hughes. At the time the company was a small manufacturer with 11 distribution depots.

The company's watershed transition began in 1976, when Jeremy Lancaster took over the chairmanship from his father. (In the 20 years that Lancaster was chairman, profits rose from about $6 million in 1976 to more than $350 million in 1996.) In the late 1970s the company began expanding rapidly through acquisitions. In 1982 it went public and acquired Ferguson Enterprises, a leading distributor of plumbing supplies on the US's East Coast. The acquisition marked the company's first substantial US purchase. Three years later the company formed Wolseley Centers, which distributed building products under the names Plumb Center, Controls Center, and Pipeline Center. In 1986 the company changed its name to Wolseley plc. Acquisitions that year included Carolina Builders Corporation and M.P. Harris & Co. Late 1980s acquisitions included Familian (1987), the largest plumbing supplier on the US's West Coast, and Familian Northwest (1988).

Wolseley then looked across the English Channel. In 1992 it bought Brossette, France's largest specialist distributor of plumbing supplies. The company moved further eastward in 1994, acquiring ÖAG Group (now Wolseley Austria), Austria's largest wholesale plumbing supply business. In addition to 40 Austrian branches, ÖAG also had five branches in both Hungary and Germany and four in the Czech Republic. The ÖAG deal solidified Wolseley's position as the world's #1 plumbing and heating merchant.

Wolseley turned its attention back to the US in the mid-1990s, buying a half-dozen companies, including Building Material Supply. John Young became CEO that year when Jeremy Lancaster retired from the company.

Chairman Richard Ireland became acting chief executive in June 2000 with the retirement of Young for health reasons. That year the company sold most of its manufacturing businesses. In May 2001 Ferguson Enterprises CEO Charles Banks was named group chief executive.

Also in 2001 Wolseley bought the heating and plumbing operations of Westburne Group (from France-based Rexel, a distributor of electrical equipment) for $356 million to further expand in the US. In 2002 Ireland was replaced as chairman by deputy chairman John Whybrow.

In 2003 Wolseley bought Pinault Bois & Materiaux (now PB & M), which distributes lumber and building supplies in France, from Pinault-Printemps-Redoute. Wolseley acquired three North American businesses, JM Lumber, Liberty Equipment & Supply, and Nuroc Plumbing and Heating Supplies, in 2003.

Wolseley expanded its Irish business through the 2004 acquisition of Brooks Group, an Irish building supply company, from UPM-Kymmene. Capping an acquisitive year, Wolseley also acquired Parnell-Martin Management and Record Supply Company in the US.

In 2007 Wolseley purchased Davidson Pipe Company in the US, gaining access to the New York metropolitan market. In 2009 Wolseley sold a 51% stake in Stock Building Supply to The Gores Group, LLC, a US private equity firm.

EXECUTIVES

Chairman: John W. Whybrow, age 63
Group Chief Executive and Board Member:
Ian K. Meakins, age 53, $99,414 total compensation
CFO and Board Member: John Martin, age 43
Board Member; Chief Executive, North America:
Frank W. Roach, age 58, $1,002,055 total compensation
Secretary, General Counsel, and Board Member:
Richard Shoylekov, age 44
Managing Director, Italy: Nicola Gasparoni
Managing Director, UK Lightside: Keith H. D. Jones
Managing Director, UK: Steve Ashmore, age 45
Managing Director, CFM: Peter Broecker
Group HR Director: Bob Morrison
Group Treasurer and Tax: Mike Verrier
Managing Director, Wolseley France: Philippe Gardies
Director Transportation, North America Division:
Brad Marsh
Director Corporate Communications: Mark Fearon
PA to Director Group Strategy and Investor Relations:
Rose Mahoney
Auditors: PricewaterhouseCoopers LLP

LOCATIONS

HQ: Wolseley plc
Parkview 1220, Arlington Business Park
Theale, West Berkshire RG7 4GA, United Kingdom
Phone: 44-118-929-8700 **Fax:** 44-118-929-8701
Web: www.wolseley.com

2010 Sales

	% of total
North America	45
UK & Ireland	19
Nordic region	15
France	14
Central & Eastern Europe	7
Total	**100**

2010 Outlets

	No.
Europe	2,657
North America	1,461
Total	**4,118**

PRODUCTS/OPERATIONS

Selected Subsidiaries

Brossette SA (plumbing, heating, bathroom products, pipes, valves, fittings; France)
CFM (heating appliances; Luxembourg)
DT Group (building materials; Denmark)
Ferguson Enterprises Inc. (wholesale distribution of plumbing, heating, and piping products; US)
Manzardo SpA (heating and plumbing equipment; Italy)
OAG AG (heating and plumbing products; Austria)
PB&M (building materials and wood distribution; France)
Tobler (heating and plumbing products; Switzerland)
Wasco Holding BV (heating equipment; The Netherlands)
Wolseley Canada (wholesale distribution of plumbing, heating, ventilation products; Canada)
Wolseley France (building materials, plumbing, heating products; France)
Wolseley UK Limited (construction products; UK)
Woodcote Group (construction materials; Czech Republic)

COMPETITORS

84 Lumber	Lowe's
B&Q	MPS Builders and
Castorama Dubois	Merchants
Emco Corporation	MSC Industrial Direct
Focus (DIY)	Noland
Grafton Group	Saint-Gobain Building
HD Supply	Distribution
Hewden Stuart	SIG plc
HSS Hire	Speedy Hire
Interline Brands	Thermador Groupe
Jewson	Travis Perkins
Kingfisher	Waxman

HISTORICAL FINANCIALS

Company Type: Public

Income Statement

FYE: July 31

	REVENUE ($ mil.)	NET INCOME ($ mil.)	NET PROFIT MARGIN	EMPLOYEES
7/10	20,650	(532)	—	48,226
7/09	23,927	(1,944)	—	55,132
7/08	29,354	147	0.5%	75,943
7/07	32,943	963	2.9%	78,948
7/06	26,403	1,002	3.8%	65,223
Annual Growth	(6.0%)	—	—	(7.3%)

2010 Year-End Financials

Debt ratio: —	No. of shares (mil.): 284
Return on equity: —	Dividends
Cash ($ mil.): 1,040	Yield: 0.0%
Current ratio: —	Payout: —
Long-term debt ($ mil.): —	Market value ($ mil.): 6,396

Stock History

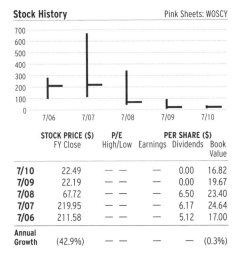

Pink Sheets: WOSCY

	STOCK PRICE ($) FY Close	P/E High/Low	PER SHARE ($) Earnings	Dividends	Book Value
7/10	22.49	— —	—	0.00	16.82
7/09	22.19	— —	—	0.00	19.67
7/08	67.72	— —	—	6.50	23.40
7/07	219.95	— —	—	6.17	24.64
7/06	211.58	— —	—	5.12	17.00
Annual Growth	(42.9%)	— —	—	—	(0.3%)

Wolters Kluwer

This publisher is focused on the basics in life: death and taxes. One of Europe's leading professional publishers, Wolters Kluwer disseminates information on tax, accounting, and legal affairs; corporate and financial services; and health. The company publishes content through print and electronic formats, serving lawyers, doctors, nurses, tax advisors, and business executives. Its operations include businesses and brands such as CCH (tax and accounting), Ovid Technologies (medical research), Lippincott Williams (health care), CT Corporation (corporate compliance), and Aspen Publishers (legal information).

The company faces challenges in advertising and subscription sales amid a weak economy that has hit the publishing industry particularly hard. In response, it implemented a cost-saving program in 2009 called the Springboard operational excellence program. The program includes standardizing technology platforms and consolidating IT infrastructure, streamlining content manufacturing processes, expanding global sourcing programs, creating offshore service centers for software development and testing, and content production and back-office support functions.

These cost reductions, in combination with a recovery in its health care and financial units, resulted in a positive financial outcome considering the difficult market. Though revenues were flat in the first half of 2010, the company saw its earnings before taxes and amortization (EBITA) reach €328 million ($423.4 million), up from €320 million ($412.4 million) a year earlier. Wolters expects that European markets will remain challenging, while the markets in North America and Asia will continue to recover.

In order to grow its global presence, the company has been making acquisitions in these recovering North American and Asian markets. In 2010 it purchased Tax Compliance Software products from Ernst & Young Australia. The previous year Wolters acquired AXENTIS, a US-based provider of enterprise-wide governance, risk, and compliance management solutions, in order to beef up its tax and accounting holdings.

Wolters has been financing these acquisitions in part with funding it received from selling its Education division to Bridgepoint Capital Limited for €774 million ($997.6 million) in 2007.

HISTORY

A pioneer of the Dutch publishing industry, J. B. Wolters founded his publishing house in 1836 to provide instructional material for Netherlands schools. The company later merged with educational publisher Noordhoff (founded in 1858). J. B. Wolters had no children, so the business went to his brother-in-law E. B. Horst in 1860. Dutch academic Anthony Schepman took over the management of Wolters-Noordhoff in 1917 and led the business' expansion. In 1920 it opened an office in the Dutch colony of Indonesia.

Wolters-Noordhoff and Information and Communication Union (ICU) merged in 1972. ICU had been formed by the 1970 merger of Samson (founded by Nicholaas Samson in 1883 to print government publications) and publisher A. W. Sijthoff. After the Wolters-Noordhoff-ICU merger, the resulting company initially took the ICU name, but in 1983 it became the Wolters Samson Group. That year it began exploring a merger with Kluwer.

Abele Kluwer, a former assistant schoolteacher, became a publisher in 1889. His publishing house specialized in educational products and children's books. The company expanded its range in the 1920s with a growing number of up-to-date publications regarding new laws, regulations, court decisions, and scholarly texts. Kluwer hired its first non-family managing director, J. M. Gorter, in 1957 and went public in 1967.

Reed Elsevier (now called Reed Elsevier Group plc) made a bid to acquire Kluwer in 1987, buying a minority stake in the company. The Anglo-Dutch concern was rebuffed by the subsequent merger of Wolters Samson with Kluwer that year, however, and was left with about a third of the shares in the new Wolters Kluwer. Despite Reed Elsevier's repeated advances to work closely with Wolters Kluwer, the company pursued an independent growth strategy. In 1990 it acquired J.B. Lippincott, a US health care publisher. That year Reed Elsevier sold its stake in the firm.

In the early 1990s Wolters Kluwer began acquiring several midsized European companies and in 1995 bought Commerce Clearing House (with roots dating back to 1892). In 1997 it agreed to an $8.8 billion acquisition deal from Reed Elsevier; however, the deal fell apart the following year. (Both companies blamed regulatory hurdles for the pact's failure.) Meanwhile, Wolters Kluwer bought Waverly (medical and scientific books and magazines) and Plenum Publishing (scientific and technical trade books and journals). It also bought Ovid Technologies, a provider of electronic information retrieval services to the academic, medical, and scientific markets.

The following year Wolters Kluwer acquired US professional information publisher Bureau of Business Practice and search and retrieval service Accusearch. In late 1999 internal candidate Casper van Kempen replaced C.J. Brakel as chairman; he was out six months later, having clashed with the board over the company's Web strategy. Deputy chairman Robert Pieterse was tapped to replace him. The company divested itself of its professional training business that year.

Wolters Kluwer sold the health care book division of its Aspen Publishing unit in late 2002 to Jones and Bartlett Publishers. In addition,

Wolters Kluwer sold its academic publishing unit (Kluwer Academic Publishers) for $582 million to two London-based equity firms. The company bought US financial services and information firm GainsKeeper Inc. in 2002.

Pieterse left the company in 2003 and was replaced by board member Nancy McKinstry. The company made two acquisitions in 2003: CEDAM, an Italian legal publisher, and TyMerix, a legal e-billing service in the US. In 2004 the company's corporate and financial services unit acquired software maker Summation Legal Technologies.

In 2005 the company announced it would group all of its financial businesses under the name Wolters Kluwer Financial Services. Acquisitions in 2005 included Italian publishers De Agostini Professionale and Utet Professionale, as well as Romanian legal publisher EON.

Under the direction of CEO Nancy McKinstry, the company focused on regaining its financial health after battling a multiyear advertising slump. Wolters Kluwer cut some 1,500 jobs at the company as part of a three-year restructuring plan, which it completed in 2006. That year, it acquired ProVation Medical, a provider of medical documentation, coding, and workflow tools.

EXECUTIVES

Chairman, Supervisory Board: Adri Baan, age 68
Deputy Chairman, Supervisory Board: Peter N. Wakkie, age 61
Chairman, Executive Board and CEO: Nancy McKinstry, age 51, $3,208,538 total compensation
Executive Board Member and CFO: Boudewijn J. L. M. Beerkens, age 47, $1,683,223 total compensation
Executive Board Member: John J. (Jack) Lynch Jr., age 51, $1,501,338 total compensation
EVP Global Business Process Outsourcing and Sourcing: Punnika Kharas
SVP Human Resources: Kathy Baker
SVP Strategy: Andres Sadler
SVP Mergers and Acquisitions: Jheroen Muste
SVP and Head Corporate Development and Mergers and Acquisitions North America: Elizabeth Satin
VP Corporate Communications: Caroline Wouters
VP Investor Relations: Jon Teppo
VP, Company Secretary, and General Counsel: Maarten Thompson
President, Wolters Kluwer Tax and Accounting Asia Pacific: Russell Evans
President and CEO, Wolters Kluwer Health, Clinical Solutions: Arvind Subramanian
President and CEO, Wolters Kluwer Health, Medical Research: Karen Abramson
President and CEO, Wolters Kluwer Law & Business, North America: Mark Dorman
President and CEO, Wolters Kluwer Tax and Accounting: Kevin Robert
President and CEO, Wolters Kluwer Health, Professional, and Education: Susan Driscoll
President and CEO, Wolters Kluwer Health and Pharma Solutions: Robert (Bob) Becker
Auditors: KPMG Accountants N.V.

LOCATIONS

HQ: Wolters Kluwer nv
Zuidpoolsingel 2
2400 BA Alphen aan den Rijn, The Netherlands
Phone: 31-0-172-641-400 **Fax:** 31-0-172-474-889
Web: www.wolterskluwer.com

2009 Sales

	% of total
Europe	45
North America	50
Asia/Pacific	4
Other regions	1
Total	**100**

PRODUCTS/OPERATIONS

2009 Sales

	% of total
Legal, Tax & Regulatory Europe	38
Tax, Accounting & Legal	26
Health	22
Corporate & Financial Services	14
Total	**100**

2009 Sales

	% of total
Electronic	
Internet	31
Software	21
Print	34
Services	14
Total	**100**

Selected Brands

Corporate and Financial Services
  BizFilings
  CT Corporation
  Uniform Forms
Health and Pharma
  Adis
  Lippincott Williams
  Ovid
  UpToDate
Tax, Accounting, and Legal
  Aspen Publishers
  CCH
  CorpSystems
  TaxWise

COMPETITORS

Advanstar
Bureau of National Affairs
Dow Jones
Editis
IHS
Informa
John Wiley
McGraw-Hill
Nielsen Holdings
Pearson plc
Reed Elsevier Group
Thomson Reuters
United Business Media
Verlagsgruppe Georg von Holtzbrinck

HISTORICAL FINANCIALS

Company Type: Public

Income Statement

FYE: December 31

	REVENUE ($ mil.)	NET INCOME ($ mil.)	NET PROFIT MARGIN	EMPLOYEES
12/09	4,909	169	3.4%	19,341
12/08	4,756	444	9.3%	19,271
12/07	5,024	1,351	26.9%	19,544
12/06	4,872	424	8.7%	19,901
12/05	3,996	308	7.7%	17,419
Annual Growth	**5.3%**	**(13.9%)**	**—**	**2.7%**

2009 Year-End Financials

Debt ratio: 141.8%
Return on equity: 8.7%
Cash ($ mil.): 586
Current ratio: 0.63
Long-term debt ($ mil.): 2,710

No. of shares (mil.): —
Dividends
  Yield: 3.6%
  Payout: 138.6%
Market value ($ mil.): —

Stock History   Pink Sheets: WTKWY

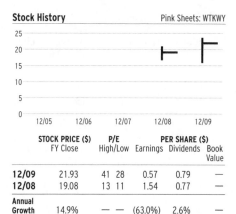

	STOCK PRICE ($) FY Close	P/E High/Low		PER SHARE ($) Earnings	Dividends	Book Value
12/09	21.93	41	28	0.57	0.79	—
12/08	19.08	13	11	1.54	0.77	—
Annual Growth	**14.9%**	**—**	**—**	**(63.0%)**	**2.6%**	**—**

Woolworths Limited

Chow Down Under with Australia's #1 food retailer (ahead of Coles) — Woolworths (aka "Woolies"). The firm operates more than 3,100 supermarkets and general merchandise and electronics stores in Australia and New Zealand. (Its 1,000 supermarkets and 1,150-plus liquor stores account for about 85% of sales.) In addition, Woolworths sells gasoline and leverages its distribution network to provide wholesale merchandise for third-party supermarkets. Woolworths' 150-plus general merchandise discount stores operate under the Big W name. It also runs about 435 consumer electronics shops under the Dick Smith Electronics, PowerHouse, and Tandy brand names. The retailer's Taverner Hotel Group operates some 280 hotels.

Woolworths (which has no relation to the five-and-dime chain once operated in the US) is trying not to choke on its own success, but it's hard to be humble. The company has overtaken archrival Coles at home and is looking to expand both internationally and further into consumer electronics and hardware. To that end, the Australian retailer has formed a partnership with India's Tata Group to open a chain of consumer electronics stores in India. Woolworths is supplying Tata's chain of Croma stores there.

Woolworths is taking on the big-box home improvement market in partnership with the #2 home improvement chain in the US — Lowe's Companies. In a joint venture two-thirds owned by Woolworths, the two plan to begin opening Lowe's-style stores in Australia in 2011. To that end, in August the joint venture launched a takeover bid for Australia's second-largest hardware distributor, Danks Holdings.

The supermarket leader has been looking to get in on other sectors of the grocery business, including organic and gourmet retailing. The company announced in 2009 that it would be acquiring organic grocer Macro Wholefoods. Snapping up the chain of nearly 10 independent stores would allow Woolworths to focus on organic offerings, which its other supermarkets don't generally carry.

In a bid to fend off rival Coles Group's entry into the food-and-fuel market, Woolworths has formed a joint venture with Caltex Australia to expand its network of discount fuel outlets to 535. Also, the retailer has overhauled its supply chain operations to become a low-cost operator after studying systems at US retail giant Wal-Mart and the UK's Tesco. To that end, the company sold its distribution centers to Australian Prime Property Fund for about $626 million in a leaseback deal.

In a bid to increase liquor sales — which are growing faster than general merchandise or grocery sales — Woolworths and millionaire pubs owner Bruce Mathieson beat out Coles in a takeover battle for Australia's biggest pub operator, Australian Leisure & Hospitality (ALH).

HISTORY

Harold Percival Christmas first tried a mail-order dress business before opening the popular Frock Salon retail store. Christmas and his partners opened a branch store in the Imperial Arcade in Sydney in 1924, renaming it "Woolworths Stupendous Bargain Basement" and luring customers with advertisements calling it "a handy place where good things are cheap . . . you'll want to live at Woolworths." The company borrowed the name from Frank Woolworth's successful US chain, after determining that chain had no plans to open stores in Australia. Woolworths was listed on the Australian stock exchange in 1924.

Food sales came more than 30 years later. Woolworths opened its first freestanding, full-line supermarket in 1960, then diversified into specialty retail, buying the Rockmans women's clothing store chain the next year (sold in 2000). It expanded into discounting with the Big W chain in 1976 and further diversified when it bought 60% of the Dick Smith Electronics store chain in 1981 (buying the remainder in 1983).

The purchase of the Safeway grocery chain (the Australian operations of the US-based chain) put Woolworths on the top of the supermarket heap in 1985. But the company was hurting (it lost $13 million in 1985-86) because of a restructuring in the early 1980s that had weakened management by bulking up the front offices and dividing responsibilities. Woolworths got a shot in the arm from Paul Simons, who returned to the company in 1987 after running competitor Franklins. He cleaned house in the front offices, closed unprofitable stores, and began the successful "Fresh Food People" marketing strategy.

Industrial Equity Limited (IEL) bought the company in 1989; IEL then became part of Adelaide Steamship group, which spun off Woolworths as a public company in 1993. The following year, career Woolworths manager Reg Clairs took over as CEO, following the untimely death (on a golf course) in 1993 of Harry Watts, who was being groomed for the job. As a result, the company has an unwritten rule of avoiding CEOs older than 60.

Clairs took the company in a variety of new directions. Woolworths began supplying fresh food to neighbor Asia in 1995. The company added Plus Petrol outlets adjacent to Woolworths Supermarkets in 1996. It also started a superstore concept for its Dick Smith Electronics chain (Power House) that year. In 1997 the company launched its Woolworths Metro store chain, which targets commuters and other on-the-run shoppers in urban areas, and it aggressively jumped into wholesaling to independent grocers.

Clairs (who was turning 60 in 1999) stepped down in late 1998 and Roger Corbett took over as CEO. In 2001 Woolworths acquired two liquor store chains (Liberty Liquor, Booze Bros), more than 200 Tandy Electronics stores, and 72

Franklins supermarkets from Hong Kong-based Dairy Farm International Holdings.

In the fall of 2004 the board of directors of Australia's biggest pub owner, Australian Leisure & Hospitality (ALH), recommended the company accept a $985 million takeover bid by Woolworths and The Bruce Mathieson Group. Previously, the duo had acquired a 16% stake in ALH. In mid-2005 the company acquired the New Zealand supermarkets of Foodland Associated and 22 Action stores in Western Australia, Queensland, and New South Wales for about $1.8 billion.

Corbett retired as CEO in 2006. He was succeeded by Michael Luscombe, the company's long-serving director of supermarkets. That year the company announced it had purchased a 10% stake in New Zealand's The Warehouse retail chain. In 2008 Woolworths offered about $1.7 billion to buy the rest of The Warehouse Group. The purchase, however, was blocked by that country's competition regulator. An attempt to take over Australia's JB Hi-Fi, a chain of home entertainment products stores, also failed.

EXECUTIVES

Chairman: James A. Strong, age 66
CEO and Director: Michael G. Luscombe, age 54
Finance Director: Thomas (Tom) Pockett
CIO: Dan Beecham
Chief Logistics Officer: Julie Coates
Group General Counsel and Company Secretary: Peter Horton
Director Corporate and Public Affairs: Andrew Hall
Director Human Resources: Kim Schmidt
Director Food and Liquor: Naum J. Onikul
General Manager Liquor: Steve Greentree
General Manager Consumer Electronics: Debra Singh
General Manager Special Projects: Bert Van der Velde
General Manager Logistics: Geoff Thomas
General Manager Global Sourcing: Ian McDonald
General Manager Marketing, Supermarkets, and Corporate: Luke Dunkerley
General Manager Petrol: Ramik Narsey
General Manager Supermarket Operations: Marty Hamnett
General Manager Business Development: Grant O'Brien
General Manager Business Planning and Corporate Finance: Mark Fleming
General Manager Customer Engagement: Richard Umbers
CEO, ALH Group: Bruce Mathieson
Auditors: Deloitte Touche Tohmatsu

LOCATIONS

HQ: Woolworths Limited
1 Woolworths Way
Bella Vista, New South Wales 2153, Australia
Phone: 61-2-8885-0000
Web: www.woolworthslimited.com.au

2010 Sales

	% of total
Australia	91
New Zealand	9
Total	**100**

2010 Supermarkets

	No.
Australia	823
New Zealand	206
Total	**1,029**

PRODUCTS/OPERATIONS

2010 Sales

	% of total
Supermarkets	86
General merchandise	12
Hotels	2
Total	**100**

Selected Operations

Food stores
  Safeway
  Woolworths Metro
  Woolworths Supermarkets
General merchandise stores
  BIG W
Liquor stores
  BWS (neighborhood stores)
  Dan Murphy's (destination outlets)
  Woolworths Liquor (attached to supermarkets)
Specialty retail
  Dick Smith Electronics
  PowerHouse
  Tandy Electronics
Other
  Caltex/WOW Petrol (gas stations)
  GreenGrocer.com.au (online grocery store)
  Woolworths Ezy Banking
  Woolworths HomeShop (online grocery and liquor store)

COMPETITORS

ALDI
BP
Harris Scarfe Holdings
Harvey Norman Holdings
Metcash
Pick'n Pay
Royal Dutch Shell
Wesfarmers

HISTORICAL FINANCIALS

Company Type: Public

Income Statement

FYE: June 30

	REVENUE ($ mil.)	NET INCOME ($ mil.)	NET PROFIT MARGIN	EMPLOYEES
6/10	44,510	1,745	3.9%	191,000
6/09	40,128	1,496	3.7%	190,000
6/08	45,471	1,586	3.5%	190,000
6/07	36,262	1,113	3.1%	180,000
6/06	27,732	0	—	175,000
Annual Growth	**12.6%**	**—**	**—**	**2.2%**

2010 Year-End Financials

Debt ratio: —
Return on equity: 29.2%
Cash ($ mil.): 611
Current ratio: 0.73
Long-term debt ($ mil.): —
No. of shares (mil.): 1,212
Dividends
  Yield: 4.0%
  Payout: 66.4%
Market value ($ mil.): 28,051

Stock History

Australian: WOW

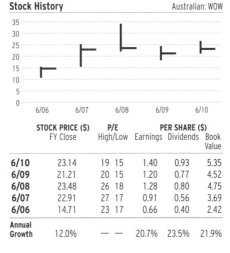

	STOCK PRICE ($) FY Close	P/E High/Low		PER SHARE ($) Earnings	Dividends	Book Value
6/10	23.14	19	15	1.40	0.93	5.35
6/09	21.21	20	15	1.20	0.77	4.52
6/08	23.48	26	18	1.28	0.80	4.75
6/07	22.91	27	17	0.91	0.56	3.69
6/06	14.71	23	17	0.66	0.40	2.42
Annual Growth	**12.0%**	**—**	**—**	**20.7%**	**23.5%**	**21.9%**

WPP plc

Marketing and advertising services bind this group together. WPP is one of the world's largest media and communications services conglomerates, with operations in 2,400 offices in more than 100 countries. Its advertising agency networks, including 24/7 Real Media, Grey Worldwide, JWT, Ogilvy & Mather, and Young & Rubicam, offer creative campaign development and brand management services. WPP's holdings also include public relations firms, media buying and planning agencies, and many specialized marketing and communications units. In addition, its Kantar Group division is one of the world's leading market research organizations. In a huge move to fortify Kantar's operations, WPP bought rival TNS in late 2008.

WPP is focused on increasing its market share in the key growing markets of the Asia/Pacific, Africa and the Middle East, Latin America, and Central and Eastern Europe. It is also centered on boosting the amount of revenue its marketing services segment brings in, primarily in the digital marketing arena. Over the years WPP has counted on long-standing client relationships with some of the biggest companies in the world. Its 10 largest clients — including GlaxoSmithKline, IBM, Johnson & Johnson, Ford Motor, Procter & Gamble, Microsoft, and Unilever, among others — account for about 18% of total revenue.

WPP often restructures its sprawling operating organization in order to optimize its flexibility and efficiency. After the combined Kantar Group and TNS created one of the largest global market research firms in the world, WPP restructured Kantar into four main operating segments: Kantar Media, Kantar Healthcare, Kantar Retail, and Kantar Worldpanel. WPP made adjustments to its health care public relations operations in mid-2010 when it combined two of its former health care marketing networks, CommonHealth and Ogilvy Healthworld, to form Ogilvy CommonHealth Worldwide. The restructuring created a giant in its industry, operating though some 65 offices spanning more than 30 countries. About the same time, the company increased its animal health marketing capabilities when it acquired Geoff Howe Marketing Communications, with offices in Prague and London, as well as Kansas City, Missouri.

HISTORY

WPP Group began as Wire and Plastic Products, a maker of grocery baskets and other goods founded in 1958 by Gordon Sampson (who retired from the company in 2000). Investors led by former Saatchi & Saatchi advertising executive (and current WPP CEO) Martin Sorrell bought the company in 1985 and began acquiring marketing firms under the shortened name of WPP. In 1987 Sorrell used revenue from these businesses (and a sizable loan) to buy US advertising warhorse J. Walter Thompson (now JWT).

JWT was founded by William James Carlton as the Carlton & Smith agency in 1864. The New York City-based firm was bought by James Walter Thompson in 1877 and was later responsible for Prudential Insurance's Rock of Gibraltar symbol (1896). It began working for Ford (which is still a client) in 1943. JWT went public in 1969.

Following its acquisition of JWT, WPP formed European agency Conquest in 1988. The company (and its debt) grew the next year when it bought the Ogilvy Group (founded by David Ogilvy in 1948) for $860 million, making WPP the world's largest advertising company. But its acquisition frenzy also positioned the company for a fall in 1991, when depressed economies in the US and the UK slowed advertising spending. Saddled with debt, WPP nearly went into receivership before recovering the next year.

WPP began a period of controlled growth with no major acquisitions in 1993. It expanded internationally in 1994, opening new offices in South America, Europe, the Middle East, and Asia. Winning IBM's $500 million international advertising contract that year also aided WPP's financial recovery. However, this led to the loss of business from IBM's rivals, including AT&T, Compaq's European division (Compaq was purchased by Hewlett-Packard in 2002), and Microsoft.

By 1997 the company was again ready to flex its acquisition muscle. The firm bought 21 companies that year, including a stake in IBOPE (a market research firm in Latin America) and a share of Batey Holdings (the majority owner of Batey Ads, a prominent ad agency in the Asia/Pacific region). That year WPP also created its media planning unit MindShare.

More acquisitions followed in 1998, including a 20% stake in Asatsu (the #3 advertising agency in Japan). The next year the company bought Texas-based market research firm IntelliQuest Information Group, which was merged with WPP's Millward Brown unit. Along with its acquisitions, WPP snagged some significant new accounts in 1998 and 1999, lining up business with Kimberly-Clark, Merrill Lynch, and the embattled International Olympic Committee.

In 2000 the company bought US-based rival Young & Rubicam for about $4.7 billion — one of the largest advertising mergers ever. The move catapulted WPP to the top spot among the world's advertising firms. As if that wasn't enough, its MindShare unit later snagged the $700 million media planning account of consumer products giant Unilever. WPP also took a 49% stake in UniWorld Group, the largest African-American-owned ad agency in the US.

Hamish Maxwell, chairman since 1996, retired in 2001 and was replaced by Philip Lader, the former US ambassador to the UK. That year, however, WPP's top ranking was stolen away by Interpublic Group following its acquisition of True North Communications. It later sparked a bidding war with Havas Advertising when it offered $630 million to buy UK media services firm Tempus Group. WPP grudgingly completed its acquisition of Tempus in 2002. The following year the company acquired Cordiant Communications.

WPP positioned itself for both short- and long-term growth in 2005 when it completed a $1.75 billion acquisition of US-based rival Grey Group, beating out bids from private equity players (including Kohlberg Kravis Roberts & Co.) and rival advertising firm Havas.

Throughout 2008 market research rival TNS rejected several unsolicited takeover bids from WPP (including a $2.1 billion offer in July). However, TNS eventually acquiesced to the proposal, once more than 60% of its shareholders accepted WPP's offer in October. The deal greatly enhanced WPP's Kantar operations and created a global market research juggernaut.

Also in late 2008 WPP shortened its legal name from WPP Group plc to WPP plc.

EXECUTIVES

Chairman: Philip Lader, age 64
CEO and Director: Sir Martin S. Sorrell, age 65
Group Finance Director and Board Member:
Paul W. G. Richardson, age 52
Strategy Director and Board Member; CEO, WPP Digital: Mark Read, age 43
EVP Public Relations and Public Affairs:
Howard G. Paster, age 64
Worldwide Creative Director: John O'Keeffe, age 47
Chief Talent Officer: Mark Linaugh
Secretary: Marie W. Capes
Group Chief Counsel: Andrea Harris
Group Communications Director: Feona McEwan
Deputy Group Finance Director: Chris Sweetland
Head of Corporate Responsibility: Vanessa Edwards
Director Compensation and Benefits: Adrian Jackson
Director Global Procurement: Tom Kinnaird
Worldwide CEO, Maxus Global: Kelly Clark
Chairman and CEO, Grey Group:
James R. (Jim) Heekin III
Worldwide Chairman and CEO, JWT: Bob Jeffrey
Chairman and CEO, Kantar: Eric Salama
CEO Worldwide, Burson-Marsteller and CEO, Penn Schoen Berland: Mark J. Penn
Global CEO, Ogilvy Public Relations Worldwide:
Christopher (Chris) Graves, age 51
Director Investor Relations: Francis S. (Fran) Butera
Auditors: Deloitte LLP

LOCATIONS

HQ: WPP plc
6 Ely Place
Dublin, Ireland
Phone: 353-1169-0333   **Fax:** 353-1669-0334
US HQ: 125 Park Ave., New York, NY 10017
US Phone: 212-632-2200   **US Fax:** 212-632-2222
Web: www.wpp.com

2009 Sales

	% of total
North America	34
Asia/Pacific, Latin America, Africa, Middle East & Central & Eastern Europe	27
Western Continental Europe	27
UK	12
Total	**100**

PRODUCTS/OPERATIONS

2009 Sales

	% of total
Advertising & media services	39
Branding & health care communications	26
Consumer insight	26
Public relations & public affairs	9
Total	**100**

COMPETITORS

Aegis Group	Interpublic Group
Arbitron	Ipsos
Dentsu	Nielsen Holdings
GfK	Omnicom
GfK NOP	Publicis Groupe
Havas	

HISTORICAL FINANCIALS

Company Type: Public

Income Statement

FYE: December 31

	REVENUE ($ mil.)	NET INCOME ($ mil.)	NET PROFIT MARGIN	EMPLOYEES
12/09	13,831	697	5.0%	105,318
12/08	10,821	636	5.9%	112,000
12/07	12,315	928	7.5%	90,000
12/06	11,577	854	7.4%	79,352
12/05	9,264	627	6.8%	74,631
Annual Growth	**10.5%**	**2.7%**	**—**	**9.0%**

2009 Year-End Financials

Debt ratio: 68.0%
Return on equity: 7.9%
Cash ($ mil.): 2,654
Current ratio: 0.91
Long-term debt ($ mil.): 6,386
No. of shares (mil.): 252
Dividends
 Yield: 1.6%
 Payout: 44.1%
Market value ($ mil.): 19,497

Stock History   NASDAQ (GS): WPPGY

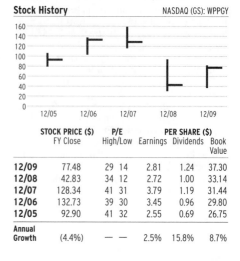

	STOCK PRICE ($) FY Close	P/E High/Low		PER SHARE ($) Earnings	Dividends	Book Value
12/09	77.48	29	14	2.81	1.24	37.30
12/08	42.83	34	12	2.72	1.00	33.14
12/07	128.34	41	31	3.79	1.19	31.44
12/06	132.73	39	30	3.45	0.96	29.80
12/05	92.90	41	32	2.55	0.69	26.75
Annual Growth	**(4.4%)**	**—**	**—**	**2.5%**	**15.8%**	**8.7%**

Yamaha Corporation

Yamaha Corporation doesn't produce records, but it does help people make plenty of music. The company is a leading maker worldwide of musical instruments, including pianos, electronic keyboards, and synthesizers. It also manufactures and distributes a wide variety of wind and percussion instruments, as well as guitars, violins, and other string instruments. In addition, Yamaha also is a leading manufacturer of home audio and video equipment and makes a line of professional audio gear. It also makes semiconductors and other electronic components. Yamaha Corporation is motorcycle manufacturer Yamaha Motor Co.'s largest shareholder.

Facing a rocky business environment with heated competition and an uncertain economic future in the US and abroad, Yamaha kick-started a plan, called the Yamaha Growth Plan 2010, in 2008 that will help it weather the storm and right the way toward growth and prosperity. As part of the two-year management plan, the company has reorganized its operations into a pair of businesses: The Sound Company and the Diversification unit. The Sound Company comprises musical instruments, music entertainment, audio, audiovisual and information technology, and semiconductors. Within this business, Yamaha is looking to boost its management ranks as it ramps up for expansion. The company's Diversification sector spans lifestyle-related products, recreation, and metallic molds and components.

The growth plan's strategy is primarily focused on The Sound Company to extend the reach of its business globally. Its objective is to maintain an operation that's nimble, while leveraging its expertise in craftsmanship and digital technology. What's helping to fund Yamaha's plan for The Sound Company's ascent is its sale of a portion of Yamaha Motor. Yamaha cut its 23% stake in the motorcycle maker in 2007 to about 15%

to reduce the influence of the larger firm's earnings on its own. (Yamaha Motor was once a fully owned division of Yamaha Corp.)

Still, musical instruments are the soul of the company's identity. Yamaha is expanding its operations in emerging markets. It plans to extend its operations into Brazil, China, India, and Russia. Yamaha intends to beef up sales in China by expanding its retail network there from 200 retailers to 350 and doubling the number of "Yamaha piano corners" to 200.

While musical instruments has traditionally been Yamaha's largest businesses segment, its components business has been the top performer in terms of profits. Sales of digital signal processing chips for use in mobile phones has been the big driver in this segment, but Yamaha is expanding into new applications for its chips, such as automobile components.

Yamaha continues to invest in its music instruction schools as a way to create future consumers for its products. In China, Yamaha boasts schools in Shanghai, Beijing, and Guangzhou, and is planning to open more schools in large cities and within sales outlets for musical instruments.

HISTORY

Torakusu Yamaha first repaired medical instruments. But while repairing a broken organ, he decided he could make his own. His first attempt did not have good sound, but continuous work over a four-month period led to a new organ — completed in 1887 — that was highly praised. He established Yamaha Organ Manufacturing Company in 1889. In 1897, as production grew, Yamaha incorporated the company as Nippon Gakki (Japan Musical Instruments). Nippon Gakki began producing upright pianos in 1900 and grand pianos in 1902.

In 1920 the company diversified into the production of wooden airplane propellers (based on woodworking skills used in making pianos), and added pipe organs (1932) and guitars (1946) to its line of musical instruments. Genichi Kawakami, whose father had managed the company since 1927, took over in 1950.

The company formed its first overseas subsidiary, Yamaha de Mexico, in 1958. Under Kawakami's leadership, Nippon Gakki became the world's largest producer of musical instruments, developing Japan's first electronic organ, the Electone, in 1959. Kawakami conducted the company's movements into wind instruments (1965), stereos (1968), microchips (1971), and furniture (1975). He established the Yamaha Music Foundation in 1966 to oversee the company's music schools. By 1982 people in the Americas, Europe, and Asia could buy Yamaha-brand products locally.

Nippon Gakki undertook further diversification, particularly into customized chips for CD players. In 1983 it introduced a powerful, but affordable synthesizer. The company changed its name to Yamaha in 1987. It opened a facility in China two years later. Yamaha emphasized exports of electronic instruments and the production of integrated circuits.

Until 1992 three generations of the Kawakami family dominated Yamaha. After a failed attempt by heir apparent Hiroshi Kawakami to cut back Yamaha's workforce through early retirement, the manufacturer's in-house labor union revolted. Kawakami was replaced by Seisuke Ueshima, a Yamaha veteran who set out to work on a combination of product innovation and corporate restructuring. Ueshima made a pact with the unions to keep most factory workers, lay off 30% of its Japanese administrative staff, and cut overseas employees.

In 1997 the company launched a joint licensing program with Stanford University for the Sondius-XG sound synthesis technology; the two institutions agreed to share royalties from the technology, which provides realistic sound quality for musical instruments and computer games.

With sluggish sales of electronic parts, in 1999 Yamaha stopped producing magnetic heads for hard disk drives, shut down a semiconductor plant, and trimmed its workforce by giving 11% of its employees early retirement. In 2000 the company introduced a bamboo guitar that could help slow the depletion of hardwoods. That same year, Shuji Ito was named president of Yamaha. The company launched a high-resolution projector for home theater use in 2001. Genichi Kawakami, the 90-year-old former president of Yamaha, died in 2002.

In 2003 the company decided to exit from the CD recorder market to focus more on high-end home theater systems. To strengthen its position in the music-creation market, Yamaha acquired Steinberg Media Technologies in 2004.

In 2008 Yamaha bought out the founders of NEXO, a leading French manufacturer and seller of professional acoustic speaker systems. It also sold off several of its resorts after having logged deep sales drops in its recreation segment.

EXECUTIVES

President and Representative Director: Mitsuru Umemura, age 59
Senior Executive Officer: Yoshihiro (Yoshi) Doi
Senior Executive Officer: Masao Kondo
Senior Executive Officer: Masaaki Koshiba
Senior Executive Officer: Tsutomu Sasaki
Senior Executive Officer: Takuya Nakata
Managing Executive Officer, Corporate Planning Group and Director: Motoki Takahashi, age 58
Managing Executive Officer, Musical Instruments Business Group and Director: Hiroo Okabe, age 58
Executive Officer Productive Technology Business Group, Process Management Group, Golf Products Division, and Director: Yasushi Yahata, age 56
Executive Officer and General Manager, Human Resources Division: Masahito Hosoi
Executive Officer, General Manager Sound Network Division, and Director: Takuya Tamaru
Executive Officer and General Manager Innovative Technology: Koji Niimi
Executive Officer and General Manager Semiconductor Division: Tatsumi Ohara
Sales and Marketing Manager, Consumer Products: Cliff DeManty
Manager, New Marketing Content: Jeff Hawley
Manager, Resort Management Division: Hisashi Yabe, age 60
Auditors: Ernst & Young ShinNihon

LOCATIONS

HQ: Yamaha Corporation
10-1, Nakazawa-cho, Naka-ku
Hamamatsu, Shizuoka 430-8650, Japan
Phone: 81-53-460-2800   **Fax:** 81-53-460-2802
US HQ: 6600 Orangethorpe Ave., Buena Park, CA 90620
US Phone: 714-522-9011   **US Fax:** 714-522-9961
Web: www.global.yamaha.com

2010 Sales

	% of total
Japan	55
Europe	17
North America	14
Asia, Oceania & other regions	14
Total	**100**

PRODUCTS/OPERATIONS

2010 Sales

	% of total
Musical instruments	66
Audiovisual & information technology	13
Lifestyle-related products	9
Electronic devices	5
Other	7
Total	**100**

COMPETITORS

CASIO COMPUTER	Roland Corporation
Creative Technology	Samick
Epson	Samsung Electronics
Fender Musical	Sharp Corp.
Instruments	Sony
Gibson Guitar	Steinway
Harman International	TDK
Hoshino Gakki	TEAC
Kawai	Toshiba
Panasonic Corp	Victor Company of Japan
Philips Electronics	Young Chang
Pioneer Corporation	

HISTORICAL FINANCIALS

Company Type: Public

Income Statement

FYE: March 31

	REVENUE ($ mil.)	NET INCOME ($ mil.)	NET PROFIT MARGIN	EMPLOYEES
3/10	4,475	2	0.0%	19,275
3/09	4,721	(212)	—	26,803
3/08	3,179	625	19.6%	26,517
3/07	4,669	236	5.1%	25,992
3/06	4,543	239	5.3%	25,298
Annual Growth	**(0.4%)**	**(69.4%)**	**—**	**(6.6%)**

2010 Year-End Financials

Debt ratio: —
Return on equity: 0.1%
Cash ($ mil.): 641
Current ratio: 2.57
Long-term debt ($ mil.): —

No. of shares (mil.): 197
Dividends
Yield: 1.4%
Payout: —
Market value ($ mil.): 2,568

Stock History

Tokyo: 79510

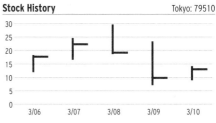

	STOCK PRICE ($) FY Close	P/E High/Low		PER SHARE ($) Earnings	Dividends	Book Value
3/10	13.02	— —		(0.27)	0.19	13.77
3/09	9.84	— —		(1.07)	0.05	12.98
3/08	19.20	15 10		1.93	—	17.34
3/07	22.31	— —		—	—	14.90
3/06	17.69	— —		—	—	13.63
Annual Growth	**(7.4%)**	— —		—	**280.0%**	**0.3%**

YPF S.A.

The largest company in Argentina answers to a Spanish parent: Integrated oil company YPF is a subsidiary of Repsol YPF (formerly Repsol), Spain's largest oil concern. YPF has proved reserves (primarily in Argentina) of about 623 million barrels of oil and 3.7 trillion cu. ft. of natural gas. It produces, refines, and markets petroleum, natural gas, and petrochemicals. The company's three Argentine refineries have an annual capacity of about 116 million barrels. It also has a joint venture refinery (Refinor) with Petrobras Energía. YPF distributes oil to its more than 1,690 service stations in Argentina. In addition, the company has a limited number of exploration and production ventures in the US.

YPF also produces electricity and distributes liquefied petroleum gas (LPG), and through joint venture Profertil, it is a leading producer of urea in the Southern Cone.

In 2020 the company formed a new oil services company (YPF Servicios Petroleros) to support its exploration and production activities in South America.

Before its acquisition by Repsol (in 1999) YPF had transformed itself from an inefficient state-owned firm into a streamlined international player. It has benefited from the Mercosur agreement, which set up an economic union in South America to promote regional trade.

In 2008 Repsol YPF sold a 15% stake in YPF to Argentine energy company Petersen Energía, S.A. to provide capital and strengthen its Argentine connections.

HISTORY

An Argentine government team discovered oil while drilling for water in 1907. Determined to keep the oil under Argentine control, the government formed the world's first state-owned oil company, Direccion Nacional de los Yacimientos Petroliferos Fiscales (YPF), in 1922 to operate the newly discovered field. However, YPF lacked drilling equipment, capital, and staff; it found that the only way to increase domestic oil production was to allow in foreign oil companies. Although YPF's activities ebbed in the 1920s, it made major oil discoveries across Argentina in the 1930s.

A major turning point came with Juan Perón's rise to power in 1945. Perón extended state control over broad sections of the economy, including oil. He nationalized British and US oil holdings and gave YPF a virtual monopoly. In 1945 YPF accounted for 68% of the country's oil production; by 1955 it produced 84%. The company discovered a huge gas field two years later in western Argentina, making YPF — and Argentina — a major gas producer.

However, YPF's production failed to keep pace with the demands of the growing economy, and imports still dominated Argentina's oil market. Over the next 30 years, YPF experienced radical swings in government policy as ultranationalist military regimes alternated with liberal, reformist governments. YPF grew into a bloated and inefficient conglomerate. Between 1982 and 1989, despite a World Bank-financed program to modernize YPF's refineries, the firm lost more than $6 billion.

In 1989 Carlos Menem became Argentina's president, and YPF was privatized as part of his economic reform plan to cut loose 50 state-owned companies. To prepare YPF for its IPO, the president brought in a former head of Baker Hughes, José Estenssoro, to draft a plan for privatization. The plan was so impressive that Menem gave him the job as CEO of the company in 1990. Estenssoro cut 87% of YPF's staff and sold off $2 billion of noncore assets. By 1993 YPF was profitable and went public as YPF Sociedad Anónima, selling 45% of its shares to raise $3 billion.

A year later YPF began expanding beyond Argentina by shipping crude oil to Chile through a new 300-mile pipeline. It bought woebegone Texas oil company Maxus Energy in 1995 and turned it around at great expense. Estenssoro and three other YPF executives died in a plane crash that year; in 1997 YPF selected Roberto Monti, who had headed Maxus, as its CEO.

In 1997 YPF and Astra C.A.P.S.A. — in which Spanish oil firm Repsol had a controlling stake — jointly purchased a 67% stake in Mexpetrol Argentina (an affiliate of Mexican state oil company PEMEX). Repsol was aggressively moving overseas. In 1998 Repsol lobbied hard to buy part of YPF; Spain's King Juan Carlos himself phoned up Menem to promote Repsol's interests.

A year later the Argentine government auctioned off a 15% stake in YPF to Repsol for $2 billion; Repsol then bought another 83% of the company for $13.2 billion. Repsol became Repsol YPF, while Monti was named VC and COO.

Monti retired the next year, after Repsol YPF increased its stake in YPF from 98% to 99%.

EXECUTIVES

Chairman: Antonio Brufau Niubó, age 62
Vice Chairman: Enrique Eskenazi, age 84
CEO and Executive Vice Chairman: Sebastián Eskenazi, age 46
COO: Ignacio C. Moran, age 39
CFO and Market Relations Officer: Guillermo Reda
General Counsel: Mauro Dacomo
Director Institutional Affairs: Juan Bautista Ordoñez
Director Chemicals: Rafael López Revuelta, age 61
Director Marketing: Alfredo Pochintesta, age 57
Director Exploration and Production: Tomás García Blanco, age 45
Director Human Resources: Fernando Dasso, age 49
Assistant Director to the CEO and Board Member: Antonio Gomis Sáez, age 58
Auditors: Deloitte & Co. S.R.L.

LOCATIONS

HQ: YPF S.A.
Avenida Presidente Roque Sáenz Peña 777
C.P. 1364 Buenos Aires, Argentina
Phone: 54-11-4329-2000 **Fax:** 54-11-4329-2113
Web: www.repsol-ypf.com/es_es

PRODUCTS/OPERATIONS

2009 Sales

	% of total
Refining & marketing	54
Exploration & production	39
Chemicals	5
Other	2
Total	**100**

COMPETITORS

BP	PETROBRAS
CBPI	Petróleos de Venezuela
COPEC	Pioneer Natural Resources
Exxon Mobil	Royal Dutch Shell
Imperial Oil	TOTAL
PEMEX	

HISTORICAL FINANCIALS

Company Type: Public

Income Statement

FYE: December 31

	REVENUE ($ mil.)	NET INCOME ($ mil.)	NET PROFIT MARGIN	EMPLOYEES
12/09	8,982	912	10.2%	12,140
12/08	10,089	1,053	10.4%	11,319
12/07	9,242	1,297	14.0%	11,534
12/06	8,346	1,451	17.4%	11,059
12/05	7,529	1,754	23.3%	10,574
Annual Growth	**4.5%**	**(15.1%)**	**—**	**3.5%**

2009 Year-End Financials

Debt ratio: 11.3%
Return on equity: 16.8%
Cash ($ mil.): 175
Current ratio: 0.84
Long-term debt ($ mil.): 560
No. of shares (mil.): 393
Dividends
Yield: 28.5%
Payout: 140.9%
Market value ($ mil.): 4,503

Stock History

NYSE: YPF

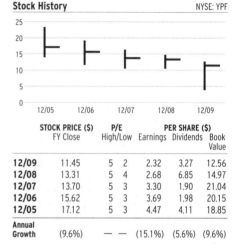

	STOCK PRICE ($) FY Close	P/E High/Low		PER SHARE ($) Earnings	Dividends	Book Value
12/09	11.45	5	2	2.32	3.27	12.56
12/08	13.31	5	4	2.68	6.85	14.97
12/07	13.70	5	3	3.30	1.90	21.04
12/06	15.62	5	3	3.69	1.98	20.15
12/05	17.12	5	3	4.47	4.11	18.85
Annual Growth	**(9.6%)**	**—**	**—**	**(15.1%)**	**(5.6%)**	**(9.6%)**

Zurich Financial Services

It's a wonder anyone would leave Zurich, nestled as it is in the beautiful Swiss Alps. But the business interests of Zurich Financial Services (Zurich) have crossed over the mountains and spread around the globe. Serving approximately 170 countries worldwide, the company is a leading provider of general corporate insurance. Focused on markets in Europe and North America, the company's General Insurance segment offers commercial and personal property/casualty and specialty coverage, while its Global Life segment offers life insurance, annuities, and other investment policies. Zurich's Farmers Group division offers personal property/casualty insurance policies in the US.

A five-year strategic reorganization sought to refocus the company's operations around its principal lines of business (including insurance underwriting and reserving, risk management, and investment management) and consolidate Zurich's General Insurance and Global Life businesses under the Zurich brand. In 2009 the company promoted chief investment officer Martin

Senn into the CEO role, replacing retiring executive James Schiro.

Zurich has benefited from its efforts to expand into markets deemed "under-represented." Specific geographic areas of expansion have included China, Spain, and Taiwan. Zurich Financial entered the Turkish market through the acquisition of TEB Sigorta in 2008. It also acquired a majority stake in Russian insurance firm NASTA for $260 million. In 2009 the company purchased two Brazilian insurance firms, and in 2010 it agreed to purchase Lebanese general insurance firm Compagnie Libanaise D'Assurances to accelerate its expansion in the Middle East.

The General Insurance segment provides property/casualty and specialty insurance to a variety of clients. Its Global Corporate unit focuses on risk management for large international and domestic clients. The Europe General Insurance division provides property/casualty and specialty lines for businesses and individuals; key markets are Germany, Italy, Spain, Switzerland, and the UK. In the US, Zurich Financial provides commercial and specialty property/casualty policies for small to midsized business customers.

Zurich Financial's Global Life segment offers life, investment, pension, and savings plans for individuals and groups. Global Life operates through regional subsidiaries to provide localized services to its clients. Its businesses include Farmers New World Life in the US, Openwork in the UK, and other subsidiaries and partnerships in Europe.

Farmers Group provides personal auto and homeowners coverage in the US, as well as small business insurance. To build up Farmers Group, Zurich Financial spent $1.9 billion to acquire 21st Century Insurance, the personal auto insurance arm of AIG, in 2009. The addition of 21st Century helped push Farmers Group into the top tier of US auto insurers.

HISTORY

The roots of Zurich Financial Services (ZFS) stretch back to the 1872 founding of a reinsurer for Switzerland Transport Insurance. The company soon branched out into accident, travel, and workers' compensation insurance and in 1875 it changed its name to Transport and Accident Insurance plc Zurich to reflect the changes. It then expanded into Berlin (the jumping-off point for its expansion into Scandinavia and Russia) and Stuttgart, Germany. The company exited marine lines in 1880; it later left the reinsurance business and expanded into liability insurance; in 1894 it changed its name to Zurich General Accident and Liability Insurance.

In 1912 Zurich crossed the Atlantic, expanding operations into the US. It agreed in 1925 to provide insurance for Ford cars at favorable terms. Zurich's business was hard hit during the war years of the late 1930s and 1940s. In 1955 the company changed its name to Zurich Insurance.

Starting in the 1960s, Zurich began buying other insurers, including Alpina (1965, Switzerland), Agrippina (1969, Germany), and Maryland Casualty Group (1989, US). It also bought the property liability operations of American General.

In the early 1990s the company shifted its strategy, expanding into what it deemed underrepresented markets in the UK and the US. Being big wasn't enough; Zurich needed to find a focus.

In 1995 Zurich bought struggling Chicago-based asset manager Kemper and in 1997 bought lackluster mutual fund manager Scudder Stevens & Clark, forming Scudder Kemper. That year it also bought failed Hong Kong investment bank Peregrine Investment Holdings.

In 1998 Zurich merged with the financial services businesses of B.A.T Industries, formerly known as the British-American Tobacco Co., created in 1902 as a joint venture between UK-based Imperial Tobacco and American Tobacco. As public disapproval of smoking grew in the 1970s, British-American Tobacco began diversifying; it changed its name to B.A.T Industries in 1976 and moved into insurance. In 1984 it rescued UK insurer Eagle Star from a hostile offer by German insurance giant Allianz. Moving into the large US market in 1988, B.A.T bought Farmers Insurance Group.

While B.A.T battled the antismoking army of the 1990s, the insurance industry struggled with stagnant growth. In 1997 Europe's largest insurance firms were named as defendants in class action lawsuits that sought recovery for unpaid claims on Holocaust-era insurance policies. In 1998 Zurich became a founding member of the International Commission on Holocaust Era Insurance Claims (ICHEIC).

Also in 1998 Zurich and B.A.T's insurance units merged to create Zurich Financial Services. In 1999 Zurich spun off its real estate holdings into PSP Swiss Property and, at the turn of the century, it focused on expansion, buying the new business of insurer Abbey Life.

In 2002 Zurich completed the spinoff of reinsurance unit Zurich Re, which became Converium. The write-off of assets and strengthening of non-life reserves resulted in Zurich posting a $3.4 billion loss for 2002. Rolf Hüppi, Zurich's legendary chairman and CEO, stepped down while the company's asset management unit tumbled and investors pulled out. James Schiro, previously with PricewaterhouseCoopers, was named as the new chief executive and began guiding a turnaround at the company.

Schiro launched a restructuring initiative in 2004. The company began its "The Zurich Way" rebranding efforts the following year, which began a financial turnaround for the company. In 2009, after five years of successful restructuring efforts, Schiro retired and chief investment officer Martin Senn took over the CEO role.

EXECUTIVES

Chairman: Manfred Gentz, age 67
CEO: Martin Senn, age 53
Group Head Operations: Kristof Terryn, age 42
Group Head Human Resources: Peter Goerke, age 48
Group Chief Economist: Daniel M. Hofmann
Global Chief Underwriting Officer and Head Organizational Transformation Management: Inga K. Beale, age 46
Chief Risk Officer: Axel P. Lehmann, age 51
Chief Investment Officer: Cecilia Reyes, age 52
Chief Information Technology Officer: Markus Nordlin, age 46
Chief Life Actuary: William J. (Bill) Robertson
Chief Administrative Officer: Richard P. Kearns, age 60
Global Head Mergers and Acquisitions and Chief Underwriting Officer of Directors and Officers Liability and Employment Practices Liability Insurance, Global Corporate: Paul Schiavone
Head Investor Relations and Rating Agency Management: Debra Broek, age 48
Head Global Corporate Communications and Climate Office: Francis Bouchard, age 44
Regional Chairman, Americas; Chairman, Farmers Group: Paul N. Hopkins, age 54
Public Relations Director, United States: Steve McKay
Auditors: PricewaterhouseCoopers AG

LOCATIONS

HQ: Zurich Financial Services AG
Mythenquai 2
8022 Zurich, Switzerland
Phone: 44-625-25-25   **Fax:** 44-625-35-55
US HQ: Zurich Towers, 1400 American Ln.
Schaumburg, IL 60196
US Phone: 847-605-6000   **US Fax:** 847-413-5187
Web: www.zurich.com

PRODUCTS/OPERATIONS

2009 Sales

	% of total
General Insurance	45
Global Life	38
Farmers	12
Other	5
Total	**100**

Selected Subsidiaries

Farmers Group, Inc. (property/casualty, US)
  21st Century Insurance Company (property/casualty, US)
  Farmers New World Life Insurance Company (life insurance, US)
  Foremost Insurance Company (specialty insurance, US)
  Bristol West Holdings, Inc. (specialty insurance, US)
  Zurich American Insurance Company (general insurance, US)
Zurich Insurance plc (general insurance, UK)
Zurich International Life Limited (life insurance, UK)

COMPETITORS

AEGON	ING
AIG	MetLife
Allianz	Mitsui Sumitomo
Aviva	Insurance
AXA	Prudential
CNA Financial	Prudential plc
GEICO	State Farm
Generali	Travelers Companies
The Hartford	

HISTORICAL FINANCIALS

Company Type: Public

Income Statement   FYE: December 31

	ASSETS ($ mil.)	NET INCOME ($ mil.)	INCOME AS % OF ASSETS	EMPLOYEES
12/09	368,914	3,236	0.9%	60,000
12/08	327,944	3,116	1.0%	60,000
12/07	389,344	5,626	1.4%	60,000
12/06	373,855	4,625	1.2%	52,286
12/05	339,612	3,214	0.9%	52,010
Annual Growth	2.1%	0.2%	—	3.6%

2009 Year-End Financials

Equity as % of assets: —   Long-term debt ($ mil.): —
Return on assets: 0.9%   Sales ($ mil.): 70,272
Return on equity: —

Net Income History   Swiss: ZURN

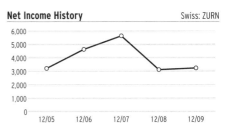

Hoover's Handbook of

World Business

The Indexes

Index by Industry

Index by Headquarters

Index of Executives

A

Aagaard, Hans Christian 46
Aakio, Seppo 192
Aasheim, Hilde M. 251
Abbott, John 299
Abdul Hamid, Mohamed Ishak 319
Abdul Rahman, Norzilah Megawati 319
Abdulla Al Qubaisi, Khadem 258
Abe, Daisaku 232
Abe, Ken 231
Abello, Vincent 94
Abenante, Frank 45
Abet, Maurizio 271
Abramson, Karen 389
Abravanel, Isaac 354
Abril Pérez, Luis 344
Achleitner, Paul 40
Ackermann, Josef 121, 317
Adachi, Toshio 315
Adachi, Yoroku 90
Adam, Bart 312
Adami, Norman J. 301
Adamitis, Thomas J. 45
Adams, Michael A. 292
Adams, Rowan 340
Adiba, Patrick 50
Adl, Manuela 386
Advani, Asheesh 377
Advani, Deepak 209
Agarwal, Bhikam C. 48
Agata, Atsunobu 29
Agata, Tetsuo 366
Agius, Marcus 63
Agnelli, Roger 374
Agnellini, Victor 37
Agnew, Nathan 32
Agon, Jean-Paul 214
Agrawal, Vineet 387
Agrusti, Raffaele 155
Aguilar Ramírez, Oscar L. 345
Ahizoune, Abdeslam 378
Ahlers, Bernd 351
Ahmed, Javed 340
Ahmed, Riaz E. 362
Aho, Esko 249
Ahrens, Oliver 23
Ahrnell, Jan H. 349
Aijala, Ainar D. Jr. 116
Ainley, John 53
Aizawa, Naoki 335
Akbas, Hakan 160
Akhurst, Bruce J. 350
Akimoto, Masami 359
Akiyoshi, Mitsuru 223
Äkräs, Juha 249
Akseli, Ari 192
Al Kuwaiti, Alyazia Ali Saleh 258
Alács, Lajos 233
Alalauri, Hannu 333
Alamouti, Siavash M. 380
Alary, Pierre 77
Ala-Seppälä, Heikki 192
Al-Aydh, Salim S. 310

Alazraki Pfeffer, Mauricio 267
Albanel, Christine 147
Albanese, Tom 288
Albrecht, Karl 38
Al-Buainain, Khalid G. 310
Alcala, Angel 182
Alcide, Peter 25
Alciturri, José Luis G. 59
Áldott, Zoltán 233
Aldridge, Gary L. 177
Alejo, Francisco S. III 306
Alekperov, Vagit Y. 217
Alemany, Ellen 298
Alexander, Craig 362
Alexopoulos, George 163
Al-Falih, Khalid A. 310
Alfonsi, Davide 181
Alford, Brad 240
Alix, Didier 325
Al-Judaimi, Abdulaziz 310
Al-Khayyal, Abdulaziz F. 310
Allen, Ken 122
Allen, Paula 53
Alm, Thomas 322
Almeida, Ann 170
Almeida, David 45
Almeida, Donald V. 275
Al-Naimi, Ali I. 310
Al-Othman, Abdullatif A. 310
Alphandéry, Edmond 105
Altavilla, Alfredo 140
Altendorfer-Zwerenz, Angelika 258
Alvarado, Cristóbal Valderas 24
Álvarez, José A. 59
Álvarez Fernández, Carlos J. 151
Álvarez-Pallete López, José M. 344
Alves, Nuno 132
Al-Wuhaib, Abdulrahman F. 310
Ambe Attar, Isidoro 345
Amblard, Guillaume 76
Ambrose, Brian 198
Amemiya, Hiroshi 357
Ames, Richard J. 203
Amine, James L. 110
Amos, Louise 106
Ananenkov, Alexander G. 153
Anders, Bettina 135
Andersen, Carsten P. 46
Andersen, Nils Smedegaard 46
Andersen, Ulrik 93
Anderson, J. Trevor 68
Anderson, Jeremy 198
Anderson, Ron 125
Ando, Goron 254
Andrade, Miguel S. 132
Andree, Timothy P. 119
Andres, Juan 253
Ang, Ramon S. 306
Anjolras, Pierre 376
Annunziato, Paolo 343
Ansaharju, Aulis 333
Ansaldo, Guillermo P. 344
Antinori, Thierry 216
Antonanzas, Miguel 134
Antoñanzas, Miguel 134

Antonietti, Francesco 150
Aoki, Shoichi 201
Aoki, Yasushi 190
Aoki, Yoshihisa 185
Aouani, Hakim L. 95
Apoita Gordo, Juan Ignacio 67
Apotheker, Léo 311
Appel, Frank 122
Arai, Masuji 34
Arakawa, Shoshi 81
Aranaz Zuza, Luis Javier 174
Aranda Moreno, Sergio 151
Aranguren Escobar, José E. 139
Araujo Ramírez, Félix José 347
Araya, Shinichi 341
Arbizu Lostao, Eduardo 67
Arbola, Gérald 332
Arditti, Gilles 50
Arentz Rostrup, Jørgen C. 251
Argüelles Díaz González, Raúl 384
Ariano, Lucia 181
Aricò, Luigi 181
Arikawa, Sadahiro 287
Armato, Francesco 343
Armengol Calvo, Domingo 67
Armour, Mark H. 283
Arnault, Bernard 103, 218
Arndt, Frank-Peter 75
Arnold, David 89
Arnoldussen, Ludger 234
Arnstad, Marit 331
Arrago, André 161
Arteaga Carlebach, Maximiliano 347
Artemiev, Anton 93
Arthur, John 386
Aruga, Shuji 313
Asada, Teruo 223
Asai, Yutaka 257
Asakawa, Osamu 39
Asami, Hiroyasu 256
Ashabolu, Ahmet 195
Ashby, Ian R. 72
Ashmore, Steve 388
Ashton, Guy 121
Ashworth, Julian 283
Aspar, Gérard 303
Asúa Madariaga, Juan 67
Atack, Jonathan 180
Atay, Temel K. 195
Athanas, Evan C. 45
Atlas, Ilana 386
Atsumi, Masanori 335
Attal, Laurent 214
Attinger, Per-Olof 291
Auguste, Georges 332
Auque, François 126
Auriemma, Marco 140
Austin, Neil D. 198
Avenía, Cesare 136
Ayyoubi, Silvia 291
Azagra Blázquez, Pedro 174
Azcárraga Jean, Emilio Fernando 347
Azema, David 324
Azuma, Kazunori 287

B

Baan, Adri 389
Babe, Gregory S. 65
Babeau, Emmauel 311
Bacardi, Facundo L. 56
Bacardit, Ramón 164
Bacchetta, Paolo 133
Bacher, Lars C. 331
Bachmann, Jay 204
Bacon, Ian 340
Badinter, Elisabeth 277
Badlishah, Dato' Tunku Putra 319
Badré, Bertrand 109
Badrinath, Vivek 147
Bae, Ho-Won 304
Bae, Yong-Tae 304
Bagattini, Roy 93
Bagel-Trah, Simone 164
Bague, Hugo 288
Baier, Horst 369
Bailey, George 329
Baines, John 298
Baker, Deborah 86
Baker, Kathy 389
Baksaas, Jon F. 346
Baladrón, Daniel Vega 24
Balakrishnan, V. 179
Balbinot, Sergio 155
Balcarcel Santa Cruz, Joaquín 347
Balcom, Robert A. 156, 213
Balcunas, Mark 182
Baldi, Alessandro 140
Ballantyne, Gordon S. 350
Baltazar Rodríguez, Miguel 384
Balz, Manfred 123
Banerjee, Gautam 275
Bänziger, Hugo 121
Barahona, Pedro 67
Baraibar, Gonzalo Gomez-Zamalloa 24
Baranes Cohen, Florence 94
Barbaroux, Olivier 375
Barbassa, Almir G. 265
Barbé, Pierre 365
Barber, Ralph G. 170
Barbier, Francois 143
Baril, Thierry 33
Barkov, Anatoly A. 217
Barnabé, Pierre 37
Barnett, Lee 42
Barr Goyder, Richard J. 385
Barreiro Hernández, Jose 67
Barrie, Sidney 142
Barrientos Fernández, Wilmer 266
Barron, Laurence 33
Barthélemy, Bertrand 91
Bartolotta, Peter 209
Basolas Tena, Antonio 151
Bassien, Jean-Claude 109
Bastón Patiño, José A. 347
Batchelor, Lance 352
Bäte, Oliver 40
Bättig, Alois 110
Baudin, Remí 326

Talma, Arja 192
Talotta, Alessandro 343
Tamagnini, Andrea 181
Tamai, Kouichi 148
Tamakoshi, Ryosuke 230
Tamaru, Takuya 393
Tamba, Toshihito 185
Tamura, Minoru 335
Tan, Chik Quee 320
Tan, Ethel M. L. 320
Tan, Paul W. L. 320
Tan, Pee Teck 320
Tan, William S. K. 320
Tanabe, Hiroyuki 328
Tanaka, Akihito 29
Tanaka, Hiroshi 250
Tanaka, Hisao 363
Tanaka, Masaaki 230
Tanaka, Nobuyoshi 90
Tanaka, Norio 287
Tanaka, Seiichi 231
Tanaka, Takashi 256
Tanaka, Toshizo 90
Tanehashi, Makio 232
Tang, Chengjian 321
Tanigawa, Kazuo 363
Taniguchi, Nobuyuki 315
Taniguchi, Shinichi (Nippon Steel) 245
Taniguchi, Shinichi (Sojitz) 328
Tank Uzun, Ali 195
Tansey, Robert 86
Tanzi, Francesco 271
Tarantini, Riccardo 140
Targett, Greg 386
Tassan, Franck 94
Tata, Ratan N. 339
Tate, G. Truett 212
Tate, John 85
Tavares, Carlos 247
Tavernier, Jacques 376
Tawada, Etsuji 194
Taylor, Aileen 298
Taylor, Jeff 262
Taylor, Joseph M. 261
Taylor, Peter 84
Tchernonog, Alain 375
Tear, Kristian 329
Techar, Franklin J. 61
Teerlink, Ron 298
Teh, Ping Choon 320
Tejón, José M. 59
ten Brinke, Henk Jan 295
Teodorani-Fabbri, Pio 139
Teoh, Tee Hooi 320
Teppo, Jon 389
Terada, Toshifumi 244
Terajima, Yoshinori 244
Terao, Minoru 238
Teraoka, Kazunori 328
Terato, Ichiro 241
Térisse, Pierre-André 114
Ternert, Bertil 309
Terrett, Mike J. 294
Terryn, Kristof 395
Testut, Cédric 147
Tetrault, Lynn 49
Teulie, Pierre Alexandre 94
Tew, Beverley 85
Teyssen, Johannes 134
Tezuka, Kazuo 194
Thérond, Valérie 147
Thiam, Tidjane C. 276
Thibaud, Laure 307
Thibault, Alain P. 362
Thiébaud, Françoise 336
Thielen, Gunter 71
Thodey, David 350
Thoemmes, Otmar 116
Thoeng, Tjhoen Onn 320
Thomas, Claire 157
Thomas, Geoff 391
Thomas, Patrick W. 65
Thomas, Uwe 290
Thomasen, Jakob 46

Thomas-Graham, Pamela A. 110
Thomé, Claudia 55
Thompson, Drew 159
Thompson, John M. 270, 362
Thompson, Maarten 389
Thompson, Mark 85
Thompson, Norman 32
Thomsen, Mads K. 254
Thomson, Caroline 85
Thomson, David K. R. 355
Thomson, Philip 157
Thorburn, Andrew 236
Thoresen, Otto 28
Thormahlen, Sven 114
Thormann, Dominique 285
Thorne, Grant 288
Thoumyre, Hervé 94
Thouvard, Charlotte 22
Thurneysen, Peter 370
Thurston, Paul A. 170
Thurston, Richard 337
Thygesen, Jan E. 346
Tible, Phillippe 193
Tikkas, Pantelis 163
Tilger, Carsten 164
Timmermans, Koos 180
Tizatto, Mariângela M. 265
Tjaarda, Francis 162
Tobin, James J. Sr. 220
Tod, Mike 32
Todt, Jean 140
Toevs, Alden 106
Togashi, Kazuo 287
Toivanen, Martti 192
Tokuda, Hiromi 117
Tokunaga, Shunichi 184
Toledano, Sidney 103
Tolle, Rolf 211
Tolot, Jérôme 154
Toma, Ihab 368
Tomas, Veneranda M. 306
Tomiyama, Takuji 238
Tonelli, Louis 220
Tong, Carlson 198
Tonne, Hilde M. 346
Tonnel, David A. 368
Tookey, Tim J. W. 212
Toomey, Mary 41
Torigoe, Takeshi 200
Toriyama, Eiichi 202
Torres, Alberto 249
Torres Vila, Carlos 67
Toselli, Damiano 343
Toshikuni, Nobuyuki 200
Tostivin, Jean-Claude 79
Touyama, Masahiko 112
Toya, Hiromichi 39
Toyama, Takashi 261
Toyoda, Akio 366
Toyoda, Kanshiro 34
Toyoda, Takahiro 328
Toyoshima, Masaaki 29
Travesedo Loring, Luis 139
Treble, Nick 41
Treschow, Michael 136, 372
Tretton, Jack 329
Treviño, Rodrigo 99
Tricoire, Jean-Pascal 311
Triffitt, Mark 385
Tripp, Eric C. 61
Tronchetti Provera, Marco 271
Tronchetti Provera, Raffaele Bruno 271
Troy, Dan 157
Truchi, Daniel 325
Truschinger, John L. 368
Tsai, N. S. 337
Tsai, Rick 337
Tseng, C. L. 144
Tseng, F. C. 337
Tso, Stephen T. 337
Tsokanos, Jim 278
Tsubouchi, Kazuto 256
Tsuchida, Osamu 111
Tsuchiya, Mitsuko 29

Tsuchiya, Sojiro 117
Tsuda, Toru 81
Tsuga, Kazuhiro 261
Tsujimura, Kiyoyuki 256
Tsukamoto, Takashi 232
Tsukioka, Ryozo 184
Tsunakawa, Satoshi 363
Tsuneishi, Tetsuo 359
Tsuzumi, Norio 358
Tsygankov, Stanislav E. 153
Tu, Che-Min 23
Tuchler, Dave 340
Tucker, Stephen 236
Tufano, Paul J. 37
Tun Musa, Hitam 319
Tunnacliffe, Paul D. 125
Turcke, Mary Ann 68
Turcotte, Martine 68
Turf, Barbara A. 260
Turicchi, Antonino 332
Turley, James S. 138
Turner, Cathy (Barclays) 63
Turner, David J. 106
Turner, Gerhard 290
Turner, Kathryn A. (Imperial Tobacco) 177
Turner, Nigel 216
Turner-Laing, Sophie 86
Turrini, Régis 378
Tweddle, Terrie L. 292
Tworek, Christopher W. 30
Tyler, David A. 186
Tzeng, M. C. 337

U

Uchida, Kohzoh 245
Uchida, Takafumi 316
Uchida, Tsuneji 90
Uchiyamada, Takeshi 366
Ude, Hermann 122
Uebber, Bodo 113, 126
Ueda, Ryoichi 228
Uehara, Haruya 230
Uemura, Hiroyuki 341
Uenoyama, Makoto 261
Ugari, Takenori 201
Uji, Noritaka 246
Ujiie, Junichi 250
Ulbrich, Thomas 381
Ulissi, Roberto 133
Ullmer, Michael J. 236
Ulrich, Rolf 135
Umbers, Richard 391
Umemoto, Kazunori 29
Umemura, Kazumasa 201
Umemura, Mitsuru 393
Umezawa, Toshinori 223
Undeli, Johnny 251
Underhill, Kerry 295
Uno, Ikuo 244
Unoura, Hiroo 246
Uramoto, Kengo 90
Urano, Takashi 81
Ureña-Raso, Domingo 33, 126
Urquijo, Gonzalo 48
Urquiza, José M. 384
Ushida, Kazuo 241
Ushijima, Noboru 313
Usuba, Yo 247
Usui, Minoru 313
Utsler, Mike 80
Utsuda, Shoei 231

V

Vacassin, Priscilla 276
Vajsman, Claude 269
Valencia Martínez, María del Carmen 384
Valentine, Debra A. 288

Valet, Didier 325
Vallance, Patrick 157
Vallaude, Jean-Pierre 285
Vallbona Vadell, Pablo 24
Valle, Gustavo 114
Vallejo, Carlos 266
Valther Pallesen, Lisbeth 207
van Beeck, Hans 337
van Boxmeer, Jean-François M. L. 162
Van Bylen, Hans 164
Van Dam, Jan 295
van Damme, Niek Jan 123
van de Laarschot, Jochem 295
van den Acker, Laurens G. 285
van den Bergh, Lodewijk Hijmans 295
van den Brink, Dolf 162
van der Hoeven, Eric 189
van der Hulst, Els 35
van der Laan, Sander 295
van der Lee, Charles W. 292
van der Linden, Hans 280
van der Meijden, Erik 199
van der Noordaa, Hans 180
van der Steur, Christine 87
van der Veer, Jeroen 372
Van der Velde, Bert 391
van der Zanden, Tim 35
van Dijk, Frits 240
Van Duijl, Milko 208
Van Hassel, Gilbert 180
van Innis, Emmanuel 154
van Iperen, Gert 290
van Kralingen, Tony 301
van Lede, Cees 162
van Maasakker, Steven 162
Van Meirvenne, Dirk 65
Van Odijk, Gerard W. M. 354
van Ool, Marjo 35
van Raemdonck, Geoffroy 218
Van Saun, Bruce W. 298
van Schijndel, Piet 280
van Veenendaal, Jan 280
van Weede, Marc A. 28
van Wijk, Leo M. 31
van Woerkom, Floris 162
Van Wyk, Steve 180
Vanaselja, Siim A. 68
Vanhainen, Juha 333
Vanot, Jean-Philippe 147
Vanselow, Alex 72
Vardas, Theodoros 163
Vareberg, Terje 251
Varin, Philippe 269
Varley, John S. 63
Varvel, Eric 110
Vasdeboncoeur, Bernard 227
Vasella, Daniel L. 253
Vasilyeva, Elena A. 153
Vasino, Christian 25
Vaswani, Suresh 387
Vaux, Robert G. 156
Vauzanges, Jean-Pierre 109
Vázquez del Mercado Benshimol, Andrés R. 345
Veihmeyer, John B. 198
Velasco, Pedro 174
Velasco Paulín, Raymundo 345
Velasco Ruiz, Roque 384
Vellano, Enrico 139
Venn, Richard E. 89
Veracierta, Nicolás 266
Verbeek, D. P. M. 280
Verdes, Marcelino Fernández 24
Verdier, Damien 311
Vermeer, A. J. A. M. 280
Vernerey, Laurent 311
Vernieri, Marco 181
Verrier, Mike 388
Verwaayen, Bernardus J. 37
Vestberg, Hans 136
Vetter, Jürgen 135
Vettese, Frank 116
Veyrier, Olivier 269
Viana, Miguel 132